Office for
National Statistics

Annual Abstract
of Statistics

No 144
2008 Edition

Editor: Ian Macrory
Office for National Statistics

palgrave
macmillan

ISBN 978-0-230-54560-1
ISSN 0072-5730

A National Statistics publication

National Statistics are produced to high professional standards set out in the National Statistics Code of Practice. They are produced free from political influence. Not all the statistics contained within this publication are national statistics because it is a compilation from various sources.

About us

The Office for National Statistics

The Office for National Statistics (ONS) is the executive office of the UK Statistics Authority, a non-ministerial department which reports directly to Parliament. ONS is the UK government's single largest statistical producer. It compiles information about the UK's society and economy which provides evidence for policy and decision-making and in the allocation of resources.

The Director of ONS is also the National Statistician.

Palgrave Macmillan

This publication first published 2008 by Palgrave Macmillan, Houndmills, Basingstoke, Hampshire RG21 6XS and 175 Fifth Avenue, New York, NY 10010, USA

Companies and representatives throughout the world.

Palgrave Macmillan is the global academic imprint of the Palgrave Macmillan division of St. Martin's Press, LLC and of Palgrave Macmillan Ltd. Macmillan® is a registered trademark in the United States, United Kingdom and other countries. Palgrave is a registered trademark in the European Union and other countries.

A catalogue record for this book is available from the British Library.

10 9 8 7 6 5 4 3 2 1
17 16 15 14 13 12 11 10 09 08

Contacts

This publication

For information about the content of this publication, contact the ONS Core Table Unit
Tel: 01633 455851
Email: ctu@ons.gsi.gov.uk

Other customer and media enquiries

ONS Customer Contact Centre
Tel: 0845 601 3034
International: +44 (0)845 601 3034
Minicom: 01633 812399
Email: info@statistics.gsi.gov.uk
Fax: 01633 652747

Post: Room 1015, Government Buildings,
Cardiff Road, Newport, South Wales NP10 8XG
www.statistics.gov.uk

Publication orders

To obtain the print version of this publication, contact Palgrave Macmillan, tel: 01256 302611
www.palgrave.com/ons

Copyright and reproduction

Printing

This book is printed on paper suitable for recycling and made from fully managed and sustained forest sources. Logging, pulping and manufacturing processes are expected to conform to the environmental regulations of the country of origin.
Printed and bound in Great Britain by Hobbs the Printer Ltd, Totton, Southampton

Typeset by Kerrypress Typesetters Ltd, Luton, Bedfordshire

Contents

Contents

Contents

Contents

16: National accounts

		Page	Type*

17: Prices

18: Government finance

Central government

Contents

		Page	Type*

22: Production

Contents

* This publication contains a mixture of 'National Statistics' and 'Other Official Statistics'. Statistics accredited as 'National Statistics' (NS) are fully compliant with the National Statistics Code of Practice, and carry the National Statistics Kitemark. Statistics labelled as 'Other Official Statistics' (Non NS) follow many of the best practice principles set out in the Code but have not been accredited as fully compliant.

Contributors and acknowledgements

The editor would like to thank the following people for their help in producing this book:

Production team: Angela Collin

Marc Evans

Dilys Rosen

Andrew White

Contributors

The editor also wishes to thank all his colleagues in ONS, the rest of the Government Statistical Service and all contributors in other organisations for their generous support and helpful comments, without whose help this publication would not be possible.

Design: ONS Design
Typesetting: Kerrypress Typesetters Ltd
Publishing management: Mark Bristow

Units of measurement

Length

1 millimetre (mm)		= 0.03937 inch
1 centimetre (cm)	= 10 millimetres	= 0.3937 inch
1 metre (m)	= 1,000 millimetres	= 1.094 yards
1 kilometre (km)	= 1,000 metres	= 0.6214 mile
1 inch (in.)		= 25.40 millimetres or 2.540 centimetres
1 foot (ft.)	= 12 inches	= 0.3048 metre
1 yard (yd.)	= 3 feet	= 0.9144 metre
1 mile	= 1,760 yards	= 1.609 kilometres

Area

1 square millimetre (mm2)		= 0.001550 square inch
1 square metre (m2)	= 1 million square millimetres	= 1.196 square yards
1 hectare (ha)	= 10,000 square metres	= 2.471 acres
1 square kilometre (km2)	= 1 million square metres	= 247.1 acres
1 square inch (sq. in.)		= 645.2 square millimetres or 6.452 square centimetres
1 square foot (sq. ft.)	= 144 square inches	= 0.09290 square metre or 929.0 square centimetres
1 square yard (sq. yd.)	= 9 square feet	= 0.8361 square metre
1 acre	= 4,840 square yards	= 4,046 square metres or 0.4047 hectare
1 square mile (sq. mile)	= 640 acres	= 2.590 square kilometres or 259.0 hectares

Volume

1 cubic centimetre (cm3)		= 0.06102 cubic inch
1 cubic decimetre (dm3)	= 1,000 cubic centimetres	= 0.03531 cubic foot
1 cubic metre (m3)	= one million cubic centimetres	= 1.308 cubic yards
1 cubic inch (cu.in.)		=16.39 cubic centimetres
1 cubic foot (cu. ft.)	= 1,728 cubic inches	= 0.02832 cubic metre or 28.32 cubic decimetres
1 cubic yard (cu. yd.)	= 27 cubic feet	= 0.7646 cubic metre

Capacity

1 litre (l)	= 1 cubic decimetre	= 0.2200 gallon
1 hectolitre (hl)	= 100 litres	= 22.00 gallons
1 pint		= 0.5682 litre
1 quart	= 2 pints	= 1.137 litres
1 gallon	= 8 pints	= 4.546 litres
1 bulk barrel	= 36 gallons (gal.)	= 1.637 hectolitres

Weight

1 gram (g)		= 0.03527 ounce avoirdupois
1 hectogram (hg)	= 100 grams	= 3.527 ounces or 0.2205 pound
1 kilogram (kg)	= 1,000 grams or 10 hectograms	= 2.205 pounds
1 tonne (t)	= 1,000 kilograms	= 1.102 short tons or 0.9842 long ton
1 ounce avoirdupois (oz.)	= 437.5 grains	= 28.35 grams
1 pound avoirdupois (lb.)	= 16 ounces	= 0.4536 kilogram
1 hundredweight (cwt.)	= 112 pounds	= 50.80 kilograms
1 short ton	= 2,000 pounds	= 907.2 kilograms or 0.9072 tonne
1 long ton (referred to as ton)	= 2,240 pounds	= 1,016 kilograms or 1.016 tonnes
1 ounce troy	= 480 grains	= 31.10 grams

Energy

British thermal unit (Btu)	= 0.2520 kilocalorie (kcal) = 1.055 kilojoule (kj)
Therm	= 105 British thermal units = 25,200 kcal = 105,506 kj
Megawatt hour (MWh)	= 106 watt hours (Wh)
Gigawatt hour (GWh)	= 106 kilowatt hours = 34,121 therms

Food and drink

Butter	23,310 litres milk	= 1 tonne butter (average)
Cheese	10,070 litres milk	= 1 tonne cheese
Condensed milk	2,550 litres milk	= 1 tonne full cream condensed milk
	2,953 litres skimmed milk	= 1 tonne skimmed condensed milk
Milk	1 million litres	= 1,030 tonnes
Milk powder	8,054 litres milk	= 1 tonne full cream milk powder
	10,740 litres skimmed milk	= 1 tonne skimmed milk powder
Eggs	17,126 eggs	= 1 tonne (approximate)
Sugar	100 tonnes sugar beet	= 92 tonnes refined sugar
	100 tonnes cane sugar	= 96 tonnes refined sugar

Shipping

Gross tonnage	= The total volume of all the enclosed spaces of a vessel, the unit of measurement being a 'ton' of 100 cubic feet.
Deadweight tonnage	= Deadweight tonnage is the total weight in tons of 2,240 lb that a ship can legally carry, that is the total weight of cargo, bunkers, stores and crew.

Introduction

Introduction

Welcome to the 2008 edition of the *Annual Abstract of Statistics*. This compendium draws together statistics from a wide range of official and other authoritative sources. Their help is gratefully acknowledged.

Regional information, supplementary to the national figures in *Annual Abstract,* appear in *Regional Trends.* The latest edition of *Regional Trends* is available electronically on the National Statistics website free of charge. This can be accessed from the *Regional Trends* entry under the Compendia and Reference theme, or directly at: www.statistics.gov.uk/regionaltrends. Earlier editions are available via Palgrave Macmillan.

Current data for many of the series appearing in this *Annual Abstract* are contained in other ONS publications, such as *Economic & Labour Market Review, Population Trends, Health Statistics Quarterly* and *Financial Statistics.* All are published by Palgrave Macmillan.

Other Office for National Statistics (ONS) publications which contain related data are the *Monthly Digest of Statistics* and *Social Trends*; these are also published by Palgrave Macmillan or can be found directly at:

www.statistics.gov.uk/statbase/product.asp?vlnk=611

www.statistics.gov.uk/statbase/product.asp?vlnk=5748

The name (and telephone number, where this is available) of the organisation providing the statistics are shown under each table. In addition, a list of sources is given at the back of the book, which sets out the official publications or other sources to which further reference can be made.

Identification codes

The four-letter identification code at the top of each data column, or at the side of each row, is the ONS reference for this series of data on our database. Please quote the relevant code if you contact us requiring any further information about the data. On some tables it is not possible to include these codes, so please quote the table number in these cases.

Definitions and classification

Time series

So far as possible annual totals are given throughout, but quarterly or monthly figures are given where these are more suitable to the type of series.

Explanatory notes

Most sections are preceded by explanatory notes which should be read in conjunction with the tables. Definitions and explanatory notes for many of the terms occurring in the *Annual Abstract* are also given in the *Annual Supplement to the Monthly Digest of Statistics*, published annually in the January edition. Detailed notes on items which appear in both the *Abstract* and *Financial Statistics* are given in an annual supplement to the latter entitled *Financial Statistics Explanatory Handbook*. The original sources listed in the sources may also be consulted.

Standard Industrial Classification

A Standard Industrial Classification (SIC) was first introduced into the UK in 1948 for use in classifying business establishments and other statistical units by the type of economic activity in which they are engaged. The classification provides a framework for the collection, tabulation, presentation and analysis of data about economic activities. Its use promotes uniformity of data collected by various government departments and agencies. Since 1948 the classification has been revised in 1958, 1968, 1980, 1992, 2003 and 2007. One of the principal objectives of the 1980 revision was to eliminate differences from the activity classification issued by the Statistical Office of the European Communities (Eurostat) and entitled 'Nomenclature générale des activités économiques dans les Communautés Européennes', usually abbreviated to NACE. In 1990, the European Communities introduced a new statistical classification of economic activities (NACE Rev 1) by regulation. The regulation made it obligatory for the UK to introduce a new Standard Industrial Classification SIC(92), based on NACE Rev 1. UK SIC(92) was based exactly on NACE Rev 1 but, where it was thought necessary or helpful, a fifth digit was added to form subclasses of the NACE 1 four digit system. Classification systems need to be revised periodically because, over time, new products, processes and industries emerge. In January 2003, a minor revision of NACE Rev 1, known as NACE Rev 1.1, was published in the Official Journal of the European Communities.

Consequently, the UK was obliged to introduce a new Standard Industrial Classification (SIC(2003)) consistent with NACE Rev 1.1. The UK took the opportunity of the 2003 revision to also update the national Subclasses. Full details are available in *UK Standard Industrial Classification of Economic Activities 2003* and the Indexes to the *UK Standard Industrial Classification of Economic Activities 2003*. These are the most recent that are currently used. The most up to date version is the *UK Standard Industrial Classification of Economic activities 2007* (SIC2007). It will be implemented in five stages and came into effect on 1 January 2008.

- For reference year 2008, the Annual Business Inquiry
  (parts 1 & 2) will be based on SIC 2007

- Products of the European Community will also be based on SIC 2007 from reference year 2008

- Other annual outputs will be based on SIC 2007 from reference year 2009, unless otherwise determined by regulation

- Quarterly and monthly surveys will be based on SIC 2007 from the first reference period in 2010, unless otherwise determined by regulation

- National Accounts will move to SIC 2007 in September 2011

ONS is currently working on a detailed implementation plan for the introduction of the new classification, covering all of our surveys and outputs.
For further information see
www.statistics.gov.uk/statbase/Product.asp?vlnk=14012

Revisions to contents

Some of the figures, particularly for the latest year, are provisional and may be revised in a subsequent issue of the *Annual Abstract*.

Symbols and conventions used

Change of basis
Where consecutive figures have been compiled on different bases and are not strictly comparable, a footnote is added indicating the nature of the difference.

Geographic coverage
Statistics relate mainly to the UK. Where figures relate to other areas, this is indicated on the table.

Units of measurement
The various units of measurement used are listed following the Contents.

Rounding of figures
In tables where figures have been rounded to the nearest final digit, the constituent items may not add up exactly to the total.

Symbols
The following symbols have been used throughout:

.. = not available or not applicable (also information supressed to avoid disclosure)

- = nil or less than half the final digit shown

National Statistics Online: www.statistics.gov.uk

Web-based access to time series, cross sectional data and metadata from across the Government Statistical Service (GSS) is available using the site search and index functions from the homepage. Users can also download many datasets, in whole or in part, or consult directory information for all GSS statistical resources, including censuses, surveys, periodicals and enquiry services. Information is posted as PDF electronic documents or in XLS and CSV formats, compatible with most spreadsheet packages. Complete copies of this publication are available to download free of charge on the following web page: www.statistics.gov.uk/statbase/product.asp?vlnk=94.

Contact point

The ONS welcomes any feedback on the content of the *Annual Abstract*, including comments on the format of the data and the selection of topics. Comments and requests for general information should be addressed to:

Core Table Unit
Social and Economic Micro-Analysis and Reporting Division
Room 2.101
Office for National Statistics
Government Buildings
Cardiff Road
Newport
South Wales NP10 8XG

or

email: info@statistics.gsi.gov.uk
July 2008

Area

Chapter 1

Area

The UK comprises Great Britain and Northern Ireland. Great Britain comprises England, Wales and Scotland.

Physical Features

The UK constitutes the greater part of the British Isles. The largest of the islands is Great Britain. The next largest comprises Northern Ireland and the Irish Republic. Western Scotland is fringed by the large island chain known as the Hebrides, and to the north east of the Scottish mainland are the Orkney and Shetland Islands. All these, along with the Isle of Wight, Anglesey and the Isles of Scilly, form part of the UK. The Isle of Man, in the Irish Sea, and the Channel Islands, between Great Britain and France, are largely self-governing and are not part of the UK. The UK is one of the 27 member states of the European Union following the accession of Bulgaria and Romania on 1 January 2007. With an area of about 243,000 sq km (about 94,000 sq miles), the UK is just under 1,000 km (about 600 miles) from the south coast to the extreme north of Scotland and just under 500 km (around 300 miles) across at the widest point.

- Highest mountain: Ben Nevis, in the highlands of Scotland, at 1,343 m (4,406 ft)

- Longest river: the Severn, 354 km (220 miles) long, which rises in central Wales and flows through Shrewsbury, Worcester and Gloucester in England to the Bristol Channel

- Largest lake: Lough Neagh, Northern Ireland, at 396 sqkm (153 sq miles)

- Deepest lake: Loch Morar in the Highlands of Scotland, 310 m (1,017 ft) deep

- Highest waterfall: Eas a'Chual Aluinn, from Glas Bheinn, in the highlands of Scotland, with a drop of 200 m (660 ft)

- Deepest cave: Ogof Ffynnon Ddu, Wales, at 308 m (1,010 ft) deep

- Most northerly point on the British mainland: Dunnet Head, north-east Scotland

- Most southerly point on the British mainland: Lizard Point, Cornwall

- Closest point to mainland continental Europe: Dover, Kent. The Channel Tunnel, which links England and France, is a little over 50 km (31 miles) long, of which nearly 38 km (24 miles) are actually under the Channel

1.1 Area of the United Kingdom[1,2], 2006

	sq km		sq km
		Shropshire	3 197
United Kingdom	242 495	Staffordshire	2 620
		Warwickshire	1 975
Great Britain[3]	228 919	West Midlands (Met County)	902
		Worcestershire	1 741
England and Wales	151 013		
		East	19 109
		Luton UA	43
England	130 279	Peterborough UA	343
		Southend-on-Sea UA	42
North East	8 573	Thurrock UA	163
Darlington UA	197	Bedfordshire	1 192
Hartlepool UA	94	Cambridgeshire	3 046
Middlesbrough UA	54	Essex	3 465
Redcar and Cleveland UA	245	Hertfordshire	1 643
Stockton-on-Tees UA	204	Norfolk	5 371
		Suffolk	3 800
Durham	2 226		
Northumberland	5 013	**London**	1 572
Tyne and Wear (Met County)	540		
		Inner London	319
North West	14 106	Outer London	1 253
Blackburn with Darwen UA	137	**South East**	19 069
Blackpool UA	35		
Halton UA	79	Bracknell Forest UA	109
Warrington UA	181	Brighton and Hove UA	83
		Isle of Wight UA	380
Cheshire	2 083	Medway UA	192
Cumbria	6 768	Milton Keynes UA	309
Greater Manchester (Met County)	1 276	Portsmouth UA	40
Lancashire	2 903	Reading UA	40
Merseyside (Met County)	645	Slough UA	33
		Southampton UA	50
Yorkshire and The Humber	15 408	West Berkshire UA	704
		Windsor and Maidenhead UA	197
East Riding of Yorkshire UA	2 408	Wokingham UA	179
Kingston upon Hull, City of UA	71		
North East Lincolnshire UA	192	Buckinghamshire	1 565
North Lincolnshire UA	846	East Sussex	1 709
York UA	272	Hampshire	3 679
		Kent	3 544
North Yorkshire	8 038	Oxfordshire	2 605
South Yorkshire (Met County)	1 552	Surrey	1 663
West Yorkshire (Met County)	2 029	West Sussex	1 991
East Midlands	15 607	**South West**	23 837
Derby UA	78	Bath and North East Somerset UA	346
Leicester UA	73	Bournemouth UA	46
Nottingham UA	75	Bristol, City of UA	110
Rutland UA	382	North Somerset UA	374
		Plymouth UA	80
Derbyshire	2 547	Poole UA	65
Leicestershire	2 083	South Gloucestershire UA	497
Lincolnshire	5 921	Swindon UA	230
Northamptonshire	2 364	Torbay UA	63
Nottinghamshire	2 085		
		Cornwall and the Isles of Scilly	2 563
West Midlands	12 998	Devon	6 564
		Dorset	2 542
Herefordshire, County of UA	2 180	Gloucestershire	2 653
Stoke-on-Trent UA	93	Somerset	3 451
Telford and Wrekin UA	290	Wiltshire	3 255

Area

1.1 Area of the United Kingdom[1,2], 2006

continued

	sq km		sq km
Wales	20 733	Dumfries & Galloway	6 426
		Dundee City	60
Blaenau Gwent	109	East Ayrshire	1 262
Bridgend	251	East Dunbartonshire	175
Caerphilly	277	East Lothian	679
Cardiff	140		
Carmarthenshire	2 371	East Renfrewshire	174
		Edinburgh, City of	264
Ceredigion	1 785	Eilean Siar[4]	3 071
Conwy	1 126	Falkirk	297
Denbighshire	837	Fife	1 325
Flintshire	438		
Gwynedd	2 535	Glasgow City	175
		Highland	25 659
Isle of Anglesey	711	Inverclyde	160
Merthyr Tydfil	111	Midlothian	354
Monmouthshire	849	Moray	2 238
Neath Port Talbot	441		
Newport	190	North Ayrshire	885
Pembrokeshire	1 619	North Lanarkshire	470
		Orkney Islands	990
Powys	5 181	Perth & Kinross	5 286
Rhondda, Cynon, Taff	424	Renfrewshire	261
Swansea	378	Scottish Borders	4 732
Torfaen	126		
The Vale of Glamorgan	331	Shetland Islands	1 466
Wrexham	504	South Ayrshire	1 222
		South Lanarkshire	1 772
		Stirling	2 187
Scotland	77 925	West Dunbartonshire	159
		West Lothian	427
Aberdeen City	186		
Aberdeenshire	6 313		
Angus	2 182	**Northern Ireland**	13 576
Argyll & Bute	6 909		
Clackmannanshire	159		

1 Figures relate to land area only.
2 The area measurements are a definitive set derived from boundaries maintained by Ordnance Survey and Ordnance Survey of Northern Ireland. The current measurements may differ from those published previously in tables, publications or other statistical outputs, even allowing for boundary changes or changes to the physical structure of the land because of improvements to the source of the data.
3 Excludes inland water for all countries.
4 Formerly known as the Western Isles.

Source: Office for National Statistics

Parliamentary elections

Chapter 2

Elections

2.1 Parliamentary elections[1]
United Kingdom

Thousands and percentages

		15 Oct 1964	31 Mar 1966	18 June 1970[1]	28 Feb 1974		10 Oct 1974	3 May 1979	9 June 1983	11 June 1987	9 April 1992	1 May 1997	7 June 2001	5 May 2005
United Kingdom														
Electorate	DZ5P	35 894	35 957	39 615	40 256	DZ6V	40 256	41 573	42 704	43 666	43 719	43 846	44 403	44 246
Average-electors per seat	DZ5T	57.0	57.1	62.9	63.4	DZ6R	63.4	65.5	66.7	67.2	67.2	66.5	67.4	68.5
Valid votes counted	DZ5X	27 657	27 265	28 345	31 340	DZ6N	29 189	31 221	30 671	32 530	33 614	31 286	26 367	27 149
As percentage of electorate	DZ63	77.1	75.8	71.5	77.9	DZ6J	72.5	75.1	71.8	74.5	76.7	71.4	59.4	61.4
England and Wales														
Electorate	DZ5Q	31 610	31 695	34 931	35 509	DZ6W	35 509	36 695	37 708	38 568	38 648	38 719	39 228	39 266
Average-electors per seat	DZ5U	57.8	57.9	63.9	64.3	DZ6S	64.3	66.5	67.2	68.8	68.8	68.0	68.9	69.0
Valid votes counted	DZ5Y	24 384	24 116	24 877	27 735	DZ6O	25 729	27 609	27 082	28 832	29 897	27 679	23 243	24 097
As percentage of electorate	DZ64	77.1	76.1	71.2	78.1	DZ6K	72.5	75.2	71.8	74.8	77.5	71.5	59.3	61.4
Scotland														
Electorate	DZ5R	3 393	3 360	3 659	3 705	DZ6X	3 705	3 837	3 934	3 995	3 929	3 949	3 984	3 840
Average-electors per seat	DZ5V	47.8	47.3	51.5	52.2	DZ6T	52.2	54.0	54.6	55.5	54.6	54.8	55.3	65.1
Valid votes counted	DZ5Z	2 635	2 553	2 688	2 887	DZ6P	2 758	2 917	2 825	2 968	2 931	2 817	2 313	2 334
As percentage of electorate	DZ65	77.6	76.0	73.5	77.9	DZ6L	74.5	76.0	71.8	74.3	74.2	71.3	58.1	60.8
Northern Ireland														
Electorate	DZ5S	891	902	1 025	1 027	DZ6Y	1 037	1 028	1 050	1 090	1 141	1 178	1 191	1 140
Average-electors per seat	DZ5W	74.2	75.2	85.4	85.6	DZ6U	86.4	85.6	61.8	64.1	67.1	65.4	66.2	63.3
Valid votes counted	DZ62	638	596	779	718	DZ6Q	702	696	765	730	785	791	810	718
As percentage of electorate	DZ66	71.7	66.1	76.0	69.9	DZ6M	67.7	67.7	72.9	67.0	68.8	67.1	68.0	62.9
Members of Parliament elected: (numbers)	DZV7	630	630	630	635	DZV8	635	635	650	650	651	659	659	646
Conservative	DZ67	303	253	330	296	DZ6D	276	339	396	375	336	165	166	198
Labour	DZ68	317	363	287	301	DZ6E	319	268	209	229	271	418	412	355
Liberal Democrat[2]	DZ69	9	12	6	14	DZ6F	13	11	23	22	20	46	52	62
Scottish National Party	DZ6A	–	–	1	7	DZ6G	11	2	2	3	3	6	5	6
Plaid Cymru	DZ6B	–	–	–	2	DZ6H	3	2	2	3	4	4	4	3
Other[3]	DZ6C	1	2	6	15	DZ6I	13	13	18	18	17	20	20	22

1 The Representation of the People Act 1969 lowered the minimum voting age from 21 to 18 years with effect from 16 February 1970.
2 Liberal before 1992. The figures for 1983 and 1987 include six and five MPs respectively who were elected for the Social Democratic Party.
3 Including the Speaker.

Sources: British Electoral Facts 1832-2006.;
University of Plymouth for the Electoral Commission: 01752 233207

2.2 Parliamentary by-elections
United Kingdom

	May 1997 - June 2001	General[1,2] Election May 1997	June 2001 - November 2004	General[1] Election June 2001	May 2005 - July 2007	General[1] Election May 2005
Numbers of by-elections	17		6		7	
Votes recorded						
By party (percentages)						
Conservative	27.0	25.1	17.7	21.2	20.5	22.6
Labour	29.7	40.1	40.8	58.3	29.1	38.1
Liberal Democrat	22.1	14.4	31.3	13.7	29.0	21.7
Scottish National Party	6.0	4.1	-	-	7.6	5.8
Plaid Cymru	2.5	2.3	2.7	2.1	0.8	0.3
Other	12.7	14.1	7.4	4.7	13.0	11.6
Total votes recorded (percentages)	100.0	100.0	100.0	100.0	100.0	100.0
(thousands)	435	723	140	205	222	304

1 Votes recorded in the same seats in the previous General Election.
2 Proportions of 'other' votes inflated by the fact that votes were cast for the retiring Speaker as 'The Speaker seeking re-election' and not as a party candidate.

Source: University of Plymouth for the Electoral Commission: 01752 233207

2.3 Devolved assembly elections
Wales and Scotland

Thousands and percentages

		6 May 1999	1 May 2003	3 May 2007
Welsh Assembly				
Electorate	E28K	2 205	2 230	2 248
Average-electors per seat[1]	E28N	55.1	55.7	56.2
Valid votes counted	E28Q	1 023	850	978
As percentage of electorate	E28T	46.4	38.1	43.5
Members elected:[2] (numbers)	E2XI	60	60	60
Conservative	E2WG	9	11	12
Labour	E2WU	28	30	26
Liberal Democrat	E2WW	6	6	6
Plaid Cymru	E2X3	17	12	15
Other	E2WY	–	1	1
Scottish Parliament				
Electorate	E28L	4 024	3 879	3 899
Average-electors per seat[1]	E28O	55.1	53.1	53.4
Valid votes counted	E28R	2 342	1 916	2 017
As percentage of electorate	E28U	58.2	49.4	51.7
Members elected:[3] (numbers)	E2XJ	129	129	129
Conservative	E2WH	18	18	17
Labour	E2WV	56	50	46
Liberal Democrat	E2WX	17	17	16
Scottish National Party	E2X4	35	27	47
Other	E2WZ	3	17	3

1 This is the average in each first-past-the-post constituency. Additional members are then elected on the basis of a regional 'list' vote.
2 Comprising 40 from constituencies and 20 from the regional 'list'.
3 Comprising 73 from constituencies and 56 from the regional 'list'.

Sources: British Electoral Facts 1832-2006;
University of Plymouth for the Electoral Commission: 01752 233207

2.4 Devolved assembly elections
Northern Ireland

Thousands and percentages

		25 June 1998	26 Nov 2003	8 Mar 2007
Electorate	E28M	1 179	1 098	1 108
Average-electors per seat[1]	E28P	65.5	61.0	61.6
Valid votes counted	E28S	810	702	690
As percentage of electorate	E28V	68.7	64.0	63.0
Members elected: (numbers)	E2XK	108	108	108
Alliance Party	E2X5	6	6	7
SDLP	E2X6	24	18	16
Sinn Fein	E2X7	18	24	28
Democratic Unionist Party	E2X8	20	30	36
UK Unionist Party	E2X9	5	1	–
Ulster Unionist Party	E2XA	28	27	18
Other	E2X2	7	2	3

1 This is the average in each Westminster constituency. Six members are elected by single transferable vote (STV) in each constituency.

Sources: British Electoral Facts 1832-2006;
University of Plymouth for the Electoral Commission: 01752 233207

International development

Chapter 3

International development

Overseas development assistance

(Tables 3.1 and 3.2)

The Department for International Development (DFID) is the UK government department with lead responsibility for overseas development. DFID's aim is to eliminate poverty in poorer countries through achievement of the Millennium Development Goals (MDGs) by 2015. Statistics relating to international development are published on a financial year basis and on a calendar year basis. Statistics on a calendar year basis allow comparisons of aid expenditure with other donor countries. Aid flows can be measured before (gross) or after (net) deductions of repayments of principal on past loans. These tables show only the gross figures.

Aid is provided in two main ways: bilateral funding is provided directly to partner countries, while multilateral funding is provided through international organisations.

Funds can only be classified as multilateral if the organisation managing them is registered with the Development Assistance Committee (DAC) of the Organisation for Economic Co-operation and Development (OECD). The list held by the DAC also highlights some bodies that might appear to be multilateral but are actually bilateral (in particular this latter category includes some international non-governmental organisations such as the International Committee of the Red Cross and some Public-Private Partnerships such as the Global Alliance for Vaccines and Immunisation). The DAC list of multilaterals is updated annually based on members nominations and organisations must be engaged in development work to be classified as multilateral aid channels.[1]

While core funding to multilateral organisations is always classified as multilateral expenditure, additional funding channelled through multilaterals is often classified as bilateral expenditure. This would be the case in circumstances where a DFID country office transfers some money to a multilateral organisation such as the United Nations (UN) agency for a particular programme in that country or region. That is where DFID has control over what the money is being spent on and/or where it is being spent. Likewise, if DFID responds to an emergency appeal from an agency for a particular country

or area, the funds will be allocated as bilateral spend to that country or region. As a result, some organisations, such as UN agencies, have some of their DFID funding classified as bilateral and some as multilateral.

DFID is planning to introduce a new activity reporting system between 2007/08 and 2009/10. The new system will integrate all DFID's current financial and project management systems. To coincide with the introduction of the new system, DFID is reviewing how it classifies its aid delivery types. The outcome of this review may lead to the introduction of a new set of classifications which may result in changes to format in future publications.

Table 3.1 shows the main groups of multilateral agencies, the International Development Association being the largest in the World Bank Group.

Bilateral assistance takes various forms:

Financial Aid – Poverty Reduction Budget Support (PRBS) – funds provided to developing countries for them to spend in support of their expenditure programmes whose long-term objective is to reduce poverty. Funds are spent using the overseas governments' own financial management, procurement and accountability systems to increase ownership and long term sustainability. PRBS can take the form of a general contribution to the overall budget – general budget support – or support with a more restricted focus which is earmarked for a specific sector – sector budget support.

Other Financial Aid – funding of projects and programmes such as Sector Wide Programmes not classified as PRBS. Financial aid in its broader sense covers all bilateral aid expenditure other than technical cooperation and administrative costs, but Statistics on International Development (SID) separately categorises Humanitarian Assistance, DFID Debt Relief, and 'other bilateral aid'. Aid and Trade Provision which was previously identified in SID has now been merged into 'other financial aid' as it is a rapidly declining flow.

Technical Co-operation – activities designed to enhance the knowledge, intellectual skills, technical expertise or the productive capability of people in recipient countries. It also covers funding of services which contribute to the design or implementation of development projects and programmes.

This assistance is mainly delivered through research and development, the use of consultants, training (generally overseas partners visiting the UK or elsewhere for a training programme) and employment of 'other personnel' (non-DFID experts on fixed term contracts). This latter category is growing less significant over time as existing contracted staff reach the end of their assignments.

---

[1] Money may be classified as bilateral while a case is being made for a new multilateral organisation to be recognised.

Other Bilateral Aid – This category comprises support to the development work of UK and international voluntary organisations, grants to the British Council and for other development work by UK institutions and non-emergency special appeals through multilateral agencies. The remaining element of 'other bilateral aid' is made up of a number of categories including, for example, DFID's contributions to two multi-donor trust funds for Sudan, the Development Awareness Fund and the provision of books, equipment and other supplies.

Humanitarian Assistance – provides food, aid and other humanitarian assistance including shelter, medical care and advice in emergency situations and their aftermath. Work of the conflict pools[1] is also included.

DFID Debt Relief – This includes sums for debt relief on DFID aid loans and cancellation of debt under the Commonwealth Debt Initiative (CDI). The non-CDI DFID debt relief is reported on the basis of the 'benefit to the recipient country'. This means that figures shown represent the money available to the country in the year in question that would otherwise have been spent on debt servicing. The CDI debt cancellation is reported on a 'lump sum' basis where all outstanding amounts on a loan are shown at the time the agreement to cancel is made.

CDC Investments – CDC Group plc (or CDC) replaced the former Commonwealth Development Corporation in 1999. CDC was founded in 1948 and is now the UK government's instrument for investing in the private sector in developing economies (it does so through fund management companies, of whom the largest is Actis Capital Limited Liability Partnership (LLP) as in PLC etc. CDC has activities in more than 50 developing countries. CDC provides equities and concessional loans to companies in some aid-eligible countries and these disbursements and repayments are included as UK flows. Although CDC no longer provides loans to governments, it did in the past and these existing loans can become eligible for debt relief.

Non-DFID Debt Relief – Comprises CDC Debt and Export Credit Guarantee Department (ECGD) Debt. CDC has a portfolio of loans to governments which can become eligible for debt relief under the HIPC (Heavily Indebted Poor Countries) or other debt relief deals. In 2005/06 £90 million of debts owed to CDC were reorganised. ECGD is an agency of the Department for Business, Enterprise and Regulatory Reform which provides insurance for exporters against the main risks in selling overseas and guarantees to

banks providing export finance. It also negotiates debt relief arrangements on commercial debt.

Other – This includes contributions from other government departments to Central Statistics Offices, British Council and Global Conflict Pool, and small amounts of drug related assistance funded by the Home Office and British Foreign and Commonwealth Office.

Further details on the UK's development assistance can be found in the Department for International Developments publication, Statistics on International Development, which can be found on the website www.dfid.gov.uk/pubs/files/sid2007/contents.asp. International Comparisons are available in the OECD Development Assistance Committee's annual report.

---

[1] Conflict pools are unstable regions (such as Sierra Leone) identified by the Foreign Office as requiring assistance in the form of food, shelter and military care.

3.1 Gross public expenditure on aid (GPEX)[1]
United Kingdom

£ Thousand

		1998/99	1999/00	2000/01	2001/02	2002/03	2003/04	2004/05	2005/06	2006/07
Bilateral Assistance										
Department for International Development										
Poverty Reduction Budget Support (General)	LUJS	10 000	15 000	239 900	245 500	184 500	288 750	286 500	347 320	297 553
Poverty Reduction Budget Support (Sector)	I4UJ	10 000	11 000	24 098	22 718	23 685	20 724	60 492	125 732	163 464
Other Financial Aid	LUJW	298 105	327 648	206 113	264 905	319 145	407 898	423 549	472 792	481 927
Technical Co-operation Projects	LUOS	452 253	457 188	455 401	473 519	508 574	459 755	462 633	481 052	522 722
Other Bilateral Aid	LUOT	214 027	222 123	243 834	294 386	394 669	431 881	530 435	628 325	692 082
Humanitarian Assistance	LUOU	113 711	224 700	222 431	192 446	294 981	310 602	332 318	405 978	336 473
DFID Debt Relief	LUOV	25 659	23 140	20 367	17 682	20 364	15 531	14 932	40 789	67 579
CDC Investments	LUOX	166 716	268 518	201 427	159 352	237 324	350 356	238 279	172 808	278 787
Debt Relief	EQ4B	64 926	70 101	79 850	242 097	399 844	163 059	627 402	1 588 414	1 866 591
Other	LUOY	22 221	30 620	66 978	67 795	79 459	111 197	143 564	153 535	196 122
Total	LUOZ	1 377 619	1 650 037	1 760 400	1 980 400	2 462 546	2 559 752	3 120 103	4 416 746	4 903 300
Multilateral Assistance										
European Community[2]	LUPA	754 548	752 472	727 684	748 022	901 058	1 085 594	1 224 066	1 193 806	1 125 390
World Bank Group	LUPB	173 753	167 298	243 162	220 233	222 228	382 740	206 561	273 339	592 304
IMF Poverty Reduction and Growth Facility	LUPC	18 000	17 000	–	11 147	11 434	9 417	1 767	23 728	15
Global Environmental Assistance	EQ4C	15 320	17 095	21 144	25 337	27 338	61 213	52 445	53 460	50 260
HIPC Trust Funds	EQ4D	..	..	27 518	23 400	17 855	22 910	42 123	11 094	18 666
UN Agencies	LUPD	143 894	186 146	250 835	238 551	206 659	225 657	235 008	336 350	356 527
Regional Development Banks	LUPE	66 295	67 179	54 784	75 383	90 648	80 391	82 166	77 759	123 591
Other	LUPF	17 128	18 053	18 213	19 316	66 086	41 516	60 535	36 072	70 836
Total	LUPG	1 188 939	1 225 243	1 343 341	1 361 390	1 543 307	1 909 439	1 904 671	2 005 608	2 337 590
Administrative costs	LUPH	105 481	117 561	138 261	134 214	154 127	248 698	227 769	256 451	245 893
Total Gross Public Expenditure on Aid	LUPI	2 672 038	2 992 842	3 242 002	3 476 004	4 159 979	4 717 890	5 252 544	6 678 804	7 486 783

1 See chapter text.
2 The institution, not the member states of the European Union.

Source: Department for International Development: 01355 843764.

3.2 Total bilateral gross public expenditure on aid (GPEX): by main recipient countries and regions[1]
United Kingdom

£ Thousand

		1998/99	1999/00	2000/01	2001/02	2002/03	2003/04	2004/05	2005/06	2006/07
Main recipients										
Nigeria	C227	11 127	14 395	15 940	20 561	29 287	32 630	73 076	1 227 717	1 750 694
India	LUPJ	108 968	104 016	126 700	198 576	182 708	242 736	267 510	270 065	293 706
Afghanistan	C224	3 873	5 452	7 465	50 027	76 018	99 595	98 959	126 949	123 011
Pakistan	LUPY	26 937	23 472	15 890	44 838	46 852	66 299	55 277	97 688	118 150
Cameroon	I53M	3 589	7 005	5 467	3 652	28 971	7 764	16 547	3 170	115 408
Tanzania	LUPK	77 904	74 709	110 590	203 830	102 614	162 372	130 009	114 134	115 023
Sudan	EU5S	24 201	3 189	4 912	5 598	19 222	24 663	83 964	117 114	109 917
Bangladesh	LUPM	66 494	69 670	75 005	60 375	73 246	155 364	149 152	128 258	109 313
Serbia	I53N	273	6 393	15 670	11 531	305 036	7 552	6 431	51 890	98 892
Ethiopia	C225	9 793	7 299	16 484	12 088	44 224	43 665	73 044	62 562	90 507
Malawi	LUPP	52 572	49 058	54 648	46 651	49 266	54 437	56 429	68 653	88 686
Ghana	LUPL	62 868	51 887	74 700	54 479	86 294	73 448	145 336	96 249	80 001
Congo, Dem Rep	C223	1 546	2 132	6 752	10 262	15 574	148 695	36 585	58 832	79 283
Uganda	LUPN	64 251	89 978	98 352	68 091	54 041	59 694	62 928	72 064	79 035
Iraq	C222	5 749	6 585	9 545	7 760	18 853	214 313	391 507	426 249	71 829
Kenya	EU5W	42 027	32 665	62 620	34 227	63 404	28 647	37 824	65 086	67 053
Zambia	LUPO	33 537	46 657	93 345	59 203	45 140	32 304	163 537	101 707	63 412
Indonesia	LUPZ	25 494	58 812	28 405	18 232	42 613	17 449	34 526	58 553	62 290
China	LUPS	39 190	26 246	56 740	50 266	44 386	42 406	42 476	36 854	60 086
Mozambique	LUPV	28 902	70 643	43 876	134 133	39 101	36 713	47 941	56 540	56 273
Total	LUQD	689 295	750 261	923 108	1 094 379	1 366 848	1 550 745	1 973 057	3 240 334	3 632 570
Total other countries	LUQE	688 324	899 776	837 292	886 021	1 095 698	1 009 008	1 147 046	1 176 412	1 270 730
Regional totals										
Africa	LUQF	574 450	628 719	774 692	865 317	891 954	1 051 958	1 280 003	2 423 279	2 991 871
America	LUQG	169 174	237 961	180 165	166 949	221 526	103 358	126 063	85 265	109 631
Asia	LUQH	347 776	375 839	413 294	534 954	609 138	967 820	1 241 408	1 355 615	1 072 286
Europe	LUQI	83 099	191 697	113 859	97 609	384 240	74 871	62 294	90 086	135 305
Pacific	LUQJ	20 249	7 248	5 029	6 885	5 362	4 484	3 272	3 823	2 670
World unallocated[2]	LUQK	182 871	208 574	273 363	308 686	350 327	357 262	407 063	458 678	591 537
Total Bilateral GPEX	LUQL	1 377 619	1 650 037	1 760 400	1 980 400	2 462 546	2 559 753	3 120 103	4 416 746	4 903 300

1 See chapter text.
2 Includes grants to VSO, CSOs, Research Institutions and Commonwealth Organisations based in the UK.

Source: Department for International Development: 01355 843764.

Defence

Chapter 4

Defence

This section includes figures on defence expenditure, on the size and role of the Armed Forces, and on related support activities.

Much of the material in this section can be found in *UK Defence Statistics 2007* (The Stationery Office).

Defence expenditure

(Table 4.1)

UK Defence Expenditure – the move from cash to resource accounting

Up until financial year 1998/99, government expenditure was accounted for on a cash basis. In April 1999 the introduction of Resource Accounting and Budgeting (RAB) brought in an accruals-based accounting system, although government departments were still controlled on a cash basis. This transitional accounting regime remained for two financial years. Government expenditure has been accounted for on a resource basis only since 2001/02.

The main difference arising from the adoption of RAB is that costs are accounted for as they are incurred (the principle of accruals), rather than when payment is made (the principle of cash). This gives rise to timing differences in accounting between the cash and RAB systems and also to the recognition of depreciation, which expends the cost of an asset over its useful economic life, and the cost of capital charge, equivalent to an interest charge on the net assets held on the balance sheet. At the time that RAB was introduced the cost of capital charge was 6 per cent of the net value of assets, although this was reduced to 3.5 per cent in 2003/04.

The change from cash-based accounting to resource (accruals)-based accounting, and the two-stage introduction of RAB (outlined below), has affected the time series comparability of the data.

Please refer to UK Defence Statistics 2007 Chapter 1 – Resource Accounting and Budgeting (RAB) section for a summary of the key events leading to the introduction of RAB. Back copies of this publication are available at: www.dasa.mod.uk/natstats/natstatsindex.html

Control regime

Under Resource Accounting, government departments are accountable for their spending against Resource and Capital Departmental Expenditure Limits (DELs). Spending against the Resource DEL includes current items, which are explained in the following two paragraphs. The Capital DEL, while part of the overall DEL, reflects investment spending that will appear on the department's balance sheet and be consumed over a number of years, net of the receipts from sale of assets. Departments are also responsible for Annually Managed Expenditure (AME). This spending is demand led (for example, payment of war pensions) and therefore cannot be controlled by departments in the same way.

In Stage 1 of RAB, which was introduced at the start of financial year 2001/02, the Resource DEL covered current costs such as in year personnel costs, equipment, maintenance of land and buildings. Non-cash costs, such as depreciation and the cost of capital charge, fell within Annually Managed Expenditure (AME) and were not controlled to the same degree as DELs. This allowed departments an interim period to gain experience of managing the new non-cash costs and to review their holdings of stocks and fixed assets, which impact the non-cash costs, prior to the charge impacting on the more tightly controlled DELs.

Stage 2 of RAB was introduced at the start of the financial year 2003/04. This involved the movement of the primary non-cash costs (depreciation and the cost of capital charge) from AME into the Resource DEL, and reduced the cost of capital charge to 3.5 per cent of the net value of assets.

The change in definition of the DELs, combined with volatile non-cash costs over the Stage 1 period, make time series comparisons over the period 2001/02–2003/04 complex.

From 2006/07, the MOD has transferred ownership of fixed assets into two Top Level Budgets (TLBs): Defence Estates (DE) for Land and Buildings, and Defence Equipment & Support (DE&S) for Plant and Machinery, Transport, IT and Communications equipment, and Single Use Military Equipment (SUME).

Factors affecting Cash to RAB data consistency

- There are timing differences as to when payments are recognised

- The movement of non-cash items of expenditure from AME into the Resource DEL from 2003/04 onwards has the 'apparent' effect of inflating the Resource DEL

- In financial year 2003/04 the rate of interest used to calculate the cost of capital charge was reduced from 6 per cent to 3.5 per cent

- The discount rate for provisions was changed from 3.5 per cent real to 2.2 per cent real with effect from

1 April 2005

- The discount rate for pension's liabilities was changed from 2.8 per cent real to 1.8 per cent real with effect from 1 April 2007

Resource DEL includes expenditure under the following headings:

- Equipment support: internal and contracted out costs for equipment repair and maintenance

- Stock consumption: consumption of armament, medical, dental, veterinary, oil, clothing and general stores

- Property management: estate and facilities management services and costs for building maintenance

- Movements: cost of transportation of freight and personnel

- Accommodation and utilities: charges include rent, rates, gas, electricity, water and sewerage costs

- Professional fees: fees, such as legal costs paid to professional organisations

- Fuel: relates to fuel consumption by military vehicles, ships and aircraft

- Other costs: includes stock and fixed assets written off, research and expensed development and rentals paid under operating leases

Expenditure on fixed asset categories in Capital DEL includes:

- Intangible assets: comprise the development costs of major equipment projects and Intellectual Property Rights

- Single Use Military Equipment (SUME): prior to 2004/05, this category was called Fighting Equipment. The category contains assets which only have a military use, such as tanks and fighter aircraft. Dual use items, such as those that also have a civilian use, are recorded under the other categories

- Assets under Construction: largely consist of major weapons platforms under construction in the Defence Procurement Agency, and a smaller element of buildings under construction. Once construction is complete, those platforms will transfer to the relevant Top Level Budget TLB holder as Single Use Military Equipment SUME on their balance sheets

- Transport/Capital Spares: from 2004/05 transport has been recorded as a separate category and Capital Spares has been removed as a category, with the costs previously recorded here being incorporated into Transport or SUME

- Other Costs: include, amongst others, items of Capital DEL and capital income

Annual Managed Expenditure includes:

- Other: for 2001/02 and 2002/03, AME included depreciation and the cost of capital charge. Under Stage 2 of RAB, this category now contains only demand led payments, such as cash release and cost of capital credit on nuclear provisions and QinetiQ loan repayments

In order to give a single measure of spending on public services under full resource budgeting, the Defence Spending line is presented as the sum of the resource and capital budgets, net of depreciation and impairments. This reflects the resources required plus the net investment in them, but avoids double counting the writing down of the existing capital stock and the cash outlay on new assets. Control is exercised separately on gross Capital and Resource DEL.

Service personnel

(Tables 4.2, 4.4, 4.5, 4.8 and 4.10)

The Regular Forces consist entirely of volunteer members serving on a whole-time basis, figures for which include both trained and untrained personnel and exclude Gurkhas, Full Time Reserve Service personnel, the Home Service battalions of the Royal Irish Regiment, mobilised reservists and Naval Activated Reservists.

Locally Entered Personnel are recruited outside the UK for whole-time service in special formations with special conditions of service and normally restricted locations. The Brigade of Gurkhas is an example.

The Regular Forces are supported by Reserves and Auxiliary Forces. There are both regular and volunteer Reserves. Regular Reserves consist of former Service personnel with a Reserve liability. Volunteer Reserves are open to both former service personnel and civilians. The call out liabilities of the various reserve forces differ in accordance with their roles.

All three services run cadet forces for young people and the Combined Cadet Force, which is found in certain schools where education is continued to the age of 17 or above, may operate sections for any or all of the services.

Defence

Full-Time Reserve Service personnel represent reserves serving full-time in regular posts. This was made possible by the Reserve Forces Act 1996. None existed before 1998. FTRS figures include Full Commitment (FC), Home Commitment (HC) and Limited Commitment (LC) individuals.

Home Service battalions of the Royal Irish Regiment. Up until 1 July 1992, this was the Ulster Defence Regiment. The figures for the Territorial Army include Officer Training Corps and non-regular permanent staff.

The figures for cadet forces for each service include the Combined Cadet Force. Naval Service figures include officers and civilian instructors. The Army and Royal Air Force figures exclude officers and civilian instructors.

Intake of UK regular forces from civilian life: by service

(Table 4.2)

This table shows all intakes to UK Regular Forces including re-enlistments and rejoined reservists.

Formation of the armed forces

(Table 4.3)

This table shows the number of units which comprise the 'teeth' elements of the Armed Forces and excludes supporting units.

Outflow of UK regular forces: by service

(Table 4.4)

This table does not include promotions to officer from other ranks and miscellaneous outflow.

Civilian personnel

(Table 4.6)

In previous years, the Ministry of Defence civilian workforce definition has reflected the historical requirement to understand the number of civil servants being directly funded. However, with changes in employment legislation and the requirement to plan the future of the civilian workforce there was a need to change the definition to a more inclusive one, better reflecting modern human resources methods and policies. In the longer term it will be used for skills planning, ensuring that the Ministry of Defence (MOD) has a well-equipped workforce able to provide the best support to the UK Armed Forces.

In summary, the change over previous years is the addition of two further categories of individuals:

> Casual personnel - those employed on a short-term casual contract

> Those not directly funded – personnel who are employed by the Ministry of Defence, but whose salaries are paid for by another department or agency. This includes personnel on loan to other government departments or working for NATO, as well as those on a career break or long term sickness absence.

These additions allow two levels of definition to be established:

> Definition - Level 1 This includes permanent and casual personnel, Royal Fleet Auxiliaries, but excludes Trading Funds. This is generally used for internal reporting and planning.

> Definition - Level 0 This contains all those at Level 1 plus Trading Funds and Locally Engaged Civilians. This is used for external reporting, including National Statistics publications CPS1 and UKDS, and Parliamentary business.

For more information on the revised civilian workforce definition, visit:
www.dasa.mod.uk/natstats/consultation/consultation.html

As from 1 April 2000 a new top level budget was formed in the centre called Defence Logistics Organisation, replacing the top level budgets CinC Fleet Support, Quarter Master General and RAF Logistics Command.

At 1 April 2007, Chief of Defence Logistics and Defence Procurement Agency merged to form Defence Equipment and Support.

The QinetiQ portion of the Defence Evaluation and Research Agency was established as a private company in July 2001. The War Pensions Agency transferred from the Department of Work and Pensions in 2001. The Clyde Dockyards were contractorised in 2002.

Data on manually paid personnel before 1999 is not available, so estimates are used. Totals and subtotals have been rounded separately and so may not appear to be the sums of their parts.

Family accommodation and defence land holdings

(Table 4.7)

In November 1996 most of the MOD's housing stock

in England and Wales was sold to a private company, Annington Homes. The homes, retained for use by service families, were leased back with the condition that the MOD releases a certain number of houses each year for disposal by Annington. The proceeds of the sale are being used to upgrade the housing stock.

The table also presents statistics of land and foreshore in the UK owned or leased by the MOD or over which it has limited rights under grants or licences. Land declared as surplus to Defence requirements is also included.

Location of Service personnel

(Table 4.8)

The figures for service personnel in England, Wales, Scotland and Northern Ireland are obtained from a different source from that used to compile the UK total. Consequently the sum of the national figures can differ from the UK total. The figures for Northern Ireland include all personnel who are serving on emergency tours of duty but exclude the former Ulster Defence Regiment, now the Home Services element of the Royal Irish Regiment. The figures for overseas countries include service personnel who are on loan to countries in the areas shown. Royal Navy and Royal Marines personnel on board ship are included in the UK figure if the ship was in home waters on the situation date or otherwise against the appropriate overseas area. All Defence Attaches and Advisers and their staffs are included under 'Other Locations' and not identified within specific areas. From 2001 the grouping of overseas locations has been changed to give a more relevant overview.

The table reports personnel against their stationed location (where they are normally based). It does not show the location of troops on operational deployments.

UK regular forces - deaths

(Table 4.9)

Rates have been standardised to 2004 Tri-Service age and gender structure. In previous publications, deaths among the Brigade of Gurkhas were excluded, even though they belong to the regular Army, owing to the lack of reliable data on date of birth from which to calculate mortality rates. Gurkhas have been included in the number of deaths provided in Table 4.9. However, they have been excluded from calculations for age and gender standardised rates.

Uniformed medical staff

(Table 4.10)

The services operate a number of hospitals in this country and in areas abroad where there is a significant British military presence. These hospitals take as patients, members of all three services and their dependants. In addition, the hospitals in the UK take civilian patients under arrangements agreed with the National Health Service. Medical support is also supplied by service medical staff at individual units, ships and stations.

Defence services and the civilian community

(Table 4.11)

Search & Rescue (SAR)

This table covers incidents attended by military Search and Rescue units. The Royal Air Force (RAF) and Royal Navy (RN) provide an essential service to the Search and Rescue (SAR) effort around the UK, forming part of the national UK SAR coverage throughout the year for air, land and maritime operations. The military SAR teams primary purpose is to recover aircrew from crashed military aircraft although, each year, over 90 per cent of callouts are to civilian incidents. The SAR force currently consists of six RAF and two RN SAR Sea King helicopter units, and four RAF mountain rescue teams operating from bases around the UK, plus specially equipped RAF Nimrod aircraft based in RAF Kinloss in Scotland.

The table also includes urgent medical incidents in which the military SAR facilities gave assistance (such as inter-hospital transfers). More than one SAR unit may be called to the same incident; consequently the number of callouts is likely to be greater than the number of incidents.

Persons moved involves moving people from a hostile environment to a safe environment or to a medical facility to receive urgent medical attention. People assisted by RAF mountain rescue teams, but subsequently transported from the scene by helicopter, are recorded as having been rescued by the helicopter unit concerned.

Fisheries Protection

The Royal Navy Fishery Protection squadron operates within the British fishery limits under contract to the Department for Environment, Food and Rural Affairs. Boardings carried out by vessels of the Scottish Executive Environment and Rural Affairs Department and the Department of Agriculture for Northern Ireland are not included.

Defence

4.1 United Kingdom defence expenditure[1]

Inclusive of non-recoverable VAT at current prices (£ million)

		2001 /02	2002 /03	2003 /04	2004 /05	2005 /06	2006 /07
Defence Spending	C228	..	..	30 861	32 515	33 164	34 045
Departmental Expenditure Limits (DEL)	SNKJ	24 456	26 148	37 174	38 323	39 751	40 654
Resource DEL	E2XV	18 905	19 944	31 266	31 798	32 911	33 457
Expenditure on personnel	SNKK	9 456	9 969	10 435	10 996	11 255	11 204
of which: Armed forces	SNKL	7 014	7 385	7 974	8 047	8 263	8 423
of which: Civilians	SNKM	2 442	2 584	2 461	2 948	2 992	2 781
Depreciation/impairments	SNKN	..	..	6 313	5 808	6 587	6 609
Cost of capital	SNKO	..	..	2 770	3 026	3 106	3 242
Equipment support	SNKP	2 419	3 135	3 804	3 623	3 542	3 793
Stock consumption	SNKQ	1 294	1 222	1 060	1 079	1 039	1 140
Property management	SNKR	1 222	1 453	1 393	1 509	1 367	1 258
Movements	SNKS	718	505	491	711	729	774
Accommodation and utilities	SNKT	573	544	643	581	735	786
Professional fees	SNKU	559	468	549	565	553	483
Fuel	SNKV	160	185	161	239	369	416
Hospitality & Entertainment	I4SS	7	7	8	6	5	4
PFI Service Charges	I4ST	..	..	..	..	870	1 148
IT & Communications	I4SU	527	628	738	678	643	719
Other costs	SNKW	1 970	1 827	2 900	2 977	2 111	1 882
Capital DEL	E2XW	5 551	6 204	5 908	6 525	6 840	7 197
Expenditure on fixed asset categories							
Intangible assets	SNKX	1 054	1 756	1 665	1 580	1 550	1 744
Land and buildings	SNKY	54	96	54	389	31	45
Single Use Military Equipment	SNKZ	42	42	90	434	402	404
Plant, machinery and vehicles	SNLA	96	45	78	124	64	32
IT and communications equipment	SNLB	87	96	183	134	180	206
Assets under construction	SNLC	4 444	3 986	3 931	4 335	4 879	5 099
Transport	E2XX	..	..	..	73	13	33
Capital spares	SNLD	360	467	581	..	..	..
Capital loan repayment	E2XY	–	–	–28	–25	–53	–8
Other Costs	E2Y3	–586	–284	–646	–519	–225	–358
Annually Managed Expenditure (AME)	SNLF	14 962	19 293	1 011	908	890	582
War pensions	SNLG	1 237	1 166	1 116	1 110	1 067	1 039
Other	SNLH	13 725	18 127	–105	–202	–177	–457

1 See chapter text. Where rounding has been used, totals and sub-totals have been rounded separately and so may not equal the sums of their rounded parts.

Sources: Ministry of Defence/DASA (Economic Statistics); 0117 913 4529/30

4.2 Intake of United Kingdom regular forces from civilian life: by service[1]

Numbers

		1996 /97	1997[2] /98	1998 /99	1999 /00	2000 /01	2001 /02	2002 /03	2003 /04	2004 /05	2005 /06	2006[3] /07
All services:												
Male	KCJB	19 230	20 190	22 560	22 390	20 410	20 950	23 040	20 760	15 660	16 410	17 830
Female	KCJC	2 940	3 340	3 440	3 160	2 610	2 700	3 240	2 710	1 900	1 740	1 960
Total	KCJA	22 170	23 530	26 000	25 550	23 020	23 650	26 280	23 470	17 560	18 150	19 790
Naval service:												
Male	KCJE	3 400	3 970	4 110	4 250	3 990	4 270	4 420	3 530	3 240	3 480	3 300
Female	KCJF	560	630	660	700	630	740	800	580	460	460	460
Total	KCJD	3 960	4 600	4 770	4 950	4 620	5 010	5 220	4 120	3 690	3 940	3 770
Army:												
Male	KCJJ	13 580	13 390	15 010	14 750	13 450	13 620	15 060	13 930	10 780	11 740	13 160
Female	KCJK	1 940	2 010	1 980	1 750	1 320	1 240	1 550	1 260	910	990	1 140
Total	KCJI	15 520	15 400	16 990	16 500	14 770	14 850	16 610	15 190	11 690	12 730	14 300
Royal Air Force:												
Male	KCJM	2 250	2 830	3 450	3 380	2 980	3 070	3 550	3 290	1 640	1 190	1 370
Female	KCJN	430	700	800	710	660	720	890	870	530	290	360
Total	KCJL	2 680	3 530	4 250	4 100	3 630	3 780	4 450	4 160	2 180	1 480	1 720

1 See chapter text.
2 The definitions of intake used have been standardised from 1997/98 to give a more consistent picture across the three services.
3 Due to ongoing validation of data from the new Personnel Administration System, Naval Service statistics from 1 October 2006, Army statistics from 1 April 2007 and RAF statistics from 1 May 2007 are provisional and subject to review.

Source: Ministry of Defence/DASA (Quad-Service): 020 7218 1470

4.3 Formation of the United Kingdom armed forces[1]
As at 1 April

Numbers

				1997	1998	1999	2000	2001	2002	2003	2004	2005	2006	2007
			Front Line Units											
Royal Navy[2]														
Submarines	KCGA		Vessels	15	15	15	16	16	16	16	15	15	14[3]	13[4]
Carriers and assault ships	KCGB		"	5	5	6	6	6	4	4	5	6	5[5]	5
Destroyers and frigates	KCGC		"	35	35	35	32	32	32	31	31	28	25[6]	25
Mine counter-measure	KCGE		"	19	19	20	21	23	22	22	19	16	16	16
Patrol ships and craft	KCGF		"	34	28	24	23	23	23	22	26	26	22[7]	22
Fixed wing aircraft[8]	KCGG		Squadrons	3	3	3	1	1	1	1	1	1	1	1
Helicopters[9]	KCGH		"	15	12	12	9	9	8	8	5	6	6	7
Royal Marines	KCGI		Commandos	3	3	3	3	3	3	3	3	3	3	3
Regular Army														
Royal Armoured Corps[10]	KCGJ		Regiments	11	11	11	10	10	10	10	10	10	10	10
Royal Artillery	KCGK		"	15	15	15	15	15	15	15	14	14	14	14
Royal Engineers[11]	KCGL		"	10	10	10	11	11	11	11	11	11	11	11
Infantry	KCGM		Battalions	40	40	40	40	40	40	40	40	40	36	36
Special Air Service	KCGN		Regiments	1	1	1	..	..	..	..	..	..	..	..
Army Air Corps[9]	KCGO		"	5	5	5	..	..	..	..	..	..	..	..
Royal Air Force														
Strike/attack	KCGP		Squadrons	6	6	5	5	5	5	5	5	5)		
Offensive support[8]	KCGQ	ZIZM	"	5	5	5	2	2	2	2	2	1)	11[12]	11[13]
Reconnaissance	KCGT		"	5	5	5	5	5	5	5	5	5)		
Air defence	KCGR		"	6	6	5	5	5	5	4	4	4	4	4
Maritime patrol	KCGS		"	3	3	3	3	3	3	3	3	3	2[14]	2
Airborne early warning[15]	KCGU		"	2	2	2	2	2	2	2	2	2	2	2
Air transport and tankers and helicopters[9]	KCGV		"	13	14	14	8	9	9	9	9	9	8	8
Search and rescue	KCGX		"	2	2	2	2	2	2	2	2	2	2	2
RAF FP Wg	GHN7		HQs	..	..	..	..	4	4	4	4	4	6	6
RAF Ground based air defence	GHN8		Squadrons	..	..	..	..	4	4	4	4	4	3	2
RAF Regiment Field[16]	GJ2F		"	..	..	..	..	6	6	6	6	6	6	6
RAF Regt (Jt CBRN)	I63Y		"	..	..	..	..	..	..	..	..	..	..	1
Tactical Provost Wg	GJ2G		HQs	–	–	–	–	–	–	–	–	–	1	1
Tactical Provost	GJ2H		Squadrons	–	–	–	–	–	–	–	–	–	2	1
Joint Helicopter Command														
Royal Navy Helicopter	JUAT		"	..	..	..	4	4	4	4	4	4	4	4
Army Aviation	JUAU		Regiments	..	..	..	5	5	5	5	5	5	5	5
Royal Air Force Helicopter	JUAV		Squadrons	..	..	..	6	6	6	6	6	6	6	5
Joint Force Harrier														
Royal Navy	JUAW		"	..	..	..	3	3	3	3	2	1	1	2[17]
Royal Air Force	JUAX		"	..	..	..	3	3	3	3	3	3	2	2

1 See chapter text.
2 Only active vessels are shown.
3 HMS Spartan was withdrawn from service during the year.
4 HMS Sovereign was withdrawn from the service during the year.
5 HMS Invincible went into Extended Readiness in late 2005.
6 HMS Cardiff, HMS Marlborough and HMS Grafton were withdrawn from service during the year.
7 HMS Leeds Castle and the NI Squadron, consisting of HMS Brecon, HMS Cottesmore and HMS Dulverton, were withdrawn from service during the year.
8 From 2000 excludes aircraft transferred to the Joint Force Harrier squadron
9 From 2000 excludes helicopters transferred to the Joint Helicopter command.

10 From 2000 includes one Armoured Regiment which is committed to the new Joint Nuclear Biological and Chemical Regiment.
11 Figure for 2000 includes an additional Close Support Regiment formed as a result of the Stategic Defence Review.
12 From 2006, these squadrons are multi-roled.
13 Includes 6 Sqn (Jag) disbanded 30 Apr 07 but not Typhoon as no Offensive capability was held on 1 Apr 07.
14 206 Sqn was disbanded on 1 Apr 05.
15 Figure for 2001 includes an embedded Operational Conversion Unit at the Sentry Operation Establishments.
16 In UKDS editions 2003 and 2004, Ground Based Air Defence and Field Squadrons for years 2001 to 2004 were also included under Regular Air Force
17 The Fleet Air Arm Strike Wing, the equivalent to an RAF Squadron, comprises 800 and 801 Naval Air Squadrons.

Source: Ministry of Defence/DASA (Tri-Service): 020 7218 0390

4.4 Outflow of United Kingdom regular forces: by service[1]

Numbers

		1996 /97	1997[2] /98	1998 /99	1999 /00	2000 /01	2001 /02	2002 /03	2003 /04	2004 /05	2005 /06	2006[3] /07
All Services:												
Male	KDNA	29 320	21 860	24 500	23 870	22 520	22 360	21 770	21 200	21 330	21 290	22 980
Female	KDNB	3 680	2 490	2 970	2 750	2 430	2 350	2 340	2 200	2 100	1 980	2 160
Total	KDNC	33 000	24 350	27 470	26 620	24 950	24 710	24 100	23 400	23 430	23 260	25 140
Naval Service:												
Male	KDND	6 190	4 650	4 920	5 160	4 480	5 110	4 680	4 230	4 150	4 000	3 820
Female	KDNE	940	620	610	630	550	690	620	540	490	480	490
Total	KDNF	7 130	5 270	5 530	5 800	5 040	5 800	5 300	4 770	4 630	4 490	4 310
Army:												
Male	KDNI	13 760	13 190	15 320	14 620	13 900	13 290	13 420	13 500	13 990	13 240	14 660
Female	KDNJ	1 600	1 280	1 730	1 580	1 330	1 090	1 140	1 090	1 080	950	1 110
Total	KDNK	15 350	14 470	17 050	16 200	15 230	14 380	14 560	14 600	15 070	14 190	15 770
Royal Air Force:												
Male	KDNL	9 380	4 020	4 250	4 080	4 140	3 960	3 670	3 470	3 200	4 050	4 500
Female	KDNM	1 140	590	640	540	540	570	580	570	530	540	560
Total	KDNN	10 520	4 610	4 890	4 620	4 680	4 530	4 250	4 040	3 730	4 590	5 070

1 See chapter text. Comprises all those who left the Regular Forces and includes deaths.

2 The definitions of outflow used have been standardised from 1997/98 to give a more consistent picture across the three services.

3 Due to ongoing validation of data from the new Personnel Administration System, Naval Service statistics from 1 October 2006, Army statistics from 1 April 2007 and RAF statistics from 1 May 2007 are provisional and subject to review.

Source: Ministry of Defence/DASA (Quad-Service): 020 7218 1470

4.5 United Kingdom Defence: service manpower strengths[1]
As at 1 April

Thousands

		1997	1998	1999	2000	2001	2002	2003	2004	2005	2006	2007
UK service personnel												
Full-time trained strength[2]	ZBTR	197.2	194.0	191.1	190.3	189.1	187.1	188.5	190.2	188.1	183.2	177.8
Trained Naval Service	ZBTS	41.7	40.5	39.3	38.9	38.5	37.5	37.6	37.5	36.4	35.6	34.9
UK regulars	ZBTT	41.7	40.4	39.1	38.5	38.0	36.8	36.6	36.4	35.5	34.9	34.3
Full-time reserve service	ZBTU	..	0.1	0.3	0.3	0.5	0.7	1.0	1.1	0.9	0.7	0.6
Trained Army[2]	ZBTV	101.4	100.9	99.8	100.2	100.4	100.4	102.0	103.6	102.4	100.6	99.3
UK regulars	ZBTW	97.8	97.5	96.3	96.5	96.3	96.0	97.6	99.4	98.5	96.8	95.4
Full-time reserve service[2]	ZBTX	..	..	0.2	0.5	0.7	0.9	1.0	0.7	0.4	0.5	0.7
Gurkhas	ZBTY	3.8	3.4	3.4	3.4	3.5	3.4	3.4	3.4	3.5	3.3	3.3
Trained Royal Air Force	ZBTZ	54.2	52.7	51.9	51.2	50.1	49.2	48.9	49.1	49.2	46.9	43.6
UK regulars	ZBUA	54.2	52.7	51.8	51.0	49.8	48.9	48.5	48.7	48.8	46.6	43.2
Full-time reserve service	ZBUB	..	..	0.1	0.2	0.3	0.3	0.4	0.4	0.4	0.3	0.3
Untrained UK regulars	ZBUC	17.2	19.7	21.5	21.6	21.5	23.0	24.2	22.5	18.3	17.5	17.5
Naval Service	ZBUD	3.5	4.1	4.6	4.3	4.4	4.9	5.0	4.5	4.4	4.5	4.5
Army	ZBUE	11.1	12.4	13.4	13.6	13.2	14.0	14.5	13.3	10.8	10.9	10.8
Royal Air Force	ZBUF	2.7	3.2	3.5	3.7	3.9	4.1	4.7	4.7	3.0	2.1	2.2
Locally Entered Personnel (excluding Gurkhas)	ZBUG	0.4	0.4	0.4	0.4	0.3	0.4	0.4	0.4	0.4	0.4	0.4
Royal Irish Regiment Home Service batallions	ZBUH	4.8	4.6	4.4	4.2	3.8	3.6	3.5	3.4	3.2	3.1	2.1
Reserve personnel	ZBUI	323.5	319.4	307.0	294.8	284.2	273.4	259.7	246.7	235.6	..	..
Regular Reserves	ZBUJ	259.4	254.9	247.6	241.6	234.9	224.9	212.6	201.4	191.5	..	..
Naval Services	ZBUK	24.1	24.8	24.7	24.2	23.5	23.5	23.2	22.8	22.2	..	..
Army[3]	ZBUL	190.1	186.2	180.5	175.5	169.8	161.1	151.5	141.9	134.2	127.6	121.8
of which mobilised:	SNEO	..	0.2	0.1	0.3	0.2	0.3	0.4	0.1	0.2	0.3	0.1
Royal Air Force	ZBUM	45.3	43.9	42.4	41.9	41.5	40.2	37.7	36.4	35.0	34.4	33.4
of which mobilised:	SNEP	..	..	–	–	–	–	–	–	–	–	–
Volunteer Reserves	ZBUN	62.6	64.5	59.4	53.2	47.3	46.3	44.9	43.4	42.3	..	42.7
Royal Naval Reserve and Royal Marine Reserve	ZBUO	4.3	4.4	4.5	4.8	4.8	5.0	4.9	4.5	4.4	..	3.0
of which mobilised:	SNEQ	..	..	..	..	..	..	0.4	0.1	..	..	0.1
Territorial Army[3]	ZBUP	57.7	57.6	52.3	45.6	41.7	40.7	39.3	38.1	37.3	38.5	36.8
of which mobilised:	SNER	..	0.6	0.5	0.8	0.4	0.5	4.1	2.9	1.5	1.1	1.0
Royal Auxilliary Air Force	ZBUQ	1.4	2.5	2.6	2.7	1.6	1.5	1.5	1.4	1.4	1.4	1.3
of which mobilised:	SNES	..	..	–	–	–	0.1	0.8	–	..	0.1	0.2
Cadet Forces	ZBUR	151.0	150.2	151.0	154.5	151.0	152.3	155.6	155.6	153.1	..	150.5
Naval Service	ZBUS	26.3	25.9	24.5	24.1	23.8	23.8	23.2	22.6	21.9	..	18.2
Army[3]	ZBUT	74.1	73.9	74.6	77.4	75.4	75.8	78.7	80.5	80.9	81.7	81.9
Royal Air Force	ZBUU	50.7	50.5	51.9	53.0	51.8	52.7	53.7	52.5	50.3	51.0	50.4

1 See chapter text.

2 Data between 1997 and 2005 have been revised due to re-examination of data.

3 Due to ongoing validation of data from a new Personnell Administration. System, 2007 Reserve data for Army are as at March 2007.

Source: Ministry of Defence/DASA (Quad-Service): 020 7218 1470

4.6 United Kingdom defence: civilian manpower strengths[1]
As at 1 April

Thousands: Full-time Equivalent

		1997	1998	1999	2000	2001	2002	2003	2004	2005	2006	2007
Ministry of Defence civilians												
MOD Head Office, HQ and centrally managed expenditure[2,3]												
Non-industrial	KDQE	22.9	22.2	21.5	19.7	19.1	20.0	21.2	22.7	24.0	24.6	19.8
Industrial	KDQF	1.2	1.1	1.0	0.9	0.9	0.8	0.7	0.6	0.7	0.8	0.8
Defence Logistics Organisation[3]												
Non-industrial	ZBTJ	..	..	..	19.7	17.8	17.3	16.4	16.5	16.5	14.1	..
Industrial	ZBTK	..	..	..	11.5	8.4	6.3	4.4	4.3	4.1	3.9	..
Defence Equipment & Support[3]												
Non-industrial	I6P5	..	..	..	..	..	..	..	..	..	..	17.3
Industrial	I6P6	..	..	..	..	..	..	..	..	..	..	3.6
Naval Service												
Non-industrial	KYCW	12.5	12.0	11.3	3.0	3.0	2.9	2.7	2.9	2.6	2.3	2.3
Industrial	KYCX	7.6	6.6	5.3	1.0	0.9	0.8	0.8	0.8	0.7	0.6	0.6
Royal Fleet Auxiliary	EQS9	2.2	2.4	2.4	2.4	2.4	2.4	2.5	2.3	2.3	2.3	2.4
Army												
Non-industrial	KDQK	22.4	21.7	21.6	16.3	16.4	16.0	16.0	14.7	14.5	13.4	12.7
Industrial	KDQL	13.8	12.1	10.6	5.8	5.7	5.5	5.4	5.6	5.5	5.2	5.3
Royal Air Force												
Non-industrial	KDQM	11.5	11.7	12.2	7.1	7.0	7.1	7.0	7.3	7.0	6.7	6.0
Industrial	KDQN	7.8	7.3	7.1	4.5	4.4	4.3	4.4	4.4	4.0	4.0	3.0
Level 1 Total	C7PE	101.9	97.1	94.1	91.9	86.0	83.6	81.5	82.2	82.0	78.1	73.8
Non-industrial	C7PF	69.4	67.6	66.6	65.8	63.4	63.4	63.3	64.1	64.7	61.3	58.1
Industrial	C7PG	30.3	27.1	25.1	23.7	20.2	17.8	15.7	15.7	15.0	14.5	13.3
Royal Fleet Auxiliary	EQT2	2.2	2.4	2.4	2.4	2.4	2.4	2.5	2.3	2.3	2.3	2.4
Locally engaged overseas	KDQA	15.9	15.2	14.9	14.8	13.3	14.1	13.8	15.4	15.7	15.1	14.2
Non-industrial	KDQT	7.0	6.7	6.7	6.7	6.3	6.5	6.5	7.3	..	..	..
Industrial	KDQU	8.9	8.4	8.1	8.2	7.0	7.6	7.4	8.1	..	..	..
Trading funds	GQHI	15.5	14.0	14.0	14.5	18.8	12.4	12.2	11.4	10.8	10.7	10.1
Level 0 Total	C7PH	133.3	126.3	123.0	121.3	118.2	110.1	107.6	109.0	108.5	103.9	98.0

1 See chapter text. Individuals on temporary and geographic (T&G) promotion are classed as non-industrial. From 2004, personnel who cannot be correctly allocated to Top Level Budgets (TLBs) are included with the Centre figures (numbering approx 200 in 2006).
2 The MOD Head Office, HQ and centrally managed expenditure budgetary area was formerly referred to as Centre.
3 At 1 April 2007, the Defence Logistics Organisation and the Defence Procurement Agency (formerly part of the MOD Head Office, HQ and centrally managed expenditure budgetary area) merged to form Defence Equipment & Support.

Source: Ministry of Defence/DASA (Quad-Service): 020 7218 5236

4.7 Family accommodation and defence land holdings[1]
As at 1 April

Thousands and thousand hectares

		1997	1998	1999	2000	2001	2002	2003	2004	2005	2006	2007
Family accommodation (thousands)												
United Kingdom: Total	KDPA	68.6	67.3	65.5	64.8	59.2	55.8	53.8	52.8	51.9	51.8	51.1
Land holdings												
United Kingdom												
Land[2]	KDPF	221.0	220.0	220.2	219.9	224.3	222.4	221.4	221.3	222.1	222.0	222.0
Foreshore[2]	KDPH	18.6	18.6	18.6	18.6	18.6	18.6	18.6	18.6	18.6	18.6	18.6
Rights held	KDPJ	124.5	124.5	124.8	124.8	124.8	124.9	131.1	131.1	124.9	124.9	124.9
Defence land[3]												
Used for agricultural purposes	KDPL	96.2	103.5	114.5	92.2	98.6	91.8	103.0	100.5	106.3	..[3]	..[3]
Used for grazing only	KDPM	51.9	59.6	65.5	50.3	66.6	60.0	70.2	68.3	71.0	..	..
Full agricultural use	KDPN	44.3	43.9	49.0	41.9	32.0	31.8	32.8	32.2	35.3	..	..

1 See chapter text.
2 Freehold and leasehold.
3 Following changes in the tenancies of agricultural land, these data are no longer available. Alternative data are being sought.

Sources: Ministry of Defence/Defence Housing Executive: 020 7305 3051;
Ministry of Defence/Defence Estates: 0121 311 3818

Defence

4.8 Location of United Kingdom service personnel[1]
As at 1 July

Thousands

		1997	1998	1999	2000	2001	2002	2003	2004	2005	2006	2007[12]
UK Service personnel, Regular Forces:												
UK distribution[2,3]												
In United Kingdom[4]	KDOB	171.6	173.4	171.7	170.3	172.0	..	..	..	169.7	167.3	161.4
England	KDOC	142.6	144.6	144.3	143.0	144.1	..	..	..	145.0	142.1	141.4
Wales	KDOD	3.3	3.2	3.3	3.2	2.6	..	..	..	2.9	3.3	2.6
Scotland	KDOE	13.9	14.2	14.9	15.1	14.5	..	..	..	13.2	13.5	12.6
Northern Ireland	KDOF	11.5	11.0	9.0	8.4	9.4	..	..	..	7.0	6.8	4.8
Global location[2,3]												
United Kingdom	MKCN	167.5	165.0	161.0	163.1	162.8	..	..	..	169.7	167.3	161.4
Overseas	KDOG	42.6	43.1	47.1	43.0	40.9	..	..	..	29.2	28.5	28.0
Mainland European States[4,5]	KDOI	6.2	6.9	15.2	8.2	8.6	..	..	..	27.0	26.6	26.2
Germany[6]	KDOH	21.2	20.3	18.0	19.5	17.3	..	..	..	22.2	22.0	21.7
Balkans	MKCO	..	..	..	..	..	..	..	..	0.1	–	0.1
Mediterranean[7,8]	KDOM	0.3	1.2	1.3	1.1	2.3	..	..	..	..	..	..
Gibraltar	KDOJ	0.5	0.5	0.6	0.6	0.5	..	..	..	0.4	0.3	0.3
Cyprus	KDOL	3.9	3.6	3.6	3.5	3.5	..	..	..	3.2	3.0	3.0
Far East/Asia[9]	MKCT	1.5	0.3	0.3	1.0	0.3	..	..	..	0.3	0.3	0.2
Africa[10]	MKCP	..	..	..	..	–	..	..	..	0.6	0.6	0.5
North America	MKCQ	..	..	..	..	2.5	..	..	..	0.7	0.7	0.7
Central/South America	MKCR	..	..	..	..	–	..	..	..	0.1	0.1	0.1
Falkland Islands	MKCS	..	..	..	..	0.8	..	..	..	0.3	0.3	0.3
Other locations, including unallocated	KDOQ	9.0	10.4	8.2	9.1	5.1	..	..	..	1.1	1.0	1.1
Locally entered service personnel:[11]												
United Kingdom	KDOS	2.1	2.1	2.0	2.1	2.3	2.6	2.6	2.6	2.1	2.2	2.4
Gibraltar	KDOT	0.2	0.4	0.4	0.3	0.4	0.4	0.4	0.4	0.4	0.4	0.4
Hong Kong	KDOV	0.7	..	..	..	..	..	..	..	..	..	..
Brunei	KDOW	1.0	0.9	0.8	0.8	0.8	0.8	0.8	0.7	0.8	0.8	0.8
India/Nepal	KDOX	0.9	0.5	0.5	0.5	0.4	0.3	0.4	0.4	0.3	0.3	0.1
Total	KDOK	4.7	4.0	3.7	3.7	3.9	4.2	4.1	4.1	3.3	3.7	3.7

1 See chapter text.
2 Prior to 2003, figures for UK distribution and global location are collated from seperate sources. Comparison is therefore not possible between the two sets of UK personnel figures.
3 Includes personnel within the UK whose location is unknown.
4 Includes the Balkans until 2002.
5 Post 2002 Mainland European States figure includes Germany, Balkans, Mediterranean, Gibraltar and Cyprus.
6 Prior to 1996, figures for the Federal Republic of Germany and Mainland European States were combined.

7 Includes Med Near East and Middle East until 2002.
8 Post 2002 Mediterranean figure is not shown separately but is included in Mainland European States figure.
9 Prior to 1997 figures include personnel serving in Hong Kong.
10 Post 2002 Africa figure includes Middle East.
11 Including Gurkhas.
12 All data for 2007 is provisional.

Source: Ministry of Defence/DASA (Quad-Service): 020 7218 1470

4.9 United Kingdom regular forces: deaths[1]

Numbers and rates per thousand

		1997	1998	1999	2000	2001	2002	2003	2004	2005	2006
Deaths											
Total	SNIA	164	165	141	147	142	147	173	169	158	190
Male	SNIB	155	157	138	143	139	138	166	163	150	183
Female	SNIC	9	8	3	4	3	9	7	6	8	7
Rates per thousand[2]											
Tri-service	SNIH	0.81	0.78	0.66	0.71	0.69	0.71	0.82	0.81	0.78	0.96
Navy	SNII	0.87	0.62	0.60	0.63	0.79	0.66	0.90	0.92	0.69	0.84
Army	SNIJ	0.93	0.87	0.72	0.78	0.70	0.82	0.79	0.78	0.81	0.93
RAF	SNIK	0.47	0.65	0.49	0.61	0.48	0.51	0.70	0.63	0.71	0.83

1 See chapter text.
2 Rates age and gender standarised to 2005 Tri-Service strengths structure.

Source: Ministry of Defence/DASA (Health Information): 01225 468615

4.10 Strength of uniformed United Kingdom medical staff[1]

As at 1 April

Numbers

		1997	1998	1999	2000	2001	2002	2003	2004	2005	2006	2007[8]
Qualified doctors:[2]												
Naval Service	KDMA	210	210	210	210	220	220	230	240	260	260	290
Army[3]	KDMB	430	440	450	460	470	490	550	600	610	650	550
Royal Air Force	KDMC	220	210	200	180	180	180	190	200	220	230	220
All Services	KDMD	870	850	860	860	870	890	970	1 040	1 090	1 140	1 060
Qualified dentists:[2]												
Naval Service	KDME	60	60	60	60	60	60	60	60	60	60	50
Army[3]	KDMF	140	140	140	140	150	140	150	150	150	140	130
Royal Air Force	KDMG	90	80	80	80	80	70	70	80	70	70	60
All Services	KDMH	290	280	290	280	290	280	270	290	280	270	240
Support staff:[4]												
Naval Service[5]	KDMI	1 020	990	970	1 000	1 030	1 010	1 060	1 110	1 110	1 120	1 130
Nursing services[5]	ZBTL	..	..	200	210	210	220	250	280	290	300	300
Support[5]	ZBTM	..	..	770	790	820	790	810	840	820	820	830
Army[3]	KDMJ	3 020	3 090	3 120	3 210	3 260	3 320	3 410	3 560	..	..	3 000
Nursing services[3,4,6]	ZBTN	..	..	520	570	610	650	710	770	770	800	790
Support[3]	ZBTO	..	..	2 600	2 640	2 650	2 670	2 700	2 800	..	..	2 210
Royal Air Force	KDMK	1 210	1 190	1 360	1 460	1 480	1 500	1 600	1 680	1 660	1 550	1 340
Nursing services[7]	ZBTP	..	..	330	400	420	450	470	480	510	480	490
Support	ZBTQ	..	..	1 030	1 060	1 070	1 050	1 130	1 200	1 160	1 070	850
All Services	KDML	5 260	5 230	5 540	5 760	5 800	5 930	6 180	6 440	..	..	..

1 See chapter text. Includes staff employed at units (including ships) and in hospitals.

2 The Medical and Dental Officers are trained only and exclude Late Entry Personnel. For 2007 includes all those individuals who hold a basic registrable qualification but may not necessarily be fully trained in their speciality. "Qualified" Doctors and Dentists refers to personnel who hold a basic registrable qualification, but may not necessarily have completed their career directed professional training, and as such may not necessarily be fully trained in their speciality.

3 Due to a change in source data, Army figures prior to 2005 cannot be verified.

4 Includes all members of the Nursing Services/Nursing Corps. From 1999, figures for support staff have been split so that nurses are separate from other support staff. From 2007, includes all medical support staff which the Defence Medical Services Department collects in its tri-service return.

5 From 2007, includes trained and untrained.

6 The 2006 Nursing Services figure is trained and untrained Soldiers with Nursing trades in the QARANC and all trained Officers in QARANC. From 2007, includes trained and untrained.

7 From 2007, includes trained and untrained.

8 Figures from 2007 provided by DMSD.

Source: Ministry of Defence/DASA (Tri- Service): 020 7218 1470

4.11 United Kingdom defence services and the civilian community[1]

Numbers

		1997	1998	1999	2000	2001	2002	2003	2004	2005	2006	2007
Military Search and rescue operations at home												
Call outs: total	GPYC	1 941	1 898	1 912	1 941	1 763	1 684	1 714	1 638	1 702	1 875	1 973
Royal Navy helicopters	GPXO	495	463	499	499	502	436	424	453	478	497	592
Royal Air Force helicopters	GPXP	1 258	1 257	1 235	1 278	1 115	1 122	1 173	1 079	1 114	1 258	1 258
Contractorised and other helicopters	GPXQ	16	20	–	–	–	–	–	–	–	1	
Royal Air Force Nimrod aircraft	GPXR	79	71	65	71	54	46	37	37	37	32	21
Other fixed wing aircraft[2]	GPXS	2	2	–	1	1	1	–	2	–	1	–
HM ships and auxilliary vessels[2]	KCMG	3	3	–	–	–	–	–	–	–	–	–
Royal Air Force mountain rescue teams	KCMH	88	82	113	92	91	79	80	67	73	86	102
Persons moved: total	KCMI	1 226	1 243	1 204	1 316	1 182	1 224	1 273	1 412	1 384	1 463	1 767
Persons moved by rescue service												
Royal Navy helicopters	GPXT	328	283	355	360	386	314	320	416	380	479	507
Royal Air Force helicopters	GPXU	877	937	832	934	781	900	922	978	907	968	1 219
Royal Air Force mountain rescue teams	GPXV	15	12	17	22	15	10	31	17	97	16	41
Other	GPXW	6	11	–	–	–	–	–	1	–	–	–
Persons moved by type of assistance												
Rescue[3]	GPXX	219	317	307	276	281	343	280	494	408	384	582
Medrescue[4]	GPXY	721	667	640	713	629	654	779	672	778	830	946
Medevac[5]	GPXZ	224	209	216	241	228	201	174	195	143	175	198
Recovery[6]	GPYA	54	43	32	29	36	21	25	33	31	43	24
Airlift[7]	GPYB	8	7	9	57	8	5	15	18	24	31	17
Search and rescue incidents: total	KCMM	1 750	1 697	1 714	1 781	1 608	1 544	1 600	1 504	1 584	1 703	1 803

Source: Ministry of Defence/DASA (Logistics): 01225 67144/72112

		1997 /98	1998 /99	1999 /00	2000 /01	2001 /02	2002 /03	2003 /04	2004 /05	2005 /06	2006 /07
Fishery protection											
Vessels boarded	KCMO	1 715	1 879	1 716	1 603	1 464	1 375	1 709	1 747	1 371	1 335

Source: Fisheries Protection - Ministry of Defence

1 See chapter text.
2 Not permanently on stand-by.
3 Rescue: Moving an uninjured person from a hostile to a benign environment.
4 Medrescue: Moving an injured casualty from a hostile environment to a medical facility.

5 Medtransfer (formerly Medevac): Moving a sick person between medical facilities such as a hospital or occasionally to move transplant organs.
6 Recovery: Moving people declared dead on scene or confirmed dead on arrival by a qualified doctor.
7 Transfer (formerly Airlift): Moving military personnel, or their families, on compassionate grounds.

Population and vital statistics

Chapter 5

Population and vital statistics

This section begins with a summary of population figures for the UK and constituent countries for 1851 to 2026, and for Great Britain from 1801 (Table 5.1). Table 5.2 analyses the components of population change. Table 5.3 gives details of the national sex and age structures for years up to the present date, with projected figures up to the year 2026. Legal marital condition of the population is shown in Table 5.4. The distribution of population at regional and local levels is summarised in Table 5.5.

In the main, historical series relate to census information, while mid-year estimates, which make allowance for under-enumeration in the census, are given for the recent past and the present (from 1961 onwards).

Population

(Tables 5.1–5.3)

Figures shown in these tables relate to the population enumerated at successive censuses (up to 1951), mid-year estimates (from 1961 to 2006) and population projections (up to 2026). Further information can be found on the National Statistics website: www.statistics.gov.uk/popest.

Population projections are 2006-based and were published by the Office for National Statistics (ONS) on 23 October 2007. Further information can be found at: www.statistics.gov.uk/cci/nugget.asp?id=1352

Definition of resident population

The estimated resident population of an area includes all people who usually live there, whatever their nationality. Members of HM and US Armed Forces in England and Wales are included on a residential basis wherever possible. HM Forces stationed outside England and Wales are not included. Students are taken to be resident at their term time address.

The projections of the resident population of the UK and constituent countries were prepared by the National Statistics Centre for Demography within ONS, in consultation with the Registrars General, as a common framework for use in national planning in a number of different fields. New projections are made every second year on assumptions regarding future fertility, mortality and migration which seem most appropriate on the basis of the statistical evidence available at the time.

The population projections in Tables 5.1 – 5.3 are based on the estimates of the population of the UK at mid-2006 made by the Registrars General.

Marital condition (de jure): estimated population

(Table 5.4)

This table shows population estimates by marital status.

Geographical distribution of the population

(Table 5.5)

The population enumerated in the censuses for 1911-1951, and the mid-year population estimates for later years, are provided for standard regions of the UK, for metropolitan areas, for broad groupings of local authority districts by type within England and Wales, and for some of the larger cities. Projections of future sub-national population levels are prepared from time to time by the Registrar General, but are not shown in this publication.

Migration into and out of the UK

(Tables 5.7–5.9)

A migrant is defined as a person who changes his or her country of usual residence for a period of at least a year, so that the country of destination effectively becomes the country of usual residence.

The main source of international migration data is the International Passenger Survey (IPS). This is a continuous voluntary sample survey that provides information on passengers entering and leaving the UK by the principal air, sea and tunnel routes. Being a sample survey, the IPS is subject to some uncertainty; therefore it should be noted that international migration estimates, in particular the difference between inflow and outflow, may be subject to large sampling errors. The IPS excludes routes between the Channel Islands and Isle of Man and the rest of the world.

The IPS data are supplemented with three types of additional information in order to provide a full picture of total international migration:

1. The IPS is based on intentions to migrate and intentions are liable to change. Adjustments are made for visitor switchers (those who intend to stay in the UK or abroad for less than one year but subsequently stay for longer and become migrants) and for migrant switchers (those who intend to stay in the UK or abroad for one year or more but then return earlier so are no longer migrants).

These adjustments are primarily based on IPS data but for years prior to 2001, Home Office data on short-term visitors who were subsequently granted an extension of stay for a year or longer for other reasons have been incorporated.

2. Home Office data on applications for asylum and dependants of asylum seekers entering the UK are used to estimate inflows of asylum seekers and dependants not already captured by the IPS. In addition, Home Office data on removals and refusals are used to estimate outflows of failed asylum seekers not identified by the IPS.

3. Migration flows between the UK and the Irish Republic are added to these data, as the IPS did not cover this route until recently and the quality of these data are still being assessed. Migration flows are obtained mainly from the Quarterly National Household Survey and are agreed between the Irish Central Statistics Office and ONS.

The international migration estimates in Table 5.7 are derived from all these sources and represent total international migration. The estimates in Tables 5.8 and 5.9 are based on the IPS only (without the three adjustments outlined above).

Grants for settlement in the United Kingdom

(Table 5.10)

This table presents in geographic regions, the statistics of individual nationalities, arranged alphabetically within each region. The figures are on a different basis from those derived from IPS (Tables 5.8 and 5.9) and relate only to people subject to immigration control. Persons granted settlements are allowed to stay indefinitely in the UK. They exclude temporary migrants such as students and generally relate only to non-European Economic Area nationals. Settlement can occur several years after entry to the country.

Applications received for asylum in the UK, excluding dependants

(Table 5.11)

This table shows statistics of applications for asylum in the UK. Figures are shown for the main applicant nationalities by geographic region. The basis of assessing asylum applications, and hence of deciding whether to grant asylum in the UK, is the 1951 United Nations Convention on Refugees.

Marriages

(Table 5.12)

The figures in this table relate to marriages solemnised in the constituent countries of the UK. They take no account of the growing trend towards marrying abroad.

Divorces

(Tables 5.13 and 5.14)

A marriage may be either dissolved following a petition for divorce and the granting of a decree absolute, or annulled following a petition for nullity and the awarding of a decree of nullity. The first group of decrees are known as dissolutions of marriage and the second as annulments of marriage. In Table 5.13 the term 'divorce' includes both types of decrees, although strictly speaking, it should refer only to dissolutions.

Births

(Tables 5.15–5.17)

For Scotland and Northern Ireland the number of births relate to those registered during the year. For England and Wales the figures up to and including 1930–32 are for those registered, while later figures relate to births occurring in each year.

All data for England and Wales and for Scotland include births occurring in those countries to mothers not usually resident in them. Data for Northern Ireland, and hence the UK, prior to 1981 include births occurring in Northern Ireland to non-resident mothers; from 1981, such births are excluded.

Deaths

(Tables 5.19 and 5.21)

The figures relate to the number of deaths registered during each calendar year.

Infant and maternal mortality

(Table 5.20)

On 1 October 1992 the legal definition of a stillbirth was altered from a baby born dead after 28 completed weeks gestation or more, to one born after 24 completed weeks of gestation or more. The 258 stillbirths of 24 to 27 weeks gestation that which occurred between 1 October and 31 December 1992 are excluded from this table.

Population and vital statistics

Life tables

(Table 5.22)

The current set of interim life tables are constructed from the estimated populations in 2004–2006 and corresponding data on births, infant deaths and deaths by individual age occurring in those years.

The estimates used in these interim life tables are the estimates, or revised estimates, issued on the following dates:

Mid-year population estimates	England	Wales	Scotland	Northern Ireland
2004	August 2007	August 2007	July 2007	July 2005
2005	August 2007	August 2007	July 2007	October 2006
2006	August 2007	August 2007	July 2007	July 2007

Adoptions

(Tables 5.23)

The figures shown within these tables relate to the date the adoption was entered in the Adopted Children Register. Figures based on the date of court order are available for England and Wales in the volume Marriage, divorce and adoption statistics 2003 (no. 31 in the FM2 series) available on the National Statistics website www.statistics.gov.uk, or from the enquiry point in the ONS shown at the foot of the tables.

5.1 Population summary: by country and sex

Thousands

	United Kingdom			England and Wales			Wales	Scotland			Northern Ireland		
	Persons	Males	Females	Persons	Males	Females	Persons	Persons	Males	Females	Persons	Males	Females
Enumerated population: Census figures													
1801	..	..	..	8 893	4 255	4 638	587	1 608	739	869	..	..	..
1851	22 259	10 855	11 404	17 928	8 781	9 146	1 163	2 889	1 376	1 513	1 442	698	745
1901	38 237	18 492	19 745	32 528	15 729	16 799	2 013	4 472	2 174	2 298	1 237	590	647
1911	42 082	20 357	21 725	36 070	17 446	18 625	2 421	4 761	2 309	2 452	1 251	603	648
1921[1]	44 027	21 033	22 994	37 887	18 075	19 811	2 656	4 882	2 348	2 535	1 258	610	648
1931[1]	46 038	22 060	23 978	39 952	19 133	20 819	2 593	4 843	2 326	2 517	1 243	601	642
1951	50 225	24 118	26 107	43 758	21 016	22 742	2 599	5 096	2 434	2 662	1 371	668	703
1961	52 709	25 481	27 228	46 105	22 304	23 801	2 644	5 179	2 483	2 697	1 425	694	731
Resident population: mid-year estimates													
	DYAY	BBAB	BBAC	BBAD	BBAE	BBAF	KGJM	BBAG	BBAH	BBAI	BBAJ	BBAK	BBAL
1971	55 928	27 167	28 761	49 152	23 897	25 255	2 740	5 236	2 516	2 720	1 540	755	786
1972	56 097	27 259	28 837	49 327	23 989	25 339	2 755	5 231	2 513	2 717	1 539	758	782
1973	56 223	27 332	28 891	49 459	24 061	25 399	2 773	5 234	2 515	2 719	1 530	756	774
1974	56 236	27 349	28 887	49 468	24 075	25 393	2 785	5 241	2 519	2 722	1 527	755	772
1975	56 226	27 361	28 865	49 470	24 091	25 378	2 795	5 232	2 516	2 716	1 524	753	770
1976	56 216	27 360	28 856	49 459	24 089	25 370	2 799	5 233	2 517	2 716	1 524	754	770
1977	56 190	27 345	28 845	49 440	24 076	25 364	2 801	5 226	2 515	2 711	1 523	754	769
1978	56 178	27 330	28 849	49 443	24 067	25 375	2 804	5 212	2 509	2 704	1 523	754	770
1979	56 240	27 373	28 867	49 508	24 113	25 395	2 810	5 204	2 505	2 699	1 528	755	773
1980	56 330	27 411	28 919	49 603	24 156	25 448	2 816	5 194	2 501	2 693	1 533	755	778
1981	56 357	27 412	28 946	49 634	24 160	25 474	2 813	5 180	2 495	2 685	1 543	757	786
1982	56 291	27 364	28 927	49 582	24 119	25 462	2 804	5 165	2 487	2 677	1 545	757	788
1983	56 316	27 371	28 944	49 617	24 133	25 484	2 803	5 148	2 479	2 669	1 551	759	792
1984	56 409	27 421	28 989	49 713	24 185	25 528	2 801	5 139	2 475	2 664	1 557	761	796
1985	56 554	27 489	29 065	49 861	24 254	25 606	2 803	5 128	2 470	2 658	1 565	765	800
1986	56 684	27 542	29 142	49 999	24 311	25 687	2 811	5 112	2 462	2 649	1 574	768	805
1987	56 804	27 599	29 205	50 123	24 371	25 752	2 823	5 099	2 455	2 644	1 582	773	809
1988	56 916	27 652	29 265	50 254	24 434	25 820	2 841	5 077	2 444	2 633	1 585	774	812
1989	57 076	27 729	29 348	50 408	24 510	25 898	2 855	5 078	2 443	2 635	1 590	776	814
1990	57 237	27 819	29 419	50 561	24 597	25 964	2 862	5 081	2 444	2 637	1 596	778	818
1991	57 439	27 909	29 530	50 748	24 681	26 067	2 873	5 083	2 445	2 639	1 607	783	824
1992	57 585	27 977	29 608	50 876	24 739	26 136	2 878	5 086	2 445	2 640	1 623	792	831
1993	57 714	28 039	29 675	50 986	24 793	26 193	2 884	5 092	2 448	2 644	1 636	798	837
1994	57 862	28 108	29 754	51 116	24 853	26 263	2 887	5 102	2 453	2 649	1 644	802	842
1995	58 025	28 204	29 821	51 272	24 946	26 326	2 889	5 104	2 453	2 650	1 649	804	845
1996	58 164	28 287	29 877	51 410	25 030	26 381	2 891	5 092	2 447	2 645	1 662	810	851
1997	58 314	28 371	29 943	51 560	25 113	26 446	2 895	5 083	2 442	2 641	1 671	816	856
1998	58 475	28 458	30 017	51 720	25 201	26 519	2 900	5 077	2 439	2 638	1 678	819	859
1999	58 684	28 578	30 106	51 933	25 323	26 610	2 901	5 072	2 437	2 635	1 679	818	861
2000	58 886	28 690	30 196	52 140	25 438	26 702	2 907	5 063	2 432	2 631	1 683	820	862
2001	59 113	28 832	30 281	52 360	25 574	26 786	2 910	5 064	2 434	2 630	1 689	824	865
2002[2]	59 323	28 964	30 359	52 572	25 704	26 868	2 920	5 055	2 432	2 623	1 697	829	868
2003[2]	59 557	29 109	30 449	52 797	25 841	26 956	2 931	5 057	2 435	2 623	1 703	833	870
2004[2]	59 846	29 278	30 568	53 057	25 995	27 062	2 946	5 078	2 446	2 632	1 710	836	874
2005[2]	60 238	29 497	30 741	53 419	26 197	27 223	2 954	5 095	2 456	2 639	1 724	844	880
2006	60 587	29 694	30 893	53 729	26 371	27 358	2 966	5 117	2 469	2 647	1 742	853	888
Resident population: projections (mid-year)[3]													
	C59J	C59K	C59L	C59M	C59N	C59O	C59P	C59Q	C59R	C59S	C59T	C59U	C59V
2011	62 761	30 893	31 868	55 744	27 482	28 262	3 038	5 206	2 520	2 685	1 812	890	921
2016	64 975	32 088	32 887	57 837	28 610	29 226	3 113	5 270	2 557	2 713	1 868	921	947
2021	67 191	33 252	33 938	59 943	29 717	30 226	3 186	5 326	2 587	2 739	1 922	949	973
2026	69 260	34 313	34 946	61 931	30 737	31 194	3 248	5 363	2 605	2 758	1 966	972	994
2031	71 100	35 243	35 857	63 727	31 646	32 081	3 296	5 374	2 609	2 765	1 999	988	1 011

1 Figures for Northern Ireland are estimated. The population at the Census of 1926 was 1 257 thousand (608 thousand males and 649 thousand females).
2 Mid 2002 to mid 2005 population estimates for the UK and England & Wales have been updated to include the latest revised revised estimates that take into account improved estimates of international migration.
3 These projections are 2006-based. See chapter text for more detail.

Sources: Office for National Statistics: 01329 813233;
General Register Office for Scotland;
Northern Ireland Statistics and Research Agency

Population and vital statistics

5.2 Population changes: by country

	Population[1] at start of period	Average annual change				
		Overall annual change	Births	Deaths[2]	Natural change	Net migration and other changes
United Kingdom						
1901 - 1911	38 237	385	1 091	624	467	-82
1911 - 1921	42 082	195	975	689	286	-92
1921 - 1931	44 027	201	824	555	268	-67
1931 - 1951	46 038	213	793	603	190	22
1951 - 1961	50 225	258	839	593	246	12
1961 - 1971	52 807	312	962	638	324	-12
1971 - 1981	55 928	42	736	666	69	-27
1981 - 1991	56 357	108	757	655	103	5
1991 - 2001	57 439	161	731	631	100	61
2001 - 2005[3]	59 113	281	692	600	92	189
2001 - 2006	59 113	295	701	595	106	189
2011 - 2021	62 761	443	802	551	252	191
England and Wales						
1901 - 1911	32 528	354	929	525	404	-50
1911 - 1921	36 070	182	828	584	244	-62
1921 - 1931	37 887	207	693	469	224	-17
1931 - 1951	39 952	193	673	518	155	38
1951 - 1961	43 758	244	714	516	197	47
1961 - 1971	46 196	296	832	560	272	23
1971 - 1981	49 152	48	638	585	53	-5
1981 - 1991	49 634	111	664	576	89	23
1991 - 2001	50 748	155	647	556	92	63
2001 - 2005[3]	52 360	265	618	528	90	175
2001 - 2006	52 360	274	626	524	102	172
2011 - 2021	55 744	420	722	484	238	182
Scotland						
1901 - 1911	4 472	29	131	76	54	-25
1911 - 1921	4 761	12	118	82	36	-24
1921 - 1931	4 882	-4	100	65	35	-39
1931 - 1951	4 843	13	92	67	25	-12
1951 - 1961	5 096	9	95	62	34	-25
1961 - 1971	5 184	5	97	63	34	-30
1971 - 1981	5 236	-6	70	64	6	-11
1981 - 1991	5 180	-7	66	63	3	-10
1991 - 2001	5 083	-2	60	60	-1	-1
2001 - 2005	5 064	8	53	57	-5	12
2001 - 2006	5 064	11	53	57	-4	14
2011 - 2021	5 206	12	56	52	3	9
Northern Ireland						
1901 - 1911	1 237	1	31	23	8	-6
1911 - 1921	1 251	1	29	22	7	-6
1921 - 1931	1 258	-2	30	21	9	-11
1931 - 1951	1 243	6	28	18	10	-4
1951 - 1961	1 371	6	30	15	15	-9
1961 - 1971	1 427	11	33	16	17	-6
1971 - 1981	1 540	-	28	17	11	-11
1981 - 1991	1 543	6	27	16	12	-5
1991 - 2001	1 607	8	24	15	9	-
2001 - 2005	1 689	9	22	14	7	1
2001 - 2006	1 689	10	22	14	8	3
2011 - 2021	1 812	11	25	14	10	1

1 Census enumerated population up to 1951; mid-year estimates of resident population from 1961 to 2001 and mid-2006-based projections of resident population thereafter.

2 Including deaths of non-civilians and merchant seamen who died outside the country. These numbered 577 000 in 1911-1921 and 240 000 in 1931-1951 for England and Wales; 74 000 in 1911-1921 and 34 000 in 1931-1951 for Scotland; and 10 000 in 1911-1926 for Northern Ireland.

3 Mid-2005 population estimates for the United Kingdom and England & Wales have been updated to include the latest revised estimates that take into account improved estimates of international migration.

Sources: Office for National Statistics: 01329 813233;
General Register Office for Scotland;
Northern Ireland Statistics and Research Agency

5.3 Age distribution of the resident population: by sex and country

Thousands

		United Kingdom																
		Population enumerated in Census			Estimated mid-year resident population									Projected mid-year resident population[1]			
		1901	1931	1951	1971	1981	1991[2]	2001[3]	2002	2003	2004	2005	2006	2011	2016	2021	2026
Persons: All ages	KGUA	38 237	46 038	50 225	55 928	56 357	57 439	59 114	59 323	59 557	59 846	60 238	60 587	62 761	64 975	67 191	69 260
Under 1	KGUK	938	712	773	899	730	790	663	661	680	705	716	732	794	799	802	790
1 - 4	KABA	3 443	2 818	3 553	3 654	2 726	3 077	2 819	2 753	2 706	2 686	2 713	2 765	3 104	3 191	3 217	3 188
5 - 9	KGUN	4 106	3 897	3 689	4 684	3 677	3 657	3 735	3 688	3 650	3 608	3 554	3 490	3 515	3 915	4 006	4 035
10 - 14	KGUO	3 934	3 746	3 310	4 232	4 470	3 485	3 890	3 915	3 896	3 867	3 819	3 751	3 499	3 523	3 922	4 013
15 - 19	KGUP	3 826	3 989	3 175	3 862	4 735	3 719	3 678	3 757	3 856	3 921	3 957	3 996	3 827	3 570	3 593	3 992
20 - 29	KABB	6 982	7 865	7 154	7 968	8 113	9 138	7 499	7 418	7 400	7 496	7 691	7 880	8 787	8 888	8 431	8 198
30 - 44	KABC	7 493	9 717	11 125	9 797	10 956	12 125	13 405	13 493	13 506	13 460	13 419	13 302	12 699	12 691	13 492	14 132
45 - 59	KABD	4 639	7 979	9 558	10 202	9 540	9 500	11 168	11 307	11 412	11 507	11 616	11 744	12 295	13 094	12 986	12 398
60 - 64	KGUY	1 067	1 897	2 422	3 222	2 935	2 888	2 884	2 892	2 949	3 027	3 114	3 240	3 746	3 450	3 842	4 293
65 - 74	KBCP	1 278	2 461	3 689	4 764	5 195	5 067	4 947	4 967	5 001	5 028	5 046	5 029	5 519	6 375	6 591	6 742
75 - 84	KBCU	470	844	1 555	2 159	2 677	3 119	3 296	3 344	3 398	3 431	3 420	3 416	3 539	3 827	4 362	5 135
85 and over	KGVD	61	113	224	485	603	873	1 130	1 127	1 104	1 111	1 174	1 243	1 436	1 653	1 947	2 342
School ages (5-15)	KBWU	..	13 120	7 649	9 704	9 086	7 818	8 381	8 371	8 334	8 254	8 159	8 041	7 745	8 106	8 668	8 850
Under 18	KGUD	..	10 557	13 248	15 798	14 472	13 120	13 357	13 311	13 259	13 219	13 176	13 120	13 139	13 494	14 133	14 420
Pensionable ages [5]	KFIA	2 387	4 421	6 828	9 123	10 035	10 557	10 845	10 916	11 012	11 117	11 232	11 344	12 184	12 493	12 900	13 431
Males: All ages	KGWA	18 492	22 060	24 118	27 167	27 412	27 909	28 832	28 964	29 109	29 278	29 497	29 694	30 893	32 088	33 252	34 313
Under 1	KGWK	471	361	397	461	374	403	338	338	349	362	367	374	406	409	410	404
1 - 4	KBCV	1 719	1 423	1 818	1 874	1 400	1 572	1 445	1 408	1 384	1 376	1 389	1 416	1 585	1 630	1 643	1 628
5 - 9	KGWN	2 052	1 967	1 885	2 401	1 889	1 871	1 913	1 891	1 870	1 847	1 819	1 785	1 798	1 998	2 045	2 060
10 - 14	KGWO	1 972	1 892	1 681	2 175	2 295	1 784	1 993	2 006	1 998	1 985	1 962	1 924	1 795	1 807	2 007	2 053
15 - 19	KGWP	1 898	1 987	1 564	1 976	2 424	1 905	1 879	1 935	1 989	2 018	2 030	2 060	1 975	1 842	1 854	2 054
20 - 29	KBCW	3 293	3 818	3 509	4 024	4 103	4 578	3 744	3 713	3 709	3 773	3 878	3 978	4 483	4 563	4 330	4 210
30 - 44	KBCX	3 597	4 495	5 461	4 938	5 513	6 045	6 645	6 686	6 695	6 669	6 655	6 597	6 313	6 335	6 789	7 157
45 - 59	KBUU	2 215	3 753	4 493	4 970	4 711	4 732	5 534	5 594	5 646	5 691	5 745	5 804	6 060	6 450	6 392	6 116
60 - 64	KGWY	490	894	1 061	1 507	1 376	1 390	1 412	1 414	1 440	1 479	1 522	1 584	1 824	1 679	1 870	2 079
65 - 74	KBWL	565	1 099	1 560	1 999	2 264	2 272	2 308	2 325	2 347	2 365	2 380	2 379	2 636	3 052	3 153	3 230
75 - 84	KBWM	196	335	617	716	922	1 146	1 308	1 338	1 369	1 392	1 400	1 413	1 535	1 716	1 991	2 357
85 and over	KGXD	23	36	70	126	141	212	312	315	312	321	350	379	483	608	770	965
School ages (5-15)	KBWV	..	6 711	3 895	4 982	4 666	4 001	4 294	4 291	4 273	4 233	4 185	4 122	3 969	4 148	4 431	4 525
Under 18	KGWD	..	3 630	6 753	8 108	7 430	6 711	6 845	6 823	6 799	6 780	6 756	6 727	6 733	6 910	7 231	7 376
Pensionable ages[5]	KFIB	785	1 471	2 247	2 841	3 327	3 630	3 928	3 978	4 028	4 078	4 130	4 171	4 654	5 376	5 913	6 173
Females: All ages	KGYA	19 745	23 978	26 107	28 761	28 946	29 530	30 281	30 359	30 449	30 568	30 741	30 893	31 868	32 887	33 938	34 946
Under 1	KGYK	466	351	376	437	356	387	324	323	331	343	349	357	388	390	392	386
1 - 4	KBWN	1 724	1 397	1 735	1 779	1 327	1 505	1 375	1 346	1 322	1 310	1 324	1 349	1 519	1 561	1 574	1 560
5 - 9	KGYN	2 054	1 930	1 804	2 283	1 788	1 786	1 822	1 798	1 781	1 761	1 735	1 705	1 717	1 917	1 962	1 976
10 - 14	KGYO	1 962	1 854	1 629	2 057	2 175	1 701	1 897	1 909	1 897	1 882	1 857	1 827	1 704	1 716	1 915	1 960
15 - 19	KGYP	1 928	2 002	1 611	1 887	2 311	1 815	1 799	1 822	1 867	1 903	1 927	1 936	1 852	1 728	1 739	1 939
20 - 29	KBWO	3 690	4 047	3 644	3 945	4 009	4 560	3 755	3 705	3 691	3 723	3 813	3 902	4 304	4 325	4 101	3 989
30 - 44	KBWP	3 895	5 222	5 663	4 859	5 442	6 080	6 760	6 807	6 811	6 792	6 764	6 706	6 386	6 356	6 703	6 975
45 - 59	KBWR	2 424	4 226	5 065	5 231	4 829	4 769	5 634	5 713	5 766	5 816	5 871	5 940	6 235	6 645	6 594	6 282
60 - 64	KGYY	577	1 003	1 361	1 715	1 559	1 498	1 473	1 478	1 509	1 548	1 591	1 656	1 922	1 770	1 972	2 215
65 - 74	KBWS	713	1 361	2 127	2 765	2 931	2 795	2 640	2 642	2 654	2 662	2 666	2 650	2 883	3 323	3 438	3 512
75 - 84	KBWT	274	509	937	1 443	1 756	1 972	1 987	2 006	2 029	2 040	2 020	2 002	2 005	2 111	2 372	2 778
85 and over	KGZD	38	77	154	359	462	661	817	811	792	789	825	864	953	1 045	1 177	1 378
School ages (5-15)	KBWW	..	6 409	3 753	4 722	4 421	3 817	4 087	4 080	4 061	4 022	3 974	3 919	3 776	3 958	4 237	4 326
Under 18	KGYD	..	6 927	6 495	7 690	7 042	6 409	6 512	6 487	6 460	6 439	6 419	6 393	6 406	6 585	6 903	7 044
Pensionable ages[5]	KFIC	1 601	2 950	4 580	6 282	6 708	6 927	6 917	6 938	6 984	7 039	7 102	7 172	7 531	7 117	6 986	7 258

5.3 Age distribution of the resident population: by sex and country

continued

Thousands

		England										Wales								
		Estimated mid-year resident population							Projected population[1]			Estimated mid-year resident population							Projected population[1]	
		1991[2]	2001[3]	2002[4]	2003[4]	2004[4]	2005[4]	2006	2011	2026		1991[2]	2001[3]	2002[4]	2003[4]	2004[4]	2005[4]	2006	2011	2026
Persons: All ages	KCCI	47 875	49 450	49 652	49 866	50 111	50 466	50 763	52 706	58 682	KERY	2 873	2 910	2 920	2 931	2 946	2 954	2 966	3 038	3 248
Under 1	KCCJ	660	558	559	576	597	606	620	677	681	KFAC	38	32	30	31	32	32	33	35	34
1 - 4	KCCK	2 560	2 366	2 313	2 275	2 262	2 289	2 335	2 639	2 741	KFBX	153	136	132	129	127	126	127	139	139
5 - 9	KCCL	3 019	3 121	3 084	3 055	3 020	2 976	2 922	2 966	3 452	KFCA	186	185	183	180	178	175	172	164	182
10 - 14	KCCM	2 865	3 238	3 264	3 250	3 225	3 185	3 130	2 925	3 418	KFCB	177	196	197	197	195	193	189	175	186
15 - 19	KCCN	3 067	3 045	3 115	3 203	3 261	3 297	3 334	3 195	3 391	KFCC	187	186	190	196	199	200	202	194	186
20 - 29	KCEG	7 651	6 307	6 244	6 232	6 315	6 483	6 633	7 420	7 008	KFCD	415	336	333	334	340	348	359	401	356
30 - 44	KCEH	10 147	11 257	11 347	11 369	11 337	11 318	11 230	10 770	12 097	KFCE	583	608	610	608	606	599	590	547	608
45 - 59	KCEQ	7 920	9 327	9 439	9 522	9 591	9 675	9 777	10 241	10 486	KFCF	486	572	578	582	586	589	592	605	568
60 - 64	KCEW	2 399	2 395	2 399	2 445	2 509	2 586	2 697	3 117	3 580	KFCG	154	154	156	161	166	171	177	204	218
65 - 74	KCGD	4 222	4 113	4 129	4 155	4 175	4 189	4 171	4 585	5 576	KFCH	284	264	265	268	270	271	273	306	362
75 - 84	KCJG	2 626	2 764	2 803	2 850	2 875	2 865	2 860	2 955	4 289	KFCI	164	183	185	187	188	186	186	189	286
85 and over	KCKJ	739	959	956	936	942	996	1 055	1 214	1 964	KFCK	45	59	59	59	60	63	67	78	125
School ages (5-15)	KCWX	6 439	6 985	6 984	6 960	6 895	6 817	6 719	6 502	7 552	KFCL	397	420	419	417	413	407	401	375	404
Under 18	KCWY	10 840	11 146	11 119	11 089	11 064	11 036	10 997	11 068	12 326	KFCM	662	662	659	654	651	646	641	625	651
Pensionable ages[5]	KEAA	8 827	9 055	9 111	9 188	9 273	9 370	9 462	10 161	11 175	KFEB	573	584	589	595	602	608	615	665	732
Males: All ages	KEAB	23 291	24 166	24 290	24 419	24 563	24 758	24 926	25 995	29 134	KFEI	1 391	1 409	1 414	1 423	1 432	1 439	1 445	1 487	1 603
Under 1	KEAC	336	285	286	296	306	310	317	346	348	KFEJ	20	16	16	16	16	17	17	18	17
1 - 4	KEAD	1 307	1 212	1 182	1 163	1 159	1 172	1 196	1 348	1 400	KFEK	78	69	68	66	65	65	65	71	71
5 - 9	KEAE	1 545	1 599	1 581	1 564	1 546	1 522	1 493	1 517	1 762	KFEL	95	95	94	92	91	90	88	84	93
10 - 14	KEAF	1 467	1 658	1 672	1 667	1 657	1 638	1 606	1 500	1 750	KFFA	91	101	101	101	100	99	97	90	95
15 - 19	KECA	1 572	1 558	1 607	1 654	1 679	1 691	1 720	1 650	1 746	KFFN	95	94	97	100	102	103	104	99	95
20 - 29	KECB	3 835	3 155	3 130	3 126	3 182	3 270	3 349	3 785	3 594	KFHA	207	166	164	166	170	176	181	206	185
30 - 44	KECC	5 064	5 600	5 644	5 658	5 639	5 637	5 591	5 372	6 132	KFHB	289	297	297	296	295	292	287	267	309
45 - 59	KECD	3 957	4 624	4 673	4 715	4 748	4 791	4 839	5 063	5 198	KFHW	242	283	285	287	288	290	291	295	274
60 - 64	KECE	1 159	1 176	1 176	1 197	1 228	1 267	1 320	1 518	1 741	KFQO	74	75	77	79	82	84	87	100	105
65 - 74	KECF	1 900	1 928	1 942	1 958	1 972	1 984	1 981	2 194	2 678	KFQV	128	124	125	127	128	129	130	147	174
75 - 84	KECG	970	1 103	1 128	1 154	1 172	1 179	1 190	1 289	1 972	KFUK	60	73	74	75	76	77	77	83	133
85 and over	KECH	181	267	269	267	274	298	324	411	814	KFUL	11	16	16	16	17	19	20	26	52
School ages (5-15)	KECI	3 295	3 578	3 580	3 569	3 536	3 497	3 444	3 331	3 862	KFUV	204	215	215	214	212	209	206	193	207
Under 18	KECJ	5 545	5 712	5 699	5 686	5 675	5 658	5 638	5 672	6 306	KFVE	339	340	338	336	335	332	329	321	333
Pensionable ages[5]	KECK	3 050	3 298	3 339	3 379	3 419	3 461	3 494	3 894	5 148	KFVF	198	212	215	218	221	224	227	256	339
Females: All ages	KEJV	24 584	25 284	25 362	25 448	25 548	25 708	25 837	26 711	29 549	KFVL	1 482	1 502	1 506	1 508	1 514	1 515	1 521	1 550	1 645
Under 1	KEJW	324	273	273	280	291	296	303	331	332	KFYW	19	15	15	15	15	16	16	17	16
1 - 4	KEJX	1 253	1 154	1 131	1 112	1 103	1 117	1 139	1 291	1 341	KFZJ	75	66	65	63	62	61	62	68	68
5 - 9	KEKP	1 474	1 522	1 503	1 490	1 474	1 454	1 428	1 450	1 690	KGCK	91	90	89	88	87	85	84	80	89
10 - 14	KEKQ	1 399	1 580	1 591	1 583	1 569	1 547	1 523	1 425	1 669	KGCM	86	95	96	95	95	94	92	85	91
15 - 19	KEKR	1 495	1 487	1 508	1 549	1 582	1 606	1 615	1 545	1 646	KGCN	91	92	93	95	97	97	98	94	91
20 - 29	KEKS	3 816	3 152	3 114	3 106	3 133	3 213	3 284	3 635	3 414	KGCO	208	170	168	167	170	172	178	195	171
30 - 44	KENR	5 083	5 657	5 703	5 711	5 699	5 682	5 638	5 397	5 965	KGCP	294	312	313	312	311	307	303	280	299
45 - 59	KEOQ	3 964	4 702	4 767	4 808	4 843	4 885	4 938	5 179	5 289	KGGZ	244	289	293	295	298	299	301	310	293
60 - 64	KEOZ	1 239	1 219	1 223	1 248	1 280	1 319	1 377	1 599	1 839	KGIY	80	78	80	82	84	87	90	104	113
65 - 74	KEQJ	2 323	2 185	2 187	2 197	2 203	2 206	2 190	2 391	2 898	KGKR	156	141	140	141	142	142	143	158	189
75 - 84	KEQK	1 656	1 661	1 676	1 696	1 703	1 686	1 670	1 666	2 316	KGTQ	104	110	111	112	112	110	108	106	153
85 and over	KEQL	558	692	687	669	667	697	731	803	1 150	KGTZ	34	43	43	42	42	44	47	52	73
School ages (5-15)	KEQM	3 143	3 406	3 404	3 392	3 359	3 320	3 275	3 171	3 690	KGVG	194	204	204	203	201	198	195	183	198
Under 18	KEQN	5 295	5 434	5 419	5 403	5 389	5 377	5 358	5 396	6 020	KGVH	323	323	321	318	317	314	311	304	318
Pensionable ages[5]	KEQO	5 777	5 757	5 772	5 809	5 854	5 908	5 968	6 267	6 027	KGVK	375	372	374	377	380	383	387	408	393

5.3 Age distribution of the resident population: by sex and country
continued

Thousands

		Scotland Estimated mid-year resident population							Scotland Projected population[1]			Northern Ireland Estimated mid-year resident population							Northern Ireland Projected population[1]	
		1991[2]	2001[3]	2002	2003	2004	2005	2006	2011	2026		1991	2001[3]	2002	2003	2004	2005	2006	2011	2026
Persons: All ages	KGVP	5 083	5 064	5 055	5 057	5 078	5 095	5 117	5 206	5 363	KIOY	1 607	1 689	1 697	1 703	1 710	1 724	1 742	1 812	1 966
Under 1	KHAQ	66	52	51	52	54	54	55	57	52	KIOZ	26	22	22	21	22	23	23	25	23
1 - 4	KHCT	258	224	217	212	210	211	213	228	214	KIPA	106	93	91	89	87	88	89	97	95
5 - 9	KHDN	320	306	299	294	290	285	279	271	278	KIPN	131	123	122	121	120	119	117	113	124
10 - 14	KHDQ	313	323	323	320	319	315	308	281	285	KIPP	129	132	131	129	128	126	125	118	124
15 - 19	KHDT	337	318	319	324	328	327	329	314	294	KIPQ	128	130	132	133	133	132	131	124	121
20 - 29	KHDU	820	630	619	614	617	630	649	700	606	KIPR	253	225	222	221	224	230	239	265	228
30 - 44	KHDV	1 080	1 163	1 158	1 150	1 140	1 124	1 107	1 019	1 032	KIPS	315	376	378	378	378	377	375	364	396
45 - 59	KHFK	853	979	993	1 008	1 025	1 042	1 058	1 104	992	KIPT	241	290	296	301	305	310	316	345	352
60 - 64	KHOZ	265	262	262	265	270	273	280	331	376	KIPU	70	74	75	78	81	84	87	93	120
65 - 74	KHTU	441	447	449	452	455	457	456	482	612	KIPV	120	123	125	126	127	128	130	147	191
75 - 84	KHUO	259	272	276	281	286	286	287	306	428	KIPW	69	77	79	81	82	83	83	89	132
85 and over	KHUQ	70	89	88	86	85	91	95	111	194	KIPX	19	23	24	24	24	25	26	33	59
School ages (5-15)	KHVV	697	694	687	679	672	664	653	611	621	KIPY	285	282	281	278	274	271	268	256	273
Under 18	KIMT	1 150	1 098	1 086	1 074	1 067	1 059	1 050	1 019	1 003	KIQL	467	451	447	443	437	435	432	427	440
Pensionable ages[5]	KIMU	912	944	950	958	968	975	983	1 048	1 163	KIQM	246	262	266	271	275	280	284	310	361
Males: All ages	KIMV	2 445	2 434	2 432	2 435	2 446	2 456	2 469	2 520	2 605	KIQN	783	824	829	833	836	844	853	890	972
Under 1	KIMW	34	26	26	26	28	28	28	29	27	KIQO	13	11	11	11	11	12	12	13	12
1 - 4	KIMX	132	115	111	108	107	107	109	117	109	KIQP	54	48	47	46	45	45	46	49	48
5 - 9	KIMY	164	156	153	151	149	146	143	139	142	KIQQ	67	63	63	62	62	61	60	58	63
10 - 14	KIMZ	161	166	165	164	163	161	157	144	145	KIQR	66	68	67	66	65	64	64	61	64
15 - 19	KINA	171	161	163	166	168	168	169	161	150	KIQS	66	66	68	68	68	68	67	64	62
20 - 29	KINB	410	311	308	306	309	317	327	356	312	KIQT	127	113	111	111	112	116	121	136	119
30 - 44	KINC	535	563	560	556	550	542	534	495	516	KIQU	156	185	186	186	185	185	184	178	200
45 - 59	KIND	415	483	490	496	503	511	517	533	474	KIQV	118	144	147	149	151	153	156	169	170
60 - 64	KINE	124	125	125	126	129	131	135	160	176	KIQW	32	35	36	38	39	41	42	45	57
65 - 74	KINR	192	200	202	204	207	208	208	225	287	KIRJ	53	56	56	57	58	59	60	69	92
75 - 84	KINS	91	103	106	108	111	112	113	126	192	KIRK	26	30	31	31	32	32	33	37	60
85 and over	KINT	16	23	23	23	23	25	27	35	75	KIRL	5	6	6	7	7	7	8	10	24
School ages (5-15)	KINU	357	356	352	348	344	340	334	313	317	KIRM	146	145	144	142	141	139	138	131	139
Under 18	KINV	588	562	556	550	546	543	538	522	512	KIRN	239	231	229	227	225	223	222	219	225
Pensionable ages[5]	KINW	299	327	331	336	341	345	349	386	521	KIRO	83	92	94	95	97	99	101	117	165
Females: All ages	KINX	2 639	2 630	2 623	2 623	2 632	2 639	2 647	2 685	2 758	KIRP	824	865	868	870	874	880	888	921	994
Under 1	KINY	32	26	25	25	26	26	27	28	25	KIRQ	13	10	11	10	11	11	11	12	11
1 - 4	KINZ	126	109	106	104	103	103	104	112	105	KIRR	52	45	44	43	42	43	43	47	46
5 - 9	KIOA	157	149	146	143	141	139	136	133	136	KIRS	64	60	59	59	58	58	57	55	61
10 - 14	KIOB	153	157	157	156	156	154	151	137	140	KIRT	63	65	64	63	62	62	61	57	61
15 - 19	KIOC	166	156	156	158	160	159	160	153	143	KIRU	62	64	65	65	65	64	64	60	59
20 - 29	KIOO	411	319	311	307	308	314	322	344	295	KISH	126	113	111	110	111	114	118	129	108
30 - 44	KIOP	545	600	598	595	590	583	573	524	515	KISI	159	191	192	193	192	192	191	185	196
45 - 59	KIOQ	437	496	504	512	521	531	541	571	518	KISJ	123	146	149	152	154	157	160	175	182
60 - 64	KIOR	141	137	137	139	141	142	145	171	200	KISK	38	38	39	40	42	43	45	48	63
65 - 74	KIOS	249	246	247	248	248	249	247	257	326	KISL	67	68	68	68	69	69	69	77	100
75 - 84	KIOT	168	169	171	173	175	174	174	180	236	KISM	44	47	48	49	50	50	51	52	72
85 and over	KIOU	54	66	65	63	62	65	68	76	119	KISN	14	17	17	17	17	18	18	22	36
School ages (5-15)	KIOV	340	339	335	331	328	324	319	298	304	KISO	139	138	137	135	134	132	130	124	134
Under 18	KIOW	562	536	530	524	520	516	512	497	491	KISP	228	220	218	215	213	212	210	208	215
Pensionable ages[5]	KIOX	612	617	619	622	627	630	634	662	642	KISQ	163	170	173	175	178	181	183	193	196

1 2006 based national population projections . See explanatory notes at be-ginning of chapter for further details.

2 Data for mid 1991 for UK, England and Wales and Scotland were revised in light of the results of the 2001 Census.

3 Data for mid-2001 was revised as a result of local authority population stu-dies

4 England & Wales population estimates for mid-2002 to mid-2005 were re-vised in August 2007 to take account of improved estimates of international migration

5 The pensionable age population is that over state retirement age. These fig-ures take account of the forthcoming changes in state retirement age between April 2010 and March 2020 from 65 for men and 60 for women to 65 for both sexes; and a further increase to 66 for both sexes between April 2024 and March 2026.

Sources: Office for National Statistics: 01329 813318;
General Register Office for Scotland;
General Register Office for Northern Ireland

5.4 Marital condition (*de jure*): estimated population: by age and sex
England and Wales

Thousands

		Males								Females						
		1991[1]	2001	2002[2]	2003[2]	2004[2]	2005[2]	2006		1991[1]	2001	2002[2]	2003[2]	2004[2]	2005[2]	2006
All ages:																
Single	KRPL	11 131	12 270	12 432	12 596	12 778	12 978	13 188	KUBS	9 824	10 917	11 048	11 190	11 342	11 537	11 730
Married	KRPM	11 636	11 090	11 008	10 929	10 851	10 801	10 723	KVCC	11 833	11 150	11 075	11 000	10 935	10 882	10 812
Widowed	KRPN	727	733	730	727	724	722	720	KVCD	2 951	2 745	2 710	2 669	2 629	2 589	2 549
Divorced	KRPO	1 187	1 482	1 534	1 589	1 642	1 696	1 739	KVCE	1 459	1 975	2 036	2 096	2 156	2 215	2 266
Age groups:																
0 - 14: Single	KRPP	4 939	5 036	4 999	4 967	4 941	4 912	4 880	KVCF	4 720	4 796	4 763	4 726	4 696	4 670	4 648
15 - 19: Single	KRPQ	1 659	1 645	1 698	1 749	1 778	1 792	1 822	KVCG	1 554	1 560	1 587	1 632	1 667	1 694	1 706
Married	KRPR	8	5	4	4	3	2	2	KVCH	32	16	13	12	11	9	7
Widowed	KRPS	–	1	1	1	–	–	–	KVCI	–	1	1	1	–	–	–
Divorced	KRPT	–	1	1	1	–	–	–	KVCJ	–	1	1	–	–	–	–
20 - 24: Single	KRPU	1 717	1 501	1 533	1 573	1 639	1 700	1 749	KVCK	1 421	1 390	1 430	1 465	1 497	1 547	1 599
Married	KRPV	242	74	69	68	69	66	59	KVCL	490	178	167	161	157	150	138
Widowed	KRPW	–	1	1	1	1	1	1	KVCM	1	1	1	1	2	2	1
Divorced	KRPX	12	3	3	3	3	3	3	KVCN	29	8	8	8	8	8	7
25 - 34: Single	KRPY	1 652	2 227	2 245	2 260	2 285	2 345	2 409	KVCO	1 135	1 770	1 796	1 826	1 866	1 934	1 997
Married	KRPZ	2 028	1 391	1 293	1 205	1 129	1 068	998	KVCP	2 488	1 768	1 662	1 568	1 483	1 421	1 347
Widowed	KRQA	2	3	3	3	3	3	3	KVCQ	8	10	9	8	8	7	7
Divorced	KRQB	237	136	131	126	121	115	107	KVCR	312	231	219	208	196	185	173
35 - 44: Single	KRQC	477	963	1 031	1 089	1 141	1 195	1 249	KVEH	280	692	751	804	858	910	965
Married	KRQD	2 632	2 494	2 490	2 471	2 441	2 417	2 371	KVEI	2 760	2 649	2 650	2 631	2 613	2 583	2 543
Widowed	KRQE	11	12	12	12	11	11	11	KVEJ	34	36	35	34	32	31	30
Divorced	KRQF	384	411	424	435	443	450	448	KVEK	444	558	572	583	593	597	595
45 - 54: Single	KRQG	251	419	432	451	474	501	534	KVEL	144	256	271	289	310	335	365
Married	KUAR	2 347	2 511	2 429	2 377	2 347	2 334	2 337	KVEM	2 322	2 548	2 475	2 426	2 398	2 385	2 390
Widowed	KUBA	31	37	35	34	33	32	31	KVEN	118	111	105	99	96	93	90
Divorced	KUBB	290	448	454	466	481	499	518	KVEO	332	557	566	578	594	613	636
55 - 59: Single	KUBC	101	128	141	150	158	165	170	KVEP	69	74	81	86	91	97	102
Married	KUBD	1 050	1 156	1 237	1 276	1 285	1 281	1 265	KVEQ	982	1 125	1 212	1 255	1 270	1 270	1 258
Widowed	KUBE	34	34	36	37	37	37	37	KVER	136	112	115	114	112	109	106
Divorced	KUBF	95	174	194	210	221	231	239	KVES	107	210	235	255	270	282	291
60 - 64: Single	KUBG	104	97	97	100	104	108	114	KVET	80	62	61	62	63	65	69
Married	KUBH	997	980	976	990	1 011	1 037	1 074	KVEU	908	906	910	931	958	987	1 028
Widowed	KUBI	63	50	49	48	47	48	49	KVEV	250	178	172	167	163	160	159
Divorced	KUBJ	70	125	131	138	148	158	170	KVEW	82	151	159	169	181	194	210
65 - 74: Single	KUBK	150	155	154	153	152	151	149	KMGN	176	130	126	123	120	117	113
Married	KUBL	1 574	1 569	1 580	1 594	1 605	1 612	1 608	KMGO	1 317	1 322	1 336	1 356	1 373	1 388	1 392
Widowed	KUBM	229	188	183	179	175	171	166	KMGP	879	697	675	655	634	611	584
Divorced	KUBN	74	139	149	158	169	179	188	KMGQ	107	177	190	204	218	232	243
75 and over: Single	KUBO	81	99	101	103	106	109	112	KMGR	246	188	182	177	173	169	166
Married	KUBP	759	909	928	944	961	984	1 010	KMGS	536	639	651	661	673	689	709
Widowed	KUBQ	357	407	411	414	417	420	423	KMGT	1 526	1 598	1 597	1 590	1 583	1 576	1 571
Divorced	KUBR	25	44	48	51	56	61	66	KMGU	46	81	86	90	96	103	110

1 Mid-1991 marital status estimates are revised in light of the 2001 Census
2 Mid-2002 to Mid-2005 marital status estimates for England and Wales have been updated to include the latest revised estimates that take into account improved estimates of international migration.

Source: Office for National Statistics: 01329 813318

5.5 Geographical distribution of the population

Thousands

		Population enumerated in Census			Mid-year population estimates							
		1911	1931	1951	1971	1981	1991	2001	2002[1]	2003[1]	2004[1]	2005[1]	2006
United Kingdom	KIUR	42 082	46 074	50 225	55 928	56 357	57 439	59 113	59 323	59 557	59 846	60 238	60 587
Great Britain	KISR	40 831	44 795	48 854	54 388	54 815	55 831	57 424	57 627	57 855	58 136	58 514	58 846
England	KKOJ	33 650	37 359	41 159	46 412	46 821	47 875	49 450	49 652	49 866	50 111	50 466	50 763
Standard Regions													
North	KKNA	2 729	2 938	3 009	3 152	3 117	3 073	3 028	3 029	3 033	3 037	3 045	3 052
Yorkshire and Humberside	KKNB	3 896	4 319	4 567	4 902	4 918	4 936	4 977	5 002	5 028	5 064	5 108	5 142
East Midlands	KKNC	2 467	2 732	3 118	3 652	3 853	4 011	4 190	4 222	4 254	4 291	4 328	4 364
East Anglia	KKND	1 191	1 231	1 381	1 688	1 894	2 068	2 181	2 195	2 220	2 242	2 268	2 287
South East	KKNE	11 613	13 349	14 877	17 125	17 011	17 511	18 566	18 646	18 706	18 783	18 936	19 069
South West	KKNF	2 818	2 984	3 479	4 112	4 381	4 688	4 943	4 973	5 005	5 042	5 087	5 124
West Midlands	KKNG	3 277	3 743	4 423	5 146	5 187	5 230	5 281	5 295	5 312	5 327	5 351	5 367
North West	KKNH	5 659	6 062	6 305	6 634	6 459	6 357	6 285	6 290	6 309	6 325	6 344	6 357
Government Office Regions													
North East	JZBU	..	–	–	2 679	2 636	2 587	2 540	2 541	2 541	2 542	2 550	2 556
North West (including Merseyside)	JZBV	..	–	–	7 108	6 940	6 843	6 773	6 778	6 800	6 820	6 840	6 853
Yorkshire and The Humber	JZBX	..	–	–	4 902	4 918	4 936	4 977	5 002	5 028	5 064	5 108	5 142
East Midlands	JZBY	..	–	–	3 652	3 853	4 011	4 190	4 222	4 254	4 291	4 328	4 364
West Midlands	JZBZ	..	–	–	5 146	5 187	5 230	5 281	5 295	5 312	5 327	5 351	5 367
South West	JZCA	..	–	–	4 112	4 381	4 688	4 943	4 973	5 005	5 042	5 087	5 124
East of England	JZCB	..	–	–	4 454	4 854	5 121	5 400	5 433	5 475	5 511	5 563	5 607
London	JZCC	..	–	–	7 529	6 806	6 829	7 322	7 362	7 364	7 389	7 456	7 512
South East	JZCD	..	–	–	6 830	7 245	7 629	8 023	8 047	8 087	8 125	8 185	8 238
Wales	KKNI	2 421	2 593	2 599	2 740	2 813	2 873	2 910	2 920	2 931	2 946	2 954	2 966
Scotland	KGJB	4 761	4 843	5 096	5 236	5 180	5 083	5 064	5 055	5 057	5 078	5 095	5 117
Northern Ireland[4]	KGJC	1 251	1 280	1 371	1 540	1 543	1 607	1 689	1 697	1 703	1 710	1 724	1 742
Greater London	KKNJ	7 161	8 110	8 197	7 529	6 806	6 829	7 322	7 362	7 364	7 389	7 456	7 512
Inner London[2]	KISS	4 998	4 893	3 679	3 060	2 550	2 599	2 859	2 886	2 891	2 907	2 944	2 973
Outer London[2]	KITF	2 162	3 217	4 518	4 470	4 255	4 230	4 463	4 475	4 473	4 482	4 512	4 539
Metropolitan areas of England and Wales	KITG	9 716	10 770	11 365	11 862	11 353	11 085	10 888	10 907	10 930	10 956	11 010	11 049
Tyne and Wear	KGJN	1 105	1 201	1 201	1 218	1 155	1 124	1 087	1 087	1 085	1 083	1 086	1 088
West Yorkshire	KGJP	1 852	1 939	1 985	2 090	2 067	2 062	2 083	2 094	2 103	2 119	2 142	2 161
South Yorkshire	KGJO	963	1 173	1 253	1 331	1 317	1 289	1 266	1 270	1 273	1 279	1 288	1 293
West Midlands	KGJQ	1 780	2 143	2 547	2 811	2 673	2 619	2 568	2 574	2 578	2 582	2 594	2 600
Greater Manchester	KGJR	2 638	2 727	2 716	2 750	2 619	2 554	2 516	2 518	2 528	2 534	2 543	2 554
Merseyside	KGJS	1 378	1 587	1 663	1 662	1 522	1 438	1 368	1 364	1 362	1 359	1 357	1 354
Principal Metropolitan Cities[2]	KITH	3 154	3 906	3 915	3 910	3 550	3 415	3 344	3 356	3 364	3 382	3 417	3 441
Newcastle	KGJT	267	286	292	312	284	275	266	267	267	267	270	270
Leeds	KGJX	446	483	505	749	718	707	716	720	723	729	741	750
Sheffield	KGJV	455	512	513	579	548	520	513	514	513	517	522	526
Birmingham	KGKF	526	1 003	1 113	1 107	1 021	1 005	985	989	992	996	1 003	1 007
Manchester	KGKJ	714	766	703	554	463	433	423	426	431	436	445	452
Liverpool	KGKM	746	856	789	610	517	476	442	441	439	437	437	436
Other metropolitan districts[2]	KITI	6 562	6 864	7 450	7 952	7 803	7 670	7 544	7 551	7 565	7 574	7 593	7 608
Non-metropolitan districts of England and Wales	KITJ	19 194	21 072	24 196	29 761	31 475	32 834	31 239	31 383	31 572	31 766	32 000	32 201
Non-metropolitan cities[2,3]	KITK	..	–	–	4 715	4 617	–						
Incl. Kingston-upon-Hull	KKNZ	278	314	299	288	274	263	250	250	251	253	255	256
Leicester	KKOA	227	239	285	285	283	281	283	282	282	283	286	290
Nottingham	KKNX	260	269	308	302	278	279	269	272	275	279	283	286
Bristol	KKNV	357	397	443	433	401	392	390	391	394	397	406	410
Plymouth	KITL	207	215	225	249	253	251	241	242	242	244	246	248
Stoke-on-Trent	KKOD	235	277	275	265	252	249	240	239	239	239	239	240
Cardiff	KKOB	182	224	244	291	281	297	310	311	310	312	314	318
Newport	IFX3	84	89	106	137	132	135	138	139	139	139	140	140
Industrial districts[2,3]	KITM	..	–	–	6 486	6 713	..	–	–	–	–	–	–
New Towns[2,3]	KITN	..	–	–	1 895	2 194	..	–	–	–	–	–	–
Resort, port and retirement districts[2,3]	KITO	..	–	–	3 184	3 368	–	–	–	–	–	–	–
Urban and mixed urban/rural districts[2,3]	KITP	..	–	–	8 821	9 446	–	–	–	–	–	–	–
Remoter, mainly rural districts[2,3]	KITQ	..	–	–	4 661	5 137	–	–	–	–	–	–	–
City of Edinburgh local government district	KGKU	320	439	467	478	446	436	449	448	448	455	458	464
City of Glasgow local government district	KGKT	784	1 088	1 090	983	774	629	579	577	577	578	579	581
Belfast[4]	KGKV	387	438	444	–	316	293	277	274	272	269	268	267

1 Mid 2002 to mid 2005 population estimates for the UK and England & Wales have been updated to include the latest revised estimates that take improved estimates of international migration into account.

2 Details of the classification by broad area type are given in recent issues of the ONS annual reference volume *Key Population and Vital Statistics; local and health authority areas* (Series VS). The ten broad area types include all local authorities in England and Wales.

3 The breakdown of non-metropolitan districts by area type has not been provided from mid-2001 onwards. This is because the effect of boundary changes due to the major local government reorganisation on 1 April 1995 and 1 April 1996 (particularly in Wales) make the comparison of 2001 data with data for earlier years invalid.

4 1931 figures shown for Northern Ireland and the City of Belfast relate to the 1937 Census.

Sources: Office for National Statistics: 01329 813318;
General Register Office for Scotland;
Northern Ireland Statistics and Research Agency

35

Population and vital statistics

5.6 Population: by ethnic group and age, January - December 2006
United Kingdom

Percentages and thousands

	0 to 4	5 to 9	10 to 14	15 to 19	20 to 24	25 to 29	30 to 34	35 to 44	45 to 59	60 to 74	75 and over	All ages (=100%) (thousands)
White												
British	5	6	6	7	6	6	6	15	21	15	8	48 424
Other	4	4	4	4	8	11	10	17	18	13	7	2 940
Mixed												
White and Black Caribbean	18	18	17	15	10	5	5	7	4	1	0	230
White and Black African	15	15	13	13	9	9	4	11	8	2	1	76
White and Asian	24	17	15	8	8	6	5	12	4	2	0	158
Other Mixed	19	16	12	9	6	8	6	15	7	3	1	141
Asian												
Indian	7	6	6	6	8	12	10	15	19	8	2	1 136
Pakistani	12	10	10	9	11	10	9	13	11	5	1	857
Bangladeshi	12	12	10	9	11	9	9	12	9	5	1	345
Other Asian	9	8	6	6	8	9	13	19	16	5	1	394
Black												
Black Caribbean	7	6	7	8	7	5	6	22	17	11	4	615
Black African	13	10	10	8	8	10	10	19	10	3	0	714
Black Other	12	12	9	9	5	8	7	17	11	8	3	55
Chinese	4	5	6	7	15	12	10	18	18	6	1	211
Other	7	8	7	6	9	10	12	18	14	5	2	836
All[1]	6	6	6	7	6	6	7	15	20	14	7	58 855

1 Includes those who did not state their ethnic origin.

Source: Office for National Statistics, Annual Population Survey

5.7 Total international migration estimates: citizenship[1,2]
United Kingdom

Citizenship by country of next or last residence

Thousands[3]

	All citizenships	British	Non-British	European Union[4]	Commonwealth Old	Commonwealth New[5]	Other foreign[6]
Inflow							
	C58E	C58H	C58K	C58N	C58Q	C58T	C58W
1998	391	104	287	82	54	51	101
1999	454	115	338	66	55	68	150
2000	479	99	379	63	56	91	169
2001	479	110	370	57	65	84	164
2002	513	97	416	59	63	92	201
2003	508	99	409	64	62	105	177
2004	586	88	498	128	73	141	155
2005	563	96	466	149	62	117	137
2006	591	81	510	167	62	139	142
Outflow							
	C58F	C58I	C58L	C58O	C58R	C58U	C58X
1998	251	126	126	49	20	13	44
1999	291	139	152	59	29	12	52
2000	321	161	160	57	32	15	55
2001	306	158	149	49	32	19	49
2002	358	185	174	52	42	16	64
2003	361	191	171	50	42	17	62
2004	342	195	147	42	33	19	52
2005	359	185	174	54	37	23	59
2006	400	207	194	66	42	24	61
Balance							
	C58G	C58J	C58M	C58P	C58S	C58V	C58Y
1998	140	−22	162	33	34	38	57
1999	163	−24	187	8	26	56	98
2000	158	−62	220	6	24	76	114
2001	173	−48	221	8	33	65	115
2002	154	−87	242	7	21	77	137
2003	147	−91	238	14	20	88	115
2004	244	−107	351	85	40	122	104
2005	204	−89	293	95	25	94	78
2006	191	−126	316	100	20	115	81

1 These data have been revised following changes to the TIM methodology. Therefore they may not agree with previously published estimates.
2 Based mainly on data from the IPS. Includes adjustments for (1) those whose intended length of stay changes so that their migrant status changes; (2) asylum seekers and their dependants not identified by the IPS; and (3) flows between the UK and the Republic of Ireland.
3 Estimates of international migration flows are shown rounded to the nearest thousand, rather than nearest hundred, as they are considered less reliable at the more detailed level.

4 Up to and including 2003, estimates sre shown for the EU15 (Cyprus, Czech Republic, Estonia, Hungary, Latvia, Lithuania, Malta, Poland, Slovakia and Slovenia). These countries are included in the definition for the whole of 2004, whether migration occurred before or after 1 May. These estimates do not include the 2 new member states international migration estimates.
5 For 2004 onwards, the New Commonwealth excludes Malta and Cyprus.
6 For 2004 onwards, Other foreign excludes the eight Central and Eastern European member states that joined the EU in May 2004.

Source: Office for National Statistics: 01329 813255

5.8 Estimates of migration into and out of the United Kingdom by usual occupation[1,2] and sex

Thousands

	Total			Professional and managerial			Manual and clerical			Not gainfully employed[3]		
	Persons	Males	Females	Persons	Males	Females	Persons	Males	Females	Persons	Males	Females
Inflow												
	KGOA	KGOB	KGOC	KGOD	KGOE	KGOF	KGOG	KGOH	KGOI	KGOJ	KGOK	KGOL
1998	318	160	158	112	65	47	71	35	35	136	60	76
1999	354	181	173	131	77	54	75	40	35	148	63	84
2000	359	188	171	162	98	64	64	33	31	133	57	76
2001	372	187	185	138	77	62	77	39	38	157	72	85
2002	386	200	186	139	78	62	83	45	38	163	77	87
2003	427	211	215	146	76	71	92	46	46	189	90	99
2004	518	261	257	175	102	73	132	66	65	212	92	119
2005	496	273	223	168	97	71	145	90	55	184	86	98
2006	529	280	249	154	82	72	136	79	57	239	120	119
Outflow												
	KGPA	KGPB	KGPC	KGPD	KGPE	KGPF	KGPG	KGPH	KGPI	KGPJ	KGPK	KGPL
1998	206	103	103	82	48	34	42	22	21	82	33	48
1999	245	132	114	97	60	38	69	32	37	79	41	39
2000	278	154	124	128	80	48	59	36	23	90	37	53
2001	250	135	115	102	66	36	60	30	30	88	39	49
2002	305	161	144	123	79	45	80	40	40	102	42	59
2003	314	165	149	108	60	49	103	59	44	102	46	57
2004	310	152	158	114	65	49	73	40	33	123	47	76
2005	328	187	141	137	88	50	83	47	37	108	53	55
2006	369	208	162	125	77	48	119	73	46	126	58	68
Balance												
	KGRA	KGRB	KGRC	KGRD	KGRE	KGRF	KGRG	KGRH	KGRI	KGRJ	KGRK	KGRL
1998	113	57	55	30	17	13	28	13	15	54	27	27
1999	109	49	60	34	18	16	6	8	−2	69	23	46
2000	82	35	47	34	18	16	5	−3	8	43	20	23
2001	122	52	70	36	11	25	17	9	8	70	33	36
2002	81	39	42	16	−1	17	3	5	−2	62	34	27
2003	113	47	67	38	16	22	−11	−13	2	86	44	42
2004	208	109	99	61	37	24	58	26	32	89	45	43
2005	168	86	82	31	9	21	61	43	18	76	34	43
2006	160	72	87	29	5	24	17	6	11	113	62	51

1 See chapter text.
2 These data have been revised in line with recent changes to the weightings used to gross up the IPS data. Therefore they may not agree with previous estimates that have been published.
3 Includes housepersons, students, children and retired persons.

Source: Office for National Statistics: 01329 813255

Population and vital statistics

5.9 Estimates of migration into and out of the United Kingdom[1] by citizenship and country of last or next residence

Thousands

	All migrants Total	British citizens Total	British citizens — Country of last/next residence					European Union citizens[1] (excluding British) Total	European Union citizens[1] (excluding British) — Country of last/next residence		
			European Union[1]	Old Common-wealth	New Common-wealth[2]	United States of America	Other countries[3]		European Union[1]	Other Europe[3]	Other countries[4]
Inflow											
	KEZR	KGLA	KGLB	KGLC	KGLD	KGLE	KGLF	KGLG	KGLH	KGLI	KGLJ
1998	318	104	28	29	15	16	17	70	64	–	5
1999	354	115	30	37	15	13	20	59	54	–	5
2000	359	99	28	29	14	8	20	59	52	–	6
2001	372	110	26	34	18	10	22	53	50	–	3
2002	386	97	30	23	10	9	25	55	50	2	3
2003	427	99	37	25	11	10	15	61	54	1	6
2004	518	84	21	23	15	9	16	106	99	–	6
2005	496	91	35	24	14	8	11	118	110	2	7
2006	529	77	32	16	7	4	18	136	129	1	7
Outflow											
	KEZS	KGMA	KGMB	KGMC	KGMD	KGME	KGMF	KGMG	KGMH	KGMI	KGMJ
1998	206	114	37	36	8	15	19	26	21	1.0	4
1999	245	115	37	41	8	14	14	47	41	–	6
2000	278	141	41	48	9	19	24	46	39	1.0	6
2001	250	133	41	47	7	15	22	40	34	1.0	5
2002	305	164	68	44	10	18	24	42	38	–	4
2003	314	170	71	55	9	13	22	42	33	3.0	5
2004	310	184	68	62	12	16	27	34	30	1.0	3
2005	328	174	74	62	6	10	22	47	42	1.0	4
2006	369	196	71	69	10	16	30	59	52	–	7
Balance											
	KEZT	KGNA	KGNB	KGNC	KGND	KGNE	KGNF	KGNG	KGNH	KGNI	KGNJ
1998	113	−10	−10	−6	7	1	−2	44	43	−1	1
1999	109	..	−8	−4	7	−2	6	12	13	–	−1
2000	82	−42	−14	−19	6	−11	−3	13	14	−1	–
2001	122	−23	−15	−13	11	−5	–	13	16	−1	−2
2002	81	−66	−37	−21	–	−9	1	13	11	2	−1
2003	113	−70	−34	−29	2	−2	−7	19	21	−3	1
2004	208	−100	−47	−39	3	−7	−11	72	69	−1	3
2005	168	−83	−39	−38	8	−2	−12	72	67	1	3
2006	160	−119	−39	−53	−3	−12	−12	78	78	1	–

These data have been revised in line with recent changes to the weightings used to gross up the IPS data. Therefore they may not agree with previous estimates that have been published.

1 Up to and including 2003, estimates are shown for the EU15 (Austria, Belgium, Denmark, Finland, France, Germany, Greece, the Irish Republic, Italy, Luxembourg, Netherlands, Portugal, Spain and Sweden). From 2004 onwards , the estimates are for the EU25 (EU15 plus the 10 countries of Cyprus, the Czech Republic, Estonia, Hungary, Latvia, Lithuania, Malta, Poland, Slovakia and Slovenia). These estimates do not include the 2 new member states admitted to the EU in January 2007. These will be included in the 2007 international migration estimates.

2 From 2004 onwards, the New Commonwealth excludes Malta and Cyprus.

3 From 2004 onwards these categories exclude the 8 central and Eastern

4 From 2004 onwards Other countries excludes Malta and cyprus.

5.9
Estimates of migration into and out of the United Kingdom[1] by citizenship and country of last or next residence
continued

Thousands

| | Commonwealth[6] citizens | | | | | | | | Other foreign citizens[4] | | | | |
| | Country of last/next residence | | | | | | | | Country of last/next residence | | | | |
	Total	Aust-ralia	Canada	New Zealand	South Africa	Indian[2] sub-continent	Other African Common-wealth	Other[3] count-ries	Total	Euro-pean Union[5]	Other Europe[6]	United States of America	Other coun-tries
Inflow													
	KGLK	KGLL	KGLM	KGLN	KTDK	IBH3	KGLQ	IBH4	KGLU	KGLV	KGLW	KGLX	KGLY
1998	88	24	5	13	11	13	10	12	56	4	7	18	27
1999	101	27	2	12	12	22	14	12	79	3	18	15	43
2000	113	22	6	11	13	30	13	18	89	2	11	13	63
2001	120	30	4	9	13	31	17	17	89	1	13	12	63
2002	121	20	4	9	20	33	22	11	113	2	11	16	84
2003	142	21	5	7	20	46	24	18	124	2	22	17	84
2004	204	24	5	8	30	77	38	21	125	1	12	14	98
2005	172	22	4	11	23	74	24	13	115	3	13	14	85
2006	193	29	6	8	16	95	17	21	122	9	13	15	86
Outflow													
	KGMK	KGML	KGMM	KGMN	KTDL	IBH5	KGMQ	IBH7	KGMU	KGMV	KGMW	KGMX	KGMY
1998	30	9	1	3	4	3	2	7	35	2	7	9	18
1999	38	11	2	6	4	2	1	11	45	–	9	14	21
2000	43	12	3	8	5	3	2	10	48	3	11	9	24
2001	44	15	3	6	5	4	2	9	33	1	9	7	16
2002	52	18	6	9	5	5	2	7	47	2	12	16	18
2003	53	19	2	8	9	5	2	8	48	2	12	8	26
2004	50	17	4	5	7	4	3	12	42	5	2	8	28
2005	59	15	4	8	9	13	2	7	49	1	7	14	28
2006	65	17	5	7	13	11	3	8	50	3	7	11	29
Balance													
	KGNK	KGNL	KGNM	KGNN	KTDM	IBH6	KGNQ	IBH8	KGNU	KGNV	KGNW	KGNX	KGNY
1998	59	15	3	10	7	10	8	6	21	2	1	9	9
1999	63	16	–	5	8	20	13	1	34	3	8	2	21
2000	70	10	4	2	9	26	10	8	41	–1	–	4	38
2001	76	15	1	3	8	27	14	8	56	–	3	6	47
2002	69	2	–1	–	15	29	21	4	66	–	–1	–	66
2003	89	2	3	–1	11	41	23	10	76	–1	10	9	57
2004	153	7	1	3	23	74	35	10	83	–4	10	7	71
2005	113	7	1	3	14	61	22	7	66	2	7	1	57
2006	128	13	2	1	3	84	14	12	72	5	6	4	57

These data have been revised in line with recent changes to the weightings used to gross up the IPS data. Therefore they may not agree with previous estimates that have been published.

1 From 2004 onwards, the Commonwealth excludes Malta and Cyprus.
2 The Indian sub-contitent consists of Bangladesh, India, Sir Lanka and Pakistan.
3 From 2004 onwards Other countries includes Malta and Cyprus.
4 From 2004 onwards Other foreign citizens excludes the 8 Central and Eastern European countries that joined the EU in 2004.
5 Up to and including 2003, estimates are shown for the EU15 (UK, Austria, Belgium, Denmark, Finland, France, Germany, Greece, the Irish Republic, Italy, Luxembourg, Netherlands, Portugal, Spain and Sweden). From 2004 onwards, the estimates are for the EU25 (EU15 plus the 8 Central and Eastern European countries, Malta and Cyprus). These do not include the 2 new member states admitted to the EU in January 2007. These will be included in the 2007 international migration estimates.
6 From 2004 onwards Other Europe excludes the 8 Central and Eastern European countries that joined the EU in 2004.

Source: Office for National Statistics: 01329 813255

Population and vital statistics

5.10 Grants of settlement by nationality[1,2]
United Kingdom

Geographical region and nationality		2004[3]	2005	2006[7]
All nationalities	KGFA	139 210	179 120	134 430
Europe[1]				
Accession States				
Cyprus	KGFN	160	..	..
Czech Republic	LQLS	520	..	..
Estonia	LQLU	165	..	..
Hungary	KGFZ	100	..	..
Latvia	I8RF	210	..	..
Lithuania	LQLW	610	..	..
Malta	KGFP	25	..	..
Poland	KGGA	1 220	..	..
Slovakia	LQLT	255	..	..
Slovenia	LQMB	5	..	..
Accession States	EL2O	3 275	..	..
Remainder of Europe				
Albania	I4UK	1 105	1 015	1 185
Bulgaria	KGFW	625	1 225	4 250
Croatia	LQMA	985	625	185
Romania	KGGB	560	955	1 620
Russia	LQLX	1 620	1 795	1 380
Serbia & Montenegro	LQMC	9 590	6 805	2 185
Turkey	KGFT	6 060	5 330	3 095
Ukraine	LQLY	1 050	1 195	860
Other former USSR	LQLZ	830	1 015	635
Other former Yugoslavia	LQMD	285	385	295
Other Europe	KOSO	595	470	115
Remainder of Europe	EL2P	23 310	20 810	15 800
Europe[1]	KOSP	26 585	20 810	15 800
Americas				
Argentina	KGGF	95	145	125
Barbados	KGGG	145	120	130
Brazil	KGGH	565	645	850
Canada	KGGI	1 225	1 215	1 125
Chile	KGGJ	65	50	105
Colombia	KGGK	1 745	1 555	880
Guyana	KGGM	170	235	165
Jamaica	KGGN	2 930	2 780	2 900
Mexico	KGGO	130	140	220
Peru	KGGP	110	220	200
Trinidad and Tobago	KGGQ	565	505	375
USA	KGGR	4 120	4 350	3 845
Venezuela	KGGT	85	155	145
Other Americas	KOSR	2 175	1 790	1 065
Americas	KGGU	14 130	13 905	12 130
Africa				
Algeria	KGGV	1 005	940	750
Angola	KOSS	1 090	1 695	980
Congo (Dem. Rep.)[4]	KOST	2 410	2 960	1 190
Egypt	KGGW	485	615	510
Ethiopia	KGGX	520	735	370
Ghana	KGGY	2 305	2 880	2 910
Kenya	KGHA	2 255	2 690	1 685
Libya	KGHB	465	360	260
Mauritius	KGHC	530	860	675
Morocco	KGHD	305	390	390
Nigeria	KGHE	4 620	5 310	4 510
Sierra Leone	KGHF	1 805	3 420	1 160

Geographical region and nationality		2004[3]	2005	2006[7]
Africa (continued)				
Somalia	KGHG	3 825	8 255	2 125
South Africa	KGHH	7 560	9 385	5 675
Sudan	KGHI	745	730	405
Tanzania	KGHJ	570	700	490
Tunisia	KGHK	115	135	195
Uganda	KGHL	960	1 065	685
Zambia	KGHM	500	830	455
Zimbabwe	KGHN	3 765	4 520	3 420
Other Africa	KOSU	3 585	5 600	3 380
Africa	KGHO	39 430	54 080	32 230
Asia				
Indian sub-continent				
Bangladesh	KGHP	3 115	3 085	2 860
India	KGHQ	11 100	16 720	11 220
Pakistan	KGHR	10 020	9 185	11 000
Indian sub-continent	KGHS	24 235	28 990	25 080
Middle East				
Iran	KGHT	1 725	2 055	1 050
Iraq	KGHU	1 725	4 675	6 875
Israel	KGHV	505	590	340
Jordan	KGHW	250	310	150
Kuwait	KGHX	90	70	20
Lebanon	KGHY	490	535	270
Saudi Arabia	KGHZ	60	70	60
Syria	KGIA	255	295	220
Yemen	KOSV	420	410	320
Other Middle East	KOSW	525	380	110
Middle East	KGIB	6 045	9 395	9 405
Remainder of Asia				
Afghanistan	I4UL	1 405	9 215	7 410
China[5]	KGIC	2 515	4 215	3 365
Hong Kong[6]	KOSX	540	805	1 065
Indonesia	KGID	195	300	255
Japan	KGIE	1 360	1 540	1 260
Malaysia	KGIF	955	1 945	1 785
Nepal	I4UM	515	3 610	6 940
Philippines	KGIG	8 200	14 710	6 325
Singapore	KGIH	305	290	205
South Korea	KOTE	570	815	620
Sri Lanka	KGII	4 870	5 475	3 135
Thailand	KGIJ	985	1 945	2 425
Other Asia	KOSZ	405	490	525
Remainder of Asia	KGIL	22 815	45 355	35 305
Asia	KGIM	53 095	83 740	69 795
Oceania				
Australia	KGIN	3 240	3 740	2 645
New Zealand	KGIO	2 370	2 505	1 405
Other Oceania	KOTA	85	90	165
Oceania	KGIP	5 690	6 335	4 215
British Overseas citizens	KGIQ	75	95	65
Nationality unknown	KGIS	205	160	190
All nationalities	KGFA	139 210	179 120	134 430

1 Excluding European Economic Area and Swiss nationals throughout the period covered.

2 Data from 2003 also excludes dependants of EEA and Swiss nationals in confirmed relationships granted permanent residence.

3 Includes nationals of the Czech Republic, Cyprus, Estonia, Hungary, Latvia, Lithuania, Malta, Poland, Slovakia and Slovenia before 1 May, but excludes them from this date.

4 Formerly known as Zaire.

5 Includes Taiwan.

6 Hong Kong (Special Administrative Region of China) includes British overseas territories citizens and stateless persons from Hong Kong and British Nationals (overseas).

7 Provisional

Source: Home Office: 020 8760 8341

5.11 Applications[1] received for asylum in the United Kingdom, excluding dependants, by nationality

Number of principal applicants

		1998	1999[2]	2000[2]	2001	2002	2003	2004	2005	2006[3]
Europe										
Albania	LQME	560	1 310	1 490	1 065	1 150	595	295	175	155
Macedonia	PTDW	50	90	65	755	310	60	15	5	–
Moldova	VQHP	25	180	235	425	820	380	170	115	45
Romania	KEAV	1 015	1 985	2 160	1 400	1 210	550	295	115	75
Russia	ZAEQ	185	685	1 000	450	295	280	190	130	115
Serbia & Montenegro	ZAFA	7 395	11 465	6 070	3 230	2 265	815	290	155	70
Turkey	KEAW	2 015	2 850	3 990	3 695	2 835	2 390	1 230	755	425
Ukraine	ZAER	370	775	770	445	365	300	120	55	50
E U Accession States	GH5T	4 975	5 350	3 745	2 025	3 200	310	75	10	10
Other Former USSR	ZAES	300	875	1 050	485	615	520	315	265	220
Europe Other	ZAEU	855	2 715	2 310	245	175	85	35	35	45
Total	KEAZ	17 745	28 280	22 880	14 215	13 235	6 295	3 025	1 810	1 210
Americas										
Colombia	KEBZ	425	1 000	505	365	420	220	120	70	60
Ecuador	KYDB	280	610	445	255	315	150	35	10	15
Jamaica	PTDX	105	180	310	525	1 310	965	455	325	215
Americas Other	PTDY	165	240	155	170	240	230	130	100	95
Total	KECT	975	2 025	1 420	1 315	2 290	1 560	740	505	385
Africa										
Algeria	KOTB	1 260	1 385	1 635	1 140	1 060	550	490	255	225
Angola	KECU	150	545	800	1 015	1 420	850	400	145	95
Burundi	PTDZ	215	780	620	610	700	650	265	90	35
Cameroon	VQHU	95	245	355	380	615	505	360	290	260
Congo	PTEA	150	450	485	540	600	320	150	65	45
Dem. Rep. Congo	KEEH	660	1 240	1 030	1 370	2 215	1 540	1 475	1 080	570
Eritrea	PTEC	345	565	505	620	1 180	950	1 105	1 760	2 585
Ethiopia	KECW	345	455	415	610	700	640	540	385	200
Gambia	DMMA	45	30	50	65	130	95	100	90	110
Ghana	KECX	225	195	285	190	275	325	355	230	130
Ivory Coast	DMLZ	95	190	445	275	315	390	280	210	170
Kenya	KOTC	885	485	455	305	350	220	145	100	95
Liberia	C53K	70	65	55	115	450	740	405	175	50
Nigeria	KECY	1 380	945	835	810	1 125	1 010	1 090	1 025	790
Rwanda	ZAEV	280	820	760	530	655	260	75	40	20
Sierra Leone	KOTD	565	1 125	1 330	1 940	1 155	380	230	135	125
Somalia	KECZ	4 685	7 495	5 020	6 420	6 540	5 090	2 585	1 760	1 845
Sudan	KEEE	250	280	415	390	655	930	1 305	885	670
Tanzania	DMMC	80	80	60	80	40	30	20	20	15
Uganda	KEEG	210	420	740	480	715	705	405	205	165
Zimbabwe	GRFS	80	230	1 010	2 140	7 655	3 295	2 065	1 075	1 650
Africa Other	PTEB	305	400	615	555	845	895	910	615	480
Total	KEEJ	12 380	18 435	17 920	20 590	29 390	20 370	14 745	10 640	10 340
Middle East										
Iran	KEEK	745	1 320	5 610	3 420	2 630	2 875	3 455	3 150	2 375
Iraq	KEEL	1 295	1 800	7 475	6 680	14 570	4 015	1 695	1 415	945
Libya	GH5U	115	115	155	140	200	145	160	125	90
Syria	GH5V	65	95	140	110	70	110	350	330	160
Middle East Other	ZAEX	565	835	1 035	915	850	825	870	715	735
Total	KEGY	2 785	4 165	14 415	11 265	18 315	7 970	6 525	5 730	4 305
Asia										
Afghanistan	DMLY	2 395	3 975	5 555	8 920	7 205	2 280	1 395	1 580	2 400
Bangladesh	ZAEY	460	530	795	510	720	735	510	425	440
China	KEGZ	1 925	2 625	4 000	2 390	3 675	3 450	2 365	1 730	1 945
India	KEIL	1 030	1 365	2 120	1 850	1 865	2 290	1 405	940	680
Pakistan	KEIM	1 975	2 615	3 165	2 860	2 405	1 915	1 710	1 145	965
Sri Lanka	KEIN	3 505	5 130	6 395	5 510	3 130	705	330	395	525
Vietnam	VQIB	35	105	180	400	840	1 125	755	380	90
Asia Other	PTEE	615	1 120	1 025	1 040	915	655	375	320	275
Total	KEJO	11 940	17 465	23 230	23 480	20 755	13 155	8 850	6 915	7 320
Nationality not known	KEJP	190	785	450	160	145	55	70	105	50
Grand Total	KEJQ	46 015	71 160	80 315	71 025	84 130	49 405	33 960	25 710	23 610

1 Figures rounded to the nearest 5.
2 May exclude some cases lodged at Local Enforcement Offices between January 1999 and March 2000.
3 Provisional figures.

Source: Home Office: 020 8760 8274

5.12 Marriages: by previous marital status, sex, age and country

Numbers

		1996	1997	1998	1999	2000	2001	2002	2003	2004	2005	2006
United Kingdom[1]												
Marriages	KKAA	317 514	310 218	304 797	301 083	305 912	286 129	293 021	308 623	313 551	286 826	275 140
Persons marrying per 1,000 resident population	KKAB	10.9	10.6	10.4	10.3	10.4	9.7	9.9	10.4	10.5	9.5	9.1
Previous marital status												
Single men[2]	KKAC	221 826	216 237	214 005	211 820	213 777	202 690	206 196	217 534	221 477	201 791	195 089
Divorced men	KKAD	87 113	85 625	82 977	81 750	84 771	76 852	80 040	84 011	85 210	78 537	73 885
Widowers	KKAE	8 575	8 356	7 815	7 513	7 364	6 587	6 785	7 078	6 864	6 498	6 163
Single women[2]	KKAF	221 697	216 776	215 399	213 246	215 865	205 048	208 385	219 828	224 344	205 569	199 291
Divorced women	KKAG	87 618	85 648	82 016	80 816	83 166	74 807	78 182	82 181	82 559	75 120	69 921
Widows	KKAH	8 199	7 794	7 382	7 021	6 881	6 274	6 454	6 614	6 648	6 137	5 925
First marriage for both partners	KMGH	185 293	181 135	180 404	178 759	180 020	171 912	174 374	184 661	188 517	173 123	168 535
First marriage for one partner	KMGI	72 937	70 743	68 596	67 548	69 602	63 914	65 833	68 040	68 787	61 114	57 320
Remarriage for both partners	KMGJ	59 284	58 340	55 797	54 776	56 290	50 303	52 814	55 922	56 247	52 589	49 292
Males												
Under 21 years	KKAI	5 497	5 126	5 173	5 234	5 019	4 625	4 396	4 340	4 233	3 262	2 770
21-24	KKAJ	42 488	36 875	32 723	29 390	28 467	25 840	26 293	27 155	27 223	22 355	20 586
25-29	KKAK	101 647	97 345	94 696	90 412	85 870	78 687	74 858	75 580	74 873	67 943	65 577
30-34	KKAL	69 867	70 904	71 096	72 129	73 809	70 657	72 592	75 892	75 705	68 453	64 013
35-44	KKAM	56 513	58 292	59 838	62 114	68 019	65 242	69 747	75 695	79 510	74 343	71 837
45-54	KKAN	26 252	26 472	26 118	26 581	28 791	26 122	27 801	30 387	31 851	30 737	30 592
55 and over	KKAO	15 250	15 204	15 153	15 223	15 937	14 956	17 334	19 574	20 156	19 733	19 772
Females												
Under 21 years	KKAP	18 485	17 254	16 793	16 082	15 938	13 874	13 194	13 510	12 878	9 113	8 004
21-24	KKAQ	66 191	59 549	54 645	50 350	48 578	45 687	45 789	47 400	46 891	39 482	36 633
25-29	KKAR	99 651	97 932	97 181	94 703	92 753	85 647	82 892	84 066	84 714	79 579	77 698
30-34	KKAS	57 752	58 589	59 349	60 446	62 478	59 859	62 279	65 979	66 508	61 047	57 312
35-44	KKAT	45 969	47 267	47 721	50 136	54 697	52 209	56 997	61 682	65 007	60 969	58 766
45-54	KKAU	21 025	21 038	20 708	20 822	22 621	20 459	22 187	24 721	25 846	24 982	24 903
55 and over	KKAV	8 441	8 589	8 400	8 544	8 847	8 394	9 683	11 265	11 707	11 654	11 821
England and Wales[1]												
Marriages	KKBA	278 975	272 536	267 303	263 515	267 961	249 227	255 596	270 109	273 069	247 805	236 980
Persons marrying per 1,000 resident population	KKBB	10.9	10.6	10.3	10.1	10.3	9.5	9.7	10.2	10.3	9.3	8.8
Previous marital status												
Single men[2]	KKBC	193 306	188 268	186 329	184 266	186 113	175 721	179 121	189 470	191 956	173 413	167 200
Divorced men	KKBD	78 003	76 839	74 029	72 617	75 378	67 678	70 506	74 397	75 129	68 672	64 400
Widowers	KKBE	7 666	7 429	6 945	6 632	6 470	5 828	5 969	6 242	5 984	5 720	5 380
Single women[2]	KKBF	192 707	188 457	187 391	185 328	187 717	177 506	180 675	191 170	194 348	176 505	170 710
Divorced women	KKBG	78 939	77 098	73 330	71 971	74 092	66 120	69 234	73 071	72 875	65 915	61 100
Widows	KKBH	7 329	6 981	6 582	6 216	6 152	5 601	5 687	5 868	5 846	5 385	5 170
First marriage for both partners	KMGK	160 680	156 907	156 539	155 027	156 140	148 642	151 014	160 283	163 007	148 405	144 120
First marriage for one partner	KMGL	64 653	62 911	60 642	59 540	61 550	55 943	57 768	60 074	60 290	53 108	49 680
Remarriage for both partners	KMGM	53 642	52 718	50 122	48 948	50 271	44 642	46 814	49 752	49 772	46 292	43 190
Males												
Under 21 years	KKBI	4 877	4 574	4 608	4 629	4 536	4 160	3 952	3 885	3 803	2 883	2 470
21-24	KKBJ	36 713	31 907	28 389	25 424	24 764	22 436	22 961	23 802	23 873	19 430	17 820
25-29	KKBK	88 338	84 644	82 135	78 364	74 367	67 934	64 619	65 568	64 701	58 066	55 950
30-34	KKBL	61 582	62 265	62 323	63 212	64 611	61 409	62 998	66 060	65 510	58 830	54 920
35-44	KKBM	50 038	51 654	52 812	54 528	59 834	56 872	61 196	66 364	69 364	64 394	61 960
45-54	KKBN	23 661	23 688	23 385	23 676	25 470	22 949	24 336	26 785	27 830	26 679	26 300
55 and over	KKBO	13 766	13 804	13 651	13 682	14 379	13 467	15 534	17 645	17 988	17 523	17 570
Females												
Under 21 years	KKBP	16 510	15 439	15 065	14 379	14 421	12 467	11 916	12 270	11 667	8 182	7 180
21-24	KKBQ	57 296	51 766	47 446	43 691	42 265	39 746	39 968	41 567	40 962	34 185	31 760
25-29	KKBR	86 838	85 352	84 399	82 250	80 312	73 799	71 540	72 790	73 072	68 062	66 310
30-34	KKBS	50 799	51 405	51 982	52 721	54 649	51 865	53 970	57 348	57 592	52 369	49 030
35-44	KKBT	40 889	41 838	42 245	44 199	48 245	45 672	49 984	54 103	56 660	52 758	50 550
45-54	KKBU	18 992	18 938	18 575	18 572	20 083	18 071	19 535	21 858	22 648	21 811	21 550
55 and over	KKBV	7 651	7 798	7 591	7 703	7 986	7 607	8 683	10 173	10 468	10 438	10 600

5.12 Marriages: by previous marital status, sex, age and country
continued

Numbers

		1996	1997	1998	1999	2000	2001	2002	2003	2004	2005	2006
Scotland												
Marriages	KKCA	30 242	29 611	29 668	29 940	30 367	29 621	29 826	30 757	32 154	30 881	29 898
Persons marrying per 1,000 resident population	KKCB	11.9	11.7	11.7	11.8	12.0	11.7	11.8	12.2	12.7	12.1	11.7
Previous marital status												
Single men[2]	KKCC	21 454	20 994	20 987	21 052	21 201	20 737	20 671	21 477	22 526	21 421	20 912
Divorced men	KKCD	8 048	7 845	7 934	8 142	8 427	8 238	8 475	8 574	8 930	8 796	8 330
Widowers	KKCE	740	772	747	746	739	646	680	706	698	664	656
Single women[2]	KKCF	21 799	21 303	21 241	21 308	21 608	21 223	21 180	21 974	22 884	21 991	21 460
Divorced women	KKCG	7 718	7 621	7 754	7 949	8 141	7 825	8 008	8 157	8 622	8 244	7 802
Widows	KKCH	725	687	673	683	618	573	638	626	648	646	636
First marriage for both partners	KEZV	18 071	17 751	17 677	17 680	17 864	17 468	17 426	18 232	19 039	18 221	17 922
First marriage for one partner	KEZW	7 111	6 795	6 874	7 000	7 081	7 024	6 999	6 987	7 332	6 970	6 528
Remarriage for both partners	KEZX	5 060	5 065	5 117	5 260	5 422	5 129	5 401	5 538	5 783	5 690	5 448
Males												
Under 21 years	KKCI	452	406	421	490	364	371	367	361	336	304	228
21-24	KKCJ	4 191	3 494	3 147	2 853	2 720	2 489	2 395	2 507	2 501	2 120	2 012
25-29	KKCK	10 056	9 495	9 439	9 031	8 536	7 949	7 468	7 219	7 365	6 981	6 795
30-34	KKCL	6 574	6 911	6 988	7 179	7 419	7 464	7 692	7 752	7 992	7 516	6 935
35-44	KKCM	5 412	5 649	5 945	6 470	7 018	7 215	7 328	8 007	8 553	8 390	8 234
45-54	KKCN	2 288	2 459	2 412	2 575	2 960	2 816	3 033	3 213	3 503	3 588	3 772
55 and over	KKCO	1 269	1 197	1 316	1 342	1 350	1 317	1 543	1 698	1 904	1 982	1 922
Females												
Under 21 years	KKCP	1 423	1 302	1 289	1 322	1 171	1 111	996	1 007	954	724	635
21-24	KKCQ	6 474	5 568	5 248	4 778	4 581	4 343	4 171	4 199	4 358	3 772	3 473
25-29	KKCR	9 818	9 574	9 764	9 539	9 495	8 994	8 520	8 321	8 528	8 339	8 230
30-34	KKCS	5 675	5 927	6 036	6 433	6 463	6 618	6 832	7 110	7 235	7 016	6 511
35-44	KKCT	4 378	4 722	4 726	5 150	5 633	5 712	6 115	6 583	7 163	7 083	7 003
45-54	KKCU	1 794	1 844	1 900	1 994	2 279	2 147	2 322	2 589	2 821	2 862	2 975
55 and over	KKCV	680	674	705	724	745	696	870	948	1 095	1 085	1 071
Northern Ireland												
Marriages	KKDA	8 297	8 071	7 826	7 628	7 584	7 281	7 599	7 757	8 328	8 140	8 259
Persons marrying per 1,000 resident population	KKDB	10.0	9.7	9.3	9.1	9.0	8.6	9.0	9.1	9.7	9.4	8.0
Previous marital status												
Single men[2]	KKDC	7 066	6 975	6 689	6 502	6 463	6 232	6 404	6 587	6 995	6 957	6 977
Divorced men	KKDD	1 062	941	1 014	991	966	936	1 059	1 040	1 151	1 069	1 155
Widowers	KKDE	169	155	123	135	155	113	136	130	182	114	127
Single women[2]	KKDF	7 191	7 016	6 767	6 610	6 540	6 319	6 530	6 684	7 112	7 073	7 121
Divorced women	KKDG	961	929	932	896	933	862	940	953	1 062	961	1 019
Widows	KKDH	145	126	127	122	111	100	129	120	154	106	119
First marriage for both partners	KEZY	6 542	6 477	6 188	6 052	6 016	5 802	5 934	6 146	6 471	6 497	6 493
First marriage for one partner	KEZZ	1 173	1 037	1 080	1 008	971	947	1 066	979	1 165	1 036	1 112
Remarriage for both partners	KFBI	582	557	558	568	597	532	599	632	692	607	654
Males												
Under 21 years	KKDI	168	146	144	115	119	94	77	94	94	75	72
21-24	KKDJ	1 584	1 474	1 187	1 113	983	915	937	846	849	805	754
25-29	KKDK	3 253	3 206	3 122	3 017	2 967	2 804	2 771	2 793	2 807	2 896	2 832
30-34	KKDL	1 711	1 728	1 785	1 738	1 779	1 784	1 902	2 080	2 203	2 107	2 158
35-44	KKDM	1 063	989	1 081	1 116	1 167	1 155	1 223	1 324	1 593	1 559	1 643
45-54	KKDN	303	325	321	330	361	357	432	389	518	470	520
55 and over	KKDO	215	203	186	199	208	172	257	231	264	228	280
Females												
Under 21 years	KKDP	552	513	439	381	346	296	282	233	257	207	189
21-24	KKDQ	2 421	2 215	1 951	1 881	1 732	1 598	1 650	1 634	1 571	1 525	1 400
25-29	KKDR	2 995	3 006	3 018	2 914	2 946	2 854	2 832	2 955	3 114	3 178	3 158
30-34	KKDS	1 278	1 257	1 331	1 292	1 366	1 376	1 477	1 521	1 681	1 662	1 771
35-44	KKDT	702	707	750	787	819	825	898	996	1 184	1 128	1 213
45-54	KKDU	239	256	233	256	259	241	330	274	377	309	378
55 and over	KKDV	110	117	104	117	116	91	130	144	144	131	150

1 Figures for 2006 are rounded and provisional.
2 Single men and single women are those who have never been married.

Sources: Office for National Statistics: 01329 444110;
General Register Office for Scotland;
Northern Ireland Statistics and Research Agency

5.13 Divorce: by duration of marriage, age of wife and country

Numbers

		1996	1997	1998	1999	2000	2001	2002	2003	2004	2005	2006
United Kingdom												
Decrees absolute granted[1,2,5]												
Number	ZBRL	171 729	161 087	160 057	158 746	154 628	156 814	160 726	166 737	167 138	155 052	148 141
Duration of marriage												
0-4 years	ZBRM	37 016	33 719	33 087	31 047	28 933	28 306	28 591	28 781	28 746	26 549	25 005
5-9 years	ZBRN	48 670	45 040	44 243	43 357	41 621	42 360	42 924	43 558	42 855	39 070	37 116
10-14 years	ZBRO	30 159	29 085	29 706	30 270	30 166	30 849	31 257	32 564	31 775	29 007	27 647
15-19 years	ZBRP	21 379	20 211	20 078	20 147	19 902	20 568	21 881	23 119	23 898	22 593	21 244
20 years and over	ZBRQ	34 487	33 020	32 935	33 916	34 000	34 729	36 073	38 713	39 844	37 824	37 116
Not stated	ZBRR	18	12	8	9	6	2	..	2	20	9	13
Age of wife at marriage												
16-19 years	ZBRS	33 590	28 987	27 627	25 440	23 505	22 558	22 107	22 367	20 948	18 507	16 707
20-24 years	ZBRT	78 075	72 971	71 416	69 509	66 215	66 282	66 264	67 070	65 671	58 829	55 085
25-29 years	ZBRU	33 634	33 452	34 195	35 585	36 009	37 418	39 116	41 464	42 544	40 143	38 812
30-34 years	ZBRV	13 122	12 968	13 719	14 420	14 892	15 842	17 374	18 658	19 729	19 366	19 419
35-39 years	ZBRW	6 470	6 155	6 571	6 848	6 993	7 417	8 070	8 742	9 456	9 275	9 261
40-44 years	ZBRX	3 507	3 375	3 360	3 557	3 568	3 778	4 104	4 404	4 550	4 703	4 677
45 years and over	ZBRY	3 239	3 094	3 086	3 291	3 352	3 429	3 572	3 917	4 093	4 042	3 985
Not stated	ZBRZ	92	85	83	96	94	90	119	115	147	187	195
Age of wife at divorce												
16-24 years	ZBSA	9 298	7 371	6 758	5 671	5 115	4 874	4 998	5 092	4 885	4 388	3 739
25-29 years	ZBSB	32 808	28 814	26 968	24 120	21 280	19 635	18 340	17 633	16 972	14 870	14 216
30-34 years	ZBSC	39 497	37 257	36 795	36 052	34 356	34 194	33 555	32 774	30 754	26 431	23 641
35-39 years	ZBSD	31 497	30 641	31 688	32 605	32 588	33 997	35 050	36 465	35 894	32 722	30 567
40-44 years	ZBSE	22 843	22 246	22 810	23 614	23 879	25 579	27 564	30 154	31 372	30 359	29 412
45 years and over	ZBSF	35 684	34 662	34 947	36 578	37 311	38 442	41 102	44 498	47 108	46 085	46 352
Not stated	ZBSG	102	96	91	106	99	93	117	121	153	197	214
Divorces in which there were[3,4]												
No children aged under 16	ZBSH	..	..	..	..	..	..	..	..	..	..	..
One or more children aged under 16	ZBSI	..	..	..	..	..	..	..	..	..	..	..
England and Wales												
Decrees absolute granted[1,2]												
Number	KKEA	157 107	146 689	145 214	144 556	141 135	143 818	147 735	153 490	153 399	141 750	132 562
Rate per 1,000 married couples	KKEB	13.8	13.0	12.9	12.9	12.7	12.9	13.4	14.0	14.1	13.0	12.2
Duration of marriage												
0-4 years	KKEC	34 924	31 767	31 136	29 307	27 474	26 987	27 344	27 511	27 389	25 345	23 427
5-9 years	KKED	44 609	41 260	40 239	39 676	38 206	39 079	39 730	40 599	39 779	36 161	33 864
10-14 years	KKEE	27 332	26 215	26 698	27 384	27 459	28 176	28 592	29 831	29 086	26 394	24 680
15-19 years	KKEF	19 321	18 027	17 934	18 072	17 870	18 603	19 784	20 923	21 591	20 363	18 792
20 years and over	KKEG	30 912	29 408	29 199	30 108	30 120	30 971	32 285	34 624	35 554	33 478	31 786
Not stated	KKEH	9	12	8	9	6	2	–	2	–	9	13
Age of wife at marriage												
16-19 years	KKEI	29 927	25 579	24 276	22 486	20 930	20 218	19 828	20 063	18 709	16 519	14 478
20-24 years	KKEJ	71 123	66 167	64 453	62 853	59 874	60 211	60 353	61 057	59 548	53 041	48 550
25-29 years	KKEK	31 396	31 022	31 533	32 867	33 282	34 759	36 387	38 722	39 575	37 103	35 177
30-34 years	KKEL	12 335	12 094	12 788	13 507	13 972	14 890	16 339	17 567	18 545	18 138	17 834
35-39 years	KKEM	6 051	5 767	6 153	6 432	6 562	6 956	7 623	8 249	8 912	8 755	8 560
40-44 years	KKEN	3 254	3 156	3 135	3 331	3 378	3 559	3 841	4 154	4 274	4 421	4 318
45 years and over	KKEO	3 021	2 904	2 876	3 080	3 137	3 225	3 364	3 678	3 836	3 773	3 645
Age of wife at divorce												
16-24 years	KKEP	8 615	6 871	6 298	5 318	4 839	4 643	4 808	4 867	4 658	4 216	3 525
25-29 years	KKEQ	30 075	26 435	24 586	22 173	19 650	18 231	17 227	16 539	15 867	13 905	13 182
30-34 years	KKER	36 274	33 967	33 446	32 837	31 420	31 489	30 982	30 345	28 368	24 381	21 409
35-39 years	KKES	28 727	27 715	28 605	29 663	29 820	31 164	32 282	33 519	33 013	29 864	27 479
40-44 years	KKET	20 774	20 125	20 521	21 325	21 469	23 190	25 017	27 610	28 558	27 570	26 128
45 years and over	KKEU	32 633	31 564	31 750	33 231	33 931	35 099	37 419	40 608	42 935	41 805	40 826
Not stated	KKEV	9	12	8	9	6	2	–	2	–	9	13
Divorces in which there were[3]												
No children aged under 16	ZBSJ	70 174	66 019	64 738	65 258	64 359	64 541	66 738	69 681	71 382	88 349	62 667
One or more children aged under 16	ZBSK	86 933	80 670	80 476	79 298	76 776	79 277	80 997	83 809	82 017	75 340	69 895

5.13 Divorce: by duration of marriage, age of wife and country
continued

Numbers

		1996	1997	1998	1999	2000	2001	2002	2003	2004	2005	2006
Scotland												
Decrees absolute granted[2]												
Number	KKFA	12 308	12 222	12 384	11 864	11 143	10 631	10 826	10 928	11 227	10 940	13 014
Rate per 1,000 married couples	KKFB	10.9	11.0	11.3	10.9	10.3	9.7	10.0	10.2	10.5	10.3	12.3
Duration of marriage												
0-4 years	KKFC	1 914	1 793	1 766	1 588	1 304	1 159	1 128	1 141	1 204	1 089	1 444
5-9 years	KKFD	3 432	3 224	3 360	3 095	2 890	2 721	2 689	2 450	2 536	2 403	2 759
10-14 years	KKFE	2 310	2 385	2 456	2 368	2 168	2 163	2 183	2 222	2 173	2 113	2 418
15-19 years	KKFF	1 709	1 804	1 729	1 686	1 622	1 562	1 705	1 773	1 810	1 789	2 033
20 years and over	KKFG	2 934	3 016	3 073	3 127	3 159	3 026	3 121	3 342	3 504	3 546	4 360
Not stated	ZBSL	9	–	–	–	–	–	–	–	–	–	–
Age of wife at marriage												
16-19 years	ZBSM	2 939	2 749	2 654	2 374	2 043	1 839	1 845	1 816	1 753	1 557	1 764
20-24 years	ZBSN	5 822	5 714	5 744	5 453	5 142	4 873	4 823	4 869	4 892	4 721	5 373
25-29 years	KKFJ	1 933	2 151	2 314	2 333	2 318	2 233	2 316	2 307	2 462	2 515	3 075
30-34 years	KKFK	697	791	824	829	805	827	895	958	1 025	1 065	1 387
35-39 years	KKFL	393	360	382	379	378	401	407	432	489	455	619
40-44 years	KKFM	234	199	198	208	170	193	235	219	252	252	325
45 years and over	KKFN	198	173	185	192	193	175	186	212	221	232	312
Not stated	KKFO	92	85	83	96	94	90	119	115	133	143	159
Age of wife at divorce												
16-24 years	KKFP	583	426	377	301	232	182	180	191	192	148	190
25-29 years	KKFQ	2 269	2 021	1 957	1 597	1 330	1 109	974	884	869	777	877
30-34 years	KKFR	2 708	2 736	2 767	2 642	2 381	2 215	2 174	1 943	1 918	1 641	1 837
35-39 years	KKFS	2 307	2 469	2 562	2 450	2 298	2 311	2 281	2 388	2 278	2 304	2 544
40-44 years	KKFT	1 761	1 819	1 951	1 929	1 999	1 963	2 110	2 106	2 341	2 330	2 751
45 years and over	KKFU	2 587	2 667	2 687	2 848	2 810	2 760	2 990	3 297	3 496	3 596	4 650
Not stated	KKFV	93	84	83	97	93	91	117	119	133	144	165
Divorces in which there were[3,4]												
No children aged under 16	KKFW	..	..	..	..	..	..	..	..	..	..	..
One or more children under 16	KKFX	..	..	..	..	..	..	..	..	..	..	..
Northern Ireland												
Decrees absolute granted:[2,5]												
Number	ZBSO	2 314	2 176	2 459	2 326	2 350	2 365	2 165	2 319	2 512	2 362	2 565
Duration of marriage												
0-4 years	ZBSP	178	159	185	152	155	160	119	129	153	115	134
5-9 years	ZBSQ	629	556	644	586	525	560	505	509	540	506	493
10-14 years	ZBSR	517	485	552	518	539	510	482	511	516	500	549
15-19 years	ZBSS	349	380	415	389	410	403	392	423	497	441	419
20 years and over	ZBST	641	596	663	681	721	732	667	747	786	800	970
Not stated[5]	EK8B	–	–	–	–	–	–	–	–	20	–	..
Age of wife at marriage												
16-19 years	ZBSU	724	659	697	580	532	501	434	488	486	431	465
20-24 years	ZBSV	1 130	1 090	1 219	1 203	1 199	1 198	1 088	1 144	1 231	1 067	1 162
25-29 years	ZBSW	305	279	348	385	409	426	413	435	507	525	560
30-34 years	ZBSX	90	83	107	84	115	125	140	133	159	163	198
35-39 years	ZBSY	26	28	36	37	53	60	40	61	55	65	82
40-44 years	ZBSZ	19	20	27	18	20	26	28	31	24	30	34
45 years and over	ZBTA	20	17	25	19	22	29	22	27	36	37	28
Not stated[6]	EK8C	–	–	–	–	–	–	–	–	14	44	..
Age of wife at divorce												
16-24 years	ZBTB	100	74	83	52	44	49	10	34	35	24	24
25-29 years	ZBTC	464	358	425	350	300	295	139	210	236	188	157
30-34 years	ZBTD	515	554	582	573	555	490	399	486	468	409	395
35-39 years	ZBTE	463	457	521	492	470	522	487	558	603	554	544
40-44 years	ZBTF	308	302	338	360	411	426	437	438	473	459	533
45 years and over	ZBTG	464	431	510	499	570	583	693	593	677	684	876
Not stated[6]	EK8D	–	–	–	–	–	–	–	–	20	44	36
Divorces in which there were[3]												
No children aged under 16	ZBTH	1 676	1 573	1 807	1 649	1 051	1 054	972	1 050	1 218	982	662
One or more children aged under 16	ZBTI	638	603	652	677	1 299	1 311	1 193	1 269	1 282	1 380	1 903
Not stated[6]	EK8E	–	–	–	–	–	–	–	–	12	–	..

1 Data for 2006 are provisional.
2 Includes decrees of nullities.
3 Children of the family as defined by the Matrimonial Causes Act 1973.
4 Data not available in Scotland.
5 Marital estimates are not available for Northern Ireland - no divorce rate for UK/Northern Ireland.
6 Due to some incomplete records.

Sources: Office for National Statistics: 01329 444410;
General Register Office for Scotland;
Northern Ireland Statistics and Research Agency

5.14 Divorce proceedings: by country

Numbers

		1996	1997	1998	1999	2000	2001	2002	2003	2004	2005	2006
United Kingdom												
Dissolution of marriage[1,4]												
Decree absolute/decree granted	ZBXR	171 309	160 733	159 688	158 418	154 273	156 562	160 528	166 536	166 937	154 879	147 989
On grounds of:												
Adultery	ZBXS	41 127	38 652	37 302	35 545	34 082	33 452	33 389	33 844	32 586	28 411	25 293
Behaviour	ZBXT	72 581	68 546	68 685	67 851	65 687	66 818	68 499	70 866	70 879	66 824	63 782
Desertion	ZBXU	1 101	956	828	748	722	718	727	697	675	612	516
Separation (2 years and consent)	ZBXV	42 265	39 398	39 627	40 368	39 763	40 699	42 579	44 012	44 819	41 433	36 917
Separation(5 years)	ZBXW	13 547	12 552	12 697	13 389	13 653	14 575	15 076	16 831	17 714	17 101	15 297
Combination of more than one ground and other	ZBXX	688	629	549	517	366	300	258	286	264	498	601
Separation[2]												
1 year and consent	IE9T	..	..	..	..	..	..	..	..	..	..	1 456
2 years	IE9U	..	..	..	..	..	..	..	..	..	..	4 217
Decree absolute/decree granted to:												
the wife	ZBXY	119 569	111 910	111 555	109 824	106 957	107 345	108 104	114 664	113 970	105 008	100 003
the husband	ZBXZ	51 247	48 393	47 764	48 236	47 069	49 015	52 251	51 691	52 793	49 725	47 847
both	ZBYA	493	430	369	358	247	202	173	181	174	146	139
Nullity of marriage												
Decree absolute/decree granted	ZBYB	420	354	369	328	355	252	198	201	201	173	152
England and Wales												
Dissolution of marriage[4]												
Petitions filed[3]	KKGA	177 970	163 769	165 870	162 137	157 809	172 341	177 224	173 265	167 340	151 824	148 564
Decree nisi granted[3]	KKGM	157 588	148 310	144 231	143 446	143 729	163 146	170 980	168 037	166 334	150 917	145 242
Decree absolute granted	KKGN	156 692	146 339	144 851	144 233	140 783	143 568	147 538	153 294	153 199	141 583	132 418
On grounds of:												
Adultery	KKGB	40 012	37 592	36 319	34 584	33 310	32 839	32 829	33 331	32 035	27 992	24 936
Behaviour	KKGC	68 986	65 047	65 257	64 816	63 182	64 768	66 480	68 944	68 859	65 169	62 234
Desertion	KKGD	1 030	912	790	713	680	689	681	665	654	593	499
Separation (2 years and consent)	KKGE	35 422	32 638	32 394	33 482	32 820	33 703	35 476	36 931	37 543	34 388	31 794
Separation(5 years)	KKGF	10 626	9 592	9 616	10 193	10 498	11 355	11 896	13 239	13 933	13 196	12 628
Combination of more than one ground and other	ZBYC	616	558	475	445	293	214	176	184	175	245	327
Decree absolute granted to:												
the wife	ZBYD	109 489	102 173	101 583	100 469	98 227	98 992	102 676	106 208	105 381	96 855	90 587
the husband	ZBYE	46 712	43 739	42 902	43 413	42 311	44 378	44 694	46 915	47 651	44 583	41 702
both	ZBYF	491	427	366	351	245	198	168	171	167	145	129
Nullity of marriage												
Petitions filed[3]	KKGO	702	485	505	549	452	492	443	463	495	440	406
Decree nisi granted[3]	KKGR	332	248	281	495	274	160	216	204	308	260	240
Decree absolute granted	KKGS	415	350	363	323	352	250	197	196	200	167	144
Judicial separation												
Petitions filed[4]	KKGT	1 584	1 078	916	882	650	1 078	1 001	826	745	697	613
Decrees granted[4]	KKGW	1 199	589	519	696	540	925	560	467	419	387	353

5.14 Divorce proceedings: by country
continued

Numbers

		1996	1997	1998	1999	2000	2001	2002	2003	2004	2005	2006
Scotland												
Dissolution of marriage[1]												
Decree granted	ZBYG	12 307	12 220	12 383	11 860	11 142	10 631	10 825	10 927	11 226	10 939	13 013
On grounds of:												
Adultery	ZBYH	943	909	832	770	610	473	428	401	413	327	263
Behaviour	ZBYI	3 184	3 081	3 005	2 611	2 099	1 639	1 656	1 537	1 546	1 344	1 215
Desertion	ZBYJ	61	33	28	18	34	24	42	23	15	17	15
Separation (2 years and consent)	ZBYK	5 835	5 773	6 121	5 908	5 878	5 943	6 101	6 016	6 122	5 989	4 014
Separation(5 years)	ZBYL	2 284	2 424	2 397	2 553	2 521	2 552	2 598	2 950	3 130	3 262	1 923
Separation[2]												
1 year and consent	IE9T	..	..	..	..	..	..	..	..	..	..	1 456
2 years	IE9U	..	..	..	..	..	..	..	..	..	..	4 217
Decree granted to[2]												
the wife	ZBYM	8 558	8 266	8 328	7 770	7 190	6 775	6 800	6 926	6 938	6 653	7 750
the husband	ZBYN	3 749	3 954	4 055	4 090	3 952	3 856	4 025	4 001	4 288	4 286	5 263
Nullity of marriage												
Decree granted	ZBYO	1	2	1	4	1	–	1	1	1	1	1
Northern Ireland												
Dissolution of marriage												
Petitions filed	ZBYP	2 695	2 808	2 760	2 414	3 005	2 869	2 929	3 192	2 808	3 299	3 098
Decree nisi granted	ZBYQ	2 419	2 532	2 904	2 393	2 456	2 615	2 454	2 616	2 697	2 594	2 607
Decree absolute granted	ZBYR	2 310	2 174	2 454	2 325	2 348	2 363	2 165	2 315	2 512	2 357	2 558
On grounds of:												
Adultery	ZBYS	172	151	151	191	162	140	132	112	138	92	94
Behaviour	ZBYT	411	418	423	424	406	411	363	385	474	311	333
Desertion	ZBYU	10	11	10	17	8	5	3	9	6	2	2
Separation (2 years and consent)	ZBYV	1 010	991	1 112	978	1 065	1 053	1 002	1 065	1 154	1 056	1 109
Separation(5 years)	ZBYW	637	536	684	643	634	668	582	642	651	643	746
Combination of more than one ground and other	ZBYX	70	67	74	72	73	86	83	102	89	253	274
Decree absolute granted to:												
the wife	ZBYY	1 522	1 473	1 644	1 585	1 540	1 578	1 405	1 530	1 651	1 500	1 666
the husband	ZBYZ	786	698	807	733	806	781	755	775	854	856	882
both	ZBZA	2	3	3	7	2	4	5	10	7	1	10
Nullity of marriage												
Petitions filed	ZBZB	5	7	5	1	2	1	5	4	8	9	–
Decree nisi granted	ZBZC	5	2	6	2	5	2	2	5	3	3	3
Decree absolute granted	ZBZD	4	2	5	1	2	2	–	4	–	5	7
Judicial separation												
Petitions filed	ZBZE	63	70	64	50	54	40	27	35	18	3	7
Decrees granted	ZBZF	22	34	40	31	23	25	15	22	12	4	8

1 The terms petition filed, decree nisi granted, decree absolute and judicial separation are not used in Scotland. Decree absolute granted to 'both' and 'Combination of more than one ground and other' are not procedures used in Scotland.

2 New categories introduced with effect from 4 May 2006 by the Family Law (Scotland) Act 2006. These replace the two 'non-cohabitation' categories (non-cohabiation is a category that is used in Scotland only) of 2 years with consent and 5 years.

3 Data supplied by Ministry of Justice (12 February 2008) see Judicial and Court Statistics 2006.

4 2006 data are provisional.

Sources: Office for National Statistics: 01329 444410;
General Register Office for Scotland;
Northern Ireland Statistics and Research Agency;
Ministry of Justice (England & Wales);
Scottish Courts Administration;
Northern Ireland Courts Administration

Population and vital statistics

5.15 Births:[1] by country and sex

	Live births				Rates				
	Total	Male	Female	Sex ratio[2]	Crude birth rate[3]	General fertility rate[4]	TFR[5]	Still- births[6]	Still- birth rate[6]
United Kingdom[7]									
1900 - 02	1 095	558	537	1 037	28.6	115.1	..	..	..
1910 - 12	1 037	528	508	1 039	24.6	99.4	..	..	..
1920 - 22	1 018	522	496	1 052	23.1	93.0	..	..	..
1930 - 32	750	383	367	1 046	16.3	66.5	..	..	..
1940 - 42	723	372	351	1 062	15.0	..	1.89	..	..
1950 - 52	803	413	390	1 061	16.0	73.7	2.21	..	..
1960 - 62	946	487	459	1 063	17.9	90.3	2.80	18.6	19.2
1970 - 72	880	453	427	1 064	15.8	82.5	2.36	11.3	12.7
1980 - 82	735	377	358	1 053	13.0	62.5	1.83	5.0	6.8
1990 - 92	790	405	385	1 051	13.8	63.7	1.81	3.6	4.6
2000 - 02	672	345	328	1 052	11.4	54.7	1.64	3.6	5.4
	BBCA	KBCZ	KBCY	KMFW	KBCT	KBCS	KBCR	KBCQ	KMFX
1996	733	376	357	1 055	12.6	60.2	1.73	4.1	5.5
1997	727	372	354	1 051	12.6	59.6	1.72	3.9	5.3
1998	717	367	350	1 052	12.3	58.8	1.71	3.9	5.4
1999	700	359	341	1 056	11.9	57.3	1.68	3.7	5.3
2000	679	348	331	1 051	11.5	55.4	1.64	3.6	5.3
2001	669	343	326	1 050	11.3	54.3	1.63	3.6	5.3
2002	669	343	326	1 054	11.3	54.2	1.64	3.8	5.6
2003	696	357	339	1 052	11.7	56.2	1.71	4.0	5.7
2004	716	368	348	1 055	12.0	57.7	1.77	4.1	5.7
2005	723	370	353	1 050	12.0	57.8	1.78	3.9	5.3
2006	749	383	366	1 047	12.4	59.7	1.84	4.0	5.3
England and Wales									
1900 - 02	932	475	458	1 037	28.6	114.7	..	..	..
1910 - 12	884	450	433	1 040	24.5	98.6	..	..	..
1920 - 22	862	442	420	1 051	22.8	91.1	..	..	..
1930 - 32	632	323	309	1 047	15.8	64.4	..	27.0	..
1940 - 42	607	312	295	1 057	15.6	61.3	1.81	22.0	..
1950 - 52	683	351	332	1 058	15.6	72.1	2.16	16.0	..
1960 - 62	812	418	394	1 061	17.6	88.9	2.77	15.6	18.9
1970 - 72	764	394	371	1 061	15.6	81.4	2.31	9.7	12.5
1980 - 82	639	328	311	1 053	12.9	61.8	1.81	4.3	6.7
1990 - 92	698	358	340	1 051	13.8	63.8	1.82	3.2	4.5
2000 - 02	598	307	292	1 052	11.4	55.2	1.65	3.2	5.4
	BBCB	KMFY	KMFZ	KMGA	KMGB	KMGC	KMGD	KMGE	KMGF
1996	649	333	316	1 055	12.6	60.6	1.74	3.5	5.4
1997	643	330	314	1 051	12.5	60.0	1.73	3.4	5.3
1998	636	326	310	1 051	12.3	59.2	1.72	3.4	5.3
1999	622	319	303	1 055	12.0	57.8	1.70	3.3	5.3
2000	604	310	295	1 050	11.6	55.9	1.65	3.2	5.3
2001	595	305	290	1 050	11.4	54.7	1.63	3.2	5.3
2002	596	306	290	1 055	11.3	54.7	1.65	3.4	5.6
2003	621	318	303	1 051	11.8	56.8	1.73	3.6	5.8
2004	640	328	311	1 054	12.1	58.2	1.78	3.7	5.7
2005	646	331	315	1 049	12.1	58.3	1.79	3.5	5.4
2006	670	342	327	1 047	12.5	60.2	1.86	3.6	5.4

5.15 Births:[1] by country and sex
continued

Thousands

	Live births				Rates				
	Total	Male	Female	Sex ratio[2]	Crude birth rate[3]	General fertility rate[4]	TFR[5]	Still-births[6]	Still-birth rate[6]
Scotland									
1900 - 02	132	67	65	1 046	29.5	120.6	..	..	..
1910 - 12	123	63	60	1 044	25.9	107.4	..	..	..
1920 - 22	125	64	61	1 046	25.6	105.9	..	..	..
1930 - 32	93	47	45	1 040	19.1	78.8	..	..	..
1940 - 42	89	46	43	1 051	18.5	73.7	..	4.0	..
1950 - 52	91	47	44	1 060	17.9	81.4	2.41	2.0	..
1960 - 62	102	53	50	1 060	19.7	97.8	2.98	2.2	20.8
1970 - 72	84	43	41	1 057	16.1	83.3	2.46	1.1	13.5
1980 - 82	68	35	33	1 051	13.1	62.2	1.80	0.4	6.3
1990 - 92	66	34	32	1 052	13.0	59.2	1.68	0.4	5.7
2000 - 02	52	27	26	1 046	10.3	48.6	1.48	0.3	5.6
	BBCD	KMEU	KMEV	KMEW	KMEX	KMEY	KMEZ	KMFM	KMFN
1996	59	31	29	1 061	11.6	54.1	1.56	0.4	6.4
1997	59	31	29	1 055	11.7	54.4	1.58	0.3	5.3
1998	57	29	28	1 060	11.3	52.7	1.55	0.4	6.1
1999	55	28	27	1 050	10.9	50.9	1.51	0.3	5.2
2000	53	27	26	1 051	10.5	49.2	1.48	0.3	5.6
2001	53	27	26	1 041	10.4	48.8	1.49	0.3	5.7
2002	51	26	25	1 047	10.1	48.1	1.48	0.3	5.4
2003	52	27	26	1 054	10.4	49.4	1.54	0.3	5.6
2004	54	28	26	1 060	10.6	51.0	1.60	0.3	5.8
2005	54	28	26	1 068	10.7	51.5	1.62	0.3	5.3
2006	56	28	27	1 046	10.9	52.8	1.67	0.3	5.3
Northern Ireland[7]									
1900 - 02	..	..	..	..	..	..	..	..	..
1910 - 12	..	..	..	..	..	..	..	..	..
1920 - 22	31	16	15	1 048	24.2	105.9	..	..	..
1930 - 32	26	13	12	1 047	20.5	78.8	..	..	..
1940 - 42	27	14	13	1 078	20.8	73.7	..	..	..
1950 - 52	29	15	14	1 066	20.9	81.4	..	..	..
1960 - 62	31	16	15	1 068	22.5	111.5	3.47	0.7	22.0
1970 - 72	31	16	15	1 074	20.4	105.7	3.13	0.5	14.3
1980 - 82	28	14	13	1 048	18.0	87.5	2.59	0.2	8.4
1990 - 92	26	13	13	1 051	16.1	74.8	2.15	0.1	4.6
2000 - 02	22	11	11	1 054	12.8	58.8	1.78	0.1	5.0
	BBCE	KMFO	KMFP	KMFQ	KMFR	KMFS	KMFT	KMFU	KMFV
1996	24	12	12	1 032	14.7	67.8	1.95	0.2	6.2
1997	24	12	12	1 048	14.4	66.4	1.93	0.1	5.4
1998	24	12	12	1 039	14.1	65.0	1.90	0.1	5.1
1999	23	12	11	1 084	13.7	62.9	1.86	0.1	5.7
2000	22	11	10	1 070	12.8	58.7	1.75	0.1	4.3
2001	22	11	11	1 058	13.0	59.7	1.80	0.1	5.1
2002	21	11	11	1 035	12.6	58.1	1.77	0.1	5.7
2003	22	11	10	1 081	12.7	59.0	1.81	0.1	5.0
2004	22	11	11	1 059	13.0	60.6	1.87	0.1	5.0
2005	22	11	11	1 032	12.9	60.4	1.87	0.1	4.0
2006	23	12	11	1 066	13.4	62.5	1.94	0.1	3.8

1 See chapter text.
2 Males per 1,000 females (calculated using whole numbers).
3 Rate per 1,000 population (calculated using whole numbers).
4 Rate per 1,000 women aged 15 - 44.
5 Total fertility rate is the average number of children which would be born to a woman if she experienced the age-specific fertility rates of the period in question throughout her child-bearing life span. UK figures for the years 1970-72 and earlier are estimates.
6 On 1 October 1992 the legal definition of a stillbirth was changed from a baby born dead after 28 completed weeks gestation or more to one born

dead after 24 completed weeks gestation or more. Between 1 October and 31 December 1992 in the UK there were 258 babies born dead between 24 and 27 completed weeks gestation (216 in England and Wales, 35 in Scotland and 7 in Northern Ireland). If these babies were included in the stillbirth figures given, the stillbirth rate would be 4.7 for the UK and England and Wales, while Scotland and Northern Ireland stillbirth rate would remain as stated.
7 From 1981, data for the United Kingdom and Northern Ireland have been revised to exclude births in Northern Ireland to non-residents of Northern Ireland.

Sources: Office for National Statistics: 01329 444410;
General Register Office for Scotland;
Northern Ireland Statistics and Research Agency

5.16 Birth occurrence inside and outside marriage by age of mother

Thousands

	Inside marriage						Outside marriage					
	All ages	Under 20	20 - 24	25 - 29	Over 30	Mean[1] age (Years)	All ages	Under 20	20 - 24	25 - 29	Over 30	Mean[1] age (Years)
United Kingdom[2]												
	KKEY	KKEZ	KKFY	KKFZ	KKGX	KKGY	KKGZ	KKIC	KKID	KKIE	KKIF	KKIG
1961	890	55	273	280	282	27.7	54	13	17	10	13	25.5
1971	828	70	301	271	185	26.4	74	24	25	13	12	23.8
1981	640	36	193	231	180	27.3	91	30	33	16	13	23.4
1986	596	21	159	231	185	27.9	158	45	60	31	22	23.7
1987	598	18	153	235	192	28.1	178	48	68	37	26	23.9
1988	589	16	144	234	195	28.2	198	51	76	42	29	24.1
1989	570	14	130	228	198	28.4	207	49	79	46	32	24.3
1990	576	13	121	233	209	28.6	223	51	83	53	37	24.5
1991	556	10	109	224	213	28.9	236	50	87	58	41	24.8
1992	540	9	98	216	218	29.1	241	46	86	62	46	25.1
1993	520	8	87	204	221	29.3	242	44	84	64	50	25.4
1994	510	7	78	194	231	29.6	240	41	80	65	55	25.7
1995	486	6	69	180	232	29.8	246	42	79	66	60	25.9
1996	473	6	61	170	237	30.1	260	45	80	69	66	26.0
1997	460	6	55	159	240	30.3	267	47	79	71	71	26.1
1998	447	6	51	149	243	30.5	270	49	77	70	74	26.2
1999	428	6	47	136	239	30.7	272	49	77	68	77	26.3
2000	411	5	44	126	237	30.9	268	47	77	66	78	26.4
2001	401	5	44	116	236	30.9	268	45	77	64	82	26.7
2002	397	5	44	109	239	31.1	272	44	80	62	85	26.7
2003	407	5	44	110	249	31.2	288	45	86	65	92	26.8
2004	413	4	44	110	255	31.3	303	47	90	69	97	26.9
2005	412	4	43	111	254	31.4	310	47	93	72	98	26.9
2006	422	3	43	115	260	31.4	327	48	99	78	102	26.9
Great Britain												
	KKIH	KKII	KKIJ	KKIK	KKIL	KKIM	KKIN	KKIO	KKIP	KKIQ	KKIR	KKIS
1961	859	53	264	270	272	27.7	53	13	17	10	13	25.5
1971	797	68	293	261	176	26.4	73	24	25	13	12	23.8
1981	614	34	186	223	171	27.2	89	29	32	16	13	23.3
1986	572	20	153	222	177	27.9	155	44	59	30	22	22.9
1987	574	17	147	227	184	28.0	174	46	66	36	25	23.4
1988	566	16	138	226	186	28.2	194	49	74	42	29	23.6
1989	549	13	125	220	190	28.4	202	48	77	45	32	24.2
1990	554	12	116	225	201	28.6	218	49	81	52	36	24.6
1991	535	10	105	216	205	28.9	231	48	85	57	41	24.8
1992	520	9	94	208	210	29.1	235	45	84	61	46	25.1
1993	500	7	84	196	213	29.3	236	42	82	62	49	25.4
1994	492	7	75	188	222	29.6	235	41	78	63	53	25.7
1995	468	6	66	173	223	29.8	240	40	77	65	59	25.9
1996	455	6	59	163	227	30.1	254	44	78	68	65	26.0
1997	442	6	53	152	231	30.3	261	46	76	69	69	26.2
1998	430	6	49	143	233	30.5	263	48	74	68	73	26.3
1999	412	6	46	131	230	30.7	265	48	74	67	76	26.4
2000	396	5	43	121	228	30.9	261	46	74	65	77	26.5
2001	386	5	43	112	227	30.9	261	44	75	62	80	26.6
2002	383	5	43	105	230	31.1	265	43	77	61	84	26.7
2003	393	4	43	106	239	31.2	281	44	83	64	90	26.9
2004	399	4	43	106	245	31.3	295	45	88	67	95	26.9
2005	398	4	42	107	245	31.4	302	45	90	70	97	26.9
2006	407	3	42	111	251	31.4	318	46	96	76	100	26.9

1 The mean ages presented in this table are unstandardised and therefore take no account of the age structure of the population.
2 From 1981, data for the United Kingdom have been revised to exclude births in Northern Ireland to non-residents of Northern Ireland.

Sources: Office for National Statistics: 01329 444410;
General Register Office for Scotland;
Northern Ireland Statistics and Research Agency

5.17 Live births: by age of mother and country

Numbers

	All ages	Under 20	20 - 24	25 - 29	30 - 34	35 - 39	40 - 44	45 and over
United Kingdom								
All live births[1,2]								
	KMBZ	KMDV	KMDW	KMDX	KMDY	KMDZ	KMES	KMET
1996	733 163	50 793	141 090	238 857	210 490	78 335	12 832	638
1997	726 622	52 851	133 257	229 429	212 162	84 508	13 731	618
1998	716 888	54 822	127 230	218 072	212 876	88 729	14 453	640
1999	699 976	54 921	124 036	204 808	208 986	91 272	15 210	695
2000	679 029	52 059	120 305	191 583	202 893	95 400	16 032	708
2001	669 123	50 157	121 664	179 776	202 017	97 379	17 271	831
2002	668 777	49 165	123 844	171 852	203 261	101 379	18 273	968
2003	695 549	49 874	129 867	175 473	210 071	109 038	20 233	933
2004	715 996	50 752	134 614	179 050	213 620	114 852	22 107	975
2005	722 549	50 396	135 891	183 513	211 076	116 902	23 518	1 176
2006	748 563	51 066	142 171	192 800	212 333	123 867	24 999	1 288
Age-specific fertility rates[3]								
	KMBY	KMBR	KMBS	KMBT	KMBU	KMBV	KMBW	KMBX
1996	60.2	29.6	75.7	106.6	89.6	37.2	6.8	0.3
1997	59.6	30.2	74.9	104.2	89.8	39.1	7.1	0.3
1998	58.8	30.8	73.6	101.4	90.4	40.0	7.4	0.3
1999	57.3	30.7	71.8	98.0	89.4	40.2	7.6	0.4
2000	55.4	29.2	68.7	93.9	87.7	41.0	7.8	0.4
2001	54.3	27.9	68.0	91.5	88.0	41.3	8.2	0.4
2002	54.2	27.0	68.0	91.3	89.7	42.6	8.4	0.5
2003	56.2	26.7	70.2	95.4	94.6	45.9	9.1	0.5
2004	57.7	26.7	71.5	97.3	99.2	48.6	9.7	0.5
2005	57.8	26.2	70.4	97.4	100.5	50.0	10.6	0.6
2006	59.7	26.4	72.0	100.1	104.6	53.4	10.6	0.6
England and Wales								
All live births								
	KGSH	KGSA	KGSB	KGSC	KGSD	KGSE	KGSF	KGSG
1996	649 485	44 667	125 732	211 103	186 377	69 503	11 516	587
1997	643 095	46 372	118 589	202 792	187 528	74 900	12 332	582
1998	635 901	48 285	113 537	193 144	188 499	78 881	12 980	575
1999	621 872	48 375	110 722	181 931	185 311	81 281	13 617	635
2000	604 441	45 846	107 741	170 701	180 113	84 974	14 403	663
2001	594 634	44 189	108 844	159 926	178 920	86 495	15 499	761
2002	596 122	43 467	110 959	153 379	180 532	90 449	16 441	895
2003	621 469	44 236	116 622	156 931	187 214	97 386	18 205	875
2004	639 721	45 094	121 072	159 984	190 550	102 228	19 884	909
2005	645 835	44 830	122 145	164 348	188 153	104 113	21 155	1 091
2006	669 601	45 509	127 828	172 642	189 407	110 509	22 512	1 194
Age-specific fertility rates[3]								
	KGSP	KGSI	KGSJ	KGSK	KGSL	KGSM	KGSN	KGSO
1996	60.6	29.7	77.0	106.6	89.8	37.5	6.9	0.3
1997	60.0	30.2	76.0	104.3	89.8	39.4	7.3	0.3
1998	59.2	30.9	74.9	101.5	90.6	40.4	7.5	0.3
1999	57.8	30.9	73.0	98.3	89.6	40.6	7.7	0.4
2000	55.9	29.3	70.0	94.3	87.9	41.4	8.0	0.4
2001	54.7	28.0	69.0	91.7	88.0	41.5	8.4	0.5
2002	54.7	27.0	69.1	91.5	89.9	43.0	8.6	0.5
2003	56.8	26.9	71.1	95.8	94.9	46.4	9.3	0.5
2004	58.2	26.9	72.8	97.6	99.6	48.8	9.9	0.5
2005	58.3	26.3	71.6	97.9	100.7	50.3	10.8	0.6
2006	60.2	26.6	73.2	100.6	104.8	53.8	10.8	0.6

5.17 Live births: by age of mother and country

continued

Numbers

	All ages	Under 20	20 - 24	25 - 29	30 - 34	35 - 39	40 - 44	45 and over
Scotland								
All live births[1]								
	KGTH	KGTA	KGTB	KGTC	KGTD	KGTE	KGTF	KGTG
1996	59 296	4 544	11 026	19 511	17 038	6 126	891	32
1997	59 440	4 835	10 607	18 782	17 455	6 740	936	19
1998	57 319	4 802	9 804	17 477	17 207	6 893	1 027	43
1999	55 147	4 755	9 440	16 011	16 722	7 034	1 096	41
2000	53 076	4 599	8 962	14 676	16 233	7 395	1 133	29
2001	52 527	4 444	9 121	13 763	16 206	7 701	1 224	40
2002	51 270	4 195	9 267	12 694	16 038	7 727	1 267	47
2003	52 432	4 155	9 626	12 725	16 085	8 310	1 432	39
2004	53 957	4 172	9 950	13 131	16 085	8 912	1 631	50
2005	54 386	4 171	10 008	13 229	15 962	9 179	1 694	66
2006	55 690	4 130	10 399	13 876	15 878	9 535	1 775	58
Age-specific fertility rates[3]								
	KGTP	KGTI	KGTJ	KGTK	KGTL	KGTM	KGTN	KGTO
1996	54.1	29.7	64.5	98.5	81.9	31.4	5.2	0.2
1997	54.4	31.0	65.5	97.4	83.9	34.0	5.3	0.1
1998	52.7	30.6	62.8	94.3	83.2	34.1	5.7	0.3
1999	50.9	30.3	61.0	90.4	82.0	34.3	5.9	0.2
2000	49.2	29.3	57.6	86.5	81.3	35.6	6.0	0.2
2001	48.8	28.4	57.8	85.1	82.2	36.9	6.3	0.2
2002	48.1	26.8	58.3	83.3	83.6	37.1	6.4	0.3
2003	49.4	26.3	60.1	86.5	86.8	40.0	7.1	0.2
2004	51.0	26.1	61.8	89.4	90.3	43.3	7.9	0.3
2005	51.5	26.2	60.9	88.6	93.2	45.4	8.1	0.3
2006	52.8	25.8	61.9	90.2	97.1	47.8	8.4	0.3
Northern Ireland								
All live births[2]								
	KMDM	KMDF	KMDG	KMDH	KMDI	KMDJ	KMDK	KMDL
1996	24 382	1 582	4 332	8 243	7 075	2 706	425	19
1997	24 087	1 644	4 061	7 855	7 179	2 868	463	17
1998	23 668	1 735	3 889	7 451	7 170	2 955	446	22
1999	22 957	1 791	3 874	6 866	6 953	2 957	497	19
2000	21 512	1 614	3 602	6 206	6 547	3 031	496	16
2001	21 962	1 524	3 699	6 087	6 891	3 183	548	30
2002	21 385	1 502	3 619	5 779	6 691	3 203	565	26
2003	21 648	1 483	3 619	5 817	6 772	3 342	596	19
2004	22 318	1 486	3 592	5 935	6 985	3 712	592	16
2005	22 328	1 395	3 738	5 936	6 961	3 610	669	19
2006	23 272	1 427	3 944	6 282	7 048	3 823	712	36
Age-specific fertility rates[2,3]								
	KMDU	KMDN	KMDO	KMDP	KMDQ	KMDR	KMDS	KMDT
1996	67.8	25.7	73.8	129.4	108.3	45.4	8.4	0.4
1997	66.4	26.4	71.1	124.2	109.2	46.6	8.8	0.3
1998	65.0	27.8	69.6	119.0	108.4	47.2	8.2	0.4
1999	62.9	28.6	70.6	112.3	105.6	46.1	8.9	0.4
2000	58.7	25.6	66.0	103.9	100.4	46.2	8.5	0.3
2001	59.7	23.9	67.5	105.1	106.0	48.0	9.1	0.6
2002	58.1	23.3	66.0	102.9	104.2	48.2	9.2	0.5
2003	59.0	22.9	65.5	106.8	107.0	50.2	9.8	0.3
2004	60.6	23.0	62.8	109.8	112.6	56.1	9.5	0.3
2005	60.4	21.7	63.2	108.6	114.8	55.0	10.2	0.3
2006	62.5	22.5	63.6	112.0	119.2	58.2	10.8	0.6

1 The 'All ages' figure for Scotland includes births to mothers whose age was not known. There were 128 such births in 1996, 66 in 1997, 66 in 1998, 48 in 1999, 49 in 2000, 28 in 2001, 35 in 2002, 60 in 2003, 26 in 2004, 77 in 2005 and 39 in 2006.

2 From 1981 data for the United Kingdom and Northern Ireland have been revised to exclude births in Northern Ireland to non residents in Northern Ireland.

3 The rates for women of all ages, under 20, and 45 and over are based upon the populations of women aged 15-44, 15-19 and 45 respectively.

Sources: Office for National Statistics: 01329 444410;
General Register Office for Scotland;
Northern Ireland Statistics and Research Agency

5.18 Legal abortions[1]: by age for residents

Numbers

	All ages	Under 15	15	16 - 19	20 - 24	25 - 29	30 - 34	35 - 39	40 - 44	45 and over	Not stated
England and Wales											
	C53Z	C542	C543	C544	C545	C546	C547	C548	C549	C54A	C54B
1986	147 619	924	2 970	33 819	45 316	28 656	18 005	12 977	4 521	409	22
1987	156 191	907	2 858	35 167	49 256	31 243	18 960	12 639	4 757	390	14
1988	168 298	859	2 709	37 928	54 067	34 584	20 000	12 681	5 047	412	11
1989	170 463	803	2 580	36 182	54 880	36 604	21 284	12 713	5 020	388	9
1990	173 900	873	2 549	35 520	55 281	38 770	22 431	12 956	5 104	404	12
1991	167 376	886	2 272	31 130	52 678	38 611	23 445	13 035	4 901	408	10
1992	160 501	905	2 095	27 589	49 052	38 430	23 870	13 252	4 844	452	12
1993	157 846	964	2 119	25 806	46 846	38 139	24 690	13 885	4 889	494	14
1994	156 539	1 080	2 166	25 223	44 871	38 081	25 507	14 156	5 008	440	7
1995	154 315	946	2 324	24 945	43 394	37 254	25 759	14 352	4 868	457	16
1996	167 916	1 098	2 547	28 790	46 356	39 311	28 228	16 118	5 027	428	13
1997	170 145	1 020	2 414	29 947	44 960	40 159	28 892	16 858	5 413	482	..
1998	177 871	1 103	2 656	33 236	45 766	40 366	30 449	18 174	5 576	511	34
1999	173 701	1 066	2 537	32 807	45 004	38 492	29 139	18 341	5 755	502	58
2000	175 542	1 048	2 700	33 218	47 099	37 852	28 735	18 589	5 794	459	48
2001	176 364	1 066	2 592	33 431	48 267	36 506	28 782	19 146	6 094	456	24
2002	175 932	1 075	2 658	32 985	48 359	35 795	28 503	19 450	6 531	457	119
2003	181 582	1 171	2 796	34 247	51 201[2]	36 018	28 749	19 868	7 032	500	–
2004	185 415	1 034	2 722	35 386	52 701[2]	37 759	28 064	19 820	7 422	507	–
2005	186 416	1 083	2 703	35 313	53 342[2]	38 330	27 836	19 782	7 459	568	–
2006	193 737	1 042	2 948	37 296	55 340[2]	40 396	28 153	20 074	7 825	663	–
Scotland											
	C54C	C54D	C54E	C54F	C54G	C54H	C54I	C54J	C54K	C54L	EVH4
1986	9 611	74	236	2 526	2 984	1 740	1 080	702	247	22	–
1987	9 449	70	210	2 415	2 991	1 728	1 082	695	241	17	–
1988	10 111	65	217	2 526	3 299	1 965	1 105	662	257	15	–
1989	10 191	53	209	2 554	3 199	1 967	1 225	704	266	14	–
1990	10 198	54	185	2 536	3 235	2 061	1 157	698	253	19	–
1991	11 046	77	203	2 567	3 479	2 247	1 443	740	262	28	–
1992	10 791	73	173	2 368	3 383	2 283	1 444	798	252	17	–
1993	11 059	92	193	2 297	3 365	2 443	1 489	889	262	29	–
1994	11 371	78	214	2 311	3 480	2 427	1 640	876	315	30	–
1995	11 131	79	233	2 168	3 395	2 437	1 606	885	295	33	–
1996	11 957	87	234	2 360	3 569	2 595	1 798	957	330	27	–
1997	12 087	85	204	2 429	3 438	2 644	1 849	1 091	322	25	–
1998	12 458	73	213	2 703	3 419	2 740	1 801	1 148	339	22	–
1999	12 145	69	182	2 629	3 351	2 548	1 807	1 178	358	23	–
2000	11 979	93	181	2 608	3 349	2 400	1 765	1 174	381	28	–
2001	12 114	66	210	2 718	3 461	2 317	1 816	1 126	377	23	–
2002	11 840	79	194	2 646	3 447	2 165	1 731	1 166	382	29	1
2003	12 267	71	242	2 781	3 673	2 224	1 725	1 112	411	28	–
2004	12 349	101	206	2 887	3 666	2 250	1 652	1 171	382	32	2
2005	12 543	93	247	2 949	3 745	2 319	1 678	1 091	396	25	–
2006[3]	13 028	90	272	3 071	3 943	2 417	1 605	1 192	410	28	–

1 Refers to therapeutic abortions notified in accordance with the Abortion Act 1967.
2 Records with missing ages were assigned to the 20 - 24 age group.
3 Provisional.

Sources: Department of Health; Information Services Division Scotland

5.19 Deaths: by sex and age[1]

Numbers

	All ages[2]	Under 1 year	1-4	5-9	10-14	15-19	20-24	25-34	35-44	45-54	55-64	65-74	75-84	85 and over
United Kingdom														
Males														
1900 - 02	340 664	87 242	37 834	8 429	4 696	7 047	8 766	19 154	24 739	30 488	37 610	39 765	28 320	6 563
1910 - 12	303 703	63 885	29 452	7 091	4 095	5 873	6 817	16 141	21 813	28 981	37 721	45 140	29 397	7 283
1920 - 22	284 876	48 044	19 008	6 052	3 953	5 906	6 572	13 663	19 702	29 256	40 583	49 398	34 937	7 801
1930 - 32	284 249	28 840	11 276	4 580	2 890	5 076	6 495	12 327	16 326	29 376	47 989	63 804	45 247	10 022
1940 - 42	314 643	24 624	6 949	3 400	2 474	4 653	4 246	11 506	17 296	30 082	57 076	79 652	59 733	12 900
1950 - 52	307 312	14 105	2 585	1 317	919	1 498	2 289	5 862	11 074	27 637	53 691	86 435	79 768	20 131
1960 - 62	318 850	12 234	1 733	971	871	1 718	1 857	3 842	8 753	26 422	63 009	87 542	83 291	26 605
1970 - 72	335 166	9 158	1 485	1 019	802	1 778	2 104	3 590	7 733	24 608	64 898	105 058	82 905	30 027
1980 - 82	330 495	4 829	774	527	652	1 999	1 943	3 736	6 568	19 728	54 159	105 155	98 488	31 936
1990 - 92	312 521	3 315	623	372	396	1 349	2 059	4 334	6 979	15 412	40 424	87 849	106 376	43 032
2000 - 02	288 261	2 065	365	233	326	1 032	1 502	4 270	7 181	15 370	32 328	66 808	98 363	58 419
	KHUA	KHUB	KHUC	KHUD	KHUE	KHUF	KHUG	KHUH	KHUI	KHUJ	KHUK	KHUL	KHUM	KHUN
1995	308 982	2 575	454	323	380	1 095	1 832	4 804	6 734	15 556	35 922	85 013	102 650	51 644
1996	306 466	2 575	484	268	369	1 087	1 689	4 709	6 807	15 777	35 078	81 746	102 546	53 331
1997	301 713	2 414	465	301	366	1 134	1 738	4 558	6 678	15 770	33 910	78 121	101 817	54 441
1998	299 655	2 315	465	297	361	1 145	1 651	4 782	6 893	15 836	33 673	75 608	101 066	55 563
1999	299 235	2 323	459	260	333	1 088	1 548	4 647	6 930	15 862	33 181	73 457	101 327	57 820
2000	291 337	2 136	390	263	305	1 068	1 595	4 491	7 168	15 458	32 661	69 707	98 398	57 697
2001	287 942	2 052	358	230	369	1 106	1 518	4 459	7 275	15 668	32 135	66 257	98 041	58 474
2002	289 083	2 050	382	224	327	1 071	1 575	4 345	7 362	15 222	32 509	65 140	99 387	59 489
2003	289 185	2 047	356	228	308	1 013	1 586	4 041	7 530	14 692	32 895	63 520	100 900	60 069
2004	278 918	2 033	345	206	282	975	1 484	3 831	7 454	14 510	31 660	60 760	98 466	56 912
2005	277 349	2 117	339	194	312	1 022	1 449	3 660	7 454	14 241	31 645	58 828	95 641	60 447
2006	274 201	2 078	328	213	299	1 008	1 482	3 712	7 485	14 406	32 012	56 319	92 532	62 327
Females														
1900 - 02	322 058	68 770	36 164	8 757	5 034	6 818	8 264	18 702	21 887	25 679	34 521	42 456	34 907	10 099
1910 - 12	289 608	49 865	27 817	7 113	4 355	5 683	6 531	15 676	19 647	24 481	32 813	46 453	37 353	11 828
1920 - 22	274 772	35 356	17 323	5 808	4 133	5 729	6 753	14 878	18 121	24 347	34 026	48 573	45 521	14 203
1930 - 32	275 336	21 072	9 995	3 990	2 734	4 721	5 931	12 699	15 373	24 695	39 471	59 520	56 250	18 886
1940 - 42	296 646	17 936	5 952	2 743	2 068	4 180	5 028	11 261	14 255	23 629	42 651	70 907	71 377	24 658
1950 - 52	291 597	10 293	2 098	880	625	1 115	1 717	5 018	8 989	18 875	37 075	75 220	92 848	36 844
1960 - 62	304 871	8 887	1 334	627	522	684	811	2 504	6 513	16 720	36 078	73 118	105 956	51 117
1970 - 72	322 968	6 666	1 183	654	459	718	900	2 110	5 345	15 594	36 177	75 599	109 539	68 024
1980 - 82	330 269	3 561	585	355	425	733	772	2 099	4 360	12 206	32 052	72 618	117 760	82 743
1990 - 92	328 218	2 431	485	259	255	520	714	1 989	4 340	9 707	25 105	61 951	115 467	104 994
2000 - 02	317 356	1 586	283	188	208	446	536	1 877	4 426	10 270	20 549	47 324	101 650	128 012
	KIUA	KIUB	KIUC	KIUD	KIUE	KIUF	KIUG	KIUH	KIUI	KIUJ	KIUK	KIUL	KIUM	KIUN
1995	332 730	1 937	376	220	266	457	611	2 123	4 201	10 375	22 012	60 667	109 501	119 984
1996	332 430	1 921	366	220	217	488	599	2 170	4 229	10 290	21 476	58 156	110 215	122 083
1997	330 804	1 863	336	221	236	489	587	1 953	4 320	10 451	21 103	55 947	108 777	124 521
1998	327 937	1 744	339	221	233	511	554	2 015	4 316	10 441	20 819	54 048	106 703	125 993
1999	330 241	1 736	346	195	244	487	567	1 963	4 359	10 400	20 963	52 098	106 323	130 560
2000	319 242	1 677	288	181	215	468	573	1 975	4 488	10 477	20 620	49 138	102 052	127 090
2001	316 451	1 639	299	218	200	447	557	1 895	4 475	10 354	20 479	47 138	101 135	127 615
2002	318 962	1 488	280	181	229	456	556	1 838	4 380	10 080	20 707	46 094	102 503	130 170
2003	322 900	1 639	309	182	237	441	563	1 869	4 506	9 870	20 974	45 374	105 182	131 754
2004	305 873	1 626	279	160	201	480	572	1 765	4 486	9 463	20 500	43 118	100 775	122 448
2005	305 615	1 555	256	153	216	450	557	1 684	4 432	9 492	20 655	41 839	98 338	125 988
2006	298 023	1 659	303	151	201	437	520	1 604	4 434	9 474	20 855	40 290	92 877	125 218

5.19 Deaths: by sex and age[1]

continued

Numbers

	All ages[2]	Under 1 year	1-4	5-9	10-14	15-19	20-24	25-34	35-44	45-54	55-64	65-74	75-84	85 and over
England and Wales														
Males														
1900 - 02	288 886	76 095	32 051	7 066	3 818	5 611	7 028	15 869	21 135	26 065	31 600	33 568	23 835	5 144
1910 - 12	257 253	54 678	24 676	5 907	3 348	4 765	5 596	13 603	18 665	24 820	32 217	38 016	24 928	6 036
1920 - 22	240 605	39 796	15 565	5 151	3 314	4 901	5 447	11 551	17 004	25 073	34 639	42 025	29 685	6 455
1930 - 32	243 147	23 331	9 099	3 844	2 435	4 354	5 580	10 600	14 041	25 657	41 581	54 910	39 091	8 624
1940 - 42	268 876	19 393	5 616	2 834	2 051	3 832	3 156	9 484	14 744	25 983	50 058	68 791	51 779	11 158
1950 - 52	266 879	11 498	2 131	1 087	778	1 248	1 947	4 990	9 489	23 815	46 948	75 774	69 496	17 677
1960 - 62	278 369	10 157	1 444	812	742	1 523	1 624	3 278	7 524	22 813	54 908	77 000	73 180	23 364
1970 - 72	293 934	7 818	1 259	860	677	1 524	1 788	3 079	6 637	21 348	56 667	92 389	73 365	26 522
1980 - 82	290 352	4 168	657	452	555	1 716	1 619	3 169	5 590	16 909	47 144	92 485	87 338	28 551
1990 - 92	275 550	2 926	545	325	338	1 157	1 757	3 717	6 057	13 258	34 977	77 063	94 672	38 757
2000 - 02	253 706	1 836	323	200	282	862	1 244	3 619	6 104	13 184	27 696	58 114	87 481	52 761
	KHVA	KHVB	KHVC	KHVD	KHVE	KHVF	KHVG	KHVH	KHVI	KHVJ	KHVK	KHVL	KHVM	KHVN
1995	272 709	2 285	398	278	332	890	1 555	4 099	5 860	13 399	30 827	74 524	91 617	46 645
1996	269 825	2 285	436	237	308	908	1 405	4 027	5 861	13 546	30 111	71 459	91 164	48 078
1997	266 164	2 160	421	268	327	970	1 468	3 915	5 718	13 565	29 110	68 275	90 659	49 308
1998	264 202	2 058	415	254	309	962	1 404	4 111	5 886	13 606	28 947	65 989	90 048	50 213
1999	263 166	2 080	408	221	289	905	1 265	3 978	5 918	13 633	28 532	64 017	89 963	51 957
2000	256 698	1 902	345	227	263	898	1 328	3 849	6 135	13 355	28 003	60 801	87 449	52 143
2001	253 608	1 818	329	192	320	927	1 276	3 830	6 184	13 424	27 599	57 638	87 238	52 833
2002	254 390	1 831	329	198	286	912	1 310	3 665	6 255	13 011	27 807	56 584	88 493	53 709
2003	254 433	1 827	310	203	263	852	1 348	3 478	6 440	12 697	28 291	55 064	89 596	54 064
2004	245 208	1 809	303	174	252	833	1 257	3 281	6 360	12 417	27 117	52 709	87 367	51 329
2005	243 870	1 877	297	166	272	856	1 217	3 146	6 362	12 158	27 292	51 019	84 661	54 547
2006	240 888	1 863	292	187	261	844	1 212	3 132	6 315	12 256	27 551	48 881	81 912	56 182
Females														
1900 - 02	269 432	60 090	30 674	7 278	4 010	5 265	6 497	15 065	18 253	21 474	28 424	35 307	29 118	7 977
1910 - 12	242 079	42 642	23 335	5 883	3 519	4 522	5 256	12 742	16 363	20 611	27 571	38 489	31 363	9 782
1920 - 22	229 908	29 178	14 174	4 928	3 456	4 719	5 533	12 244	15 142	20 580	28 633	41 010	38 439	11 871
1930 - 32	233 915	16 929	8 013	3 338	2 293	3 969	5 039	10 716	13 022	21 190	33 798	50 844	48 531	16 234
1940 - 42	253 702	14 174	4 726	2 265	1 695	3 426	4 198	9 470	12 093	20 413	36 814	60 987	61 891	21 550
1950 - 52	252 176	8 367	1 727	732	520	893	1 365	4 131	7 586	16 161	31 875	65 087	81 154	32 579
1960 - 62	266 849	7 409	1 103	527	444	591	700	2 147	5 576	14 389	31 083	63 543	93 548	45 789
1970 - 72	284 181	5 677	1 020	562	396	620	806	1 814	4 585	13 417	31 222	65 817	96 952	61 293
1980 - 82	290 026	3 064	511	301	365	635	670	1 821	3 740	10 420	27 606	63 023	103 676	74 194
1990 - 92	288 851	2 161	420	227	217	455	625	1 718	3 765	8 347	21 466	53 783	101 752	93 914
2000 - 02	279 482	1 412	251	168	182	382	455	1 629	3 805	8 893	17 659	40 734	89 387	114 525
	KIVA	KIVB	KIVC	KIVD	KIVE	KIVF	KIVG	KIVH	KIVI	KIVJ	KIVK	KIVL	KIVM	KIVN
1995	293 193	1 683	339	192	226	390	521	1 842	3 642	8 987	18 810	52 666	96 416	107 479
1996	293 182	1 704	331	181	189	425	517	1 882	3 672	8 841	18 314	50 462	97 316	109 348
1997	291 888	1 664	300	183	206	428	503	1 711	3 734	9 055	18 053	48 553	96 009	111 489
1998	289 233	1 547	301	185	207	432	466	1 768	3 705	9 077	17 872	46 742	94 281	112 650
1999	290 366	1 555	308	168	219	399	484	1 707	3 773	8 999	17 949	44 958	93 360	116 487
2000	281 179	1 497	257	160	191	403	504	1 702	3 853	9 108	17 722	42 318	89 651	113 813
2001	278 890	1 449	272	198	171	386	472	1 665	3 858	8 984	17 608	40 639	89 036	114 152
2002	280 966	1 337	240	160	204	391	467	1 597	3 767	8 689	17 807	39 645	90 213	116 449
2003	284 718	1 479	278	159	209	370	485	1 636	3 884	8 554	18 001	39 001	92 694	117 968
2004	269 042	1 462	251	140	173	410	494	1 536	3 855	8 139	17 649	37 041	88 404	109 488
2005	269 123	1 371	222	134	189	379	478	1 481	3 805	8 175	17 797	35 913	86 309	112 870
2006	261 711	1 505	267	135	169	381	444	1 382	3 802	8 098	17 948	34 502	81 210	111 868

5.19 Deaths: by sex and age[1]
continued

Numbers

	All ages[2]	Under 1 year	1-4	5-9	10-14	15-19	20-24	25-34	35-44	45-54	55-64	65-74	75-84	85 and over
Scotland														
Males														
1900 - 02	40 224	9 189	4 798	1 083	672	1 069	1 292	2 506	2 935	3 591	4 597	4 531	3 117	834
1910 - 12	35 981	7 510	3 935	962	595	826	910	1 969	2 469	3 325	4 356	5 113	3 182	813
1920 - 22	34 649	6 757	2 847	710	489	747	791	1 616	2 128	3 314	4 785	5 624	3 928	911
1930 - 32	32 476	4 426	1 771	610	365	568	706	1 352	1 848	2 979	5 095	6 906	4 839	1 010
1940 - 42	36 384	3 973	1 011	449	321	668	888	1 643	2 090	3 348	5 728	8 556	6 317	1 337
1950 - 52	32 236	1 949	349	175	105	200	265	693	1 267	3 151	5 574	8 544	8 094	1 871
1960 - 62	32 401	1 578	222	121	102	146	185	456	1 013	2 986	6 682	8 505	7 980	2 425
1970 - 72	32 446	944	168	119	93	178	233	396	875	2 617	6 641	10 176	7 383	2 624
1980 - 82	31 723	451	80	56	71	206	233	423	776	2 280	5 601	10 152	8 804	2 591
1990 - 92	29 421	287	57	34	40	137	230	485	744	1 730	4 402	8 611	9 311	3 353
2000 - 02	27 526	165	30	23	30	119	196	523	882	1 775	3 781	7 038	8 535	4 430
	KHWA	KHWB	KHWC	KHWD	KHWE	KHWF	KHWG	KHWH	KHWI	KHWJ	KHWK	KHWL	KHWM	KHWN
1995	28 791	197	37	30	30	152	195	563	698	1 746	4 144	8 449	8 604	3 946
1996	29 223	206	41	23	46	139	212	556	755	1 845	4 087	8 259	8 926	4 128
1997	28 305	186	32	22	27	114	208	521	788	1 794	3 876	7 909	8 791	4 037
1998	28 132	183	37	34	39	134	200	524	843	1 796	3 828	7 746	8 585	4 183
1999	28 605	161	31	23	33	138	215	545	818	1 820	3 773	7 569	8 908	4 571
2000	27 511	173	33	24	28	115	198	512	842	1 716	3 789	7 224	8 523	4 334
2001	27 324	155	22	27	35	131	179	510	902	1 820	3 751	6 950	8 433	4 409
2002	27 743	167	34	17	27	111	211	546	901	1 789	3 804	6 940	8 648	4 548
2003	27 832	146	35	15	31	122	186	469	893	1 634	3 787	6 797	8 994	4 723
2004	26 775	160	29	21	23	105	181	449	889	1 676	3 629	6 507	8 733	4 373
2005	26 522	159	33	19	30	106	150	385	882	1 654	3 478	6 352	8 691	4 583
2006	26 251	145	21	18	21	112	206	461	938	1 697	3 567	5 966	8 353	4 746
Females														
1900 - 02	39 891	7 143	4 477	1 162	747	1 058	1 246	2 625	2 732	3 130	4 485	5 273	4 305	1 508
1910 - 12	36 132	5 854	3 674	981	618	836	910	2 149	2 473	2 909	3 960	5 636	4 588	1 552
1920 - 22	34 449	5 029	2 602	687	489	711	889	1 947	2 266	2 828	4 157	5 587	5 443	1 814
1930 - 32	32 377	3 319	1 602	527	339	568	666	1 508	1 812	2 731	4 380	6 630	6 178	2 117
1940 - 42	33 715	2 852	921	373	283	595	656	1 382	1 672	2 528	4 630	7 674	7 613	2 536
1950 - 52	31 525	1 432	284	115	84	185	293	714	1 127	2 188	4 204	8 157	9 310	3 431
1960 - 62	30 559	1 107	170	80	63	72	87	287	762	1 897	4 115	7 752	9 991	4 177
1970 - 72	30 978	694	118	69	46	73	74	231	608	1 769	4 036	7 823	10 112	5 324
1980 - 82	32 326	337	49	37	44	74	73	213	493	1 456	3 565	7 781	11 333	6 871
1990 - 92	31 747	190	45	20	29	49	72	218	458	1 093	2 966	6 630	11 079	8 898
2000 - 02	30 235	123	24	14	21	50	64	199	493	1 110	2 341	5 326	9 785	10 685
	KIWA	KIWB	KIWC	KIWD	KIWE	KIWF	KIWG	KIWH	KIWI	KIWJ	KIWK	KIWL	KIWM	KIWN
1995	31 709	178	26	16	26	50	70	231	435	1 100	2 601	6 449	10 452	10 075
1996	31 448	159	24	31	21	49	67	218	453	1 172	2 573	6 206	10 256	10 219
1997	31 189	130	23	28	21	43	71	199	496	1 128	2 480	5 985	10 164	10 421
1998	31 032	137	26	28	19	55	68	198	485	1 106	2 416	5 955	9 913	10 626
1999	31 676	115	26	20	17	65	58	201	467	1 128	2 431	5 837	10 198	11 113
2000	30 288	132	20	10	21	46	56	222	510	1 086	2 324	5 512	9 875	10 474
2001	30 058	135	20	16	21	47	71	189	480	1 111	2 361	5 235	9 695	10 677
2002	30 360	103	32	15	20	58	65	185	489	1 134	2 339	5 232	9 784	10 904
2003	30 640	119	24	18	20	57	64	181	489	1 062	2 446	5 194	9 977	10 989
2004	29 412	106	19	15	22	52	62	179	492	1 065	2 291	4 924	9 924	10 261
2005	29 225	125	27	11	18	55	58	163	506	1 073	2 316	4 841	9 620	10 412
2006	28 842	103	26	11	17	40	58	170	497	1 090	2 351	4 722	9 303	10 454

5.19 Deaths: by sex and age[1]
continued

Numbers

	All ages[2]	Under 1 year	1-4	5-9	10-14	15-19	20-24	25-34	35-44	45-54	55-64	65-74	75-84	85 and over
Northern Ireland														
Males														
1900 - 02	11 554	1 958	985	280	206	367	446	779	669	832	1 413	1 666	1 368	585
1910 - 12	10 469	1 697	841	222	152	282	311	569	679	836	1 148	2 011	1 287	434
1920 - 22	9 622	1 491	596	191	150	258	334	496	570	869	1 159	1 749	1 324	435
1930 - 32	8 626	1 083	406	126	90	154	209	375	437	740	1 313	1 988	1 317	388
1940 - 42	9 383	1 258	322	117	102	153	202	379	462	751	1 290	2 305	1 637	405
1950 - 52	8 197	658	105	55	36	50	77	179	318	671	1 169	2 117	2 178	583
1960 - 62	8 080	499	67	38	27	49	48	108	216	623	1 419	2 037	2 131	816
1970 - 72	8 786	396	58	40	32	76	83	115	221	643	1 590	2 493	2 157	881
1980 - 82	8 420	211	37	20	26	77	92	144	202	539	1 414	2 518	2 346	795
1990 - 92	7 550	102	21	13	18	55	73	132	178	423	1 044	2 175	2 393	922
2000 - 02	7 029	64	13	11	14	50	62	128	195	411	851	1 656	2 347	1228
	KHXA	KHXB	KHXC	KHXD	KHXE	KHXF	KHXG	KHXH	KHXI	KHXJ	KHXK	KHXL	KHXM	KHXN
1995	7 482	93	19	15	. 18	53	82	142	176	411	951	2 040	2 429	1 053
1996	7 418	84	7	8	15	40	72	126	191	386	880	2 028	2 456	1 125
1997	7 244	68	12	11	12	50	62	122	172	411	924	1 937	2 367	1 096
1998	7 321	74	13	9	13	49	47	147	164	434	898	1 873	2 433	1 167
1999	7 464	82	20	16	11	45	68	124	194	409	876	1 871	2 456	1 292
2000	7 128	61	12	12	14	55	69	130	191	387	869	1 682	2 426	1 220
2001	7 010	79	7	11	14	48	63	119	189	424	785	1 669	2 370	1 232
2002	6 950	52	19	9	14	48	54	134	206	422	898	1 616	2 246	1 232
2003	6 920	74	11	10	14	39	52	94	197	361	817	1 659	2 310	1 282
2004	6 935	64	13	11	7	37	46	101	205	417	914	1 544	2 366	1 210
2005	6 957	81	9	9	10	60	82	129	210	429	875	1 457	2 289	1 317
2006	7 062	70	15	8	17	52	64	119	232	453	894	1 472	2 267	1 399
Females														
1900 - 02	12 735	1 537	1 013	317	277	495	521	1 012	902	1 075	1 612	1 876	1 484	614
1910 - 12	11 397	1 369	808	249	218	325	365	785	811	961	1 282	2 328	1 402	494
1920 - 22	10 415	1 149	547	193	188	299	331	687	713	939	1 236	1 976	1 639	518
1930 - 32	9 044	824	380	125	102	184	226	475	539	774	1 293	2 046	1 541	535
1940 - 42	9 229	910	305	105	90	159	174	409	490	688	1 207	2 246	1 873	572
1950 - 52	7 896	494	87	33	21	37	59	173	276	526	996	1 976	2 384	834
1960 - 62	7 463	371	61	20	15	21	24	70	175	434	880	1 823	2 417	1 151
1970 - 72	7 809	295	45	23	17	25	20	65	152	408	919	1 959	2 475	1 407
1980 - 82	7 917	160	26	17	17	23	29	65	127	329	881	1 813	2 752	1 678
1990 - 92	7 620	80	20	12	9	16	17	53	117	267	672	1 538	2 636	2 182
2000 - 02	7 638	50	9	7	5	13	17	49	129	266	548	1 263	2 479	2 802
	KIXA	KIXB	KIXC	KIXD	KIXE	KIXF	KIXG	KIXH	KIXI	KIXJ	KIXK	KIXL	KIXM	KIXN
1995	7 828	76	11	12	14	17	20	50	124	288	601	1 552	2 633	2 430
1996	7 800	58	11	8	7	14	15	70	104	277	589	1 488	2 643	2 516
1997	7 727	69	13	10	9	18	13	43	90	268	570	1 409	2 604	2 611
1998	7 672	60	12	8	7	24	20	49	126	258	531	1 351	2 509	2 717
1999	8 199	66	12	7	8	23	25	55	119	273	583	1 303	2 765	2 960
2000	7 775	48	11	11	3	19	13	51	125	283	·574	1 308	2 526	2 803
2001	7 503	55	7	4	8	14	14	41	137	259	510	1 264	2 404	2 786
2002	7 636	48	8	6	5	7	24	56	124	257	561	1 217	2 506	2 817
2003	7 542	41	7	5	8	14	14	52	133	254	527	1 179	2 511	2 797
2004	7 419	58	9	5	6	18	16	50	139	259	560	1 153	2 447	2 699
2005	7 267	59	7	8	9	16	21	40	121	244	542	1 085	2 409	2 706
2006	7 470	51	10	5	15	16	18	52	135	286	556	1 066	2 364	2 896

1 See chapter text.
2 In some years the totals include a small number of persons whose age was not stated.

Sources: Office for National Statistics: 020 7533 5249; General Register Office for Scotland; Northern Ireland Statistics and Research Agency

5.20 Infant and maternal mortality[1]
(i) - By country. (ii) - Infant mortality by country, type of death and sex

	Deaths of Infants under 1 year of age per thousand live births												Maternal deaths per thousand live births[3]			
	United Kingdom			England and Wales[2]			Scotland			Northern Ireland			United Kingdom	England and Wales	Scotland	Northern Ireland
	Total	Males	Females	Total	Males	Females	Total	Males	Females	Total	Males	Females				
1900 - 02	142	156	128	146	160	131	124	136	111	113	123	103	4.71	4.67	4.74	6.03
1910 - 12	110	121	98	110	121	98	109	120	97	101	110	92	3.95	3.67	5.65	5.28
1920 - 22	82	92	71	80	90	69	94	106	82	86	95	77	4.37	4.03	6.36	5.62
1930 - 32	67	75	58	64	72	55	84	94	73	75	83	66	4.54	4.24	6.40	5.24
1940 - 42	59	66	51	55	62	48	77	87	66	80	89	70	3.29	2.74	4.50	3.79
1950 - 52	30	34	26	29	33	25	37	42	32	40	45	36	0.88	0.79	1.09	1.09
1960 - 62	22	25	19	22	24	19	26	30	22	27	30	24	0.36	0.36	0.37	0.43
1970 - 72	18	20	16	18	20	15	19	22	17	22	24	20	0.17	0.17	0.17	0.12
1980 - 82	12	13	10	11	13	10	12	13	10	13	15	12	0.09	0.09	0.14	0.06
1990 - 92	7	8	6	7	8	6	7	8	6	7	8	6	0.07	0.07	0.10	-
2000 - 02	5	6	5	5	6	5	5	6	5	5	6	5	0.07	0.06	0.12	0.05
	KKAW	KKAX	KKAY	KKAZ	KKBW	KKBX	KKBY	KKBZ	KKCW	KKCX	KKCY	KKCZ	KKDW	KKDX	KKDY	KKDZ
1995	6.2	6.9	5.4	6.1	6.9	5.3	6.2	6.4	6.1	7.1	7.5	6.6	0.07	0.07	0.10	–
1996	6.1	6.8	5.4	6.1	6.9	5.4	6.2	6.7	5.5	5.8	6.7	4.8	0.07	0.07	0.10	0.04
1997	5.8	6.4	5.3	5.9	6.5	5.3	5.3	6.1	4.5	5.6	5.5	5.8	0.06	0.06	0.07	–
1998	5.7	6.3	5.0	5.7	6.4	5.0	5.6	6.2	4.9	5.6	6.1	5.1	0.07	0.07	0.09	0.04
1999	5.8	6.4	5.1	5.8	6.5	5.1	5.0	5.7	4.3	6.4	6.8	5.9	0.05	0.05	0.13	–
2000	5.6	6.1	5.0	5.6	6.1	5.1	5.7	6.4	5.1	5.1	5.5	4.6	0.07	0.06	0.15	–
2001	5.5	6.0	5.0	5.4	5.9	4.9	5.5	5.8	5.2	6.1	7.0	5.2	0.07	0.07	0.11	0.09
2002	5.2	5.9	4.5	5.2	5.9	4.5	5.3	6.4	4.1	4.7	4.8	4.6	0.06	0.06	0.10	0.05
2003	5.3	5.7	4.9	5.3	5.7	4.9	5.1	5.4	4.7	5.2	6.5	3.9	0.10	0.07	0.10	0.14
2004	5.0	5.5	4.6	5.0	5.5	4.6	4.9	5.8	4.0	5.3	5.4	5.2	0.07	0.07	0.11	0.04
2005	5.1	5.7	4.5	5.0	5.7	4.4	5.2	5.7	4.8	6.1	7.0	5.3	0.06	0.06	0.07	0.04
2006	5.0	5.4	4.5	5.0	5.4	4.6	4.5	5.1	3.8	5.2	5.8	4.5	0.07	0.06	0.13	0.13

5.20
continued

Infant and maternal mortality[1]
(i) - By country. (ii) - Infant mortality by country, type of death and sex

Deaths per thousand live births

		1996	1997	1998	1999	2000	2001	2002	2003	2004	2005	2006
Total												
United Kingdom:												
Stillbirths[4]	KHNQ	5.5	5.3	5.4	5.3	5.3	5.3	5.6	5.7	5.7	5.3	5.3
Perinatal[4]	KHNR	8.7	8.3	8.3	8.2	8.1	8.0	8.3	8.5	8.3	8.0	7.9
Neonatal	KHNS	4.1	3.9	3.8	3.9	3.9	3.6	3.5	3.6	3.4	3.5	3.5
Post neonatal	KHNT	2.0	2.0	1.9	1.9	1.7	1.8	1.7	1.7	1.6	1.6	1.5
England and Wales:												
Stillbirths[4]	KHNU	5.4	5.3	5.3	5.3	5.3	5.3	5.6	5.7	5.7	5.4	5.4
Perinatal[4]	KHNV	8.6	8.3	8.2	8.2	8.2	8.0	8.3	8.5	8.4	8.0	8.0
Neonatal	KHNW	4.1	3.9	3.8	3.9	3.9	3.6	3.6	3.6	3.5	3.4	3.5
Post neonatal	KHNX	2.0	2.0	1.9	1.9	1.7	1.9	1.7	1.7	1.6	1.6	1.5
Scotland:												
Stillbirths[4]	KHNY	6.4	5.3	6.1	5.2	5.6	5.7	5.4	5.6	5.8	5.3	5.3
Perinatal[4]	KHNZ	9.2	7.8	8.7	7.6	8.4	8.5	7.6	8.0	8.1	7.7	7.4
Neonatal	KHOA	3.9	3.2	3.6	3.3	4.0	3.8	3.2	3.4	3.1	3.5	3.5
Post neonatal	KHOB	2.2	2.1	2.0	1.7	1.8	1.7	2.1	1.7	1.9	1.7	1.5
Northern Ireland:												
Stillbirths[4]	KHOC	6.3	5.4	5.1	5.7	4.3	5.1	5.7	4.9	5.0	4.0	3.8
Perinatal[4]	KHOD	9.4	8.2	8.1	10.0	7.3	8.5	8.9	8.0	8.0	8.1	7.1
Neonatal	KHOE	3.7	4.2	3.9	4.8	3.8	4.5	3.5	3.9	3.6	4.9	4.1
Post neonatal	KHOF	2.0	1.4	1.7	1.6	1.3	1.6	1.2	1.3	1.7	1.3	1.4
Males												
United Kingdom:												
Perinatal[4]	KHOG	9.1	8.7	8.8	8.7	8.7	8.6	8.9	8.8	8.8	8.3	8.3
Neonatal	KHOH	4.6	4.2	4.2	4.3	4.2	4.0	4.0	3.9	3.8	3.9	3.9
Infant mortality	KHOI	6.8	6.4	6.3	6.4	6.1	6.0	5.9	5.7	5.5	5.7	5.5
England and Wales:												
Perinatal[4]	KHOK	9.0	8.7	8.8	8.6	8.7	8.5	8.9	8.9	8.8	8.4	8.3
Neonatal	KHOL	4.6	4.2	4.3	4.3	4.2	3.9	4.0	3.8	3.8	3.8	3.8
Infant mortality	KHOM	6.9	6.5	6.4	6.5	6.1	5.9	5.9	5.7	5.5	5.7	5.4
Scotland:												
Perinatal[4]	KHOO	10.0	8.1	9.6	8.4	9.5	9.2	7.9	8.4	8.8	7.6	7.7
Neonatal	KHOP	4.3	3.4	4.0	3.8	4.5	4.0	3.7	3.6	3.6	3.8	4.0
Infant mortality	KHOQ	6.7	6.1	6.2	5.7	6.4	5.8	6.4	5.4	5.8	5.7	5.6
Northern Ireland:												
Perinatal[4]	KHOS	10.1	8.5	8.9	10.5	8.0	9.8	10.0	8.2	8.2	9.2	7.5
Neonatal	KHOT	4.3	4.3	4.4	5.5	4.2	5.3	3.8	4.6	3.7	5.5	5.0
Infant mortality	KHOU	6.7	5.5	6.1	6.8	5.5	7.0	4.8	6.5	5.4	7.0	5.8
Females												
United Kingdom:												
Perinatal[4]	KHOW	8.2	7.9	7.7	7.8	7.5	7.4	7.7	8.2	7.9	7.6	7.5
Neonatal	KHOX	3.6	3.5	3.3	3.4	3.5	3.3	3.1	3.4	3.1	3.1	3.2
Infant mortality	KHOY	5.4	5.3	5.0	5.1	5.0	5.0	4.5	4.9	4.6	4.5	4.5
England and Wales:												
Perinatal[4]	KHPA	8.2	7.9	7.7	7.8	7.6	7.3	7.7	8.2	8.0	7.6	7.6
Neonatal	KHPB	3.6	3.6	3.3	3.5	3.5	3.2	3.1	3.4	3.1	3.0	3.2
Infant mortality	KHPC	5.4	5.3	5.0	5.1	5.1	4.9	4.5	4.9	4.6	4.4	4.6
Scotland:												
Perinatal[4]	KHPE	8.4	7.5	7.9	6.7	7.2	7.8	7.2	7.7	7.3	7.9	7.1
Neonatal	KHPF	3.5	2.9	3.2	2.8	3.5	3.5	2.6	3.1	2.5	3.2	2.9
Infant mortality	KHPG	5.5	4.5	4.9	4.3	5.1	5.2	4.1	4.7	4.0	4.8	3.8
Northern Ireland:												
Perinatal[4]	KHPI	8.6	8.0	7.3	9.5	6.5	7.0	7.8	7.8	7.8	6.9	6.6
Neonatal	KHPJ	3.1	4.0	3.4	4.1	3.4	3.6	3.1	3.2	3.5	4.2	3.1
Infant mortality	KHPK	4.8	5.8	5.1	5.9	4.6	5.2	4.6	3.9	5.2	5.3	4.5

1 See chapter text.
2 From 1937 to 1956 death rates are based on the births to which they relate in the current and preceding years.
3 Deaths in pregnancy and childbirth.
4 Deaths per 1,000 live and stillbirths. See chapter introduction.

Sources: Office for National Statistics;
General Register Office for Scotland;
General Register Office (Northern Ireland)

5.21 Death rates by sex and age[1]
United Kingdom

Rates per 1,000 population

	All ages	0-4	5-9	10-14	15-19	20-24	25-34	35-44	45-54	55-64	65-74	75-84	85 and over
Males													
1900 - 02	18.4	57.0	4.1	2.4	3.7	5.0	6.6	11.0	18.6	35.0	69.9	143.6	289.6
1910 - 12	14.9	40.5	3.3	2.0	3.0	3.9	5.0	8.0	14.9	29.8	62.1	133.8	261.5
1920 - 22	13.5	33.4	2.9	1.8	2.9	3.9	4.5	6.9	11.9	25.3	57.8	131.8	259.1
1930 - 32	12.9	22.3	2.3	1.5	2.6	3.3	3.5	5.7	11.3	23.7	57.9	134.2	277.0
1940 - 42	..	..	..	..	..	..	..	..	..	..	..	..	..
1950 - 52	12.6	7.7	0.7	0.5	0.9	1.4	1.6	3.0	8.5	23.2	55.2	127.6	272.0
1960 - 62	12.5	6.4	0.5	0.4	0.9	1.1	1.1	2.5	7.4	22.2	54.4	123.4	251.0
1970 - 72	12.4	4.6	0.4	0.4	0.9	1.0	1.0	2.4	7.3	20.9	52.9	116.3	246.1
1980 - 82	12.1	3.2	0.3	0.3	0.8	0.9	0.9	1.9	6.3	18.2	46.7	107.1	224.9
1990 - 92	11.2	2.0	0.2	0.2	0.7	0.9	1.0	1.8	4.6	14.2	38.6	93.0	201.4
2000 - 02	10.0	1.4	0.1	0.2	0.5	0.8	1.0	1.6	4.0	10.4	28.9	75.2	187.7
	KHZA	KHZB	KHZC	KHZD	KHZE	KHZF	KHZG	KHZH	KHZJ	KHZK	KHZL	KHZM	KHZN
1995	11.0	1.6	0.2	0.2	0.6	0.9	1.0	1.7	4.2	12.6	36.7	90.0	202.1
1996	10.8	1.6	0.1	0.2	0.6	0.9	1.0	1.7	4.2	12.3	35.2	86.0	199.6
1997	10.6	1.5	0.2	0.2	0.6	1.0	1.0	1.7	4.1	11.8	33.9	83.2	196.7
1998	10.5	1.5	0.1	0.2	0.6	0.9	1.1	1.7	4.1	11.6	33.0	81.8	193.6
1999	10.5	1.5	0.1	0.2	0.6	0.9	1.0	1.7	4.1	11.2	32.2	80.9	195.7
2000	10.1	1.4	0.1	0.2	0.6	0.8	1.0	1.6	4.0	10.7	30.3	76.8	187.9
2001	9.9	1.3	0.1	0.2	0.6	0.8	1.0	1.6	4.0	10.4	28.6	74.8	186.9
2002	9.9	1.4	0.1	0.2	0.5	0.8	1.0	1.6	4.0	10.1	27.8	74.1	188.2
2003	9.9	1.4	0.1	0.1	0.5	0.8	1.0	1.6	3.9	9.9	27.0	73.6	191.7
2004	9.5	1.4	0.1	0.1	0.5	0.7	0.9	1.6	3.8	9.3	25.5	70.6	176.3
2005	9.5	1.4	0.1	0.1	0.5	0.7	0.9	1.6	3.7	9.3	24.8	68.7	187.8
2006	9.2	1.3	0.1	0.2	0.5	0.7	0.9	1.6	3.7	9.1	23.7	65.5	164.5
Females													
1900 - 02	16.3	47.9	4.3	2.6	3.5	4.3	5.8	9.0	14.4	27.9	59.3	127.0	262.6
1910 - 12	13.3	34.0	3.3	2.1	2.9	3.4	4.4	6.7	11.5	23.1	50.7	113.7	234.0
1920 - 22	11.9	26.9	2.8	1.9	2.8	3.4	4.1	5.6	9.3	19.2	45.6	111.5	232.4
1930 - 32	11.5	17.7	2.1	1.5	2.4	2.9	3.3	4.6	8.3	17.6	43.7	110.1	246.3
1940 - 42	..	..	..	..	..	..	..	..	..	..	..	..	..
1950 - 52	11.2	6.0	0.5	0.4	0.7	1.0	1.4	2.3	5.3	12.9	35.5	98.4	228.8
1960 - 62	11.2	4.9	0.3	0.3	0.4	0.5	0.8	1.8	4.5	11.0	30.8	87.3	218.5
1970 - 72	11.3	3.6	0.3	0.2	0.4	0.4	0.6	1.6	4.5	10.5	27.5	76.7	196.1
1980 - 82	11.4	2.3	0.2	0.2	0.3	0.4	0.5	1.3	3.9	9.9	24.8	67.2	179.5
1990 - 92	11.1	1.5	0.1	0.2	0.3	0.3	0.4	1.1	2.9	8.4	22.1	58.7	157.2
2000 - 02	10.5	1.1	0.1	0.1	0.2	0.3	0.4	1.0	2.6	6.4	17.9	51.1	157.3
	KHZO	KHZP	KHZQ	KHZR	KHZS	KHZT	KHZU	KHZV	KHZW	KHZX	KHZY	KHZZ	KHZI
1995	11.2	1.2	0.1	0.1	0.3	0.3	0.5	1.1	2.8	7.5	21.7	57.8	161.4
1996	11.1	1.2	0.1	0.1	0.3	0.3	0.5	1.1	2.7	7.3	21.0	56.4	159.4
1997	11.0	1.2	0.1	0.1	0.3	0.3	0.4	1.1	2.7	7.1	20.5	55.2	160.3
1998	11.0	1.2	0.1	0.1	0.3	0.3	0.4	1.0	2.7	7.0	20.2	54.4	159.8
1999	11.0	1.2	0.1	0.1	0.3	0.3	0.4	1.0	2.7	6.9	19.6	54.2	163.7
2000	10.5	1.1	0.1	0.1	0.3	0.3	0.5	1.0	2.7	6.6	18.5	51.6	155.8
2001	10.4	1.1	0.1	0.1	0.2	0.3	0.4	1.0	2.6	6.4	17.8	50.8	155.8
2002	10.5	1.0	0.1	0.1	0.2	0.3	0.4	1.0	2.6	6.2	17.4	51.0	160.3
2003	10.6	1.2	0.1	0.1	0.2	0.3	0.4	1.0	2.6	6.1	17.1	51.8	166.4
2004	10.0	1.1	0.1	0.1	0.2	0.3	0.4	1.0	2.4	5.8	16.2	49.3	155.2
2005	10.0	1.1	0.1	0.1	0.2	0.3	0.4	0.9	2.5	5.9	15.8	48.2	160.1
2006	9.6	1.1	0.1	0.1	0.2	0.3	0.4	0.9	2.4	5.7	15.2	46.4	144.9

1 See chapter text.

Sources: Office for National Statistics;
General Register Office for Scotland;
Northern Ireland Statistics and Research Agency

5.22 Interim life tables, 2004-06

Age(x)	United Kingdom				England and Wales			
	Males		Females		Males		Females	
	l_x	e^0_x	l_x	e^0_x	l_x	e^0_x	l_x	e^0_x
0 years	100 000	76.9	100 000	81.3	100 000	77.2	100 000	81.5
5 years	99 347	72.4	99 462	76.7	99 350	72.7	99 461	76.9
10 years	99 291	67.4	99 417	71.7	99 295	67.7	99 417	71.9
15 years	99 216	62.5	99 362	66.8	99 221	62.7	99 364	67.0
20 years	98 972	57.6	99 245	61.9	98 988	57.9	99 250	62.0
25 years	98 608	52.8	99 103	56.9	98 644	53.1	99 112	57.1
30 years	98 201	48.0	98 928	52.0	98 255	48.3	98 940	52.2
35 years	97 687	43.3	98 689	47.2	97 764	43.5	98 707	47.3
40 years	97 023	38.6	98 320	42.3	97 131	38.8	98 350	42.5
45 years	96 100	33.9	97 748	37.6	96 243	34.1	97 793	37.7
50 years	94 693	29.4	96 819	32.9	94 886	29.6	96 886	33.1
55 years	92 504	25.0	95 373	28.3	92 757	25.2	95 475	28.5
60 years	89 284	20.8	93 211	23.9	89 622	21.0	93 364	24.1
65 years	84 083	16.9	89 852	19.7	84 567	17.1	90 097	19.9
70 years	76 420	13.4	84 658	15.8	77 043	13.5	85 031	15.9
75 years	65 210	10.2	76 589	12.2	65 966	10.3	77 114	12.2
80 years	49 706	7.6	63 976	9.0	50 508	7.6	64 627	9.1
85 years	31 432	5.5	46 476	6.5	32 094	5.5	47 152	6.5
90 years	14 886	3.9	26 341	4.4	15 313	3.9	26 856	4.5

Age(x)	Scotland				Northern Ireland			
	Males		Females		Males		Females	
	l_x	e^0_x	l_x	e^0_x	l_x	e^0_x	l_x	e^0_x
0 years	100 000	74.6	100 000	79.6	100 000	76.1	100 000	81.0
5 years	99 348	70.1	99 488	75.0	99 274	71.6	99 410	76.4
10 years	99 282	65.1	99 444	70.0	99 198	66.7	99 358	71.5
15 years	99 206	60.2	99 382	65.1	99 112	61.8	99 279	66.5
20 years	98 890	55.4	99 230	60.2	98 750	57.0	99 150	61.6
25 years	98 363	50.6	99 052	55.3	98 240	52.3	98 998	56.7
30 years	97 788	45.9	98 841	50.4	97 770	47.5	98 812	51.8
35 years	97 009	41.3	98 533	45.5	97 235	42.7	98 595	46.9
40 years	96 023	36.7	98 044	40.7	96 528	38.0	98 204	42.1
45 years	94 751	32.1	97 349	36.0	95 581	33.4	97 606	37.3
50 years	92 907	27.7	96 201	31.4	94 011	28.9	96 693	32.7
55 years	90 186	23.5	94 427	26.9	91 717	24.6	95 204	28.1
60 years	86 188	19.4	91 749	22.7	88 263	20.4	93 035	23.7
65 years	79 701	15.8	87 549	18.6	82 601	16.6	89 560	19.5
70 years	70 712	12.5	81 187	14.9	75 142	13.0	84 393	15.6
75 years	58 395	9.6	71 840	11.4	63 605	9.9	76 135	12.0
80 years	42 599	7.2	58 075	8.5	47 641	7.3	63 548	8.8
85 years	25 588	5.3	40 308	6.2	29 567	5.3	46 058	6.2
90 years	11 199	3.9	21 688	4.3	13 263	3.8	25 737	4.2

Note Column l_x shows the number who would survive to exact **age**(x), out of 100,000 born, who were subject throughout their lives to the death rates experienced in the three-year period indicated. Column e^0_x is 'the expectation of life', that is, the average future lifetime which would be lived by a person aged exactly x if likewise subject to the death rates experienced in the three-year period indicated. See introductory notes.

Source: Office for National Statistics: 020 7533 5222

Population and vital statistics

5.23 Adoptions by date of entry in Adopted Children Register: by sex, age and country

Numbers and Percentages

	All ages		Under 1		1-4		5-9		10-14		15-17	
	Numbers	Percentages	Numbers	Percentages	Numbers	Percentages	Numbers	Percentages	Numbers	Percentages	Numbers	Percentages
United Kingdom **Persons**												
	VOXI	VOXJ	VOXK	VOXL	VOXM	VOXN	VOXO	VOXP	VOXQ	VOXR	VOXS	VOXT
2001	6 588	100	272	4	2 874	44	2 047	31	1 103	17	290	4
2002	6 239	100	313	5	2 737	44	1 937	31	999	16	253	4
2003	5 426	100	212	4	2 481	46	1 716	32	789	15	228	4
2004	6 116	100	274	5	2 843	46	1 856	30	847	14	269	4
2005	6 151	100	242	4	3 127	51	1 757	29	798	13	227	4
2006	5 539	100	216	4	2 788	50	1 608	29	696	13	226	4
Males												
	VOXU	VOXV	VOXW	VOXX	VOXY	VOXZ	VOYA	VOYB	VOYC	VOYD	VOYE	VOYF
2001	3 314	100	138	4	1 483	45	1 006	30	547	17	139	4
2002	3 140	100	176	6	1 425	45	935	30	488	16	116	4
2003	2 634	100	104	4	1 224	46	844	32	351	13	111	4
2004	3 051	100	145	5	1 426	47	936	31	418	14	126	4
2005	3 072	100	121	4	1 566	51	910	30	370	12	105	3
2006	2 708	100	97	4	1 377	51	806	30	314	12	113	4
Females												
	VOYG	VOYH	VOYI	VOYJ	VOYK	VOYL	VOYM	VOYN	VOYO	VOYP	VOYQ	VOYR
2001	3 274	100	134	4	1 391	42	1 041	32	556	17	151	5
2002	3 099	100	137	4	1 312	42	1 002	32	511	16	137	4
2003	2 792	100	108	4	1 257	45	872	31	438	16	117	4
2004	3 065	100	129	4	1 417	46	920	30	456	15	143	5
2005	3 079	100	121	4	1 561	51	847	28	428	14	122	4
2006	2 831	100	119	4	1 411	50	802	28	382	13	113	4
England and Wales[1] **Persons**												
	GQTP	GQTQ	GQTR	GQTS	GQTT	GQTU	GQTV	GQTW	GQTX	GQTY	GQTZ	GQUA
2001	5 981	100	246	4	2 648	44	1 845	31	983	16	257	4
2002	5 680	100	287	5	2 532	45	1 748	31	900	16	213	4
2003	4 818	100	183	4	2 260	47	1 503	31	683	14	189	4
2004	5 562	100	253	5	2 627	47	1 651	30	786	14	245	4
2005	5 565	100	222	4	2 906	52	1 555	28	683	12	199	4
2006	4 980	100	197	4	2 592	52	1 406	28	585	12	195	4
Males												
	GQUB	GQUC	GQUD	GQUE	GQUF	GQUG	GQUH	GQUI	GQUJ	GQUK	GQUL	GQUM
2001	3 011	100	124	4	1 370	45	904	30	494	16	118	4
2002	2 871	100	160	6	1 324	46	846	29	443	15	98	3
2003	2 339	100	91	4	1 115	48	737	32	301	13	95	4
2004	2 777	100	132	5	1 327	48	831	30	373	13	114	4
2005	2 791	100	112	4	1 461	52	808	29	320	11	90	3
2006	2 446	100	95	4	1 282	52	707	29	267	11	94	4
Females												
	GQUN	GQUO	GQUP	GQUQ	GQUR	GQUS	GQUT	GQUU	GQUV	GQUW	GQUX	GQUY
2001	2 970	100	122	4	1 278	43	941	32	489	16	139	5
2002	2 809	100	127	5	1 208	43	902	32	457	16	115	4
2003	2 479	100	92	4	1 145	46	766	31	382	15	94	4
2004	2 785	100	121	4	1 300	47	820	29	413	15	131	5
2005	2 774	100	110	4	1 445	52	747	27	363	13	109	4
2006	2 534	100	102	4	1 310	52	699	28	318	13	101	4

5.23
continued

Adoptions by date of entry in Adopted Children Register: by sex, age and country

Numbers and Percentages

	All ages		Under 1		1-4		5-9		10-14		15-17	
	Numbers	Percentages	Numbers	Percentages	Numbers	Percentages	Numbers	Percentages	Numbers	Percentages	Numbers	Percentages

Scotland[1]
Persons

	GQUZ	GQVA	GQVB	GQVC	GQVD	GQVE	GQVF	GQVG	GQVH	GQVI	GQVJ	GQVK
2001	468	100	18	4	176	38	161	34	92	20	21	4
2002	385	100	13	3	143	37	130	34	73	19	26	7
2003	468	100	25	5	153	33	170	36	88	19	32	7
2004	393	100	21	5	144	37	143	36	67	17	18	5
2005	439	100	18	4	162	37	155	35	81	18	23	5
2006	418	100	16	4	153	37	150	36	73	17	26	6

Males

	GQVL	GQVM	GQVN	GQVO	GQVP	GQVQ	GQVR	GQVS	GQVT	GQVU	GQVV	GQVW
2001	241	100	11	5	93	39	83	34	40	17	14	6
2002	193	100	8	4	75	39	60	31	37	19	13	7
2003	228	100	11	5	78	34	85	37	43	19	11	5
2004	200	100	13	7	67	34	77	39	34	17	9	5
2005	217	100	9	4	80	37	79	36	36	17	13	6
2006	194	100	2	1	72	37	78	40	25	13	17	9

Females

	GQVX	GQVY	GQVZ	GQWA	GRFK	GRFL	GRFM	GRFN	GRFO	GRFP	GRFQ	GRFR
2001	227	100	7	3	83	37	78	34	52	23	7	3
2002	192	100	5	3	68	35	70	36	36	19	13	7
2003	240	100	14	6	75	31	85	35	45	19	21	9
2004	193	100	8	4	77	40	66	34	33	17	9	5
2005	222	100	9	4	82	37	76	34	45	20	10	5
2006	224	100	14	6	81	36	72	32	48	22	9	4

Northern Ireland
Persons

	VOYS	VOYT	VOYU	VOYV	VOYW	VOYX	VOYY	VOYZ	VOZA	VOZB	VOZC	VOZD
2001	139	100	8	6	50	36	41	29	28	20	12	9
2002	174	100	13	7	62	36	59	34	26	15	14	8
2003	140	100	4	3	68	49	43	31	18	13	7	5
2004	161	100	–	2	72	43	62	38	21	12	6	4
2005	147	100	2	4	59	38	47	32	34	21	5	4
2006	141	100	2	2	44	31	52	36	38	27	5	4

Males

	VOZE	VOZF	VOZG	VOZH	VOZI	VOZJ	VOZK	VOZL	VOZM	VOZN	VOZO	VOZP
2001	62	100	3	5	20	32	19	31	13	21	7	11
2002	76	100	8	11	26	34	29	38	8	11	5	7
2003	67	100	2	3	31	46	22	33	7	10	5	7
2004	74	100	–	–	32	43	28	38	11	15	3	4
2005	64	100	–	–	25	39	23	36	14	22	2	3
2006	68	100	–	–	23	35	21	29	22	32	2	3

Females

	VOZQ	VOZR	VOZS	VOZT	VOZU	VOZV	VOZW	VOZX	VOZY	VOZZ	VPAA	VPVD
2001	77	100	5	6	30	39	22	29	15	19	5	6
2002	98	100	5	5	36	37	30	31	18	18	9	9
2003	73	100	2	3	37	51	21	29	11	15	2	3
2004	87	100	–	–	40	46	34	39	10	11	3	3
2005	83	100	2	2	34	41	24	29	20	24	3	4
2006	73	100	3	4	20	27	31	42	16	22	3	4

1 England & Wales: number of persons aged over 17 (counted into 'All ages')

Year	Persons	Male	Female
2001	2	1	1
2006	5	1	4

Scotland: number of persons aged over 17 (counted into 15-17 age group)

Year	Persons	Male	Female
2001	1	1	-
2002	4	1	3
2003	4	3	1
2004	3	-	3
2006	5	5	-

Sources: Office for National Statistics: 01329 444410;
General Register Office for Scotland;
Northern Ireland Statistics and Research Agency

Education

Chapter 6

Education

Educational establishments in the UK are administered and financed in several ways. Most schools are controlled by local authorities (LAs), which are part of the structure of local government, but some are 'assisted', receiving grants direct from central government sources and being controlled by governing bodies that have a substantial degree of autonomy. Completely outside the public sector are non maintained schools run by individuals, companies or charitable institutions.

For the purposes of UK education statistics, schools fall under the following broad categories:

Mainstream state schools (grant-aided mainstream schools in Northern Ireland)

These schools work in partnership with other schools and LAs and they receive funding from LAs. Since 1 September 1999, the categories (typically in England) are:

Community - schools formerly known as 'county' plus some former grant-maintained (GM) schools

Foundation - most former GM schools

Voluntary Aided - schools formerly known as 'aided' and some former GM schools

Voluntary Controlled - schools formerly known as 'controlled'

Non-maintained mainstream schools consisting of

(a) Independent schools

Schools which charge fees and may also be financed by individuals, companies or charitable institutions. These include Direct Grant schools, where the governing bodies are assisted by departmental grants and a proportion of the pupils attending them do so free or under an arrangement by which LAs meet tuition fees. City Technology Colleges (CTCs) and Academies (applicable in England only) are also included as independent schools.

(b) Non-maintained schools

Run by voluntary bodies which may receive some grant from central government for capital work and for equipment, but the current expenditure is met primarily from the fees charged to the LAs for pupils placed in schools.

Special schools

Provide education for children with Special Educational Needs (SEN) (Record of Needs or a Coordinated Support Plan in Scotland) who cannot be educated satisfactorily in an ordinary school. Maintained special schools are run by LAs, while non-maintained special schools are financed as shown at (b) above.

Pupil Referral Units

Pupil Referral Units (PRUs) operate in England and Wales and provide education outside of a mainstream or special school setting, to meet the needs of difficult or disruptive children.

Schools in Scotland are categorised as Education Authority, Grant-Aided, Opted-out/Self-governing (these three being grouped together as 'Publicly funded' schools), Independent schools and Partnership schools.

The home government departments dealing with education statistics are:

Department for Children, Schools and Families (DCSF)

Department for Innovation, Universities and Skills (DIUS)

Welsh Assembly Government (WAG)

Scottish Government (SG)

Northern Ireland Department of Education (DENI)

Northern Ireland Department for Employment and Learning (DELNI)

Each of the home education departments in Great Britain, along with the Northern Ireland Department of Education, have overall responsibility for funding the schools sectors in their own country.

Up to March 2001, further education (FE) courses in FE sector colleges in England and in Wales were largely funded through grants from the respective Further Education Funding Councils. In April 2001, however, the Learning and Skills Council (LSC) took over the responsibility for funding the FE sector in England, and the National Council for Education and Training for Wales (part of Education and Learning Wales (ELWa)) did so for Wales. The LSC in England is also responsible for funding provision for FE and some non-prescribed higher education in FE sector colleges; it also funds some FE provided by LA maintained and other institutions referred to as 'external institutions'. In Wales, the National Council – ELWa funds FE provision made by FE institutions via a third party or sponsored arrangements. The Scottish Further

Education Funding Council (SFEFC) funds FE colleges in Scotland, while the Department for Employment and Learning funds FE colleges in Northern Ireland.

Higher education (HE) courses in higher education establishments are largely publicly funded through block grants from the HE funding councils in England and Scotland, the Higher Education Council – ELWa in Wales - and the Department for Employment and Learning in Northern Ireland. In addition, some designated HE (mainly HND/HNC Diplomas and Certificates of HE) courses are also funded by these sources. The FE sources mentioned above fund the remainder.

Statistics for the separate systems obtained in England, Wales, Scotland and Northern Ireland are collected and processed separately in accordance with the particular needs of the responsible departments. Since 1994/95 the Higher Education Statistics Agency (HESA) has undertaken the data collection for all higher education institutions (HEIs) in the UK. This includes the former Universities Funding Council (UFC) funded UK universities previously collected by the Universities Statistical Record. There are some structural differences in the information collected for schools, further and higher education in each of the four home countries and in some tables the GB/UK data presented are amalgamations from sources that are not entirely comparable.

Stages of education

There are five stages of education: early years, primary, secondary, FE and HE, and education is compulsory for all children between the ages of five (four in Northern Ireland) and 16. The non-compulsory fourth stage, FE, covers non-advanced education, which can be taken at further (including tertiary) education colleges, HEIs and increasingly in secondary schools. The fifth stage, HE, is study beyond GCE A levels and their equivalent which, for most full-time students, takes place in universities and other HEIs.

Early years education

Children under five attend a variety of settings including state nursery schools, nursery classes within primary schools and, in England and Wales, reception classes within primary schools, as well as settings outside the state sector such as voluntary pre-schools or privately run nurseries. In recent years there has been a major expansion of early years education, and the *Education Act 2002* extended the National Curriculum for England to include the foundation stage.The foundation stage was introduced in September 2000, and covers children's education from the age of three to the end of the reception year, when

most are just five and some almost six years old. The Early Years Foundation Stage (EYFS), which is due to come into force in September 2008, will be a single framework for care, learning and development for children in all registered early years settings from birth to five.

Children born in Scotland between March and December are eligible for early years education at the time the Pre-School Education and Day Care Census is carried out. In Scotland, early years education is called ante-pre-school education for those aged three to four years old, and pre-school education for those aged four.

Primary education

The primary stage covers three age ranges: nursery (under five), infant (five to seven or eight) and junior (up to 11 or 12), but in Scotland and Northern Ireland there is generally no distinction between infant and junior schools. Most public sector primary schools take both boys and girls in mixed classes. It is usual to transfer straight to secondary school at the age of 11 (in England, Wales and Northern Ireland) or 12 (in Scotland), but in England some children make the transition via middle schools catering for various age ranges between eight and 14. Depending on their individual age ranges, middle schools are classified as either primary or secondary.

Secondary education

Public provision of secondary education in an area may consist of a combination of different types of school, the pattern reflecting historical circumstance and the policy adopted by the local authority. Comprehensive schools largely admit pupils without reference to ability or aptitude and cater for all the children in a neighbourhood, but in some areas they co-exist with grammar, secondary modern or technical schools.

In 2005/06, 88 per cent of secondary pupils in England attended comprehensive schools, while all secondary schools in Wales are comprehensive schools. The majority of education authority secondary schools in Scotland are comprehensive in character and offer six years of secondary education; however in remote areas there are several two-year and four-year secondary schools. In Northern Ireland, post primary education is provided by grammar schools and non-selective secondary schools.

In England, the Specialist Schools Programme helps schools, in partnership with private sector sponsors and supported by additional government funding, to establish distinctive identities through their chosen specialisms and achieve their targets to raise standards. Specialist schools have a special focus on their chosen subject area but must meet the National Curriculum requirements and deliver a broad and balanced education to all pupils. Any maintained secondary school in England can apply to be designated as a specialist school in one of ten specialist areas: arts, business and enterprise, engineering, humanities, languages, mathematics and computing, music, science, sports and technology. Schools can also combine any two specialisms.

Academies, operating in England, are publicly funded independent local schools that provide free education. They are all ability schools established by sponsors from business, faith or voluntary groups working with partners from the local community. The DCSF Secretary of State announced in July 2007 that future academies would be required to follow the National Curriculum programmes of study in English, mathematics, science and information and communication technology (ICT). This is different to the previous model whereby academies had to teach English, mathematics, science and ICT to all pupils and the curriculum had to be broad and balanced.

Special schools

Special schools (day or boarding) provide education for children who require specialist support to complete their education, for example because they have physical or other difficulties. Many pupils with special educational needs are educated in mainstream schools. All children attending special schools are offered a curriculum designed to overcome their learning difficulties and to enable them to become self-reliant. Since December 2005, special schools have also been able to apply for the Special Educational Needs (SEN) specialism, under the Specialist Schools Programme. They can apply for a curriculum specialism, but not for both the SEN and a curriculum specialism.

Further education

The term further education may be used in a general sense to cover all non-advanced courses taken after the period of compulsory education, but more commonly it excludes those staying on at secondary school and those in higher education, such as courses in universities and colleges leading to qualifications above GCE A Level, SCE H Grade, GNVQ/NVQ level 3, and their equivalents. Since 1 April 1993, sixth form colleges in England and Wales have been included in the further education sector.

Higher education

Higher education is defined as courses that are of a standard that is higher than GCE A level, the Higher

Grade of the Scottish Certificate of Education/National Qualification, GNVQ/NVQ level 3 or the Edexcel (formerly BTEC) or SQA National Certificate/Diploma. There are three main levels of HE course:

(i)   Postgraduate courses leading to higher degrees, diplomas and certificates (including postgraduate certificates of education (PGCE) and professional qualifications), which usually require a first degree as entry qualification

(ii)   undergraduate courses which includes first degrees, first degrees with qualified teacher status, enhanced first degrees, first degrees obtained concurrently with a diploma, and intercalated first degrees (where first degree students, usually in medicine, dentistry or veterinary medicine, interrupt their studies to complete a one-year course of advanced studies in a related topic)

(iii)   other undergraduate courses which includes all other higher education courses, for example HND's and Diplomas in HE

As a result of the *1992 Further and Higher Education Act*, former polytechnics and some other HEIs were designated as universities in 1992/93. Students normally attend HE courses at HEIs, but some attend at FE colleges. Some also attend institutions which do not receive public grant (such as the University of Buckingham) and these numbers are excluded from the tables; however, the University of Buckingham is included in Table 6.10.

6.1 Number of schools by type and establishments of further and higher education
Academic years

Numbers

		1995/96	2001/02	2002/03	2003/04	2004[1]/05	2005[1]/06	2006/07
United Kingdom:								
Public sector mainstream								
Nursery[2,3]	KBFK	1 486	3 227	3 394	3 438	3 425	3 349	3 326
Primary	KBFA	23 441	22 800	22 638	22 509	22 343	22 156	21 968
Secondary[4]	KBFF	4 463	4 306	4 284	4 255	4 230	4 206	4 176
of which 6th form colleges	KPGM	..	..	..	..	..	..	..
Non-maintained mainstream[5]	KBFU	2 500	2 407	2 380	2 524	2 476	2 493	2 542
Special - all	KBFP	1 560	1 483	1 473	1 465	1 436	1 416	1 391
maintained	KPVX	1 456	1 387	1 369	1 362	1 329	1 311	1 285
non maintained	KPGO	104	96	104	103	107	105	106
Pupil referral units	KXEP	315	340	390	457	478	481	489
Universities (including Open University)[6]	KAHG	96	97	96	114	119	123	124
All other further and higher education institutions	KJPQ	609	541	520	520	527	519	504
Higher education institutions	KPVY	66	58	54	55	47	43	45
Further education institutions	KSNY	543	483	466	465	480	476	459
of which 6th form colleges	KPGP	110	101	103	102	102	102	96
England:								
Public sector mainstream								
Nursery	KBAK	547	494	475	468	456	453	446
Primary	KBAA	18 480	17 985	17 861	17 762	17 642	17 504	17 361
Secondary[4]	KBAF	3 594	3 457	3 436	3 409	3 385	3 367	3 343
of which 6th form colleges	KPGS	..	..	..	..	..	..	..
Non-maintained[5]	KBAU	2 266	2 206	2 180	2 330	2 283	2 301	2 342
Special - all	KBAP	1 263	1 161	1 160	1 148	1 122	1 105	1 078
maintained	KPGT	1 191	1 098	1 088	1 078	1 049	1 033	1 006
non maintained	KPGU	72	63	72	70	73	72	72
Pupil referral units	KXEQ	291	312	360	426	447	449	448
Universities (including Open University)[6]	KAHM	72	73	72	90	96	100	100
All other further and higher education institutions	KJPR	503	441	422	422	414	422	409
Higher education institutions	KPXA	50	45	41	42	34	31	32
Further education institutions	KPWC	453	396	381	380	395	391	377
of which 6th form colleges	KPGV	110	101	103	102	102	102	96
Wales:								
Public sector mainstream								
Nursery	KBBK	52	40	37	34	34	33	31
Primary	KBBA	1 681	1 624	1 602	1 588	1 572	1 555	1 527
Secondary	KBBF	228	227	227	227	227	224	224
of which 6th form colleges	KPGY	..	..	..	..	..	..	..
Non-maintained	KBBU	62	56	59	60	58	56	66
Special (Maintained)	KBBP	54	44	43	43	43	43	44
Pupil referral units	KZBF	24	28	30	31	31	32	41
Universities	KAHS	9	9	9	9	8	8	8
All other further and higher education institutions	KJQP	31	28	27	27	27	27	27
Higher education institutions	KSNZ	5	4	4	4	4	4	4
Further education institutions	KPGZ	26	24	23	23	23	23	23
Scotland:								
Public sector mainstream								
Nursery[2]	KBDK	796	2 597	2 782	2 836	2 836	2 763	2 750
Primary	KBDA	2 332	2 271	2 258	2 248	2 217	2 194	2 184
Secondary	KBDF	405	387	386	386	386	385	381
Non-maintained	KBDU	151	120	119	117	118	117	116
Special - all	KBDP	196	230	223	227	226	223	224
maintained	KYCZ	164	197	191	194	192	190	190
non-maintained	KYDA	32	33	32	33	34	33	34
Universities	KAHX	13	13	13	13	13	13	14
All other further and higher education institutions	KJRA	56	53	53	53	53	52	50
Higher education institutions	KPWE	9	7	7	7	7	6	7
Further education institutions	KPHB	47	46	46	46	46	46	43
Northern Ireland:								
Grant aided mainstream								
Nursery[3]	KBEK	91	96	100	100	99	100	99
Primary	KBEA	948	920	917	911	912	903	896
Secondary	KBEF	236	235	235	233	232	230	228
Non-maintained	KBEU	21	25	22	17	17	19	18
Special (Maintained)	KBEP	47	48	47	47	45	45	45
Universities	KIAD	2	2	2	2	2	2	2
Colleges of education	KIAE	2	2	2	2	2	2	2
Further education colleges	KIAG	17	17	16	16	16	16	16

1 Includes revised data.
2 Nursery schools figures for Scotland prior to 1998/99 only include data for Local Authority pre-schools. Data thereafter include partnership pre-schools. From 2005/06, figures exclude pre-school education centres not in partnership with the Local Authority.
3 Excludes voluntary and private pre-school education centres in Northern Ireland (372 in total in 2006/07).

4 From 1995/96, includes Specialist schools in England, operational from September of the first year shown (2,611 in total in 2006/07).
5 From 2002/03, includes Acadamies in England (46 in total in 2006/07).
6 From 2003/04, universities includes the members of the University of London separately. For earlier years, its member institutions are counted as one institution.

Source: Education Departments: 01325 392754

Education

6.2 Full-time and part-time pupils in school[1] by age and sex[2]
United Kingdom
All schools at January[3]

Thousands

		1997	1998	1999	2000	2001	2002	2003	2004	2005	2006[4]	2007[5]
Age at previous 31 August[8]												
Number (thousands)												
England[7]	KBIA	8 195	8 261	8 310	8 346	8 374	8 369	8 367	8 335	8 274	8 216	8 149
Wales	KBIB	510	513	513	512	512	511	509	506	501	495	490
Scotland	KBIC	848	850	844	874	882	876	874	866	851	850	844
Northern Ireland[2]	KBID	354	352	352	349	348	346	345	341	337	333	329
United Kingdom	KBIE	9 907	9 975	10 020	10 081	10 116	10 102	10 095	10 048	9 963	9 893	9 813
Boys and girls												
2 - 4[8]	KBIF	1 148	1 149	1 154	1 184	1 187	1 180	1 189	1 145	1 138	1 130	1 139
5 - 10	KBIG	4 628	4 668	4 661	4 629	4 597	4 537	4 489	4 403	4 378	4 321	4 264
11	KBIH	744	746	762	783	771	783	791	784	758	756	739
12 - 14	KBII	2 151	2 182	2 211	2 256	2 297	2 320	2 343	2 355	2 369	2 344	2 309
15	KBIK	716	701	706	705	732	737	751	775	764	777	786
16	KBIL	289	288	283	285	287	298	290	314	304	304	314
17	KBIM	206	217	218	213	219	223	217	238	226	235	234
18 and over	KBIN	22	24	25	27	27	23	24	32	27	26	28
Boys												
14	KBIO	365	368	367	381	384	391	401	394	402	407	404
15	KBIP	365	358	361	359	374	377	384	394	390	397	401
16	KBIQ	141	140	137	138	139	145	140	150	146	146	150
17	KBIR	100	104	104	101	105	107	104	112	107	111	110
18 and over	KBIS	12	13	13	14	15	13	13	17	14	15	15
Girls												
14	KBIT	349	350	352	364	365	373	384	378	384	388	385
15	KBIU	351	343	345	346	358	360	368	379	375	380	385
16	KBIV	148	149	146	147	148	153	150	161	159	159	164
17	KBIW	107	113	114	111	114	116	113	124	119	123	124
18 and over	KBIX	10	11	11	13	12	11	11	15	12	12	13

1 From 1 April 1993 excludes 6th form colleges in England and Wales which were reclassified as further education colleges.
2 In Northern Ireland, a gender split is not collected by age but is available by year group and so this is used as a proxy.
3 In Scotland, as at the previous September.
4 Includes revised figures for pre-school education in Scotland.
5 Provisional.
6 1 July for Northern Ireland and 31 December for non-maintained primary and secondary schools pupils in Scotland and age at census date in January for pre-school education in Scotland.
7 From 1992, figures for independent schools in England include pupils aged less than 2.
8 Includes the so-called "rising 5s" (i.e. those pupils who become 5 during the autumn term).

Source: Education Departments: 01325 392754

6.3 Number of pupils and teachers, and pupil:teacher ratios:[1] by school type
United Kingdom
At January[2]

Numbers

		2002	2003	2004	2005[3]	2006[3,4]	2007[4,5]
All schools or departments							
Total							
Pupils (thousands)							
Full-time and full-time							
equivalent of part-time	KBCA	9 858.1	9 852.2	9 812.6	9 686.7	9 613.9	9 527.6
Teachers[6] (thousands)	KBCB	558.3	561.6	561.4	562.6	568.6	570.1
Pupils per teacher[6]:							
United Kingdom	KBCC	17.7	17.6	17.6	17.3	17.0	16.8
England	KBCD	18.0	17.9	17.8	17.5	17.2	17.1
Wales	KBCE	18.1	18.0	18.0	18.0	17.6	17.6
Scotland	KBCF	15.4	14.9	15.0	14.3	13.8	13.0
Northern Ireland	KBCG	16.4	16.3	16.5	16.5	16.7	16.8
Public sector mainstream schools or departments							
Nursery							
Pupils (thousands)							
Full-time and full-time							
equivalent of part-time	KBFM	85.6	84.8	83.9	29.1	29.1	29.4
Teachers[6] (thousands)	KBFN	3.6	3.6	3.5	1.7	1.7	1.7
Pupils per teacher[6]	KBFO	23.6	23.6	23.7	17.6	17.3	17.7
Primary[7]							
Pupils (thousands)							
Full-time and full-time							
equivalent of part-time	KBFB	5 083.4	5 021.9	4 953.9	4 896.6	4 831.9	4 778.8
Teachers[6] (thousands)	KBFD	231.5	228.9	224.9	224.2	226.6	226.3
Pupils per teacher[6]	KBFE	22.0	21.9	22.0	21.8	21.3	21.1
Secondary[8]							
Pupils (thousands)							
Full-time and full-time							
equivalent of part-time	KBFG	3 948.0	3 994.0	4 014.1	4 001.9	3 987.1	3 941.3
Teachers[6] (thousands)	KBFH	241.2	243.3	243.8	246.6	248.5	247.6
Pupils per teacher[6]	KBFI	16.4	16.4	16.5	16.2	16.0	15.9
Special schools							
Pupils (thousands)							
Full-time and full-time							
equivalent of part-time	KPGE	105.4	104.5	102.2	100.4	99.5	99.4
Teachers[6] (thousands)	KPGG	17.0	17.0	16.9	16.8	17.0	17.0
Pupils per teacher[6]	KPGI	6.2	6.1	6.1	6.0	5.9	5.9

1 'All schools' pupil:teacher ratios exclude Pupil Referral Units and non-maintained special schools.
2 In Scotland, as at the previous September.
3 Excluding nursery school figures for Scotland as FTE pupils numbers are not available.
4 Nursery schools for Scotland, from 2005/06 exclude pre-school education centres not in partnership with Local Authority.
5 Provisional
6 Figures of teachers and of pupil/teacher ratios take account of the full-time equivalent of part-time teachers.

7 Includes grammar schools in Northern Ireland
8 Includes grammar schools in Northern Ireland.
9 England and Scotland only.

Source: Education Departments: 01325 392754

6.4 Full-time and part-time pupils with special educational needs (SEN)[1], 2006/07[2]
United Kingdom
By type of school

Thousands and percentages

	United Kingdom	England[3]	Wales	Scotland	Northern Ireland
All schools					
Total pupils	9 819.5	8 149.2	489.6	845.0	335.7
SEN pupils with statements	270.6	229.1	15.3	13.7	12.5
Incidence (%)[4]	2.8	2.8	3.1	1.6	3.7
Maintained schools[5]					
Nursery[6]					
Total pupils[7]	163.5	37.6	1.8	111.7	12.4
SEN pupils with statements	2.1	0.3	-	1.7	0.1
Incidence (%)[4]	1.3	0.8	0.8	1.5	0.5
Placement (%)[8]	0.8	0.1	0.1	12.3	0.5
Primary[9]					
Total pupils	4 921.9	4 107.7	263.3	382.8	168.2
SEN pupils without statements	817.8	727.7	49.8	12.8	27.4
SEN pupils with statements	73.9	61.3	5.0	3.2	4.4
Pupils with statements -incidence (%)[4]	1.5	1.5	1.9	0.8	2.6
Pupils with statements - placement (%)[8]	27.3	26.7	33.0	23.1	35.5
Secondary					
Total pupils	3 941.6	3 268.5	210.4	313.0	149.8
SEN pupils without statements	587.3	529.8	32.3	9.3	15.9
SEN pupils with statements	83.1	69.5	5.8	3.9	3.8
Pupils with statements - incidence (%)[4]	2.1	2.1	2.7	1.3	2.6
Pupils with statements - placement (%)[8]	30.7	30.3	37.8	28.8	30.8
Special[10,11]					
Total pupils	100.2	84.7	4.0	7.0	4.6
SEN pupils with statements	95.3	82.5	4.0	4.7	4.2
Incidence (%)[4]	95.1	97.4	100.0	66.9	91.2
Placement (%)[8]	35.2	36.0	26.2	34.1	33.3
Pupil referral units[10,12]					
Total pupils	15.7	15.2	0.6	..	..
SEN pupils with statements	2.1	2.0	0.2	..	..
Incidence (%)[4]	13.6	13.1	27.2	..	..
Placement (%)[8]	0.8	0.9	1.0	..	..
Other schools					
Independent					
Total pupils	670.8	630.8	9.7	29.4	0.8
SEN pupils with statements	9.3	8.9	0.3	0.1	..
Incidence (%)[4]	1.4	1.4	3.0	0.2	..
Placement (%)[8]	3.4	3.9	1.9	0.4	..
Non-maintained special[10]					
Total pupils	5.8	4.7	..	1.1	..
SEN pupils with statements	4.8	4.6	..	0.2	..
Incidence (%)[4]	82.4	97.7	..	16.9	..
Placement (%)[8]	1.8	2.0	..	1.4	..

1 For Scotland, a Coordinating Support Plan, including some who also had an Individualised Education Programme (IEP)

2 Provisional.

3 Includes new codes for recording SEN status following the introduction of a new SEN Code of Practice from January 2002.

4 Incidence of pupils - as a proportion of the total number of people on roll in each school type.

5 Grant-Aided schools in Northern Ireland.

6 Includes 6,327 pupils in Voluntary and Private Pre-School Centres in Northern Ireland funded under the Pre-School Expansion Programme which began in 1998/99.

7 In Scotland, on pupils in centres providing pre-school education as a Local Authority centre or in partnership with the Local Authority only. Children are counted once for each centre they are registered with.

8 Placement of pupils - the number of pupils with statements within each school type expressed as a proportion of the number of pupils with statements in all schools.

9 Includes nursery classes (except for Scotland, where they are included with Nursery schools) and reception classes in Primary schools.

10 England and Wales figures exclude dually registered pupils.

11 Including general and hospital special schools.

12 England and Wales only.

Source: Education Departments: 01325 392754

6.5 GCE, GCSE and SCE/NQ[1] and vocational qualifications obtained by pupils and students

United Kingdom

Percentages and thousands

| | Pupils in their last year of compulsory education[2] | | | | | Pupils/students in education[3] | |
| | | | | | | % achieving GCE A Levels and equivalent[4,5] | |
	5 or more grades A*-C[6]	1-4 grades A*-C[6]	Grades D-G[7] only	No graded results	Total (=100%) (Thousands)	2 or more passes[8]	Population aged 17 (thousands)
2000/01							
All	51.0	24.1	19.4	5.5	729.7	37.4	717.9
Males	45.7	24.6	23.1	6.5	372.1	33.4	366.6
Females	56.5	23.6	15.5	4.4	357.6	41.6	351.3
2001/02[9]							
All	52.5	23.7	18.4	5.4	732.5	37.4	739.0
Males	47.2	24.3	22.0	6.4	374.0	33.0	379.8
Females	58.0	23.1	14.6	4.3	358.5	42.0	359.2
2002/03							
All	53.5	23.1	18.2	5.2	750.2	38.4	771.2
Males	48.3	23.6	21.8	6.3	382.7	33.9	397.2
Females	58.8	22.7	14.4	4.1	367.6	43.2	374.0
2003/04							
All	54.2	22.7	18.8	4.4	772.0	39.2	769.5
Males	49.2	23.1	22.4	5.3	392.6	34.7	395.8
Females	59.3	22.2	15.0	3.4	379.4	44.0	373.7
2004/05[9]							
All	57.0	22.1	17.9	3.0	759.1	38.3	788.5
Males	52.1	22.8	21.4	3.7	385.5	33.8	405.2
Females	62.1	21.4	14.2	2.3	373.5	43.1	383.4
2005/06[10]							
All	59.0	21.4	16.9	2.7	773.8	37.3	807.3
Males	54.3	22.1	20.3	3.3	394.2	32.7	415.5
Females	63.9	20.6	13.5	2.1	379.6	42.1	391.8

1 From 1999/00, National Qualifications (NQ) were introduced in Scotland but are not all shown until 2001/01. NQs include Standard Grades, Intermediate 1 & 2 and Higher Grades. The figures for Higher Grades combine the new NQ Higher and the old SCE Higher and include Advanced Highers.

2 Pupils aged 15 at the start of the acadamic year, pupils in Year S4 in Scotland. From 2004/05, pupils at the end of Key Stage 4 in England.

3 Pupils in schools and students in further education institutions generally aged 16-18 at the start of the academic year in England, Wales and Northern Ireland as a percentage of the 17 year old population. Data from 2002/03 for Wales and Northern Ireland however, relate to schools only. Pupils in Scotland generally sit Highers one year earlier than their A level counterparts and the figures relate to the results of pupils in Year S5/S6.

4 Figures, other than for Scotland, include Vocational Certificates of Education (VCE) and, previously, Advanced level GNVQ which is equivalent to 2 GCE A level or AS equivalents.

5 2 AS levels or 2 Highers/1Adavanced Higher or 1 each in Scotland, count as 1 A level pass.

6 Standard Grades 1-3/Intermediate 2 A-C/Intermediate 1 A in Scotland.

7 Grades D-G at GCSE and Scottish Standard Grades 4-6/Intermediate 1 B and C/Access 3 (pass).

8 3 or more SCE/NQ Higher Grades/2 or more Advanced Highers/1 Advanced Higher with 2 or more Higher Passes in Scotland.

9 Includes revised data.

10 Provisional.

Source: Source: Education Departments: 01325 392754

6.6 Students in further[1] education: by country, mode of study,[2] sex and age,[3] during 2005/06[4]

United Kingdom (home and overseas students)

Thousands

	United Kingdom		England[5]		Wales		Scotland[6]		Northern Ireland	
	Full-time	Part-time	Full-time	Part-time	Full-time	Part-time	Full-time	Part-time	Full-time	Part-time
All										
Age under 16	4.4	55.3	2.0	10.2	0.8	4.9	1.5	32.8	0.1	7.4
16	305.3	72.9	274.7	46.4	13.5	3.0	8.7	12.1	8.4	11.4
17	265.6	81.4	235.3	54.4	11.7	3.6	9.7	14.9	8.9	8.5
18	121.3	86.7	103.3	65.4	5.5	4.6	6.9	11.4	5.6	5.3
19	49.0	78.3	41.1	61.6	2.3	4.0	3.3	9.0	2.2	3.6
20	27.7	75.9	23.3	61.9	1.3	3.8	2.1	7.2	1.0	3.0
21	19.6	75.7	16.8	63.6	0.8	3.6	1.4	5.9	0.5	2.6
22	16.8	79.5	14.7	67.4	0.7	4.0	1.1	5.4	0.4	2.7
23	14.9	81.4	13.2	69.3	0.5	4.1	1.0	5.4	0.3	2.6
24	13.5	84.5	12.0	72.5	0.4	4.2	0.9	5.4	0.2	2.4
25	12.9	87.0	11.7	75.1	0.4	4.2	0.7	5.2	0.1	2.5
26	11.7	82.3	10.6	71.2	0.3	3.9	0.6	4.9	0.1	2.2
27	10.5	75.9	9.5	65.6	0.3	3.5	0.6	4.7	0.1	2.0
28	9.4	71.8	8.6	62.1	0.3	3.4	0.4	4.3	0.1	2.0
29	9.1	72.1	8.3	62.6	0.3	3.5	0.5	4.3	0.1	1.8
30+	162.6	2 218.7	151.8	1 884.9	4.0	134.7	5.8	153.4	1.1	45.7
Unknown	0.7	16.0	0.7	12.2	0.1	3.4	-	-	-	0.4
All ages	1 055.0	3 395.4	937.5	2 806.5	43.3	196.4	45.1	286.2	29.2	106.2
Males										
Age under 16	2.5	30.3	1.2	5.2	0.4	2.8	0.8	17.4	0.1	4.9
16	149.4	37.2	133.2	24.4	6.8	1.4	4.6	5.8	4.9	5.5
17	127.2	41.1	112.2	27.6	5.6	2.0	4.6	7.7	4.8	3.8
18	61.1	43.3	52.2	31.3	2.7	2.5	3.2	7.1	3.0	2.4
19	26.6	37.7	22.3	28.2	1.3	2.1	1.7	5.6	1.3	1.7
20	15.1	34.9	12.7	27.6	0.7	1.8	1.1	4.1	0.6	1.3
21	10.1	32.5	8.7	26.8	0.4	1.6	0.7	3.0	0.3	1.1
22	8.3	32.8	7.3	27.5	0.3	1.7	0.5	2.5	0.2	1.1
23	7.1	32.9	6.3	27.9	0.2	1.7	0.4	2.3	0.1	1.0
24	6.4	33.6	5.8	28.9	0.2	1.7	0.4	2.2	0.1	0.8
25	6.2	35.0	5.7	30.2	0.2	1.7	0.3	2.1	0.1	0.9
26	5.5	32.9	5.0	28.6	0.1	1.6	0.3	2.0	-	0.8
27	4.8	30.3	4.5	26.3	0.1	1.5	0.2	1.8	-	0.8
28	4.4	28.9	4.1	25.1	0.1	1.4	0.2	1.7	-	0.7
29	4.3	29.6	4.0	25.8	0.1	1.4	0.2	1.7	-	0.7
30+	77.3	805.2	73.8	684.0	1.2	50.0	1.8	55.5	0.5	15.8
Unknown	0.5	6.6	0.5	5.1	-	1.3	-	-	-	0.2
All Ages	516.8	1 324.7	459.4	1 080.5	20.5	78.2	20.9	122.5	16.0	43.6
Females										
Age under 16	1.9	24.9	0.9	4.9	0.4	2.1	0.7	15.3	-	2.5
16	155.9	35.7	141.5	22.0	6.7	1.5	4.1	6.3	3.6	5.9
17	138.4	40.3	123.1	26.8	6.1	1.7	5.0	7.2	4.1	4.7
18	60.2	43.3	51.1	34.0	2.8	2.2	3.7	4.3	2.7	2.9
19	22.4	40.6	18.8	33.4	1.1	2.0	1.7	3.4	0.8	1.9
20	12.6	41.0	10.6	34.3	0.6	1.9	1.1	3.1	0.4	1.7
21	9.6	43.3	8.1	36.8	0.4	2.0	0.8	2.9	0.2	1.5
22	8.5	46.7	7.4	39.9	0.4	2.2	0.6	2.9	0.2	1.7
23	7.8	48.5	6.8	41.4	0.3	2.4	0.5	3.1	0.1	1.6
24	7.1	50.9	6.2	43.7	0.3	2.5	0.5	3.2	0.1	1.6
25	6.7	52.0	6.0	44.9	0.3	2.4	0.4	3.1	0.1	1.6
26	6.2	49.3	5.6	42.7	0.2	2.3	0.3	2.9	0.1	1.5
27	5.7	45.6	5.0	39.3	0.2	2.1	0.4	2.9	0.1	1.3
28	5.0	42.9	4.5	37.0	0.2	2.0	0.3	2.7	-	1.3
29	4.8	42.6	4.3	36.8	0.2	2.0	0.3	2.6	-	1.1
30+	85.3	1 413.5	77.9	1 200.9	2.8	84.8	4.0	98.0	0.6	29.8
Unknown	0.2	9.4	0.2	7.1	-	2.1	-	-	-	0.2
All ages	538.2	2 070.6	478.0	1 726.0	22.8	118.2	24.2	163.8	13.2	62.7

1 Further education (FE) institution figures are whole year counts. Higher education (HE) institution figures are based on the HESA 'standard registration' count.
2 Full-time includes sandwich. Part-time comprises both day and evening, including block release and open/distance learning.
3 Ages as at 31 August 2005 (1 July in Northern Ireland and 31 December in Scotland).
4 Provisional.

5 Further education institution figures for England include LSC funded students only.
6 Figures for Scotland further education colleges are vocational course enrolments rather than headcounts.

Source: Education Departments: 01325 392754

6.7 Students in further education:[1] by country, mode of study,[2] sex and area[3] 2005/06

United Kingdom - Home and overseas students

Thousands

	United Kingdom		England[5]		Wales		Scotland[6]		Northern Ireland	
	Full-time	Part-time	Full-time	Part-time	Full-time	Part-time	Full-time	Part-time	Full-time	Part-time
All persons										
Health, Public Services and Care	146.5	579.6	135.9	510.6	-	-	7.4	60.1	3.3	8.9
Science and Mathematics	60.8	57.1	56.3	40.3	-	-	1.7	6.3	2.8	10.5
Agriculture, Horticulture and Animal Care	22.8	47.1	21.4	37.4	-	-	1.2	8.9	0.2	0.7
Engineering and Manufacturing Technologies	54.9	142.3	47.6	113.9	-	0.1	4.9	22.9	2.4	5.5
Construction, Planning and the Built Environment	49.8	90.6	40.0	69.4	-	-	4.2	15.0	5.6	6.3
Information & Communication Technology	60.5	555.1	55.4	487.3	-	-	3.1	51.9	2.0	15.9
Retail and Commercial Enterprise	68.1	140.1	64.5	125.5	-	-	0.1	4.3	3.5	10.3
Leisure,Travel and Tourism	63.4	96.9	56.9	64.9	-	-	4.6	31.0	1.9	1.0
Arts, Media and Publishing	117.2	170.3	109.5	146.8	-	-	4.8	19.5	2.9	4.0
History, Philosophy and Theology	14.9	27.5	14.5	27.1	-	-	-	-	0.4	0.4
Social Sciences	19.2	12.3	18.2	10.3	-	-	-	-	1.0	1.9
Languages, Literature and Culture	30.3	217.0	27.4	178.7	-	2.9	2.6	23.5	0.4	12.0
Education and Training	4.6	96.9	4.3	83.2	-	-	-	-	0.3	13.7
Preparation for Life and Work	167.3	638.2	166.9	633.1	-	-	-	-	0.4	5.0
Business Adiminstration & Law	63.1	195.3	57.1	163.3	-	0.1	4.0	21.8	2.0	10.2
Other subjects[7] / Unknown	111.5	329.1	61.7	114.6	43.2	193.3	6.6	21.1	-	-
All subjects	1 055.0	3 395.4	937.5	2 806.5	43.3	196.4	45.1	286.2	29.2	106.2
Males										
Health, Public Services and Care	51.5	164.2	50.0	141.2	-	-	1.3	21.4	0.2	1.6
Science and Mathematics	27.4	17.8	25.7	11.6	-	-	0.5	2.6	1.2	3.7
Agriculture, Horticulture and Animal Care	11.1	22.7	10.3	17.1	-	-	0.7	5.4	0.1	0.3
Engineering and Manufacturing Technologies	51.2	110.7	44.2	86.7	-	0.1	4.6	18.9	2.4	4.9
Construction, Planning and the Built Environment	48.0	83.5	38.5	64.2	-	-	4.0	13.8	5.5	5.6
Information & Communication Technology	43.2	208.4	39.5	184.0	-	-	2.0	18.5	1.6	5.9
Retail and Commercial Enterprise	10.5	41.3	9.8	35.6	-	-	0.1	3.7	0.6	2.1
Leisure, Travel and Tourism	36.7	47.5	33.2	35.8	-	-	2.4	11.1	1.0	0.6
Arts Media and Publishing	53.8	47.7	50.0	39.9	-	-	2.2	6.6	1.6	1.3
History, Philosophy and Theology	6.4	8.9	6.3	8.7	-	-	-	-	0.2	0.2
Social Sciences	7.7	3.6	7.3	2.9	-	-	-	-	0.4	0.7
Languages, Literature and Culture	10.5	77.7	9.3	62.4	-	1.0	1.1	9.2	0.1	5.1
Education and Training	1.7	25.9	1.5	20.2	-	-	-	-	0.2	5.7
Preparation for Life and Work	80.3	267.2	80.0	246.3	-	-	-	-	0.3	2.9
Business Administration & Law	28.6	70.2	27.1	60.1	-	-	0.9	7.1	0.6	3.0
Other Subjects[7]/Unknown	48.2	127.3	26.7	45.9	20.5	77.2	1.1	4.2	-	-
All subjects	516.8	1 324.7	459.4	1 080.5	20.5	78.2	20.9	122.5	16.0	43.6
Females										
Health, Public Services and Care	95.1	415.3	85.9	369.5	-	-	6.0	38.6	3.1	7.2
Science and Mathematics	33.4	39.2	30.6	28.7	-	-	1.1	3.7	1.7	6.8
Agriculture, Horticulture and Animal Care	11.8	24.4	11.1	20.4	-	-	0.5	3.6	0.1	0.4
Engineering and Manufacturing Technologies	3.7	31.6	3.3	27.2	-	-	0.3	3.9	0.1	0.5
Construction, Planning and the Built Environment	1.8	7.1	1.5	5.1	-	-	0.3	1.2	0.1	0.7
Information & Communication Technology	17.3	346.7	15.8	303.3	-	-	1.1	33.4	0.4	10.0
Retail and Commercial Enterprise	57.6	98.8	54.7	89.9	-	-	-	0.7	2.9	8.2
Leisure, Travel and Tourism	26.7	49.4	23.7	29.1	-	-	2.2	19.9	0.9	0.4
Arts, Media and Publishing	63.3	122.6	59.5	106.9	-	-	2.5	12.9	1.3	2.7
History, Philosophy and Theology	8.5	18.7	8.2	18.4	-	-	-	-	0.2	0.2
Social Sciences	11.5	8.7	10.9	7.5	-	-	-	-	0.6	1.2
Language, Literature and Culture	19.8	139.3	18.1	116.3	-	2.0	1.5	14.2	0.2	6.9
Education and Training	2.9	71.0	2.8	63.1	-	-	-	-	0.1	8.0
Preparation for Life and Work	87.1	370.9	86.9	368.8	-	-	-	-	0.1	2.1
Business Administration & Law	34.6	125.1	30.0	103.3	-	-	3.1	14.6	1.4	7.2
Other subjects[7]/Unknown	63.2	201.8	35.0	68.7	22.8	116.2	5.5	16.9	-	-
All subjects	538.2	2 070.6	478.0	1 726.0	22.8	118.2	24.2	163.8	13.2	62.7

1 Further education (FE) institution figures are whole year counts. Higher education (HE) institution figures are based on the HESA 'standard registration' count.

2 Full-time includes sandwich. Part-time comprises both day and evening including block release and open/distance learning.

3 Data are shown by sector subject area and not directly comparable with previous years.

4 Provisional.

5 Further education institution figures for England include LSC funded students only.

6 Figures for Scotland further education colleges are vocational course enrolments rather than headcounts.

7 For UK higher education institutions, includes the previous subject groups not allocated to specific sector subject areas, i e. medicine & dentistry, subjects allied to medicine, biological, veterinary, physical, mathematical and computer sciences and creative arts & design.

Source: Education Departments/DIUS: 01325 392754

Education

6.8 Students in higher[1] education by level, mode of study,[2] sex and age,[3] 2005/06[4,5,6]
United Kingdom (home and overseas students)

Thousands

| | Postgraduate level | | | | | | First degree | | Other undergraduate | | Total higher education[7] | |
| | PhD and equivalent | | Masters and others | | Total Postgraduate | | | | | | | |
	Full-time	Part-time	Full-time	Part-time	Full-time	Part-time	Full-time	Part-time	Full-time	Part-time	Full-time	Part-time
All												
Age under 16	-	-	-	-	-	-	-	-	-	0.4	-	0.4
16	-	-	-	-	-	-	0.3	-	0.5	3.3	0.8	3.3
17	-	-	-	-	-	-	10.0	0.1	4.4	2.6	14.4	2.7
18	-	-	-	-	-	-	180.3	1.3	20.7	6.8	201.1	8.1
19	-	-	0.1	-	0.1	-	231.5	4.2	24.8	11.2	256.5	15.5
20	-	-	1.5	0.3	1.5	0.3	237.8	6.8	19.7	12.9	259.0	20.1
21	0.6	-	16.2	1.8	16.8	1.8	155.6	9.0	13.5	12.2	186.0	23.0
22	2.7	0.1	27.7	5.9	30.4	6.0	76.2	9.2	10.0	13.4	116.7	28.6
23	5.0	0.2	27.5	10.1	32.5	10.4	40.4	8.7	7.9	14.4	80.8	33.5
24	6.3	1.0	21.1	12.0	27.3	12.9	25.0	8.2	6.7	15.2	59.0	36.3
25	5.8	2.4	16.2	12.7	22.0	15.1	17.8	8.0	5.9	15.8	45.6	38.8
26	4.8	2.8	12.3	12.2	17.2	15.0	13.1	7.3	4.9	15.4	35.2	37.7
27	3.7	2.3	9.2	11.3	12.9	13.7	9.9	6.5	4.2	13.9	27.0	34.1
28	3.1	2.2	7.6	10.6	10.7	12.8	7.9	6.1	3.6	13.3	22.2	32.2
29	2.5	2.0	6.0	10.2	8.5	12.3	6.9	5.8	3.4	13.2	18.9	31.3
30+	15.2	31.3	39.5	183.9	54.7	215.2	69.6	131.1	48.6	342.7	173.0	689.6
Unknown	-	0.1	0.1	1.7	0.2	1.7	0.2	0.2	0.2	6.6	0.5	8.5
All ages	49.9	44.4	185.1	272.8	234.9	317.2	1 082.6	212.3	179.0	513.3	1 497.0	1 043.8
Males												
Age under 16	-	-	-	-	-	-	-	-	-	0.2	-	0.2
16	-	-	-	-	-	-	0.1	-	0.2	1.4	0.4	1.4
17	-	-	-	-	-	-	4.4	0.1	1.9	1.3	6.3	1.3
18	-	-	-	-	-	-	80.1	0.6	9.0	3.8	89.1	4.4
19	-	-	-	-	-	-	104.9	2.0	11.0	6.1	116.1	8.2
20	-	-	0.7	0.1	0.7	0.1	107.7	3.4	8.6	6.7	117.0	10.2
21	0.3	-	6.6	0.6	6.9	0.6	75.2	4.4	5.7	5.9	87.9	10.9
22	1.6	-	11.8	2.3	13.3	2.3	39.1	4.4	4.1	5.7	56.6	12.5
23	2.8	0.1	12.4	4.0	15.1	4.1	21.0	4.1	3.1	5.6	39.2	13.8
24	3.5	0.5	10.0	4.8	13.5	5.2	12.5	3.4	2.6	5.6	28.7	14.3
25	3.2	1.4	7.8	4.9	11.0	6.3	8.5	3.1	2.1	5.5	21.7	14.9
26	2.6	1.6	6.2	4.9	8.8	6.5	6.2	2.8	1.8	5.5	16.7	14.8
27	2.0	1.3	4.7	4.7	6.7	6.0	4.5	2.5	1.5	5.0	12.6	13.5
28	1.7	1.2	3.8	4.4	5.6	5.6	3.4	2.3	1.2	4.8	10.2	12.7
29	1.4	1.1	3.2	4.4	4.6	5.5	3.1	2.2	1.1	4.6	8.8	12.3
30+	8.8	17.0	20.5	80.5	29.3	97.5	23.1	47.0	12.6	115.0	65.1	259.7
Unknown	-	-	0.1	0.7	0.1	0.7	0.1	0.1	0.1	2.3	0.3	3.1
All ages	28.0	24.3	87.8	116.2	115.8	140.4	493.9	82.3	66.7	185.0	676.7	408.2
Females												
Age under 16	-	-	-	-	-	-	-	-	-	0.2	-	0.2
16	-	-	-	-	-	-	0.2	-	0.3	1.9	0.5	1.9
17	-	-	-	-	-	-	5.5	0.1	2.6	1.3	8.1	1.4
18	-	-	-	-	-	-	100.2	0.7	11.8	3.0	112.0	3.7
19	-	-	-	-	0.1	-	126.6	2.1	13.8	5.1	140.4	7.3
20	-	-	0.8	0.3	0.8	0.3	130.1	3.4	11.1	6.2	142.0	9.9
21	0.3	-	9.6	1.2	9.9	1.2	80.4	4.6	7.8	6.3	98.1	12.1
22	1.1	-	16.0	3.7	17.1	3.7	37.1	4.7	5.8	7.7	60.1	16.1
23	2.2	0.1	15.2	6.2	17.4	6.3	19.4	4.6	4.8	8.8	41.6	19.7
24	2.8	0.5	11.1	7.2	13.8	7.7	12.5	4.7	4.1	9.6	30.4	22.0
25	2.6	1.0	8.4	7.7	11.0	8.8	9.2	4.9	3.7	10.3	23.9	23.9
26	2.2	1.2	6.1	7.3	8.4	8.5	7.0	4.5	3.1	9.9	18.5	22.9
27	1.8	1.0	4.5	6.6	6.3	7.7	5.4	4.0	2.7	9.0	14.4	20.6
28	1.4	1.0	3.7	6.2	5.1	7.2	4.5	3.8	2.4	8.5	12.0	19.5
29	1.1	0.9	2.8	5.9	3.9	6.8	3.9	3.7	2.3	8.6	10.1	19.0
30+	6.4	14.3	19.0	103.4	25.4	117.7	46.6	84.1	35.9	227.7	107.9	429.9
Unknown	-	-	0.1	1.0	0.1	1.0	0.1	0.1	0.1	4.3	0.3	5.4
All ages	21.9	20.2	97.3	156.6	119.2	176.8	588.6	130.0	112.3	328.3	820.3	635.6

1 Includes Open University students. Part-time figures include dormant modes, those writing up at home and on sabbaticals.
2 Full-time includes sandwich. Part-time comprises both day and evening, including block release and open/distance learning.
3 Ages as at 31 August 2005 (1 July in Northern Ireland and 31 December in Scotland).
4 Provisional.
5 Figures for higher education (HE) institutions are based on the HESA 'standard registration' count. Figure for further education (FE) institutions are whole year enrolments.
6 FE institution figures for England include Learning and Skills Council (LSC) funded students only.
7 Includes data for higher education students in further education institutions in Wales which cannot be split by level.

Source: Education Departments: 01325 392754

6.9 Students in higher[1] education by level, mode of study[2], sex and subject group[3], 2005/06[4,5,6]

United Kingdom - Home and overseas students

Thousands

	Postgraduate level						First degree		Other undergraduate		Total higher education[7]	
	PhD and equivalent		Masters and others		Total Postgraduate							
	Full-time	Part-time	Full-time	Part-time	Full-time	Part-time	Full-time	Part-time	Full-time	Part-time	Full-time	Part-time
All persons												
Medicine & Dentistry	3.5	4.0	3.3	7.6	6.8	11.6	40.7	0.1	0.4	0.2	47.8	11.8
Subjects Allied to Medicine	2.4	3.0	6.8	34.5	9.2	37.5	83.5	34.3	69.4	78.1	162.1	149.9
Biological Sciences	7.8	4.5	7.1	9.6	14.9	14.1	101.3	15.9	3.5	5.8	119.8	35.8
Vet. Science, Agriculture & related	0.7	0.6	1.4	1.2	2.1	1.8	11.3	0.6	4.1	5.5	17.5	7.9
Physical Sciences	7.2	3.3	6.0	3.8	13.2	7.1	48.9	7.1	1.0	5.6	63.2	19.8
Mathematical and Computing Sciences	4.0	2.6	12.1	10.5	16.1	13.1	79.9	15.8	9.2	23.8	105.2	52.7
Engineering & Technology	7.6	4.2	14.1	13.0	21.7	17.3	70.9	10.0	9.6	23.7	102.3	50.9
Architecture, Building & Planning	0.8	0.7	5.0	8.8	5.7	9.5	25.1	7.3	3.7	12.7	34.5	29.5
Social Sciences (inc Law)	5.2	5.2	31.0	27.6	36.3	32.8	154.4	31.6	8.4	36.9	199.1	101.2
Business & Administrative Studies	2.1	3.2	38.5	66.0	40.6	69.2	141.6	20.1	24.5	99.0	206.6	188.3
Mass Communication & Documentation	0.4	0.4	5.1	4.3	5.5	4.7	33.3	2.0	5.3	5.9	44.1	12.5
Languages	2.9	2.7	6.8	5.4	9.6	8.1	73.8	9.0	2.4	38.8	85.8	56.0
Historical and Philosophical Studies	2.9	3.5	4.6	7.7	7.5	11.2	52.3	14.4	1.1	19.8	60.9	45.4
Creative Arts & Design	1.0	1.4	8.2	5.5	9.2	7.0	113.7	4.6	16.3	13.9	139.2	25.5
Education[8]	1.1	4.8	35.1	65.1	36.2	70.0	40.8	9.5	3.8	50.0	80.8	129.4
Other subjects[9]	0.1	0.2	0.2	2.2	0.3	2.4	11.2	30.1	16.1	93.7	27.6	126.1
Unknown[7]	-	-	-	-	-	-	-	-	0.1	-	0.6	1.0
All subjects	49.9	44.4	185.1	272.8	234.9	317.2	1 082.6	212.3	179.0	513.3	1 497.0	1 043.8
of which overseas students	23.3	15.2	93.4	39.9	116.7	55.1	121.7	9.1	13.5	19.2	252.0	83.4
Males												
Medicine and Dentistry	1.5	2.2	1.3	3.4	2.8	5.6	16.7	-	-	-	19.5	5.6
Subjects Allied to Medicine	1.0	1.2	2.2	9.6	3.2	10.7	18.0	4.9	8.7	10.2	29.9	25.9
Biological Sciences	3.0	1.9	2.6	2.9	5.7	4.8	37.3	4.2	1.8	2.1	44.7	11.1
Vet. Science, Agriculture & related	0.3	0.3	0.7	0.6	1.0	0.9	3.3	0.2	1.6	2.7	5.9	3.8
Physical Sciences	4.6	2.2	3.3	2.0	7.9	4.2	28.7	4.0	0.5	2.9	37.1	11.1
Mathematical and Computing Sciences	3.1	2.0	9.4	7.8	12.5	9.8	61.4	11.8	7.7	13.4	81.6	35.0
Engineering & Technology	6.0	3.4	11.3	10.7	17.4	14.0	60.0	9.0	8.5	21.6	85.8	44.6
Architecture, Building & Planning	0.5	0.5	3.0	5.5	3.5	6.0	17.6	5.7	2.9	10.2	23.9	21.9
Social Sciences (inc Law)	2.7	2.7	13.6	10.9	16.2	13.6	62.2	10.8	2.5	9.6	80.9	33.9
Business & Administrative Studies	1.2	1.9	20.4	33.5	21.6	35.4	72.5	8.6	11.5	35.1	105.7	79.2
Mass Communication & Documentation	0.2	0.2	1.8	1.3	2.0	1.5	14.2	1.0	3.9	3.6	20.1	6.1
Languages	1.2	1.1	2.2	1.7	3.4	2.8	21.5	2.2	1.2	15.0	26.1	20.0
Historical and Philosophical Studies	1.7	2.0	2.2	3.7	3.9	5.8	24.7	5.6	0.4	6.8	29.0	18.2
Creative Arts & Design	0.5	0.7	3.2	2.3	3.7	3.0	44.7	1.6	6.8	4.4	55.2	9.0
Education[8]	0.4	2.0	10.5	19.3	10.9	21.3	7.0	1.3	0.8	13.4	18.7	36.0
Other subjects[9]	0.1	0.1	0.1	1.0	0.2	1.1	4.2	11.4	7.8	33.7	12.2	46.2
Unknown[7]	-	-	-	-	-	-	-	-	0.1	-	0.3	0.5
All subjects	28.0	24.3	87.8	116.2	115.8	140.4	493.9	82.3	66.7	185.0	676.7	408.2
of which overseas students	13.9	8.8	49.5	22.1	63.4	30.9	61.5	4.5	6.7	8.3	131.6	43.7
Females												
Medicine & Dentistry	2.0	1.9	1.9	4.2	4.0	6.1	24.0	-	0.3	0.1	28.3	6.2
Subjects Allied to Medicine	1.4	1.9	4.6	24.9	6.0	26.8	65.4	29.4	60.7	67.9	132.2	124.1
Biological Sciences	4.8	2.6	4.5	6.7	9.3	9.3	64.1	11.7	1.7	3.7	75.1	24.6
Vet. Science, Agriculture & related	0.4	0.3	0.7	0.6	1.1	0.9	8.0	0.4	2.5	2.7	11.6	4.1
Physical Sciences	2.6	1.1	2.7	1.8	5.3	2.9	20.3	3.1	0.5	2.7	26.1	8.7
Mathematical and Computing Sciences	0.9	0.6	2.7	2.7	3.6	3.3	18.4	4.0	1.6	10.3	23.6	17.7
Engineering & Technology	1.6	0.9	2.8	2.4	4.4	3.2	11.0	1.0	1.1	2.1	16.5	6.3
Architecture, Building & Planning	0.3	0.2	2.0	3.3	2.3	3.5	7.5	1.6	0.8	2.5	10.6	7.6
Social Sciences (inc Law)	2.6	2.5	17.5	16.7	20.1	19.2	92.2	20.8	5.9	27.3	118.2	67.3
Business & Administrative Studies	0.8	1.2	18.1	32.6	18.9	33.8	69.1	11.5	12.9	63.9	100.9	109.1
Mass Communication & Documentation	0.2	0.2	3.3	2.9	3.5	3.1	19.1	1.0	1.4	2.2	24.0	6.4
Languages	1.6	1.6	4.6	3.7	6.2	5.4	52.2	6.8	1.3	23.9	59.7	36.0
Historical and Philosophical Studies	1.3	1.5	2.4	4.0	3.6	5.4	27.6	8.8	0.7	13.0	31.9	27.3
Creative Arts & Design	0.5	0.7	5.0	3.3	5.5	4.0	69.0	3.0	9.5	9.5	84.0	16.5
Education[8]	0.7	2.8	24.6	45.9	25.3	48.7	33.8	8.1	3.0	36.5	62.1	93.4
Other subjects[9]	0.1	0.1	0.1	1.2	0.2	1.3	7.0	18.7	8.2	59.9	15.4	79.9
Unknown[7]	-	-	-	-	-	-	-	-	-	-	0.2	0.5
All subjects	21.9	20.2	97.3	156.6	119.2	176.8	588.6	130.0	112.3	328.3	820.3	635.6
of which overseas students	9.4	6.3	43.9	17.8	53.3	24.1	60.2	4.6	6.8	10.9	120.3	39.7

1 Higher Education Statistics Agency (HESA) higher education institutions include Open University students. Part-time figures include dormant modes, those writing up at home and on sabbaticals.

2 Full-time includes sandwich. Part-time comprises both day and evening, including block release and open/distance learning.

3 For HE students in further education institutions in England, includes those subject sector areas which cannot be allocated to specific subject groups shown.

4 Provisional.

5 FE institution figures for England include Learning and Skills Council (LSC) funded students only.

6 Figures for higher education (HE) institutions are based on the HESA 'Standard registration ' count. Figures for further education (FE) institutions are whole year enrolments. Students starting courses after these dates will not therefore be counted. Figures for Scotland and England, however, are whole year (not snapshot) enrolments (rather than headcounts).

7 Includes data for higher education students in further education institutions in Wales which cannot be split by level.

8 Including ITT and INSET.

9 Includes Combined and general categories.

Source: Education Departments: 01325 392754

6.10 Students[1,2] obtaining higher education qualifications[3,4]: by level, sex and subject group, 2005/06

United Kingdom

Thousands

	Sub-degree[3]	First degree	Postgraduate			Total higher education
			PhD and equivalent	Other	Total	
All persons						
Subject group						
Medicine & Dentistry	0.1	7.7	1.7	3.4	5.2	13.0
Subjects Allied to Medicine	44.9	29.8	0.9	9.8	10.7	85.4
Biological Sciences	3.3	27.8	2.5	6.6	9.1	40.2
Vet. Science, Agriculture & related	1.3	2.8	0.3	1.2	1.5	5.6
Physical Sciences	2.3	12.9	2.3	4.0	6.3	21.5
Mathematical & Computer Sciences	7.5	24.3	1.2	9.3	10.5	42.3
Engineering & Technology	4.8	19.8	2.2	11.0	13.2	37.8
Architecture, Building & Planning	2.8	7.4	0.2	5.4	5.6	15.7
Social Studies (inc Law)	14.7	45.2	1.5	27.6	29.1	89.0
Business & Administrative Studies	13.0	42.4	0.7	40.4	41.1	96.5
Mass Communication & Documentation	1.3	9.1	0.1	4.6	4.7	15.1
Languages	4.3	20.2	0.9	5.5	6.4	30.9
Historical and Philosophical Studies	2.2	15.8	1.0	4.5	5.5	23.5
Creative Arts & Design	5.9	31.3	0.3	6.8	7.2	44.4
Education[5]	15.9	12.3	0.6	41.6	42.1	70.4
Combined, general	2.2	7.1	0.1	0.1	0.2	9.5
All subjects	126.6	316.0	16.5	181.8	198.3	640.8
Males						
Subject group						
Medicine and Dentistry	-	3.2	0.8	1.5	2.3	5.5
Subjects Allied to Medicine	5.7	5.3	0.4	2.5	2.8	13.9
Biological Sciences	1.4	9.6	1.0	2.1	3.1	14.1
Vet. Science, Agriculture & related	0.6	0.9	0.2	0.6	0.7	2.2
Physical Sciences	1.4	7.3	1.5	2.1	3.6	12.2
Mathematical & Computer Sciences	5.5	18.2	0.9	7.0	7.9	31.6
Engineering & Technology	4.4	16.6	1.7	8.7	10.5	31.4
Architecture, Building & Planning	2.0	5.2	0.1	3.3	3.4	10.6
Social Studies (inc Law)	4.3	17.7	0.8	11.9	12.7	34.7
Business & Administrative Studies	5.9	20.1	0.4	20.8	21.2	47.2
Mass Communication & Documentation	0.7	3.5	-	1.5	1.6	5.8
Languages	1.5	5.5	0.4	1.7	2.1	9.1
Historical and Philosophical Studies	0.9	7.2	0.6	2.1	2.7	10.7
Creative Arts & Design	2.5	12.0	0.2	2.7	2.9	17.4
Education[5]	3.9	1.9	0.2	12.0	12.3	18.1
Combined, general	0.8	3.0	-	0.1	0.1	3.9
All subjects	41.5	137.1	9.4	80.4	89.8	268.4
Females						
Subject group						
Medicine & Dentistry	0.1	4.5	0.9	1.9	2.9	7.5
Subjects Allied to Medicine	39.2	24.5	0.5	7.4	7.9	71.6
Biological Sciences	1.9	18.2	1.5	4.4	5.9	26.0
Vet. Science, Agriculture & related	0.7	1.9	0.1	0.6	0.7	3.4
Physical Sciences	1.0	5.6	0.8	1.9	2.7	9.3
Mathematical & Computer Sciences	2.0	6.1	0.3	2.4	2.6	10.7
Engineering & Technology	0.5	3.2	0.5	2.3	2.7	6.4
Architecture, Building & Planning	0.8	2.2	0.1	2.1	2.2	5.2
Social Studies (inc Law)	10.4	27.5	0.7	15.7	16.4	54.3
Business & Administrative Studies	7.0	22.4	0.3	19.6	19.9	49.3
Mass Communication & Documentation	0.6	5.5	0.1	3.1	3.2	9.3
Languages	2.8	14.7	0.5	3.8	4.3	21.8
Historical and Philosophical Studies	1.4	8.6	0.4	2.4	2.8	12.8
Creative Arts & Design	3.4	19.4	0.1	4.1	4.2	27.0
Education[5]	12.0	10.4	0.3	29.6	29.9	52.3
Combined, general	1.4	4.2	-	0.1	0.1	5.6
All subjects	85.1	178.9	7.1	101.4	108.5	372.5

1 Includes students on Open University courses.
2 Includes students qualifying on all modes of study.
3 Includes higher education in higher education institutions in the UK only. Excludes qualifications from the private sector, except for the University of Buckingham who returned data to HESA in 2005/06, and higher education qualifications in further education institutions (approximately 8% of the total number of students).

4 Excludes students who successfully completed courses for which formal qualifications are not awarded.
5 Includes ITT and INSET.

Source: Education Departments: 01325 392754

6.11 Qualified teachers: by type of school and sex[1]

Thousands

	Public sector mainstream schools		Non-maintained mainstream schools	All special schools	Total[3]
	Nursery and primary	Secondary[2]			
All full-time teachers					
United Kingdom					
1990/91[4]	208.8	233.1	44.9	19.0	505.7
1995/96[4,5]	211.8	222.1	48.6	17.2	499.7
2000/01[6,7]	211.2	225.7	52.3	16.5	505.7
2001/02	211.2	227.1	52.8	16.3	507.3
2002/03[8]	210.5	229.7	53.6	19.8	513.6
2003/04[9]	210.6	229.7	55.8	19.8	516.0
2004/05[9]	208.5	232.5	56.3	19.9	517.2
2005/06[10]	208.4	233.8	57.2	20.4	519.8
of which:					
England and Wales[1]	178.9	200.1	54.5	17.5	451.0
Scotland	21.7	23.7	2.6	2.1	50.1
Northern Ireland	7.9	10.0	0.1	0.7	18.7
Full-time male teachers					
United Kingdom					
1990/91[4]	37.7	120.7	20.6	5.9	184.9
1995/96[4,5]	35.5	107.9	21.1	5.4	169.8
2000/01[6,7]	32.1	102.9	21.3	5.0	161.3
2001/02	31.8	102.6	21.5	4.9	160.8
2002/03[8]	31.7	101.6	21.6	5.9	160.8
2003/04[9]	31.7	101.5	22.7	5.9	161.9
2004/05[9]	31.2	101.6	22.9	5.9	161.6
2005/06[10]	31.0	100.8	23.5	6.0	161.4
of which:					
England and Wales[1]	28.0	86.6	22.4	5.4	142.5
Scotland	1.6	10.3	1.0	0.5	13.4
Northern Ireland	1.4	3.9	-	0.1	5.4
Full-time female teachers					
United Kingdom					
1990/91[4]	171.1	112.3	24.3	13.1	320.8
1995/96[4,5]	176.3	114.2	27.4	11.8	329.9
2000/01[6,7]	179.1	122.8	30.9	11.6	344.4
2001/02	179.4	124.5	31.2	11.4	346.5
2002/03[8]	178.8	128.2	32.0	13.9	352.8
2003/04[9]	178.9	128.2	33.0	13.9	354.0
2004/05[9]	177.3	130.9	33.4	14.0	355.6
2005/06[10]	177.4	133.1	33.7	14.3	358.4
of which:					
England and Wales[1]	150.8	113.4	32.1	12.1	308.5
Scotland	20.1	13.5	1.5	1.6	36.6
Northern Ireland	6.5	6.2	0.1	0.6	13.3
All full time equivalents (FTE) of part-time teachers					
United Kingdom					
1990/91	..	..	..	..	30.0
1995/96[4,5]	19.1	17.7	8.9	1.5	47.2
2000/01[6,7]	21.9	16.7	10.2	1.6	50.4
2001/02	23.4	17.4	10.4	1.8	53.0
2002/03[8]	23.8	17.8	11.1	1.7	54.4
2003/04[9]	26.4	19.5	11.4	1.9	59.3
2004/05[9]	27.5	20.6	11.5	1.9	61.4
2005/06[10]	30.4	21.5	11.6	2.0	65.5

1 Public sector teachers numbers in England & Wales have been provided from the 618G survey and gender split has been calculated by using the proportions from the Database of Teacher Records (DTR).

2 From 1993/94 excludes sixth form colleges in England and Wales which were reclassified as further education colleges on 1 April 1993.

3 Excludes Pupil Referral Units (PRUs).

4 Figures for non-maintained mainstream schools refer to Great Britain.

5 Includes 1994/95 data for Northern Ireland.

6 Includes 1999/00 pre-school data for Scotland.

7 Includes 2001/02 data for Northern Ireland.

8 Includes 2001/02 pre-school and 2003/04 school data for Scotland.

9 Includes revised data.

10 Provisional.

Source: Education Departments: 01325 392754

Labour market

Chapter 7

Labour market

Labour Force Survey

(Tables 7.1–7.3, 7.6, 7.9, 7.10–7.11, 7.13 and 7.16–7.18)

The impact of Census 2001 on LFS data

(Tables 7.1–7.3, 7.6, 7.9, 7.10–7.11, 7.16–7.18)

The first results of the 2001 Census, published on 30 September 2002, showed that previous estimates of the total UK population were about one million too high. Please see the Introduction of this publication for more details. Estimates of employment and unemployment levels from the Labour Force Survey (LFS) released before 30 October 2002 are therefore too high, with rates also affected. This has led to the LFS needing to reweight their estimates to the new population figures.

The Office for National Statistics (ONS) has published interim reweighted LFS estimates for the UK, which have been used in this chapter. The interim reweighted figures only cover top-level seasonally adjusted series published in the ONS Labour Market Statistics First Release. The non-seasonally adjusted series, used in previous editions of the *Annual Abstract of Statistics*, were not available in time for this publication.

Future editions of the *Annual Abstract of Statistics* will continue to show seasonally adjusted data for these tables, in line with other headline publications. These figures are not directly comparable to the non-seasonally adjusted figures previously published in the *Annual Abstract of Statistics*.

Background

The LFS is the largest regular household survey in the UK LFS interviews are conducted continuously throughout the year. In any three-month period, a nationally representative sample of approximately 102,000 people aged 16 or over in around 52,000 households are interviewed. Each household is interviewed five times, at three-monthly intervals. The initial interview is done face-to-face by an interviewer visiting the address. The other interviews are done by telephone wherever possible. The survey asks a series of questions about respondents' personal circumstances and their labour market activity. Most questions refer to activity in the week before the interview.

The concepts and definitions used in the LFS are agreed by the International Labour Organisation (ILO) – an agency of the United Nations. The definitions are used by European Union member countries and members of the Organisation for Economic Co-operation and Development (OECD).

The LFS was carried out every two years from 1973 to 1983. The ILO definition was first used in 1984. This was also the first year in which the survey was conducted on an annual basis with results available for every spring quarter (representing an average of the period from March to May). The survey moved to a continuous basis in spring 1992 in Great Britain and in winter 1994/95 in Northern Ireland, with average quarterly results published four times a year for seasonal quarters: spring (March to May), summer (June to August), autumn (September to November) and winter (December to February). From April 1998, results are published 12 times a year for the average of three consecutive months.

The LFS collects information on a sample of the population. To convert this information to give estimates for the population the data must be grossed. This is achieved by calculating weighting factors (often referred to simply as weights) which can be applied to each sampled individual in such a way that the weighted-up results match estimates or projections of the total population in terms of age distribution, sex, and region of residence.

Strengths and limitations of the LFS

The LFS produces coherent labour market information on the basis of internationally standard concepts and definitions. It is a rich source of data on a wide variety of labour market and personal characteristics. It is the most suitable source for making comparisons between countries. The LFS is designed so that households interviewed in each three month period constitute a representative sample of UK households. The survey covers those living in private households and nurses in National Health Service accommodation. Students living in halls of residence have been included since 1992 as information about them is collected at their parents' address.

However the LFS has its limitations. It is a sample survey and is therefore subject to sampling variability. The survey does not include people living in institutions such as hostels or residential homes. 'Proxy' reporting (when members of the household are not present at the interview, another member of the household answers the questions on their behalf) can affect the quality of information on topics such as earnings, hours worked, benefit receipt and qualifications. Around one-third of interviews are conducted 'by proxy', usually by a spouse or partner but sometimes by a parent or other near relation.

Sampling variability

Survey estimates are prone to *sampling variability*. The easiest way to explain this concept is by example. In the September to November 1997 period, ILO unemployment in Great Britain (seasonally adjusted) stood at 1,847,000. If we drew another sample for the same period we could get a different result, perhaps 1,900,000 or 1,820,000.

In theory, we could draw many samples, and each would give a different result. This is because each sample would be made up of different people who would give different answers to the questions. The spread of these results is the sampling variability. Sampling variability is determined by a number of factors including the sample size, the variability of the population from which the sample is drawn and the sample design. Once we know the sampling variability we can calculate a range of values about the sample estimate that represents the expected variation with a given level of assurance. This is called a confidence interval. For a 95 per cent confidence interval we expect that in 95 per cent of the samples (19 times out of 20) the confidence interval will contain the true value that would be obtained by surveying the entire population. For the example given above, we can be 95 per cent confident that the true value was in the range 1,791,000 to 1,903,000.

Unreliable estimates

Very small estimates have relatively wide confidence intervals making them unreliable. For this reason, ONS does not publish LFS estimates below 10,000.

Non-response

Non-response can introduce bias to a survey, particularly if the people not responding have characteristics that are different from those who do respond. The LFS has a response rate of around 80 per cent to the first interview, and over 90 per cent of those who are interviewed once go on to complete all five interviews. These are relatively high levels for a household survey. Any bias from non-response is minimised by *weighting* the results.

Weighting (or grossing) converts sample data to represent the full population. In the LFS, the data are weighted separately by age, sex and area of residence to population estimates based on the census. Weighting also adjusts for people not in the survey and thus minimises non-response bias.

LFS concepts and definitions

Discouraged workers – a sub-group of the economically inactive population, defined as those neither in employment nor unemployed (on the ILO measure) who said they would like a job and whose main reason for not seeking work was because they believed there were no jobs available.

Economically active – people aged 16 and over who are either in employment or ILO unemployed.

Economic activity rate – the percentage of people aged 16 and over who are economically active.

Economically inactive – people who are neither in employment nor unemployed. This group includes, for example, all those who were looking after a home or retired.

Employment – people aged 16 or over who did at least one hour of paid work in the reference week (whether as an employee or self-employed); those who had a job that they were temporarily away from (on holiday, for example); those on government-supported training and employment programmes (from spring 1983); and those doing unpaid family work (from spring 1992).

Employees – the division between employees and self-employed is based on survey respondents' own assessment of their employment status.

Full Time – the classification of employees, self-employed and unpaid family workers in their main job as full-time or part-time is on the basis of self-assessment. Up until autumn 1995, people who were on government work-related training programmes are classified as full-time or part-time according to whether their usual hours of work per week were over 30 or 30 and under; from winter 1995/96 onwards, the full-time/part-time classification for this group has been changed to self-assessment, in line with the other groups outlined above. People on government-supported training and employment programmes who are at college in the survey reference week are classified, by convention, as part-time.

Government-supported training and employment programmes – comprise all people aged 16 and over participating in one of the government's employment and training programmes (Youth Training, Training for Work and Community Action), together with those on similar programmes administered by Training and Enterprise Councils in England and Wales, or Local Enterprise Companies in Scotland.

Hours worked – respondents to the LFS are asked a series of questions enabling the identification of both their usual hours and their actual hours. Total hours include overtime (paid and unpaid) and exclude lunchbreaks.

Unemployment – Unemployment figures from the LFS, which are based upon the ILO definition, were re-labelled 'unemployment' rather than 'ILO unemployment' in January 2003. This emphasises that the LFS figures provide the official and only internationally comparable measure of unemployment in the UK. For more details see the National Statistics website at: www.statistics.gov.uk/cci/nugget.asp?id=251

The ILO measure of unemployment used throughout this publication refers to people without a job who were available to start work in the two weeks following their LFS interview and who had either looked for work in the four weeks prior to interview or were waiting to start a job they had already obtained. This definition of unemployment is in accordance with that adopted by the 13th International Conference of Labour Statisticians, further clarified at the 14th ICLS, and promulgated by the ILO in its publications.

Unemployment (rate) – the percentage of economically active people who are unemployed on the ILO measure.

Unemployment (duration) – defined as the shorter of the following two periods:

- duration of active search for work

- length of time since employment

Part-time – see full-time.

Second jobs – jobs which LFS respondents hold in addition to a main full-time or part-time job.

Self-employment – See Employees.

Temporary employees – in the LFS these are defined as those employees who say that their main job is non permanent in one of the following ways: fixed period contract; agency temping; casual work; seasonal work; other temporary work.

Unpaid family workers – the separate identification from spring 1992 of this group in the LFS is in accordance with international recommendations. The group comprises persons doing unpaid work for a business they own or for a business that a relative owns.

Distribution of workforce

(Table 7.4)

Claimant unemployed – those people who were claiming unemployment-related benefits (contributions or income related Jobseeker's Allowance and/or National Insurance credits) at Jobcentre Plus local offices on the day of the monthly count. The seasonally adjusted claimant unemployment series allows for all relevant changes

which, unless adjusted for, would distort comparisons over time.

Workforce jobs (formerly workforce in employment) – comprises employee jobs, self-employment jobs (from the LFS), HM Forces and government-supported trainees.

HM Forces (provided by Ministry of Defence) – represent the total number of UK service personnel, male and female, in HM Regular. Full Time Reserve personnel, mobilised reservists, the Ghurkhas and the Home Service battalions of the Royal Irish Regiment, wherever serving and including those on leave.

Self-employed jobs – estimates are based on the results of the Labour Force Survey. The Northern Ireland estimates are not seasonally adjusted.

Government-supported trainees – include all participants on government training and employment programmes who are receiving some work experience on their placement but who do not have a contract of employment (those with a contract are included in the employee jobs series). The numbers are not subject to seasonal adjustment.

International Employment Comparisons

(Table 7.7)

All employment rates for European Union (EU) countries published by Eurostat (including the rate for the UK) are based on the population aged 15–64. The rates for Canada and Japan are also based on the population aged 15–64, but the rate for the US is for those aged 16–64. The employment rate for the UK published by ONS is based on the working age population aged 16–64 (men) and 16–59 (women) and therefore takes into account both the current school leaving age and state pension ages.

The unemployment rate published by Eurostat for most EU countries (but not for the UK), are calculated by extrapolating from the most recent LFS data using monthly registered unemployment data. A standard population basis (15–74) is used by Eurostat except for Spain and the UK (16–74). The unemployment rate for the US is based on those aged 16 and over, but the rates for Canada and Japan are for those aged 15 and over. All unemployment rates are seasonally adjusted.

The unemployment rate for the UK published by Eurostat is based on the population aged 16–74 while the unemployment rate for the UK published by ONS is based on those aged 16 and over. There are other minor definitional differences.

Persons employed in local authorities

(Table 7.9)

The full-time equivalents for local authorities are derived by applying factors to the numbers of part-time workers in three groups based on average hours worked in each group nationally.

Jobseekers allowance claimant count

(Tables 7.14 and 7.15)

This is a count of all those people who are claiming Jobseeker's Allowance (JSA) at Jobcentre Plus local offices. People claiming JSA must declare that they are:

- out of work
- capable of work
- available for work
- actively seeking work

during the week in which the claim is made.

All people claiming JSA on the day of the monthly count are included in the claimant count, irrespective of whether they are actually receiving benefits. Also see table 10.6 in Social protection chapter.

Labour disputes

(Table 7.19)

These figures exclude details of stoppages involving fewer than ten workers or lasting less than one day except any in which the aggregate number of working days lost is 100 or more. There may be some under-recording of small or short stoppages; this would have much more effect on the total of stoppages than of working days lost. Some stoppages which affected more than one industry group have been counted under each of the industries but only once in the totals. Stoppages have been classified using the *Standard Industrial Classification (SIC) 1992*.

The figures for working days lost and workers involved have been rounded and consequently the sum of the constituent items may not agree with the totals. Classifications by size are based on the full duration of stoppages where these continue into the following year. Working days lost per thousand employees are based on the latest available mid-year (June) estimates of employee jobs.

Earnings

(Tables 7.20 to 7.25)

The total gross remuneration employees receive before any statutory deductions (tax, national insurance). Income in kind and pension funds are excluded.

Annual Survey of Hours and Earnings

(Tables 7.20, 7.21, 7.24 and 7.25)

The Annual Survey of Hours and Earnings (ASHE) is a new survey that has been developed to replace the New Earnings Survey (NES). The ASHE includes improvements to the coverage of employees and to the weighting of earnings estimates. The data variables collected remain broadly the same, although an improved questionnaire was introduced for the 2005 survey. The change in methodology means that statistics on pay and hours published from the ASHE, including the calculation of ONS's low pay statistics, are discontinuous with previous NES surveys.

To improve coverage and make the survey more representative, supplementary information was collected for the 2004 ASHE survey on businesses not registered for VAT and for people who changed or started new jobs between sample selection and the survey reference period. The 2004 ASHE results are therefore discontinuous with the results for 2003, for which no supplementary information was collected. However, for 2004 two sets of results are available; the headline results that include supplementary information and results that exclude this information. These second set of results are given solely for comparison to earlier results.

The ASHE methodology includes imputation and weighting, the main impact of these changes when applied to existing NES data for 1997 to 2003 are:

- to increase the estimates of the level of average weekly pay over estimates published from the NES

- for males the increase in estimates of earnings is more than the increase for females. In particular this affects hourly pay excluding overtime, which is used in the calculation of ONS's preferred measure of the gender pay gap. The estimate of hourly pay for males is increased more then the estimate for females, which widens the estimate of the gap between male and female hourly pay

- estimates of the level of earnings for people working in London are increased more than estimates for other regions. This widens the estimate of the difference in pay between London and other regions of the UK

For information about methodological changes to the 2007 ASHE survey see: www.statistics.gov.uk/downloads/theme_labour/ASHE/ChangeInASHE07.pdf

Average Earnings Index

(Tables 7.22 and 7.23)

The Average Earnings Index (AEI) is designed to measure changes in the level of earnings, that is, wage inflation in Great Britain. Average earnings are calculated as the total wages and salaries paid by firms, divided by the number of employees paid. Like all indices, changes are measured against a base year, whose index value is set to 100. The current base year is 2000 for Tables 7.22 and 7.23.

Users should note that the data contained in Table 7.23 of the *Annual Abstract of Statistics* since 2003 are not comparable with that published up until 2002. Table 7.23 now shows the set of 20 industry sectors. That better reflect the current state of the economy, and supersedes the previous set of 26 industry sectors. The new series are available in the format of excluding bonus index, including bonus index, and an annual percentage change for including and excluding bonuses. An article covering the reasons for the change can be found on the National Statistics website: www.statistics.gov.uk/labour.

The AEI is published monthly in the ONS Labour Market Statistics First Release. The main indicator of growth, the headline rate, is based on the annual change in the seasonally adjusted index values for the latest three months compared with the same period a year ago. The use of a three-month average reduces the level of volatility seen in the data on a month-on-month basis.

Strengths of the AEI

The AEI, based on monthly survey data, is a timely indicator of changes in the level of earnings.

Limitations of the AEI

The index is not adjusted for any changes in the composition of the workforce such as changes in the share of full-time and part-time workers, or in the share of skilled and unskilled workers. Similarly, the index does not account for changes in the number of hours worked, or any temporary factors that affect earnings.

The sample of the Monthly Wages and Salaries Survey on which the AEI is based is not designed to provide information on the level of earnings. The sample is not completely representative of the economy as firms with fewer than 20 employees are excluded, as are the earnings of self-employed persons.

The AEI only covers earnings in Great Britain as earnings information is not collected for Northern Ireland and regional data are not available.

Trade unions

(Table 7.26)

The statistics relate to all organisations of employees known to Certification Officer with head offices in the UK that fall within the appropriate definition of a trade union in the Trade Union and Labour Relations (Consolidation) Act 1992. Included in the data are home and overseas membership figures of contributory and non-contributory members. Employment status of members is not provided and the figures may therefore include some people who are self-employed, unemployed or retired.

The membership part of this table was revised in 2001, so that statistics presented here are on a consistent basis with the Great Britain table produced by the Certification Officer in his Annual Report and with tables produced in the annual Trade Union membership article published by the Department for Business, Enterprise & Regulatory Reform (BERR). There is a break in the time series for the figures in this table between the years 1988 (contained within previous publications) and 1989. Great Britain data for 1989–95 are BERR analyses of annual returns, with 1996–1999 as published in the Certification Officer's Annual Report. Data for Northern Ireland for 1989–1991 are BERR analyses of annual returns, with 1992–1999 from the Certification Officer's Annual Report.

7.1 Labour force summary:[1] by sex
United Kingdom
At Quarter 2 each year[2]. Seasonally adjusted

Thousands and percentages

	All aged 16 and over					Percentages			
	Total[3]	Total economically active	Total in employment	Total unemployed	Economically inactive	Economic activity rate 16-59/64[4]	Employment rate all aged 16 and over[5]	Employment rate 16-59/64[6]	Unemployment rate[7]
All Persons									
	MGSL	MGSF	MGRZ	MGSC	MGSI	MGSO	MGSR	MGSU	MGSX
1997	45 509	28 561	26 513	2 048	16 949	78.6	58.3	72.9	7.2
1998	45 675	28 509	26 721	1 788	17 166	78.3	58.5	73.3	6.3
1999	45 880	28 833	27 090	1 743	17 047	78.7	59.0	73.9	6.0
2000	46 128	29 061	27 461	1 599	17 067	78.8	59.5	74.4	5.5
2001	46 441	29 167	27 694	1 472	17 274	78.6	59.6	74.5	5.0
2002	46 727	29 422	27 906	1 516	17 305	78.6	59.7	74.5	5.2
2003	47 016	29 656	28 192	1 464	17 361	78.7	60.0	74.8	4.9
2004	47 361	29 857	28 423	1 434	17 504	78.5	60.0	74.7	4.8
2005	47 787	30 163	28 727	1 435	17 624	78.6	60.1	74.7	4.8
2006	48 185	30 670	28 983	1 687	17 515	79.0	60.2	74.6	5.5
2007	48 590	30 814	29 153	1 661	17 776	78.8	60.0	74.4	5.4
Male									
	MGSM	MGSG	MGSA	MGSD	MGSJ	MGSP	MGSS	MGSV	MGSY
1997	21 883	15 707	14 442	1 265	6 175	84.8	66.0	77.9	8.1
1998	21 968	15 650	14 576	1 074	6 318	84.1	66.4	78.3	6.9
1999	22 081	15 790	14 731	1 059	6 291	84.5	66.7	78.7	6.7
2000	22 213	15 854	14 897	957	6 359	84.4	67.1	79.2	6.0
2001	22 393	15 876	14 994	882	6 518	83.9	67.0	79.2	5.6
2002	22 565	15 981	15 071	910	6 584	83.8	66.8	79.0	5.7
2003	22 735	16 184	15 298	886	6 551	84.2	67.3	79.5	5.5
2004	22 930	16 212	15 369	843	6 719	83.6	67.0	79.2	5.2
2005	23 166	16 342	15 507	835	6 824	83.4	66.9	79.1	5.1
2006	23 391	16 595	15 618	978	6 796	83.7	66.8	78.7	5.9
2007	23 618	16 735	15 785	951	6 883	83.6	66.8	78.8	5.7
Female									
	MGSN	MGSH	MGSB	MGSE	MGSK	MGSQ	MGST	MGSW	MGSZ
1997	23 627	12 853	12 071	783	10 773	72.0	51.1	67.5	6.1
1998	23 707	12 859	12 144	715	10 847	72.0	51.2	67.9	5.6
1999	23 799	13 043	12 359	684	10 756	72.6	51.9	68.7	5.2
2000	23 915	13 207	12 565	642	10 708	72.9	52.5	69.3	4.9
2001	24 047	13 291	12 700	591	10 756	72.9	52.8	69.5	4.4
2002	24 162	13 440	12 835	606	10 721	73.1	53.1	69.7	4.5
2003	24 281	13 471	12 894	578	10 810	72.9	53.1	69.7	4.3
2004	24 431	13 646	13 054	592	10 785	73.1	53.4	69.8	4.3
2005	24 620	13 820	13 220	600	10 800	73.4	53.7	70.0	4.3
2006	24 794	14 075	13 366	709	10 719	74.0	53.9	70.1	5.0
2007	24 972	14 079	13 369	710	10 893	73.6	53.5	69.7	5.0

1 See chapter text. In August 2007, ONS published the mid-year population estimates for 2006. These estimates have now been incorporated into the LFS estimates from 2001 onwards. Further details can be found at http://www.statistics.gov.uk/cci/article.asp?id=1919

2 The Labour Force Survey has now moved to calendar quarters from May 2006. More information can be found on page 5 of the Concepts and Definitions.pdf by following this link:- www.statistics.gov.uk/downloads/theme_labour/Concepts_Definitions_HQS.pdf

3 Population aged 16 and over in private households and student halls of residence.

4 Economically active of working age as a percentage of all persons of working age (men 16-64, women 16-59).

5 Total employed as a percentage of all persons aged 16 and over.

6 Total employed of working age as a percentage of all persons of working age (men 16-64, women 16-59).

7 Total unemployed as a percentage of all economically active.

Sources: Labour Force Survey, Office for National Statistics;
Helpline: 01633 456901

7.2 Employment status: full-time, part-time and temporary employees[1]
United Kingdom
At Quarter 2 each year[2]. Seasonally adjusted

Thousands

	All in employment[3]					Total employment[3]		Employees[3]		Self-employed[3]			
	Total	Employees	Self employed	Unpaid family workers	Government supported training and employment programmes[4]	Full-time	Part-time	Full-time	Part-time	Full-time	Part-time	Workers with second jobs[5]	Temporary employees
All Persons													
	MGRZ	MGRN	MGRQ	MGRT	MGRW	YCBE	YCBH	YCBK	YCBN	YCBQ	YCBT	YCBW	YCBZ
1997	26 513	22 709	3 470	115	218	19 832	6 680	16 948	5 761	2 730	740	1 242	1 787
1998	26 721	23 088	3 368	100	164	20 000	6 721	17 261	5 827	2 616	752	1 197	1 711
1999	27 090	23 509	3 324	100	156	20 288	6 802	17 593	5 916	2 590	735	1 299	1 673
2000	27 461	23 948	3 255	113	146	20 524	6 937	17 897	6 051	2 519	736	1 167	1 705
2001	27 694	24 177	3 276	96	145	20 718	6 976	18 037	6 141	2 580	697	1 185	1 717
2002	27 906	24 366	3 337	97	106	20 779	7 127	18 147	6 219	2 561	775	1 133	1 590
2003	28 192	24 453	3 559	88	92	20 919	7 273	18 135	6 317	2 722	837	1 110	1 489
2004	28 423	24 523	3 678	98	123	21 062	7 361	18 154	6 369	2 828	850	1 073	1 504
2005	28 727	24 878	3 635	101	114	21 394	7 334	18 496	6 381	2 815	820	1 077	1 443
2006	28 983	25 068	3 727	93	94	21 632	7 352	18 711	6 357	2 859	869	1 049	1 456
2007	29 153	25 108	3 829	103	114	21 729	7 424	18 753	6 355	2 914	915	1 106	1 505
Male													
	MGSA	MGRO	MGRR	MGRU	MGRX	YCBF	YCBI	YCBL	YCBO	YCBR	YCBU	YCBX	YCCA
1997	14 442	11 734	2 538	35	135	13 164	1 278	10 794	940	2 275	263	536	810
1998	14 576	11 984	2 456	30	107	13 282	1 294	11 030	953	2 173	283	511	765
1999	14 731	12 154	2 439	34	103	13 373	1 358	11 143	1 012	2 165	273	550	775
2000	14 897	12 413	2 360	37	87	13 529	1 368	11 389	1 025	2 076	284	489	775
2001	14 994	12 459	2 404	34	97	13 623	1 371	11 411	1 048	2 142	262	485	769
2002	15 071	12 537	2 442	31	61	13 593	1 478	11 427	1 110	2 125	317	473	742
2003	15 298	12 607	2 607	32	52	13 708	1 590	11 411	1 195	2 257	351	455	683
2004	15 369	12 555	2 702	41	72	13 742	1 627	11 348	1 206	2 343	359	451	696
2005	15 507	12 727	2 673	37	70	13 865	1 642	11 476	1 251	2 336	337	463	686
2006	15 618	12 816	2 711	36	54	13 947	1 671	11 554	1 263	2 356	355	450	649
2007	15 785	12 890	2 794	39	63	14 048	1 737	11 614	1 276	2 396	398	460	697
Female													
	MGSB	MGRP	MGRS	MGRV	MGRY	YCBG	YCBJ	YCBM	YCBP	YCBS	YCBV	YCBY	YCCB
1997	12 071	10 975	932	80	84	6 668	5 403	6 154	4 821	455	478	706	976
1998	12 144	11 105	912	71	58	6 718	5 426	6 231	4 873	443	469	685	945
1999	12 359	11 355	886	66	53	6 915	5 444	6 451	4 904	424	461	749	897
2000	12 565	11 534	895	76	60	6 995	5 569	6 508	5 026	443	452	679	930
2001	12 700	11 719	872	62	48	7 095	5 605	6 626	5 093	438	434	700	948
2002	12 835	11 829	895	65	45	7 185	5 649	6 720	5 109	436	459	660	848
2003	12 894	11 846	952	57	39	7 211	5 683	6 724	5 122	465	487	655	806
2004	13 054	11 969	976	58	51	7 320	5 734	6 806	5 163	485	491	622	808
2005	13 220	12 151	962	64	44	7 529	5 691	7 021	5 130	479	483	614	757
2006	13 366	12 252	1 016	57	41	7 685	5 681	7 158	5 095	503	513	599	807
2007	13 369	12 218	1 036	64	51	7 681	5 687	7 139	5 079	518	518	646	808

1 See chapter text. In August 2007, ONS published the mid-year population estimates for 2006. These estimates have now been incorporated into the LFS estimates from 2001 onwards. Further details can be found at http://www.statistics.gov.uk/cci/article.asp?id=1919
2 The Labour Force Survey has now moved to calendar quarters from May 2006. More information can be found on page 5 of the Concepts and Definitions.pdf by following this link:- www.statistics.gov.uk/downloads/theme_labour/Concepts_Definitions_HQS.pdf
3 People whose main job is full or part-time and based on respondents' self assessment.
4 Those on employment and training programmes are classified as in employment. Some of those on programmes may consider themselves to be employees or self employed so appear in other categories.
5 Second jobs reported in LFS in addition to person's main full or part-time job.

Sources: Labour Force Survey, Office for National Statistics;
Helpline: 01633 456901

7.3 Employment: by sex and age[1]
United Kingdom
At Quarter 2 each year[2]. Seasonally adjusted

Thousands and percentages

	All aged 16 and over	16-59/64	16-17	18-24	25-34	35-49	50-64 (m) 50-59 (f)	65+ (m) 60+ (f)
Thousands								
All Persons								
	MGRZ	YBSE	YBTO	YBTR	YBTU	YBTX	MGUW	MGUZ
2001	27 694	26 863	669	3 321	6 738	10 212	5 924	831
2002	27 906	27 025	647	3 386	6 544	10 423	6 025	881
2003	28 192	27 263	650	3 381	6 397	10 585	6 249	928
2004	28 423	27 413	631	3 514	6 309	10 690	6 269	1 010
2005	28 727	27 669	627	3 523	6 309	10 851	6 360	1 059
2006	28 983	27 829	560	3 578	6 297	10 941	6 453	1 154
2007	29 153	27 942	519	3 616	6 284	11 021	6 503	1 211
Male								
	MGSA	YBSF	YBTP	YBTS	YBTV	YBTY	MGUX	MGVA
2001	14 994	14 721	330	1 746	3 684	5 441	3 520	273
2002	15 071	14 779	323	1 765	3 583	5 549	3 559	292
2003	15 298	14 968	320	1 788	3 510	5 647	3 704	330
2004	15 369	15 030	306	1 870	3 423	5 713	3 718	340
2005	15 507	15 153	304	1 868	3 435	5 773	3 773	354
2006	15 618	15 227	261	1 876	3 433	5 821	3 835	391
2007	15 785	15 381	241	1 925	3 458	5 880	3 876	403
Female								
	MGSB	YBSG	YBTQ	YBTT	YBTW	YBTZ	MGUY	MGVB
2001	12 700	12 143	339	1 575	3 053	4 771	2 404	558
2002	12 835	12 246	324	1 621	2 960	4 874	2 466	589
2003	12 894	12 295	330	1 594	2 887	4 939	2 546	598
2004	13 054	12 383	325	1 645	2 885	4 977	2 551	671
2005	13 220	12 515	323	1 654	2 874	5 077	2 587	705
2006	13 366	12 602	298	1 702	2 864	5 120	2 618	763
2007	13 369	12 561	277	1 690	2 826	5 140	2 627	808
Percentages[3]								
All Persons								
	MGSR	MGSU	YBUA	YBUD	YBUG	YBUJ	YBUM	YBUP
2001	59.6	74.5	45.4	67.9	80.0	81.7	67.7	8.0
2002	59.7	74.5	42.9	68.0	79.6	82.1	68.0	8.4
2003	60.0	74.8	42.7	66.2	79.6	82.2	70.0	8.8
2004	60.0	74.7	40.6	67.0	79.9	82.0	69.8	9.5
2005	60.1	74.7	39.9	65.6	80.3	82.3	70.4	9.8
2006	60.2	74.6	35.7	65.1	80.5	82.2	70.8	10.6
2007	60.0	74.4	32.7	64.4	80.6	82.2	71.2	11.0
Male								
	MGSS	MGSV	YBUB	YBUE	YBUH	YBUK	YBUN	YBUQ
2001	67.0	79.2	43.8	71.6	88.4	88.0	69.8	7.2
2002	66.8	79.0	41.8	70.8	88.0	88.4	70.0	7.6
2003	67.3	79.5	40.8	69.6	88.2	88.7	72.2	8.4
2004	67.0	79.2	38.4	70.6	87.5	88.7	71.9	8.6
2005	66.9	79.1	37.8	68.7	88.2	88.6	72.2	8.8
2006	66.8	78.7	32.5	67.3	88.4	88.4	72.6	9.7
2007	66.8	78.8	29.6	67.4	89.2	88.8	72.5	9.8
Female								
	MGST	MGSW	YBUC	YBUF	YBUI	YBUL	YBUO	YBUR
2001	52.8	69.5	47.1	64.2	71.8	75.5	64.7	8.5
2002	53.1	69.7	44.2	65.2	71.4	75.9	65.4	8.9
2003	53.1	69.7	44.5	62.7	71.2	75.9	67.1	9.0
2004	53.4	69.8	42.9	63.4	72.4	75.5	67.0	10.0
2005	53.7	70.0	42.1	62.4	72.5	76.2	67.8	10.4
2006	53.9	70.1	39.0	62.8	72.7	76.0	68.4	11.2
2007	53.5	69.7	36.1	61.2	72.1	75.8	69.4	11.6

1 See chapter text. In August 2007, ONS published the mid-year population estimates for 2006. These estimates have now been incorporated into the LFS estimates from 2001 onwards. Further details can be found at http://www.statistics.gov.uk/cci/article.asp?id=1919

2 The Labour Force Survey has now moved to calendar quarters from May 2006. More information can be found on page 5 of the Concepts and Definitions.pdf by following this link:- www.statistics.gov.uk/downloads/theme_labour/Concepts_Definitions_HQS.pdf

3 Total in employment as a percentage of all persons in the relevant group.

Sources: Labour Force Survey, Office for National Statistics;
Helpline: 01633 456901

7.4 Distribution of the workforce:[1,2] by sex

At mid-June each year. Seasonally adjusted

Thousands

		1997	1998	1999	2000	2001	2002	2003	2004	2005	2006	2007
United Kingdom												
Claimant count	BCJD	1 584.5	1 347.8	1 248.1	1 088.4	969.9	946.6	933.0	853.3	861.7	944.7	863.9
Males	DPAE	1 214.9	1 029.4	955.0	831.6	739.6	717.1	700.3	636.2	639.7	697.3	630.9
Females	DPAF	369.6	318.4	293.1	256.8	230.3	229.6	232.8	217.1	222.0	247.4	233.0
Workforce jobs	DYDC	28 705	28 835	29 165	29 604	29 923	30 078	30 375	30 683	31 040	31 294	31 536
Males	KAMS	15 149	15 338	15 681	15 795	16 001	16 002	16 256	16 372	16 497	16 668	16 775
Females	KAMT	13 556	13 496	13 484	13 810	13 921	14 075	14 118	14 311	14 542	14 625	14 762
HM Forces	KAMU	220	219	218	217	214	214	223	218	209	203	197
Males	KAMV	204	203	201	199	196	197	203	199	191	185	179
Females	KAMW	16	17	17	18	18	18	19	19	18	18	18
Self-employment jobs	DYZN	3 854	3 699	3 692	3 583	3 608	3 677	3 894	3 974	3 962	4 072	4 216
Males	KAMZ	2 753	2 647	2 647	2 556	2 596	2 640	2 797	2 874	2 856	2 893	2 990
Females	KANA	1 101	1 052	1 045	1 028	1 011	1 036	1 098	1 100	1 106	1 179	1 226
Employees jobs	BCAJ	24 460	24 786	25 125	25 685	26 002	26 096	26 165	26 383	26 771	26 953	27 068
Males	KANC	12 087	12 413	12 754	12 967	13 147	13 111	13 201	13 233	13 392	13 552	13 573
Females	KAND	12 373	12 373	12 371	12 719	12 855	12 986	12 964	13 149	13 379	13 401	13 495
of whom												
Total, production and construction industries	KANF	5 398	5 525	5 382	5 349	5 194	4 952	4 748	4 594	4 474	4 422	4 361
Total, all manufacturing industries	KANG	4 191	4 208	4 059	3 959	3 805	3 599	3 411	3 246	3 103	2 973	2 917
Government-supported trainees	KANH	171	131	131	119	99	91	92	108	97	65	55
Males	KANI	105	76	81	73	62	55	55	65	58	38	33
Females	KANJ	66	55	50	46	38	36	37	44	38	27	22
Great Britain												
Claimant count	DPAG	1 521.1	1 290.3	1 197.3	1 046.3	930.5	910.2	898.5	822.5	833.1	916.9	839.5
Males	ZSDP	1 165.0	984.6	915.7	799.6	709.7	689.3	673.9	612.8	618.0	676.5	612.5
Females	ZSDQ	356.1	305.7	281.6	246.8	220.8	220.9	224.6	209.8	215.1	240.4	227.0
Workforce jobs	KANQ	27 990	28 112	28 432	28 853	29 158	29 305	29 583	29 884	30 217	30 458	30 692
Males	KANR	14 761	14 946	15 285	15 388	15 588	15 590	15 833	15 945	16 058	16 220	16 324
Females	KANS	13 229	13 165	13 146	13 465	13 570	13 715	13 750	13 939	14 158	14 238	14 368
HM Forces	BCAH	220	219	218	217	214	214	223	218	209	203	197
Males	KANU	204	203	201	199	196	197	203	199	191	185	179
Females	KANV	16	17	17	18	18	18	19	19	18	18	18
Self-employment jobs	KANW	3 752	3 603	3 596	3 484	3 502	3 576	3 784	3 863	3 842	3 949	4 097
Males	KANX	2 672	2 569	2 569	2 474	2 509	2 558	2 706	2 784	2 758	2 794	2 894
Females	KANY	1 080	1 035	1 026	1 010	993	1 018	1 078	1 079	1 084	1 155	1 202
Employee jobs	KANZ	23 862	24 172	24 499	25 043	25 350	25 431	25 491	25 701	26 075	26 246	26 350
Males	KAOA	11 790	12 108	12 442	12 649	12 826	12 785	12 873	12 902	13 055	13 207	13 222
Females	KAOB	12 072	12 064	12 056	12 394	12 524	12 646	12 618	12 799	13 020	13 039	13 127
of whom												
Total, production and construction industries	KAOC	5 256	5 383	5 239	5 205	5 052	4 813	4 615	4 463	4 344	4 288	4 223
Total, all manufacturing industries	KAOD	4 083	4 101	3 954	3 856	3 704	3 501	3 318	3 157	3 015	2 886	2 828
Government-supported trainees	KAOE	157	117	120	110	92	84	86	102	90	59	48
Males	KAOF	96	67	73	67	57	50	51	60	54	34	28
Females	KAOG	61	50	47	43	35	34	35	42	36	25	20

Note. Because the figures have been rounded independently totals may differ from the sum of the components. Also the totals may include some employees whose industrial classification could not be ascertained.

1 The data in this table have not been adjusted to reflect the 2001 Census population data. See chapter text.

2 There is a discontinuity in the employee jobs series between December 2005 and September 2006 due to improvements to the annual benchmark. Further information can be found at:
http://www.statistics.gov.uk/statbase/product.asp?vlnk=9765

Sources: Employment, Earnings and Innovations Division, Office for National Statistics;
Customer Helpline: 01633 456776

7.5 Employee jobs: by industry[1,2,3]
Standard Industrial Classification 2003
At June each year. Not seasonally adjusted

Thousands

		SIC 2003	United Kingdom						Great Britain				
			2003	2004	2005	2006	2007		2003	2004	2005	2006	2007
All sections	KAOH	A - O	26 139	26 351	26 376	26 916	27 030	LMAB	25 466	25 671	26 042	26 212	26 313
Index of production and construction industries	KAOI	C - F	4 738	4 583	4 462	4 409	4 348	LMAH	4 606	4 453	4 332	4 276	4 210
Index of production industries	KAOJ	C - E	3 594	3 413	3 258	3 133	3 084	LMAF	3 497	3 320	3 166	3 041	2 991
of which, manufacturing industries	KAOK	D	3 409	3 245	3 102	2 973	2 917	KAPQ	3 317	3 156	3 015	2 886	2 829
Service industries	KAOL	G - O	21 172	21 543	22 036	22 280	22 443	LMAJ	20 647	21 007	21 484	21 722	21 875
Agriculture, hunting and forestry and fishing	KAOM	A/B	228	226	239	227	240	KAPS	213	211	225	215	228
Agriculture hunting and forestry	KPHI	A	221	219	233	220	233	KOVW	207	204	220	208	221
Agriculture hunting & related activities	KPHJ	01	210	209	223	211	224	KOVX	196	195	210	199	212
Fishing	KPHK	B	7	7	5	7	7	KOVY	7	7	5	7	7
Mining and quarrying	KPHL	C	62	58	57	58	60	KOVZ	60	56	55	56	58
Mining and quarrying of energy producing materials	KPHM	CA	38	35	34	35	38	KOWA	37	35	34	35	38
Mining	KAPG	10/12	..	..	..	..	..	KOWB	10	9	7	6	7
Extraction of crude petroleum	KPHN	11	..	..	..	..	..	KOWC	27	25	27	29	30
Mining and quarrying except of energy producing materials	KPHO	CB(13/14)	24	23	23	22	22	KOWD	23	22	21	20	20
Energy and water supply industries	KAOO	C/E	185	168	156	160	167	LMAM	180	163	151	155	162
Manufacturing	KPHP	D	3 409	3 245	3 102	2 973	2 917	LMAD	3 317	3 156	3 015	2 886	2 829
Manufacture of food products Beverages and tobacco	KPHQ	DA	456	443	428	418	411	LMAN	437	424	409	399	393
Of food	KPHR	151 to 158	..	..	..	..	..	KOWH	387	375	364	355	351
Of beverages and tobacco	KPHS	159/16	..	..	..	..	..	KOWI	50	48	45	44	42
Manufacture of textiles and textile products	KPHT	DB	163	142	123	107	98	KOWJ	154	135	118	103	95
Of textiles	KPHU	17	106	95	84	74	69	KOWK	101	90	81	71	67
Of made-up textile articles except apparel	KPHV	174	..	..	..	..	..	KOWL	31	29	27	25	24
Of textiles excluding made-up textile	KPHW	Rest of 17	..	..	..	..	..	KOWM	70	61	54	46	42
Of wearing apparel,dressing and dyeing of fur	KPHX	18	57	47	39	33	29	KOWN	54	45	38	31	28
Manufacture of leather and leather products including footwear	KPHY	DC	14	12	11	11	12	KOWO	14	12	11	11	12
Of leather and leather goods	KPHZ	191/192	..	..	..	..	..	KOWP	6	6	5	7	7
Of footwear	KPIA	193	..	..	..	..	..	KOWQ	8	6	5	5	5
Manufacture of wood and wood products	KPIB	DD(20)	83	83	81	77	79	LMAP	79	79	77	73	75
Manufacture of pulp paper and paper products, publishing and printing	KPIC	DE	426	412	400	381	366	LMAQ	420	406	394	375	361
Of pulp paper and paper products	KPID	21	87	82	77	71	68	KOWT	85	80	76	70	66
Publishing printing and reproduction of recorded media	KPIE	22	339	330	322	310	299	KOWU	335	326	318	305	294
Manufacture of coke refined petroleum products and nuclear fuel	KPIF	DF(23)	25	24	23	23	23	KOWV	25	23	23	23	23
Manufacture of chemicals, chemical products and man-made fibres	KPIG	DG(24)	226	210	199	193	189	LMAR	222	207	196	190	186
Manufacture of rubber and plastics	KPIH	DH(25)	214	212	203	196	194	LMAS	206	205	196	189	187
Manufacture of other non-metallic mineral products	KPII	DI(26)	121	118	111	107	104	KOWZ	115	112	105	101	98
Manufacture of basic metals and fabricated metal products	KPIJ	DJ	443	417	398	387	381	KOXA	436	409	391	379	374
Of basic metals	KPIK	27	92	81	74	73	71	KOXB	91	81	73	72	71
except machinery	KPIL	28	351	335	325	314	310	KOXC	344	328	317	307	303

7.5
Employee jobs: by industry[1,2,3]
Standard Industrial Classification 2003
At June each year. Not seasonally adjusted   Thousands

			United Kingdom						Great Britain				
			2003	2004	2005	2006	2007		2003	2004	2005	2006	2007
		SIC 2003											
Manufacture of Machinery and Equipment not elsewhere classified	KPIM	DK(29)	301	285	280	270	270	LMAU	294	279	273	263	263
Manufacture of electrical and optical equipment	KPIN	DL	380	351	333	315	305	LMAV	370	341	324	305	295
Of office machinery and computers	KPIO	30	37	33	30	26	23	KOXF	34	30	28	23	20
Of electrical machinery and apparatus	KPIP	31	138	127	122	117	116	KOXG	135	123	118	113	112
Of electric motors etc control apparatus and insulated cable	KPIQ	311 to 313	..	..	..	..	..	KOXH	74	66	63	61	61
Of accumulators, primary cells, batteries, lamps and electrical equipment	KPIR	314 to 316	..	..	..	..	..	KOXI	61	58	56	52	51
Radio television and communication equipment	KPIS	32	81	74	66	61	60	KOXJ	79	72	64	59	58
Of electronic components	KPIT	321	..	..	..	..	..	KOXK	29	29	27	24	23
Of radio TV and telephone apparatus, sound and video recorders	KPIU	322/323	..	..	..	..	..	KOXL	49	42	37	35	34
Of medical precision and optical equipment, watches	KPIV	33	124	118	116	111	107	KOXM	122	116	114	109	106
Manufacture of transport equipment	KPIW	DM	356	343	329	315	308	LMAW	345	333	320	306	299
Of motor vehicles and trailers	KPIX	34	205	196	184	171	162	KOXO	200	193	180	168	159
Of other transport equipment	KPIY	35	151	146	146	144	146	KOXP	145	140	139	138	140
Manufacturing not elsewhere classified	KPIZ	DN(36/37)	203	197	182	175	176	KOXQ	199	193	178	170	170
Electricity gas and water supply	KPJA	E	123	110	99	102	107	KOXR	120	107	96	99	104
Electricity gas steam and hot water supply	KPJB	40	..	..	..	..	..	KOXT	90	82	73	73	76
Collection purification and distribution of water	KPJC	41	..	..	..	..	..	KOXU	30	25	24	26	28
Construction	KPJD	F(45)	1 145	1 169	1 204	1 276	1 264	LMAY	1 109	1 133	1 166	1 235	1 219
Services	KPJE	G - O	21 172	21 543	22 036	22 280	22 443	KOXX	20 647	21 007	21 484	21 722	21 875
Wholesale and retail trade; Repair of motor vehicles, motorcycles and personal household goods	KPJF	G (50 - 52)	4 535	4 562	4 597	4 554	4 582	LMAZ	4 422	4 445	4 478	4 432	4 459
Sale maintenance and repair of motor vehicles, retail of automotive fuel	KPJG	50	563	561	565	565	566	KOXZ	548	546	550	549	549
Sale of motor vehicles, motorcycles and parts, motorcycle repair and sale of automotive fuel	KPJH	501/503 - 505	..	..	..	..	..	KOYA	381	379	380	374	377
Maintenance and repair of motor vehicles	KPJI	502	..	..	..	..	..	KOYB	167	168	169	175	172
Wholesale trade and commission trade except motor vehicles	KPJJ	51	1 127	1 119	1 131	1 127	1 131	KOYC	1 104	1 095	1 108	1 103	1 107
Wholesale on a fee of contract basis	KPJK	511	..	..	..	..	..	KOYD	59	60	61	66	70
Wholesale agricultural raw materials and live animals	KPJL	512	..	..	..	..	..	KPLD	23	23	22	19	19
Wholesale food beverages & tobacco	KPJM	513	..	..	..	..	..	KPLE	190	188	190	195	196
Wholesale household goods	KPJN	514	..	..	..	..	..	KPLF	264	267	274	272	269
Wholesale of non-agricultural intermediate products waste & scrap	KPJO	515	..	..	..	..	..	KPLG	232	232	232	230	236
Wholesale machinery eqpt. & supplies	KPJP	516	..	..	..	..	..	KPLH	238	230	238	232	230
Other wholesale	KPJQ	517	..	..	..	..	..	KPLI	98	95	91	89	87
Retail trade except of motor vehicles and motorcycles;repair of personal and household goods	KPJR	52	2 845	2 882	2 901	2 862	2 886	KPLJ	2 770	2 804	2 820	2 781	2 804
Non-specialised stores selling mainly food beverages & tobacco	KPJS	5211/5221-4,5227	..	..	..	..	..	KPLK	1 143	1 120	1 140	1 111	1 107
Other non-specialised stores second hand shops & sales not in stores	KPJT	5212/525-526	..	..	..	..	..	KPLL	365	360	353	338	335

7.5

Employee jobs: by industry[1,2,3]
Standard Industrial Classification 2003

continued At June each year. Not seasonally adjusted

Thousands

		SIC 2003	United Kingdom						Great Britain				
			2003	2004	2005	2006	2007		2003	2004	2005	2006	2007
Alcoholic & other beverages, tobacco	KPJU	5225 to 5226	..	..	..	..	..	KPLM	56	54	49	46	43
Pharmaceutical & medical goods cosmetics & toilet articles	KPJV	523	..	..	..	..	..	KPLN	93	99	103	105	106
Clothing footwear & leather goods	KPJW	5242/5243	..	..	..	..	..	KPLO	369	409	415	417	431
Textile furniture lighting equipment electrical household appliances radio and TV paints glass hardware and household goods not elsewhere classified	KPJX	5241/5244-46	..	..	..	..	..	KPLP	296	304	299	296	302
Books newspapers and stationery, other retail in specialised stores	KPJY	5247/5248	..	..	..	..	..	KPLQ	421	432	435	447	457
Repair of personal and household goods	KPJZ	527	..	..	..	..	..	KPLR	27	26	26	22	22
Hotels and restaurants	KPKA	H	1 792	1 839	1 855	1 844	1 843	LMBA	1 751	1 798	1 813	1 801	1 800
Hotels camp sites short-stay accom.	KPKB	551/552	..	..	..	..	..	KPLT	369	379	386	384	393
Restaurants	KPKC	553	..	..	..	..	..	KPLU	575	594	614	633	637
Bars	KPKD	554	..	..	..	..	..	KPLV	540	558	552	542	531
Canteens and catering	KPKE	555	..	..	..	..	..	KPLW	267	267	261	243	239
Transport, storage and communication	KPKF	I	1 587	1 570	1 594	1 581	1 563	KPLX	1 559	1 542	1 565	1 552	1 532
Land transport, transport via pipelines	KPKG	60	518	519	534	546	547	KPLY	505	505	521	533	533
Transport via railways	KPKH	601	..	..	..	..	..	KPLZ	49	50	53	52	52
Other land transport and via pipelines	KPKI	602/603	..	..	..	..	..	KPMA	457	456	468	481	482
Water transport	KPKJ	61	17	17	19	18	16	KPMB	16	17	18	17	16
Air transport	KPKK	62	90	85	88	90	88	KPMC	90	85	88	89	87
Supporting and auxiliary transport activities, activities of travel agents	KPKL	63	412	440	453	442	440	KPMD	406	435	447	437	434
Travel agencies and tour operators	KPKM	633	..	..	..	..	..	KPME	124	133	120	107	105
Post and telecommunications	KPKN	64	551	509	500	485	472	LMBC	542	500	491	476	462
National post and courier activities	KPKO	641	..	..	..	..	..	KPMG	297	275	275	266	254
Telecommunications	KPKR	6420	..	..	..	..	..	KPMJ	245	225	216	210	208
Financial intermediation	KPKS	J	1 104	1 073	1 062	1 047	1 044	LMBD	1 087	1 056	1 044	1 029	1 025
Financial intermediation except insurance and pension funding	KPKT	65	639	621	609	593	584	KPML	627	609	596	580	571
Insurance and pension funding except compulsory social security	KPKU	66	215	197	183	181	181	KPMM	213	196	181	179	179
Activities auxiliary to financial intermediation	KPKV	67	249	255	271	273	279	KPMN	246	252	267	270	275
Except insurance and pension funding	KPKW	671	..	..	..	..	..	KPMO	113	123	136	137	143
Auxiliary to insurance and pension funding	KPKX	672	..	..	..	..	..	KPMP	133	129	131	132	132
Real estate renting & business activities	KPKY	K	3 996	4 129	4 336	4 546	4 680	KPMQ	3 938	4 065	4 268	4 476	4 608
Real estate activities	KPKZ	70	381	409	449	451	457	LMBE	378	402	441	442	449
Activities with own property, letting of own property	KPLA	701/702	..	..	..	..	..	KPMS	224	236	252	248	250
Activities on a fee or contract basis	KPLB	703	..	..	..	..	..	KPMT	154	166	189	194	199

93

7.5
continued

Employee jobs: by industry[1,2,3]
Standard Industrial Classification 2003
At June each year. Not seasonally adjusted

Thousand

		SIC 2003	United Kingdom						Great Britain				
			2003	2004	2005	2006	2007		2003	2004	2005	2006	2007
Renting of machinery and equipment without operator & of personal & household goods	KPLC	71	151	153	157	161	162	KPMU	149	150	155	158	159
Construction and civil engineering machinery	KOUU	7132	..	..	..	..	..	KPMV	42	41	42	45	46
All other goods and equipment	KOUV	Rest of 71	..	..	..	..	..	KPMW	107	109	113	114	113
Computer and related equipment	KOUW	72	501	488	493	522	520	KPMX	495	482	486	515	512
Research and development	KOUX	73	106	101	104	109	113	KPMY	105	100	103	107	111
Other business activities	KOUY	74	2 857	2 978	3 133	3 304	3 428	KPMZ	2 811	2 930	3 083	3 253	3 376
Legal, accounting, book-keeping & auditing activities	KOUZ	741	..	..	..	..	..	KPNA	..	840	889	962	993
Legal activities	KOVA	7411	..	..	..	..	..	KPNB	250	254	260	280	295
Accounting, book-keeping auditing, tax consultancy	KOVB	7412	..	..	..	..	..	KPNC	191	194	203	216	215
Market research business and consultancy activities	KOVC	7413/7414	..	..	..	..	..	KPND	272	291	316	357	374
Management activities of holding companies[4]	KOVD	7415	..	..	..	..	..	KPNE	..	101	110	109	109
Architectural engineering activities and related technical consultancy, technical testing	KOVE	742/743	..	..	..	..	..	KPNF	332	340	347	373	399
Advertising	KOVF	744	..	..	..	..	..	KPNG	83	80	84	81	90
Industrial cleaning	KOVG	747	..	..	..	..	..	KPNH	418	414	436	448	451
Public administration and defence, compulsory social security	KOVH	L(75)	1 469	1 496	1 520	1 518	1 514	LMBG	1 405	1 435	1 460	1 458	1 454
Education	KOVI	M(80)	2 229	2 307	2 355	2 390	2 394	LMBH	2 160	2 238	2 282	2 318	2 322
Health and social work	KOVJ	N	3 079	3 180	3 300	3 361	3 390	LOJV	2 973	3 072	3 189	3 249	3 275
Human health, veterinary activities	KOVK	851/852	..	..	..	..	..	KPNL	1 965	2 027	2 103	2 113	2 124
Social work activities	KOVL	853	..	..	..	..	..	KPNM	1 009	1 045	1 086	1 135	1 151
Other community social and personal service activities, private households with employed persons, extra-territorial organisations and bodies	KOVM	O	1 383	1 388	1 417	1 440	1 432	LMBK	1 351	1 357	1 385	1 408	1 400
Sewage and refuse disposal; sanitation	KOVN	90	96	100	104	108	114	KPNO	93	97	101	105	111
Activities of membership organisations	KOVO	91	224	212	215	225	232	KPNP	216	204	206	217	224
Recreational cultural and sporting activities	KOVP	92	741	762	779	783	764	KPNQ	725	747	764	767	748
Motion picture video radio TV news agencies and entertainment activities	KOVQ	921 to 924	..	..	..	..	..	KPNR	220	225	221	223	206
Other service activities, private households with employed persons, extra territorial organisations	KOVT	93/95/99	322	314	318	324	322	KPNU	317	309	313	319	317
Washing, dry cleaning of textile and fur products	KOVU	9301	..	..	..	..	..	KPNV	46	42	40	42	42
Hairdressing, other beauty treatment, physical and well-being activities	KOVV	9302/9304	..	..	..	..	..	KPNW	104	105	114	122	121

Note. Because the figures have been rounded independently totals may differ from the sum of the components. Also the totals may include some employees whose industrial classification could not be ascertained.

1 See chapter text. The data in this table have not been adjusted to reflect the 2001 Census population data.

2 All figures have been revised. For further information see: http://www.statistics.gov.uk/cci/article.asp?id=1340

3 There is a discontinuity in the employee jobs series between December 2005 and September 2006 due to improvements to the annual benchmark. Further information can be found at: http://www.statistics.gov.uk/Statbase/Product.asp?vlnk=9765

4 Head office and holding company local units were reclassified to Class 74.15 (within Section K) from December 2003 as a result of the SIC 2003 update.

Sources: Department of Manpower Services (Northern Ireland);;
Employment, Earnings and Innovations Division, ONS: 01633 456776

7.6 Weekly hours worked: by sex[1,2]
United Kingdom
At Quarter 2 each year[3]. Seasonally adjusted

Hours

| | All workers' weekly hours[4,5] | | Average actual weekly hours of work[5] | | |
	Total (millions)	Average	Full-time employment[4,6]	Part-time employment[6]	Second jobs[7]
All Persons					
	YBUS	YBUV	YBUY	YBVB	YBVE
1997	877.2	33.2	38.6	15.2	9.4
1998	884.5	33.2	38.6	15.2	9.2
1999	890.3	32.9	38.2	15.3	9.0
2000	895.2	32.7	38.0	15.4	9.0
2001	906.0	32.8	38.0	15.7	9.3
2002	897.9	32.2	37.4	15.5	9.4
2003	908.1	32.2	37.5	15.6	9.2
2004	908.5	32.0	37.3	15.6	8.8
2005	919.4	32.0	37.2	15.7	9.6
2006	928.1	32.1	37.2	15.6	9.5
2007	937.6	32.2	37.4	15.6	9.4
Male					
	YBUT	YBUW	YBUZ	YBVC	YBVF
1997	558.7	38.8	40.6	15.0	10.6
1998	563.0	38.7	40.6	14.8	9.8
1999	562.2	38.3	40.2	15.1	9.8
2000	564.7	38.0	39.9	15.1	9.7
2001	568.7	38.0	39.9	15.5	10.2
2002	558.9	37.1	39.2	15.0	10.3
2003	567.1	37.1	39.2	15.5	10.2
2004	566.6	36.9	39.1	15.4	9.7
2005	570.6	36.8	39.0	15.6	10.6
2006	573.0	36.7	38.9	15.4	10.2
2007	581.9	36.9	39.2	15.7	10.3
Female					
	YBUU	YBUX	YBVA	YBVD	YBVG
1997	318.5	26.4	34.5	15.3	8.4
1998	321.4	26.5	34.6	15.3	8.8
1999	328.1	26.6	34.5	15.4	8.5
2000	330.5	26.3	34.2	15.5	8.5
2001	337.3	26.6	34.3	15.7	8.7
2002	339.0	26.4	34.1	15.7	8.7
2003	340.9	26.5	34.2	15.7	8.6
2004	341.9	26.2	33.8	15.7	8.1
2005	348.8	26.4	33.8	15.7	8.8
2006	355.1	26.6	34.0	15.7	8.9
2007	355.7	26.7	34.1	15.6	8.7

1 See chapter text. In August 2007, ONS published the mid-year population estimates for 2006. These estimates have now been incorporated into the LFS estimates from 2001 onwards. Further details can be found at http://www.statistics.gov.uk/cci/article.asp?id=1919
2 Average hours actually worked in the reference week which includes hours worked in second jobs.
3 The Labour Force Survey has now moved to calendar quarters from May 2006. More information can be found on page 5 of the Concepts and Definitions.pdf by following this link:- www.statistics.gov.uk/downloads/theme_labour/Concepts_Definitions_HQS.pdf
4 Main and second job.
5 Includes both paid and unpaid overtime.

6 People whose main job is full-time or part-time and based on respondents' self assessment.
7 Second jobs reported in the LFS in addition to persons' main full time job.

Sources: Labour Force Survey, Office for National Statistics;
Helpline: 01633 456901

7.7 International comparisons
Employment and unemployment rates[1,2]

		2005 Q1	2005 Q2	2005 Q3	2005 Q4	2006 Q1	2006 Q2	2006 Q3	2006 Q4	2007 Q1	2007 Q2	2007 Q3	2007 Q4
EUROSTAT Employment rates													
Austria	YXSN	67.6	68.4	69.8	68.8	68.2	70.0	71.9	70.6	70.3	71.5	72.5	71.3
Belgium	YXSO	60.9	61.0	61.2	61.2	60.3	60.4	61.2	62.1	61.7	61.6	62.1	62.7
Bulgaria	A495	53.0	56.2	57.9	56.0	55.5	59.1	60.3	59.8	59.7	61.6	62.7	62.9
Cyprus	A4AC	68.4	68.7	68.7	68.1	68.2	69.5	70.4	70.4	69.8	71.2	71.3	71.5
Czech Republic	A4AD	64.1	64.7	65.2	65.2	64.8	65.3	65.4	65.6	65.5	66.0	66.3	66.5
Denmark	YXSP	75.2	75.5	76.1	76.8	76.5	76.9	78.2	77.9	76.7	77.3	77.1	77.4
Estonia	A4AE	63.2	64.9	64.7	65.0	67.4	68.8	67.9	68.1	68.6	69.7	70.2	69.1
Finland	YXSQ	66.7	69.2	69.6	68.0	67.7	69.9	70.8	69.0	68.3	71.3	71.7	69.9
France	YXSR	63.5	64.1	64.3	63.5	63.2	63.8	64.4	63.9	63.8	64.6	65.1	64.9
Germany	YXSS	65.4	65.8	66.3	66.5	66.4	67.4	68.1	68.3	68.4	69.1	69.9	70.0
Greece	YXST	59.5	60.3	60.3	60.3	60.4	61.0	61.5	61.0	60.8	61.5	61.8	61.5
Hungary	A4AF	56.4	56.8	57.3	57.1	56.7	57.3	57.6	57.6	56.9	57.6	57.7	57.1
Ireland	YXSU	66.8	67.1	68.8	67.8	68.0	68.1	69.6	68.7	68.5	68.9	69.9	69.0
Italy	YXSV	57.3	57.8	57.4	57.8	57.9	58.9	58.4	58.5	57.9	58.9	59.1	58.7
Latvia	A4AG	62.5	63.0	63.8	63.9	64.3	65.5	68.0	67.4	66.4	67.6	69.0	70.3
Lithuania	A4AH	61.4	62.6	63.4	63.1	63.0	63.7	64.2	63.5	63.9	65.4	66.1	64.4
Luxembourg	YXSW	63.6	63.6	63.6	63.6	63.6	63.6	63.6	63.6	63.0	63.0	64.1	64.0
Malta	A4AI	54.6	53.6	53.5	53.8	54.4	54.3	55.5	55.1	55.1	55.7	56.1	55.7
Netherlands	YXSX	72.5	73.2	73.6	73.6	73.5	74.2	74.7	75.0	75.0	76.0	76.5	76.4
Poland	A4AJ	51.5	52.2	53.7	53.7	52.6	53.9	55.6	55.7	55.4	56.8	57.8	58.1
Portugal	YXSY	67.3	67.6	67.5	67.4	67.6	68.1	68.2	67.6	67.4	67.6	68.1	68.1
Romania	A494	56.6	58.7	57.8	57.2	57.2	59.6	60.9	57.4	57.2	59.6	60.5	57.9
Slovak Republic	A4AK	56.9	57.4	58.0	58.5	58.3	59.3	59.9	60.2	60.1	60.4	60.7	61.6
Slovenia	A4AL	65.2	66.0	66.6	66.0	65.9	67.1	67.2	66.0	66.0	68.3	69.0	67.7
Spain	YXSZ	62.1	63.2	63.9	64.0	64.0	64.7	65.2	65.2	65.1	65.8	66.0	65.5
Sweden	YXTA	70.7	72.6	72.6	72.3	71.5	73.1	74.7	73.2	72.7	74.3	75.7	74.0
United Kingdom	ANZ6	71.8	71.5	71.9	71.6	71.4	71.3	71.7	71.5	70.9	71.1	71.4	71.7
Total EU[3]	A496	62.9	63.5	63.9	63.8	63.5	64.4	65.0	64.8	64.5	65.4	65.9	65.7
Eurozone[3]	YXTC	63.3	63.9	64.2	64.1	64.0	64.8	65.2	65.1	64.9	65.8	66.2	66.0
National Statistical Offices Employment Rates													
Canada	IUUK	71.0	72.8	73.5	72.6	71.3	73.4	74.0	73.0	72.1	74.0	74.6	73.8
Japan	YXTF	68.2	69.6	69.8	69.4	69.1	70.4	70.3	70.1	69.7	71.3	70.8	70.9
United Kingdom	MGSU	74.9	74.7	74.8	74.5	74.6	74.6	74.5	74.5	74.3	74.4	74.4	74.7
United States	YXTE	71.3	71.5	71.7	71.5	71.9	71.9	72.0	72.2	72.1	71.8	71.6	71.5

		2007 Feb	2007 Mar	2007 Apr	2007 May	2007 Jun	2007 Jul	2007 Aug	2007 Sep	2007 Oct	2007 Nov	2007 Dec	2008 Jan	2008 Feb	2008 Mar
EUROSTAT Unemployment rates															
Austria	ZXDS	4.5	4.5	4.5	4.4	4.4	4.4	4.4	4.3	4.3	4.3	4.2	4.2	4.1	4.1
Belgium	ZXDI	7.8	7.7	7.9	7.8	7.6	7.3	7.3	7.1	7.1	7.0	7.0	7.0	6.9	6.9
Bulgaria	A492	7.7	7.5	7.3	7.1	7.0	6.9	6.7	6.5	6.3	6.0	5.9	6.1	6.0	5.9
Cyprus	A4AN	4.1	4.1	4.0	4.0	3.9	3.9	3.9	3.7	3.8	3.8	3.8	3.7	3.7	3.7
Czech Republic	A4AO	5.8	5.6	5.6	5.6	5.4	5.3	5.1	5.0	5.0	4.9	4.7	4.7	4.6	4.5
Denmark	ZXDJ	4.1	4.1	3.8	3.8	3.7	4.1	3.9	3.8	3.5	3.4	3.3	3.2	3.1	..
Estonia	A4AP	4.8	4.9	4.9	5.0	4.8	4.5	4.5	4.7	4.5	4.6	4.6	5.3	5.4	5.5
Finland	ZXDU	7.1	7.0	6.9	6.9	6.9	6.9	6.8	6.8	6.7	6.6	6.5	6.4	6.3	6.3
France	ZXDN	8.7	8.6	8.5	8.5	8.4	8.3	8.2	8.1	8.0	7.9	7.9	7.9	7.8	7.8
Germany	ZXDK	8.7	8.6	8.5	8.5	8.4	8.4	8.3	8.2	8.1	8.0	7.8	7.6	7.4	7.3
Greece	ZXDL	8.6	8.6	8.4	8.4	8.4	8.2	8.2	8.2	7.9	7.9	7.9	..	..	..
Hungary	A4AQ	7.2	7.3	7.1	7.1	7.2	7.3	7.4	7.3	7.7	7.8	7.9	7.6	7.6	7.6
Ireland	ZXDO	4.4	4.6	4.6	4.7	4.6	4.6	4.6	4.6	4.7	4.8	5.1	5.2	5.4	5.6
Italy	ZXDP	6.1	6.1	6.0	6.0	6.0	6.1	6.1	6.1	6.1	6.1	6.1	..	..	..
Latvia	A4AR	6.6	6.4	5.9	5.9	5.8	6.2	6.0	5.8	5.5	5.4	5.4	5.4	5.3	5.3
Lithuania	A4AS	4.8	4.6	4.5	4.2	3.9	4.2	4.1	4.1	4.1	4.2	4.3	4.6	4.5	4.5
Luxembourg	ZXDQ	4.9	4.9	4.8	4.7	4.7	4.7	4.7	4.6	4.7	4.7	4.6	4.6	4.7	4.5
Malta	A4AT	6.6	6.6	6.5	6.5	6.4	6.3	6.4	6.3	6.3	6.1	5.8	5.8	5.7	5.6
Netherlands	ZXDR	3.5	3.4	3.3	3.3	3.2	3.1	3.1	3.0	2.9	2.8	2.8	2.7	2.6	2.6
Poland	A4AU	10.8	10.3	10.1	9.9	9.6	9.5	9.3	9.0	8.9	8.6	8.2	8.3	8.0	7.7
Portugal	ZXDT	8.2	8.2	8.2	8.1	8.1	8.1	8.0	7.9	7.7	7.6	7.6	7.5	7.5	7.4
Romania	A48Z	6.6	6.6	6.6	6.6	6.6	6.3	6.3	6.3	6.2	6.2	6.2	..	..	..
Slovak Republic	A4AV	11.5	11.3	11.5	11.4	11.3	11.3	11.2	11.1	10.6	10.4	10.3	10.1	9.9	9.8
Slovenia	A4AW	5.4	5.2	4.8	4.7	4.7	4.7	4.7	4.5	4.6	4.5	4.5	4.5	4.4	4.3
Spain	ZXDM	8.1	8.1	8.1	8.1	8.2	8.3	8.3	8.3	8.5	8.6	8.7	9.0	9.1	9.3
Sweden	ZXDV	6.6	6.6	6.4	6.3	5.8	5.7	5.8	6.0	6.0	6.0	5.8	5.7	5.6	5.6
United Kingdom	ZXDW	5.5	5.5	5.3	5.3	5.3	5.3	5.3	5.2	5.1	5.0	5.0	5.1	..	..
Total EU[3]	A493	7.4	7.3	7.2	7.2	7.1	7.1	7.1	7.0	6.9	6.8	6.8	6.8	6.7	6.7
Eurozone[3]	ZXDH	7.6	7.5	7.5	7.5	7.4	7.4	7.4	7.3	7.3	7.2	7.2	7.1	7.1	7.1
National Statistical Offices Unemployment Rates															
Canada	ZXDZ	6.1	6.1	6.2	6.0	6.1	6.0	6.0	5.9	5.8	5.9	6.0	5.8	5.8	6.0
Japan	ZXDY	4.0	4.0	3.8	3.8	3.7	3.6	3.8	4.0	4.0	3.8	3.8	3.8	3.9	3.8
United Kingdom	MGSX	5.5	5.5	5.4	5.4	5.4	5.4	5.4	5.3	5.3	5.2	..	..	..	..
United States	ZXDX	4.5	4.4	4.5	4.5	4.6	4.7	4.7	4.7	4.8	4.7	5.0	4.9	4.8	5.1

1 See chapter text.
2 The UK employment rate as published by the Office for National Statistics is seasonally adjusted. All other employment and unemployment rates are not seasonally adjusted.

3 The "Total EU" series consists of all 27 EU countries. The Eurozone series consists of the following EU countries: Austria, Belgium, Cyprus, Finland, France, Germany, Greece, Ireland, Italy, Luxembourg, Malta, Netherlands, Portugal, Slovenia and Spain.

Sources: Office for National Statistics; Eurostat; StatsBLS; StatCan; Stat.go.JP; Labour Market Statistics Helpline: 01633 456901

7.8 Civil Service employment by department[1]
Great Britain

Full-time equivalents, not seasonally adjusted

		2006 Q4	2007 Q1	2007 Q2	2007 Q3	2007 Q4
Attorney General's Departments	GB3F	9 590	9 520	9 480	9 770	9 750
Cabinet Office	BBGD	1 660	1 410	1 430	1 270	1 270
Other Cabinet Office Agencies	GB3G	780	1 020	900	920	920
HM Treasury	GB3H	1 110	1 130	1 170	1 170	1 140
Chancellor's other departments	GB3I	5 170	5 050	4 970	4 760	4 800
Charity Commission	GB3J	500	500	490	460	460
Communities and Local Government	YEGA	5 520	5 400	5 370	5 390	5 350
Ministry of Justice	GB3K	33 640	33 550	83 210	83 560	83 880
Culture, Media and Sport	DMTC	630	620	620	610	600
Defence	BCDW	84 670	83 120	82 300	81 150	80 250
Education and Skills (former)	LNFW	3 940	3 850	3 840	–	–
Children, Schools and Families	I44Z	..	..	–	3 320	3 290
Innovation, Universities and Skills	I452	..	..	–	1 770	1 850
Environment, Food and Rural Affairs	LNFX	11 580	12 120	12 240	11 870	11 580
Export Credits Guarantee Department	GB3L	270	260	260	250	240
Foreign and Commonwealth	BCDK	6 050	6 060	6 120	6 070	6 030
Health	BAKR	5 870	3 610	3 630	3 480	3 520
Food Standards Agency	H6NX	..	810	810	800	790
Meat Hygiene Service	H6NY	..	1 390	1 360	1 330	1 270
HM Revenue and Customs	GB3M	94 880	93 320	91 060	89 210	88 420
Home Office	BCDL	73 490	74 270	24 990	24 920	24 760
International Development	DMUA	1 750	1 720	1 730	1 680	1 660
Northern Ireland Office	BBGG	140	140	140	130	130
Office for Standards in Education	GB3N	2 370	2 190	2 550	2 520	2 480
Security and Intelligence Services	GB3O	4 960	4 960	5 000	5 060	5 070
Business, Enterprise and Regulatory Reform	BCDQ	10 110	9 870	9 580	8 380	8 440
Transport	BCDR	18 780	18 790	18 810	18 880	18 910
Work and Pensions	LNGA	115 530	112 070	110 570	109 000	107 960
Central Governments Departments Total	GB3P	493 000	486 740	482 610	477 730	474 820
Scottish Executive	GB3Q	15 830	15 930	16 040	15 940	15 780
Welsh Assembly	GB3R	6 410	6 380	5 950	5 840	5 720
TOTAL	BCDX	515 240	509 050	504 600	499 510	496 320

1 Numbers are rounded to the nearest ten.

Source: Office for National Statistics

7.9 Unemployment: number by sex and age group[1]
United Kingdom

At Quarter 2 each year[2]. Seasonally adjusted

Thousands

	All aged 16 and over	16-59/64	16-17	18-24	25-34	35-49	50-64 (m) 50-59 (w)	65+ (m) 60+ (w)
All Persons								
	MGSC	YBSH	YBVH	YBVN	YCGM	YCGS	MGVL	MGVO
2001	1 472	1 458	152	377	340	387	202	14
2002	1 516	1 493	161	386	341	385	220	22
2003	1 464	1 446	176	400	310	345	215	18
2004	1 434	1 417	172	404	291	353	197	17
2005	1 435	1 418	176	438	278	335	193	17
2006	1 687	1 659	178	522	333	415	211	27
2007	1 661	1 632	195	521	302	390	223	29
Male								
	MGSD	YBSI	YBVI	YBVO	YCGN	YCGT	MGVM	MGVP
2001	882	875	91	221	203	213	147	..
2002	910	900	92	242	192	225	149	10
2003	886	877	98	244	175	213	147	..
2004	843	834	98	232	177	187	139	..
2005	835	828	100	264	153	183	127	..
2006	978	966	104	314	183	228	137	11
2007	951	937	109	313	160	205	151	13
Female								
	MGSE	YBSJ	YBVJ	YBVP	YCGO	YCGU	MGVN	MGVQ
2001	591	584	62	156	138	174	55	..
2002	606	593	69	145	149	160	70	13
2003	578	569	78	156	136	131	68	..
2004	592	583	74	172	113	166	58	..
2005	600	591	76	173	124	151	66	..
2006	709	693	74	208	150	187	74	16
2007	710	695	87	209	142	185	72	15

1 See chapter text. In August 2007, ONS published the mid-year population estimates for 2006. These estimates have now been incorporated into the LFS estimates from 2001 onwards. Further details can be found at http://www.statistics.gov.uk/cci/article.asp?id=1919

2 The LFS has now moved to calendar quarters from May 2006. More information is on page 5 of the Concepts and Definitions.pdf : www.statistics.gov.uk/downloads/theme_labour/Concepts_Definitions_HQS.pdf

Source: LFS, Office for National Statistics; Helpline: 01633 456901

7.10 Unemployment: percentage by sex and age group[1,2]
United Kingdom

At Quarter 2 each year[3]. Seasonally adjusted   Percentages

	All aged 16 and over	16-59/64	16-17	18-24	25-34	35-49	50-64 (m) 50-59 (w)	65+ (m) 60+ (w)
All Persons								
	MGSX	YBTI	YBVK	YBVQ	YCGP	YCGV	MGXE	MGXH
2000	5.5	5.6	19.7	10.7	5.1	3.9	4.2	2.1
2001	5.0	5.1	18.5	10.2	4.8	3.7	3.3	1.6
2002	5.2	5.2	19.9	10.2	5.0	3.6	3.5	2.4
2003	4.9	5.0	21.3	10.6	4.6	3.2	3.3	1.9
2004	4.8	4.9	21.5	10.3	4.4	3.2	3.0	1.7
2005	4.8	4.9	21.9	11.1	4.2	3.0	2.9	1.6
2006	5.5	5.6	24.1	12.7	5.0	3.7	3.2	2.3
2007	5.4	5.5	27.4	12.6	4.6	3.4	3.3	2.3
Male								
	MGSY	YBTJ	YBVL	YBVR	YCGQ	YCGW	MGXF	MGXI
2000	6.0	6.1	21.3	12.1	5.3	4.1	5.1	..
2001	5.6	5.6	21.6	11.2	5.2	3.8	4.0	..
2002	5.7	5.7	22.2	12.0	5.1	3.9	4.0	3.2
2003	5.5	5.5	23.5	12.0	4.7	3.6	3.8	..
2004	5.2	5.3	24.3	11.1	4.9	3.2	3.6	..
2005	5.1	5.2	24.7	12.4	4.3	3.1	3.3	..
2006	5.9	6.0	28.4	14.4	5.1	3.8	3.4	2.8
2007	5.7	5.7	31.0	14.0	4.4	3.4	3.8	3.2
Female								
	MGSZ	YBTK	YBVM	YBVS	YCGR	YCGX	MGXG	MGXJ
2000	4.9	5.0	18.1	9.1	4.7	3.6	3.0	1.9
2001	4.4	4.6	15.4	9.0	4.3	3.5	2.2	..
2002	4.5	4.6	17.6	8.2	4.8	3.2	2.8	2.1
2003	4.3	4.4	19.0	8.9	4.5	2.6	2.6	..
2004	4.3	4.5	18.6	9.5	3.8	3.2	2.2	..
2005	4.3	4.5	19.1	9.5	4.1	2.9	2.5	..
2006	5.0	5.2	19.9	10.9	5.0	3.5	2.8	2.1
2007	5.0	5.2	23.8	11.0	4.8	3.5	2.7	1.9

Note: Where figure denoted as .. it is not shown as it is based on a small sample size and is subject to a margin of uncertainty.

1 See chapter text. In August 2007, ONS published the mid-year population estimates for 2006. These estimates have now been incorporated into the LFS estimates from 2001 onwards. Further details can be found at http://www.statistics.gov.uk/cci/article.asp?id=1919

2 Total unemployment as a percentage of all economically active persons in the relevant age group.

3 The Labour Force Survey has now moved to calendar quarters from May 2006. More information can be found on page 5 of the Concepts and Definitions.pdf by following this link:- www.statistics.gov.uk/downloads/theme_labour/Concepts_Definitions_HQS.pdf

Sources: Labour Force Survey, Office for National Statistics;
Helpline: 01633 456901

7.11 Duration of unemployment: by sex[1,2]
United Kingdom
At Quarter 2 each year[3]. Seasonally adjusted

Thousands

		1997	1998	1999	2000	2001	2002	2003	2004	2005	2006	2007
All Persons												
All unemployed[4]	MGSC	2 048	1 788	1 743	1 599	1 472	1 516	1 464	1 434	1 435	1 687	1 661
Duration of unemployment												
Less than 6 months	YBWF	1 009	980	986	920	878	977	947	923	912	1 026	1 000
6 months & less than 1 year	YBWG	298	252	268	240	219	218	205	228	215	304	265
1 year or more	YBWH	741	556	490	439	376	320	312	284	308	357	396
1 year or more as % of total	YBWI	*36.2*	*31.1*	*28.1*	*27.5*	*25.5*	*21.1*	*21.3*	*19.8*	*21.5*	*21.2*	*23.8*
Male												
All unemployed[4]	MGSD	1 265	1 074	1 059	957	882	910	886	843	835	978	951
Duration of unemployment												
Less than 6 months	MGYK	550	518	536	500	481	537	537	504	488	548	528
6 months & less than 1 year	MGYM	178	160	165	140	131	147	131	141	138	177	154
1 year or more	MGYO	538	396	359	317	269	227	218	198	210	252	269
1 year or more as % of total	YBWJ	*42.5*	*36.9*	*33.9*	*33.1*	*30.5*	*24.9*	*24.6*	*23.5*	*25.1*	*25.8*	*28.3*
Female												
All unemployed[4]	MGSE	783	715	684	642	591	606	578	592	600	709	710
Duration of unemployment												
Less than 6 months	MGYL	459	462	450	420	396	441	410	419	425	478	473
6 months & less than 1 year	MGYN	121	93	102	100	87	71	74	86	77	126	111
1 year or more	MGYP	203	160	131	122	107	94	94	86	98	105	127
1 year or more as % of total	YBWK	*26.0*	*22.4*	*19.2*	*19.0*	*18.1*	*15.4*	*16.3*	*14.6*	*16.3*	*14.8*	*17.8*

1 All aged 16 and over. See chapter text.
2 In August 2007, ONS published the mid-year population estimates for 2006. These estimates have now been incorporated into the LFS estimates from 2001 onwards. Further details can be found at http://www.statistics.gov.uk/cci/article.asp?id=1919
3 The Labour Force Survey has now moved to calendar quarters from May 2006. More information can be found on page 5 of the Concepts and Definitions.pdf by following this link:- www.statistics.gov.uk/downloads/theme_labour/Concepts_Definitions_HQS.pdf
4 Totals include people who did not state their duration of unemployment.

Sources: Labour Force Survey, Office for National Statistics;
Helpline: 01633 456901

7.12 Claimant count:[1] by age and duration
Computerised claims only

United Kingdom. Seasonally adjusted

Thousands

		2001	2002	2003	2004	2005	2006	2007
Annual averages								
Males								
All ages								
All durations	AGNG	733.6	708.3	693.0	630.7	635.0	694.0	628.7
Up to 6 months	AGXK	449.4	457.4	451.2	408.8	423.4	438.5	405.1
Over 6 and up to 12 months	ELNP	125.4	124.2	127.1	113.7	113.3	136.4	111.2
All over 12 months	ELON	158.8	126.7	114.7	108.2	98.3	119.0	112.3
All over 24 months	IKBS	77.5	50.7	37.6	34.6	33.1	34.5	33.8
Aged 18 to 24								
All durations	JLGC	167.9	168.1	171.9	161.8	174.5	195.5	176.9
Up to 6 months	JLGD	141.4	141.0	143.8	134.3	143.6	154.9	145.8
Over 6 and up to 12 months	JLGE	23.4	23.8	24.5	23.3	25.9	33.0	25.3
All over 12 months	JLGF	3.1	3.3	3.6	4.2	5.0	7.5	5.8
All over 24 months	JLGH	0.3	0.3	0.4	0.5	0.6	0.9	1.1
Aged 25 to 49								
All durations	AGMA	445.9	421.8	404.8	362.3	357.5	387.5	352.5
Up to 6 months	JLHG	248.2	254.9	248.0	221.3	225.9	228.9	211.4
Over 6 and up to 12 months	JLHH	83.1	80.9	82.9	72.9	70.3	83.4	69.6
All over 12 months	JLHI	114.7	86.1	73.8	68.1	61.2	75.2	71.5
All over 24 months	JLHK	52.4	29.2	17.0	14.1	14.2	15.2	14.5
Aged 50 and over								
All durations	JLHL	119.8	118.4	116.3	106.7	103.0	111.0	99.3
Up to 6 months	JLHM	59.9	61.6	59.4	53.2	53.8	54.7	48.0
Over 6 and up to 12 months	JLHN	18.9	19.6	19.7	17.5	17.0	20.0	16.3
All over 12 months	JLHO	41.0	37.3	37.2	35.9	32.1	36.3	35.0
All over 24 months	JLHQ	24.8	21.1	20.2	19.9	18.3	18.4	18.2
Females								
All ages								
All durations	JLGI	227.9	226.8	230.1	214.7	220.0	245.9	231.9
Up to 6 months	JLGK	160.4	163.6	166.3	153.2	159.2	171.5	164.3
Over 6 and up to 12 months	JLGJ	35.1	35.5	37.2	34.9	35.6	43.6	37.5
All over 12 months	JLGL	32.5	27.6	26.5	26.7	25.2	30.8	30.1
All over 24 months	JLGN	13.9	9.7	8.1	8.0	7.9	8.4	8.4
Aged 18 to 24								
All durations	JLGO	73.4	75.0	77.3	74.0	79.0	90.1	85.4
Up to 6 months	JLGP	62.1	62.9	64.9	61.5	65.3	72.2	70.9
Over 6 and up to 12 months	JLGQ	9.8	10.4	10.6	10.4	11.4	14.6	12.0
All over 12 months	JLGR	1.4	1.8	1.8	2.1	2.3	3.3	2.5
All over 24 months	JLGT	0.2	0.2	0.3	0.3	0.4	0.5	0.5
Aged 25 to 49								
All durations	JLHR	113.3	111.4	112.1	102.1	101.8	111.8	105.1
Up to 6 months	JLHS	74.4	76.7	77.3	69.0	70.3	73.6	69.3
Over 6 and up to 12 months	JLHT	18.6	18.5	19.9	18.2	17.7	21.2	18.8
All over 12 months	JLHU	20.4	16.2	14.9	14.9	13.8	16.9	17.0
All over 24 months	JLHW	8.2	4.7	3.1	2.9	3.0	3.3	3.2
Aged 50 and over								
All durations	JLHX	41.3	40.4	40.7	38.7	39.1	44.0	41.4
Up to 6 months	JLHY	23.9	24.1	24.1	22.7	23.6	25.6	24.1
Over 6 and up to 12 months	JLHZ	6.7	6.6	6.8	6.3	6.5	7.8	6.8
All over 12 months	JLIA	10.7	9.7	9.8	9.7	9.1	10.6	10.6
All over 24 months	JLIC	5.5	4.8	4.7	4.8	4.5	4.7	4.7

1 Count of claimants of unemployment-related benefits.

Source: Office for National Statistics: 01633 456901

7.13 Unemployment rates: by region[1,2,3]
At Quarter 2 each year[4]. Seasonally adjusted[5]

Percentages

		1997	1998	1999	2000	2001	2002	2003	2004	2005	2006	2007
North East	YCNC	9.8	8.3	9.6	8.9	7.4	6.5	6.1	5.5	6.8	6.1	6.5
North West	YCND	7.1	6.9	6.3	5.3	5.3	5.5	5.0	4.4	4.4	5.3	5.8
Yorkshire and The Humber	YCNE	7.5	7.3	6.3	6.1	5.5	5.3	5.1	4.6	4.8	5.8	5.7
East Midlands	YCNF	5.9	4.9	5.4	4.8	5.0	4.6	4.3	4.2	4.2	5.4	5.0
West Midlands	YCNG	6.8	5.9	6.9	6.1	5.5	5.7	5.6	5.5	4.7	5.7	6.8
East	YCNH	6.3	4.9	4.3	3.7	3.6	3.7	3.9	3.8	3.9	5.0	4.6
London	YCNI	9.3	8.6	7.5	7.4	6.2	6.8	7.2	7.0	7.1	7.8	7.4
South East	YCNJ	5.3	4.4	4.0	3.3	3.2	3.8	3.9	3.7	3.8	4.7	4.2
South West	YCNK	5.8	4.8	4.5	4.3	3.6	3.7	3.4	3.7	3.2	3.7	4.0
Wales	YCNM	8.3	7.0	7.5	6.1	6.1	5.7	4.5	4.2	4.6	5.7	5.6
Scotland	YCNN	8.6	7.4	7.1	7.1	6.3	6.3	5.3	6.0	5.4	5.4	4.5
Northern Ireland	ZSFB	8.1	6.9	7.6	6.7	6.1	5.6	5.2	5.1	4.9	4.2	3.7

1 Total unemployed as a percentage of all economically active persons.
2 All aged 16 and over. See chapter text.
3 In August 2007, ONS published the mid-year population estimates for 2006. These estimates have now been incorporated into the LFS estimates from 2001 onwards. Further details can be found at http://www.statis-tics.gov.uk/cci/article.asp?id=1919
4 The Labour Force Survey has now moved to calendar quarters from May 2006. More information can be found on page 5 of the Concepts and Defini-tions.pdf by following this link:- www.statistics.gov.uk/downloads/theme_la-bour/Concepts_Definitions_HQS.pdf
5 Previously not seasonally adjusted data was shown.

Sources: Labour Force Survey, Office for National Statistics;
Helpline: 01633 456901

7.14 Claimant count rates: by region[1]
Seasonally adjusted annual averages

Percentages

		1997	1998	1999	2000	2001	2002	2003	2004	2005	2006	2007
United Kingdom	BCJE	5.3	4.5	4.1	3.6	3.1	3.1	3.0	2.7	2.7	2.9	2.8
North East	DPDM	7.9	7.0	6.9	6.2	5.6	5.0	4.5	4.0	3.9	4.1	4.3
North West	IBWC	5.7	5.0	4.6	4.1	3.7	3.5	3.2	2.8	2.9	3.3	3.2
Yorkshire and the Humber	DPBI	6.0	5.4	5.0	4.3	3.9	3.6	3.3	2.8	2.9	3.3	3.2
East Midlands	DPBJ	4.6	3.9	3.6	3.3	3.1	2.9	2.8	2.5	2.5	2.8	2.8
West Midlands	DPBN	5.2	4.5	4.4	4.0	3.7	3.5	3.5	3.3	3.4	3.9	3.8
East	DPDP	4.0	3.2	2.9	2.4	2.0	2.1	2.1	2.0	2.1	2.3	2.2
London	DPDQ	6.2	5.1	4.4	3.7	3.3	3.5	3.6	3.5	3.4	3.4	3.1
South East	DPDR	3.3	2.6	2.3	1.8	1.5	1.6	1.7	1.6	1.6	1.8	1.6
South West	DPBM	4.1	3.4	3.0	2.5	2.1	1.9	1.9	1.6	1.6	1.8	1.6
England	VASQ	5.1	4.3	3.9	3.4	3.0	2.9	2.9	2.6	2.6	2.9	2.7
Wales	DPBP	6.1	5.4	5.0	4.4	3.9	3.5	3.3	3.0	3.0	3.1	3.1
Scotland	DPBQ	5.9	5.3	5.0	4.5	3.9	3.8	3.7	3.4	3.2	3.2	2.9
Northern Ireland	DPBR	8.0	7.3	6.3	5.3	4.9	4.4	4.1	3.6	3.3	3.2	2.9
Great Britain	DPAJ	5.2	4.4	4.0	3.5	3.1	3.0	3.0	2.7	2.7	2.9	2.8

1 The number of unemployment-related benefit claimants as a percentage of the estimated total workforce (the sum of claimants, employee jobs, self-em-ployed, participants on work-related government training programmes and HM Forces) at mid-year. Excluded are claimants under 18, consistent with current coverage. See chapter text.

Source: Office for National Statistics: 01633 456901

7.15 Claimant count:[1] by region
Seasonally adjusted

Thousands

	North East	North West	Yorkshire and the Humber	East Midlands	West Midlands	East	London	South East	South West	England	Wales	Scotland	Great Britain	Northern Ireland	United Kingdom
	DPDG	IBWA	DPAX	DPAY	DPBC	DPDJ	DPDK	DPDL	DPBB	IBWK	DPBE	DPBF	DPAG	DPBG	BCJD
1992 Jan	133.9	325.4	222.7	160.4	250.6	183.3	389.8	258.4	188.4	2 112.6	121.3	228.0	2 462.2	102.2	2 564.4
Apr	135.7	332.8	227.6	168.0	260.0	196.0	409.6	277.7	199.0	2 205.5	123.4	231.8	2 561.6	103.4	2 665.0
Jul	136.7	335.2	232.4	172.1	266.1	205.1	426.2	288.9	206.6	2 268.9	124.1	235.2	2 628.6	104.6	2 733.2
Oct	141.4	343.6	240.2	178.8	277.4	218.6	448.0	308.4	215.3	2 371.1	129.2	242.4	2 743.3	105.1	2 848.4
1993 Jan	146.2	348.3	247.5	185.2	286.2	229.5	464.6	325.2	222.6	2 454.4	131.4	245.3	2 832.0	105.5	2 937.5
Apr	148.0	345.2	246.5	183.6	285.1	228.2	469.5	321.4	220.0	2 446.6	130.3	243.2	2 821.0	104.5	2 925.5
Jul	148.5	338.0	240.9	180.8	278.7	223.5	466.3	314.0	214.4	2 404.4	129.3	241.2	2 775.6	102.5	2 878.1
Oct	147.5	331.1	237.8	177.8	271.5	216.6	460.4	306.6	208.4	2 356.8	127.8	236.6	2 722.1	101.8	2 823.9
1994 Jan	145.6	325.1	233.7	174.7	262.3	210.0	451.4	296.7	203.6	2 302.3	126.7	236.0	2 665.8	100.2	2 766.0
Apr	141.6	314.5	227.4	170.7	252.0	200.4	440.4	280.9	194.5	2 221.7	123.3	231.7	2 577.4	98.9	2 676.3
Jul	139.1	304.2	222.7	166.3	242.3	191.0	428.1	268.1	188.1	2 148.8	119.0	227.4	2 496.3	97.2	2 593.5
Oct	136.0	291.7	215.9	160.1	230.5	180.5	415.4	251.1	178.9	2 059.0	112.9	218.1	2 391.1	93.8	2 484.9
1995 Jan	133.0	280.1	210.6	153.2	218.5	172.3	401.4	237.9	171.4	1 977.5	108.3	209.3	2 296.0	91.3	2 387.3
Apr	130.0	270.8	206.8	148.1	211.0	167.1	395.0	229.7	166.0	1 923.8	106.2	200.3	2 231.0	88.6	2 319.6
Jul	128.2	266.1	204.6	145.3	206.9	165.0	390.2	225.1	162.5	1 892.8	106.7	195.3	2 195.9	87.6	2 283.5
Oct	126.4	260.9	200.7	142.3	201.3	160.7	383.2	219.1	159.4	1 852.7	105.4	193.5	2 152.9	85.8	2 238.7
1996 Jan	123.1	255.8	197.0	140.0	196.5	157.2	376.8	213.3	155.6	1 814.6	104.0	193.2	2 112.5	85.9	2 198.4
Apr	121.7	254.9	195.7	137.7	194.2	153.5	367.9	207.6	152.3	1 785.1	104.6	194.9	2 085.0	86.1	2 171.1
Jul	116.9	248.2	188.8	131.8	187.6	146.8	357.5	198.9	146.8	1 722.5	101.8	191.9	2 017.0	86.4	2 103.4
Oct	110.5	238.4	181.1	124.9	177.8	138.5	341.6	185.5	137.9	1 635.0	98.2	186.3	1 920.7	81.7	2 002.4
1997 Jan	101.0	218.5	166.4	111.8	160.1	123.5	312.6	163.3	126.0	1 483.2	90.3	173.8	1 747.3	71.1	1 818.4
Apr	95.2	201.3	154.7	102.4	147.3	110.6	284.9	144.4	112.1	1 352.9	82.5	162.2	1 597.6	65.0	1 662.6
Jul	92.4	188.9	148.2	95.0	138.0	102.5	264.3	131.0	100.7	1 261.0	78.1	153.6	1 492.7	61.4	1 554.1
Oct	90.4	177.6	142.0	87.6	131.7	94.3	246.4	120.4	93.0	1 183.4	73.6	146.5	1 403.5	60.6	1 464.1
1998 Jan	87.6	170.6	137.2	82.8	126.1	88.5	234.3	112.3	88.7	1 128.1	70.9	141.6	1 340.6	59.9	1 400.5
Apr	84.1	165.4	134.1	79.9	122.3	85.2	229.4	108.0	85.1	1 093.5	69.3	138.7	1 301.5	57.9	1 359.4
Jul	81.8	163.7	133.3	80.0	121.4	83.7	225.2	105.5	84.1	1 078.7	68.6	139.4	1 286.7	57.3	1 344.0
Oct	82.1	160.9	130.9	79.9	121.4	82.0	219.3	102.5	81.8	1 060.8	68.1	136.9	1 265.8	56.1	1 321.9
1999 Jan	82.6	159.5	129.5	79.0	122.6	80.3	214.5	101.2	81.2	1 050.4	67.8	135.6	1 253.8	55.9	1 309.7
Apr	82.5	157.2	127.0	78.2	123.1	79.1	207.8	98.8	78.4	1 032.1	67.1	133.9	1 233.1	55.0	1 288.1
Jul	80.3	153.8	122.4	75.9	120.2	76.6	202.2	94.4	74.9	1 000.7	63.8	130.2	1 194.7	50.0	1 244.7
Oct	76.7	150.0	118.3	73.6	115.9	73.6	196.5	91.1	71.4	967.1	61.0	126.1	1 154.2	46.5	1 200.7
2000 Jan	75.7	145.7	114.6	73.2	112.1	70.3	189.4	87.2	68.0	936.2	59.3	123.2	1 118.7	44.2	1 162.9
Apr	73.6	139.9	108.9	70.0	108.1	66.9	181.6	81.3	63.8	894.1	57.8	119.0	1 070.9	42.4	1 113.3
Jul	72.0	135.4	104.9	68.7	107.2	62.5	172.0	77.5	61.1	861.3	57.1	115.1	1 033.5	41.2	1 074.7
Oct	69.5	131.0	102.5	67.7	106.5	60.7	165.0	74.3	58.1	835.3	56.4	111.7	1 003.4	41.3	1 044.7
2001 Jan	66.2	127.4	99.9	66.6	104.0	57.2	158.2	69.7	54.9	804.1	54.9	108.8	967.8	40.8	1 008.6
Apr	63.2	124.9	97.6	65.1	100.8	54.8	151.8	66.1	53.6	777.9	52.4	105.3	935.6	39.9	975.5
Jul	61.4	121.5	95.1	63.0	97.4	53.7	151.0	65.1	52.1	760.3	49.8	102.4	912.5	39.3	951.8
Oct	61.5	121.4	93.2	61.6	95.7	54.3	156.3	65.9	51.1	761.0	49.2	104.2	914.4	38.6	953.0
2002 Jan	60.9	121.3	91.4	60.6	95.4	55.4	163.1	68.6	51.1	767.8	48.1	104.3	920.2	38.0	958.2
Apr	59.2	119.4	89.4	59.4	93.6	56.4	166.2	71.0	50.9	765.5	47.5	104.4	917.4	37.5	954.9
Jul	58.5	118.1	89.1	58.6	93.4	57.5	167.3	72.3	50.1	764.9	46.8	101.9	913.6	36.4	950.0
Oct	55.9	116.1	87.6	57.9	93.7	57.2	167.6	72.3	49.3	757.6	46.7	100.1	904.4	35.1	939.5
2003 Jan	54.8	115.9	87.0	58.0	94.3	57.4	168.6	72.9	48.9	757.8	46.3	100.2	904.3	35.0	939.3
Apr	53.5	112.7	84.1	58.8	94.7	58.5	171.3	75.6	48.6	757.8	45.2	99.1	902.1	34.0	936.1
Jul	52.6	112.5	84.2	59.9	94.9	58.7	171.7	76.4	49.1	760.0	45.0	100.6	905.6	34.6	940.2
Oct	51.1	108.7	81.6	58.8	94.2	57.3	170.2	76.0	47.4	745.3	43.1	98.9	887.3	34.7	922.0
2004 Jan	49.8	104.6	78.3	56.2	93.0	56.7	167.8	75.0	45.3	726.7	42.0	97.0	865.7	33.5	899.2
Apr	47.5	101.3	75.6	53.7	89.7	56.0	165.5	72.3	42.7	704.3	41.4	94.4	840.1	31.8	871.9
Jul	45.4	96.7	71.6	51.1	86.7	54.6	162.0	68.5	40.4	677.0	39.5	90.0	806.5	29.9	836.4
Oct	45.1	96.5	71.1	50.9	86.0	55.0	158.8	69.2	40.6	673.2	39.2	89.5	801.9	29.6	831.5
2005 Jan	43.9	94.5	70.1	50.8	85.6	55.3	158.6	68.3	40.8	667.9	38.9	87.4	794.2	29.1	823.3
Apr	44.9	97.9	73.2	51.8	87.6	56.3	162.2	70.1	41.3	685.3	39.5	86.1	810.9	28.8	839.7
Jul	46.2	102.0	76.2	54.6	96.6	58.9	162.2	71.6	42.6	710.9	41.7	84.7	837.3	28.4	865.7
Oct	47.3	105.9	79.7	56.5	99.3	60.1	165.7	73.6	43.0	731.1	42.9	85.3	859.3	28.1	887.4
2006 Jan	47.2	109.1	84.0	58.7	102.6	62.3	168.0	78.0	44.0	753.9	43.8	84.9	882.6	28.3	910.9
Apr	49.7	115.0	87.1	61.9	108.7	65.5	167.8	81.7	47.9	785.3	45.2	88.3	918.8	28.3	947.1
Jul	50.5	116.8	88.4	62.7	109.3	65.8	168.3	83.7	49.2	794.7	44.2	88.5	927.4	27.7	955.1
Oct	51.2	118.1	88.7	63.2	109.8	67.4	165.9	82.7	49.2	796.2	44.0	87.2	927.4	27.7	955.1
2007 Jan	51.0	115.3	85.8	61.7	109.5	66.2	158.9	77.8	47.2	773.4	42.2	81.4	897.0	26.1	923.1
Apr	50.3	111.6	83.5	60.2	104.3	63.4	151.4	74.7	44.6	744.0	41.2	79.2	864.4	25.3	889.7
Jul	49.3	109.0	81.1	58.6	101.1	61.0	144.5	71.5	42.2	718.3	40.4	74.8	833.5	23.6	857.1
Oct	47.9	107.3	77.6	55.9	99.4	57.5	136.0	67.4	39.8	688.8	39.7	72.4	800.9	23.2	824.1

1 The figures are based on the number of claimants receiving unemployment related benefits and are adjusted for seasonality and discontinuities to be consistent with current coverage. See chapter text.

The latest national and regional seasonally adjusted claimant count figures are provisional and subject to revision in the following month.

Source: Office for National Statistics: 01633 456901

7.16

Economic activity: by sex and age[1]
United Kingdom
At Quarter 2 each year[2]. Seasonally adjusted

Thousands and percentages

	All aged 16 and over	16-59/64	16-17	18-24	25-34	35-49	50-64 (m) 50-59 (w)	65+ (m) 60+ (w)
Thousands								
All Persons								
	MGSF	YBSK	YBZL	YBZO	YBZR	YBZU	YBZX	YCAD
2001	29 167	28 322	821	3 698	7 078	10 599	6 125	845
2002	29 422	28 519	808	3 773	6 885	10 808	6 245	903
2003	29 656	28 709	826	3 781	6 707	10 930	6 464	946
2004	29 857	28 830	803	3 919	6 599	11 043	6 466	1 028
2005	30 163	29 087	803	3 960	6 586	11 185	6 553	1 075
2006	30 670	29 488	738	4 100	6 630	11 356	6 665	1 182
2007	30 814	29 574	714	4 137	6 586	11 411	6 726	1 240
Male								
	MGSG	YBSL	YBZM	YBZP	YBZS	YBZV	YBZY	YCAE
2001	15 876	15 595	421	1 966	3 887	5 654	3 667	280
2002	15 981	15 680	415	2 007	3 776	5 774	3 708	302
2003	16 184	15 845	418	2 031	3 685	5 860	3 851	339
2004	16 212	15 863	404	2 102	3 601	5 900	3 857	348
2005	16 342	15 981	404	2 133	3 588	5 957	3 900	361
2006	16 595	16 193	365	2 191	3 616	6 048	3 972	402
2007	16 735	16 319	350	2 238	3 618	6 085	4 027	417
Female								
	MGSH	YBSM	YBZN	YBZQ	YBZT	YBZW	YBZZ	YCAF
2001	13 291	12 726	401	1 731	3 191	4 945	2 459	565
2002	13 440	12 839	393	1 766	3 109	5 034	2 536	601
2003	13 471	12 864	408	1 750	3 023	5 070	2 613	607
2004	13 646	12 966	400	1 816	2 999	5 143	2 609	679
2005	13 820	13 106	399	1 828	2 998	5 229	2 653	714
2006	14 075	13 295	372	1 909	3 014	5 308	2 693	779
2007	14 079	13 256	364	1 899	2 968	5 326	2 699	823
Percentages[3]								
All Persons								
	MGWG	MGSO	YCAG	YCAJ	YCAM	YCAP	MGWP	MGWS
2001	62.8	78.6	55.8	75.6	84.1	84.8	70.0	8.1
2002	63.0	78.6	53.6	75.7	83.8	85.1	70.5	8.6
2003	63.1	78.7	54.2	74.0	83.5	84.9	72.4	9.0
2004	63.0	78.5	51.7	74.7	83.6	84.7	72.0	9.6
2005	63.1	78.6	51.1	73.7	83.8	84.8	72.5	10.0
2006	63.7	79.0	47.0	74.6	84.7	85.3	73.1	10.9
2007	63.4	78.8	45.0	73.6	84.5	85.1	73.6	11.2
Male								
	MGWH	MGSP	YCAH	YCAK	YCAN	YCAQ	MGWQ	MGWT
2001	70.9	83.9	55.8	80.7	93.3	91.5	72.8	7.3
2002	70.8	83.8	53.7	80.5	92.7	92.0	72.9	7.8
2003	71.2	84.2	53.4	79.1	92.6	92.1	75.1	8.7
2004	70.7	83.6	50.7	79.3	92.0	91.6	74.6	8.8
2005	70.5	83.4	50.2	78.4	92.1	91.4	74.7	9.0
2006	70.9	83.7	45.4	78.6	93.1	91.9	75.1	9.9
2007	70.9	83.6	42.9	78.4	93.3	91.9	75.3	10.2
Female								
	MGWI	MGSQ	YCAI	YCAL	YCAO	YCAR	MGWR	MGWU
2001	55.3	72.9	55.7	70.6	75.0	78.2	66.2	8.6
2002	55.6	73.1	53.6	71.0	75.0	78.4	67.2	9.1
2003	55.5	72.9	55.0	68.9	74.6	77.9	68.9	9.1
2004	55.9	73.1	52.7	70.0	75.3	78.0	68.5	10.1
2005	56.1	73.4	52.0	68.9	75.6	78.4	69.5	10.6
2006	56.8	74.0	48.7	70.5	76.5	78.8	70.3	11.4
2007	56.4	73.6	47.3	68.7	75.8	78.5	71.3	11.8

1 See chapter text. In August 2007, ONS published the mid-year population estimates for 2006. These estimates have now been incorporated into the LFS estimates from 2001 onwards. Further details can be found at http://www.statistics.gov.uk/cci/article.asp?id=1919

2 The Labour Force Survey has now moved to calendar quarters from May 2006. More information can be found on page 5 of the Concepts and Definitions.pdf by following this link:- www.statistics.gov.uk/downloads/theme_labour/Concepts_Definitions_HQS.pdf

3 Total economically active as a percentage of all persons in the relevant age group.

Sources: Labour Force Survey, Office for National Statistics;
Helpline: 01633 456901

Labour Market

7.17 Economically inactive: by sex and age[1]
United Kingdom

At Quarter 2 each year[2]. Seasonally adjusted

Thousands and percentages

	All aged 16 and over	16-59/64	16-17	18-24	25-34	35-49	50-64 (m) 50-59 (w)	65+ (m) 60+ (w)
Thousands								
All Persons								
	MGSI	YBSN	YCAS	YCAV	YCAY	YCBB	MGWA	MGWD
2001	17 274	7 717	652	1 192	1 342	1 901	2 629	9 557
2002	17 305	7 743	699	1 208	1 333	1 888	2 615	9 562
2003	17 361	7 755	698	1 327	1 327	1 943	2 460	9 606
2004	17 504	7 879	751	1 327	1 298	1 988	2 516	9 624
2005	17 624	7 940	768	1 412	1 274	2 000	2 486	9 684
2006	17 515	7 830	832	1 394	1 195	1 961	2 449	9 684
2007	17 776	7 965	872	1 482	1 210	1 993	2 410	9 811
Male								
	MGSJ	YBSO	YCAT	YCAW	YCAZ	YCBC	MGWB	MGWE
2001	6 518	2 983	333	471	280	526	1 373	3 535
2002	6 584	3 022	358	486	296	502	1 380	3 561
2003	6 551	2 980	365	535	296	505	1 279	3 571
2004	6 719	3 109	393	548	313	539	1 316	3 610
2005	6 824	3 178	400	586	308	561	1 323	3 646
2006	6 796	3 150	440	595	269	532	1 314	3 646
2007	6 883	3 201	466	618	260	534	1 323	3 682
Female								
	MGSK	YBSP	YCAU	YCAX	YCBA	YCBD	MGWC	MGWF
2001	10 756	4 734	319	721	1 062	1 375	1 256	6 022
2002	10 721	4 721	341	722	1 037	1 386	1 235	6 001
2003	10 810	4 775	334	792	1 031	1 437	1 182	6 034
2004	10 785	4 771	358	779	985	1 449	1 200	6 014
2005	10 800	4 762	368	825	966	1 439	1 163	6 038
2006	10 719	4 681	392	799	926	1 429	1 135	6 039
2007	10 893	4 764	405	864	950	1 459	1 087	6 129
Percentages[3]								
All Persons								
	YBTC	YBTL	LWEX	LWFA	LWFD	LWFG	LWFJ	LWFM
2001	37.2	21.4	44.2	24.4	15.9	15.2	30.0	91.9
2002	37.0	21.4	46.4	24.3	16.2	14.9	29.5	91.4
2003	36.9	21.3	45.8	26.0	16.5	15.1	27.6	91.0
2004	37.0	21.5	48.3	25.3	16.4	15.3	28.0	90.4
2005	36.9	21.4	48.9	26.3	16.2	15.2	27.5	90.0
2006	36.3	21.0	53.0	25.4	15.3	14.7	26.9	89.1
2007	36.6	21.2	55.0	26.4	15.5	14.9	26.4	88.8
Male								
	YBTD	YBTM	LWEY	LWFB	LWFE	LWFH	LWFK	LWFN
2001	29.1	16.1	44.2	19.3	6.7	8.5	27.2	92.7
2002	29.2	16.2	46.3	19.5	7.3	8.0	27.1	92.2
2003	28.8	15.8	46.6	20.9	7.4	7.9	24.9	91.3
2004	29.3	16.4	49.3	20.7	8.0	8.4	25.4	91.2
2005	29.5	16.6	49.8	21.6	7.9	8.6	25.3	91.0
2006	29.1	16.3	54.6	21.4	6.9	8.1	24.9	90.1
2007	29.1	16.4	57.1	21.6	6.7	8.1	24.7	89.8
Female								
	YBTE	YBTN	LWEZ	LWFC	LWFF	LWFI	LWFL	LWFO
2001	44.7	27.1	44.3	29.4	25.0	21.8	33.8	91.4
2002	44.4	26.9	46.4	29.0	25.0	21.6	32.8	90.9
2003	44.5	27.1	45.0	31.1	25.4	22.1	31.1	90.9
2004	44.1	26.9	47.3	30.0	24.7	22.0	31.5	89.9
2005	43.9	26.6	48.0	31.1	24.4	21.6	30.5	89.4
2006	43.2	26.0	51.3	29.5	23.5	21.2	29.7	88.6
2007	43.6	26.4	52.7	31.3	24.2	21.5	28.7	88.2

1 See chapter text. In August 2007, ONS published the mid-year population estimates for 2006. These estimates have now been incorporated into the LFS estimates from 2001 onwards. Further details can be found at http://www.statistics.gov.uk/cci/article.asp?id=1919

2 The Labour Force Survey has now moved to calendar quarters from May 2006. More information can be found on page 5 of the Concepts and Definitions.pdf by following this link:- www.statistics.gov.uk/downloads/theme_labour/Concepts_Definitions_HQS.pdf

3 Total economically inactive as a percentage of all persons in the relevant age group.

Sources: Labour Force Survey, Office for National Statistics;
Helpline: 01633 456901

7.18 Economically inactive:[1,2] by reason and sex
United Kingdom
At Quarter 2 each year[3]. Seasonally adjusted

Thousands and percentages

	Economic inactivity by reason:							by:		All economically inactive
	Student	Looking after family/home	Temporary sick	Long-term sick	Discouraged workers[4]	Retired	Other	Does not want a job	Wants a job	

Thousands

All Persons

	BEDZ	BEEC	BEBK	BEBN	YCFO	BEEI	BEEL	YBVZ	YBWC	YBSN
2000	1 433	2 371	187	2 149	69	553	810	5 258	2 314	7 571
2001	1 505	2 391	192	2 212	34	593	790	5 526	2 191	7 717
2002	1 519	2 384	177	2 228	32	584	818	5 495	2 248	7 743
2003	1 645	2 400	193	2 110	38	569	801	5 612	2 143	7 755
2004	1 697	2 341	191	2 171	35	598	845	5 858	2 021	7 879
2005	1 786	2 335	189	2 151	33	624	822	5 860	2 080	7 940
2006	1 809	2 306	189	2 087	36	592	811	5 754	2 076	7 830
2007	1 896	2 355	199	2 045	35	621	815	5 878	2 088	7 965

Male

	BEEX	BEAQ	BEDI	BEDL	YCFP	BEDR	BEDU	YBWA	YBWD	YBSO
2000	705	163	88	1 202	38	383	299	1 939	939	2 878
2001	731	180	91	1 242	21	405	313	2 078	905	2 983
2002	750	182	87	1 242	21	396	343	2 086	936	3 022
2003	819	181	88	1 150	20	389	333	2 065	915	2 980
2004	858	188	94	1 185	23	410	350	2 252	857	3 109
2005	887	193	100	1 191	21	427	357	2 335	843	3 178
2006	897	197	94	1 143	26	437	354	2 254	895	3 150
2007	948	207	89	1 144	21	453	339	2 313	888	3 201

Female

	BEBL	BEBO	BEEG	BEEJ	YCFQ	BEEP	BEES	YBWB	YBWE	YBSP
2000	729	2 207	99	947	31	170	511	3 319	1 375	4 694
2001	774	2 212	101	970	13	188	477	3 449	1 285	4 734
2002	769	2 202	90	986	11	187	475	3 409	1 312	4 721
2003	826	2 218	105	960	18	180	468	3 548	1 228	4 775
2004	839	2 153	97	986	12	188	495	3 606	1 165	4 771
2005	899	2 142	89	960	12	196	464	3 524	1 237	4 762
2006	911	2 109	94	944	10	154	457	3 500	1 181	4 681
2007	948	2 148	110	901	14	168	475	3 564	1 200	4 764

Percentages[5]

All Persons

	BEDJ	BEDM	BEDP	BEDS	BEDV	BEDY	BEEB	BEEE	BEBM	BEAR
2000	18.9	31.3	2.5	28.4	0.9	7.3	10.7	69.4	30.6	100.0
2001	19.5	31.0	2.5	28.7	0.4	7.7	10.2	71.6	28.4	100.0
2002	19.6	30.8	2.3	28.8	0.4	7.5	10.6	71.0	29.0	100.0
2003	21.2	30.9	2.5	27.2	0.5	7.3	10.3	72.4	27.6	100.0
2004	21.5	29.7	2.4	27.6	0.4	7.6	10.7	74.3	25.7	100.0
2005	22.5	29.4	2.4	27.1	0.4	7.9	10.3	73.8	26.2	100.0
2006	23.1	29.5	2.4	26.7	0.5	7.6	10.4	73.5	26.5	100.0
2007	23.8	29.6	2.5	25.7	0.4	7.8	10.2	73.8	26.2	100.0

Male

	BEEH	BEEK	BEEN	BEEQ	BEET	BEEW	BEEZ	BEAS	BEGT	BEBP
2000	24.5	5.7	3.0	41.8	1.3	13.3	10.4	67.4	32.6	100.0
2001	24.5	6.0	3.1	41.6	0.7	13.6	10.5	69.7	30.3	100.0
2002	24.8	6.0	2.9	41.1	0.7	13.1	11.3	69.0	31.0	100.0
2003	27.5	6.1	3.0	38.6	0.7	13.0	11.2	69.3	30.7	100.0
2004	27.6	6.1	3.0	38.1	0.7	13.2	11.3	72.4	27.6	100.0
2005	27.9	6.1	3.2	37.5	0.7	13.4	11.2	73.5	26.5	100.0
2006	28.5	6.3	3.0	36.3	0.8	13.9	11.2	71.6	28.4	100.0
2007	29.6	6.5	2.8	35.7	0.6	14.2	10.6	72.3	27.7	100.0

Female

	BEGZ	BEHC	BEHF	BEHI	BEHL	BEHO	BEBQ	BEHR	BEHU	BEGW
2000	15.5	47.0	2.1	20.2	0.7	3.6	10.9	70.7	29.3	100.0
2001	16.4	46.7	2.1	20.5	0.3	4.0	10.1	72.8	27.2	100.0
2002	16.3	46.7	1.9	20.9	0.2	4.0	10.1	72.2	27.8	100.0
2003	17.3	46.5	2.2	20.1	0.4	3.8	9.8	74.3	25.7	100.0
2004	17.6	45.1	2.0	20.7	0.3	3.9	10.4	75.6	24.4	100.0
2005	18.9	45.0	1.9	20.2	0.3	4.1	9.8	74.0	26.0	100.0
2006	19.5	45.1	2.0	20.2	0.2	3.3	9.8	74.8	25.2	100.0
2007	19.9	45.1	2.3	18.9	0.3	3.5	10.0	74.8	25.2	100.0

1 All persons aged 16-59(women)/ 64 (men). See chapter text.
2 In August 2007, ONS published the mid-year population estimates for 2006. These estimates have now been incorporated into the LFS estimates from 2001 onwards. Further details can be found at http://www.statistics.gov.uk/cci/article.asp?id=1919
3 The Labour Force Survey has now moved to calendar quarters from May 2006. More information can be found on page 5 of the Concepts and Definitions.pdf by following this link:- www.statistics.gov.uk/downloads/theme_labour/Concepts_Definitions_HQS.pdf
4 People whose reason for not seeking work was that they believed no jobs were available.
5 Reasons for inactivity as a percentage of all economically inactive.

Sources: Labour Force Survey, Office for National Statistics; Helpline: 01633 456901

7.19 Labour disputes: by industry[1]
United Kingdom
Standard Industrial Classification 2003

Thousands and numbers

		2000	2001	2002	2003	2004	2005	2006
Working days lost through all stoppages in progress (thousands)	KBBZ	499	525	1 323	499	905	157	755
Analysis by industry								
Mining, quarrying, electricity, gas and water	DMME	3	25	–	–	5	6	12
Manufacturing	BBFX	52	43	21	63	31	16	18
Construction	DMMG	49	10	17	14	–	2	15
Transport, storage and communication	BBFY	97	107	96	126	44	33	41
Public administration and defence	BBFZ	50	216	488	138	437	23	627
Education	BBGA	50	43	376	131	379	43	31
Health and social work	BBGB	122	73	148	15	4	–	5
Other community, social and personal services	DMML	36	4	107	10	4	6	2
All other industries and services	DMMM	40	4	70	2	2	29	5
Analysis by number of working days lost in each stoppage								
Under 250 days	KBFC	12	9	7	6	7	5	7
250 and under 500 days	KBFJ	9	11	8	6	5	4	8
500 and under 1,000 days	KBFL	21	15	15	13	12	7	8
1,000 and under 5,000 days	KBFY	71	59	47	69	51	80	66
5,000 and under 25,000 days	KBFZ	85	140	104	46	59	61	69
25,000 and under 50,000 days	KBGS	–	72	122	112	–	–	–
50,000 days and over	KBGT	301	220	1 021	248	770	–	597
Working days lost per 1 000 employees all industries and services	KBHA	20	20	51	19	34	6	28
Workers directly and indirectly involved (thousands)	KBHB	183	180	943	151	293	93	713
Analysis by industry								
Mining, quarrying, electricity, gas and water	DMMN	1	3	–	–	1	6	1
Manufacturing	DMMO	28	17	10	18	14	3	11
Construction	DMMP	16	3	17	2	–	1	2
Transport, storage and communications	DMMQ	39	69	33	52	12	13	14
Public administration and defence	DMMR	29	46	171	56	207	15	654
Education	DMMS	17	34	388	15	55	43	28
Health and social work	DMMT	28	6	144	3	1	–	2
Other community, social and personal services	DMMU	13	1	103	3	3	6	1
All other industries and services	DMMV	12	1	76	1	1	5	2
Analysis by duration of stoppage								
Not more than 5 days	KBHM	82	98	828	78	222	89	706
Over 5 but not more than 10 days	KBHN	9	43	57	23	47	3	5
Over 10 but not more than 20 days	KBJQ	8	4	3	31	1	1	2
Over 20 but not more than 30 days	KBJR	–	–	1	–	3	–	1
Over 30 but not more than 50 days	KBJS	83	6	1	–	–	1	–
Over 50 days	KBJT	1	30	55	20	20	–	–
Numbers of stoppages in progress: total	KBLG	212	194	146	133	130	116	158
Analysis by industry								
Mining, quarrying, electricity, gas and water	DMMW	3	3	2	1	3	2	2
Manufacturing	DMMX	38	32	33	43	30	19	25
Construction	DMMY	16	9	3	4	1	3	5
Transport, storage and communications	DMMZ	116	94	51	45	46	42	30
Public administration and defence	DMNA	7	22	20	12	19	13	18
Education	DMNB	18	16	16	15	16	22	53
Health and social work	DMNC	10	12	14	7	4	1	4
Other community, social and personal services	DMND	13	10	11	9	12	5	8
All other industries and services	DMNE	5	9	12	4	4	10	13
Analysis of number of stoppages by duration								
Not more than 5 days	KBNH	187	162	118	113	111	102	126
Over 5 but not more than 10 days	KBNI	14	15	16	10	10	8	19
Over 10 but not more than 20 days	KBNJ	5	7	3	5	4	3	10
Over 20 but not more than 30 days	KBNK	1	1	3	1	2	–	1
Over 30 but not more than 50 days	KBNL	3	4	1	1	1	3	2
Over 50 days	KBNM	2	5	5	3	2	–	–

1 See chapter text.

Source: Labour Market Statistics, Office for National Statistics: 01633 819205

7.20 Average earnings and hours of full-time employees by industry division:[1] by sex
United Kingdom

At April. Standard Industrial Classification 1992

	Agriculture, Hunting and Forestry	Fishing	Mining and Quarrying	Manufacturing	Electricity, Gas and Water Supply	Construction	Wholesale and Retail Trade; repair of motor vehicles, cycles, personal and household goods
All employees							
Weekly earnings							
	C9EG	C9EI	C9EK	C9EM	C9EO	C9EP	C9EQ
2004[2]	362.5	419.0	633.5	493.1	591.9	509.4	433.3
	355.8	415.7	617.1	485.0	579.2	505.1	421.3
2005	364.7	440.6	657.9	508.0	612.2	524.6	425.2
2006[3]	379.9	450.7	753.4	526.8	625.8	554.2	447.5
	379.7	445.1	749.9	524.2	624.8	553.4	445.6
2007	397.0	359.4	757.6	539.3	630.8	567.9	459.5
Total hours worked							
	C5TJ	C5TK	C5TL	C5TV	C5TW	C5TX	C5U3
2004[2]	44.5	43.5	43.4	41.0	40.0	43.1	40.4
		43.8	43.2			43.2	
2005	43.7	43.1	43.5	40.6	39.3	43.0	40.3
2006[3]	44.1	42.3	42.6	40.7	40.3	43.1	40.3
		42.2					40.4
2007	43.9	43.6	44.1	40.9	39.7	43.0	40.3
Hourly earnings excluding overtime							
	C9HV	C9HX	C9HZ	C9I3	C9I5	C9I7	C9IA
2004[2]	8.03	9.57	14.97	12.01	14.61	11.81	10.74
	7.87	9.41	14.60	11.80	14.29	11.68	10.44
2005	8.27	10.14	15.56	12.50	15.33	12.15	10.57
2006[3]	8.53	10.72	18.17	12.94	15.23	12.82	11.12
		10.60	18.08	12.87	15.19	12.80	11.07
2007	8.96	7.92	17.67	13.18	15.66	13.16	11.43
Male employees							
Weekly earnings							
	C9FZ	C9F4	C9F6	C9F8	C9FA	C9FC	C9FE
2004[2]	375.4	433.2	653.7	519.4	626.1	521.5	483.2
	368.8	426.6	637.1	511.2	607.9	517.8	470.3
2005	381.9	445.7	675.4	533.8	647.3	537.6	469.5
2006[3]	395.2	433.6	787.6	553.0	668.8	570.0	493.3
		428.2	783.4	551.4	666.5	569.8	491.1
2007	409.2	313.9	773.0	568.7	678.4	582.6	504.8
Total hours worked							
	C5W8	C5WE	C5WH	C5WK	C5WN	C5WQ	C5WT
2004[2]	45.6	45.4	44.4	41.6	40.5	43.7	41.4
		45.5	44.2			43.8	
2005	44.7	43.4	44.4	41.2	39.9	43.5	41.2
2006[3]	44.9	43.3	43.6	41.3	41.1	43.6	41.3
	45.0	43.2					
2007	44.6	44.2	45.0	41.5	40.3	43.6	41.2
Hourly earnings excluding overtime							
	C9IS	C9IU	C9IW	C9IY	C9J2	C9J4	C9J6
2004[2]	8.11	9.47	15.16	12.49	15.29	11.95	11.71
	7.96	9.26	14.80	12.28	14.82	11.83	11.38
2005	8.46	10.13	15.72	12.98	15.96	12.30	11.42
2006[3]	8.71	10.01	18.66	13.42	15.90	13.04	12.00
	8.70	9.91	18.55	13.38	15.89	13.02	11.94
2007	9.11	6.64	17.71	13.72	16.61	13.34	12.27
Female employees							
Weekly earnings							
	C9G6	C9G8	C9GA	C9GC	C9GE	C9GG	C9GI
2004[2]	297.5	–	511.0	388.1	453.0	403.8	339.3
	290.9		496.3	380.8	464.8	392.8	330.9
2005	287.6	–	552.5	404.3	490.2	411.5	343.2
2006[3]	316.1	–	581.4	420.9	490.7	419.3	364.1
			580.3	415.9	486.5	415.7	361.8
2007	337.1	–	661.5	423.8	474.7	438.0	375.5
Total hours worked							
	C7NN	C7NP	C7NR	C7NT	C7NV	C7OA	C7OC
2004[2]	39.2	36.5	37.2	38.7	38.1	38.2	38.5
			37.3			38.3	
2005	39.0	42.2	38.1	38.4	37.3	38.0	38.5
2006[3]	40.6	–	37.7	38.6	37.8	38.6	38.7
	40.5						
2007	40.8	–	38.0	38.6	37.9	38.2	38.4
Hourly earnings excluding overtime							
	C9JO	C9JQ	C9JS	C9JU	C9JW	C9JY	C9K2
2004[2]	7.55	–	13.73	10.02	11.83	10.55	8.82
	7.38		13.31	9.84	12.17	10.25	8.60
2005	7.35	–	14.54	10.51	13.13	10.82	8.92
2006[3]	7.77	–	15.54	10.93	12.98	10.87	9.45
	7.78			10.80	12.87	10.78	9.39
2007	8.24	–	17.44	10.99	12.50	11.46	9.78

7.20
continued

Average earnings and hours of full-time employees by industry division:[1] by sex
United Kingdom
At April. Standard Industrial Classification 1992

	Hotels and restaurants	Transport, Storage and Communication	Financial Inter-mediation	Real Estate, Renting and Business	Public Administration and Defence; compulsory social security	Educa-tion	Health and Social work	Other community, social and personal service activities
All employees								
Weekly earnings								
	C9ER	C9ES	C9ET	C9EU	C9EV	C9EW	C9EX	C9EY
2004[2]	323.8	504.3	696.3	590.6	496.6	493.6	474.9	515.4
	319.1	494.4	667.5	573.9	497.6	495.9	478.9	499.5
2005	323.5	508.0	701.3	589.3	525.0	518.6	503.2	503.8
2006[3]	344.0	526.5	723.0	616.0	540.4	533.1	518.4	525.9
	343.3	523.4	719.7	612.8	536.6	532.2	515.9	524.1
2007	349.2	546.5	757.0	632.0	549.7	544.8	528.0	512.5
Total hours worked								
	C5U4	C5U5	C5U6	C5U7	C5U8	C5V5	C5V8	C5VU
2004[2]	41.1	42.6	36.3	39.3	39.2	35.6	38.6	39.8
	41.2	42.7			39.1			
2005	40.9	42.9	36.0	39.1	39.2	35.5	38.7	40.0
2006[3]	41.0	42.2	36.1	39.3	39.2	35.6	38.6	39.9
		42.3						
2007	41.0	42.2	36.2	39.2	39.0	35.7	38.4	39.6
Hourly earnings excluding overtime								
	C9IC	C9IE	C9IG	C9II	C9IK	C9IM	C9IO	C9IQ
2004[2]	7.86	11.99	19.25	15.10	12.57	13.90	12.29	13.02
	7.74	11.73	18.44	14.67	12.62	13.96	12.39	12.60
2005	7.93	11.89	19.54	15.14	13.28	14.64	12.99	12.65
2006[3]	8.39	12.56	20.07	15.75	13.72	15.03	13.44	13.28
	8.38	12.47	19.96	15.67	13.63	14.99	13.38	13.23
2007	8.52	13.02	20.98	16.18	14.05	15.31	13.77	12.99
Male employees								
Weekly earnings								
	C9FO	C9FQ	C9FS	C9FU	C9FW	C9FY	C9G2	C9G4
2004[2]	352.5	522.0	869.2	652.5	547.9	536.3	614.8	593.1
	345.9	514.0	829.8	635.3	549.0	542.2	624.3	572.8
2005	357.2	527.7	872.4	654.9	583.6	568.4	669.5	563.6
2006[3]	381.7	544.3	888.2	683.7	593.0	589.9	695.6	582.8
	381.4	541.8	884.9	681.6	589.4	589.2	692.7	582.5
2007	382.0	565.7	928.4	702.8	609.8	603.7	699.3	570.1
Total hours worked								
	C5WW	C5WZ	C7MU	C7MW	C7NF	C7NH	C7NJ	C7NL
2004[2]	42.1	43.5	36.4	40.2	40.1	36.6	39.5	40.9
		43.6			40.0			
2005	41.8	43.8	36.2	39.9	40.1	36.5	39.7	41.1
2006[3]	41.8	43.2	36.3	40.2	40.0	36.6	39.5	40.7
		43.3						40.8
2007	42.0	43.2	36.3	40.1	39.8	36.7	39.4	40.5
Hourly earnings excluding overtime								
	C9J8	C9JA	C9JC	C9JE	C9JG	C9JI	C9JK	C9JM
2004[2]	8.38	12.20	23.99	16.39	13.56	14.79	15.57	14.68
	8.23	11.97	22.88	15.94	13.62	14.88	15.82	14.14
2005	8.56	12.12	24.19	16.52	14.43	15.64	16.91	13.83
2006[3]	9.14	12.71	24.54	17.14	14.76	16.21	17.64	14.44
	9.13	12.63	24.43	17.08	14.68	16.18	17.56	14.42
2007	9.11	13.19	25.63	17.65	15.24	16.55	17.78	14.17
Female employees								
Weekly earnings								
	C9GK	C9GM	C9HJ	C9HL	C9HN	C9HP	C9HR	C9HT
2004[2]	287.2	439.0	492.5	474.5	418.9	460.2	417.9	405.7
	283.8	423.1	474.1	461.0	420.8	461.8	419.7	398.4
2005	282.4	432.8	500.0	472.8	440.2	484.0	440.3	417.9
2006[3]	296.8	463.3	524.2	494.3	463.4	495.7	451.4	441.8
	295.9	458.1	519.6	490.2	460.0	494.8	448.9	438.3
2007	309.4	476.5	550.3	502.5	469.3	506.5	463.1	424.9
Total hours worked								
	C7OE	C7OG	C7OI	C7OK	C7OM	C7OO	C7OQ	C7OS
2004[2]	39.9	39.3	36.2	37.7	37.9	34.9	38.2	38.2
	40.0	39.4	36.1					38.3
2005	39.7	39.3	35.7	37.6	37.9	34.8	38.4	38.4
2006[3]	40.0	38.7	35.9	37.7	38.1	34.9	38.3	38.7
						35.0	38.2	
2007	39.8	38.6	36.0	37.6	37.8	35.0	38.0	38.2
Hourly earnings excluding overtime								
	C9K4	C9K6	C9K8	C9KG	C9KI	C9KK	C9KS	C9KU
2004[2]	7.16	11.22	13.62	12.58	11.01	13.22	10.93	10.60
	7.07	10.80	13.10	12.22	11.07	13.26	10.97	10.39
2005	7.12	10.99	14.00	12.59	11.57	13.92	11.49	10.90
2006[3]	7.42	12.02	14.62	13.14	12.14	14.22	11.83	11.51
	7.39	11.89	14.48	13.03	12.07	14.19	11.77	11.41
2007	7.77	12.35	15.30	13.36	12.40	14.48	12.22	11.13

1 See chapter text. Employees on adult rates whose pay for the survey period was not affected by absence.

2 For 2004, two sets of figures are shown. The first does not include supplementary information and therefore is comparable with earlier years. The second includes supplementary information and so is discontinuous with previous years (where the two figures are equal, only one appears).

3 In 2006 additional methodology was introduced. Therefore the bottom data is comparable with 2007, whilst the top data is comparable with earlier years (where the two figures are equal, only one appears).

Sources: Annual Survey of Hours and Earnings; Office for National Statistics: 01633 819024

7.21 Average earnings and hours of full-time employees:[1] by sex
United Kingdom

At April

£ and numbers

	All Industries				Manufacturing industries			
	Average weekly earnings	Total hours worked (numbers)	Average hourly earnings		Average weekly earnings	Total hours worked (numbers)	Average hourly earnings	
			including overtime	excluding overtime			including overtime	excluding overtime
All employees								
	C7Q5	C7QX	C7Q7	C7Q9	C7PU	C7QL	C7PV	C7PW
2002	472.2	39.6	11.94	11.98	455.6	41.0	11.12	11.09
2003	487.1	39.5	12.32	12.34	476.5	40.9	11.65	11.62
2004[2]	506.1	39.5	12.80	12.84	493.1	41.0	12.03	12.01
	498.2		12.60	12.63	485.0		11.83	11.80
2005	516.5	39.4	13.11	13.15	508.0	40.6	12.51	12.50
2006[3]	537.5	39.4	13.63	13.68	526.8	40.7	12.94	12.94
	535.0		13.56	13.61	524.2		12.87	12.87
2007	549.9	39.4	13.96	14.00	539.3	40.9	13.19	13.18
Male employees								
	C7QA	C7QZ	C7QC	C7QE	C7PX	C7QT	C7PY	C7PZ
2002	523.4	40.8	12.83	12.92	482.9	41.6	11.62	11.62
2003	539.3	40.8	13.21	13.28	503.2	41.5	12.13	12.12
2004[2]	557.4	40.8	13.67	13.76	519.4	41.6	12.50	12.49
	548.1		13.44	13.51	511.2		12.30	12.28
2005	568.1	40.6	13.98	14.05	533.8	41.2	12.97	12.98
2006[3]	592.0	40.7	14.56	14.64	553.0	41.3	13.40	13.42
	589.8		14.50	14.58	551.4		13.36	13.38
2007	606.1	40.7	14.90	14.98	568.7	41.5	13.71	13.72
Female employees								
	C7QF	C7SA	C7QH	C7QJ	C7Q2	C7QV	C7Q3	C7Q4
2002	386.8	37.5	10.32	10.32	350.8	38.8	9.04	9.03
2003	400.7	37.4	10.71	10.70	372.8	38.7	9.64	9.62
2004[2]	422.1	37.5	11.26	11.27	388.1	38.7	10.02	10.02
	416.8		11.11	11.12	380.8		9.83	9.84
2005	435.7	37.4	11.64	11.65	404.3	38.4	10.52	10.51
2006[3]	453.0	37.5	12.06	12.10	420.9	38.6	10.91	10.93
	450.0		11.99	12.02	415.9		10.78	10.80
2007	462.8	37.4	12.38	12.40	423.8	38.6	10.99	10.99

1 See chapter text. Employees on adult rates whose pay for the survey period was not affected by absence.
2 For 2004, two sets of figures are shown. The first does not include supplementary information and therefore is comparable with earlier years. The second includes supplementary information and so is discontinuous with previous years (where the two figures are equal, only one appears).

3 In 2006 additional methodology was introduced. Therefore the bottom data is comparable with 2007, whilst the top data is comparable with earlier years (where the two figures are equal, only one appears).

Sources: Annual Survey of Hours and Earnings;
Office for National Statistics: 01633 819024

7.22 Average earnings index:[1] all employees by main industrial sectors
Great Britain

Analyses by industry based on Standard Industrial Classification 1992

Indices (2000=100)

Not seasonally adjusted

	Annual averages	January	February	March	April	May	June	July	August	September	October	November	December
Whole economy (Divisions 01 - 93)													
LNMM													
2005	121.4	123.3	124.9	127.5	119.9	119.2	120.4	120.5	119.0	118.8	119.1	119.9	124.6
2006	126.4	127.2	131.6	133.2	124.1	124.5	126.4	125.2	123.5	123.7	123.9	124.6	129.4
2007	131.5	133.3	138.8	137.8	128.0	129.0	130.5	129.7	128.7	128.8	128.2	130.2	134.4
Manufacturing industries (Divisions 15 - 37)													
LNMN													
2005	120.1	116.3	119.2	126.6	120.0	117.5	118.2	119.9	118.1	119.2	120.4	120.5	125.1
2006	126.2	121.9	125.5	133.0	126.8	124.1	125.2	125.5	124.4	125.6	126.5	126.1	130.0
2007	130.7	125.9	130.1	137.8	130.8	129.6	130.4	131.1	127.9	128.6	130.0	130.8	135.6
Production industries (Divisions 10 - 41)													
LNMO													
2005	120.0	116.3	119.6	126.6	120.2	117.4	118.5	119.6	117.9	118.9	120.1	120.1	125.3
2006	126.0	121.7	125.2	133.0	126.9	124.1	125.6	125.3	124.0	125.2	126.0	125.9	129.4
2007	130.9	125.7	129.7	138.8	131.0	129.7	131.0	131.3	127.9	128.8	130.0	131.1	135.2
Service industries (Divisions 50 - 93)													
LNMP													
2005	121.6	125.0	126.4	127.6	119.8	119.4	120.7	120.5	119.2	118.3	118.5	119.4	123.8
2006	126.5	128.6	133.4	133.5	123.5	124.6	126.6	125.1	123.5	123.3	123.4	124.2	129.1
2007	131.7	135.3	141.4	137.8	127.5	129.0	130.6	129.5	129.1	128.7	127.9	129.8	133.9
Private sector services (Divisions 50-99)													
JJGF													
2005	120.1	125.9	127.8	129.1	117.9	116.3	118.7	118.8	116.7	115.7	115.9	116.9	122.1
2006	125.2	129.2	135.1	135.3	121.5	121.6	125.1	123.0	121.0	120.8	121.0	121.7	127.3
2007	130.7	136.7	144.6	139.8	125.5	126.1	129.1	128.1	127.0	126.8	125.7	127.1	131.9

Seasonally adjusted

	Annual averages	January	February	March	April	May	June	July	August	September	October	November	December
Whole economy (Divisions 01 - 93)													
LNMQ													
2005	121.5	119.4	119.7	120.3	120.6	120.8	121.0	122.1	122.2	122.5	122.6	123.2	123.9
2006	126.5	123.3	125.2	125.3	125.5	126.0	127.0	126.7	126.8	127.4	128.0	127.9	128.8
2007	131.5	129.3	131.3	129.7	129.8	130.5	131.1	131.5	132.1	132.7	132.7	133.2	133.5
Manufacturing industries (Divisions 15 - 37)													
LNMR													
2005	120.2	117.9	118.4	119.6	118.9	118.4	119.4	120.1	120.9	121.4	121.9	122.4	123.3
2006	126.4	124.0	124.6	125.1	126.2	125.2	126.3	125.8	127.3	128.2	128.4	128.1	128.0
2007	130.8	128.4	129.1	129.5	130.2	130.7	131.2	131.1	130.9	131.1	131.6	132.6	133.4
Production industries (Divisions 10 - 41)													
LNMS													
2005	120.0	117.9	118.5	118.7	118.8	118.5	119.0	119.8	120.6	121.1	121.6	121.8	123.6
2006	126.0	123.7	124.2	124.3	125.9	125.4	125.9	125.4	126.9	127.6	127.9	127.7	127.6
2007	130.7	128.1	128.6	129.5	129.9	130.6	131.1	131.2	130.9	131.1	131.7	132.7	133.3
Service industries (Divisions 50 - 93)													
LNMT													
2005	121.7	119.5	119.9	120.4	121.3	121.2	121.2	122.5	122.2	122.4	122.5	123.3	123.8
2006	126.6	123.1	125.2	126.0	125.5	126.2	127.0	127.0	126.8	127.4	128.0	128.2	129.1
2007	131.8	129.5	131.9	130.1	130.0	130.6	131.1	131.8	132.6	133.2	133.1	133.6	133.7
Private sector services (Divisions 50-93)													
JJGH													
2005	120.4	118.3	118.6	119.2	120.2	119.5	120.0	121.4	121.1	121.2	121.1	121.9	122.5
2006	125.5	121.5	124.0	124.9	124.5	125.0	126.4	125.8	125.7	126.3	127.1	127.2	128.2
2007	131.0	128.7	131.6	129.1	129.0	129.7	130.4	131.1	131.9	132.6	132.3	132.8	132.8

1 See chapter text.
2 Provisional.

Source: Office for National Statistics: 01633 819024

7.23 Average earnings index:[1] all employee jobs: by industry
Great Britain
Not seasonally adjusted

Indices (2000=100)

Excluding bonuses

	Agriculture, forestry and fishing	Mining and quarrying	Food products, beverages and tobacco	Textiles, leather and clothing	Chemicals and man-made fibres	Basic metals and metal products	Engineering and allied industries	Other manufacturing	Electricity, gas and water supply	Construction
SIC 1992	(A,B)	(C)	(DA)	(DB,DC)	(DG)	(DJ)	(DK, DL,DM)	(DD,DE,DF, DH,DI,DN)	(E)	(F)
	JVUZ	JVVA	JVVB	JVVC	JVVD	JVVE	JVVF	JVVG	JVVH	JVVI
2006	134.5	129.1	127.6	122.5	122.8	127.4	126.6	126.5	116.0	127.9
2007	127.4	139.1	128.6	125.4	127.2	130.8	133.0	132.2	121.3	130.6
2005 Jul	122.2	122.1	121.2	119.1	118.5	122.2	122.7	120.3	115.3	125.1
Aug	122.5	122.5	122.0	117.0	119.7	122.2	121.7	121.0	115.2	123.3
Sep	131.7	123.5	122.6	118.9	119.2	123.2	122.5	122.1	113.7	125.7
Oct	130.3	125.2	123.1	121.6	119.4	122.9	123.6	122.3	115.2	126.2
Nov	126.8	125.6	125.2	121.9	121.1	122.1	123.1	122.9	116.1	128.1
Dec	127.6	125.1	126.2	122.4	121.3	120.0	123.6	124.2	117.8	126.4
2006 Jan	129.0	127.4	125.0	122.1	121.3	124.0	123.0	124.1	115.7	126.6
Feb	132.0	124.9	124.3	123.1	121.6	124.5	124.7	124.7	116.3	127.6
Mar	133.0	126.1	125.2	121.4	121.1	125.7	125.2	125.1	115.2	127.0
Apr	141.3	127.6	129.4	122.5	122.1	125.2	126.4	125.2	114.2	126.6
May	140.2	128.1	128.4	123.2	122.0	126.9	126.3	125.9	118.3	127.2
Jun	141.4	128.4	127.8	124.0	123.0	129.5	126.5	126.9	118.2	127.9
Jul	137.2	128.7	128.3	122.8	121.6	128.4	126.4	126.5	118.7	128.2
Aug	139.9	129.0	128.2	120.1	122.5	127.9	126.2	127.1	116.2	126.7
Sep	135.7	131.0	128.1	122.1	124.3	129.3	127.7	127.7	114.6	128.5
Oct	130.3	131.3	128.2	122.0	125.1	129.2	128.8	127.8	113.0	129.5
Nov	123.8	131.7	127.7	122.4	123.9	129.9	129.1	128.8	116.6	130.0
Dec	130.5	134.7	130.0	124.4	125.2	127.9	128.6	128.6	114.9	129.3
2007 Jan	129.5	133.1	126.7	124.2	123.2	128.0	129.6	128.7	114.3	130.6
Feb	121.7	132.5	125.2	125.6	124.9	129.4	130.6	129.8	115.1	129.7
Mar	129.8	134.0	125.4	123.5	125.6	130.0	132.6	131.4	118.9	131.5
Apr	133.3	139.6	127.5	123.0	125.0	130.3	133.3	131.7	118.6	129.8
May	132.0	140.4	130.2	124.2	127.5	128.4	133.0	131.3	122.2	129.5
Jun	124.5	141.7	128.0	129.1	128.7	131.6	133.6	132.3	122.9	130.2
Jul	124.9	140.3	128.2	127.6	127.8	130.8	134.3	132.6	124.4	131.6
Aug	127.7	141.6	128.8	127.8	127.1	130.9	132.8	132.2	121.5	129.3
Sep	126.6	140.3	129.1	126.4	126.6	131.5	133.1	133.2	122.5	130.8
Oct	128.1	142.3	130.3	126.6	129.2	132.8	134.2	134.4	124.3	131.3
Nov	126.3	140.8	130.3	124.4	129.5	133.5	134.5	134.7	127.3	132.0
Dec	125.0	143.2	133.2	122.2	131.0	132.5	134.3	134.2	123.3	131.0
2008 Jan	125.4	145.4	129.3	125.2	127.9	135.0	134.3	133.7	122.3	131.3
Feb	125.5	146.0	129.9	123.3	130.8	134.9	134.7	134.7	122.5	133.1

Percentage change on the year

	JVVT	JVVU	JVVV	JVVW	JVVX	JVVY	JVVZ	JVWA	JVWB	JVWC
2006 Jul	12.2	5.5	5.8	3.1	2.6	5.1	3.0	5.1	2.9	2.4
Aug	14.2	5.3	5.1	2.7	2.3	4.7	3.7	5.1	0.8	2.8
Sep	3.0	6.1	4.5	2.7	4.3	5.0	4.2	4.6	0.8	2.2
Oct	–	4.9	4.1	0.4	4.9	5.1	4.3	4.5	-1.9	2.7
Nov	-2.4	4.8	2.0	0.4	2.3	6.4	4.9	4.8	0.4	1.5
Dec	2.2	7.6	3.0	1.6	3.2	6.6	4.0	3.5	-2.4	2.3
2007 Jan	0.4	4.5	1.3	1.8	1.6	3.3	5.4	3.7	-1.2	3.1
Feb	-7.8	6.1	0.7	2.0	2.7	4.0	4.7	4.1	-1.0	1.7
Mar	-2.5	6.3	0.2	1.7	3.7	3.5	5.9	5.0	3.2	3.5
Apr	-5.7	9.4	-1.5	0.4	2.4	4.1	5.5	5.2	3.8	2.6
May	-5.8	9.5	1.4	0.8	4.5	1.1	5.3	4.3	3.2	1.9
Jun	-11.9	10.4	0.1	4.1	4.6	1.6	5.6	4.3	4.0	1.8
Jul	-8.9	9.0	–	3.9	5.1	1.9	6.2	4.8	4.8	2.7
Aug	-8.7	9.7	0.4	6.4	3.8	2.3	5.2	4.0	4.6	2.0
Sep	-6.7	7.1	0.7	3.5	1.9	1.7	4.2	4.4	6.9	1.8
Oct	-1.7	8.4	1.7	3.8	3.3	2.8	4.2	5.1	10.0	1.4
Nov	2.0	7.0	2.0	1.7	4.5	2.8	4.2	4.6	9.2	1.6
Dec	-4.2	6.3	2.5	-1.8	4.7	3.6	4.5	4.4	7.2	1.3
2008 Jan	-3.2	9.2	2.1	0.8	3.8	5.5	3.6	3.9	7.0	0.6
Feb	3.1	10.2	3.8	-1.8	4.7	4.3	3.1	3.8	6.4	2.6

7.23
continued

Average earnings index:[1] all employee jobs: by industry
Great Britain
Not seasonally adjusted

Indices (2000=100)

	Wholesale trade	Retail trade and repairs	Hotels and restaurants	Transport, storage and communication	Financial interm-ediation	Real estate renting and business activities	Public admini-stration	Education	Health and social work	Other services
Excluding bonuses										
SIC 1992	(G:51)	(G:50,52)	(H)	(I)	(J)	(K)	(L)	(M)	(N)	(O)
	JVVJ	JVVK	JVVL	JVVM	JVVN	JVVO	JVVP	JVVQ	JVVR	JVVS
2006	121.9	118.8	133.2	126.8	125.3	127.8	128.3	128.7	137.5	121.8
2007	127.2	122.3	140.3	130.0	128.6	133.7	130.7	134.0	142.7	126.0
2005 Jul	118.0	117.8	127.1	123.9	121.8	123.5	124.3	124.5	133.0	121.3
Aug	118.1	118.3	127.3	123.4	121.1	123.0	124.7	126.1	132.9	118.8
Sep	118.0	115.8	126.2	125.8	119.5	123.2	125.3	126.8	132.9	118.6
Oct	119.1	116.0	126.7	124.9	121.0	123.7	125.4	126.3	133.2	115.4
Nov	119.1	115.2	127.4	125.2	121.3	124.3	125.7	124.9	135.0	116.8
Dec	119.3	115.4	132.5	126.4	123.3	124.7	126.9	125.4	134.7	119.8
2006 Jan	119.8	117.9	127.2	124.9	123.9	126.3	126.0	124.8	135.3	120.0
Feb	119.8	115.8	127.8	124.6	123.1	125.4	129.5	125.0	135.9	118.8
Mar	119.8	116.6	130.9	125.3	123.9	126.2	127.5	125.8	136.2	120.2
Apr	120.9	117.9	131.8	127.2	126.4	127.3	127.9	127.8	136.5	122.0
May	120.9	120.0	133.1	127.5	126.5	127.3	127.9	127.1	137.2	122.3
Jun	122.1	118.5	132.1	127.9	125.7	128.0	128.4	127.6	138.7	124.6
Jul	122.0	119.2	134.0	126.8	125.8	128.0	128.5	128.8	138.7	123.0
Aug	122.1	120.1	134.1	126.8	125.6	128.1	127.2	131.6	137.7	122.7
Sep	122.4	120.5	134.7	128.3	124.9	128.3	128.4	132.2	137.7	121.4
Oct	123.6	120.5	136.2	127.0	126.3	129.3	128.2	131.3	137.8	121.2
Nov	124.4	118.7	136.1	127.4	125.8	129.4	128.8	130.9	139.4	122.3
Dec	125.3	119.7	139.8	128.0	125.8	130.1	131.4	131.4	139.2	123.3
2007 Jan	124.8	122.0	135.9	127.7	127.1	130.9	129.2	130.4	139.8	124.1
Feb	125.0	119.6	137.2	127.7	127.5	131.5	129.6	130.2	139.3	123.1
Mar	126.3	120.9	138.1	128.2	126.3	132.5	129.4	130.5	139.8	122.7
Apr	126.8	123.7	137.6	129.0	127.7	132.6	130.2	132.6	141.0	123.3
May	127.0	122.7	140.6	130.0	128.6	133.9	130.2	132.5	142.0	125.8
Jun	127.5	122.2	141.0	131.0	129.0	134.0	130.0	132.8	142.8	127.9
Jul	128.0	122.4	141.4	130.6	129.2	134.2	130.0	133.8	142.0	127.8
Aug	126.9	124.1	142.4	131.4	128.6	134.5	131.6	136.2	142.8	128.1
Sep	127.2	123.5	141.4	130.4	129.2	133.9	131.3	137.3	143.2	127.3
Oct	128.0	122.8	141.4	130.3	129.8	134.9	130.8	135.9	144.5	126.4
Nov	128.4	122.1	142.8	131.4	130.3	135.3	132.1	137.5	148.8	127.2
Dec	130.1	122.1	143.5	132.6	130.2	136.5	133.4	138.8	146.9	128.2
2008 Jan	129.4	125.7	141.2	131.0	130.7	137.0	133.4	134.7	146.2	129.7
Feb	129.6	124.0	141.6	131.7	132.0	138.2	134.3	134.3	145.8	129.2
Percentage change on the year										
	JVWD	JVWE	JVWF	JVYJ	JVYK	JVYL	JVYM	JVYN	JVYO	JVYP
2006 Jul	3.3	1.2	5.4	2.4	3.3	3.7	3.4	3.5	4.3	1.3
Aug	3.4	1.5	5.4	2.8	3.8	4.1	2.0	4.3	3.6	3.3
Sep	3.7	4.0	6.8	1.9	4.5	4.2	2.5	4.3	3.6	2.4
Oct	3.8	3.9	7.5	1.7	4.4	4.5	2.3	3.9	3.4	5.0
Nov	4.4	3.1	6.8	1.8	3.7	4.1	2.4	4.8	3.3	4.6
Dec	5.0	3.7	5.5	1.3	2.0	4.4	3.5	4.7	3.3	2.9
2007 Jan	4.1	3.4	6.8	2.2	2.6	3.6	2.6	4.4	3.3	3.5
Feb	4.3	3.2	7.4	2.5	3.5	4.9	0.1	4.2	2.5	3.7
Mar	5.4	3.7	5.5	2.4	1.9	5.0	1.5	3.7	2.7	2.1
Apr	4.9	4.9	4.4	1.4	1.0	4.2	1.8	3.8	3.3	1.1
May	5.0	2.3	5.6	2.0	1.7	5.2	1.8	4.2	3.5	2.8
Jun	4.4	3.1	6.8	2.5	2.7	4.7	1.3	4.1	2.9	2.7
Jul	5.0	2.7	5.5	3.0	2.7	4.8	1.2	3.9	2.4	3.9
Aug	4.0	3.3	6.2	3.6	2.4	5.0	3.4	3.5	3.7	4.4
Sep	3.9	2.5	4.9	1.7	3.5	4.3	2.2	3.8	4.0	4.8
Oct	3.6	1.9	3.8	2.6	2.8	4.3	2.0	3.5	4.8	4.3
Nov	3.2	2.8	4.9	3.1	3.6	4.6	2.6	5.0	6.7	4.1
Dec	3.9	2.0	2.6	3.6	3.5	4.9	1.6	5.7	5.5	4.0
2008 Jan	3.7	3.0	3.9	2.6	2.8	4.6	3.2	3.3	4.6	4.5
Feb	3.7	3.7	3.2	3.1	3.5	5.1	3.6	3.1	4.6	4.9

7.23
continued

Average earnings index:[1] all employee jobs: by industry
Great Britain

Not seasonally adjusted

Indices (2000=100)

Including bonuses

	Agriculture, forestry and fishing	Mining and quarrying	Food products, beverages and tobacco	Textiles, leather and clothing	Chemicals and man-made fibres	Basic metals and metal products	Engineering and allied industries	Other manufacturing	Electricity, gas and water supply	Construction
SIC 1992	(A,B)	(C)	(DA)	(DB,DC)	(DG)	(DJ)	(DK, DL,DM)	(DD,DE,DF, DH,DI,DN)	(E)	(F)
	JVUF	JVUG	JVUH	JVUI	JVUJ	JVUK	JVUL	JVUM	JVUN	JVUO
2006	132.7	134.9	123.2	124.9	119.7	132.5	129.0	123.3	117.6	125.8
2007	129.0	144.4	122.0	131.7	123.6	138.6	135.0	128.2	126.1	129.3
2005 Jul	119.4	117.8	117.8	120.0	115.5	126.9	121.7	116.8	115.0	124.4
Aug	120.1	120.1	116.6	117.2	115.6	122.8	119.3	115.8	112.7	120.9
Sep	143.4	125.6	118.0	118.1	115.8	125.2	120.3	116.7	110.2	124.3
Oct	127.5	121.8	115.3	126.6	115.1	128.8	121.8	118.1	112.7	124.9
Nov	125.6	123.5	116.2	121.3	116.1	124.9	122.5	119.0	111.4	127.6
Dec	125.9	124.6	122.9	126.6	122.0	124.5	126.9	124.2	130.8	132.9
2006 Jan	126.1	130.8	117.0	123.7	117.4	127.8	123.4	120.4	113.7	123.9
Feb	129.2	131.0	120.8	123.6	121.2	125.4	132.1	121.0	115.7	125.2
Mar	130.5	160.6	132.4	125.5	146.2	130.5	135.4	127.2	118.8	130.3
Apr	138.9	150.4	127.2	124.4	121.1	132.3	130.4	121.8	116.9	122.8
May	137.3	130.3	122.0	124.4	112.9	130.2	126.7	122.3	121.3	123.0
Jun	139.0	128.8	122.5	125.6	115.4	131.8	127.0	124.1	129.6	125.8
Jul	134.5	126.8	122.5	125.4	114.8	135.2	127.4	123.6	119.2	125.1
Aug	137.2	126.6	120.4	121.8	114.7	130.4	126.3	124.0	115.6	121.6
Sep	133.0	130.6	125.1	122.7	117.8	135.6	127.6	121.9	114.4	125.1
Oct	127.6	130.2	121.6	125.1	116.5	139.6	129.6	122.6	114.3	125.1
Nov	121.2	136.8	121.4	125.5	114.5	133.2	130.5	123.4	116.5	127.8
Dec	138.2	135.7	125.7	131.2	123.5	138.2	132.3	127.3	115.1	133.8
2007 Jan	127.6	137.7	117.9	128.1	116.0	132.0	130.7	123.9	114.3	126.7
Feb	120.0	141.5	119.4	130.4	120.1	135.3	138.2	126.3	115.7	128.3
Mar	135.4	177.0	128.3	134.4	152.2	135.1	141.1	134.6	136.2	135.9
Apr	133.6	147.6	125.4	126.7	124.8	140.2	134.6	127.1	124.3	125.9
May	134.9	140.1	121.2	127.7	119.1	137.5	134.0	128.1	126.4	126.6
Jun	124.9	144.1	119.1	133.9	123.1	143.0	133.6	128.0	135.8	128.3
Jul	125.3	139.0	121.0	137.2	120.0	141.9	134.3	129.9	130.2	128.2
Aug	130.8	138.3	119.9	134.7	118.6	134.8	132.3	125.5	122.9	124.2
Sep	128.4	143.0	122.6	136.6	120.1	135.4	132.3	125.5	124.9	130.0
Oct	128.7	138.6	121.2	131.4	119.8	140.6	133.9	127.6	126.9	126.8
Nov	128.8	143.0	120.0	130.6	121.5	138.8	135.4	129.4	130.7	132.5
Dec	129.3	143.3	128.5	128.8	127.8	148.6	139.1	132.1	125.0	138.3
2008 Jan	130.3	143.7	119.6	135.2	121.1	142.3	134.2	128.6	125.1	..
Feb	127.0	149.7	126.6	128.5	126.1	142.3	139.8	131.3	126.0	..

Percentage change on the year

	JVYQ	JVYR	JVYS	JVYT	JVYU	JVYV	JVYW	JVYX	JVYY	JVYZ
2006 Jul	12.6	7.7	4.0	4.5	−0.6	6.5	4.7	5.8	3.6	0.6
Aug	14.2	5.4	3.3	3.9	−0.8	6.2	5.8	7.1	2.5	0.6
Sep	−7.3	4.0	6.0	3.9	1.7	8.3	6.0	4.5	3.8	0.6
Oct	0.1	6.9	5.4	−1.2	1.2	8.4	6.4	3.7	1.4	0.2
Nov	−3.5	10.7	4.4	3.5	−1.4	6.6	6.5	3.7	4.6	0.1
Dec	9.8	8.9	2.3	3.7	1.2	10.9	4.3	2.4	−12.1	0.7
2007 Jan	1.2	5.3	0.8	3.6	−1.2	3.3	5.9	3.0	0.5	2.2
Feb	−7.2	8.0	−1.1	5.5	−0.9	7.9	4.6	4.4	−	2.5
Mar	3.8	10.2	−3.1	7.1	4.1	3.5	4.2	5.8	14.7	4.2
Apr	−3.8	−1.9	−1.4	1.8	3.1	6.0	3.2	4.3	6.4	2.5
May	−1.7	7.5	−0.7	2.6	5.6	5.6	5.8	4.7	4.2	2.9
Jun	−10.2	11.9	−2.8	6.6	6.6	8.5	5.2	3.1	4.8	2.0
Jul	−6.8	9.6	−1.2	9.4	4.5	5.0	5.5	5.1	9.2	2.5
Aug	−4.7	9.3	−0.4	10.6	3.4	3.4	4.8	1.2	6.4	2.2
Sep	−3.5	9.5	−2.0	11.3	2.0	−0.1	3.7	2.9	9.2	3.9
Oct	0.8	6.5	−0.3	5.0	2.8	0.7	3.3	4.1	11.1	1.4
Nov	6.2	4.6	−1.2	4.0	6.1	4.2	3.8	4.9	12.2	3.7
Dec	−6.5	5.6	2.2	−1.9	3.5	7.6	5.1	3.8	8.7	3.4
2008 Jan	2.1	4.3	1.4	5.5	4.4	7.8	2.6	3.7	9.4	−
Feb	5.9	5.8	6.1	−1.4	5.0	5.2	1.2	4.0	8.9	−0.9

7.23
continued

Average earnings index:[1] all employee jobs: by industry
Great Britain
Not seasonally adjusted

Indices (2000=100)

	Wholesale trade	Retail trade and repairs	Hotels and restaurants	Transport, storage and communication	Financial interm-ediation	Real estate renting and business activities	Public admini-stration	Education	Health and social work	Other services
Including bonuses										
SIC 1992	(G:51)	(G:50,52)	(H)	(I)	(J)	(K)	(L)	(M)	(N)	(O)
	JVUP	JVUQ	JVUR	JVUS	JVUT	JVUU	JVUV	JVUW	JVUX	JVUY
2006	124.0	119.4	137.1	127.5	123.9	123.8	129.1	128.4	137.5	123.2
2007	132.6	123.7	143.8	131.5	130.2	129.5	131.2	133.8	142.6	129.5
2005 Jul	118.7	117.2	130.2	125.5	97.0	120.7	124.2	124.3	133.0	122.2
Aug	115.3	116.9	130.9	121.4	96.1	117.1	126.4	125.9	133.0	120.3
Sep	115.5	114.1	128.5	122.8	94.8	115.3	124.6	126.5	132.8	119.7
Oct	119.9	115.6	129.8	122.0	93.1	116.0	125.2	126.0	133.4	116.3
Nov	121.3	114.3	131.7	123.6	96.4	117.1	125.6	124.5	134.9	117.2
Dec	123.8	116.1	140.5	130.4	108.1	122.8	129.0	125.1	134.8	122.8
2006 Jan	121.1	118.0	129.9	123.6	168.7	120.9	125.5	124.4	135.2	121.1
Feb	121.4	115.6	134.7	124.1	209.8	121.1	129.1	124.8	135.9	121.1
Mar	129.6	122.2	136.5	125.7	175.6	129.8	127.5	125.5	137.1	123.3
Apr	121.0	119.3	134.5	124.3	105.4	122.9	127.9	127.4	136.4	123.2
May	120.2	119.7	138.4	139.0	103.4	122.3	127.7	126.8	137.0	125.4
Jun	123.0	120.8	134.7	138.2	113.2	124.7	129.1	127.3	138.5	124.9
Jul	123.9	121.3	136.5	127.5	103.4	124.9	131.2	128.7	138.5	123.9
Aug	121.3	119.0	136.9	124.6	99.3	122.2	130.1	131.3	137.4	123.2
Sep	121.9	119.6	137.6	124.6	96.7	122.3	128.6	131.9	137.4	121.6
Oct	124.6	120.2	139.4	122.9	97.7	122.6	128.6	130.9	137.6	120.6
Nov	126.6	118.0	140.7	124.4	100.4	122.7	129.1	130.7	139.2	123.5
Dec	133.9	118.9	145.5	130.8	113.5	129.5	134.7	131.2	139.2	126.7
2007 Jan	129.1	120.5	139.3	125.5	195.0	125.3	128.9	130.0	139.8	126.8
Feb	133.7	120.0	142.5	127.5	243.1	127.4	129.6	129.9	139.5	125.1
Mar	140.6	128.4	146.3	129.7	176.0	134.4	129.3	130.3	140.5	129.2
Apr	129.9	126.4	139.3	126.3	105.1	127.5	130.4	132.3	140.7	127.8
May	128.8	124.1	145.8	140.9	108.0	127.2	130.3	132.1	141.7	127.8
Jun	132.3	126.3	142.5	145.2	106.4	130.0	131.1	132.4	142.5	132.4
Jul	130.2	126.7	142.6	129.0	104.3	132.1	130.4	133.8	141.8	133.0
Aug	129.0	122.8	144.6	130.7	102.7	129.9	134.4	135.8	142.5	131.0
Sep	131.1	122.4	143.0	127.9	106.4	128.1	131.1	136.9	143.1	129.3
Oct	130.4	123.6	143.8	127.7	99.0	128.1	130.6	135.9	144.2	128.4
Nov	135.4	121.0	145.8	130.0	103.9	128.7	133.0	137.5	148.6	129.9
Dec	140.4	122.3	150.4	137.0	113.1	135.0	135.6	138.9	146.8	133.0
2008 Jan	138.3	123.7	144.2	129.5	196.9	131.3	134.1	134.4	145.8	135.2
Feb	142.9	125.4	149.0	132.5	247.5	132.7	134.4	134.3	145.5	136.7
Percentage change on the year										
	JVZA	JVZB	JVZC	JVZD	JVZE	JVZF	JVZG	JVZH	JVZI	JVZJ
2006 Jul	4.3	3.5	4.9	1.6	6.6	3.5	5.7	3.5	4.1	1.4
Aug	5.2	1.8	4.6	2.6	3.3	4.3	2.9	4.3	3.3	2.4
Sep	5.5	4.8	7.0	1.5	2.0	6.1	3.1	4.2	3.5	1.6
Oct	3.9	4.0	7.4	0.7	4.9	5.8	2.7	3.9	3.2	3.8
Nov	4.4	3.3	6.9	0.6	4.2	4.8	2.8	5.0	3.2	5.4
Dec	8.1	2.3	3.6	0.3	5.0	5.4	4.5	4.8	3.2	3.1
2007 Jan	6.6	2.2	7.3	1.5	15.6	3.6	2.7	4.5	3.4	4.7
Feb	10.1	3.8	5.8	2.8	15.9	5.2	0.4	4.1	2.6	3.3
Mar	8.5	5.0	7.2	3.1	0.2	3.5	1.4	3.8	2.5	4.8
Apr	7.3	6.0	3.5	1.6	-0.3	3.7	1.9	3.8	3.1	3.7
May	7.2	3.7	5.4	1.4	4.5	4.0	2.0	4.2	3.4	1.9
Jun	7.6	4.6	5.8	5.1	-6.0	4.2	1.6	4.0	2.9	6.0
Jul	5.1	4.5	4.5	1.2	0.9	5.7	-0.6	3.9	2.4	7.3
Aug	6.3	3.2	5.6	4.9	3.4	6.4	3.3	3.4	3.7	6.3
Sep	7.6	2.3	4.0	2.7	10.0	4.8	2.0	3.8	4.1	6.3
Oct	4.6	2.8	3.2	3.9	1.3	4.5	1.6	3.8	4.8	6.5
Nov	7.0	2.5	3.6	4.6	3.5	4.9	3.1	5.2	6.7	5.1
Dec	4.8	2.9	3.4	4.8	-0.3	4.3	0.6	5.9	5.5	5.0
2008 Jan	7.1	2.6	3.5	3.2	1.0	4.8	4.0	3.4	4.4	6.6
Feb	6.9	4.5	4.6	3.9	1.8	4.2	3.7	3.4	4.3	9.3

1 See chapter text.

Source: Office for National Statistics: 01633 819024

7.24 Gross weekly and hourly earnings of full-time employees:[1] by sex
United Kingdom
At April

£

	Gross weekly earnings					Gross hourly earnings				
	Lowest decile	Lower quartile	Median	Upper quartile	Highest decile	Lowest decile	Lower quartile	Median	Upper quartile	Highest decile
All employees										
	C5U9	C5UC	C5UF	C5UI	C5UL	C5UO	C5UR	C5UU	C5V2	C5UX
2002	214.4	279.1	390.9	551.8	767.8	5.44	6.97	9.74	14.36	20.60
2003	222.7	288.0	404.0	572.6	794.2	5.68	7.23	10.07	14.82	21.27
2004[2]	231.9	301.3	422.8	595.0	827.3	5.91	7.54	10.56	15.41	22.18
	230.3	298.0	419.2	590.6	814.4	5.84	7.45	10.44	15.32	21.83
2005	235.4	305.3	431.2	611.6	850.5	6.00	7.68	10.77	15.91	22.86
2006[3]	244.1	316.2	446.4	632.5	886.2	6.24	7.96	11.20	16.46	23.63
	243.8	315.2	443.6	630.5	881.6		7.93	11.12	16.39	23.49
2007	252.3	325.8	456.7	649.5	905.9	6.47	8.21	11.45	16.87	24.18
Male employees										
	C5UA	C5UD	C5UG	C5UJ	C5UM	C5UP	C5US	C5UV	C5V3	C5UY
2002	239.0	310.2	430.1	599.9	857.5	5.78	7.41	10.40	15.32	22.56
2003	246.6	320.3	444.6	622.8	881.9	6.00	7.68	10.75	15.83	23.17
2004[2]	254.5	333.3	463.0	647.8	916.8	6.21	7.99	11.23	16.42	24.08
	250.0	329.4	460.0	640.5	900.7	6.13	7.89	11.10	16.25	23.67
2005	255.6	335.4	471.0	666.0	939.1	6.27	8.08	11.42	16.88	24.74
2006[3]	264.9	347.1	487.1	689.9	985.5	6.50	8.39	11.83	17.50	25.79
	264.5	346.0	484.3	687.5	980.5		8.37	11.76	17.38	25.64
2007	274.4	358.2	498.3	706.7	1 009.6	6.73	8.65	12.09	17.92	26.46
Female employees										
	C5UB	C5UE	C5UH	C5UK	C5UN	C5UQ	C5UT	C5UW	C5V4	C5UZ
2002	192.1	241.8	330.7	474.0	623.7	5.04	6.35	8.70	12.80	17.66
2003	201.3	251.6	343.0	490.2	645.7	5.30	6.63	9.07	13.28	18.33
2004[2]	210.8	265.3	360.8	515.5	678.8	5.53	6.96	9.57	13.96	19.19
	209.3	262.3	356.7	510.0	673.9	5.50	6.91	9.42	13.82	18.96
2005	217.5	271.6	371.4	532.8	704.7	5.71	7.16	9.85	14.45	20.01
2006[3]	226.6	282.2	385.8	554.1	728.5	5.99	7.44	10.24	15.04	20.48
	226.3	282.1	383.3	550.0	724.9	5.98	7.42	10.16	14.92	20.39
2007	233.3	289.5	394.0	563.5	747.4	6.17	7.67	10.48	15.31	20.94

1 See chapter text. Employees on adult rates whose pay for the survey period was not affected by absence.

2 For 2004, two sets of figures are shown. The first does not include supplementary information and therefore is comparable with earlier years. The second includes supplementary information and so is discontinuous with previous years (where the two figures are equal, only one appears).

3 In 2006 additional methodology was introduced. Therefore the bottom data is comparable with 2007, whilst the top data is comparable with earlier years (where the two figures are equal, only one appears).

Sources: Annual Survey of Hours and Earnings;
Office for National Statistics: 01633 819024

7.25 Median earnings by age group of full-time employees:[1] by sex, 2007
United Kingdom
At April

£ and numbers

	Median gross weekly pay excluding overtime	Median gross weekly overtime	Median weekly hours (numbers)		Median gross hourly earnings excluding overtime
			Total	Overtime	
All employees					
16 to 17	172.5	..	39.0	4.1	4.45
18 to 21	254.7	29.5	38.9	3.6	6.6
22 to 29	374.9	40.6	37.5	3.7	9.78
30 to 39	483.8	56.3	37.5	4.3	12.75
40 to 49	486.7	62.6	37.5	4.8	12.76
50 to 59	452.0	57.8	37.5	4.5	11.89
60+	391.7	57.7	38.1	5.3	10.12
All ages	431.7	53.0	37.5	4.3	11.34
Male employees					
16 to 17	167.0	..	40.0	..	4.34
18 to 21	263.9	38.7	40.0	4.3	6.65
22 to 29	383.3	48.7	39.0	4.1	9.79
30 to 39	508.8	66.0	39.0	5.0	13.10
40 to 49	535.7	74.9	39.0	5.5	13.79
50 to 59	494.0	72.0	38.9	5.5	12.78
60+	406.1	64.0	39.6	5.5	10.38
All ages	464.1	64.8	39.0	5.0	11.96
Female employees					
16 to 17	180.5	..	37.8	..	4.53
18 to 21	246.9	19.8	37.5	2.4	6.53
22 to 29	364.1	28.7	37.5	2.6	9.76
30 to 39	450.0	33.8	37.0	2.7	12.25
40 to 49	407.1	31.7	37.0	2.8	11.12
50 to 59	387.8	28.5	37.0	2.7	10.54
60+	351.6	23.9	37.0	..	9.50
All ages	385.6	29.3	37.0	2.6	10.46

1 See chapter text. Employees on adult rates whose pay for the survey period was not affected by absence.

Sources: Annual Survey of Hours and Earnings, Office for National Statistics; 01633 819024

7.26 Trade unions[1]
United Kingdom
Year ending 31st March[2]

Percentages

		1998 /99	1999 /00	2000 /01	2001 /02	2002 /03	2003 /04	2004 /05	2005 /06
Number of trade unions	KCLB	238	237	226	216	210	206	193	192
Analysis by number of members:									
Under 100 members	KCLC	16.4	18.6	22.1	19.0	19.5	19.9	17.6	17.7
100 and under 500	KCLD	21.8	20.7	18.1	18.5	19.0	17.5	20.7	18.2
500 and under 1,000	KCLE	10.9	9.3	9.3	11.6	10.5	10.7	9.3	9.9
1,000 and under 2,500	KCLF	13.0	14.3	12.4	10.2	11.0	11.7	13.0	12.5
2,500 and under 5,000	KCLG	9.7	9.7	9.3	11.6	11.0	10.7	10.9	11.5
5,000 and under 10,000	KCLH	5.90	5.10	5.30	4.20	4.80	5.30	5.70	6.25
10,000 and under 15,000	KCLI	2.1	1.7	1.8	2.8	3.3	2.4	2.1	1.6
15,000 and under 25,000	KCLJ	2.9	4.2	5.3	6.0	4.3	4.9	4.1	4.7
25,000 and under 50,000	KCLK	8.0	7.6	6.6	6.5	7.1	7.3	7.8	8.9
50,000 and under 100,000	KCLL	2.5	2.1	2.7	2.3	1.9	2.4	1.6	1.6
100,000 and under 250,000	KCLM	2.5	2.1	2.2	2.3	2.9	2.4	2.6	2.6
250,000 and over	KCLN	4.2	4.6	4.9	5.1	4.8	4.9	4.7	4.7
All sizes	KCLP	100	100	100	100	100	100	100	100
Membership									
Analysis by size of union:									
Under 100 members	KCLQ	–	–	–	–	–	–	–	–
100 and under 500	KCLR	0.2	0.2	0.2	0.2	0.2	0.1	0.1	0.1
500 and under 1,000	KCLS	0.2	0.2	0.2	0.2	0.2	0.2	0.2	0.2
1,000 and under 2,500	KCLT	0.7	0.7	0.6	0.5	0.5	0.5	0.6	0.5
2,500 and under 5,000	KCLU	1.1	1.1	1.0	1.2	1.1	1.0	1.0	1.0
5,000 and under 10,000	KCLV	1.3	1.2	1.1	0.9	0.9	1.1	1.2	1.2
10,000 and under 15,000	KCLW	0.9	0.7	0.6	0.9	1.1	0.8	0.6	0.5
15,000 and under 25,000	KCLX	1.6	2.3	2.9	3.3	2.2	2.5	1.9	2.2
25,000 and under 50,000	KCLY	8.0	7.8	6.6	6.3	6.7	6.9	7.1	8.1
50,000 and under 100,000	KCLZ	4.5	3.8	4.6	4.0	3.1	4.4	2.6	2.7
100,000 and under 250,000	KCMA	12.0	10.0	9.8	9.6	10.2	9.0	10.6	10.6
250,000 and over	KCMB	69.5	72.1	72.4	73.0	73.9	73.3	74.1	72.9
All sizes	KCMC	100	100	100	100	100	100	100	100
Total membership (thousands)	KCMD	7 851 904	7 897 519	7 779 393	7 750 990	7 735 983	7 559 062	7 473 000	7 602 842

1 See chapter text.
2 Data derived from trade union annual returns with periods which ended between October and September each year. The majority, however, ended in December. In the case of year 2004/05, for example, the data derived from annual returns with periods which ended between October 2004 and September 2005 - approximately 73% ended in December.

Source: Certification Office

Personal income, expenditure and wealth

Chapter 8

Personal income, expenditure and wealth

Distribution of total incomes

(Table 8.1)

The information shown in Table 8.1 comes from the Survey of Personal Incomes for the financial years, 2002/03, 2003/04, 2004/05 and 2005/06. This is an annual survey that covers approximately 540,000 individuals across the whole of the UK. It is based on administrative data held by HM Revenue & Customs offices on individuals who could be liable to tax.

The table relates only to those individuals who are taxpayers. The distributions cover only incomes as computed for tax purposes and above a level which for each year corresponds approximately to the single person's allowance. Incomes below these levels are not shown because the information about them is incomplete.

Investment income from which tax has been deducted at source is not always known to local tax offices. Estimates of missing bank and building society interest and dividends from UK companies are included in these tables. The missing investment income is distributed, in a manner consistent with information from the Expenditure and Food Survey and the National Accounts, to individuals for whom there is no investment income already reported by the tax office.

Superannuation contributions are estimated and included in total income. They have been distributed among earners in the Survey of Personal Incomes sample by a method consistent with information about the number of employees who are contracted in or out of the State Earnings Related Pension Scheme and the proportion of their earnings contributed.

When comparing results of these surveys across years, it should be noted that the Survey of Personal Incomes is not a longitudinal survey. However, sample sizes have increased in recent years to increase precision.

Average incomes of households

(Table 8.2)

Original income is the total income in cash of all the members of the household before receipt of state benefits or the deduction of taxes. It includes income from employment, self-

employment, investment income and occupational pensions. Gross income is original income plus cash benefits received from government (retirement pensions, child benefit, etc). Disposal income is the income available for consumption. It is equal to gross income less direct taxes which include income tax, National Insurance (NI) contributions, and council tax. By further allowing for taxes paid on goods and services purchased, such as VAT, an estimate of post-tax income is derived. These income figures are derived from estimates made by the Office for National Statistics, based largely on information from the Expenditure and Food Survey (EFS), and published each year on the National Statistics website.

For the purposes of Table 8.2, a retired household is defined as one where the combined income of retired members amounts to at least half the total gross income of the household, where a retired person is defined as anyone who describes themselves as 'retired' or anyone over the minimum NI pension age describing themselves as 'unoccupied' or 'sick or injured but not intending to seek work'.

Children are defined as persons aged under 16 or aged between 16 and 18, unmarried and receiving full-time non-advanced further education.

Expenditure and Food Survey

(Tables 8.3–8.5)

The Expenditure and Food Survey (EFS) is a sample survey of 12,096 private households in the UK, with an achieved response of around 7,000 private households. The survey was introduced in April 2001 as a result of the amalgamation of the Family Expenditure and National Food Surveys (FES and NFS). The EFS sample is representative of all regions of the UK and of different types of households. The survey is continuous with interviews spread evenly over the year to ensure that estimates are not biased by seasonal variation. The survey results show how households spend their money – how much goes on food, clothing and so on – and how spending patterns vary depending upon income, household composition, and regional location of households. From January 2006, the survey has been conducted on a calendar year basis; therefore the latest results refer to the January to December 2006 period.

One of the main purposes of the EFS is to define the 'basket of goods' for the Retail Price Index (RPI) and the Consumer Price Index (CPI). The RPI has a vital role in the up rating of state pensions and welfare benefits, while the CPI is a key instrument of the government's monetary policy. Information from the survey is also a major source for estimates of household expenditure in the UK National Accounts. In addition, many other government departments use EFS data as a basis for policy making, for example in the areas of housing and transport. The Department for Environment, Food and Rural Affairs (DEFRA) uses EFS data to report on trends in food consumption and nutrient intake within the UK. Users of the EFS outside government include independent research institutes, academic researcher and business and market researchers. Like all surveys based on a sample of the population, its results are subject to sampling variability and potentially to some bias due to non response. The results of the survey are published in an annual report, the latest being *Family Spending 2007* edition. The report includes a list of definitions used in the survey, items on which information is collected and a brief account of the fieldwork procedure.

8.1 Distribution of total income before and after tax
United Kingdom
Years ending 5 April

| | 2002/2003 Annual Survey | | | | | 2003/04 Annual Survey | | | |
| | Number of individuals (Thousands) | £ million | | | | Number of individuals (Thousands) | £ million | | |
		Total income before tax	Total tax	Total income after tax			Total income before tax	Total tax	Total income after tax
Lower limit of range of income					**Lower limit of range of income**				
All incomes[1]	28 900	624 000	108 800	515 200	All incomes[1]	28 500	624 900	110 600	514 300
Income before tax (£)					Income before tax (£)				
4 615	439	2 110	8	2 100	4 615	498	2 390	8	2 380
5 000	1 050	5 760	88	5 670	5 000	1 090	6 000	93	5 900
6 000	2 860	20 100	652	19 400	6 000	2 710	19 100	636	18 400
8 000	2 840	25 600	1 630	23 900	8 000	2 660	23 900	1 570	22 300
10 000	2 660	29 200	2 550	26 600	10 000	2 570	28 300	2 500	25 800
12 000	2 520	32 600	3 470	29 200	12 000	2 430	31 600	3 400	28 200
14 000	2 310	34 600	4 130	30 500	14 000	2 270	33 900	4 130	29 800
16 000	2 060	34 900	4 510	30 400	16 000	1 990	33 700	4 450	29 300
18 000	1 740	33 100	4 540	28 600	18 000	1 730	32 900	4 610	28 300
20 000	5 700	138 900	21 200	117 700	20 000	5 710	139 400	21 800	117 500
30 000	3 300	122 400	22 500	100 000	30 000	3 360	124 500	22 800	101 700
50 000	1 090	72 100	19 100	53 000	50 000	1 110	73 600	19 300	54 200
100 000	249	33 100	10 600	22 500	100 000	256	34 000	10 800	23 200
200 000 and over	91	39 500	13 900	25 700	200 000 and over	95	41 600	14 400	27 200
Income after tax (£)					Income after tax (£)				
4 615	488	2 350	10	2 340	4 615	545	2 620	10	2 610
5 000	1 160	6 510	109	6 400	5 000	1 220	6 820	116	6 710
6 000	3 390	24 800	983	23 800	6 000	3 190	23 500	955	22 500
8 000	3 440	33 400	2 490	30 900	8 000	3 270	31 900	2 470	29 400
10 000	3 280	40 000	4 000	36 000	10 000	3 160	38 600	3 920	34 700
12 000	2 930	43 100	5 090	38 000	12 000	2 890	42 600	5 120	37 500
14 000	2 500	43 000	5 600	37 400	14 000	2 460	42 400	5 660	36 800
16 000	2 110	41 600	5 580	35 800	16 000	2 090	41 300	5 910	35 400
18 000	1 720	38 200	5 620	32 500	18 000	1 720	38 400	5 840	32 600
20 000	4 900	140 900	22 600	118 300	20 000	4 900	141 600	23 300	118 300
30 000	2 270	105 700	23 000	82 600	30 000	2 280	106 000	22 800	83 200
50 000	578	53 800	16 000	37 900	50 000	601	55 700	16 300	39 400
100 000	113	22 800	7 690	15 100	100 000	119	23 800	7 930	15 800
200 000 and over	43	27 900	9 840	18 100	200 000 and over	45	29 600	10 200	19 300

8.1 Distribution of total income before and after tax
United Kingdom

Years ending 5 April

	2004/05 Annual Survey	£ million				2005/06 Annual Survey	£ million		
	Number of individuals (Thousands)	Total income before tax	Total tax	Total income after tax		Number of individuals (Thousands)	Total income before tax	Total tax	Total income after tax
Lower limit of range of income					**Lower limit of range of income**				
All incomes[1]	30 300	691 000	123 000	568 000	All incomes[1]	31 100	756 000	138 000	618 000
Income before tax (£)					Income before tax (£)				
4 745	329	1 600	4	1 600	4 895	112	555	-	555
5 000	1 110	6 090	80	6 010	5 000	1 040	5 750	62	5 690
6 000	2 760	19 500	600	18 900	6 000	2 540	18 000	522	17 500
8 000	2 950	26 500	1 600	24 900	8 000	2 920	26 200	1 450	24 800
10 000	2 760	30 300	2 580	27 700	10 000	2 810	30 900	2 500	28 400
12 000	2 470	32 100	3 350	28 700	12 000	2 550	33 100	3 380	29 700
14 000	2 280	34 200	4 080	30 100	14 000	2 340	35 000	4 140	30 900
16 000	2 050	34 800	4 520	30 300	16 000	2 100	35 700	4 610	31 100
18 000	1 790	34 100	4 720	29 300	18 000	1 880	35 700	4 930	30 800
20 000	6 000	146 000	22 700	124 000	20 000	6 200	152 000	23 400	128 000
30 000	4 090	152 000	27 300	125 000	30 000	4 540	170 000	29 900	140 000
50 000	1 270	83 700	21 600	62 100	50 000	1 500	98 800	25 000	73 700
100 000	300	40 000	12 600	27 400	100 000	366	49 300	15 300	34 000
200 000 and over	111	49 500	17 300	32 200	200 000 and over	144	66 000	22 900	43 000
Income after tax (£)					Income after tax (£)				
4 745	364	1 770	5	1 770	4 895	129	636	1	636
5 000	1 220	6 830	98	6 730	5 000	1 160	6 500	77	6 420
6 000	3 270	24 100	902	23 200	6 000	3 000	22 000	767	21 300
8 000	3 600	34 800	2 510	32 300	8 000	3 590	34 600	2 300	32 300
10 000	3 280	40 000	3 920	36 000	10 000	3 390	41 100	3 890	37 200
12 000	2 920	43 000	5 050	37 900	12 000	3 020	44 300	5 120	39 200
14 000	2 540	43 700	5 730	38 000	14 000	2 650	45 600	5 940	39 600
16 000	2 180	43 200	6 090	37 100	16 000	2 260	44 600	6 270	38 300
18 000	1 850	41 400	6 210	35 200	18 000	1 850	41 300	6 140	35 100
20 000	5 320	154 000	25 100	129 000	20 000	5 630	163 000	26 400	137 000
30 000	2 840	131 000	27 100	104 000	30 000	3 310	152 000	30 700	121 000
50 000	681	63 200	18 300	44 800	50 000	817	75 500	21 600	53 900
100 000	143	28 400	9 420	19 000	100 000	188	37 100	12 100	24 900
200 000 and over	53	35 500	12 500	23 000	200 000 and over	69	47 900	16 800	31 100

1 See chapter text. All figures have been independently rounded.

Sources: Survey of Personal Incomes; Board of HM Revenue & Customs:020 7438 7055

8.2 Average incomes of households before and after taxes and benefits,[1] 2005/06
United Kingdom

	Retired households		Non-retired households								
	1 adult	2 or more adults	1 adult	2 adults	3 or more adults	1 adult with children	2 adults with 1 child	2 adults with 2 children	2 adults with 3 or more children	3 or more adults with children	All house-holds
Number of households in the population (thousands)	3 489	3 195	3 621	5 287	2 076	1 422	1 859	2 088	830	933	24 799
Average per household (£ per year)											
Original income	4 533	12 810	19 698	39 954	48 887	9 933	40 256	45 548	39 451	45 388	28 224
Gross income	11 694	22 435	21 804	42 085	51 631	17 864	43 288	48 543	44 947	50 655	32 779
Disposable income	10 469	19 422	16 825	32 172	40 624	16 073	33 751	37 528	35 497	41 176	26 039
Post-tax income	8 629	15 325	13 773	26 541	33 161	12 559	28 035	30 996	28 655	33 325	21 277

1 See chapter text. Figures taken from the article "Effects of taxes and bene-fits on household income, 2005/06", published on the National Statistics website *www.statistics.gov.uk/taxesbenefits*

Source: Office for National Statistics: 020 7533 5770

8.3 Sources of gross household income[1]
United Kingdom

		1996 /97	1997 /98	1998[2] /99	1999 /00	2000 /01	2001[3] /02	2002 /03	2003 /04	2004 /05	2005 /06	2006[6]
Weighted number of households (thousands)	GH92	24 310	24 560	24 660	25 330	25 030	24 450	24 350	24 670	24 430	24 800	24 790
Number of households supplying data	KPDA	6 420	6 410	6 630	7 100	6 640	7 470	6 930	7 050	6 800	6 790	6 650
Average weekly household income by source (£)												
Wages and salaries	KPCB	256.30	280.20	309.20	315.40	336.70	369.30	373.90	383.90	409.70	414.80	432.40
Self-employment	KPCC	37.50	32.90	37.20	46.00	44.50	43.10	44.50	49.80	49.00	50.80	56.20
Investments	KPCD	17.70	18.70	18.80	21.80	20.00	20.00	18.80	16.70	16.50	19.50	21.20
Annuities and pensions (other than social security benefits)	KPCE	26.00	28.90	30.30	32.80	35.00	37.00	39.90	40.90	41.70	45.50	45.40
Social security benefits[4]	KPCF	54.10	55.00	55.80	58.00	60.10	64.50	68.50	72.50	76.90	78.00	79.90
Other sources	KPCH	5.30	5.20	5.70	5.90	6.20	6.70	6.70	6.40	6.90	7.40	6.60
Total[5]	KPCI	396.90	420.80	457.00	479.90	502.50	540.60	552.30	570.30	600.70	615.90	641.90
Sources of household income as a percentage of total household income												
Wages and salaries	KPCJ	65	67	68	66	67	68	68	67	68	67	67
Self-employment	KPCK	9	8	8	10	9	8	8	9	8	8	9
Investments	KPCL	4	4	4	5	4	4	3	3	3	3	3
Annuities and pensions (other than social security benefits)	KPCM	7	7	7	7	7	7	7	7	7	7	7
Social security benefits[4]	KPCN	14	13	12	12	12	12	12	13	13	13	12
Other sources	KPCP	1	1	1	1	1	1	1	1	1	1	1
Total[5]	KPCQ	100	100	100	100	100	100	100	100	100	100	100

1 See chapter text.
2 Based on weighted data from 1998/99.
3 From 2001/02 onwards, weighting is based on the population estimates from the 2001 census.
4 Excluding housing benefit and council tax benefit (rates rebate in Northern Ireland) and their predecessors in earlier years.
5 Does not include imputed income from owner-occupied and rent-free occupancy.
6 For the 2006 results the survey has moved onto a calendar year basis.

Sources: Expenditure and Food Survey and Family Expenditure Survey;
Office for National Statistics;
01633 455282

8.4 Household expenditure based on FES classification[1]
United Kingdom

		1995[2] /96	1996 /97	1997 /98	1998 /99	1999 /00	2000 /01	2001[3] /02	2002 /03	2003 /04	2004 /05	2005 /06	2006[4]
Weighted number of households (thousands)	GH92	24 130	24 310	24 560	24 660	25 330	25 030	24 450	24 350	24 670	24 430	24 800	24 790
Number of households supplying data	KPDA	6 800	6 420	6 410	6 630	7 100	6 640	7 470	6 930	7 050	6 800	6 790	6 650

Average weekly household expenditure on commodities and services (£)

Housing (NET)	KPEV	48.30	63.10	64.20	69.20	67.90	73.90	75.10	74.50	75.90	80.80	83.00	85.40
Fuel and power	KPEW	12.90	17.10	15.70	14.10	13.50	13.70	13.40	13.10	13.00	13.20	14.20	15.90
Food and non-alcoholic drinks	KPEX	52.90	72.30	71.20	71.30	71.00	71.60	70.50	71.80	70.50	70.90	69.70	70.40
Alcoholic drink	KPEY	11.40	16.90	17.70	16.90	18.20	17.40	16.30	16.50	16.00	15.60	15.20	14.90
Tobacco	KPEZ	5.80	8.00	7.90	7.00	7.10	7.00	6.20	6.10	5.90	5.20	4.70	4.60
Clothing and footwear	KCWC	17.20	24.10	25.30	26.30	25.00	25.40	25.50	24.50	24.30	24.70	23.00	22.90
Household goods	KCWH	23.50	34.30	33.60	35.90	36.60	37.70	37.60	37.80	38.10	37.50	34.40	34.50
Household services	KCWI	15.10	20.90	22.10	22.90	22.50	25.40	26.90	26.10	27.00	27.70	27.80	26.60
Personal goods and services	KCWJ	11.60	15.20	15.80	16.10	16.50	17.00	17.00	17.00	17.50	16.90	17.40	17.60
Motoring	KCWK	37.00	54.30	59.00	62.60	62.60	63.70	66.00	68.80	67.70	65.90	65.50	62.40
Fares and other travel costs	KCWL	6.20	9.90	10.70	10.00	10.90	10.90	10.60	10.80	10.50	10.00	11.40	11.10
Leisure goods	KCWM	13.20	20.40	21.70	21.60	22.10	22.80	22.40	22.90	23.30	22.60	19.90	19.60
Leisure services	KCWN	32.10	45.10	49.30	50.70	52.30	58.50	59.10	59.80	59.70	62.70	64.60	66.30
Miscellaneous	KCWO	2.40	1.30	1.30	1.50	1.70	0.80	2.10	2.20	2.10	2.10	2.20	2.10
Total	KCWP	289.90	402.90	415.50	426.10	427.90	445.80	448.70	451.90	451.50	455.80	453.00	454.30

Expenditure on commodity or service as a percentage of total expenditure

Housing (NET)	KPFH	17	16	15	16	16	17	17	16	17	18	18	19
Fuel and power	KPFI	4	4	4	3	3	3	3	3	3	3	3	3
Food and non-alcoholic drinks	KPFJ	18	18	17	17	17	16	16	16	16	16	15	15
Alcoholic drink	KPFK	4	4	4	4	4	4	4	4	4	3	3	3
Tobacco	KPFL	2	2	2	2	2	2	1	1	1	1	1	1
Clothing and footwear	KPFM	6	6	6	6	6	6	6	5	5	5	5	5
Household goods	KCWQ	8	9	8	8	8	8	8	8	8	8	8	8
Household services	KCWR	5	5	5	5	5	6	6	6	6	6	6	6
Personal goods and services	KCWS	4	4	4	4	4	4	4	4	4	4	4	4
Motoring	KCWT	13	13	14	15	15	14	15	15	15	14	14	14
Fares and other travel costs	KCWU	2	2	3	2	2	2	2	2	2	2	3	2
Leisure goods	KCWV	5	5	5	5	5	5	5	5	5	5	4	4
Leisure services	KCWW	11	11	12	12	12	13	13	13	13	14	14	15
Miscellaneous	KPFR	1	–	–	–	–	–	–	–	–	–	–	–
Total	KPFS	100	100	100	100	100	100	100	100	100	100	100	100

1 Data are based on the Family Expenditure Survey (FES) classification and not the Expenditure and Food Survey (EFS) standard classification: Classification of Individual Consumption by Purpose (COICOP). This has been done to preserve an historical time-series, as COICOP data are only available from 2001/02.

2 From this version of 1995-96 figures shown are based on weighted data, including children's expenditure. Weighting is based on the population figures from the 1991 and 2001 Censuses.

3 From 2001/02 onwards, weighting is based on population estimates from the 2001 census.

4 For the 2006 results the survey has moved onto a calendar year basis.

Sources: Expenditure and Food Survey and Family Expenditure Survey;
Office for National Statistics;
01633 455282

8.5 Percentage of households with certain durable goods
United Kingdom

Percentages

		1996/97	1997/98	1998[1]/99	1999/00	2000/01	2001[2]/02	2002/03	2003/04	2004/05	2005/06	2006[4]
Weighted number of households (thousands)	GH92	24 310	24 560	24 660	25 330	25 030	24 450	24 350	24 670	24 430	24 800	24 790
Number of households supplying data	KPDA	6 420	6 410	6 630	7 100	6 640	7 470	6 930	7 050	6 800	6 790	6 650
Car/van	KPDB	69	70	72	71	72	74	74	75	75	74	76
One	KPDC	43	44	44	43	44	44	44	44	42	46	44
Two	KPDD	22	21	23	21	22	23	25	25	27	23	26
Three or more	KPDE	5	5	5	6	6	6	6	6	6	5	6
Central heating, full or partial	KPDF	87	89	89	90	91	92	93	94	95	94	95
Washing machine	KPDG	91	91	92	91	92	93	94	94	95	95	96
Fridge/freezer or deep freezer	KPDI	91	90	92	91	94	95	96	96	96	97	97
Dishwasher	GPTL	20	22	23	23	25	27	29	31	33	35	38
Telephone	KPDL	93	94	95	95	93	94	94	92	93	92	91
Mobile phone	GH96	16	20	27	44	47	64	70	76	78	79	80
Home computer	KPDM	27	29	33	38	44	49	55	58	62	65	67
DVD player/Video recorder	KPDN	82	84	85	86	87	90	90	90	88	86	83
Digital television service[3]	GH97	19	26	28	32	40	43	45	49	58	65	71
Internet connection	ZBUZ	..	..	10	19	32	39	45	49	53	55	59

1 Based on weighted data from 1998/99.
2 From 2001/02 onwards, weighting is based on the population estimates from the 2001 census.
3 Includes digital, satelite and cable receivers.
4 For the 2006 results the survey has moved onto a calendar year basis.

Sources: Expenditure and Food Survey and Family Expenditure Survey;
Office for National Statistics;
01633 455282

Health

Chapter 9

Health

Hospital and family health services

(Table 9.1)

The courses of treatment are for the General Dental Services (GDS). A course of treatment is complete when the treatment that is required – or such of it that the patient is willing to undergo – has been carried out. A dentist in accepting a patient for continuing care (adults) or capitation (children), undertakes to provide the care and treatment necessary to secure and maintain oral health.

Deaths: analysed by cause

(Table 9.6)

All figures in this table for England and Wales represent the number of deaths **occurring** in each calendar year. All data for Scotland and Northern Ireland relate to the number of deaths **registered** during each calendar year. From 2001, all three constituent countries of the UK are coding their causes of death using the latest, tenth, revision of the International Statistical Classification of Diseases and Related Health Problems (ICD-10). All cause of death information from 2001 (also for 2000 for Scotland) presented in this table is based on the revised classification.

To assist users in assessing any discontinuities arising from the introduction of the revised classification, bridge-coding exercises were carried out on all deaths registered in 1999 in England and Wales and also in Scotland. For further information about ICD-10 and the bridge-coding carried out by the Office for National Statistics (ONS), see the ONS Report: 'Results of the ICD-10 bridge-coding study, England and Wales, 1999', *Health Statistics Quarterly* 14 (2002), pages 75–83 or on the National Statistics website at: www.statistics. gov.uk. For information on the Scottish bridge-coding exercise, consult the Annual Report of the General Register Office for Scotland or at: www.gro-scotland.gov.uk. No bridge-coding exercise was conducted for Northern Ireland.

Neonatal deaths and homicide and assault

For England and Wales, neonatal deaths (those at age under 28 days) are included in the number of total deaths but excluded from the cause figures. This has particular impact on the totals shown for the chapters covered by the ranges P and Q, 'Conditions originating in the perinatal period' and 'Congenital malformations, deformations and chromosomal abnormalities'. These are considerably lower than the actual number of deaths because it is not possible to assign an

underlying cause of death from the neonatal death certificate used in England and Wales. Also, for England and Wales only, the total number shown for Homicide and assault, X85–Y09, will not be a true representation because the registration of these deaths is often delayed by adjourned inquests.

Occupational ill-health

(Tables 9.8 and 9.9)

There are a number of sources of data on the extent of occupational or work-related ill-health in Great Britain. For some potentially severe lung diseases caused by exposures which are highly unlikely to be found in a non-occupational setting, it is useful to count the number of death certificates issued each year. This is also true for mesothelioma, a cancer affecting the lining of the lungs and stomach, for which the number of cases with non-occupational causes is likely to be larger (although still a minority). **Table 9.9** shows the number of deaths for mesothelioma and asbestosis (linked to exposure to asbestos), pneumoconiosis (linked to coal dust or silica), byssinosis (linked to cotton dust) and some forms of allergic alveolitis (including farmer's lung). For asbestos-related diseases the figures are derived from a special register maintained by the Health and Safety Executive (HSE).

Most conditions which can be caused or made worse by work can also arise from other factors. The remaining sources of data on work-related ill health rely on attribution of individual cases of illness to work causes. In The Health and Occupation Reporting Network (THOR), this is done by specialist doctors – either occupational physicians or those working in particular disease specialisms (covering musculoskeletal, psychological, respiratory, skin, audiological and infectious disease). **Table 9.8** presents data from THOR for the last three years. It should be noted that not all cases of occupational disease will be seen by participating specialists; for example, the number of deaths due to mesothelioma (shown in Table 9.9) is known to be greater than the number of cases reported to THOR.

Injuries at work

(Table 9.10)

The appropriate 'responsible person' is required to report injuries arising from workplace activities to HSE or the local authority under the Reporting of Injuries, Diseases and Dangerous Occurrences Regulations 1995 (RIDDOR 95). This includes fatal injuries, non-fatal major injuries, as defined by the Regulations, and other injuries causing incapacity for work for more than three days. As of 1 April 2001, reports are to be made to an Incident Centre (ICC), based at Caerphilly.

HSE gets to know about virtually all workplace fatalities. However, it is known that employers and others do not report all non-fatal reportable injuries. To estimate the level of under-reporting by employers, HSE place questions each year with the Labour Force Survey (LFS), asking respondents if they have suffered a workplace injury in the past year.

The results from the latest LFS show that in Great Britain employers report around 54 per cent of reportable injuries (2006/07). When compared to the previous year, these results also indicate a drop of in the non-fatal injury rate of 3 per cent. The self-employed report between 5 and 10 per cent of reportable non-fatal injuries.

Health

9.1 Hospital and family health services
England and Wales

			England						Wales				
			2002	2003	2004	2005	2006		2002	2003	2004	2005	2006
Hospital services[1]													
Average daily number of available beds	KNMY	Thousands	184	184	181	175	167	KNHY	14	14	14	14	14
Average daily occupation of beds:													
All departments	KNMX	"	157	158	154	148	141	KNHX	12	12	12	11	11
Psychiatric departments	KNMW	"	..	..	..	..	..	KNGZ	2	2	2	2	2
Persons waiting for admission at 31 March[2]	KNMV	"	992	906	822	809	..	KNGY	75	75	66	69	62
Finished consultant episodes[3]													
Day case admissions	KNLY	"	3 703	3 757	3 848	4 113	4 373	KNBZ	107	109	109	111	111
Ordinary admissions	KIBS	"	9 012	9 417	9 859	10 310	10 411	KNEO	493	503	499	502	514
Out-patients													
New cases	KNLX	"	12 879	13 431	13 370	..	..	KNBY	737	739	741	776	813
Total attendances	KNLW	"	43 765	45 120	44 768	..	..	KNBX	2 843	2 868	2 804	2 882	2 933
Accident and Emergency:													
New cases	KOTH	"	12 945	15 313	16 712	17 775	18 011	KTCO	889	916	937	942	980
Total attendances	KOTI	"	14 046	16 517	17 837	18 759	18 922	KTCP	1 005	1 036	1 059	1 061	1 090
Ward attendances	KOTJ	"	1 179	..	..	..	..	KTCQ	..	..	..	..	..
Family health services[4]													
Medical services:													
Doctors on the list[5]	KNKX	Numbers	..	..	..	..	..	KNBR	1 808	1 822	1 816	1 849	1 882
Number of GPs (exc. Retainers and Registrars)[6]	LQZZ	"	29 202	30 358	31 523	32 738	33 091	ZCMA	1 808	1 822	1 816	1 849	1 882
Number of patients per GP (exc. Retainers and Registrars)	KNKW	"	1 764	1 736	1 666	1 613	1 610	KNBQ	1 679	1 659	1 674	1 650	1 650
Paid to doctors[7]	KNKV	£ million	..	..	..	..	..	KNBP	241	269	..	..	..
Pharmaceutical services:[8,9]													
Number of prescription forms	KWUK	Millions	326	..	..	366	..	VQEU	..	..	..	..	..
Number of prescription items	KWUL	"	617	650	686	733	..	KNBO	49	51	54	57	59
Total cost	KWUM	£ million	7 162	..	..	8 542	..	KNBN	..	..	..	..	..
Average total cost per prescription	KWUN	£	12.0	..	..	12.0	..	KNBK	..	..	..	..	..
Income from patients	KWUO	£ million	423	..	..	368	..	KNBM	23	23	..	..	22
General Dental Services (GDS) and Personal Dental Services (PDS):													
Dentists as at 30 September[10]	KIAZ	Numbers	19 056	19 339	19 722	20 890	..	KIBG	927	919	927	928	1 186
Number of adult courses of treatment[11]	KIBA	Thousands	26 637	26 726	27 032	26 488	25 844	KIBH	1 886	1 629	1 689	..	1 643
Number of adults registered[12]	KIBB	"	17 281	17 064	17 374	17 237	17 670	KIBI	1 065	1 079	1 050	1 023	1 220
Number of children registered[12]	KIBC	"	6 982	6 841	6 964	6 891	7 044	KIBJ	400	397	384	389	423
Gross expenditure[13]	KIBD	£ million	–	..	..	..	..	KIBK	99	104	107	..	137
Paid by patients[13]	KIBE	"	–	..	..	..	..	KIBL	25	27	26	..	23
Paid out of public funds[13]	KIBF	"	–	..	..	..	..	KIBM	74	76	82	..	..
General ophthalmic services:													
Sight tests[14]	KNJL	Thousands	9 662	9 845	10 149	10 355	10 485	KNBD	647	646	656	674	676
Pairs of spectacles for which NHS vouchers redeemed	KNJK	"	3 472	3 520	3 624	3 678	3 765	KNBC	252	252	251	252	253
Cost of services (gross)[13]	KNJJ	£ million	304	..	..	..	..	KNBA	22	22	23	..	..
Paid out of public funds:[13]													
For sight testing	KNJH	"	166	..	..	..	..	KMZZ	11	11	11	..	..
For cost of vouchers[12]	WMPC	"	137	..	..	..	..	KMZX	9	9	10	..	..

1 Reflects data for the financial year commencing the year in the heading. Out-patient figures do not include accident and emergency figures or ward attenders which are given separately. Information on general practitioner maternity clinics is not collected separately in England but is included for Wales.

2 People awaiting elective admission at NHS Trusts in England and Wales, as an inpatient or a day case.

3 Finished Consultant Episode (FCE), is defined as a period of admitted patient care under one consultant within one healthcare provider. Please note that the figures do not represent the number of patients, as a person may have more than one episode of care within the year.

4 Welsh FHS expenditure and income is based upon cash payments and receipts in each financial year, as accrued gross expenditure is not available in a common format for all years shown in this series. Welsh Dental Services data excludes refunds of dental charges.

5 For Wales, all practitioners (excluding GP registrars and GP retainers) at 30 September.

6 GP's includes Contracted GP's, GMS Others and PMS Others. English GP data as at 30 September.

7 For Wales, includes PFMA but excludes GPFH drugs and payments to providers.

8 Welsh data are based on pricing bureau totals of prescriptions dispensed in a calendar year and paid during the financial year. Data shown reflects data for the year commencing the year in the heading. Financial year is from 1 April to 31 March.

9 The data cover all prescription items dispensed by community pharmacists and appliance contractors, dispensing doctors and prescriptions submitted by prescribing doctors for items personally administered. Total cost refers to the cost of the drug less discounts and includes on cost allowance, dispensing fees, container allowance, oxygen payments and VAT. Income from patients relates to financial years and from 2001/2002 is taken from HA annual accounts. Previous years taken from the Appropriation Account. Income includes charges retained by pharmacists & dispensing doctors, sales of pre-payment certificates and recoveries from patients.

10 Dentist consist of principals, assistants and trainees. Information on NHS dentistry in the community dental services, in hospitals and prisons are excluded.

11 Data shown reflect data for the financial year ending in the year in the heading.

12 Personal Dental Services (PDS) schemes had varying registrations periods. To ensure comparibility with corresponding General Dental Services (GDS) data, PDS registrations are estimated using "proxy registrations", namely the number of patients seen by PDS practices in the previous 15 months. PDS proxy registrations were not estimated for the periods before September 2003 - actual registrations were used before this date.

13 Figures for England are based on provisional outturn figures, with gross expenditure and patient figures having been adjusted from previous publications to include refunds of dental charges. For Wales, figures are for the financial year and based on the Appropriation account.

14 Number of NHS sight tests paid for by FHSAs/HAs in the period.

Sources: Department of Health;
The Information Centre for health and social care;
NHS Business Services Authority;
Welsh Assembly Government

9.2 Hospital and primary care services
Scotland

			1996	1997	1998	1999	2000	2001	2002	2003	2004	2005	2006
Hospital and community services													
In-patients:[1,2]													
Average available staffed beds	KDEA	Thousands	40.6	38.4	36.8	35.2	33.5	32.1	30.9	29.8	28.9	28.1	27.4
Average occupied beds:													
All departments	KDEB	"	32.8	30.9	29.5	28.2	26.9	25.8	25.1	24.2	23.2	22.5	22.1
Psychiatric and learning disability	KDEC	"	11.7	10.8	10.0	9.1	8.3	7.6	7.0	6.4	5.9	5.5	5.2
Discharges or deaths[3]	KDED	"	973	965	978	977	965	957	952	939	968	1 003	1 014
Outpatients:[2,4]													
New cases	KDEE	"	2 666	2 675	2 715	2 734	2 766	2 748	2 728	2 730	2 748	2 720	2 763
Total attendances	KDEF	"	6 338	6 272	6 331	6 424	6 451	6 381	6 254	6 192	6 144	5 990	6 083
Medical and dental staff:[5]	JYXO	Numbers	8 699	9 018	9 081	9 273	9 325	9 644	10 256	10 407	10 658	10 871	11 201
Whole-time	KDEG	"	6 729	7 024	7 057	7 185	7 216	7 530	8 115	8 349	8 612	8 796	9 201
Part-time	KDEH	"	1 461	1 510	1 550	1 632	1 648	1 681	1 697	1 636	1 630	1 670	1 607
Honorary	JYXN	"	534	521	506	495	495	468	468	437	431	418	411
Professional and technical staff:[6]													
Whole-time	KDEI	"	10 584	10 740	10 884	11 261	11 261	11 705	12 265	12 942	13 258	13 750	14 323
Part-time	KDEJ	"	4 370	4 738	4 928	5 218	5 483	5 852	6 273	6 708	6 968	7 440	7 990
Nursing and midwifery staff:[7]													
Whole-time	KDEK	"	32 560	32 218	32 156	32 356	32 401	33 334	34 294	34 939	35 338	36 093	37 104
Part-time	KDEL	"	29 917	29 736	29 178	29 242	29 131	29 004	29 015	29 354	29 484	29 688	29 995
Administrative and clerical staff:[8]													
Whole-time	KDEM	"	15 155	14 707	14 564	14 541	14 710	15 361	16 200	17 260	17 806	18 434	18 907
Part-time	KDEN	"	6 986	7 174	7 265	7 456	7 677	8 075	8 630	9 307	9 943	10 707	11 375
Domestic, transport, etc, staff:[9]													
Whole-time	KDEO		8 596	8 187	8 090	7 972	7 848	7 625	7 768	8 234	8 305	8 516	8 697
Part-time	KDEP		13 554	13 082	12 716	12 424	12 272	11 522	11 915	12 588	12 324	12 545	12 675
Primary care services													
Medical services													
Doctors on the list:[11]													
Principals[12]	KDET	Numbers	3 581	3 631	3 666	3 702	3 710	3 761	3 769	3 805	3 782	3 801	3 807
Assistants	KDEU	"	62	70	85	88	99	108	114	155	188	267	330
Average number of patients per principal doctor[13]	KDEV	"	1 499	1 476	1 462	1 449	1 441	1 423	1 418	1 404	1 421	1 418	1 421
Payments to doctor[14]	KDEW	£ million	333.2	356.4	365.9	377.5	404.7	429.6	467.5	519.0	628.4	701.0	699.8
Pharmaceutical services[15]													
Prescriptions dispensed	KDEX	Millions	54.62	56.64	58.52	60.36	62.34	65.56	69.13	71.83	74.66	76.74	79.03
Payments to pharmacists (gross)	KDEY	£ million	543.4	588.4	627.2	693.7	731.0	788.6	868.9	946.3	988.0	993.7	1 043.0
Average gross cost per prescription	KDEZ	£	10.0	10.4	10.7	11.5	11.7	12.0	12.6	13.2	13.2	12.9	13.2
Dental services													
Dentists on list[16]	KDFA	Numbers	1 709	1 710	1 739	1 786	1 808	1 808	1 844	1 869	1 882	1 900	1 936
Number of courses of treatment completed	KDFB	Thousands	2 711	2 825	3 406	3 388	3 389	3 359	3 420	3 359	3 375	3 348	3 387
Payments to dentists (gross)	KDFC	£ million	137.3	139.2	154.9	157.5	160.6	162.9	165.1	172.3	170.4	173.5	179.0
Payments by patients	KDFD	"	41.7	41.4	45.9	47.4	48.8	50.6	52.3	54.7	53.3	53.9	54.1
Payments out of public funds	KDFE	"	95.6	97.8	109.0	110.1	111.8	112.3	112.9	117.6	117.1	119.6	124.9
Average gross cost per course	KDFF	£	38.0	40.1	36.5	38.0	38.0	37.0	38.0	40.0	40.0	40.0	40.5
General ophthalmic services													
Number of sight tests given[17]	KDFG	Thousands	618	635	656	657	850	861	877	907	920	935	960
Number of pairs of glasses supplied[18]	KDFH	"	461	474	488	485	494	439	463	458	450	457	457
Payments out of public funds for sight testing and dispensing	KDFK	£ million	27.7	29.1	29.8	32.0	33.1	..	..	34.9	35.5	37.8	39.4

1 Excludes joint user and contractual hospitals.

2 In year to 31 March.

3 Includes transfers out and emergency inpatients treated in day bed units.

4 Including attendances at accident and emergency consultant clinics.

5 As at 30 September. Figures exclude officers holding honorary locum appointments. Part-time includes maximum part-time appointments. There is an element of double counting of "heads" in this table as doctors can hold more than one contract. For example, they may hold contracts of different type, eg part time and honorary. Doctors holding two or more contracts of the same type, eg part time, are not double counted. Doctors, whose sum of contracts amounts to whole time, are classed as such. Figures have been revised due to coding changes.

6 As at 30 September. Comprises Therapeutic, Healthcare science, Technical and Pharmacy staff.

7 As at 30 September. Includes Health Care Assistants. Figures post 2003 have been amended due to a coding error resulting in some staff previously in this group being moved to the admin and clerical group.

8 As at 30 September. Comprises Senior Management and Administrative and Clerical staff. Figures from 2003 onwards have been amended due to the inclusion of some staff previously in the nursing and midwifery staff group

9 As at 30 September. Comprises Ambulance, Works, Ancillary and Trades.

10 These figures are for Health Boards only and do not include the 2 NHS Trusts in 1995 and 47 in 1995/96. Estimated from financial years.

11 At 1 October for 1996-2004 and 30 Sept for 2005-07. Source www.isdscotland.org/workforce

12 Performer GPs only (known prior to 2004 as Unrestricted and restricted principals)

13 For 1996-2003 this group comprises salaried GPs plus associates, assistants and 'other' GPs. Terminology changed with the introduction of the new GMS contract in 2004.

14 Average number of registered patients for Performer (Principal) GPs only. Note this is based only on GP headcount, not Whole Time Equivalence (WTE). Source: ISD General Medical Practice Team.

15 For prescriptions dispensed in calendar year by all community pharmacists (including stock orders), dispensing doctors and appliance Total expenditure on General Medical Services/Primary Medical Service NHS Scotland Costs Book, "R390" tables. www.isdscotland.org/costs. Note, the contractual arrangements for payments to many general practices changed with the introduction of the new GMS contract in April 2004.

16 Comprises principals only as at 31 March only.

17 Figure represents sight tests paid for by health boards, hospital eye service referrals and GOS(s) ST (v) claimants. From 1995, data refers to financial year, (eg 1995 data is for year ending 31st March 1995). 1994 calender year data is missing.

18 Does not include hospital eye service.

Sources: ISD Scotland, NHS National Services Scotland;
0131 275 7777

9.3 Hospital and general health services
Northern Ireland

			1997	1998	1999	2000	2001	2002	2003	2004	2005	2006
Hospital services[1]												
In-patients:												
Beds available[2]	KDGA	Numbers	9 006	8 818	8 639	8 571	8 419	8 301	8 347	8 323	8 238	8 049
Average daily occupation of beds	KDGB	Percentages	*80.8*	*81.9*	*81.5*	*82.0*	*83.3*	*84.3*	*84.1*	*84.2*	*83.6*	*83.2*
Discharges or deaths[3]	KDGC	Thousands	305	335	332	333	328	327	332	337	343	359
Out-patients:[4]												
New cases	KDGD	"	952	962	984	994	997	992	1 014	1 027	1 043	1 081
Total attendances	KDGE	"	2 084	2 091	2 111	2 114	2 131	2 122	2 161	2 175	2 221	2 233
General health services												
Medical services[1]												
Doctors (principals) on the list[5,6]	KDGF	Numbers	1 039	1 042	1 054	1 066	1 073	1 076	1 076	1 078	1 084	1 100
Number of patients per doctor	KDGG	"	1 690	1 693	1 678	1 661	1 651	1 652	1 658	1 663	1 655	1 631
GrossPayments to doctors[7]	KDGH	£ thousand	69 889	71 385	78 604	82 471	84 664	88 194	96 894	..	..	..
Pharmaceutical services[8]												
Prescription forms dispensed	KDGI	Thousands	13 246	13 489	13 454	13 666	14 277	14 622	15 158	15 283	15 860	16 393
Number of prescriptions	KDGJ	"	22 047	22 754	23 249	23 985	24 705	25 501	26 656	27 401	28 417	29 599
Gross Cost[9]	KDGK	£ thousand	236 746	248 845	266 535	278 405	303 489	327 045	362 401	382 789	390 763	408 771
Charges[10]	KDGL	"	6 784	7 007	8 183	8 499	9 074	9 597	9 798	10 262	10 676	11 298
Net Cost[9]	KDGM	"	229 962	241 837	258 353	269 906	294 415	317 448	352 602	372 527	380 087	397 473
Average gross cost per prescription[9]	KDGN	£	10.74	10.94	11.46	11.61	12.28	12.82	13.60	13.97	13.75	13.81
Dental services[8,11]												
Dentists on the list[5]	KDGO	Numbers	592	612	632	661	673	689	696	720	722	751
Number of courses of paid treatment	KDGP	Thousands	1 053	1 088	1 086	1 113	1 126	1 123	1 107	1 086	1 084	1 064
Gross cost	KDGQ	£ thousand	53 735	56 835	58 712	61 237	64 454	66 201	66 910	67 294	69 480	65 172
Patients	KDGR	Thousands	12 433	13 686	14 358	15 302	16 041	930	919	907	910	900
Contributions (Net cost)	KDGS	£ thousand	41 303	43 149	44 354	46 152	48 413	49 376	50 282	50 498	52 308	50 068
Average gross cost per paid treatment	KDGT	£	50	52	54	55	57	59	60	62	64	61
Ophthalmic services[8]												
Number of sight tests given[12]	KDGU	Thousands	227	236	305	307	326	334	346	347	360	368
Number of optical appliances supplied[13]	KDGV	"	159	179	178	181	187	190	192	189	194	196
Cost of service (gross)[14]	KDGW	£ thousand	10 271	10 303	11 509	12 035	12 738	13 473	13 981	14 395	15 868	16 280
Health and social services[15]												
Medical and dental staff:												
Whole-time	KDGZ	Numbers	2 156	2 196	2 231	2 224	2 281	2 411	2 607	2 749	2 948	3 152
Part-time	KDHA	"	1 041	1 009	1 014	580	597	626	620	627	562	556
Nursing and midwifery staff:												
Whole-time	KDHB	"	10 114	10 117	10 135	9 926	9 828	10 248	10 729	11 137	11 416	11 477
Part-time	KDHC	"	9 015	8 287	8 813	7 591	7 814	8 395	8 706	8 887	9 047	9 107
Administrative and clerical staff:												
Whole-time	KDHD	"	6 915	7 019	7 230	7 373	7 536	7 966	8 370	8 846	9 047	9 113
Part-time	KDHE	"	2 708	2 776	2 910	2 972	3 136	3 372	3 609	3 858	4 190	4 249
Professional and technical staff:												
Whole-time	KDHF	"	2 933	3 014	3 177	3 642	3 762	3 975	4 163	4 528	4 695	4 772
Part-time	KDHG	"	1 060	1 146	1 226	1 283	1 369	1 499	1 616	1 731	1 827	2 032
Social services staff(excluding casual home helps):												
Whole-time	KDHH	"	3 349	3 262	3 319	3 017	3 127	3 284	3 461	3 716	3 777	3 893
Part-time	KDHI	"	2 394	2 241	2 358	868	911	986	1 105	1 207	1 297	1 429
Ancillary and other staff:												
Whole-time	KDHJ	"	3 569	3 423	3 426	3 506	3 472	3 426	3 418	3 470	3 725	3 836
Part-time	KDHK	"	3 482	3 558	3 913	4 508	4 925	5 125	5 420	5 588	5 498	5 904
Cost of services (gross)[14]	KDHL	£ thousand	1 153 741	1 292 348	1 422 920	1 576 657	1 639 283	1 868 538	2 113 453	..	..	..
Payments by recipients	KDHM	Thousands	49 498	59 484	65 533	71 411	78 478	88 860	87 999	..	..	..
Payments out of public funds	KDHN	£ thousand	1 104 243	1 232 864	1 357 387	1 505 246	1 560 805	1 779 678	2 025 454	..	..	..

1 Financial Year.
2 Average available beds in wards open overnight during the year.
3 Includes transfers to other hospitals.
4 Includes consultant outpatient clinics and Accident and Emergency departments.
5 At beginning of period for Dentists. Doctors numbers at 2002 (Oct), 2003 (Nov), 2004, 2005 & 2006 (Oct).
6 From 2003 onwards (UPE's).
7 These costs refer to the majority of non-cash limited services: further expenditure under GMS is allocated through HSS Boards on a cash limited basis. Change between 2002 and 2003 is due to advance payments being made in relation to the new GMS contract introduced in April 2004.
8 From 1995 onwards figures are taken from financial year.
9 Gross cost is defined as net ingredient costs plus on-cost, fees and other payments.
10 Excludes amount paid by patients for pre-payment certificates.
11 Due to changes in the Dental Contract which came into force in October 1990 dentists are paid under a combination of headings relating to Capitation and Continuing Care patients. Prior to this, payment was simply on an item of service basis.

12 Excluding sight tests given in hospitals and under the school health service and in the home.
13 Relates to the number of vouchers supplied and excludes repair/replace spectacles.
14 Figures relate to the costs of the hospital, community health and personal social services, and have been estimated from financial year data.
15 Workforce figures until 1999 refer to 31st December and are taken from the Trust and Board payroll system. Figures from 2000 onwards are at 30th September and are taken from the Trust and Board Human Resource Management Systems. Figures for 2000 onwards exclude all home helps and all agency/bank staff but include Ambulance and Works staff in the Ancillary & Other Staff category. As a result, backward comparison of the workforce is not advisable as definitions differ. Some figures for 2000 have been revised.

Sources: Central Services Agency Northern Ireland: 028 9032 4431;
Dept of Health, Social Services & Public Safety Northern Ireland: 028 9052 2509;
(Figures on Hospital Services: 028 9052 2800)

9.4 Health services: workforce summary[1,2], Great Britain

As at 30 September

Whole-time equivalent

		1997	1998	1999	2000	2001	2002	2003	2004	2005	2006
Health service staff and practitioners											
Medical staff: total[14]	KDBC	64 316	67 408	69 089	70 939	73 206	78 024	82 294	89 450	93 532	92 670
Hospital medical staff: total[3]	KDBD	61 937	65 088	66 812	68 767	71 107	76 122	80 537	87 641	13 452	92 284
Consultant	KDBE	21 699	23 139	24 250	25 067	26 106	27 951	29 566	31 628	33 844	33 390
Staff grade	KADJ	2 785	3 458	3 868	4 423	4 720	5 409	5 462	5 648	5 576	5 508
Associate specialist	KDBF	1 340	1 439	1 527	1 572	1 609	1 780	1 993	2 263	2 485	2 577
Registrar group[4]	KWUG	12 435	12 863	13 299	13 372	13 826	14 530	15 580	17 890	19 337	19 359
Senior house officer	KDBI	17 353	17 760	17 518	17 945	18 377	19 850	21 525	23 567	24 702	21 020
House officer[15]	KADK	4 163	4 287	4 364	4 518	4 560	4 944	4 985	5 276	5 637	4 892
Hospital practitioner[5]	KDBL	198	220	230	231	223	248	247	256	211	178
Clinical assistant[5]	KDBM	1 924	1 907	1 744	1 638	1 684	1 407	1 179	1 064	765	578
Other staff[6]	KDBK	38	16	11	1	1	3	–	50	542	197
Public health medicine and community health services medical staff[3]	KDBN	2 379	2 320	2 278	2 172	2 100	1 902	1 756	1 809	434	386
Dental staff: total[14]	KDBO	3 078	3 193	3 147	3 107	3 152	3 357	3 429	3 571	3 680	3 466
Hospital dental staff: total[3]	KDBP	1 696	1 807	1 816	1 781	1 816	1 944	1 981	2 021	357	3 135
Consultant	KDBQ	524	570	581	580	578	610	664	689	726	640
Staff grade	KADL	86	99	113	118	135	154	158	163	181	172
Associate specialist	KDBR	62	68	70	73	74	75	79	93	97	114
Registrar group[4]	LQMZ	..	309	314	295	311	339	329	344	388	373
Senior house officer	KDBU	491	531	496	497	513	572	584	580	616	480
Dental house officer	KDBV	58	59	68	60	61	60	38	31	28	36
Hospital practitioner[7]	KDBX	22	21	23	21	18	20	20	22	17	42
Clinical assistant[7]	KDBY	152	144	146	136	126	112	108	98	89	77
Other staff[6]	KDBW	6	5	6	–	–	1	–	1	1 137	1 424
Community health dental staff[3,]	KDBZ	1 382	1 386	1 331	1 326	1 336	1 413	1 448	1 550	401	1 423
Non-medical staff: total	KWUH	849 426	855 305	870 921	890 282	927 831	974 390	1 022 837	1 061 640	1 093 439	1 021 324
Nursing and midwifery staff:[8,9,10] (excluding agency): total	KDCA	407 760	409 045	415 786	423 737	437 417	455 361	474 263	485 180	492 391	485 289
of which:											
qualified	KSBR	298 483	299 654	303 644	309 682	320 685	335 313	349 701	360 910	368 276	369 453
unqualified[10]	KSBS	106 313	106 773	109 687	111 931	114 532	117 582	121 896	121 194	121 129	113 381
learners	KSBT	2 356	2 178	1 961	2 054	2 201	2 387	2 591	3 076	2 985	2 454
All Professional and Technical staff (excluding works)[11,12]	KSBM	120 439	123 902	128 116	131 943	138 348	146 804	155 507	164 419	171 326	174 091
Health care assistants	KWUI	19 268	22 026	22 746	24 919	30 047	33 301	36 027	37 829	39 272	37 876
Support staff	KWUJ	72 608	71 043	69 883	68 449	69 245	69 628	69 553	69 749	73 457	71 269
Ancillary, Works & Maintainance[13]	KSBN	26 037	25 131	24 468	23 962	23 013	23 430	23 820	24 708	23 438	23 132
Administrative and Estates staff	KSBO	183 112	184 711	190 421	197 327	209 004	224 490	241 634	256 412	269 131	262 919
Ambulance staff	KSBP	18 751	18 382	18 552	19 209	19 888	20 864	21 449	22 753	23 888	23 147
Others	KSBQ	1 079	906	780	746	711	512	584	590	535	549

1 Whole-time equivalent. Figures exclude locums and occasional seasonal staff.

2 Medical and dental data (1996-2004) have been revised for comparability purposes. Since 2005, data can no longer be split by sector (hospital and community).

3 Does not include England data as hospital and community staff are no longer split.

4 Includes Specialist Registrar (SpR), Senior Registrar and Registrar. The SpR grade was introduced formally on 1 April 1996.

5 Scottish figures not available 2005.

6 Includes Senior clinical medical officers, clinical medical officers, GDP/GMP grades (including Clinical Assistant (Para. 94 and Para. 107 appointments), Hospital Practitioner and Limited Specialist. Staff in these grades may also hold General Medical services, or General Dental Service appointments), Medical Adviser, Assistant Prescribing Adviser, Dental Adviser, Dental Officer, Senior Dental Officer, Assistant/ Chief Administrative Dental Officers, Clinical Director/Assistant Clinical Director.

7 Excludes bank nurses for Wales & Scotland.

8 Nursing total includes qualified, unqualified and others only. England & Wales.

9 Nursing total includes Registered and Unregistered nurses and midwives only. Scotland.

10 Excludes health care assistants.

11 GP Registrars were formally referred to as Trainees.

12 Include Therapeutic, Healthcare Science, Technical & Pharmacy staff.

13 Welsh figures not available 2005.

14 Only total figures ie, breakdown not available for 2006

15 For England data - " A new curriculum for doctors in training and equivalents was introduced in 2005 as part of the Modernising Medical Careers Programme. The workforce census now records two foundation programmes; foundation doctors in their 2nd year (F2) and foundation doctors in their 1st year (F1), which are added into the House Officer grade.

Sources: Information Centre for Health and Social Care; Welsh Assembly Government; ISD Scotland; NHS National Services Scotland

Health

9.5 Health and personal social services: workforce summary
Great Britain

		1997	1998	1999[3]	2000	2001	2002	2003	2004	2005	2006
Family Health services:											
General medical practitioners[1]											
All practitioners: total[2,3]	GPYL	..	..	36 954	37 583	38 172	38 656	40 021	41 322	42 531	40 634
All practitioners (excluding GP Retainees)	LQZN	35 204	35 618	35 957	36 233	36 761	37 283	38 769	40 273	41 650	39 813
GP Registrars[4]	LQZU	1 677	1 830	1 902	2 028	2 278	2 386	2 626	2 959	2 973	2 588
GP Retainees[5]	GPYM	–	–	997	1 350	1 411	1 373	1 252	1 049	903	823
General dental practitioners: total[6,7]	KDCQ	19 598	20 216	20 833	21 316	21 929	22 194	22 507	22 997	24 123	2 301
General Dental Service	GPYN	19 598	20 216	20 750	21 124	21 462	21 538	21 701	20 826	17 943	2 301
Personal Dental Service	GPYO	..	..	83	192	467	656	806	2 171	5 149	..
Ophthalmic medical practitioners [8]	KDCT	833	863	827	819	754	686	644	614	498	439
Ophthalmic opticians [8]	KDCU	7 790	8 024	8 423	8 742	8 650	8 761	9 123	9 349	9 599	10 228
Personal Social Services staff: total[9]	KDDE	283 000	276 000	274 000	269 400	264 000	263 300	274 000	278 300	283 600	279 400
of which:											
Home help service	KSBU	53 600	50 500	47 200	42 900	40 200	37 800	34 900	34 400	38 200	31 700
Field Social Workers	KSBX	33 000	33 400	33 900	34 700	35 200	35 900	37 100	37 800	40 800	40 100
Day care establishments staff	KADV	30 800	30 300	30 800	30 800	29 500	29 500	28 800	28 600	30 600	27 300
Residential care staff	KADW	65 400	62 100	59 200	56 600	53 800	51 500	51 300	49 000	52 200	46 400

Note Scotland GPs figures included in this totals will be slightly different to GPs 'headcount' figures published on the ISD Scotland website as GPs holding more than one contract will be counted in this table by the 'number of contracts held' in each year rather than the 'headcount' of GPs.

1 All GP data as at 1 October except England and Wales as at 30 September from 2000 and Scotland from 2005.

2 The 'All practitioners' totals do not equal the sum of their parts, having been adjusted in respect of some Scottish GPs who have posts in two separate categories.

3 All Practitioners data for1997-1999 does not include Scotland retainees as these were first collected in April 2000.

4 GP Registrars were formerly referred to as Trainees. From 2004 GP Registrars are known as Performer Registrars in Scotland and these data include Performer Registrars working in 2C practices.

5 From 2004 GP Retainees are known as Performer Retainees in Scotland and these data include Performer Retainees working in 2C practices.

6 Includes principals, assistants and trainees. Prison contracts and salaried dentists are excluded. A small proportion of dentists work in both the GDS and PDS. These dentists have been counted only within GDS figures to avoid double counting. (Data at 30th Sept for 1997-2005)

7 The methodology for reporting dental workforce information in England and Wales since the introduction of the new dental contract on 1 April 2006 is currently under review. No update on workforce figures for England and Wales will be available until this review has been completed.

8 Figures for Scotland are as at 31 March, and figures for England and Wales are as at 31 December, of that year. Count of OMPs and OOs holding contracts with FHSAs/HA's/LHBs and/ or Scottish NHS Boards to carry out NHS Sight Tests. Practitioners with contracts in both England and Scotland are counted twice for these statistics. The OMP figure for 2003 (644) includes an estimate of 22 OMP's for Scotland, the OMP figure for Scotland being unavailable for 2003.

9 Split of Personal Social Services staff are for England only.

Sources: The NHS Information Centre for health and social care;
Dental Practice Board;
Welsh Assembly Government;
ISD Scotland;
NHS National Services Scotland

9.6 Deaths: by cause
International Statistical Classification of Diseases, Injuries and Causes of Death[1]
Tenth Revision 2001

Numbers

		England and Wales				
	ICD-10 code	2002	2003	2004	2005	2006
Total deaths		533 527	538 254	512 541	512 692	502 599
Deaths from natural causes	A00-R99	515 262	519 297	493 835	494 054	482 745
Certain infectious and parasitic diseases	A00-B99	4 330	4 763	5 009	6 141	7 632
Intestinal infectious diseases	A00-A09	847	1 063	1 382	2 221	3 630
Respiratory and other tuberculosis including late effects	A15-A19,B90	443	451	388	406	432
Meningococcal infection	A39	115	118	72	86	52
Viral hepatitis	B15-B19	170	209	197	205	205
AIDS (HIV - disease)	B20-B24	198	224	209	230	235
Neoplasms	C00-D48	140 174	139 360	138 062	138 454	138 777
Malignant neoplasms	C00-97	136 777	135 955	134 856	135 252	135 635
Malignant neoplasm of oesophagus	C15	6 330	6 427	6 298	6 490	6 495
Malignant neoplasm of stomach	C16	5 588	5 285	5 098	4 927	4 562
Malignant neoplasm of colon	C18	9 504	9 152	9 130	9 076	8 954
Malignant neoplasm of rectum and anus	C20-C21	3 907	3 982	3 917	3 995	3 870
Malignant neoplasm of pancreas	C25	6 142	6 242	6 294	6 509	6 584
Malignant neoplasm of trachea, bronchus and lung	C33-C34	28 806	28 765	28 328	28 792	29 332
Malignant neoplasm of skin	C43	1 480	1 585	1 597	1 622	1 649
Malignant neoplasm of breast	C50	11 557	11 276	11 031	11 121	11 011
Malignant neoplasm of cervix uteri	C53	1 001	951	957	911	831
Malignant neoplasm of prostate	C61	8 973	9 166	9 169	9 042	9 057
Leukaemia	C91-C95	3 911	3 916	3 828	3 910	3 859
Diseases of the blood and blood-forming organs and certain disorders involving the immune mechanism	D50-D89	1 086	1 065	1 014	1 096	1 013
Endocrine, nutritional and metabolic diseases	E00-E90	7 897	8 016	7 519	7 433	7 153
Diabetes mellitus	E10-E14	6 192	6 316	5 837	5 677	5 490
Mental and behavioural disorders	F00-F99	14 444	14 846	14 299	14 563	14 863
Vascular and unspecified dementia	F01,F03	12 753	13 401	12 756	12 995	13 289
Alcohol abuse (inc. alcoholic psychosis)	F10	435	469	538	523	545
Drug dependence and non-dependent abuse of drugs	F11-F16,F18-F19	882	655	718	762	739
Diseases of the nervous system and sense organs	G00-H95	14 796	15 793	14 645	15 253	15 218
Meningitis (including meningococcal)	G00-G03	173	229	182	187	164
Alzheimer's disease	G30	4 771	5 055	4 821	4 914	4 901
Diseases of the circulatory system	I00-I99	209 433	205 508	190 603	183 997	174 637
Ischaemic heart diseases	I20-I25	102 833	99 790	92 528	88 271	82 619
Cerebrovascular diseases	I60-I69	59 068	57 808	52 899	50 772	48 389
Diseases of the respiratory system	J00-J99	69 900	75 138	69 213	72 517	68 599
Influenza	J10-J11	38	77	25	44	17
Pneumonia	J12-J18	32 631	34 400	30 649	31 443	28 674
Bronchitis, emphysema and other chronic obstructive pulmonary diseases	J40-J44	24 159	25 765	23 204	24 230	23 319
Asthma	J45-J46	1 264	1 284	1 243	1 186	1 082
Diseases of the digestive system	K00-K93	24 124	24 948	24 912	25 213	25 786
Gastric and duodenal ulcer	K25-K27	3 746	3 678	3 495	3 266	3 145
Chronic liver disease	K70,K73-K74	5 376	5 844	5 824	5 873	6 250
Diseases of the skin and subcutaneous tissue	L00-L99	1 470	1 661	1 670	1 788	1 812
Diseases of the musculo-skeletal system and connective tissue	M00-M99	4 647	4 634	4 393	4 378	4 238
Rheumatoid arthritis and juvenile arthritis	M05-M06,M08	966	907	794	835	743
Osteoporosis	M80-M81	1 605	1 583	1 478	1 416	1 390
Diseases of the genito-urinary system	N00-N99	8 452	9 120	9 397	10 231	10 722
Diseases of the kidney and ureter	N00-N29	4 072	4 135	4 024	3 967	3 988
Complications of pregnancy, childbirth and the puerperium	O00-O99	34	45	46	36	41
Certain conditions originating in the perinatal period (excluding neonatals)[1]	P00-P96	208	207	213	205	160
Congenital malformations, deformations and chromosomal abnormalities (excluding neonatals)[1]	Q00-Q99	1 233	1 299	1 274	1 292	1 214
Congenital malformations of the nervous system	Q00-Q07	127	142	116	123	117
Congenital malformations of the circulatory system	Q20-Q28	541	540	527	535	484
Symptoms, signs and abnormal clinical and laboratory findings not elsewhere classified	R00-R99	13 034	12 894	11 566	11 457	10 880
Senility without mention of psychosis (old age)	R54	11 645	11 394	9 905	9 785	9 169
Sudden infant death syndrome	R95	137	136	148	164	143
Deaths from external causes	V01-Y89	16 139	16 693	16 497	16 411	17 509
All accidents	V01-X59,Y85,Y86	10 382	10 979	10 735	11 053	11 824
Land transport accidents	V01-V89	2 929	2 943	2 693	2 697	2 990
Accidental falls	W00-W19	2 509	2 732	2 915	3 006	3 226
Accidental poisonings	X40-X49	814	835	927	910	1 072
Suicide and intentional self-harm	X60-X84,Y87.0	3 269	3 270	3 306	3 172	3 331
Homicide and assault[1]	X85-Y09,Y87.1	373	318	363	326	342
Event of undetermined intent	Y10-Y34, Y87.2	1 754	1 776	1 685	1 486	1 616

Health

9.6
Deaths: by cause
International Statistical Classification of Diseases, Injuries and Causes of Death[1]
continued   Tenth Revision 2001

Numbers

		Scotland				
	ICD-10 code	2002	2003	2004	2005	2006
Total deaths		58 103	58 472	56 187	55 747	55 093
Deaths from natural causes	A00-R99	55 689	56 161	53 759	53 535	52 856
Certain infectious and parasitic diseases	A00-B99	651	660	688	719	791
Intestinal infectious diseases	A00-A09	96	85	104	99	128
Respiratory and other tuberculosis including late effects	A15-A19,B90	52	59	52	49	43
Meningococcal infection	A39	13	5	8	4	6
Viral hepatitis	B15-B19	13	23	20	16	20
AIDS (HIV - disease)	B20-B24	33	33	16	31	19
Neoplasms	C00-D48	15 391	15 412	15 336	15 408	15 360
Malignant neoplasms	C00-C97	15 051	15 116	15 047	15 135	15 084
Malignant neoplasm of oesophagus	C15	763	776	801	798	765
Malignant neoplasm of stomach	C16	621	579	615	590	552
Malignant neoplasm of colon	C18	975	966	917	966	922
Malignant neoplasm of rectum and anus	C20-21	384	368	383	367	390
Malignant neoplasm of pancreas	C25	562	641	615	603	567
Malignant neoplasm of trachea, bronchus and lung	C33-34	4 039	3 893	3 923	4 009	4 062
Malignant neoplasm of skin	C43	132	146	151	158	158
Malignant neoplasm of breast	C50	1 110	1 149	1 093	1 151	1 112
Malignant neoplasm of cervix uteri	C53	100	120	102	127	92
Malignant neoplasm of prostate	C61	775	786	802	765	779
Leukaemia	C91-C95	330	367	352	351	362
Diseases of the blood and blood-forming organs and certain disorders involving the immune mechanism	D50-D89	122	148	111	118	113
Endocrine, nutritional and metabolic diseases	E00-E90	902	958	972	988	1 018
Diabetes mellitus	E10-E14	676	709	760	745	751
Mental and behavioural disorders	F00-F99	2 446	2 637	2 670	2 454	2 817
Vascular and unspecified dementia	F01,F03	1 763	1 997	1 955	1 835	2 101
Alcohol abuse (inc. alcoholic psychosis)	F10	339	356	421	343	378
Drug dependence and non-dependent abuse of drugs	F11-F16,F18-F19	294	228	238	217	293
Diseases of the nervous system and sense organs	G00-H95	1 317	1 303	1 254	1 306	1 333
Meningitis (including meningococcal)	G00-G03	6	19	25	18	15
Alzheimer's disease	G30	388	354	399	415	452
Diseases of the circulatory system	I00-I99	22 688	22 102	20 837	20 060	18 771
Ischaemic heart diseases	I20-I25	11 692	11 441	10 778	10 331	9 532
Cerebrovascular diseases	I60-I69	6 722	6 497	6 155	5 789	5 466
Diseases of the respiratory system	J00-J99	6 806	7 454	6 743	7 093	7 183
Influenza	J10-J11	6	15	3	11	2
Pneumonia	J12-J18	2 466	2 859	2 399	2 483	2 513
Bronchitis, emphysema and other chronic obstructive pulmonary diseases	J40-J44	2 840	3 014	2 752	2 857	2 848
Asthma	J45-J46	131	98	94	100	82
Diseases of the digestive system	K00-K93	3 153	3 215	3 065	3 221	3 208
Gastric and duodenal ulcer	K25-K27	350	316	305	230	262
Chronic liver disease	K70,K73-K74	1 128	1 170	1 044	1 152	1 162
Diseases of the skin and subcutaneous tissue	L00-L99	118	131	131	127	130
Diseases of the musculo-skeletal system and connective tissue	M00-M99	384	369	350	326	354
Rheumatoid arthritis and juvenile arthritis	M05-M06,M08	133	103	107	109	108
Osteoporosis	M80-M81	59	70	52	47	40
Diseases of the genito-urinary system	N00-N99	1 013	1 056	965	1 063	1 112
Diseases of the kidney and ureter	N00-N29	627	670	574	617	578
Complications of pregnancy, childbirth and the puerperium	O00-O99	5	7	6	4	7
Certain conditions originating in the perinatal period	P00-P96	155	149	151	164	139
Congenital malformations, deformations and chromasomal abnormalities	Q00-Q99	168	172	134	159	151
Congenital malformations of the nervous system	Q00-Q07	31	23	21	15	25
Congenital malformations of the circulatory system	Q20-Q28	60	63	53	58	46
Symptoms, signs and abnormal clinical and laboratory findings not elsewhere classified	R00-R99	370	388	346	325	369
Senility without mention of psychosis (old age)	R54	191	236	193	210	206
Sudden infant death syndrome	R95	32	43	28	20	27
Deaths from external causes	V01-Y89	2 414	2 311	2 428	2 212	2 237
All accidents	V01-X59,Y85,Y86	1 315	1 326	1 390	1 284	1 264
Land transport accidents	V01-V89	321	357	325	293	326
Accidental falls	W00-W19	668	668	690	676	642
Accidental poisonings	X40-X49	37	30	57	48	70
Suicide and intentional self-harm	X60-X84,Y87.0	636	560	606	547	542
Homicide and assault	X85-Y09,Y87.1	118	101	121	80	115
Event of undetermined intent	Y10-Y34, Y87.2	263	234	229	216	223

9.6
continued

Deaths: by cause
International Statistical Classification of Diseases, Injuries and Causes of Death[1]
Tenth Revision 2001

Numbers

	ICD-10 code	Northern Ireland				
		2002	2003	2004	2005	2006
Total deaths		14 586	14 462	14 354	14 224	14 532
Deaths from natural causes	A00-R99	13 949	13 912	13 711	13 463	13 679
Certain infectious and parasitic diseases	A00-B99	134	157	149	162	188
Intestinal infectious diseases	A00-A09	11	13	16	16	39
Respiratory and other tuberculosis including late effects	A15-A19,B90	10	11	13	4	7
Meningococcal infection	A39	7	4	5	1	1
Viral hepatitis	B15-B19	-	-	1	2	4
AIDS (HIV - disease)	B20-B24	3	2	-	5	-
Neoplasms	C00-D48	3 766	3 882	3 835	3 826	3 959
Malignant neoplasms	C00-C97	3 652	3 757	3 757	3 735	3 848
Malignant neoplasm of oesophagus	C15	163	154	138	162	161
Malignant neoplasm of stomach	C16	164	165	180	161	159
Malignant neoplasm of colon	C18	270	313	286	293	280
Malignant neoplasm of rectum and anus	C20-C21	90	103	94	99	99
Malignant neoplasm of pancreas	C25	194	173	152	173	194
Malignant neoplasm of trachea, bronchus and lung	C33-C34	802	810	837	824	850
Malignant neoplasm of skin	C43	38	40	36	43	48
Malignant neoplasm of breast	C50	278	291	320	307	300
Malignant neoplasm of cervix uteri	C53	25	31	37	20	29
Malignant neoplasm of prostate	C61	193	217	241	222	212
Leukaemia	C91-C95	93	85	95	92	91
Diseases of the blood and blood-forming organs and certain disorders involving the immune mechanism	D50-D89	24	37	34	36	31
Endocrine, nutritional and metabolic diseases	E00-E90	238	246	248	302	281
Diabetes mellitus	E10-E14	187	190	189	224	197
Mental and behavioural disorders	F00-F99	411	341	370	408	418
Vascular and unspecified dementia	F01,F03	329	284	298	316	335
Alcohol abuse (inc. alcoholic psychosis)	F10	74	52	68	86	79
Drug dependence and non-dependent abuse of drugs	F11-F16,F18-F19	6	3	2	2	1
Diseases of the nervous system and sense organs	G00-H95	531	481	487	484	557
Meningitis (including meningococcal)	G00-G03	5	3	1	2	1
Alzheimer's disease	G30	246	224	251	207	265
Diseases of the circulatory system	I00-I99	5 729	5 448	5 272	5 002	4 879
Ischaemic heart diseases	I20-I25	2 948	2 843	2 775	2 708	2 556
Cerebrovascular diseases	I60-I69	1 573	1 531	1 435	1 307	1 326
Diseases of the respiratory system	J00-J99	1 883	2 082	1 950	1 921	1 982
Influenza	J10-J11	1	4	1	-	1
Pneumonia	J12-J18	951	1 025	909	895	895
Bronchitis, emphysema and other chronic obstructive pulmonary diseases	J40-J44	553	660	609	596	616
Asthma	J45-J46	36	32	44	32	35
Diseases of the digestive system	K00-K93	581	587	691	584	646
Gastric and duodenal ulcer	K25-K27	62	77	70	60	57
Chronic liver disease	K70,K73-K74	166	156	189	150	171
Diseases of the skin and subcutaneous tissue	L00-L99	21	15	19	20	21
Diseases of the musculo-skeletal system and connective tissue	M00-M99	90	93	66	95	79
Rheumatoid arthritis and juvenile arthritis	M05-M06,M08	21	26	15	28	36
Osteoporosis	M80-M81	19	16	10	12	11
Diseases of the genito-urinary system	N00-N99	333	327	364	351	359
Diseases of the kidney and ureter	N00-N29	246	225	252	210	219
Complications of pregnancy, childbirth and the puerperium	O00-O99	1	3	1	1	3
Certain conditions originating in the perinatal period	P00-P96	62	62	64	81	54
Congenital malformations, deformations and chromasomal abnormalities	Q00-Q99	53	69	61	82	84
Congenital malformations of the nervous system	Q00-Q07	7	12	10	10	9
Congenital malformations of the circulatory system	Q20-Q28	17	16	17	20	19
Symptoms, signs and abnormal clinical and laboratory findings not elsewhere classified	R00-R99	92	82	100	108	138
Senility without mention of psychosis (old age)	R54	63	63	70	71	98
Sudden infant death syndrome	R95	0	-	-	2	1
Deaths from external causes	V01-Y89	637	550	643	761	853
All accidents	V01-X59,Y85,Y86	424	364	448	492	525
Land transport accidents	V01-V89	144	120	161	175	184
Accidental falls	W00-W19	60	44	63	99	117
Accidental poisonings	X40-X49	30	30	17	40	22
Suicide and intentional self-harm	X60-X84,Y87.0	162	132	128	186	249
Homicide and assault	X85-Y09,Y87.1	27	30	32	32	30
Event of undetermined intent	Y10-Y34, Y87.2	21	12	18	27	42

1 See chapter text

Sources: Office for National Statistics;
General Register Office, Scotland;
Northern Ireland Statistics and Research Agency

9.7 Notifications of infectious diseases: by country

Numbers

		1996	1997	1998	1999	2000	2001	2002	2003	2004	2005	2006
United Kingdom[1]												
Measles	KHQD	6 866	4 844	4 540	2 951	2 865	2 661	3 675	2 726	2 703	2 326	4 016
Mumps	KWNN	2 182	2 264	1 917	2 000	3 367	3 433	2 333	4 565	20 742	66 541	15 867
Rubella	KWNO	11 720	4 205	4 064	2 575	2 064	1 782	2 002	1 525	1 548	1 327	1 402
Whooping cough	KHQE	2 721	3 669	1 902	1 461	866	1 059	1 051	509	619	679	639
Scarlet fever	KHQC	6 101	4 639	4 708	2 956	2 544	2 320	2 749	3 252	2 642	2 075	2 648
Dysentery	KHQG	2 643	2 427	1 934	1 630	1 613	1 495	1 167	1 144	1 301	1 346	1 238
Food poisoning	KHQH	94 923	105 579	105 060	96 866	98 076	95 752	81 562	79 073	78 812	78 959	79 059
Typhoid and Paratyphoid fevers	KHQB	291	249	252	278	205	254	183	277	282	300	390
Hepatitis	KWNP	2 876	3 601	3 781	4 365	4 530	4 419	5 035	5 203	5 054	5 246	5 034
Tuberculosis	KHQI	6 238	6 367	6 605	6 701	7 100	7 204	7 239	6 978	7 259	8 017	8 020
Malaria	KWNQ	1 743	1 549	1 163	1 038	1 166	1 118	866	820	634	700	637
England and Wales[2]												
Measles	KHRD	5 614	3 962	3 728	2 438	2 378	2 250	3 187	2 488	2 356	2 089	3 705
Mumps	KWNR	1 747	1 914	1 587	1 691	2 162	2 741	1 997	4 204	16 367	56 256	12 841
Rubella	KWNS	9 081	3 260	3 208	1 954	1 653	1 483	1 660	1 361	1 287	1 155	1 221
Whooping cough	KHRE	2 387	2 989	1 577	1 139	712	888	883	409	504	594	550
Scarlet fever	KHRC	4 873	3 569	3 339	2 086	1 933	1 756	2 159	2 553	2 201	1 678	2 166
Dysentery	KHRG	2 312	2 274	1 813	1 538	1 494	1 388	1 087	1 047	1 203	1 237	1 122
Food poisoning	KHRH	83 233	93 901	93 932	86 316	86 528	85 468	72 649	70 895	70 311	70 407	70 603
Typhoid and Paratyphoid fevers	KHRB	276	241	243	276	204	250	175	280	280	298	386
Viral hepatitis	KWNT	2 437	3 186	3 183	3 424	3 541	3 388	3 859	4 004	3 932	4 109	4 007
Tuberculosis[3]	KHRJ	5 654	5 859	6 087	6 144	6 572	6 714	6 753	6 518	6 723	7 628	7 621
Malaria	KWNU	1 659	1 476	1 110	1 005	1 128	1 081	847	791	609	679	613
Total meningitis	KHRO	2 686	2 345	2 072	2 094	2 432	2 623	1 545	1 472	1 267	1 381	1 494
Meningococcal meningitis	KHRP	1 164	1 220	1 152	1 145	1 164	1 020	706	646	554	579	618
Meningococcal septicaemia	KWNV	1 129	1 440	1 509	1 822	1 614	1 238	842	732	691	721	657
Ophthalmia neonatorum	KHRI	246	224	198	163	176	115	91	102	85	87	100
Scotland[1]												
Measles	KHSE	1 055	762	700	434	395	315	399	181	257	186	259
Mumps	KWNW	368	282	251	216	199	155	259	181	3 595	5 698	2 821
Rubella	KWNX	2 449	818	745	548	349	234	292	130	222	141	148
Whooping cough	KHSF	186	545	225	214	93	106	99	60	87	51	61
Scarlet fever	KHSD	750	645	883	438	301	281	376	395	213	208	269
Dysentery	KHSH	176	124	103	82	95	85	73	83	90	103	109
Food poisoning[4]	KHSI	10 234	10 144	9 186	8 517	9 263	8 640	7 693	6 910	6 835	6 918	6 987
Typhoid and Paratyphoid fevers	KHSB	14	6	6	2	1	3	4	2	2	1	3
Viral hepatitis	KWNY	360	359	490	863	943	1 008	1 165	1 159	1 063	1 002	982
Tuberculosis[4]	KHSL	509	433	457	496	469	442	418	422	463	389	351
Malaria	KWUC	70	57	30	20	27	24	17	28	20	20	18
Meningococcal infection	KWUD	201	271	313	329	301	256	175	117	147	139	136
Erysipelas	KHSC	84	95	66	64	41	39	41	28	28	17	26
Northern Ireland												
Measles	KHTD	197	120	112	79	92	96	89	57	90	56	52
Mumps	KHTR	67	68	79	93	1 006	537	77	180	780	4 556	205
Rubella	KHTQ	190	127	111	73	62	65	50	34	39	31	33
Whooping cough	KHTE	148	135	100	108	61	65	69	40	28	28	28
Scarlet fever	KHTC	478	425	486	432	310	283	214	304	228	186	213
Dysentery	KHTG	155	29	18	10	24	22	7	14	8	7	7
Food poisoning	KHTH	1 456	1 534	1 942	2 033	2 285	1 644	1 220	1 268	1 666	1 409	1 469
Typhoid and Paratyphoid fevers	KHTB	1	2	3	–	–	1	4	–	–	1	1
Infective hepatitis	KHTO	79	56	108	78	46	23	11	40	59	74	45
Tuberculosis	KHTI	75	75	61	61	59	48	68	38	73	68	48
Malaria	KWUE	14	16	23	13	11	13	2	1	5	2	6
Acute encephalitis/meningitis	KHTM	105	91	64	99	130	97	98	78	64	66	58
Meningococcal septicaemia	KWUF	67	56	87	145	123	90	98	76	82	66	75
Gastro-enteritis (children under 2 years)	KHTP	745	896	1 371	1 121	1 205	1 106	882	867	697	736	718

1 The figures show the corrected number of notifications, incorporating revisions of diagnosis, either by the notifying medical practitioner or by the medical superintendent of the infectious diseases hospital. Cases notified in Port Health Authorities are included

2 Formal notifications of new cases only. The figures exclude chemoprophylaxis.

3 Scotland's food poisoning includes 'otherwise ascertained' for the first time in 1995.

4 Figures include cases of tuberculosis not notified before death.

Sources: Information and Statistics Division, NHS in Scotland; Communicable Disease Surveillance Centre (Northern Ireland); Health Protection Agency, Centre for Infections, IM&T Dept: 020 8200 6868

9.8 Estimated number of cases of work-related disease reported by specialist physicians to THOR[1]

Great Britain

Numbers

	All physicians				Disease specialist				Occupational physicians			
	2003	2004	2005	2006	2003	2004	2005	2006	2003	2004	2005	2006
Musculoskeletal disorders					MOSS				OPRA			
Upper limb	3 359	4 189	3 654	3 324	1 477	1 534	1 521	1 499	1 882	2 655	2 133	1 825
Spine/ back	1 997	2 028	1 761	1 348	501	394	447	392	1 496	1 634	1 314	956
Lower limb	352	580	441	406	40	175	122	158	312	405	319	248
Other	176	252	221	204	68	29	33	55	108	223	188	149
Total number of diagnoses	5 981	7 161	6 205	5 343	2 123	2 181	2 204	2 127	3 858	4 980	4 001	3 216
Total number of individuals[2]	5 804	6 879	5 932	5 156	2 066	2 063	2 064	2 032	3 738	4 816	3 868	3 124
Mental ill health					SOSMI				OPRA			
Stress/ anxiety/ depression	6 529	6 440	6 063	5 609	1 705	1 804	1 751	1 423	4 824	4 636	4 312	4 186
Other	880	869	912	908	604	663	702	660	276	206	210	248
Total number of diagnoses	7 409	7 309	6 975	6 517	2 309	2 467	2 453	2 083	5 100	4 842	4 522	4 434
Total number of individuals[2]	6 747	6 801	6 396	5 879	2 175	2 282	2 223	1 975	4 572	4 519	4 173	3 904
Respiratory disease					SWORD				OPRA			
Asthma	667	555	492	592	351	386	374	448	316	169	118	144
Malignant mesothelioma	875	830	762	636	869	819	754	632	6	11	8	4
Benign pleural disease	1 094	1 132	1 496	1 258	1 082	1 120	1 481	1 246	12	12	15	12
Other	820	837	906	537	549	567	620	479	271	270	286	58
Total number of diagnoses	3 456	3 342	3 656	3 023	2 851	2 892	3 229	2 805	605	450	427	218
Total number of individuals[2]	3 357	3 249	3 609	2 977	2 764	2 799	3 207	2 760	593	450	402	217
Skin disease					EPIDERM				OPRA			
Contact dermatitis	2 617	2 374	2 285	2 395	1 668	1 750	1 698	1 799	949	624	587	596
Skin neoplasia	361	616	434	760	361	615	434	760	-	1	-	-
Other	419	325	361	389	220	215	176	295	199	110	185	94
Total number of diagnoses	3 397	3 315	3 080	3 544	2 249	2 580	2 308	2 854	1 148	735	772	690
Total number of individuals[2]	3 331	3 281	3 045	3 495	2 183	2 546	2 275	2 817	1 148	735	770	678
Audiological disease					OSSA				OPRA			
Sensorineural hearing loss	488	291	315	264	212	33	53	28	276	258	262	236
Other	170	41	48	31	146	12	22	15	24	29	26	16
Total number of diagnoses	658	332	363	295	358	45	75	43	300	287	288	252
Total number of individuals[2]	529	321	340	280	229	34	54	28	300	287	286	252
Infections					SIDAW				OPRA			
Diarrhoeal diseases	962	916	1 429	1 408	959	915	1 396	1 408	3	1	33	-
Other	181	192	149	168	160	123	121	165	75	69	28	3
Total number of diagnoses	1 143	1 108	1 578	1 576	1 065	1 038	1 517	1 573	78	70	61	3
Total number of individuals[2]	1 143	1 108	1 578	1 576	1 065	1 038	1 517	1 573	78	70	61	3

1 THOR: The Health and Occupation Reporting Network (formerly know as ODIN) comprises of the following schemes: MOSS: Musculoskeletal Occupation Surveillance Scheme; SOSMI: Surveillance of Occupational Stress and Mental Illness; SWORD: Surveillance or Work-related and Occupational Respiratory Disease; EPIDERM: Occupational Skin Disease Surveillance by Dermatologists; OSSA: Occupational Surveillance Scheme for Audiologists; SIDAW: Surveillance of Infectious Disease at Work.
2 Individuals may have more than one diagnosis.

Sources: Health and Safety Executive: 0151 951 4842/4604; statisticsrequestteam@hse.gsi.gov.uk

Health

9.9 Deaths due to occupationally related lung disease
Great Britain

Numbers

		1995	1996	1997	1998	1999	2000	2001	2002	2003	2004	2005
Asbestosis (without mesothelioma)[1,3]	KADY	166	196	191	165	171	186	233	234	235	266	301
Mesothelioma[2]	KADZ	1 317	1 322	1 367	1 541	1 615	1 633	1 862	1 868	1 886	1 978	2 037
Pneumoconiosis (other than asbestosis)	KAEA	287	223	230	268	321	279	240	271	231	214	194
Byssinosis	KAEB	6	3	5	5	6	4	2	–	3	4	3
Farmer's lung and other occupational allergic alveolitis	KAEC	10	1	5	8	9	7	7	6	7	5	13
Total	KAED	1 786	1 745	1 798	1 987	2 122	2 109	2 344	2 373	2 362	2 467	2 548

1 By definition every case of asbestosis is due to asbestos; the association with mesothelioma is also very strong, though there is thought to be a low natural background incidence.
2 For the inclusion into the Mesothelioma register the cause of death on the death certificate must mention the word Mesothelioma.
3 For inclusion into the Asbestosis register the cause of death on the death certificate must mention the word Asbestosis.

Sources: Office for National Statistics;
Health and Safety Executive: 0151 951 4842/4604;
statisticsrequestteam@hse.gsi.gov.uk

9.10 Injuries to workers:[1] by industry and severity of injury
Great Britain

As reported to all enforcing authorities

Numbers

				Fatal			Major			Over 3 Days[2]		
		Section	SIC (92)	2004 /05	2005 /06	2006 /07	2004 /05	2005 /06	2006 /07	2004 /05	2005 /06	2006 /07
Agriculture, hunting, forestry and fishing[3]	KSYS	A,B	01,02,05	42	34	34 KSZN	586	538	487 KTAZ	933	893	856
Energy and water supply industries	KSYT	C,E	10-14,40/41	2	5	10 KSZO	411	402	395 KTBH	1 565	1 344	1 347
Mining and quarrying	KSYU	C	10-14	2	4	9 KSZP	235	220	197 KTBI	722	589	605
Mining and quarrying of energy producing materials	KSON	CA	10-12	1	2	7 KSZQ	141	128	118 KTBJ	484	362	377
Mining and quarrying except energy producing materials	KSOO	CB	13/14	1	2	2 KSZR	94	92	79 KTBK	238	227	228
Electricity, gas and water supply	KSOP	E	40/41	–	1	1 KSZS	176	182	198 KTBL	843	755	742
Manufacturing	KSOQ	D	15-37	43	45	35 KSZT	6 201	5 525	5 175 KTBM	26 408	24 220	21 769
of food products; beverages and tobacco	KSOR	DA	15/16	3	4	5 KSZU	1 133	1 060	922 KTBN	6 523	5 987	5 232
of textile and textile products	KSOS	DB	17/18	1	2	– KSZV	157	132	128 KTBO	618	525	437
of leather and leather products	KSOT	DC	19	–	–	– KSZW	13	8	5 KTBP	38	30	24
of wood and wood products	KSOU	DD	20	3	4	3 KSZX	288	231	226 KTBQ	678	690	697
of pulp, paper and paper products; publishing and printing	KSOV	DE	21/22	2	1	2 KSZY	398	311	341 KTBR	1 600	1 520	1 317
of coke, refined petroleum products and nuclear fuel	KSOW	DF	23	–	–	1 KSZZ	16	22	21 KTBS	40	52	49
of chemicals, chemical products and man-made fibres	KSOX	DG	24	3	3	2 KTAE	327	261	216 KTBT	1 230	1 063	979
of rubber and plastic products	KSOY	DH	25	9	4	– KTAF	444	388	367 KTBU	1 959	1 747	1 522
of other non-metallic mineral products	KSOZ	DI	26	4	7	1 KTAG	331	280	268 KTBV	1 349	1 171	977
of basic metals and fabricated metal products	KSYV	DJ	27/28	7	5	9 KTAH	1 301	1 220	1 203 KTBW	4 122	3 921	3 846
of machinery and equipment not elsewhere classified	KSYW	DK	29	3	2	7 KTAI	332	313	323 KTBX	1 604	1 415	1 370
of electrical and optical equipment	KSYX	DL	30-33	1	–	– KTAJ	221	187	197 KTBY	1 180	1 021	936
of transport equipment	KSYY	DM	34/35	5	5	3 KTAK	534	474	470 KTBZ	2 725	2 541	2 377
Manufacturing not elsewhere classified	KSYZ	DN	36/37	2	8	2 KTAL	706	638	487 KTCA	2 742	2 537	2 006
Construction	KSZA	F	45	69	60	77 KTAM	4 496	4 472	4 430 KTCB	8 288	8 384	7 857
Total service industries	KSZB	G-Q	50-99	67	73	85 KTAN	20 008	19 280	18 964 KTCC	85 728	85 427	82 393
Wholesale and retail trade, and repairs	KSZC	G	50-52	11	16	6 KTAO	3 967	3 759	3 648 KTCD	15 355	15 020	14 067
Hotel and restaurants	KSZD	H	55	3	3	4 KTAP	1 256	1 190	1 092 KTCE	4 001	4 068	4 088
Transport, storage and communication[4]	KSZE	I	60-64	22	20	34 KTAQ	3 782	3 541	3 331 KTCF	22 303	22 035	20 439
Financial intermediation	KSZF	J	65-67	–	1	– KTAR	326	250	274 KTCG	895	747	726
Real estate, renting and business activities	KSZG	K	70-74	8	19	14 KTAS	2 694	2 573	2 471 KTCH	7 248	7 182	7 157
Public administration and defence	KSZH	L	75	9	2	5 KTAT	3 280	3 393	3 377 KTCI	16 951	16 873	16 290
Education	KSZI	M	80	1	1	2 KTAU	1 042	1 073	1 151 KTCJ	2 625	2 679	2 881
Health and social work	KSZJ	N	85	–	2	5 KTAV	2 339	2 334	2 385 KTCK	13 266	13 812	13 807
Other community, social and personal services activities	KSZK	O-Q	90-99	13	9	15 KTAW	1 322	1 167	1 235 KTCL	3 084	3 011	2 938
All industries	KSZM			223	217	241 KTAY	31 702	30 217	29 450 KTCN	122 922	120 268	114 222

1 See chapter text.
2 Injuries causing incapacity for normal work for more than 3 days.
3 Excludes sea fishing.

4 Injuries arising from shore based services only. Excludes incidents reported under merchant shipping legislation.

Sources: Health and Safety Executive (HSE): 0151 951 4842/4604;
statisticsrequestteam@hse.gsi.gov.uk

Social protection

Chapter 10

Social protection

(Tables 10.2 to 10.11, 10.13 and 10.15 to 10.19)

Tables 10.2 to 10.6, 10.9 to 10.11 and 10.13 to 10.19 give details of contributors and beneficiaries under the National Insurance and Industrial Injury Acts, supplementary benefits and war pensions.

There are four classes of National Insurance Contributions (NICs):

Class 1   Earnings-related contributions paid on earnings from employment. Employees pay primary Class 1 contributions and employers pay secondary Class 1 contributions. Payment of Class 1 contributions builds up entitlement to contributory benefits which include Basic State Pension; Additional State Pension (State Earnings Related Pension Scheme SERPS and from April 2002, State Second Pension, S2P); Contribution Based Jobseeker's Allowance; Bereavement Benefits; and Incapacity Benefit.

Primary class 1 contributions stop at State Pension age, but not Class 1 secondary contributions paid by employers.

There are reduced contribution rates where the employee contracts out of S2P (previously SERPS). They still receive a Basic State Pension but an Occupational or Personal Pension instead of the Additional State Second Pension.

Class 2   Flat rate contributions paid by the self-employed whose profits are above the small earnings exception. Payment of Class 2 contributions builds up entitlement to the contributory benefits, which include Basic State Pension, Bereavement Benefits, Maternity Allowance and Incapacity Benefit, but not Additional State Second Pension or Contribution Based Jobseeker's Allowance (JSA).

Class 2 contributions stop at State Pension age.

Class 3   Flat rate voluntary contributions, which can be paid by someone whose contribution record is insufficient. Payment of Class 3 contributions builds up entitlement to contributory benefits which include Basic State Pension and Bereavement Benefits.

Class 4   Profit-related contributions paid by the self employed in addition to Class 2 contributions. Class 4 contributions stop at State Pension age.

Under some circumstances people who are not in employment do not have to make voluntary contributions to accrue a qualifying year for Basic State Pension.

Home Responsibilities Protection

Home Responsibilities Protection (HRP) helps to protect the basic State Pension of those precluded from regular employment because they are caring for children or a sick or disabled person at home. To be entitled to HRP, a person must have been precluded from regular employment for a full tax year. HRP reduces the amount of qualifying years a person would otherwise need for a Basic State Pension.

National Insurance Credits

In addition to paying, or being treated as having paid contributions, a person can be credited with National Insurance. Contribution credits help to protect people's rights to State Retirement Pension and other Social Security Benefits.

A person is likely to be entitled to contributions credits if they are: a student in full time education or training, in receipt of Jobseeker's Allowance, unable to work due to sickness or disability, entitled to Statutory Maternity Pay or Statutory Adoption Pay, or they have received Carer's Allowance.

Credits are automatically awarded for men aged 60 to 65 provided they are not liable to pay Class 1 or 2 NICs, and to young people for the tax years containing their 16th, 17th and 18th birthdays.

Jobseeker's Allowance

(Table 10.6)

Jobseeker's Allowance JSA replaced Unemployment Benefit and Income Support for unemployed claimants on 7 October 1996. It is a unified benefit with two routes of entry: contribution-based, which depends mainly upon National Insurance contributions, and income-based, which depends mainly upon a means test. Some claimants can qualify by either route. In practice they receive income-based JSA but have an underlying entitlement to the contribution-based element.

Sickness Benefit, Invalidity Benefit and Incapacity Benefit

(Tables 10.7 and 10.8)

Incapacity Benefit replaced Sickness Benefit and Invalidity Benefit from 13 April 1995. The first condition for entitlement to these contributory benefits is that the claimants are incapable of work because of illness or disablement. The second is that they satisfy the contribution conditions which depend on contributions paid as an employed (Class 1) or self-employed person (Class 2). Under Sickness and Invalidity Benefits the contribution conditions were automatically treated as satisfied if a person was incapable of work because of an industrial accident or prescribed disease. Under Incapacity Benefit those who do not satisfy the contribution conditions in this case do not have them treated as satisfied. Class 1A contributions paid by employers are in respect of the benefit of cars provided for the private use of employees, and the free fuel provided for private use. These contributions do not provide any type of benefit cover.

Since 6 April 1983, most people working for an employer and paying National Insurance contributions as employed persons receive Statutory Sick Pay (SSP) from their employer when they are off work sick. SSP was payable for a maximum of eight weeks until 5 April 1986, and 28 weeks thereafter. People who do not work for an employer, and employees who are excluded from the SSP scheme, or those who have run out of SSP before reaching the maximum of 28 weeks and are still sick, can claim benefit. Any period of SSP is excluded from the tables.

Spells of incapacity of three days or less do not count as periods of interruption of employment and are excluded from the tables. Exceptions are where people are receiving regular weekly treatment by dialysis or treatment by radiotherapy, chemotherapy or plasmapheresis where two days in any six consecutive days make up a period of interruption of employment, and those whose incapacity for work ends within three days of the end of SSP entitlement.

At the beginning of a period of incapacity, benefit is subject to three waiting days, except where there was an earlier spell of incapacity of more than three days in the previous eight weeks. Employees entitled to SSP for less than 28 weeks and who are still sick can get Sickness Benefit or Incapacity Benefit Short Term (Low) until they reach a total of 28 weeks provided they satisfy the conditions. After 28 weeks SSP and/or Sickness Benefit (SB), Invalidity Benefit (IVB) was payable up to pension age for as long as the incapacity lasts. From pension age IVB was paid at the person's State Pension rate, until entitlement ceases when SP is paid or at deemed pension age (70 for a man, 65 for a woman). For people on Incapacity Benefit under

State Pension age there are two short-term rates: the lower rate is paid for the first 28 weeks of sickness and the higher rate for weeks 29 to 52. From week 53 the Long Term rate Incapacity Benefit is payable. The Short Term rate Incapacity Benefit is based on State Pension entitlement for people over State Pension age and is paid for up to a year if incapacity began before pension age.

The long-term rate of Incapacity Benefit applies to people under State Pension age who have been sick for more than a year. People with a terminal illness, or who are receiving the higher rate care component of Disability Living Allowance, will get the Long Term rate. The Long Term rate is not paid for people over pension age.

Under Incapacity Benefit, for the first 28 weeks of incapacity, people previously in work will be assessed on the 'own occupation' test – the claimant's ability to do their own job. Otherwise, incapacity will be based on a personal capability assessment, which will assess ability to carry out a range of work-related activities. The test will apply after 28 weeks of incapacity or from the start of the claim for people who did not previously have a job. Certain people will be exempted from this test.

The tables exclude all men aged over 65 and women aged over 60 who are in receipt of State Pension, and all people over deemed pension age (70 for a man and 65 for a woman), members of the armed forces, mariners while at sea, and married women and certain widows who have chosen not to be insured for sickness benefit. The tables include a number of individuals who were unemployed prior to incapacity.

The Short Term (Higher) and Long Term rates of Incapacity Benefit are treated as taxable income. There were transitional provisions for people who were on Sickness or Invalidity Benefit on 12 April 1995. They were automatically transferred to Incapacity Benefit, payable on the same basis as before. Former IVB recipients continue to get Additional Pension entitlement, but frozen at 1994 levels. Also their IVB is not subject to tax. If they were over State Pension age on 12 April 1995 they may get Incapacity Benefit for up to five years beyond pension age.

Child Benefits

(Table 10.9)

Child Benefit (CB) is paid to those responsible for children (aged under 16) or qualifying young people. The latter includes:

a) a person under the age of 19 in full-time non-advanced education or (from April 2006) on certain approved vocational training programmes

b) a person who is aged 19 who began their course of full-time, non-advanced education or approved training before reaching age 19 (note: those reaching 19 up to 9 April 2006 ceased to qualify on their 19th birthdays)

c) a person who has reached the age of 16 until the 31 August following their 16th birthday

d) a person aged 16 or 17 who has left education and training who is registered with the Careers service or with Connexions and is awaiting a placement in employment or training for the limited period of up to 20 weeks from the date they left education or training

Entitlement for a qualifying young person continues until the terminal date following the date they leave full-time education or approved training. The terminal dates are at the end of August, November, February and May (there is a slight variation for Scotland). Entitlement is also maintained for a person who is entered for external examinations connected with their course throughout the period between a person leaving education or training and completing those examinations.

Entitlement in all cases ceases when a person reaches the age of 20.

Guardian's Allowance is an additional allowance for people bringing up a child because one or both of their parents has died. They must be getting Child Benefit (CB) for the child.

The table shows the number of families in the UK in receipt of CB. The numbers shown in the table are estimates based on a random 5 per cent sample of awards current at 31 August, and are therefore subject to sampling error. The figures take no account of new claims, or revisions to claims that were received or processed after 31 August, even if they are backdated to start before 31 August.

Family Credit/ Working Families' Tax Credit

(Table 10.10)

Working Families' Tax Credit (WFTC) replaced Family Credit from 5 October 1999.

Family Credit was, and Working Families' Tax Credit is, available to families with at least one adult in remunerative work for at least 16 hours per week and who is responsible for at least one child under 16 (under 19 if in full time education up to A-level or equivalent standard). The rate of payment of WFTC depends on the number of such children and expenditure incurred on eligible childcare. It is also higher if the worker works for at least 30 hours per week, or if there are disabled children or severely disabled adults in the family.

It is tapered away above an income threshold. Further details can be obtained from the Inland Revenue.

Child and Working Tax Credits (New Tax Credits)

(Table 10.11)

Child and Working Tax Credits (CTC and WTC) replaced Working Families' Tax Credit (WFTC) from 6th April 2003.

CTC and WTC are claimed by individuals, or jointly by couples, whether or not they have children.

CTC provides support to families for the children (up to the 31 August after their 16th birthdays) and the 'qualifying' young people (in full-time non-advanced education until their 19th birthdays) for which they are responsible. It is paid in addition to CB.

WTC tops up the earnings of families on low or moderate incomes. People working for at least 16 hours a week can claim it if they: (a) are responsible for at least one child or qualifying young person, (b) have a disability which puts them at a disadvantage in getting a job, or (c) in the first year of work, having returned to work aged at least 50 after a period of at least six months receiving out-of-work benefits. Other adults also qualify if they are aged at least 25 and work for at least 30 hours a week.

Widow's Benefit and Bereavement Benefit

(Table 10.12 and 10.13)

Widow's Benefit is payable to women widowed on or after 11 April 1988 and up to and including 8 April 2001. There are three types of Widow's Benefits: Widow's Payment, Widowed Mother's Allowance and Widow's Pension. Women widowed before 11 April 1988 continue to receive Widow's Benefit based on the rules that existed before that date. Bereavement Benefit was introduced on 9 April 2001 as a replacement of Widow's Benefit, payable to both men and women widowed on or after 9 April 2001. There are three types of Bereavement Benefits available: Bereavement Payment, Widowed Parent's Allowance and Bereavement Allowance.

Government expenditure on social services and housing

(Table 10.20 to 10.25)

The tables of general government expenditure on social services and housing in the UK comprise a summary table followed by separate tables for each of the social services and housing categories. The definition of government expenditure used in the tables is consistent with Table 5.2.4S and Table 11.2 of the *Blue Book* 2006 Edition, and covers both current and capital expenditure of central government (including the National Insurance Fund) and local authorities.

The figures in the tables have been compiled based on the United Nations Classification of the Functions of Government (COFOG) and are consistent with the European System of Accounts 1995 (ESA95). The format of the tables was revised in the 2007 edition. As such they may not be comparable with earlier editions of the Annual Abstract of Statistics, which were based on data information supplied directly by government departments. This information from government departments is generally no longer available, as such the tables are compiled under the categories of National Accounts.

Useful links

National Accounts *Blue Book* www.statistics.gov.uk/statbase/Product.asp?vlnk=1143

UN CoFoG classification http://unstats.un.org/unsd/cr/registry/regcst.asp?Cl=4

The main categories of expenditure now used are:

Final Consumption Expenditure – The expenditure on goods and services that are used for the direct satisfaction of individual needs or the collective needs of members of the community as distinct from their purchase for use in the productive process. It may be contrasted with actual final consumption, which is the value of goods consumed but not necessarily purchased by that sector.

Compensation of Employees – Total remuneration payable to employees in cash or in kind. Includes the value of social contributions payable by the employer

Net Procurement – current expenditure less receipts for sales and charges.

Gross Capital Formation – acquisition less disposals of fixed assets and the improvement of land.

Subsidies – current unrequited payments made by general government or the European Union to enterprises. Those made on the basis of a quantity or value of goods or services are classified as 'subsidies on products'. Other subsidies based on levels of productive activity (e.g. numbers employed) are designated Other subsidies on production.

Capital Transfers – transfers which are related to the acquisition or disposal of assets by the recipient or payer. They may be in cash or kind, and may be imputed to reflect the assumption or forgiveness of debt.

Non-produced financial or non financial assets – assets produced either through production or otherwise of a non-financial nature.

Non-market capital consumption – output of own account production of goods and services provided free or at prices that are not economically significant. Non-market output is produced mainly by the general government and Non Profit Institutions Serving Households sectors.

Education

(Table 10.21)

Table 10.21 includes expenditure by the education departments, local education authorities and the University Grants Committee on education in schools, training colleges, technical institutions and universities. Compensation of employees figures are based on revenue outturn returns produced by Department for Communities and Local Government, Welsh Assembly Government and the Scottish Government.

National Health Service

(Table 10.22)

Table 10.22 includes expenditure by central government on hospital and community health, family practitioner and other health services. The figures are based on departmental expenditure reported to HM Treasury.

Welfare services

(Table 10.23)

Personal social services: this table covers local authority and central government expenditure, on such things as the aged, handicapped, homeless, child care, care of mothers and young children, mental health, domestic help, etc.

Social security

(Table 10.24)

Table 10.24 comprises both benefits under the Social Security schemes and non-contributory benefits and allowances, administered by the Department for Work and Pensions. Benefits paid overseas are also included, as are unfunded social benefits such as voluntary employer social contributions. The analysis by type of Income Support is not exact; the estimates are derived from average numbers in receipt of benefit and average amounts paid. War pensions which are now administered by the Ministry of Defence are included in this table. Child and Working Tax Credits (NTC's) replaced Working Families' Tax Credit (WFTC) from 6 April 2003 and are administered by the HMRC.

Housing

(Table 10.25)

The table shows government expenditure on housing. It includes expenditure made by the central and local government sectors, but excludes expenditure by public corporations. The Housing Revenue Account is classified as a quasi-public corporation, so that most of its current and capital expenditure and income is included in the corporate rather than government sector. All overhead and administration expenses are included in final current expenditure. Non-capitalised support for public corporations and other market bodies relating to housing is recorded as subsidies. Capital transfers are paid mainly by local government to individuals for repair and improvement of privately owned housing. Current transfers paid include insurance premiums. Gross capital formation includes that of the council houses administered by the Housing Revenue Account. This is net of any sales of housing either through Right to Buy or Large Scale Voluntary Transfers. Housing benefit in the form of rent rebates and rent allowances is not included in the table, as they are regarded as forms of social security.

10.1 National Insurance Fund
(Great Britain and Northern Ireland)
Years ended 31 March

£ million

		1998/99	1999/00	2000/01	2001/02	2002/03	2003/04	2004/05	2005/06	2006/07
Receipts										
Opening balance	KJFB	9 763	12 625	14 909	19 868	24 177	27 267	27 816	29 804	34 940
Contributions	JXVM	50 023	51 852	55 627	58 050	59 658	59 827	62 863	67 786	69 599
State Scheme Premiums[1]	C59W	..	..	..	..	194	147	115	117	76
Grant from Consolidated Fund	KOTF	3	2	..	..	..	..	..	..	..
Compensation for SSP/SMP	KJQM	576	625	688	710	775	1 346	1 470	1 392	1 197
Transfers from Great Britian	KOTG	315	230	200	110	350	260	270	185	630
Income from investments	KJFE	667	724	884	1 146	1 457	1 292	1 288	1 399	1 867
Other receipts	KJFF	92	127	112	67	80	82	72	66	54
Redundancy receipts	KIBQ	21	21	23	22	24	28	32	38	43
Total	JYJO	61 462	66 206	72 442	79 972	86 716	90 249	93 926	100 787	108 406
Expenditure										
Total benefits	JYJP	46 822	50 026	50 960	54 550	54 201	56 255	58 572	61 304	63 695
Jobseeker's Allowance (Contributory)	LUQW	489	475	449	478	519	512	455	497	493
Incapacity	JYXL	7 574	7 206	6 982	7 074	7 104	7 116	6 910	7 028	7 009
Maternity	KETY	39	40	46	57	70	128	153	128	180
Bereavement Benefits	KEWU	1 008	1 020	1 008	1 132	1 142	1 033	946	903	826
Guardian's allowances and Child's special allowance[2]	KJFK	2	2	2	2	2	2	1	2	2
Retirement pensions[3]	JYJV	38 072	41 157	42 350	45 677	45 240	47 339	49 979	52 578	55 053
Pensioners' lump sum payments	KAAW	128	126	123	131	124	125	128	168	131
Other payments	KAAZ	18	19	21	29	27	34	30	33	40
Administration	KABE	1 053	847	1 197	873	1 280	1 794	1 521	1 464	1 473
Transfers to Northern Ireland	KABF	315	230	200	110	350	260	270	185	630
Redundancy payments	KIBR	140	174	195	232	255	243	222	295	248
Personal Pensions	C59X	..	..	..	..	3 336	3 847	3 508	2 566	3 076
Total	JYJU	48 837	51 297	52 574	55 795	59 449	62 433	64 123	65 847	69 161
Accumulated funds	KABH	12 625	14 909	19 868	24 177	27 267	27 816	29 804	34 940	39 245

1 State Scheme Premiums are payable in respect of employed persons who cease to be covered, in certain circumstances, by a contracted out pension scheme.
2 Includes Child's special allowance for Northern Ireland
3 Includes personal pensions up to 2001/02.

Sources: HM Revenue and Customs: 01702 367480;
Department for Work and Pensions: 01253 856123 Ext 62436

10.2 Persons[1] who paid National Insurance contributions[2] in a tax year:[3] by sex
United Kingdom

Millions

		Total				Men				Women		
		2003/04	2004/05	2005/06		2003/04	2004/05	2005/06		2003/04	2004/05	2005/06
Total[4]	KABI	28.51	28.31	28.26	KEYF	15.68	15.55	15.50	KEYP	12.84	12.76	12.76
Class 1	KABJ	25.18	25.00	25.10	KEYG	13.34	13.22	13.25	KEYQ	11.84	11.78	11.85
Not contracted out[5]	KABK	16.42	16.83	17.10	KEYH	9.09	9.31	9.49	KEYR	7.33	7.52	7.61
Contracted out	KABL	7.36	6.96	6.85	KEYI	3.64	3.39	3.26	KEYS	3.72	3.57	3.58
Mixed contracted in/out[6]	KABM	1.41	1.21	1.15	KEYJ	0.61	0.51	0.50	KEYT	0.80	0.69	0.66
Class 1 Reduced rate (including standard rate)	KABO	0.07	0.06	0.04	KEYL	..	..	..	KEYV	0.07	0.06	0.04
Class 2 exclusively[7]	KABP	2.32	2.36	2.34	KEYM	1.78	1.79	1.76	KEYW	0.54	0.56	0.58
Mixed Class 1 and Class 2	KABQ	0.66	0.67	0.67	KEYN	0.45	0.45	0.45	KEYX	0.21	0.22	0.23
Class 3 exclusively[8]	KABR	0.18	0.15	0.10	KEYO	0.08	0.07	0.04	KEYY	0.10	0.08	0.06
Mixed Class 1 and Class 3	I6CF	0.08	0.05	0.01	I6CI	0.02	0.01	−	I6CL	0.05	0.04	0.01
Mixed Class 2 and Class 3	I6CG	0.02	0.02	−	I6CJ	0.01	0.01	−	I6CM	0.01	0.01	−
Mixed Class 1, 2 and 3	I6CH	..	..	..	I6CK	..	..	..	I6CN	..	..	..

1 Based on all persons making contributions and not only if they have a qualifying year.
2 Estimates obtained from DWP Information Directorate: Lifetime Labour Market Data Tabulation Tool which uses a 1% sample of the National Insurance Recording System (NIRS2) July 2007 extract.
3 The tax year commences on 6 April and ends on 5 April the following year.
4 Components may not sum to totals as a result of rounding.

5 Includes those persons with an Appropriate Personal Pension (such persons pay contributions at the not contracted out rate but then receive a rebate paid directly to their scheme).
6 Not included in the above rows.
7 Persons who paid a mixture of Class 2 contributions and others are not included in this category.
8 Persons who paid a mixture of Class 3 contributions and others are not included in this category.

Sources: Department for Work and Pensions: 020 7122 2444;
HM:Revenue and Customs

10.3 National Insurance contributions
United Kingdom

	Employee's standard contibutions[1]		Employer's standard contributions[1]	
	not contracted-out rate	contracted-out rate[2]	not contracted-out rate	contracted-out rate[3]
Class 1				
Weekly earnings				
2001/02				
Below 72.00 (LEL)	-	-	-	-
72.00-87.00 (PT/ST)	-	See note 4	-	See note 5
87.01-575.00 (UEL)	10.0%	8.4%	11.9%	8.9%
Above 575.00 (UEL)	£48.80	£40.75	11.9%	11.9%
2002/03				
Below 75.00 (LEL)	-	-	-	-
75.00-89.00 (PT/ST)	-	See note 4	-	See note 6
89.01-585.00 (UEL)	10.0%	8.4%	11.8%	8.3%
Above 585.00 (UEL)	£49.60	£41.44	11.8%	11.8%
2003/04				
Below 77.00 (LEL)	-	-	-	-
77.00-89.00 (PT/ST)	-	See note 4	-	See note 6
89.01-595.00 (UEL)	11.0%	9.4%	12.8%	9.3%
	£55.66	£47.37		
Above 595.00 (UEL)	1%	1%	12.8%	12.8%
2004/05				
Below 79.00 (LEL)	-	-	-	-
79.00-91.00 (PT/ST)	-	See note 4	-	See note 6
91.01-610.00 (UEL)	11.0%	9.4%	12.8%	9.3%
	£57.09	£48.59		
Above 610.00(UEL)	1.0%	1.0%	12.8%	12.8%
2005/06				
Below 82.00 (LEL)	-	-	-	-
82.00-94.00 (PT/ST)	-	See note 4	-	See note 6
94.01-630.00 (UEL)	11.0%	9.4%	12.8%	9.3%
	£58.96	£50.38		
Above 630.00(UEL)	1.0%	1.0%	12.8%	12.8%
2006/07				
Below 84.00 (LEL)	-	-	-	-
84.00-97.00 (PT/ST)	-	See note 4	-	See note 6
97.01-645.00 (UEL)	11.0%	9.4%	12.8%	9.3%
	£60.28	£51.51		
Above 645.00(UEL)	1.0%	1.0%	12.8%	12.8%
2007/08				
Below 87.00 (LEL)	-	-	-	-
87.00-100.00 (PT/ST)	-	See note 4	-	See note 7
100.01-670.00 (UEL)	11.0%	9.4%	12.8%	9.1%
	£62.70	£53.58		
Above 670.00(UEL)	1.0%	1.0%	12.8%	12.8%

	2001/02	2002/03	2003/04	2004/05	2005/06	2006/07	2007/08
Class 2							
Flat rate weekly	£2.00	£2.00	£2.00	£2.05	£2.10	£2.10	£2.20
Small earnings exception[8] (per annum)	£3,955	£4,025	£4,095	£4,215	£4,345	£4,465	£4,635
Class 3							
Flat-rate voluntary weekly contributions	£6.75	£6.85	£6.95	£7.15	£7.35	£7.55	£7.80
Class 4 (Self-employed; profit-related)							
Rate on profits between LPL and UPL	7.0%	7.0%	8.0%	8.0%	8.0%	8.0%	8.0%
Rate on profits above UPL	..	..	1.0%	1.0%	1.0%	1.0%	1.0%
Lower profits limit (LPL)	£4,535	£4,615	£4,615	£4,745	£4,895	£5,035	£5,225
Upper profits limit (UPL)	£29,900	£30,420	£30,940	£31,720	£32,760	£33,540	34,840

Note: LEL: Lower Earnings Limit; UEL: Upper Earnings Limit. PT: Primary Threshold; ST: Secondary Threshold.

1 Married women opting to pay contributions at the reduced rate at 3.85% before 2003-04 and 4.85% from 2003-04 earn no entitlement to contributory National Insurance benefits as a result of these contributions. No women have been allowed to exercise this option since 1977, but around 70,000 women who have been continually married or widowed and in the labour market since that time have retained their right to pay the reduced rate.

2 The contracted-out rebate for employees' contributions is applied only between LEL and UEL. Earnings below LEL are charged at the appropriate not contracted-out rate (which depends on total earnings). Earnings above the UEL are not subject to employee NICs before 2003-04.

3 The rates shown only apply to Contracted-Out Salary Related schemes (COSR). Earnings below the LEL and above the UEL are charged at the appropriate

not-contracted out rate. The employers' contracted-out rate applies only between the LEL and the UEL.

4 The contracted-out rebate for primary contributions is 1.6% of earnings between the LEL and the UEL for all forms of contracting-out.

5 The contracted-out rebate for secondary contributions is 3.0% of earnings between the LEL and the UEL.

6 The contracted-out rebate for secondary contributions is 3.5% of earnings between the LEL and the UEL up to 2006-07.

7 Since 2007-08 the contracted-out rebate for secondary contributions is 3.7% of earnings between the LEL and UEL.

8 If earnings from self-employment are below this annual limit and the contributor applies for and is granted a small earnings exception Class 2 contributions need not be paid. Class 2 or 3 contributions may be paid voluntarily.

Source: HM Revenue and Customs: 020 7147 3045

10.4 Weekly rates of principal social security benefits[1]
Great Britain
At April

£

		1997	1998	1999	2000	2001	2002	2003	2004	2005	2006	2007
Jobseeker's Allowance:												
Personal allowances												
Single												
Aged under 18	KXDH	29.60	30.30	30.95	31.45	31.95	32.50	32.90	33.50	33.85	34.60	35.65
Aged 18 - 24	KXDJ	38.90	39.85	40.70	41.35	42.00	42.70	43.25	44.05	44.50	45.50	46.85
Aged 25 or over	KXDK	49.15	50.35	51.40	52.20	53.05	53.95	54.65	55.65	56.20	57.45	59.15
Lone parent												
Aged under 18 - usual rate	F92E	..	..	..	31.45	31.95	32.50	32.90	33.50	33.85	34.60	36.65
Aged under 18 - higher rate payable in specific circumstances	F92F	..	..	..	41.35	42.00	42.70	43.25	44.05	44.50	45.50	46.85
Aged 18 or over	F92G	..	..	..	52.20	53.05	53.95	54.65	55.65	56.20	57.45	59.15
Couple												
Both aged under 18[2]	KXDL	58.70	30.30	30.95	31.45	31.95	32.50	32.90	33.50	33.85	34.60	35.65
Both under 18, one disabled	KXDI	38.90	39.85	40.70	41.35	42.00	42.70	43.25	44.05	44.50	45.50	46.85
Both under 18, with a child	F92H	..	..	..	62.35	63.35	64.45	65.30	66.50	67.15	68.65	70.70
One under 18, one 18 - 24	KXDI	38.90	39.85	40.70	41.35	42.00	42.70	43.25	44.05	44.50	45.50	46.85
One under 18, one 25+	F92I	..	..	..	52.20	53.05	53.95	54.65	55.65	56.20	57.45	59.15
Both aged 18 or over	KXDM	77.15	79.00	80.65	81.95	83.25	84.65	85.75	87.30	88.15	90.10	92.80
Dependant children and young people												
Aged under 11 - 16	KXDN	16.90	17.30	20.20	26.60	31.45	33.50	38.50	42.27	43.88	45.58	47.45
Aged 16 - 18	KXDP	29.60	30.30	30.95	31.75	32.25	34.30	38.50	42.27	43.88	45.58	47.45
Invalidity allowance												
High rate	KJND	13.15	13.60	14.05	14.20	14.65	14.90	15.15	15.55	16.05	16.50	17.10
Middle rate	KJNE	8.30	8.60	8.90	9.00	9.30	9.50	9.70	10.00	10.30	10.60	11.00
Low rate	KJNF	4.15	4.30	4.45	4.50	4.65	4.75	4.85	5.00	5.15	5.30	5.50
Increase for dependants												
Adult	KJNG	37.35	38.70	39.95	40.40	41.75	42.45	43.15	44.35	45.70	46.95	48.65
Each child[3]	KJNH	11.20	11.30	11.35	11.35	11.35	11.35	11.35	11.35	11.35	11.35	11.35
Incapacity Benefit:												
Short term (Lower) Under pension age	KOSB	47.10	48.80	50.35	50.90	52.60	53.50	54.40	55.90	57.65	59.20	61.35
Increase for adult dependant	KOSC	29.15	30.20	31.15	31.50	32.55	33.10	33.65	34.60	35.65	36.60	37.90
Short term (Lower) Over pension age	KOSD	59.90	62.05	64.05	64.75	66.90	68.05	69.20	71.15	73.35	75.35	78.05
Increase for adult dependant	KOSE	35.90	37.20	38.40	38.80	40.10	42.45	41.50	42.65	43.95	45.15	46.80
Short term (Higher)	KOSF	55.70	57.70	59.55	60.20	62.20	63.25	64.35	66.15	68.20	70.05	72.55
Increase for dependants:												
Adult	KOSG	29.15	30.20	31.15	31.50	32.55	33.10	33.65	34.60	35.65	36.60	37.90
Child[3]	KOSH	11.20	11.30	11.35	11.35	11.35	11.35	11.35	11.35	11.35	11.35	11.35
Long term	KOSI	62.45	64.70	66.75	67.50	69.75	70.95	72.15	74.15	76.45	78.50	81.35
Increase for dependants:												
Adult	KOSJ	37.35	38.70	39.95	40.40	41.75	42.45	43.15	44.35	45.70	46.95	48.65
Child[3]	KOSK	11.20	11.30	11.35	11.35	11.35	11.35	11.35	11.35	11.35	11.35	11.35
Incapacity age addition:[4]												
Higher rate	KOSL	13.15	13.60	14.05	14.20	14.65	14.90	15.15	15.55	16.05	16.50	17.10
Lower rate	KOSM	6.60	6.80	7.05	7.10	7.35	7.45	7.60	7.80	8.05	8.25	8.55
Attendance Allowance:												
Higher rate	KJNI	49.50	51.30	52.95	53.55	55.30	56.25	57.20	58.80	60.60	62.25	64.50
Lower rate	KJNJ	33.10	34.30	35.40	35.80	37.00	37.65	38.30	39.35	40.55	41.65	43.15
Disability Living Allowance:												
Care component												
Higher rate	KXDC	49.50	51.30	52.95	53.55	55.30	56.25	57.20	58.80	60.60	62.25	64.50
Middle rate	KXDD	33.10	34.30	35.40	35.80	37.00	37.65	38.30	39.35	40.55	41.65	43.15
Lower rate	KXDE	13.15	13.60	14.05	14.20	14.65	14.90	15.15	15.55	16.05	16.50	17.10
Mobility component												
Higher rate	KXDF	34.60	35.85	37.00	37.40	38.65	39.30	39.95	41.05	42.30	43.45	45.00
Lower rate	KXDG	13.15	13.60	14.05	14.20	14.65	14.90	15.15	15.55	16.05	16.50	17.10

10.4
Weekly rates of principal social security benefits[1]
Great Britain

At April

£

		1997	1998	1999	2000	2001	2002	2003	2004	2005	2006	2007
Maternity Benefit:												
Maternity allowances for insured women[5]												
Higher rate	KOSN	55.70	57.70	59.55	60.20	..	..	..	..	..	..	..
Lower rate[6]	KJNL	48.35	50.10	51.70	52.25	..	..	..	..	..	..	..
Standard rate[7]	GPTJ	..	..	..	..	62.20	75.00	100.00	102.80	106.00	108.85	112.75
Threshold[8]	GPTK	..	..	..	..	30.00	30.00	30.00	30.00	30.00	30.00	30.00
Guardian's Allowance	KJNN	11.20	11.30	11.35	11.35	11.35	11.35	11.55	11.85	12.20	12.50	12.95
Widow's Benefit:												
Widow's pension	KJNO	62.45	64.70	66.75	67.50	72.50	75.50	77.45	79.60	82.05	84.25	87.30
Widowed mother's allowance	KJNP	62.45	64.70	66.75	67.50	72.50	75.50	77.45	79.60	82.05	84.25	87.30
Addition for each child	KJNQ	11.20	11.30	11.35	11.35	11.35	11.35	11.35	11.35	11.35	11.35	11.35
Bereavement Benefit:												
Bereavement allowance	WMPF	..	..	..	..	72.50	75.50	77.45	79.60	82.05	84.25	87.30
Widowed parent's allowance	WMOZ	..	..	..	..	72.50	72.50	77.45	79.60	82.05	84.25	87.30
Addition for each child	WMPA	..	..	..	..	11.35	11.35	11.35	11.35	11.35	11.35	11.35
State Pension contributory:[9]												
Single person	KJNR	62.45	64.70	66.75	67.50	72.50	75.50	77.45	79.60	82.05	84.25	87.30
Married couple	KJNS	99.80	103.40	106.70	107.90	115.90	120.70	122.80	127.25	131.20	134.75	139.60
State Pension non contributory:												
Man or woman	KJNT	37.35	38.70	39.95	40.40	43.40	45.20	45.45	47.65	49.15	50.50	52.30
Married woman	KJNU	22.35	23.15	23.90	24.15	24.95	27.00	27.70	28.50	29.40	30.20	31.30
Industrial Injuries Benefit:												
Disablement pension at 100 per cent rate	KJNW	101.10	104.70	108.10	109.30	112.90	114.80	116.80	120.10	123.80	127.10	131.70
Widow's or widower's pension	KJNX	62.45	..	..	..	..	..	..	..	..	..	..
Child Benefit:												
First child	KJOA	11.05	11.45	14.40	15.00	15.50	15.75	16.05	16.50	17.00	17.45	18.10
Subsequent children	KETZ	9.00	9.30	9.60	10.00	10.35	10.55	10.75	11.05	11.40	11.70	12.10
Family Credit[10]												
(maximum awards payable):[11]												
Families with 1 child												
Birth to September following 11th birthday	KJOB	59.70	61.15	64.95	..	..	..	..	..	..	..	..
From September following 11th birthday to September following 16th birthday	KJOC	67.60	69.25	70.70	..	..	..	..	..	..	..	..
From September following 16th birthday to day before 19th birthday	KJOD	72.45	74.20	75.95	..	..	..	..	..	..	..	..
Increase for each additional child												
Birth to September following 11th birthday	KJOF	12.05	12.35	15.15	..	..	..	..	..	..	..	..
From September following 11th birthday to September following 16th birthday	KJOG	19.95	20.45	20.90	..	..	..	..	..	..	..	..
From September following 16th birthday to day before 19th birthday	KJOH	24.80	25.40	25.95	..	..	..	..	..	..	..	..
War pension:												
Ex-private (100 per cent assessment)	KJOJ	107.20	111.10	114.70	116.00	119.80	121.80	127.38	130.16	123.90	133.63	138.40
War widow	KJOK	81.00	83.90	86.60	87.55	90.45	92.00	92.69	95.27	98.08	100.76	104.26

10.4

Weekly rates of principal social security benefits[1]
Great Britain

continued   At April

£

		1997	1998	1999	2000	2001	2002	2003	2004	2005	2006	2007
Income Support:												
Personal allowances[12]												
Single												
aged 16-17 usual rate	KJOW	29.60	30.30	30.95	31.45	31.95	32.50	32.90	33.50	33.85	34.60	35.65
aged 16-17 higher rate in specific circumstances	KABS	38.90	39.85	40.70	41.35	42.00	42.70	43.25	44.05	44.50	45.50	46.85
aged 18-24	KJOX	38.90	39.85	40.70	41.35	42.00	42.70	43.25	44.05	44.50	45.50	46.85
aged 25 or over	KJOY	49.15	50.35	51.40	52.20	53.05	53.95	54.65	55.65	56.20	57.45	59.15
Couple												
both aged under 18[2]	KJOZ	..	..	..	31.45	31.95	32.50	32.90	33.50	33.85	34.60	35.65
both aged under 18, one disabled	F92J	..	..	..	41.35	42.00	42.70	43.25	44.05	44.50	45.50	46.85
both aged under 18, with a child	F92K	..	..	..	62.35	63.35	64.45	65.30	66.50	67.15	68.65	70.70
One aged under 18, one 18-24	F92L	..	..	..	41.35	42.00	42.70	43.25	44.05	44.50	45.50	46.85
One aged under 18, one 25+	F92M	..	..	..	52.20	53.05	53.95	54.65	55.65	56.20	57.45	59.15
Both aged 18 or over	KJPA	77.15	79.00	80.65	81.95	83.25	84.65	85.75	87.30	88.15	90.10	92.80
Lone parent												
aged 16-17 usual rate	KJPB	29.60	30.30	30.95	31.45	31.95	32.50	32.90	33.50	33.85	34.60	35.65
aged 16-17 higher rate in specific circumstances	KABT	38.90	39.85	40.70	41.35	42.00	42.70	43.25	44.05	44.50	45.50	46.85
aged 18 or over	KJPC	49.15	50.35	51.40	52.20	53.05	53.95	54.65	55.65	56.20	57.45	59.15
Dependant children and young people[12]												
From 1997 to 1999												
Birth to September following												
11th birthday	KXDQ	16.90	17.30	20.20	..	..	..	..	..	..	..	..
From September following												
11th birthday to September following 16th	KXDR	24.75	25.35	25.90	..	..	..	..	..	..	..	..
From September following												
16th birthday to day before 19th	KXDS	29.60	30.30	30.95	..	..	..	..	..	..	..	..
Dependant children and young people - from 2000												
Birth to September following 16th birthday	WMOD	..	..	..	26.60	31.45	33.50	38.50	42.27	43.88	45.58	47.45
From September following 16th birthday to day before 19th	WMOP	..	..	..	31.75	32.25	34.30	38.50	42.27	43.88	45.58	47.45
Pension Credit[13]												
Standard minimum guarantee:												
single	C59Y	..	..	..	..	..	..	102.10	105.45	109.45	114.05	119.05
couple	C59Z	..	..	..	..	..	..	155.80	160.95	167.05	174.05	181.70
Additional amount for severe disability												
single	C5A2	..	..	..	..	..	..	42.95	44.15	45.50	46.75	48.45
couple (one qualifies)	C5A3	..	..	..	..	..	..	42.95	44.15	45.50	46.75	48.45
couple (both qualifies)	C5A4	..	..	..	..	..	..	85.90	88.30	91.00	93.50	96.90
Additional amount for carers	C5A8	..	..	..	..	..	..	25.10	25.55	25.80	26.35	27.15
savings credit												
threshold single	C5A9	..	..	..	..	..	..	77.45	79.60	82.05	84.25	87.30
threshold couple	C5AA	..	..	..	..	..	..	123.80	127.25	131.20	134.75	139.60
maximum single	C5AB	..	..	..	..	..	..	14.79	15.51	16.44	17.88	19.05
maximum couple	C5AC	..	..	..	..	..	..	19.20	20.22	21.51	23.58	25.26

1 See chapter text
2 From 12 April 1999 the personal allowance for couples where both members are not yet 18 or one of the couples is aged 18 or over depends on the couple's circumstances. They may be entitled to a couple allowance or a single person's allowance dependant on certain criteria.
3 For the first child only the Child Dependency increase is reduced by £1.30 to £9.90 because of child benefit.
4 The rate of age addition depends on age at date of onset of incapacity: higher rate for under age 35 and lower rate for age 35-44.
5 Following a EU Directive, employee's maternity benefit is aligned with the state benefit they would receive if off work sick.
6 Women who were either not employed or self-employed received the lower rate.

7 New Standard rate introduced from April 2000.
8 MA Earnings Threshold introduced April 2000.
9 Retirement pensioners over 80 receive 25p addition.
10 Family credit was replaced by In-work Families with Child or Working Child Tax Credit awards. Some children have protected rights. Further information is available from the Department for Work and Pensions.
11 Maximum award does not include the 30 hour credit.
12 In addition to personal allowances, a claimant may also be entitled to premiums. The types of premiums are family, lone parent, pensioner, higher pensioner, disability, severe disability and disabled child.
13 Pension Credit replaced Minimum Income Guarantee (MIG) for Income Support for those aged 60 and over on 6th Ocotober 2003.

Sources: Department for Work and Pensions;
Information and Analysis Directorate : 0191 225 7373;
HM Revenue and Customs: 020 7438 7370;
Ministry of Defence/DASA (Pay & Pensions): 020 7218 4271

10.5 Social Security Acts: number of persons receiving benefit[1]
Great Britain

At any one time

Thousands

		1997	1998	1999	2000	2001	2002	2003	2004	2005	2006	2007
Persons receiving:												
Jobseeker's Allowance	JYXM	1 406.30	1 181.20	1 105.80	1 060.40	936.40	906.06	914.52	806.35	830.11	930.86	837.50
Incapacity benefit	KXDT	1 749.20	1 671.20	1 557.10	2 352.50	2 420.90	2 471.14	2 494.89	2 508.77	2 490.85	2 449.99	2 417.70
Attendance Allowance[2]	KXDU	1 183.20	1 225.60	1 243.80	1 556.10	1 570.90	1 290.77	1 315.64	1 377.35	1 419.42	1 465.59	1 507.50
Disability Living Allowance[2]	KXDW	1 886.50	1 995.90	2 061.30	2 193.10	2 306.40	2 424.35	2 547.09	2 644.28	2 729.72	2 799.16	2 881.80
Widows' Benefits[3]	KJHF	296.40	278.70	267.60	265.10	255.00	223.41	191.50	163.43	138.96	117.65	96.90
Bereavement Benefits[3]	VQAA	..	..	..	..	..	41.49	47.68	51.18	55.24	57.66	58.50
National Insurance												
State pension contributory[3]:												
Males	KJHH	3 786.50	3 880.40	3 956.30	4 039.40	4 083.90	4 149.16	4 211.37	4 275.67	4 336.81	4 374.18	4 432.30
Females	KJHL	6 783.20	6 850.70	6 886.30	6 928.00	6 959.70	6 972.20	7 037.15	7 117.78	7 197.92	7 245.71	7 391.10
Total	KJHG	10 569.70	10 731.10	10 842.60	10 967.40	11 043.60	11 121.35	11 248.52	11 393.45	11 534.73	11 619.89	11 823.40
State pension non contributory[3]:												
Males	KJHI	5.60	5.50	5.10	5.20	5.10	5.26	5.37	5.39	5.34	5.36	5.68
Females	KJHJ	20.90	19.80	18.80	18.00	18.20	18.06	17.73	17.31	16.74	16.58	17.34
Total	KJHK	26.50	25.20	23.90	23.20	23.30	23.32	23.10	22.70	22.08	21.94	23.03
Industrial Injuries Disablement												
Pensions assessments[4]	KJHN	257.80	269.10	278.20	274.60	275.40	273.70	267.13	266.48	267.12	266.45	264.88
Reduced Earnings Allowance/												
Retirement Allowance assessments[5,6]	KEYC	155.60	152.80	153.50	82.90	82.60	81.00	76.22	74.81	73.15	71.38	69.36
Income Support (Excluding MIG)[7]	KABV	3 958.00	3 853.10	3 814.40	2 237.10	2 260.60	2 238.76	2 236.38	2 192.64	2 139.78	2 114.77	2 117.70
Pension Credit[7]	C5AP	..	..	..	..	..	..	..	2 490.76	2 682.73	2 717.39	2 733.50
Housing Benefit and Council Tax Benefit[8,9]												
Housing Benefit Total	EW3X	4 639.40	4 474.70	4 313.10	4 033.30	3 874.40	3 812.60	3 796.40	3 879.40	3 957.10	3 990.00	4 039.75
Social Landlord[10]	KABY	2 792.30	2 664.10	2 518.50	3 218.40	3 131.10	3 093.80	3 081.67	3 135.49	3 165.89	3 152.25	3 146.30
Private Landlord	KABZ	1 847.10	1 810.60	1 794.60	815.00	743.30	718.83	714.75	743.93	790.93	837.79	893.40
Council tax benefit[11]	KJPO	5 498.30	5 325.70	5 166.10	4 830.10	4 673.40	4 601.73	4 627.78	4 800.22	4 959.69	5 049.97	5 096.60
War pensions[12]	KADG	324.64	317.65	306.06	295.67	284.33	272.78	260.79	247.59	235.30	223.85	212.54

1 See chapter text. Figures as at May each year unless otherwise stated. Taken from DWP 100% Work and Pensions Longitudinal Study (WPLS) data.
2 AA and DLA figures based on WPLS data from 2002. Prior to 2002 a consistent series for caseload, based on WPLS levels, has been created by combining older information, available from the previously published 5% sample data, with the WPLS data.
3 Includes overseas cases up to 2002.
4 Figures for IIDB include those receiving both IIDB and REA, at March.
5 Figures show REA only from 2000, at March.
6 Figures from 2000 to 2001 are based on 10% data at March, 2002 and 2003 are at March from 100% data, from 2004 are as at May.
7 Pension Credit replaced MIG on 6th October 2003 and extended Income Support entitlement to customers aged 60+. MIG claimants have been excluded from the IS figures in order to keep the series consistent.
8 Housing Benefit figures excludes any Extended Payment cases.
9 As at February.
10 Social landlord figures include registered social landlord tenants.
11 Figure excludes Second Adult Rebate Claims.
12 Includes overseas cases. As at end of March.

Sources: Department for Work and Pensions; Information and Analysis Directorate : 0191 225 7373; HM Revenue and Customs: 020 7438 7370; Ministry of Defence/DASA (Pay & Pensions): 020 7218 4271

10.6 Jobseeker's Allowance[1,2,3] claimants: by benefit entitlement
Great Britain
As at May

Thousands

		2001	2002	2003	2004	2005	2006	2007
All Persons								
All with benefit - total	KXDX	843.2	816.2	823.8	725.7	755.1	843.7	758.1
Contribution-based JSA only	KXDY	146.1	160.4	165.6	135.9	144.6	139.8	117.8
Contribution based JSA & income-based JSA	KXDZ	18.1	19.1	18.7	14.0	14.0	13.5	12.4
Income-based JSA only payment	KXEA	679.0	636.7	639.5	575.8	596.4	690.4	627.9
No benefit in payment	KXEB	93.2	89.8	90.7	80.7	75.0	87.1	79.3
Total	KXEC	936.4	906.1	914.5	806.3	830.1	930.9	837.5
Males								
All with benefit - total	KXED	655.4	626.0	625.3	546.9	565.4	630.4	557.9
Contribution-based JSA only	KXEE	103.8	114.4	117.8	97.3	103.1	99.6	82.6
Contribution based JSA & income-based JSA	KXEF	16.6	17.3	16.4	12.7	13.1	12.4	11.1
Income-based JSA only payment	KXEG	534.9	494.3	491.1	436.8	449.2	518.4	464.2
No benefit in payment	KXEH	61.5	61.4	62.3	54.7	51.6	58.8	53.6
Total	KXEI	716.9	687.4	687.6	601.6	617.0	689.3	611.5
Females								
All with benefit - total	KXEJ	187.8	190.3	198.5	178.8	189.7	213.3	200.2
Contribution-based JSA only	KXEK	42.3	46.0	47.8	38.6	41.5	40.3	35.3
Contribution based JSA & income-based JSA	KXEL	1.5	1.8	2.3	1.3	0.9	1.0	1.3
Income-based JSA only payment	KXEM	144.0	142.4	148.4	139.0	147.3	172.0	163.7
No benefit in payment	KXEN	31.7	28.4	28.5	26.0	23.4	28.3	25.7
Total	KXEO	219.5	218.6	227.0	204.8	213.1	241.6	225.9

1 See chapter text. Jobseeker's Allowance (JSA) has two routes of entry: contribution-based which depends mainly upon national insurance contributions and income-based which depends mainly on a means test. Some claimants can qualify by either route. In practice they receive income-based JSA but have an underlying entitlement to the contribution-based element.
2 Figures are given at May each year and have been derived by applying 5% proportions to 100% totals taken from the DWP 100% Work and Pensions Longitudinal Study (WPLS).
3 Figures are rounded to the nearest hundred.

Sources: Department for Work and Pensions; Information and Analysis Directorate: 0191 225 7373

10.7 Sickness Benefit, Invalidity Benefit and Incapacity Benefit[1,2] claimants: by sex, age and duration of spell

Great Britain. At end of May

Thousands

		2002	2003	2004	2005	2006	2007
Males							
All durations: All ages	KJJA	1 526.17	1 525.02	1 517.62	1 492.38	1 455.52	1 428.65
Under 20	KJJB	21.79	21.81	22.04	21.45	19.95	18.66
20-29	KJJC	133.83	138.54	142.68	143.24	141.80	146.07
30-39	KJJD	250.79	254.30	253.32	245.61	233.70	224.29
40-49	KJJE	304.47	311.85	318.04	320.77	319.77	320.24
50-59	KJJF	478.01	472.03	463.37	451.93	439.54	418.26
60-64	KJJG	337.22	326.45	318.12	309.36	300.73	301.10
65 and over	KJJH	0.05	0.05	0.05	0.04	0.02	0.03
Over six months: All ages	KJJI	1 346.80	1 359.53	1 359.08	1 347.43	1 323.20	1 291.32
Under 20	KJJJ	6.91	13.40	13.78	13.51	12.85	11.70
20-29	KJJK	96.61	105.72	110.85	114.57	115.21	117.83
30-39	KJJL	213.19	217.05	217.81	213.91	205.36	195.22
40-49	KJJM	271.25	278.53	285.90	290.72	291.36	289.94
50-59	KJJN	438.55	434.04	427.06	418.60	409.46	387.76
60-64	KJJO	320.26	310.75	303.64	296.10	288.93	288.85
65 and over	KJJP	0.03	0.03	0.04	0.02	0.02	0.03
Females							
All durations: All ages	KJJQ	944.44	969.44	990.84	998.20	994.33	988.93
Under 20	KJJR	21.51	21.49	21.48	20.51	18.92	17.86
20-29	KJJS	96.66	100.78	105.02	108.61	109.73	114.42
30-39	KJJT	175.37	177.70	177.91	173.45	167.36	162.39
40-49	KJJU	252.82	262.20	270.90	276.62	279.32	283.45
50-59	KJJV	398.06	407.24	415.52	418.99	418.99	410.80
60 and over	KJJW	0.03	0.03	0.02	0.02	0.02	0.02
Over six months: All ages	KJJX	825.25	858.03	880.52	894.57	896.33	885.69
Under 20	KJJY	7.41	12.35	12.40	12.10	11.13	10.20
20-29	KJJZ	72.32	79.63	84.02	88.98	90.99	93.60
30-39	KJKA	151.59	154.19	154.95	152.48	148.00	142.28
40-49	KJKB	225.65	234.71	243.52	250.11	253.50	255.99
50-59	KJKC	368.25	377.12	385.61	390.88	392.69	383.60
60 and over	KJKD	0.03	0.03	0.02	0.02	0.02	0.02
Unknown Gender							
All durations	EW44	0.54	0.44	0.31	0.26	0.15	0.13
Over 6 months	EW45	0.29	0.21	0.16	0.13	0.10	0.09

1 See chapter text. Figures are given at May each year and are based on 100% Work and Pensions Longitudinal Study (WPLS) data.
2 Figures will Include a small number of overseas cases.

Sources: Department for Work and Pensions; Information and Analysis Directorate: 0191 225 7373

10.8 Sickness, Invalidity and Incapacity Benefit: days of certified incapacity

Great Britain analysis by age at end of period[1]

Years starting on first Monday in April[2]

Millions

		1992 /93	1993 /94	1994[3] /95	1995 /96	1996 /97	1997 /98	1998 /99	1999 /00	2000 /01	2001 /02	2002 /03
Age at 31 March[4]												
Males: All ages	KJKH	445.5	468.8	507.9	596.2	576.3	563.5	538.6	526.7	531.7	536.1	540.3
Under 20	KJKI	1.5	1.6	1.8	3.4	3.1	3.5	3.7	3.3	2.6	3.5	5.4
20 - 29	KJKJ	24.5	27.0	30.4	43.7	42.4	43.2	41.7	38.3	38.9	40.4	44.3
30 - 39	KJKK	41.4	46.6	56.0	72.3	73.9	77.7	78.2	75.8	81.3	84.0	85.1
40 - 49	KJKL	64.6	72.7	78.9	98.5	98.5	97.7	97.6	98.0	103.9	106.0	106.8
50 - 59	KJKM	121.7	129.8	141.4	172.0	170.7	172.2	170.0	161.9	165.9	168.5	168.1
60 - 64	KJKN	102.4	107.3	112.6	127.9	127.8	126.7	124.3	126.0	125.8	120.2	116.3
65 and over	KJKO	80.4	83.9	86.8	78.4	59.9	41.7	23.0	23.4	13.3	13.4	14.4
Females: All ages	KJKP	190.7	211.4	237.5	279.5	285.8	292.8	294.8	315.0	325.1	338.7	344.6
Under 20	KJKQ	2.1	2.4	2.6	4.8	4.1	4.4	4.5	4.0	3.5	3.9	5.4
20 - 29	KJKR	22.1	22.1	23.9	31.9	32.0	32.1	31.3	30.7	30.3	32.3	34.4
30 - 39	KJKS	28.5	32.7	37.6	48.0	49.8	51.4	53.4	54.9	58.9	59.9	61.3
40 - 49	KJKT	46.6	51.5	58.9	72.1	74.0	75.8	77.1	79.1	82.8	88.9	89.8
50 - 59	KJKU	71.3	79.1	88.4	101.0	107.5	115.3	120.0	134.3	142.2	145.9	146.0
60 and over	KJKV	20.1	23.6	26.1	21.7	18.4	13.8	8.4	12.0	7.3	7.9	7.7

1 See chapter text. The end of the statistical year up to 1993/94 was the Saturday before the first Monday in April.
2 Up to and including 1994/95 years start first Monday in April. The 1995/96 year started 13 April and ended 31 March. From 1996/97 years start 1 April.
3 The statistical year for 1994/95 was extended to 12 April 1995, the day before the introduction of the new Incapacity Benefit which replaced Sickness and Invalidity Benefit.
4 Until 1995/96 then at 1 March.

Sources: Department for Work and Pensions; Taken from 1% extract; Information and Analysis Directorate: 0191 225 7373

10.9 Child benefits[1]

Thousands

		Great Britain As at 31 December				United Kingdom As at 31 August							
		1997[2]	1998[2]	1999		2000	2001	2002	2003	2004	2005	2006	2007
Families receiving allowances:													
Total	KJMU	6 956	6 976	7 102	VOWX	7 340	7 335	7 336	7 342	7 353	7 375	7 441	7 530
With 1 child	KJMV	..	..	3 015	VOWY	3 128	3 143	3 162	3 189	3 219	3 260	3 329	3 414
2 children	KJMW	..	..	2 822	VOWZ	2 898	2 891	2 894	2 890	2 885	2 882	2 884	2 893
3 children	KJMX	..	..	943	VOXA	977	970	954	942	931	920	917	911
4 children	KJMY	..	..	241	VOXB	251	247	242	239	235	233	231	231
5 or more children	KJMZ	..	..	82	VOXC	86	84	83	82	82	80	80	81
Families receiving Guardian's Allowance	VOXG	2.3	2.3	2.3	VOXH	2.5	2.3	2.5	2.6	2.9	2.8	3.2	3.3

1 See chapter text.
2 Figures provided by Child Benefit Centre Management Information Statistics as a new scan was being developed.

Source: HM Revenue and Customs: 020 7147 3021

10.10 Family Credit/ Working Families' Tax Credit[1,2]

Thousands

		Great Britain As at 31 December						United Kingdom As at 30 November			
		1994	1995	1996	1997	1998		1999	2000	2001	2002
Families in receipt:											
Total	KJTO	578.0	646.5	716.7	751.4	779.7	ZCMK	965.3	1 167.8	1 293.7	1 377.3
Two-parent families: total	KJTP	324.6	356.9	390.2	388.0	383.4	ZCML	467.6	565.9	617.2	639.8
With 1 child	KJTQ	80.1	89.7	98.6	96.6	95.4	ZCMM	116.8	144.8	151.6	159.0
2 children	KJTR	122.4	135.1	146.1	144.4	141.7	ZCMN	178.4	220.1	243.5	252.7
3 children	KJTS	76.4	83.4	91.1	91.4	89.1	ZCMO	107.8	129.2	142.9	147.3
4 children or more children	ZIYM	45.8	48.6	54.4	55.6	57.3	ZCMP	64.6	71.8	79.2	80.8
One-parent families: total	KJTW	253.4	289.6	326.5	363.4	396.3	ZIYI	497.8	601.8	676.5	737.6
With 1 child	KJTX	133.8	152.2	170.4	189.3	203.4	ZIYJ	259.6	313.7	349.5	381.2
2 children	KJTY	86.0	99.1	111.2	121.8	136.1	ZIYK	169.6	207.6	238.7	261.6
3 or more children	KJTZ	33.5	38.3	45.0	52.3	56.9	ZIYL	68.6	80.5	88.3	94.8

1 See chapter text. Family Credit was replaced by Working Families Tax Credit (WFTC) in October 1999. The WFTC figures for December 1999 include Family Credit awards made before October 1999 and still current (both FC and WFTC awards last for 26 weeks).
2 WFTC was replaced by Child Credit and Working Tax Credit on 6th April 2003. See table 10.11.

Sources: Board of Inland Revenue: 020 7438 7370;
Department for Work and Pensions;
Information and Analysis Directorate: 0191 225 7373

10.11 In-work families with Child Tax Credit or Working Tax Credit awards
United Kingdom
As at December

Thousands

		2003[1]	2004	2005	2006	2007
In-work families with positive award:	C5PF	4 423	4 519	4 538	4 526	4 541
With children	C5PG	4 208.0	4 261.0	4 218.0	4 204.0	4 189.0
Receiving Working Tax Credit and Child Tax Credit	C5PH	1 548.0	1 492.0	1 497.0	1 596.0	1 650.0
Receiving Child Tax Credit only	C5PI	2 660.0	2 769.0	2 721.0	2 608.0	2 539.0
Without children						
Working Tax Credit only	C5PL	215.0	258.0	320.0	323.0	352.0

1 Child and Working Tax Credits replaced Working Families' Tax Credit on 6th April 2003. Figures for 2003 are based on awards current at 5th January 2004. All other figures at December each year. See chapter text.

Source: HM Revenue and Customs: 020 7147 3083

10.12 Widows' Benefit (excluding bereavement payment[1,2,3]): by type of benefit
Great Britain
Number in receipt of windows benefit as at May 2007

Thousands

		2002	2003	2004	2005	2006	2007
All Widows' Benefit (excluding bereavement allowance)							
All ages	KJGA	223.40	191.50	163.40	139.00	117.70	96.89
Unknown Age	EW4O	0.20	0.10	–	–	–	0.02
18 - 24	EW4P	0.1	–	–	–	..	..
25 - 29	EW4Q	0.50	0.30	0.20	0.10	0.10	0.04
30 - 34	EW4R	2.30	1.70	1.20	0.80	0.50	0.32
35 - 39	EW4S	6.40	5.10	3.90	2.90	2.10	1.53
40 - 44	EW4T	10.80	9.10	7.50	6.10	4.90	3.93
45 - 49	EW4U	20.10	16.30	13.20	11.00	9.10	7.58
50 - 54	EW4V	50.20	40.60	33.30	26.90	21.80	17.69
55 - 59	EW4W	103.40	90.90	77.70	66.90	57.30	45.78
60 - 64	EW4X	29.50	27.40	26.40	24.30	21.80	20.01
Widowed parents' allowance - with dependant children							
All ages	KJGG	40.7	34.2	28.2	23.2	19.0	15.6
Unknown Age	EW4Y	0.1	0.1	–	–	..	..
18 - 24	EW4Z	0.1	–	–	–	..	..
25 - 29	EW52	0.50	0.30	0.20	0.10	0.10	0.03
30 - 34	EW53	2.30	1.60	1.10	0.80	0.50	0.31
35 - 39	EW54	6.20	4.90	3.80	2.80	2.10	1.49
40 - 44	EW55	10.00	8.40	7.00	5.70	4.60	3.75
45 - 49	EW56	10.80	9.30	7.80	6.70	5.60	4.71
50 - 54	EW57	7.60	6.60	5.70	4.80	4.10	3.58
55 - 59	EW58	3.00	2.70	2.30	2.00	1.80	1.57
60 - 64	EW59	0.20	0.30	0.30	0.30	0.20	0.17
Widowed parents' allowance - without dependant children							
All ages	KJGM	2.30	1.80	1.40	1.10	0.80	0.69
Unknown Age	EW5A	–	–	–	–	..	..
18 - 24	EW5B	–	–	–	–	..	..
25 - 29	EW5C	–	–	–	–	..	..
30 - 34	EW5D	0.10	–	–	–	–	0.01
35 - 39	EW5E	0.20	0.20	0.10	0.10	0.10	0.04
40 - 44	EW5F	0.50	0.40	0.30	0.20	0.20	0.13
45 - 49	EW5G	0.60	0.50	0.40	0.30	0.20	0.21
50 - 54	EW5H	0.60	0.50	0.30	0.30	0.20	0.17
55 - 59	EW5I	0.40	0.30	0.20	0.20	0.10	0.11
60 - 64	EW5J	0.10	0.10	–	–	–	0.02
Age -related bereavement allowance							
All ages	KJGS	138.70	124.30	110.10	96.60	84.00	70.13
Unknown Age	EW5K	–	–	–	–	–	0.01
18 - 24	EW5L	–	–	–	–	..	..
25 - 29	EW5M	–	–	–	–	..	..
30 - 34	EW5N	–	–	–	–	..	..
35 - 39	EW5O	–	–	–	–	..	..
40 - 44	EW5P	0.30	0.20	0.20	0.20	0.10	0.06
45 - 49	EW5Q	8.70	6.60	5.10	4.00	3.30	2.66
50 - 54	EW5R	41.00	32.80	26.70	21.40	17.20	13.75
55 - 59	EW5S	77.70	73.50	66.30	59.00	50.90	40.57
60 - 64	EW5T	11.00	11.20	11.90	12.00	12.50	13.08
Bereavement allowance (Not age related)							
All ages	KJGW	41.70	31.30	23.70	18.10	13.90	10.47
Unknown Age	EW5U	–	–	–	–	..	..
18 - 24	EW5V	–	–	–	–	..	..
25 - 29	EW5W	–	–	–	–	..	..
30 - 34	EW5X	–	–	–	–	..	..
35 - 39	EW5Y	–	–	–	–	..	..
40 - 44	EW5Z	–	–	–	–	..	..
45 - 49	EW62	–	–	–	–	..	..
50 - 54	EW63	1.1	0.8	0.6	0.5	0.3	0.2
55 - 59	EW64	22.40	14.40	8.80	5.60	4.40	3.53
60 - 64	EW65	18.20	16.00	14.20	12.00	9.10	6.74

1 Definitions and Conventions: "-" Nil or Negligible; "." Not applicable; Caseload figures are rounded to the nearest hundred and displayed in thousands.

2 Caseload (Thousands) All Claimants of Widows Benefit are female. No new claims for WB have been accepted since April 2001 when it was replaced by Bereavement Benefit.

3 Figures include overseas cases.

Sources: DWP Information Directorate: Work and Pensions Longitudinal Study 100% data;
Information and Analysis Directorate: 0191 225 7373

10.13 Bereavement Benefit[1,2] (excluding bereavement payment): by sex, type of benefit and age of widow/er

Great Britain.   Thousands

		Males				Females		
		2005	2006	2007		2005	2006	2007
All Bereavement Benefit (excluding bereavement allowance)								
All ages	WLSX	17.60	17.97	17.77	WLTC	37.64	39.69	40.77
18 - 24	EVW9	..	..	..	EVY2	0.10	0.09	0.07
25 - 29	EVX2	0.05	0.05	0.05	EVY3	0.48	0.49	0.53
30 - 34	EVX3	0.38	0.33	0.28	EVY4	1.58	1.67	1.63
35 - 39	EVX4	1.24	1.20	1.15	EVY5	3.49	3.82	4.05
40 - 44	EVX5	2.48	2.60	2.50	EVY6	5.66	6.49	7.01
45 - 49	EVX6	3.31	3.46	3.61	EVY7	7.39	8.14	8.92
50 - 54	EVX7	3.35	3.43	3.47	EVY8	7.99	8.32	8.65
55 - 59	EVX8	3.63	3.70	3.43	EVY9	10.96	10.67	9.90
60 - 64	EVX9	3.16	3.20	3.29	EVZ2	–	..	..
Widowed parents' allowance - with dependant children								
All ages	WLUD	10.69	11.05	11.27	WLUH	21.36	24.40	26.86
18 - 24	EVZ3	–	..	..	EW24	0.09	0.09	0.07
25 - 29	EVZ4	0.05	0.05	0.05	EW25	0.48	0.47	0.52
30 - 34	EVZ5	0.37	0.33	0.28	EW26	1.55	1.65	1.61
35 - 39	EVZ6	1.23	1.20	1.14	EW27	3.43	3.77	4.01
40 - 44	EVZ7	2.47	2.58	2.48	EW28	5.56	6.41	6.93
45 - 49	EVZ8	2.81	2.94	3.13	EW29	5.40	6.31	7.23
50 - 54	EVZ9	2.14	2.25	2.36	EW2A	3.39	4.04	4.61
55 - 59	EW22	1.19	1.24	1.29	EW2B	1.46	1.67	1.89
60 - 64	EW23	0.43	0.46	0.53	EW2C	–	..	..
Widowed parents' allowance - without dependant children								
All ages	WLVK	0.06	0.06	0.05	WMMR	0.40	0.37	0.34
18 - 24	EW2D	–	..	..	EW2M	–	..	..
25 - 29	EW2E	–	..	..	EW2N	0.01	0.01	0.01
30 - 34	EW2F	–	..	..	EW2O	0.03	0.03	0.02
35 - 39	EW2G	0.01	0.01	0.01	EW2P	0.06	0.05	0.05
40 - 44	EW2H	0.02	0.02	0.02	EW2Q	0.10	0.08	0.08
45 - 49	EW2I	0.01	0.02	0.01	EW2R	0.09	0.08	0.08
50 - 54	EW2J	0.01	0.01	0.01	EW2S	0.08	0.07	0.06
55 - 59	EW2K	0.01	0.01	0.01	EW2T	0.05	0.04	0.04
60 - 64	EW2L	–	..	..	EW2U	–	..	..
Age-related bereavement allowance								
All ages	WMOB	1.87	1.87	1.17	WMOC	7.08	6.58	6.17
18 - 24	EW2V	–	..	..	EW36	–	..	..
25 - 29	EW2W	–	..	..	EW37	–	..	..
30 - 34	EW2X	–	..	..	EW38	–	..	..
35 - 39	EW2Y	–	..	..	EW39	–	..	..
40 - 44	EW2Z	–	..	..	EW3A	–	..	..
45 - 49	EW32	0.49	0.50	0.46	EW3B	1.90	1.75	1.61
50 - 54	EW33	1.20	1.17	1.10	EW3C	4.52	4.21	3.97
55 - 59	EW34	0.18	0.20	0.15	EW3D	0.66	0.62	0.58
60 - 64	EW35	–	..	..	EW3E	–	..	..
Bereavement allowance (not age related)								
All ages	WMOX	4.97	4.98	4.74	WMOY	8.79	8.34	7.39
18 - 24	EW3F	–	..	..	EW3O	–	..	..
25 - 29	EW3G	–	..	..	EW3P	–	..	..
30 - 34	EW3H	–	..	..	EW3Q	–	..	..
35 - 39	EW3I	–	..	..	EW3R	–	..	..
40 - 44	EW3J	–	..	..	EW3S	–	..	..
45 - 49	EW3K	–	..	..	EW3T	–	..	..
50 - 54	EW3L	–	..	..	EW3U	–	..	..
55 - 59	EW3M	2.25	2.24	1.98	EW3V	8.79	8.34	7.39
60 - 64	EW3N	2.72	2.74	2.76	EW3W	–	..	..

1 Figures include overseas cases.
2 Figures are given at May each year and are taken from the DWP 100% Work and Pensions Longitudinal Study (WPLS).

Source: DWP Information Directorate: 0191 225 7874

10.14 Contributory and non-contributory retirement pensions:[1] by sex and age of claimant

Great Britain. Numbers in payment at end of May

Thousands and percentages

		2003	2004	2005	2006	2007
Men:						
Age-groups:						
65-69	KJSB	1 330.2	1 354.3	1 364.1	1 341.5	1 332.8
Percentage	KJSC	*31.5*	*31.6*	*31.4*	*30.6*	*30.0*
70-74	KJSD	1 136.6	1 140.3	1 150.0	1 160.1	1 178.0
Percentage	KJSE	*27.0*	*26.6*	*26.5*	*26.5*	*26.5*
75-79	KJSF	867.1	875.0	887.1	903.0	918.5
Percentage	KJSG	*20.6*	*20.4*	*20.4*	*20.6*	*20.7*
80-84	KJSH	565.3	593.7	593.3	596.9	604.7
Percentage	KJSI	*13.4*	*13.9*	*13.7*	*13.6*	*13.6*
85-89	KJSJ	225.9	221.4	246.4	273.1	296.4
Percentage	KJSK	*5.4*	*5.2*	*5.7*	*6.2*	*6.7*
90 and over	KJSL	90.6	95.5	100.2	103.6	106.1
Percentage	KJSM	*2.1*	*2.2*	*2.3*	*2.4*	*2.4*
Unknown age	EW3Y	1.0	0.8	1.1	1.2	1.5
Percentage	EW3Z	*–*	*–*	*–*	*–*	*–*
Total all ages	KJSA	4 216.7	4 281.1	4 342.2	4 379.5	4 438.0
Women:						
Age-groups:						
60-64	KJSO	1 402.7	1 451.3	1 498.7	1 524.0	1 628.2
Percentage	KJSP	*19.9*	*20.3*	*20.8*	*21.0*	*22.0*
65-69	KJSQ	1 429.7	1 452.7	1 464.2	1 453.1	1 456.1
Percentage	KJSR	*20.3*	*20.4*	*20.3*	*20.0*	*19.7*
70-74	KJSS	1 329.1	1 319.2	1 314.5	1 312.7	1 322.1
Percentage	KJST	*18.8*	*18.5*	*18.2*	*18.1*	*17.8*
75-79	KJSU	1 161.9	1 156.7	1 158.6	1 165.5	1 168.9
Percentage	KJSV	*16.5*	*16.2*	*16.1*	*16.0*	*15.8*
80-84	KJSW	939.4	973.9	951.6	933.3	923.7
Percentage	KJSX	*13.3*	*13.6*	*13.2*	*12.9*	*12.5*
85-89	KJSY	491.3	473.1	511.0	552.7	587.9
Percentage	KJSZ	*7.0*	*6.6*	*7.1*	*7.6*	*7.9*
90 and over	KJTA	298.8	307.2	314.9	319.4	319.9
Percentage	KJTB	*4.2*	*4.3*	*4.4*	*4.4*	*4.3*
Unknown age	EW42	2.0	1.1	1.3	1.5	1.7
Percentage	EW43	*–*	*–*	*–*	*–*	*–*
Total all ages	KJSN	7 054.9	7 135.1	7 214.7	7 262.3	7 408.4

1 See chapter text. Including pensions payable to persons residing overseas.

Sources: Department for Work and Pensions;
Work and Pensions Longitudinal Study (WPLS);
Information and Analysis Directorate: 0191 225 7373

10.15 War pensions: estimated number of pensioners[1]
Great Britain

At 31 March each year
Thousands

		1997	1998	1999	2000	2001	2002	2003	2004	2005	2006[2]	2007
Disablement	KADH	264.59	259.16	248.93	240.76	231.62	221.80	212.18	201.55	191.75	182.80	173.85
Widows and dependants	KADI	60.05	58.49	55.85	54.92	52.71	50.98	48.61	46.04	43.55	41.05	38.69
Total	KADG	324.64	317.65	306.06	295.67	284.33	272.78	260.79	247.59	235.30	223.85	212.54

1 See chapter text. From 1914 war, 1939 war and later service.
2 The discontinuity between 2005 and 2006 is due to improvements in data processing.

Source: Ministry of Defence/DASA (Health Information): 01225 467801

10.16 Income support[1] (excluding MIG)[2] by statistical group[3]: number of claimants receiving weekly payment
Great Britain

Thousands[4]

		2002	2003	2004	2005	2006	2007
All income support claimants (excluding MIG)[5]	F8YY	2 238.8	2 236.4	2 192.6	2 139.8	2 114.8	2 117.7
Incapacity Benefits	F8YZ	1 197.9	1 215.1	1 205.2	1 193.8	1 183.2	1 184.7
Lone Parent	F8Z2	865.9	853.3	823.3	789.3	774.9	765.6
Carer	F8Z3	75.70	77.50	78.40	79.00	80.20	82.80
Others on Income Related Benefits	F8Z4	99.30	90.50	85.90	77.70	76.50	84.60

1 Figures are given at May each year and are taken from the DWP 100% Work and Pensions Longitudinal Study (WPLS).
2 Figures exclude MIG claimants. Pension Credit replaced MIG on 6th October 2003 and extended Income Support entitlements to customers aged 60 and over.
3 Statistical groups are defined as follows:
Incapacity Benefits- claimants aged under 60 on Incapacity Benefit or Severe Disablement Allowance;
Lone Parent - single claimants aged under 60 with dependants not in receipt of IB/SDA;
Carer- claimants aged under 60 entitled to Carer's Allowance;
Other Income Related Benefit- claimants not in one of the above categories.
4 Figures are rounded to the nearest hundred and quoted in thousands.
5 Totals may not sum due to rounding.

Sources: Department for Work and Pensions; Information and Analysis Directorate: 0191 225 7373

10.17 MIG/Pension Credit[1,2]: number of claimants
Great Britain

End of May
Thousands[3]

		2002[4]	2003[4]	2004[5]	2005[5]	2006[5]	2007[5]
All Pension Credit	F8Z5	..	..	2 490.8	2 682.7	2 717.4	2 733.5
Guarantee Credit Only	F8Z6	..	..	735.0	767.3	775.6	805.7
Guarantee Credit Only and Savings Credit	F8Z7	..	..	1 269.5	1 321.7	1 343.2	1 330.1
Savings Credit	F8Z8	..	..	486.0	593.7	598.6	597.7
(Residual)[6] MIG Case	F8Z9	1 737.5	1 777.8	0.3	–	–	–

1 Source: DWP 100% Work and Pensions Longitudinal study (WPLS).
2 Pension Credit was introduced on 6th October 2003 and replaced Monthly Income Guarantee (Income Support for people aged 60 or over). The vast majority of people who were in receipt of MIG transferred to PC in October 2003.
3 Figures are rounded to the nearest hundred and expressed in thousands.
4 Columns 2002 - 2003 represent MIG caseloads.
5 Columns 2004 onwards represent Pension Credit Caseloads.
6 When MIG was replaced by Pension Credit in October 2003 some cases continued to be MIG cases. These were cases where the partner aged under 60 continued as the claimant. These cases are minimal and are reducing each quarter.

Sources: Department for Work and Pensions; Information and Analysis Directorate: 0191 225 7373

Social protection

10.18 Income support: average weekly amounts of benefit[1,2]
Great Britain
As at May

£ per week

		2002	2003	2004	2005	2006	2007
All income support claimants (excluding MIG)[3]	F8ZF	84.83	91.07	91.14	85.81	83.41	82.29
Incapacity benefits[4]	F8ZG	72.32	76.10	77.70	76.93	78.12	79.78
Lone Parent[4]	F8ZH	105.85	116.52	114.96	102.85	94.88	89.70
Carer[4]	F8ZI	71.50	76.63	76.78	72.42	70.40	69.97
Others on income related benefits[4]	F8ZJ	62.45	64.43	64.25	62.69	62.62	62.33

1 Figures are given at May each year and are taken from the DWP 100% Work and Pensions Longitudinal Study (WPLS).
2 Average amounts are rounded to the nearest penny.
3 Figures exclude MIG claimants. Pension Credit replaced MIG on 6 October 2003 and extended Income Support entitlement to customers aged 60 and over.
4 Statistical groups are defined as follows:
Incapacity Benefits- claimants under 60 on incapacity benefit or Severe Disablement Allowance;
Lone Parent- single claimants aged under 60 with dependants not in receipt of IB/SDA;
Carer- claimants aged under 60 entitled to Carer's Allowance;
Other Income Related Benefit- claimants not in one of the above categories.

Sources: Department for Work and Pensions; Information and Analysis Directorate: 0191 225 7373

10.19 MIG/Pension Credit: average weekly amounts of benefit[1,2]
Great Britain
As at May

£ per week[3]

		2002[4]	2003[4]	2004[5]	2005[5]	2006[5]	2007[5]
All Pension Credit	F8ZA	..	..	42.30	43.62	46.75	50.04
Guarantee Credit Only	F8ZB	..	..	71.91	75.43	79.56	83.74
Guarantee Credit and Savings Credit	F8ZC	..	..	37.51	39.87	43.11	46.11
Savings Credit only	F8ZD	..	..	10.03	10.83	12.39	13.36
(Residual) MIG Case[6]	F8ZE	49.45	50.37	47.49	68.89	110.60	110.49

1 Figures are given in each May from 2000 - 2005 and are taken from the DWP 100% Work and Pensions Longitudinal Study (WPLS).
2 Pension Credit was introduced on 6th October 2003 and replaced Minimum Income Guarantee (Income Support for people aged 60 or over).
3 Average amounts are shown as pounds per week and rounded to the nearest penny.
4 Columns 2002-2003 represent MIG average amounts.
5 Columns 2004 onwards represent Pension Credit Average amounts.
6 When MIG replaced pension credit in October 2003 some cases continued to be MIG cases. These were cases where the partner aged under 60 continued as the claimant. These cases are minimal and are reducing each quarter.

Sources: Department for Work and Pensions; Information and Analysis Directorate: 0191 225 7373

10.20 Summary of government expenditure on social services and housing[1]
Years ended 31 March

£ million

		1999 /00	2000 /01	2001 /02	2002 /03	2003 /04	2004 /05	2005 /06	2006 /07
Final Consumption Expenditure									
Education	QYWZ	43 044	46 933	52 752	57 475	61 983	65 653	70 087	75 632
Health	QYXA	52 901	57 362	62 727	69 065	75 585	83 989	90 394	96 889
Personal social services	GB7F	12 659	13 717	15 033	17 232	19 930	21 922	23 239	24 217
Social benefits	GG5O	106 998	110 417	121 098	126 345	135 571	141 612	145 616	150 614
Housing	QYXD	6 168	6 387	6 590	7 236	10 802	11 222	12 294	13 707
Total government expenditure	GH2K	221 770	234 816	258 200	277 353	303 871	324 398	341 630	361 059
Total government expenditure on social services and housing as a percentage of GDP	GGN7	24.1	24.4	25.6	26.1	27.0	27.2	27.8	27.4

1 See chapter text.

Source: Office for National Statistics: 0207 014 2125

10.21 Summary of Government expenditure on education[1]
Years ended 31 March

£ million

		1999 /00	2000 /01	2001 /02	2002 /03	2003 /04	2004 /05	2005 /06	2006 /07
Education									
Final consumption expenditure									
Current expenditure									
Compensation of employees									
Local Authorities[2]									
Nursery and primary schools	G8ZX	8 396	9 092	10 079	10 740	11 955	13 132	13 879	14 638
Secondary schools	G8ZY	7 991	8 652	9 592	10 356	11 570	13 115	13 891	14 651
Special schools	G8ZZ	858	929	1 030	1 164	1 145	1 362	1 746	1 842
Central Government									
Northern Ireland wages and salaries	HMPM	666	709	769	841	928	959	997	1 251
Other wages and salaries[3]	GB7H	275	297	463	529	610	661	703	872
Total Central Government expenditure	MMTF	941	1 006	1 232	1 370	1 538	1 620	1 700	2 123
Tertiary Education & Other Education[4]	G922	3 284	3 569	3 840	4 127	3 728	2 553	2 524	2 332
Total Compensation of employees	QYSA	21 470	23 248	25 773	27 757	29 936	31 782	33 740	35 586
Net procurement									
Local Government Net procurement[5]	QTKJ	5 839	6 154	6 407	7 620	7 785	8 418	9 741	10 726
Central Government Net procurement[6]	QTLN	1 560	1 737	1 623	1 787	1 933	2 020	2 186	2 445
Nursery/Primary schools									
secondary schools									
Tertiary education									
Total	QYSB	7 399	7 891	8 030	9 407	9 718	10 438	11 927	13 171
Non-market capital consumption	QYSD	1 108	1 142	1 200	1 248	1 305	1 409	1 568	1 778
Total final consumption expenditure	QYSE	29 977	32 281	35 003	38 412	40 959	43 629	47 235	50 535
Other current transfers	QZNU	11 061	12 123	14 315	15 407	17 050	17 862	17 321	18 531
Gross capital formation	QYVD	1 843	2 188	2 863	2 753	2 936	3 094	3 853	4 766
Non-produced non-financial assets	QYWM	−167	−151	−187	−191	−206	−217	−229	−240
Capital transfers	QZKJ	330	492	758	1 094	1 244	1 285	1 907	2 040
Total Central Government Expediture	G924	15 584	17 411	20 623	22 239	24 519	25 690	26 769	30 705
Total Local Government Expediture	G925	27 460	29 522	32 129	35 236	37 464	39 963	43 318	44 927
Total government expenditure	QYWZ	43 044	46 933	52 752	57 475	61 983	65 653	70 087	75 632
Total government education expenditure as a percentage of GDP	GGN8	4.7	4.9	5.2	5.4	5.5	5.5	5.7	5.8

1 See chapter text.
2 Based on pay figures published by Dept for Communities and Local Government , Scottish Executive and National Assembly for Wales.
3 Includes wages/salaries for Scotland, Wales and Non-Departmental Public Bodies (NDPBs).
4 Includes Higher, Further, Adult and Continuing education.
5 Net of VAT.
6 Includes Central Government Net Procurement on NDPBs, Scotland, Wales, Northern Ireland and Education in Healthcare.

Sources: Office for National Statistics: 0207 014 2125;
Department for Communities and Local Government;
Scottish Government;
Welsh Assembly Government

Social protection

10.22 Summary of Government expenditure on Health[1]
Years ended 31 March

£ million

		1999 /00	2000 /01	2001 /02	2002 /03	2003 /04	2004 /05	2005 /06	2006 /07
Final Consumption expenditure[2]									
Current expenditure[3]									
Compensation of employees	QWWQ	26 560	28 794	31 470	34 954	38 140	42 574	45 069	46 430
non-market capital consumption	QYOB	1 492	1 593	1 574	1 680	1 787	1 884	2 113	2 342
other	QTLP	22 413	23 954	26 155	28 407	31 218	34 446	38 149	42 383
Total Final consumption expenditure	QYOT	50 465	54 341	59 199	65 041	71 145	78 904	85 331	91 155
Subsidies	CBRA	–	28	34	33	21	21	21	38
other current transfers	QZMR	931	1 277	1 312	1 171	1 220	1 248	1 658	1 452
Grosss capital formation	QYVE	1 440	1 643	2 067	2 581	3 049	3 727	3 215	4 063
Non produced non financial assets	QYWN	–	–	–	–	–	–	–	–
Capital transfers	HMSF	65	73	115	239	150	89	169	181
total outlays	QYXA	52 901	57 362	62 727	69 065	75 585	83 989	90 394	96 889
Total NHS expenditure as a percentage of GDP	GGN9	5.8	5.9	6.2	6.5	6.7	7.1	7.2	7.3

1 See chapter text.
2 Figures are based on Departmental Expenditure reported to HM Treasury Statistics database.
3 Includes expenditure by Dept. of Health, NHS Trusts, Scottish Government, Welsh Assembly Government and Northern Ireland Executive.

Source: Office for National Statistics: 0208 014 2125

10.23 Summary of Government expenditure on personal social services[1]
Years ended 31 March

£ million

		1999 /00	2000 /01	2001 /02	2002 /03	2003 /04	2004 /05	2005 /06	2006 /07
Personal social services									
Central government Current Expenditure									
Compensation of employees	ADQ7	282	318	331	376	462	482	508	541
Net Procurement	ADR2	252	311	343	532	489	667	410	395
Total	GB7D	534	629	674	908	951	1 149	918	936
Local Authorities Current Expenditure									
Compensation of employees	CFCR	5 735	5 760	5 936	6 385	6 960	7 506	7 959	8 278
Net Procurement	QWSB	6 326	7 259	8 349	9 859	11 934	13 165	14 244	14 863
Total	GB7E	12 061	13 019	14 285	16 244	18 894	20 671	22 203	23 141
Capital Expenditure	GDZU	64	69	74	80	85	102	118	140
Total Final Consumption Expenditure	GB7F	12 659	13 717	15 033	17 232	19 930	21 922	23 239	24 217
Total government expenditure as a percentage of GDP	GGO2	1.4	1.4	1.5	1.6	1.8	1.8	1.9	1.8

1 See chapter text.

Source: Office for National Statistics: 0208 014 2125

10.24 Summary of Government expenditure on social security benefits[1] and administration

Years ended 31 March

£ million

		1999 /00	2000 /01	2001 /02	2002 /03	2003 /04	2004 /05	2005 /06	2006 /07
Social benefits									
Social security benefits in cash									
National Insurance fund									
Retirement pensions	CSDG	37 965	38 923	42 157	44 590	46 701	48 969	51 579	53 766
Widows and Guardians allowances	CSDH	989	980	1 099	1 093	1 006	923	873	792
Unemployment Benefit	CSDI	−1	−1	–	−2	–	–	−3	–
Jobseeker's Allowance	CJTJ	462	435	470	520	506	445	486	474
Incapacity Benefit	CUNL	6 896	6 677	6 678	6 839	6 801	6 754	6 635	6 563
Maternity Benefit	CSDL	41	45	56	69	124	152	164	175
Statutory sick pay	CSDQ	29	29	22	18	72	75	80	85
Statutory maternity pay	GTKZ	577	635	665	737	1 261	1 339	1 295	1 303
Payment in lieu of benefits foregone	GTKV	–	–	–	–	–	–	–	–
Total national insurance fund benefits	ACHH	46 958	47 723	51 147	53 864	56 471	58 657	61 109	63 158
Redundancy fund benefit	GTKN	147	168	205	280	240	186	253	205
Maternity fund benefit	GTKO	–	–	–	–	–	–	–	–
Social fund benefit	GTLQ	1 024	1 784	1 883	1 925	2 159	2 200	2 249	2 279
Benefits paid to overseas residents	FJVZ	1 112	1 176	1 262	1 357	1 445	1 522	1 607	1 724
Total social security benefits in cash	QYRJ	49 241	50 851	54 497	57 426	60 315	62 565	65 218	67 366
Total unfunded social benefits[2]:	QYJT	12 148	12 445	13 728	14 539	15 962	15 676	18 083	19 365
Social assistance benefits in cash									
War pensions and allowances[3]	CSDD	1 254	1 201	1 200	1 186	1 100	1 114	1 009	983
Income Support	CSDE	12 227	13 076	14 100	14 527	15 106	16 356	15 506	15 616
Income tax credits and reliefs	RYCQ	2 623	4 654	5 745	6 711	9 485	11 566	12 938	14 316
Child benefit	EKY3	10 167	8 532	8 795	8 955	9 414	9 565	9 756	10 132
Non-contributory job seekers allowance	EKY4	2 813	2 442	2 124	2 118	2 062	1 780	1 890	2 082
Care allowances	EKY5	2 834	2 955	5 096	5 214	5 445	5 714	6 218	6 487
Disability benefits	EKY6	5 653	6 021	7 310	7 863	8 389	8 900	9 376	9 997
Other benefits	EKY7	4 242	4 360	4 387	3 924	4 473	4 554	5 574	4 222
Benefits paid to overseas residents	RNNF	59	54	55	48	48	48	48	48
Total social assistance benefits in cash	NZGO	41 872	43 295	48 812	50 546	55 522	59 597	62 315	63 883
Total social benefits	NMDR	103 261	106 591	117 037	122 511	131 799	137 838	145 616	150 614
Administration[4]	KJEE	3 737	3 826	4 061	3 834	3 772	3 774	–	–
Total benefits and administration	GG5O	106 998	110 417	121 098	126 345	135 571	141 612	145 616	150 614
Total government benefit expenditure as a percentage of GDP	GGO3	11.7	11.5	11.2	11.9	12.0	11.9	11.7	11.4

1 See chapter text. Figures are based on table 5.2.4s of the Blue Book 2007. They are not fully comparable with earlier editions of the Annual Abstract.
2 Includes Civil & Defence, voluntary employer social contributions, teachers & NHS inflationary pensions increase payments.
3 From 2002/03 War Pensions are administered by the Ministry of Defence.
4 Figures published by HM Treasury in Public Expenditure Statistical Analyses. A separate figure for administration is no longer published.

*Sources: Office for National Statistics: 0208 014 2125;
Department for Work and Pensions;
HM Treasury*

Social protection

10.25 Summary of Government expenditure on housing[1]
Years ended 31 March

£ million

		1999 /00	2000 /01	2001 /02	2002 /03	2003 /04	2004 /05	2005 /06	2006 /07
Housing									
Final consumption expenditure									
Compensation of employees	QYSV	748	776	851	985	1 077	1 172	1 359	1 599
Other current expenditure on goods and services	QYSW	709	935	1 068	1 295	3 023	2 940	3 636	4 195
Capital consumption	QYSY	1 117	1 181	1 301	1 407	1 454	1 632	1 563	1 596
Total	QYSZ	2 574	2 892	3 220	3 687	5 554	5 744	6 558	7 390
Subsidies	QYVP	798	759	613	611	495	302	478	554
Other current transfers	QZNY	30	42	129	93	539	119	227	249
Gross Fixed Capital Formation	QYVH	312	434	497	552	1 184	1 408	1 458	1 598
Non-produced financial assets	QYWQ	–	–	–	–	–	–	–	–
Capital transfers	GVFX	2 454	2 260	2 131	2 293	3 030	3 649	3 573	3 916
Total government expenditure	QYXD	6 168	6 387	6 590	7 236	10 802	11 222	12 294	13 707
Total public sector housing expenditure as a percentage of GDP	GGO4	0.7	0.7	0.7	0.7	1.0	1.0	1.0	1.0

1 See chapter text.

Source: Office for National Statistics: 0208 014 2125

Crime and Justice

Chapter 11

Crime and Justice

There are differences in the legal and judicial systems of England and Wales, Scotland and Northern Ireland which make it impossible to provide tables covering the UK as a whole in this section. These differences concern the classification of offences, the meaning of certain terms used in the statistics, the effects of the several Criminal Justice Acts and recording practices.

Recorded crime statistics

(Table 11.3)

Crimes recorded by the police provide a measure of the amount of crime committed. The statistics are based on counting rules, revised with effect from 1 April 1998, which are standard for all the police forces in England, Wales and Northern Ireland and now include all indictable and triable-either-way offences together with a few summary offences which are closely linked to these offences. The new rules have changed the emphasis of measurement more towards one crime per victim, and have also increased the coverage of offences. These changes have particularly impacted on the offence groups of violence against the person, fraud and forgery, drugs offences and other offences.

For a variety of reasons many offences are either not reported to the police or not recorded by them. The changes in the number of offences recorded do not necessarily provide an accurate reflection of changes in the amount of crime committed.

In order to further improve the consistency of recorded crime statistics and to take a more victim oriented approach to crime recording, the National Crime Recording Standard (NCRS) was introduced in England, Wales and Northern Ireland from 1 April 2002. Some police forces implemented the principles of NCRS in advance of its implementation across all forces in April 2002. The NCRS had the effect of increasing the number of offences recorded by the police.

Similarly, the Scottish Crime Recording Standard (SCRS) was introduced by the eight Scottish police forces with effect from 1 April 2004. This means that no corroborative evidence is required initially to record a crime related incident as a crime if so perceived by the victim. Again, the introduction of this new recording standard was expected to increase the numbers of minor crimes recorded by the police, such as minor crimes of vandalism and minor thefts and offences of petty assault and breach of the peace. However, it was expected that the SCRS would not have much impact on the figures for the more serious crimes such as serious assault, sexual assault, robbery or housebreaking.

The Sexual Offences Act 2003 introduced in May 2004 altered the definition and coverage of sexual offences. In particular, it redefined indecent exposure as a sexual offence which is likely to account for much of the increase in sexual offences.

Further information is available from the Home Office: *Crime in England and Wales 2006/2007*, editors: Sian Nicholas, Chris Kershaw and Alison Walker.

Court proceedings and police cautions

(Tables 11.4–11.8, 11.13–11.17, 11.20–11.22)

The statistical basis of the tables of court proceedings is broadly similar in England and Wales, Scotland and Northern Ireland; the tables show the number of persons found guilty, recording a person under the heading of the principal offence of which he is found guilty, excluding additional findings of guilt at the same proceedings. A person found guilty at a number of separate court proceedings is included more than once.

The statistics on offenders cautioned in England and Wales cover only those who, on admission of guilt, were given a formal caution by, or on the instructions of, a senior police officer as an alternative to prosecution. Written warnings by the police for motor offences and persons paying fixed penalties for certain motoring offences are excluded. Formal cautions are not issued in Scotland. There are no statistics on cautioning available for Northern Ireland.

The Crime and Disorder Act 1998 created provisions in relation to reprimands and final warnings, new offences and orders which have been implemented nationally since 1 June 2000. They replace the system of cautioning for offenders aged under 18. Reprimands can be given to first-time offenders for minor offences. Any further offending results in either a final warning or a charge.

For persons proceeded against in Scotland, the statistics relate to the High Court of Justiciary, the Sheriff Court and the District Court. The High Court deals with serious solemn (that is, Jury) cases and has unlimited sentencing power. The Sheriff Court is limited to imprisonment of three years for solemn cases, or three months (six months when specified in legislation for second or subsequent offences and 12 months for certain statutory offences) for summary (that is, non-Jury) cases. The District Court deals only with summary cases and is limited to 60 days imprisonment and level 4 fines. Stipendiary Magistrates sit in Glasgow District Court and have the summary sentencing powers of a Sheriff.

In England and Wales, indictable offences are offences which are:

- triable only on indictment. These offences are the most serious breaches of the criminal law and must be tried at the Crown Court. 'Indictable-only' offences include murder, manslaughter, rape and robbery

- triable either way. These offences may be tried at the Crown Court or Magistrates' Court

The Criminal Justice Act 1991 led to the following main changes in the sentences available to the courts in England and Wales:

- introduction of combination orders

- introduction of the 'unit fine scheme' at Magistrates' courts

- abolishing the sentence of detention in a young offender institution for 14 year old boys and changing the minimum and maximum sentence lengths for 15 to 17 year olds to ten and 12 months respectively

- abolishing partly suspended sentences of imprisonment and restricting the use of a fully suspended sentence

The Criminal Justice Act 1993 abolished the 'Unit Fine Scheme' in Magistrates' courts which had been introduced under the Criminal Justice Act 1991.

A charging standard for assault was introduced in England and Wales on 31 August 1994 with the aim to promote consistency between the police and prosecution on the appropriate level of charge to be brought.

The Criminal Justice and Public Order Act 1994 created several new offences in England and Wales, mainly in the area of Public Order, but also including male rape (there is no statutory offence of 'male rape' in Scotland, although such a crime may be charged as serious assault). The Act also:

- extended the provisions of section 53 of the Children and Young Persons Act 1993 for ten to 13 year olds

- increased the maximum sentence length for 15 to 17 year olds to two years

- increased the upper limit from £2,000 to £5,000 for offences of criminal damage proceeded against as if triable only summarily

- introduced provisions for the reduction of sentences for early guilty pleas

- increased the maximum sentence length for certain firearm offences

Provisions within the Crime (Sentences) Act 1997 (as amended by the Powers of Criminal Courts Sentencing Act 2000), in England and Wales, and the Crime and Punishment (Scotland) Act 1997, in Scotland, included:

- an automatic life sentence for a second serious violent or sexual offence unless there are exceptional circumstances (this provision has not been enacted in Scotland)

- a minimum sentence of seven years for an offender convicted for a third time of a class A drug trafficking offence unless the court considers this to be unjust in all the circumstances, and in England and Wales

- the new section 38A of the Magistrates' Courts' Act 1980 extending the circumstances in which a magistrates' court may commit a person convicted of an offence triable either way to the Crown Court for sentence. It was implemented in conjunction with section 49 of the Criminal Procedure and Investigations Act 1996, which involves the magistrates' courts in asking defendants to indicate plea before the mode of trial decision is taken and compels the court to sentence or commit for sentence any defendant who indicates a guilty plea

Under the Criminal Justice and Court Service Act 2000 new terms were introduced for certain orders. Community rehabilitation order is the new name for a probation order. A community service order is now known as a community punishment order. Finally, the new term for a combination order is community punishment and rehabilitation order. In April 2000 the secure training order was replaced by the detention and training order. Section 53 of the Children and Young Persons Act 1993 was repealed on 25 August 2000 and its provisions were transferred to Sections 90–92 of the Powers of Criminal Courts (Sentencing) Act 2000. Reparation and Action plan order were implemented nationally from 1 June 2000. Drug treatment and testing order was implemented in England, Scotland and Wales from October 2000. Referral order was implemented in England, Scotland and Wales from April 2000. These changes are now reflected in Table 11.8.

The system of Magistrates' courts and Crown Courts in Northern Ireland operates in a similar way to that in England and Wales. A particularly significant statutory development, however, has been the Criminal Justice (NI) Order 1996 which introduces a new sentencing regime into Northern Ireland, largely replicating that which was introduced into England and Wales by the Criminal Justice Acts of 1991 and 1993. The order makes many changes to both community and custodial sentences, while introducing new orders such as the combination order, the custody probation order and orders for release on licence of sexual offenders.

Expenditure on penal establishments in Scotland

(Table 11.19)

The results shown in this table are reported on a cash basis for financial years 1996–97 to 2000–01 in line with funding arrangements. Financial year 2001–02 is reported on a resource accounting basis in line with the introduction of Resource Budgeting. Capital Charges were introduced with Resource Accounting and Budgeting.

11.1

Police force strength[1]: by country and sex
As at 31 March

Numbers

		1997	1998	1999	2000	2001	2002	2003	2004	2005	2006	2007
England and Wales												
Regular Police(FTE)												
Strength:												
Men	KERB	106 271	105 145	103 956	101 801	102 321	104 483	106 996	110 150	110 597	109 327	108 118
Women	KERC	18 780	19 611	19 885	20 155	21 155	22 784	24 430	26 956	28 898	30 307	31 914
Seconded:[2,3]												
Men	KERD	1 882	1 836	2 017	2 077	1 914	2 031	1 689	1 811	1 514	1 545	422
Women	KERE	225	222	238	307	292	305	251	284	222	203	60
Additional Officers:[4]												
Men	KERF	200	267	324	361	493	567	375	394	522	676	657
Women	KERG	158	514	582	519	509	564	709	969	1 042	1 213	1 203
Special constables												
Strength:[5]												
Men	KERH	12 886	11 977	10 860	9 623	8 630	8 014	7 718	7 645	8 074	8 829	9 327
Women	KERI	6 988	6 279	5 624	4 724	4 108	3 584	3 319	3 343	3 844	4 350	4 694
Scotland												
Regular police												
Strength:[6]												
Men	KERK	12 752	12 753	12 545	12 374	12 547	12 513	12 590	12 685	12 798	12 820	12 687
Women	KERL	2 037	2 227	2 265	2 325	2 602	2 738	2 897	2 898	3 203	3 401	3 547
Central service:[7]												
Men	KERM	85	85	88	95	87	116	131	166	195	171	153
Women	KERN	4	6	9	13	10	12	17	29	29	25	28
Seconded:[8]												
Men	KERO	101	101	85	130	140	133	166	192	216	200	195
Women	KERP	13	10	12	18	14	18	24	30	31	27	3
Additional regular police:												
Men	HFVM	71	88	85	80	83	80	79	88	79	85	107
Women	HFVN	1	9	6	4	5	12	10	13	21	15	12
Special constables												
Strength:												
Men	KERS	1 336	1 286	1 229	981	924	812	711	773	718	888	1 428[9]
Women	KERT	450	437	422	355	336	307	280	328	437	432	..
Northern Ireland												
Regular police[10,11]												
Strength:												
Men	KERU	7 562	7 523	7 406	6 844	6 227	6 057	6 171	6 108	6 016	5 992	5 957
Women	KERV	923	933	987	966	1 009	1 080	1 266	1 418	1 547	1 534	1 605
Reserve[12]												
Strength:												
Men	KERW	3 587	3 469	3 199	2 962	2 629	2 223	1 983	1 824	1 431	1 424	1 212
Women	KERX	719	705	641	607	556	510	453	485	410	402	400

1 Figures for England and Wales excluding those on career breaks or maternity/paternity leave. From 1999, figures for Northern Ireland reflect the position at the end of the financial year, prior to this figures were as at 31 December.

2 Figures exclude secondments outside the police service in England and Wales (eg to the private sector or to law enforcement agencies overseas).

3 From 31 March 2007 onwards details of officers seconded to NCIS and NCS will no longer appear following the launch of Serious Organised Crime Agency (SOCA) in April 2006.

4 Figures include those officers on career breaks or maternity/paternity leave. Prior to 2003, these figures were not collected centrally.

5 Special constable figures are given as a headcount measure.

6 'Strength' is WTE police strength, only excluding special constables.

7 Instructors at Training Establishments, etc, formerly shown as secondments.

8 Includes Scottish Crime and Drug Enforcement Agency .

9 Split between Male and Female special constables is unavailable for 2007.

10 Does not include officers on secondment.

11 Also includes student officers.

12 Includes part-time reserve and full-time reserve, FTR -745 as at 31 March 2007 (693 males and 52 females). PTR - 867 as at 31 March 2007 (519 males and 348 females).

Sources: Home Office: 020 7035 0289;
Scottish Government Justice Analytical Services: 0131 244 2226;
The Police Service of Northern Ireland: 028 9065 0222 ext 24070

Crime and justice

11.2 Prison Population[1] international comparisons

Country	2000	2001	2002	2003	2004	2005	2006	% change 2005-2006	Rate[15] per 100,000 population in 2006
England & Wales[2]	65 666	67 056	71 324	72 992	75 057	76 896	79 085	3	147
Northern Ireland[3]	1 068	910	1 026	1 160	1 274	1 301	1 433	10	82
Scotland[3]	5 869	6 137	6 404	6 524	6 805	6 792	7 111	5	139
Austria	6 896	6 915	7 511	7 816	9 000	8 767	8 780	0	106
Belgium[4]	8 688	8 544	8 605	9 308	9 245	9 375	9 635	3	92
Bulgaria[5]	10 147	8 971	8 994	9 422	10 066	10 871	11 436	5	148
Croatia[5]	2 027	2 623	2 584	2 732	2 803	3 022	3 485	15	78
Cyprus	288	369	345	355	546	536	599	12	77
Czech Republic[6]	21 538	19 320	16 213	17 277	18 343	18 937	18 578	-2	181
Denmark	3 279	3 150	3 439	3 577	3 762	4 132	3 759	-9	69
Estonia[5]	4 679	4 803	4 775	4 352	4 576	4 565	4 411	-3	328
Finland[6]	2 887	3 110	3 469	3 463	3 535	3 883	3 477	-10	66
France[7]	48 835	47 005	53 463	57 440	56 271	56 595	55 754	-1	88
Germany[8]	79 507	80 333	74 904	81 176	81 166	80 410	78 581	-2	95
Greece[9]	8 038	8 343	8 284	8 555	8 760	9 589	10 113	5	91
Hungary[6]	15 539	17 275	17 838	16 507	16 543	15 720	14 824	-6	147
Iceland	82	110	107	112	115	119	119	0	39
Ireland (Eire)	2 887	3 025	3 028	2 986	3 083	3 022	3 080	2	72
Italy[6]	55 242	57 203	56 723	56 845	56 068	59 523	39 005	-34	66
Latvia[5]	8 815	8 831	8 531	8 366	8 179	7 646	6 965	-9	303
Lithuania[5]	14 412	9 516	11 566	11 070	8 063	8 125	8 137	0	239
Luxembourg	394	357	380	498	548	693	756	9	163
Malta	246	257	283	278	277	298	346	16	85
Netherlands	13 847	15 246	16 239	18 242	20 075	21 826	20 463	-6	125
Norway	2 643	2 666	2 662	2 914	2 975	3 097	3 164	2	68
Poland[2]	65 336	80 004	80 610	80 692	79 344	82 656	87 669	6	230
Portugal[6]	12 944	13 260	13 918	13 835	13 152	12 889	12 636	-2	119
Romania[10]	48 267	49 841	48 075	42 815	39 031	36 505	34 542	-5	160
Russian Federation[5]	1 060 404	925 072	980 151	877 393	847 004	763 115	823 451	8	577
Slovakia[6]	8 873	7 433	7 758	8 873	8 422	8 897	8249	-7	153
Slovenia	1 136	1 155	1 120	1 099	1 126	1 132	1 301	15	65
Spain	45 044	46 962	50 994	55 244	59 224	61 269	64 120	5	145
Sweden[11]	5 678	6 089	6 506	6 755	7 332	7 054	7 175	2	79
Switzerland[12]	6 390	5 137	4 937	5 214	5 977	6 137	5 888	-4	79
Turkey	71 860	61 336	60 091	64 051	71 148	-	67 795	25	93
Ukraine	220 306	198 885	198 946	198 386	193 489	179 519	165 716	-8	356
Australia[13]	21 714	22 458	22 492	23 555	24 171	25 353	25 790	2	125
Canada[14]	35 552	35 533	35 841	36 070	34 096	34 244	-	-	107 (2005)
Japan[5]	56 134	61 242	65 508	69 502	73 734	76 413	79 052	3	62
Korea(Rep. of)[3]	62 959	62 235	61 084	58 945	57 184	52 403	46 721	-11	97
Mexico[6]	154 765	165 687	172 888	182 530	193 889	205 821	214 452	4	197
New Zealand[3]	5 720	5 887	5 738	6 059	6 556	7 100	7 595	7	183
South Africa[8]	171 462	170 959	178 998	189 748	189 748	187 394	150 302	-20	316
U.S.A.[13]	1 935 753	1 961 247	2 033 331	2 081 580	2 129 802	2 186 230	2 245 189	3	750
European Union 25	507 631	522 608	535 256	555 285	560 776	572 528	556 039	-3	120

1 At 1 September: number of prisoners, including pre-trial detainees.
2 At 31 August.
3 Annual averages. Countries calculate these on the basis of daily, weekly or monthly figures.
4 At 1 March.
5 At 1 January.
6 At 31 December.
7 Metropolitan and overseas departments and territories.
8 At 31 March
9 At 1 September (2000-03, 2005-06). At 16 December (2004).
10 At 31 December (2000-05). At 28 November (2006)
11 At 1 October.
12 At third Wednesday in March (2000-01). At first Wednesday in September (2002-06).
13 At 30 June.
14 Annual averages by financial year (1 April - 31 March).
15 Based on estimates of national population.

Sources: Ministries responsible for prisons, national prison administrations,; national statistical offices, Council of Europe Annual Penal Statistics (SPACE),; World Prison Population List and World Prison Brief; (International Centre for Prison Studies King's College, London)

11.3 Recorded crime statistics: by offence group[1]
England and Wales

Thousands

		1996	1997	1998[2,3]/99		1998[3]/99	1999/00	2000/01	2001[4]/02	2002[4,6]/03	2003/04	2004/05	2005/06	2006[8]/07
Violence against the person	BEAB	239.3	250.8	230.8	LQMP	502.8	581.0	600.9	650.3	845.1	967.2	1 048.1	1 059.6	1 046.4
Sexual offences[7]	BEAC	31.4	33.2	34.9	LQMQ	36.2	37.8	37.3	41.4	58.9	62.5	62.9	62.1	57.5
Burglary	BEAD	1 164.6	1 015.1	951.9	LQMR	953.2	906.5	836.0	878.5	890.1	820.0	680.4	645.1	622.0
Robbery	BEAE	74.0	63.1	66.2	LQMS	66.8	84.3	95.2	121.4	110.3	103.7	91.0	98.2	101.4
Theft and handling stolen goods (of which):	BEAF	2 383.9	2 165.0	2 126.7	LQMT	2 191.4	2 223.6	2 145.4	2 267.0	–	–	–	–	–
Offences against vehicles					I8RM	..	..	..	..	1 074.7	985.0	820.1	792.8	765.1
Other theft offences					I8RN	..	..	..	..	1 336.9	1 327.9	1 247.6	1 226.2	1 181.0
Fraud and forgery	BEAG	136.2	134.4	173.7	LQMU	279.5	334.8	319.3	314.9	331.1	319.6	280.1	232.8	199.8
Criminal damage	BEAH	951.3	877.0	834.4	LQMV	879.6	945.7	960.1	1 064.5	1 120.6	1 218.5	1 197.5	1 184.3	1 185.1
Drug offences[5]	LQMO	..	..	21.3	LQYT	135.9	121.9	113.5	121.4	143.3	143.5	145.8	178.5	194.3
Other offences[5]	BEAI	33.6	36.6	42.0	LQYU	63.6	65.7	63.2	65.7	64.0	65.7	64.0	75.6	75.6
Total	BEAA	5 036.6	4 598.3	4 481.8	LQYV	5 109.1	5 301.2	5 170.8	5 525.0	5 975.0	6 013.8	5 637.5	5 555.2	5 428.3

1 See chapter text.
2 Estimates.
3 Figures from this period are not directly comparable with data prior to 1998/99 and from 2002/03 onwards.
4 The National Crime Recording Standard (NCRS) was introduced in England and Wales from 1 April 2002. These figures are not directly comparable with those for earlier years. For more details about the inflationary effects of the NCRS on the 2001/02 and 2002/03 figures see chapter text. A detailed explanation for the NCRS can be accessed via the following Home Office Research Development and Statistics website http://www.homeoffice.gov.uk/rds/countrules.html

5 Prior to 1 April 1998 the offence of drug trafficking was included in the 'Other offences' group. From 1 April 1999, under the new counting rules, drug trafficking became part of a new 'Drug offences' group which, now also includes possession and other drug offences. For 1998/99 under the old counting rules, drug trafficking has been separated out and listed under drugs offences.
6 Includes the British Transport Police (BTP) from 2002/03 onwards.
7 The Sexual Offences Act 2003, introduced in May 2004, altered the
8 The offence groupings were revised in 2006/07 and backdated to 2002/03.

Source: Home Office: 020 7035 0307

11.4 Offenders found guilty: by offence group[1,2,3],
England and Wales
Magistrates' courts and the Crown Court

Thousands

		1996	1997	1998	1999	2000	2001	2002	2003	2004	2005	2006
All ages[4]												
Indictable offences												
Violence against the person:	KJEJ	30.0	34.6	35.7	34.4	34.0	35.3	37.7	38.0	39.1	40.9	41.9
Murder	KESB	0.3	0.3	0.3	0.3	0.3	0.3	0.3	0.3	0.4	0.4	0.4
Manslaughter	KESC	0.3	0.3	0.3	0.3	0.3	0.3	0.3	0.2	0.3	0.3	0.2
Wounding	KESD	28.3	32.7	35.2	33.9	33.5	33.5	35.7	35.9	36.9	38.6	39.8
Other offences of violence against the person	KESE	1.2	1.3	1.3	1.3	1.3	1.2	1.4	1.5	1.3	1.3	1.2
Sexual offences	KESF	4.4	4.5	4.6	4.3	3.9	3.8	4.4	4.4	4.8	4.8	4.9
Burglary	KESG	32.2	31.7	30.8	29.3	26.2	24.8	26.7	25.7	24.3	23.0	23.0
Robbery	KESH	5.9	5.6	5.5	5.6	6.0	6.8	7.7	7.3	7.5	7.1	8.1
Theft and handling stolen goods	KESI	114.5	118.4	125.7	131.2	128.0	127.0	127.3	119.1	110.6	103.8	99.0
Fraud and forgery	KESJ	16.3	17.0	19.8	20.3	19.2	18.3	18.1	18.0	18.1	18.5	18.2
Criminal damage	KESK	9.8	10.5	10.9	10.9	10.2	10.7	11.0	11.2	11.7	11.7	12.7
Drugs	KBWX	34.1	40.7	48.8	48.7	44.6	45.6	49.0	51.2	54.5	39.1	39.6
Other offences (excluding motoring)	KESL	43.5	47.6	49.6	47.9	44.5	44.2	48.0	51.4	54.7	53.1	50.0
Motoring offences	KESM	9.9	9.5	9.0	8.1	7.6	7.7	8.2	8.7	8.0	6.6	5.9
Total	KESA	300.6	320.1	341.7	342.0	325.5	324.2	338.3	335.1	317.8	308.5	303.2
Summary offences												
Assaults	KESO	30.0	32.0	35.3	37.5	37.4	37.7	40.7	45.6	53.4	60.4	64.5
Betting and gaming	KESP	–	–	–	–	–	–	–	–	–	–	–
Offences with pedal cycles	KBWY	1.3	1.5	2.1	1.3	0.8	0.6	0.5	0.6	0.7	0.7	0.7
Other Highways Acts offences	KBWZ	2.8	3.2	3.1	2.9	2.7	2.4	2.2	1.9	1.8	2.0	2.1
Breach of local or other regulations	KESQ	5.9	6.4	5.8	6.5	5.0	4.3	3.9	3.4	3.1	2.6	1.9
Intoxicating Liquor Laws: Drunkenness	KESR	24.2	28.8	30.8	28.7	27.2	26.2	26.9	27.7	21.1	16.1	15.7
Other offences	KESS	0.5	0.6	0.6	0.5	0.4	0.3	0.4	0.7	0.8	1.0	1.2
Education Acts	KEST	3.5	3.7	5.0	5.1	5.1	5.6	5.8	5.8	6.5	6.4	7.4
Game Laws	KESU	0.4	0.3	0.4	0.3	0.2	0.2	0.3	0.2	0.2	0.4	–
Labour Laws	KESV	–	0.1	0.1	0.1	0.1	–	–	–	–	–	–
Summary offences of criminal damage and malicious damage	KESW	23.4	24.7	26.5	27.9	28.0	26.9	28.3	29.8	31.5	31.1	30.2
Offences by prostitutes	KESX	6.6	6.6	6.0	4.0	4.1	3.7	4.2	3.9	2.9	2.2	1.6
Railway offences	KESY	9.1	11.4	12.6	15.2	17.4	22.6	29.4	34.8	35.0	40.2	44.6
Revenue Laws	KESZ	139.1	143.5	174.7	165.8	175.0	146.9	167.8	172.5	175.5	130.5	104.4
Vagrancy Acts	KETB	2.0	2.0	2.2	2.7	3.3	3.2	3.8	3.8	2.9	2.2	2.2
Wireless Telegraphy Acts	KETC	164.9	77.0	76.6	55.8	105.7	83.8	96.6	79.9	89.3	105.0	115.6
Other summary offences	KETD	74.7	74.7	80.9	79.3	78.1	77.8	76.4	82.9	97.9	108.2	103.6
Motoring offences (summary)	KETA	649.0	649.3	665.2	632.9	607.5	583.3	595.8	662.6	707.9	667.1	622.5
Total	KESN	1 137.4	1 065.8	1 128.0	1 066.5	1 098.2	1 025.5	1 083.0	1 156.1	1 230.7	1 175.9	1 118.2
Persons aged 10 to under 18[5]												
Indictable offences												
Violence against the person:	KETF	5.3	5.9	5.9	6.2	6.4	6.9	6.9	6.6	6.9	7.4	7.5
Murder	KBXA	–	–	–	–	–	–	–	–	–	–	–
Manslaughter	KBXB	–	–	–	0.2	–	–	–	–	–	–	–
Wounding	KBXC	5.3	5.8	5.9	5.9	6.3	6.8	6.8	6.5	6.5	7.3	7.4
Other offences of violence against the person	KCAA	–	0.1	0.1	–	0.1	0.1	0.1	0.1	0.3	0.2	0.1
Sexual offences	KETG	0.4	0.5	0.5	0.5	0.5	0.5	0.6	0.4	0.6	0.6	0.5
Burglary	KETH	8.6	8.6	8.5	7.8	6.8	6.3	6.4	5.8	5.9	6.0	6.2
Robbery	KETI	2.4	2.3	2.2	2.0	2.2	2.8	2.8	2.6	3.0	3.1	3.7
Theft and handling stolen goods	KETJ	19.0	19.6	21.9	22.7	21.0	20.6	18.4	16.5	16.8	17.1	16.3
Fraud and forgery	KETK	0.7	0.8	1.0	1.1	1.0	1.0	1.2	0.8	0.8	0.7	0.6
Criminal damage	KETL	2.2	2.3	2.3	2.7	2.6	2.9	2.9	2.9	3.2	3.3	3.7
Drugs	KCAB	1.6	1.8	2.7	3.1	3.7	4.3	5.0	5.1	4.5	4.6	4.5
Other offences (excluding motoring)	KETM	3.8	4.2	4.2	4.3	4.4	4.4	4.4	4.3	4.6	4.5	4.1
Motoring	KETN	0.4	0.4	0.4	0.4	0.6	0.7	0.8	0.8	0.7	0.6	0.5
Total	KETE	44.4	46.4	49.7	50.6	49.2	50.3	49.1	46.0	47.0	47.8	47.6
Summary offences												
Offences with pedal cycles	KETP	0.2	0.2	0.3	0.3	0.2	0.2	0.2	0.2	0.2	0.3	0.2
Breach of local or other regulations	KETR	0.3	0.2	0.2	0.2	0.2	0.2	0.1	0.1	0.1	0.1	0.1
Summary offences of criminal damage and malicious damage	KETS	3.9	4.4	5.2	6.1	6.7	6.9	7.0	7.2	8.3	8.8	8.6
Railway offences	KETT	0.4	0.5	0.5	0.5	0.4	0.4	0.4	0.3	0.4	0.4	0.4
Other summary offences	KETU	8.8	16.6	19.4	20.0	20.2	20.8	20.6	20.9	23.1	24.0	24.7
Motoring offences (summary)	KCAC	10.8	10.8	11.3	12.6	14.5	16.7	17.1	17.8	17.0	14.8	12.1
Total	KETO	30.3	22.0	36.8	39.6	42.2	45.2	45.4	46.6	49.2	48.3	46.1

1 See chapter text.
2 Data provided on the principal offence basis.
3 Every effort is made to ensure that the figures presented are accurate and complete. However, it is important to note that these data have been extracted from large administrative data systems generated by the courts and police forces. As a consequence, care should be taken to ensure data collection processes and their inevitable limitations are taken into account when those data are used.
4 Includes 'Companies', etc .
5 Figures for persons aged 10 to under 18 are included in the totals above.

Source: Office for Criminal Justice Reform: 020 7035 4955

11.5 Offenders cautioned: by offence group[1,2,3]
England and Wales

Thousands

		1996	1997	1998	1999	2000	2001	2002	2003	2004	2005	2006
All ages[4]												
Indictable offences												
Violence against the person	KELB	21.8	23.6	23.5	21.2	19.9	19.5	23.6	28.8	36.6	51.0	57.3
Murder	KCAD	–	–	–	–	–	–	–	–	–	–	–
Manslaughter	KCAE	–	–	–	–	–	–	–	–	–	–	–
Wounding	KCAF	21.4	23.3	22.9	20.6	19.3	18.9	22.9	27.9	35.4	49.6	55.7
Other violence against the person	KCAG	0.4	0.4	0.6	0.6	0.6	0.6	0.7	0.8	1.2	1.4	1.5
Sexual offences	KELC	2.0	1.9	1.7	1.5	1.3	1.2	1.2	1.4	1.6	1.8	1.9
Burglary	KELD	10.2	9.4	8.4	7.7	6.6	6.4	5.8	5.6	5.6	6.5	7.7
Robbery	KELE	0.6	0.7	0.6	0.6	0.6	0.5	0.4	0.4	0.5	0.6	0.7
Theft and handling stolen goods	KELF	93.6	82.8	83.6	75.4	67.6	63.5	54.2	54.5	61.9	67.6	72.4
Fraud and forgery	KELG	7.5	7.2	7.4	7.2	6.2	5.8	5.3	5.5	6.0	6.9	8.0
Criminal damage	KELH	3.1	2.8	2.7	3.0	3.2	3.4	3.1	3.7	5.5	7.2	9.0
Drug offences	KCAI	47.5	56.0	58.7	49.4	41.1	39.4	44.9	45.7	32.6	34.4	37.4
Other offences	KELI	4.4	5.0	5.0	4.6	4.4	4.1	4.4	5.3	6.0	6.9	9.3
All offenders cautioned	KELA	190.8	189.4	191.7	170.6	150.9	143.9	142.9	150.7	156.3	182.9	203.7
Summary offences												
Assaults	KELK	9.1	9.1	13.2	17.0	17.2	18.2	17.3	19.8	26.1	40.8	64.6
Betting and gaming	KELL	–	–	–	–	–	–	–	–	–	–	–
Offences with pedal cycles	KCAK	0.9	0.9	0.8	0.7	0.3	0.2	0.1	0.1	0.3	0.3	0.3
Other Highways Acts offences	KCAL	0.8	0.8	0.8	0.7	0.4	0.3	0.2	0.3	0.3	0.2	0.3
Breach of local or other regulations	KELM	0.8	0.9	0.9	0.7	0.5	0.3	0.3	0.2	0.2	0.2	0.1
Intoxicating Liquor Laws:												
Drunkenness	KELN	25.9	25.7	22.8	20.3	18.1	16.6	16.2	18.1	13.5	8.6	5.8
Other offences	KELO	0.9	0.9	0.7	0.4	0.3	0.3	0.3	0.3	0.3	0.3	0.2
Education Acts	KELP	–	–	–	–	–	–	–	0.1	0.1	0.1	0.1
Game Laws	KELQ	0.1	0.1	0.1	0.1	–	–	–	–	–	–	–
Labour Laws	KELR	–	–	–	–	–	–	–	–	–	–	–
Summary offences of criminal damage and malicious damage	KELS	27.7	27.6	28.3	28.7	26.8	26.7	24.7	27.6	33.3	38.0	43.2
Offences by prostitutes	KELT	3.5	3.5	3.5	2.1	1.3	1.0	1.8	1.3	1.6	1.4	1.2
Railway offences	KELU	0.2	0.1	–	–	–	–	–	–	–	0.1	0.1
Revenue Laws	KELV	0.1	0.1	0.1	0.1	–	–	–	–	–	–	–
Vagrancy Acts	KELX	0.6	0.6	1.2	0.8	0.4	0.3	0.3	0.3	0.2	0.3	0.4
Wireless Telegraphy Acts	KELY	–	–	–	–	–	–	–	–	–	–	–
Other summary offences	KELZ	24.7	22.3	37.0	24.1	22.5	21.9	21.0	22.9	23.4	25.2	29.2
All offenders cautioned	KELJ	95.4	92.7	96.2	95.6	88.1	85.9	82.4	91.1	99.5	115.5	145.6
Persons aged 10 to under 18[5]												
Indictable offences												
Violence against the person	KEMB	9.4	9.6	9.5	8.5	8.3	8.7	9.3	11.0	13.6	16.5	16.6
Murder	KCAN	–	–	–	–	–	–	–	–	–	–	–
Manslaughter	KCAO	–	–	–	–	–	–	–	–	–	–	–
Wounding	KCAP	9.4	9.6	9.4	8.4	8.2	8.6	9.2	10.9	13.5	16.4	16.5
Other violence against the person	KCCE	–	–	0.1	0.1	0.1	0.1	0.1	0.1	0.1	0.1	0.1
Sexual offences	KEMC	0.7	0.7	0.6	0.6	0.5	0.5	0.4	0.5	0.5	0.6	0.6
Burglary	KEMD	8.2	7.5	6.7	6.1	5.4	5.3	4.6	4.4	4.2	4.6	5.0
Robbery	KEME	0.6	0.6	0.5	0.5	0.5	0.5	0.4	0.4	0.4	0.5	0.6
Theft and handling stolen goods	KEMF	48.2	40.9	44.0	39.6	36.9	35.2	28.1	28.3	33.1	36.8	39.4
Fraud and forgery	KEMG	1.5	1.4	1.6	1.7	1.5	1.3	1.1	1.0	1.0	1.1	1.3
Criminal damage	KEMH	2.0	1.8	1.7	1.9	2.1	2.3	1.9	2.3	3.1	3.9	4.7
Drug offences	KCCF	7.9	9.7	11.0	9.6	7.9	8.5	9.5	9.6	8.3	7.8	7.1
Other offences	KEMI	1.3	1.5	1.5	1.4	1.3	1.3	1.3	1.4	1.6	1.6	1.9
All offenders cautioned	KEMA	79.9	73.7	77.2	69.8	64.3	63.5	56.6	58.7	65.9	73.4	77.1
Summary offences												
Offences with pedal cycles	KEMK	0.5	0.5	0.4	0.3	0.2	0.1	0.1	0.1	0.2	0.2	0.2
Breach of local or other regulations	KEMM	0.3	0.3	0.3	0.2	0.2	0.1	0.1	0.1	0.1	0.1	0.1
Summary offences of criminal damage and malicious damage	KEMN	13.8	13.5	14.2	14.7	14.4	15.2	12.6	14.3	17.1	19.8	21.9
Railway offences	KEMO	0.1	0.1	–	–	–	–	–	–	–	–	–
Other summary offences	KEMP	10.8	16.4	17.7	19.0	18.4	19.1	17.1	18.8	21.7	25.1	29.6
All offenders cautioned	KEMJ	33.2	30.8	32.5	34.2	33.2	34.5	29.9	33.3	39.1	45.1	51.7

1 See chapter text.
2 Data provided on the principal offence basis.
3 Every effort is made to ensure that the figures presented are accurate and complete. However, it is important to note that these data have been extracted from large administrative data systems generated by police forces. As a consequence, care should be taken to ensure data collection processes and their inevitable limitations are taken into account when those data are used.
4 Includes 'Companies', etc.
5 Figures for persons aged 10 to under 18 are included in the totals above.

Source: Office for Criminal Justice Reform: 020 7035 4955

11.6 Offenders found guilty of offences: by age and sex[1,2,3]
England and Wales
Magistrates' courts and the Crown Court

Thousands

		1996	1997	1998	1999	2000	2001	2002	2003	2004	2005	2006
Males												
Indictable offences												
All ages	KEFA	261.1	276.5	292.9	291.7	276.5	275.5	287.1	283.4	268.4	261.3	258.4
10 and under 15 years	KEFB	6.6	7.1	8.1	8.9	8.7	9.0	8.8	8.0	8.5	8.6	8.3
15 and under 18 years	KEFC	32.5	33.6	35.2	35.1	33.8	34.4	33.7	31.4	31.8	32.0	32.5
18 and under 21 years	KEFD	46.3	48.4	51.8	52.6	49.9	48.2	46.6	43.8	39.9	38.5	39.0
21 years and over	KEFE	175.6	187.3	197.9	195.0	184.0	183.9	198.0	200.2	188.2	182.2	178.7
Summary offences												
All ages	KEFF	903.6	880.9	929.0	886.6	881.0	826.6	866.4	937.1	990.0	931.2	877.7
10 and under 15 years	KEFG	2.8	3.0	3.9	5.1	5.8	6.2	6.1	6.1	6.7	7.2	7.0
15 and under 18 years	KEFH	24.6	25.9	28.5	30.3	32.2	34.5	34.6	35.3	36.4	34.6	32.3
18 and under 21 years	KEFI	88.4	91.0	96.3	94.8	93.0	92.2	94.7	99.9	98.2	89.4	85.1
21 years and over	KEFJ	787.9	761.0	800.3	756.5	750.0	693.6	731.0	795.8	848.8	800.1	753.4
Females												
Indictable offences												
All ages	KEFK	38.0	42.2	47.3	49.0	47.7	47.4	50.0	50.2	48.4	46.1	43.7
10 and under 15 years	KEFL	1.0	1.0	1.4	1.4	1.5	1.6	1.6	1.6	1.7	1.7	1.7
15 and under 18 years	KEFM	4.2	4.6	5.1	5.2	5.2	5.3	5.1	4.9	5.0	5.5	5.1
18 and under 21 years	KEFN	5.7	6.3	7.1	7.6	7.5	7.0	6.9	6.2	5.7	5.3	4.8
21 years and over	KEFO	27.2	30.4	33.7	34.7	33.5	33.5	36.5	37.5	35.9	33.6	32.1
Summary offences												
All ages	KEFP	222.9	174.9	188.3	171.0	208.3	190.2	208.7	210.5	231.2	236.6	233.9
10 and under 15 years	KEFQ	0.4	0.5	0.6	0.8	0.9	0.9	1.1	1.2	1.4	1.6	1.6
15 and under 18 years	KEFR	2.6	3.4	3.8	3.4	3.3	3.6	3.6	4.0	4.6	4.9	5.2
18 and under 21 years	KEFS	12.1	11.1	12.1	10.8	11.8	11.1	11.6	12.6	13.0	13.5	14.2
21 years and over	KEFT	207.9	160.0	171.7	155.4	192.3	174.7	192.4	192.7	212.1	216.6	212.9
Companies, etc												
Indictable offences	KEFU	1.5	1.3	1.5	1.3	1.3	1.3	1.2	1.4	1.1	1.1	1.0
Summary offences	KEFV	10.9	10.0	10.7	8.9	8.8	8.6	7.9	8.6	9.4	8.1	6.6

1 See chapter text.
2 These data are on the principal offence basis.
3 Every effort is made to ensure that the figures presented are accurate and complete. However, it is important to note that these data have been extracted from large administrative data systems generated by the courts and police forces. As a consequence, care should be taken to ensure data collection processes and their inevitable limitations are taken into account when those data are used.

Source: Office for Criminal Justice Reform: 020 7035 4955

11.7 Persons cautioned by the police: by age and sex[1,3,4]
England and Wales

Thousands

		1996	1997	1998	1999	2000	2001	2002	2003	2004	2005	2006
Males												
Indictable offences												
All ages	KEGA	142.6	143.3	142.9	126.1	109.7	103.8	104.4	109.8	110.0	129.9	147.6
10 and under 15 years[2]	KEGB	25.1	22.9	23.7	22.0	20.3	19.7	16.7	16.9	18.7	21.0	21.7
15 and under 18 years[2]	KEGC	33.0	32.0	32.0	28.7	25.0	24.5	23.3	24.1	25.9	28.0	30.2
18 and under 21 years	KEGD	24.3	25.2	25.7	22.7	20.1	18.5	18.9	19.4	16.7	19.8	22.9
21 years and over	KEGE	60.2	63.2	61.5	52.7	44.3	41.2	45.6	49.4	48.7	61.1	72.8
Summary offences												
All ages	KEGF	79.2	75.7	76.9	76.1	69.6	68.0	63.8	70.9	76.0	87.6	112.0
10 and under 15 years[2]	KEGG	10.3	9.9	10.6	11.7	12.0	12.7	10.3	10.9	12.6	15.5	17.9
15 and under 18 years[2]	KEGH	18.0	16.1	16.1	16.1	14.9	15.2	13.3	15.1	17.2	18.6	21.3
18 and under 21 years	KEGI	13.0	12.9	13.2	13.0	11.9	11.0	11.0	12.4	12.3	12.2	15.0
21 years and over	KEGJ	37.9	36.9	37.0	35.3	30.9	29.0	29.2	32.5	33.9	41.2	57.8
Females												
Indictable offences												
All ages	KEGK	48.2	46.0	48.8	44.5	41.2	40.1	38.5	41.0	46.3	53.0	56.2
10 and under 15 years[2]	KEGL	10.8	9.2	11.1	9.8	10.0	10.1	8.4	8.6	10.6	12.2	12.5
15 and under 18 years[2]	KEGM	10.9	9.5	10.3	9.3	9.0	9.3	8.3	9.1	10.7	12.2	12.7
18 and under 21 years	KEGN	5.6	5.7	5.9	5.7	5.2	4.9	4.8	4.9	5.2	5.8	6.2
21 years and over	KEGO	20.9	21.5	21.4	19.6	17.0	15.9	17.0	18.4	19.9	22.8	24.7
Summary offences												
All ages	KEGP	16.2	17.0	19.2	9.4	18.5	18.0	18.6	20.2	23.5	28.5	34.2
10 and under 15 years[2]	KEGQ	1.8	1.7	2.1	2.5	2.8	2.9	2.7	3.0	3.9	5.1	5.6
15 and under 18 justice[2]	KEGR	3.2	3.2	3.7	3.9	3.7	3.8	3.6	4.3	5.4	6.2	7.1
18 and under 21 years	KEGS	2.1	2.3	2.6	2.7	2.5	2.3	2.4	2.7	2.9	3.3	4.1
21 years and over	KEGT	9.1	9.9	10.8	10.3	9.6	9.0	9.8	10.2	11.3	13.9	17.4

1 See chapter text.
2 From 1 June 2000 the Crime and Disorder Act 1998 came into force nationally and removed the use of cautions for persons under 18 and replaced them with reprimands and final warnings.
3 These data are on the principal offence basis.
4 Every effort is made to ensure that the figures presented are accurate and complete. However, it is important to note that these data have been extracted from large administrative data systems generated by police forces. As a consequence, care should be taken to ensure data collection processes and their inevitable limitations are taken into account when those data are used.

Source: Office for Criminal Justice Reform:020 7035 4955

11.8 Sentence or order passed on persons sentenced for indictable offences: by sex[1]
England and Wales
Magistrates' courts and the Crown Court

Percentages and thousands

		1996	1997	1998	1999	2000	2001	2002	2003	2004	2005	2006
Males												
Sentence or order												
Absolute discharge	KEJB	0.8	0.7	0.7	0.6	0.6	0.6	0.8	0.9	0.8	0.7	0.7
Conditional discharge	KEJC	15.6	15.5	15.3	15.0	14.1	13.4	12.4	13.0	12.2	11.9	11.3
Fine	KEJF	28.6	28.2	28.4	27.7	25.7	24.5	23.9	24.0	20.9	19.4	17.4
Community rehabilitation order	KEJD	9.9	10.0	10.0	10.1	10.1	10.7	10.6	10.1	9.5	5.6	0.8
Supervision order	KEJE	2.9	2.7	2.7	2.7	2.4	2.3	2.1	1.8	2.0	2.1	2.3
Community punishment order	KEJG	9.9	9.5	9.3	9.3	9.5	9.0	8.6	8.3	8.8	6.3	1.2
Attendance centre order	KEJH	1.9	1.8	1.7	1.8	1.5	1.2	0.7	0.6	0.6	0.6	0.6
Community punishment and rehabilitation order	KIJW	3.5	3.7	3.8	3.7	3.6	2.6	2.6	2.6	2.8	2.1	0.5
Curfew order	LUJP	0.1	0.1	0.2	0.3	0.5	0.7	1.1	1.6	2.7	2.3	1.3
Reparation order	SNFI	..	..	..	..	0.7	1.3	0.8	0.4	0.4	0.5	0.6
Action plan order	SNFJ	..	..	..	..	0.9	1.7	1.1	0.7	0.8	0.8	0.8
Drug treatment and testing order	SNFK	..	..	..	..	0.1	1.2	1.4	1.9	2.3	1.6	0.1
Referral order	SNFL	..	..	..	..	..	..	3.0	4.0	4.4	5.2	5.2
Community order[2]	GN7P	..	..	..	..	..	..	..	..	..	8.7	19.8
Suspended sentence order	KEJL	0.8	0.8	0.7	0.6	0.7	0.6	0.5	0.5	0.6	1.7	6.7
Imprisonment												
Sec 90-92	LUJQ	0.2	0.3	0.2	0.2	0.2	0.2	0.2	0.2	0.2	0.2	0.2
Detention and training order	LUJR	..	..	..	..	1.4	1.9	1.8	1.5	1.6	1.6	1.7
Young offender institution	KEJK	6.1	6.1	6.0	6.2	5.2	4.5	4.2	3.6	3.8	3.7	3.6
Unsuspended imprisonment	KEJM	17.2	17.9	18.2	18.7	19.9	20.0	20.9	20.6	21.5	21.2	20.4
Other sentence or order	KEJN	2.4	3.0	2.6	3.1	3.1	3.4	3.3	3.5	4.1	3.9	4.4
Total number of males (thousands) = 100 per cent	KEJA	260.8	275.4	292.4	291.3	277.1	274.6	285.6	282.3	267.5	259.4	258.4
Females												
Sentence or order												
Absolute discharge	KEKB	0.9	0.8	0.7	0.7	0.6	0.6	0.9	1.0	0.8	0.8	0.7
Conditional discharge	KEKC	30.6	29.4	28.7	26.9	24.9	23.9	22.0	22.5	21.8	20.7	20.1
Fine	KEKF	22.5	21.8	21.3	20.8	20.1	18.6	17.9	18.5	16.7	15.2	12.8
Community rehabilitation order	KEKD	19.0	19.1	19.1	19.4	19.6	19.1	19.2	17.0	15.4	9.0	1.4
Supervision order	KEKE	2.9	2.9	3.1	2.9	2.8	2.7	2.1	2.1	2.1	2.4	2.5
Community punishment order	KEKG	6.5	6.5	6.5	7.1	7.5	7.3	6.8	6.6	7.6	6.1	1.6
Attendance centre order	KEKH	1.0	1.0	0.9	0.9	0.8	0.6	0.4	0.3	0.3	0.3	0.5
Community punishment and rehabilitation order	KIJX	3.0	3.2	3.4	3.3	3.0	2.1	2.1	1.8	1.9	1.5	0.5
Curfew order	LUJT	–	0.1	0.1	0.3	0.4	0.6	0.8	1.4	2.2	2.3	1.1
Reparation order	SNFX	..	..	..	..	0.8	1.6	0.8	0.4	0.5	0.5	0.5
Action plan order	SNFZ	..	..	..	..	1.0	2.0	1.2	0.8	0.8	1.0	0.9
Drug treatment and testing order	SNGA	..	..	..	..	0.1	1.4	1.7	2.4	3.2	2.1	0.2
Referral order	SNGB	..	..	..	..	..	..	3.9	5.1	5.6	6.7	6.9
Community order[2]	GN7Q	..	..	..	..	..	..	..	..	..	9.9	23.3
Suspended sentence order	KEKL	1.5	1.6	1.5	1.3	1.3	1.2	1.1	1.0	1.3	2.5	7.8
Imprisonment												
Sec 90-92	LUJU	0.1	0.1	..	0.1	0.1	0.1	0.1	0.1	0.1	0.1	–
Detention and training order	LUJV	..	..	..	..	0.6	0.8	0.8	0.7	0.7	0.8	0.7
Young offender institution	KEKK	1.8	1.9	2.2	2.4	2.2	2.0	1.9	1.7	1.4	1.6	1.6
Unsuspended imprisonment	KEKM	8.4	9.4	10.0	11.0	11.5	12.1	12.7	12.8	13.2	12.6	12.8
Other sentence or order	KEKN	2.0	2.2	2.5	3.0	2.9	3.5	3.4	3.8	4.3	3.8	4.3
Total number of females (thousands) = 100 per cent	KEKA	38.0	42.1	47.2	49.0	47.8	47.3	49.9	50.2	48.3	46.1	43.7

1 See chapter text. Every effort is made to ensure that the figures presented are accurate and complete. However, it is important to note that these data have been extracted from large administrative data systems generated by the courts and police forces. As a consequence, care should be taken to ensure data collection processes and their inevitable limitations are taken into account when those data are used.

2 The community order was introduced on 4 April 2005 and applies to offences committed on or after that date.

Source: Office for Justice Reform: 020 7035 4955

11.9 Persons sentenced to life imprisonment[1] : by sex and age
England and Wales

Number of Persons

		1996	1997	1998	1999	2000	2001	2002	2003	2004	2005	2006
Males												
All ages	I28G	329	346	380	465	446	484	536	489	548	594	531
10 - 17 years	I28D	27	24	11	26	19	28	21	11	15	27	16
18 - 20 years	I28E	32	29	25	38	9	27	21	47	24	50	46
21 years and over	I28F	270	293	344	401	418	429	494	431	509	517	469
Females												
All ages	I28K	10	21	14	19	21	19	19	24	22	31	16
10 - 17 years	I28H	–	3	1	3	2	1	1	–	1	1	–
18 - 20 years	I28I	1	2	–	2	1	3	2	4	2	4	2
21 years and over	I28J	9	16	13	14	18	15	16	20	19	26	14
All persons												
All ages	I28O	339	367	394	484	467	503	555	513	570	625	547
10 - 17 years	I28L	27	27	12	29	21	29	22	11	16	28	16
18 - 20 years	I28M	33	31	25	40	10	30	23	51	26	54	48
21 years and over	I28N	279	309	357	415	436	444	510	451	528	543	483

1 Includes detention under the Powers of Criminal Courts (Sentencing) Act 2000, Secs 90-92 (Childrens and Young Persons Act 1993, Secs 53(1) & (2) prior to Aug 2000) (persons aged 10-17), custody for life under the Powers of Criminal Courts (Sentencing) Act 2000, Sec 93 and 94 (1) (persons aged 18 - 20), mandatory life sentences under the Powers of Criminal Courts (Sentencing) Act 2000 Sec 109 (persons aged 18 and over) and immediate imprisonment (persons aged 21 and over). Indeterminate sentences for public protection under the Criminal Justice Act 2003 are excluded.

Source: Office for Criminal Justice Reform:020 8760 1404

11.10 Receptions and average population in custody
England and Wales

		1996	1997	1998	1999	2000	2001	2002	2003	2004	2005	2006
Receptions												
Type of inmate:												
Untried	KEDA	58 888	62 066	64 697	64 572	54 892	53 467	58 708	58 696	54 556	55 455	55 809
Convicted, unsentenced	KEDB	34 987	36 424	43 387	45 893	43 889	46 851	53 301	53 246	50 115	49 104	47 995
Sentenced	KEDE	82 861	87 168	91 282	93 965	93 671	91 978	94 807	93 495	95 161	92 452	90 038
Immediate custodial sentence	KEDF	74 306	80 832	85 908	90 238	91 195	90 523	93 615	92 245	93 326	90 414	88 134
Young offenders	KEDG	17 593	18 743	19 599	21 020	21 333	20 969	20 236	18 179	18 264	17 819	17 985
Up to 12 months	KEDH	11 285	11 867	12 942	14 330	14 639	14 234	12 891	11 850	11 855	11 610	11 526
12 months up to 4 years	KEDJ	5 497	5 949	5 921	5 904	5 877	5 856	6 355	5 412	5 426	5 243	5 317
4 years up to and including life	KEDL	811	927	736	786	817	879	990	917	983	966	1 142
Adults	KFBO	56 713	62 089	66 309	69 218	69 862	69 554	73 379	74 066	75 062	72 595	70 149
Up to 12 months	KEDV	34 864	38 702	42 513	45 662	46 759	46 146	47 870	48 962	49 814	48 190	45 768
12 months up to 4 years	KEDW	16 560	17 546	18 100	17 751	17 290	17 116	18 313	17 968	17 988	17 397	16 970
4 years up to and including life	KEDX	5 289	5 841	5 696	5 805	5 813	6 292	7 196	7 136	7 260	7 008	7 411
Committed in default of payment												
of a fine	KEDY	8 555	6 336	5 374	3 727	2 476	1 455	1 192	1 250	1 835	1 876	1 904
Young offenders	KEEA	885	555	568	366	216	138	110	116	155	162	118
Adults	KAFQ	7 670	5 781	4 806	3 361	2 260	1 317	1 082	1 134	1 680	1 714	1 786
Non-criminal prisoners	KEDM	3 128	3 204	3 290	3 271	3 153	4 630	2 674	3 142	3 669	3 668	4 734
Immigration Act 1971	KEDN	1 857	2 122	2 348	2 443	2 455	4 035	2 093	2 457	3 041	3 093	4 073
Others	KEDO	1 271	1 082	942	828	698	595	581	685	628	575	661
Average population												
Total in custody	KEDP	55 281	61 114	65 298	64 771	64 602	66 301	70 861	73 038	74 657	75 979	78 150
Total in prison service												
establishments	KFBQ	55 281	61 114	65 298	64 771	64 602	66 301	70 778	73 038	74 657	75 979	78 127
Police cells[2]	KFBN	–	–	–	–	–	–	83	–	–	–	22
Untried	KEDQ	8 374	8 453	8 157	7 947	7 098	6 924	7 727	7 862	7 735	8 088	8 293
Convicted, unsentenced	KEDR	3 238	3 678	4 411	4 571	4 177	4 314	5 064	5 060	4 750	4 806	4 967
Sentenced	KEDU	43 043	48 413	52 176	51 691	52 685	54 051	57 222	59 007	61 071	61 991	63 504
Immediate custodial sentence	KFBR	42 863	48 272	52 045	51 596	52 620	54 006	57 184	58 959	61 012	61 925	63 429
Young offenders	KFBS	6 700	7 821	8 490	8 336	8 435	8 558	8 777	8 421	8 290	8 239	8 535
Determinate sentence	I7IJ	6 614	7 707	8 363	8 197	8 288	8 408	8 616	8 262	8 123	8 030	8 141
Indeterminate sentence	I7IL	86	114	127	139	147	150	161	159	167	209	394
Adults	KFCO	36 162	40 451	43 556	43 261	44 185	45 448	48 408	50 536	52 721	53 686	54 894
Determinate sentence	I7IK	32 756	36 838	39 733	39 183	39 779	40 768	43 411	45 278	47 264	47 914	47 885
Indeterminate sentence	I7IM	3 406	3 613	3 823	4 078	4 406	4 680	4 997	5 258	5 457	5 772	7 009
Committed in default of payment												
of a fine	KFCS	180	141	131	95	64	45	37	48	59	71	82
Young offenders	KFEW	22	13	15	9	4	6	2	3	4	3	3
Adults	KFEX	158	128	116	86	59	39	35	45	54	68	79
Non-criminal prisoners	KEEB	627	572	554	558	641	1 012	847	1 107	1 100	1 087	1 355
Immigration Act 1971	KEEC	516	485	474	485	576	955	777	1 041	1 033	1 022	1 288
Others	KEED	111	87	79	73	63	57	69	67	68	65	65
Accommodation[3]	I7IQ	53 152	56 329	61 253	62 369	63 436	63 757	64 232	66 104	67 576	69 443	70 585

1 The components do not always add up to the totals as they have been rounded independently.
2 Mostly untried prisoners.
3 In use certified normal accomodation at 30 June.

Source: Ministry of Justice: 020 7210 0638

11.11 Prison population serving sentences: by age and offence[1,2]
England and Wales

Numbers

	15 - 17	18 - 20	21 - 24	25 - 29	30 - 39	40 - 49	50 - 59	60 and over	Total
				Age in years					
At 30 June 2001									
Offences									
Males									
Total	1 918	5 864	9 051	9 964	14 538	6 044	2 723	1 211	51 313
Violence against the person	343	1 180	1 810	1 997	3 432	1 631	702	252	11 347
Sexual offences	53	145	265	406	1 368	1 172	953	686	5 048
Burglary	383	1 176	2 039	2 190	2 158	389	61	15	8 410
Robbery	429	1191	1 436	1 309	1 652	360	60	12	6 449
Theft, handling, fraud and forgery	318	742	1 086	1 080	1 362	510	217	55	5 370
Drugs offences	47	423	1 126	1 686	2 828	1 278	479	113	7 980
Other offences	285	840	1 146	1 163	1 541	616	213	66	5 868
Offences not known	61	165	143	133	196	90	40	13	841
Females									
Total	63	305	493	589	906	406	119	18	2 899
Violence against the person	18	63	55	72	123	81	24	6	441
Sexual offences	-	2	1	1	7	10	2	2	25
Burglary	9	29	44	29	36	5	2	-	153
Robbery	10	53	63	54	55	13	1	-	248
Theft, handling, fraud and forgery	12	53	100	155	178	64	29	4	594
Drugs offences	3	72	183	215	411	193	49	4	1130
Other offences	8	27	40	50	82	32	9	2	249
Offences not known	3	7	8	14	14	9	4	-	59
At 30 June 2002									
Offences									
Males									
Total	1 986	5 821	9 722	10 196	15 415	6 630	2 832	1 365	53 967
Violence against the person	336	1 187	1 942	1 937	3 490	1 769	749	267	11 678
Sexual offences	58	167	262	406	1 347	1 241	996	794	5 270
Burglary	396	1 130	2 159	2 331	2 379	448	58	15	8 917
Robbery	503	1 285	1 647	1 390	1 865	443	66	10	7 208
Theft, handling, fraud and forgery	302	570	1 055	1 105	1 416	480	213	62	5 203
Drugs offences	43	431	1 255	1 763	3 142	1 496	495	129	8 754
Other offences	275	875	1 195	1 103	1 555	640	205	73	5 921
Offences not known	72	174	207	162	222	113	50	15	1 016
Females									
Total	103	356	596	662	1 030	439	134	19	3 339
Violence against the person	27	67	73	85	163	84	33	6	538
Sexual offences	-	1	-	1	11	6	3	1	23
Burglary	9	37	58	54	68	12	1	-	239
Robbery	19	63	89	65	60	14	3	1	314
Theft, handling, fraud and forgery	22	56	103	139	168	68	20	4	581
Drugs offences	8	94	206	256	474	216	60	6	1 319
Other offences	12	32	52	50	73	34	9	1	262
Offences not known	6	7	16	13	13	5	4	-	63
At 30 June 2003									
Offences									
Males									
Total	1 724	5 740	10 112	10 441	16 304	7 252	2 975	1 413	55 962
Violence against the person	310	1 257	2 112	2 068	3 733	1 932	780	290	12 482
Sexual offences	42	183	310	390	1 376	1 353	1 023	838	5 514
Burglary	289	919	2 003	2 204	2 555	527	71	11	8 579
Robbery	436	1 370	1 910	1 546	2 022	514	69	12	7 879
Theft, handling, fraud and forgery	291	543	1 020	1 060	1 437	472	201	45	5 069
Drugs offences	43	452	1 256	1 791	3 215	1 579	528	127	8 993
Other offences	271	884	1 329	1 218	1 760	787	263	69	6 581
Offences not known	42	133	172	164	205	89	40	21	865
Females									
Total	57	305	670	702	1 100	492	123	28	3 477
Violence against the person	10	61	91	66	155	82	32	7	506
Sexual offences	-	-	2	1	11	7	3	2	26
Burglary	1	24	64	60	77	12	2	-	240
Robbery	21	60	105	100	93	24	4	-	407
Theft, handling, fraud and forgery	10	56	117	128	199	70	18	11	609
Drugs offences	6	73	226	271	453	253	54	8	1 343
Other offences	7	27	58	66	108	39	6	-	311
Offences not known	2	3	8	10	5	4	4	-	36

11.11

Prison population serving sentences: by age and offence[1,2]
England and Wales

continued

Numbers

	Age in years								Total
	15 - 17	18 - 20	21 - 24	25 - 29	30 - 39	40 - 49	50 - 59	60 and over	
At 30 June 2004									
Offences									
Males									
Total	1 706	5 585	10 095	10 738	17 021	7 858	3 013	1 508	57 523
Violence against the person	326	1 353	2 247	2 272	3 965	2 107	799	304	13 373
Sexual offences	55	193	329	424	1 433	1 416	1 030	865	5 747
Burglary	242	855	1 807	2 141	2 662	608	71	11	8 397
Robbery	449	1 254	1 865	1 691	2 127	583	70	17	8 056
Theft, handling, fraud and forgery	272	502	903	1 045	1 479	573	180	63	5 017
Drugs offences	51	471	1 383	1 789	3 258	1 615	537	150	9 256
Other offences	286	848	1 390	1 249	1 895	868	284	87	6 908
Offences not known	25	108	171	126	202	87	41	10	769
Females									
Total	58	300	632	727	1 056	507	152	20	3 453
Violence against the person	15	70	98	89	192	95	36	9	603
Sexual offences	-	-	3	3	8	7	4	2	27
Burglary	6	19	59	83	56	22	3	-	247
Robbery	8	65	93	90	114	20	2	-	392
Theft, handling, fraud and forgery	11	28	100	140	171	67	25	1	543
Drugs offences	6	78	197	245	392	246	65	6	1 235
Other offences	11	37	75	72	108	44	13	2	361
Offences not known	2	3	8	7	15	7	4	-	46
At 30 June 2005									
Offences									
Males									
Total	1 782	5 595	9 937	10 969	16 843	8 731	3 256	1 594	58 707
Violence against the person	366	1 493	2 553	2 553	4 015	2 402	840	319	14 541
Sexual offences	65	186	397	505	1 436	1 552	1 084	922	6 147
Burglary	285	719	1 559	1 947	2 570	669	78	17	7 844
Robbery	422	1 307	1 819	1 705	2 035	649	83	15	8 035
Theft, handling, fraud and forgery	240	433	858	1 074	1 449	650	238	55	4 997
Drugs offences	76	491	1 332	1 834	3 263	1 741	544	148	9 429
Other offences	310	870	1 306	1 245	1 902	987	360	99	7 079
Offences not known	18	96	113	106	173	81	29	19	635
Females									
Total	55	269	614	680	1 073	585	179	24	3 479
Violence against the person	23	68	109	85	190	114	40	9	638
Sexual offences	-	2	3	4	12	8	7	3	39
Burglary	4	18	50	62	79	23	3	-	239
Robbery	16	59	61	82	102	20	3	-	343
Theft, handling, fraud and forgery	4	35	105	119	202	88	27	3	583
Drugs offences	3	54	195	255	366	268	84	9	1 234
Other offences	5	30	84	68	117	56	14	-	374
Offences not known	-	3	7	5	5	8	1	-	29
At 30 June 2006									
Offences									
Males									
Total	1 814	5 716	9 612	11 349	16 828	9 349	3 511	1 719	59 898
Violence against the person	381	1 563	2 616	2 977	4 109	2 609	935	348	15 537
Sexual offences	67	213	452	560	1 497	1 683	1 118	971	6 561
Burglary	275	707	1 363	1 838	2 554	715	97	15	7 563
Robbery	486	1 413	1 739	1 674	1 975	706	91	16	8 100
Theft, handling, fraud and forgery	200	451	830	1 093	1 598	707	214	54	5 147
Drugs offences	68	492	1 232	1 913	3 153	1 829	623	174	9 484
Other offences	327	835	1 326	1 231	1 838	1 040	406	129	7 129
Offences not known	12	43	55	64	105	60	28	10	378
Females									
Total	50	271	551	707	1 094	604	189	39	3 506
Violence against the person	11	75	111	101	205	118	48	9	678
Sexual offences	1	3	2	2	8	13	5	3	37
Burglary	7	13	39	63	80	24	2	-	228
Robbery	17	48	67	76	86	18	2	-	315
Theft, handling, fraud and forgery	3	30	97	171	232	106	24	7	671
Drugs offences	4	62	158	217	354	253	88	17	1 163
Other offences	7	36	61	72	120	67	19	3	385
Offences not known	1	5	5	4	9	5	1	-	30

1 The data presented in this table are drawn from administrative IT systems. Where figures in the table have been rounded to the nearest whole number, the rounded components do not always add to the totals, which are calculated and rounded independently. Reconciliation exercises with published Home Office figures may demonstrate differences due to rounded components. A programme of work is currently being undertaken to audit the quality of the data and to identify priorities for improvements.
2 Excludes persons committed in default of payment of a fine.

Source: Ministry of Justice: 020 7210 0630

11.12 Expenditure on prisons
England and Wales
Operating cost and total capital employed, years ending 31 March

£ thousand

		2000 /01	2001 /02	2002 /03	2003 /04	2004 /05	2005 /06	2006 /07
Expenditure								
Staff costs	KWUV	1 094 500	1 138 400	1 259 502	1 364 193	1 439 882	1 498 446	1 586 126
Accommodation costs	KXCO	153 700	193 100	200 000	194 000	185 400	150 270	138 322
Other operating costs	KXCP	654 200	706 100	756 198	653 007	694 618	528 529	498 913
Depreciation	KXCQ	117 200	128 100	132 600	129 600	143 800	7 974	11 044
Cost of capital	KXCR	259 900	284 900	292 700	164 400	170 300	279	905
Total expenditure	KXCS	2 279 500	2 450 600	2 641 000	2 505 200	2 634 000	2 185 498	2 235 310
Income								
Contributions from industries	KXCT	−10 600	−11 600	−10 100	−11 000	−10 600	−11 154	−7 698
Other operating income	KXCU	−10 300	−13 100	−15 500	−21 000	−38 400	−41 323	−45 411
Income from Other Government Departments[1]	GDPM	−123 900	−180 600	−210 200	−368 000	−381 500	−302 549	−245 917
Total income	KXCV	−144 800	−205 300	−235 800	−400 000	−430 500	−355 026	−299 026
Net operating costs	KXCW	2 134 700	2 245 300	2 405 200	2 105 200	2 203 500	1 830 472	1 936 284
Total capital employed	KXCX	4 726 200	4 859 600	4 821 500	5 228 600	5 116 700	5 716	−52 207

1 Income from the Youth Justice Board (a non-departmental public body of the
Home Office) for the provision of juvenile custody within the Prison Service,
Department for Education and Skills for the provision of education services
and Department of Health and PCTs for the provision of healthcare.

Source: Ministry of Justice

11.13 Crimes and offences recorded by the police: by crime group[1]
Scotland

Thousands

		1997 /98	1998 /99	1999 /00	2000 /01	2001 /02	2002 /03	2003 /04	2004[3] /05	2005 /06	2006 /07
Non-sexual crimes of violence											
against the person	BEBC	13.4	14.7	15.8	14.8	15.7	16.1	15.2	14.7	13.7	14.1
Serious assault, etc	KAFS	6.2	6.7	7.3	6.9	7.5	7.6	7.5	7.8	7.2	7.5
Robbery	KAFU	4.6	5.0	4.9	4.3	4.6	4.6	4.2	3.7	3.6	3.6
Other	KAFV	2.6	3.0	3.6	3.6	3.5	3.8	3.5	3.2	3.0	3.0
Crimes involving indecency	BEBD	7.4	7.1	5.9	5.7	6.0	6.6	6.8	7.3	6.6	6.7
Rape and attempted rape[1]	OXBQ	0.8	0.8	0.8	0.7	0.8	0.9	1.0	1.1	1.2	1.1
Indecent assault[1]	OXBR	1.3	1.3	1.1	1.0	1.2	1.4	1.4	1.5	1.5	1.7
Lewd and indecent behaviour	KAFY	3.0	2.9	2.3	2.4	2.4	2.8	2.6	2.8	2.7	2.6
Other	KAFZ	2.4	2.1	1.7	1.6	1.6	1.6	1.7	1.9	1.2	1.4
Crimes involving dishonesty	BEBE	266.9	277.0	275.6	253.3	242.9	224.8	211.0	210.4	187.8	183.8
Housebreaking	KAGB	55.6	55.8	52.9	47.7	45.5	40.6	36.4	35.0	31.3	30.6
Theft by opening lockfast places	KAGC	10.5	12.1	11.6	10.6	8.2	7.8	7.4	7.9	8.3	7.4
Theft from a motor vehicle (OLP)	EPI4	39.8	39.5	38.0	32.0	32.7	30.4	26.8	20.4	16.5	16.1
Theft of a motor vehicle	KAGD	27.9	29.3	28.9	25.6	23.1	20.9	17.6	15.6	14.0	15.0
Shoplifting	KAGE	27.0	30.8	32.1	32.3	31.6	28.3	27.9	28.5	28.2	28.8
Other theft	KAGF	80.0	80.1	81.2	76.6	76.0	73.2	72.5	77.6	72.1	70.2
Fraud	KAGG	16.2	18.4	20.6	20.0	17.4	15.8	15.3	18.3	11.1	9.3
Other	KAGH	9.9	11.1	10.3	8.4	8.4	7.9	7.0	7.1	6.3	6.4
Fire-raising, vandalism, etc	BEBF	81.0	77.6	81.2	85.8	94.9	97.6	103.7	128.6	127.9	129.7
Fire-raising	KAGJ	2.7	2.5	2.3	2.4	2.9	3.8	4.2	4.7	4.9	5.0
Vandalism, etc	KAGK	78.3	75.2	78.9	83.4	92.0	93.8	99.6	123.9	123.0	124.8
Other crimes	BEBG	52.3	57.7	57.0	58.9	66.8	73.2	77.5	77.1	81.8	84.9
Crimes against public justice	KAGM	16.6	17.7	18.4	18.6	20.9	22.7	25.8	25.6	27.7	32.1
Handling offensive weapons[2]	KAFT	6.2	7.1	8.1	8.1	9.0	9.4	9.3	9.5	9.6	10.1
Drugs	KAGN	29.4	32.8	30.4	32.1	36.8	40.9	42.3	41.8	44.2	42.4
Other	KAGO	0.1	0.1	0.1	0.1	0.1	0.2	0.2	0.2	0.3	0.4
Total crimes	KAGQ	421.0	434.1	435.5	418.5	426.2	418.3	414.2	438.1	417.8	419.3
Miscellaneous offences	BEBH	156.6	153.3	151.9	154.9	163.5	169.6	181.0	214.3	219.5	232.4
Minor assault	KAGS	50.2	51.6	54.6	54.1	55.4	55.0	57.4	73.7	72.3	78.2
Breach of the peace	KAGT	73.3	71.7	71.3	70.2	72.7	74.7	77.9	90.0	89.6	93.4
Drunkenness	KAGU	9.6	8.4	7.6	7.8	7.8	7.3	7.5	7.2	7.0	6.7
Other	KAGV	23.4	21.6	18.4	22.8	27.6	32.6	38.2	43.4	50.6	54.2
Motor vehicle offences	BEBI	339.6	367.2	347.5	341.2	368.5	354.6	434.9	424.3	380.4	375.0
Dangerous and careless driving	KAGX	16.2	15.8	13.2	12.0	12.2	12.7	12.0	13.1	13.0	13.6
Drunk driving	KAGY	11.1	10.6	10.9	10.8	11.5	11.8	11.6	11.1	11.3	11.7
Speeding	KAGZ	95.6	119.7	123.4	113.9	126.8	117.2	199.2	210.1	167.7	162.9
Unlawful use of a motor vehicle	KAHA	77.3	76.0	80.7	84.3	94.6	99.5	99.5	76.7	75.1	73.1
Vehicle defect offences	KAHB	62.3	63.8	48.0	46.8	45.5	46.5	37.2	27.0	23.9	21.2
Other	KAHC	77.0	81.3	71.2	73.3	77.9	66.9	75.4	86.3	89.4	92.6
Total offences	KAHD	496.2	520.5	499.4	496.1	532.0	524.1	615.9	638.6	600.0	607.4
Total crimes and offences	BEBB	917.2	954.6	934.9	914.6	958.1	942.4	1 030.1	1 076.7	1 017.7	1 026.7

1 See chapter text.
2 'Handling offensive weapons' used to be included in the group 'non-sexual crimes of violence'.
3 The introduction of the Scottish Crime Recording Standard on 1 April 2004 has increased the number of minor crimes recorded, such as minor crimes of theft, vandalism, petty assault and breach of the peace.

Source: The Scottish Government Justice Department: 0131 244 2635

11.14 Persons with a charge proved: by crime group[1,2]
Scotland

Numbers

		1995/96	1996/97	1997/98	1998/99	1999/00	2000/01	2001/02	2002/03	2003/04	2004/05	2005[4]/06
Non-sexual crimes of violence	KEHC	1 812	2 002	2 039	2 000	2 003	1 976	2 092	2 381	2 596	2 422	2 083
Homicide	KEHD	125	119	104	92	105	100	103	99	131	143	106
Serious assault, etc	KEHE	847	954	1 039	1 036	1 053	1 089	1 171	1 360	1 475	1 371	1 274
Robbery	KEHG	640	720	666	652	659	603	627	682	689	609	443
Other violence	KEHH	200	209	230	220	186	184	191	240	301	299	260
Crimes of indecency	KEHI	1 259	938	1 329	1 280	790	633	614	562	666	810	838
Rape and attempted rape	HFVU	56	57	55	58	48	52	67	55	58	69	60
Indecent assault	KEHJ	73	67	91	83	84	60	48	65	93	88	84
Lewd and libidinous practices	KEHK	300	292	343	320	302	256	298	273	297	321	314
Other indecency	KEHL	830	522	840	819	356	265	201	169	218	332	380
Crimes of dishonesty	KEHM	27 626	26 779	25 272	24 726	22 652	20 571	21 536	21 700	19 887	19 659	17 485
Housebreaking	KEHN	4 249	3 736	3 174	3 071	2 860	2 676	2 672	2 752	2 508	2 373	1 989
Theft by opening lockfast places	KEHO	2 394	2 362	1 940	1 770	1 614	1 504	1 478	1 448	1 288	1 194	922
Theft of motor vehicle	KEHP	2 402	2 313	2 006	1 882	1 536	1 426	1 386	1 486	1 268	1 098	957
Shoplifting	KEHQ	6 648	7 197	7 313	7 559	7 753	7 345	8 366	8 826	8 123	8 424	7 928
Other theft	KEHR	6 177	6 031	5 866	5 796	5 026	4 303	4 234	3 783	3 521	3 550	3 096
Fraud	KEHS	2 215	1 956	1 992	1 920	1 595	1 448	1 479	1 459	1 444	1 354	1 185
Other dishonesty	KEHT	3 541	3 184	2 981	2 728	2 268	1 869	1 921	1 946	1 735	1 666	1 408
Fire-raising, vandalism, etc	KEHU	4 870	5 211	4 871	4 591	3 979	3 942	4 051	4 212	4 759	5 026	4 801
Fire-raising	KEHV	132	146	112	125	102	109	125	147	169	192	173
Vandalism, etc	KEHW	4 738	5 065	4 759	4 466	3 877	3 833	3 926	4 065	4 590	4 834	4 628
Other crime	KEHX	15 172	15 061	14 551	13 698	12 888	12 558	13 823	13 954	15 453	16 792	16 385
Crime against public justice	KFBK	7 362	6 553	5 096	4 776	4 589	4 929	5 257	5 048	5 290	5 764	5 598
Handling offensive weapons	KEHF	1 867	2 309	2 173	2 033	2 118	2 340	2 633	2 771	2 875	3 447	3 392
Drugs offences	KFBL	5 912	6 162	7 236	6 861	6 158	5 279	5 913	6 111	7 258	7 550	7 288
Other	KFBM	31	37	46	28	23	10	20	24	30	31	107
Total crimes	KEHB	50 739	49 991	48 062	46 295	42 312	39 680	42 116	42 809	43 361	44 709	41 592
Miscellaneous offences	KEHZ	46 305	45 599	45 816	39 241	34 189	33 262	34 661	37 007	39 631	42 803	42 380
Common assault	KEIA	11 926	12 387	12 441	11 677	10 749	10 270	10 823	11 745	12 317	13 571	13 956
Breach of the peace	KEIB	18 451	19 292	19 355	17 156	14 023	13 031	13 950	14 384	15 050	16 168	16 346
Drunkenness	KEIC	1 270	1 028	937	626	454	430	374	370	418	311	290
Breach of social work orders	HFVT	2 842	3 260	3 765	4 217	4 684	4 611	4 509	4 945	5 095	5 317	4 141
Other miscellaneous offences	KEID	11 816	9 632	9 318	5 565	4 279	4 920	5 005	5 563	6 751	7 436	7 647
Motor vehicle offences	KEIE	57 987	55 975	55 456	51 638	51 603	40 264	44 821	47 956	50 622	47 497	44 483
Dangerous and careless driving	KEIF	4 847	4 825	4 577	3 764	3 431	2 561	3 319	3 628	4 118	3 810	3 568
Drunk driving	KEIG	7 578	8 367	8 173	7 290	7 366	6 265	6 538	9 508	8 158	8 001	7 884
Speeding[3]	KEIH	14 546	12 141	12 220	12 971	15 293	9 427	9 988	9 832	12 700	13 537	12 111
Unlawful use of vehicle	KEII	19 609	19 870	20 052	18 662	16 950	15 987	18 553	19 192	19 563	16 690	14 402
Vehicle defect offences	KEIJ	3 259	3 221	3 198	2 470	2 075	1 302	1 252	1 510	1 859	1 791	1 633
Other motor vehicle offences	KEIK	8 148	7 551	7 236	6 481	6 488	4 722	5 171	4 286	4 224	3 668	4 885
Total offences	KEHY	104 292	101 574	101 272	90 879	85 792	73 526	79 482	84 963	90 253	90 300	86 863
Total crimes and offences	KEHA	155 031	151 565	149 334	137 174	128 104	113 206	121 598	127 772	133 614	135 009	128 455

1 See chapter text. Data as at 18 February 2008.
2 All figures are now reported as financial years.
3 Includes motorway and clearway offences.

4 Figures for 2005-06 for some categories dealt with by the High Court - including homicide, rape and major drug cases - may be underestimated slightly due to late recording of disposals on SCRO.

Source: Scottish Government Justice Department: 0131 244 2229

11.15 Persons with a charge proved: by court procedure[1,2]
Scotland

Numbers

		1995/96	1996/97	1997/98	1998/99	1999/00	2000/01	2001/02	2002/03	2003/04	2004/05	2005/06
Court procedure												
High Court[3]	KEIQ	1 093	1 086	1 126	1 062	1 183	1 099	1 142	1 205	1 228	978	863
Sheriff Court	KEIU	84 327	84 973	82 150	78 362	74 913	70 043	76 244	84 835	85 043	86 032	82 011
District Court[4]	KEIV	60 188	56 803	57 500	50 953	46 228	38 580	38 665	41 732	47 340	47 998	45 579
Stipendiary Magistrate Court[4]	KEIW	9 420	8 703	8 556	6 797	5 779	3 482	5 543	..	..	..	..
Total called to court[5]	KEIZ	155 031	151 565	149 334	137 174	128 104	113 206	121 598	127 772	133 614	135 009	128 455

1 See chapter text.
2 All figures are now reported as financial years.
3 Including cases remitted to the High Court from the Sheriff Court. Figure for 2004/05 may be an underestimate due to late recording of disposals on SCRO.

4 District Court figures from 2002/03 include the Stipendiary Magistrate Court.
5 Includes court type not known.

Source: Scottish Government Justice Department: 0131 244 2229

11.16 Persons with charge proved: by main penalty[1,2]
Scotland

Numbers

Main penalty		1995 /96	1996 /97	1997 /98	1998 /99	1999 /00	2000 /01	2001 /02	2002 /03	2003 /04	2004 /05	2005 /06
Restriction of liberty order[3]	ZBRE	..	..	..	125	230	189	193	743	1 048	1 312	1 198
Supervised attendance order[4]	ZBRF	..	11	93	78	97	64	58	54	38	43	108
Drug treatment and testing order[5]	OEWA	..	..	..	..	5	147	327	428	696	787	801
Absolute discharge	KEXA	927	1 045	1 046	914	991	978	1 055	1 020	1 102	1 209	1 050
Admonition or caution	KEXB	15 972	15 582	14 707	13 841	12 647	11 649	12 176	12 828	13 445	14 271	13 725
Probation	KEXC	6 176	6 604	6 817	7 464	7 258	7 344	8 496	9 438	8 902	9 433	9 033
Remit to children's hearing	KEXD	189	194	208	176	120	116	159	230	196	221	246
Community service order	KEXE	5 399	5 705	5 605	5 254	4 776	4 744	4 726	5 279	4 881	5 432	5 342
Fine	KEXF	108 525	103 969	103 091	91 904	84 778	71 104	76 641	78 957	84 797	83 764	79 458
Compensation order	KEXG	1 494	1 367	1 308	1 261	1 171	1 087	1 164	1 362	1 789	1 716	1 413
Insanity, hospital, guardianship order	KYAN	143	151	160	130	136	128	104	105	132	94	97
Prison	KEXI	11 593	12 070	11 754	11 456	11 519	11 390	12 418	13 560	13 153	13 498	12 731
Young offenders' institution	KEXJ	4 576	4 823	4 521	4 547	4 363	4 253	4 067	3 741	3 406	3 196	3 225
Detention of child	KEXM	37	44	24	24	13	13	14	25	25	20	23
Total persons with charge proved[6]	KEXO	155 031	151 565	149 334	137 174	128 104	113 206	121 598	127 772	133 614	135 009	128 455

1 See chapter text.
2 All figures are now reported as financial years.
3 A community sentence introduced by Section 5 of the Crime and Punishment (Scotland) Act 1995 and available on a pilot basis to 3 Scottish sheriff courts since August 1998. This sentence was made available to High Court, Sheriff Courts and Stipendiary Magistrates court from 1 May 2002.
4 The pilot scheme under the Crime and Punishment (S) Act 1995, where fines for 16 & 17 year olds were replaced by supervised attendance orders, was discontinued in December 1999. The majority of supervised attendance orders recorded from the year 2000-01 onwards were disposals relating to the breach of an existing order.

5 Drug treatment and testing orders are new measures made available on a pilot basis to the High Court and to Sheriff Courts for residents in Glasgow (from October 1999), Fife (from July 2000) and Aberdeen/Aberdeenshire (from December 2001). They are now available to all Sheriff courts and the High Court.
6 Totals from 2002/03 include a small number of cases where penalty is unknown.

Source: Scottish Government Justice Department: 0131 244 2229

11.17 Persons with charge proved[1]: by age and sex
Scotland

Numbers

		1995 /96	1996 /97	1997 /98	1998 /99	1999 /00	2000 /01	2001 /02	2002 /03	2003 /04	2004 /05	2005 /06
Males	KEWA	131 710	130 331	128 079	118 583	110 742	96 917	104 785	108 456	112 292	112 947	108 202
Under 16	KEWB	160	150	136	112	75	56	79	132	97	108	128
16 to 20	KEWC	30 114	31 871	30 742	29 145	26 489	23 632	25 153	25 423	24 925	24 543	24 287
21 to 30	KEWD	53 321	51 687	50 105	45 055	41 768	36 992	40 251	41 371	42 133	41 389	38 587
Over 30	KEWE	47 007	45 506	46 096	43 354	41 597	35 555	39 011	41 511	45 132	46 901	45 197
Age not known	KEWF	1 108	1 117	1 000	917	813	682	291	19	5	6	3
Females	KEWG	22 413	20 452	20 535	17 923	16 784	15 915	16 469	18 961	20 854	21 564	19 902
Under 16	KEWH	16	12	14	2	5	10	4	5	18	18	7
16 to 20	KEWI	3 104	3 358	3 426	3 401	3 278	2 952	2 906	3 013	3 045	3 016	2 941
21 to 30	KEWJ	9 297	8 090	8 183	7 121	6 506	6 155	6 528	7 309	7 939	8 082	7 402
Over 30	KEWK	9 405	8 394	8 497	7 091	6 734	6 555	6 960	8 630	9 850	10 448	9 552
Age not known	KEWL	591	598	415	308	261	243	71	4	2	–	–
Males and Females	KEWM	154 123	150 783	148 614	136 506	127 526	112 832	121 254	127 417	133 146	134 511	128 104
Under 16	KEWN	176	162	150	114	80	66	83	137	115	126	135
16 to 20	KEWO	33 218	35 229	34 168	32 546	29 767	26 584	28 059	28 436	27 970	27 559	27 228
21 to 30	KEWP	62 618	59 777	58 288	52 176	48 274	43 147	46 779	48 680	50 072	49 471	45 989
Over 30	KEWQ	56 412	53 900	54 593	50 445	48 331	42 110	45 971	50 141	54 982	57 349	54 749
Age not known	KEWR	1 699	1 715	1 415	1 225	1 074	925	362	23	7	6	3
Companies	KEWS	905	772	718	659	562	316	320	343	451	480	343
Total persons with charge proved[2]	KEWT	155 031	151 565	149 334	137 174	128 104	113 206	121 598	127 772	133 614	135 009	128 455

1 See chapter text.
2 Includes sex unknown.

Source: Scottish Government Justice Department: 0131 244 2229

11.18 Penal establishments: average daily population and receptions
Scotland

Numbers

		1997/98	1998/99	1999/00	2000/01	2001/02	2002/03	2003/04	2004/05	2005/06	2006/07
Average daily population											
Male	KEPB	5 874	5 830	5 765	5 676	5 929	6 193	6 307	6 447	6 523	6 830
Female	KEPC	186	199	210	207	257	282	314	332	334	353
Total	KEPA	6 059	6 029	5 975	5 883	6 186	6 475	6 621	6 779	6 857	7 183
Analysis by type of custody											
Remand	KEPD	927	971	976	881	1 019	1 247	1 246	1 216	1 242	1 567
Persons under sentence: total	KEPE	5 129	5 056	4 997	5 001	5 165	5 226	5 375	5 561	5 614	5 615
Adult prisoners	KEPF	4 357	4 347	4 317	4 346	4 537	4 624	4 802	5 001	4 989	4 970
Young offenders	KEPI	773	708	679	655	628	601	573	560	625	645
Persons recalled from supervision/licence[1]	KEPN	51	78	100	145	202	250	310	356	400	519
Others[1]	KEPO	18	21	28	36	37	6	6	5	1	–
Persons sentenced by court martial[1]	KEPP	1	–	2	–	–	–	–	1	–	–
Civil prisoners[1]	KEPQ	2	1	1	1	1	2	–	1	1	1
Receptions to penal establishments											
Remand	KEPR	14 685	15 713	14 626	14 062	15 725	19 198	18 963	18 892	19 593	23 181
Male	KEPS	13 677	14 527	13 450	13 042	14 402	17 455	17 111	17 085	17 796	21 129
Female	KEPT	1 008	1 186	1 176	1 020	1 323	1 743	1 852	1 807	1 797	2 052
Persons under sentence: total	KEPU	21 910	22 376	20 336	19 136	18 953	20 084	19 357	18 584	19 477	20 403
Male	KEPV	20 698	20 952	19 125	17 953	17 755	18 779	18 013	17 272	18 161	19 018
Female	KEPW	1 212	1 424	1 211	1 183	1 198	1 305	1 344	1 312	1 316	1 385
Imprisoned: Adults:											
directly	KEPX	9 697	9 887	9 217	8 943	9 470	10 571	10 255	10 299	10 746	11 684
in default of fine[2]	KEPY	7 650	7 907	7 030	6 450	5 882	6 081	6 063	5 404	5 442	5 265
Sentenced to young offenders' institution:											
directly	KEQA	2 811	2 824	2 582	2 436	2 312	2 207	1 949	1 908	2 170	2 286
in default of fine[2]	KEQB	1 695	1 606	1 328	1 116	1 109	1 016	825	694	771	698
Persons recalled from supervision/licence[3]	JYYD	57	152	179	191	180	209	265	279	348	470
Persons sentenced by court martial	KEQH	6	2	3	2	2	3	1	5	–	–
Civil prisoners[2]	KEQI	22	10	17	10	8	11	10	7	4	4

1 Persons recalled from supervision/licence and others are included in persons under sentence. Persons sentenced by court martial and civil prisoners are not included in persons under sentence.

2 Includes in default of compensation orders.
3 Now covers all recalls from supervised release orders.

Source: The Scottish Government Justice Department: 0131 244 8740

11.19 Expenditure on penal establishments[1]
Scotland

Years ended 31 March

£ thousand

		1996/97	1997/98	1998/99	1999/00	2000/01	2001/02	2002/03	2003/04	2004/05	2005/06	2006/07
Departmental Expenditure												
Manpower and Associated Services	KPHC	143 107	137 890	144 660	170 347	160 242	172 490	168 593	169 784	181 931	200 742	199 854
Prisoner and Associated Costs	KPHD	13 377	16 313	18 891	22 930	23 501	24 652	23 363	51 070	42 767	28 582	41 821
Capital Expenditure	KPHE	22 577	22 136	23 697	28 918	24 283	24 955	36 519	34 617	72 812	70 406	81 818
Gross Expenditure	KPHF	179 061	176 339	187 248	222 195	208 026	222 097	228 475	255 471	297 510	299 730	323 493
Less Receipts	KPHG	2 600	2 810	8 160	6 668	8 380	8 194	3 485	3 298	3 312	2 872	–2 178
Net Departmental Expenditure	KPHH	176 461	173 529	179 088	215 527	199 646	213 903	224 990	252 173	294 198	296 858	321 315
Plus Annually Managed Expenditure Capital Charges	DSJI	..	..	..	..	..	31 341	40 432	41 728	48 497	52 840	41 816
Total Net Expenditure	DSNX	176 461	173 529	179 088	215 527	199 646	245 244	265 422	293 901	342 695	349 698	363 131

1 See chapter text.

Source: The Scottish Government Justice Department: 0131 244 2225

11.20 Recorded crime statistics: by offence group[1]
Northern Ireland

Thousands

		Old counting rules					New counting rules							
		1995	1996	1997	1998 /99		1999 /00	2000 /01	2001 /02	2002 /03	2003 /04	2004 /05	2005 /06	2006 /07
Violence against the person	RVCP	5.2	5.6	5.2	6.6	RVCQ	21.4	21.4	26.1	28.5	29.0	29.3	31.0	31.8
Sexual offences	RVCR	1.7	1.7	1.4	1.5	RVCS	1.3	1.2	1.4	1.5	1.8	1.7	1.7	1.8
Burglary	RVCT	16.5	16.1	14.3	15.5	RVCU	16.1	15.8	17.1	18.7	16.4	13.4	12.8	11.6
Robbery	RVCV	1.5	1.7	1.7	1.4	RVCW	1.4	1.8	2.2	2.5	2.0	1.5	1.7	1.6
Theft	RVCX	33.5	32.8	29.5	34.6	RVCY	37.0	36.9	41.7	41.9	35.7	31.1	29.5	27.8
Fraud and forgery	RVCZ	4.9	4.1	3.8	5.3	RVDA	7.9	8.0	8.6	8.8	6.3	5.2	5.1	4.5
Criminal damage	RVDB	3.8	4.8	4.7	9.8	RVDC	31.2	32.3	40.0	36.6	32.4	31.4	34.8	36.3
Offences against the state	RVDD	0.3	0.4	0.5	0.5	RVDE	0.7	0.8	1.2	1.8	1.3	1.2	1.3	1.3
Other notifiable offences	RVDF	1.5	1.2	1.1	1.5	RVDG	2.1	1.7	1.4	2.4	3.2	3.3	5.3	4.5
of which drug offences	RVDH	1.4	1.1	1.0	1.4	RVDI	1.7	1.5	1.1	1.9	2.6	2.6	2.9	2.4
Total	RVDR	68.8	68.5	62.2	76.6	RVDS	119.1	119.9	139.8	142.5	128.0	118.1	123.2	121.1

1 See chapter text.

Source: The Police Service of Northern Ireland

11.21 Persons found guilty at all courts: by offence group[1]
Northern Ireland

Numbers

		1995	1996	1997	1998	1999	2000	2001	2002	2003	2004	2005
Violence against the person	KYCT	1 685	1 597	1 594	1 596	1 699	1 858	1 621	1 790	1 965	2 012	2 009
Sexual offences	KEVG	182	184	130	128	90	130	112	84	108	137	136
Burglary	KYBW	951	801	715	647	703	703	496	595	602	620	557
Robbery	KYBX	195	161	166	134	129	122	121	152	192	159	135
Theft	KYBY	3 128	2 765	2 596	2 342	1 995	2 111	1 831	1 695	1 803	1 819	1 819
Fraud and forgery	KYBZ	533	467	491	426	476	403	398	362	314	359	330
Criminal damage	KYCA	1 008	1 076	1 163	1 043	931	1 060	917	957	1 034	1 094	1 168
Offences against the state	KYCB	166	147	165	198	178	174	158	215	274	252	270
Other indictable[2]	KYCC	863	899	739	936	943	700	495	453	527	636	722
Total indictable[3]	KYCD	8 711	8 097	7 759	7 450	7 144	7 261	6 149	6 303	6 819	7 088	7 146
Summary[4]	KYCE	4 137	4 402	4 435	4 062	3 598	3 967	3 735	3 453	3 514	3 622	3 575
Motoring[5]	KYCF	20 124	18 177	18 770	15 369	15 782	15 390	14 466	14 344	16 342	17 215	15 534
All offences	KYCG	32 972	30 676	30 964	26 881	26 524	26 618	24 350	24 100	26 675	27 925	26 255

1 See chapter text.
2 1998 and 1999 figures include 'dangerous driving' (a triable-either-way offence).
3 From 2000, includes 'indictable-only' motoring offences.

4 Excludes motoring offences.
5 Prior to 2000, includes all motoring offences (except for note 2 above). From 2000, includes summary and triable-either-way motoring offences.

Source: Northern Ireland Office: 028 9052 7157

11.22 Juveniles found guilty at all courts:[1] by offence group
Northern Ireland

Numbers

		1995	1996	1997	1998	1999	2000	2001	2002	2003	2004	2005
Violence against the person	KYCH	51	75	49	97	73	77	66	82	75	78	146
Sexual offences	KAHF	7	4	8	12	12	4	1	6	5	7	9
Burglary	KYCI	170	137	124	108	117	125	73	77	89	66	113
Robbery	KYCJ	22	13	18	4	7	15	8	14	10	6	8
Theft	KYCK	345	338	334	304	227	254	244	212	173	183	291
Fraud and forgery	KYCL	21	14	11	4	10	2	9	3	7	2	6
Criminal damage	KYCM	116	121	136	139	102	143	152	132	162	129	241
Offences against the state	KYCN	9	6	10	11	12	8	10	20	26	18	19
Other indictable[2]	KYCO	14	24	10	20	17	10	12	7	19	22	46
Total indictable[3]	KYCP	755	732	700	699	577	638	575	553	566	511	879
Summary[4]	KYCQ	180	182	198	187	163	180	203	194	174	135	296
Motoring[5]	KYCR	74	58	57	98	97	82	102	89	94	76	280
All offences	KYCS	1 009	972	955	984	837	900	880	836	834	722	1 455

1 See chapter text. For the purpose of criminal proceedings, prior to 30 August 2005, a juvenile refers to a person aged 10 years or more but under 17. From 30 August 2005, the youth justice system was extended to include those under the age of 18. The number of juveniles convicted in 2005 refers to those aged 10-17, while the term juvenile refers to 10-16 year olds for the years prior to this.

2 1998 and 1999 figures include 'dangerous driving'.
3 From 2000, includes 'indictable-only' motoring offences.
4 Excludes motoring offences.
5 Prior to 2000 includes all motoring offences (except for note 2 above). From 2000, includes summary and triable-either-way motoring offences.

Source: Northern Ireland Office: 028 9052 7157

11.23 Disposals given to those convicted by court
Northern Ireland

Numbers

		1995	1996	1997	1998	1999	2000	2001	2002	2003	2004	2005
Magistrates court - all offences												
Prison[1]	KYAO	1 046	1 003	989	996	1 278	1 356	1 048	1 107	1 133	1 101	977
Custody Probation Order[1]	EOG9	..	..	..	..	..	..	..	..	7	7	9
Young offenders centre	KYAP	483	443	430	326	243	191	209	288	395	456	416
Training school[2]	KYAQ	169	147	148	136	13	..	..	..	..	..	..
Juvenile Justice Centre order[2]	OEUX	..	..	..	..	22	78	72	58	48	50	50
Total immediate custody	KYAR	1 698	1 593	1 567	1 458	1 556	1 625	1 329	1 453	1 583	1 614	1 452
Prison suspended	KYAS	1 674	1 722	1 506	1 025	1 080	1 247	1 215	1 278	1 407	1 469	1 584
YOC suspended	KYAT	385	444	461	139	104	93	77	100	201	372	375
Attendance centre	KYAU	101	91	66	55	14	20	37	84	91	108	127
Probation/supervision[3]	KYAV	1 137	1 134	1 155	1 473	1 246	1 096	1 070	1 005	974	991	977
Community service order	KYAW	547	591	561	622	678	726	587	643	623	647	628
Combination order	OEUZ	..	..	..	38	7	48	24	36	96	78	106
Fine[4]	KYAX	22 726	20 614	21 313	17 956	18 076	17 716	16 439	15 968	17 546	18 520	17 231
Recognizance	KYAY	1 001	1 203	1 267	1 134	1 089	1 357	810	912	1 091	913	853
Conditional discharge	KYAZ	1 928	1 679	1 597	1 538	1 439	1 286	1 559	1 497	1 526	1 524	1 326
Absolute discharge	KYBA	608	509	424	303	223	242	209	163	201	183	148
Youth conference order[5]	GGL8	..	..	..	..	..	..	..	..	..	21	74
Community responsibility order	GGL9	..	..	..	..	..	..	..	..	..	1	32
Other	KYBC	10	15	8	123	221	57	61	104	215	190	122
Total	KYBD	31 815	29 595	29 925	25 864	25 733	25 513	23 417	23 243	25 554	26 631	25 035
Crown court - all offences												
Prison[1]	KYBE	533	469	475	520	386	521	407	410	238	259	248
Custody Probation Order[1]	EOH2	..	..	..	..	..	..	..	..	331	332	370
Young offenders centre	KYBF	76	106	111	63	67	32	42	23	51	47	41
Training school[2]	KYBG	6	–	4	2	–	..	..	..	..	..	..
Juvenile Justice Centre order[2]	VQEV	..	..	..	–	–	–	–	2	–	–	–
Total immediate custody	KYBH	615	575	590	585	453	553	449	435	620	638	659
Prison suspended	KYBI	265	253	220	199	185	313	262	220	240	262	260
YOC suspended	KYBJ	63	71	60	49	41	48	37	35	50	72	45
Attendance centre	KYBK	–	–	–	–	–	–	–	1	–	–	–
Probation/supervision[3]	KYBL	60	49	47	70	43	68	48	49	63	93	79
Community service order	KYBM	60	54	37	33	24	29	45	25	27	33	31
Combination order	ZAEP	..	..	..	13	6	7	5	18	34	33	40
Fine[4]	KYBN	27	39	40	25	20	40	38	32	49	108	57
Recognizance	KYBO	–	7	10	7	–	4	11	12	8	6	9
Conditional discharge	KYBR	64	30	31	23	17	38	36	20	24	45	28
Absolute discharge	KYBS	1	–	1	6	–	3	–	6	1	1	6
Other	KYBU	2	3	3	7	2	2	2	4	5	3	6
Total	KYBV	1 157	1 081	1 039	1 017	791	1 105	933	857	1 121	1 294	1 220

1 Custody Probation Orders cannot be separately identified from 'prison' sentences from 1998 to 2002. Thus during this timeframe, figures for prison include custody probation orders.

2 The Juvenile Justice Centre order replaced the training school order from 31st January 1999.

3 Supervision orders were abolished with the introduction of the Criminal Justice (Children) Northern Ireland Order 1998.

4 From 2000, fine incorporates 'fine plus disqualification' and 'fine plus penalty points'.

5 Refers to the number of youth conference orders completed.

Source: Northern Ireland Office: 028 9052 7157

11.24 Prisons and Young Offenders Centres
Northern Ireland
Receptions and average population

Numbers

		1996	1997	1998	1999	2000	2001	2002	2003	2004	2005	2006
Receptions:												
Reception of untried prisoners	KEOA	2 292	2 188	2 284	2 497	2 197	1 922	2 337	2 439	2 440	2 776	3 193
Reception of sentenced prisoners:												
Imprisonment under sentence of immediate custody[1]	KEOB	1 070	1 062	949	963	1 001	791	916	1 032	975	966	1 075
Imprisonment in default of payment of a fine	KEOC	1 374	1 513	1 530	1 423	1 261	1 090	990	1 140	1 296	1 437	1 569
Total	KEOD	2 444	2 575	2 479	2 386	2 262	1 881	1 906	2 172	2 271	2 403	2 644
Reception into Young Offender Centres:												
Detention under sentence of immediate custody	KEOE	362	331	347	346	282	252	315	268	287	222	229
Detention in default of payment of a fine	KEOF	373	366	385	417	389	303	250	313	351	377	382
Total	KEOG	735	697	732	763	671	555	565	581	638	599	611
Other receptions[2]	KEOL	27	42	70	38	56	58	57	117	106	134	24
Daily average population:												
Unconvicted[3]	KEON	337	376	383	377	317	272	347	393	456	450	531
Convicted[4]	KEOP	1 302	1 256	1 124	867	751	638	679	767	818	851	902
Total	KEOM	1 639	1 632	1 507	1 244	1 068	910	1 026	1 160	1 274	1 301	1 433

1 Includes those detained under Section 73 of the Children and Young Persons (NI) Act 1968.
2 Non-criminal prisioners including those imprisoned for non-payment of maintenance, non-payment of debt, contempt of court or are being held under the terms of an Immigration Act.

3 Prisoners on remand or awaiting trial and prisoners committed by civil process.
4 Includes those sentenced to immediate custody and fine defaulters.

Sources: The Northern Ireland Prison Population in 2006;
Northern Ireland Office: 028 9052 7534

Lifestyles

Chapter 12

Lifestyles

Expenditure by the Department for Culture, Media and Sport

(Table 12.1)

The figures in this table are taken from the Department's Annual Report and are outturn figures for each of the headings shown (later figures are the estimated outturn). The Department's planned expenditure for future years is also shown.

Cinema statistics

(Table 12.4)

This table now includes data from CAA, Gallup and Nielsen EDI which replaces the previous Office for National Statistics (ONS) inquiry data which are no longer collected.

Domestic tourism

(Table 12.6)

The figures in this table are compiled using data from the United Kingdom Tourism Survey (UKTS) and represent trips of one or more nights away from home. The UKTS changed survey methodology in 2000 and 2005. Data from 1995 to 1999 were reworked to allow comparisons to be made with 2000-04 data. Data from 2004 should be used and interpreted with caution. Data from 2005 is not comparable with previous years.

International tourism and holidays abroad

(Tables 12.7 and 12.8)

The figures in these tables are compiled using data from the International Passenger Survey. A holiday abroad is a visit made for holiday purposes. Business trips and visits to friends and relatives are excluded.

Attendances at leisure and cultural activities

(Table 12.9)

The definitions used in this table differ from those normally used to define regular attendees by the Department for Culture, Media and Sport.

Gambling

(Table 12.10)

The National Lottery figures in this table are the latest figures at the time of going to press which have been released by the National Lottery Commission, and represent ticket sales (money staked) for each of the games which comprise the lottery. The figures have been adjusted to real terms using the Retail Prices Index (RPI).

The National Lottery commenced on the 19 November 1994, with the first instant ticket being sold in March 1995. Various other games have been started since, the latest shown in the table being the Euromillions game. The sum of the individual games may not agree exactly with the figures for total sales. Total sales also include the Easy Play games which commenced in 1998, but were dropped in 1999.

The other gambling figures in this table are obtained from the Gaming Board and H.M. Revenue and Customs. The figures have been adjusted to real terms using the RPI.

The money staked at bingo clubs refers to licensed clubs only.

Most popular boy and girl baby names

(Table 12.11)

The list comprises of the most popular names from England, Wales and Scotland. This is taken from the publications produced by ONS (England and Wales) and General Register Office Scotland.

12.1 Expenditure by the Department for Culture, Media and Sport[1]

£ million

	Museums, galleries and libraries[2]	The arts (England)	Sports (UK)	Architect-ure and the Historic Environ-ment (England)	The Royal Parks (UK)	Tourism (UK)	Broad-casting and media (UK)	Admin-istration and research	Gambling and the National Lottery[3]	Comme-morative services (Queen's Golden Jubilee)	Regional Cultural Consortiu-ms	Unallocat-ed Provision	Total Resource Budget
	GQIF	KWFP	KWFQ	KWFR	LQYY	KWFS	KWFT	GQIG	SNKA	SNKB	GLZ8	GLZ9	GM22
2000/01	407	239	52	137	24	48	2 490	29	801	–	–	–	4 228
2001/02	302	254	67	133	42	68	2 337	33	897	–	–	–	4 134
2002/03	425	286	123	143	26	75	2 638	38	654	6	–	–	4 413
2003/04	764	329	67	348	26	52	2 559	42	664	–	–	–	4 851
2004/05	443	367	106	162	27	51	2 610	42	611	–	2	–	4 421
2005/06	483	407	121	146	31	51	2 659	49	797	–	2	5	4 750
2006/07[4]	596	424	155	179	20	52	2 843	55	726	–	2	9	5 060
2007/08[5]	548	421	170	159	19	54	2 931	51	631	–	2	17	5 003

1 See chapter text.
2 Includes museums and galleries (England), libraries (UK) and museums library archives (UK).
3 DCMS and Treasury undertook a complete overhaul of the way Lottery expenditure is recorded.
4 Data is estimated.
5 Data are forecasts.

Source: Department for Culture, Media and Sport: 020 7211 6121

12.2 Employment in tourism
United Kingdom

Non seasonally adjusted. At June each year

Thousands

	Hotels and other tourist accommodation	Restaurants, bars and canteens	Transport	Travel agents, tour operators	Recreation services	Rest of the economy	All tourism related industries		
								Of which:	
							All	Employee jobs	Self-employment jobs
	EUR7	EUR8	EUR9	EUS2	EUS3	EUS4	EUS5	EUS6	EUS7
2000	230.0	556.1	132.2	135.2	73.2	205.2	1 331.9	1 214.4	117.5
2001	229.3	578.9	136.7	146.5	76.6	213.0	1 380.9	1 261.9	119.0
2002	225.4	601.1	135.5	140.0	82.1	213.8	1 397.8	1 278.0	119.8
2003	228.4	616.4	137.7	134.4	81.2	215.4	1 413.4	1 294.4	119.0
2004	238.0	634.0	136.0	144.0	87.2	217.2	1 456.5	1 326.9	129.6
2005	234.7	635.9	138.7	131.8	89.9	219.8	1 450.9	1 330.7	120.2
2006	235.3	632.9	143.5	118.1	93.3	221.6	1 444.7	1 317.8	126.9
2007	246.3	629.3	141.6	114.8	93.4	223.4	1 448.9	1 316.5	132.4

Sources: Department for Culture, Media and Sport: 020 7211 6451; using data from Labour Force Survey, Office for National Statistics

Lifestyles

12.3 Employment in creative industries
Great Britain

Thousands

	Advertising	Architecture	Crafts	Design and designer fashion	Film, video and photography	Music and the visual and performing arts	Publishing	Software computer games and electronic publishing	Television and radio	Art/antiques	All
	EUS8	EUS9	EUT2	EUT3	EUT4	EUT5	EUT6	EUT7	EUT8	EUT9	EUU2
1998	204.2	101.5	119.8	88.8	64.1	217.8	317.1	426.0	101.5	19.8	1 660.7
1999	200.9	101.5	96.8	93.5	61.9	255.7	317.0	488.6	92.5	20.8	1 729.3
2000	206.0	102.6	111.3	98.5	67.5	224.3	283.9	544.6	109.8	20.9	1 769.4
2001	220.5	103.4	115.1	103.0	75.5	224.6	293.3	567.7	104.1	20.9	1 828.1
2002	215.4	102.9	114.1	115.0	68.9	240.8	286.8	556.7	108.8	21.4	1 830.7
2003	213.8	103.1	108.7	113.2	74.3	245.8	305.2	581.2	110.9	22.5	1 878.8
2004	200.0	102.6	112.9	110.4	65.5	232.3	274.3	593.9	110.6	22.5	1 825.0
2005	223.4	108.2	95.5	115.5	63.8	236.3	253.3	596.8	108.7	22.9	1 824.4
2006	230.3	111.3	99.3	118.7	57.5	257.2	269.7	631.3	109.4	21.7	1 906.3

Sources: Creative Industries Economic Estimates Statistical Bulletin;
Department for Culture, Media and Sport

12.4 Cinema statistics[1,2]
United Kingdom

	Sites (numbers)	Screens (numbers)	Total number of admissions[3] (millions)	Gross box office takings[4] (£ million)	Revenue per admission[3] (£)	Revenue per screen (£ thousand)
	JMHX	JMHY	JMHZ	JMIA	JMIB	JMIC
1998	761	2 638	135.2	504.9	3.73	191.4
1999	751	2 825	139.1	549.7	3.95	194.6
2000	754	3 017	142.4	572.8	4.02	189.9
2001	766	3 248	155.9	645.0	4.14	198.6
2002	775	3 402	175.9	755.3	4.29	222.0
2003	776	3 433	167.3	742.0	4.44	216.1
2004	773	3 475	171.3	769.1	4.49	221.3
2005	771	3 486	164.7	768.3	4.66	220.4
2006	783	3 569	156.6	767.0	4.90	214.9
2007	775	3 596	162.4	823.4	5.10	229.0

1 See chapter text.
2 Includes Isle of Man and the Channel Islands.
3 Admissions are based on all cinemas taking advertising.
4 Box office takings are for UK only

Source: CAA/Nielsen EDI

12.5 Films
United Kingdom

Numbers and £ million

	Production of UK films		Expenditure on feature films (Current prices)				
	Films produced in the UK (numbers)	Production costs (1998 prices)	UK box office	Video rental	Video retail[1]	Subscriptions to movie channels	Box office, video, subscription channels
	KWGD	KWGE	KWHU	KWHV	KWHW	KWHX	KWHY
1996	128	726.0	411	382	733	1 319	2 930
1997	116	558.0	489	369	784	..	1 733
1998	88	487.0	547	437	896	..	1 892
1999	100	570.0	563	408	878	..	1 896
2000	98	793.0	583	444	1 100	..	2 176
2001	96	..	645	465	1 417	..	..
2002	119	550.0	755	476	1 895	..	..
2003	173	1 158.0	742	450	2 244	..	..
2004	133	812.0	770	461	2 478	..	..
2005	131	577.0	770	399	2 317	..	..
2006	134	842.0	762	340	2 161	..	..

1 In 2005 the British Video Association changed its methodology for producing market value which has necessitated a change to historical figures quoted.

Source: UK Film Council

12.6 Domestic tourism[1]
United Kingdom

	Number of trips (millions)	Number of nights spent (millions)	Expenditure at current prices (£ million)	Average nights spent (numbers)	Average expenditure per trip (£)
	GQGY	GQGZ	GQHA	GQHB	GQHC
1997	162.2	555.3	24 137	3.4	148.8
1998	148.8	516.0	22 814	3.5	153.3
1999	173.1	568.6	25 635	3.3	148.1
2000	175.4	576.4	26 133	3.3	149.0
2001	163.1	529.6	26 094	3.2	160.0
2002	167.3	531.9	26 699	3.2	159.6
2003	151.0	490.5	26 482	3.2	175.4
2004[2]	126.6	408.9	24 357	3.2	192.4
2005[3]	138.7	442.3	22 667	3.2	163.4
2006	126.3	400.1	20 965	3.2	165.9

1 See chapter text.
2 There were concerns that data for 2004 was not truly representative of the United Kingdom population. Data for 2004 should be used and interpreted with caution.

3 The UKTS underwent a methodological change in 2005 and results should not be compared with previous years. The survey did not run between Jan-April 2005, as a result full-year estimates were made using Jan-April 2003 data.

Source: United Kingdom Tourism Survey, VisitBritain: 020 8563 3317

12.7 International tourism[1]

Thousands and £ million

	Visits to the UK by overseas residents (thousands)	Spending in the UK by overseas residents		Visits overseas by UK residents (thousands)	Spending overseas by UK residents	
		Current prices	Constant 1995 prices		Current prices	Constant 1995 prices
	GMAA	GMAK	CQPR	GMAF	GMAM	CQPS
1997	25 515	12 244	11 542	45 957	16 931	18 652
1998	25 745	12 671	11 573	50 872	19 489	21 847
1999	25 394	12 498	11 133	53 881	22 020	24 676
2000	25 209	12 805	11 102	56 837	24 251	27 281
2001	22 835	11 306	9 528	58 281	25 332	27 710
2002	24 180	11 737	9 641	59 377	26 962	29 311
2003	24 715	11 855	9 451	61 424	28 550	28 677
2004	27 755	13 047	10 146	64 194	30 285	30 444
2005	29 970	14 248	10 714	66 441	32 154	30 954
2006	32 713	16 002	11 637	69 536	34 411	30 904
2007	32 558	15 955	11 462	70 029	35 475	32 953

1 See chapter text.

Sources: International Passenger Survey, Office for National Statistics; 01633 455277

12.8 Holidays abroad:[1] by destination

Percentages

		1971	1981	1991	2000	2001	2002	2003	2004	2005	2006	2007
Spain[2]	JTKC	34.30	29.80	21.30	27.80	27.90	28.50	29.80	28.40	27.20	27.80	26.20
France	JTKD	15.90	18.10	25.80	18.30	18.30	19.00	18.10	17.30	16.60	15.90	16.50
Greece	JTKF	4.50	6.60	7.60	6.80	7.80	7.00	6.60	5.70	5.10	5.00	5.00
United States	JTKE	1.00	5.50	6.80	7.30	6.30	5.40	5.50	6.10	6.00	5.10	5.30
Italy	JTKG	9.20	5.00	3.50	4.20	4.30	4.60	5.00	5.00	5.40	5.40	5.50
Ireland	JTKI	–	3.70	3.00	4.60	4.10	4.10	3.70	3.80	3.80	4.00	3.30
Portugal	JTKH	2.60	4.00	4.80	3.90	3.60	4.00	4.00	3.50	3.60	3.70	4.10
Cyprus	JTKL	1.00	2.70	2.40	3.30	3.50	3.00	2.70	2.60	2.80	2.40	2.40
Netherlands	JTKK	3.60	2.60	3.50	2.20	2.60	2.80	2.60	2.60	2.50	2.70	2.40
Turkey	JTKJ	–	2.30	0.70	1.80	2.00	2.20	2.30	2.30	2.70	2.70	2.80
Belgium	JTKM	–	2.20	2.10	1.80	2.10	2.00	2.20	1.80	1.90	2.00	2.20
Germany	JTKN	3.40	1.20	2.70	1.70	1.40	1.50	1.20	1.60	1.70	1.70	2.00
Austria	JTKP	5.50	1.10	2.40	1.00	1.10	1.40	1.10	1.40	1.30	1.20	1.20
Malta	JTKO	–	1.00	1.70	1.10	1.00	1.00	1.00	1.00	1.10	1.00	0.90
Other countries	JTKQ	19.00	14.20	11.80	14.10	13.80	13.60	14.20	16.80	18.40	19.70	20.30

1 See chapter text.
2 Excludes the Canary Islands prior to 1981.

Sources: International Passenger Survey, Office for National Statistics; 01633 455277

12.9 Attendance at leisure and cultural activities[1]
Great Britain

At Spring | | | | | | | | | | | Percentages

		1996/97	1997/98	1998/99	1999/00	2000/01	2001/02	2002/03	2003/04	2004/05	2005/06	2006/07
Attendance by men at:												
Cinema	JSPR	55	55	57	57	57	57	62	59	64	59	59
Plays	JSPS	21	20	19	21	21	20	22	23	23	25	25
Art galleries and exhibitions	JSPT	22	20	20	21	22	22	23	24	24	27	26
Classical music	JSPU	12	11	10	11	11	12	12	13	12	15	15
Ballet	JSPV	4	4	4	4	4	4	5	5	5	5	5
Opera	JSPW	6	6	6	6	6	5	6	6	6	7	7
Contemporary dance	JSPX	3	4	3	3	3	3	3	5	4	4	5
Taking part in sporting events - regularly[2]	EU5X	..	..	..	50	53	50	51	51	54	54	54
Watching sporting events	JSPY	87	87	86	85	81	76	76	74	77	75	70
Pop/rock concerts	C3Q8	..	..	..	..	..	..	25	26	25	29	30
Attendance by women at:												
Cinema	JSQA	52	54	57	55	54	56	60	62	63	61	61
Plays	JSQB	26	25	24	25	24	26	26	27	27	33	32
Art galleries and exhibitions	JSQC	23	22	22	22	22	23	24	24	25	30	29
Classical music	JSQD	12	13	13	12	12	13	13	14	14	17	17
Ballet	JSQE	9	8	8	8	8	8	9	10	10	12	12
Opera	JSQF	7	7	7	7	7	7	7	8	8	10	9
Contemporary dance	JSQG	5	5	5	5	5	6	6	7	7	9	8
Taking part in sporting events - regularly[2]	EU5Y	..	..	..	38	40	39	41	41	40	43	43
Watching sporting events	JSQH	69	67	66	66	58	56	57	55	62	61	55
Pop/rock concerts	C3Q9	..	..	..	..	..	..	21	23	24	26	28
Attendance by all persons at:												
Cinema	JSQJ	54	55	57	56	55	56	61	61	63	60	60
Plays	JSQK	24	22	22	23	23	23	24	25	25	29	29
Art galleries and exhibitions	JSQL	22	21	21	22	22	22	23	24	25	29	27
Classical music	JSQM	12	12	12	12	11	12	13	13	13	16	16
Ballet	JSQN	7	6	6	6	6	6	7	8	7	9	9
Opera	JSQO	7	6	6	6	6	6	7	8	7	9	8
Contemporary dance	JSQP	4	5	4	4	4	5	5	6	5	7	7
Taking part in sporting events - regularly[2]	EU5Z	..	..	..	44	46	44	46	46	47	48	49
Watching sporting events	JSQQ	78	77	76	75	69	66	66	64	69	68	62
Pop/rock concerts	C3QA	..	..	..	..	..	..	23	25	24	27	29

1 Percentage of resident population aged 15 and over attending 'these days'.
  See chapter text.
2 From 2002 the question asked to the respondent was changed.

Source: Target Group Index, BMRB International: 020 8433 4125

12.10 Gambling[1]
United Kingdom

											£ million at 2005/06 prices[2]

		1996/97	1997/98	1998/99	1999/00	2000/01	2001/02	2002/03	2003/04	2004/05	2005/06	2006/07
Money staked on gambling												
National Lottery - Total[3]	C229	5 603	6 325	5 809	5 450	5 315	5 029	4 670	4 614	4 757	5 000	4 911
Lotto including on-line	C3PU	4 564	5 408	5 064	4 641	4 416	4 038	3 479	3 225	3 225	3 021	2 858
Instants[4]	C3PV	1 039	917	744	612	590	606	592	641	729	804	943
Thunderball	C3PW	..	..	..	197	257	254	287	351	343	355	329
Lottery Extra[7]	C3PX	..	..	..	..	51	131	90	78	77	57	12
HotPicks	C3PY	..	..	..	..	..	..	222	244	219	228	222
Christmas draw	C3PZ	..	..	..	..	..	..	..	15	..	..	..
Euromillions	C3Q2	..	..	..	..	..	..	..	15	104	427	464
Daily Play	C3Q3	..	..	..	..	..	..	..	45	59	54	49
Dream Numbers[8]	I67H	..	..	..	..	..	..	..	..	..	..	59
Lotteries (excluding the National Lottery)[5]	C3Q4	136	144	179	114	114	114	134	127	141	139	137
Bingo clubs	C3Q5	1 148	1 170	1 159	1 179	1 190	1 221	1 256	1 381	1 783	1 826	1 820
Football pools	C3Q6	548	400	286	221	185	151	124	112	109	90	88
Off-course betting[6]	C3Q7	7 972	7 869	7 916	7 996	7 689	9 969	17 985	32 265	44 971	44 437	36 553

1 See chapter text.
2 Adjusted to real terms using the Retail Prices Index.
3 Includes Easy Play tickets which are not shown separately.
4 From 2003/04 includes Inter-active games.
5 From 2002/03 includes Hotspot lotteries.
6 From 2001/02 includes Fixed Odds Betting Terminals.
7 Discontinued July 2006
8 Started July 2006

Sources: National Lottery Commission;
Gaming Board for Great Britain: 020 7306 6253;
Department for Culture, Media and Sport: 020 7211 6451

12.11 Most Popular Boy and Girl Baby Names 2007
Great Britain[1]

Rank	Names Boys	Rank	Names Boys	Rank	Names Girls	Rank	Names Girls
1	Jack	51	Isaac	1	Grace	51	Isabel
2	Thomas	52	Finlay	2	Olivia	52	Paige
3	Oliver	53	Rhys	3	Emily	53	Anna
4	Joshua	54	Noah	4	Ruby	54	Eleanor
5	Harry	55	Mason	5	Jessica	55	Lola
6	James	56	Kieran	6	Sophie	56	Libby
7	Daniel	57	Toby	7	Chloe	57	Isla
8	Charlie	58	Charles	8	Lily	58	Niamh
9	William	59	Alex	9	Ella	59	Sarah
10	Samuel	60	Riley	10	Lucy	60	Lilly
11	Alfie	61	David	11	Ellie	61	Skye
12	Lewis	62	Louis	12	Amelia	62	Isobel
13	George	63	Kai	13	Charlotte	63	Amelie
14	Joseph	64	Reece	14	Mia	64	Maisie
15	Benjamin	65	Brandon	15	Hannah	65	Rosie
16	Ethan	66	Freddie	16	Evie	66	Aimee
17	Dylan	67	Kian	17	Katie	67	Zara
18	Callum	68	John	18	Megan	68	Matilda
19	Jake	69	Bradley	19	Amy	69	Maddison
20	Mohammed	70	Aidan	20	Emma	70	Eve
21	Alexander	71	Harley	21	Erin	71	Sienna
22	Luke	72	Luca	22	Isabella	72	Zoe
23	Ryan	73	Bailey	23	Millie	73	Gracie
24	Matthew	74	Sam	24	Abigail	74	Tia
25	Jacob	75	Robert	25	Isabelle	75	Abbie
26	Adam	76	Mohammad	26	Freya	76	Alisha
27	Liam	77	Leon	27	Daisy	77	Nicole
28	Tyler	78	Evan	28	Holly	78	Harriet
29	Cameron	79	Theo	29	Molly	79	Courtney
30	Max	80	Andrew	30	Poppy	80	Maya
31	Jayden	81	Christopher	31	Caitlin	81	Faith
32	Jamie	82	Hayden	32	Jasmine	82	Sofia
33	Harvey	83	Taylor	33	Phoebe	83	Layla
34	Harrison	84	Joe	34	Imogen	84	Madeleine
35	Connor	85	Ashton	35	Ava	85	Lacey
36	Archie	86	Ellis	36	Keira	86	Shannon
37	Nathan	87	Joel	37	Madison	87	Julia
38	Ben	88	Jay	38	Rebecca	88	Lydia
39	Lucas	89	Zachary	39	Leah	39	Martha
40	Henry	90	Sean	40	Elizabeth	90	Francesca
41	Kyle	91	Sebastian	41	Sophia	91	Lexie
42	Owen	92	Billy	42	Lauren	92	Hollie
43	Michael	93	Elliot	43	Georgia	93	Maria
44	Logan	94	Reuben	44	Brooke	94	Alexandra
45	Aaron	95	Gabriel	45	Eva	95	Rose
46	Leo	96	Zak	46	Summer	96	Alicia
47	Muhammad	97	Morgan	47	Alice	97	Victoria
48	Oscar	98	Corey	48	Scarlett	98	Sara
49	Edward	99	Louie	49	Amber	99	Evelyn
50	Finlay	100	Dominic	50	Bethany	100	Tilly

1 Great Britain compiled from Top 100 names from England & Wales and most popular names Scotland publications. See chapter text.

Sources: Office for National Statistics;
General Register Office Scotland

Environment

Chapter 13

Environment

Environmental Taxes

(Table 13.1)

In 2006, government revenue from environmental taxes was £35.4 billion. As a proportion of Gross Domestic Product (GDP) this amounts to 2.7 per cent, and as a proportion of total taxes and social contributions, environmental taxes were 7.3 per cent in 2006. These proportions are lower than in previous years because growth in the economy and total taxes and social contributions has exceeded that of environmental taxes.

Air emissions

(Table 13.2 to 13.8)

Emissions of air pollutants arise from a wide variety of sources. The National Atmospheric Emissions Inventory (NAEI) is prepared annually for the Government and the devolved administrations by AEA Energy and Environment, with the work being co-ordinated by the Department for Food and Rural Affairs (Defra). Information is available for a range of point sources, including the most significant polluters. However, a different approach has to be taken for diffuse sources, such as transport and domestic emissions, where this type of information is not available and estimates for these are derived from statistical information and from research on emission factors for stationary and mobile sources. Although for any given year considerable uncertainties surround the emission estimates for each pollutant, trends over time are likely to be more reliable.

UK national emission estimates are updated annually and any developments in methodology are applied retrospectively to earlier years. Adjustments in the methodology are made to accommodate new technical information and to improve international comparability.

Three different classification systems are used in the tables presented here: a National Accounts basis (Table 13.2); the format required by the Inter-governmental Panel on Climate Change (IPCC) (Table 13.3); and the National Communications (NC) categories (Tables 13.6-13.8).

The NC source categories are detailed below, together with details of the main sources of these emissions:

Energy supply total: power stations, petroleum refining, manufacture of solid fuels and other energy industries,

fossil fuel exploration, production, transport and offshore oil – venting and flaring.

Business total: iron and steel – combustion, other industrial combustion and miscellaneous industrial and commercial combustion.

Transport total: road transport – passenger cars, light duty vehicles, buses, HGVs, mopeds, motorcycles; gasoline evaporation from vehicles, tyre and brake wear.

Other transport: civil aviation (domestic cruise, take off and landing cycles), railway locomotives, railway – stationary combustion, shipping, national navigation, fishing vessels, and other mobile sources including agricultural machinery; gardening, construction and aircraft support equipment and mobile industrial equipment powered by diesel or petrol engines.

Residential total: residential plant, household and gardening (mobile).

Agriculture total: stationary combustion, manure liquid systems, manure solid storage and dry lot, other manure management, direct soil emission, field burning of agricultural wastes.

Industrial process total: industrial process sinter production, iron and steel – flaring, nitric acid production, adipic acid production and metal production.

Solvent and other product use: paint application, degreasing and dry cleaning, chemical products, manufacture and processing wood impregnation and tyre manufacture.

Land-use change: emissions from managed and unmanaged forests, and forest and grassland conversion.

Waste management total: treatment of domestic, industrial and other waste, including landfill and waste incineration.

Estimated atmospheric emissions on a National Accounts basis

(Table 13.2)

The National Accounts figures in Table 13.2 differ from those on an IPCC basis in that they include estimated emissions from fuels purchased by UK resident households and companies either at home or abroad. These include emissions from UK international shipping and aircraft operators, and exclude emissions in the UK resulting from the activities of non-residents.

Greenhouse gases include carbon dioxide, methane, nitrous oxide, hydro-fluorocarbons, perfluorocarbons and sulphur hexafluoride which are expressed in thousand tonnes of carbon dioxide equivalent.

Acid rain precursors include sulphur dioxide, nitrogen oxides and ammonia which are expressed as thousand tonnes of sulphur dioxide equivalent.

PM_{10} are carbon particles in the air arising from incomplete combustion.

Estimated total emissions of greenhouse gases on an IPCC basis

(Table 13.3)

The IPCC classification is used to report greenhouse gas emissions under the Framework Convention on Climate Change and includes land use change and all emissions from domestic aviation and shipping, but excludes international marine and aviation bunker fuels. Estimates of the relative contribution to global warming of the main greenhouse gases, or classes of gases, is presented weighted by their global warming potential.

Average number of days of moderate or higher air pollution

(Table 13.4)

The air quality indicator is one of the 68 indicators of the Government's Sustainable Development Strategy. The indicator is split into two parts covering: (a) measures annual levels of pollution from particulates (PM_{10}) and ozone (O_3), the two pollutants thought to have the greatest health impacts; and (b) the number of days on which levels of any one of a basket of five pollutants were 'moderate or higher'.

Table 13.4 details the second part of this indicator according to the Air Pollution Information Service bandings used in the air pollution forecasting. At a moderate level, the effects of pollution may start to be noticeable to sensitive people. There is no clear trend in the number of pollution days, due to the effects of variability in weather patterns from year to year.

The bandings are based on five pollutants consisting of carbon monoxide, nitrogen oxide, ozone, particulates and sulphur dioxide. These are recognised as the most important for causing short-term health effects. The main causes of days of moderate or higher air pollution at urban sites are ozone and particulates (PM_{10}). Sulphur dioxide also used to make a significant contribution but has now fallen to relatively very low levels. Carbon monoxide and nitrogen oxide have rarely

reached moderate or higher levels since the urban index began in 1992.

Emissions of carbon dioxide

(Table 13.6)

Carbon dioxide is the main man-made contributor to global warming. The UK contributes about 2 per cent to global man-made emissions, which, according to the IPCC, was estimated to be 38 billion tonnes carbon dioxide in 2004. Carbon dioxide accounted for about 85 per cent of the UK's man-made greenhouse gas emissions in 2006.

Emissions of methane

(Table 13.7)

Weighted by global warming potential, methane accounted for about 7.5 per cent of the UK's greenhouse gas emissions in 2006. Methane emissions, excluding those from natural sources, were 53 per cent below 1990 levels. In 2006, the main sources of methane were landfill sites (40 per cent of total) and agriculture (38 per cent). Emissions from landfill have reduced by 61 per cent and emissions from agriculture by 13 per cent since 1990.

Emissions of nitrous oxide

(Table 13.8)

Weighted by global warming potential, nitrous oxide emissions accounted for about 6 per cent of the UK's man-made greenhouse gas emissions in 2006. Nitrous oxide emissions fell by 40 per cent between 1990 and 2006. The largest reductions were in emissions from adipic acid production between 1998 and 1999. This leaves agriculture as the main source, accounting for over two thirds of emissions, mainly from agricultural soils. Nitrous oxide emissions from road transport were more than five times higher in 2006 than in 1990, increasing from 2 per cent of the total to 14 per cent in 2006. This is a result of the introduction of the three way catalytic converters, which significantly reduce emissions of various other harmful gases such as carbon monoxide, hydrocarbons and nitrogen oxides, but have a side-effect of producing higher emissions of nitrous oxide.

Annual Rainfall

(Table 13.9)

Regional rainfall is derived by the Met Office's National Climate Information Centre for the National Hydrological

Enviroment

Monitoring Programme at the Centre for Ecology and Hydrology. These monthly area rainfalls are based initially on a subset of rain gauges (circa 350) but are updated after four to five months with figures using the majority of the UK's rain gauge network.

The regions of England shown in this table correspond to the original nine English regions of the National Rivers Authority (NRA). The NRA became part of the Environment Agency upon its creation in April 1996. The figures in this table relate to the country of Wales, not the Environment Agency Welsh Region.

UK Weather Summary

(Table 13.10)

For 2007 data these initial averages use data available from about 180 observing sites available on 1 January 2008. They represent an initial assessment of the weather that was experienced across the UK during 2007 and how it compares with the 1961 to 1990 average.

For all other years, these final averages use quality controlled data from the UK climate network of observing stations. They show the Met Office's best assessment of the weather that was experienced across the UK during the years and how it compares with the 1961 to 1990 average. The columns headed 'Anom' (anomaly) show the difference from, or percentage of, the 1961 to 1990 long-term average.

Biological and chemical quality of rivers and canals

(Table 13.11)

The chemical quality of river and canal waters is monitored in a series of separate national surveys in England and Wales and Northern Ireland. The General Quality Assessment (GQA) Scheme used in the surveys provides a rigorous and objective method for assessing the basic chemical quality of rivers and canals based on three determinants: dissolved oxygen, biochemical oxygen demand and ammoniacal nitrogen. The GQA grades river stretches into six categories (A-F) of chemical quality, and these in turn have been grouped into four broader groups: good (classes A and B), fair (C and D), poor (E) and bad (F).

To provide a more comprehensive picture of the health of rivers and canals, biological testing has also been carried out. The biological grading is based on the monitoring of tiny animals (invertebrates) which live in or on the bed of the river. Research has shown that there is a relationship between species composition and water quality. Using a procedure known as the River Invertebrate Prediction and Classification System, species groups recorded at a site were compared

with those which would be expected to be present in the absence of pollution, allowing for the different environmental characteristics in different parts of the country. Two different summary statistics (known as ecological quality indices) were calculated and then the biological quality was assigned to one of six bands based on a combination of these two statistics.

It should be noted that the monitoring network only covers stretches the Environment Agency are required to monitor, that is rivers and streams with a flow greater than $1m^3$/second. On this basis, 40,000km of river network are monitored in England and Wales out of an estimated total river length of 150,000km. No canals are classified in Northern Ireland.

Biological and chemical quality of rivers and canals Scotland

(Table 13.12)

In Scotland, river and canal water quality is based on the Scottish River Classification Scheme of 20 June 1997, which combines chemical, biological, nutrient and aesthetic quality using the following classes: excellent (A1), good (A2), fair (B), poor (C) and seriously polluted (D). The figures in the table are also rounded to the nearest 10km and may not sum to totals.

During 2000 a new digitised river network (DRN) was developed, based on 1:50,000 ordnance survey data digitised by the Institute of Hydrology. The new network ensures consistency between all Scottish Environment Protection Agency areas and includes the Scottish Islands which were not previously covered. Data based on this network are published for the first time in the 2004 edition of Annual Abstract and are not consistent with data which have previously been published. The DRN includes:

> All mainland and islands rivers with a catchment area of 10 km² or more. This is known as the 'baseline network'

> Mainland and islands stream stretches with a catchment of less than 10 km² which are classified as fair, poor or seriously polluted and have been monitored. These are added to the baseline network to give a 'classification network'

It is intended that future emphasis will be placed on the baseline network, which will be the reportable network for the purposes of the European Commission Water Framework Directive. Efforts to improve the quality of the downgraded smaller streams will continue, but once this has been sustainably achieved, their monitoring may be reduced. Many of these streams are the subject of current attention because of their influence on the quality of larger classification network rivers.

Using the DRN scheme, data for every routine sampling point are automatically applied to an identified river stretch of predetermined length. The loss in total river length in moving to the DRN (that is despite the first time inclusion of islands rivers) arises mainly from the exclusion from classification of thousands of small remote headwater streams which were never monitored, but assumed to be of excellent quality. The smaller reduction in length of downgraded waters arises mainly from using 1:50,000 maps for the DRN; in the former system lengths were hand measured from 1:10,000 maps, so more minor channel bends were included.

Reservoir stocks in England and Wales

(Table 13.13)

Data are collected for a network of major reservoirs (or reservoir groups) in England and Wales for the National Hydrological Monitoring Programme at the Centre for Ecology and Hydrology. Figures of usable capacity are supplied by the Water Plcs and the Environment Agency at the start of each month and are aggregated to provide an index of the total reservoir stocks for England and Wales.

Water industry expenditure

(Table 13.14)

The table is informed by the annual and regulatory accounts of water and sewerage companies and water companies of England and Wales. The elements which make up operating expenditure are as follows: manpower costs, other costs of employment, power, agencies, associated companies, Environment Agency charges, bulk supply imports, general and support, customer services, scientific services, other business activities, local authority rates, water charges, local authority sewerage agencies, materials and consumables, hired and contracted services, charge for bad and doubtful debts, depreciation, infrastructure renewals expenditure, infrastructure renewals accrual, exceptional items and other operating costs. Capital expenditure figures are the addition to tangible fixed assets including management and general expenditure but excluding infrastructure renewals expenditure. Adopted assets at nil cost are also included.

Water pollution incidents

(Table 13.15)

The Environment Agency responds to complaints and reported incidents of pollution in England and Wales. Each incident is then logged and categorised according to its severity. The category describes the impact of each incident on our water,

land and air. The impact of an incident on each medium is considered and reported separately. If no impact has occurred for a particular medium, the incident is reported as a category 4. Before 1999, the reporting system was used only for water pollution incidents; thus the total number of substantiated incidents was lower, as it did not include incidents not relating to the water environment.

Bathing waters

(Table 13.16)

Under the EC Bathing Water Directive 76/160/EEC, 11 physical, chemical and microbiological parameters are measured including total and faecal coliforms which are generally considered to be the most important indicators of the extent to which water is contaminated by sewage. The mandatory value for total coli forms is 10,000 per 100 ml, and for faecal coli forms 2,000 per 100 ml. For a bathing water to comply with the coli form standards, the Directive requires that at least 95 per cent of samples taken for each of these parameters over the bathing season are less than or equal to the mandatory values. In the UK a minimum of 20 samples are normally taken at each site. In practice this means that where 20 samples are taken, a maximum of only one sample may exceed the mandatory value for the bathing water to comply, and where less than 20 samples are taken none may exceed the mandatory value for the bathing water to comply.

The bathing water season is from mid-May to end-September in England and Wales, but shorter in Scotland and Northern Ireland. Bathing waters which are closed for the season are excluded for that year.

The table shows Environment Agency regions for England and Wales, the boundaries of which are based on river catchment areas and not county borders. In particular, the figures shown for Wales are the Environment Agency Welsh Region, the boundary of which does not coincide with the boundary of Wales.

Surface and groundwater abstractions

(Table 13.17)

Significant changes in the way data is collected and/or reported were made in 1991 (due to Water Resources Act 1991) and 1999 (commission of National Abstraction Licensing Database). Figures are therefore not strictly comparable with those in previous/intervening years. From 1999, data has been stored and retrieved from one system nationally and is therefore more accurate and reliable. Some regions report licensed and actual abstracts for financial rather than calendar years. As figures represent an average for the whole year expressed as daily amounts, differences between amounts reported for financial and calendar years are small.

Under the Water Act 2003, abstraction of less than 20m³/ day became exempt from the requirement to hold a licence as of 1 April 2005. As a result over 22,000 licences were deregulated, mainly for agricultural or private water supply purposes. However, due to the small volumes involved, this has had a minimal affect on the estimated licensed and actual abstraction totals.

The following changes have occurred in the classification of individual sources:

Spray irrigation: this category includes small amounts of non-agricultural spray irrigation

Mineral washing: from 1999 this was not reported as a separate category; licences for 'Mineral washing' are now contained in 'Other industry'

Private water supply: was shown as separate category from 1992 and includes private abstractions for domestic use and individual households

Fish farming, cress growing, amenity ponds: Includes amenity ponds, but excludes miscellaneous from 1991

Estimates of remaining recoverable oil and gas reserves

(Table 13.18)

The latest oil and gas data for 2006 shows that UK reserves of oil were estimated to be around 2.9 billion tonnes, while UK gas reserves were around 2016 billion cubic meters. Of these, proven reserves of oil were 0.5 billion tonnes and proven reserves of gas were 412 billion cubic meters. Compared with a year earlier, proven reserves were 7.2 per cent lower for oil and 14.3 per cent lower for gas. The monetary value of oil reserves increased from £100.1 billion in 2005 to £114.2 billion in 2006, a rise of 14.1 per cent reflecting rising oil prices. At £85.3 billion, the vale of gas reserves increased by 30.4 per cent from £65.4 billion between 2005 and 2006.

Municipal waste disposal

(Table 13.19)

Municipal waste includes household and non-household waste that is collected and disposed of by local authorities. It includes regular household collections, specific recycling collections, special collections of bulky items, waste received at civic amenity sites, and waste collected from non-household sources that come under the control of local authorities.

Amounts of different materials from household sources collected for recycling

(Table 13.20)

Household recycling includes those materials collected for recycling, composting or reuse by local authorities and those collected from household sources by 'private/voluntary' organisations where this material comes under the possession or control of local authorities. It includes residual waste from the household stream which was diverted for recycling by sorting or further treatment.

'Bring sites' are facilities where members of the public can bring recyclable materials (such as paper, glass, cans, textiles, shoes, etc). These are often located at supermarkets or similar locations, but exclude civic amenity sites.

'Civic Amenity sites' refers to household waste collected at sites provided by local authorities for the disposal of excess household and garden waste free of charge, as required by the Refuse Disposal (Amenity) Act 1978. These are also known as Household Waste Recycling Centres.

Noise incidents

(Table 13.21)

The table shows trends in the number of incidents reported by local authority Environmental Health Officers (EHO). The figures are from those authorities making returns and are calculated per million people based on the population of the authorities making returns. Environmental health has changed from calculating complaints per million of population to incidents per million of the population in 2004/05. The reason for asking about incidents is to better reflect both the local noise environment and investigatory workloads during the reporting year, while avoiding the double counting which occurs with complaints (i.e. multiple complaints about the same incident). As a result the data does reflect this change by a drop in numbers across all categories.

Most complaints about traffic noise are addressed to highways authorities or Department for Transport (DfT) Regional Directors, and will not necessarily be included in the figures. Similarly, complaints about noise from civil aircraft are generally received by aircraft operators, the airport companies, the DfT or Civil Aviation Authority. Complaints about military flying are dealt with either by Station Commanding Officers or by Ministry of Defence headquarters. It is also true that railway noise will be reported elsewhere. Thus the figures in this table will not necessarily include these complaints and are likely to be considerably understated. Therefore, the information reported to the EHO is considered to give, at best, only a very approximate indication of the trend in noise complaints from these sources.

Over time some of the categories shown in this table have changed. These have included, up until 1996/97, Section 62 of the Control of Pollution Act 1974 covered noise in the streets; it primarily included the chimes of ice-cream vendors and the use of loudspeakers other than for strictly defined purposes. From 1997/98, all complaints about noise in the street are included with 'vehicles machinery and equipment in streets'. From 1997/98, complaints about road works are included with 'vehicles machinery and equipment in streets'.

Material flows

(Table 13.22)

Economy-wide material flow accounts record the total mass of natural resources and products that are used by the UK economy, either directly in the production and distribution of products and services, or indirectly through the movement of materials which are displaced in order for production to take place.

The direct movement of materials into the economy derives primarily from domestic extraction that is from biomass (agricultural harvest, timber, fish and animal grazing), fossil fuel extraction (such as coal, crude oil and natural gas) and mineral extraction (metal ores, industrial minerals such as pottery clay, and construction material such as crushed rock, sand and gravel). This domestic extraction is supplemented by the imports of products, which may be of raw materials such as unprocessed agricultural products, but can also be of semi-manufactured or finished products. In a similar way the UK produces exports of raw materials, semi-manufactured and finished goods which can be viewed as inputs to the production and consumption of overseas economies.

Indirect flows of natural resources consist of the unused material resulting from domestic extraction, such as mining and quarrying overburden and the soil removed during construction and dredging activities. They also include the movement of used and unused material overseas which is associated with the production and delivery of imports. Water, except for that included directly in products, is excluded from the accounts.

There are three main indicators used to measure inputs. The Direct Material Input measures the input of used materials into the economy, that is all materials which are of economic value and are used in production and consumption activities (including the production of exports). Domestic Material Consumption measures the total amount of material directly used in the economy, that is it includes imports but excludes

exports. The Total Material Requirement (TMR) measures the total material basis of the economy, that is the total primary resource requirements of all the production and consumption activities. It includes not only the direct use of resources for producing exports, but also indirect flows from the production of imports and the indirect flows associated with domestic extraction. Although TMR is widely favoured as a resource use indicator, the estimates of indirect flows are less reliable than those for materials directly used by the economy, and the indicator therefore needs to be considered alongside other indicators.

13.1 Government revenues from environmental taxes
United Kingdom

£ million

		1993	1995	1998	1999	2000	2001	2002	2003	2004	2005	2006
Energy												
Duty on hydrocarbon oils	GTAP	12 497	15 360	20 996	22 391	23 041	22 046	22 070	22 476	23 412	23 346	23 448
including												
Unleaded petrol[1]	GBHE	4 242	5 901	9 897	11 952	11 573	1 938	–	–	–	–	–
Leaded petrol/LRP[2]	GBHL	4 502	4 088	2 984	1 630	1 115	661	310	320	75	20	15
Ultra low sulphur petrol	ZXTK	–	–	–	–	976	10 285	12 453	11 891	12 171	11 723	11 354
Diesel[3]	GBHH	3 484	5 127	7 088	1 274	23	66	–	–	–	–	–
Ultra low sulphur diesel	GBHI	–	–	806	7 338	9 086	8 633	9 137	9 579	10 298	10 808	10 811
VAT on duty	CMYA	2 187	2 688	3 674	3 918	4 032	3 858	3 862	3 933	4 097	4 086	4 103
Fossil fuel levy	CIQY	1 331	1 306	181	104	56	86	32	–	–	–	–
Gas levy	GTAZ	240	161	32	–	–	–	–	–	–	–	–
Climate change levy	LSNT	–	–	–	–	–	585	825	828	756	747	711
Hydro-benefit	LITN	22	27	32	35	42	46	44	44	40	10	–
Road vehicles												
Vehicle excise duty	CMXZ	3 482	3 954	4 631	4 873	4 606	4 102	4 294	4 720	4 763	4 762	5 010
Other environmental taxes												
Air passenger duty	CWAA	–	339	823	884	940	824	814	781	856	896	963
Landfill tax	BKOF	–	–	333	430	461	502	541	607	672	733	808
Aggregates levy	MDUQ	–	–	–	–	–	–	213	340	328	327	325
Total environmental taxes	JKVW	19 755	23 835	30 702	32 635	33 178	32 049	32 695	33 729	34 924	34 907	35 358
Environmental taxes as a % of:												
Total taxes and social contributions	JKVX	9.0	9.3	9.7	9.7	9.3	8.6	8.7	8.5	8.3	7.7	7.3
Gross domestic product	JKVY	3.1	3.3	3.5	3.6	3.5	3.2	3.1	3.0	2.9	2.8	2.7

1 Unleaded petrol includes superunleaded petrol.
2 Lead Replacement Petrol (the alternative to 4-Star leaded petrol introduced in 2000) is lead-free.
3 Duty incentives have concentrated production on ultra low sulphur varieties.

Sources: ONS, Department for Business Enterprise & Regulatory Reform;
environment.accounts@ons.gsi.gov.uk

13.2 Estimated atmospheric emissions on a National Accounts basis[1], 2005
United Kingdom

Thousand tonnes

	Greenhouse gases[2]	Acid rain precursors[3]	Emissions affecting air quality					Lead (Tonnes)	Cadmium (Tonnes)	Mercury (Tonnes)
			PM$_{10}$	Carbon monoxide	Volatile organic compounds[4]	Benzene	Butadiene			
Agriculture	51 302	555.78	22.30	49.07	83.26	0.23	0.09	0.41	0.030	0.032
Mining and quarrying	29 155	87.09	12.80	38.75	111.86	0.37	0.02	0.26	0.064	0.021
Manufacturing	119 745	436.76	32.95	573.56	347.25	2.37	0.47	86.70	2.049	3.586
Electricity, gas and water supply	188 216	638.72	10.09	75.01	49.23	0.52	0.01	9.66	0.709	2.272
Construction	11 302	49.98	9.50	59.64	65.07	0.25	0.12	0.37	0.042	0.020
Wholesale and retail trade	18 809	54.39	6.66	75.67	60.93	0.28	0.18	12.90	0.096	0.035
Transport and communication	104 466	1003.96	68.97	160.51	58.88	3.62	0.73	4.86	3.716	0.211
Financial intermediation	7 066	14.17	1.99	52.40	4.70	0.11	0.04	0.14	0.034	0.006
Public administration	9 226	39.79	2.01	44.45	4.96	0.28	0.05	0.54	0.030	0.044
Education, health and social work	11 029	15.29	1.10	13.13	2.29	0.06	0.01	0.43	0.021	0.039
Other services	27 159	44.40	1.51	97.31	28.97	1.80	0.20	0.36	0.030	1.352
Domestic	155 972	271.43	36.89	1 258.95	257.22	7.34	0.76	4.84	0.439	0.135
Total	733 446	3 211.75	206.77	2 498.45	1 074.62	17.24	2.68	121.47	7.26	7.752
Of which, emissions from road transport	128 057	415.50	34.34	1 139.79	121.10	2.94	1.64	2.11	0.42	0.004

1 See chapter text.
2 Thousand tonnes of carbon dioxide equivalent.
3 Thousand tonnes of sulphur dioxide equivalent.
4 Excluding methane, but including benzene and 1,3-butadiene.

Sources: National Environmental Technology Centre;
Office for National Statistics: 020 7014 2079;
environment.accounts@ons.gsi.gov.uk

13.3 Estimated emissions of greenhouse gases on an IPCC basis[1,2,3,6,7]
United Kingdom

Million tonnes (Carbon dioxide equivalent[4])

		1990	1995	1996	1997	1998	1999	2000	2001	2002	2003	2004	2005	2006
Net CO_2 emissions/removals	JZCK	592.4	549.8	571.0	548.1	549.9	540.3	548.6	559.4	542.7	554.7	555.1	555.2	554.5
Methane(CH_4)	GXDO	103.5	90.2	87.8	82.9	78.2	73.0	68.4	62.4	59.4	53.4	51.6	49.6	49.1
Nitrous oxide(N_2O)	GXDP	63.8	53.0	53.4	54.8	54.5	44.2	43.6	41.5	40.1	39.8	40.6	39.8	38.3
Hydrofluorocarbons(HFCs)	JZCN	11.4	15.5	16.7	19.2	17.3	10.9	9.1	9.7	9.9	10.2	8.9	9.2	9.2
Perfluorocarbons(PFCs)	JZCO	1.4	0.5	0.5	0.4	0.4	0.4	0.5	0.4	0.3	0.3	0.3	0.3	0.3
Sulphur hexafluoride(SF_6)	JZCP	1.0	1.2	1.3	1.2	1.3	1.4	1.8	1.4	1.5	1.3	1.1	1.1	0.9
Kyoto greenhouse gas basket[5]	F92X	770.8	709.0	729.5	705.6	700.9	669.5	671.4	674.4	653.8	659.5	657.9	655.5	652.3

1 Net emissions weighted by global warming potential. Emissions inventories based on the methodology developed by the Intergovernmental Panel on Climate Change (IPCC) are used to report UK emissions to the Climate Change Convention.
2 See chapter text.
3 Figures for each individual gas include the Land use, Land-Use Change and Forestry sector (LULUCF) but exclude emissions from UK overseas territories
4 Emissions are presented as carbon dioxide equivalent in line with international reporting and carbon trading. To convert Carbon Dioxide into carbon equivalents, divide figures by 44 /12.

5 Kyoto basket total differs slightly from sum of individual pollutants above as the basket uses a narrower definition for the Land Use Change and Forestry sector, and includes emissions from UK Overseas Territories.
6 The entire time series is revised each year to take account of methodological improvements in the UK emissions inventory.
7 Figures shown do not include any adjustment for the effect of the EU Emissions Trading Scheme (EUETS), which was introduced in 2005.

Sources: AEA Energy & Environment; for Department for Environment, Food and Rural Affairs 020 7238 4908

13.4 Average number of days of moderate or higher air pollution per site[1] caused by each of the basket of 5 pollutants
United Kingdom

		1993	1994	1995	1996	1997	1998	1999	2000	2001	2002	2003	2004	2005	2006	2007[2]
Ozone	I6B3	5	13	24	17	16	10	25	13	17	14	36	18	16	33	12
Nitrogen dioxide	I6B4	–	–	1	–	1	–	–	–	–	–	–	–	1	–	1
Carbon monoxide	I6B5	–	–	–	–	–	–	–	–	–	–	–	–	–	–	–
Sulphur dioxide	I6B6	20	13	12	6	4	3	1	1	–	–	–	–	–	–	–
Particulates	I6B7	43	27	28	30	23	13	9	7	8	6	17	4	6	10	11

1 See chapter text.
2 2007 data is provisional.

Sources: AEA Energy & Environment; Environment Agency; for Department for Environment, Food and Rural Affairs: 020 7238 4908

13.5 Road Transport Emissions by Pollutant
United Kingdom

Thousand tonnes

		1995	1996	1997	1998	1999	2000	2001	2002	2003	2004	2005
Pollutant												
Greenhouse gases[1]	I6BZ	114 693	119 617	122 215	122 293	123 915	123 363	123 477	126 205	126 249	127 489	128 057
of which												
Carbon dioxide	I6C2	111 971	116 540	118 775	118 484	119 746	118 929	118 776	121 224	121 113	122 189	122 724
Methane	I6C3	479	453	417	383	349	311	274	243	214	189	169
Nitrous oxide	I6C4	2 244	2 624	3 023	3 426	3 820	4 124	4 427	4 738	4 922	5 111	5 164
Acid rain precursors[2]	I6C5	844	816	774	735	685	619	566	524	483	452	415
of which												
Sulphur dioxide	I6C6	52	38	28	23	14	6	3	3	3	3	2
Nitrogen oxides	I6C7	775	756	724	688	648	589	539	498	458	429	395
Ammonia	I6C8	17	22	22	23	23	24	24	23	22	20	18
PM10	I6C9	54	52	48	46	44	40	39	38	37	36	34
Carbon monoxide	I6CA	4 197	4 018	3 689	3 369	3 038	2 532	2 155	1 878	1 617	1 385	1 140
NMVOCs	I6CB	637	563	510	442	381	308	253	214	178	147	121
Benzene	I6CC	29	26	23	20	17	6	5	5	4	3	3
1,3-Butadiene	I6CD	7	7	6	5	5	4	3	3	2	2	2

1 Greenhouse gases are made up of carbon dioxide, methane & nitrous oxide. Weight in carbon dioxide equivalent.
2 Acid rain precursors are made of sulphur dioxide, nitrogen oxide & ammonia. weight in sulphur dioxide equivalent.

Sources: AEA Energy & Environment; Environment Agency; Office for National Statistics 020 7014 2079; environment.accounts@ons.gsi.gov.uk

Environment

13.6 Estimated emissions[1] of carbon dioxide (CO_2)
United Kingdom

Million tonnes as CO_2

		1970	1980	1990	1995	1996	1997	1998	1999	2000	2001	2002	2003	2004	2005	2006
By source NC category																
Energy Supply Total	I6AH	260.07	261.75	242.30	207.52	209.28	195.04	199.01	189.27	199.76	209.75	207.91	215.87	214.68	217.64	220.83
Business Total	I6AI	204.08	131.34	108.87	103.73	105.88	104.08	103.07	104.08	104.17	104.08	93.72	95.28	93.31	93.36	91.86
Transport Total	I6AJ	72.00	90.17	122.46	122.09	126.84	128.08	126.87	127.60	126.60	126.25	128.36	129.20	130.68	131.88	133.55
Public	I6AK	23.71	19.67	13.48	13.17	14.22	13.80	12.61	12.39	11.66	12.09	10.28	10.14	11.09	10.94	10.46
Residential Total	I6AL	96.24	84.40	79.77	81.15	92.26	85.21	87.20	86.30	86.96	89.16	85.92	86.83	88.36	84.64	81.27
Agriculture Total	I6AM	6.19	5.22	5.15	5.28	5.35	5.24	5.05	5.05	4.72	4.80	4.76	4.72	4.62	4.47	4.28
Industrial Process Total	I6AN	21.08	14.31	16.30	14.88	15.43	15.59	15.59	15.44	14.67	13.37	12.41	13.35	13.80	13.94	13.87
Land-use change	I6AO	–	–	2.89	1.16	0.90	0.57	−0.03	−0.31	−0.44	−0.58	−1.14	−1.17	−1.92	−2.08	−2.02
Waste treatment	I6AP	1.40	1.40	1.20	0.87	0.88	0.50	0.50	0.46	0.46	0.50	0.48	0.46	0.45	0.44	0.42
Total	I6AQ	684.76	608.25	592.42	549.83	571.04	548.11	549.87	540.29	548.55	559.41	542.71	554.70	555.08	555.22	554.52

1 See chapter text. Data are for the UK and exclude overseas territories

Source: Department for Environment, Food and Rural Affairs: 020 7238 4908

13.7 Estimated emissions[1] of methane (CH_4)
United Kingdom

Thousand tonnes

		1990	1995	1996	1997	1998	1999	2000	2001	2002	2003	2004	2005	2006
By source NC category														
Energy Supply Total	I6AR	1 368.22	1 067.40	1 011.10	962.49	875.32	786.37	720.30	691.23	680.84	542.09	528.30	474.46	441.47
Business Total	I6AS	15.79	15.96	16.35	16.46	16.13	15.91	15.60	14.53	13.29	14.13	13.74	13.63	13.60
Transport Total	I6AT	29.78	23.10	21.87	20.10	18.43	16.81	15.01	13.24	11.75	10.37	9.23	8.32	7.62
Public	I6AU	1.27	1.38	1.46	1.37	1.26	1.22	1.13	1.18	1.00	0.98	1.07	1.06	1.01
Residential Total	I6AV	68.99	38.41	41.51	38.38	39.90	42.66	32.47	29.21	24.24	22.58	21.23	18.85	18.91
Agriculture Total	I6AW	1 023.99	995.36	1 003.85	991.74	989.78	987.29	954.19	899.26	890.52	893.32	894.68	873.97	886.45
Industrial Process Total	I6AX	10.02	8.29	9.48	8.00	6.10	5.24	4.78	4.14	3.97	4.15	4.19	4.58	4.48
Land Use Change	I6AY	0.80	1.41	1.02	1.20	0.91	0.83	1.19	1.47	1.27	1.21	1.18	1.01	1.37
Waste Management Total	I6AZ	2 409.04	2 142.70	2 072.48	1 908.54	1 778.19	1 618.83	1 512.62	1 318.44	1 202.30	1 056.25	982.89	967.69	964.87
Total	I6B2	4 927.90	4 294.00	4 179.09	3 948.28	3 726.01	3 475.16	3 257.29	2 972.70	2 829.17	2 545.07	2 456.51	2 363.57	2 339.80

1 See chapter text. Data are for the UK and exclude overseas territories

Source: Department for Environment, Food and Rural Affairs: 020 7238 4908

13.8 Estimated emissions[1] of nitrous oxide (N_2O)
United Kingdom

Thousand tonnes

		1990	1995	1996	1997	1998	1999	2000	2001	2002	2003	2004	2005	2006
By source NC Category														
Energy Supply Total	I6A7	6.2	4.8	4.6	4.1	4.2	3.7	4.1	4.4	4.2	4.4	4.3	5.3	5.4
Business Total	I6A8	5.1	4.7	4.6	4.4	4.3	4.3	4.2	4.3	4.1	4.1	4.1	4.2	4.2
Transport Total	I6A9	4.3	8.2	9.4	10.7	12.0	13.2	14.2	15.2	16.1	16.8	17.4	17.6	18.0
Public Total	I6AA	0.2	0.1	0.1	0.1	0.1	0.1	0.1	0.1	–	–	–	–	–
Residential Total	I6AB	0.9	0.7	0.8	0.7	0.7	0.7	0.6	0.6	0.5	0.5	0.4	0.4	0.4
Agriculture Total	I6AC	105.8	100.8	101.3	104.4	101.3	99.1	95.3	89.6	91.3	89.1	88.8	87.4	83.4
Industrial Processes Total	I6AD	79.7	48.2	47.9	48.5	49.4	17.5	18.1	15.7	8.8	9.3	11.7	9.2	7.8
Land-use change	I6AE	–	–	–	–	–	–	–	–	–	–	–	–	–
Waste Management Total	I6AF	3.5	3.5	3.6	3.9	4.0	3.8	4.0	4.1	4.1	4.1	4.1	4.1	4.2
Total	I6AG	205.9	171.0	172.2	176.9	175.9	142.5	140.5	133.9	129.2	128.3	130.9	128.3	123.5

1 See chapter text. Data are for the UK and exclude overseas territories

Source: Department for Environment, Food and Rural Affairs: 020 7238 4908

13.9 Annual rainfall: by region
United Kingdom

Millimetres and percentages

		Annual rainfall as a percentage of the 1961-1990 average										
		1997	1998	1999	2000	2001	2002	2003	2004	2005	2006	2007[3]
Region[1]	1961 - 1990 rainfall average (= 100%) millimetres											
United Kingdom JSJB	1 080	95	117	115	124	97	119	83	112	100	109	111
North West JSJC	1 201	90	115	109	129	92	118	84	113	94	112	108
Northumbria JSJD	853	93	120	103	129	103	121	78	117	108	98	102
Severn Trent JSJE	754	95	116	121	133	105	120	82	111	93	103	124
Yorkshire JSJF	821	92	114	109	135	99	124	81	113	95	109	114
Anglian JSJG	596	95	120	115	130	125	120	87	117	90	103	120
Thames JSLK	688	89	119	113	140	118	130	83	105	80	108	120
Southern JSLL	778	98	110	106	149	115	130	85	97	79	101	107
Wessex JSLM	839	101	119	121	140	103	136	86	102	92	103	117
South West JSLN	1 173	100	122	117	132	95	125	80	101	93	94	112
England JSLO	823	94	116	112	133	105	122	82	108	91	103	114
Wales[2] JSLP	1 355	94	122	117	135	100	120	84	110	96	108	111
Scotland JSLQ	1 436	95	117	116	113	91	113	84	117	110	115	110
Northern Ireland JSLR	1 059	98	119	117	115	85	133	88	103	101	109	104

1 The regions of England shown in this table correspond to the original nine English regions of the National Rivers Authority (NRA); the NRA became part of the Environment Agency upon its creation in April 1996.
2 The figures in this table relate to the country of Wales, not the Environment Agency Welsh Region.

3 Data from September 2007 are provisional and subject to revision.

Sources: The Met Office;
Centre for Ecology and Hydrology: 01491 838800

13.10 UK Annual Weather Summary

	Max Temp		Min Temp		Mean Temp		Sunshine		Rainfall	
	Actual (degrees celsius)	Anomaly (degrees celsius)	Actual (degrees celsius)	Anomaly (degrees celsius)	Actual (degrees celsius)	Anomaly (degrees celsius)	Actual (hours/ day)	Anomaly (%)	Actual (mm)	Anomaly (%)
	WLRL	WLRM	WLRO	WLRP	WLRR	WLRS	WLRX	WLRY	WLSH	WLSI
1987	11.4	−0.4	4.7	−0.2	8.1	−0.3	1 249.5	93.4	1 034.6	94.1
1988	12.2	0.3	5.4	0.6	8.8	0.5	1 324.3	99.0	1 131.2	102.9
1989	13.1	1.2	5.5	0.7	9.3	1.0	1 563.8	116.9	1 018.5	92.6
1990	13.1	1.2	5.8	0.9	9.4	1.1	1 490.7	111.4	1 172.8	106.7
1991	12.1	0.3	5.1	0.2	8.6	0.3	1 302.0	97.3	998.2	90.8
1992	12.3	0.4	5.2	0.4	8.7	0.4	1 290.8	96.5	1 186.8	107.9
1993	11.8	−0.1	5.0	0.1	8.4	−	1 218.6	91.1	1 121.1	102.0
1994	12.4	0.5	5.5	0.6	8.9	0.6	1 366.9	102.2	1 184.7	107.7
1995	13.0	1.1	5.4	0.6	9.2	0.9	1 588.5	118.7	1 023.7	93.1
1996	11.7	−0.1	4.7	−0.1	8.2	−0.2	1 403.5	104.9	916.6	83.4
1997	13.1	1.3	5.8	1.0	9.4	1.1	1 430.3	106.9	1 024.0	93.1
1998	12.6	0.8	5.8	1.0	9.1	0.8	1 268.4	94.8	1 265.1	115.1
1999	13.0	1.1	5.9	1.0	9.4	1.1	1 419.4	106.1	1 237.2	112.5
2000	12.7	0.8	5.6	0.8	9.1	0.8	1 367.5	102.2	1 335.6	121.5
2001	12.4	0.6	5.3	0.5	8.8	0.5	1 411.9	105.5	1 049.9	95.5
2002	13.0	1.1	6.0	1.2	9.5	1.2	1 304.0	97.5	1 280.5	116.5
2003	13.5	1.6	5.6	0.7	9.5	1.2	1 587.4	118.7	901.5	82.0
2004	13.0	1.2	6.0	1.2	9.5	1.2	1 361.4	101.8	1 210.1	110.1
2005	13.1	1.2	5.9	1.1	9.5	1.1	1 399.2	104.6	1 083.0	98.4
2006	13.4	1.5	6.1	1.3	9.7	1.4	1 495.9	111.8	1 175.9	106.8
2007	13.2	1.4	6.0	1.1	9.6	1.3	1 453.2	109.0	1 197.0	109.0

Anomalies are with respect to the 1961-90 averaging period.

Source: Met Office

13.11 Biological[1] and chemical[2] water quality of rivers and canals[3]
England, Wales and Northern Ireland

Length surveyed (Kilometres)[5] and percentages

| | | Length surveyed | | | | | | | Percentage of total | |
| | | Good | | Fair | | | | | | |
	Years	A	B	C	D	Poor E	Bad F	Total	Good or fair	Poor or bad
Biological quality										
North East	1990	1 358	1 223	551	377	364	259	4 132	85	15
	2006	2 186	1 726	851	503	296	79	5 641	93	7
North West	1990	470	1 251	656	367	770	508	4 022	68	32
	2006	994	1 847	1 020	649	427	68	5 005	90	10
Midlands	1990	493	929	1 405	673	229	83	3 811	92	8
	2006	1 480	2 416	1 585	642	356	129	6 607	93	7
Anglian	1990	813	1 665	1 287	266	120	19	4 170	97	3
	2006	1 685	1 894	771	152	79	7	4 587	98	2
Thames	1990	851	1 027	623	312	228	52	3 093	91	9
	2006	1 215	1 193	750	255	141	14	3 568	96	4
Southern	1990	426	490	366	102	27	8	1 419	97	3
	2006	1 007	729	347	74	43	2	2 202	98	2
South West	1990	2 348	2 223	655	154	107	59	5 547	97	3
	2006	3 606	1 714	376	72	29	27	5 824	99	1
England[4]	1990	6 984	9 006	5 642	2 297	1 853	988	26 771	89	11
	2006	12 534	11 489	5 754	2 352	1 374	325	33 828	95	5
Wales	1990	1 239	1 377	477	181	52	5	3 331	98	2
	2006	1 379	2 397	687	99	42	-	4 603	99	1
Northern Ireland	1991	713	952	415	100	10	-	2 190	100	-
	2006	891	2 048	1 845	566	110	-	5 460	98	2
Chemical quality										
North East	1990	840	1 603	557	441	607	176	4 224	81	19
	2006	1 980	2 508	952	420	297	32	6 188	95	5
North West	1990	719	598	556	436	648	204	3 161	73	27
	2006	2 354	1 408	1 083	592	393	49	5 880	92	8
Midlands	1990	450	1 519	1 619	968	956	131	5 643	81	19
	2006	1 891	2 620	1 395	594	467	27	6 993	93	7
Anglian	1990	36	759	1 691	1 189	786	102	4 564	81	19
	2006	583	1 693	1 320	698	501	9	4 803	89	11
Thames	1990	293	992	1 098	519	618	42	3 563	81	19
	2006	971	1 471	718	365	267	16	3 808	93	7
Southern	1990	238	713	672	292	238	33	2 186	88	12
	2006	384	874	563	224	174	11	2 229	92	8
South West	1990	1 644	2 700	1 301	695	363	68	6 771	94	6
	2006	2 679	2 363	640	202	176	3	6 063	97	3
England[4]	1990	4 197	9 164	7 670	4 643	4 297	772	30 742	84	16
	2006	10 842	12 936	6 672	3 095	2 273	146	35 964	93	7
Wales	1990	1 825	1 209	269	130	57	27	3 518	98	2
	2006	3 724	830	100	33	80	10	4 777	98	2
Northern Ireland	1991	103	642	682	174	64	18	1 685	95	5
	2006	1 264	2 401	881	205	156	23	4 930	96	4

1 Based on the River Invertebrate Prediction and Classification System (RIVPACS).
2 Based on the General Quality Assessment (GQA) Scheme.
3 See chapter text.
4 Figures for the English regions will not add to the national figure for England because a small amount of river lengths which are located along the border between England and Wales are counted in both the national figures for England and Wales.
5 Lengths are rounded to the nearest 1 km and may not exactly sum to totals.

Sources: Environment Agency;
Environment and Heritage Service

13.12 Chemical and biological water quality of rivers and canals[1]
Scotland

Kilometres and percentages

			Length surveyed					Percentage of total	
	Excellent A1	Good A2	Unclassified assumed good	Fair B	Poor C	Seriously polluted D	Total	Good or fair[2]	Poor or seriously polluted

Scottish Environment Protection Agency Regions

North

	DYO4	DYO5	DYO6	DYO7	DYO8	DYO9	DYP2	DYP3	DYP4
2001	1 420	1 560	7 950	380	90	20	11 420	99	1
2002	2 020	3 480	5 140	660	90	10	11 400	99	1
2003	2 610	4 310	3 950	430	90	10	11 390	99	1
2004	3 330	5 010	2 570	370	110	10	11 390	99	1
2005	3 110	6 240	1 390	550	90	–	11 390	99	1
2006	2 970	6 500	1 360	470	100	–	11 390	99	1

South East Scotland

	DYP5	DYP6	DYP7	DYP8	DYP9	DYQ2	DYQ3	DYQ4	DYQ5
2001	1 520	2 450	1 670	1 000	520	20	7 170	93	7
2002	2 260	2 800	610	980	510	10	7 160	93	7
2003	2 570	2 810	430	990	360	10	7 160	95	5
2004	2 550	2 810	300	1 170	310	20	7 160	95	5
2005	2 830	2 760	260	950	340	10	7 160	95	5
2006	2 770	2 820	250	980	340	10	7 160	95	5

South West Scotland

	DYQ6	DYQ7	DYQ8	DYQ9	DYR2	DYR3	DYR4	DYR5	DYR6
2001	930	2 320	2 340	960	320	40	6 920	95	5
2002	1 000	2 370	2 230	930	310	40	6 880	95	5
2003	1 630	2 430	1 530	960	300	40	6 880	95	5
2004	1 780	2 790	940	1 050	300	30	6 880	95	5
2005	2 040	3 020	510	980	290	40	6 880	95	5
2006	2 130	3 010	470	980	270	20	6 880	96	4

Scotland

	DZ38	DZ39	DZ3A	DZ3B	DZ3C	DZ3D	DZ3E	DZ3F	DZ3G
2001	3 870	6 320	11 960	2 340	930	80	25 510	96	4
2002	5 280	8 660	7 990	2 560	900	60	25 440	96	4
2003	6 820	9 540	5 900	2 370	750	50	25 440	97	3
2004	7 660	10 610	3 810	2 590	720	50	25 430	97	3
2005	8 000	12 050	2 130	2 470	720	50	25 430	97	3
2006	7 860	12 330	2 080	2 430	700	40	25 430	97	3

1 See chapter text.
2 Classes A1, A2, B and unclassified.

Source: Scottish Environment Protection Agency: 01786 457700

13.13 Reservoir stocks in England and Wales:[1] by month

Percentages

		1997	1998	1999	2000	2001	2002	2003	2004	2005	2006	2007
January	JTAS	79.1	90.5	95.8	95.8	94.8	86.5	95.1	79.9	91.2	85.9	92.2
February	JTAT	75.6	93.1	97.0	95.9	94.4	93.7	95.0	93.8	92.3	88.7	93.7
March	JTAU	91.6	92.3	96.5	97.4	95.0	95.5	92.1	92.1	92.1	91.2	96.7
April	JTAV	92.3	96.9	96.9	95.2	95.5	94.5	92.3	94.4	93.6	96.2	95.2
May	JTAW	87.1	97.0	97.0	97.0	96.7	91.9	88.6	94.7	95.0	93.4	91.9
June	JTAX	87.7	93.9	95.4	95.7	91.9	97.0	93.1	90.5	93.0	94.4	91.1
July	JTAY	87.8	95.1	92.0	93.8	85.1	94.9	87.0	84.8	85.6	88.4	94.4
August	JTAZ	81.3	93.5	82.6	88.5	80.7	91.1	81.1	78.5	77.9	77.2	93.5
September	JTBA	73.8	88.3	76.9	83.2	77.9	85.9	69.9	82.4	71.5	70.7	88.3
October	JTBB	70.6	86.6	79.7	88.0	77.0	77.3	60.4	84.2	67.4	67.8	86.1
November	JTBC	69.1	93.3	81.7	95.2	85.5	82.9	53.0	87.5	77.2	80.0	81.2
December	JTBD	76.4	93.1	84.9	96.7	87.9	91.8	60.9	86.2	83.8	89.8	82.4

1 Reservoir stocks are the percentage of useable capacity based on a representative selection of reservoirs; the percentages relate to the beginning of each month.

Sources: Water PLCs;
Environment Agency;
Centre for Ecology and Hydrology: 01491 838800

207

13.14 Water industry expenditure[1]
England and Wales

£ million

		1996/97	1997/98	1998/99	1999/00	2000/01	2001/02	2002/03	2003/04	2004/05	2005/06	2006/07
Operating expenditure												
Water supply	KQQX	2 314.9	2 339.3	2 386.1	2 448.1	2 391.0	2 426.9	2 544.2	2 676.5	2 690.7	2 942.7	3 118.6
Sewerage services	KQQY	1 780.7	1 854.6	1 971.3	2 069.8	2 087.1	2 167.6	2 265.2	2 319.4	2 499.3	2 708.1	2 876.2
Capital expenditure												
Water supply	KQSX	1 314.3	1 467.2	1 294.1	1 290.0	935.0	1 132.5	1 347.1	1 346.4	1 309.0	1 282.5	1 681.7
Sewerage	KQSY	479.9	455.2	507.5	488.5	352.0	362.4	507.2	617.6	601.4	476.1	585.3
Sewage treatment and disposal	KQSZ	959.4	1 296.3	1 374.5	1 440.8	1 040.9	996.0	1 066.2	1 235.6	1 185.6	1 046.2	1 289.6

1 See chapter text.

Source: Office of Water Services: 0121 625 1300

13.15 Water pollution incidents[1, 3]
United Kingdom

Numbers

		1996	1997	1998		1999[2]	2000[2]	2001[2]	2002[2]	2003[2]	2004[2]	2005[2]	2006[2]
Categories 1 to 3													
Environment Agency Regions													
North West	JZIA	2 818	2 160	2 201	MKDB	1 668	1 757	1 734	1 805	1 534	1 091	1 056	913
North East	JZIB	2 143	2 404	1 993	MKDC	1 828	1 822	1 952	1 789	1 971	1 692	1 448	1 132
Midlands	JZKR	4 305	4 411	4 061	MKDD	2 804	3 106	2 862	2 843	2 464	1 955	1 890	1 914
Anglian	JZKS	2 417	2 411	2 163	MKDE	1 726	1 369	1 606	1 716	1 616	1 418	1 290	1 223
Thames	JZKT	1 959	1 917	1 819	MKDF	1 208	1 379	1 510	1 630	1 447	1 211	1 203	1 159
Southern	JZKU	1 189	1 174	1 138	MKDG	1 317	1 540	1 585	1 511	1 543	1 218	955	1 020
South West	JZKV	3 042	2 847	2 603	MKDH	2 463	2 294	2 292	1 929	1 882	1 689	1 744	1 539
Welsh	JZKW	2 285	2 247	1 885	MKDI	1 360	1 395	1 475	1 287	1 356	1 309	1 260	1 202
England and Wales	JZKX	20 158	19 571	17 863	MKDJ	14 374	14 662	15 016	14 510	13 813	11 583	10 846	10 102
Scotland[3]	JZKY	2 878	3 356	2 329	MKDK	2 306	2 345	1 829	1 409	1 708	1 480	1 377	1 641
Northern Ireland	JZKZ	2 087	1 826	1 644	MKDL	1 507	1 705	1 546	1 510	1 551	1 227	1 174	1 133
By category in England and Wales													
Category 1	MKCW	156	194	128	MKDM	90	77	118	82	94	114	99	86
Category 2	MKCX	1 510	1 354	1 238	MKDN	863	758	860	784	685	594	562	519
Category 3	MKCY	18 492	18 023	16 497	MKDO	13 421	13 827	14 038	13 644	13 034	10 875	10 185	9 497
Category 4[2,4]	MKCZ	..	..	..	MKDP	16 548	21 744	18 706	15 370	15 813	13 613	12 658	11 932
Total substantiated incidents[4]	MKDA	20 158	19 571	17 863	MKDQ	30 922	36 406	33 722	29 880	29 626	25 196	23 504	32 136

1 See chapter text. Substantiated incidents to water, unless otherwise specified.
2 From 1999, categories 1-3 do not include all substantiated incidents to water. An additional category (Category 4) was introduced which includes all incidents which were substantiated, but which had no impact on the water environment. Therefore, data are not comparable to previous years.
3 Data for all years refer to financial years.
4 Category 4 and Total substantiated incidents include incidents to other media (air, land), which did not involve the water environment.

Sources: Environment Agency;
Scottish Environment Protection Agency;
Environment and Heritage Service

13.16 Bathing water:[1] by region
United Kingdom

Numbers and percentages

		Compliance with EC Bathing Water Directive coliform standards during the bathing season													Percentage complying
		Identified bathing waters (numbers)						Numbers complying							
		2003	2004	2005	2006	2007		2003	2004	2005	2006	2007			2007
Coastal bathing waters															
Environment Agency Regions															
United Kingdom	GPKA	554	556	559	561	567	GPKN	545	543	550	559	547	GPLA		97
North East	GPKB	55	55	55	55	55	GPKO	53	53	53	54	52	GPLB		95
North West	GPKC	34	34	34	33	32	GPKP	33	33	32	33	29	GPLC		91
Anglian	GPKE	38	38	39	39	39	GPKR	38	38	39	39	39	GPLE		100
Thames	GPKF	8	8	8	8	8	GPKS	8	8	8	8	8	GPLF		100
Southern	GPKG	79	79	79	78	81	GPKT	79	78	79	78	81	GPLG		100
South West	GPKH	188	190	190	191	190	GPKU	186	187	189	191	187	GPLH		98
England	GPKI	402	404	405	404	405	GPKV	397	397	400	403	396	GPLI		98
Wales	GPKJ	78	78	80	80	80	GPKW	77	78	80	79	78	GPLJ		98
Scotland	GPKL	58	58	58	61	59	GPKY	55	54	55	61	52	GPLL		88
Northern Ireland	GPKM	16	16	16	16	23	GPKZ	16	14	15	16	21	GPLM		91
Inland bathing waters															
United Kingdom	JTIG	11	11	11	11	11	JTIH	11	11	11	10	11	JTII		100

1 See chapter text.

Sources: Environment Agency;
Scottish Environment Protection Agency;
Environment and Heritage Service, Northern Ireland

13.17 Estimated abstractions from all surface and groundwater sources: by purpose[1]
England and Wales

Megalitres per day

		1995	1996	1997	1998	1999	2000	2001	2002	2003	2004	2005
Public water supply	JZLA	17 346	17 453	16 820	16 765	16 255	16 990	16 231	16 938	16 920	17 210	17 370
Spray irrigation	JZLB	352	369	292	282	325	291	259	248	315	225	226
Agriculture (excl spray irrigation)[4]	JZLC	103	136	108	111	142	152	108	120	132	122	60
Electricity supply industry[2]	JZLD	29 510	31 294	33 307	34 587	29 490	31 546	32 263	35 447	31 378	30 568	30 021
Other industry[3]	JZLE	3 808	4 960	4 352	4 964	5 428	5 433	4 772	4 883	6 623	6 585	6 339
Mineral washing	JZLF	262	250	297	223	..	..	..	..	..	..	..
Fish farming, cress growing, amenity ponds	JYXG	4 268	4 338	4 211	5 495	4 867	4 709	4 657	3 215	3 077	4 068	3 654
Private water supply	JZLG	98	171	162	175	91	102	92	54	61	30	26
Other	JZLH	223	531	408	289	526	559	108	77	86	77	60
Total	JZLI	55 970	59 503	59 957	62 891	57 123	59 782	58 489	60 981	58 593	58 885	57 757

1 See chapter text.
2 Increased electricity supply abstraction from 2002 due to increased production from power station in Anglian Region and two new licences issued in Southern Region.

3 Three abstraction licences re-assigned to other industry from electricty supply in Midlands Region (2003).
4 Reduction in agricultural abstraction due to deregulation of licences with effect from 1 April 2005

Source: Environment Agency

Environment

13.18 Estimates of remaining recoverable oil and gas reserves
United Kingdom

		1995	1998	1999	2000	2001	2002	2003	2004	2005	2006
Oil (Million tonnes)											
Reserves											
Proven	JKOV	605	685	665	630	605	593	571	533	516	479
Probable	JKOW	765	575	455	380	350	327	286	283	300	298
Proven plus Probable	JKOX	1 370	1 260	1 120	1 010	955	920	857	816	816	776
Possible	JKOY	520	540	545	480	475	425	410	512	451	478
Maximum	JKOZ	1 890	1 800	1 665	1 490	1 430	1 344	1 267	1 328	1 267	1 254
Range of undiscovered resources											
Lower	JKNY	380	275	250	225	205	272	323	396	346	438
Upper	JKNZ	2 920	2 550	2 600	2 300	1 930	1 770	1 826	1 830	1 581	1 637
Range of total reserves											
Lower[1]	JKOA	985	960	915	855	810	865	894	929	862	917
Upper[2]	JKOB	4 810	4 350	4 265	3 790	3 360	3 115	3 093	3 158	2 848	2 892
Expected level of reserves[3]											
Opening stocks	JKOC	1 975	1 675	1 535	1 370	1 235	1 160	1 192	1 180	1 212	1 162
Extraction[5]	JKOD	−130	−132	−137	−126	−117	−117	−106	−95	−85	−77
Other volume changes	JKOE	−95	−8	−28	−9	42	149	94	127	35	130
Closing stocks	JKOF	1 750	1 535	1 370	1 235	1 160	1 192	1 180	1 212	1 162	1 215
Life expectancy[4] (years)	JKOG	13	12	10	10	10	10	11	13	14	16
Gas (billion cubic metres)											
Reserves											
Proven	JKOH	700	755	760	735	695	628	590	531	481	412
Probable	JKOI	780	585	500	460	445	369	315	296	247	272
Proven plus Probable	JKOJ	1 480	1 340	1 260	1 195	1 140	998	905	826	728	684
Possible	JKOK	435	455	490	430	395	331	336	343	278	283
Maximum	JKOL	1 915	1 795	1 750	1 630	1 535	1 329	1 241	1 169	1 006	967
Range of undiscovered resources											
Lower	JKOM	395	440	355	325	290	238	279	293	226	301
Upper	JKON	1 412	1 595	1 465	1 440	1 680	1 386	1 259	1 245	1 035	1 049
Range of total reserves											
Lower[1]	JKOO	1 095	1 195	1 115	1 060	985	866	869	824	707	713
Upper[2]	JKOP	3 327	3 390	3 215	3 065	3 215	2 714	2 500	2 415	2 041	2 016
Expected level of reserves[3]											
Opening stocks	JKOQ	1 945	1 885	1 780	1 615	1 520	1 430	1 235	1 184	1 120	954
Extraction[5]	JKOR	−70	−89	−99	−108	−104	−102	−102	−95	−86	−78
Other volume changes	JKOS	−	−16	−66	13	14	−93	51	31	−80	109
Closing stocks	JKOT	1 875	1 780	1 615	1 520	1 430	1 235	1 184	1 120	954	985
Life expectancy[4] (years)	JKOU	27	20	16	14	14	12	12	12	11	13

1 The lower end of the range of total reserves has been calculated as the sum of proven reserves and the lower end of the range of undiscovered reserves.

2 The upper end of the range of total reserves is the sum of proven, probable and possible reserves and the upper end of the range of undiscovered reserves.

3 Expected reserves are the sum of proven reserves, probable reserves and the lower end of the range of undiscovered reserves.

4 Based on expected level of reserves at year end and current extraction rates (source: ONS).

5 Negative extraction is shown here for the purposes of the calculation only. Of itself, extraction should be considered as a positive value.

*Sources: ONS and Department for Business Enterprise & Regulatory Reform;
environment.accounts@ons.gsi.gov.uk*

13.19 Municipal waste disposal: by method
United Kingdom

Thousand tonnes

		2000 /01	2001 /02	2002 /03	2003 /04	2004 /05	2005 /06	2006 /07
England								
Household								
Disposed	I6EB	22 270	22 327	22 092	20 927	19 873	18 658	17 799
Recycled/composted	I6EC	2 809	3 197	3 740	4 521	5 785	6 796	7 976
Total	I6ED	25 079	25 524	25 832	25 448	25 658	25 454	25 775
Non Household								
Disposed	I6EE	2 342	2 656	2 730	2 650	2 795	2 289	2 408
Recycled/composted	I6EF	636	724	832	1 016	1 167	1 003	961
Total	I6EG	2 978	3 380	3 562	3 666	3 962	3 292	3 369
Total Municipal Waste								
Disposed	I6EH	24 612	24 983	24 822	23 577	22 668	20 947	20 207
Recycled/composted	I6EI	3 445	3 921	4 572	5 537	6 952	7 799	8 937
Total	I6EJ	28 057	28 905	29 394	29 114	29 619	28 745	29 144
Wales								
Household								
Disposed	I6EK	1 314	1 330	1 309	1 271	1 298	1 210	1 153
Recycled/composted	I6EL	90	126	179	252	286	332	419
Total	I6EM	1 404	1 456	1 488	1 522	1 585	1 542	1 572
Non Household								
Disposed	I6EN	223	244	238	227	213	204	132
Recycled/composted	I6EO	25	18	43	71	131	152	130
Total	I6EP	247	262	281	298	344	356	262
Total Municipal Waste								
Disposed	I6EQ	1 537	1 573	1 547	1 498	1 511	1 414	1 285
Recycled/composted	I6ER	115	144	222	323	418	484	549
Total	I6ES	1 652	1 718	1 769	1 820	1 928	1 898	1 834
Scotland								
Household								
Disposed	I6ET	2 405	2 472	2 477	2 375	2 276	2 221	..
Recycled/composted	I6EU	122	149	206	330	522	665	..
Total	I6EV	2 527	2 621	2 683	2 705	2 798	2 886	..
Non Household								
Disposed	I6EW	662	619	602	545	584	508	..
Recycled/composted	I6EX	22	27	60	66	125	265	..
Total	I6EY	684	646	663	611	709	773	..
Total Municipal Waste								
Disposed	I6EZ	3 067	3 091	3 079	2 920	2 860	2 729	..
Recycled/composted	I6F2	145	176	267	397	647	930	..
Total	I6F3	3 211	3 267	3 345	3 317	3 506	3 658	..

		1999 /00	2001	2002	2003	2004 /05	2005 /06	2006 /07
Northern Ireland								
Household								
Disposed	I6F4	776	785	813	786	746	708	679
Recycled/composted	I6F5	55	94	90	112	173	235	260
Total	I6F6	831	879	902	898	919	937	939
Non Household								
Disposed	I6F7	..	..	119	116	114	106	108
Recycled/composted	I6F8	..	..	2	13	18	20	12
Total	I6F9	173	178	121	129	132	126	125
Total Municipal Waste								
Disposed	I6FA	..	..	932	902	860	813	787
Recycled/composted	I6FB	..	..	92	125	191	250	272
Total	I6FC	1 004	1 056	1 023	1 027	1 051	1 064	1 064

Sources: Department for Environment, Food and Rural Affairs 020 7238 4908;
Welsh Assembly Government 029 2082 6822;
Scottish Environment Protection Agency 01786 457700;
Environment & Heritage Services Northern Ireland 028 9069 429

13.20 Amounts of different materials from household sources collected for recycling by collection method 2005/06[1]

United Kingdom

Thousand tonnes

	Paper & Card	Glass	Compost	Scrap Metal & White Goods	Textiles	Cans	Plastics	Co-Mingled	Other	Total
England[2]										
Kerbside collection	1 043	373	1 324	29	11	56	22	930	47	3 834
Bring site collection	219	325	12	3	34	8	10	6	6	623
Civic Amenity site collection	188	57	1 104	502	24	9	6	4	455	2 349
Private/voluntary collection schemes[3]	27	6	4	1	18	1	-	2	5	64
Total	**1 477**	**760**	**2 444**	**534**	**87**	**74**	**39**	**942**	**514**	**6 870**
Wales										
Kerbside collection	59	24	41	2	1	5	6	5	4	148
Bring site collection	19	13	3	-	2	1	1	-	-	39
Civic Amenity site collection	10	3	57	27	1	-	1	-	38	138
Private/voluntary collection schemes[3]	2	1	1	-	-	-	-	-	3	7
Total	**90**	**42**	**102**	**30**	**4**	**6**	**8**	**5**	**45**	**332**
Scotland										
Kerbside collection	80	14	158	8	-	2	2	72	13	349
Bring site & Civic Amenity collection	30	39	65	33	12	1	1	24	91	296
Private/voluntary collection schemes[3]	14	2	-	1	-	-	-	1	2	20
Total	**124**	**55**	**223**	**42**	**12**	**3**	**3**	**97**	**106**	**665**
Northern Ireland										
Kerbside collection	56	3	30	-	-	3	7	3	1	103
Bring site collection	2	4	-	-	1	-	-	-	-	7
Civic Amenity site collection	8	6	86	17	1	-	1	1	4	125
Total	**66**	**13**	**116**	**17**	**3**	**3**	**8**	**4**	**6**	**235**

1 See chapter text.
2 Total amount of household waste collected for recycling is greater than that sent for recycling as some material is subsequently rejected during sorting or by the reprocessor.
3 Includes household waste collected from municipal parks, community skips and other methods of capture for recycling/composting.

Sources: Department for Environment Food and Rural Affairs 020 7238 4908;
Welsh Assembly Government 029 2082 6822;
Scottish Environment Protection Agency 01786 457700;
Environment & Heritage Services 028 9069 429.

13.21 Noise incidents[1] received by Environmental Health Officers[2]

England and Wales

Number per million people

		2000 /01	2001 /02	2002 /03	2003 /04	2004 /05	2005 /06	2006 /07
Not controlled by the Environmental Protection Act 1990:								
Road traffic	JZLJ	44	37	36	32	..	..	..
Aircraft	JZLK	26	101	104	120	..	..	..
Railway	JTHH	16	12	18	21	..	..	..
Total	JUZR	86	150	158	173	..	..	..
Controlled by the Environmental Protection Act 1990:								
Industrial/commercial premises	JZLN	1 381	1 273	1 315	1 480	1 260	936	1 036
Industrial	EAC3	..	..	301	284	219	191	176
Commercial/leisure[3]	EAC4	..	..	1 014	1 196	1 041	745	860
Construction/Demolition sites	SNLE	325	347	325	335	343	212	246
Domestic premises	JZLP	5 001	5 540	5 573	5 973	5 903	4 058	4 409
Vehicles, machinery and equipment in streets	JZLQ	365	372	377	346	330	181	205
Traffic	I4SR	..	..	..	..	..	116	154
Miscellaneous[4]	EAC2	..	..	..	..	433	265	414
Total	JZLR	7 072	7 532	7 590	8 134	8 269	5 838	5 620

1 From 2004/05 Data reported is for incidents per million where previously complaints per million was reported.
2 See chapter text.
3 Includes railway noise and airports (non aircraft).
4 From 2004/05 includes 'traffic' which consists of commercial vehicles, cars motorbikes, fixed-wing aircraft in flight and helicopters in flight. From 2005/06 this data is recorded separately as 'traffic'.

Sources: The Chartered Institute of Environmental Health;
020 7827 6322

13.22 Material flows[1]
United Kingdom

Million tonnes

		1970	1975	1980	1985	1990	1995	2000	2001	2002	2003	2004	2005	2006
Domestic extraction														
Biomass														
Agricultural harvest	JKUN	42	38	47	47	46	47	51	45	51	48	48	47	45
Timber	JKUO	3	3	4	5	6	8	8	8	8	8	8	9	8
Animal grazing	JKUP	49	49	49	48	47	45	43	43	43	43	43	43	43
Fish	JKUQ	1	1	1	1	1	1	1	1	1	1	1	1	1
Total	JKUR	96	92	101	100	101	100	102	97	102	100	101	100	98
Minerals														
Ores	JKUS	12	5	1	1	–	–	–	–	–	–	–	–	–
Clay	JKUT	38	33	25	23	21	18	15	14	14	14	15	14	13
Other industrial minerals	JKUU	14	11	11	11	11	10	8	9	8	9	8	8	8
Sand and gravel	JKUV	122	131	110	112	128	106	106	105	98	95	102	99	97
Crushed stone	JKUW	156	169	150	160	212	200	176	183	173	170	175	169	171
Total	JKUX	342	349	298	307	373	334	305	311	293	288	300	290	289
Fossil fuels														
Coal	JKUY	149	129	130	94	94	53	31	32	30	28	25	20	19
Natural gas	JKUZ	11	37	39	37	43	71	109	106	104	103	96	88	80
Crude oil	JKVA	–	2	80	128	92	130	126	117	116	106	95	85	77
Total	JKVB	161	168	249	259	229	254	266	255	250	237	217	193	175
Total domestic extraction	JKVC	598	608	648	666	702	688	673	663	645	626	618	583	562
Imports														
Biomass	JKVD	38	33	30	31	38	40	42	46	47	49	50	50	50
Minerals	JKVE	30	32	24	34	41	50	51	54	55	55	60	58	59
Fossil fuels	JKVF	123	111	74	76	89	73	83	99	95	102	127	137	148
Other products	JKVG	6	7	14	15	19	23	34	34	32	34	36	35	35
Total	JKVH	197	184	141	157	187	188	210	232	228	240	273	280	292
Exports														
Biomass	JKVI	3	5	8	11	13	15	17	13	15	19	18	19	20
Minerals	JKVJ	17	20	26	22	25	39	44	43	42	44	48	48	50
Fossil fuels	JKVK	23	19	60	102	67	103	115	118	120	104	98	88	83
Other products	JKVL	5	7	8	11	12	17	21	21	20	21	21	21	21
Total	JKVM	47	51	101	146	117	173	198	194	197	189	185	177	174
Indirect flows														
From domestic extraction,[2] excluding soil erosion	JKVN	576	575	633	627	693	634	567	572	564	549	547	519	487
Of which:														
Unused biomass	JKVO	25	23	32	35	37	37	40	35	40	38	38	37	36
Fossil fuels	JKVP	169	202	287	274	309	276	231	241	225	209	204	178	149
Minerals and ores	JKVQ	185	155	120	120	144	116	97	95	101	100	104	101	99
Soil excavation and dredging	JKVR	197	195	195	199	203	204	199	202	199	202	201	203	203
From production of imports	JKVS	394	395	368	423	457	527	614	711	648	671	692	752	792
Summary aggregates														
Physical Trade Balance (export - imports)[3]	F8YL	−150	−133	−40	−11	−70	−14	−13	−38	−32	−52	−88	−103	−117
Direct material input (Domestic extraction + imports)	JKVT	796	792	789	822	889	876	884	896	874	866	891	863	855
Domestic material consumption (Domestic extraction + imports - exports)	JKVU	748	741	688	677	772	703	686	701	677	677	706	686	680
of which														
Biomass	G9A8	131	119	123	120	125	126	127	130	134	130	133	131	128
Minerals	G9A9	355	361	296	319	389	346	312	322	307	298	312	300	298
Fossil fuels	G9AA	261	260	263	233	250	224	234	236	225	236	246	241	240
Total material requirement (Direct material input + indirect flows)	JKVV	1 765	1 762	1 790	1 872	2 039	2 036	2 064	2 179	2 086	2 086	2 130	2 134	2 134

1 See chapter text. Components may not sum to totals due to rounding.
2 Indirect flows from domestic extraction relate to unused material which is moved during extraction, such as overburden from mining and quarrying.
3 A negative physical trade balance indicates a net import of material into the UK.

Sources: Office for National Statistics: 020 7014 2079; environment.accounts@ons.gsi.gov.uk

Housing

Chapter 14

Housing

Permanent dwellings

(Table 14.1, 14.3)

Local housing authorities include the Commission for the New Towns and New Towns Development Corporations, Communities Scotland and the Northern Ireland Housing Executive. The figures shown for housing associations include dwellings provided by housing associations other than the Communities Scotland and the Northern Ireland Housing Executive and provided or authorised by government departments for the families of police, prison staff, the armed forces and certain other services.

Households in Temporary Accommodation under homelessness provisions

(Table 14.9)

Comprises households in accommodation arranged by local authorities pending enquiries or after being accepted as owed a main duty under homelessness legistation under the 1996 Act (includes residual cases awaiting re-housing under the 1985 Act). Excludes 'homeless at home' cases.

14.1 Stock of dwellings: [1] by tenure and country

Thousands

		1996	1997	1998	1999	2000	2001	2002	2003	2004	2005	2006
England												
Owner occupied	JUTY	13 865	14 041	14 237	14 433	14 635	14 818	14 956	15 110	15 261	15 325	15 442
Rented	JUUC	6 603	6 582	6 541	6 495	6 440	6 388	6 381	6 371	6 375	6 480	6 547
Local Authority	JUTZ	3 470	3 401	3 309	3 178	3 012	2 812	2 706	2 457	2 335	2 166	2 086
Privately	JUUA	2 191	2 196	2 192	2 171	2 155	2 152	2 208	2 293	2 375	2 497	2 611
Registered Social Landlords	JUUB	942	985	1 040	1 146	1 273	1 424	1 467	1 621	1 665	1 817	1 850
All dwellings	JUUD	20 468	20 622	20 778	20 927	21 075	21 207	21 337	21 481	21 636	21 804	21 989
Wales												
Owner occupied	JUUE	878	891	888	915	903	905	932	925	946	951	955
Rented	JUUI	104	100	112	94	117	127	110	130	125	133	137
Local Authority	JUUF	207	204	201	197	193	188	183	177	162	158	156
Privately	JUUG	104	105	106	108	109	111	112	113	125	133	137
Registered Social Landlords	JUUH	45	48	50	52	54	55	57	57	65	65	66
All dwellings	JUUJ	1 233	1 243	1 252	1 259	1 267	1 275	1 282	1 290	1 298	1 306	1 314
Scotland[4]												
Owner occupied	JUUK	1 327	1 366	1 400	1 435	1 472	1 468	1 496	1 548	1 580	1 614	..
Rented	JUUO	921	899	883	869	849	855	847	814	805	793	..
Local Authority	JUUL	668	630	608	583	557	535	514	388	377	363	..
Privately	JUUM	154	154	154	155	155	176	175	177	178	178	..
Registered Social Landlords	JUUN	99	115	121	131	137	144	158	249	250	252	..
All dwellings	JUUP	2 248	2 266	2 283	2 303	2 322	2 323	2 343	2 363	2 385	2 407	..
Northern Ireland[2]												
Owner occupied	JUUQ	422	434	446	455	489	–	481	491	501	505	508
Rented	JUUU	186	183	180	180	184	–	187	188	183	193	198
Local Authority	JUUR	148	142	137	131	130	–	120	113	100	102	100
Privately	JUUS	23	26	27	32	34	–	47	54	61	69	75
Registered Social Landlords	JUUT	15	15	16	17	20	–	20	21	22	22	23
All dwellings	JUUV	608	618	626	636	674	–	668	679	684	698	706
United Kingdom[3]												
Owner occupied	JUVY	16 492	16 726	16 977	17 225	17 507	17 206	17 873	18 107	18 280	18 360	18 522
Rented	JUWC	8 065	8 021	7 961	7 901	7 829	7 597	7 752	7 698	7 699	7 833	7 890
Local Authority	JUVZ	4 493	4 377	4 255	4 089	3 892	3 535	3 520	3 131	2 985	2 803	2 704
Privately	JUWA	2 472	2 481	2 479	2 466	2 453	2 439	2 529	2 618	2 713	2 876	2 995
Registered Social Landlords	JUWB	1 101	1 163	1 227	1 346	1 484	1 623	1 703	1 949	2 001	2 154	2 191
All dwellings	JUWD	24 557	24 749	24 938	25 125	25 338	24 804	25 625	25 806	25 980	26 912	26 412

1 At 31 March for England and Wales and at 31 December for Scotland. At 31 March for Northern Ireland, but data prior to 2002 are at 31 December.
2 To include estimates for vacants in the tenure figures the total dwelling stock figures in Northern Ireland have been apportioned according to the % of occupied dwellings.
3 Calculated from data for England, Wales and Northern Ireland for the current year with Scotland data for the previous year, except for 2001 and earlier where Northern Ireland data for the previous year are used.
4 Figures for 2006 for Scotland unavailable.

Sources: Communities and Local Government;
National Assembly for Wales;
Scottish Government;
Department for Social Development (Northern Ireland)

14.2 Type Of Accommodation by Tenure [1], 2006 Great Britain

Weighted Percentages

	Type of accommodation[2]							
	Detached House	Semi-detached house	Terraced	All Houses	Purpose-built flat or maisonette	Converted flat maisonette/rooms	All flats
Owner-occupied							
Owned outright	36	34	21	91	7	2	9
Owned with mortgage	27	34	31	91	7	2	9
All owners	31	34	27	91	7	2	9
Rented from social sector							
Council[3]	1	24	28	54	45	1	46
Housing association[4]	1	19	34	54	41	5	46
All rented from social sector	1	22	30	54	43	3	46
Rented privately[6]							
Unfurnished[5]	14	24	34	71	16	13	29
Furnished	8	13	29	50	30	20	50
Private renters[6]	12	21	32	65	20	15	35
All Tenures	**23**	**30**	**28**	**81**	**15**	**3**	**19**

1 Results for 2006 include longitudinal data
2 Tables for type of accommodation exclude households living in caravans
3 Council includes local authority
4 Since 1996, housing associations are more correctly described as Registered Social Landlords (RSLs)
5 Unfurnished includes the answer 'partly furnished'
6 Tenants whose accommodation goes with the job of someone in the households have been allocated to 'rented privately'. Squatters are also included.

Source: General Household Survey, Office for National Statistics

14.3 Permanent dwellings completed:[1] by tenure and country

Numbers

	United Kingdom				England and Wales			
	All dwellings	Local authorities[2]	Private enterprise	Registered Social Landlords[3][4]	All dwellings	Local authorities[2]	Private enterprise	Registered Social Landlords[3][4]
	KAAD	KAAE	KAAF	KAAG	KAAH	KAAI	KAAJ	KAAK
1980	242 017	88 534	131 989	21 494	214 934	78 539	116 179	20 216
1981	206 915	68 554	118 647	19 714	180 147	58 633	104 069	17 445
1982	181 894	40 091	128 088	13 715	159 407	33 544	113 893	11 970
1983	207 496	39 161	151 638	16 697	181 391	31 625	134 901	14 865
1984	220 414	37 573	165 555	17 286	191 112	31 338	145 263	14 511
1985	205 938	30 420	161 828	13 690	178 284	24 359	142 020	11 905
1986	214 471	25 377	175 905	13 189	187 710	20 496	156 056	11 158
1987	226 167	21 833	191 250	13 084	198 732	17 435	169 895	11 402
1988	242 233	21 448	207 423	13 362	214 156	16 921	185 733	11 502
1989	221 494	19 323	187 542	14 629	190 990	15 332	163 344	12 314
1991/92	191 849	10 027	160 664	21 158	165 553	7 447	139 583	18 523
1992/93	178 872	4 433	144 367	30 072	152 452	2 706	123 045	26 701
1993/94	185 960	3 611	145 914	36 435	157 813	1 726	122 779	33 308
1994/95	197 169	2 970	156 547	37 652	168 301	997	133 002	34 302
1995/96	198 212	3 045	156 696	38 471	164 581	954	130 891	32 736
1996/97	185 654	1 538	153 165	30 951	156 334	474	128 682	27 178
1997/98	190 748	1 519	160 675	28 554	157 987	325	134 327	23 335
1998/99	178 700	865	154 968	22 867	148 445	207	128 084	20 154
1999/00	185 315	317	160 685	24 313	150 752	58	132 576	18 118
2000/01	156 957	291	134 916	21 750	141 851	226	124 293	17 332
2001/02	173 585	221	151 771	21 593	138 265	131	123 321	14 813
2002/03	183 061	390	162 796	19 875	146 287	205	132 217	13 865
2003/04	190 340	199	170 935	19 206	152 254	207	137 959	14 088
2004/05	205 327	116	182 821	22 390	164 385	131	147 118	17 136
2005/06[5]	215 024	326	190 305	24 393	171 655	326	152 820	18 509
2006/07[6]	218 543	251	191 050	27 242	176 911	245	154 371	22 295

	Scotland				Northern Ireland			
	All dwellings	Local authorities[2]	Private enterprise	Registered Social Landlords[3]	All dwellings	Local authorities[2]	Private enterprise	Registered Social Landlords[3]
	BLFI	BAEZ	BLFK	BLFO	BLGI	BAFA	BLGK	BLGO
1979	23 782	4 755	15 175	3 852	7 312	3 507	3 574	231
1980	20 611	7 488	12 242	881	6 456	2 563	3 568	325
1981	20 011	7 062	11 021	1 928	6 827	3 082	3 557	188
1982	16 423	3 733	11 523	1 167	7 033	3 032	3 606	395
1983	17 929	3 492	13 166	1 271	9 698	4 093	4 971	634
1984	18 838	2 647	14 115	2 076	10 464	3 594	6 177	693
1985	18 411	2 828	14 435	1 148	10 770	3 235	6 940	595
1986	18 637	2 301	14 870	1 466	10 197	2 580	7 082	535
1987	17 707	2 634	13 904	1 169	9 795	1 764	7 451	580
1988	18 272	2 815	14 179	1 278	9 931	1 715	7 511	705
1989	20 190	2 283	16 287	1 620	10 283	1 708	7 911	664
1991/92	18 787	1 495	15 483	1 809	7 318	971	5 553	794
1992/93	18 994	773	15 620	2 601	7 559	992	5 759	808
1993/94	22 107	976	18 314	2 817	7 083	907	5 642	534
1994/95	21 812	1 127	17 894	2 791	7 212	877	5 859	476
1995/96	24 694	722	19 195	4 777	8 990	1 325	6 750	915
1996/97	20 695	241	17 491	2 963	6 420	668	5 035	717
1997/98	22 586	114	17 983	4 489	10 181	1 080	8 371	730
1998/99	20 657	120	18 784	1 753	9 618	538	8 120	960
1999/00	24 220	69	19 048	5 103	10 349	190	9 067	1 092
2000/01	23 478	112	18 048	5 318	11 670	46	10 512	1 112
2001/02	23 585	65	18 041	5 479	13 487	29	12 072	1 386
2002/03	23 416	94	18 627	4 695	14 415	2	13 387	1 026
2003/04	23 812	–	20 085	3 727	14 511	–	13 951	560
2004/05	26 411	–	21 659	4 752	15 768	–	14 940	828
2005/06	25 959	–	20 857	5 102	17 410	–	16 628	782
2006/07	23 684	6	20 058	3 620	17 948	–	16 621	1 327

1 See chapter text.
2 Including the Commission for the New Towns Development Corporations, Communities Scotland, the Northern Ireland Housing Executive.
3 Dwellings provided by housing associations other than Communities Scotland and the Northern Ireland Housing Trust and provided or authorised by government departments for families of police, prison staff, the armed forces and certain other services.
4 Includes non-registered social landlords
5 Reviseed
6 Provisional

Sources: Communities and Local Government;
Scottish Government;
Welsh Assembly Government;
Department for Social Development, Northern Ireland

14.4 Stock of dwellings: Estimated annual gains and losses
England

Thousands of dwellings

		1995 /96	1996 /97	1997 /98	1998 /99	1999 /00	2000[2] /01	2001 /02	2002 /03	2003 /04	2004 /05	2005 /06
Dwelling stock at start of financial year	GRWM	20 305	20 468	20 622	20 778	20 927	21 075	21 207	21 337	21 481	21 636	21 804
Gains to dwelling stock:												
Housebuilding completions	GRWN	154.6	146.2	149.6	138.6	141.4	133.1	129.8	137.7	144.0	155.9	163.4
Conversions (net gain)[1]	GRWO	8.9	8.6	2.8	4.2	3.5	2.8	..	..	..	..	..
Change of use	GRWP	..	..	11.6	15.9	13.9	10.1	..	..	..	..	..
Non-permanent dwellings additions	GRWQ	..	..	0.2	0.2	0.3	0.3	..	..	..	..	..
Losses from dwelling stock:												
Slum clearance (non LA owned dwelling demolished)	GRWR	2.7	2.9	1.3	1.3	1.4	1.7	..	..	..	..	..
Other demolitions[1]	GRWS	4.8	4.1	12.8	13.2	15.8	18.3	..	..	..	..	..
Change of use	GRWT	..	..	0.7	1.4	0.8	0.7	..	..	..	..	..
Non-permanent dwelling losses	GRWU	..	..	0.1	0.2	0.1	0.3	..	..	..	..	..
New gain in year	GRWV	156.0	147.8	149.3	143.0	140.9	125.3	130.5	143.7	154.8	167.9	185.3
Adjustment[3]	VQDN	6.6	6.6	6.6	6.6	6.6	6.6	..	..	..	..	..
Dwelling stock at end of financial year	GRWW	20 468	20 622	20 778	20 927	21 075	21 207	21 337	21 481	21 636	21 804	21 989

1 Conversion figures prior to 1997/98 include change of use.
2 Figures for 2000/01 conversions, change of use and non permanent dwellings are based on reported figures and do not include estimates for missing returns.

3 Series has been adjusted so that the 2000/01 estimates matches the 2001 Census.

Source: Communities and Local Government - 020 7944 4178

14.5 Housebuilding completions: by number of bedrooms

Percentages

		1996 /97	1997 /98	1998 /99	1999 /00	2000 /01	2001[1] /02	2002[1] /03	2003[1] /04	2004[1] /05	2005[1] /06	2006[1] /07
England												
1 bedroom	JUWJ	8	7	7	7	7	7	6	8	10	10	11
2 bedrooms	JUWK	29	27	27	26	27	25	29	33	38	42	42
3 bedrooms	JUWL	36	38	36	35	34	31	30	29	28	27	27
4 or more bedrooms	JUWM	26	28	30	32	32	37	34	30	23	21	20
All houses and flats	JUWN	100	100	100	100	100	100	100	100	100	100	100
Wales												
1 bedroom	JUWO	5	4	3	5	5	4	6	6	7	9	11
2 bedrooms	JUWP	27	24	21	19	18	19	18	20	21	27	28
3 bedrooms	JUWQ	47	46	46	43	42	39	35	37	35	35	33
4 or more bedrooms	JUWR	21	26	31	34	34	38	41	37	37	30	28
All houses and flats	JUWS	100	100	100	100	100	100	100	100	100	100	100

1 Figures for 2001/02 onwards are based on just NHBC figures, so there is some degree of variability owing to partial coverage.

Sources: Communities and Local Government;
Welsh Assembly Government

14.6 County Court mortgage possession actions:[1] by region

Thousands

		1997	1998	1999	2000	2001	2002	2003	2004	2005	2006	2007
Claims Issued[3]												
England and Wales	JURS	67.1	84.8	77.9	70.4	65.9	63.2	65.9	77.3	114.8	131.2	137.6
North East[3]	JURT	3.0	4.3	4.0	4.0	3.5	3.2	3.1	3.4	5.5	7.1	8.1
North West	JURU	11.0	14.2	14.1	12.7	12.1	11.1	10.0	10.6	15.3	19.2	21.7
Yorkshire and the Humber	JURV	6.9	8.2	8.8	7.8	7.1	6.1	5.9	6.6	10.1	12.0	13.7
East Midlands[4]	JURW	4.9	6.4	6.5	5.7	5.2	4.7	4.8	5.8	8.6	10.2	10.7
West Midlands[4]	JURX	6.7	8.1	8.5	8.2	7.5	6.8	7.2	8.6	12.2	14.8	16.2
East[5]	JURY	6.7	8.5	6.8	6.2	5.6	5.5	6.4	7.8	11.2	12.0	12.4
London	JURZ	9.2	11.4	8.7	7.0	7.6	8.7	10.5	13.4	21.1	21.9	20.1
South East	JUSA	9.1	11.2	9.9	9.0	8.4	8.3	9.3	11.4	16.5	17.4	16.9
South West	JUSB	5.7	7.3	5.7	4.9	4.4	4.3	4.5	5.4	7.8	8.5	8.6
England	JUSC	63.1	79.4	72.9	65.4	61.3	58.7	61.7	72.9	108.3	123.0	128.4
Wales	JUSD	3.9	5.4	5.0	5.0	4.6	4.5	4.2	4.3	6.5	8.2	9.2
Northern Ireland[2]	JUSE	..	..	1.9	1.7	1.6	1.6	1.7	2.2	2.6	2.5	..
Suspended orders												
England and Wales	JUSF	34.6	40.8	32.9	31.1	29.4	25.1	24.5	26.6	38.1	44.5	43.9
North East[3]	JUSG	1.6	2.3	2.0	2.0	1.8	1.4	1.3	1.3	1.9	2.6	7.0
North West	JUSH	5.5	6.5	6.2	5.7	5.5	4.9	4.0	3.8	5.0	6.7	7.2
Yorkshire and the Humber	JUSI	3.5	4.3	3.9	3.6	3.4	2.5	2.3	2.4	3.5	4.3	..
East Midlands[4]	JUSJ	2.6	3.1	2.8	2.5	2.5	1.9	1.8	2.1	2.9	3.4	8.9
West Midlands[4]	JUSK	3.4	3.8	3.7	3.7	3.7	2.9	2.9	3.1	4.3	5.2	..
East[5]	JUSL	3.0	3.9	2.8	2.6	2.3	2.2	2.3	2.7	3.8	4.0	9.1
London	JUSM	4.7	5.3	3.3	2.7	2.7	2.8	3.3	4.0	6.5	6.9	6.0
South East	JUSN	5.4	5.8	4.0	3.8	3.5	3.1	3.3	3.8	5.4	5.9	..
South West	JUSO	2.7	3.0	2.3	2.2	1.9	1.6	1.7	1.9	2.7	2.9	2.6
England	JUSP	32.3	38.0	30.9	28.7	27.3	23.2	22.8	25.1	36.0	41.9	40.9
Wales	JUSQ	2.4	2.8	2.0	2.3	2.1	1.9	1.7	1.5	2.2	2.7	3.0
Northern Ireland[2]	JUSR	..	..	0.3	0.2	0.2	0.2	0.3	0.4	0.5	0.4	..
Orders made												
England and Wales	JUSS	22.5	25.3	23.0	19.9	18.6	16.7	16.5	20.1	32.8	46.0	51.5
North East[3]	JUST	1.0	1.2	1.3	1.2	1.2	0.9	0.8	0.9	1.4	2.5	8.1
North West	JUSU	3.3	3.7	4.3	4.0	3.7	3.2	2.6	2.7	4.1	6.5	7.9
Yorkshire and the Humber	JUSV	2.3	3.1	2.7	2.4	2.3	1.8	1.6	1.7	2.8	4.2	..
East Midlands[4]	JUSW	1.7	1.7	2.0	1.6	1.6	1.4	1.2	1.5	2.6	3.8	10.1
West Midlands[4]	JUSX	2.0	2.4	2.3	2.1	2.2	1.8	1.7	2.2	3.3	5.0	..
East[5]	JUSY	2.5	2.6	1.9	1.6	1.4	1.3	1.5	2.0	3.2	4.4	11.1
London	JUSZ	3.4	3.5	2.5	1.8	1.9	2.2	2.7	3.8	6.6	8.3	7.9
South East	JUTA	3.1	3.4	2.6	2.2	1.9	1.9	2.2	2.9	4.6	5.7	..
South West	JUTB	1.9	2.1	1.8	1.3	1.1	1.0	1.0	1.4	2.3	2.9	3.1
England	JUTC	21.3	23.6	21.4	18.3	17.2	15.4	15.4	19.0	31.0	43.3	48.2
Wales	JUTD	1.3	1.7	1.6	1.6	1.4	1.3	1.1	1.1	1.8	2.7	3.2
Northern Ireland[2]	JUTE	..	..	0.7	0.6	0.7	0.5	0.6	0.7	0.9	0.9	..

Note In 1999 the data extraction method changed. From 1999 the data are collected electronically from Caseman, the main administrative system in the county courts. Previously they were collected from Stats Module, a manual form completed monthly by all county courts.

1 Suspended possession/suspended possession combined final orders
2 Possession/sale & possession final orders
3 Orders figures for North East in 2007 include those for Yorkshire and the Humber.
4 Orders figures for the Midlands in 2007 are combined.
5 Orders figures for the East in 2007 include those for South East

*Sources: Ministry of Justice 0207 210 8846;
Northern Ireland Court Service: 028 9032 8594*

14.7 Mortgages
United Kingdom

		1997	1998	1999	2000	2001	2002	2003	2004	2005	2006	2007
Mortgages[1] (Thousands)	JUTH	10 738	10 821	10 982	11 173	11 270	11 364	11 448	11 511	11 604	11 742	11 822
Arrears and repossessions[1] (Thousands)												
Loans in arrears at end-period												
By 6-12 months	JUTI	74	74	57	48	42	34	31	30	39	36	41
By over 12 months	JUTJ	45	35	30	21	18	17	13	11	15	16	16
Properties repossessed in period	JUTK	33	34	30	23	18	12	9	8	15	22	27
Type of mortgage for house purchase[2] (Percentages)												
Standard repayment	JUTL	39.6	42.6	46.2	60.1	72.0	82.8	81.7	79.0	69.8	65.1	61.1
Endowment	JUTM	36.0	33.7	27.0	17.5	9.6	5.4	4.2	4.4	4.2	7.2	8.5
Other[3]	JUTN	24.4	23.6	26.8	22.5	18.3	11.4	14.1	16.6	25.9	27.6	30.3

1 Estimates cover only members of the Council of Mortgage Lenders; these account for 98 per cent of all mortgages outstanding.
2 Includes new mortgages advanced by building societies, banks and other major lenders. Includes sitting tenants.
3 Includes interest only, PEP/ISA and pension.

4 Figures are estimates of arrears on first charge loans held by CML members. They do not include arrears relating relating to other secured lending or to firms that are not CML members.
5 Figures are subject to revision as better information about rates of growth and performance in different parts of the market is received, or lenders report for the first time or re-submit earlier figures.

Source: Council of Mortgage Lenders

14.8 Sales and transfers of local authority dwellings
Great Britain

Thousands

		1996	1997	1998	1999	2000	2001	2002	2003	2004	2005	2006
Right to buy sales	JUQV	45.0	58.1	56.0	66.8	71.3	66.6	78.5	94.1	74.7	41.6	26.1
Large scale voluntary transfers[1]	JUQW	29.9	21.1	36.9	88.7	111.4	100.8	102.5	104.6	67.9	81.7	82.7
Other sales and transfers[2]	JUQX	3.0	3.4	2.7	3.3	2.4	1.6	1.4	0.6	0.5	0.3	3.7
Total sales and transfers	JUQY	77.9	82.6	95.5	158.8	185.2	168.9	182.4	199.4	143.1	123.6	105.6

1 Except for 2003 large scale and voluntary transfers are included in other sales and transfers for Wales.
2 Excludes new town and Scottish Homes sales and transfers.

Sources: Communities and Local Government;
Welsh Assembly Government;
Scottish Governmant

14.9 Households in Temporary Accommodation[1]
Great Britain
As at 31st March of each year

Households

		1997/98	1998/99	1999/00	2000/01	2001/02	2002/03	2003/04	2004/05	2005/06	2006/07
Bed and breakfast hotels	JUWF	5 269	7 062	9 254	11 436	13 404	13 654	8 985	9 100	7 288	6 253
Hostels/women's refuges	JUWG	11 356	11 567	12 068	12 273	11 128	11 707	12 753	12 205	10 979	9 580
Social sector accommodation[2]	JXVN	16 077	20 686	23 510	27 826	30 310	31 719	31 821	31 295	27 758	23 463
Private sector accommodation and other[3]	JXVO	19 282	21 934	25 067	28 533	30 391	38 715	52 456	58 129	61 086	58 586
All accommodation[4]	JUWI	52 070	61 393	70 100	80 334	85 665	96 015	107 146	111 960	108 092	99 436

1 Households in temporary accommodation arranged by the local authority pending enquiries, or after being accepted as owed a main duty under homelessness legislation. Excludes 'homeless at home' cases who have remained in their existing accommodation after acceptance but have the same rights to suitable alternative housing as those in accommodation arranged directly by authorities.
2 Local authorities' and Registered Social Landlords' own stock.

3 Includes private sector properties leased by social sector landlords, households placed directly with a private sector landlord and other accommodation. From 2002 some self-contained B&B Annexe-style units, previously recorded under B&B have been more appropriately attributed to private sector accommodation.
4 Includes 'homeless at home' for Wales.

Sources: Communities and Local Government;
Welsh Assembly Government;
Scottish Executive

Transport and communications

Transport and communications

Road data

(Tables 15.4, 15.5, 15.6 and 15.7)

The Department for Transport has undertaken significant development work over the last two years to improve its traffic estimates and measurement of traffic flow on particular stretches of the road network. This work has previously been outlined in a number of publications (Road Traffic Statistics: 2001 SB(02)23, Traffic in Great Britain Q4 2002 Data SB(03)5 and Traffic in Great Britain Q1 2003 SB(03)6).

The main point to note is that figures for 1993 to 2004 have been calculated on a different basis from years prior to 1993. Therefore, figures prior to 1993 are not directly comparable with estimates for later years. Estimates on the new basis for 1993 and subsequent years were first published by the Department on 8 May 2003 in Traffic in Great Britain Q1 2003 SB(03)6. A summary of the main methodological changes to take place over the last couple of years appears below.

Traffic estimates are now disaggregated for roads in urban and rural areas rather than between built-up and non built-up roads. Built-up roads were defined as those with a speed limit of 40mph or lower. This created difficulties in producing meaningful disaggregated traffic estimates because an increasing number of clearly rural roads were subject to a 40mph speed limit for safety reasons. The urban/rural split of roads is largely determined by whether roads lie within the boundaries of urban areas with a population of 10,000 or more with adjustments in some cases for major roads at the boundary.

Traffic estimates are based on the results of many 12-hour manual counts in every year, which are grossed up to estimates of annual average daily flows using expansion factors based on data from automatic traffic counters on similar roads. These averages are needed so that traffic in off-peak times, at weekends and in the summer and winter months (when only special counts are undertaken) can be taken into account when assessing the traffic at each site. For this purpose roads are now sorted into 22 groupings (previously there were only seven) and this allows a better match of manual count sites with our automatic count sites. These groupings are based on a detailed analysis of the results from all the individual automatic count sites and take into account regional groupings, road category (that is both the

urban/rural classification of the road and the road class) and traffic flow levels. The groupings range from lightly-trafficked, rural minor roads in holiday areas such as Cornwall and Devon, to major roads in central London.

With the increasing interest in sub-regional statistics, we have undertaken a detailed study of traffic counts on minor roads carried out in the last ten years. This has been done in conjunction with a Geographic Information System to enable us to establish general patterns of minor road traffic in each local authority. As a result of this, we have been able to produce more reliable estimate of traffic levels in each authority in our base year of 1999. This in turn has enabled us to produce better estimates of traffic levels back to 1993, as well as more reliable estimates for 1999 onwards.

The Department created a database for major roads based on a Geographic Information System and Ordnance Survey data. This was checked by local authorities and discussed with Government Regional Offices and the Highways Agency to ensure that good local knowledge supplemented the available technical data.

Road class

(Tables 15.5 and 15.6)

Urban major and minor roads, from 1993 onwards, are defined as being within an urban area with a population of more than 10,000 people, based on the 2001 urban settlements. The definition for urban settlement can be found on the Communities and Local Government website at:

www.communities.gov.uk/planningandbuilding/ planningbuilding/planningstatistics/urbanrural.

Rural major and minor roads, from 1993 onwards, are defined as being outside an urban settlement.

New vehicle registrations

(Table 15.9)

Special concession group

Various revisions to the vehicle taxation system were introduced on 1 July 1995 and on 29 November 1995. Separate taxation classes for farmers' goods vehicles were abolished on 1 July 1995; after this date new vehicles of this type were registered as Heavy Goods Vehicles (HGVs). The total includes 5,900 vehicles registered between 1 January and 30 June in the (now abolished) agricultural and special machines group in classes which were not eligible to register in the special concession group. The old agricultural and special machines taxation group was abolished at end June 1995. The group includes agricultural and mowing machines, snow ploughs and gritting vehicles. Electric vehicles are also included in this group and are no longer exempt from Vehicle Excise Duty (VED). Steam propelled vehicles were added to this group from November 1995.

Other licensed vehicles

Includes three wheelers, pedestrian controlled vehicles, general haulage and showmen's tractors and recovery vehicles. Recovery vehicle tax class introduced January 1988.

Special vehicles group

The special vehicles group was created on 1 July 1995 and consists of various vehicle types over 3.5 tonnes gross weight but not required to pay VED as heavy goods vehicles. The group includes mobile cranes, work trucks, digging machines, road rollers and vehicles previously taxed as showman's goods and haulage. Figure shown for 1995 covers period from 1 July to 31 December only.

National Travel Survey data

(Tables 15.1, 15.11)

The National Travel Survey (NTS) is designed to provide a databank of personal travel information for Great Britain. It has been conducted as a continuous survey since July 1988, following ad hoc surveys since the mid-1960s. The survey is designed to identify long-term trends and is not suitable for monitoring short-term trends.

For the first time, the 2005 NTS results were based on weighted data, and data from 1995 onwards have now been weighted. The weighting methodology adjusts for non-response bias and also adjusts for the drop-off in the number of trips recorded by respondents during the course of the travel week. All results now published for 1995 onwards are based on weighted data, and direct comparisons cannot be made to earlier years or previous publications.

During 2005, over 8,400 households provided details of their personal travel by filling in travel diaries over the course of a week. The drawn sample size from 2002 was nearly trebled compared with previous years following recommendations in a National Statistics Review of the NTS. This enables most results to be presented on a single year basis from 2002.

Travel included in the NTS covers all trips by British residents within Great Britain for personal reasons, including travel in the course of work. A trip is defined as a one-way course of travel having a single main purpose. It is the basic unit of

personal travel defined in the survey. A round trip is split into two trips, with the first ending at a convenient point about half-way round as a notional stopping point for the outward destination and return origin. A stage is that portion of a trip defined by the use of a specific method of transport or of a specific ticket (a new stage being defined if either the mode or ticket changes). The main mode of a trip is that used for the longest stage of the trip. With stages of equal length the mode of the latest stage is used. Walks of less than 50 yards are excluded.

Travel details provided by respondents include trip purpose, method of travel, time of day and trip length. The households also provided personal information, such as their age, sex, working status, driving licence holding, and details of the cars available for their use.

Because estimates made from a sample survey depend on the particular sample chosen, they generally differ from the true values of the population. This is not usually a problem when considering large samples (such as all car trips in Great Britain), but it may give misleading information when considering data from small samples even after weighting.

The most recent editions of all NTS publications are available on the DfT website at: www.dft.gov.uk/transtat/personaltravel. Bulletins of key results are published annually. The most recent bulletin is National Travel Survey: 2005.

Households with regular use of cars

(Table 15.12)

The mid-year estimates of the percentage of households with regular use of a car or van are based on combined unweighted data from the NTS, the Expenditure and Food Survey (previously the Family Expenditure Survey) and the General Household Survey, where available data by area type are based on weighted data from the NTS only.

Continuing Survey of Road Goods Transport

(Tables 15.3, 15.18, 15.19)

The estimates are derived from the Continuing Survey of Road Goods Transport (CSRGT) which in 2005 was based on an average weekly returned sample of some 330 HGVs. The samples are drawn from the computerised vehicle licence records held by the Driver and Vehicle Licensing Agency. Questionnaires are sent to the registered keepers of the sampled vehicles asking for a description of the vehicle and its activity during the survey week. The estimates are grossed to the vehicle population, and at the overall national level have a 2 per cent margin of error (at 95 per cent confidence level). Further details and results are published in Road Freight Statistics 2005, and previously in Transport of Goods by Road in Great Britain.

Methodological changes

A key component of National Statistics outputs is a programme of quality reviews carried out at least every five years to ensure that such statistics are fit for purpose and that their quality and value continue to improve. A quality review of the Department for Transport's road freight surveys, including the CSRGT, was carried out in 2003. A copy of the report can be accessed at:

www.statistics.gov.uk/nsbase/methods_quality/quality_review/downloads/NSQR30FinalReport.doc

The quality review made a number of recommendations about the CSRGT. The main methodological recommendation was that, to improve the accuracy of survey estimates, the sample strata should be amended to reflect current trends in vehicle type, weight and legislative groups. These new strata are described more fully in Appendix C of the survey report. For practical and administrative reasons, changes were also made to the sample selection methodology (see Appendix B of the report). These changes have resulted in figures from 2004 not being fully comparable with those for 2003 and earlier years. Detailed comparisons should therefore be made with caution.

Railways: permanent way and rolling stock

(Table 15.22)

1. Locomotives – locos owned by Northern Ireland Railways (NIR), does not include those from the Republic of Ireland Railway System.

2. Diesel electric etc rail motor vehicles – powered passenger carrying vehicles, includes diesel electric (DE) power cars and all Construcciones y Auxiliar de Ferocarriles (CAF) vehicles. (Note: only 16 of the CAF sets were delivered to NIR at the time.)

3. Loco hauled coaches – NIR owned De Dietrich plus Gatwick but not including gen van.

4. Rail car trailers – 80 class and 450 class trailers. Not CAF, they are all powered.

5. Rolling stock for maintenance and repair – a 'standalone' figure – may or may not be included in the above totals. Anything listed as 'repair' or 'workshop' in the motive power sheets is included. Also, those CAF vehicles not yet delivered at the time.

6. The information is a 'snapshot' taken from the motive power sheets at end of March, together with any other known information.

Activity at civil aerodromes

(Table 15.28)

Figures exclude Channel Island airports. Other covers local pleasure flights, scheduled service, positioning flights and non-transport charter flights for reward (for example: aerial survey work, crop dusting and delivery of empty aircraft). Non-commercial covers test and training flights, private, aeroclub, military and official flights, and business aviation, etc.

Roll-on/roll-off enquiry

(Table 15.30)

Statistics on the number of lorries and unaccompanied trailers travelling from Great Britain to mainland Europe and Ireland are compiled from quarterly returns provided by roll-on/roll-off ferry operators and Eurotunnel. (Unaccompanied trailers are not carried on the Eurotunnel freight service.) The results are broken down by country of vehicle registration, by country of disembarkation and by Great Britain port group. Separate figures are given for powered vehicles and unaccompanied trailers. The statistics presented in Table 15.30 refer to vehicles travelling to mainland Europe only and exclude those to Ireland.

Powered vehicles comprise rigid vehicles, lorries with semi-trailers (articulated units) and lorries with drawbar trailers. (Some vehicles under 3.5 tonnes gross vehicle weight are also included.) Unaccompanied trailers are trailers and semi-trailers not accompanied on the ferry by a powered unit. Up until 1978 inward traffic was also recorded, but because it was similar to outward traffic, the data requirement was discontinued to save respondent effort.

More detailed analyses are provided in the Department's quarterly publication Road Goods Vehicles Travelling to Mainland Europe, available on the Department's website.

Postal services and television licences

(Table 15.31)

Letters posted category includes printed papers, newspapers, postcards and sample packets, where airmail includes letters without special charge for air transport. Business reply and freepost is now known as Response Services.

15.1

Trips per person per year: by sex, main mode and trip purpose[1], 2006
Great Britain

Numbers

Males

	Car	Walk	Bus and coach	Rail[2]	Other[3]	All modes
Social/entertainment	154	44	11	5	12	226
Shopping	123	49	13	2	6	193
Other escort	82	10	2	0	1	95
Other personal business	66	22	5	1	4	99
Commuting	131	15	11	13	14	185
Education	20	27	10	2	6	64
Escort education	17	8	0	0	0	25
Business	37	3	0	2	2	45
Holiday/day trip	28	2	2	1	5	38
Other, including just walk	0	43	0	0	0	44
All purpose (=100%) (number)	659	225	53	27	50	1014
Base						
Unweighted Base(Trips)	114,000	40,000	9,000	4,000	8,000	175,000

Females

	Car	Walk	Bus and coach	Rail[2]	Other[3]	All modes
Social/entertainment	165	48	13	4	9	239
Shopping	149	60	26	3	5	243
Other escort	82	13	2	0	1	99
Other personal business	71	29	8	1	3	111
Commuting	87	19	14	9	5	135
Education	18	26	10	1	3	60
Escort education	34	25	1	0	1	62
Business	19	4	1	1	1	26
Holiday/day trip	30	3	2	1	3	39
Other, including just walk	1	45	0	0	0	46
All purposes (numbers)	657	272	77	22	32	1060
Base						
Unweighted Base(Trips)	119,000	52,000	14,000	4,000	6,000	194,000

All persons

	Car	Walk	Bus and coach	Rail[2]	Other[3]	All modes
Social/entertainment	160	46	12	5	11	233
Shopping	136	55	20	2	6	219
Other escort	82	12	2	0	1	97
Other personal business	69	26	6	1	3	105
Commuting	109	17	12	11	10	160
Education	19	27	10	2	5	62
Escort education	26	17	1	0	0	44
Business	28	3	1	2	1	35
Holiday/daytrip	29	2	2	1	4	38
Other, including just walk	1	44	0	0	0	45
All purposes (numbers)	658	249	65	24	40	1037
Base						
Unweighted Base(Trips)	233,000	92,000	22,000	8,000	14,000	369,000

1 Main mode is that used for the longest part of the trip.
2 Includes London Underground.
3 Includes bicycles, two-wheeled motor vehicles, motorcaravans, taxis/ mini-cabs, domestic air travel and other private and public transport.

Source: National Travel Survey, Department for Transport 020 7944 3097

15.2 Retail Prices Index: transport components: 1996 - 2006
Great Britain

Indices (1996=100)

| | All items | Motor vehicles | | | | | Rail fares | Bus fares | Fares & other travel costs |
		Purchase	Maintenance	Petrol and oil	Tax and insurance	All motoring			
	ENX3	ENX4	ENX5	ZCFV	ENX6	ZCFW	ZCFX	ENX7	ENX8
1996	100.0	100.0	100.0	100.0	100.0	100.0	100.0	100.0	100.0
1997	103.1	102.4	105.4	110.0	104.1	105.3	102.3	103.6	103.4
1998	106.7	101.3	109.8	115.4	113.3	108.6	106.6	106.9	105.6
1999	108.3	97.0	114.0	125.1	122.5	111.2	110.4	110.8	108.9
2000	111.5	91.7	118.8	141.6	135.6	115.5	112.3	115.3	112.5
2001	113.5	90.4	124.6	134.4	142.7	114.8	116.6	120.2	116.1
2002	115.4	88.6	131.0	130.1	144.8	113.9	119.3	123.8	119.4
2003	118.7	86.2	138.9	134.8	151.1	115.4	121.3	129.0	127.8
2004	122.3	83.5	147.3	142.3	151.8	116.6	126.0	135.6	132.2
2005	125.7	79.1	156.2	154.8	149.8	117.3	131.1	144.6	137.7
2006	129.7	77.0	165.8	163.3	151.8	119.0	136.3	146.6	140.1

Source: Consumer Prices and Inflation Division, ONS: 020 7944 4442

15.3 Domestic freight transport: by mode
Great Britain

		1996	1997	1998	1999	2000	2001	2002	2003	2004	2005	2006
Goods moved (billion tonnes kilometres)												
Petroleum products												
Road[1]	ZBZP	6.1	5.8	5.2	5.0	6.4	5.8	5.2	5.5	5.7	5.5	5.7
Rail[2]	ZBZQ	..	..	1.6	1.5	1.4	1.2	1.2	1.2	1.2[7]	1.2[7]	1.5
Water[3]	ZBZR	45.9	38.3	45.2	48.6	52.7	43.5	51.7	46.9	46.9	47.2	37.8
of which: coastwise	ZBZS	38.7	33.8	36.4	33.3	26.0	23.1	24.2	23.3	26.6	30.3	22.8
Pipeline	ZBZT	11.6	11.2	11.7	11.6	11.4	11.5	10.9	10.5	10.7	10.8	10.8
All modes	ZBZU	63.6[4]	55.3[4]	63.7	66.7	71.9	62.0	69.0	64.1	64.5	64.7	..
Coal and coke												
Road[1]	ZBZV	2.5	2.7	2.0	2.2	1.5	2.1	1.5	1.5	1.2	1.5	1.3
Rail[2]	ZBZW	3.8	4.4	4.5	4.8	4.8	6.2	5.7	5.8	6.7[7]	8.3[7]	8.8
Water[3]	ZBZX	0.6	0.6	0.5	0.5	0.2	0.5	0.3	0.5	0.3	0.4	0.5
All modes	ZBZY	6.9	7.7	7.0	7.5	6.5	8.8	7.5	7.9	8.5	10.2	..
Other traffic												
Road[1]	ZBZZ	145.3	148.9	153.1	150.5	151.5	150.6	152.7	154.7	155.6	156.4	159.9
Rail[2]	ZCAA	11.3	12.5	11.2	11.9	11.9	12.0	11.7	11.9	12.5[7]	12.2[7]	11.8
Water[3]	ZCAB	8.70	9.20	11.20	9.60	14.60	14.80	15.20	13.50	12.30	13.30	13.49
All modes	ZCAC	165.3	170.6	175.5	172.0	178.0	177.4	179.6	180.0	180.4	181.9	..
All traffic												
Road[1]	KCTA	153.9	157.4	160.3	157.7	159.4	158.5	159.4	161.7	162.5[5]	163.4[5]	166.9[5]
Rail[2]	KCTB	15.1	16.9	17.3	18.2	18.1	19.4	18.5	18.9	20.4[7]	21.7[7]	22.1
Water[3]	ZCAD	55.30	48.10	56.90	58.70	67.40	58.80	67.20	60.90	59.50	61.00	51.85
Pipeline	KCTE	11.6	11.2	11.7	11.6	11.4	11.5	10.9	10.5	10.7	10.8	10.8
All modes	KCTF	235.9	233.6	246.2	246.2	256.3	248.2	256.0	252.0	253.0	256.9	251.7
Percentage of all traffic												
Road[1]	ZCAE	65	67	65	64	62	64	62	64	64	64	66
Rail[2]	ZCAF	6	7	7	7	7	8	7	7	8	8	9
Water[3]	ZCAG	23	21	23	24	26	24	26	24	23	24	21
Pipeline	ZCAH	5	5	5	5	4	5	4	4	4	4	4
All modes	ZCAI	100	100	100	100	100	100	100	100	100	100	100
Goods lifted (million tonnes)												
Petroleum products												
Road[1]	ZCAJ	75	73	61	61	75	74	59	64	67	70	69
Rail[2]	ZCAK	..	..	..	..	..	..	..	..	..	..	..
Water[3]	ZCAL	71	69	76	72	72	60	67	64	63	66	57
of which: coastwise	ZCAM	54	52	55	52	40	34	36	35	38	42	34
Pipeline	ZCAN	157	148	153	155	151	151	146	141	158	168	159
All modes	ZCAO	303[4]	290[4]	290[4]	288[4]	298[4]	285[4]	272[4]	269[4]	288[4]	304[4]	..
Coal and coke												
Road[1]	ZCAP	32	37	26	28	22	21	17	22	14	21	15
Rail[2]	ZCAQ	52	50	45	36[8]	35	40	34	35	44[6]	49	49
Water[3]	ZCAR	3	4	3	3	3	3	2	2	1	2	2
All modes	ZCAS	87	91	70	75	60	64	53	59	67	72	..
Other traffic												
Road[1]	ZCAT	1 623	1 630	1 640	1 575	1 596	1 587	1 658	1 667	1 782	1 777	1 852
Rail[2]	ZCAU	50	55	57	61	60	55	53	54	57	59	60
Water[3]	ZCAV	67	69	70	70	62	68	70	67	63	65	66
All modes	ZCAW	1 740	1 754	1 767	1 706	1 718	1 710	1 781	1 788	1 902	1 901	..
All traffic												
Road[1]	KCTG	1 730	1 740	1 727	1 664	1 693	1 682	1 734	1 753	1 863[5]	1 868[5]	1 936[5]
Rail[2]	KCTH	102	105	102	97[8]	96	94	87	89	101[6]	108	108
Water[3]	ZCAX	142.0	142.0	149.0	144.0	137.0	131.0	139.0	133.0	127.0	133.0	126.3
Pipeline	KCTK	157.0	148.0	153.0	155.0	151.0	151.0	146.0	141.0	158.0	168.0	159.1
All modes	KCTL	2 131	2 135	2 131	2 060	2 077	2 058	2 106	2 116	2 250	2 277	2 330
Percentage of all traffic												
Road[1]	ZCAY	81	81	81	81	82	82	82	83	83	82	83
Rail[2]	ZCAZ	5	5	5	5[8]	5	5	4	4	4	5	5
Water[3]	ZCBA	7	7	7	7	7	6	7	6	6	6	5
Pipeline	ZCBB	7	7	7	8	7	7	7	7	7	7	7
All modes	ZCBC	100	100	100	100	100	100	100	100	100	100	100

1 All goods vehicles, including those up to 3.5 tonnes gross vehicle weight.
2 Figures for rail are for financial years e.g 1996/97 etc
3 Figures for water are for UK traffic.
4 Excludes rail.
5 Figures for 2004, 2005 and 2006 are not fully comparable with those for 2003 and earlier years. Detailed comparisons should therefore be made with caution.
6 Break in the series increase largely due to changes in coverage.
7 There have been revisions to data since the last TSGB publication
8 Goods lifted data from 1999 onwards have been revised since the last TSGB publication

Sources: Department for Transport;
Rail: 020 7944 4977;
Road 020 7944 4261;
Water: 020 7944 3087;
Pipeline : 020 7215 2718;
Sources - Rail : ORR;
Pipeline : Department for Business Enterprise and Regulatory Reform

Transport and communications

15.4 Passenger transport by mode
Great Britain

		1996	1997	1998	1999	2000	2001	2002	2003	2004	2005	2006
Billion passenger kilometres												
Road												
Buses and coaches	GRXK	43	44	45	46	47	47	47	47	48	49	50
Cars, vans and taxis	GRXG	622	632	636	642	640	654	677	673	678	674	686
Motor cycles	GRXH	4	4	4	5	5	5	5	6	6	6	6
Pedal cycles	GRXI	4	4	4	4	4	4	4	5	4	4	5
All road	GRXJ	674	685	689	697	695	710	733	731	736	733	747
Rail[1]	KCTN	39	42	44	46	47	47	48	49	50	52	55
Air	KCTM	6	7	7	7	8	8	8	9	10	10	10
All modes[2]	GRXM	719	733	740	751	749	765	790	789	796	795	812
Percentages												
Road												
Buses and coaches	GRXN	6	6	6	6	6	6	6	6	6	6	6
Cars, vans and taxis	GRXO	87	86	86	86	85	85	86	85	85	85	85
Motor cycles	GRXP	1	1	1	1	1	1	1	1	1	1	1
Pedal cycles	GRXQ	1	1	1	1	1	1	1	1	–	1	1
All road	GRXR	94	93	93	93	93	93	93	93	92	92	92
Rail[1]	ZCBJ	5	6	6	6	6	6	6	6	6	7	7
Air	ZCBK	1	1	1	1	1	1	1	1	1	1	1
All modes[2]	GRXU	100	100	100	100	100	100	100	100	100	100	100

1 Financial years. National Rail, urban metros and modern trams
2 Excluding travel by water

Sources: Department for Transport;
Bus & coach: 020 7944 3076;
Car, m/cycle & pedal cycle: 020 7944 3097;
Rail: 020 7944 8874;
Air: 020 7944 3088

15.5 Motor vehicle traffic: by road class: 1996-2006
Great Britain

Billion vehicle kilometres

		1996	1997	1998	1999	2000[1]	2001[2]	2002	2003	2004	2005	2006
Motorways	JSZV	78.3	82.1	85.7	87.8	88.4	90.8	92.6	93.0	96.6	97.0	99.2
Rural 'A' roads[3]												
Trunk[5]	JSZW	60.4	62.5	63.3	64.7	64.2	65.9	64.6	61.5	59.7	58.0	59.2
Principal[5]	JSZX	63.1	64.1	65.4	66.0	65.8	67.4	71.8	77.7	81.6	83.3	84.6
All rural 'A' roads	JSZY	123.5	126.6	128.7	130.7	130.0	133.3	136.4	139.3	141.3	141.3	143.8
Urban 'A' roads[4]												
Trunk[5]	JSZZ	13.9	13.8	13.8	14.0	14.0	7.6	7.4	6.7	6.0	5.5	5.6
Principal[5]	JTAA	67.0	67.1	67.5	67.9	67.7	74.2	74.8	75.1	76.8	76.2	76.7
All urban 'A' roads	JTAB	80.9	80.9	81.3	81.9	81.7	81.8	82.2	81.7	82.8	81.7	82.2
All Major Roads	I45C	282.7	289.6	295.7	300.4	300.0	305.9	311.2	314.0	320.7	320.1	325.3
Minor roads												
Minor rural roads	JTAC	58.9	60.0	60.4	61.3	61.5	61.6	64.5	64.4	65.9	66.8	68.5
Minor urban roads	JTAD	99.6	100.7	102.4	105.3	105.5	106.9	110.8	111.9	112.0	112.5	112.6
All minor roads	JTAE	158.5	160.7	162.8	166.6	167.0	168.5	175.3	176.4	177.9	179.3	181.1
All roads	JTAF	441.1	450.3	458.5	467.0	467.1	474.4	486.5	490.4	498.6	499.4	506.4

1 The decline in the use of cars and taxis in 2000 was due to the fuel dispute.
2 Figures affected by the impact of Foot and Mouth disease during 2001.
3 Rural roads; Major and minor roads, from 1993 onwards, are defined as being outside an urban area. (see definition below).
4 Urban roads; Major and minor roads, from 1993 onwards, are defined as within an urban area with a population of 10,000 or more. These are based on the 2001 urban settlements. The definition for 'urban settlement' is in Urban and Rural area definitions: a user guide which can be found on the Department for Communities and Local Government web site at: http:/www.communities.gov.uk/index.asp?id=1147748
5 Figures for trunk and principal 'A' roads in England, from 2001 onwards are affected by the detrunking programme.

Source: Department for Transport: 020 7944 3095

15.6 Public road length:[1] by road type
Great Britain

Kilometres

		1996	1997	1998	1999	2000	2001	2002	2003	2004	2005	2006
Trunk motorway	JSZD	3 253	3 333	3 376	3 404	3 422	3 431	3 433	3 432	3 478	3 466	3 503
Principal motorway	JSZE	45	45	44	45	45	45	45	46	46	54	53
Rural 'A' roads[2]:												
Trunk[3]	JSZF	10 598	10 690	10 585	10 611	10 627	10 607	9 973	9 027	8 641	8 239	8 277
Principal[3]	JSZG	24 592	24 636	24 783	24 852	24 866	24 915	25 559	26 498	26 889	27 312	27 336
All rural 'A' roads	JSZH	35 190	35 326	35 369	35 463	35 493	35 522	35 532	35 525	35 530	35 550	35 612
Urban 'A' roads[4]:												
Trunk[3]	JSZI	1 117	1 108	1 096	1 087	1 074	762	705	587	506	444	446
Principal[3]	JSZJ	9 885	9 923	9 931	10 019	10 040	10 370	10 436	10 539	10 632	10 663	10 696
All urban 'A' roads	JSZK	11 002	11 031	11 027	11 106	11 114	11 132	11 141	11 127	11 138	11 107	11 143
Minor rural roads[5]:												
B roads	JSZL	24 603	24 594	24 586	24 579	24 570	24 562	24 554	24 547	24 640	24 639	23 950
C roads	JSZM	73 218	73 312	73 405	73 500	73 593	73 688	73 783	73 878	73 363	73 581	72 985
Unclassified	JSZN	110 698	110 915	111 132	111 350	111 568	111 787	112 006	112 231	109 561	109 426	113 826
All minor rural roads	JSZO	208 518	208 820	209 123	209 429	209 731	210 037	210 343	210 656	207 565	207 646	210 761
Minor urban roads[5]:												
B roads	JSZP	5 615	5 618	5 622	5 626	5 630	5 633	5 638	5 641	5 538	5 550	6 209
C roads	JSZQ	10 943	10 966	10 986	11 009	11 031	11 054	11 076	11 098	10 859	10 878	11 514
Unclassified	JSZR	112 417	112 754	113 093	113 432	113 772	114 114	114 456	114 816	113 520	113 757	119 556
All minor urban roads	JSZS	128 975	129 338	129 702	130 068	130 432	130 802	131 169	131 556	129 917	130 186	137 279
All major roads	GG5B	49 490	49 735	49 816	50 018	50 074	50 130	50 152	50 130	50 192	50 176	50 310
All minor roads[5]	JSZT	337 494	338 158	338 825	339 496	340 163	340 838	341 512	342 212	337 482	337 832	348 040
All roads	JSZU	386 983	387 893	388 641	389 515	390 237	390 969	391 663	392 342	387 674	388 008	398 350

1 A number of minor revisions have been made to the lengths of major roads from 1993 onwards.
2 Rural roads: Major and minor roads, from 1993 onwards, are defined as being outside an urban area.
3 Figures for trunk and principal 'A' roads in England, from 2001 onwards, are affected by the detrunking programme.

4 Urban roads: Major and minor roads, from 1993 onwards, are defined as within an urban area with a population of 10,000 or more. These are based on the 2001 urban settlements. The definition for 'urban settlement' is in Urban and rural area definitions : a user guide can be found on the Department for Communities and Local Government web site at : http://www.communities.gov.uk/index.asp?id=1147748
5 New information from 2004 and from 2006 has enabled better estimates of minor road lengths to be made

Sources: National Road Traffic Survey;
Department for Transport 020 7944 3095

15.7 Road traffic: by type of vehicle
Great Britain

Billion vehicle kilometres

		1996	1997	1998	1999	2000[1]	2001[2]	2002	2003	2004	2005	2006
Cars and taxis	JTAH	359.9	365.8	370.6	377.4	376.8	382.8	392.9	393.1	398.1	397.2	402.4
Motor cycles etc.	JTAI	3.8	4.0	4.1	4.5	4.6	4.8	5.1	5.6	5.2	5.4	5.2
Larger buses and coaches	JTAJ	5.0	5.2	5.2	5.3	5.2	5.2	5.2	5.4	5.2	5.2	5.4
Light vans[3]	JTAK	46.2	48.6	50.8	51.6	52.3	53.7	55.0	57.9	60.8	62.6	64.3
Goods vehicles[4]:												
2 axles rigid	JTAL	10.9	11.0	11.1	11.6	11.7	11.5	11.6	11.7	11.7	11.5	11.3
3 axles rigid	JTAM	1.6	1.6	1.9	1.7	1.7	1.8	1.8	1.8	1.9	1.9	1.9
4 or more axles rigid	JTAN	1.5	1.5	1.6	1.5	1.5	1.5	1.5	1.6	1.6	1.7	1.7
3 and 4 axles artic	JTAO	3.3	3.2	3.0	3.0	2.7	2.5	2.3	2.2	2.2	2.0	1.9
5 axles artic	JTAP	6.6	7.1	7.3	7.2	6.7	6.4	6.4	6.2	6.5	6.4	6.5
6 or more axles artic	JTAQ	2.3	2.5	2.9	3.3	4.1	4.5	4.8	5.0	5.4	5.5	5.7
All	JTAR	26.2	26.9	27.7	28.1	28.2	28.1	28.3	28.5	29.4	29.0	29.1
All motor vehicles	JURA	441.1	450.3	458.5	467.0	467.1	474.4	486.5	490.4	498.6	499.4	506.4
Pedal cycles	JURB	4.1	4.1	4.0	4.1	4.2	4.2	4.4	4.5	4.2	4.4	4.6

1 The decline in the use of cars and taxis in 2000 was due to the fuel dispute.
2 Figures affected by the impact of Foot and Mouth disease during 2001.
3 Not exceeding 3,500 kgs gross vehicle weight.
4 Over 3,500 kgs gross vehicle weight.

Sources: National Road Traffic Survey;
Department for Transport 020 7944 3095

Transport and communications

15.8 Motor vehicles currently licenced
Great Britain

At end of year

Thousands

	Private and light goods										Body type cars	
	Private cars	Other vehicles	Motor cycles, scooters and mopeds	Public transport vehicles[1]	Goods vehicles	Special machines/ special conces- sionary[1]	Other vehicles	Crown and exempt vehicles[1]	Special vehicles group	All vehicles[4]	All	Percent- age of company cars
	BMBJ	BMBK	BMBB	BMBE	BMBD	KSBY	BMBF	BMBL	KSBZ	BMBI	ZCGR	ZCGS
1996	21 172	2 267	609	77	413	254	40	1 424	48	26 302	22 238	10.3
1997	21 681	2 317	626	79	414	249	38	1 522	48	26 974	22 832	10.5
1998	22 115	2 362	684	80	412	243	37	1 558	47	27 538	23 293	10.4
1999	22 785	2 427	760	84	415	241	36	1 573	47	28 368	23 975	10.0
2000	23 196	2 469	825	86	418	233	34	1 590	46	28 898	24 406	10.3
2001	23 899	2 544	882	89	422	233	33	1 602	45	29 747	25 126	9.7
2002	24 543	2 622	941	92	425	243	32	1 855	46	30 557	25 782	9.0
2003	24 985	2 730	1 005	96	426	258	32	1 887	47	31 207	26 240	8.4
2004	25 754	2 900	1 060	100	434	–	32	1 929	50	32 259	27 028	8.5
2005	26 208	3 019	1 075	103	433	–	31	1 978	51	32 897	27 520	8.8
2006	26 508	3 137	1 094	107	446	–	31	1 991	54	33 369	27 830	8.7

1 The 'Special concession' vehicles form part of the 'Crown and exempt' taxation class from 2002

Source: Department for Transport 020 7944 3077

15.9 New vehicle registrations by taxation class
Great Britain

Thousands

		1996	1997	1998	1999	2000	2001	2002	2003	2004	2005	2006
Cars	BMAA	1 888.4	2 015.9	2 123.5	2 100.4	2 174.9	2 431.8	2 528.8	2 497.1	2 437.4	2 266.3	2 161.0
Other Vehicles	BMAE	205.0	228.4	244.5	241.6	254.9	277.9	286.8	323.5	347.3	337.2	338.0
Motor Cycles, Scooters and Mopeds	BMAL	89.6	121.3	143.3	168.4	182.9	177.1	162.2	157.3	133.7	132.3	132.0
Goods	BBJY	45.5	41.8	49.1	48.3	50.4	48.6	44.9	48.4	48.0	51.2	48.0
Buses	BBJZ	6.5	6.6	7.4	8.0	7.5	6.8	7.8	8.4	8.3	8.9	8.0
Special machines/special concessionary[1]:	DMNR	8.1	8.6	7.6	7.6	6.5	7.0	7.2	8.1	7.6	8.0	8.0
Other Vehicles[2]	I8B3	150.0	162.0	157.0	174.0	176.0	169.0	192.0	189.0	204.0	218.0	219.0
All Vehicles	BBKD	2 410.1	2 597.7	2 740.3	2 765.8	2 870.9	3 137.7	3 229.4	3 231.9	3 185.4	3 021.4	2 914.0

1 From 2002 the Special Concessionary group was abolished and became part of the exempt category.
2 Includes crown and exempt vehicles, three wheelers, and others. From 2002 the former 'special concessionary group ' vehicles are also included.

Source: Department for Transport: 020 7944 3077

15.10

Driving test pass rates: by sex and type of vehicle licence
Great Britain

Percentages

		1989/90	1991/92	1998/99	2000/01	2001/02	2002/03	2003/04	2004/05	2005/06	2006/07
Males											
Motorcycle	JTRB	72	69	69	68	67	66	67	66	66	67
Car	JTRC	58	57	51	48	47	47	46	46	46	46
Bus	JTTG	–	–	48	47	46	44	46	46	43	43
Lorry	JTTH	–	–	52	53	50	50	49	47	45	46
All males	JTTI	–	–	–	51	50	49	48	47	47	48
Females											
Motorcycle	JTTJ	68	63	63	56	55	54	53	53	52	54
Car	JTTK	47	46	42	40	40	40	40	39	40	41
Bus	JTTL	–	–	47	45	40	40	45	46	47	49
Lorry	JTTM	–	–	50	53	47	46	48	45	45	47
All females	JTTN	–	–	–	41	41	40	40	40	40	41
All											
Motorcycle	JTTO	–	–	68	66	66	65	65	64	64	65
Car	JTTP	–	–	46	44	43	43	43	42	42	43
Bus	JTTQ	–	–	48	48	45	44	46	44	43	44
Lorry	JTTR	–	–	52	54	56	49	49	46	45	46
All persons	JTTS	–	–	–	46	46	45	44	43	44	44

Source: Driving Standards Agency - info.rsis@dsa.gov.uk

15.11

Full car driving licence holders by sex and age[1]
Great Britain

Percentages and millions

	All aged 17+	17-20	21-29	30-39	40-49	50-59	60-69	70 and over	Estimated number of licence holders (millions)
All adults									
1975/76	48	28	59	67	60	50	35	15	19.4
1985/86	57	33	63	74	71	60	47	27	24.3
1989/91	64	43	72	77	78	67	54	32	27.8
1992/94	67	48	75	82	79	72	57	33	29.3
1995/97[2]	69	43	74	81	81	75	63	38	30.3
1998/00	71	41	75	84	83	77	67	39	31.4
	GB9O	C98J	C98K	C98L	C98M	C98N	C98O	C98P	C98Q
2003	70	29	67	82	83	80	72	44	32.1
2004	70	27	65	82	83	80	72	46	32.2
2005	72	32	66	82	84	82	74	51	33.3
2006	72	34	67	82	84	82	76	50	33.7
Males									
1975/76	69	36	78	85	83	75	58	32	13.4
1985/86	74	37	73	86	87	81	72	51	15.1
1989/91	80	52	82	88	89	85	78	58	16.7
1992/94	81	54	83	91	88	88	81	59	17.0
1995/97[2]	81	50	80	88	89	89	83	65	17.2
1998/00	82	44	80	89	91	88	83	65	17.4
	GB9P	C98R	C98S	C98T	C98U	C98V	C98W	C98X	C98Y
2003	81	33	73	87	90	91	87	69	17.8
2004	79	30	68	87	89	90	86	72	17.7
2005	81	37	69	86	90	90	88	73	18.1
2006	81	37	71	86	89	91	90	76	18.4
Females									
1975/76	29	20	43	48	37	24	15	4	6.0
1985/86	41	29	54	62	56	41	24	11	9.2
1989/91	49	35	64	67	66	49	33	15	11.1
1992/94	54	42	68	73	70	57	37	16	12.2
1995/97[2]	57	36	67	74	73	62	45	21	13.1
1998/00	60	38	69	78	76	67	53	22	14.0
	GB9Q	C98Z	C992	C993	C994	C995	C996	C997	C998
2003	61	25	62	77	77	70	58	26	14.3
2004	61	24	62	77	77	71	58	28	14.5
2005	63	27	62	77	79	73	61	35	15.2
2006	63	31	63	78	79	74	63	31	15.3

1 See chapter text.
2 Figures for 1995 onwards are based on weighted data.

Source: National Travel Survey, Department for Transport 020 7944 3097

15.12 Households with regular use of cars[1]
Great Britain

Percentages and millions

	No car	One car	Two cars	Three or more cars	Total (millions)
	ZCGA	ZCGB	ZCGC	ZCGD	ZCGE
1995	30	45	21	4	22.9
1996	30	45	21	4	23.0
1997	30	45	21	5	23.1
1998	28	44	23	5	23.3
1999	28	44	22	5	23.4
2000	27	45	23	5	23.6
2001	26	45	23	5	23.9
2002	26	44	24	5	24.1
2003	26	44	25	5	24.4
2004	25	44	25	5	24.6
2005	25	44	26	5	24.8

	No car	One car	Two or more cars	Total
Government Office Regions, 2005[1,2]				
Great Britain	25	44	31	100
North East	35	42	23	100
North West	26	43	30	100
Yorkshire and The Humber	27	44	29	100
East Midlands	22	44	34	100
West Midlands	23	43	34	100
East	17	44	38	100
London	35	44	21	100
South East	18	43	39	100
South West	17	47	36	100
England	24	44	32	100
Wales	23	47	31	100
Scotland	31	44	25	100
Northern Ireland	24	45	31	100

	No car	One car	Two or more cars	Total
Area type, 2006				
Great Britain	25	44	32	100
London	38	46	16	100
Metropolitan areas	31	42	26	100
Other urban areas with population:				
Over 250,000	23	45	32	100
25,000 - 250,000	24	45	31	100
10,000 - 25,000	23	45	33	100
3,000 - 10,000	20	42	38	100
Rural areas	11	38	51	100

1 Includes cars and light vans normally available to the household.
2 Based on combined survey data sources - Family Expenditure Survey, ONS, General Household Survey, ONS, National Survey DfT.

Sources: Office for National Statistics;
Department for Transport 020 7944 3097

15.13 Vehicles with current licences[1]
Northern Ireland

Numbers

		1996	1997	1998	1999	2000	2001[5]	2002	2003	2004	2005	2006
Private light goods, etc	KNKA	540 083	575 923	584 706	608 316	615 180	644 968	666 731	711 913	737 198	765 061	800 969
Motorcycles, Scooters and mopeds	KNKB	10 026	10 932	11 663	13 087	14 116	15 205	17 598	23 820	24 533	25 998	27 083
Public road passenger vehicles[2]:												
Taxis,buses,coaches	KNKD	..	..	..	..	..	..	..	..	−	..	..
Buses, coaches (9 seats or more)	KNKE	2 090	2 144	2 175	2 204	2 266	2 315	2 322	2 353	2 378	2 566	2 670
Total	KNKC	2 090	2 144	2 175	2 204	2 266	2 315	2 322	2 353	2 378	2 566	2 670
General (HGV) goods vehicles:	KNKF	17 401	18 172	18 312	17 075	17 864	19 415	20 244	22 100	23 062	23 517	24 806
Agricultural tractors and engines, etc[3]	KNKM	5 911	6 378	5 906	5 505	5 048	4 901	5 731	7 503	8 674	9 584	10 586
Other	KNKN	1 019	1 188	1 193	1 446	1 287	1 366	1 347	1 671	1 794	1 898	2 039
Vehicles exempt from duty:												
Government owned	KNKP	3 753	3 705	3 785	4 032	3 822	6 427	6 383	6 172	6 116	6 367	7 315
Other:												
Ambulances	KNKQ	371	389	425	417	452	318	299	325	355	355	388
Fire engines	KNKR	292	291	285	286	290	181	174	170	178	179	166
Other exempt[4]	KNKS	58 340	64 447	66 981	68 277	70 405	72 209	73 648	76 715	78 973	81 874	82 655
Total	KNKO	62 756	68 832	71 476	73 012	74 969	79 135	80 504	83 382	85 622	88 775	90 524
Total	KNKT	639 286	683 569	695 431	720 645	730 730	767 305	794 477	852 742	883 261	917 399	958 677

1 Licences current at 31 December.
2 Tax class change from 'Hackney' to 'Bus' with effect from July 2005. Only Vehicles with 9 or more seats are included in 'Bus' class. Vehicles with 8 seats or less previously recorded in ' Hackney ' class moved into 'Private Light Goods' class.
3 Owned by a farmer and availalble for hauling produce and requisites for his farm.
4 Changes in the Mobility Allowance (DWP) have contributed to the increase in Other exempt.
5 Taxation classes have been revised.

Source: Driver and Vehicle Agency: 028 7034 6903

15.14 New vehicle registrations
Northern Ireland

Numbers

		1996	1997	1998	1999	2000	2001	2002	2003	2004	2005	2006
Private cars	KNLA	77 817	83 968	91 141	89 078	84 973	88 592	83 402	87 506	85 190	86 366	91 224
Motorcycles	KNLB	2 803	3 376	4 307	5 310	6 010	5 591	5 596	6 804	4 601	4 648	4 289
Public road passenger vehicles	KNLC	724	714	486	568	565	451	439	609	467	621	677
Goods vehicles:												
General haulage vehicles:												
Under 3.5 tonnes	KNLH	7 232	8 468	10 107	11 054	12 617	13 274	12 007	11 492	11 090	12 300	13 457
3.5 tonnes and over	KNLJ	3 492	3 521	3 572	3 697	3 502	4 534	3 669	4 059	3 987	3 768	4 080
Agricultural tractors[1]	KNLM	1 292	1 364	971	987	1 313	301	1	9	2	2	8
Vehicles exempt from duty	KNLR	10 520	10 885	10 718	11 083	10 789	12 126	12 515	11 907	12 881	13 987	13 031
General haulage and special types	JTAG	..	..	..	..	..	..	15	12	11	16	32
Total	KNLS	103 880	112 296	121 302	121 777	119 769	124 869	117 644	122 398	118 229	121 708	126 798

1 Agricultural tractors driven on public roads. From April 2001 tractors were exempt.

Source: Driver and Vehicle Agency : 028 7034 6903

Transport and communications

15.15 Local bus services: passenger journeys by area: 1995/96-2005/06[1]

Millions

		1996/97	1997/98	1998/99	1999/00	2000/01	2001/02	2002/03	2003/04	2004/05	2005/06	2006/07
Great Britain	ZCET	4 455	4 429	4 350	4 376	4 420	4 455	4 550	4 681	4 737	4 791	4 972
London	KILS	1 230	1 281	1 266	1 294	1 347	1 422	1 527	1 692	1 802	1 881	1 993
English Metropolitan Counties	KILT	1 310	1 292	1 256	1 213	1 203	1 196	1 182	1 162	1 128	1 111	1 109
English other areas	KILU	1 304	1 286	1 286	1 297	1 292	1 263	1 255	1 233	1 210	1 204	1 269
All outside London	ZCES	3 225	3 148	3 084	3 082	3 073	3 033	3 023	2 989	2 935	2 910	2 979
England	ZCER	3 844	3 859	3 808	3 804	3 842	3 881	3 964	4 087	4 140	4 196	4 371
Scotland	KILV	478	448	424	455	458	466	471	478	479	477	482
Wales	KILW	133	122	118	117	119	108	115	116	118	118	119

1 Previous years figures have been revised.

Source: Department for Transport 020 7944 3076

15.16 Local bus services: fare indices: by area
Current prices

Indices (1995=100)

		1996/97	1997/98	1998/99	1999/00	2000/01	2001/02	2002/03	2003/04	2004/05	2005/06	2006/07
Great Britain	KNEU	106.2	112.1	117.1	121.8	126.4	130.6	134.5	139.2	146.5	157.5	159.0
London	KNEP	105.5	109.4	113.8	117.2	117.3	115.5	114.8	116.9	126.8	139.7	151.5
English Metropolitan Counties	KILD	106.4	112.8	117.9	123.5	128.6	135.5	140.7	146.7	153.3	166.0	168.3
English other areas	KILE	106.2	112.0	117.3	122.6	129.2	136.1	142.4	149.0	155.9	166.2	159.5
All outside London	ZCEQ	106.5	112.9	118.2	123.2	129.0	135.1	140.4	146.0	152.3	162.2	160.7
England	ZCEP	106.0	111.5	116.4	121.4	125.8	130.3	134.3	139.4	147.2	159.4	160.1
Scotland	KILF	107.8	116.2	121.2	124.1	129.1	131.1	133.8	136.1	140.0	143.9	151.0
Wales	KILG	103.6	109.6	116.0	121.9	128.4	135.7	142.3	147.2	153.7	159.9	169.7
Retail Prices Index (1995=100)	KNEV	103.1	106.5	109.9	111.6	114.9	116.6	119.1	122.4	126.2	129.5	134.4

Source: Department for Transport 020 7944 3076

15.17 Road accident casualties: by road user type and severity
Great Britain

Numbers

		1996	1997	1998	1999	2000	2001	2002	2003	2004	2005	2006
Child pedestrians[1]:												
Killed	ZCDH	131	138	103	107	107	107	79	74	77	63	71
Killed or seriously injured	KIJS	4 132	3 954	3 737	3 457	3 226	3 144	2 828	2 381	2 339	2 134	2 025
All severities	ZCDI	18 510	18 407	17 971	16 876	16 184	15 819	14 231	12 544	12 234	11 250	10 131
Adult pedestrians[2]:												
Killed	ZCDJ	858	835	803	760	750	712	688	695	589	604	602
Killed or seriously injured	KIJT	7 300	6 925	6 592	6 221	6 112	5 745	5 644	5 422	5 005	4 847	4 894
All severities	ZCDK	26 827	26 223	25 827	24 806	24 481	23 463	23 258	22 531	21 404	20 725	19 774
Child pedal cyclists[1]:												
Killed	ZCDL	54	33	32	36	27	25	22	18	25	20	31
Killed or seriously injured	KIJU	1 231	1 016	915	950	758	674	594	595	577	527	503
All severities	ZCDM	8 217	7 899	6 930	7 290	6 260	5 451	4 809	4 769	4 682	4 286	3 765
Adult pedal cyclists[2]:												
Killed	ZCDN	148	150	126	135	98	111	107	95	109	127	115
Killed or seriously injured	KIJV	2 517	2 542	2 345	2 172	1 954	1 951	1 801	1 776	1 697	1 787	1 898
All severities	ZCDO	15 778	16 181	15 326	14 834	13 630	12 974	11 712	11 643	11 366	11 637	11 911
Motorcyclists[3] and passengers:												
Killed	ZCDP	440	509	498	547	605	583	609	693	585	569	599
Killed or seriously injured	ZCDQ	6 208	6 446	6 442	6 908	7 374	7 305	7 500	7 652	6 648	6 508	6 484
All severities	BMDH	23 133	24 492	24 610	26 192	28 212	28 810	28 353	28 411	25 641	24 824	23 326
Car drivers and passengers:												
Killed	ZCDS	1 806	1 795	1 696	1 687	1 665	1 749	1 747	1 769	1 671	1 675	1 612
Killed or seriously injured	ZCDT	24 048	23 191	21 676	20 368	19 719	19 424	18 728	17 291	16 144	14 617	14 254
All severities	ZCDU	205 336	211 448	210 474	205 735	206 799	202 802	197 425	188 342	183 858	178 302	171 000
Bus/coach drivers and passengers:												
Killed	ZCDV	11	14	18	11	15	14	19	11	20	9	19
Killed or seriously injured	KCUZ	695	601	631	611	578	562	551	500	488	363	426
All severities	ZCDW	9 345	9 439	9 839	10 252	10 088	9 884	9 005	9 068	8 820	7 920	7 253
LGV drivers and passengers:												
Killed	ZCDX	61	64	67	65	66	64	70	72	62	54	52
Killed or seriously injured	ZCDY	989	928	949	867	813	811	780	765	631	587	564
All severities	ZCDZ	7 215	7 476	7 672	7 124	7 007	7 304	7 007	6 897	6 166	6 048	5 914
HGV drivers and passengers:												
Killed	ZCEA	63	45	60	52	55	54	63	44	47	55	39
Killed or seriously injured	ZCEB	555	573	560	540	571	500	524	429	406	395	383
All severities	ZCEC	3 245	3 302	3 444	3 484	3 597	3 388	3 178	3 061	2 883	2 843	2 530
All road users[4]:												
Killed	BMDC	3 598	3 599	3 421	3 423	3 409	3 450	3 431	3 508	3 221	3 201	3 172
Killed or seriously injured	ZCEE	48 097	46 583	44 255	42 545	41 564	40 560	39 407	37 215	34 351	32 155	31 845
All severities	BMDA	320 578	327 803	325 212	320 310	320 283	313 309	302 605	290 607	280 840	271 017	258 404

1 Casualities aged 0 - 15.
2 Casualties aged 16 and over.
3 Includes mopeds and scooters.
4 Includes other motor or non-motor vehicle users, and unknown road user type and casualty age.

Source: Department for Transport 020 7944 3078

15.18 Freight transport by road: goods moved by goods vehicles over 3.5 tonnes[1]
Great Britain

Billion tonne kilometres

		1996	1997	1998	1999	2000	2001	2002	2003	2004[2]	2005[2]	2006[2]
By mode of working												
Mainly public haulage	KNND	109.1	112.2	114.3	110.9	113.0	114.7	110.6	114.3	110.8	109.7	112.1
Mainly own account	KNNC	37.7	37.4	37.6	38.3	37.5	34.7	39.2	37.4	41.4	43.0	43.6
All modes	KNNB	146.8	149.6	151.9	149.2	150.5	149.4	149.8	151.7	152.2	152.7	155.8
By gross weight of vehicle												
Rigid vehicles:												
Over 3.5 tonnes to 17 tonnes	ZCIL	19.5	19.2	17.8	17.9	15.8	13.1	11.9	10.1	9.1	8.1	7.3
Over 17 tonnes to 25 tonnes	ZCIM	5.3	4.7	4.2	4.3	4.8	5.7	6.3	6.8	7.9	8.3	8.7
Over 25 tonnes	ZCIN	13.5	14.3	14.7	15.3	15.4	15.6	17.3	18.3	18.9	20.3	20.9
All rigids	ZCIO	38.3	38.1	36.6	37.5	36.0	34.5	35.6	35.2	35.9	36.7	36.8
Articulated vehicles:												
Over 3.5 tonnes to 33 tonnes	ZCIP	15.9	14.3	14.4	14.0	14.0	12.8	9.9	8.8	7.0	6.3	6.2
Over 33 tonnes	ZCIQ	92.6	97.1	100.9	97.7	100.4	102.1	104.4	107.7	109.4	109.7	112.8
All articulated vehicles	ZCIR	108.5	111.4	115.3	111.7	114.4	114.9	114.3	116.5	116.4	116.0	118.9
All vehicles												
Over 3.5 tonnes to 25 tonnes	ZCIS	25.3	24.3	22.5	22.7	21.3	19.3	18.7	17.3	17.3	16.7	16.4
Over 25 tonnes	KNNG	121.5	125.2	129.4	126.5	129.2	130.1	131.1	134.4	134.9	136.0	139.4
All weights	ZCIT	146.8	149.6	151.9	149.2	150.5	149.4	149.8	151.7	152.2	152.7	155.8
By commodity												
Food, drink and tobacco	ZCIU	39.3	40.8	42.5	41.5	44.3	41.4	43.1	42.2	41.7	40.6	42.0
Wood, timber and cork	ZCIV	3.8	3.5	3.6	3.8	3.7	3.9	3.8	4.1	4.5	4.7	4.1
Fertiliser	ZCIW	1.5	1.3	1.2	1.4	1.2	1.2	1.2	1.2	0.8	1.1	0.8
Crude minerals	ZCIX	13.5	13.6	13.3	12.7	12.4	13.0	13.9	13.8	14.1	14.8	15.6
Ores	ZCIY	1.3	1.1	1.1	1.3	1.2	1.2	1.1	1.2	1.4	1.7	1.3
Crude materials	ZCIZ	2.1	2.1	2.6	2.6	2.6	2.3	2.7	2.3	3.3	2.4	2.7
Coal and coke	ZCJA	2.5	2.7	2.0	2.2	1.5	2.1	1.5	1.5	1.2	1.5	1.3
Petrol and petroleum products	ZCJB	6.1	5.8	5.2	5.0	6.4	5.8	5.2	5.5	5.7	5.5	5.7
Chemicals	ZCJC	7.7	8.2	7.9	7.4	6.8	7.2	6.5	6.8	6.3	7.6	6.1
Building materials	ZCJD	9.6	11.1	10.7	10.6	10.6	11.7	10.9	12.0	12.1	10.9	11.6
Iron and steel products	ZCJE	7.2	7.9	7.7	6.8	6.8	5.7	5.3	5.4	5.4	5.2	4.7
Other metal products	ZCJF	1.7	1.5	1.7	1.7	1.7	1.4	1.5	1.5	1.9	2.1	2.2
Machinery and transport equipment	ZCJG	7.7	8.4	9.1	8.7	9.1	8.9	8.5	8.7	8.9	9.3	9.4
Miscellaneous manufactures	ZCJH	14.2	14.2	15.9	15.7	15.1	15.4	16.2	15.8	16.3	15.5	16.3
Miscellaneous transactions	ZCJI	28.4	26.8	27.5	27.9	27.1	28.2	28.4	29.5	28.8	29.8	31.8
All commodities	ZCJJ	146.8	149.6	151.9	149.2	150.5	149.4	149.8	151.7	152.2	152.7	155.8

1 Rigid vehicles or articulated vehicles (tractive unit and trailer) with gross vehicle weight over 3.5 tonnes.

2 Figures for 2004 , 2005 and 2006 are not fully comparable with those for 2003 and earlier years. Detailed comparisons should therefore be made with caution.

Source: Department for Transport 020 7944 3093

15.19 Freight transport by road: goods lifted by goods vehicles over 3.5 tonnes[1]
Great Britain

Million tonnes

		1996	1997	1998	1999	2000	2001	2002	2003	2004[2]	2005[2]	2006[2]
By mode of working												
Mainly public haulage	ZCJK	1 011	1 044	1 041	991	1 038	1 052	1 019	1 053	1 101	1 079	1 123
Mainly own account	ZCJL	618	599	589	576	556	529	608	590	643	667	686
All modes	ZCJM	1 628	1 643	1 630	1 567	1 593	1 581	1 627	1 643	1 744	1 746	1 810
By gross weight of vehicle												
Rigid vehicles:												
Over 3.5 tonnes to 17 tonnes	ZCJN	306	294	268	254	229	203	188	159	160	135	130
Over 17 tonnes to 25 tonnes	ZCJO	133	120	106	86	87	86	90	100	113	118	121
Over 25 tonnes	ZCJP	371	380	401	408	424	443	491	506	539	559	597
All rigids	ZCJQ	811	793	776	748	741	733	768	765	812	812	849
Articulated vehicles:												
Over 3.5 tonnes to 33 tonnes	ZCJR	138	124	125	113	107	97	81	69	60	51	51
Over 33 tonnes	ZCJS	679	726	729	706	746	751	778	809	872	883	910
All articulated vehicles	ZCJT	817	850	854	819	852	848	859	878	932	934	961
All vehicles												
Over 3.5 tonnes to 25 tonnes	ZCJU	447	419	382	346	325	294	283	265	277	257	257
Over 25 tonnes	ZCJV	1 181	1 224	1 248	1 221	1 268	1 287	1 343	1 378	1 467	1 489	1 553
All weights	ZCJW	1 628	1 643	1 630	1 567	1 593	1 581	1 627	1 643	1 744	1 746	1 810
By commodity												
Food, drink and tobacco	ZCJX	326	342	346	333	346	321	339	333	351	339	358
Wood, timber and cork	ZCJY	27	26	27	28	26	28	28	32	42	36	30
Fertiliser	ZCJZ	13	10	9	11	10	9	11	12	7	14	7
Crude minerals	ZCKA	320	329	327	297	308	298	333	327	364	370	381
Ores	ZCKB	18	25	18	20	16	16	17	21	22	23	19
Crude materials	ZCKC	18	17	20	20	18	20	21	19	25	22	23
Coal and coke	ZCKD	32	37	26	28	22	21	17	22	14	21	15
Petrol and petroleum products	ZCKE	75	73	61	61	75	74	59	64	67	70	69
Chemicals	ZCKF	51	53	53	47	49	50	41	47	46	53	48
Building materials	ZCKG	142	156	161	159	165	165	167	165	185	169	180
Iron and steel products	ZCKH	52	55	54	48	49	44	39	41	43	42	41
Other metal products	ZCKI	15	16	18	17	16	14	14	16	19	19	22
Machinery and transport equipment	ZCKJ	59	71	73	67	69	70	68	66	70	76	79
Miscellaneous manufactures	ZCKK	88	90	96	91	97	97	105	98	111	109	112
Miscellaneous transactions	ZCKL	393	343	342	340	328	353	367	379	378	384	426
All commodities	ZCKM	1 628	1 643	1 630	1 567	1 593	1 581	1 627	1 643	1 744	1 746	1 810

1 Rigid vehicles or articulated vehicles (tractive unit and trailer) with gross vehicle weight over 3.5 tonnes.

2 Figures for 2004, 2005 and 2006 are not fully comparable with those for 2003 and earlier years. Detailed comparison should therefore be made with caution.

Source: Department for Transport 020 7944 3093

15.20 Rail systems summary

		1996/97	1997/98	1998/99	1999/00	2000/01	2001/02	2002/03	2003/04	2004/05	2005/06	2006/07
Passenger journeys (millions)												
National Rail network[1]	ZCKN	801	846	892	931	957	960	976	1 012	1 045	1 082	1 164
London Underground	KNOE	772	832	866	927	970	953	942	948	976	970	1 040
Docklands Light Railway	ZCKO	17	21	28	31	38	41	46	48	50	54	64
Glasgow Underground	ZCKP	14	14	15	15	14	14	13	13	13	13	13
Tyne and Wear Metro[2]	ZCKQ	35	35	34	33	33	33	37	38	37	36	38
Blackpool trams[3]	EL9L	5	5	4	4	4	5	4	4	4	4	3
Manchester Metrolink[4]	ZCKS	13	14	13	14	17	18	19	19	20	20	20
Midland Metro[5]	ZCKR	–	–	–	5	5	5	5	5	5	5	5
Croydon Tramlink[6]	GEOE	–	–	–	–	15	18	19	20	22	23	25
Sheffield Supertram	ZCKT	8	9	10	11	11	11	12	12	13	13	14
Nottingham NET[7]	C3MI	–	–	–	–	–	–	–	–	8	10	10
All rail	ZCKU	1 665	1 776	1 862	1 971	2 065	2 059	2 072	2 119	2 193	2 229	2 396
All light rail	GENZ	92	98	104	113	138	146	154	160	172	177	192
Passenger revenue (£ million at current prices)												
National Rail network	KNDL	2 573	2 821	3 089	3 368	3 413	3 548	3 663	3 901	4 158	4 493	5 038
London Underground	KNOA	797	899	977	1 058	1 129	1 151	1 138	1 161	1 241	1 309	1 417
Docklands Light Railway	ZCKV	12	14	20	22	29	32	36	37	40	46	54
Glasgow Underground	ZCKW	8	9	9	10	10	10	10	10	11	11	14
Tyne and Wear Metro	ZCKX	21	22	23	24	24	25	29	31	33	34	40
Blackpool trams	EL9M	4	5	4	4	4	5	5	4	4	4	5
Manchester Metrolink	ZCKZ	13	14	..	..	18	20	20	21	22	23	24
Midland Metro	ZCKY	–	–	–	..	3	4	5	5	5	6	7
Croydon Tramlink	GEOF	–	–	–	–	12	13	15	16	18	19	21
Sheffield Supertram	ZCLA	5	6	6	7	7	8	10	9	11	10	13
Nottingham NET	C3MJ	–	–	–	–	–	–	–	..	6	7	8
All rail	ZCLB	3 433	3 790	4 128	4 493	4 650	4 815	4 931	5 197	5 550	5 963	6 640
All light rail	GEOA	63	70	62	68	108	117	130	135	151	161	185
Passenger kilometres (millions)												
National Rail network	KNDZ	32 100	34 700	36 280	38 472	38 179	39 141	39 678	40 937	41 762	43 211	46 497
London Underground	KNOI	6 153	6 479	6 716	7 171	7 470	7 451	7 367	7 340	7 606	7 586	7 947
Docklands Light Railway	ZCLC	86	103	144	172	200	207	232	235	245	257	301
Glasgow Underground	ZCLD	40	45	47	47	46	44	43	43	43	42	42
Tyne and Wear Metro	ZCLE	254	249	238	230	229	238	275	284	283	279	295
Blackpool trams	EL9N	..	..	..	13	13	15	14	11	12	11	10
Manchester Metrolink	ZCLG	86	88	117	126	152	161	167	169	204	206	208
Midland Metro	ZCLF	–	–	–	50	56	50	50	54	52	54	51
Croydon Tramlink	GEOG	–	–	–	–	96	99	100	105	112	117	128
Sheffield Supertram	ZCLH	29	34	35	37	38	39	40	42	44	44	42
Nottingham NET	C3MK	–	–	–	–	–	–	–	2	37	42	43
All rail	ZCLI	38 748	41 698	43 577	46 318	46 479	47 446	47 965	49 222	50 401	51 849	55 564
All light rail	GEOB	495	519	581	675	830	854	920	945	1 033	1 052	1 120
Route kilometres open for passenger traffic (numbers)												
National Rail network[8]	ZCLJ	15 034	15 024	15 038	15 038	15 042	15 042	15 042	14 883	14 328	14 356	14 353
London Underground	ZCLK	392	392	392	408	408	408	408	408	408	408	408
Docklands Light Railway	ZCLM	22	22	22	26	26	26	26	26	26	30	31
Glasgow Underground	ZCLN	11	11	11	11	11	11	11	11	11	10	10
Tyne and Wear Metro	ZCLO	59	59	59	59	59	78	78	78	78	78	78
Blackpool trams	EL9O	18	18	18	18	18	18	18	18	18	18	18
Manchester Metrolink	ZCLQ	31	31	31	39	39	39	39	39	39	39	39
Midland Metro	ZCLP	–	–	–	20	20	20	20	20	20	20	20
Croydon Tramlink	GEOH	–	–	–	–	28	28	28	28	28	28	28
Sheffield Supertram	ZCLR	29	29	29	29	29	29	29	29	29	29	29
Nottingham NET	C3ML	–	–	–	–	–	–	–	14	14	15	14
All rail	ZCLS	15 596	15 586	15 600	15 648	15 680	15 699	15 699	15 554	14 999	15 032	15 028
All light rail	GEOC	170	170	170	202	230	249	249	263	263	268	267
Stations served (numbers)												
National Rail network	ZCLT	2 498	2 495	2 499	2 503	2 508	2 508	2 508	2 507	2 508	2 510	2 520
London Underground	KNOO	245	245	246	253	253	253	253	253	253	253	253
Docklands Light Railway	ZCLU	28	29	29	34	34	34	34	34	34	38	34
Glasgow Underground	ZCLV	15	15	15	15	15	15	15	15	15	15	15
Tyne and Wear Metro	ZCLW	46	46	46	46	46	58	58	58	58	59	59
Blackpool trams	EL9P	124	124	124	124	124	124	124	124	124	124	121
Manchester Metrolink	ZCLY	26	26	26	36	36	36	37	37	37	37	37
Midland Metro	ZCLX	–	–	–	23	23	23	23	23	23	23	23
Croydon Tramlink	GEOI	–	–	–	–	38	38	38	38	38	39	39
Sheffield Supertram	ZCLZ	45	46	47	47	47	48	48	48	48	48	48
Nottingham NET	C3MM	–	–	–	–	–	–	–	23	23	23	23
All rail	ZCLL	3 027	3 026	3 032	3 081	3 124	3 137	3 138	3 160	3 161	3 169	3 172
All light rail	GSOC	284	286	287	325	363	376	377	400	400	406	399

1 Franchised train operating companies from Feb 1996 after privatisation.
2 Tyne & Wear Metro extension to Sunderland opened in March 2002.
3 Blackpool Trams shown as a self-contained system.
4 Transfer of 20 stations from the rail network to Manchester Metrolink.
5 Midland Metro opened in 1999.
6 Croydon Tramlink opened in 2000.
7 Nottingham Express Transit opened in March 2004.
8 Break in series due to change in methodology.

Sources: Department for Transport: 020 7944 3076;
Network Rail, former Railtrack, ORR, TfL, light rail operators and PTEs

15.21 National railways freight
Great Britain

Billion tonne kilometres

		1996[2] /97	1997 /98	1998 /99	1999 /00	2000 /01	2001 /02	2002 /03	2003 /04	2004 /05	2005 /06	2006 /07
Freight moved by commodity[1]												
Coal	ZCGG	3.9	4.4	4.5	4.8	4.8	6.2	5.7	5.8	6.7	8.3	8.8
Metals	ZCGH	..	..	2.1	2.2	2.1	2.4	2.7	2.4	2.6	2.2	2.1
Construction	ZCGI	..	..	2.1	2.0	2.4	2.8	2.5	2.7	2.9	2.9	2.7
Oil and petroleum	ZCGJ	..	..	1.6	1.5	1.4	1.2	1.2	1.2	1.2	1.2	1.5
Other traffic	ZCGK	11.2	12.5	7.1	7.6	7.4	6.7	6.6	6.8	7.0	7.1	7.0
All traffic	VOXD	15.1	16.9	17.3	18.2	18.1	19.4	18.5	18.9	20.4	21.7	22.1

Million tonnes

		1996 /97	1997 /98	1998 /99	1999 /00	2000 /01	2001 /02	2002 /03	2003 /04	2004 /05	2005 /06	2006 /07
Freight lifted by commodity[6]												
Coal	ZCGL	52.2	50.3	45.3	35.9[3]	35.3	39.5	34.0	35.2	44.0[4]	48.9[5]	48.8
Metals	ZCGM	..	..	..	..	..	..	..	..	..	..	..
Construction	ZCGN	..	..	..	..	..	..	..	..	..	..	..
Oil and petroleum	ZCGO	..	..	..	..	..	..	..	..	..	..	..
Other traffic	ZCGP	49.6	55.1	56.8	60.6[3]	60.3	54.5	53.0	53.7	57.1[4]	58.7[5]	59.6
All traffic	VOXE	101.8	105.4	102.1	96.5[3]	95.6	93.9	87.0	88.9	101.1[4]	107.6[5]	108.4

1 Revised series on new basis from 1998/99.
2 Owing to changes in the way freight traffic has been estimated following privatisation, data since 1996/97 are not comparable to those for previous years. Freight excludes parcels and materials carried for rail infrastructure..
3 Break in series from 1999/2000.
4 Break in series, increase largely due to changes in data collection method.
5 Break in series due to change in coverage.
6 Goods lifted data from 1999 onwards have been revised since last TSGB publication.

Source: Department for Transport: 020 7944 4977

15.22 Railways: permanent way and rolling stock
Northern Ireland

At end of year

Numbers

		1996	1997	1998	1999	2000	2001	2002	2003	2004	2005	2006
Length of road open for traffic[1] (Km)	KNRA	335	335	335	335	356	334	334	334	299	299	299
Length of track open for traffic (Km)												
Total	KNRB	506	506	526	526	547	480	480	480	445	445	445
Running lines	KNRC	464	464	484	484	505	464	464	464	427	427	427
Sidings (as single track)	KNRD	42	42	42	42	42	16	16	16	18	18	18
Locomotives												
Diesel-electrics	KNRE	8	6	5	6	6	6	6	5	6	5	5
Passenger carrying vehicles												
Total	KNRF	112	112	120	105	105	106	100	100	102	124	125
Rail motor vehicles:												
Diesel-electric, etc	KNRG	30	30	28	30	30	29	28	28	28	70	85
Trailer carriages:												
Total locomotive hauled	KNRH	28	28	38	21	21	25	22	22	22	22	22
Ordinary coaches	KNRI	26	26	36	19	19	23	20	20	20	20	20
Restaurant cars	KNRJ	2	2	2	2	2	2	2	2	2	2	2
Rail car trailers	KNRK	54	54	54	54	54	52	50	50	52	32	18
Rolling stock for maintenance and repair	KNRT	41	41	26	18	18	18	18	39	46	48	48

1 The total length of railroad open for traffic irrespective of the number of tracks comprising the road.

Sources: Department for Regional Development;
Northern Ireland: 028 9054 0800

Transport and communications

15.23 Operating statistics of railways
Northern Ireland

		Unit	1996	1997	1998	1999	2000	2001	2002	2003	2004	2005	2006
Maintenance of way and works													
Material used:													
Ballast	KNSA	Thousand m²	27.0	51.3	38.5	40.0	47.0	80.0	40.0	130.0	70.0	90.0	30.0
Rails	KNSB	Thousand tonnes	2.1	0.4	2.5	3.0	3.5	2.5	1.0	4.5	1.0	3.2	1.0
Sleepers	KNSC	Thousands	27.5	5.1	32.0	30.0	40.0	50.0	5.0	40.0	28.0	45.0	2.0
Track renewed	KNSD	Km	20.0	2.4	22.5	7.0	29.0	15.0	5.0	25.8	2.0	29.0	1.0
New Track laid	KPGD	Km	–	–	–	–	21.0	–	–	–	–	–	–
Engine kilometres													
Total[1]	KNSE	Thousand Km	4 100	4 100	4 100	4 100	4 100	4 056	4 056	4 170	4 110	3 610	3 900
Train kilometres:													
Total	KNSF	"	3 670	3 670	3 670	3 670	3 670	3 626	3 626	3 704	3 610	3 610	3 900
Coaching	KNSG	"	3 666	3 666	3 666	3 666	3 666	3 622	3 622	3 700	3 610	3 610	3 900
Freight	KNSH	"	4	4	4	4	4	4	4	4	–	–	–

1 Including shunting, assisting, light, departmental, maintenance and repair.

Sources: Department for Regional Development;
Northern Ireland: 028 9054 0800

15.24 Main output of United Kingdom airlines

Available tonne kilometres (millions)

		1997	1998	1999	2000	2001	2002	2003	2004	2005	2006	2007
All services	KNTA	35 538	40 021	42 002	43 379	42 370	40 550	42 784	43 883	48 186	50 391	54 181
Percentage growth on previous year	KNTB	10.3	12.5	5.0	3.6	–2.4	–4.3	5.5	2.6	9.8	4.4	7.5
Scheduled services	KNTC	26 504	29 756	31 815	32 938	31 866	30 433	31 513	32 422	36 937	38 590	40 971
Percentage growth on previous year	KNTD	11.4	12.3	6.9	3.5	–3.3	–4.5	3.6	2.9	13.9	4.5	6.2
Non-scheduled services	KNTE	9 034	10 265	10 186	10 440	10 505	10 117	11 271	11 461	11 249	11 801	13 209
Percentage growth on previous year	KNTF	7.3	13.3	–0.7	4.1	0.6	–3.7	11.4	1.7	–1.8	4.3	11.9

Source: Civil Aviation Authority: 020 7453 6246

15.25 Air traffic between the United Kingdom and abroad[1]

Thousands

		1997	1998	1999	2000	2001	2002	2003	2004	2005	2006	2007
Flights												
United Kingdom airlines												
Scheduled services	KNUA	410.3	443.7	480.9	520.3	536.7	531.3	517.7	546.5	584.2	596.3	621.9
Non-scheduled services	KNUB	208.2	218.7	212.6	216.2	208.5	218.6	211.0	198.6	200.6	209.6	207.1
Overseas airlines[2]												
Scheduled services	KNUC	399.6	426.4	467.6	467.6	496.8	487.5	487.0	544.2	584.5	629.5	656.9
Non-scheduled services	KNUD	32.5	34.8	31.7	31.7	26.0	36.7	27.1	28.8	33.7	28.4	27.2
Total	KNUE	1 050.6	1 123.6	1 192.8	1 235.8	1 268.0	1 274.1	1 242.8	1 318.1	1 403.0	1 463.8	1 513.1
Passengers carried												
United Kingdom airlines												
Scheduled services	KNUF	41 854.7	46 747.7	50 148.5	54 522.8	53 591.7	54 360.0	56 476.7	63 216.1	69 106.2	72 196.4	76 959.9
Non-scheduled services	KNUG	28 699.5	31 616.6	32 603.8	33 185.9	34 009.1	33 935.7	33 385.6	32 195.7	30 179.4	29 725.5	28 524.0
Overseas airlines[2]												
Scheduled services	KNUH	39 900.7	42 554.5	46 628.0	46 627.9	51 107.8	51 317.6	54 504.0	60 278.0	67 634.9	74 670.8	79 820.1
Non-scheduled services	KNUI	4 413.0	4 569.7	4 156.5	4 156.5	3 966.1	3 956.3	3 947.1	4 068.3	4 169.1	4 107.7	3 803.3
Total	KNUJ	114 867.9	125 488.5	133 536.8	138 493.1	142 674.7	143 569.6	148 313.4	159 758.1	171 089.6	180 700.4	189 107.3

1 Excludes travel to and from the Channel Islands.
2 Includes airlines of overseas UK Territories.

Source: Civil Aviation Authority: 020 7453 6246

15.26

Operations and traffic on scheduled services: revenue traffic
United Kingdom airlines[1]

		Unit	1997	1998	1999	2000	2001	2002	2003	2004	2005	2006	2007
All services													
Aircraft stage flights:													
Number	KNFA	Numbers	749 806	797 682	835 031	878 582	921 556	911 518	895 095	926 498	1 016 354	1 037 729	1 052 799
Average length	KNFB	Kilometres	1 079	1 111	1 134	1 156	1 138	1 149	1 215	1 227	1 304	1 349	1 400
Aircraft-kilometres flown	KNFC	Millions	809	886	947	1 016	1 049	1 047	1 088	1 137	1 325	1 400	1 474
Passengers uplifted	KNFD	"	56	62	65	70	70	72	76	83	94	98	102
Seat-kilometres used	KNFE	"	136 388	151 969	160 336	170 469	158 651	156 494	164 806	173 722	200 460	213 442	227 720
Cargo uplifted:[2]	KNFF	Tonnes	782 855	831 436	860 291	897 184	742 705	768 736	800 645	842 912	921 412	946 365	941 421
Tonne-kilometres used:		Millions											
Passenger	KNFH	"	13 287	14 755	15 518	16 507	15 258	15 035	15 419	15 580	15 044	16 090	17 246
Freight	KNFI	"	4 454	4 663	4 925	5 160	4 548	4 941	5 187	5 297	5 998	6 213	6 199
Mail	KNFJ	"	172	178	153	179	102	57	55	75	90	99	112
Total	KNFG	"	17 913	19 596	20 596	21 846	19 908	20 032	20 660	20 952	21 133	22 402	23 557
Domestic services													
Aircraft stage flights:													
Number	KNFK	Numbers	336 218	352 936	354 864	353 525	365 881	359 400	345 954	373 858	394 069	399 438	383 591
Average length	KNFL	Kilometres	330	333	337	344	350	350	357	360	374	371	367
Aircraft-kilometres flown	KNFM	Millions	111	118	120	121	128	126	123	135	147	148	140
Passengers uplifted	KNFN	"	16	17	17	18	18	20	21	22	23	23	22
Seat-kilometres used	KNFO	"	6 646	6 948	7 184	7 542	7 645	8 322	8 904	9 263	9 795	9 800	9 449
Cargo uplifted:[2]	KNFP	Tonnes	30 679	31 879	25 964	24 644	19 498	16 755	17 248	14 862	10 015	8 498	7 099
Tonne-kilometres used:		Millions											
Passenger	KNFR	"	569	593	610	640	649	703	738	757	784	759	733
Freight	KNFS	"	6	6	6	6	4	4	3	3	3	2	2
Mail	KNFT	"	6	6	4	4	4	3	3	3	–	1	1
Total	KNFQ	"	581	605	620	650	656	709	744	762	787	762	735
International services													
Aircraft stage flights:													
Number	KNFU	Numbers	413 588	444 746	480 167	525 057	555 675	552 118	549 141	552 640	622 285	638 291	669 208
Average length	KNFV	Kilometres	1 688	1 729	1 723	1 704	1 656	1 670	1 758	2 148	1 893	1 960	1 993
Aircraft-kilometres flown	KNFW	Millions	698	769	827	895	921	921	965	1 002	1 178	1 251	1 333
Passengers uplifted	KNFX	"	40	45	48	52	52	52	56	61	71	75	80
Seat-kilometres used	KNFY	"	129 743	145 022	153 153	162 927	151 006	148 172	155 903	164 459	190 666	203 642	218 271
Cargo uplifted:[2]	KNFZ	Tonnes	752 176	799 557	834 327	872 540	723 206	751 975	783 397	828 051	911 398	937 868	934 323
Tonne-kilometres used:		Millions											
Passenger	KNJX	"	12 718	14 162	14 908	15 867	14 610	14 332	14 681	14 824	14 260	15 331	16 513
Freight	KNJY	"	4 448	4 657	4 919	5 154	4 544	4 937	5 184	5 294	5 995	6 383	6 197
Mail	KNJZ	"	166	172	149	176	98	54	51	72	90	99	111
Total	KNJW	"	17 333	18 991	19 976	21 197	19 252	19 322	19 916	20 190	20 345	21 813	22 822

1 Includes services of British Airways and other UK private companies.
2 Cargo has re-defined as freight and mail.

Source: Civil Aviation Authority: 020 7453 6246

15.27 Accidents on scheduled fixed wing passenger-carrying services[1]
United Kingdom airlines

	Number of fatal accidents	Passenger casualties		Crew casualties		Thousand aircraft stage flights per fatal accident	Million aircraft-kms. flown per fatal accident	Thousand passengers carried per passenger killed	Million passenger kms. flown per passenger killed	Fatal accidents		Passengers killed per hundred million passenger-kms.
		Killed	Seriously injured	Killed	Seriously injured					per 100 000 aircraft stage flights	per hundred million aircraft-kms.	
1950-54	7	194	9	28	4	107.4	61.8	46.1	50.1	0.93	1.62	2.00
1955-59	7	123	28	29	8	158.3	92.1	155.2	158.5	0.63	1.09	0.63
1960-64	5	104	35	21	6	303.7	182.2	373.4	390.6	0.33	0.55	0.26
1965-69	6	273	2	32	2	282.7	194.9	222.2	255.2	0.35	0.51	0.39
1970-74	2	167	5	14	2	889.5	737.1	464.3	657.7	0.11	0.14	0.15
1975-79	1	54	6	9	-	1 773.0	1 523.5	1 688.2	3 239.9	0.06	0.07	0.03
1980-84	-	-	4	-	1	-	-	-	-	-	-	-
1985-89	2	47	79	1	8	1 220.0	1 014.5	3031.0	6 262.9	0.08	0.10	0.02
1990-94	-	-	1	-	9	-	-	-	-	-	-	-
1995-99	1	9	1	3	3	3 699.9	4 026.0	31 265.6	76 539.4	0.03	0.02	0.001
	KCVN	KCVO	KCVP	KCVQ	KCVR							
2000	-	-	1	-	-	-	-	-	-	-	-	-
2001	-	-	-	-	-	-	-	-	-	-	-	-
2002	-	-	-	-	3	-	-	-	-	-	-	-
2003	-	-	1	-	1	-	-	-	-	-	-	-
2004	-	-	2	-	-	-	-	-	-	-	-	-
2005	-	-	-	-	-	-	-	-	-	-	-	-
2006	-	-	-	-	1	-	-	-	-	-	-	-

1 Excluding accidents involving the deaths of third parties only.

Source: Civil Aviation Authority: 01293 573446

15.28 Activity at civil aerodromes
United Kingdom[1]

Thousands and tonnes

		1998	1999	2000	2001	2002	2003	2004	2005	2006	2007
Movement of civil aircraft (thousands)											
Commercial											
Transport	KNQC	1 871	1 959	2 045	2 095	2 094	2 160	2 277	2 406	2 451	2 494
Other[2]	KNQD	162	159	159	150	120	117	116	120	129	124
Total	KNQB	2 033	2 118	2 204	2 245	2 214	2 277	2 393	2 526	2 580	2 609
Non-commercial[3]	KNQE	1 343	1 263	1 186	1 207	1 100	1 186	1 135	1 129	1 059	1 033
Total	KNQA	3 376	3 381	3 390	3 452	3 314	3 463	3 528	3 655	3 639	3 637
Passengers handled											
Terminal	KNQG	158 856	168 363	179 885	181 231	188 761	199 950	215 681	228 214	235 139	240 722
Transit	KNQH	1 226	1 156	1 167	1 087	1 054	990	950	984	1 016	963
Total	KNQF	160 082	169 519	181 052	182 318	189 815	200 940	216 631	229 198	236 155	241 685
Commercial freight handled[4] (tonnes)											
Set down	KNQJ	1 072 127	1 135 065	1 174 635	1 093 142	1 124 026	1 172 552	1 267 411	1 282 724	1 277 177	1 316 359
Picked up	KNQK	1 008 358	1 053 902	1 139 292	1 052 379	1 071 407	1 035 680	1 103 539	1 080 620	1 038 261	1 009 414
Total	KNQI	2 080 485	2 188 967	2 313 927	2 145 521	2 195 433	2 208 232	2 370 950	2 363 344	2 315 438	2 325 773
Mail handled											
Set down	KNQM	88 766	92 974	101 743	98 690	90 738	86 415	108 481	102 344	91 535	102 027
Picked up	KNQN	113 993	114 752	123 352	117 389	99 747	93 096	112 424	110 576	98 391	105 755
Total	KNQL	202 759	207 726	225 095	216 079	190 485	179 511	220 905	212 920	189 926	207 790

1 Figures exclude Channel Island Airports.
2 Local pleasure flights for reward (eg aerial survey work, crop dusting and delivery of empty aircraft) and empty positioning flights.
3 Test and Training flights, Other flights by Air Transport Operators, Aero-club, Private, Official, Military & Business Aviation.

4 With effect from 2001, passengers, freight and mail handled exclude traffic carried on air taxi operations.

Source: Civil Aviation Authority: 020 7453 6258

15.29 United Kingdom ports: foreign, coastwise and one-port traffic

Thousand tonnes

		1996	1997	1998	1999	2000	2001	2002	2003	2004	2005	2006
Foreign												
Liquid bulk traffic												
Imports	EL9Q	59 309	61 060	61 346	56 528	70 788	74 495	62 811	66 447	75 897	76 988	85 530
Exports	EL9R	106 169	104 654	106 041	110 591	118 509	110 321	107 516	100 772	95 974	87 995	82 883
All	EL9S	165 478	165 714	167 387	167 120	189 297	184 816	170 327	167 218	171 871	164 983	168 412
Dry bulk traffic												
Imports	EL9T	63 905	68 208	68 333	65 219	65 652	77 360	67 575	72 644	76 625	87 546	92 846
Exports	EL9U	19 549	19 596	20 840	18 905	19 739	17 206	18 026	20 559	18 098	18 010	18 113
All	EL9V	83 454	87 805	89 173	84 124	85 391	94 565	85 600	93 203	94 722	105 557	110 959
Container and roll-on traffic												
Imports	EL9W	52 008	58 822	61 191	64 272	64 753	65 721	68 371	69 199	75 520	77 431	80 288
Exports	EL9X	43 711	48 805	49 029	49 616	49 323	47 334	47 313	47 291	49 869	51 045	52 801
All	EL9Y	95 719	107 628	110 220	113 889	114 076	113 054	115 685	116 490	125 390	128 476	133 089
Semi-bulk traffic												
Imports	EL9Z	15 987	16 097	16 878	15 967	17 174	17 059	18 523	17 284	18 413	16 766	16 706
Exports	ELA2	5 267	5 142	4 897	4 519	4 411	3 737	3 613	3 848	4 342	5 287	5 299
All	ELA3	21 253	21 239	21 775	20 486	21 584	20 796	22 136	21 131	22 755	22 054	22 005
Conventional traffic												
Imports	ELA4	1 493	1 506	1 531	1 595	2 500	3 730	3 645	3 699	3 990	3 529	3 555
Exports	ELA5	1 094	1 100	854	735	1 145	1 786	1 705	1 535	1 314	1 393	1 456
All	ELA6	2 587	2 607	2 385	2 330	3 645	5 515	5 349	5 234	5 304	4 922	5 012
All foreign traffic												
Imports	ELA7	192 702	205 694	209 279	203 581	220 866	238 364	220 924	229 273	250 445	262 261	278 925
Exports	ELA8	175 790	179 298	181 661	184 367	193 127	180 383	178 173	174 003	169 597	163 731	160 552
All	ELA9	368 492	384 992	390 940	387 948	413 993	418 747	399 097	403 276	420 042	425 992	439 477
Coastwise traffic												
Liquid bulk traffic												
Inwards	ELB2	52 354	49 981	51 514	48 164	36 677	37 008	38 694	36 973	39 236	41 308	35 487
Outwards	ELB3	57 146	53 753	52 622	51 966	41 696	36 049	37 535	35 371	38 788	42 477	33 941
All	ELB4	109 501	103 734	104 136	100 131	78 373	73 058	76 229	72 344	78 024	83 786	69 428
Dry bulk traffic												
Inwards	ELB5	7 613	6 678	7 599	6 792	8 243	8 032	7 245	7 956	6 453	6 717	7 914
Outwards	ELB6	7 942	6 963	7 882	7 229	8 201	7 112	7 785	8 438	7 814	8 366	8 675
All	ELB7	15 555	13 642	15 480	14 021	16 444	15 144	15 030	16 395	14 268	15 083	16 589
Container and roll-on traffic												
Inwards	ELB8	9 623	10 522	11 236	11 542	12 186	11 797	11 854	11 788	12 510	13 241	13 236
Outwards	ELB9	9 716	10 786	10 660	11 396	11 506	11 064	11 341	11 426	12 026	12 995	12 988
All	ELC2	19 339	21 307	21 895	22 938	23 692	22 861	23 195	23 214	24 537	26 236	26 224
Semi-bulk traffic												
Inwards	ELC3	187	166	176	203	247	364	324	373	320	217	351
Outwards	ELC4	251	188	477	221	311	570	546	544	519	565	373
All	ELC5	438	354	653	424	558	934	870	917	838	783	725
Conventional traffic												
Inwards	ELL6	139	161	212	274	96	74	99	194	73	278	167
Outwards	ELM5	261	314	306	285	139	131	124	368	518	451	482
All	ELN2	400	475	518	559	236	206	223	562	591	729	649
All coastwise traffic												
Inwards	ELN3	69 917	67 508	70 736	66 975	57 448	57 276	58 215	57 285	58 592	61 761	57 156
Outwards	ELN4	75 316	72 004	71 946	71 098	61 853	54 926	57 331	56 147	59 665	64 854	56 459
All	ELN5	145 233	139 512	142 682	138 073	119 302	112 202	115 546	113 432	118 257	126 615	113 614

15.29 United Kingdom ports: foreign, coastwise and one-port traffic

continued

Thousand tonnes

		1996	1997	1998	1999	2000	2001	2002	2003	2004	2005	2006
One-port traffic												
Liquid bulk traffic												
Inwards	ELN6	10 861	6 871	10 587	20 220	24 937	18 245	25 886	22 328	19 152	16 169	14 171
Outwards	ELN7	8 847	8 560	4 365	126	485	647	693	563	361	421	336
All	ELN8	19 708	15 431	14 951	20 346	25 422	18 892	26 579	22 892	19 513	16 590	14 506
Dry bulk traffic												
Inwards	ELN9	13 260	14 123	14 436	15 051	12 503	14 362	15 197	14 389	13 821	13 476	14 189
Outwards	ELO2	98	106	98	41	41	68	67	70	28	52	32
All	ELO3	13 357	14 229	14 534	15 092	12 544	14 430	15 264	14 460	13 849	13 529	14 221
Non-oil traffic with UK off-shore installations												
Inwards	ELO4	984	851	1 063	1 136	589	643	606	490	414	724	672
Outwards	ELO5	3 468	3 515	4 332	3 019	1 199	1 452	1 234	1 112	995	1 470	1 249
All	ELO6	4 453	4 366	5 394	4 155	1 789	2 095	1 840	1 602	1 409	2 194	1 921
All one-port traffic												
Inwards	ELO7	25 105	21 844	26 085	36 407	38 030	33 250	41 688	37 208	33 388	30 369	29 031
Outwards	ELO8	12 413	12 181	8 794	3 186	1 725	2 167	1 994	1 745	1 383	1 944	1 617
All	ELO9	37 518	34 026	34 880	39 593	39 755	35 417	43 682	38 953	34 771	32 313	30 648
Foreign and domestic traffic												
Liquid bulk traffic												
Inwards	ELP2	122 524	117 912	123 446	124 913	132 402	129 748	127 391	125 748	134 285	134 465	135 187
Outwards	ELP3	172 163	166 967	163 028	162 684	160 690	147 017	145 744	136 706	135 123	130 894	117 159
All	ELP4	294 687	284 879	286 474	287 597	293 092	276 765	273 134	262 454	269 408	265 359	252 347
Dry bulk traffic												
Inwards	ELP5	84 778	89 009	90 367	87 062	86 398	99 754	90 016	94 990	96 899	107 739	114 949
Outwards	ELP6	27 588	26 666	28 820	26 175	27 981	24 386	25 878	29 067	25 940	26 429	26 820
All	ELP7	112 366	115 675	119 187	113 237	114 379	124 140	115 894	124 057	122 839	134 168	141 769
Container and roll-on traffic												
Inwards	ELP8	61 631	69 344	72 427	75 814	76 939	77 518	80 225	80 987	88 030	90 672	93 524
Outwards	ELP9	53 427	59 591	59 689	61 013	60 829	58 398	58 654	58 717	61 896	64 040	65 789
All	ELQ2	115 058	128 935	132 115	136 827	137 768	135 915	138 879	139 704	149 926	154 712	159 313
Semi-bulk traffic												
Inwards	ELQ3	16 174	16 263	17 054	16 170	17 421	17 423	18 847	17 657	18 733	16 984	17 057
Outwards	ELQ4	5 518	5 330	5 374	4 740	4 721	4 307	4 159	4 392	4 860	5 853	5 672
All	ELQ5	21 692	21 593	22 428	20 910	22 142	21 730	23 006	22 049	23 593	22 836	22 729
Conventional traffic												
Inwards	ELQ6	1 632	1 667	1 744	1 869	2 596	3 804	3 744	3 893	4 063	3 807	3 722
Outwards	ELQ7	1 355	1 414	1 159	1 020	1 284	1 917	1 828	1 903	1 832	1 843	1 938
All	ELQ8	2 987	3 082	2 903	2 889	3 880	5 721	5 572	5 796	5 895	5 651	5 660
Non-oil traffic with UK off-shore installations												
Inwards	ELQ9	984	851	1 063	1 136	589	643	606	490	414	724	672
Outwards	ELR2	3 468	3 515	4 332	3 019	1 199	1 452	1 234	1 112	995	1 470	1 249
All	ELR3	4 453	4 366	5 394	4 155	1 789	2 095	1 840	1 602	1 409	2 194	1 921
All foreign and domestic traffic												
Inwards	ELR4	287 724	295 046	306 100	306 963	316 344	328 890	320 828	323 766	342 425	354 391	365 112
Outwards	ELR5	263 519	263 484	262 402	258 651	256 706	237 477	237 497	231 896	230 645	230 529	218 627
All	ELR6	551 243	558 530	568 502	565 614	573 050	566 366	558 325	555 662	573 070	584 919	583 739

Source: Department for Transport; 020 7944 3087

15.30 Roll-on/roll-off ferry and Channel Tunnel traffic; road goods vehicles outward to mainland Europe: by country of registration

Thousands

		1996	1997	1998	1999	2000	2001	2002	2003	2004	2005	2006
Powered vehicles:												
United Kingdom	ZCGT	531.1	543.2	544.3	562.7	544.8	517.6	493.3	473.9	493.1	517.4	524.5
Austria	ZCGU	8.6	5.3	10.1	14.7	17.1	42.0	45.8	42.9	30.0	27.0	26.2
Belgium/Luxembourg	ZCGV	41.0	53.6	72.7	96.7	114.1	119.3	121.4	104.3	112.3	112.4	119.2
Denmark	ZCGW	4.6	5.5	7.3	8.7	9.5	12.0	16.9	13.7	17.1	17.7	22.0
Finland	ZCGX	0.2	0.1	0.6	0.7	0.9	3.1	2.0	1.1	0.1	0.2	0.5
Germany	ZCGY	30.4	39.3	52.4	73.1	111.5	132.0	148.2	155.7	164.7	168.3	186.8
France	ZCGZ	181.7	234.2	272.4	319.1	338.8	352.4	363.1	363.2	388.0	361.4	367.2
Greece	ZCHA	2.1	2.6	1.9	2.6	2.9	2.6	2.8	3.6	4.0	3.6	3.4
Irish Republic	ZCHB	30.1	32.3	38.8	44.7	48.5	46.6	44.6	30.8	27.6	31.9	42.7
Italy	ZCHC	28.8	30.4	35.3	45.8	67.8	91.1	127.8	132.4	120.1	96.9	79.6
Netherlands	ZCHD	87.2	107.0	125.4	153.3	185.1	187.5	186.3	210.2	252.1	253.2	257.9
Spain	ZCHE	39.4	45.1	56.3	67.7	81.8	93.9	102.2	105.9	109.8	105.1	111.4
Sweden	ZCHF	0.9	8.9	10.3	1.0	1.4	1.8	1.8	1.4	1.4	1.3	1.7
Portugal	ZCHG	3.1	5.1	6.7	9.2	10.7	10.2	11.0	9.4	8.9	9.5	13.3
EU15 (excluding UK)	ZCHH	458.1	569.5	692.1	837.3	990.0	1 094.5	1 173.9	1 174.6	1 236.2	1 188.5	1 231.8
Cyprus[1]	GG5P	..	..	..	0.1	0.2	0.1	0.2	0.2	0.1	0.1	0.1
Czech Republic[1]	GG5Q	..	..	..	5.4	5.2	6.8	7.8	13.1	25.0	40.6	45.0
Estonia[1]	GG5R	..	..	..	–	0.1	0.2	0.3	0.3	0.8	1.6	3.1
Hungary[1]	GG5S	..	..	..	6.9	8.0	11.1	12.4	12.7	24.6	38.0	45.0
Latvia[1]	GG5T	..	..	..	0.3	0.3	0.1	0.2	0.2	0.2	1.3	1.2
Lithuania[1]	GG5U	..	..	..	0.9	1.4	1.0	0.7	1.6	2.9	7.5	13.0
Malta[1]	GG5V	..	..	..	0.2	0.3	0.3	0.3	0.2	0.1	0.1	0.1
Poland[1]	GG5W	..	..	..	7.0	10.4	12.5	12.0	14.2	31.0	54.5	73.4
Slovakia[1]	GG5X	..	..	..	0.2	0.2	0.4	1.0	2.4	8.0	12.7	18.9
Slovenia[1]	GG5Y	..	..	..	1.5	1.9	3.5	4.7	4.7	10.0	10.8	13.2
NMS10[1]	GG5Z	..	..	..	22.5	28.0	36.2	39.5	49.5	102.9	167.2	213.0
Non-European Union	ZCHI	26.3	28.0	33.3	24.9	24.9	43.2	76.7	97.6	107.6	116.5	68.0
Unknown	ZCHJ	2.2	5.7	4.8	6.3	17.7	20.5	18.1	19.1	17.0	31.8	36.4
All countries	ZCHK	1 017.7	1 146.4	1 274.8	1 453.7	1 605.4	1 711.9	1 801.5	1 814.7	1 956.8	2 021.4	2 073.9
Unaccompanied trailers	ZCHL	626.4	740.0	737.5	737.8	712.9	686.4	726.0	780.4	782.2	756.0	786.2
Powered vehicles and unaccompanied trailers	ZCHM	1 644.1	1 886.4	2 012.3	2 191.4	2 318.3	2 398.3	2 527.5	2 595.1	2 739.0	2 777.4	2 860.1

1 New Member State countries that joined the EU on 1st May 2004. There is no individual breakdown available before 1999 for these countries.

Source: Department for Transport; 0117 372 8484

15.31 Postal services and television licences[1]
United Kingdom

Millions and thousands

		1997	1998	1999	2000	2001	2002	2003	2004	2005	2006	2007
Letters, etc posted (millions)	KMRA	18 101	18 350	18 878	19 711	20 076	20 648	21 979	22 837	24 341	24 880	24 089
of which:												
Registered and insured	KMRB	25.6	28.7	31.6	30.2	32.3	36.1	38.5	41.4	45.3	45.3	44.7
Airmail (Commonwealth and foreign)	KMRC	684.5	658.4	693.2	672.3	659.2	600.7	541.6	512.0	457.9	502.2	541.0
Business reply and freepost items	KMRD	505.8	524.7	503.6	475.3	487.4	486.2	434.4	397.7	401.1	402.3	373.7
Postal orders												
Total issued (thousands)[2]	KMRH	33 404	31 907	30 289	30 153	30 931	29 150	28 666	28 888	29 344	20 489	19 714
Television licences (thousands)												
In force on 31 March	KMQL	21 305	21 723	22 240	22 625	22 839	23 157	23 486	23 899	24 162	24 419	24 546
of which:												
Colour	KMQM	20 849	21 344	21 944	22 413	22 684	23 040	23 392	23 824	24 103	24 370	24 505

1 See chapter text.
2 Excluding those issued on HM ships, in many British possessions and in other places abroad. Up to 1998 includes Postal Orders issued Overseas and by Ministry of Defence.

Sources: Royal Mail: 0207 2502890;
Capita Business Services Limited: 0117 3021003;
Post Office Limited: 0207 3207424

National accounts

Chapter 16

National accounts

National accounts

(Tables 16.1 to 16.22)

The tables which follow are based on those in the *Blue Book* 2007 Edition. Some of the figures are provisional and may be revised later; this applies particularly to the figures for 2005 and 2006.

The accounts are based on the European System of Accounts 1995 (ESA95). The *Blue Book* contains an introduction to the system of the UK accounts outlining some of the main concepts and principles of measurement used. It explains how key economic indicators are derived from the sequence of accounts and how the figures describing the whole economy are broken down by sector and by industry. A detailed description of the structure for the accounts is provided in a separate Office for National Statistics publication *United Kingdom National Accounts: Concepts, Sources and Methods* (TSO 1998). Further information on the financial accounts is given in the *Financial Statistics Explanatory Handbook*.

In the tables in this chapter on national income, analyses by industry are based, as far as possible, on the Standard Industrial Classification Revised 1992. The principal aggregate measured in these tables is the Gross Domestic Product (GDP). This is a concept of the value of the total economic activity taking place in UK territory. It can be viewed as incomes earned, as expenditures incurred, or as production. Adding all primary incomes received from the rest of the world and deducting all primary incomes payable to non-residents produces Gross National Income (GNI) (previously known as Gross National Product). This is a concept of the value of all incomes earned by UK residents.

ESA95, the internationally compatible accounting framework, provides a systematic and detailed description of the UK economy. It includes the sector accounts which provide, by institutional sector, a description of the different stages of the economic process from production through income generation, distribution and use of income to capital accumulation and financing; and the input-output framework, which describes the production process in more detail. It contains all the elements required to compile such aggregate measures as GDP, GNI and saving.

Gross Domestic Product and Gross National Income

(Tables 16.1, 16.2, 16.3)

Table 16.1 shows the main national accounts aggregates, both at current prices and chained volume measures.

Table 16.2 shows the various money flows which generate the GDP and GNI. The output approach to GDP shows the total output of goods and services, the use of goods and services in the production process (intermediate consumption) and taxes and subsidies on products. The expenditure approach to GDP shows consumption expenditure by households and government, gross capital formation and expenditure on UK exports by overseas purchasers. The sum of these items overstates the amount of income generated in the UK by the value of imports of goods and services. This item is therefore subtracted to produce GDP at market prices.

The income approach to GDP shows gross operating surplus, mixed income and compensation of employees (previously known as income from employment). Taxes are added and subsidies are deducted to produce the total of the income based components at market prices.

Table 16.2 also shows the primary incomes received from the rest of the world, which are added to GDP, and primary incomes payable to non-residents, which are deducted from GDP, to arrive at GNI. Primary income comprises compensation of employees, taxes less subsidies on production, and property and entrepreneurial income.

Table 16.3 shows the expenditure approach to the chained volume measure of GDP. When looking at the change in the economy over time the main concern is usually whether more goods and services are actually being produced now than at some time in the past. Over time changes in current price GDP show changes in the monetary value of the components of GDP and, as these changes in value can reflect changes in both price and volume, it is difficult to establish how much of an increase in the series is due either to increased activity in the economy or to an increase in the price level. As a result, when looking at the real growth in the economy over time, it is useful to look at volume estimates of GDP. In chained volume series, volume measures for each year are produced in prices of the previous year. These volume measures are then 'chain-linked' together to produce a continuous time series.

Industrial analysis

(Tables 16.4, 16.5)

The analysis of gross value added by industry at current prices shown in Table 16.4 reflects the estimates based on the Standard Industrial Classification, revised 1992 (SIC92). The table is based on current price data reconciled through the input-output process for 1992 to 2004. The estimates are valued at basic prices, that is, the only taxes included in the price will be taxes paid as part of the production process, such as business rates, and not any taxes specifically levied on the production of a unit of output, for example Value Added Tax. Table 16.5 shows chained volume measures of gross value added at basic prices by industry. Chained volume measures of gross value added (output approach) provides the lead indicator of economic change in the short term. The output analysis of gross value added is estimated in terms of change and expressed in index number form. It is therefore inappropriate to show as a statistical adjustment any divergence of an output measure of GDP derived from it from other measures of GDP. Such an adjustment does, however, exist implicitly.

Sector analysis – Distribution of income accounts and capital account

(Tables 16.6 to 16.13)

The National Accounts accounting framework includes the sector accounts which provide, by institutional sector, a description of the different stages of the economic process, from production through income generation, distribution and use of income to capital accumulation and financing.

Tables 16.6 to 16.12 show the allocation of primary income account and the secondary distribution of income account for the non-financial corporations, financial corporations, government and households sectors. Additionally, Table 16.12 shows the use of income account for the households sector and Table 16.13 provides a summary of the capital account. The full sequence of accounts is shown in the *Blue Book*.

The allocation of primary income account shows the resident units and institutional sectors as recipients rather than producers of primary income. It demonstrates the extent to which operating surpluses are distributed to the owners of the enterprises. The resources side of the allocation of primary income accounts includes the components of the income approach to measurement of GDP. The balance of this account is the gross balance of primary income (B.5g) for each sector, and if the gross balance is aggregated across all sectors of the economy the result is Gross National Income.

The secondary distribution of income account describes how the balance of income for each sector is allocated by redistribution; through transfers such as taxes on income, social contributions and benefits and other current transfers. The balancing item of this account is Gross Disposable Income (GDI) (B.6g). For the households sector, the chained volume measure of GDI is shown as real household disposable income.

Table 16.12 shows, for the households sector, the use of disposable income where the balancing item is saving (B.8g). For the non-financial corporations sector the balancing item of the secondary distribution of income account, GDI (B.6g), is equal to saving (B.8g).

The summary capital account (Table 16.13) brings together the saving and investment of the several sectors of the economy. It shows saving, capital transfers, gross capital formation and net acquisition of non-financial assets for each of the four sectors.

Household and non-profit institutions serving households consumption expenditure at current market prices and chained volume measures

(Tables 16.14 to 16.17)

Household and non-profit institutions serving households (NPISH) consumption expenditure is a major component of the expenditure measure of GDP, both at current prices (Table 16.2) and chained volume measures (Table 16.3).

Household final consumption expenditure includes the value of income-in-kind and imputed rent of owner-occupied dwellings, but excludes business expenditure allowed as deductions in computing income for tax purposes. It includes expenditure on durable goods, for instance motor cars, which from the point of view of the individual might more appropriately be treated as capital expenditure. The only exceptions are the purchase of land and dwellings and costs incurred in connection with the transfer of their ownership and expenditure on major improvements by occupiers, which are treated as personal capital expenditure.

The estimates of household consumption expenditure include purchases of second-hand as well as new goods, *less* the proceeds of sales of used goods.

The most detailed figures are published quarterly in *Consumer Trends* (available as a web-only publication on the National Statistics website: www.statistics.gov.uk).

Change in inventories (previously known as value of physical increase in stocks and work in progress)

(Table 16.18)

This table gives a broad analysis by industry and, for manufacturing industry, by asset, of the value of entries less withdrawals and losses of inventories (stocks).

Gross fixed capital formation

(Table 16.19 to 16.22)

Gross fixed capital formation comprises expenditure on the replacement of, and additions to, fixed capital assets located in the UK, including all ships and aircraft of UK ownership.

16.1 United Kingdom national and domestic product[1]
Main aggregates
At current prices and chained volume measures, reference year 2003

Indices (2003=100) and £ million

		1999	2000	2001	2002	2003	2004	2005	2006	2007
INDICES (2003=100)										
VALUES AT CURRENT PRICES										
Gross domestic product at current market prices ("money GDP")	YBEU	81.6	85.8	89.7	94.4	100.0	105.9	110.3	116.6	123.8
Gross value added at current basic prices	YBEX	81.1	85.2	89.5	94.3	100.0	105.9	110.4	116.7	124.0
CHAINED VOLUME MEASURES										
Gross domestic product at market prices	YBEZ	89.7	93.1	95.3	97.3	100.0	103.3	105.2	108.2	111.5
Gross national disposable income at market prices	YBFP	87.6	90.7	93.7	97.1	100.0	103.4	104.2	105.7	109.1
Gross value added at basic prices	CGCE	90.2	93.6	95.6	97.3	100.0	103.3	105.2	108.4	111.5
PRICES										
Implied deflator of GDP at market prices	YBGB	90.9	92.1	94.1	97.0	100.0	102.6	104.9	107.7	111.1
VALUES AT CURRENT PRICES (£ million)										
Gross measures (before deduction of fixed capital consumption) at current market prices										
Gross Domestic Product ("money GDP")	YBHA	911 945	958 931	1 003 297	1 055 793	1 118 245	1 184 296	1 233 976	1 303 915	1 384 823
Employment, property and entrepreneurial income from the rest of the world (receipts *less* payments)	YBGG	1 270	4 540	11 664	23 443	24 646	26 596	25 734	18 555	..
Subsidies (receipts) *less* taxes (payments) on products from/to the rest of the world	-QZOZ	-3 438	-4 098	-3 920	-2 890	-2 596	-1 640	-4 260	-4 496	..
Other subsidies on production from/to the rest of the world	-IBJL	309	292	298	519	..	..	..	..	..
Gross National Income (GNI)	ABMX	910 115	959 708	1 011 623	1 076 865	1 140 887	1 209 844	1 258 192	1 310 399	1 388 315
Current transfers from the rest of the world (receipts *less* payments)	-YBGF	-4 435	-6 253	-3 426	-6 711	-8 130	-9 920	-11 087	-10 697	..
Gross National Disposable Income	NQCO	905 680	953 455	1 008 197	1 070 154	1 132 757	1 199 924	1 247 102	1 299 703	1 376 183
Adjustment to current basic prices										
Gross Domestic Product (at current market prices)	YBHA	911 945	958 931	1 003 297	1 055 793	1 118 245	1 184 296	1 233 976	1 303 915	1 384 823
Adjustment to current basic prices (*less* taxes *plus* subsidies on products)	-NQBU	-105 956	-112 248	-114 234	-118 470	-124 738	-132 362	-137 347	-144 658	-152 831
Gross Value Added (at current basic prices)	ABML	805 989	846 683	889 063	937 323	993 507	1 051 934	1 096 629	1 159 257	..
Net measures (after deduction of fixed capital consumption) at current market prices	-NQAE	-105 507	-111 251	-115 796	-121 914	-125 553	-135 184	-138 354	-147 720	..
Net domestic product	NHRK	810 890	852 559	892 863	939 786	999 006	1 055 869	1 102 883	1 165 686	..
Net national income	NSRX	809 060	853 336	901 189	960 858	1 021 648	1 081 417	1 127 629	1 183 020	..
Net national disposable income	NQCP	804 625	847 083	897 763	954 147	1 013 518	1 071 497	1 116 542	1 172 323	..
CHAINED VOLUME MEASURES (Reference year 2003, £ million)										
Gross measures (before deduction of fixed capital consumption) at market prices										
Gross Domestic Product	ABMI	1 003 370	1 041 517	1 066 217	1 088 108	1 118 245	1 154 685	1 175 916	1 210 288	1 246 895
Terms of trade effect ("Trading gain or loss")	YBGJ	-5 461	-8 007	-9 966	-2 932	–	1 226	-6 950	-11 474	..
Real gross domestic income	YBGL	997 909	1 033 510	1 056 251	1 085 176	1 118 245	1 155 911	1 168 966	1 197 870	..
Real employment, property and entrepreneurial income from the rest of the world (receipts *less* payments)	YBGI	1 386	4 880	12 256	24 081	24 646	25 981	24 398	17 121	..
Subsidies (receipts) *less* taxes (payments) on production from/to the rest of the world	-QZPB	-2 701	-3 686	-3 393	-2 624	-2 596	-1 762	-2 140	-2 664	..
Other subsidies on production from/to the rest of the world	-IBJN	298	305	590	707	592	661	669	664	..
Gross National Income (GNI)	YBGM	996 838	1 034 615	1 065 447	1 107 294	1 140 887	1 180 791	1 191 893	1 212 991	..
Real current transfers from the rest of the world (receipts *less* payments)	-YBGP	-4 842	-6 722	-3 600	-6 894	-8 130	-9 691	-10 511	-9 870	..
Gross National Disposable Income	YBGO	992 000	1 027 891	1 061 855	1 100 401	1 132 757	1 171 100	1 180 876	1 197 868	1 235 349
Adjustment to basic prices										
Gross Domestic Product (at market prices)	ABMI	1 003 370	1 041 517	1 066 217	1 088 108	1 118 245	1 154 685	1 175 916	1 210 288	1 246 895
Adjustment to basic prices (*less* taxes *plus* subsidies on products)	-NTAQ	-107 873	-112 020	-116 584	-121 657	-124 738	-128 660	-130 432	-133 966	..
Gross Value Added (at basic prices)	ABMM	895 795	929 802	949 755	966 449	993 507	1 026 025	1 045 484	1 076 520	1 108 182
Net measures (after deduction of fixed capital consumption) at market prices	-CIHA	-110 533	-114 722	-118 072	-123 405	-125 553	-133 203	-133 706	-139 227	..
Net national income at market prices	YBET	893 158	926 314	953 482	989 809	1 021 648	1 054 226	1 064 967	1 094 122	..
Net national disposable income at market prices	YBEY	888 326	919 584	949 906	982 918	1 013 518	1 044 535	1 054 456	1 084 252	..

1 See chapter text.

Source: Office for National Statistics: 020 7014 2083

16.2 United Kingdom gross domestic product and national income[1]
Current prices

£ million

		1999	2000	2001	2002	2003	2004	2005	2006	2007
Gross domestic product: Output										
Gross value added, at basic prices										
Output of goods and services	NQAF	1 681 412	1 778 350	1 859 652	1 944 508	2 046 891	2 159 602	..	..	..
less intermediate consumption	-NQAJ	-875 423	-931 667	-970 589	-1 007 185	-1 053 384	-1 107 668	..	..	..
Total Gross Value Added	ABML	805 989	846 683	889 063	937 323	993 507	1 051 934	1 096 629	1 159 257	..
Value added taxes (VAT) on products	QYRC	61 512	64 189	67 097	71 059	77 335	81 540	83 382	87 679	..
Other taxes on products	NSUI	50 512	54 086	52 845	53 945	54 813	58 102	59 076	62 752	..
less subsidies on products	-NZHC	-6 068	-6 027	-5 708	-6 534	-7 410	-7 280	-5 111	-5 768	..
Gross Domestic Product at market prices	YBHA	911 945	958 931	1 003 297	1 055 793	1 118 245	1 184 296	1 233 976	1 303 915	1 384 823
Gross domestic product: Expenditure										
Final consumption expenditure										
Actual individual consumption										
Household final consumption expenditure	ABPB	567 994	600 826	632 496	664 562	697 160	732 531	760 869	793 675	838 285
Final consumption expenditure of NPISH	ABNV	21 874	23 169	24 720	25 968	27 185	28 953	31 585	33 966	36 674
Individual government final consumption expenditure	NNAQ	102 742	109 297	118 458	130 816	143 954	155 811	167 399	175 306	184 502
Total actual individual consumption	NQEO	692 610	733 292	775 674	821 346	868 299	917 295	959 853	1 002 947	1 059 461
Collective government final consumption expenditure	NQEP	66 778	72 554	76 045	81 648	88 745	94 897	101 502	111 049	115 675
Total final consumption expenditure	ABKW	759 388	805 846	851 719	902 994	957 044	1 012 192	1 061 355	1 113 996	1 175 136
Households and NPISH	NSSG	589 868	623 995	657 216	690 530	724 345	761 484	792 454	827 641	874 959
Central government	NMBJ	103 580	110 807	118 762	130 326	142 639	152 325	162 751	174 701	182 764
Local government	NMMT	65 940	71 044	75 741	82 138	90 060	98 383	106 150	111 654	117 413
Gross capital formation										
Gross fixed capital formation	NPQX	161 722	167 172	171 782	180 551	186 700	202 260	211 862	231 762	251 486
Changes in inventories	ABMP	6 060	5 271	6 189	2 909	3 983	4 856	4 071	2 463	7 575
Acquisitions less disposals of valuables	NPJO	229	3	396	214	-37	-37	-377	285	538
Total gross capital formation	NQFM	168 011	172 446	178 367	183 674	190 646	207 079	215 556	234 510	259 599
Exports of goods and services	KTMW	239 782	267 602	273 140	276 511	285 397	298 694	326 790	370 788	359 281
less imports of goods and services	-KTMX	-255 236	-286 963	-299 929	-307 386	-314 842	-333 669	-370 968	-417 320	-408 480
External balance of goods and services	KTMY	-15 454	-19 361	-26 789	-30 875	-29 445	-34 975	-44 178	-46 532	-49 199
Statistical discrepancy between expenditure components and GDP	RVFD	–	–	–	–	–	–	1 243	1 941	-713
Gross Domestic Product at market prices	YBHA	911 945	958 931	1 003 297	1 055 793	1 118 245	1 184 296	1 233 976	1 303 915	1 384 823
Gross domestic product: Income										
Operating surplus, gross										
Non-financial corporations										
Public non-financial corporations	NRJT	7 678	7 188	6 892	6 657	7 265	6 653	8 494	9 872	..
Private non-financial corporations	NRJK	183 283	189 745	191 062	195 548	208 945	226 203	234 129	246 767	264 941
Financial corporations	NQNV	17 010	13 555	13 242	33 614	41 419	47 324	39 697	44 741	54 007
Adjustment for financial services	-NSRV	-29 468	-33 465	-33 648	-41 136	-45 370	-50 165	-51 922	-53 065	..
General government	NMXV	9 262	9 542	9 796	10 289	10 807	11 681	12 605	13 597	14 523
Households and non-profit institutions serving households	QWLS	51 195	53 960	59 083	62 544	67 935	72 709	77 791	82 112	87 599
Total operating surplus, gross	ABNF	238 960	240 525	246 427	267 516	291 001	314 405	320 794	343 934	376 486
Mixed income	QWLT	55 734	57 805	62 121	65 771	69 122	71 958	75 675	78 863	83 951
Compensation of employees	HAEA	495 793	532 179	564 194	587 396	616 893	648 717	686 805	723 260	754 422
Taxes on production and imports	NZGX	128 527	135 358	137 507	143 117	150 665	158 587	162 059	171 518	..
less subsidies	-AAXJ	-7 069	-6 936	-6 952	-8 007	-9 436	-9 371	-10 441	-11 827	..
Statistical discrepancy between income components and GDP	RVFC	–	–	–	–	–	–	-916	-1 478	2 193
Gross Domestic Product at market prices	YBHA	911 945	958 931	1 003 297	1 055 793	1 118 245	1 184 296	1 233 976	1 303 915	1 384 823

16.2 United Kingdom gross domestic product and national income[1]
Current prices

continued

		1999	2000	2001	2002	2003	2004	2005	2006	2007
Gross Domestic Product at market prices	YBHA	911 945	958 931	1 003 297	1 055 793	1 118 245	1 184 296	1 233 976	1 303 915	1 384 823
Compensation of employees										
receipts from the rest of the world	KTMN	960	1 032	1 087	1 121	1 116	1 171	974	1 058	1 105
less payments to the rest of the world	-KTMO	−759	−882	−1 021	−1 054	−1 057	−1 100	−1 584	−1 803	−1 727
Total	KTMP	201	150	66	67	59	71	−610	−745	−622
less Taxes on products paid to the rest of the world										
plus Subsidies received from the rest of the world	-QZOZ	−3 438	−4 098	−3 920	−2 890	−2 596	−1 640	−4 260	−4 496	..
Other subsidies on production	-IBJL	309	292	298	519	..	..	..	..	..
Property and entrepreneurial income										
receipts from the rest of the world	HMBN	101 952	134 114	139 848	123 505	124 881	141 030	186 259	234 143	281 674
less payments to the rest of the world	-HMBO	−100 883	−129 724	−128 250	−100 129	−100 294	−114 505	−160 445	−225 638	−275 772
Total	HMBM	1 069	4 390	11 598	23 376	24 587	26 525	25 814	8 505	5 902
Gross National Income at market prices	ABMX	910 115	959 708	1 011 623	1 076 865	1 140 887	1 209 844	1 258 192	1 310 399	1 388 315

1 See chapter text.

Source: Office for National Statistics: 020 7014 2083

16.3 United Kingdom gross domestic product[1]
Chained volume measures, reference year 2003

£ million

		1999	2000	2001	2002	2003	2004	2005	2006	2007
Gross domestic product: expenditure approach										
Final consumption expenditure										
Actual individual consumption										
Household final consumption expenditure	ABPF	606 648	633 662	653 326	676 833	697 160	721 434	732 005	745 737	768 397
Final consumption expenditure of non-profit institutions serving households	ABNU	25 023	27 177	27 155	27 130	27 185	27 327	28 167	29 858	31 079
Individual government final consumption expenditure	NSZK	109 554	111 763	114 159	117 238	120 288	..	..	..	..
Total actual individual consumption	YBIO	760 172	792 076	815 286	843 504	868 299	897 055	911 168	929 237	..
Collective government final consumption expenditure	NSZL	76 926	80 829	82 502	85 331	88 745	91 835	95 531	99 097	..
Total final consumption expenditure	ABKX	837 119	872 899	897 801	928 849	957 044	988 890	1 006 699	1 028 334	..
Gross capital formation										
Gross fixed capital formation	NPQR	169 117	173 710	178 203	184 701	186 700	197 655	200 654	215 985	229 423
Changes in inventories	ABMQ	5 803	4 648	5 577	2 289	3 982	4 597	3 611	2 416	6 523
Acquisitions less disposals of valuables	NPJP	−	−28	342	183	−37	−42	−354	290	525
Total gross capital formation	NPQU	175 118	178 660	184 462	187 374	190 646	202 210	203 911	220 491	..
Gross domestic final expenditure	YBIK	1 012 457	1 051 600	1 082 333	1 116 239	1 147 690	1 191 099	1 210 610	1 244 916	1 291 263
Exports of goods and services	KTMZ	247 289	269 830	277 694	280 593	285 397	299 289	323 749	358 356	339 434
Gross final expenditure	ABME	1 259 336	1 321 604	1 360 205	1 396 862	1 433 087	1 490 388	1 534 359	1 603 272	1 630 698
less imports of goods and services	-KTNB	−257 809	−281 081	−294 449	−308 706	−314 842	−335 703	−359 626	−394 789	−383 162
Statistical discrepancy between expenditure components and GDP	GIXS	−	−	−	−	−	−	1 183	1 805	−639
Gross Domestic Product at market prices	ABMI	1 003 370	1 041 517	1 066 217	1 088 108	1 118 245	1 154 685	1 175 916	1 210 288	1 246 895
of which External balance of goods and services	KTNC	−10 520	−11 251	−16 755	−28 113	−29 445	−36 414	−35 877	−36 433	−43 728

1 See chapter text.

Source: Office for National Statistics: 020 7014 2083

16.4 Gross value added at current basic prices: by industry[1,2]
United Kingdom

£ million

		1998	1999	2000	2001	2002	2003	2004	2005	2006
Agriculture, hunting, forestry and fishing	EWSH	9 457	9 270	8 789	8 566	9 218	10 031	10 323	..	..
Production										
Mining and quarrying										
Mining and quarrying of energy producing materials										
Mining of coal	QTOQ	817	642	611	548	534	468	385	370	334
Extraction of mineral oil and natural gas	QTOR	13 054	14 694	22 283	20 940	20 006	19 542	19 845	23 082	26 144
Other mining and quarrying	QTOS	1 645	1 716	1 795	1 760	1 474	1 524	1 646	1 656	1 615
Total mining and quarrying	EWSL	15 516	17 053	24 689	23 251	22 012	21 534	21 876	..	..
Manufacturing										
Food; beverages and tobacco	QTOU	20 047	20 220	20 261	20 914	21 052	21 654	22 288	22 890	23 048
Textiles and textile products	QTOV	6 803	6 270	5 863	5 390	4 857	4 318	3 823	3 685	3 448
Leather and leather products	QTOW	822	808	750	650	594	463	347	347	360
Wood and wood products	QTOX	2 329	2 248	2 336	2 369	2 516	2 694	2 904	3 063	3 109
Pulp, paper and paper products; publishing and printing	QTOY	18 781	19 619	20 207	20 155	19 988	19 698	20 157	19 648	19 099
Coke, petroleum products and nuclear fuel	QTOZ	2 524	2 569	2 361	2 493	2 433	2 358	2 420	2 837	2 833
Chemicals, chemical products and man-made fibres	QTPA	14 873	15 136	14 982	15 979	15 984	15 980	16 233	17 082	17 228
Rubber and plastic products	QTPB	8 026	7 794	7 692	7 730	7 627	7 569	7 824	8 219	8 707
Other non-metal mineral products	QTPC	5 028	4 952	5 013	5 084	5 333	5 452	5 686	5 870	6 077
Basic metals and fabricated metal products	QTPD	17 633	16 675	16 023	15 637	14 957	14 807	15 097	15 963	16 713
Machinery and equipment not elsewhere classified	QTPE	13 591	12 731	12 343	12 265	12 056	12 071	12 198	12 923	13 137
Electrical and optical equipment	QTPF	19 826	20 442	20 414	18 382	16 501	15 529	15 625	14 530	14 794
Transport equipment	QTPG	16 179	16 064	16 016	16 100	16 136	15 801	16 318	16 038	16 735
Manufacturing not elsewhere classified	QTPH	6 282	6 422	6 555	6 704	6 588	6 438	6 548	6 710	6 958
Total manufacturing	EWSP	152 744	151 951	150 819	149 852	146 621	144 830	147 468	..	..
Electricity, gas and water supply	EWST	15 887	15 784	15 942	15 826	16 084	16 482	17 103	..	..
Total production	QTPK	184 146	184 791	191 452	188 928	184 706	182 844	186 443	199 977	211 861
Construction	EWSX	39 970	42 511	45 975	50 903	55 020	59 855	64 747	..	..
Service industries										
Wholesale and retail trade (including motor trade); repair of motor vehicles, personal and household goods	QTPM	93 572	99 981	103 910	110 658	113 988	120 605	127 520	132 784	139 795
Hotels and restaurants	QTPN	22 547	24 476	26 004	27 384	29 023	30 509	33 074	32 707	35 573
Transport, storage and communication										
Transport and storage	QTPO	40 072	41 138	42 648	43 360	44 633	47 108	49 516	53 237	55 263
Communication	QTPP	22 297	23 935	26 652	27 142	28 346	29 376	29 762	28 960	27 679
Total	EWTF	62 369	65 073	69 299	70 502	72 980	76 485	79 279	..	..
Financial intermediation	QTPR	46 952	46 229	46 093	46 956	68 120	77 852	86 145	96 686	108 869
Adjustment for financial services (FISIM)	-NSRV	−27 658	−29 468	−33 465	−33 648	−41 136	−45 370	−50 165	−51 922	−53 065
Real estate, renting and business activities										
Letting of dwellings including imputed rent of owner occupiers	QTPS	56 741	60 501	63 176	68 802	72 531	77 913	83 037	83 332	87 806
Other real estate, renting and business activities	QTPT	108 523	119 892	131 348	142 806	150 399	162 851	175 333	187 440	198 443
Total	QTPU	165 264	180 393	194 525	211 608	222 930	240 765	258 370	270 772	286 249
Public administration and defence (PAD)	EWTN	39 561	40 909	42 712	45 025	47 528	51 302	55 280	..	..
Education	QTPW	41 687	44 879	48 069	51 616	55 025	58 246	61 786	63 286	64 692
Health and social work	QTPX	48 800	51 688	55 390	59 623	64 552	70 630	75 817	..	..
Other social and personal services, private households with employees and extra-territorial organisations	EWTV	37 011	39 881	42 228	44 629	48 331	51 802	55 543	..	..
Total service industries	QTPZ	530 106	564 043	594 765	634 354	681 342	732 825	782 647	821 083	866 597
All industries	ABML	768 594	805 989	846 683	889 063	937 323	993 507	1 051 934	1 096 629	1 159 257

1 See chapter text. Components may not sum to totals as a result of rounding.
2 Because of differences in the annual and monthly production inquiries, estimates of current price output and value added by industry derived from the current price input-output supply-use balances are not consistent with the equivalent measures of constant price growth given in Table 16.5. These differences do not affect GDP totals. For further information see "Experimental Constant Price Input-Output Supply-Use Balances: An approach to improving the quality of the national accounts" Nadim Ahmad, *Economic Trends*, July 1999 (No. 548).

Source: Office for National Statistics: 020 7014 2083

16.5 Gross value added at basic prices: by industry[1,2,3,4]
Chained volume indices
United Kingdom

Indices (2003=100)

	Weight per 1000[1] 2003		1999	2000	2001	2002	2003	2004	2005	2006	2007
Agriculture, hunting, forestry and fishing	9.9	GDQA	101.1	100.3	90.9	102.1	100.0	99.0	103.3	106.2	107.2
Production											
Mining and quarrying											
Mining and quarrying of energy producing materials											
Mining of coal	0.6	CKZP	132.5	113.1	112.6	105.9	100.0	85.8	67.2	63.0	56.4
Extraction of mineral oil and natural gas	25.1	CKZO	117.7	113.6	107.3	105.9	100.0	91.6	82.0	74.3	72.4
Other mining and quarrying	2.0	CKZQ	82.6	85.8	80.4	98.7	100.0	101.4	110.0	115.0	123.1
Total mining and quarrying	27.7	CKYX	114.8	111.1	105.0	105.4	100.0	92.1	83.7	76.7	75.7
Manufacturing											
Food; beverages and tobacco	23.8	CKZA	97.5	96.7	98.0	100.0	100.0	101.6	102.5	101.6	100.8
Textiles and textile products	6.3	CKZB	125.3	122.4	107.2	99.7	100.0	91.8	90.2	91.2	89.1
Leather and leather products	0.7	CKZC	156.2	137.7	140.0	122.5	100.0	74.6	69.8	74.4	74.1
Wood and wood products	2.7	CKZD	94.1	96.5	96.6	99.2	100.0	101.8	97.8	93.0	96.2
Pulp, paper and paper products; publishing and printing	23.2	CKZE	101.1	101.5	101.3	101.4	100.0	99.1	94.0	93.8	93.8
Coke, petroleum products and nuclear fuel	2.9	CKZF	107.2	112.9	106.9	108.3	100.0	105.8	110.1	103.4	107.2
Chemicals, chemical products and man-made fibres	18.4	CKZG	88.9	93.6	99.3	99.1	100.0	103.4	103.5	106.1	104.9
Rubber and plastic products	9.0	CKZH	107.0	107.0	103.2	99.2	100.0	98.5	95.1	97.7	97.3
Other non-metallic mineral products	5.8	CKZI	92.8	95.6	96.0	94.5	100.0	105.8	105.4	107.2	108.3
Basic metals and fabricated metal products	17.8	CKZJ	101.4	103.5	101.4	102.4	100.0	103.1	102.4	102.0	102.8
Machinery and equipment not elsewhere classified	13.9	CKZK	102.4	102.3	104.2	98.3	100.0	105.8	108.7	115.1	120.2
Electrical and optical equipment	21.3	CKZL	111.5	128.2	118.7	102.6	100.0	101.8	97.3	97.8	99.2
Transport equipment	18.1	CKZM	103.8	99.7	97.9	94.8	100.0	105.8	104.9	112.3	112.0
Manufacturing not elsewhere classified	7.6	CKZN	101.6	100.4	99.9	100.5	100.0	99.3	100.2	100.7	103.6
Total manufacturing	171.6	CKYY	101.4	103.8	102.5	99.8	100.0	102.0	100.8	102.4	103.0
Electricity, gas and water supply	18.2	CKYZ	92.1	95.0	98.0	98.4	100.0	101.1	100.7	98.7	98.7
Total production	217.6	CKYW	101.9	103.8	102.3	100.3	100.0	100.8	98.8	99.1	99.4
Construction	56.7	GDQB	89.8	90.2	92.2	95.5	100.0	104.0	105.6	106.7	109.2
Service industries											
Wholesale and retail trade (including motor trade); repair of motor vehicles, personal and household goods	125.5	GDQC	85.9	89.0	92.3	96.9	100.0	105.3	106.7	109.6	113.9
Hotels and restaurants	33.3	GDQD	88.3	89.4	91.3	94.4	100.0	104.5	105.6	112.4	116.9
Transport, storage and communication											
Transport and storage	49.8	GDQF	90.5	95.6	97.7	99.2	100.0	103.4	108.4	114.1	118.9
Communication	31.3	GDQG	73.4	88.8	96.0	96.5	100.0	101.2	104.6	106.3	111.2
Total	81.0	GDQH	83.4	92.9	97.0	98.2	100.0	102.5	106.9	111.1	115.9
Financial intermediation	48.5	GDQI	82.0	87.1	90.2	93.7	100.0	107.6	113.8	124.4	138.3
Adjustment for financial services (FISIM)	−38.1	GDQJ	73.7	81.7	86.3	89.2	100.0	113.0	123.3	138.8	162.9
Real estate, renting and business activities											
Letting of dwellings, including imputed rent of owner occupiers	77.8	GDQL	93.3	95.2	96.5	97.7	100.0	101.5	102.9	105.1	105.6
Other real estate, renting and business activities	160.4	GDQK	80.6	87.6	92.9	94.7	100.0	107.7	114.8	122.8	132.0
Total	238.3	GDQM	84.5	89.9	94.0	95.7	100.0	105.7	111.0	117.1	123.5
Public administration and defence (PAD)[4]	55.6	GDQO	91.4	91.9	93.0	95.3	100.0	101.9	102.8	103.4	103.6
Education	58.7	GDQP	95.7	96.9	97.6	99.3	100.0	100.4	101.5	101.7	101.8
Health and social work[4]	62.3	GDQQ	86.3	89.6	92.8	96.3	100.0	103.9	107.0	110.2	114.0
Other social and personal services, private households with employees and extra-territorial organisations	51.0	GDQR	91.5	94.7	98.5	100.1	100.0	101.3	103.0	106.0	109.4
Total service industries	715.8	GDQS	87.2	91.3	94.5	96.9	100.0	103.9	106.9	110.8	115.0
All industries	1 000.0	CGCE	90.2	93.6	95.6	97.3	100.0	103.3	105.2	108.4	111.5

1 See chapter text. The weights are in proportion to total gross value added (GVA) in 2003 and are used to combine the industry output indices to calculate the totals for 2004 and 2005. For 2003 and earlier, totals are calculated using the equivalent weight for the previous year (eg totals for 2002 use 2001 weights).

2 As GVA is expressed in index number form, it is inappropriate to show as a statistical adjustment any divergence from the other measures of GDP. Such an adjustment does, however, exist implicitly.

3 See footnote 2 to Table 16.4.

4 The GVA for PAD, education and Health and social work in this table follows the SIC(92) and differs from that used in Table 2.3 in *United Kingdom National Accounts* (the *Blue Book*) which is based on Input-Output groups. The administration costs of the NHS are included in PAD in this table but are included in Health and social work in Table 2.3.

Source: Office for National Statistics: 020 7014 2083

16.6 Non-financial corporations[1]
Allocation of primary income account[2]
United Kingdom. ESA95 sector S.11

£ million

		1999	2000	2001	2002	2003	2004	2005	2006	2007
Resources										
Operating surplus, gross	NQBE	190 961	196 933	197 954	202 205	216 210	232 856	242 623	256 549	275 515
Property income, received										
Interest	EABC	10 794	14 427	12 860	9 338	9 032	11 428	15 040	18 547	..
Distributed income of corporations	EABD	21 501	26 631	36 868	32 210	..	..	..	..	..
Reinvested earnings on direct foreign investment	HDVR	16 214	20 118	22 950	26 893	12 492	24 181	33 199	36 426	40 664
Attributed property income of insurance policy-holders	FAOF	338	489	280	302	..	..	..	..	..
Rent	FAOG	117	117	117	118	..	..	..	..	..
Total	FAKY	48 935	61 471	73 796	67 240	72 370	80 188	95 498	99 842	109 789
Total resources	FBXJ	239 896	258 404	271 750	269 445	288 580	313 044	338 121	356 391	385 304
Uses										
Property income, paid										
Interest	EABG	31 857	38 389	40 056	37 134	36 445	42 002	49 725	62 369	..
Distributed income of corporations	NVCS	87 100	83 202	100 810	91 868	..	..	..	..	..
Reinvested earnings on direct foreign investment	HDVB	2 776	7 348	1 699	1 614	3 955	6 729	4 983	16 802	20 390
Rent	FBXO	564	1 319	1 896	1 853	..	..	..	..	..
Total	FBXK	123 593	133 583	149 517	130 849	140 764	149 298	163 317	183 468	199 278
Balance of primary incomes, gross	NQBG	116 303	124 821	122 233	138 596	147 816	163 746	174 804	172 923	186 026
Total uses	FBXJ	239 896	258 404	271 750	269 445	288 580	313 044	338 121	356 391	385 304
After deduction of fixed capital consumption	-DBGF	−60 263	−62 465	−64 028	−65 775	−67 438	−69 979	−71 335	−72 737	..
Balance of primary incomes, net	FBXQ	56 040	62 356	58 205	72 821	80 378	93 767	103 659	111 062	..

1 See chapter text.
2 Before deduction of fixed capital formation.

Source: Office for National Statistics: 020 7014 2014

16.7 Non-financial corporations[1]
Secondary distribution of income account
United Kingdom. ESA95 sector S.11

£ million

		1999	2000	2001	2002	2003	2004	2005	2006	2007
Resources										
Balance of primary incomes, gross	NQBG	116 303	124 821	122 233	138 596	147 816	163 746	174 804	172 923	186 026
Social contributions										
Imputed social contributions	NSTJ	3 845	4 175	4 357	4 575	4 229	3 864	3 612	3 490	3 508
Current transfers other than taxes, social contributions and benefits										
Non-life insurance claims	FCBP	4 151	4 456	4 565	7 789	..	..	..	..	..
Miscellaneous transfers	NRJY	611	622	619	616	..	..	..	..	..
Total	NRJB	4 260	6 008	5 122	5 599	6 595	6 619	7 248	8 524	6 335
Total resources	FCBR	124 408	135 004	131 712	148 770	158 640	174 229	185 664	184 937	195 869
Uses										
Current taxes on income, wealth etc.										
Taxes on income	FCBS	22 948	24 497	23 177	24 038	23 702	27 348	33 610	37 182	40 882
Social benefits other than social transfers in kind	NSTJ	3 845	4 175	4 357	4 575	4 229	3 864	3 612	3 490	3 508
Current transfers other than taxes, social contributions and benefits										
Net non-life insurance premiums	FCBY	4 151	4 456	4 565	7 789	..	..	..	..	..
Miscellaneous current transfers	FDBI	569	413	411	422	434	446	..	..	..
Total, other current transfers	FCBX	4 860	6 476	5 506	5 932	6 933	7 042	7 736	9 001	6 823
Gross Disposable Income	NRJD	92 755	99 856	98 672	114 225	123 776	135 975	140 706	135 264	144 656
Total uses	FCBR	124 408	135 004	131 712	148 770	158 640	174 229	185 664	184 937	195 869
After deduction of fixed capital consumption	-DBGF	−60 263	−62 465	−64 028	−65 775	−67 438	−69 979	−71 335	−72 737	..
Disposable income, net	FCCF	32 492	37 391	34 644	48 450	56 338	65 996	69 564	73 364	..

1 See chapter text.

Source: Office for National Statistics: 020 7014 2014

16.8 General government[1]
Allocation of primary income account
United Kingdom. ESA95 sector S.13 Unconsolidated

£ million

		1999	2000	2001	2002	2003	2004	2005	2006	2007
Resources										
Operating surplus, gross	NMXV	9 262	9 542	9 796	10 289	10 807	11 681	12 605	13 597	14 523
Taxes on production and imports, received										
Taxes on products										
Value added tax (VAT)	NZGF	57 713	59 998	63 525	68 258	74 603	79 761	81 416	85 586	89 645
Taxes and duties on imports excluding VAT										
Import duties	NMXZ	–	–	–	–	–	–	–	–	..
Taxes on imports excluding VAT and import duties	NMBT	–	–	–	–	–	–	..	..	..
Taxes on products excluding VAT and import duties	NMYB	48 442	51 956	50 745	52 001	52 858	55 932	56 815	60 480	64 234
Total taxes on products	NVCC	106 143	111 941	114 267	120 252	127 453	135 683	138 198	146 066	153 879
Other taxes on production	NMYD	16 503	17 083	17 565	18 113	18 517	18 945	19 601	20 841	21 654
Total taxes on production and imports, received	NMYE	122 646	129 024	131 832	138 365	145 970	154 628	157 799	166 907	175 533
less Subsidies, paid										
Subsidies on products	-NMYF	–3 625	–3 791	–3 953	–4 672	–5 311	–4 961	–5 111	–5 904	–5 779
Other subsidies on production	-LIUF	–663	–574	–662	–954	–1 434	–1 499	–2 058	–2 943	–3 771
Total	-NMRL	–4 288	–4 365	–4 615	–5 626	–6 745	–6 460	–7 169	–8 863	..
Property income, received										
Total Interest	NMYL	7 335	7 340	7 332	6 624	7 053	6 280	6 318	7 081	7 972
Distributed income of corporations	NMYM	7 303	7 777	6 910	6 156	8 073	7 869	2 585	2 461	3 048
Property income attributed to insurance policy holders	NMYO	33	54	24	22	19	17	27	25	16
Rent										
from sectors other than general government	NMYR	529	1 289	1 919	1 901	1 565	1 422	1 352	1 235	1 242
Total	NMYU	15 200	16 460	16 185	14 703	16 710	15 588	10 282	10 802	12 278
Total resources	NMYV	142 820	150 661	153 198	157 731	166 742	175 437	173 517	182 459	192 784
Uses										
Property income, paid										
Total interest	NRKB	30 699	30 639	27 965	25 463	26 955	27 050	29 449	30 421	..
Total	NMYY	30 699	30 639	27 965	25 463	26 955	27 050	29 449	30 444	34 267
Balance of primary incomes, gross	NMZH	112 121	120 022	125 233	132 268	139 787	148 387	144 068	152 015	158 517
Total uses	NMYV	142 820	150 661	153 198	157 731	166 742	175 437	173 517	182 459	192 784
After deduction of fixed capital consumption	-NMXO	–9 262	–9 542	–9 796	–10 289	–10 807	–11 681	–12 605	–13 597	..
Balance of primary incomes, net	NMZI	102 859	110 480	115 437	121 979	128 980	136 706	131 463	138 371	..

1 See chapter text.

Source: Office for National Statistics: 020 7014 2122

16.9

General government[1]
Secondary distribution of income account

United Kingdom. ESA95 sector S.13 Unconsolidated

£ million

		1999	2000	2001	2002	2003	2004	2005	2006	2007
Resources										
Balance of primary incomes, gross	NMZH	112 121	120 022	125 233	132 268	139 787	148 387	144 068	152 015	158 517
Current taxes on income, wealth etc.										
Taxes on income	NMZJ	129 553	140 002	147 264	142 842	144 234	154 717	172 619	192 805	200 068
Other current taxes	NVCM	19 519	20 287	22 068	23 664	26 016	27 718	29 253	30 906	32 643
Total	NMZL	149 072	160 289	169 332	166 506	170 250	182 435	201 872	223 711	232 711
Social contributions										
Actual social contributions										
Employers' actual social contributions	NMZM	33 401	36 397	38 460	38 780	45 067	49 602	52 904	56 024	59 834
Employees' social contributions	NMZN	26 645	27 293	28 725	29 568	34 376	38 150	41 538	44 378	46 380
Social contributions by self- and non-employed persons	NMZO	1 883	2 049	2 183	2 318	2 595	2 727	2 825	2 930	2 890
Total	NMZP	61 929	65 739	69 368	70 666	82 038	90 479	97 267	103 332	109 104
Imputed social contributions	NMZQ	6 927	7 395	7 577	8 348	6 456	5 928	7 282	7 283	7 698
Total	NMZR	68 856	73 134	76 945	79 014	88 494	96 407	104 549	110 615	116 802
Other current transfers										
Non-life insurance claims	NMZS	410	403	353	400	296	285	328	373	275
Current transfers within general government	NMZT	64 446	66 187	72 522	77 592	85 224	91 910	100 224	110 297	112 789
Current international cooperation	NMZU	3 176	2 084	4 568	3 112	3 570	3 604	3 668	3 674	3 559
Miscellaneous current transfers										
from sectors other than general government	NMZX	392	447	460	502	562	610	627	589	591
Other current transfers	NNAA	68 424	69 121	77 903	81 606	89 652	96 409	104 847	114 933	117 214
Total resources	NNAB	398 473	422 566	449 413	459 394	488 183	523 638	555 336	601 274	625 244
Uses										
Social benefits other than social transfers in kind	NNAD	117 685	120 163	129 591	136 801	146 066	154 216	161 979	167 243	177 179
Other current transfers										
Net non-life insurance premiums	NNAE	410	403	353	400	296	285	328	373	275
Current transfers within general government	NNAF	64 446	66 187	72 522	77 592	85 224	91 910	100 224	110 297	112 789
Current international cooperation	NNAG	1 667	2 418	2 434	2 573	2 720	3 180	3 300	3 640	4 066
Miscellaneous current transfers										
to sectors other than general government	NNAI	18 466	20 913	22 131	27 351	30 275	32 550	34 947	34 708	36 019
Of which: GNP based fourth own resource	NMFH	4 632	4 379	3 858	5 335	6 772	7 549	8 732	8 521	8 323
Other current transfers	NNAN	84 989	89 921	97 440	107 916	118 515	127 925	138 799	149 018	153 149
Gross Disposable Income	NNAO	194 938	211 622	221 480	213 801	222 760	240 660	253 561	283 938	293 805
Total uses	NNAB	398 473	422 566	449 413	459 394	488 183	523 638	555 336	601 274	625 244
After deduction of fixed capital consumption	-NMXO	−9 262	−9 542	−9 796	−10 289	−10 807	−11 681	−12 605	−13 597	..
Disposable income, net	NNAP	185 676	202 080	211 684	203 512	211 953	228 979	240 956	268 305	..

1 See chapter text.

Source: Office for National Statistics: 020 7014 2122

16.10 Households and non-profit institutions serving households[1]
Allocation of primary income account
United Kingdom. ESA95 sectors S.14 and S.15

£ million

		1999	2000	2001	2002	2003	2004	2005	2006	2007
Resources										
Operating surplus, gross	QWLS	51 195	53 960	59 083	62 544	67 935	72 709	77 791	82 112	87 599
Mixed income, gross	QWLT	55 734	57 805	62 121	65 771	69 122	71 958	75 675	78 863	83 951
Compensation of employees										
Wages and salaries	QWLW	431 795	462 505	491 044	508 681	527 689	550 654	578 300	606 710	636 205
Employers' social contributions	QWLX	64 199	69 824	73 216	78 782	89 263	98 134	107 895	115 805	117 595
Total	QWLY	495 994	532 329	564 260	587 463	616 952	648 788	686 195	722 515	753 800
Property income										
Interest	QWLZ	24 147	28 239	26 823	20 878	20 966	26 242	31 422	32 824	40 937
Distributed income of corporations	QWMA	40 411	44 408	49 881	43 695	44 843	46 239	51 628	49 154	46 856
Attributed property income of insurance policy holders	QWMC	56 303	56 048	56 109	55 057	54 997	54 589	63 725	66 960	72 984
Rent	QWMD	105	105	105	106	108	110	110	112	106
Total	QWME	120 966	128 800	132 918	119 736	120 914	127 180	146 885	149 050	160 883
Total resources	QWMF	723 889	772 894	818 382	835 514	874 923	920 635	986 546	1 032 540	1 086 233
Uses										
Property income										
Interest	QWMG	47 434	52 875	52 141	51 513	53 576	62 677	69 497	73 381	86 326
Rent	QWMH	215	215	215	216	220	224	224	224	230
Total	QWMI	47 649	53 090	52 356	51 729	53 796	62 901	69 721	73 605	86 556
Balance of primary incomes, gross	QWMJ	676 240	719 804	766 026	783 785	821 127	857 734	916 825	958 935	999 677
Total uses	QWMF	723 889	772 894	818 382	835 514	874 923	920 635	986 546	1 032 540	1 086 233
After deduction of										
fixed capital consumption	-QWLL	−27 976	−30 518	−32 908	−36 043	−36 903	−42 509	−43 257	−48 623	..
Balance of primary incomes, net	QWMK	648 264	689 287	733 117	747 742	784 224	815 368	874 204	916 423	..

1 See chapter text.

Source: Office for National Statistics: 020 7014 2131

16.11 Households and non-profit institutions serving households[1]
Secondary distribution of income account
United Kingdom. ESA95 sectors S.14 and S.15

£ million

		1999	2000	2001	2002	2003	2004	2005	2006	2007
Resources										
Balance of primary incomes, gross	QWMJ	676 240	719 804	766 026	783 785	821 127	857 734	916 825	958 935	999 677
Imputed social contributions	RVFH	450	476	502	530	505	495	500	508	516
Social benefits other than social transfers in kind	QWML	157 647	162 833	171 814	182 673	193 596	202 074	213 858	222 618	232 143
Other current transfers										
Non-life insurance claims	QWMM	13 762	16 150	15 607	17 177	14 824	15 494	17 172	20 729	15 371
Miscellaneous current transfers	QWMN	24 392	27 520	29 080	33 041	34 687	36 284	38 489	38 742	39 782
Total	QWMO	38 154	43 670	44 687	50 218	49 511	51 778	55 661	59 471	55 153
Total resources	QWMP	872 491	926 783	983 029	1 017 206	1 064 739	1 112 081	1 186 844	1 241 532	1 287 489
Uses										
Current taxes on income, wealth etc										
Taxes on income	QWMQ	96 528	105 299	111 888	112 171	113 087	120 253	130 342	139 962	151 574
Other current taxes	NVCO	18 658	19 427	21 166	22 788	25 174	26 881	28 256	29 831	31 532
Total	QWMS	115 186	124 726	133 054	134 959	138 261	147 134	158 598	169 793	183 106
Social contributions										
Actual social contributions										
Employers' actual social contributions	QWMT	52 529	57 288	60 296	64 805	77 571	87 347	95 997	104 016	105 361
Employees' social contributions	QWMU	57 434	58 806	60 599	62 458	66 490	69 576	78 033	83 495	87 548
Social contributions by self and non-employed	QWMV	1 883	2 049	2 183	2 318	2 595	2 727	2 825	2 930	2 890
Total	QWMW	111 846	118 143	123 078	129 581	146 656	159 650	176 855	189 696	..
Imputed social contributions	QWMX	11 670	12 536	12 920	13 977	11 692	10 787	11 898	11 789	12 234
Total	QWMY	123 516	130 679	135 998	143 558	158 348	170 437	188 753	202 230	208 033
Social benefits other than social transfers in kind	QWMZ	922	948	977	1 006	987	984	994	1 004	1 012
Other current transfers										
Net non-life insurance premiums	QWNA	13 762	16 150	15 607	17 177	14 824	15 494	17 172	20 729	15 371
Miscellaneous current transfers	QWNB	10 117	10 865	11 081	11 458	11 930	12 349	13 340	13 269	13 550
Total	QWNC	23 879	27 015	26 688	28 635	26 754	27 843	30 512	33 998	28 921
Gross Disposable Income[2]	QWND	608 988	643 415	686 312	709 048	740 389	765 683	807 987	834 507	866 417
Total uses	QWMP	872 491	926 783	983 029	1 017 206	1 064 739	1 112 081	1 186 844	1 241 532	1 287 489
After deduction of fixed capital consumption	-QWLL	−27 976	−30 518	−32 908	−36 043	−36 903	−42 509	−43 257	−48 623	..
Disposable income, net	QWNE	581 012	612 898	653 403	673 005	703 486	723 317	765 366	793 314	..

1 See chapter text.
2 Gross household disposable income revalued by the implied households and NPISH's final consumption expenditure deflator. For more details see table 6.1.4 on page 217 in *United Kingdom National Accounts* (the *Blue book*).

Source: Office for National Statistics: 020 7014 2131

16.12 Households and non-profit institutions serving households[1]
Use of disposable income account
United Kingdom. ESA95 sectors S.14 and S.15

£ million and percentages

		1999	2000	2001	2002	2003	2004	2005	2006	2007
Resources										
Disposable income, gross	QWND	608 988	643 415	686 312	709 048	740 389	765 683	807 987	834 507	866 417
Adjustment for the change in net equity of households in pension funds	NSSE	14 016	14 164	16 041	17 783	21 377	25 108	31 210	35 043	34 955
Total resources	NSSF	623 004	657 579	702 353	726 831	761 766	790 791	839 197	869 550	901 372
Uses										
Final consumption expenditure										
Individual consumption expenditure	NSSG	589 868	623 995	657 216	690 530	724 345	761 484	792 454	827 641	874 959
Saving, gross	NSSH	33 136	33 584	45 137	36 301	37 421	29 307	46 743	41 909	26 413
Total uses	NSSF	623 004	657 579	702 353	726 831	761 766	790 791	839 197	869 550	901 372
Saving ratio (percentages)	RVGL	5.3	5.1	6.4	5.0	4.9	3.7	5.6	4.8	2.9

1 See chapter text.

Source: Office for National Statistics: 020 7014 2131

16.13

The sector accounts: key economic indicators[1]
United Kingdom

£ million and indices (2003=100)

		1999	2000	2001	2002	2003	2004	2005	2006	2007
Net lending/borrowing by:										
Non-financial corporations	EABO	−13 157	−7 541	−10 509	6 529	18 181	26 255	21 040	13 796	7 556
Financial corporations	NHCQ	−14 185	−27 457	−22 800	7 018	19 335	26 479	7 830	3 226	25 592
General government	NNBK	8 749	13 338	6 727	−20 164	−37 013	−40 144	−41 969	−33 307	−40 095
Households and NPISH's	NSSZ	−4 112	−4 205	2 938	−11 841	−14 687	−32 241	−13 954	−28 565	−50 464
Rest of the world	NHRB	20 970	23 130	20 566	15 581	13 455	17 265	29 494	49 872	55 336
Private non-financial corporations										
Gross trading profits										
Continental shelf profits	CAGJ	13 864	21 458	20 397	18 742	..	..	..	..	..
Others	CAED	160 743	160 153	159 134	167 068	181 339	199 272	202 699	210 125	231 637
Rental of buildings	FCBW	10 821	11 747	12 394	12 904	13 891	14 864	15 404	16 005	16 787
less Holding gains of inventories	-DLQZ	−1 800	−2 941	438	−2 856	−4 266	−6 158	−6 619	−5 486	−6 306
Gross operating surplus	NRJK	183 283	189 745	191 062	195 548	208 945	226 203	234 129	246 767	264 941
Households and NPISH										
Household gross disposable income	QWND	608 988	643 415	686 312	709 048	740 389	765 683	807 987	834 507	866 417
Implied deflator of household and NPISH individual consumption expenditure indicies (2003=100)	YBFS	93.4	94.4	96.6	98.1	100.0	101.7	104.2	106.7	109.4
Real household disposable income:										
Chained volume measures (Reference year 2003)	RVGK	652 060	681 249	710 531	722 823	740 389	752 890	775 072	782 029	791 672
Indices (2003=100)	OSXR	88.1	92.0	96.0	97.6	100.0	101.7	104.7	105.7	106.9
Gross saving	NSSH	33 136	33 584	45 137	36 301	37 421	29 307	46 743	41 909	26 413
Households total resources	NSSJ	725 746	766 876	820 811	857 647	905 720	946 602	1 006 596	1 044 856	1 085 874
Saving ratio (percentages)	RVGL	*5.3*	*5.1*	*6.4*	*5.0*	*4.9*	*3.7*	*5.6*	*4.8*	*2.9*

1 See chapter text.

Source: Office for National Statistics: 020 7014 2083

16.14 Household final consumption expenditure: by purpose[1]
Current market prices
United Kingdom

£ million

		1999	2000	2001	2002	2003	2004	2005	2006	2007
Durable goods										
Furnishings, household equipment and routine maintenance of the house	LLIJ	16 566	18 006	19 275	20 470	21 595	22 363	22 535	23 192	24 426
Health	LLIK	1 881	1 997	2 109	2 411	2 604	2 727	2 710	3 091	3 220
Transport	LLIL	31 888	33 291	35 864	36 574	38 016	38 792	38 319	38 646	39 827
Communication	LLIM	512	601	636	644	810	859	958	935	978
Recreation and culture	LLIN	14 262	14 878	15 970	16 471	17 752	19 373	19 593	20 297	21 003
Miscellaneous goods and services	LLIO	3 398	3 403	3 750	4 204	4 284	4 539	4 357	4 540	4 542
Total durable goods	UTIA	68 507	72 176	77 604	80 774	85 061	88 653	88 472	90 701	93 996
Semi-durable goods										
Clothing and footwear	LLJL	32 661	34 759	36 092	38 351	40 389	42 006	43 170	45 213	47 041
Furnishings, household equipment and routine maintenance of the house	LLJM	10 577	11 677	12 400	13 361	13 932	14 462	13 641	14 273	14 706
Transport	LLJN	3 018	2 772	2 783	3 112	3 423	3 381	3 537	3 785	3 821
Recreation and culture	LLJO	19 049	20 405	21 606	23 910	26 009	28 228	28 692	29 810	30 987
Miscellaneous goods and services	LLJP	1 926	2 018	2 427	2 886	3 356	3 754	3 432	3 299	3 471
Total semi-durable goods	UTIQ	67 231	71 631	75 308	81 620	87 109	91 831	92 472	96 380	100 026
Non-durable goods										
Food & drink	ABZV	57 040	58 628	59 804	61 310	63 174	65 521	67 539	70 929	76 505
Alcohol & tobacco	ADFL	24 458	24 617	25 158	25 966	27 297	27 713	28 073	28 522	29 780
Housing, water, electricity, gas and other fuels	LLIX	21 800	22 265	23 076	23 444	24 241	27 011	28 441	32 789	35 101
Furnishings, household equipment and routine maintenance of the house	LLIY	2 657	2 786	2 972	3 169	3 338	3 391	3 456	3 681	3 652
Health	LLIZ	3 111	3 268	3 613	3 855	3 938	4 023	3 815	3 852	3 879
Transport	LLJA	18 210	19 987	19 391	19 129	20 072	21 873	23 689	23 843	23 818
Recreation and culture	LLJB	12 665	12 959	13 107	13 392	13 507	13 650	13 831	14 088	14 559
Miscellaneous goods and services	LLJC	9 121	9 463	9 884	11 272	12 602	13 486	14 108	14 347	15 674
Total non-durable goods	UTII	149 062	153 973	157 005	161 537	168 169	176 668	182 952	192 051	202 968
Total goods	UTIE	284 800	297 780	309 917	323 931	340 339	357 152	363 896	379 132	396 990
Services										
Clothing and footwear	LLJD	714	720	730	741	766	786	843	902	929
Housing, water, electricity, gas and other fuels	LLJE	81 393	85 785	92 829	97 794	104 810	111 029	118 484	125 572	134 803
Furnishings, household equipment and routine maintenance of the house	LLJF	3 046	3 206	3 327	3 448	3 601	3 813	4 013	4 142	4 200
Health	LLJG	3 783	3 943	4 254	4 512	4 793	5 182	5 577	5 533	6 108
Transport	LLJH	34 121	37 002	38 397	41 332	43 058	45 167	47 393	49 909	52 533
Communication	LLJI	11 493	12 755	13 521	14 031	14 844	15 589	15 814	15 993	16 691
Recreation and culture	LLJJ	21 505	21 912	22 769	25 349	27 118	29 806	32 003	33 524	35 325
Education	ADIE	8 943	9 534	9 409	9 381	9 610	9 990	10 409	10 998	12 157
Restaurants and hotels	ADIF	64 387	68 557	71 620	76 426	78 902	83 595	88 934	92 012	96 442
Miscellaneous goods and services	LLJK	48 431	52 691	56 199	57 054	57 161	58 381	61 454	63 999	69 327
Total services	UTIM	277 816	296 105	313 055	330 068	344 663	363 338	384 924	402 584	428 515
Final consumption expenditure in the UK by resident and non-resident households (domestic concept)	ABQI	562 616	593 885	622 972	653 999	685 002	720 490	748 820	781 716	825 505
Final consumption expenditure outside the UK by UK resident households	ABTA	19 690	21 654	22 907	24 435	26 314	27 739	29 209	30 564	32 362
less Final consumption expenditure in the UK by households resident in the rest of the world	CDFD	−14 312	−14 713	−13 383	−13 872	−14 156	−15 698	−17 160	−18 605	−19 582
Final consumption expenditure by UK resident households in the UK and abroad (national concept)	ABPB	567 994	600 826	632 496	664 562	697 160	732 531	760 869	793 675	838 285

1 See chapter text. Additional detail is published in *Consumer Trends* and table A7 of *UK Economic Accounts*, available from the National Statistics website *www.statistics.gov.uk/statbase/Product.asp?vlnk=1904*.

Source: Office for National Statistics: 020 7014 2116

16.15 Household final consumption expenditure: by purpose[1]
Chained volume measures, reference year 2003

United Kingdom

£ million

		1999	2000	2001	2002	2003	2004	2005	2006	2007
Durable goods										
Furnishings, household equipment and routine maintenance of the house	LLME	16 764	18 442	19 542	20 603	21 595	22 030	21 892	22 228	22 641
Health	LLMF	2 585	2 455	2 337	2 421	2 604	2 612	2 562	2 938	3 010
Transport	LLMG	29 455	31 680	35 100	36 057	38 016	39 107	39 571	40 364	41 453
Communication	LLMH	428	536	582	640	810	883	1 082	1 133	1 427
Recreation and culture	LLMI	9 657	11 243	13 344	14 911	17 752	21 381	24 909	28 982	35 010
Miscellaneous goods and services	LLMJ	3 656	3 618	3 932	4 360	4 284	4 445	4 227	4 146	3 984
Total durable goods	UTIC	61 603	67 366	74 551	78 825	85 061	90 458	94 243	99 791	107 525
Semi-durable goods										
Clothing and footwear	LLNG	27 921	30 969	33 712	37 727	40 389	43 327	45 637	48 279	50 892
Furnishings, household equipment and routine maintenance of the house	LLNH	10 177	11 473	12 221	13 215	13 932	14 426	13 862	14 615	14 888
Transport	LLNI	3 136	2 856	2 880	3 172	3 423	3 313	3 369	3 486	3 474
Recreation and culture	LLNJ	17 229	19 175	20 339	23 040	26 009	29 115	30 179	31 868	32 765
Miscellaneous goods and services	LLNK	1 932	2 053	2 438	2 920	3 356	3 771	3 354	3 175	3 255
Total semi-durable goods	UTIS	60 277	66 478	71 563	80 058	87 109	93 952	96 401	101 423	105 274
Non-durable goods										
Food & drink	ADIP	59 904	61 944	61 048	62 143	63 174	65 181	66 231	67 970	70 453
Alcohol & tobacco	ADIS	27 623	26 704	26 497	26 884	27 297	27 444	27 325	26 900	27 347
Housing, water, electricity, gas and other fuels	LLMS	22 594	23 189	23 958	23 881	24 241	25 723	24 743	24 445	24 312
Furnishings, household equipment and routine maintenance of the house	LLMT	2 492	2 666	2 878	3 101	3 338	3 519	3 582	3 687	3 593
Health	LLMU	3 314	3 397	3 686	3 895	3 938	4 043	3 830	3 930	3 894
Transport	LLMV	19 691	19 114	19 550	19 825	20 072	20 731	20 719	19 809	19 233
Recreation and culture	LLMW	13 713	13 657	13 537	13 681	13 507	13 463	13 571	13 483	13 770
Miscellaneous goods and services	LLMX	8 669	9 248	9 586	11 124	12 602	13 631	14 399	15 146	16 137
Total non-durable goods	UTIK	157 573	159 677	160 597	164 482	168 169	173 735	174 400	175 370	178 739
Total goods	UTIG	277 468	292 390	306 198	323 179	340 339	358 145	365 044	376 584	391 538
Services										
Clothing and footwear	LLMY	819	805	790	775	766	760	773	791	777
Housing, water, electricity, gas and other fuels	LLMZ	101 184	102 168	102 778	104 106	104 810	105 767	107 013	108 882	110 118
Furnishings, household equipment and routine maintenance of the house	LLNA	3 874	3 821	3 718	3 646	3 601	3 602	3 595	3 548	3 433
Health	LLNB	4 531	4 612	4 683	4 665	4 793	4 954	5 244	5 124	5 489
Transport	LLNC	41 413	43 153	40 971	42 611	43 058	43 459	43 657	44 277	45 111
Communication	LLND	10 527	12 167	13 877	14 158	14 844	15 478	16 038	16 222	17 408
Recreation and culture	LLNE	24 795	25 101	25 960	26 216	27 118	28 930	29 935	29 874	30 336
Education	ADMJ	11 394	11 489	10 692	10 091	9 610	9 541	9 476	9 480	9 757
Restaurants and hotels	ADMK	74 191	76 252	76 434	78 303	78 902	81 796	83 893	83 648	84 763
Miscellaneous goods and services	LLNF	53 735	55 696	57 368	57 336	57 161	56 232	55 739	55 843	57 241
Total services	UTIO	325 416	334 699	337 218	341 883	344 663	350 519	355 363	357 689	364 433
Final consumption expenditure in the UK by resident and non-resident households (domestic concept)	ABQJ	600 627	625 437	642 595	664 790	685 002	708 664	720 407	734 273	755 971
Final consumption expenditure outside the UK by UK resident households	ABTC	21 899	24 189	24 897	26 376	26 314	28 068	27 750	28 419	29 658
less Final consumption expenditure in the UK by households resident in the rest of the world	CCHX	−16 031	−16 038	−14 164	−14 292	−14 156	−15 298	−16 152	−16 955	−17 232
Final consumption expenditure by UK resident households in the UK and abroad (national concept)	ABPF	606 648	633 662	653 326	676 833	697 160	721 434	732 005	745 737	768 397

1 See chapter text. Additional detail is published in *Consumer Trends* and table A7 of *UK Economic Accounts*, available from the National Statistics website *www.statistics.gov.uk/statbase/Product.asp?vlnk=1904*.

Source: Office for National Statistics: 020 7014 2116

16.16 Individual consumption expenditure: by households, NPISHs and general government[1] Current market prices

United Kingdom. Classified by function (COICOP/COPNI/COFOG)[2]

£ million

		1999	2000	2001	2002	2003	2004	2005	2006	2007
FINAL CONSUMPTION EXPENDITURE OF HOUSEHOLDS										
Food and non-alcoholic beverages	ABZV	57 040	58 628	59 804	61 310	63 174	65 521	67 539	70 929	76 505
Food	ABZW	50 685	51 905	52 742	53 984	55 507	57 357	59 366	61 817	66 767
Non-alcoholic beverages	ADFK	6 355	6 723	7 062	7 326	7 667	8 164	8 173	9 112	9 738
Alcoholic beverages and tobacco	ADFL	24 458	24 617	25 158	25 966	27 297	27 713	28 073	28 522	29 780
Alcoholic beverages	ADFM	10 166	10 395	10 700	11 344	12 027	12 213	12 344	12 417	13 140
Tobacco	ADFN	14 292	14 222	14 458	14 622	15 270	15 500	15 729	16 105	16 640
Clothing and footwear	ADFP	33 375	35 479	36 822	39 092	41 155	42 792	44 013	46 115	47 970
Clothing	ADFQ	28 932	31 048	32 103	33 927	35 689	37 112	38 351	40 381	41 997
Footwear	ADFR	4 443	4 431	4 719	5 165	5 466	5 680	5 662	5 734	5 973
Housing, water, electricity, gas and other fuels	ADFS	103 193	108 050	115 905	121 238	129 051	138 040	146 925	158 361	169 904
Actual rentals for housing	ADFT	22 584	23 595	25 302	25 828	27 610	28 784	30 286	32 500	35 133
Imputed rentals for housing	ADFU	51 401	54 378	59 581	63 279	68 458	73 160	78 502	82 388	87 807
Maintenance and repair of the dwelling	ADFV	10 234	10 512	11 340	12 306	12 615	13 379	13 440	13 920	15 357
Water supply and miscellaneous dwelling services	ADFW	5 201	5 033	5 059	5 222	5 438	5 698	6 389	6 936	7 353
Electricity, gas and other fuels	ADFX	13 773	14 532	14 623	14 603	14 930	17 019	18 308	22 617	24 254
Furnishings, household equipment and routine maintenance of the house	ADFY	32 846	35 675	37 974	40 448	42 466	44 029	43 645	45 288	46 984
Furniture, furnishings, carpets and other floor coverings	ADFZ	12 437	13 758	14 362	15 591	16 789	17 645	17 616	18 353	18 997
Household textiles	ADGG	3 972	4 465	4 636	5 086	5 452	5 680	5 326	5 409	5 692
Household appliances	ADGL	5 038	5 156	5 758	5 715	5 578	5 563	5 560	5 806	6 039
Glassware, tableware and household utensils	ADGM	3 722	4 231	4 609	4 710	4 701	4 635	4 591	4 762	4 990
Tools and equipment for house and garden	ADGN	2 586	2 722	2 977	3 355	3 589	3 919	3 670	3 674	3 904
Goods and services for routine household maintenance	ADGO	5 091	5 343	5 632	5 991	6 357	6 587	6 882	7 284	7 362
Health	ADGP	8 775	9 208	9 976	10 778	11 335	11 932	12 102	12 476	13 207
Medical products, appliances and equipment	ADGQ	4 992	5 265	5 722	6 266	6 542	6 750	6 525	6 943	7 099
Out-patient services	ADGR	2 107	2 178	2 344	2 422	2 553	2 752	3 007	2 996	3 498
Hospital services	ADGS	1 676	1 765	1 910	2 090	2 240	2 430	2 570	2 537	2 610
Transport	ADGT	87 237	93 052	96 435	100 147	104 569	109 213	112 938	116 183	119 999
Purchase of vehicles	ADGU	31 888	33 291	35 864	36 574	38 016	38 792	38 319	38 646	39 827
Operation of personal transport equipment	ADGV	34 450	37 059	37 028	38 816	40 507	42 915	45 683	47 256	48 177
Transport services	ADGW	20 899	22 702	23 543	24 757	26 046	27 506	28 936	30 281	31 995
Communication	ADGX	12 005	13 356	14 157	14 675	15 654	16 448	16 772	16 928	17 669
Postal services	CDEF	899	873	870	878	890	892	926	894	941
Telephone & telefax equipment	ADWO	512	601	636	644	810	859	958	935	978
Telephone & telefax services	ADWP	10 594	11 882	12 651	13 153	13 954	14 697	14 888	15 099	15 750
Recreation and culture	ADGY	67 481	70 154	73 452	79 122	84 386	91 057	94 119	97 719	101 874
Audio-visual, photographic and information processing equipment	ADGZ	16 312	17 034	17 580	18 051	19 408	21 820	21 586	21 773	22 281
Other major durables for recreation and culture	ADHL	3 582	3 944	4 325	4 672	5 126	5 428	5 737	6 265	6 581
Other recreational items and equipment; flowers, garden and pets	ADHZ	17 655	18 636	20 216	22 475	23 894	25 041	25 605	26 930	28 687
Recreational and cultural services	ADIA	19 876	20 272	21 034	23 555	25 278	27 772	29 888	31 251	32 728
Newspapers, books and stationery	ADIC	10 056	10 268	10 297	10 369	10 680	10 996	11 303	11 500	11 597
Package holidays[3]	ADID	–	–	–	–	–	–	–	–	–
Education										
Education services	ADIE	8 943	9 534	9 409	9 381	9 610	9 990	10 409	10 998	12 157
Restaurants and hotels	ADIF	64 387	68 557	71 620	76 426	78 902	83 595	88 934	92 012	96 442
Catering services	ADIG	55 164	59 019	62 449	66 701	68 839	72 837	77 046	78 837	81 926
Accommodation services	ADIH	9 223	9 538	9 171	9 725	10 063	10 758	11 888	13 175	14 516
Miscellaneous goods and services	ADII	62 876	67 575	72 260	75 416	77 403	80 160	83 351	86 185	93 014
Personal care	ADIJ	13 229	13 883	14 626	16 444	18 181	19 558	20 328	20 623	22 223
Personal effects not elsewhere classified	ADIK	4 673	4 748	5 455	6 140	6 462	6 866	6 581	6 818	6 907
Social protection	ADIL	8 446	8 643	8 963	9 219	9 501	9 821	10 124	10 285	11 294
Insurance	ADIM	20 257	22 238	25 423	25 456	24 373	23 178	24 393	24 854	26 548
Financial services not elsewhere classified	ADIN	10 009	11 974	11 708	11 982	12 529	14 208	15 166	16 839	18 523
Other services not elsewhere classified	ADIO	6 262	6 089	6 085	6 175	6 357	6 529	6 759	6 766	7 519
Final consumption expenditure in the UK by resident and non-resident households (domestic concept)	ABQI	562 616	593 885	622 972	653 999	685 002	720 490	748 820	781 716	825 505
Final consumption expenditure outside the UK by UK resident households	ABTA	19 690	21 654	22 907	24 435	26 314	27 739	29 209	30 564	32 362
less Final consumption expenditure in the UK by households resident in the rest of the world	CDFD	–14 312	–14 713	–13 383	–13 872	–14 156	–15 698	–17 160	–18 605	–19 582
Final consumption expenditure by UK resident households in the UK and abroad (national concept)	ABPB	567 994	600 826	632 496	664 562	697 160	732 531	760 869	793 675	838 285

16.16
continued

Individual consumption expenditure: by households, NPISHs and general government[1] Current market prices

United Kingdom. Classified by function (COICOP/COPNI/COFOG)[2]

£ million

		1999	2000	2001	2002	2003	2004	2005	2006	2007
FINAL CONSUMPTION EXPENDITURE OF UK RESIDENT HOUSEHOLDS										
Final consumption expenditure of UK resident households in the UK and abroad	ABPB	567 994	600 826	632 496	664 562	697 160	732 531	760 869	793 675	838 285
FINAL INDIVIDUAL CONSUMPTION EXPENDITURE OF NPISH										
Final individual consumption expenditure of NPISH	ABNV	21 874	23 169	24 720	25 968	27 185	28 953	31 585	33 966	36 674
FINAL INDIVIDUAL CONSUMPTION EXPENDITURE OF OF GENERAL GOVERNMENT										
Health	QYOT	50 254	53 236	58 032	63 388	69 888	76 855	83 579	85 331	..
Recreation and culture	QYSU	3 736	3 898	4 049	4 335	4 513	4 272	..	..	..
Education	QYSE	29 484	31 521	33 900	37 535	39 876	42 727	11 058	47 235	..
Social protection	QYSP	16 843	18 055	19 441	22 464	25 517	28 028	..	..	..
Housing	QYXO	–	–	–	–	..	..	..	..	..
Final individual consumption expenditure of general government	NNAQ	102 742	109 297	118 458	130 816	143 954	155 811	167 399	175 306	184 502
Total, individual consumption expenditure/ actual individual consumption	NQEO	692 610	733 292	775 674	821 346	868 299	917 295	959 853	1 002 947	1 059 461

1 See chapter text.
2 "Purpose" or "function" classifications are designed to indicate the "socio-economic objectives" that institutional units aim to achieve through various kinds of outlays. COICOP is the Classification of Individual Consumption by Purpose and applies to households. COPNI is the Classification of the Purposes of Non-Profit Institutions Serving Households and COFOG the Classification of the Functions of Government. The introduction of ESA95 coincides with the redefinition of these classifications and data will be available on a consistent basis for all European Union member states.
3 Package holidays data are dispersed between components (transport etc).

Source: Office for National Statistics: 020 7014 2116

16.17 Individual consumption expenditure: by households, NPISHs and general government[1] Chained volume measures, reference year 2003

United Kingdom. Classified by function (COICOP/COPNI/COFOG)[2]

£ million

		1999	2000	2001	2002	2003	2004	2005	2006	2007
FINAL CONSUMPTION EXPENDITURE OF HOUSEHOLDS										
Food and non-alcoholic beverages	ADIP	59 904	61 944	61 048	62 143	63 174	65 181	66 231	67 970	70 453
Food	ADIQ	53 697	55 255	53 992	54 835	55 507	56 946	57 997	59 124	61 317
Non-alcoholic beverages	ADIR	6 260	6 725	7 063	7 312	7 667	8 235	8 234	8 846	9 136
Alcoholic beverages and tobacco	ADIS	27 623	26 704	26 497	26 884	27 297	27 444	27 325	26 900	27 347
Alcoholic beverages	ADIT	10 309	10 476	10 831	11 516	12 027	12 369	12 590	12 471	13 136
Tobacco	ADIU	17 541	16 341	15 716	15 380	15 270	15 075	14 735	14 429	14 211
Clothing and footwear	ADIW	28 689	31 744	34 485	38 499	41 155	44 087	46 410	49 070	51 669
Clothing	ADIX	24 424	27 394	29 827	33 315	35 689	38 407	40 606	43 106	45 522
Footwear	ADIY	4 324	4 360	4 660	5 185	5 466	5 680	5 804	5 964	6 147
Housing, water, electricity, gas and other fuels	ADIZ	123 662	125 299	126 749	127 979	129 051	131 490	131 756	133 327	134 430
Actual rentals for housing	ADJA	27 366	27 345	27 418	27 084	27 610	27 555	27 782	28 838	29 193
Imputed rentals for housing	ADJB	64 980	65 704	66 495	67 872	68 458	69 617	70 651	71 089	71 474
Maintenance and repair of the dwelling	ADJC	11 791	11 675	12 139	12 702	12 615	13 007	12 683	12 735	13 407
Water supply and miscellaneous dwelling services	ADJD	5 228	5 386	5 379	5 424	5 438	5 412	5 522	5 615	5 599
Electricity, gas and other fuels	ADJE	14 363	15 149	15 277	14 891	14 930	15 899	15 118	15 050	14 757
Furnishings, household equipment and routine maintenance of the house	ADJF	33 130	36 305	38 310	40 552	42 466	43 577	42 931	44 078	44 555
Furniture, furnishings, carpets and other floor coverings	ADJG	13 120	14 514	14 860	15 896	16 789	17 206	16 715	17 016	16 928
Household textiles	ADJH	3 743	4 361	4 534	5 043	5 452	5 604	5 375	5 577	5 927
Household appliances	ADJI	4 648	4 922	5 549	5 566	5 578	5 649	5 735	6 158	6 264
Glassware, tableware and household utensils	ADJJ	3 699	4 266	4 655	4 717	4 701	4 620	4 674	4 856	4 955
Tools and equipment for house and garden	ADJK	2 435	2 590	2 856	3 238	3 589	3 972	3 796	3 723	3 889
Goods and services for routine household maintenance	ADJL	5 556	5 708	5 859	6 092	6 357	6 526	6 636	6 748	6 592
Health	ADJM	10 362	10 421	10 697	10 980	11 335	11 609	11 636	11 992	12 393
Medical products, appliances and equipment	ADJN	5 839	5 819	6 020	6 315	6 542	6 655	6 392	6 868	6 904
Out-patient services	ADJO	2 556	2 528	2 560	2 492	2 553	2 685	2 903	2 797	3 172
Hospital services	ADJP	1 976	2 082	2 122	2 173	2 240	2 269	2 341	2 327	2 317
Transport	ADJQ	92 969	96 209	98 485	101 621	104 569	106 610	107 316	107 936	109 271
Purchase of vehicles	ADJR	29 455	31 680	35 100	36 057	38 016	39 107	39 571	40 364	41 453
Operation of personal transport equipment	ADJS	39 617	39 124	39 225	40 668	40 507	40 578	40 225	39 437	38 711
Transport services	ADJT	24 661	25 913	24 214	24 965	26 046	26 925	27 520	28 135	29 107
Communication	ADJU	10 948	12 698	14 452	14 796	15 654	16 361	17 120	17 355	18 835
Postal services	CCGZ	960	916	901	906	890	866	941	995	1 146
Telephone & telefax equipment	ADQF	428	536	582	640	810	883	1 082	1 133	1 427
Telephone & telefax services	ADQG	9 604	11 264	12 978	13 254	13 954	14 612	15 097	15 227	16 262
Recreation and culture	ADJV	63 601	68 038	72 552	77 597	84 386	92 889	98 594	104 207	111 881
Audio-visual, photographic and information processing equipment	ADJW	11 178	13 022	14 690	16 301	19 408	24 316	27 665	31 332	37 022
Other major durables for recreation and culture	ADJX	3 798	4 182	4 560	4 817	5 126	5 261	5 489	5 974	6 296
Other recreational items and equipment; flowers, gardens and pets	ADJY	16 190	17 455	18 980	21 642	23 894	25 585	26 490	28 302	29 873
Recreational and cultural services	ADJZ	22 827	23 206	24 049	24 333	25 278	26 993	28 012	27 891	28 160
Newspapers, books and stationery	ADKM	11 242	11 181	10 910	10 756	10 680	10 734	10 938	10 708	10 530
Package holidays[3]	ADMI	–	–	–	–	–	–	–	–	–
Education										
Education services	ADMJ	11 394	11 489	10 692	10 091	9 610	9 541	9 476	9 480	9 757
Restaurants and Hotels	ADMK	74 191	76 252	76 434	78 303	78 902	81 796	83 893	83 648	84 763
Catering services	ADML	63 354	65 644	66 815	68 462	68 839	71 244	72 812	71 945	72 304
Accommodation services	ADMM	10 851	10 610	9 620	9 843	10 063	10 552	11 081	11 703	12 459
Miscellaneous goods and services	ADMN	67 867	70 524	73 239	75 715	77 403	78 079	77 719	78 310	80 617
Personal care	ADMO	13 497	14 251	14 719	16 526	18 181	19 482	20 113	20 709	21 756
Personal effects not elsewhere classified	ADMP	4 871	4 922	5 607	6 289	6 462	6 791	6 428	6 371	6 236
Social protection	ADMQ	10 778	10 357	10 058	9 760	9 501	9 306	9 033	8 638	9 142
Insurance	ADMR	22 511	23 526	25 453	24 880	24 373	22 776	22 399	22 175	21 813
Financial services not elsewhere classified	ADMS	8 966	10 421	10 694	11 733	12 529	13 678	13 815	14 793	15 622
Other services not elsewhere classified	ADMT	7 937	7 336	6 827	6 536	6 357	6 046	5 931	5 624	6 048
Final consumption expenditure in the UK by resident and non-resident households (domestic concept)	ABQJ	600 627	625 437	642 595	664 790	685 002	708 664	720 407	734 273	755 971
Final consumption expenditure outside the UK by UK resident households	ABTC	21 899	24 189	24 897	26 376	26 314	28 068	27 750	28 419	29 658
less Final consumption expenditure in the UK by households resident in the rest of the world	CCHX	−16 031	−16 038	−14 164	−14 292	−14 156	−15 298	−16 152	−16 955	−17 232
Final consumption expenditure by UK resident households in the UK and abroad (national concept)	ABPF	606 648	633 662	653 326	676 833	697 160	721 434	732 005	745 737	768 397

16.17
continued

Individual consumption expenditure: by households, NPISHs and general government[1] Chained volume measures, reference year 2003

United Kingdom. Classified by function (COICOP/COPNI/COFOG)[2]

£ million

		1999	2000	2001	2002	2003	2004	2005	2006	2007
FINAL CONSUMPTION EXPENDITURE OF UK RESIDENT HOUSEHOLDS										
Final consumption expenditure of UK resident households in the UK and abroad	ABPF	606 648	633 662	653 326	676 833	697 160	721 434	732 005	745 737	768 397
FINAL INDIVIDUAL CONSUMPTION EXPENDITURE OF NPISH										
Final individual consumption expenditure of NPISH	ABNU	25 023	27 177	27 155	27 130	27 185	27 327	28 167	29 858	31 079
FINAL INDIVIDUAL CONSUMPTION EXPENDITURE OF GENERAL GOVERNMENT										
Health	EMOA	56 805	58 517	61 019	63 272	65 611	68 758	..	..	..
Recreation and culture	QYXK	3 930	4 051	3 968	4 470	4 717	..	..	..	..
Education	EMOB	36 520	36 876	37 100	37 535	37 732	37 944	..	..	..
Social protection	QYXM	23 359	23 454	23 645	24 864	25 843	26 811	26 698	27 323	..
Housing	QYXN	–	–	–	–	–	..	..	..	..
Final individual consumption expenditure of general government	NSZK	109 554	111 763	114 159	117 238	120 288	..	..	..	..
Total, individual consumption expenditure/ actual individual consumption	YBIO	760 172	792 076	815 286	843 504	868 299	897 055	911 168	929 237	..

1 See chapter text.
2 "Purpose" or "function" classifications are designed to indicate the "socio-economic objectives" that institutional units aim to achieve through various kinds of outlays. COICOP is the Classification of Individual Consumption by Purpose and applies to households. COPNI is the Classification of the Purposes of Non-Profit Institutions Serving Households (NPISH) and COFOG the Classification of the Functions of Government. The introduction of ESA95 coincides with the redefinition of these classifications and data will be available on a consistent basis for all European Union member states.
3 Package holidays data are dispersed between components (transport etc).

Source: Office for National Statistics: 020 7014 2116

16.18

Change in inventories[1,2]
Chained volume measures, reference year 2003

United Kingdom

Reference year 2003, £ million

	Mining and quarrying	Manufacturing industries				Electricity, gas and water supply	Distributive trades		Other industries[4]	Change in inventories
		Materials and fuel	Work in progress	Finished goods	Total		Wholesale[3]	Retail[3]		
	FADO	FBID	FBIE	FBIF	DHBH	FADP	FAJM	FBYH	DLWV	ABMQ
1998	367	537	−703	317	151	−163	666	1 186	2 636	4 291
1999	−325	503	−259	−430	−186	−167	1 743	1 722	3 464	5 803
2000	−263	543	358	418	1 319	202	1 939	1 480	−283	4 648
2001	87	−513	369	160	16	16	887	1 113	3 458	5 577
2002	−37	−496	−149	−372	−1 017	−132	788	1 716	971	2 289
2003	−66	−198	−650	−138	−986	−13	407	1 241	3 399	3 982
2004	−46	7	−614	−296	−903	8	304	1 000	4 234	4 597
2005	−47	−179	863	56	740	586	978	−412	1 766	3 611
2006	−58	−273	598	−234	91	210	490	677	1 006	2 416
2007	−104	280	−398	633	515	−270	293	1 995	4 093	6 523

1 See chapter text. Estimates are given to the nearest £ million but cannot be regarded as accurate to this degree.
2 Components may not sum to totals due to rounding.
3 Wholesaling and retailing estimates exclude the motor trades.
4 Quarterly alignment adjustment included in this series.

Source: Office for National Statistics 020 7014 2083

16.19 Gross fixed capital formation at current purchasers' prices: by broad sector and type of asset[1,2]

United Kingdom. Total economy

£ million

		1999	2000	2001	2002	2003	2004	2005	2006	2007
Private sector										
New dwellings, excluding land	DFDF	23 921	25 604	27 085	31 455	34 804	40 927	44 398	49 628	52 492
Other buildings and structures	EQBU	31 828	31 966	32 730	33 580	35 366	36 994	39 575	43 429	..
Transport equipment	EQBV	13 919	12 859	13 897	15 637	14 708	13 735	14 030	14 831	..
Other machinery and equipment and cultivated assets	EQBW	57 957	61 236	58 062	53 498	50 228	52 359	52 923	56 169	..
Intangible fixed assets	EQBX	3 624	4 048	4 285	4 674	4 894	5 258	5 594	..	..
Costs associated with the transfer of ownership of non-produced assets	EQBY	9 784	11 174	12 697	15 399	16 385	20 752	19 901	24 611	27 445
Total	EQBZ	141 033	146 887	148 756	154 243	156 385	170 025	177 123	..	..
Public non-financial corporations										
New dwellings, excluding land	DEER	1 529	1 421	2 387	2 837	3 509	3 235	3 574	4 049	4 202
Other buildings and structures	DEES	1 692	1 775	1 854	2 304	2 236	1 493	2 111	1 819	..
Transport equipment	DEEP	155	178	171	110	126	193	334	235	..
Other machinery and equipment and cultivated assets	DEEQ	617	600	628	787	1 037	1 042	16 478	1 192	..
Intangible fixed assets	DLXJ	625	551	397	556	623	737	754	769	..
Costs associated with the transfer of ownership of non-produced assets	DLXQ	−1 906	−2 171	−2 254	−2 764	−5 674	−5 440	−2 675	−2 375	−2 227
Total	FCCJ	2 712	2 354	3 183	3 830	1 857	1 260	20 576	5 440	6 079
General government										
New dwellings, excluding land	DFHW	250	369	334	207	149	137	71	6	..
Other buildings and structures	EQCH	9 414	9 434	10 348	11 678	14 693	15 866	18 884	21 204	..
Transport equipment	EQCI	609	540	588	567	758	1 011	610	431	..
Other machinery and equipment and cultivated assets	EQCJ	2 096	1 699	2 239	2 867	3 176	3 652	−12 438	2 580	..
Intangible fixed assets	EQCK	396	367	334	358	384	400	304	515	..
Costs associated with the transfer of ownership of non-produced assets	EQCL	−166	−182	−310	−225	1 349	2 140	−301	−589	..
Total	NNBF	12 599	12 227	13 533	15 452	20 509	23 206	7 130	23 667	26 128
Total gross fixed capital formation	NPQX	161 722	167 172	171 782	180 551	186 700	202 260	211 862	231 762	251 486

1 See chapter text.
2 Components may not sum to totals due to rounding.

Source: Office for National Statistics: 020 7014 2083

16.20 Gross fixed capital formation at current purchasers' prices: by type of asset[1,2]

United Kingdom. Total economy

£ million

		1999	2000	2001	2002	2003	2004	2005	2006	2007
Tangible fixed assets										
New dwellings, excluding land	DFDK	25 700	27 394	29 806	34 499	38 462	44 299	48 043	53 686	56 725
Other buildings and structures	DLWS	42 934	43 175	44 932	47 562	52 295	54 353	60 570	66 452	..
Transport equipment	DLWZ	14 683	13 577	14 656	16 314	15 592	14 939	14 974	15 436	15 772
Other machinery and equipment and cultivated assets	DLXI	60 670	63 535	60 929	57 152	54 441	57 053	56 963	59 344	66 171
Total	EQCQ	143 987	147 681	150 323	155 527	160 790	170 644	180 550	197 519	..
Intangible fixed assets	DLXP	10 023	10 670	11 326	12 614	13 850	14 164	14 387	15 531	16 475
Costs associated with the transfer of ownership of non-produced assets	DFBH	7 712	8 821	10 133	12 410	12 060	17 452	16 925	21 587	..
Total gross fixed capital formation	NPQX	161 722	167 172	171 782	180 551	186 700	202 260	211 862	231 762	251 486

1 See chapter text.
2 Components may not sum to totals due to rounding.

Source: Office for National Statistics: 020 7014 2083

16.21

Gross fixed capital formation: by broad sector and type of asset[1,2,3]
Chained volume measures, reference year 2003
United Kingdom. Total economy   £ million

		1999	2000	2001	2002	2003	2004	2005	2006	2007
Private sector										
New dwellings, excluding land	DFDP	30 928	31 041	31 318	33 748	34 804	38 245	38 845	41 930	43 702
Other buildings and structures	EQCU	33 931	33 206	33 251	33 406	35 366	35 786	38 155	41 754	..
Transport equipment	EQCV	13 778	12 713	13 863	15 708	14 708	13 704	13 831	14 446	..
Other machinery and equipment and cultivated assets	EQCW	49 522	53 869	54 140	52 405	50 228	53 997	54 572	59 100	..
Intangible fixed assets	EQCX	10 185	10 702	11 228	11 680	12 843	13 043	13 072	13 916	..
Costs associated with the transfer of ownership of non-produced assets	EQCY	16 821	16 293	16 173	17 369	16 385	19 616	16 773	18 437	18 656
Total	EQCZ	154 580	158 347	160 569	164 304	164 334	174 391	175 248	189 559	..
Public non-financial corporations										
New dwellings, excluding land	DEEW	1 747	1 552	2 521	2 898	3 509	3 161	3 423	3 807	3 779
Other buildings and structures	DEEX	1 890	1 939	1 961	2 342	2 236	1 426	1 928	1 568	..
Transport equipment	DEEU	164	186	180	114	126	193	326	230	..
Other machinery and equipment and cultivated assets	DEEV	504	516	588	765	1 037	1 063	16 173	1 230	..
Intangible fixed assets	EQDE	684	586	415	572	623	716	711	710	..
Costs associated with the transfer of ownership of non-produced assets	EQDF	−3 141	−3 093	−2 825	−3 092	−5 674	−5 561	−2 813	−1 869	−1 823
Total	EQDG	1 796	1 695	2 424	3 019	1 857	998	19 748	5 610	..
General government										
New dwellings, excluding land	DFID	286	404	354	213	149	135	69	6	..
Other buildings and structures	EQDI	10 792	10 513	11 107	12 115	14 693	14 877	16 506	17 283	..
Transport equipment	EQDJ	676	606	672	586	758	809	751	809	..
Other machinery and equipment and cultivated assets	EQDK	1 632	1 424	2 063	2 801	3 176	3 757	−11 906	3 189	..
Intangible fixed assets	EQDL	241	219	196	211	384	698	294	495	..
Costs associated with the transfer of ownership of non-produced assets	EQDM	−1 728	−542	−548	−261	1 349	1 991	−56	−282	..
Total	EQDN	13 059	12 665	13 980	15 740	20 509	22 266	5 658	21 338	22 307
Total gross fixed capital formation	NPQR	169 117	173 710	178 203	184 701	186 700	197 655	200 654	215 985	229 423

1 See chapter text.
2 For the years before 2003, the total differs from the sum of their components.
3 Components may not sum to totals due to rounding.

Source: Office for National Statistics: 020 7014 2083

16.22

Gross fixed capital formation: by type of asset[1,2,3]
Chained volume measures, reference year 2003
United Kingdom. Total economy   £ million

		1999	2000	2001	2002	2003	2004	2005	2006	2007
Tangible fixed assets										
New dwellings, excluding land	DFDV	32 863	32 888	34 172	36 839	38 462	41 541	42 337	45 746	47 508
Other buildings and structures	EQDP	46 738	45 780	46 413	47 913	52 295	52 089	56 589	60 605	..
Transport equipment	DLWJ	14 602	13 489	14 698	16 414	15 592	14 706	14 908	15 361	15 631
Other machinery and equipment and cultivated assets	DLWM	51 667	55 774	56 780	55 971	54 441	58 817	58 839	62 878	69 745
Total	EQDS	145 621	148 509	152 571	157 257	160 790	167 152	172 672	185 300	..
Intangible fixed assets	EQDT	11 079	11 445	11 742	12 371	13 850	14 457	14 077	14 979	15 521
Costs associated with the transfer of ownership of non-produced assets	DFDW	13 088	12 810	12 960	14 097	12 060	16 046	13 904	16 247	..
Total gross fixed capital formation	NPQR	169 117	173 710	178 203	184 701	186 700	197 655	200 654	215 985	229 423

1 See chapter text.
2 For the years before 2003, the total differs from the sum of their components.
3 Components may not sum to totals due to rounding.

Source: Office for National Statistics: 020 7014 2083

Prices

Chapter 17

Prices

Producer price index numbers

(Tables 17.1 and 17.2)

The producer price indices (PPIs) were published for the first time in August 1983, replacing the former wholesale price indices. Full details of the differences between the two indices were given in an article published in *British Business*, 15 April 1983. The producer price indices are calculated using the same general methodology as that used by the wholesale price indices.

The high level index numbers in Tables 17.1 and 17.2 are constructed on a net sector basis. That is to say, they are intended to measure only transactions between the sector concerned and other sectors. Within sector transactions are excluded. Index numbers for the whole of manufacturing are thus not weighted averages of sector index numbers.

The index numbers for selected industries in Tables 17.1 and 17.2 are constructed on a gross sector basis, that is, all transactions are included in deriving the weighting patterns, including sales within the same industry.

All the index numbers are compiled exclusive of value-added tax. Excise duties on cigarettes, manufactured tobacco and alcoholic liquor are included, as is the duty on hydrocarbon oils.

The indices relate to the average prices for a year. The movement in these prices are weighted to reflect the relative importance of the composite products in a chosen year (known as the base year), currently 2000.

Since July 1995, PPIs have been published fully reclassified to the 1992 version of the Standard Industrial Classification (SIC).

Further details are available from the National Statistics website: www.statistics.gov.uk/ppi.

Purchasing power of the pound

(Table 17.3)

Changes in the internal purchasing power of a currency may be defined as the 'inverse' of changes in the levels of prices; when prices go up, the amount which can be purchased with a given sum of money goes down. Movements in the internal purchasing power of the pound are based on the consumers' expenditure deflator (CED) prior to 1962 and on the General index of retail prices (RPI) from January 1962 onwards. The CED shows the movement in prices implied by the national accounts estimates of consumers' expenditure valued at current and at constant prices, while the RPI is constructed directly by weighting together monthly movements in prices according to a given pattern of household expenditure derived from the Expenditure and Food Survey. If the purchasing power of the pound is taken to be 100p in a particular month (quarter, year), the comparable purchasing power in a subsequent month (quarter, year) is:

$$100 \quad \times \quad \frac{\text{earlier period price index}}{\text{later period price index}}$$

where the price index used is the CED for years 1946–1961 and the RPI for periods after 1961.

Consumer prices index

(Table 17.4)

The consumer prices index (CPI) is the main UK domestic measure of inflation for macro-economic purposes. Like the RPI (see below) it measures the average change from month to month in the prices of consumer goods and services purchased in the UK, but there are differences in coverage and methodology. A detailed description of these differences is given in the paper entitled 'The New Inflation Target: the Statistical Perspective'. This paper is available on the National Statistics website at: www.statistics.gov.uk/StatBase/Product.asp?vlnk=10913.

Since 10 December 2003, the Government inflation target for the UK has been defined in terms of the CPI measure of inflation. Prior to that the CPI had been published in the UK as the harmonised index of consumer prices (HICP); the two shall remain one and the same index.

The HICPs are calculated in each Member State of the European Union (EU), according to rules specified in a series of European Regulations developed by the EU statistical office in conjunction with the EU Member States. The HICPs are used to compare inflation rate across the EU. Since January 1999 it has also been used by the European Central Bank (ECB) as the measure of price stability across the euro area. Additional information on HICPs is available from the National Statistics website at: www.statistics.gov.uk/hicp

CPI inflation rates prior to 1997 and index levels prior to 1996 are estimated. See article on National Statistics website at: www.statistics.gov.uk/cci/article.asp?ID=31. Also the coverage of CPI categories for health, education and miscellaneous goods and services have been extended between 2000 and 2002. Details are given in articles available on the National

Statistics website at: www.statistics. gov.uk/cci/searchres2. asp?ct=6&term=HICP

Further details on the CPI are available from the National Statistics website at: www.statistics.gov.uk/cpi

Retail prices index

(Table 17.5)

The retail prices index (RPI) is the most familiar general purpose measure of inflation in the UK, measuring the percentage changes month by month in the average level of prices of the goods and services purchased by the great majority of households in the UK. The uses of the RPI include indexation of pensions, state benefits and index-linked gilts. The expenditure pattern on which the index is based is revised each year using information from the Expenditure and Food Survey. The expenditure of certain higher income households and households of retired people dependent mainly on social security benefits is excluded.

The index covers a large and representative selection of more than 650 separate goods and services, for which price movements are regularly measured in around 150 locations throughout the country. Around 120,000 separate price quotations are used in compiling the index.

Further details are available from the National Statistics website: www.statistics.gov.uk/rpi

Tax and price index (TPI)

(Table 17.6)

The purpose and methodology of the TPI were described in an article in the August 1979 issue (No. 310) of *Economic Trends*. The TPI measures the change in gross taxable income needed for taxpayers to maintain their purchasing power, allowing for changes in retail prices. The TPI thus takes account of the changes to direct taxes (and employees' National Insurance (NI) contributions) facing representative cross-section of taxpayers as well as changes in the retail prices index (RPI).

When direct taxation or employees' NI contributions change, the TPI will rise by less than or more than the RPI according to the type of changes made. Between Budgets, the monthly increase in the TPI is normally slightly larger than that in the RPI, since all the extra income needed to offset any rise in retail prices is fully taxed.

Index numbers of agricultural prices

(Tables 17.7 and 17.8)

The indices of producer prices of agricultural products are currently based on the calendar year 2000. They are designed to provide short-term and medium-term indications of movements in these prices. All annual series are base-weighted Laspeyres type, using value weights derived from the Economic Accounts for Agriculture prepared for the Statistical Office of the European Union. Prices are measured exclusive of VAT. For Table 17.7, it has generally been necessary to measure the prices of materials (inputs) ex-supplier. For Table 17.8, it has generally been necessary to measure the prices received by producers (outputs) at the first marketing stage. The construction of the indices enables them to be combined with similar indices for other member countries of the EU to provide an overall indication of trends within the Union which appears in the Union's Eurostat series of publications.

Index numbers at a more detailed level and for earlier based series are available from the Department for Environment, Food and Rural Affairs, SSP, Room 146 Foss House, Kingspool 1–2 Peasholme Green, York, YO1 7PX, tel 01904 455249.

Prices

17.1 Producer price index of materials and fuels purchased: by all manufacturing and selected industries SIC(92)[1]

United Kingdom: Annual averages

Indices (2000=100)

			2000	2001	2002	2003	2004	2005	2006	2007
Net sector										
Materials and fuel purchased by manufacturing industry[2]	RNNK	6292000050	100.0	98.8	94.4	95.7	99.5	111.1	121.8	125.8
Materials	PLKX	6292000010	100.0	98.1	93.7	95.2	98.7	108.1	116.1	121.2p
Fuels[2]	RNNL	6292000060	100.0	107.1	103.4	102.1	109.9	152.1	198.7	187.9
Materials and fuels purchased by manufacturing industry-seasonally adjusted[2]	RNPE	6292008950	100.0	98.8	94.4	95.7	99.5	111.0	121.8r	125.9#
Materials and fuels purchased by manufacturing industry other than food, beverages, petroleum and tobacco[2]	RNNQ	6292990050	100.0	98.7	94.0	93.7	95.4	103.0	111.1	113.9p
Materials	RWCJ	6292990010	100.0	98.1	93.2	93.0	94.2	98.9	103.8	107.7
Fuel[2]	RNNS	6292990060	100.0	106.8	103.1	101.8	109.6	151.6	198.3	187.7
Materials and fuels purchased by manufacturing industries other than food, beverages, petroleum and tobacco-seasonally adjusted[2]	RNPF	6292998950	100.0	98.7	94.0	93.7	95.4	103.0	111.1r	113.9#
Gross sector[3]										
All manufacturing	RBBO	6192000000	100.0	99.3	97.1	98.4	102.1	109.7	116.9	121.3
Other mining and quarrying products[4]	RABE	6112140000	100.0	96.9	92.3	93.1	96.0	107.6	114.5	116.5p
Manufacture of food products	RBBQ	6192151600	100.0	103.2	102.3	105.2	108.5	109.3	113.6	120.1p
Food products and beverages	RABF	6112150000	100.0	103.3	102.3	105.2	108.6	109.3	113.6	120.2#
Tobacco products	RABG	6112160000	100.0	100.0	101.2	106.9	107.0	107.9	110.9	112.2p
Manufacture of textiles	RBBR	6192171800	100.0	100.5	98.4	99.2	99.6	103.3	106.4	107.5#
Textiles	RABH	6112170000	100.0	100.5	98.6	99.8	100.0	105.4	109.3	110.3p
Wearing apparel	RABI	6112180000	100.0	100.4	97.8	98.0	98.7	99.8	101.4	102.6p
Manufacture of leather	RBBS	6192190000	100.0	101.9	100.0	101.1	102.0	105.7	109.5	112.0p
Manufacture of wood and wood products	RBBT	6192200000	100.0	99.2	96.5	96.8	99.5	104.1	109.5	119.9p
Manufacture of pulp, paper, publishing and printing	RBBU	6192212200	100.0	100.9	99.2	99.4	100.4	103.8	108.0	110.3p
Pulp and paper products	RABL	6112210000	100.0	100.7	97.5	96.5	96.9	100.7	106.5	108.9p
Printed matter and recording material	RABM	6112220000	100.0	101.0	100.0	100.8	102.2	105.3	108.8	111.0p
Manufacture of coke	RBBV	6192230000	100.0	92.0	89.2	95.4	109.1	150.9	175.6	180.4p
Manufacture of chemical products	RBBW	6192240000	100.0	101.1	99.4	103.0	105.5	114.4	120.6	122.2p
Manufacture of rubber products	RBBX	6192250000	100.0	99.1	97.7	99.5	102.6	110.8	116.2	118.7p
Manufacture of other non-metallic mineral products	RBBY	6192260000	100.0	100.5	99.6	100.7	103.0	111.8	120.0	121.4#
Manufacture of basic metals	RBBZ	6192272800	100.0	98.5	96.6	99.8	111.8	123.0	137.3	147.5#
Basic metals	RABV	6112270000	100.0	98.6	96.8	101.3	115.7	127.0	144.8	157.0#
Fabricated metal products	RABW	6112280000	100.0	98.4	96.4	98.6	108.4	119.5	130.9	139.4p
Manufacture of machinery and equipment not elsewhere classified	RBCA	6192290000	100.0	98.9	97.1	97.8	102.4	109.3	116.7	122.0p
Manufacture of electrical and optical equipment	RBCB	6192303300	100.0	97.2	92.5	88.8	87.7	90.1	93.9	95.4#
Office machinery and computers	RABY	6112300000	100.0	95.5	87.4	80.7	78.5	79.3	81.1	78.5#
Electrical machinery and apparatus not elsewhere classified	RACB	6112310000	100.0	98.5	95.8	94.5	96.1	101.5	108.8	111.8#
Radio, television and communication equipment	RACC	6112320000	100.0	98.1	94.5	92.1	92.4	96.6	103.5	107.1#
Medical, precision, optical instruments and clocks	RACD	6112330000	100.0	98.2	95.2	92.3	90.6	93.3	97.0	97.3#
Manufacture of transport equipment	RBCC	6192343500	100.0	99.1	97.3	98.1	100.1	105.3	110.4	115.0p
Motor vehicles, trailers and semi-trailers	RACE	6112340000	100.0	99.3	98.1	99.3	101.5	106.8	111.6	116.6p
Other transport equipment	RACF	6112350000	100.0	98.7	95.4	95.5	97.0	102.0	107.7	111.4p
Manufacturing not elsewhere classified	RBCD	6192363700	100.0	99.1	97.8	99.9	104.4	109.9	116.4	122.9p
Electricity including Climate Change Levy	RCVR	7167850000	100.0	96.2	92.5	89.3	95.2	127.5	173.2	175.9
Gas including Climate Change Levy	RCVW	7167860000	100.0	140.7	136.5	141.3	155.5	231.8	286.9	230.5
Collected and purified water	PQNB	7167870000	100.0	101.6	103.4	107.0	113.9	131.1	144.5	155.1

1 See chapter text.
2 These indices include the Climate Change Levy which was introduced in April 2001.
3 The Climate Change Levy is excluded from the detailed industry input index.
4 These indices include the Aggregates Levy which was introduced in April 2002.

Source: Office for National Statistics: 01633 815783

17.2 Producer price index of output: by all manufacturing and selected industries SIC(92)[1]

United Kingdom: Annual averages

Indices (2000=100)

			2000	2001	2002	2003	2004	2005	2006	2007
Net sector										
Output of manufactured products	PLLU	7209200000	100.0	99.7	99.8	101.3	103.8	106.7	109.3	112.6p
All manufacturing excluding duty	PVNP	7209200010	100.0	99.7	99.7	101.2	103.7	106.8	109.7	112.9p
All manufacturing excluding duty - seasonally adjusted	PVNQ	7209200890	100.0	99.7	99.8	101.2	103.7	106.8	109.7r	113.0#
Products of manufacturing industries other than the food, beverages, petroleum and tobacco manufacturing industries - not seasonally adjusted	PLLV	7209299000	100.0	99.4	99.3	100.6	102.5	104.7	107.1	109.6p
All manufacturing excluding food, beverages, tobacco and petroleum - seasonally adjusted	PLLW	7209299890	100.0	99.4	99.3	100.6	102.5	104.7	107.1	109.7
Gross sector										
Manufactured products excluding duty	POKE	7109200000	100.0	99.4	99.1	100.8	104.0	108.8	112.6	116.1
Manufactured products excluding food, drink, tobacco and petroleum	POKF	7109299000	100.0	99.4	99.3	100.5	103.0	106.2	109.2	112.4
Other mining and quarrying products[2]	ROFV	7112148000	100.0	104.4	120.3	126.9	129.1	129.9	133.4	137.6
Food products, beverages and tobacco excluding duty	POKH	7111151600	100.0	101.9	103.3	104.6	106.9	108.4	110.7	116.0
Food products, beverages and tobacco including duty	RBGA	7111151680	100.0	102.0	103.3	104.7	107.2	108.9	111.2	116.0
Food products and beverages including duty	RPUN	7112150080	100.0	101.5	102.6	103.6	105.9	107.1	109.0	113.6
Food products excluding beverages	RBGD	7112159900	100.0	101.7	102.7	103.7	106.0	107.1	108.8	113.8
Alcoholic beverages including duty	RPUX	7113159080	100.0	101.6	103.1	103.7	106.8	108.2	110.2	113.3
Tobacco products including duty	RPUS	7112160080	100.0	105.0	107.8	111.2	115.3	119.8	124.7	130.7
Textiles and textile products	POKI	7111171800	100.0	99.2	98.8	98.7	98.5	100.0	101.2	102.4
Textiles	POKZ	7112170000	100.0	99.4	99.2	99.4	99.2	101.2	102.7	104.4
Wearing apparel: Furs	POLA	7112180000	100.0	99.0	97.9	97.2	97.0	97.4	98.1	98.4
Leather and leather products	POKJ	7111190000	100.0	102.5	102.7	102.9	102.9	104.5	106.5	107.0
Wood and wood products	POKK	7111200000	100.0	99.9	100.0	101.8	105.2	110.0	113.0	123.6
Pulp, paper and paper products, recorded media and printing services	POKL	7111212200	100.0	101.5	102.1	104.0	106.0	108.6	110.7	112.9
Pulp, paper and paper products	POLD	7112210000	100.0	101.0	100.3	100.1	99.7	99.0	100.8	104.3
Printed matter and recorded media	POLE	7112220000	100.0	101.7	102.7	105.5	108.4	112.2	114.3	116.1
Chemicals, chemical, products and manmade fibres	POKN	7111240000	100.0	100.2	100.5	103.9	106.7	111.6	115.8	118.4
Rubber and plastic products	POKO	7111250000	100.0	100.3	100.4	100.5	101.5	106.4	109.8	111.1
Other non-metallic mineral products	POKP	7111260000	100.0	101.9	105.0	107.8	109.6	113.9	118.2	123.7
Base metals and fabricated metal products	POKQ	7111272800	100.0	99.9	99.5	101.3	108.8	118.4	125.4	132.7
Base metals	POLJ	7112270000	100.0	98.4	96.0	99.2	113.1	126.6	141.5	154.9
Fabricated metal products, except machinery and equipment	POLK	7112280000	100.0	100.6	101.1	102.3	106.8	114.6	118.0	122.5
Machinery and equipment not elsewhere classified	POKR	7111290000	100.0	100.9	101.8	101.9	103.3	106.5	109.2	112.5
Electrical and optical equipment	POKS	7111343500	100.0	94.7	90.0	87.5	86.6	85.9	86.8	86.6
Office machinery and computers	POLM	7112300000	100.0	75.2	64.6	57.1	52.2	46.7	44.3	41.6
Electrical machinery and apparatus not elsewhere classified	POLN	7112310000	100.0	99.9	100.4	100.6	102.8	106.2	111.5	115.0
Radio, television and communication equipment and apparatus	POLO	7112320000	100.0	97.3	88.0	84.3	82.1	80.1	79.3	76.9
Medical precision and optical instruments, watches and clocks	POLP	7112330000	100.0	101.1	102.4	103.3	103.6	104.1	104.8	105.1
Transport equipment	POKT	7111343500	100.0	98.4	98.8	99.2	100.3	102.4	103.9	105.2
Motor vehicles, trailers and semi-trailers	POLQ	7112340000	100.0	96.6	96.3	96.1	97.2	98.6	99.5	99.5
Other transport	POLR	7112350000	100.0	102.3	103.8	105.8	107.0	110.5	113.2	117.3
Furniture: other manufactured goods not elsewhere classified	POLS	7112360000	100.0	100.3	100.9	103.8	104.4	104.5	105.7	108.1

1 See chapter text.
2 These indices include the Aggregates Levy which was introduced in April 2002. These indices do not feed into Net Sector output (PLLU).

Source: Office for National Statistics: 01633 815783

17.3 Internal purchasing power of the pound[1,2]
United Kingdom

Pence

Year in which purchasing power was 100p

	1988	1989	1990	1991	1992	1993	1994	1995	1996	1997	1998	1999	2000	2001	2002	2003	2004	2005	2006	2007
	BAMU	BAMV	BAMW	BASX	CZVM	CBXX	DOFX	DOHR	DOLM	DTUL	CDQG	JKZZ	ZMHO	IKHI	FAUI	SEZH	C687	E9AO	GB4Y	HT4R
1988	100	108	118	125	130	132	135	139	143	147	152	155	159	162	165	170	175	180	185	193
1989	93	100	109	116	120	122	125	129	133	137	141	144	148	150	153	157	162	167	172	179
1990	85	91	100	106	110	112	114	118	121	125	129	131	135	137	140	144	148	152	157	164
1991	80	86	94	100	104	105	108	112	114	118	122	124	128	130	132	136	140	144	148	155
1992	77	83	91	96	100	102	104	108	110	114	118	119	123	125	127	131	135	139	143	149
1993	76	82	90	95	98	100	102	106	109	112	116	118	121	123	125	129	133	136	141	147
1994	74	80	88	93	96	98	100	103	106	109	113	115	118	120	122	126	130	133	137	143
1995	72	77	85	90	93	94	97	100	102	106	109	111	114	116	118	122	125	129	133	139
1996	70	75	83	87	91	92	94	98	100	103	107	108	112	113	115	119	122	126	130	135
1997	68	73	80	85	88	89	92	95	97	100	103	105	108	110	112	115	119	122	126	131
1998	66	71	77	82	85	86	88	92	94	97	100	102	105	106	108	111	115	118	122	127
1999	65	70	76	81	84	85	87	90	92	95	98	100	103	105	107	110	113	116	120	125
2000	63	68	74	78	81	83	85	88	90	92	96	97	100	102	103	106	110	113	116	121
2001	62	66	73	77	80	81	83	86	88	91	94	95	98	100	102	105	108	111	114	119
2002	61	65	72	76	79	80	82	85	87	89	92	94	97	98	100	103	106	109	112	117
2003	59	64	70	74	76	78	79	82	84	87	90	91	94	96	97	100	103	106	109	114
2004	57	62	68	72	74	75	77	80	82	84	87	89	91	93	94	97	100	103	106	111
2005	56	60	66	70	72	73	75	78	80	82	85	86	89	90	92	94	97	100	103	108
2006	54	58	64	67	70	71	73	75	77	80	82	83	86	87	89	92	94	97	100	104
2007	52	56	61	65	67	68	70	72	74	76	79	80	82	84	85	88	90	93	96	100

1 See chapter text. These figures are calculated by taking the inverse ratio of the respective annual averages of the Retail Prices Index (RPI).

2 To find the purchasing power of the pound in 1995, given that it was 100 pence in 1990, select the column headed 1990 and look at the 1995 row. The result is 85 pence.

Source: Office for National Statistics: 020 7533 5874

17.4 Consumer Prices Index:[1] detailed figures by division
United Kingdom

Indices (2005=100)

	Food and non-alcoholic beverages	Alcoholic beverages and tobacco	Clothing and footwear	Housing, water, electric-ity, gas & other fuels	Furniture, household equipment & routine mainte-nance	Health	Transport	Commun-ication	Recreation and culture	Education	Restaur-ants and hotels	Miscell-aneous goods and services	CPI (overall index)
COICOP Division	01	02	03	04	05	06	07	08	09	10	11	12	
Weights 2006	102	44	65	108	73	24	155	25	147	17	134	106	1000
	D7BU	D7BV	D7BW	D7BX	D7BY	D7BZ	D7C2	D7C3	D7C4	D7C5	D7C6	D7C7	D7BT
2005 Sep	99.7	100.3	99.9	100.7	100.2	100.7	102.2	99.8	99.6	100.8	100.8	100.8	100.6
Oct	99.5	100.7	99.9	101.7	99.4	101.0	102.0	99.5	99.7	103.3	101.2	101.2	100.7
Nov	100.1	100.7	100.5	102.3	100.5	101.0	100.4	99.6	99.5	103.3	101.2	101.4	100.7
Dec	100.7	100.2	100.1	102.8	102.8	100.3	100.7	99.4	99.5	103.3	101.4	101.5	101.0
2006 Jan	100.4	101.0	96.0	103.3	97.8	101.0	101.2	100.9	98.6	103.3	101.5	102.0	100.5
Feb	101.0	100.8	95.9	103.6	98.5	101.1	101.4	101.0	99.4	103.3	101.9	102.1	100.9
Mar	100.4	101.1	96.5	104.5	100.3	101.0	101.4	100.9	98.9	103.3	102.2	102.4	101.1
Apr	100.2	102.3	96.5	107.3	98.5	102.2	102.9	100.9	99.1	103.3	102.5	103.3	101.7
May	101.7	102.5	97.2	108.8	99.3	102.6	103.5	99.7	98.9	103.3	103.0	103.4	102.2
Jun	102.4	103.6	96.7	109.7	100.2	102.5	103.5	100.0	98.7	103.3	103.1	103.9	102.5
Jul	102.6	103.4	92.2	110.5	98.1	103.0	105.5	99.8	98.4	103.3	103.5	104.0	102.5
Aug	103.0	103.8	94.4	110.9	99.1	103.4	105.8	99.2	98.4	103.3	103.6	104.5	102.9
Sep	103.6	103.7	96.4	111.5	100.6	103.6	102.9	99.6	98.6	107.9	103.8	104.7	103.0
Oct	104.2	103.9	96.6	112.7	99.0	104.2	101.5	100.4	98.6	117.8	104.2	105.0	103.2
Nov	105.1	103.4	97.2	113.7	100.0	104.1	101.1	100.3	98.7	117.8	104.5	105.0	103.4
Dec	105.4	103.0	96.0	114.5	103.3	104.2	102.8	99.9	99.2	117.8	104.7	104.9	104.0
2007 Jan	104.4	104.5	92.0	114.9	98.3	104.8	102.1	99.0	98.3	117.8	104.9	105.1	103.2
Feb	105.4	105.1	91.9	115.1	99.6	104.9	102.8	98.1	98.4	117.8	105.2	105.8	103.7
Mar	106.0	105.6	92.8	115.0	102.9	104.8	103.1	98.1	98.2	117.8	105.7	106.2	104.2
Apr	106.2	107.0	93.7	115.7	100.7	105.5	104.5	97.2	98.3	117.8	106.3	105.8	104.5
May	106.7	106.8	93.7	115.0	101.8	105.8	106.1	96.6	98.0	117.8	106.6	105.7	104.8
Jun	107.3	107.1	93.6	114.5	104.0	106.1	106.8	96.1	97.6	117.8	106.9	105.8	105.0
Jul	105.5	106.9	89.8	114.3	99.7	106.6	108.0	94.8	97.0	117.8	107.2	106.1	104.4
Aug	106.1	107.0	91.1	114.0	100.3	106.8	108.6	97.2	97.5	117.8	107.4	105.6	104.7
Sep	107.4	107.1	92.5	114.0	102.1	107.1	105.7	96.6	97.6	122.9	107.6	105.8	104.8
Oct	109.1	106.8	92.5	114.3	100.8	107.5	106.6	96.2	97.7	133.2	107.9	106.4	105.3
Nov	110.1	106.4	92.9	114.6	101.6	107.3	107.0	96.3	97.6	133.2	108.0	106.6	105.6
Dec	111.1	105.7	92.2	114.7	104.2	107.6	108.7	96.2	98.0	133.2	108.3	106.8	106.2

Percentage change on a year earlier

	D7G8	D7G9	D7GA	D7GB	D7GC	D7GD	D7GE	D7GF	D7GG	D7GH	D7GI	D7GJ	D7G7
2005 Sep	2.0	1.4	−5.3	6.5	−0.2	3.1	6.0	−1.2	−1.6	4.7	3.7	5.1	2.5
Oct	1.5	1.9	−5.3	6.5	−0.2	3.0	5.8	−1.6	−1.5	4.7	3.7	4.2	2.3
Nov	1.7	2.5	−5.1	6.5	0.1	2.9	4.1	−1.2	−1.5	4.7	3.5	4.3	2.1
Dec	1.7	2.5	−4.2	6.4	−	2.4	2.8	−1.0	−1.7	4.7	3.5	4.2	1.9
2006 Jan	1.2	2.3	−4.7	6.3	−0.8	2.3	5.1	0.5	−2.1	4.7	3.4	3.5	1.9
Feb	1.1	1.6	−4.7	6.4	−0.5	2.3	4.2	0.4	−0.8	4.7	3.5	3.6	2.0
Mar	−0.4	2.5	−4.7	7.0	−0.4	2.1	3.5	0.5	−1.4	4.7	3.6	3.7	1.8
Apr	0.3	2.5	−4.4	7.7	−0.8	2.7	4.4	0.3	−1.6	4.7	3.0	4.0	2.0
May	1.1	2.2	−3.7	9.0	−0.8	2.9	4.0	−0.4	−1.6	4.7	3.2	4.1	2.2
Jun	1.8	3.3	−3.9	9.8	−0.1	2.7	3.9	−0.3	−1.6	4.7	3.2	4.4	2.5
Jul	3.2	2.8	−4.5	10.0	−1.3	2.4	3.3	0.3	−1.4	4.7	3.2	3.6	2.4
Aug	3.4	3.3	−3.9	10.5	−0.5	2.6	2.4	−0.7	−0.9	4.7	3.0	3.9	2.5
Sep	4.0	3.4	−3.5	10.7	0.3	2.8	0.6	−0.2	−1.0	7.1	2.9	3.9	2.4
Oct	4.7	3.2	−3.3	10.8	−0.4	3.1	−0.5	0.9	−1.1	14.0	3.0	3.8	2.4
Nov	5.0	2.7	−3.2	11.1	−0.5	3.1	0.8	0.7	−0.7	14.0	3.2	3.5	2.7
Dec	4.6	2.7	−4.1	11.4	0.6	3.9	2.1	0.5	−0.3	14.0	3.2	3.3	3.0
2007 Jan	3.9	3.5	−4.1	11.2	0.5	3.8	0.9	−1.8	−0.3	14.0	3.3	3.1	2.7
Feb	4.4	4.2	−4.2	11.1	1.2	3.7	1.4	−2.8	−1.0	14.0	3.3	3.6	2.8
Mar	5.6	4.4	−3.9	10.1	2.7	3.7	1.6	−2.8	−0.7	14.0	3.4	3.7	3.1
Apr	6.0	4.5	−2.8	7.9	2.2	3.2	1.5	−3.7	−0.8	14.0	3.8	2.4	2.8
May	5.0	4.2	−3.6	5.7	2.5	3.1	2.5	−3.2	−0.8	14.0	3.5	2.2	2.5
Jun	4.8	3.4	−3.2	4.3	3.8	3.4	3.2	−3.9	−1.1	14.0	3.7	1.8	2.4
Jul	2.8	3.4	−2.6	3.5	1.6	3.4	2.4	−5.0	−1.4	14.0	3.6	2.0	1.9
Aug	3.0	3.1	−3.5	2.8	1.2	3.3	2.6	−2.0	−0.9	14.0	3.6	1.1	1.8
Sep	3.7	3.2	−4.0	2.3	1.5	3.4	2.7	−3.0	−1.0	13.9	3.7	1.0	1.8
Oct	4.7	2.7	−4.3	1.4	1.8	3.2	5.1	−4.2	−0.9	13.2	3.5	1.3	2.1
Nov	4.8	2.9	−4.4	0.8	1.7	3.1	5.8	−4.0	−1.1	13.2	3.4	1.6	2.1
Dec	5.4	2.7	−3.9	0.2	0.9	3.3	5.8	−3.8	−1.3	13.2	3.4	1.9	2.1

1 See chapter text. Prior to 10 December 2003, the consumer prices index (CPI) was published in the UK as the harmonised index of consumer prices (HICP).

Source: Office for National Statistics: 020 7533 5874

Prices

17.5 Retail Prices Index[1]
United Kingdom

Indices (13 January 1987=100)

| | All items (RPI) | All items excluding | | | | | Food and catering | Alcohol and tobacco | Housing and household expenditure | Personal expenditure | Travel and leisure | Consumer durables | All items excluding mortgage interest payments & indirect taxes (RPIY)[3] |
		mortgage interest payments (RPIX)	mortgage interest payments and depreciation	housing	food	seasonal food[2]							
Weights													
	CZGU	CZGY	DOGZ	CZGX	CZGV	CZGW	CBVV	CBVW	CBVX	CBVY	CBVZ	CBWA	
1999	1 000	958	928	807	872	980	179	100	358	95	268	127	
2000	1 000	960	924	805	882	982	170	95	355	101	279	126	
2001	1 000	954	914	795	884	982	169	97	362	96	276	125	
2002	1 000	964	924	801	886	980	166	99	363	94	278	126	
2003	1 000	961	919	797	891	983	160	98	365	92	285	126	
2004	1 000	961	914	791	889	981	160	97	367	93	283	121	
2005	1 000	950	901	776	890	981	159	96	387	89	269	122	
2006	1 000	950	906	778	895	983	155	96	392	90	267	117	
2007	1 000	945	895	762	895	981	152	95	408	83	262	109	
Annual averages													
	CHAW	CHMK	CHON	CHAZ	CHAY	CHAX	CHBS	CHBT	CHBU	CHBV	CHBW	CHBY	CBZW
1999	165.4	164.3	163.6	158.9	169.4	166.5	155.4	202.6	167.7	139.6	165.6	112.3	157.1
2000	170.3	167.7	166.4	161.3	175.1	171.4	156.7	210.3	176.2	137.2	170.3	108.0	159.9
2001	173.3	171.3	169.5	163.7	178.0	174.3	162.2	216.9	180.0	135.7	172.0	105.0	163.7
2002	176.2	175.1	172.5	166.0	181.1	177.2	164.8	222.3	184.6	133.2	174.2	101.9	167.5
2003	181.3	180.0	176.2	168.9	186.7	182.4	167.9	228.0	194.3	133.2	177.0	99.8	172.0
2004	186.7	184.0	179.1	170.9	192.8	187.9	170.0	233.6	207.4	131.5	178.1	97.7	175.5
2005	192.0	188.2	182.6	173.7	198.7	193.3	172.9	239.8	219.4	131.0	179.2	95.3	179.4
2006	198.1	193.7	187.8	178.3	205.2	199.5	176.9	247.1	231.8	131.7	181.1	94.0	184.8
2007	206.6	199.9	193.3	183.2	213.9	207.9	184.3	256.2	248.1	132.9	183.8	93.3	190.8
Monthly figures													
2004 Dec	189.9	186.4	180.9	172.5	196.4	191.2	171.2	234.7	215.6	131.8	178.6	99.1	177.9
2005 Jan	188.9	185.2	179.8	171.2	195.2	190.1	171.6	236.0	214.3	129.4	177.1	94.5	176.7
Feb	189.6	185.9	180.4	171.9	195.9	190.8	172.4	236.9	214.9	130.2	177.6	95.0	177.4
Mar	190.5	186.8	181.4	173.0	196.8	191.6	173.4	236.8	216.3	131.4	178.1	96.7	178.3
Apr	191.6	187.8	182.4	173.3	198.2	192.9	172.7	239.4	218.3	131.4	179.3	95.6	179.0
May	192.0	188.2	182.7	173.7	198.6	193.2	173.7	240.2	219.0	131.4	179.1	95.9	179.4
Jun	192.2	188.3	182.8	173.8	198.8	193.4	173.6	240.5	219.7	131.4	178.9	95.8	179.5
Jul	192.2	188.3	182.7	173.5	199.1	193.7	172.4	241.0	220.2	128.8	180.2	94.0	179.5
Aug	192.6	188.6	183.0	173.8	199.5	194.1	172.7	241.0	220.5	130.3	180.2	94.1	179.8
Sep	193.1	189.3	183.7	174.6	200.0	194.5	172.7	241.1	220.7	131.6	181.0	95.1	180.5
Oct	193.3	189.5	183.8	174.7	200.4	194.8	172.7	241.8	221.4	131.8	180.8	94.7	180.7
Nov	193.6	189.7	184.0	174.9	200.5	195.0	173.4	241.9	222.5	132.2	179.6	95.4	180.9
Dec	194.1	190.2	184.5	175.5	201.0	195.5	174.1	241.6	224.5	131.9	179.0	97.0	181.5
2006 Jan	193.4	189.4	183.7	174.5	200.3	194.8	174.1	242.5	223.0	129.1	179.4	92.4	180.7
Feb	194.2	190.1	184.4	175.2	201.0	195.6	174.9	242.8	224.0	130.0	179.9	93.5	181.4
Mar	195.0	190.8	185.2	176.0	202.0	196.4	174.3	243.8	225.8	131.1	180.0	95.1	182.2
Apr	196.5	192.3	186.7	177.0	203.8	198.0	174.2	245.8	228.3	131.7	181.6	93.6	183.2
May	197.7	193.6	187.8	178.2	204.9	199.1	176.1	246.8	230.0	132.7	182.1	94.3	184.5
Jun	198.5	194.2	188.4	178.9	205.7	199.8	176.8	248.3	231.6	132.6	181.9	94.7	185.2
Jul	198.5	194.2	188.3	178.7	205.6	199.9	177.1	248.3	231.5	129.4	183.3	91.8	185.2
Aug	199.2	194.9	188.9	179.3	206.4	200.7	177.6	249.1	232.6	131.3	183.3	93.0	186.0
Sep	200.1	195.3	189.2	179.6	207.4	201.5	178.1	249.2	235.9	133.0	181.2	94.8	186.4
Oct	200.4	195.5	189.3	179.7	207.5	201.7	179.1	249.7	237.3	133.4	179.6	93.7	186.7
Nov	201.1	196.2	190.0	180.4	208.2	202.4	180.2	249.6	238.7	133.7	179.8	94.5	187.5
Dec	202.7	197.4	191.2	181.7	210.1	204.1	180.6	249.4	242.7	132.9	181.0	96.7	188.6
2007 Jan	201.6	196.1	189.8	180.0	208.9	203.0	180.0	251.3	240.6	130.1	180.8	91.1	187.3
Feb	203.1	197.1	190.7	181.1	210.4	204.4	181.2	252.4	243.0	131.3	181.4	92.1	188.4
Mar	204.4	198.3	191.9	182.4	211.7	205.7	182.1	253.8	245.3	132.5	181.6	95.1	189.5
Apr	205.4	199.3	192.9	182.7	212.8	206.8	182.7	256.8	245.7	133.8	183.1	93.5	190.0
May	206.2	200.0	193.6	183.4	213.6	207.5	183.6	257.0	246.5	134.0	184.3	94.4	190.7
Jun	207.3	200.7	194.1	184.0	214.7	208.6	184.5	257.5	248.9	133.9	184.5	95.8	191.4
Jul	206.1	199.4	192.7	182.2	213.7	207.6	182.7	257.6	247.2	131.2	184.7	91.0	190.1
Aug	207.3	200.1	193.3	182.9	215.0	208.7	183.5	257.9	249.4	132.2	185.2	91.9	190.9
Sep	208.0	200.8	193.8	183.5	215.5	209.4	185.2	258.2	251.3	133.7	183.7	93.7	191.6
Oct	208.9	201.6	194.6	184.3	216.2	210.2	187.3	257.7	251.9	134.1	184.7	92.8	192.3
Nov	209.7	202.4	195.4	185.1	216.9	211.0	188.8	257.3	253.0	134.3	185.4	93.2	193.2
Dec	210.9	203.5	196.6	186.3	218.0	212.2	190.2	256.9	254.8	134.0	186.8	94.8	194.4

1 See chapter text.
2 Seasonal food is defined as items of food the prices of which show significant seasonal variations. These are fresh fruit and vegetables, fresh fish, eggs and home-killed lamb.

3 There are no weights available for RPIY.

Source: Office for National Statistics: 020 7533 5874

17.6 Tax and Price Index[1]
United Kingdom

Indices and percentages

Tax and Price Index: (January 1988=100)

DQAB

	1993	1994	1995	1996	1997	1998	1999	2000	2001	2002	2003	2004	2005	2006	2007
January	128.7	132.1	137.2	141.6	143.6	147.1	150.5	152.7	156.7	156.5	161.4	166.9	172.1	175.9	183.3
February	129.6	132.9	138.2	142.3	144.2	147.9	150.8	153.7	157.6	157.0	162.3	167.6	172.8	176.7	184.8
March	130.2	133.4	138.8	143.0	144.6	148.4	151.2	154.6	157.8	157.7	163.0	168.4	173.7	177.4	186.1
April	131.3	135.3	140.3	141.7	143.8	149.7	151.2	155.7	156.3	158.6	164.9	168.9	174.1	178.3	186.3
May	131.8	135.8	141.0	142.0	144.4	150.6	151.7	156.3	157.4	159.1	165.2	169.7	174.5	179.5	187.1
June	131.7	135.8	141.2	142.1	145.0	150.5	151.7	156.7	157.6	159.1	165.0	170.0	174.7	180.3	188.2
July	131.4	135.1	140.4	141.5	145.0	150.1	151.1	156.1	156.5	158.8	165.0	170.0	174.7	180.3	187.0
August	132.1	135.8	141.3	142.2	146.0	150.8	151.5	156.1	157.2	159.3	165.4	170.6	175.1	181.0	188.2
September	132.7	136.1	142.0	143.0	146.9	151.5	152.3	157.3	157.8	160.6	166.3	171.3	175.6	181.9	188.9
October	132.6	136.4	142.2	143.0	147.1	151.6	152.6	157.2	157.5	160.9	166.4	171.8	175.8	182.2	189.8
November	132.4	136.5	141.2	143.1	147.2	151.5	152.8	157.7	156.8	161.2	166.5	172.2	176.1	182.8	190.6
December	132.7	137.2	142.1	143.6	147.6	151.5	153.4	157.8	156.6	161.5	167.3	173.1	176.6	184.4	191.8

Retail Prices Index: (January 1988=100)

CHAW

	1993	1994	1995	1996	1997	1998	1999	2000	2001	2002	2003	2004	2005	2006	2007
January	137.9	141.3	146.0	150.2	154.4	159.5	163.4	166.6	171.1	173.3	178.4	183.1	188.9	193.4	201.6
February	138.8	142.1	146.9	150.9	155.0	160.3	163.7	167.5	172.0	173.8	179.3	183.8	189.6	194.2	203.1
March	139.3	142.5	147.5	151.5	155.4	160.8	164.1	168.4	172.2	174.5	179.9	184.6	190.5	195.0	204.4
April	140.6	144.2	149.0	152.6	156.3	162.6	165.2	170.1	173.1	175.7	181.2	185.7	191.6	196.5	205.4
May	141.1	144.7	149.6	152.9	156.9	163.5	165.6	170.7	174.2	176.2	181.5	186.5	192.0	197.7	206.2
June	141.0	144.7	149.8	153.0	157.5	163.4	165.6	171.1	174.4	176.2	181.3	186.8	192.2	198.5	207.3
July	140.7	144.0	149.1	152.4	157.5	163.0	165.1	170.5	173.3	175.9	181.3	186.8	192.2	198.5	206.1
August	141.3	144.7	149.9	153.1	158.5	163.7	165.5	170.5	174.0	176.4	181.6	187.4	192.6	199.2	207.3
September	141.9	145.0	150.6	153.8	159.3	164.4	166.2	171.7	174.6	177.6	182.5	188.1	193.1	200.1	208.0
October	141.8	145.2	149.8	153.8	159.5	164.5	166.5	171.6	174.3	177.9	182.6	188.6	193.3	200.4	208.9
November	141.6	145.3	149.8	153.9	159.6	164.4	166.7	172.1	173.6	178.2	182.7	189.0	193.6	201.1	209.7
December	141.9	146.0	150.7	154.4	160.0	164.4	167.3	172.2	173.4	178.5	183.5	189.9	194.1	202.7	210.9

Percentage changes on one year earlier[1]

	1994	1995	1996	1997	1998	1999	2000	2001	2002	2003	2004	2005	2006	2007
Tax and Price Index[1]														
January	2.6	3.9	3.2	1.4	2.4	2.3	1.5	2.6	−0.1	3.1	3.4	3.1	2.2	4.2
February	2.5	4.0	3.0	1.3	2.6	2.0	1.9	2.5	−0.4	3.4	3.3	3.1	2.3	4.6
March	2.5	4.0	3.0	1.1	2.6	1.9	2.2	2.1	−0.1	3.4	3.3	3.1	2.1	4.9
April	3.0	3.7	1.0	1.5	4.1	1.0	3.0	0.4	1.5	4.0	2.4	3.1	2.4	4.5
May	3.0	3.8	0.7	1.7	4.3	0.7	3.0	0.7	1.1	3.8	2.7	2.8	2.9	4.2
June	3.1	4.0	0.6	2.0	3.8	0.8	3.3	0.6	1.0	3.7	3.0	2.8	3.2	4.4
July	2.8	3.9	0.8	2.5	3.5	0.7	3.3	0.3	1.5	3.9	3.0	2.8	3.2	3.7
August	2.8	4.1	0.6	2.7	3.3	0.5	3.0	0.7	1.3	3.8	3.1	2.6	3.4	4.0
September	2.6	4.3	0.7	2.7	3.1	0.5	3.3	0.3	1.8	3.5	3.0	2.5	3.6	3.8
October	2.9	3.5	1.3	2.9	3.1	0.7	3.0	0.2	2.2	3.4	3.2	2.3	3.6	4.2
November	3.1	3.4	1.3	2.9	2.9	0.9	3.2	−0.6	2.8	3.3	3.4	2.3	3.8	4.3
December	3.4	3.6	1.1	2.8	2.6	1.3	2.9	−0.8	3.1	3.6	3.5	2.0	4.4	4.0
Retail Prices Index														
January	2.5	3.3	2.9	2.8	3.3	2.4	2.0	2.7	1.3	2.9	2.6	3.2	2.4	4.2
February	2.4	3.4	2.7	2.7	3.4	2.1	2.3	2.7	1.0	3.2	2.5	3.2	2.4	4.6
March	2.3	3.5	2.7	2.6	3.5	2.1	2.6	2.3	1.3	3.1	2.6	3.2	2.4	4.8
April	2.6	3.3	2.4	2.4	4.0	1.6	3.0	1.8	1.5	3.1	2.5	3.2	2.6	4.5
May	2.6	3.4	2.2	2.6	4.2	1.3	3.1	2.1	1.1	3.0	2.8	2.9	3.0	4.3
June	2.6	3.5	2.1	2.9	3.7	1.3	3.3	1.9	1.0	2.9	3.0	2.9	3.3	4.4
July	2.3	3.5	2.2	3.3	3.5	1.3	3.3	1.6	1.5	3.1	3.0	2.9	3.3	3.8
August	2.4	3.6	2.1	3.5	3.3	1.1	3.0	2.1	1.4	2.9	3.2	2.8	3.4	4.1
September	2.2	3.9	2.1	3.6	3.2	1.1	3.3	1.7	1.7	2.8	3.1	2.7	3.6	3.9
October	2.4	3.2	2.7	3.7	3.1	1.2	3.1	1.6	2.1	2.6	3.3	2.5	3.7	4.2
November	2.6	3.1	2.7	3.7	3.0	1.4	3.2	0.9	2.6	2.5	3.4	2.4	3.9	4.3
December	2.9	3.2	2.5	3.6	2.8	1.8	2.9	0.7	2.9	2.8	3.5	2.2	4.4	4.0

1 See chapter text.

Source: Office for National Statistics: 020 7533 5874

Prices

17.7 Index of purchase prices of the means of agricultural production[1]
United Kingdom
Annual averages

Indices (2000=100)

		Weights	1997	1998	1999	2000	2001	2002	2003	2004	2005	2006	2007
Goods and services currently consumed[2]	C3FU	100	105.5	99.5	98.1	100.0	104.3	103.7	106.5	113.7	116.0	120.7	132.5
Seeds	C3FV	3.3	119.2	119.2	109.0	100.0	109.2	105.5	116.0	110.3	108.2	104.0	153.6
Energy, lubricants	C3FW	8.1	82.1	75.1	82.4	100.0	96.7	92.4	100.5	108.8	137.4	154.4	158.0
Fuels for heating	C3FX	1.0	77.3	61.6	66.6	100.0	95.5	87.2	104.5	118.3	158.9	185.0	203.0
Motor fuel	C3FY	5.1	73.1	66.7	77.8	100.0	96.7	91.6	100.7	110.3	143.4	157.6	159.7
Electricity	C3FZ	1.8	109.6	104.8	102.9	100.0	96.9	96.2	96.5	98.9	110.7	132.0	132.0
Lubricants	C3G2	0.2	86.2	88.5	98.1	100.0	101.2	106.2	112.7	113.1	113.1	113.1	113.1
Fertilisers and soil improvers	C3G3	9.1	106.6	95.3	93.3	100.0	115.8	110.3	119.0	130.5	143.3	151.4	170.1
Straight nitrogen	C3G4	3.9	104.4	87.0	82.9	100.0	129.1	120.2	133.1	148.5	168.7	181.8	187.7
Compound fertilisers	C3G5	4.6	109.6	101.9	101.3	100.0	106.7	103.0	109.1	118.4	126.0	130.4	160.0
Other fertiliser (mainly lime and chalk)	C3G6	0.4	93.5	95.9	96.7	100.0	100.5	104.0	103.4	103.8	105.6	109.1	116.1
Plant protection products	C3G7	7.2	116.6	108.2	105.8	100.0	96.8	95.8	95.7	100.6	102.9	103.4	104.9
Animal feedstuffs	C3G8	26.4	125.4	106.5	99.1	100.0	107.4	103.5	104.9	111.6	103.0	108.1	130.4
Feed wheat	C3G9	2.2	133.8	113.8	110.7	100.0	110.9	97.3	106.5	119.4	97.6	111.9	156.2
Whole barley	C3GA	2.1	125.3	108.5	111.5	100.0	101.8	89.5	103.2	112.8	97.8	108.8	157.1
Whole oats	C3GB	0.2	123.3	98.0	104.7	100.0	97.8	90.7	85.1	94.3	94.6	102.6	125.8
Maize glutten feed	C3GC	0.4	117.8	95.3	100.2	100.0	110.0	102.9	122.9	123.8	110.1	124.6	165.8
Oilcake	C3GD	2.1	131.5	91.9	83.5	100.0	109.4	100.4	109.5	112.0	100.0	100.6	127.0
White fish meal	C3GE	0.4	125.3	137.9	93.2	100.0	115.1	134.7	129.1	120.3	126.6	182.6	173.7
Other straight feedstuffs	C3GF	3.3	121.7	98.2	91.8	100.0	114.1	109.3	109.9	115.1	109.8	109.1	142.3
All straight feedstuffs	C3GG	10.6	127.3	104.1	97.1	100.0	109.7	101.3	108.2	114.9	102.9	110.5	146.3
Feedstuffs non-concentrates	C3GH	0.1	127.3	104.1	97.1	100.0	109.7	101.3	108.2	114.9	102.9	110.5	146.3
Compound feedstuffs for:	C3GI	15.8	124.1	108.1	100.4	100.0	105.8	104.9	102.7	109.4	103.1	106.5	119.8
Cattle and calves	C3GJ	6.2	122.0	105.0	99.9	100.0	106.4	105.9	102.5	108.1	103.9	105.4	117.2
Pigs	C3GK	3.5	130.5	112.8	101.9	100.0	105.9	103.5	101.0	107.7	100.2	105.3	117.7
Poultry	C3GL	5.0	121.7	108.7	100.6	100.0	105.9	104.5	104.9	112.8	104.5	109.7	126.3
Sheep	C3GM	1.1	126.5	108.3	98.0	100.0	102.2	106.2	99.4	105.9	101.6	101.5	112.0
Maintenance and repair of plant	C3GN	7.9	91.0	93.4	96.6	100.0	104.3	109.4	116.0	122.5	130.3	137.8	143.4
Maintenance and repair of buildings	C3GO	3.6	97.3	98.5	97.7	100.0	101.9	105.1	108.3	113.4	118.1	125.1	134.3
Veterinary services	C3GP	3.2	100.1	101.1	101.2	100.0	98.6	97.8	101.6	104.6	103.9	111.1	112.5
Other goods and services	C3GQ	31.2	95.6	98.5	99.9	100.0	102.5	105.5	105.2	114.0	114.5	115.5	119.7
Goods and services contributing to investment in agriculture	C3GR	100	98.1	99.8	100.2	100.0	99.0	100.0	101.5	104.4	108.7	111.7	115.4
Materials	C3GS	71.5	100.5	101.6	101.7	100.0	97.3	97.0	97.5	99.4	103.4	105.3	107.2
Machinery and other equipment	C3GT	28.4	95.0	97.7	99.2	100.0	97.4	95.7	95.1	96.1	103.8	108.2	114.0
Machinery and plant for cultivation	C3GU	8.0	93.3	97.7	99.1	100.0	99.6	98.6	98.7	103.8	109.4	111.0	115.9
Machinery and plant for harvesting	C3GV	14.3	96.8	98.4	100.0	100.0	92.3	88.8	88.2	87.3	97.9	105.4	113.2
Farm machinery and installations	C3GW	6.0	93.2	96.1	97.5	100.0	106.3	108.2	106.8	107.0	110.2	111.2	113.2
Tractors	C3GX	28.6	101.0	101.6	102.4	100.0	96.8	98.4	101.4	106.1	110.5	111.8	111.8
Other vehicles	C3GY	14.5	110.0	109.1	105.1	100.0	98.3	96.7	94.4	92.4	88.6	86.7	84.9
Buildings	C3GZ	19.5	93.2	95.6	96.6	100.0	103.3	107.8	112.1	118.1	123.7	130.9	140.0
Engineering and soil improvement operations	C3H2	9.0	89.8	94.8	96.9	100.0	101.4	107.2	110.3	113.3	118.0	118.8	124.7

1 See chapter text.
2 The sum of the percentages of categories included does not add up to 100% due to the exclusion of some minor categories.

Source: Department for Environment, Food and Rural Affairs: 01904 455249

17.8 Index of producer prices of agricultural products[1]
United Kingdom
Annual averages

Indices (2000=100)

		Weights	1997	1998	1999	2000	2001	2002	2003	2004	2005	2006	2007
All products[2]	C3H6	100	117.1	107.0	103.6	100.0	108.3	103.3	109.9	113.3	109.7	114.2	129.3
All crop products	C3H7	40.2	108.9	111.7	109.0	100.0	112.0	104.0	110.7	115.1	108.6	118.1	143.9
Cereals (including cereal seeds)	C3H8	13.3	132.4	113.8	111.0	100.0	107.8	95.0	105.2	114.2	99.1	110.5	163.7
Wheat for:													
breadmaking	C3H9	1.1	139.5	122.8	112.9	100.0	109.6	101.4	110.6	120.8	102.1	107.4	172.6
other milling	C3HA	1.5	133.7	116.0	110.9	100.0	107.5	92.9	104.1	116.8	96.6	108.6	177.1
feeding	C3HB	6.4	135.4	114.0	110.5	100.0	110.5	96.7	105.6	117.6	98.2	112.0	154.1
Barley for:													
feeding	C3HC	2.5	123.9	109.2	112.9	100.0	102.6	89.1	103.7	110.8	98.7	108.4	159.8
malting	C3HD	1.4	128.2	115.1	108.9	100.0	104.8	96.5	107.1	101.6	104.5	112.8	199.1
Oats for:													
milling	C3HE	0.1	128.8	104.9	109.9	100.0	109.8	89.0	90.7	96.3	104.9	113.8	149.6
feeding	C3HF	0.2	119.0	97.0	106.1	100.0	98.5	91.2	86.7	94.4	96.3	104.3	130.5
Potatoes:	C3HG	4.5	63.5	138.8	143.5	100.0	131.0	90.0	105.6	140.3	109.2	141.7	161.1
early	C3HH	0.4	46.3	100.7	51.9	100.0	114.5	73.0	90.0	124.8	98.0	131.8	102.1
main crop	C3HI	4.1	63.4	141.1	151.5	100.0	132.5	90.6	106.0	141.6	109.7	143.1	166.5
Industrial crops	C3HJ	4.3	127.9	118.4	103.4	100.0	111.9	114.4	120.3	121.6	114.3	118.3	124.0
Oilseed rape (non set-aside)	C3HK	1.2	135.6	140.0	102.0	100.0	119.2	121.2	140.3	136.1	112.9	134.5	158.8
Sugar beet	C3HL	2.2	124.9	111.4	108.7	100.0	107.3	114.8	112.1	115.4	117.1	112.6	86.6
Fresh vegetables	C3HM	7.7	97.4	105.2	99.2	100.0	113.6	112.7	125.5	113.7	120.3	129.7	143.5
Cauliflowers	C3HN	0.4	79.1	87.9	82.4	100.0	103.9	117.7	119.8	102.4	127.1	123.2	166.2
Lettuce	C3HO	0.7	114.0	98.6	102.9	100.0	129.2	128.6	151.5	130.2	140.7	151.7	150.2
Tomatoes	C3HP	0.7	86.9	91.8	100.3	100.0	100.1	107.6	135.6	99.8	117.7	124.3	126.6
Carrots	C3HQ	0.7	88.1	125.4	119.3	100.0	166.5	150.4	157.2	144.7	170.5	184.2	208.9
Cabbage	C3HR	0.4	83.2	94.5	94.2	100.0	123.0	109.8	119.7	109.3	122.6	133.1	161.7
Beans	C3HS	0.2	87.3	107.8	102.8	100.0	124.3	118.0	119.1	128.7	127.2	172.5	188.6
Onions	C3HT	0.5	122.8	165.8	104.7	100.0	128.6	126.7	136.1	138.8	113.1	150.8	196.7
Mushrooms	C3HU	1.3	99.1	98.9	98.1	100.0	91.0	95.9	100.6	94.4	83.4	81.3	70.9
Fresh fruit	C3HV	1.9	109.1	105.4	100.0	100.0	99.0	113.9	124.2	112.4	120.1	114.6	126.7
Dessert apples	C3HW	0.3	124.7	110.5	104.3	100.0	109.8	111.3	124.6	120.7	116.4	122.5	140.4
Dessert pears	C3HX	0.1	118.2	110.4	108.7	100.0	128.7	124.8	115.3	114.6	115.0	123.0	122.9
Cooking apples	C3HY	0.2	135.6	150.9	100.7	100.0	105.6	109.4	152.1	142.5	118.8	129.7	144.1
Strawberries	C3HZ	0.7	106.9	93.7	102.4	100.0	94.5	121.7	124.4	97.1	111.8	106.5	113.2
Raspberries	C3I2	0.2	103.3	114.3	104.9	100.0	102.9	128.9	125.7	114.3	152.9	133.4	158.6
Seeds (excluding cereal seeds)	C3I3	0.5	130.9	98.6	97.7	100.0	104.0	95.7	113.6	112.9	114.1	113.1	113.1
Flowers and plants	C3I4	5.9	102.4	103.1	105.3	100.0	105.3	106.8	107.9	105.3	105.6	108.8	115.3
Other crop products	C3I5	0.7	122.2	98.7	97.0	100.0	106.0	98.9	108.6	109.7	110.8	110.6	114.0
Animals and animal products	C3I6	59.8	122.6	103.9	99.9	100.0	105.8	102.7	109.4	112.0	110.4	111.6	119.5
Animals for slaughter	C3I7	35.3	118.0	97.2	95.2	100.0	101.3	103.2	109.3	111.7	110.3	113.8	115.8
Calves	C3I8	0.1	179.3	149.4	115.1	100.0	94.2	120.2	143.9	140.8	108.3	131.5	135.9
Clean cattle	C3I9	9.7	107.1	95.0	101.7	100.0	100.8	103.8	106.7	113.4	114.6	123.9	125.9
Clean pigs	C3IA	7.0	117.5	85.8	83.4	100.0	103.6	98.7	109.0	109.3	109.8	110.9	114.3
Sows and boars	C3IB	0.2	157.1	81.1	81.0	100.0	107.4	94.0	103.2	123.9	124.1	126.1	99.8
Clean sheep and lambs	C3IC	5.2	131.0	97.1	90.2	100.0	101.3	118.5	132.5	131.4	122.9	125.5	111.7
Ewes and rams	C3ID	0.4	198.5	116.3	81.3	100.0	152.4	149.6	188.2	182.5	148.9	158.9	155.4
All poultry	C3IE	11.5	116.8	103.3	99.0	100.0	98.6	97.2	99.4	101.2	100.8	99.4	108.2
Chickens	C3IF	7.9	126.6	105.9	101.3	100.0	100.1	99.5	100.2	103.4	102.0	100.0	107.5
Turkeys	C3IG	2.9	89.5	91.3	90.0	100.0	94.4	89.5	97.8	95.0	94.7	94.0	108.6
Cows' milk	C3IH	20.1	130.6	114.4	108.3	100.0	113.7	101.0	106.4	109.0	109.0	106.0	122.4
Eggs	C3II	3.2	121.1	109.4	98.0	100.0	104.9	109.5	130.7	135.1	121.0	127.4	144.3
Other animal products:	C3IJ	1.1	129.4	108.0	103.0	100.0	107.7	100.0	107.4	110.4	107.5	93.5	111.1
Wool (clip)	C3IK	0.2	150.1	98.6	93.5	100.0	87.0	96.4	108.4	107.3	92.3	33.6	71.7

1 See chapter text.
2 The sum of the percentages of all the categories does not add up to 100% due to the exclusion of some minor categories.

Source: Department for Environment, Food and Rural Affairs: 01904 455249

17.9 Commodity price trends[1]
United Kingdom

			1997	1998	1999	2000	2001	2002	2003	2004	2005	2006	2007[16]
Wheat £ per tonne	KVAA	Average ex-farm price[2,3]	91.8	77.8	75.4	68.1	76.9	65.6	77.3	..	..	..	..
Barley £ per tonne	KVAB	Average ex-farm price[2,3]	86.3	79.2	74.2	70.1	72.1	64.8	75.5	..	..	..	..
Oats £ per tonne	KVAC	Average ex-farm price[2,3]	82.3	66.4	71.1	65.0	67.7	56.6	62.1	..	..	..	..
Rye £ per tonne	KVAD	Average ex-farm price[2]	..	..	..	..	78.10	61.40	71.80	86.40	..	..	..
Hops £ per tonne	KVAE	Average farm-gate price	3 550	3 500	4 000	4 017	4 081	3 255	3 212	2 496	3 277	3 241	..
Potatoes £ per tonne	KVAF	Average farm-gate price[4]	66.10	121.50	119.10	83.30	111.40	81.10	102.50	123.20	100.60	128.90	143.50
Sugar beet £ per tonne	KVAG	Producer price[5]	29.70	29.80	26.40	27.80	30.80	29.60	30.50	30.80	30.90	24.10	22.80
Oilseed rape £ per tonne	KVAH	Average market price[6]	160.20	164.30	112.90	120.40	148.40	148.20	171.60	..	..	..	..
Apples £ per tonne	KPUE	Dessert average farm-gate price[7]	525.0	480.3	436.8	357.8	352.2	385.2	460.3	412.2	418.6	433.6	491.9
" "	KVAI	Dessert average market price	462.0	431.5	405.4	408.7	418.2	453.1	551.3	526.1	471.5	..	..
" "	KVAJ	Culinary average market price	517.7	575.5	384.1	378.1	422.4	419.4	652.6	592.0	458.7	..	..
" "	KPUJ	Culinary average farm-gate price	335.1	341.4	248.9	215.3	175.7	285.7	471.7	359.1	316.5	378.7	377.1
Pears £ per tonne	KPUG	Average farm-gate price	441.9	405.1	426.4	283.3	352.1	402.9	344.0	349.2	350.3	392.1	387.4
" "	KVAK	Average market price	429.5	413.3	396.8	374.0	412.5	463.6	443.0	437.2	426.3	..	..
Tomatoes £ per tonne	LQMH	Average farm-gate price[7]	546.9	594.6	576.5	751.6	724.9	793.7	1 042.3	751.6	870.8	989.7	1 009.9
" "	KVAL	Average market price[7]	549.3	636.0	583.6	629.7	651.3	736.3	824.8	647.2	754.8	..	..
Cauliflowers £ per tonne	KPUI	Average farm-gate price[7]	236.76	216.28	211.33	274.10	285.30	329.60	331.70	296.31	344.40	331.10	376.76
" "	KVAM	Average market price[7]	309.8	284.8	242.5	282.9	304.9	365.6	368.2	330.8	408.3	..	..
Cattle (rearing) £ per head	KVAN	1st quality Hereford/cross bull calves[8,9,10]	147.00	107.90	88.20	79.50	..	84.90	112.70	113.70	81.50	73.40	93.10
"	KVAO	1st quality beef/ cross yearling steers[9,10]	427.00	369.00	382.00	400.05	..	403.85	451.54	395.90	429.10	..	..
Cattle (fat) p per kg liveweight	KVAP	Clean cattle[11]	96.89	86.10	92.12	89.68	87.53	91.38	95.15	101.18	102.22	..	..

17.9 Commodity price trends[1]
United Kingdom
continued

			1997	1998	1999	2000	2001	2002	2003	2004	2005	2006	2007[16]
Sheep (store) £ per head	KVAQ	1st quality lambs, hoggets and tegs[8]	53.42	31.28	28.62	34.50	..	..	36.03	37.70	30.52	..	..
Sheep (fat) p per kg estimated dressed carcase weight	KVAR KVAS	Great Britain[12] Northern Ireland[13]	239.02 228.23	192.46 179.06	180.27 165.71	196.44 182.67	.. ..	233.40 228.80	271.08 239.91	262.55 227.83	250.10 223.75	.. ..	.. ..
Pigs £ per kg deadweight	KVAT	Average price clean pigs	110.80	80.60	78.60	95.08	97.75	93.32	102.64	102.85	102.08	..	..
Broilers p per kg carcass weight	KVAU	Average producer price	86.2	76.7	72.1	70.7	70.6	68.8	68.6	73.6	73.2	..	..
Milk p per litre	KVAV	Average net return to producers[14]	22.12	19.37	18.35	16.93	19.26	17.10	18.03	18.47	18.47	..	..
Eggs p per dozen	KVAW	Average producer price[15]	39.33	36.35	34.45	39.28	40.72	42.08	45.95	48.92	45.27	..	..
Wool p per kg	KHWQ	Average producer price for clip paid to producers by the British Wool Marketing Board	74.90	48.00	46.60	51.30	47.00	50.00	55.70	53.10	50.20	..	..

1 This table gives indications of the movement in commodity prices at the first point of sale. The series do not always show total receipts by farmers; for some commodities additional premiums or deficiency payments are made to achieve support price levels.
2 Weighted average ex-farm prices of United Kingdom cereals.
3 Data from 1997 onwards have been revised and are not directly comparable with earlier years.
4 Weighted average price paid to growers for early and main crop potatoes in the United Kingdom (includes all potatoes and a value for sacks).
5 Returns to growers figures since 1986 prices per 'adjusted' tonne at 16% sugar content.
6 Typical contract price adjusted to delivered basis and 40 per cent oil content.
7 Weighted average wholesale prices for England and Wales. Average farmgate price for England and Wales, crop year (June-May).

8 Average prices at representative markets in England and Wales.
9 Consists of Hereford/cross, Charolais/cross, Limousin/cross, Simmental/cross, Belgian/cross, other continental cross, other beef/dairy cross, other beef/beef cross.
10 From 2002 no differentiation between class 1 and class 2 animals.
11 Based on Meat and Livestock Commission all clean cattle prices.
12 Average of Great Britain weekly market prices as used to determine the level of ewe premium.
13 Average of Northern Ireland weekly market prices used to determine the level of ewe premium.
14 Derived by dividing total value of output by the total quantity of output available for human consumption.
15 Average price of all Class A eggs weighted according to quantity in each grade.
16 Provisional.

Source: Department for Environment, Food and Rural Affairs: 01904 455332

Government finance

Chapter 18

Government finance

Public sector

(Tables 18.1 to 18.3 and 18.5)

In Table 18.1 the term public sector describes the consolidation of central government, local government and public corporations. General government is the consolidated total of central government and local government. The table shows details of the key public sector finances' indicators, consistent with the European System of Accounts 1995 (ESA95), by sub sector.

The concepts in Table 18.1 are consistent with the format for public finances in the Economic and Fiscal Strategy Report (EFSR), published by HM Treasury on 11 June 1998, and The Budget. The public sector current budget is equivalent to net saving in national accounts plus capital tax receipts. Net investment is gross capital formation, plus payments less receipts of investment grants, less depreciation. Net borrowing is net investment less current budget. Net borrowing differs from the net cash requirement (see below) in that it is measured on an accruals basis whereas the net cash requirement is mainly a cash measure which includes some financial transactions. Table 18.2 shows the public sector key fiscal balances. The table shows the component detail of the public sector key fiscal balance by economic category. The tables are consistent with the budget.

Table 18.3 shows public sector net debt. Public sector net debt consists of the public sector's financial liabilities at face value, minus its liquid assets – mainly foreign currency exchange reserves and bank deposits. General government gross debt (consolidated) in Table 18.3 is consistent with the definition of general government gross debt reported to the European Commission under the requirements of the Maastricht Treaty.

More information on the concepts in Table 18.1, 18.2 and 18.3 can be found in a guide to monthly public sector finance statistics, GSS Methodology Series No 12, the Office for National Statistics First Release 'Public Sector Finances' and *Financial Statistics Explanatory Handbook*.

Table 18.5 shows the taxes and National Insurance contributions paid to central government, local government, and to the institutions of the European Union. The table is the same as table 11.1 of the National Accounts *Blue Book*. More information on the data and concepts in the table can be found in Chapter 11 of the *Blue Book*.

Consolidated Fund and National Loans Fund

(Tables 18.4, 18.6 and 18.7)

The central government embraces all bodies for whose activities a Minister of the Crown, or other responsible person, is accountable to Parliament. It includes, in addition to the ordinary government departments, a number of bodies administering public policy, but without the substantial degree of financial independence which characterises the public corporations. It also includes certain extra-budgetary funds and accounts controlled by departments.

The government's financial transactions are handled through a number of statutory funds or accounts. The most important of these is the Consolidated Fund, which is the government's main account with the Bank of England. Up to 31 March 1968 the Consolidated Fund was virtually synonymous with the term 'Exchequer', which was then the government's central cash account. From 1 April 1968 the National Loans Fund, with a separate account at the Bank of England, was set up by the National Loans Act, 1968. The general effect of this Act was to remove from the Consolidated Fund most of the government's domestic lending and the whole of the government's borrowing transactions, and to provide for them to be brought to account in the National Loans Fund.

Revenue from taxation and miscellaneous receipts, including interest and dividends on loans made from votes, continue to be paid into the Consolidated Fund.

After meeting the ordinary expenditure on Supply Services and the Consolidated Fund Standing Services, the surplus or deficit of the Consolidated Fund (Table 18.4), is payable into or met by the National Loans Fund. Table 18.4 also provides a summary of the transactions of the National Loans Fund. The service of the National Debt, previously borne by the Consolidated Fund, is now met from the National Loans Fund which receives:

(a) interest payable on loans to the nationalised industries, local authorities and other bodies, whether the loans were made before or after 1 April 1968, and

(b) the profits of the Issue Department of the Bank of England, mainly derived from interest on government securities, which were formerly paid into the Exchange Equalisation Account. The net cost of servicing the National Debt after applying these interest receipts and similar items is a charge on the Consolidated Fund as part of the standing services. Details of National Loans Fund loans outstanding are shown in Table 18.7. Details of borrowing and repayments of debt, other than loans from the National Loans Fund, are shown in Table 18.6.

Income tax

(Table 18.9, 18.10)

Following the introduction of Independent Taxation from 1990–91, the Married Couple's Allowance was introduced. It is payable in addition to the Personal Allowance and between 1990–91 and 1992–93 went to the husband unless the transfer condition was met. The condition was that the husband was unable to make full use of the allowance himself and in that case he could transfer only part or all of the Married Couple's Allowance to his wife. In 1993–94 all or half of the allowance could be transferred to the wife if the couple had agreed beforehand. The wife has the right to claim half the allowance. The Married Couple's Allowance, and allowances linked to it, were restricted to 20 per cent in 1994–95 and to 15 per cent from 1995–96. From 2000–01 only people born before 6 April 1935 are entitled to Married Couple's Allowance.

The age allowance replaces the single allowance, provided the taxpayer's income is below the limits shown in the table. From 1989–90, for incomes in excess of the limits, the allowance is reduced by £1 for each additional £2 of income until the ordinary limit is reached (before it was £2 for each £3 of additional income). The relief is due where the taxpayer is aged 65 or over in the year of assessment.

The additional Personal Allowance could be claimed by a single parent (or by a married man if his wife was totally incapacitated) who maintained a resident child at his or her own expense. Widow's Bereavement Allowance was due to a widow in the year of her husband's death and in the following year provided the widow had not remarried before the beginning of that year. Both the additional Personal Allowance and the Widow's Bereavement Allowance were abolished from April 2000.

The Blind Person's Allowance may be claimed by blind persons (in England and Wales, registered as blind by a local authority) and surplus Blind Person's Allowance may be transferred to a husband or wife. Relief on life assurance premiums is given by deduction from the premium payable. From 1984–85, it is confined to policies made before 14 March 1984.

From 1993–94 until 1998–99 a number of taxpayers with taxable income in excess of the lower rate limit only paid tax at the lower rate. This was because it was only their dividend income and (from 1996–97) their savings income which took their taxable income above the lower rate limit but below the basic rate limit, and such income was chargeable to tax at the lower rate and not the basic rate.

In 1999–2000 the 10 per cent starting rate replaced the lower rate and taxpayers with savings or dividend income at the basic rate of tax are taxed at 20 per cent and 10 per cent respectively. Before 1999–2000 these people would have been classified as lower rate taxpayers.

Rateable values

(Table 18.11)

Major changes to local government finance in England and Wales took effect from 1 April 1990. These included the abolition of domestic rating – replaced by the Community Charge (replaced in 1993 by the Council Tax), the revaluation of all non-domestic properties, and the introduction of the Uniform Business Rate. Also in 1990, a new classification scheme was introduced which has resulted in differences in coverage. Further differences are caused by legislative changes which have changed the treatment of certain types of property. There was little change in the total rateable value of non-domestic properties when all these properties were revalued in April 1995. Rateable values for offices fell and there was a rise for all other property types shown in the table.

With effect from 1 April 2000, all non-domestic properties were revalued. Overall there was an increase in rateable values of over 25 per cent compared to the last year of the 1995 list. The largest proportionate increase was for offices and cinemas, with all property types given in the table showing rises.

The latest revaluation affecting all non domestic properties took effect from 1 April 2005. In this revaluation the overall increase in rateable values between 1 April of the first year of the new list and the same day on the last year of the 2000 list was 17 per cent. The largest proportionate increase was for theatres and music halls with again, all property types in the table showing rises.

Local authority capital expenditure and receipts

(Table 18.15)

Capital spending by local authorities is mainly for buying, constructing or improving physical assets such as:

– buildings – schools, houses, libraries and museums, police and fire stations.

– land – for development, roads, playing fields; vehicles, plant and machinery – including street lighting and road signs. It also includes grants and advances made to the private sector or the rest of the public sector for capital purposes, such as advances to Registered Social Landlords

Government finance

Local authority capital expenditure has risen by almost 42 per cent since 2002–03.

Capital expenditure by local authorities in England was £16.3 billion in 2006–07 compared with £16.6 billion in 2005–06, a decrease of 2 per cent. The refinancing of the National Exhibition Centre in Birmingham and major rail development funded by the Greater London Authority (GLA) in 2005–06 account for most of the decrease between 2005–06 and 2006–07.

New construction, conversion and renovation forms the major part of capital spending.

Local authority capital expenditure on social services has risen by 83 per cent since 2002–03, although it remains a small proportion of total spending.

Education and Transport sectors have maintained their share of total spending over the last four years.

Other spending (mainly relating to libraries and the arts, fire service, parks, waste collection, general administration, planning and development) rose by 77 per cent over the same period, increasing its share of total spending to 30 per cent.

Housing's share of spending fell from 34 per cent to 28 per cent over this period.

Local authority financing for capital expenditure

(Table 18.16)

Authorities finance capital spending in a number of ways, including use of their own revenue funds, borrowing or grants and contributions from elsewhere. Up until 31 March 2004, the capital finance system laid down in Part 4 of the Local Government and Housing Act 1989 (the '1989 Act') provided the framework within which authorities were permitted to finance capital spending from sources other than revenue – that is by the use of borrowing, long-term credit or capital receipts.

Up until 31 March 2004, capital spending could be financed by:

- revenue resources – either the General Fund Revenue Account, the Housing Revenue Account (HRA) or the Major Repairs Reserve – but an authority could not charge council tenants for spending on general services, or spending on council houses to local taxpayers

- borrowing or long-term credit as authorised by the credit approvals issued by central government. Credit approvals were normally accompanied by an element of Revenue Support Grant (RSG) covering most of the costs of borrowing

- grants received from central government

- contributions or grants from elsewhere – including the National Lottery and Non-Departmental Public Bodies such as Sport England, English Heritage and Natural England, as well as private sector partners, capital receipts (that is proceeds from the sale of land, buildings or other fixed assets) and sums set aside as Provision for Credit Liabilities (PCL). This required the use of a credit approval, unless the authority was debt-free.

From 1 April 2004, capital spending can be financed in the same ways, except that central government no longer issues credit approvals to allow authorities to finance capital spending by borrowing. However, it continues to provide financial support in the usual way, via RSG or HRA subsidy, towards some capital spending financed by borrowing that is Supported Capital Expenditure (Revenue). Authorities are now free to finance capital spending by self-financed borrowing within limits of affordability set, having regard to the 2003 Act and the Chartered Institute of Public Finance and Accountancy Prudential Code. The concept of PCL has not been carried forward into the new system, although authorities which were debt-free and had a negative credit ceiling at the end of the old system could still spend amounts of PCL built up under the old rules.

In 2006–07 capital expenditure of almost £2.3 billion (about 14 per cent) was financed by self-financed borrowing, an increase of 2 per cent from the amount financed in 2005–06. Self-financed borrowing in 2005–06 includes a bond issued as part of the refinancing of the National Exhibition Centre in Birmingham, and if this is excluded, capital expenditure financed by self-financed borrowing in 2006–07 shows an increase of 13 per cent over 2005–06.

In 2001–02 credit approvals were the principal financing source for capital expenditure, accounting for 26 per cent of the total. By 2006–07, government grants accounted for 25 per cent of the total financing.

18.1 Sector analysis of key fiscal balances[1]
United Kingdom
Not seasonally adjusted

£ million[2]

		1997 /98	1998 /99	1999 /00	2000 /01	2001 /02	2002 /03	2003 /04	2004 /05	2005 /06	2006 /07	2007 /08
Surplus on current budget[3]												
Central Government	ANLV	920	12 529	24 456	26 836	13 906	−7 969	−17 562	−17 953	−13 686	−5 330	−7 799
Local government	NMMX	−420	−406	−2 179	−1 531	−1 657	−1 270	817	−1 846	−5 485	−2 972	..
General Government	ANLW	−746	11 086	20 878	21 996	10 861	−11 103	−19 005	−19 516	−21 569	−10 283	..
Public corporations	FDDP	−1 046	−1 220	−1 675	−1 828	−631	−2 580	−2 918	−685	5 171	4 183	..
Public sector	ANMU	−930	10 415	21 005	23 487	12 213	−11 095	−17 422	−18 965	−14 098	−4 307	−7 554
Net investment[4]												
Central government	-ANNS	7 734	8 085	9 368	8 669	13 543	17 174	18 582	20 018	19 272	26 478	30 909
Local government	-ANNT	−536	−313	−832	−1 882	−1 824	−3 595	−1 001	−230	549	−672	..
General Government	-ANNV	7 297	7 848	6 461	6 574	10 951	12 487	16 371	19 499	18 318	24 517	..
Public corporations	-ANNU	−2 080	−1 033	−2 944	−2 141	−456	−922	−2 941	−1 378	3 759	−285	..
Public sector	-ANNW	4 765	5 897	5 395	5 225	11 831	13 707	15 590	20 616	23 550	25 779	28 002
Net borrowing[5]												
Central government	-NMFJ	6 814	−4 444	−15 088	−18 167	−363	25 143	36 144	37 971	32 958	31 808	38 708
Local government	-NMOE	1 595	1 820	3 136	2 490	2 081	1 074	183	3 795	5 445	2 371	784
General Government	-NNBK	8 409	−2 624	−11 952	−15 677	1 718	26 217	36 327	41 766	38 403	34 179	39 492
Public corporations	-CPCM	−2 714	−1 894	−3 658	−2 585	−2 100	−1 415	−3 315	−2 185	−755	−4 093	−3 936
Public sector	-ANNX	5 695	−4 518	−15 610	−18 262	−382	24 802	33 012	39 581	37 648	30 086	35 556
Net cash requirement												
Central government[6]	RUUX	2 751	−6 344	−10 664	−37 251	3 366	24 214	42 717	37 454	35 908	36 891	29 593
Local government	ABEG	−820	−404	979	−611	−423	−2 715	−2 712	1 270	4 153	58	−907
General Government	RUUS	1 931	−6 748	−9 685	−37 862	2 943	21 499	40 005	38 724	40 061	36 949	28 686
Public corporations	ABEM	−669	698	1 712	1 541	1 159	3 095	−1 539	−184	270	−1 657	−2 071
Public sector	RURQ	1 262	−6 050	−7 973	−36 321	4 102	24 594	38 466	38 540	40 331	35 292	26 615
Public sector debt												
Public sector net debt (£ billion)	RUTN	352.9	351.6	345.4	312.4	315.5	347.1	382.8	423.6	463.0	499.5	527.7
Public sector net debt as a percentage of GDP	RUTO	41.3	39.2	36.4	31.4	30.3	31.5	32.8	34.7	36.0	36.6	36.7

1 National accounts entities as defined under the European System of Accounts 1995 (ESA95) consistent with the latest national accounts. See chapter text.
2 Unless otherwise stated
3 Net saving *plus* capital taxes.
4 Gross capital formation *plus* payments *less* receipts of investment grants *less* depreciation.

5 Net investment *less* surplus on current budget. A version of General government net borrowing is reported to the European Commision under the requirements of the Maastricht Treaty.
6 Central government net cash requirement (own account).

Source: Office for National Statistics: 020 7014 2124

18.2 Public sector transactions and fiscal balances[1]
United Kingdom

£ million

		1997 /98	1998 /99	1999 /00	2000 /01	2001 /02	2002 /03	2003 /04	2004 /05	2005 /06	2006 /07	2007 /08
Current receipts												
Taxes on income and wealth	ANSO	114 939	123 875	133 720	144 157	145 122	143 228	145 505	160 974	179 909	194 177	..
Taxes on production	NMYE	111 502	116 519	125 099	129 273	133 043	139 827	148 817	154 958	159 295	170 026	..
Other current taxes[2]	MJBC	16 223	17 688	18 916	19 698	21 569	23 192	25 748	27 236	28 679	30 313	..
Taxes on capital	NMGI	1 684	1 805	2 054	2 236	2 365	2 370	2 521	2 941	3 276	3 623	..
Social contributions	ANBO	51 692	54 746	56 935	62 068	63 162	63 529	75 148	80 408	85 335	90 701	..
Gross operating surplus	ANBP	16 655	16 755	16 897	16 617	16 861	17 182	18 367	18 852	22 080	23 930	..
Interest and dividends from private sector and Rest of World	ANBQ	4 809	5 232	4 307	6 175	4 891	4 541	4 506	5 696	6 613	6 126	..
Rent and other current transfers[3]	ANBS	1 084	891	1 037	2 036	2 427	2 474	2 081	2 062	1 961	1 872	..
Total current receipts	ANBT	316 383	336 218	358 965	382 260	389 458	396 343	422 693	453 127	487 148	520 768	..
Current expenditure												
Current expenditure on goods and services[4]	GZSN	150 967	159 336	172 168	185 763	198 864	217 387	237 126	254 999	274 792	288 711	..
Subsidies	NMRL	5 912	4 528	5 400	5 046	5 077	6 043	6 716	7 200	7 633	8 709	..
Social benefits	ANLY	105 881	106 585	105 555	108 010	118 269	122 636	130 873	137 492	143 083	148 273	..
Net current grants abroad[5]	GZSI	102	−847	−253	−146	−1 861	−626	−995	−579	−26	109	..
Other current grants	NNAI	14 441	16 163	16 957	19 313	21 481	27 555	31 065	33 719	34 143	34 004	..
Interest and dividends paid to private sector and Rest of World	ANLO	29 661	29 364	25 381	26 462	22 565	21 619	22 777	24 605	26 758	28 711	..
Total current expenditure	ANLT	305 490	313 801	326 172	346 177	366 273	394 614	427 562	457 436	486 364	508 449	..
Saving, gross plus capital taxes	ANSP	10 893	22 417	32 793	36 083	23 185	1 729	−4 869	−4 309	784	12 319	..
Depreciation	-ANNZ	−12 320	−12 390	−12 764	−13 092	−13 548	−14 446	−14 996	−16 044	−17 182	−18 419	..
Surplus on current budget	ANMU	−930	10 415	21 005	23 487	12 213	−11 095	−17 422	−18 965	−14 098	−4 307	−7 554
Net investment												
Gross fixed capital formation[6]	ANSQ	13 472	14 055	14 146	13 427	17 307	20 122	21 067	25 650	27 895	29 390	..
Less depreciation	-ANNZ	−12 320	−12 390	−12 764	−13 092	−13 548	−14 446	−14 996	−16 044	−17 182	−18 419	..
Increase in inventories and valuables	ANSR	139	231	−472	−126	−10	−74	107	−47	−16	5	..
Capital grants to private sector and Rest of World	ANSS	4 420	4 942	4 304	3 875	7 958	7 564	9 918	10 851	12 582	14 635	..
Capital grants from private sector and Rest of World	-ANST	−516	−367	−427	−756	−989	−1 091	−1 500	−1 222	−1 202	−1 379	..
Total net investment	-ANNW	4 765	5 897	5 395	5 225	11 831	13 707	15 590	20 616	23 550	25 779	28 002
Net borrowing[7]	-ANNX	5 695	−4 518	−15 610	−18 262	−382	24 802	33 012	39 581	37 648	30 086	35 556
Financial transactions determining net cash requirement												
Net lending to private sector and Rest of World	ANSU	−359	171	2 212	3 174	2 677	2 877	2 657	1 076	874	145	..
Net acquisition of UK company securities	ANSV	−1 336	704	−310	949	−408	765	593	408	653	−2 262	..
Accounts receivable/payable	ANSW	−747	803	8 393	−17 163	2 200	−2 921	8 975	2 630	2 357	10 618	..
Adjustment for interest on gilts	ANSX	−2 350	−2 446	−1 294	−2 630	−361	−1 444	−1 186	−2 305	−2 749	−1 279	..
Other financial transcations[8]	ANSY	359	−764	−1 364	−2 389	376	515	−4 527	−2 955	1 216	−2 153	..
Public sector net cash requirement	RURQ	1 262	−6 050	−7 973	−36 321	4 102	24 594	38 466	38 540	40 331	35 292	26 615

1 See chapter text.
2 Includes domestic rates, council tax, community charge, motor vehicle duty paid by household and some licence fees.
3 ESA95 transactions D44, D45, D74, D75 and D72-D71: includes rent of land, oil royalties, other property income and fines.
4 Includes non-trading capital consumption.
5 Net of current grants received from abroad.
6 Including net acquisition of land.
7 Net investment *less* surplus on current budget.
8 Includes statistical discrepancy, finance leasing and similar borrowing, insurance technical reserves and some other minor adjustments.

Source: Office for National Statistics: 020 7014 2124

18.3 Public sector net debt[1]
United Kingdom

£ million

		1999 /00	2000 /01	2001 /02	2002 /03	2003 /04	2004 /05	2005 /06	2006 /07	2007 /08
Central government sterling gross debt:										
British government stock										
Conventional gilts	BKPK	218 687	204 285	200 833	206 119	232 877	261 373	287 481	306 489	320 622
Index linked gilts	BKPL	65 740	70 316	70 417	75 966	78 982	86 749	98 654	113 090	132 404
Total	BKPM	284 427	274 601	271 250	282 085	311 859	348 122	386 135	419 579	453 026
Sterling Treasury bills	BKPJ	4 453	3 521	9 700	15 000	19 300	20 350	19 100	15 600	17 569
National savings	ACUA	63 331	62 611	62 275	63 087	66 522	68 504	73 365	78 929	84 735
Tax instruments	ACRV	535	491	478	376	407	350	308	353	428
Other sterling debt[2]	BKSK	28 689	30 230	28 276	32 711	35 032	32 272	36 468	41 280	39 543
Central government sterling gross debt total	BKSL	381 435	371 454	371 979	393 259	433 120	469 598	515 376	555 741	595 301
Central government foreign currency gross debt:										
US$ bonds	BKPG	4 388	4 924	2 107	–	1 632	1 587	1 730	1 530	1 509
ECU bonds	EYSJ	1 500	–	–	–	–	–	–	–	–
ECU/Euro Treasury notes	EYSV	2 701	2 486	1 225	–	–	–	–	–	–
ECU/Euro Treasury bills	EYSN	–	–	–	–	–	–	–	–	–
Other foreign currency debt	BKPH	364	291	243	172	105	57	1	–	–
Central government foreign currency gross debt total	BKPI	8 954	7 701	3 575	172	1 738	1 644	1 731	1 530	1 509
Central government gross debt total	BKPW	390 389	379 155	375 554	393 431	434 858	471 242	517 107	557 271	596 810
Local government gross debt total	EYKP	51 707	52 522	52 566	51 353	50 547	53 300	60 114	62 420	66 212
less										
Central government holdings of local government debt	-EYKZ	–46 563	–47 789	–47 530	–44 836	–41 540	–42 339	–47 384	–48 199	–51 036
Local government holdings of central government debt	-EYLA	–77	–31	–29	–184	–510	–62	–62	–	–74
General government gross debt (consolidated)	BKPX	395 456	383 857	380 561	399 764	443 355	482 141	529 775	571 492	611 912
Public corporations gross debt	EYYD	8 721	9 414	8 859	18 660	13 895	14 875	15 191	14 336	13 527
less:										
Central government holdings of public corporations debt	-EYXY	–4 307	–4 714	–4 308	–4 171	–5 188	–5 740	–6 222	–4 984	–5 092
Local government holdings of public corporations debt	-EYXZ	–123	–124	–122	–121	–120	–121	–112	–103	–105
Public corporations holdings of central government debt	-BKPZ	–6 615	–6 414	–4 638	–4 928	–4 780	–5 080	–2 822	–2 255	–4 119
Public corporations holdings of local government debt	-EYXV	–141	–106	–60	–50	–84	–100	–79	–194	–26
Public sector gross debt (consolidated)	BKQA	392 991	381 913	380 292	409 154	447 078	485 937	535 731	578 292	616 097
Public sector liquid assets:										
Official reserves	AIPD	21 498	30 423	28 055	26 387	25 266	25 813	27 835	26 631	..
Central government deposits[3]	BKSM	1 879	2 797	2 802	2 900	3 879	3 868	5 212	6 171	5 450
Other central government	BKSN	4 756	15 670	10 743	8 141	7 077	3 044	8 498	11 369	14 834
Local government deposits[3]	BKSO	10 221	11 522	13 698	14 797	16 797	18 718	20 923	23 670	28 212
Other local government short term assets	BKQG	5 468	5 719	5 990	6 061	5 573	5 057	5 381	4 709	4 975
Public corporations deposits[3]	BKSP	2 619	2 215	2 336	2 133	2 813	3 411	2 430	3 665	2 858
Other public corporations short term assets	BKSQ	1 128	1 212	1 180	1 586	2 845	2 457	2 453	2 605	2 481
Public sector liquid assets total	BKQJ	47 569	69 558	64 804	62 005	64 250	62 368	72 732	78 820	88 371
Public sector net debt	BKQK	345 422	312 355	315 488	347 149	382 828	423 569	462 999	499 472	527 726
as percentage of GDP[4]	RUTO	*36.4*	*31.4*	*30.3*	*31.5*	*32.8*	*34.7*	*36.0*	*36.6*	*36.7*

1 See chapter text.
2 Including overdraft with Bank of England.
3 Bank and building society deposits.
4 Gross domestic product at market prices from 12 months centred on the end of the month.

Source: Office for National Statistics: 020 7014 2124

18.4 Consolidated Fund and National Loans Fund:[1] revenue and expenditure; receipts and payments

United Kingdom, years ending 31 March

£ million

	Consolidated Fund													
	Revenue							Expenditure							Surplus (+) or deficit (-) of Consolidated Fund
		HM Revenue and Customs								Standing services					
	Total	Inland Revenue[1]	Customs and Excise	Vehicle excise duties	National non domestic rates	Interest and dividends	Other receipts	Total	Supply services	Service of national debt[2]	Northern Ireland	European community etc.	Contingencies Fund	Other expenditure[3]	
	1	2	3	4	5	6	7	8	9	10	11	12	13	14	15
	ACAA	EYJN	ACAC	ACAD	RUUD	ACAG	ACBC	ACAI	ACAJ	ACAK	ACAL	ACAM	ACAN	ACAO	ACAP
2003	293 885	144 533	113 520	4 613	19 975	367	10 877	338 191	317 808	14 042	–	7 405	–1 277	211	–44 308
2004	301 011	153 699	119 726	4 816	13 468	516	8 786	345 938	322 672	15 201	–	7 301	501	261	–44 926
2005	329 708	170 130	121 109	4 865	17 326	389	15 889	368 821	342 414	17 654	–	8 910	–500	344	–39 116
2006	359 954	192 715	124 219	5 055	19 597	398	17 970	401 411	373 074	19 263	–	8 858	–	212	–41 456
2007	373 040	200 127	130 808	5 355	17 334	2 610	16 806	429 078	399 947	19 959	–	8 934	3	233	–56 035
2003/04	293 052	145 555	115 660	4 712	16 580	352	10 193	335 274	313 072	14 501	–	7 494	1	203	–42 223
2004/05	313 323	158 974	120 924	4 752	15 990	578	12 105	351 237	325 541	16 966	–	8 460	–	267	–37 914
2005/06	336 031	178 707	120 845	5 001	17 762	351	13 365	382 230	355 429	18 323	–	8 139	–	340	–46 200
2006/07	369 841	195 598	125 846	5 108	19 698	2 340	21 251	400 394	371 574	19 895	–	8 685	3	232	–30 551
2007/08	378 538	205 681	132 043	5 398	..	953	15 530	427 567	398 160	19 390	–	9 786	6	224	–49 028
2003 Q2	61 171	31 634	28 296	1 191		–	50	82 949	75 030	4 760	–	2 102	1 000	56	–21 780
Q3	75 368	37 098	28 474	1 209	6 009	57	2 521	78 159	72 938	3 054	–	2 116	–	51	–2 790
Q4	66 468	30 442	30 349	1 116	3 132	32	1 397	92 836	87 567	4 130	–	1 090	–	47	–26 368
2004 Q1	90 045	46 381	28 541	1 196	7 439	263	6 225	81 330	77 537	2 557	–	2 186	–999	49	8 715
Q2	64 213	32 911	30 061	1 199		1	41	83 020	76 032	4 086	–	1 793	1 000	108	–18 808
Q3	72 074	38 847	29 840	1 239	1 316	29	803	87 069	81 009	3 884	–	2 124	–	53	–14 994
Q4	74 679	35 560	31 284	1 182	4 713	223	1 717	94 519	88 094	4 674	–	1 198	500	51	–19 839
2005 Q1	102 357	51 656	29 739	1 132	9 961	325	9 544	86 629	80 406	4 322	–	3 345	–1 500	55	15 727
Q2	67 425	36 762	29 379	1 242	–	3	39	94 409	86 970	4 426	–	1 883	1 000	132	–26 984
Q3	84 896	43 353	30 516	1 391	5 657	54	3 925	92 502	85 379	4 817	–	2 198	–	106	–7 606
Q4	75 030	38 359	31 475	1 100	1 708	7	2 381	95 281	89 659	4 089	–	1 484	–	51	–20 253
2006 Q1	108 680	60 233	29 475	1 268	10 397	287	7 020	100 038	93 421	4 991	–	2 574	–1 000	51	8 643
Q2	72 430	39 406	30 606	1 284	303	29	802	101 986	94 934	4 382	–	1 612	1 000	58	–29 555
Q3	79 869	47 921	30 571	1 348	–	–	29	99 192	91 420	5 588	–	2 132	–	49	–19 323
Q4	98 975	45 155	33 567	1 155	8 897	82	10 119	100 195	93 299	4 302	–	2 540	–	54	–1 221
2007 Q1	118 567	63 116	31 102	1 321	10 498	2 229	10 301	99 021	91 921	5 623	–	2 401	–997	71	19 548
Q2	75 241	38 704	32 917	1 394	–	89	2 137	106 166	99 627	4 005	–	1 478	1 000	56	–30 925
Q3	90 954	52 463	32 173	1 407	3 224	30	1 657	101 387	93 820	5 452	–	2 064	–	51	–10 433
Q4	88 278	45 844	34 616	1 233	3 612	262	2 711	122 504	114 579	4 879	–	2 991	–	55	–34 225
2008 Q1	124 065	68 670	32 337	1 364	..	572	9 025	97 510	90 134	5 054	–	3 253	–994	62	26 555

18.4

Consolidated Fund and National Loans Fund:[1] revenue and expenditure; receipts and payments

United Kingdom, years ending 31 March

£ million

| | National Loans Fund | | | | | | | | | Other central government funds and accounts | | | |
| | Receipts | | | | Payments | | | | | | | | |
	Surplus (+) or deficit (-) of Consolidated Fund	Total receipts	Interest receipts and profits of note issue	Service of the national debt met from Consolidated Fund	Total payments	Service of national debt	CG Transactions with issue dept for asset revaluation	Net lending[4]	Borrowing required	Surplus (+) or deficit (-) of National Insurance Fund	Departmental balances and miscellaneous	Northern Ireland central government debt[1]	Central government net cash requirement
	16	17	18	19	20	21	22	23	24	25	26	27	28
	ACAP	ACAQ	RUUC	ACAK	ACAU	ACAV	RUUB	ACAW	ACAX	ACAY	ACAZ	ACBA	RUUW
2003	−44 308	21 043	7 000	14 042	17 012	21 044	3	−4 036	40 276	−238	2 890	−9	37 615
2004	−44 926	22 659	7 455	15 201	23 242	22 658	−1	586	45 510	3 203	−890	−4	43 193
2005	−39 116	23 777	6 123	17 654	26 612	23 991	–	2 619	41 948	4 303	−2 779	−2	40 422
2006	−41 456	24 788	5 524	19 263	27 323	24 708	–	2 616	43 990	7 973	−3 592	3	39 612
2007	−56 035	25 425	5 466	19 959	27 144	25 898	–	1 246	57 758	7 593	16 391	4	33 778
2003/04	−42 223	21 968	7 465	14 501	18 691	21 969	11	−3 289	38 947	2 270	−2 724	−10	39 391
2004/05	−37 914	23 673	6 705	16 966	24 245	23 672	−7	580	38 486	1 436	−1 484	−2	38 532
2005/06	−46 200	24 164	5 842	18 323	29 455	24 379	–	5 075	51 488	7 022	3 654	1	40 813
2006/07	−30 551	25 265	5 367	19 895	26 229	25 184	–	1 046	31 516	3 996	−9 546	3	37 069
2007/08	−49 028	25 014	..	19 390	28 077	25 486	..	2 589	52 093	10 536	9 007	4	32 554
2003 Q2	−21 780	6 238	1 477	4 760	5 464	6 238	–	−775	21 005	51	3 572	−3	17 379
Q3	−2 790	4 627	1 573	3 054	3 613	4 628	14	−1 029	1 776	−1 390	−3 196	−3	6 359
Q4	−26 368	5 943	1 813	4 130	5 021	5 943	−9	−913	25 447	−868	9 909	−1	16 405
2004 Q1	8 715	5 160	2 602	2 557	4 593	5 160	6	−572	−9 281	4 477	−13 009	−3	−752
Q2	−18 808	5 637	1 550	4 086	5 464	5 637	−4	−169	18 634	−1 212	6 089	−1	13 756
Q3	−14 994	5 412	1 528	3 884	6 146	5 775	1	371	15 729	2 533	5 892	–	7 304
Q4	−19 839	6 450	1 775	4 674	7 039	6 086	−4	956	20 428	−2 595	138	–	22 885
2005 Q1	15 727	6 174	1 852	4 322	5 596	6 174	–	−578	−16 305	2 710	−13 603	−1	−5 413
Q2	−26 984	5 761	1 336	4 426	8 031	5 761	–	2 268	29 253	1 710	8 513	–	19 030
Q3	−7 606	6 183	1 365	4 817	6 793	6 359	–	434	8 215	532	−383	−1	8 065
Q4	−20 253	5 659	1 570	4 089	6 192	5 697	–	495	20 785	−649	2 694	–	18 740
2006 Q1	8 643	6 561	1 571	4 991	8 439	6 562	–	1 878	−6 765	5 429	−7 170	2	−5 022
Q2	−29 555	5 517	1 134	4 382	5 326	5 384	–	−59	29 364	1 952	4 152	1	23 261
Q3	−19 323	6 827	1 238	5 588	7 688	6 827	–	861	20 184	2 233	10 715	–	7 236
Q4	−1 221	5 883	1 581	4 302	5 870	5 935	–	−64	1 207	−1 641	−11 289	–	14 137
2007 Q1	19 548	7 038	1 414	5 623	7 345	7 038	–	308	−19 239	1 452	−13 124	2	−7 565
Q2	−30 925	5 280	1 274	4 005	4 772	5 753	–	−982	30 418	4 305	8 644	–	17 469
Q3	−10 433	6 734	1 283	5 452	8 251	6 734	–	1 518	11 951	1 628	6 964	2	3 361
Q4	−34 225	6 373	1 495	4 879	6 776	6 373	–	402	34 628	208	13 907	–	20 513
2008 Q1	26 555	6 627	..	5 054	8 278	6 626	..	1 651	−24 904	4 395	−20 508	2	−8 789

1 See chapter text.
2 Payment to National Loans Fund representing its payments for the service of the National Debt *less its receipts of interest on loans outstanding, etc.*
3 Includes net issues to Contingencies Fund.
4 Minus sign indicates a net issue repayment.

Sources: HM Treasury;
National Statistics 020 7014 2124

18.5 Taxes paid by UK residents to general government and the European Union[1]
Total economy sector S.1

£ million

		1997/98	1998/99	1999/00	2000/01	2001/02	2002/03	2003/04	2004/05	2005/06	2006/07
Generation of income											
Uses											
Taxes on production and imports											
Taxes on products and imports											
Value added tax (VAT)											
Paid to central government	NZGF	52 308	54 209	58 688	60 746	64 735	69 087	76 638	79 978	81 496	87 728
Paid to the European Union	FJKM	3 531	4 105	3 451	4 172	3 592	2 518	2 574	1 905	1 964	2 288
Total	QYRC	55 485	57 845	62 127	64 908	68 322	71 599	79 201	81 869	83 421	89 855
Taxes and duties on imports excluding VAT											
Paid to EU: import duties	FJWE	2 261	2 042	2 049	2 103	2 024	1 893	1 957	2 207	2 264	2 332
Taxes on products excluding VAT and import duties											
Paid to central government											
Customs and Excise revenue											
Beer	GTAM	2 699	2 733	2 848	2 798	2 907	2 952	3 084	3 099	3 092	3 068
Wines, cider, perry & spirits	GTAN	3 057	3 301	3 652	3 814	4 068	4 430	4 526	4 790	4 784	4 846
Tobacco	GTAO	7 622	7 551	7 796	7 638	7 639	8 046	8 092	8 113	7 952	8 146
Hydrocarbon oils	GTAP	19 451	21 553	22 510	22 630	21 916	22 147	22 780	23 313	23 438	23 585
Betting, gaming & lottery	CJQY	1 539	1 527	1 500	1 517	1 317	977	898	876	884	958
Air passenger duty	CWAA	522	845	882	956	802	804	799	872	906	1 114
Insurance premium tax	CWAD	1 179	1 248	1 511	1 751	1 921	2 189	2 313	2 353	2 349	2 317
Landfill tax	BKOF	364	322	456	475	501	545	639	673	754	837
Other	ACDN	–	–	–	–	–	–	–	–	–	–
Fossil fuel levy	CIQY	256	164	84	52	92	9	–	–	–	–
Gas levy	GTAZ	188	−44	–	–	–	–	–	–	–	–
Stamp duties	GTBC	3 456	4 623	6 898	8 165	6 983	7 549	7 544	8 966	10 918	13 386
Camelot payments to National Lottery Distribution Fund	LIYH	1 572	1 665	1 593	1 542	1 520	1 382	1 311	1 354	1 397	1 366
Hydro-benefit	LITN	32	32	38	44	44	44	43	40	–	–
Aggregates Levy	MDUQ	–	–	–	–	–	293	341	326	323	327
Climate change levy	LSNT	–	–	–	–	822	813	816	750	741	711
Renewable energy obligations	EP89	–	–	–	–	–	265	375	368	381	389
Other taxes and levies	GCSP	–	–	–	–	–	–	–	–	–	–
Total paid to central government	NMBV	42 504	45 971	49 768	51 382	50 551	52 486	53 624	55 965	57 931	61 166
Paid to the European Union											
Sugar levy	GTBA	72	44	46	43	27	25	19	24	24	–
European Coal & Steel Community levy	GTBB	–	–	–	–	–	–	–	–	–	–
Total paid to the European Union	FJWG	72	44	46	43	27	25	19	24	24	–
Total taxes on products excluding VAT & import duties	QYRA	42 080	45 613	49 814	51 425	50 578	52 511	53 643	55 989	57 945	61 050
Total taxes on products and imports	NZGW	99 826	105 500	113 990	118 436	120 924	126 003	134 801	140 065	143 630	153 236
Production taxes other than on products											
Paid to central government											
Consumer Credit Act fees	CUDB	168	158	156	171	157	200	211	223	189	234
National non-domestic rates	CUKY	13 283	13 764	14 353	15 154	16 252	16 728	16 941	17 355	18 160	19 181
Old style non-domestic rates	NSEZ	159	145	123	132	131	136	140	146	193	326
Levies paid to CG levy-funded bodies	LITK	162	171	234	213	215	190	194	218	239	244
Motor vehicle duties paid by businesses	EKED	1 405	1 503	1 559	1 230	751	736	787	802	850	869
Regulator fees	GCSQ	53	52	86	105	95	94	101	88	74	71
Total	NMBX	16 820	16 698	16 511	17 005	17 601	18 084	18 374	18 832	19 705	20 925
Paid to local government											
Old style non-domestic rates	NMYH	126	127	144	150	161	176	192	197	187	207
Total production taxes other than on products	NMYD	15 335	15 918	16 655	17 155	17 762	18 260	18 566	19 029	19 892	21 132
Total taxes on production and imports, paid											
Paid to central government	NMBY	111 376	116 054	124 727	129 536	133 199	140 152	148 758	154 963	159 265	169 819
Paid to local government	NMYH	126	127	144	150	161	176	192	197	187	207
Paid to the European Union	FJWB	5 864	6 191	5 546	6 318	5 643	4 436	4 550	4 136	4 252	4 620
Total	NZGX	117 701	124 454	133 100	137 868	141 085	144 263	153 367	159 094	163 486	174 793

18.5

Taxes paid by UK residents to general government and the European Union[1]
Total economy sector S.1

continued

£ million

		1997 /98	1998 /99	1999 /00	2000 /01	2001 /02	2002 /03	2003 /04	2004 /05	2005 /06	2006 /07
Secondary distribution of income											
Uses											
Current taxes on income, wealth etc											
Taxes on income											
Paid to central government											
Household income taxes	DRWH	81 901	89 728	96 977	106 866	108 526	110 407	112 356	121 746	130 754	141 202
Petroleum revenue tax	DBHA	963	502	853	1 518	1 310	958	1 179	1 284	2 016	2 155
Windfall tax	EYNK	2 610	2 614	–	–	–	–	–	–	–	–
Other corporate taxes	BMNX	–593	1 231	1 842	3 458	3 302	2 657	3 974	4 445	5 539	7 006
Total	NMCU	115 902	124 238	133 994	144 263	145 180	143 238	145 488	160 479	180 138	194 409
Other current taxes											
Paid to central government											
Motor vehicle duty paid by households	CDDZ	3 046	3 134	3 296	3 039	3 540	3 600	3 902	3 935	4 100	4 270
Old style domestic rates	NSFA	88	93	117	108	109	104	100	94	120	247
Licences	NSNP	11	8	8	2	–	–	–	–	–	–
National non-domestic rates paid by non-market sectors	BMNY	929	971	1 002	997	1 065	1 013	994	996	1 221	1 265
Passport fees	E8A6	–	41	89	113	139	153	198	237	285	346
Television licence fee	DH7A	2 009	2 179	2 286	2 064	2 183	2 287	2 391	2 508	2 623	2 734
Total	NMCV	3 139	5 763	6 798	6 325	7 036	7 155	7 585	7 770	8 354	8 898
Paid to local government											
Old style domestic rates	NMHK	64	62	68	76	80	85	92	111	149	157
Council tax	NMHM	10 850	12 037	12 918	14 155	15 371	16 809	18 911	20 190	21 227	22 299
Total	NMIS	10 914	12 099	12 986	14 231	15 451	16 894	19 003	20 301	21 376	22 499
Total	NVCM	17 023	18 528	19 784	20 556	22 487	24 049	26 588	28 071	29 730	31 397
Total current taxes on income, wealth etc											
Paid to central government	NMCP	119 041	130 001	140 792	150 588	152 215	150 445	153 171	168 818	188 492	203 367
Paid to local government	NMIS	10 914	12 099	12 986	14 231	15 451	16 894	19 003	20 301	21 376	22 499
Total	NMZL	129 268	139 451	150 547	161 324	166 043	167 339	172 174	189 119	209 868	225 866
Social contributions											
Actual social contributions											
Paid to central government											
(National Insurance Contributions)											
Employers' compulsory contributions	CEAN	27 761	29 779	31 705	35 212	35 816	35 476	41 459	44 576	47 302	50 283
Employees' compulsory contributions	GCSE	21 495	23 607	23 289	24 772	25 130	25 701	31 013	33 088	35 181	37 426
Self- and non-employed persons' compulsory contributions	NMDE	1 884	1 828	1 941	2 084	2 216	2 352	2 676	2 744	2 852	2 956
Total	AIIH	51 692	54 746	56 935	62 068	63 162	63 529	75 148	80 923	85 335	90 976
Capital account											
Changes in liabilities and net worth											
Other capital taxes											
Paid to central government											
Inheritance tax	GILF	1 649	1 764	2 016	2 181	2 346	2 323	2 486	2 874	..	..
Tax on other capital transfers	GILG	35	41	38	55	37	47	35	48	..	..
Development land tax and other	GCSV	–	–	–	–	–	–	–	–	–	–
Total	NMGI	1 684	1 805	2 054	2 236	2 365	2 370	2 521	2 941	3 276	3 623
Total taxes and compulsory social contributions											
Paid to central government	GCSS	283 208	303 493	324 736	344 015	350 642	355 995	379 465	406 928	436 107	467 323
Paid to local government	GCST	10 992	12 181	13 130	14 381	15 612	17 070	19 195	20 498	21 563	22 663
Paid to the European Union	FJWB	5 864	6 191	5 546	6 318	5 643	4 436	4 550	4 136	4 252	4 620
Total	GCSU	300 705	320 271	343 290	365 330	372 169	377 839	403 282	431 735	462 280	494 836
Total taxes and social contributions as percentage of GDP	GDWM	*36.2*	*36.5*	*37.0*	*37.6*	*36.7*	*35.3*	*35.5*	*36.1*	*37.0*	*37.4*

1 See chapter text.

Sources: HM Treasury;
Office for National Statistics: 020 7014 2129

18.6 Borrowing and repayment of debt[1]
United Kingdom
Years ending 31 March

£ million

		1997/98	1998/99	1999/00	2000/01	2001/02	2002/03	2003/04	2004/05	2005/06	2006/07
Borrowing											
Government securities: new issues	KQGA	28 484.4	12 048.0	26 426.5	25 789.8	43 433.4	54 068.9	53 220.9	57 290.5	80 668.9	66 233.4
National savings securities:											
National savings certificates	KQGB	4 435.2	3 028.7	1 962.7	3 086.2	2 580.7	2 434.3	1 940.4	1 696.4	1 206.8	1 464.7
Capital bonds	KQGC	619.0	469.6	35.4	29.0	40.9	107.3	65.0	25.2	34.3	20.7
Income bonds	KQGD	1 043.4	1 371.7	653.4	760.5	625.6	484.8	415.3	426.6	567.5	593.5
Deposit bonds	KQGE	..	..	..	..	..	..	–	..	..	..
British savings bonds	KQGF	..	..	..	..	..	..	..	..	..	..
Premium savings bonds	KQGG	3 158.8	3 652.8	3 449.4	3 296.0	3 859.6	4 604.5	7 530.1	5 737.8	7 817.5	8 432.5
Save As You Earn	KQGH	20.7	11.4	5.0	0.3	..	..	–	..	..	..
Yearly plan	KQGI	..	5.2	..	..	..	..	–	..	..	..
National savings stamps and gift tokens	KQGJ	..	..	..	..	..	..	–	..	..	..
National Savings Bank Investments	KQGK	1 282.3	1 085.0	901.6	955.3	864.9	1 012.4	809.9	817.5	643.6	558.4
Children's Bonus Bonds	KGVO	255.3	205.0	58.5	53.4	45.0	54.0	51.7	66.8	59.5	54.1
First Option Bonds	KIAR	1 152.9	1 001.8	34.3	..	..	..	..	..	..	..
Pensioners Guaranteed Income Bond	KJDW	1 126.9	201.0	590.7	687.2	603.5	662.9	274.2	323.9	142.7	216.4
Treasurer's account	KWNF	39.9	17.1	13.6	12.5	15.2	19.4	13.9	11.1	10.9	11.6
Individual Savings Account	ZAFC	..	..	257.8	265.9	397.8	405.6	335.4	276.4	261.3	1 015.1
Fixed Rate Savings Bonds	ZAFD	..	..	175.9	284.7	192.7	193.0	82.0	86.3	51.2	69.5
Guaranteed Equity Bonds	ECPU	..	..	..	..	27.2	274.8	227.9	317.1	81.4	62.1
Easy Access Savings Account	C3OM	..	..	..	..	..	..	126.9	903.5	608.6	513.2
Certificate of tax deposit	KQGL	84.1	66.4	121.4	76.5	77.6	59.6	145.2	114.8	110.6	100.2
Nationalised industries', etc temporary deposits	KQGM	46 375.9	39 962.4	40 343.3	56 106.6	62 150.0	55 395.1	47 958.6	25 022.0	22 039.1	35 224.0
Sterling Treasury bills (net receipt)	KQGO	..	3 546.2	..	..	..	..	–	..	..	..
ECU Treasury bills (net receipt)	KQGP	..	..	..	..	..	..	–	..	..	..
ECU Treasury notes (net receipt)	KDZZ	..	..	721.1	..	..	..	–	..	..	..
Ways and means (net receipt)	KQGQ	..	183.6	5 599.0	12 126.0	12 095.3	3 899.9	22 700.2	..	..	23 428.0
Other debt : payable in sterling :											
Interest free notes	KQGR	32.4	2 130.9	373.5	972.7	1 427.2	754.0	1 213.2	662.3	1 858.9	1 049.9
Other debt : payable in external currencies	KHCY	..	..	..	..	..	..	1 792.5	..	..	..
Total receipts	KHCZ	88 111.2	68 986.8	81 723.1	104 502.6	128 436.6	124 430.5	138 903.3	93 778.2	116 162.8	139 047.3
Repayment of debt											
Government securities: redemptions	KQGS	20 678.9	18 575.5	19 815.8	33 722.2	43 642.3	42 109.9	35 087.4	25 130.1	17 456.5	62 406.9
Statutory sinking funds	KQGT	2.1	2.0	2.0	2.0	1.9	1.9	1.8	1.8	0.4	..
Terminable annuities:											
National Debt Commissioners	KQGU	..	..	..	..	..	..	–	..	..	..
National savings securities:											
National savings certificates	KQGV	4 058.5	3 449.0	2 405.2	4 546.8	4 177.7	4 146.7	2 769.1	1 979.6	1 107.4	1 172.1
Capital bonds	KQGW	1 160.5	888.3	324.2	375.0	175.9	155.9	116.9	121.1	159.2	137.4
Income bonds	KQGX	1 148.9	880.8	1 686.3	857.0	933.8	1 144.2	977.1	879.5	724.6	719.2
Deposit bonds	KQGY	72.6	84.2	70.2	71.1	45.4	369.9	4.4	..	..	..
Yearly Plan	KQGZ	113.2	120.0	141.8	18.4	4.5	3.0	2.0	..	..	0.8
British savings bonds	KQHA	..	..	..	..	..	..	–	..	..	..
Premium savings bonds	KQHB	1 203.1	1 398.4	1 923.8	1 872.6	1 942.9	2 343.3	2 967.4	3 492.4	3 289.2	4 279.8
Save As You Earn	KQHC	68.2	37.1	34.5	22.9	8.0	3.2	0.5	..	0.5	0.5
National savings stamps and gift tokens	KQHD	..	..	..	..	..	..	–	1.2	..	..
National Savings Bank Investments (repayments)	KQHE	2 175.7	2 027.0	1 886.3	1 654.1	1 415.8	1 350.1	1 342.7	1 554.0	1 153.3	1 172.4
Children's Bonus Bonds	KGVQ	187.9	183.2	69.3	95.0	114.5	92.6	79.8	84.5	95.8	105.7
First Option Bonds	KIAS	1 283.0	1 055.5	298.1	225.2	111.6	77.4	62.2	33.4	36.1	25.6
Pensioners Guaranteed Income Bond	KPOB	318.8	897.8	935.3	2 003.8	1 640.4	703.9	538.5	445.0	428.6	452.7
Treasurer's account	KWNG	11.8	13.7	16.4	13.9	16.5	16.9	14.2	16.2	18.3	11.7
Individual Savings Account	ZAFE	..	..	12.3	39.9	70.3	105.9	157.6	202.2	194.1	193.6
Fixed Rate Savings Bonds	ZAFF	..	..	2.8	62.1	110.1	133.6	153.1	92.1	105.0	77.2
Guaranteed Equity Bonds	JUWE	..	..	..	..	..	3.9	3.3	..	0.2	3.7
Easy Access Savings Account	C3ON	..	..	..	..	..	..	126.9	189.3	400.6	509.7
Certificates of tax deposit	KQHF	229.0	199.9	159.9	120.1	91.4	161.5	113.1	171.9	152.1	56.0
Tax reserve certificates	KQHG	..	..	..	..	..	..	–	..	..	..
Nationalised industries', etc temporary deposits	KQHH	46 835.7	41 776.9	41 089.4	56 004.0	63 127.9	55 695.6	47 757.7	25 949.5	21 943.1	35 686.5
Debt to the Bank of England	KPOC	..	..	..	..	..	..	..	..	..	..
Sterling Treasury bills (net repayment)	KQHJ	1 928.5	..	3 014.8	6 194.2	..	..	–	..	..	..
ECU Treasury bills (net repayment)	KJEG	..	..	2 492.9	..	..	..	–	..	..	..
ECU Treasury notes (net repayment)	KSPA	3.3	13.2	..	1 391.9	1 359.6	1 453.1	–	..	..	..
Ways and means (net repayment)	KQHK	5 815.4	..	..	..	..	..	–	9 760.2	36 207.3	..
Other debt: payable in sterling :											
Interest free notes	KQHL	1 215.5	850.5	246.4	458.2	1 723.3	1 393.3	990.5	300.4	222.3	586.4
Other	KQHM	..	..	..	..	..	..	–	..	..	..
Other debt : payable in external currencies	KQHN	2 082.7	92.0	98.1	1 835.6	2 838.1	1 960.3	47.0	46.5	98.9	52.4
Total payments	KQHO	90 593.3	72 545.0	76 725.8	111 586.0	123 551.9	113 426.1	93 313.2	70 450.9	83 793.5	107 650.3
Net borrowing	KQHP	..	..	4 997.3	..	4 884.7	11 004.4	45 590.1	23 327.3	32 369.3	31 397.0
Net repayment	KHDD	2 482.1	3 558.2	..	7 083.4	..	..	–	..	..	..

1 See chapter text.

Source: HM Treasury: 020 7270 4761

18.7 Consolidated Fund and National Loans Fund: assets and liabilities[1]
United Kingdom
At 31 March each year

£ million

		1995	1996	1997	1998	1999	2000	2001	2002	2003
CONSOLIDATED FUND										
Total estimated assets	KQIA	33 992.4	33 809.0	36 177.4	36 061.0	36 148.0	33 932.1	35 967.9	37 458.5	39 694.1
Subscriptions and contributions to international financial organisations	KQIB	5 898.1	6 470.8	6 528.9	6 660.8	7 059.7	6 903.6	7 298.4	7 564.4	8 540.3
International Bank for Reconstruction and Development	KQIC	265.2	271.6	265.0	262.5	266.0	267.1	279.2	279.0	268.2
International Finance Corporation	KQID	62.0	73.1	74.9	72.9	75.6	76.5	85.8	85.7	77.2
International Development Association	KQIE	3 005.5	3 205.8	3 372.7	3 562.2	3 733.3	3 900.0	4 134.0	4 347.8	4 567.5
African Development Bank	KQIF	141.2	148.3	162.9	180.0	199.1	215.7	229.8	259.8	293.9
Asian Development Bank	KQIG	201.5	214.6	240.4	272.5	304.6	339.3	365.5	393.3	420.4
Caribbean Development Bank	KQIH	32.6	34.2	34.1	34.6	36.8	40.7	41.9	44.0	49.1
European Investment Bank	KQII	1 876.4	2 166.6	2 036.5	1 840.7	2 083.1	1 706.6	1 767.3	1 742.1	2 419.2
European Bank for Reconstruction and Development	KPOD	146.3	189.4	175.6	164.2	179.2	170.0	187.4	197.6	239.3
Inter-American Development Bank	KQIJ	107.2	119.6	117.5	219.3	127.8	130.6	145.7	147.3	135.6
International Fund for Agricultural Development	KQIK	42.7	44.2	46.1	48.8	51.0	53.7	56.4	59.1	62.1
Multilateral Investment Guarantee Agency	KQIL	3.2	3.4	3.2	3.1	3.2	3.3	5.4	8.7	7.8
Loans from Votes	KQIP	13 599.7	12 967.0	13 684.7	14 050.0	11 546.3	3 970.3	7 015.3	9 006.1	11 097.1
Issues of public dividend capital:	KQIQ	11 467.0	12 161.1	12 424.8	13 157.1	16 238.5	21 338.3	20 083.6	19 546.2	18 982.3
Army Base Repair Organisation (ABRO)	C3QV	..	..	..	..	..	..	..	..	19.4
Royal Mint	KQIV	7.0	7.0	7.0	7.0	7.0	7.0	7.0	5.5	5.5
Welsh Development Agency	KQIY	10.9	9.8	8.9	8.8	8.6	9.1	9.1	11.0	12.7
British Shipbuilders	KQJA	1 598.3	1 598.3	1 598.5	1 598.5	50.0	21.0	21.0	21.0	21.0
Patent Office	KIAT	6.3	6.3	6.3	6.3	6.3	6.3	6.3	6.3	6.3
NHS Trusts	KIAU	9 603.1	10 173.8	10 349.7	11 078.0	14 158.7	19 216.6	19 539.2	19 184.1	18 600.7
Companies House	KIAV	15.9	15.9	15.9	15.9	15.9	15.9	15.9	15.9	15.9
Central Office of Information	KIAW	0.3	0.3	0.3	0.3	0.3	0.3	0.3	0.3	0.3
Chessington Computer Centre	KPOE	3.5	3.5	..	..	..	..	..	..	..
OGC Buying Solutions[2]	KWNH	0.1	0.4	0.4	0.4	0.4	0.4	0.4	0.4	0.4
Defence Aviation Repair Agency	JRVU	..	..	..	..	..	..	..	50.4	42.3
Defence Evaluation and Research Agency	KWNI	128.8	253.0	274.5	274.5	275.4	275.4	275.4		..
Defence Scientific Technology Laboratory	JRVV	..	..	..	..	..	..	..	42.3	50.4
Fire Service College	KWNJ	16.7	16.7	16.7	16.7	16.7	16.7	16.7	16.7	16.7
Forensic Science Service	GPVB	..	..	..	..	–	18.0	18.0	18.0	18.0
Hydrographic Office	GPVC	..	..	..	..	..	13.3	13.3	13.3	13.3
Land Registry	KWNK	55.4	55.4	61.5	61.5	61.5	61.5	61.5	61.5	61.5
Medicines Control Agency	KWNL	1.6	1.6	1.6	1.6	1.6	1.6	1.6	1.6	..
Meteorological Office	KZAZ	..	..	58.9	58.9	58.9	58.9	58.9	58.9	58.9
NHS Estates	GPVD	..	..	..	..	..	0.4	0.4	0.4	0.4
Registers of Scotland	KZBA	..	..	4.3	4.3	4.3	..	..	..	..
Vehicle Inspectorate	KWNM	19.1	19.1	20.3	20.3	20.3	20.3	20.3	20.3	20.3
Driving Standards Agency	LQMI	..	..	..	3.5	3.5	3.5	3.5	3.5	3.5
Ordnance Survey	GPVE	..	..	..	..	..	14.0	14.0	14.0	14.0
Queen Elizabeth II Conference Centre	LQMJ	..	..	..	0.8	0.8	0.8	0.8	0.8	0.8
Contingencies Fund - capital	KQJB	447.0	297.0	977.0	577.0	277.0	277.0	277.0	277.0	..
Balance on revenue accounts	KQJC	1 433.6	1 096.1	954.9	1 546.0	1 026.5	1 442.9	1 293.6	1 064.8	1 074.4
Privatisation receipts	KIAX	1 147.0	817.0	1 607.1	70.1	..	..	..	..	..
Total liabilities	KQJD	..	333 927.9	364 803.0	364 950.8	363 625.5	354 807.7	327 180.6	341 162.2	366 453.7
Liability to balance National Loans Fund	KQJE	286 055.9	331 164.9	362 506.5	362 582.5	361 065.3	351 626.3	324 336.7	338 550.1	362 496.5
Payment from Votes:	KQJF	64.3	63.4	62.4	61.3	60.2	59.0	57.7	56.4	54.9
Married quarters for Armed Forces	KQJG	64.3	63.4	62.4	61.3	60.2	59.0	57.7	56.4	54.9
Liability to Post Office Post-war credits outstanding and interest due - estimated	KQJI	46.0	45.9	45.9	45.9	45.9	45.8	45.8	45.8	45.8
Revenue paid over in advance of collection	KQJJ	37.0	..	28.2	13.8	177.9	259.7	301.7	635.6	1 293.7
Inland Revenue	KQJK	–	–	–	–	177.9	259.7	301.7	635.6	1 293.7
Customs and Excise	KQJL	..	..	28.2	..	..	..	..	..	..
Vehicle Excise Duty	KQJN	37.0	..	..	13.8	..	..	..	..	..
Promissory notes issued by Minister of Overseas Development	KQJQ	996.7	1 005.8	1 021.9	822.1	963.1	783.1	939.9	891.9	954.7
International Development Association	KQJR	656.5	663.2	673.6	484.0	612.3	445.6	553.1	509.7	589.4
African Development Fund	KQJS	93.2	86.2	95.3	95.2	105.6	89.1	141.6	145.5	152.3
Asian Development Bank	KQJT	–	–	–	–	–	1.9	2.5	2.4	2.3
Asian Development Fund	KQJU	140.5	127.6	136.0	120.5	105.4	87.8	78.6	73.2	68.3
Caribbean Development Bank	KQJV	1.3	1.4	1.3	1.3	1.3	1.3	1.5	1.5	1.4
Special Development Fund	KQKC	9.5	10.6	13.2	15.8	16.4	16.9	15.9	13.8	17.3
Inter-American Development Bank	KQJY	1.3	2.0	1.8	1.9	1.0	2.0	1.4	0.7	0.2

18.7 Consolidated Fund and National Loans Fund: assets and liabilities[1]
United Kingdom
continued   At 31 March each year

£ million

		1998	1999	2000	2001	2002	2003	2004	2005	2006
Promissory notes issued by										
Minister of Overseas Development (continued)										
Fund for special operations	KQJZ	6.3	2.6	2.1	1.1	..	..	..	..	..
International Fund for Agricultural Development	KQKA	14.2	16.5	18.4	15.6	12.9	9.9	..	..	..
International Bank for Reconstruction and Development	KQKB	81.9	94.3	105.9	112.5	114.6	88.5	..	..	..
European Bank for Reconstruction and Development	KIAY	..	7.7	12.1	16.1	17.6	19.8	..	..	..
United Nations Environment Programme	KJEH	1.0	..	..	..	..	5.3	..	..	..
Other contributions and instalments due in respect of international subscriptions, etc	KQYX	1 425.2	1 313.1	1 669.2	1 174.0	955.1	1 608.1	..	..	..
NATIONAL LOANS FUND[3]										
Total assets	KQKD	418 444.7	421 635.7	426 239.2	425 955.6	434 544.6	448 006.3	108 243.1	94 226.5	83 227.6
Total National Loans Fund loans outstanding	KQKE	46 742.6	48 513.6	49 788.8	51 037.6	50 251.4	47 719.0	44 431.4	45 013.1	50 087.9
Loans to Public Corporations:										
Royal Mail Group plc	KQKF	..	..	..	500.0	500.0	550.0	500.0	500.0	500.0
Scottish Nuclear Ltd	KQKM	..	..	..	..	..	..	..	..	..
Railtrack	KTCR	..	..	..	..	..	..	..	..	..
European Passenger Services	KTCS	..	..	..	..	..	..	..	..	..
Civil Aviation Authority	KQKQ	420.9	365.7	342.5	92.5	9.8	8.8	8.2	7.6	11.0
British Railways Board	KQKS	573.7	546.2	518.7	481.3	..	..	..	..	..
British Waterways Board	KQKU	18.2	18.2	18.2	16.7	16.3	14.7	14.7	14.7	10.6
New Towns - Development Corporations and Commission	KQLD	36.2	8.0	8.0	8.0	8.0	7.9	7.9	7.9	7.9
Scottish Homes	KQLF	259.8	190.9	179.0	161.6	149.7	138.1	100.6	–	..
Housing Corporation (England)	KQLH	4.0	4.0	3.0	3.0	2.0	2.0	1.2	1.4	1.4
Housing for Wales	KQLI	..	..	..	..	..	..	..	..	..
Land Authority for Wales	KQLL	1.3	..	..	..	..	..	..	..	..
Scottish Enterprise	KQLM	0.1	..	..	..	..	..	..	..	..
Welsh Development Agency	KQLN	1.2	0.9	0.6	0.3	0.2	0.1	..	..	..
Land Registry Trading Fund	KPOF	..	..	..	..	..	..	..	..	..
Development Board for Rural Wales	KQLO	4.0	4.0	4.0	4.0	4.0	4.0	4.0	4.0	4.0
Royal Mint	KQLP	–	–	2.0	5.0	14.8	11.3	15.7	18.1	22.5
Crown Agents	KQLS	..	..	..	..	..	..	..	..	..
Her Majesty's Stationery Office	KQLT	..	..	..	..	..	..	..	..	..
Urban Development Corporations	KQLU	..	..	..	..	..	..	..	..	..
Harbour Authorities	KQLV	0.5	0.4	0.2	0.1	0.1	0.1	0.1	0.1	0.1
UK Atomic Energy Authority	KQLX	..	..	..	..	..	..	..	..	..
Ordnance Survey	GPVF	..	..	15.5	13.9	12.3	11.0	9.9	8.9	8.0
Central Office of Information	KJEI	..	..	..	..	..	..	..	..	..
Registers of Scotland	KZBB	5.6	5.1	4.5	4.0	3.7	3.6	3.5	3.3	3.2
East of Scotland Water Authority	KZBC	229.0	288.0	283.0	268.0	258.0	248.0	238.0	223.0	213.0
North of Scotland Water Authority	KZBD	189.2	242.0	236.5	236.5	236.5	231.5	231.5	226.5	226.5
West of Scotland Water Authority	KZBE	304.9	425.6	412.4	412.4	412.4	412.4	402.4	402.4	402.4
Loans to local authorities	KQLY	42 951.1	44 742.7	46 099.2	47 239.1	47 093.4	44 640.3	41 468.3	42 102.9	47 123.7
Loans to private sector:										
Housing associations	KGVS	0.5	0.5	0.5	0.5	..	..	..	..	..
Loans within central government:										
Northern Ireland Exchequer	KGVW	1 681.1	1 611.2	1 602.0	1 533.1	1 473.9	1 380.4	1 372.0	1 440.5	1 503.5
Married quarters for Armed Forces	KGVX	61.3	60.2	59.0	57.7	56.4	54.9	53.4	51.8	50.1
Other assets:										
Exchange Equalisation Account - Advances o/s	KGVZ	..	..	475.0	5 680.0	831.0	30.0	670.0	910.0	2 005.0
Subscriptions and contributions to international financial organisations:										
International Monetary Fund	KGXE	5 895.6	9 048.1	9 067.4	9 496.6	9 494.5	9 293.8	8 696.8	8 615.9	8 813.5
Gilt-Edged Official Operations Account -advances outstanding	KPUF	2 500.0	2 500.0	..	..	..	..	..	..	..
-surplus not paid to the National Loans Fund	KPUH	141.6	190.8	..	..	..	..	..	..	..
Borrowing included in national debt but not brought to account by 31 March	KGXF	568.6	317.9	281.6	405.9	417.5	467.1	..	..	..
Other NLF Assets	GLX9	..	..	..	..	..	..	18 545.9	18 792.0	20 735.2
NLF Debtors	GLY2	..	..	..	..	..	..	899.0	895.5	1 586.0
Debt Management Account -advances outstanding	GPVG	..	..	15 000.0	35 000.0	35 000.0	28 000.0	35 000.0	20 000.0	–
Consolidated Fund liability	KCYI	362 596.4	361 065.3	351 626.3	324 335.5	338 550.2	362 496.5	395 161.4	436 345.0	483 836.2
Total liabilities										
National Loans Fund - Gross liabilities outstanding	KCYJ	418 444.7	421 635.7	426 239.2	425 955.6	434 544.6	448 006.3	503 404.5	530 571.5	567 063.8

1 See Chapter text.
2 Formerly The Buying Agency.
3 From 2003-04 the NLF Account has been prepared on an Accruals basis. The figures from 2004 onwards reflect this accounting change.

Source: HM Treasury: 020 7270 4761

18.8 British government and government guaranteed marketable securities[1]
Nominal values of official and market holdings by maturity[2,3]

At 31 March each year

£ million

		1997	1998	1999	2000	2001	2002	2003	2004	2005	2006	2007
Total holdings	KQMO	290 259	297 366	291 788	290 629	285 915	278 808	292 777	321 051	355 553	411 525	442 862
Up to 5 years	KQMP	90 357	86 094	95 112	95 131	92 090	92 780	106 074	88 678	110 477	127 844	119 129
Over 5 and up to 15 years	KQMQ	125 401	131 758	124 603	116 910	120 101	106 044	101 465	131 665	124 754	146 309	167 274
Over 15 years (including undated)	KQMR	74 501	79 515	72 074	78 587	73 724	79 984	85 238	97 500	120 322	137 372	156 458
Official holdings:[3]												
Total	HHAW	6 858	6 345	6 394	6 204	8 210	7 558	10 650	9 118	7 432	25 391	23 282
Up to 5 years	HHAY	2 850	2 499	2 600	2 849	4 652	3 928	4 797	3 321	2 586	8 206	7 321
Over 5 and up to 15 years	HHAZ	3 041	2 726	2 989	2 567	3 009	2 844	4 115	4 015	3 245	9 622	9 502
Over 15 years (including undated)	HHBA	967	1 120	805	788	549	786	1 738	1 540	1 600	7 563	6 459
Market holdings:												
Total	HHBB	283 402	291 021	285 394	284 425	277 705	271 250	282 127	311 933	348 121	386 134	419 580
Up to 5 years	HHBD	87 508	83 595	92 512	92 282	87 438	88 852	101 277	85 357	107 891	119 638	111 808
Over 5 and up to 15 years	HHBE	122 360	129 032	121 614	114 343	117 092	103 200	97 350	127 650	121 509	136 687	157 772
Over 15 years (including undated)	HHBF	73 536	78 395	71 269	77 800	73 175	79 198	83 500	95 960	118 721	129 809	150 000

1 The government guaranteed securities of nationalised industries only. A re-latively small amount of other government guaranteed securities is exclud-ed.

2 Securities with optional redemption dates are classified according to the fi-nal redemption date. The nominal value of index-linked British Government Stock has been raised by the amount of accrued capital uplift.

3 Official holdings were changed following the introduction of the central bank sector in the UK national accounts. These holdings now principally include those of the Debt Management Office and other government departments. The Issue and Banking Departments of the Bank of England are classified within the central bank sector and are therefore part of market holdings.

Source: Office for National Statistics: 020 7014 2124

18.9 Income tax: allowances and reliefs[1]
United Kingdom

£

		1997/98	1998/99	1999/00	2000/01	2001/02	2002/03	2003/04	2004/05	2005/06	2006/07	2007/08
Personal allowances												
Personal allowance	KDZP	4 045	4 195	4 335	4 385	4 535	4 615	4 615	4 745	4 895	5 035	5 225
Married couple's (both partners under 65)[2]	KDZR	1 830	1 900	1 970	..	..	..	..	..	..	..	..
Age allowance:												
Personal (aged 65-74)	KSOH	5 220	5 410	5 720	5 790	5 990	6 100	6 610	6 830	7 090	7 280	7 550
Personal (aged 75 or over)	KSOI	5 400	5 600	5 980	6 050	6 260	6 370	6 720	6 950	7 220	7 420	7 690
Married couple's (either partner between 65-74 but neither partner 75 or over)[2,3]	KEDI	3 185	3 305	5 125	5 185	5 365	5 465	5 565	5 725	5 905	6 065	6 285
Married couple's (either partner 75 or over)[2]	KEIY	3 225	3 345	5 195	5 255	5 435	5 535	5 635	5 795	5 975	6 135	6 365
Minimum married couple's allowance	C58D	1 830	1 900	1 970	2 000	2 070	2 110	2 150	2 210	2 280	2 350	2 440
Income limit[4]	KEOO	15 600	16 200	16 800	17 000	17 600	17 900	18 300	18 900	19 500	20 100	20 900
Additional personal allowance[2]	KEPG	1 830	1 900	1 970	..	..	..	..	..	..	..	..
Widow's bereavement allowance	KEPH	1 830	1 900	1 970	..	..	..	..	..	..	..	..
Blind person's allowance												
Single or married (one spouse blind)	KSOJ	1 280	1 330	1 380	1 400	1 450	1 480	1 510	1 560	1 610	1 660	1 730
Married (both spouses blind)	KSOK	2 560	2 660	2 760	2 800	2 900	2 960	3 020	3 120	3 220	3 320	3 460
Life Assurance Relief												
Percentage of gross premium	KFDR	12.5 or Nil	12.5 or Nil	12.5 or Nil	12.5 or Nil	12.5 or Nil	12.5 or Nil	12.5 or Nil	12.5 or Nil	12.5 or Nil	12.5 or Nil	12.5 or Nil

1 See chapter text.
2 The allowance was restricted to 20 per cent in 1994-95, 15 per cent from 1995-96 and 10 per cent from 1999-00
3 At least one of the partners must be aged 65 before April 2000 to be entitled to the married couple's allowance (MCA). From 2000-01 only people born before 6 April 1935 are entitled to MCA.

4 If the total income, less allowable deductions of a taxpayer aged 65 or over exceeds the limit, the age-related allowances are reduced by £1 for each £2 of income over the aged income level until the basic levels of the personal and married couple's allowances are reached.

Source: HM Revenue & Customs: 020 7147 3045

18.10 Rates of Income tax
United Kingdom

	1998/99		1999/00		2000/01		2001/02		2002/03	
	Bands of taxable income (£)[1]	Rate of tax - Percent-ages	Bands of taxable income (£)[1]	Rate of tax - Percent-ages	Bands of taxable income (£)[1]	Rate of tax - Percent-ages	Bands of taxable income (£)[1]	Rate of tax - Percent-ages	Bands of taxable income (£)[1]	Rate of tax - Percent-ages
Lower rate or starting rate[2]	1 - 4 300	20	1 - 1 500	10[4]	1 - 1 520	10[4]	1 - 1 880	10[4]	1 - 1 920	10[4]
Basic rate	4 301 - 27 100	23[3]	1 501 - 28 000	23[5]	1 521 - 28400	22[5]	1 881 - 29 400	22[5]	1 921 - 29 900	22[5]
Higher rate	over 27 100	40	over 28 000	40[6]	over 28 400	40[6]	over 29 400	40[6]	over 29 900	40[6]

	2003/04		2004/05		2005/06		2006/07		2007/08	
	Bands of taxable income (£)[1]	Rate of tax - Percent-ages	Bands of taxable income (£)[1]	Rate of tax - Percent-ages	Bands of taxable income (£)[1]	Rate of tax - Percent-ages	Bands of taxable income (£)[1]	Rate of tax - Percent-ages	Bands of taxable income (£)[1]	Rate of tax - Percent-ages
Starting rate	1 - 1 960	10[4]	1 - 2 020	10[4]	1 - 2 090	10[4]	1 - 2 150	10[4]	1 - 2 230	10[4]
Basic rate	1 961 - 30 500	22[5]	2 021 - 31 400	22[5]	2 091 - 32 400	22[5]	2 151 - 33 300	22[5]	2 231 - 34 600	22[5]
Higher rate	over 30 500	40[6]	over 31 400	40[6]	over 32 400	40[6]	over 33 300	40[6]	over 34 600	40[6]

1 Taxable income is defined as gross income for income tax purposes less any allowances and reliefs available at the taxpayer's marginal rate.
2 In 1999/00 the starting rate replaced the lower rate.
3 The basic rate of tax on dividends and savings income is 20%.
4 The starting rate also applies to savings and dividends.
5 The basic rate of tax on dividends is 10% and savings income is 20%
6 The higher rate of tax on dividends is 32.5%.

Source: HM Revenue & Customs: 020 7147 3045

18.11 Rateable values[1]
England and Wales
At 1 April each year

		1997	1998	1999	2000	2001	2002	2003	2004	2005	2006	2007
Number of properties (Thousands)												
Commercial	KMIN	1 225	1 223	1 219	1 223	1 230	1 234	1 236	1 239	1 234	1 245	1 258
Shops and cafes	KMIO	491	488	484	478	476	473	469	466	462	459	457
Offices	KMIP	255	257	258	261	269	273	279	284	287	296	304
Other	KMIQ	479	478	477	484	485	487	488	490	485	490	497
On-licensed premises	KMIR	59	59	60	61	61	60	60	60	66	65	65
Entertainment and recreational:	KMIS	87	81	80	79	79	80	80	80	78	79	81
Cinemas	KMIT	1	1	1	1	1	1	1	1	1	1	1
Theatres and music-halls	KMIU	1	1	1	1	1	1	1	1	1	1	1
Other	KMIV	86	80	79	76	76	77	77	78	76	78	80
Public utility	KMIW	8	9	9	8	8	8	8	8	8	8	8
Educational and cultural	KMIX	41	41	41	41	42	42	42	43	45	45	45
Miscellaneous	KMIY	55	56	61	67	70	70	72	74	74	77	80
Industrial	KMIZ	249	250	250	250	251	250	250	250	252	251	252
Total	KMIH	1 725	1 719	1 720	1 729	1 740	1 745	1 749	1 754	1 756	1 771	1 788
Value of assessments (£ million)												
Commercial	KMHG	19 859	19 733	19 652	26 320	27 255	27 622	27 713	27 878	33 013	33 548	33 566
Shops and cafes	KMHH	5 959	5 860	5 840	6 801	6 972	6 953	6 863	6 845	8 257	8 311	8 289
Offices	KMHI	5 641	5 624	5 575	8 625	9 191	9 388	9 555	9 591	10 840	11 034	10 904
Other	KMHJ	8 259	8 249	8 237	10 894	11 092	11 281	11 295	11 441	13 916	14 203	14 373
On-licensed premises	KMHK	970	980	997	1 311	1 347	1 345	1 334	1 320	1 667	1 652	1 615
Entertainment and recreational	KMHL	1 033	1 040	1 045	1 310	1 369	1 430	1 416	1 362	1 467	1 483	1 481
Cinemas	KMHM	36	39	45	79	92	104	106	96	117	115	110
Theatres and music-halls	KMHN	21	21	20	24	25	26	26	26	34	35	35
Other	KMHO	975	979	980	1 207	1 252	1 300	1 284	1 240	1 316	1 333	1 337
Public utility	KMHP	3 488	3 380	3 361	3 828	3 411	3 460	3 444	3 410	3 680	3 668	3 668
Educational and cultural	KMHQ	1 894	1 773	1 672	1 829	1 872	1 902	1 895	1 904	2 359	2 411	2 407
Miscellaneous	KMHR	1 494	1 464	1 439	2 142	2 172	2 220	2 218	2 022	2 582	2 646	2 687
Industrial	KMHS	5 561	5 540	5 463	6 249	6 202	6 157	6 034	5 935	6 651	6 575	6 453
Total	KMHA	34 299	33 909	33 649	42 985	43 626	44 136	44 053	43 831	51 419	51 983	51 878

1 See chapter text.

Source: HM Revenue & Customs: 020 7147 2941

18.12 Local authorities: gross loan debt outstanding[1]
At 31 March each year

£ billion

		2003	2004	2005	2006	2007
United Kingdom						
Total debt	KQBR	51.2	50.5	52.9	59.7	62.3
Public Works Loan Board	KQBS	44.6	41.3	42.4	47.1	47.9
Northern Ireland Consolidated Fund	KQBT	0.3	0.3	0.3	..	..
Other debt	KQBU	6.3	8.8	10.5	..	..
England						
Total debt	C3OO	38.2	37.7	40.1	46.1	48.6
of which Public Works Loan Board	C3OP	33.4	31.1	32.2	36.6	37.6
Wales						
Total debt	C3OQ	3.7	3.6	3.7	3.8	3.8
of which Public Works Loan Board	C3OR	3.3	3.1	3.1	3.3	3.1
Scotland						
Total debt	KQBX	8.8	8.8	8.7	9.4	9.5
of which Public Works Loan Board	KQBY	*7.9*	*7.1*	*6.8*	*7.2*	*7.1*
Northern Ireland						
Total debt	KQBZ	0.3	0.3	0.3	0.3	0.3
of which						
Northern Ireland Consolidated Fund	KQBT	0.3	0.3	0.3	..	..

1 The sums shown exclude inter-authority loans.

Sources: Communities and Local Government: 020 7944 4176;
Public Works Loan Board: 020 7862 6610;
Department of Finance and Personnel for Northern Ireland: 028 9185 8131

18.13 Revenue expenditure of local authorities

£ million

	2004/05 outturn	2005/06 outturn	2006/07 outturn	2007/08 budget
England				
Education[1]	33 290	36 020	37 972	39 620
Transport	4 673	4 843	5 313	5 600
of which:				
Highways	2 163	2 205	2 262	2 320
Public transport	2 511	2 635	3 051	3 280
Social Services[2]	16 310	17 359	18 094	18 469
Housing (excluding HRA)[3]	13 288	14 066	14 963	15 246
Cultural, environmental and planning	8 519	9 162	9 651	9 902
of which:				
Cultural	2 835	2 967	3 158	3165
Environmental	3 864	4 248	4 519	4 872
Planning and development	1 822	1 947	1 973	1 866
Police	10 206	10 957	11 651	11 609
Fire	1 925	2 040	2 193	2 227
Courts	460	58	62	62
Central services	2 953	2 432	3 453	3 350
Other	275	206	159	248
Net current expenditure	91 902	97 142	103 513	106 333
Capital financing	2 362	2 473	2 993	3 352
Capital Expenditure charged to Revenue Account	957	891	1 106	1 245
Interest receipts	-1 125	-1 214	-1 481	-1 123
Pension Interest Costs	3 947	4 785	4 534	3 531
Other non-current expenditure[4]	3 062	3 194	3 350	3 417
Specific grants outside Aggregate External Finance (AEF)	-17 311	-18 267	-19 643	-19 444
Revenue expenditure	83 795	89 004	94 372	97 312
Specific and special grants inside AEF	-14 090	-14 785	-41 771	-43 035
Net revenue expenditure	69 705	74 219	52 601	54 277
Appropriation to/from reserves (excluding pension reserves)	1 347	816	695	-890
Appropriation to/from Pension Reserves	-4 492	-4 582	-5 890	-3 990
Other adjustments	2	24	16	0
Budget requirement	66 561	70 477	47 422	49 398
SSA reduction grant	-	-	-	-
Police grant	-4 168	-4 353	-3 936	-4 028
Revenue support grant	-26 964	-26 663	-3 378	-3 105
Central Support Protection Grant	-	-	-	-
Council Tax Benefit Subsid Limitation Scheme	-	-	-	-
Redistributed business rates	-15 004	-18 004	-17 506	-18 506
General Greater London Authority Grant	-36	-37	-38	-38
Other items	-90	-104	-111	-112
Council tax requirement	20 299	21 315	22 453	23 608
Scotland				
Net revenue expenditure on general fund	9 847	10 603	10 708	11 032

18.13 Revenue expenditure of local authorities

continued

£ million

	2004/05 outturn	2005/06 outturn	2006/07 outturn	2007/08 budget
Wales[5]				
Education	2 011.3	2 121.8	2 213.0	2 312.7
Personal social services	1 069.2	1 164.7	1 253.6	1 307.8
Housing[6]	632.4	674.6	716.7	730.7
Local environmental services[7]	289.6	318.9	353.9	358.9
Roads and transport	256.7	270.8	283.3	300.3
Libraries, culture, heritage, sport and recreation	239.4	248.3	259.9	263.0
Planning, economic development and community development	98.6	108.4	115.2	111.2
Council tax benefit and administration[8]	30.0	31.0	32.1	30.0
Debt financing costs: counties	258.8	272.4	278.0	312.9
Central administrative and other revenue expenditure: counties[9]	221.5	206.7	207.4	239.1
Total county and county borough council expenditure	5 107.3	5 417.4	5 713.1	5 966.6
Total police expenditure	538.2	557.9	601.4	616.4
Total fire expenditure	124.5	135.7	142.1	137.2
Total national park expenditure	15.7	17.0	15.8	17.1
Gross revenue expenditure	5 785.7	6 128.0	6 472.4	6 737.3
less specific and special government grants (except council tax benefit grant)	-1 380.8	-1 473.5	-1 529.7	-1 489.4
Net revenue expenditure	4 404.9	4 654.5	4 942.7	5 247.9
Putting to (+)/drawing from (-) reserves	5.7	13.5	24.6	-42.1
Budget requirement	4 410.6	4 668.0	4 967.3	5 205.9
Plus discretionary non-domestic rate relief	2.2	2.5	2.6	2.5
less revenue support grant	-2 591.0	-2 751.6	-2 951.8	-3 061.6
less police grant	-225.8	-235.0	-217.0	-225.0
less re-distributed non-domestic rates income	-672.0	-672.0	-730.0	-791.0
Council tax requirement	924.1	1 012.0	1 071.2	1 130.8
of which:				
Paid by council tax benefit grant from the Department for Work and Pensions	155.0	170.1	177.2	178.2
Paid directly by council tax payers	769.1	841.9	894.0	952.6

1 Includes mandatory student awards and inter-authority education recoupment.
2 Includes supported employment.
3 Includes mandatory rent allowances and rent rebates.
4 Includes:
  (i) Gross expenditure on council tax benefit.
  (ii) Expenditure on council tax reduction scheme.
  (iii) Discretionary (non-domestic) rate relief.
  (iv) Flood defence payments to the Environment Agency
  (v) Bad debt provision.
5 Service expenditure is shown excluding that financed by sales, fees and charges, but including that financed by specific and special government grants.
6 Includes housing benefit and private sector costs such as provision for the homeless. Includes rent rebates granted to HRA tenants which is 100% grant funded. Excludes council owned housing.

7 Includes cemeteries and crematoria, community safety, environmental health, consumer protection, waste collection/disposal and central services to the public such as birth registration and elections.
8 Excludes council tax benefit expendnditure funded by the specific grant from the Department for Work and Pensions.
9 Includes agricultural services, coastal and flood defence and community councils. Also includes central administrative costs of corporate management, democratic representation and certain costs, such as those relating to back-year or additional pension contributions which should not be allocated to individual services, capital expenditure charged to the revenue account and is net of any interest expected to accrue on balances.

Sources: Communities and Local Government: 020 7944 4158;
Scottish Government, Statistical Support for Local Government: 0131 244 7033;
Welsh Assembly Government: 029 2082 5355

18.14 Financing of revenue expenditure
England and Wales

Years ending 31 March   £ million

		1997 /98	1998 /99	1999 /00	2000 /01	2001 /02	2002 /03	2003 /04	2004 /05	2005 /06	2006 /07	2007[1] /08
England[2]												
Revenue expenditure[3]												
Cash £m	KRTN	47 256	50 189	53 651	57 329	61 952	65 898	75 244	79 303	84 422	88 482	93 321
Government grants												
Cash £m	KRTO	23 840	25 291	26 421	27 809	31 469	32 634	41 777	45 258	45 838	49 123	50 206
Percentage of revenue expenditure	KRTP	50	50	49	49	50	50	56	57	54	56	54
Redistributed business rates[4]												
Cash £m	KRTQ	12 034	12 531	13 619	15 407	15 144	16 639	15 611	15 004	18 004	17 506	18 506
Percentage of revenue expenditure	KRTR	25	25	25	27	24	25	21	19	21	20	20
Council tax												
Cash £m	KRTS	11 241	12 332	13 278	14 200	15 246	16 648	18 946	20 299	21 315	22 453	23 608
Percentage of revenue expenditure	KRTT	24	25	25	25	25	25	25	26	25	25	25
Wales												
Gross revenue expenditure[5]	ZBXH	3 121	3 246	3 424	3 605	4 350	4 709	5 243	5 786	6 128	6 472	6 737
General government grants[6]	ZBXI	1 957	2 009	2 093	2 234	2 345	2 541	2 743	2 817	2 987	3 169	3 287
Specific government grants[7]	ZBXG	75	84	80	94	601	779	1 005	1 381	1 473	1 530	1 489
Share of redistributed business rates	ZBXJ	584	612	656	638	697	643	660	672	672	730	791
Council tax income[8]	ZBXK	483	542	596	670	716	776	861	924	1 012	1 071	1 131
Other[9]	ZBXL	22	..	−1	−31	−10	−30	−25	−8	−16	−28	40

1 Budget estimates
2 Produced on a non-Financial Reporting Standard 17 (FRS17) basis.
3 The sum of government grants, business rates and local taxes does not normally equal revenue expenditure because of the use of reserves.
4 1993-94 to 2003-04 includes City of London Offset.
5 Gross revenue expenditure is total local authority expenditure on services, plus capital charges, but net of any income from sales, fees, and charges and other non-grant sources. It includes expenditure funded by specific grants. The figures have been adjusted to account for FRS17 pension costs.

6 Includes all unhypothecated grants, namely revenue support grant, police grant, council tax reduction scheme grant, transitional grant and the adjustment to reverse the transfer.
7 Comprises specific and supplementary grants, excluding police grant.
8 This includes community council precepts, and income covered by charge/council tax benefit grant, but excludes council tax reduction scheme
9 This includes use of, or contributors to, local authority reserves and other minor adjustments.

Sources: Communities and Local Government: 020 7944 4158;
Welsh Assembly Government: 029 2082 5355

18.15 Local authority capital expenditure and receipts
England
Final outturn: Years ending 31 March

£ million

		2001/02	2002/03	2003/04	2004/05	2005/06	2006/07
Expenditure[1]							
Education	KRUD	2 064	2 287	2 780	3 087	3 492	3 442
Personal Social Services	KRUE	158	199	260	285	387	364
Transport	KRUC	1 877	2 461	2 552	2 906	3 461	3 480
Housing	KRUB	3 110	3 828	3 485	3 987	4 534	4 507
Arts and libraries	GEKZ	213	208	196	227	329	296
Agriculture and fisheries	GELA	38	65	72	66	93	96
Sport and recreation	KRUH	314	307	263	305	424	415
Other[2]	GELB	1 513	1 631	2 056	2 725	3 218	3 052
Fire and civil defence	GELC	62	72	68	81	96	126
Police and probation	GELD	359	408	513	561	606	531
Magistrates courts	GELE	33	40	37	46	1	–
Total	KRUR	9 741	11 508	12 282	14 276	16 641	16 307
Receipts[3]							
Education	KRUT	146	233	221	210	217	261
Personal social services	KRUV	71	75	74	75	85	85
Transport	KRUU	138	107	92	101	87	130
Housing	KRUS	2 245	3 474	3 622	3 193	2 179	1 769
Arts and libraries	GELF	19	22	5	10	7	10
Agriculture and fisheries	GELG	42	49	53	45	63	65
Sport and recreation	KRUX	12	21	7	11	48	51
Other[2]	GELH	801	975	1 145	931	987	1 172
Fire and civil defence	GELI	7	10	18	6	8	9
Police and probation	GELJ	86	70	78	71	96	117
Magistrates court	GELK	12	4	6	8	1	–
Total	KRVB	3 579	5 040	5 322	4 661	3 777	3 671

1 Includes aquisition of share and loan capital.
2 Environmental services, consumer protection and employment services.
3 Includes disposal of share and loan capital and disposal of other investments.

Source: Department for Communities and Local Government: 020 7944 4075

18.16 Capital expenditure and income
England

£ million

Financial year	Central government grants	Other grants and contributions[1]	Use of usable capital receipts	BCA/SCE(R)Single Capital Pot	BCA/SCE(R)Separate Programme Element	Other borrowing and credit arrangements not supported by central government
	KRVM	I4V9	I4VA	I4VB	I4VC	I4VD
1991/92	1 041	159	1 305	2 327	813	..
1992/93	1 210	148	1 119	2 230	999	..
1993/94	1 279	140	1 901	1 743	1 205	..
1994/95	1 176	223	1 520	1 784	938	..
1995/96	1 484	230	1 216	1 493	771	..
1996/97	1 388	281	1 192	1 291	829	..
1997/98	1 262	389	1 184	968	1 131	..
1998/99	1 160	485	1 223	1 048	1 286	..
1999/00	1 161	571	1 599	1 051	1 250	..
2000/01	1 298	762	1 592	2 271	945	..
2001/02	2 027	757	1 975	1 173	1 378	..
2002/03	2 474	716	2 426	2 281	935	..
2003/04	2 642	869	1 988	2 583	1 326	..
2004/05	3 196	1 080	2 647	2 959	704	1 061
2005/06	3 909	1 377	2 812	2 932	947	2 251
2006/07	4 083	1 344	2 628	2 734	630	2 291

Financial year	Use of other resources[2]	Revenue financing of capital espenditure, of which: Housing revenue account	Major repairs reserve	General Fund	Total resources used
	I4VE	I4VF	I4VG	I4VH	I4VI
1991/92	–	213	..	819	6 678
1992/93	22	239	..	712	6 679
1993/94	67	314	..	571	7 219
1994/95	97	449	..	853	7 040
1995/96	236	552	..	1 039	7 021
1996/97	172	511	..	914	6 578
1997/98	196	491	..	891	6 512
1998/99	253	408	..	847	6 710
1999/00	231	327	..	808	6 998
2000/01	304	218	..	896	8 288
2001/02	387	1 505	..	825	10 028
2002/03	375	175	1 465	825	11 672
2003/04	262	212	1 388	1 055	12 326
2004/05	..	187	1 440	1 130	14 404
2005/06	..	238	1 327	1 004	16 797
2006/07	..	240	1 337	1 185	16 472

1 Includes grants and contributions for private developers, Non-Departmental
Public Bodies, National Lottery and European Structural Fund.
2 Use of monies set aside as provision for credit liabilities to finance capital
expenditure (debt free authorities).

Source: Department for Communities and Local Government: 020 7944 4075

18.17 Expenditure of local authorities
Scotland
Year ending 31 March

£ thousand

		1997/98	1998/99	1999/00	2000/01	2001/02	2002/03	2003/04	2004/05	2005/06	2006/07
Out of revenue:[1] Total	KQTA	9 566 936	10 033 985	10 439 999	10 924 634	11 553 927	12 858 533	13 658 834	14 527 867	15 746 429	15 986 751
General Fund Services:	KQTB	6 679 396	7 021 038	7 429 626	7 884 168	8 428 217	9 290 268	10 139 679	10 964 598	12 021 453	12 143 056
Education	KQTC	2 512 725	2 649 170	2 855 945	3 037 780	3 283 827	3 533 853	3 872 786	4 180 675	4 406 876	4 596 832
Libraries, museums and galleries	KQTD	121 387	124 648	131 696	134 174	138 318	152 308	160 540	161 650	168 953	164 976
Social work	KQTE	1 315 387	1 394 142	1 519 191	1 632 843	1 793 732	2 173 752	2 400 652	2 621 134	2 808 040	2 994 486
Law, order and protective services	KQTF	931 795	952 940	1 006 000	1 047 034	1 088 791	1 130 693	1 226 067	1 306 085	1 501 854	1 469 644
Roads and Transport[2]	KQTG	440 712	546 945	527 018	564 738	506 326	601 454	611 721	635 329	673 167	625 341
Environmental services	KQTH	343 565	349 413	373 050	393 333	414 975	484 177	525 556	581 220	635 475	670 308
Planning	KQTI	163 380	179 078	198 285	194 771	223 414	265 315	282 572	299 182	351 617	366 803
Leisure and recreation	KQTJ	364 853	368 023	375 579	387 115	401 904	426 495	472 120	494 237	520 612	543 047
Other services	KQTL	456 219	430 790	435 155	465 612	572 136	515 661	585 425	681 288	948 167	702 554
Other general fund expenditure[3]	KQTM	29 373	25 889	7 707	26 768	4 794	6 560	2 240	3 798	6 692	9 065
Housing	KQTN	1 658 935	1 754 686	1 821 380	1 886 189	1 954 444	2 224 209	2 295 005	2 459 146	2 609 228	2 740 592
Trading services:	KQTO	75 976	79 644	87 321	80 355	61 899	74 062	92 782	106 445	103 461	102 336
Passenger transport	KQTR	1 524	121	336	162	343	427	441	282	353	355
Ferries	KQTS	7 512	8 930	9 709	10 005	9 650	11 493	11 768	13 759	14 308	18 483
Harbours, docks and piers	KQTT	12 884	15 697	15 923	13 604	10 912	12 222	13 405	12 407	11 995	8 495
Road bridges	KQTV	16 064	16 408	8 231	8 606	6 914	7 267	11 235	13 276	12 366	16 279
Slaughterhouses	KQTW	850	228	4	..	..	..	..	..	..	..
Markets	KQTX	13 479	13 161	14 106	23 844	16 657	17 995	14 824	15 353	17 447	16 793
Other trading services	KQTY	23 663	25 099	39 012	24 134	17 423	24 658	41 109	51 368	46 992	41 931
Loan charges:[4] Total	KQTZ	1 126 637	1 152 728	1 109 379	1 100 690	1 114 161	1 269 994	1 131 368	997 678	1 012 287	1 000 767
Allocated to:											
General Fund services	KMHV	651 982	710 371	701 515	708 822	739 351	738 870	772 852	772 648	792 404	782 002
Housing	KMHW	471 274	438 556	402 936	386 512	369 943	525 201	348 180	212 440	210 856	214 395
Trading services	KMHX	3 381	3 801	4 928	5 356	4 867	5 923	10 336	12 590	9 027	4 370
On capital works:[4] Total	KQUA	813 900	815 981	816 473	802 672	929 631	972 049	1 052 310	1 264 031	1 572 281	1 952 249
General Fund Services:	KQUB	540 096	541 769	557 119	538 843	610 485	662 869	767 122	1 006 150	1 160 818	1 462 620
Education	KQUC	112 753	125 341	136 508	127 781	143 268	157 439	172 227	199 387	310 054	402 865
Libraries, museums and galleries	KQUD	9 974	13 231	10 261	5 834	8 683	19 018	12 043	24 796	22 762	24 210
Social work	KQUE	19 660	22 554	22 097	21 539	31 359	30 116	31 966	33 450	37 877	50 327
Law, order and protective services	KQUF	37 701	37 727	37 132	35 761	39 901	53 268	65 477	65 154	51 146	60 287
Roads and Transport	KQUG	108 227	113 954	108 500	117 485	147 975	147 357	200 278	258 071	308 366	418 987
Environmental services	KQUH	21 193	18 397	14 936	17 944	16 396	17 957	20 567	40 773	55 020	43 104
Planning	KQUI	69 648	50 854	52 045	47 684	33 312	40 241	36 496	61 544	76 043	66 063
Leisure and recreation	KQUJ	29 692	40 926	52 365	44 516	39 240	50 558	71 486	74 116	83 681	98 275
Administrative buildings and equipment	KQUK	45 374	35 107	35 824	34 633	53 189	68 438	48 896	64 414	84 569	113 896
Other services	KQUL	85 814	83 678	87 451	85 666	97 162	78 477	107 686	184 445	131 300	184 606
Housing	KQUM	270 005	268 135	255 019	255 189	300 054	284 418	261 715	241 107	382 697	454 838
Trading Services:	KQUN	3 799	6 077	4 335	8 640	19 092	24 762	23 473	16 774	28 766	34 791
Ferries	KQUR	770	268	1 030	23	467	1	111	608	195	547
Harbours, docks and piers	KQUS	1 175	1 626	1 389	6 192	15 898	20 361	19 503	12 024	12 899	5 855
Airports	KQUT	439	..	..	607	663	1 031	609	572	663	798
Road bridges	KQUU	973	2 791	600	964	882	2 386	2 395	442	12 106	22 865
Slaughterhouses	KQUV	69	54	12	..	40	116	82	–	–	–
Other trading services	KMHY	373	1 338	1 304	854	1 142	867	773	3 128	2 903	4 726

1 Gross expenditure *less* inter-authority and inter-account transfers.
2 Including general fund support for transport (LA and NON-LA).
3 General fund contributions to Housing and Trading services (excluding transport), are also included in the expenditure figures for these services.
4 Expenditure out of loans, government grants and other capital receipts.

Source: Scottish Government, Statistical Support for Local Government: 0131 244 7033

18.18 Income of local authorities: classified according to source
Scotland

Year ending 31 March

£ thousand

		1996/97	1997/98	1998/99	1999/00	2000/01	2001/02	2002/03	2003/04	2004/05	2005/06	2006/07
Revenue account												
Non-Domestic Rates[1]	KQXA	1 313 531	1 326 129	1 437 646	1 440 522	1 662 691	1 553 926	1 718 104	1 804 423	1 895 941	1 897 073	1 883 769
Council tax	KPUC	9 681 531	70 405	1 146 366	1 193 693	1 273 316	1 363 399	1 459 212	1 532 071	1 614 808	1 720 305	1 811 577
Government grants												
Revenue Support Grant	KQXC	3 649 694	3 520 461	3 483 815	3 537 043	3 440 842	3 935 328	4 557 867	5 037 140	5 266 054	5 567 902	5 777 204
Rate rebate grant	KQXG	496	..	..	..	..	..	..	..	..	..	..
Council tax rebate grants	KPUD	226 132	260 424	274 940	275 789	279 459	285 131	293 606	307 733	344 899	354 067	359 159
Other grants and subsidies	KQXI	1 347 706	1 480 890	1 642 045	1 778 216	1 891 839	2 061 297	2 141 543	2 479 311	2 823 820	2 940 137	3 147 497
Sales	KQXJ	59 059	46 874	39 595	43 660	49 826	..	..	..	..	..	..
Fees and charges[2]	KQXK	1 539 611	1 625 952	1 668 223	1 682 385	1 776 455	1 789 428	1 954 337	1 785 672	1 845 161	1 951 315	2 039 217
Other income	KQXL	238 985	290 427	324 932	398 894	453 458	490 574	712 423	515 897	709 226	1 003 925	961 693
Capital account												
Sale of fixed assets	KQXM	499 143	327 569	335 037	303 582	149 504	165 016	207 388	222 844	355 069	366 302	451 353
Revenue contributions to capital	KQXP	119 641	149 423	204 982	213 564	210 912	147 760	239 778	212 533	219 593	247 693	199 749
Transfer from special funds	KMHZ	2 652	36 929	26 959	125 365	27 317	37 087	39 650	52 619	82 991	72 195	20 935
Other receipts[3]	KMGV	45 067	32 118	45 028	39 014	45 351	90 360	75 846	114 745	130 575	261 872	595 722

1 This is the Distributable Amount of Non-Domestic Rates.
2 From 2001-02 onwards, fees & charges incorporates sales.
3 Figures include public sector contributions from 2001-02 onwards.

Source: Scottish Government, Statistical Support for Local Government: 0131 244 7033

18.19 Income of local authorities from government grants[1]
Scotland

Year ending 31 March

£ thousand

		1997/98	1998/99	1999/00	2000/01	2001/02	2002/03	2003/04	2004/05	2005/06	2006/07
General fund services	KQYA	557 536	690 569	818 537	935 452	1 032 591	952 692	1 029 338	1 207 912	1 358 190	1 524 829
Education	KQYB	61 960	92 368	225 668	324 340	380 726	251 333	217 743	287 226	327 905	439 678
Libraries, museums and galleries	KQYC	326	627	507	634	1 137	5 359	1 517	763	818	1 394
Social work	KQYD	59 892	62 167	71 611	78 611	86 533	114 591	205 229	240 665	236 774	222 551
Law, order and protective services	KQYE	359 811	366 961	382 246	401 485	423 636	445 275	476 681	512 501	597 322	601 593
Roads and Transport[2]	KQYF	237	97 649	68 429	57 702	49 900	57 664	27 280	35 038	31 704	49 295
Environmental services	KQYG	159	89	71	301	2 272	5 407	18 120	39 971	45 338	55 173
Planning and Economic Development	KQYH	4 885	2 695	4 311	4 375	20 351	19 434	21 517	20 767	31 293	33 750
Leisure and recreation	KQYI	1 856	1 509	1 491	2 377	3 322	2 968	3 732	5 830	6 256	9 194
Other services	KQYK	68 410	66 504	64 203	65 627	64 714	50 661	57 519	65 151	80 780	112 201
Housing	KQYL	920 700	948 232	959 276	956 239	1 028 529	1 188 626	1 449 616	1 614 976	1 580 504	1 622 049
Trading services	KQYM	..	..	403	148	177	225	357	932	1 443	619
Other trading services	KQYP	..	..	403	148	177	225	357	932	1 443	619
Grants not allocated to specific services[3]	KMGY	3 520 461	3 483 815	3 537 043	3 440 842	3 935 328	4 557 867	5 037 140	5 266 054	5 567 902	5 777 204
Total	KMGZ	4 998 697	5 122 616	5 315 259	5 332 681	5 996 625	6 699 410	7 516 451	8 089 874	8 508 039	8 924 701

1 Including grants for capital works.
2 The significant increase in 1998/99 is due to the different reporting of a grant in aid of expenditure on rail passenger services in the Strathclyde Passenger Transport area.
3 Revenue support grant.

Source: Scottish Government, Statistical Support for Local Government: 0131 244 7033

18.20 Expenditure of local authorities
Northern Ireland
Years ending 31 March

£ thousand

		1995 /96	1996 /97	1997 /98	1998 /99	1999 /00	2000 /01	2001 /02	2002 /03	2003 /04	2004 /05	2005 /06
Libraries, museums and art galleries	KQVB	8 481	10 956	13 928	14 571	19 900	23 097	24 181	32 728	30 062	30 481	33 516
Environmental health services:												
Refuse collection and disposal	KQVC	41 284	52 267	56 246	56 360	62 226	65 289	73 336	90 148	94 715	102 633	113 768
Public baths	KQVD	1 703	1 838	2 585	2 634	1 750	1 724	1 423	..	..	..	..
Parks, recreation grounds, etc	KQVE	100 418	111 884	115 302	118 396	158 304	170 999	184 406	194 224	193 617	205 734	221 298
Other sanitary services	KQVF	35 706	39 545	39 682	42 923	44 214	45 552	48 784	52 075	55 349	59 906	66 294
Housing (grants and small dwellings acquisition)	KQVG	472	489	545	358	37	28	27	12	21	18	10
Trading services:												
Cemeteries	KQVI	5 489	5 120	5 626	5 887	5 973	6 151	6 538	7 208	7 980	8 455	8 520
Other trading services (including markets, fairs and harbours)	KQVJ	4 254	8 672	7 016	10 779	9 366	7 209	7 769	18 281	17 489	18 776	19 595
Miscellaneous	KQVK	54 987	63 792	63 375	161 790	86 649	89 881	98 244	79 645	114 971	105 031	128 304
Total expenditure	KQVA	252 794	294 563	304 305	413 698	388 419	409 930	444 708	474 321	490 619	531 034	591 305
Total loan charges	KQVL	21 122	24 363	34 823	26 413	..	..	..	..	..	..	..

Source: Department of the Environment for Northern Ireland: 028 9025 6085

External trade and investment

Chapter 19

External trade and investment

External trade

(Table 19.1 and 19.3 to 19.6)

The statistics in this section are on a Balance of Payments (BoP) basis, compiled from information provided to HM Revenue and Customs by importers and exporters on an Overseas Trade Statistics (OTS) basis, which values exports 'f.o.b.' (free on board) and imports 'c.i.f.' (including insurance and freight). In addition to deducting these freight costs and insurance premiums from the OTS figures, coverage adjustments are made to convert the OTS data to a BoP basis. Adjustments are also made to the level of all exports and European Union (EU) imports to take account of estimated under-recording. The adjustments are set out and described in the annual Office for National Staistics (ONS) *Pink Book* (United Kingdom Balance of Payments). These adjustments are made to conform to the definitions in the 5th edition of the IMF Balance of Payments Manual.

Aggregate estimates of trade in goods, seasonally adjusted and on a BoP basis, are published monthly in the ONS First Release *UK Trade*. More detailed figures are available from Time Series Data on the National Statistics website and are also published in the *Monthly Review of External Trade Statistics* (Business Monitor MM24). Detailed figures for EU and non-EU trade on an OTS basis are published by The Stationery Office in *Overseas Trade Statistics of the United Kingdom*.

A fuller description of how trade statistics are compiled can be found in *Statistics on Trade in Goods* (Government Statistical Service Methodological Series).

Overseas Trade Statistics

HM Revenue and Customs provide accurate and up to date information via the website: www.uktradeinfo.com

They also produce publications 'Overseas Trade Statistics'.

Import penetration and export sales ratios

(Table 19.2)

The ratios were first introduced in the August 1977 edition of *Economic Trends* in an article 'The Home and Export Performance of United Kingdom Industries'. The article described the conceptual and methodological problems involved in measuring such variables as import penetration.

The industries are grouped according to the 1992 Standard Industrial Classification. The four different ratios are defined as follows:

Ratio 1: percentage ratio of imports to home demand

Ratio 2: percentage ratio of imports to (home demand plus exports)

Ratio 3: percentage ratio of exports to total manufacturers' sales

Ratio 4: percentage ratio of exports to (total manufacturers' sales plus imports)

Home demand is defined as total manufacturers' sales plus imports minus exports. This is only an approximate estimate as different sources are used for the total manufacturers' sales and the import and export data. Total manufacturers' sales are determined by the Products of the European Community inquiry, and import and export data are provided by HM Revenue and Customs.

Ratio 1 is commonly used to describe the import penetration of the home market. Allowance is made for the extent of a domestic industry's involvement in export markets by using Ratio 2; this reduces as exports increase.

Similarly, Ratio 3 is the measure normally used to relate exports to total sales by UK producers, and Ratio 4 makes an allowance for the extent that imports of the same product are coming into the UK.

International trade in services

(Tables 19.7 and 19.8)

These data relate to overseas trade in services and cover both production and non-production industries (excluding the public sector). In terms of types of services traded, this equates to trade in royalties, various forms of consultancy, computing and telecommunications services, advertising and market research and other business services. A separate inquiry covers the film and television industries. The surveys cover receipts from the provision of services to residents of other countries (exports) and payments to residents of other countries for services rendered (imports).

Sources of data

The International Trade in Services (ITIS) surveys (which consist of a quarterly component addressed to the largest businesses and an annual component for the remainder) are based on a sample of companies derived from the Inter-departmental Business register. The companies are asked to show the amounts for their imports and exports against the geographical area to which they were paid or from which they were received — irrespective of where they were first earned.

The purpose of the ITIS survey is to record international transactions which impact on the UK's BoP; hence companies are asked to exclude from their earnings trade expenses such as the cost of services purchased abroad. Exports and imports of services are excluded where they are included within an invoice for the import or export of goods; in this case they will already be counted in the estimate for Trade in Goods. However, earnings from third country trade — that is from arranging the sale of goods between two countries other than the UK and where the goods never physically enter the UK (known as merchanting) — are included. Earnings from commodity trading are also included. Together, these two comprise 'Trade Related Services'.

'Royalties' are the largest part of the total trade in services collected in the ITIS survey. These cover transactions for items such as printed matter, sound recordings, performing rights, patents, licences, trademarks, designs, copyrights, manufacturing rights, the use of technical 'know-how' and technical assistance.

Balance of payments

(Tables 19.9 to 19.12)

Tables 19.9 to 19.12 are derived from United Kingdom Balance of Payments 2004 edition — the ONS *Pink Book*. The following general notes to the tables provide brief definitions and explanations of the figures and terms used. Further notes are included in the *Pink Book*.

Summary of Balance of Payments

The BoP consists of the current account, the capital account, the financial account and the International Investment Position (IIP). The current account consists of trade in goods and services, income and current transfers. Income consists of investment income and compensation of employees. The capital account mainly consists of capital transfers and the financial account covers financial transactions. The IIP covers balance sheet levels of UK external assets and liabilities. Every credit entry in the balance of payments accounts should, in theory, be matched by a corresponding debit entry so that total current, capital and financial account credits should be equal to, and therefore offset by, total debits. In practice there is a discrepancy termed net errors and omissions.

The current account

Trade in goods

The goods account covers exports and imports of goods. Imports of motor cars from Japan, for example, are recorded as debits in the trade in goods account, whereas exports of vehicles manufactured in the UK are recorded as credits. Trade in goods forms a component of the expenditure measure of Gross Domestic Product (GDP).

Trade in services

The services account covers exports and imports of services (for example, civil aviation). Passenger tickets for travel on UK aircraft sold abroad, for example, are recorded as credits in the services account, whereas the purchases of airline tickets from foreign airlines by UK passengers are recorded as debits. Trade in services, along with trade in goods, forms a component of the expenditure measure of GDP.

Income

The income account consists of compensation of employees and investment income and is dominated by the latter. Compensation of employees covers employment income from cross-border and seasonal workers which is less significant in the UK than in other countries. Investment income covers earnings (for instance, profits, dividends and interest payments and receipts) arising from cross-border investment in financial assets and liabilities. For example, earnings on foreign bonds and shares held by financial institutions based in the UK are recorded as credits in the investment income account, whereas earnings on UK company securities held abroad are recorded as investment income debits. Investment income forms a component of Gross National Income (GNI) but not GDP.

Current transfers

Current transfers are composed of central government transfers (for instance, taxes and payments to, and receipts from, the EU) and other transfers (for instance, gifts in cash or kind received by private individuals from abroad or receipts from the EU, where the UK government acts as an agent for the ultimate beneficiary of the transfer). Current transfers do not form a component either of GDP or of GNI. For example, payments to the UK farming industry under the EU Agricultural Guarantee Fund are recorded as credits in the current transfers account, while payments of EU agricultural

External trade and investment

levies by the UK farming industry are recorded as debits in the current transfers account.

Capital account

Capital account transactions involve transfers of ownership of fixed assets, transfers of funds associated with acquisition or disposal of fixed assets, and cancellation of liabilities by creditors without any counterparts being received in return. The main components are migrants transfers, EU transfers relating to fixed capital formation (regional development fund and agricultural guidance fund) and debt forgiveness. Funds brought into the UK by new immigrants would, for example, be recorded as credits in the capital account, while funds sent abroad by UK residents emigrating to other countries would be recorded as debits in the capital account. The size of capital account transactions are quite minor compared with the current and financial accounts.

Financial account

While investment income covers earnings arising from cross-border investments in financial assets and liabilities, the financial account of the balance of payments covers the flows of such investments. Earnings on foreign bonds and shares held by financial institutions based in the UK are, for example, recorded as credits in the investment income account, but the acquisition of such foreign securities by UK-based financial institutions are recorded as net debits in the financial account or portfolio investment abroad. Similarly, the acquisitions of UK company securities held by foreign residents are recorded in the financial account as net credits or portfolio investment in the UK.

International Investment Position

While the financial account covers the flows of foreign investments and financial assets and liabilities, the IIP records the levels of external assets and liabilities. While the acquisition of foreign securities by UK-based financial institutions are recorded in the financial account, as net debits, the total holdings of foreign securities by UK-based financial institutions are recorded as levels of UK external assets. Similarly, the holdings of UK company securities held by foreign residents are recorded as levels of UK liabilities.

Foreign direct investment

(Tables 19.13 to 19.18)

Direct investment refers to investment that adds to, deducts from or acquires a lasting interest in an enterprise operating in an economy other than that of the investor, the investor's

purpose being to have an effective voice in the management of the enterprise. (For the purposes of the statistical inquiry, an effective voice is taken as equivalent to a holding of 10 per cent or more in the foreign enterprise.) Other investments in which the investor does not have an effective voice in the management of the enterprise are mainly portfolio investments and these are not covered here. Cross-border investment by public corporations or in property (which is regarded as direct investment in the national accounts) are not covered here, but are shown in the BoP. Similarly, foreign direct investment earnings data are shown net of tax in Tables 19.15 and 19.18 but are gross of tax in the BoP.

Direct investment is a financial concept and is not the same as capital expenditure on fixed assets. It covers only the money invested in a related concern by the parent company, and the concern will then decide how to use the money. A related concern may also raise money locally without reference to the parent company.

The investment figures are published on a net basis; that is, they consist of investments net of disinvestments by a company into its foreign subsidiaries, associate companies and branches.

Definitional changes from 1997

The new European System of Accounts (ESA(95)) definitions were introduced from the 1997 estimates. The changes were as follows:

i) Previously for the measurement of direct investment, an effective voice in the management of an enterprise was taken as the equivalent of a 20 per cent shareholding. This is now 10 per cent.

ii) The Channel Islands (Jersey, Guernsey, etc) and the Isle of Man have been excluded from the definition of the economic territory of the UK. Prior to 1987, these islands were considered to be part of the UK.

iii) Interest received or paid was replaced by interest accrued in the figures on earnings from direct investment. There is deemed to be little or no impact arising from this definitional change on the estimates.

New register sources available from 1998 have led to revisions for the figures from that year onwards. These sources gave an improved estimate of the population satisfying the criteria for foreign direct investment.

The definitional changes have been introduced from 1997 and the register changes from 1998. The data prior to these years have not been reworked in Tables 19.13 to 19.18. For clarity, the Offshore Islands are identified separately on the tables. The breaks in the series for the other definitional changes are not quantified but are relatively small. More detailed information on the effect of these changes appears in the business monitor MA4 – Foreign Direct Investment 2002, which was published in February 2003 and is available from the National Statistics website.

Sources of data

The figures in Tables 19.13 to 19.18 are based on annual inquiries into foreign direct investment for 2002. These were sample surveys which involved sending around 1,250 forms to UK businesses investing abroad, and 2,250 forms to UK businesses in which foreign parents and associates had invested. The tables also contain some revisions to 2001 as a result of new information coming to light in the course of the latest surveys. Further details from the latest annual surveys, including analyses by industry and by components of direct investment, are available in business monitor MA4. Initial figures were published on the National Statistics website in a First Release 'Foreign Direct Investment 2002' in December 2003. Data for 2003 will be published in a First Release in December 2004, followed by the full business monitor MA4 in February 2005.

Country allocation

The analysis of inward investment is based on the country of ownership of the immediate parent company. Thus, inward investment in a UK company may be attributed to the country of the intervening overseas subsidiary, rather than the country of the ultimate parent. Similarly, the country analysis of outward investment is based on the country of ownership of the immediate subsidiary. As an example, to the extent that overseas investment in the UK is channelled through holding companies in the Netherlands, the underlying flow of investment from this country is overstated and the inflow from originating countries is understated.

Further information

More detailed statistics on foreign direct investment are available on request from Simon Harrington, Office for National Statistics, Financial & Accounting Surveys Division, Room 2.301, Government Buildings, Cardiff Road, Newport, South Wales, United Kingdom, NP108XG. Telephone: 01633 813314, fax: 01633 812855, email: simon.harrington@ons. gsi.gov.uk.

External trade and investment

19.1 Trade in goods[1]
United Kingdom
Balance of payments basis

£ million and indices (2003=100)

		1997	1998	1999	2000	2001	2002	2003	2004	2005	2006	2007
Value (£ million)												
Exports of goods	BOKG	171 923	164 056	166 166	187 936	189 093	186 524	188 320	190 877	211 608	243 631	220 857
Imports of goods	BOKH	184 265	185 869	195 217	220 912	230 305	234 229	236 927	251 770	280 397	321 186	308 506
Balance on trade in goods	BOKI	−12 342	−21 813	−29 051	−32 976	−41 212	−47 705	−48 607	−60 893	−68 789	−77 555	−87 649
Price index numbers												
Exports of goods	BQKR	106.1	100.9	98.8	99.9	98.3	98.2	100.0	100.3	104.3	107.5	108.8
Imports of goods	BQKS	107.9	102.4	100.8	104.2	103.3	100.7	100.0	99.5	103.7	107.5	109.0
Terms of trade[2]	BQKT	*98.3*	*98.5*	*98.0*	*95.9*	*95.2*	*97.5*	*100.0*	*100.8*	*100.6*	*100.0*	*99.8*
Volume index numbers												
Exports of goods	BQKU	84.9	85.8	88.6	99.3	101.5	100.3	100.0	101.5	111.0	125.2	110.1
Imports of goods	BQKV	70.4	76.4	81.5	89.1	93.8	98.2	100.0	106.9	114.7	127.9	121.8

1 See chapter text. Statistics of trade in goods on a balance of payments basis are obtained by making certain adjustments in respect of valuation and coverage to the statistics recorded in the *Overseas Trade Statistics*. These adjustments are described in detail in *The Pink Book 2006*.
2 Export price index as a percentage of the import price index.

Source: Office for National Statistics: 020 7533 6064

19.2 Import penetration and export sales ratios for products of manufacturing industry[1,2]

United Kingdom: Standard Industrial Classification 1992

Ratios

			2004	2005	2006
Ratio 1 Imports/Home Demand		SIC Division			
Other mining and quarrying	BBAM	14	158	192	161
Food products and beverages	BBAN	15	26	26	27
Tobacco products	BBAO	16	17	17	15
Textiles	BAZJ	17	77	77	79
Wearing apparel: Dressing and dyeing of fur	BAZK	18	100	104	106
Tanning and dressing of leather: Luggage, handbags, saddlery, harness and footwear	BBAP	19	106	109	110
Wood products of wood and cork (except furniture) articles of straw and plaiting materials	BBAQ	20	37	35	35
Pulp, paper and paper products	BBAR	21	41	42	45
Publishing, printing and reproduction of recorded media	BBAS	22	6	6	6
Chemicals and chemical products	BAZL	24	87	91	97
Rubber and plastic products	BBAT	25	35	35	37
Other non metallic mineral products	BBAU	26	25	25	27
Basic metals	BBAV	27	81	91	92
Fabricated metal products (except machinery and equipment)	BBAW	28	25	24	26
Machinery and equipment not elsewhere classified	BBAX	29	65	67	75
Office machinery and computers	BBAY	30	142	151	223
Electrical machinery not elsewhere classified	BBAZ	31	75	68	77
Radio, television and communication equipment and apparatus	BBBA	32	123	184	..
Medical, precision and optical instruments, watches and clocks	BBBB	33	90	86	98
Motor vehicles, trailers and semi-trailers	BBBC	34	69	70	73
Other transport equipment	BBBD	35	75	76	115
Furniture and manufacturing not elsewhere classified	BBBE	36	65	68	72
Total	BAZY		58	62	..
Ratio 2 Imports/Home Demand plus Exports					
Other mining and quarrying	BBBH	14	57	62	62
Food products and beverages	BBBI	15	23	23	24
Tobacco products	BBBJ	16	11	12	12
Textiles	BAZN	17	55	56	57
Wearing apparel: Dressing and dyeing of fur	BAZO	18	80	84	85
Tanning and dressing of leather: Luggage, handbags, saddlery, harness and footwear	BBBK	19	85	86	87
Wood products of wood and cork (except furniture) articles of straw and plaiting materials	BBBL	20	35	33	34
Pulp, paper and paper products	BBBM	21	35	37	39
Publishing, printing and reproduction of recorded media	BBBN	22	5	5	5
Chemicals and chemical products	BAZP	24	45	46	46
Rubber and plastic products	BBBO	25	28	28	30
Other non metallic mineral products	BBBP	26	21	22	23
Basic metals	BBBQ	27	48	50	54
Fabricated metal products (except machinery and equipment)	BBBR	28	21	21	22
Machinery and equipment not elsewhere classified	BBBS	29	40	42	44
Office machinery and computers	BBBT	30	77	77	86
Electrical machinery not elsewhere classified	BBBU	31	46	44	47
Radio, television and communication equipment and apparatus	BBBV	32	69	70	..
Medical, precision and optical instruments, watches and clocks	BBBW	33	49	47	51
Motor vehicles, trailers and semi-trailers	BBBX	34	48	48	50
Other transport equipment	BBBY	35	40	42	50
Furniture and manufacturing not elsewhere classified	BBBZ	36	51	53	55
Total	BBBF		41	41	44

19.2

Import penetration and export sales ratios for products of manufacturing industry[1,2]

United Kingdom: Standard Industrial Classification 1992

Ratios

			2004	2005	2006
Ratio 3 Exports/Sales		SIC Division			
Other mining and quarrying	BBCM	14	148	179	161
Food products and beverages	BBCN	15	15	15	15
Tobacco products	BBCO	16	40	35	27
Textiles	BAZR	17	63	62	64
Wearing apparel: Dressing and dyeing of fur	BAZS	18	100	119	131
Tanning and dressing of leather: Luggage, handbags, saddlery, harness and footwear	BBCP	19	134	151	161
Wood products of wood and cork (except furniture) articles of straw and plaiting materials	BBCQ	20	7	6	7
Pulp, paper and paper products	BBCR	21	21	22	23
Publishing, printing and reproduction of recorded media	BBCS	22	9	9	9
Chemicals and chemical products	BAZT	24	88	92	97
Rubber and plastic products	BBCT	25	27	27	28
Other non metallic mineral products	BBCU	26	18	18	20
Basic metals	BBCV	27	78	91	90
Fabricated metal products (except machinery and equipment)	BBCW	28	19	18	20
Machinery and equipment not elsewhere classified	BBCX	29	64	65	74
Office machinery and computers	BBCY	30	202	213	436
Electrical machinery not elsewhere classified	BBDK	31	72	63	74
Radio, television and communication equipment and apparatus	BBDL	32	141	206	..
Medical, precision and optical instruments, watches and clocks	BBDM	33	90	85	98
Motor vehicles, trailers and semi-trailers	BBDN	34	59	59	62
Other transport equipment	BBDO	35	77	78	113
Furniture and manufacturing not elsewhere classified	BBDP	36	43	48	53
Total	BBCK		50	55	..
Ratio 4 Exports/Sales plus Imports					
Other mining and quarrying	BBDS	14	64	68	62
Food products and beverages	BBDT	15	11	12	12
Tobacco products	BBDU	16	36	31	23
Textiles	BAZV	17	28	28	27
Wearing apparel: Dressing and dyeing of fur	BAZW	18	20	19	20
Tanning and dressing of leather: Luggage, handbags, saddlery, harness and footwear	BBDV	19	20	20	21
Wood products of wood and cork (except furniture) articles of straw and plaiting materials	BBDW	20	5	4	4
Pulp, paper and paper products	BBDX	21	13	14	14
Publishing, printing and reproduction of recorded media	BBDY	22	9	8	8
Chemicals and chemical products	BAZX	24	48	50	52
Rubber and plastic products	BBDZ	25	19	19	20
Other non-metallic mineral products	BBEA	26	14	14	16
Basic metals	BBEB	27	40	45	41
Fabricated metal products (except machinery and equipment)	BBEC	28	15	14	15
Machinery and equipment not elsewhere classified	BBED	29	38	38	41
Office machinery and computers	BBEE	30	46	49	61
Electrical machinery not elsewhere classified	BBEF	31	39	35	39
Radio, television and communication equipment and apparatus	BBEG	32	44	62	..
Medical, precision and optical instruments, watches and clocks	BBEH	33	46	45	48
Motor vehicles, trailers and semi-trailers	BBEI	34	31	31	31
Other transport equipment	BBEJ	35	46	45	57
Furniture and manufacturing not elsewhere classified	BBEK	36	21	22	24
Total	BBDQ		30	31	35

1 See chapter text.

2 Division 13 (Mining of metal ores) has not been published since 1995. Division 23 (Coke, refined petroleum products and nuclear fuel) and SIC 24610 (Manufacture of explosives) are excluded from the analysis. SIC 27100 (Basic iron and steel and ferro-alloys) is not incorporated in PRODCOM and therefore also does not form part of the analysis.

Source: Office for National Statistics: 01633 456746

19.3 United Kingdom exports: by commodity[1,2]
Seasonally adjusted

£ million

		1998	1999	2000	2001	2002	2003	2004	2005	2006	2007
0. Food and live animals	BOGG	6 286	5 925	5 827	5 491	5 693	6 478	6 462	6 552	6 766	7 390
of which:											
01. Meat and meat preparations	BOGS	746	657	642	428	516	606	667	729	753	865
02. Dairy products and eggs	BQMS	745	689	660	614	625	760	780	718	711	805
04 & 08. Cereals and animal feeding stuffs	BQMT	1 714	1 568	1 604	1 383	1 444	1 681	1 553	1 554	1 586	1 790
05. Vegetables and fruit	BQMU	408	437	403	401	433	475	508	515	586	599
1. Beverages and tobacco	BQMZ	3 930	4 022	4 081	4 139	4 300	4 401	4 116	4 095	4 174	4 395
11. Beverages	BQNB	2 875	3 004	3 065	3 218	3 320	3 478	3 354	3 481	3 714	4 093
12. Tobacco	BQOW	1 055	1 018	1 016	921	980	923	762	614	460	302
2. Crude materials	BQOX	2 267	2 087	2 447	2 422	2 645	3 069	3 566	3 746	4 619	5 177
of which:											
24. Wood, lumber and cork	BQOY	55	66	72	70	81	106	117	131	145	145
25. Pulp and waste paper	BQOZ	47	54	78	81	106	180	244	283	338	415
26. Textile fibres	BQPA	493	447	496	440	472	492	520	516	542	497
28. Metal ores	BQPB	560	518	759	810	928	1 193	1 605	1 713	2 418	2 879
3. Fuels	BOPN	7 513	9 929	17 057	16 386	16 000	16 558	17 885	21 496	25 400	24 767
33. Petroleum and petroleum products	ELBL	7 018	9 123	15 584	14 815	14 321	14 608	16 200	19 794	23 274	22 812
32, 34 & 35. Coal, gas and electricity	BOQI	495	806	1 473	1 571	1 679	1 950	1 685	1 702	2 126	1 955
4. Animal and vegetable oils and fats	BQPI	245	197	156	149	210	266	205	235	271	330
5. Chemicals	ENDG	22 102	23 071	24 992	27 514	28 386	31 373	32 008	33 388	37 162	38 913
of which:											
51. Organic chemicals	BQPJ	4 914	5 494	5 718	6 090	5 698	6 070	6 040	6 702	8 005	7 624
52. Inorganic chemicals	BQPK	1 153	1 137	1 491	1 636	1 367	1 460	1 543	1 555	2 142	2 841
53. Colouring materials	CSCE	1 542	1 534	1 555	1 521	1 583	1 627	1 630	1 635	1 601	1 673
54. Medicinal products	BQPL	5 850	6 279	7 217	9 067	10 103	11 897	12 326	12 320	13 780	14 490
55. Toilet preparations	CSCF	2 446	2 462	2 597	2 714	2 823	3 122	3 105	3 219	3 441	3 699
57 & 58. Plastics	BQQA	3 194	3 144	3 366	3 416	3 526	3 703	3 846	4 298	4 443	4 620
6. Manufactures classified chiefly by material	BQQB	21 243	20 302	22 673	22 781	21 837	23 119	24 458	26 492	27 649	29 397
of which:											
63. Wood and cork manufactures	BQQC	253	278	255	261	270	322	291	255	273	270
64. Paper and paperboard manufactures	BQQD	2 197	2 020	2 096	2 081	2 019	2 097	1 996	2 043	2 013	2 089
65. Textile manufactures	BQQE	3 259	3 020	3 051	3 022	2 847	2 956	2 846	2 647	2 678	2 618
67. Iron and steel	BQQF	3 321	2 576	2 848	2 879	2 916	3 319	4 245	5 183	5 128	6 054
68. Non-ferrous metals	BQQG	2 433	2 130	3 171	3 033	2 552	2 567	3 229	3 862	4 825	5 788
69. Metal manufactures	BQQH	3 591	3 553	3 595	3 853	3 660	3 766	3 856	4 066	4 517	4 636
7. Machinery and transport equipment[3]	BQQI	78 011	78 875	87 812	87 240	84 395	79 650	78 377	89 379	110 346	82 669
71 - 716, 72, 73 & 74. Mechanical machinery	BQQK	22 695	21 888	22 140	24 244	22 704	24 231	23 810	25 795	28 231	28 913
716, 75, 76 & 77. Electrical machinery	BQQL	34 464	36 012	42 681	41 997	38 706	30 651	28 623	37 120	55 314	24 311
78. Road vehicles	BQQM	14 550	15 077	15 604	13 845	16 316	17 474	18 489	19 439	19 324	21 103
79. Other transport equipment	BQQN	6 302	5 898	7 387	7 154	6 669	7 294	7 455	7 025	7 477	8 342
8. Miscellaneous manufactures[3]	BQQO	20 563	20 263	21 206	21 948	21 985	22 543	22 919	25 105	25 958	26 650
of which:											
84. Clothing	CSCN	2 976	2 804	2 722	2 578	2 507	2 708	2 729	2 712	2 875	3 097
85. Footwear	CSCP	535	532	514	484	452	426	419	470	521	538
87 & 88. Scientific and photographic	BQQQ	6 705	6 732	7 333	7 775	7 212	7 281	7 041	7 245	7 339	7 044
9. Other commodities and transactions	BOQL	1 896	1 495	1 685	1 023	1 073	863	881	1 120	1 286	1 169
Total United Kingdom exports	BOKG	164 056	166 166	187 936	189 093	186 524	188 320	190 877	211 608	243 631	220 857

1 See chapter text. The numbers on the left hand side of the table refer to the code numbers of the *Standard International Trade Classification,* Revision 3, which was introduced in January 1988.
2 Balance of payments consistent basis.
3 Sections 7 and 8 are shown by broad economic category in table G2 of the *Monthly Review of External Trade Statistics.*

Source: Office for National Statistics: 020 7533 6064

19.4 United Kingdom imports: by commodity[1,2]
Seasonally adjusted

£ million

		1998	1999	2000	2001	2002	2003	2004	2005	2006	2007
0. Food and live animals	BQQR	13 223	13 336	13 310	14 269	14 874	16 452	17 208	18 593	19 814	21 291
of which:											
01. Meat and meat preparations	BQQS	2 006	2 144	2 366	2 689	2 793	3 267	3 439	3 619	3 800	4 005
02. Dairy products and eggs	BQQT	1 112	1 167	1 165	1 245	1 291	1 501	1 609	1 700	1 808	1 836
04 & 08. Cereals and animal feeding stuffs	BQQU	1 806	1 719	1 762	1 957	1 985	2 219	2 308	2 363	2 497	2 929
05. Vegetables and fruit	BQQV	4 017	4 040	3 894	4 101	4 374	4 766	4 918	5 447	5 783	6 170
1. Beverages and tobacco	BQQW	4 027	4 451	4 350	4 216	4 501	4 735	4 939	5 102	5 199	5 434
11. Beverages	EGAT	2 881	3 064	2 910	2 854	3 028	3 237	3 474	3 625	3 701	3 951
12. Tobacco	EMAI	1 146	1 387	1 440	1 362	1 473	1 498	1 465	1 477	1 498	1 483
2. Crude materials	ENVB	5 076	4 861	5 816	5 921	5 420	5 525	5 718	6 129	7 116	8 668
of which:											
24. Wood, lumber and cork	ENVC	1 100	1 088	1 193	1 168	1 236	1 366	1 337	1 358	1 453	1 805
25. Pulp and waste paper	EQAH	477	510	763	606	488	489	480	477	512	504
26. Textile fibres	EQAP	452	413	412	393	361	337	340	314	298	314
28. Metal ores	EHAA	1 314	1 308	1 811	1 997	1 448	1 430	1 648	1 999	2 672	3 794
3. Fuels	BQAT	4 892	5 428	10 016	10 795	10 279	12 311	17 547	25 921	31 627	31 262
33. Petroleum and petroleum products	ENXO	3 976	4 675	9 048	9 525	9 213	11 232	15 307	21 989	26 706	26 114
32, 34 & 35. Coal, gas and electricity	BPBI	916	753	968	1 270	1 066	1 079	2 240	3 932	4 921	5 148
4. Animal and vegetable oils and fats	EHAB	555	568	491	521	538	614	622	641	771	895
5. Chemicals	ENGA	17 379	18 619	20 633	22 745	23 987	26 139	27 927	29 208	31 727	34 831
of which:											
51. Organic chemicals	EHAC	4 508	4 788	5 374	5 529	5 673	6 102	6 801	7 183	7 692	8 629
52. Inorganic chemicals	EHAE	1 015	1 056	1 046	1 171	1 070	1 094	1 366	1 507	2 123	2 689
53. Colouring materials	CSCR	1 003	956	1 002	975	952	1 003	1 060	1 072	1 090	1 179
54. Medicinal products	EHAF	3 305	4 124	4 714	6 149	7 288	8 189	8 372	8 504	9 158	10 036
55. Toilet preparations	CSCS	1 617	1 774	2 005	2 261	2 499	2 745	2 881	3 035	3 336	3 475
57 & 58. Plastics	EHAG	3 903	3 819	4 144	4 096	4 063	4 403	4 749	5 038	5 409	5 712
6. Manufactures classified chiefly by material	EHAH	27 695	26 930	29 232	30 165	28 735	29 906	32 299	33 469	37 615	39 767
of which:											
63. Wood and cork manufactures	EHAI	1 089	1 145	1 245	1 340	1 436	1 449	1 585	1 505	1 575	1 733
64. Paper and paperboard manufactures	EHAJ	4 504	4 321	4 407	4 864	4 582	4 747	4 841	4 820	5 037	5 243
65. Textile manufactures	EHAK	4 862	4 380	4 365	4 303	4 149	4 089	4 124	3 844	4 018	4 069
67. Iron and steel	EHAL	3 205	2 473	2 731	3 051	3 047	3 237	4 198	4 402	4 981	5 946
68. Non-ferrous metals	EHAM	3 709	2 942	3 711	3 780	3 222	3 320	3 617	3 923	6 185	6 246
69. Metal manufactures	EHAN	3 721	3 789	4 065	4 324	4 501	4 765	4 977	5 355	5 852	6 548
7. Machinery and transport equipment[3]	EHAO	83 300	90 183	102 420	105 386	107 556	101 473	103 883	117 318	140 328	116 258
71 - 716, 72, 73 & 74. Mechanical machinery	EHAQ	17 156	17 313	17 867	18 618	18 901	18 951	19 725	21 848	22 614	25 713
716, 75, 76 & 77. Electrical machinery	EHAR	36 900	42 423	53 631	50 842	49 917	43 656	45 497	55 735	75 587	44 935
78. Road vehicles	EHAS	22 472	24 000	23 117	26 289	28 449	29 921	30 732	31 436	32 674	36 290
79. Other transport equipment	EHAT	6 772	6 447	7 805	9 637	10 289	8 945	7 929	8 299	9 453	9 320
8. Miscellaneous manufactures[3]	EHAU	27 917	29 042	32 798	35 023	36 889	38 168	39 820	42 175	44 919	47 811
of which:											
84. Clothing	CSDR	7 023	7 483	8 495	9 119	9 804	10 323	10 639	11 303	11 847	12 258
85. Footwear	CSDS	1 859	2 041	2 001	2 236	2 365	2 375	2 448	2 563	2 698	2 653
87 & 88. Scientific and photographic	EHAW	6 102	6 170	7 273	7 620	7 044	7 049	7 256	7 414	7 655	7 568
9. Other commodities and transactions	BQAW	1 805	1 799	1 846	1 264	1 450	1 604	1 807	1 841	2 070	2 289
Total United Kingdom imports	BOKH	185 869	195 217	220 912	230 305	234 229	236 927	251 770	280 397	321 186	308 506

1 See chapter text. The numbers on the left hand side of the table refer to the code numbers of the *Standard International Trade Classification*, Revision 3, which was introduced in January 1988.
2 Balance of payments consistent basis.
3 Sections 7 and 8 are shown by broad economic category in table G2 of the *Monthly Review of External Trade Statistics*.

Source: Office for National Statistics: 020 7533 6064

19.5 United Kingdom exports: by area[1,2]
Seasonally adjusted

£ million

		1998	1999	2000	2001	2002	2003	2004	2005	2006	2007
European Union:[3]	LGCK	99 336	101 537	112 459	114 406	114 737	111 286	111 653	121 486	152 353	127 886
EMU members:	QAKW	89 819	92 359	102 138	104 202	103 908	100 631	100 601	109 506	134 778	113 452
Austria	CHMY	1 190	1 168	1 146	1 224	1 265	1 264	1 094	1 332	1 699	1 372
Belgium & Luxembourg	CHNQ	8 445	9 241	10 322	9 893	10 552	11 374	10 511	11 394	15 081	12 150
Finland	CHMZ	1 434	1 354	1 471	1 611	1 442	1 493	1 362	1 514	1 872	1 965
France	ENYL	16 449	16 907	18 577	19 249	18 757	18 885	18 564	19 931	28 692	18 110
Germany	ENYO	20 590	20 464	22 789	23 655	22 064	20 805	21 671	23 025	27 601	24 701
Greece	CHNT	1 070	1 181	1 267	1 156	1 234	1 286	1 418	1 367	1 470	1 353
Irish Republic	CHNS	9 604	10 783	12 372	13 835	15 422	12 224	14 133	16 294	17 479	17 793
Italy	CHNO	8 608	7 831	8 429	8 404	8 506	8 603	8 401	8 790	9 494	9 170
Netherlands	CHNP	12 983	13 632	15 167	14 599	14 011	13 597	12 030	12 716	16 521	15 150
Portugal	CHNU	1 722	1 712	1 660	1 579	1 518	1 453	1 580	1 698	2 374	1 485
Spain	CHNV	7 171	7 526	8 302	8 363	8 490	8 943	9 100	10 677	12 295	10 000
Non-EMU members:[3]	BQIA	9 517	9 178	10 321	10 204	10 829	10 655	11 052	11 980	17 575	14 434
of which:											
Bulgaria	WYUF	81	76	85	122	134	154	155	220	237	204
Czech Rep	FKML	713	733	927	1 075	1 031	1 003	975	1 080	1 526	1 394
Denmark	CHNR	2 057	2 054	2 315	2 267	2 729	2 180	2 042	2 314	3 715	2 198
Hungary	QALC	498	486	613	612	750	856	933	834	855	870
Poland	ERDR	1 213	1 169	1 299	1 297	1 318	1 462	1 413	1 653	2 705	2 388
Romania	WMDB	235	242	381	341	432	509	610	647	637	663
Slovakia	BQHB	103	114	157	203	201	237	224	259	272	381
Sweden	CHNA	4 392	4 035	4 211	3 951	3 873	3 823	4 355	4 588	5 246	4 887
Other Western Europe:	HCJD	7 392	6 244	7 223	6 786	6 334	6 629	7 027	9 730	9 224	9 120
of which:											
Iceland	EPLW	158	159	193	150	131	141	167	179	188	195
Norway	EPLX	2 658	1 999	2 018	1 813	1 696	1 886	1 937	2 211	2 125	2 671
Switzerland	EPLV	2 892	2 768	3 061	3 496	3 080	2 786	2 840	4 985	4 190	3 768
Turkey	EOBA	1 562	1 198	1 800	1 150	1 287	1 638	1 903	2 160	2 426	2 242
North America:	HBZQ	24 091	27 582	33 714	33 408	32 261	32 924	32 750	35 007	36 935	36 320
of which:											
Canada	EOBC	2 147	2 532	3 487	3 203	3 107	3 239	3 339	3 277	3 895	3 259
Mexico	EPJX	516	577	675	681	704	687	629	638	747	792
USA	EOBB	21 082	24 040	29 276	29 244	28 197	28 672	28 576	30 913	32 103	32 109
Other OECD countries:	HCII	6 321	6 728	8 028	7 542	7 469	7 824	8 226	8 577	8 716	8 701
of which:											
Australia	EPMA	2 188	2 155	2 699	2 298	2 114	2 289	2 455	2 580	2 488	2 608
Japan	EOBD	3 127	3 300	3 672	3 673	3 583	3 710	3 862	3 900	4 109	3 832
New Zealand	EPMB	336	324	305	309	311	348	418	415	373	360
South Korea	ERDM	666	949	1 350	1 262	1 461	1 468	1 482	1 677	1 746	1 897
Oil exporting countries:	HDII	7 289	5 524	6 031	6 474	6 229	7 615	7 997	10 851	9 061	9 646
of which:											
Brunei	QALF	247	124	96	59	61	127	67	43	79	864
Dubai	QALI	830	790	966	1 012	940	1 383	2 019	4 657	2 830	1 914
Indonesia	FKMR	369	385	404	313	324	452	398	366	311	287
Kuwait	QATB	325	293	338	359	308	373	354	426	438	446
Nigeria	QATE	454	447	524	686	711	738	773	799	821	1 036
Saudi Arabia	ERDI	2 605	1 481	1 557	1 525	1 388	1 819	1 611	1 559	1 644	1 841
Rest of the World	HCHW	19 627	18 551	20 481	20 477	19 494	22 042	23 224	25 957	27 342	29 184
of which:											
Brazil	FKMO	899	739	775	808	880	825	790	836	918	1 099
China	ERDN	860	1 211	1 468	1 709	1 493	1 924	2 372	2 811	3 265	3 823
Egypt	QALL	505	539	498	452	463	458	667	543	578	681
Hong Kong	ERDG	2 671	2 312	2 673	2 683	2 411	2 481	2 632	3 088	2 864	2 700
India	ERDJ	1 242	1 450	2 058	1 772	1 755	2 284	2 235	2 798	2 695	2 942
Israel	ERDL	1 079	1 295	1 516	1 357	1 428	1 359	1 389	1 352	1 308	1 245
Malaysia	ERDK	677	934	907	1 029	877	1 028	995	1 088	877	965
Pakistan	FKMU	228	221	207	229	240	291	344	461	488	418
Philippines	FKMX	301	239	273	392	352	377	315	279	242	250
Russia	ERDQ	929	532	668	893	981	1 420	1 466	1 869	2 063	2 865
Singapore	ERDH	1 598	1 597	1 625	1 592	1 445	1 582	1 710	2 078	2 318	2 444
South Africa	EPME	1 520	1 281	1 413	1 534	1 597	1 766	1 877	2 073	2 184	2 223
Taiwan	ERDP	867	865	1 015	875	848	897	951	939	911	948
Thailand	ERDO	386	463	582	594	529	572	637	638	567	606

1 See chapter text.
2 Balance of payments consistent basis.
3 Includes Bulgaria and Romania after accession on 1 January 2007.

Source: Office for National Statistics: 020 7533 6064

19.6 United Kingdom imports: by area[1,2]

Seasonally adjusted

£ million

		1998	1999	2000	2001	2002	2003	2004	2005	2006	2007
European Union:[3]	LGDC	105 048	109 622	117 644	126 973	136 931	137 404	142 512	158 363	184 440	168 250
EMU members	QAKX	95 776	99 645	106 146	114 724	123 716	123 224	126 792	139 741	156 338	146 772
Austria	CHNB	1 410	1 453	1 410	1 888	2 396	2 776	2 354	2 461	2 789	2 475
Belgium & Luxembourg	CHNY	9 831	10 156	10 927	12 159	13 201	13 205	13 845	15 155	18 202	15 716
Finland	CHNC	2 327	2 365	2 765	2 965	2 791	2 663	2 336	2 431	3 119	2 559
France	ENYP	17 949	18 410	18 644	20 127	20 798	20 389	20 132	22 184	26 902	21 823
Germany	ENYS	25 086	26 812	28 462	30 192	32 442	33 667	35 380	39 169	42 709	43 944
Greece	CHOB	372	408	459	476	555	613	625	703	796	611
Irish Republic	CHOA	7 801	8 705	10 261	12 141	13 176	9 920	10 133	10 411	10 779	11 390
Italy	CHNW	9 739	9 383	9 514	9 860	10 675	11 481	12 186	12 673	12 790	13 054
Netherlands	CHNX	13 404	13 768	15 380	15 395	16 143	16 692	18 195	20 436	22 301	22 960
Portugal	CHOC	1 790	1 822	1 735	1 625	1 761	1 966	1 928	2 018	3 055	1 480
Spain	CHOD	5 732	5 966	6 141	7 360	9 190	9 247	9 120	11 450	12 156	10 445
Non-EMU members:[3]	BQIB	9 272	9 977	11 498	12 249	13 215	14 180	15 720	18 622	28 102	21 478
of which:											
Bulgaria	WYUT	76	69	85	101	116	124	150	169	208	226
Czech Rep	FKMM	560	580	802	1 097	1 250	1 412	1 291	1 883	2 989	2 918
Denmark	CHNZ	2 154	2 341	2 630	2 922	3 595	3 399	3 357	4 393	6 444	3 446
Hungary	QALD	544	668	683	710	846	1 120	1 579	1 860	2 351	2 365
Poland	ERED	668	676	905	1 166	1 265	1 545	1 834	2 320	3 625	3 609
Romania	WMDC	228	253	336	448	522	679	786	803	862	909
Slovakia	BQHC	74	102	136	177	211	259	261	370	815	1 258
Sweden	CHND	4 360	4 648	4 951	4 671	4 330	4 568	5 118	5 463	5 992	5 257
Other Western Europe:	HBTS	9 701	10 554	13 040	12 240	12 523	13 331	15 726	20 072	23 445	24 268
of which:											
Iceland	EPMW	251	282	365	281	289	296	355	346	402	414
Norway	EPMX	3 440	3 546	5 563	5 523	5 258	6 423	8 479	12 078	14 472	14 264
Switzerland	EPMV	4 755	5 341	5 485	4 544	4 595	3 759	3 439	3 882	4 376	4 726
Turkey	EOBU	1 103	1 204	1 450	1 669	2 164	2 619	3 246	3 511	3 950	4 615
North America:	HCRB	27 815	28 035	33 460	34 617	29 811	27 480	27 087	27 128	31 439	32 229
of which:											
Canada	EOBW	2 519	3 026	4 009	3 664	3 563	3 664	4 187	4 155	4 987	5 737
Mexico	EPJY	366	395	613	680	505	490	411	446	449	576
USA	EOBV	24 785	24 360	28 416	29 345	25 149	22 857	22 067	22 184	25 723	25 626
Other OECD countries:	HDJQ	13 205	13 805	15 717	14 154	13 017	12 989	13 641	14 426	13 710	13 759
of which:											
Australia	EPNA	1 363	1 338	1 543	1 776	1 688	1 789	1 868	2 100	2 119	2 228
Japan	EOBX	9 124	9 118	10 214	9 080	8 079	8 085	8 106	8 670	7 902	7 824
New Zealand	EPNB	517	565	544	542	522	552	584	592	604	659
South Korea	ERDY	2 201	2 784	3 416	2 756	2 728	2 563	3 083	3 064	3 085	3 048
Oil exporting countries:	HCPC	3 201	3 228	4 258	3 969	3 780	3 923	4 865	6 017	7 011	6 388
of which:											
Brunei	QALG	161	66	95	35	33	51	63	25	71	57
Dubai	QALJ	337	433	401	396	499	722	578	643	680	663
Indonesia	FKMS	854	931	1 081	1 128	1 006	875	917	839	960	926
Kuwait	QATC	164	121	314	296	271	313	396	367	743	696
Nigeria	QATF	121	112	89	65	90	83	106	152	206	271
Saudi Arabia	ERDU	791	783	977	933	677	715	1 158	1 714	1 234	820
Rest of the World	HCIF	26 899	29 973	36 793	38 352	38 167	41 800	47 939	54 391	61 141	63 612
of which:											
Brazil	FKMP	883	910	1 114	1 279	1 365	1 477	1 547	1 739	1 911	2 050
China	ERDZ	2 816	3 384	4 826	5 741	6 726	8 342	10 405	12 963	15 292	18 613
Egypt	QALM	277	255	411	406	416	432	496	350	665	538
Hong Kong	ERDS	4 391	4 909	5 917	5 754	5 561	5 500	5 771	6 601	7 366	6 896
India	ERDV	1 382	1 426	1 651	1 816	1 804	2 093	2 290	2 783	3 133	3 785
Israel	ERDX	875	996	1 025	939	880	861	923	1 002	967	1 040
Malaysia	ERDW	1 892	1 961	2 288	1 939	1 731	1 867	2 024	1 814	1 902	1 674
Pakistan	FKMV	340	318	363	421	472	519	554	487	512	511
Philippines	FKMY	855	983	1 155	1 155	944	713	657	712	743	714
Russia	EREC	1 406	1 324	1 496	2 047	1 950	2 454	3 511	5 009	5 760	5 224
Singapore	ERDT	2 343	2 348	2 395	2 067	1 959	2 672	3 382	3 829	3 771	4 221
South Africa	EPNE	1 351	1 636	2 553	2 841	2 685	2 949	3 277	3 938	3 919	3 041
Taiwan	EREB	2 217	2 626	3 561	2 784	2 385	2 198	2 344	2 225	2 349	2 402
Thailand	EREA	1 264	1 291	1 602	1 607	1 550	1 646	1 762	1 719	1 929	1 999

1 See chapter text.
2 Balance of payments consistent basis.
3 Includes Bulgaria and Romania after accession on 1 January 2007.

Source: Office for National Statistics: 020 7533 6064

19.7 Services supplied (exports) and purchased (imports)[1,2]: 2005

£ million

	Exports	Imports	Balances
Agricultural,Mining and On-site Processing services			
Agricultural	15	15	-
Mining	66	27	39
Waste treatment and depollution	10	19	-8
Other on-site processing services	166	39	127
Business and Professional services			
Accountancy,auditing, bookkeeping and tax consul	1 037	328	709
Advertising	1 987	914	1 073
Management consulting	1 061	370	691
Public relations services	105	31	74
Recruitment	342	151	191
Other Business Management	628	736	-108
Legal Services	2 168	429	1 739
Market research and public opinion polling	417	186	231
Operational leasing services	313	350	-36
Procurement	113	378	-265
Property management	98	31	67
Research and development	4 648	2 021	2 627
Services between related enterprises	4 749	2 899	1 850
Other business and professional services	1 108	400	708
Communications services			
Postal and courier	171	125	46
Telecommunications	1 916	1 825	90
Computer services			
Computer	4 002	1 652	2 350
Information services			
News agency services	772	138	633
Publishing services	284	107	177
Other information provision services	543	236	308
Construction Goods and Services			
Construction in the UK	131	363	-231
Construction outside the UK	538	277	262
Financial services			
Financial	5 896	1 205	4 691
Insurance Services			
Auxiliary services	1 245	47	1 198
Freight Insurance - Claims	..		..
Freigh Insurance - Premiums		11	-11
Life insurance and pension funding - Claims	..		..
Life insurance and pension funding - Premiums		10	-10
Reinsurance - Claims	-		-
Reinsurance - Premiums		20	-20
Other Direct insurance - Claims	16		16
Other Direct insurance - Premiums		141	-141
Merchanting and Other Trade related Services			
Merchanting	982		982
Other trade related services	1 925	409	1 516
Personal, Cultural and Recreational Services			
Audio-Visual and related services	265	43	221
Health services	19	8	11
Training and educational services	71	14	57
Other personal, cultural and recreational services	302	180	122
Royalties and Licenses			
Use of Franchise and similar rights fees	3 948	1 959	1 989
Other royalties and license fees	2 394	1 846	548
Purchases and sales of franchises and similar right	125	217	-92
Purchases and sales of other royalties and licenses	212	377	-164
Technical services			
Architectural	95	5	90
Engineering	3 092	1 067	2 025
Surveying	226	89	138
Other technical services	1 616	556	1 061
Other Trade in Services			
Other Trade in services	1 888	1 202	687
World Total	**51 710**	**23 451**	**28 259**

1 See chapter text.
2 Due to rounding, the sum of constituent items may not always equal the total
  shown. Data excludes the following industries: , Film and TV, Travel and
  Transport, Public Sector (including Education) and Law Society members.
3 (-) Denotes nil or less than £500,000.
4 (..) Denotes disclosive data.

Source: Office for National Statistics: 01633 456644

19.8 International trade in services:[1,2] by country, 2005

£ million

	Exports	Imports	Balances
European Union			
Austria	562	166	396
Belgium	1 128	539	589
Cyprus	69	54	15
Czech Republic	127	73	54
Denmark	414	140	274
Estonia	11	3	8
Finland	495	138	357
France	2 184	2 432	-248
Germany	3 631	2 326	1 305
Greece	323	78	244
Hungary	288	59	230
Irish Republic	3 539	1 088	2 451
Italy	1 137	821	316
Latvia	11	7	5
Lithuania	18	10	8
Luxembourg	585	103	482
Malta	19	10	9
Netherlands	3 329	971	2 358
Poland	127	70	57
Portugal	251	67	184
Slovakia	23	9	14
Slovenia	17	6	10
Spain	973	586	387
Sweden	617	724	-107
EU Institutions	15	1	14
Total European Union	**19892**	**10480**	**9412**
EFTA			
Iceland	42	5	37
Liechtenstein	30	5	26
Norway	696	267	429
Switzerland	3 040	864	2 176
Total EFTA	**3 808**	**1 141**	**2 667**
Other European countries			
Russia	319	130	189
Channel Islands	480	85	395
Isle of Man	56	7	49
Turkey	124	39	84
Rest of Europe	275	151	124
Europe Unallocated	1 776	986	790
Total Europe	**26 730**	**13 019**	**13 711**
Africa			
Nigeria	191	29	162
South Africa	339	115	225
Rest of Africa	590	221	369
Africa Unallocated	84	27	57
Total Africa	**1 204**	**392**	**812**
America			
Brazil	75	66	9
Canada	590	234	356
Mexico	118	18	101
USA	11 566	5 686	5 880
Rest of America	2 285	424	1 860
America Unallocated	213	95	117
Total America	**14 846**	**6 523**	**8 323**

19.8 International trade in services:[1,2] by country, 2005
continued

£ million

	Exports	Imports	Balances
Asia			
China	288	106	182
Hong Kong	346	182	164
India	315	278	36
Indonesia	76	33	43
Israel	267	116	150
Japan	1 542	668	874
Malaysia	139	81	58
Pakistan	74	33	41
Phillippines	27	21	6
Saudi Arabia	1 131	444	687
Singapore	1 783	276	1 507
South Korea	223	33	190
Taiwan	144	133	11
Thailand	71	51	20
Rest of Asia	1 344	610	734
Asia Unallocated	189	60	129
Total Asia	**7 959**	**3 126**	**4 833**
Australiasia and Oceania			
Australia	583	231	353
New Zealand	81	28	53
Rest of Australia and Oceania	52	21	32
Oceania Unallocated	5	5	-
Total Australasia and Oceania	**722**	**284**	**438**
Rest of World Unallocated and International orgainisations	249	106	143
World Total	**51 710**	**23 451**	**28 259**
Economic Zones			
OECD	37 685	18 453	19 232
NAFTA	11 606	5 927	5 679
Central and Eastern Europe	797	317	480
OPEC	2 142	731	1 411
ASEAN	2 117	471	1 646
CIS	823	463	361
NICs1	2 496	624	1 872
Offshore Financial centres	4 997	967	4 030
ACP	1 032	500	532

1 Due to rounding, the sum of constituent items may not always equal the total shown.
2 Data excludes the following industries: Financial, Film and TV, Travel and Transport, Public Sector (including Education) and Law Society Members
3 (-) Denotes nil or less than £500,000.

Source: Office for National Statistics: 01633 456644

327

19.9 Summary of balance of payments,[1] 2006
United Kingdom

£ million

	Credits	Debits
1. Current account		
A. Goods and services	370 788	417 320
1. Goods	243 631	321 186
2. Services	127 157	96 134
2.1. Transportation	16 704	19 426
2.2. Travel	18 313	34 291
2.3. Communications	4 259	3 969
2.4. Construction	658	529
2.5. Insurance	3 525	960
2.6. Financial	28 420	5 845
2.7. Computer and information	6 489	2 658
2.8. Royalties and licence fees	7 381	5 407
2.9. Other business	34 733	18 884
2.10. Personal, cultural and recreational	2 031	746
2.11. Government	2 073	2 677
B. Income	235 201	227 441
1. Compensation of employees	1 058	1 803
2. Investment income	234 143	225 638
2.1 Direct investment	84 339	52 013
2.2 Portfolio investment	55 114	56 885
2.3 Other investment (including earnings on reserve assets)	94 690	116 740
C. Current transfers	18 346	30 299
1. General government	4 351	13 882
2. Other sectors	13 995	16 417
Total current account	**624 335**	**675 060**
2. Capital and financial accounts		
A. Capital account	3 818	2 988
1. Capital transfers	3 393	2 358
2. Acquisition/disposal of non-produced, non-financial assets	425	630
B. Financial account	716 526	671 726
1. Direct investment	80 539	47 155
Abroad		47 155
1.1. Equity capital		25 647
1.2. Reinvested earnings		47 875
1.3. Other capital[2]		−26 287
In United Kingdom	80 539	
1.1. Equity capital	56 005	
1.2. Reinvested earnings	22 930	
1.3. Other capital[3]	1 604	
2. Portfolio investment	157 622	198 456
Assets		198 456
2.1. Equity securities		18 571
2.2. Debt securities		179 885
Liabilities	157 622	
2.1. Equity securities	−5 563	
2.2. Debt securities	163 185	
3. Financial derivatives (net)		−7 449
4. Other investment	478 365	433 990
Assets		433 990
4.1 Trade credits		1 361
4.2 Loans		117 376
4.3 Currency and deposits		315 542
4.4 Other assets		−289
Liabilities	478 365	
4.1. Trade credits	−	
4.2. Loans	142 906	
4.3. Currency and deposits	334 238	
4.4. Other liabilities	1 221	
5. Reserve assets		−426
5.1. Monetary gold		−4
5.2. Special drawing rights		51
5.3. Reserve position in the IMF		−225
5.4. Foreign exchange		62
Total capital and financial accounts	**720 344**	**674 714**
Total current, capital and financial accounts	**1 344 679**	**1 349 774**
Net errors and omissions	5 072	

1 See chapter text.
2 Other capital transaction on direct investment abroad represents claims on affiliated enterprises less liabilities to affiliated enterprises
3 Other capital transactions on direct investment in the United Kingdom represents liabilities to direct investors less claims on direct investors

Source: Office for National Statistics

19.10 Summary of balance of payments: balances (credits less debits)[1]
United Kingdom

£ million

			Current account									
	Trade in goods	Trade in services	Total goods and services	Compensation of employees	Investment income	Total income	Current transfers	Current balance	Current balance as % of GDP[2]	Capital account	Financial account	Net errors & omissions
	LQCT	KTMS	KTMY	KTMP	HMBM	HMBP	KTNF	HBOG	AA6H	FKMJ	HBNT	HHDH
1953	−244	123	−121	−25	207	182	143	204	1.2	−13	−177	−14
1954	−210	115	−95	−27	227	200	55	160	0.9	−13	−174	27
1955	−315	42	−273	−27	149	122	43	−108	−0.6	−15	34	89
1956	50	26	76	−30	203	173	2	251	1.2	−13	−250	12
1957	−29	121	92	−32	223	191	−5	278	1.3	−13	−313	48
1958	34	119	153	−34	261	227	4	384	1.7	−10	−411	37
1959	−116	118	2	−37	233	196	−	198	0.8	−5	−68	−125
1960	−404	39	−365	−35	201	166	−6	−205	−0.8	−6	−7	218
1961	−144	51	−93	−35	223	188	−9	86	0.3	−12	23	−97
1962	−104	50	−54	−37	301	264	−14	196	0.7	−12	−195	11
1963	−123	4	−119	−38	364	326	−37	170	0.6	−16	−30	−124
1964	−551	−34	−585	−33	365	332	−74	−327	−1.0	−17	392	−48
1965	−263	−66	−329	−34	405	371	−75	−33	−0.1	−18	49	2
1966	−111	44	−67	−39	358	319	−91	161	0.4	−19	22	−164
1967	−601	157	−444	−39	354	315	−118	−247	−0.6	−25	179	93
1968	−708	341	−367	−48	303	255	−119	−231	−0.5	−26	688	−431
1969	−214	392	178	−47	468	421	−109	490	1.0	−23	−794	327
1970	−18	455	437	−56	527	471	−89	819	1.6	−22	−818	21
1971	205	590	795	−63	481	418	−90	1 123	2.0	−23	−1 330	230
1972	−736	665	−71	−52	407	355	−142	142	0.2	−35	477	−584
1973	−2 573	803	−1 770	−68	1 074	1 006	−336	−1 100	−1.5	−39	1 031	108
1974	−5 241	1 118	−4 123	−92	1 184	1 092	−302	−3 333	−4.0	−34	3 185	182
1975	−3 245	1 447	−1 798	−102	518	416	−313	−1 695	−1.6	−36	1 569	162
1976	−3 930	2 532	−1 398	−140	1 100	960	−534	−972	−0.8	−12	507	477
1977	−2 271	3 306	1 035	−152	−280	−432	−889	−286	−0.2	11	−3 286	3 561
1978	−1 534	3 777	2 243	−140	138	−2	−1 420	821	0.5	−79	−2 655	1 913
1979	−3 326	4 076	750	−130	155	25	−1 777	−1 002	−0.5	−103	864	241
1980	1 329	3 829	5 158	−82	−1 683	−1 765	−1 653	1 740	0.8	−4	−2 157	421
1981	3 238	3 951	7 189	−66	−1 058	−1 124	−1 219	4 846	1.9	−79	−5 312	545
1982	1 879	3 198	5 077	−95	−1 273	−1 368	−1 476	2 233	0.8	6	−1 233	−1 006
1983	−1 618	4 076	2 458	−89	280	191	−1 391	1 258	0.4	75	−3 287	1 954
1984	−5 409	4 491	−918	−94	1 284	1 190	−1 566	−1 294	−0.4	107	−7 130	8 317
1985	−3 416	6 767	3 351	−120	−877	−997	−2 924	−570	−0.2	185	−1 657	2 042
1986	−9 617	6 403	−3 214	−156	1 850	1 694	−2 094	−3 614	−0.9	135	−122	3 601
1987	−11 698	6 813	−4 885	−174	1 091	917	−3 570	−7 538	−1.8	333	10 764	−3 559
1988	−21 553	4 450	−17 103	−64	817	753	−3 500	−19 850	−4.2	235	17 201	2 414
1989	−24 724	3 643	−21 081	−138	−654	−792	−4 448	−26 321	−5.1	270	18 001	8 050
1990	−18 707	4 337	−14 370	−110	−2 869	−2 979	−4 932	−22 281	−4.0	497	15 083	6 701
1991	−10 223	4 102	−6 121	−63	−3 244	−3 307	−1 231	−10 659	−1.8	290	5 269	5 100
1992	−13 050	5 602	−7 448	−49	177	128	−5 534	−12 854	−2.1	421	5 090	7 343
1993	−13 066	6 741	−6 325	35	−226	−191	−5 243	−11 759	−1.8	309	11 332	118
1994	−11 126	6 509	−4 617	−170	3 518	3 348	−5 369	−6 638	−1.0	33	2 126	4 479
1995	−12 023	8 957	−3 066	−296	2 460	2 164	−7 574	−8 476	−1.2	533	2 552	5 391
1996	−13 722	11 204	−2 518	93	463	556	−4 755	−6 717	−0.9	1 260	2 811	2 646
1997	−12 342	14 106	1 764	83	3 231	3 314	−5 918	−840	−0.1	958	−8 771	8 653
1998	−21 813	14 672	−7 141	−10	12 330	12 320	−8 374	−3 195	−0.4	489	9 922	−7 216
1999	−29 051	13 597	−15 454	201	1 069	1 270	−7 533	−21 717	−2.4	747	21 416	−446
2000	−32 976	13 615	−19 361	150	4 390	4 540	−10 012	−24 833	−2.6	1 703	12 604	10 526
2001	−41 212	14 423	−26 789	66	11 598	11 664	−6 759	−21 884	−2.2	1 318	17 503	3 063
2002	−47 705	16 830	−30 875	67	23 376	23 443	−9 081	−16 513	−1.6	932	7 202	8 379
2003	−48 607	19 162	−29 445	59	24 587	24 646	−10 122	−14 921	−1.3	1 466	20 507	−7 052
2004	−60 893	25 918	−34 975	71	26 525	26 596	−10 949	−19 328	−1.6	2 063	5 641	11 624
2005	−68 789	24 611	−44 178	−610	25 814	25 204	−12 011	−30 985	−2.5	1 491	33 954	−4 460
2006	−77 555	31 023	−46 532	−745	8 505	7 760	−11 953	−50 725	−3.9	853	44 800	5 072
2007	−87 649	38 450	−49 199	−622	5 902	5 280	−13 876	−57 795	−4.2	2 459	61 988	−6 652

1 See chapter text.
2 Using series YBHA: GDP at current market prices.

Source: Office for National Statistics

19.11 Balance of payments:[1] current account
United Kingdom

£ million

		1997	1998	1999	2000	2001	2002	2003	2004	2005	2006	2007
Credits												
Exports of goods and services												
Exports of goods	LQAD	171 923	164 056	166 166	187 936	189 093	186 524	188 320	190 877	211 608	243 631	220 857
Exports of services	KTMQ	62 096	67 978	73 616	79 666	84 047	89 987	97 077	107 817	115 182	127 157	138 424
Total exports of goods and services	KTMW	234 019	232 034	239 782	267 602	273 140	276 511	285 397	298 694	326 790	370 788	359 281
Income												
Compensation of employees	KTMN	1 007	840	960	1 032	1 087	1 121	1 116	1 171	974	1 058	1 105
Investment income	HMBN	95 435	103 388	101 952	134 114	139 848	123 505	124 881	141 030	186 259	234 143	281 674
Total income	HMBQ	96 442	104 228	102 912	135 146	140 935	124 626	125 997	142 201	187 233	235 201	282 779
Current transfers												
General government	FJUM	2 173	1 767	3 542	2 465	4 991	3 663	3 968	4 000	4 236	4 351	4 197
Other sectors	FJUN	10 898	10 597	9 678	8 076	9 453	8 572	8 235	8 917	13 021	13 995	11 405
Total current transfers	KTND	13 071	12 364	13 220	10 541	14 444	12 235	12 203	12 917	17 257	18 346	15 602
Total	HBOE	343 532	348 626	355 914	413 289	428 519	413 372	423 597	453 812	531 280	624 335	657 662
Debits												
Imports of goods and services												
Imports of goods	LQBL	184 265	185 869	195 217	220 912	230 305	234 229	236 927	251 770	280 397	321 186	308 506
Imports of services	KTMR	47 990	53 306	60 019	66 051	69 624	73 157	77 915	81 899	90 571	96 134	99 974
Total imports of goods and services	KTMX	232 255	239 175	255 236	286 963	299 929	307 386	314 842	333 669	370 968	417 320	408 480
Income												
Compensation of employees	KTMO	924	850	759	882	1 021	1 054	1 057	1 100	1 584	1 803	1 727
Investment income	HMBO	92 204	91 058	100 883	129 724	128 250	100 129	100 294	114 505	160 445	225 638	275 772
Total income	HMBR	93 128	91 908	101 642	130 606	129 271	101 183	101 351	115 605	162 029	227 441	277 499
Current transfers												
General government	FJUO	5 260	6 787	7 482	8 015	7 584	9 296	10 944	12 304	13 663	13 882	14 228
Other sectors	FJUP	13 729	13 951	13 271	12 538	13 619	12 020	11 381	11 562	15 605	16 417	15 250
Total current transfers	KTNE	18 989	20 738	20 753	20 553	21 203	21 316	22 325	23 866	29 268	30 299	29 478
Total	HBOF	344 372	351 821	377 631	438 122	450 403	429 885	438 518	473 140	562 265	675 060	715 457
Balances												
Trade in goods and services												
Trade in goods	LQCT	−12 342	−21 813	−29 051	−32 976	−41 212	−47 705	−48 607	−60 893	−68 789	−77 555	−87 649
Trade in services	KTMS	14 106	14 672	13 597	13 615	14 423	16 830	19 162	25 918	24 611	31 023	38 450
Total trade in goods and services	KTMY	1 764	−7 141	−15 454	−19 361	−26 789	−30 875	−29 445	−34 975	−44 178	−46 532	−49 199
Income												
Compensation of employees	KTMP	83	−10	201	150	66	67	59	71	−610	−745	−622
Investment income	HMBM	3 231	12 330	1 069	4 390	11 598	23 376	24 587	26 525	25 814	8 505	5 902
Total income	HMBP	3 314	12 320	1 270	4 540	11 664	23 443	24 646	26 596	25 204	7 760	5 280
Current transfers												
General government	FJUQ	−3 087	−5 020	−3 940	−5 550	−2 593	−5 633	−6 976	−8 304	−9 427	−9 531	−10 031
Other sectors	FJUR	−2 831	−3 354	−3 593	−4 462	−4 166	−3 448	−3 146	−2 645	−2 584	−2 422	−3 845
Total current transfers	KTNF	−5 918	−8 374	−7 533	−10 012	−6 759	−9 081	−10 122	−10 949	−12 011	−11 953	−13 876
Total (Current balance)	HBOG	−840	−3 195	−21 717	−24 833	−21 884	−16 513	−14 921	−19 328	−30 985	−50 725	−57 795

1 See chapter text.

Source: Office for National Statistics

19.12 Balance of payments:[1] summary of international investment position, financial account and investment income

United Kingdom

£ billion

		1997	1998	1999	2000	2001	2002	2003	2004	2005	2006	2007
Investment abroad												
International investment position												
Direct investment	HBWD	232.4	309.8	438.3	618.8	616.9	637.2	691.1	689.0	705.9	733.6	851.9
Portfolio investment	HHZZ	651.0	703.8	838.3	906.1	937.4	844.0	935.8	1 092.3	1 374.3	1 599.9	1 808.4
Other investment	HLXV	1 070.4	1 107.7	1 129.7	1 427.5	1 573.1	1 635.8	1 885.1	2 156.2	2 745.3	2 947.3	3 759.0
Reserve assets	LTEB	22.8	23.3	22.2	28.8	25.6	25.5	23.8	23.3	24.7	22.9	26.7
Total	HBQA	1 976.5	2 144.7	2 428.5	2 981.2	3 153.1	3 142.4	3 535.8	3 960.7	4 850.3	5 303.6	6 445.9
Financial account transactions												
Direct investment	-HJYP	37.3	73.8	125.6	155.6	42.8	35.0	40.9	53.8	44.0	47.2	114.9
Portfolio investment	-HHZC	51.9	32.1	21.4	65.6	86.6	1.0	36.3	140.9	160.3	198.5	134.2
Financial derivatives (net)	-ZPNN	-1.2	3.0	-2.7	-1.6	-8.4	-1.0	5.4	7.9	-9.6	-7.4	17.5
Other investment	-XBMM	169.4	14.9	59.6	276.0	174.1	97.2	255.9	325.6	505.0	434.0	756.3
Reserve assets	-LTCV	-2.4	-0.2	-0.6	3.9	-3.1	-0.5	-1.6	0.2	0.7	-0.4	..
Total	-HBNR	255.1	123.6	203.2	499.5	292.0	131.8	336.9	528.3	700.5	671.7	1 024.1
Investment income												
Direct investment	HJYW	29.5	29.9	33.1	45.0	46.7	51.5	55.1	64.4	79.2	84.3	86.7
Portfolio investment	HLYX	23.8	29.3	25.9	33.0	34.9	32.5	32.5	36.7	45.4	55.1	64.3
Other investment	AIOP	40.8	43.0	41.8	55.1	57.3	38.7	36.4	39.2	61.0	94.0	130.1
Reserve assets	HHCB	1.4	1.1	1.2	1.0	1.0	0.8	0.8	0.7	0.7	0.6	0.6
Total	HMBN	95.4	103.4	102.0	134.1	139.8	123.5	124.9	141.0	186.3	234.1	281.7
Investment in the UK												
International investment position												
Direct investment	HBWI	173.7	213.6	250.2	310.4	363.5	340.6	355.5	384.4	494.2	577.4	642.9
Portfolio investment	HLXW	583.3	692.7	828.8	998.2	958.5	892.3	1 047.3	1 177.8	1 426.7	1 701.1	1 878.9
Other investment	HLYD	1 274.3	1 355.0	1 403.9	1 696.4	1 889.6	1 945.8	2 177.1	2 509.4	3 108.0	3 369.0	4 275.3
Total	HBQB	2 031.3	2 261.4	2 482.9	3 005.0	3 211.5	3 178.7	3 579.9	4 071.6	5 028.9	5 647.5	6 797.2
Financial account transactions												
Direct investment	HJYU	22.9	45.1	55.1	80.6	37.3	16.8	16.8	42.4	97.8	80.5	92.9
Portfolio investment	HHZF	26.8	20.9	114.1	164.5	48.1	51.0	95.2	87.2	130.9	157.6	189.6
Other investment	XBMN	196.7	67.6	55.5	267.0	224.0	71.2	245.4	404.3	505.7	478.4	803.5
Total	HBNS	246.4	133.5	224.6	512.1	309.5	139.0	357.4	534.0	734.4	716.5	1 086.1
Investment income												
Direct investment	HJYX	14.9	8.6	17.0	27.4	21.4	16.0	21.9	27.9	36.2	52.0	49.2
Portfolio investment	HLZC	26.5	29.5	31.1	31.0	34.5	32.1	31.6	36.4	46.9	56.9	65.9
Other investment	HLZN	50.8	53.0	52.8	71.3	72.3	52.1	46.8	50.2	77.3	116.7	160.7
Total	HMBO	92.2	91.1	100.9	129.7	128.3	100.1	100.3	114.5	160.4	225.6	275.8
Net investment												
International investment position												
Direct investment	HBWQ	58.6	96.2	188.1	308.4	253.5	296.6	335.6	304.6	211.7	156.2	208.9
Portfolio investment	CGNH	67.7	11.1	9.5	-92.2	-21.1	-48.3	-111.5	-85.5	-52.4	-101.2	-70.5
Other investment	CGNG	-204.0	-247.3	-274.2	-268.9	-316.5	-310.0	-292.0	-353.2	-362.7	-421.7	-516.4
Reserve assets	LTEB	22.8	23.3	22.2	28.8	25.6	25.5	23.8	23.3	24.7	22.9	26.7
Net investment position	HBQC	-54.8	-116.7	-54.4	-23.9	-58.4	-36.3	-44.1	-110.9	-178.7	-343.8	-351.3
Financial account transactions												
Direct investment	HJYV	-14.4	-28.7	-70.5	-75.0	-5.5	-18.3	-24.1	-11.4	53.8	33.4	-21.9
Portfolio investment	HHZD	-25.2	-11.2	92.7	99.0	-38.4	50.0	59.0	-53.6	-29.5	-40.8	55.4
Financial derivatives	ZPNN	1.2	-3.0	2.7	1.6	8.4	1.0	-5.4	-7.9	9.6	7.4	-17.5
Other investment	HHYR	27.3	52.8	-4.1	-9.0	49.9	-26.0	-10.5	78.7	0.7	44.4	47.2
Reserve assets	LTCV	2.4	0.2	0.6	-3.9	3.1	0.5	1.6	-0.2	-0.7	0.4	..
Net transactions	HBNT	-8.8	9.9	21.4	12.6	17.5	7.2	20.5	5.6	34.0	44.8	62.0
Investment income												
Direct investment	HJYE	14.6	21.3	16.1	17.6	25.3	35.5	33.2	36.5	43.0	32.3	37.5
Portfolio investment	HLZX	-2.7	-0.2	-5.2	2.0	0.4	0.4	0.9	0.3	-1.6	-1.8	-1.7
Other investment	CGNA	-10.0	-10.0	-11.0	-16.2	-15.1	-13.3	-10.3	-11.0	-16.3	-22.7	-30.5
Reserve assets	HHCB	1.4	1.1	1.2	1.0	1.0	0.8	0.8	0.7	0.7	0.6	0.6
Net earnings	HMBM	3.2	12.3	1.1	4.4	11.6	23.4	24.6	26.5	25.8	8.5	5.9

1 See chapter text.

Source: Office for National Statistics

19.13 Net outward foreign direct investment by United Kingdom companies:[1,2] by area and main country

£ million

		2002	2003	2004	2005	2006
Europe	GQBX	27 300	16 600	10 814	12 105	15 965
EU25	DG7S	28 865	13 339	11 900	13 217	3 577
Austria	CBJD	797	165	1 322	−301	−107
Belgium	HIIL	1 046	−1 241	−544	970	−4 370
Cyprus	DG8D	−79	−53	18	69	98
Czech Republic	DG8O	49	142	23	24	−162
Denmark	CAUW	543	−53	569	391	1 547
Estonia	DG8E	5	4	21	2	3
Finland	CBJE	1 124	99	−37	707	106
France	CAUX	4 112	6 627	793	3 138	224
Germany	CAUY	8 473	1 552	−366	−479	3 147
Greece	CAUZ	−65	229	−253	63	14
Hungary	DG8F	163	527	336	1 821	29
Irish Republic	CAVA	1 674	985	3 325	−1 181	5 114
Italy	CAVB	572	500	667	191	−420
Latvia	DG8G	1	..	1	−1	5
Lithuania	DG8H	..	..	1	−4	..
Luxembourg	HIIM	−2 046	1 313	−1 022	−1 213	−14 664
Malta	DG8I	..	58	178	142	..
Netherlands	CAVC	13 152	728	4 805	4 821	2 195
Poland	DG8J	431	4	182	150	464
Portugal	CAVD	88	308	444	603	336
Slovakia	DG8K	−22	−11	18	21	18
Slovenia	DG8L	..	37	−5	−5	14
Spain	CAVE	288	626	1 131	564	3 130
Sweden	CBJG	−35	794	299	2 732	6 438
EFTA	CAVG	994	2 313	−6 667	547	7 011
of which						
Norway	CBJF	−329	−274	367	−831	104
Switzerland	CBJH	1 329	2 591	−7 007	1 330	6 946
Other European Countries	DG8M	−2 559	948	5 582	−1 658	5 377
of which						
Russia	GLAA	108	2 030	1 831	349	−17
UK offshore islands	GLAC	−1 249	−1 031	3 528	−2 341	4 371
The Americas	GQBZ	−5 150	15 959	24 321	20 689	21 175
of which						
Bermuda	CBKZ	−4 371	−2 613	6 242	653	908
Brazil	CBLA	17	786	386	48	356
Canada	CAVK	536	2 521	1 143	3 372	8 211
Chile	GQCA	1 021	290	675	790	25
Colombia	GQCB	−385	78	225	−687	315
Mexico	GLAD	939	261	1 386	168	334
Panama	GLAE	..	58	12	27	7
USA	CAVJ	−984	19 300	9 732	15 041	259
Asia	GQCI	5 538	3 601	7 689	5 399	8 327
Near and Middle East Countries	CBKF	376	82	486	398	1 368
of which						
Gulf Arabian countries[3]	GQCC	369	−85	293	577	483
Other Asian Countries	GQCD	5 162	3 518	7 203	5 001	6 958
of which						
China	HIIN	757	309	539	598	363
Hong Kong	CAVN	1 186	1 285	5 303	1 547	1 992
India	GLAF	276	193	274	616	282
Indonesia	GLAG	70	481	−289	−116	246
Japan	CAVM	388	338	37	247	433
Malaysia	CBKN	334	277	428	244	248
Singapore	CBKQ	1 619	−449	−161	−508	2 587
South Korea	GLAH	174	332	278	2 247	670
Thailand	GLAI	−55	155	181	228	525
Australasia and Oceania	GQCE	3 677	−1 524	1 026	423	3 631
of which						
Australia	CBJO	3 322	−492	408	444	3 243
New Zealand	CBJP	337	−1 017	258	−56	405
Africa	GQCF	2 196	3 454	5 863	5 843	293
of which						
Kenya	GLAJ	32	58	47	73	62
Nigeria	CBJY	220	19	−44	−108	40
South Africa	CAVO	2 265	2 222	3 840	4 368	1 458
Zimbabwe	CBKD	33	37	91	18	10
World Total	CDQD	33 561	38 088	49 713	44 458	49 390
OECD	GQCG	36 096	37 030	18 355	35 305	24 045
Central and Eastern Europe[4]	GQCH	654	156	36	158	76

1 See chapter text. Net investment includes re-invested earnings.
2 Minus sign indicates net disinvestment abroad.
3 Includes Abu Dhabi, Bahrain, Dubai, Iraq, Kuwait, Oman, Other Gulf States, Qatar, Saudi Arabia and Yemen.

4 From 2003 includes Albania, Bosnia & Herzegovina, Bulgaria, Croatia, FYR of Macedonia, Romiania and Serbia & Montenegro. Prior to 2003 Czech Republic, Estonia, Hungary, Latvia, Lithuania, Poland, Slovakia and Slovenia also included.

Source: ONS Foreign Direct Investments Surveys: 01633 456647; Bank of England

19.14 United Kingdom outward foreign direct international investment position: book value of net assets: by area and main country[1]

At year end

£ million

		2002	2003	2004	2005	2006
Europe	GQCJ	390 359	408 881	382 104	387 324	393 826
EU25	DG8P	343 931	354 707	348 293	339 283	306 127
Austria	CDLZ	2 679	3 339	4 102	4 005	2 388
Belgium	HIIO	10 364	8 662	7 828	13 492	4 459
Cyprus	DG8Q	84	80	64	59	561
Czech Republic	DG8R	1 088	954	793	823	656
Denmark	CDLP	3 165	3 021	5 256	5 090	7 790
Estonia	DG8S	29	21	78	7	5
Finland	CDMA	580	588	695	2 465	1 287
France	CDLQ	31 928	31 460	35 313	47 348	36 587
Germany	CDLR	13 924	13 486	12 164	20 753	17 159
Greece	CDLS	498	460	456	625	563
Hungary	DG8T	1 403	1 722	1 506	2 491	1 787
Irish Republic	CDLT	29 944	29 989	29 059	26 824	23 196
Italy	CDLU	5 505	10 178	11 322	10 872	7 954
Latvia	DG8U	51	13	25	22	28
Lithuania	DG8V	24	16	22	16	..
Luxembourg	HIIP	62 556	79 208	81 709	97 260	59 907
Malta	DG8W	−24	264	1 528	−459	..
Netherlands	CDLV	158 478	146 345	131 143	64 511	90 804
Poland	DG8X	2 809	2 900	2 316	1 974	2 594
Portugal	CDLW	629	973	1 664	2 702	3 247
Slovakia	DG8Y	261	332	103	93	138
Slovenia	DG8Z	92	128	54	3	52
Spain	CDLX	7 156	9 460	11 318	25 604	26 202
Sweden	CDMD	10 712	11 108	9 776	12 702	17 774
EFTA	CDLY	22 069	27 187	14 468	12 933	12 548
of which						
Norway	CDMC	4 904	4 900	4 934	4 498	2 107
Switzerland	CDME	17 164	21 913	9 104	7 979	10 158
Other European Countries	DG92	24 359	26 987	19 344	35 107	75 151
of which						
Russia	GQAA	744	777	1 627	1 814	6 051
UK offshore islands	GQAB	15 203	22 717	15 678	29 954	65 266
The Americas	GQCU	167 345	178 599	182 091	216 343	259 702
of which						
Bermuda	CDOA	4 929	1 554	7 561	10 604	13 890
Brazil	CDOB	2 050	2 532	3 922	3 220	2 791
Canada	CDML	8 209	8 537	8 922	12 812	19 187
Chile	GQCT	2 036	1 919	2 133	2 814	562
Colombia	GQCS	1 752	2 434	1 874	1 132	995
Mexico	GQAC	1 450	1 431	2 461	2 860	2 271
Panama	GQAD	..	153	132	166	..
USA	CDMM	131 800	150 021	140 321	164 405	184 204
Asia	GQCL	28 914	43 118	47 311	54 919	53 045
Near and Middle East Countries	CDNH	1 619	1 559	3 008	3 733	4 371
of which						
Gulf Arabian countries[2]	GQCM	1 027	1 211	2 062	3 013	2 247
Other Asian Countries	GQCR	27 295	41 559	44 303	51 187	48 674
of which						
China	HIIQ	3 212	1 809	1 882	2 685	2 230
Hong Kong	CDNN	5 872	17 221	19 165	20 432	22 388
India	GQAE	1 409	1 555	1 682	2 126	2 302
Indonesia	GQAF	1 014	1 309	1 178	1 168	1 521
Japan	CDMP	1 896	2 361	5 829	6 076	2 461
Malaysia	CDNQ	1 214	1 476	1 592	1 455	1 316
Singapore	CDNT	6 797	9 510	6 610	7 144	6 628
South Korea	GQAG	927	1 339	1 218	4 586	3 777
Thailand	GQAH	1 513	1 357	947	1 281	1 405
Australasia and Oceania	GQCN	16 652	17 486	16 888	16 694	12 646
of which						
Australia	CDMO	13 936	16 283	14 586	14 627	11 391
New Zealand	CDMQ	2 524	1 060	1 459	1 176	1 084
Africa	GQCQ	13 516	17 039	17 350	20 834	15 455
of which						
Kenya	GQAI	278	285	238	281	315
Nigeria	CDNA	1 012	1 028	950	924	1 009
South Africa	CDMR	8 765	11 250	10 964	13 733	8 630
Zimbabwe	CDNF	62	48	103	50	58
World Total	CDOO	616 786	665 123	645 744	696 113	734 674
OECD	GQCO	527 681	563 769	537 109	561 694	543 980
Central & Eastern Europe[3]	GQCP	6 449	560	534	640	519

1 See chapter text.
2 Includes Abu Dhabi, Bahrain, Dubai, Iraq, Kuwait, Oman, Other Gulf States, Qatar, Saudi Arabia and Yemen.
3 From 2003 includes Albania, Bosnia & Herzegovina, Bulgaria, Croatia, FYR of Macedonia, Romiania and Serbia & Montenegro. Prior to 2003 Czech Republic, Estonia, Hungary, Latvia, Lithuania, Poland, Slovakia and Slovenia also included.

Sources: ONS Foreign Direct Investment Surveys: 01633 456647; Bank of England

19.15 Net earnings from foreign direct investment abroad by United Kingdom companies:[1,2] by area and main country

£ million

		2002	2003	2004	2005	2006
Europe	GQCV	26 598	26 857	25 782	32 186	39 049
EU25	DG93	23 151	22 972	20 686	23 868	28 443
Austria	CBLQ	267	317	296	301	183
Belgium	HIIR	549	324	653	818	868
Cyprus	DG94	93	20	22	37	171
Czech Republic	DG95	115	165	110	108	−25
Denmark	CAWI	54	197	272	387	409
Estonia	DG96	4	9	3	..	10
Finland	CBLR	95	103	112	103	67
France	CAWJ	1 904	1 714	2 107	2 957	3 196
Germany	CAWK	2 199	1 592	2 328	2 685	2 139
Greece	CAWL	120	120	102	160	150
Hungary	DG97	232	241	202	295	82
Irish Republic	CAWM	1 553	2 197	2 461	2 835	2 515
Italy	CAWN	517	639	708	732	718
Latvia	DG98	..	−	−	..	5
Lithuania	DG99	..	−	−	−	−
Luxembourg	HIIS	1 822	1 500	2 191	4 006	7 082
Malta	DG9A	36	41	60	31	22
Netherlands	CAWO	11 395	11 691	6 651	5 344	7 897
Poland	DG9B	210	290	218	293	373
Portugal	CAWP	115	175	191	297	262
Slovakia	DG9C	21	..	..	34	24
Slovenia	DG9D	..	..	..	17	5
Spain	CAWQ	672	576	694	1 023	927
Sweden	CBLT	1 115	959	1 271	1 395	1 364
EFTA	CAWS	1 643	1 761	2 382	3 334	3 764
of which						
Norway	CBLS	293	319	297	937	334
Switzerland	CBLU	1 349	1 441	2 084	2 396	3 427
Other European Countries	DG9E	1 804	2 124	2 713	4 984	6 842
of which						
Russia	GQAJ	334	345	841	1 681	1 713
UK offshore islands	GQAK	1 127	1 332	1 602	3 017	4 526
The Americas	GQCX	14 716	17 586	21 113	26 585	27 098
of which						
Bermuda	CBNK	203	1 254	1 629	1 561	..
Brazil	CBNL	378	291	652	866	585
Canada	CAWW	1 015	1 055	1 340	1 895	1 813
Chile	GQCY	199	273	820	1 164	771
Colombia	GQCZ	200	234	379	414	274
Mexico	GQAL	295	207	485	536	548
Panama	GQAM	44	55	44	50	23
USA	CAWV	11 461	12 723	14 332	18 244	17 506
Asia	GQDA	4 755	5 108	8 001	10 975	11 828
Near and Middle East Countries	CBMS	398	461	692	1 053	1 453
of which						
Gulf Arabian countries[3]	GQDB	335	370	549	688	744
Other Asian Countries	GQDC	4 357	4 647	7 309	9 922	10 375
of which						
China	HIIT	255	278	370	580	441
Hong Kong	CAYB	610	1 083	2 541	3 553	3 878
India	GQAN	496	511	427	626	784
Indonesia	GQAO	132	184	155	226	386
Japan	CAWY	181	332	440	482	381
Malaysia	CBNA	448	477	525	508	509
Singapore	CBND	1 053	911	1 651	2 510	2 271
South Korea	GQAP	233	237	340	683	528
Thailand	GQAQ	162	160	159	171	−125
Australasia and Oceania	GQDD	2 337	2 022	3 623	3 157	3 194
of which						
Australia	CBMB	1 818	1 518	3 108	2 681	2 795
New Zealand	CBMC	488	478	279	359	388
Africa	GQDE	2 973	2 959	3 958	5 764	3 479
of which						
Kenya	GQAR	64	81	64	70	88
Nigeria	CBML	282	122	153	197	133
South Africa	CAWZ	1 784	1 693	2 706	3 768	1 612
Zimbabwe	CBMQ	37	43	87	16	10
World Total	GLAB	51 379	54 531	62 476	78 667	84 649
OECD	GQDF	40 229	41 353	43 453	52 138	56 188
Central & Eastern Europe[4]	GQDG	802	195	74	76	62

1 See chapter text. A minus sign indicates net losses.
2 Net earnings equal profits of overseas branches plus UK companies' receipts of interest and their share of profits of overseas subsidiaries and associates. Earnings are after deducting provisions for depreciation and withholding tax on profits, dividends and interest.

3 Includes Abu Dhabi, Bahrain, Dubai, Iraq, Kuwait, Oman, Other Gulf States, Qatar, Saudi Arabia and Yemen.
4 From 2003 includes Albania, Bosnia & Herzegovina, Bulgaria, Croatia, FYR of Macedonia, Romiania and Serbia & Montenegro. Prior to 2003 Czech Republic, Estonia, Hungary, Latvia, Lithuania, Poland, Slovakia and Slovenia also included.

Source: ONS Foreign Direct Investments Survey: 01633 456647; Bank of England

19.16 Net inward foreign direct investment in the United Kingdom:[1,2] by area and main country

£ million

		2002	2003	2004	2005	2006
Europe	GQDH	15 431	7 013	29 901	80 087	47 589
EU25	DG9F	15 721	5 498	26 412	71 022	41 335
Austria	CBOB	..	8	−31	171	−61
Belgium	HIIU	−333	218	1 542	23	691
Cyprus	DG9G	−3	−	−	7	18
Czech Republic	DG9H	..	−	−	−	..
Denmark	CAYQ	114	321	−11	−1 246	−232
Estonia	DG9I	−	−	−	−	−
Finland	CBOC	5	26	32	238	51
France	CAYR	1 460	414	1 703	9 643	3 205
Germany	CAYS	11 340	1 437	11 131	7 279	−1 747
Greece	CAYT	7	33	13	14	17
Hungary	DG9J	−	−	..	1	3
Irish Republic	CAYU	210	206	936	723	866
Italy	CAYV	−208	−468	1 327	−42	357
Latvia	DG9K	−	..	−	..	..
Lithuania	DG9L	..	−	..	−	−
Luxembourg	HIIV	1	−105	−115	151	−183
Malta	DG9M	..	−	−	1	2
Netherlands	CAYW	1 756	2 452	1 226	50 366	14 336
Poland	DG9N	1	−	−	1	50
Portugal	CAYX	−12	..	..	−6	9
Slovakia	DG9O	..	..	..	..	..
Slovenia	DG9P	..	..	..	..	..
Spain	CAYY	232	518	..	3 297	23 429
Sweden	CBOE	493	406	−14	393	519
EFTA	CAZB	−298	1 408	3 016	9 050	5 214
of which						
Norway	CBOD	−137	−179	−798	927	171
Switzerland	CBOF	−162	1 411	3 488	7 405	4 679
Other European Countries	DG9Q	9	107	473	15	1 040
of which						
Russia	GQAS	..	..	..	..	..
UK offshore islands	GQAT	−8	32	476	−60	950
The Americas	GQDJ	−2 051	3 396	−4 792	17 422	18 901
of which						
Brazil	HP5A	..	4	..	6	..
Canada	CAZF	562	−325	683	1 632	3 529
USA	CAZE	−2 157	2 676	−5 727	15 589	13 994
Asia	GQDK	2 551	−449	4 081	−4 168	11 805
Near and Middle East Countries	GQAU	−26	−34	384	736	5 035
Other Asian Countries	GQAV	2 579	−415	3 697	−4 904	6 770
of which						
China	HP5B	..	2	−26	13	12
Hong Kong	GQAW	63	63	..	315	103
India	HP5C	1	7	−15	138	264
Japan	CAZH	2 352	−543	817	−5 575	3 714
Singapore	GQAX	157	−76	14	46	..
South Korea	GQAY	−26	−20	193	175	−85
Australasia and Oceania	GQDL	31	310	1 420	3 396	1 835
of which						
Australia	CBOJ	14	309	1 412	3 396	1 444
New Zealand	CBOK	18	2	8	−	54
Africa	GQAZ	71	7	−43	66	138
of which						
South Africa	CAZJ	63	21	−35	25	101
World Total	CBDH	16 033	10 276	30 566	96 803	80 269
OECD	GQBA	16 194	8 984	26 762	95 187	69 151
Central & Eastern Europe[3]	GQBB	−	4	−32	..	6

1 See chapter text. Net investment includes reinvested earnings.
2 A minus sign indicates net disinvestment in the UK.
3 From 2003 includes Albania, Bosnia & Herzegovina, Bulgaria, Croatia, FYR of Macedonia, Romania and Serbia & Montenegro. Prior to 2003 Czech Republic, Estonia, Hungary, Latvia, Lithuania, Poland, Slovakia and Slovenia also included.

Sources: ONS Foreign Direct Investment Surveys: 01633 456647; Bank of England

19.17 United Kingdom inward foreign direct international investment position: book value of net liabilities: by area and main country[1]

At year end

£ million

		2002	2003	2004	2005	2006
Europe	GQDM	157 313	158 903	181 198	277 027	321 731
EU25	DG9R	142 514	142 240	161 327	244 325	289 911
Austria	CDPF	1 003	349	366	561	848
Belgium	HIIW	1 765	1 987	4 338	4 481	5 631
Cyprus	DG9S	68	67	78	100	162
Czech Republic	DG9T	3	9	6	3	..
Denmark	CDOV	2 358	2 086	2 359	1 404	4 205
Estonia	DG9U	–	–	–	–	–
Finland	CDPG	767	946	886	756	787
France	CDOW	37 195	36 565	41 100	56 309	51 862
Germany	CDOX	37 737	32 260	39 300	51 469	49 095
Greece	CDOY	89	86	100	103	121
Hungary	DG9V	8	9	12	9	12
Irish Republic	CDOZ	4 544	4 769	5 021	7 146	8 164
Italy	CDPA	5 788	4 580	6 708	6 122	4 548
Latvia	DG9W	–	..	–	..	..
Lithuania	DG9X	..	..	..	–	–
Luxembourg	HIIX	4 985	5 627	5 963	7 880	11 738
Malta	DG9Y	22	21	5	12	12
Netherlands	CDPB	39 512	46 876	47 579	95 579	118 778
Poland	DG9Z	13	10	7	21	96
Portugal	CDPC	97	115	113	111	122
Slovakia	DGA2	..	..	..	–	–
Slovenia	DGA3	..	..	..	..	..
Spain	CDPD	2 303	3 344	4 536	8 782	29 666
Sweden	CDPI	4 254	2 527	2 849	3 467	4 050
EFTA	CDPE	10 951	13 758	15 752	25 033	21 917
of which						
Norway	CDPH	1 019	831	242	1 085	969
Switzerland	CDPJ	9 717	12 439	14 685	21 624	18 592
Other European Countries	DGA4	3 849	2 906	4 120	7 670	9 903
of which						
Russia	GQBC	..	..	..	..	..
UK offshore islands	GQBD	3 393	2 361	3 500	7 059	9 133
The Americas	GQDU	138 156	145 973	140 090	174 037	207 540
of which						
Brazil	HP5D	..	5	..	77	134
Canada	CDPM	8 718	11 176	12 108	15 587	19 335
USA	CDPN	124 597	130 512	122 069	149 759	177 783
Asia	GQDO	20 323	19 869	24 800	24 101	39 490
Near and Middle East Countries	GQBE	1 697	1 627	2 765	2 970	10 158
Other Asian Countries	GQBF	18 626	18 242	22 035	21 131	29 332
of which						
China	HP5E	42	102	119	111	99
Hong Kong	GQBG	..	..	..	..	..
India	HP5F	162	194	164	518	795
Japan	CDPQ	11 791	11 949	12 300	10 513	14 809
Singapore	GQBH	1 684	830	925	1 034	4 048
South Korea	GQBI	448	635	635	638	798
Australasia and Oceania	GQDP	8 462	14 336	16 804	12 537	7 303
of which						
Australia	CDPP	8 309	14 160	16 631	12 313	7 132
New Zealand	CDPR	134	158	153	224	428
Africa	GQBJ	427	560	530	510	515
of which						
South Africa	CDPS	250	387	296	186	130
World Total	CDPZ	324 680	339 641	363 422	488 212	576 580
OECD	GQBK	307 395	324 491	340 870	458 185	531 801
Central & Eastern Europe[2]	GQBL	58	34	..	..	..

1 See chapter text.
2 From 2003 includes Albania, Bosnia & Herzegovina, Bulgaria, Croatia, FYR of Macedonia, Romiania and Serbia & Montenegro. Prior to 2003 Czech Republic, Estonia, Hungary, Latvia, Lithuania, Poland, Slovakia and Slovenia also included.

Sources: ONS Foreign Direct Investment Surveys 01633 456647;
Bank of England

19.18 Net earnings from foreign direct investment in the United Kingdom:[1,2] by area and main country

£ million

		2002	2003	2004	2005	2006
Europe	GQDQ	5 475	10 158	12 676	17 592	26 875
EU25	DGA5	4 447	9 011	11 329	15 269	23 069
Austria	CBOR	176	111	61	60	207
Belgium	HIIY	38	165	269	367	646
Cyprus	DGA6	16	24	20	24	44
Czech Republic	DGA7	–	–	–	–	..
Denmark	CBDL	253	305	311	326	184
Estonia	DGA8	–	–	–	–	–
Finland	CBOS	70	36	62	61	93
France	CBDM	1 322	2 743	3 842	5 121	5 807
Germany	CBDN	−1 109	1 754	2 900	4 037	4 044
Greece	CBDO	64	4	−4	49	70
Hungary	DGA9	–	–	–	1	3
Irish Republic	CBDP	561	578	471	724	1 015
Italy	CBDQ	−148	174	408	483	475
Latvia	DGB2	–	..	–	..	..
Lithuania	DGB3	..	–	..	1	1
Luxembourg	HIIZ	87	196	289	214	204
Malta	DGB4	–	–	–	–	3
Netherlands	CBDR	2 455	2 405	2 585	2 800	7 352
Poland	DGB5	1	–	–	1	8
Portugal	CBDS	13	49	47	30	48
Slovakia	DGB6	..	..	..	5	5
Slovenia	DGB7	..	..	..	..	..
Spain	CBDT	52	298	37	773	2 536
Sweden	CBOU	599	167	21	182	316
EFTA	CBDW	735	822	849	1 495	2 647
of which						
Norway	CBOT	40	–	−20	82	169
Switzerland	CBOV	692	794	819	1 320	2 215
Other European Countries	DGB8	293	325	499	829	1 159
of which						
Russia	GQBM	..	..	..	..	..
UK offshore islands	GQBN	267	287	468	757	1 098
The Americas	GQDV	7 314	10 013	12 278	16 460	20 845
of which						
Brazil	HP5G	..	..	1	−4	−4
Canada	CBEA	659	639	1 021	1 348	1 450
USA	CBDZ	6 623	9 054	10 981	14 156	17 480
Asia	GQDS	1 214	−781	168	937	2 692
Near and Middle East Countries	GQBO	33	114	188	354	561
Other Asian Countries	GQBP	1 182	−895	−19	583	2 131
of which						
China	HP5H	..	..	8	−63	−35
Hong Kong	GQBQ	−52	−456	..	..	−611
India	HP5I	29	55	−2	65	132
Japan	CBEC	1 022	−538	608	1 089	1 955
Singapore	GQBS	100	62	32	85	259
South Korea	GQBT	16	−54	23	72	104
Australasia and Oceania	GQDT	432	835	695	535	1 250
of which						
Australia	CBOZ	396	802	690	521	867
New Zealand	CBPA	3	4	5	13	46
Africa	GQBU	99	59	59	65	81
of which						
South Africa	CBED	97	50	26	25	31
World Total	CBEV	14 534	20 283	25 876	35 588	51 742
OECD	GQBV	13 904	19 715	25 471	33 927	47 547
Central & Eastern Europe[3]	GQBW	2	1	1	..	..

1 See chapter text. A minus sign indicates net losses.
2 Net earnings equal profits of UK branches plus overseas investors' receipts of interest and their share of the profits of UK subsidiaries and associates. Earnings are after deducting provisions for depreciation and withholding tax on profits and interest.
3 From 2003 includes Albania, Bosnia & Herzegovina, Bulgaria, Croatia, FYR of Macedonia, Romiania and Serbia & Montenegro. Prior to 2003 Czech Republic, Estonia, Hungary, Latvia, Lithuania, Poland, Slovakia and Slovenia also included.

Sources: ONS Foreign Direct Investment Surveys: 01633 456647; Bank of England

Research and development

Chapter 20

Research and development

Research and experimental development (R&D) is defined for statistical purposes as 'creative work undertaken on a systematic basis in order to increase the stock of knowledge, including knowledge of man, culture and society, and the use of this stock of knowledge to devise new applications'.

R&D is financed and carried out mainly by businesses, the Government, and institutions of higher education. A small amount is performed by non-profit-making bodies. Gross Expenditure on R&D (GERD) is an indicator of the total amount of R&D performed within the UK which, in recent years, has been approximately 2 per cent of GDP. Detailed figures are reported each year in a first release published in March and the August edition of Office for National Statistics (ONS)' *Economic and Labour Market Review*. Table 20.1 shows the main components of GERD.

ONS conducts an annual survey of expenditure and employment on R&D performed by government, and of government funding of R&D. The survey collects data on outturn and planning years. Until 1993 the detailed results were reported in the Annual Review of Government Funded R&D produced by the Department of Innovation, Universities and Skills (DIUS). From 1997, the results have appeared in DIUS' Science, Engineering and Technology Statistics publication. Table 20.2 gives some broad totals for gross expenditure by government (expenditure before deducting funds received by government for R&D). Table 20.3 gives a breakdown of net expenditure (receipts are deducted).

ONS conducts an annual survey of R&D in business. Tables 20.4 and 20.5 give a summary of the main trends up to 2006. The latest set of results from the survey became available in a first release dated 26 November 2007 and a business monitor (MA14) published on 18 January 2008.

Revisions were made to the business data for the period 2004 to 2006 and were published at the same time as the 2006 Business Enterprise R&D first release on 26th November 2007. The format of this report, similar to MA14, was used as it covers all aspects of the R&D data published by ONS.

Statistics on expenditure and employment on R&D in Higher Education Institutions (HEIs) are based on information collected by Higher Education Funding Councils and Higher Education Statistics Agency (HESA). In 1994 a new methodology was introduced to estimate expenditure on R&D

in HEIs. This is based on the allocation of various Funding Council Grants. Full details of the new methodology are contained in SET Statistics available on the Department of Innovation, Universities and Science Web Site at www.berr. gov.uk/dius/science/science-funding/set-stats/index.html

The most comprehensive international comparisons of resources devoted to R&D appear in Main Science and Technology Indicators published by the Organisation for Economic Co-operation and Development (OECD). The Statistical Office of the European Union and the United Nations also compile R&D statistics based on figures supplied by member states.

To make international comparisons more reliable, the OECD has published a series of manuals giving guidance on how to measure various components of R&D inputs and outputs. The most important of these is the Frascati Manual, which defines R&D and recommends how resources for R&D should be measured. The UK follows the Frascati Manual as far as possible.

For information on available aggregated data on Research and Development, please contact Julie Owens on 01633 456765 (e-mail Julie.Owens@ons.gsi.gov.uk).

20.1 Cost of research and development: by sector[1]
United Kingdom

£ million and percentages

	2000		2001		2002		2003		2004		2005		2006	
	£m	%	£m	%	£m	%	£m	%	£m	%	£m	%	£m	%
Sector carrying out the work **Cash terms (£ million)**														
Government	1 593	9	1 160	6	1 053	5	1 243	6	1 240	6	1 238	6	1 264	5
Research councils	647	4	674	4	713	4	825	4	930	5	1 051	5	1 054	5
Business enterprise	11 510	65	11 978	66	12 469	65	12 677	64	12 668	63	13 310	61	14 306	62
Higher education	3 691	21	4 149	22	4 618	24	4 785	24	5 004	25	5 580	26	6 062	26
Private non-profit	296	2	325	2	374	2	369	2	406	2	502	2	518	2
Total	17 736	100	18 286	100	19 228	100	19 898	100	20 248	100	21 681	100	23 204	100
Sector providing the funds **Cash terms (£ million)**														
Government	2 779	16	2 292	12	2 215	11	2 705	13	2 777	14	2 594	12	2 582	12
Research councils	1 317	8	1 512	8	1 713	9	1 947	10	2 084	10	2 574	12	2 727	12
Higher education funding councils	1 276	7	1 474	8	1 626	8	1 665	8	1 804	9	1 928	9	2 085	9
Higher education	160	1	184	1	208	1	218	1	229	1	266	1	292	1
Business enterprise[2]	8 559	49	8 329	46	8 366	44	8 394	42	8 922	44	9 119	42	10 487	45
Private non-profit	815	5	888	5	962	5	931	5	960	5	1 022	5	1 076	5
Abroad	2 830	16	3 607	20	4 138	22	4 038	20	3 472	17	4 178	19	3 954	17
Total	17 736	100	18 286	100	19 228	100	19 898	100	20 248	100	21 681	100	23 204	100

1 See chapter text.
2 Including research associations and public corporations.

Source: Office for National Statistics: 01633 456765

20.2 Gross central government expenditure on research and development[1]
United Kingdom

£ million

	2000/01		2001/02		2002/03		2003/04		2004/05		2005/06	
	Intra-mural	Extra-mural[2]	Intra-mural	Extra-mural[2]	Intra-mural	Extra-mural[2]	Intra-mural	Extra-mural[2]	Intra-mural	Extra-mural[2]	Intra-mural	Extra-mural[2]
Defence[3]	932	..	419	1 685	288	2 502	380	2 364	357	2 283	365	2 223
Research councils	667	1 024	695	1 244	725	1 457	811	1 643	874	1 752	1 004	2 038
Higher education institutes	-	1 276	-	1 474	-	1 626	-	1 665	-	1 804	-	1 928
Other programmes	283	841	282	977	297	1 163	338	1 111	327	870	316	1 542
Total (excluding NHS)	1 778	..	1 396	5 380	1 310	6 748	1 529	6 783	1 558	6 709	1 685	7 731

1 See chapter text.
2 Extramural Includes work performed overseas and excludes monies spent with other government departments.

3 .. Denotes figures no longer available due to MOD revision between the years 1997 - 2000. The details are outlined in Defence Statistics Bulletin 6, which is available at the following web address: www.dasa.mod.uk

Source: Office for National Statistics: 01633 456765

20.3 Net central government expenditure on research and development:[1] European Union objectives for research and development expenditure
United Kingdom

£ million

		1995 /96	1996 /97	1997 /98	1998 /99	1999 /00	2000 /01	2001 /02	2002 /03	2003 /04	2004 /05	2005 /06
Exploration and exploitation of the earth	KDVP	105.2	95.4	81.3	78.5	79.5	85.5	106.0	138.3	176.8	193.0	239.0
Infrastructure and general planning of land-use	KDVQ	94.1	98.8	98.9	103.5	104.4	102.4	100.3	101.0	118.7	88.0	70.0
Control of environmental pollution	KDVR	131.8	128.7	136.2	142.8	147.0	151.1	129.1	126.5	150.1	149.0	158.0
Protection and promotion of human health (ex NHS)	KDVS	416.0	427.4	444.8	450.1	519.5	530.6	571.6	597.8	1 163.7	1 227.3	1 258.0
Production, distribution and rational utilisation of energy	KDVT	52.3	43.2	41.0	28.0	29.0	31.9	36.8	40.3	28.4	35.0	21.0
Agricultural production and technology	KDVU	281.9	257.0	268.9	255.5	260.6	266.6	265.2	267.8	275.9	278.0	273.0
Industrial production and technology	KDVV	165.8	144.6	116.9	61.6	56.5	109.2	237.0	423.4	426.5	138.4	94.0
Social structures and relationships	KDVW	137.1	120.7	113.8	154.7	217.6	270.2	268.8	293.4	226.7	291.8	471.0
Exploration and exploitation of space	KDVX	153.0	164.1	164.4	142.5	142.7	146.3	139.8	155.5	168.6	168.9	192.0
Research financed from general university funds	KDVY	1 018.6	1 027.5	1 033.3	1 085.1	1 157.1	1 276.1	1 473.5	1 626.4	1 664.6	1 804.7	1 933.0
Non-oriented research	KDVZ	653.5	680.5	671.0	677.0	700.5	789.3	918.2	1 071.6	1 290.9	1 332.0	1 658.0
Other civil research	KDWA	24.7	20.5	21.6	25.8	20.6	22.3	19.7	36.3	39.9	38.4	38.0
Defence	KDWB	2 071.7	2 237.0	2 317.2	2 144.2	2 275.9	2 245.1	2 063.0	2 739.7	2 682.2	2 582.7	2 528.0
Total (Excluding NHS)	KDWC	5 305.7	5 445.4	5 509.3	5 349.3	5 710.9	6 026.6	6 329.0	7 618.0	8 413.5	8 327.0	8 932.0

1 See chapter text.

Source: Office for National Statistics: 01633 456765

20.4 Intramural expenditure on Business Enterprise research and development:[1] by industry

United Kingdom: At Current Prices and Constant 2006 Prices

£ million

		Total				Civil				Defence		
		2004	2005	2006		2004	2005	2006		2004	2005	2006
Current Prices												
Chemicals	KDWF	3 864	4 008	4 624	KDWP	..	..	..	KDWZ	..	..	..
Mechanical engineering	KDWG	838	821	874	KDWQ	492	501	564	KDXA	346	320	310
Electrical machinery	KJRT	1 222	1 273	1 216	KJTC	935	969	880	KJUL	287	305	336
Aerospace	KDWJ	1 960	2 157	1 836	KDWT	934	890	912	KDXD	1 026	1 267	924
Transport equipment	KDWK	937	892	913	KDWU	..	..	..	KDXE	..	..	..
Other manufacturing	KDWL	1 242	1 221	1 333	KDWV	1 134	1 131	1 262	KDXF	108	90	71
Manufacturing: Total	KDWE	10 064	10 372	10 796	KDWO	8 186	8 274	9 035	KDWY	1 878	2 097	1 762
Services	KDWM	2 378	2 730	3 322	KDWW	..	2 573	3 142	KDXG	..	157	180
Agriculture, hunting and forestry; fishing	HFRV	..	127	88	HFSA	..	..	88	MKFC	..	..	—
Extractive industries	HFRW	36	43	43	HFSB	36	43	43	MKFD	—	—	—
Electricity, gas and water supply	HFRX	21	15	21	HFSC	21	15	21	MKFE	—	—	—
Construction	HFRY	..	33	36	HFSE	..	..	36	MKFF	..	..	..
Other: Total	HFRU	226	208	187	HFRZ	..	208	187	MKFB	..	—	—
Total	KDWD	12 668	13 310	14 306	KDWN	10 629	11 055	12 364	KDWX	2 039	2 254	1 942
2006 Prices												
Chemicals	HFXA	4 055	4 120	4 624	HFXJ	..	..	..	HFYO	..	..	..
Mechanical engineering	HFXB	879	844	874	HFXK	516	515	564	HFYP	363	329	310
Electrical machinery	HFXC	1 282	1 308	1 216	HFYH	981	996	880	HFYQ	301	313	336
Aerospace	HFXD	2 057	2 217	1 836	HFYI	980	915	912	HFYR	1 077	1 302	924
Transport equipment	HFXE	983	917	913	HFYJ	..	..	..	HFYS	..	..	..
Other manufacturing	HFXF	1 303	1 255	1 333	HFYK	1 190	1 162	1 262	HFYT	113	93	71
Manufacturing: Total	HFWZ	10 561	10 661	10 796	HFXI	8 591	8 504	9 035	HFYN	1 971	2 155	1 762
Services	HFXG	2 496	2 806	3 322	HFYL	..	2 645	3 142	HFYU	..	161	180
Agriculture, hunting and forestry: fishing	HFSG	..	131	88	HFSL	..	..	88	MKFH	..	..	—
Extractive industries	HFSH	38	44	43	HFSM	38	44	43	MKFI	—	—	—
Electricity, gas and water supply	HFSI	22	15	21	HFSN	22	15	21	MKFJ	—	—	—
Construction	HFSJ	..	34	36	HFSO	..	..	36	MKFK	..	..	..
Other: Total	HFSF	237	214	187	HFSK	..	214	187	MKFG	..	—	—
Total	HFWY	13 294	13 681	14 306	HFXH	11 154	11 363	12 364	HFYM	2 140	2 317	1 942

1 See chapter text.

Source: Office for National Statistics: 01633 456765

20.5 Sources of funds for research and development within Business Enterprises[1]

United Kingdom

£ million and percentages

		Total				Civil				Defence		
		2004	2005	2006		2004	2005	2006		2004	2005	2006
Cash terms (£ million)												
Government funds	KDYM	1 290	1 110	1 082	KDYU	162	165	172	KDZC	1 128	945	909
Overseas funds	KDYN	2 958	3 611	3 289	KDYV	2 440	2 683	2 714	KDZD	518	928	575
Mainly own funds	KDYO	8 420	8 588	9 934	KDYW	8 027	8 207	9 477	KDZE	393	381	458
Total	KDYL	12 668	13 310	14 306	KDYT	10 629	11 055	12 364	KDZB	2 039	2 254	1 942
Percentages												
Government funds	KDYQ	10	8	8	KDYY	2	1	1	KDZG	55	42	47
Overseas funds	KDYR	23	27	23	KDYZ	23	24	22	KDZH	25	41	30
Mainly own funds	KDYS	66	65	69	KDZA	76	74	77	KDZI	19	17	24
Total	KDYP	100	100	100	KDYX	100	100	100	KDZF	100	100	100

1 See chapter text.

Source: Office for National Statistics: 01633 456765

Agriculture, fisheries and food

Chapter 21

Agriculture, fisheries and food

Output and input

(Tables 21.1 and 21.2)

For both tables, output is a net of VAT collected on the sale of non-edible products. Figures for total output include subsidies on products, but not other subsidies. Unspecified crops include turf, other minor crops and arable area payments for fodder maize. Eggs include the value of duck eggs and exports of eggs for hatching. Landlords' expenses are included within farm maintenance, miscellaneous expenditure and depreciation of buildings and works. Also included within 'other farming costs' are livestock and crop costs, water costs, insurance premia, bank charges, professional fees, rates, and other farming costs.

Other subsidies

Agri-Environment initiatives include the Environmentally and Nitrate Sensitive Areas, Countryside Stewardship, Countryside Premium, Tir Cymen, Tir Gofal, Moorland, Habitat, Farm Woodland and Organic Farming schemes. Included in 'other' subsidies are guidance premium for beef and sheep meat production, Pilot Beef and Sheep Extensification Scheme, non-agricultural horse grazing and farm accounts grant, as well as historic data for fertiliser and lime grant and payments to small scale cereal producers.

Compensation of employees and interest charges

Total compensation of employees excludes the value of work done by farm labour on own account capital formation in buildings and work. 'Interest' relates to interest charges on loans for current farming purposes and buildings and less interest on money held on short-term deposit.

Rent

Rent paid (after deductions) is the rent paid on all tenanted land including 'conacre' land in Northern Ireland, less landlords' expenses and the benefit value of dwellings on that land. Rent received (after deductions) is the rent received by farming landowners from renting of land to other farmers, less landlords' expenses and the benefit value of dwellings on that land. Total net rent is the net rent flowing out of the agricultural sector paid to non-farming landowners, including that part of tenanted land in Northern Ireland. (Although there has been some updating of the technical procedures for calculating this figure, it corresponds with the previous net rent variable.)

Agricultural censuses and surveys

(Tables 21.3, 21.5 and 21.13)

The coverage for holdings includes all main and minor holdings for each country. Northern Ireland data are now based on all active farm business.

Estimated quantity of crops and grass harvested

(Table 21.4)

The estimated yields of sugar beet and hops are obtained from production figures supplied by British Sugar plc, and the main hop producers in England and Wales. In Great Britain potato yields are estimated in consultation with the British Potato Council.

Forestry

(Table 21.6)

Statistics for state forestry are from Forestry Commission and Forest Service management information systems. For private forestry in Great Britain, statistics on new planting and restocking are based on records of grant aid and estimates of planting undertaken without grant aid, and timber removals are estimated from a survey of the largest timber harvesting companies.

Average weekly earnings and hours of agricultural and horticultural workers

(Tables 21.11 and 21.12)

Prior to 1998, data were collected from a monthly postal survey, which mainly covered male full-time workers. Between 1998 and 2002, the survey collected information on an annual basis via a telephone survey. The survey was reviewed in 2002 and it was concluded that the frequency of the survey should be increased to four times per year to enable the production of more representative annual estimates. The annual sample size has been retained and has been split between four quarterly telephone surveys.

Results for other quarters can be found on the Department for Environment, Food and Rural Affairs (DEFRA) website: www.defra.gov.uk

The survey covers seven main categories of workers and provides data which are used by the Agricultural Wages Board when considering wage claims and by in considering the cost of labour in agriculture and horticulture.

Data on earnings represents the total earnings of regular fulltime male workers, aged 20 and over. Figures include all payments-in-kind, valued where applicable in accordance with the Agricultural Wages Order. The earnings and hours of hire farm managers are excluded. Part-time workers are defined as those working less than 39 basic hours per week. Casual workers are those employed on a temporary basis.

Fisheries

(Table 21.15)

Fishing fleet information (Table 21.15) is obtained from vessel registers maintained by DEFRA in England and Wales, and the Scottish Executive Agriculture and Fisheries Department.

Estimated average household food consumption – 'Family Food' Expenditure and Food Survey

(Table 21.16)

The Expenditure and Food Survey replaced both the National Food Survey and the Family Expenditure Survey in April 2001. The new survey is a voluntary sample survey of private households throughout the UK and the results are produced for the financial year ending 31 March each year. This represents a break in the continuity of the data as results from the National Food Survey were produced for Great Britain and for the calendar year ended 31 December.

The basic unit of the survey is the household, which is defined as a group of persons living at the same address and sharing common catering arrangements. Each individual aged 16 or over in the household visited is asked to keep diary records, for a two-week period, of daily expenditure on, and weight and volume of, food and drink brought into the home and expenditure on food and drink eaten out. Children aged between 7 and 15 are asked to keep simplified diaries.

For the year 2005/06, the sample size was 12,096 households in Great Britain with a response rate of 57 per cent. In Northern Ireland the sample was 1,057 with a response rate of 50 per cent.

21.1 Production and income account at current prices[1]
United Kingdom

£ million

		1997	1998	1999	2000	2001	2002	2003	2004	2005	2006	2007[2]
Output[3]												
1.Total cereals:	C5X5	2 069.6	1 732.9	1 620.2	1 604.3	1 336.8	1 561.5	1 485.7	1 707.2	1 450.0	1 513.4	1 910.1
Wheat	KFKA	1 357.7	1 186.8	1 105.2	1 119.6	831.5	1 111.7	993.8	1 230.7	1 029.5	1 072.1	1 307.1
Rye	VQBG	3.1	2.8	1.8	1.5	1.8	1.2	1.4	1.6	1.3	1.4	1.5
Barley	KFKB	660.8	504.1	474.6	440.8	462.2	401.2	445.8	432.2	383.0	385.5	538.5
Oats and summer cereal mixtures	KFKC	47.3	38.8	37.9	41.6	40.8	46.5	43.9	41.8	35.2	53.5	62.0
Other cereals	VQBH	0.7	0.5	0.8	0.8	0.6	0.9	0.9	0.9	0.9	0.9	1.0
2.Total industrial crops	VQBI	791.2	848.2	783.3	699.4	773.8	860.0	812.8	798.8	807.9	737.1	779.1
Oilseeds	VQBJ	254.2	282.9	225.0	143.8	177.2	220.4	314.3	266.2	278.7	318.2	425.8
Oilseed rape	KFKG	239.4	262.6	194.8	139.0	171.5	217.4	303.8	256.9	261.7	310.4	421.5
Other oil seeds	KIBT	14.8	20.3	30.1	4.8	5.6	2.9	10.4	9.3	17.0	7.8	4.2
Sugar beet	KFKH	329.1	298.5	279.7	252.1	256.4	282.9	279.7	278.1	268.8	178.2	171.9
Other industrial crops	VQBK	207.9	266.8	278.7	303.4	340.3	356.7	218.9	254.4	260.4	240.6	181.5
Fibre plants	VQBL	3.2	2.6	2.3	1.3	1.7	1.0	1.8	1.3	1.0	1.2	1.2
Hops	KFKI	18.5	13.1	12.1	10.4	9.0	7.2	6.1	5.7	5.4	4.4	4.4
Others[4]	VQBM	186.3	251.1	264.2	291.7	329.6	348.4	211.0	247.5	254.0	235.1	175.9
3.Total forage plants	VQBO	93.4	71.0	75.9	80.9	103.4	90.3	103.7	93.3	94.9	85.1	104.0
4.Total vegetables and horticultural products	VQBP	1 621.1	1 627.6	1 667.5	1 561.1	1 612.6	1 591.1	1 672.6	1 621.5	1 690.3	1 760.0	1 843.7
5.Total potatoes (including seeds)	KFKO	390.0	629.4	749.0	463.7	682.1	485.0	526.4	674.1	515.0	621.1	663.9
6.Total fruit	KFKQ	198.5	258.8	256.9	232.2	238.8	251.2	310.3	315.8	388.1	382.8	444.6
7.Other crop products including seeds	VQBQ	42.3	39.4	42.0	37.7	37.5	25.5	31.6	31.0	51.9	47.9	45.1
8.Total crop output (Sum 1 to 7)	VQBR	5 206.1	5 207.2	5 194.8	4 679.3	4 785.1	4 864.5	4 943.0	5 241.6	4 998.1	5 147.5	5 790.5
9.Total livestock production	VQBS	5 555.1	4 694.3	4 326.5	4 363.8	4 260.9	4 574.9	4 825.6	4 837.1	4 891.6	5 099.5	5 241.8
Primarily for meat	KFLA	4 834.5	4 099.6	3 929.2	3 970.0	3 634.4	3 868.4	4 094.2	4 179.8	4 232.4	4 339.5	4 418.6
Cattle	KFKU	1 160.9	1 052.6	1 145.2	1 093.7	955.3	1 145.8	1 227.1	1 279.2	1 399.7	1 579.1	1 656.7
Pigs	KFKW	1 201.5	882.4	784.6	800.4	748.5	687.7	671.5	680.2	677.4	684.8	734.6
Sheep	VQBT	822.4	631.1	574.8	616.8	438.0	613.4	697.7	725.5	682.1	681.6	628.5
Poultry	KFXX	1 500.6	1 384.7	1 275.8	1 306.5	1 337.6	1 263.9	1 336.7	1 329.3	1 302.2	1 218.4	1 215.5
Other animals	KFKY	149.1	148.8	148.9	152.6	154.9	157.7	161.2	165.7	170.9	175.5	183.4
Gross fixed capital formation	KFLI	720.6	594.7	397.3	393.8	626.5	706.6	731.4	657.2	659.3	760.1	823.1
Cattle	KUJZ	378.1	296.9	206.9	192.9	371.3	392.2	447.7	337.4	411.2	490.8	520.1
Pigs	LUKB	15.2	5.7	6.9	5.6	5.3	7.5	7.1	7.5	6.3	7.9	7.1
Sheep	LUKA	196.1	155.3	56.7	63.9	122.5	177.5	146.5	176.4	111.0	130.3	153.3
Poultry	LUKC	131.1	136.8	126.8	131.4	127.4	129.3	130.1	135.9	130.8	131.1	142.6
10.Total livestock products	KFLF	3 540.3	3 067.1	2 963.0	2 711.3	3 088.1	2 834.2	3 032.1	3 040.2	3 009.5	2 917.8	3 293.5
Milk	KFLB	3 167.6	2 740.7	2 662.0	2 385.8	2 742.6	2 466.3	2 628.5	2 610.5	2 592.6	2 497.5	2 829.8
Eggs	KFLC	312.3	281.5	253.9	280.2	307.0	314.3	337.8	380.6	349.3	361.1	409.8
Raw wool	KFLD	35.1	23.9	21.4	22.7	17.3	19.1	20.8	20.2	19.6	11.5	13.5
Other animal products	KFLE	25.3	21.0	25.7	22.6	21.2	34.5	45.1	28.9	48.1	47.7	40.4
11.Total livestock output (9+10)	VQBV	9 095.4	7 761.4	7 289.5	7 075.1	7 349.0	7 409.1	7 857.8	7 877.2	7 901.1	8 017.3	8 535.2
12.Total other agricultural activities	LUOS	722.3	689.2	726.0	638.1	632.2	644.2	632.5	718.3	642.3	627.4	624.8
Agricultural services	LUKD	575.0	570.2	609.5	587.0	604.0	601.4	592.3	636.2	632.6	626.3	623.9
Leasing out quota	VQBW	147.2	119.1	116.5	51.2	28.1	42.8	40.2	82.0	9.7	1.0	0.9
13.Total inseparable non-agricultural activities	LUOT	371.6	421.1	430.4	488.3	624.0	559.8	592.3	637.3	673.5	710.3	771.1
14.Gross output at market prices (8+11+12+13)	LUOV	15 395.4	14 079.0	13 640.7	12 880.8	13 390.3	13 477.7	14 025.5	14 474.5	14 215.1	14 502.5	15 721.6
15.Total subsidies (less taxes) on product	LUOU	2 402.9	2 260.0	2 213.6	2 011.7	1 749.7	1 941.8	1 976.1	2 167.5	208.3	81.6	60.0
16.Output at basic prices (14+15)	KFLT	17 798.3	16 338.9	15 854.3	14 892.4	15 140.0	15 419.5	16 001.6	16 642.0	14 423.5	14 584.1	15 781.7
of which transactions within the agricultural industry												
Feed wheat	LUNQ	77.3	78.8	64.4	39.8	41.0	42.5	69.6	103.1	87.0	75.9	93.7
Feed barley	LUNR	192.8	163.6	147.9	136.9	148.5	146.9	148.6	147.9	137.8	147.2	193.6
Feed oats	LUNS	11.8	11.5	14.5	12.6	12.8	12.2	12.0	14.3	12.2	14.9	17.0
Seed potatoes	LUNT	9.2	12.7	28.8	6.9	14.0	12.1	4.0	9.2	12.5	16.0	7.8
Straw	LUNU	160.3	222.1	232.9	258.6	291.2	306.5	177.0	209.0	210.8	191.0	136.6
Contract work	LUNV	575.0	570.2	609.5	587.0	604.0	601.4	592.3	636.2	632.6	626.3	623.9
Leasing of quota	LUNW	147.2	119.1	116.5	51.2	28.1	42.8	40.2	82.0	9.7	1.0	0.9
Total capital formation in livestock	LUNX	720.6	594.7	397.3	393.8	626.5	706.6	731.4	657.2	659.3	760.1	823.1

21.1 Production and income account at current prices[1]
United Kingdom

continued

£ million

		1997	1998	1999	2000	2001	2002	2003	2004	2005	2006	2007[2]
Intermediate consumption												
17.Seeds	KFME	415.8	490.0	542.6	468.2	510.3	485.9	466.7	619.8	661.9	579.6	605.2
18.Energy	VQDO	629.9	598.3	621.9	697.9	683.3	647.0	600.0	669.1	780.8	820.2	874.4
Electricity	VQDQ	232.7	231.0	221.7	230.2	240.1	234.8	204.8	209.7	235.0	252.5	276.5
Fuels	VQDV	397.2	367.3	400.2	467.8	443.2	412.2	395.2	459.4	545.8	567.7	597.9
19.Fertilisers	KFMM	1 006.9	831.7	756.0	737.8	755.1	752.2	696.1	774.6	773.9	769.5	850.7
20.Pesticides	KFMN	674.6	653.7	621.0	579.4	526.2	531.2	501.1	576.3	546.6	513.8	547.1
21.Veterinary expenses	KCPC	307.8	288.0	270.0	255.8	241.2	250.1	253.4	279.3	279.9	282.8	287.3
22.Animal feed	KFMB	2 804.0	2 444.4	2 260.9	2 165.6	2 398.0	2 261.1	2 382.0	2 547.5	2 312.3	2 399.2	2 807.3
Compounds	LUNY	1 772.2	1 523.5	1 402.4	1 283.3	1 398.2	1 376.9	1 348.2	1 449.6	1 318.0	1 401.6	1 635.3
Straights	LUNZ	749.9	667.0	631.7	693.0	797.4	682.6	803.6	832.6	757.3	759.6	867.8
Feed purchased from other farms	LUOA	281.9	253.9	226.8	189.3	202.4	201.6	230.2	265.3	237.1	237.9	304.3
23.Total maintenance[5]	VQDW	1 090.5	1 023.0	1 013.7	939.7	980.4	957.6	966.6	1 012.4	994.4	1 015.6	1 048.6
Materials	KFMO	720.9	699.2	698.2	651.2	660.1	636.2	641.9	663.1	654.0	654.0	671.0
Buildings	KCPB	369.6	323.9	315.5	288.5	320.3	321.3	324.7	349.3	340.4	361.6	377.5
24.Agricultural services	LUOE	575.0	570.2	609.5	587.0	604.0	601.4	592.3	636.2	632.6	626.3	623.9
25.Other goods and services[5,6]	VQDX	2 314.7	2 251.3	2 265.8	2 083.4	2 032.0	2 061.7	2 122.6	2 362.0	2 332.4	2 297.5	2 384.0
26.Total intermediate consumption (Sum 17 to 25)	KCPM	9 819.3	9 150.6	8 961.2	8 515.0	8 730.5	8 548.1	8 580.8	9 477.3	9 314.8	9 304.6	10 028.5
27.Gross value added at market prices (14-26)	LUOG	5 576.2	4 928.4	4 679.5	4 365.8	4 659.8	4 929.5	5 444.7	4 997.2	4 900.3	5 197.9	5 693.2
28.Total consumption of Fixed Capital	KCPS	2 673.9	2 596.8	2 438.2	2 495.5	2 599.9	2 583.8	2 647.6	2 532.8	2 659.0	2 705.0	2 749.9
Equipment	KCPR	1 322.6	1 329.7	1 317.6	1 267.4	1 262.9	1 261.9	1 205.7	1 192.4	1 204.7	1 192.7	1 199.2
Buildings[5,7]	LUOH	669.2	681.5	701.3	691.1	686.1	689.0	691.7	673.1	673.6	683.4	694.5
Livestock	VQEA	682.0	585.6	419.3	537.0	650.8	632.9	750.1	667.3	780.7	829.0	856.2
Cattle	LUOI	391.3	314.8	208.2	281.1	348.4	353.2	441.2	363.6	489.6	528.7	553.2
Pigs	LUOK	14.6	8.4	7.7	8.0	6.1	8.0	7.8	8.7	7.3	7.2	7.4
Sheep	LUOJ	155.1	119.0	69.6	120.1	169.5	141.5	173.0	167.3	150.7	161.6	156.9
Poultry	LUOL	120.9	143.4	133.8	127.8	126.8	130.3	128.2	127.8	133.0	131.5	138.7
29.Net value added at market prices (27-28)	KCPT	2 902.3	2 331.6	2 241.3	1 870.3	2 059.9	2 345.7	2 797.2	2 464.4	2 241.4	2 492.9	2 943.3
30.Compensation of employees[8]	LUOR	1 929.6	1 975.0	2 028.4	1 900.3	1 949.8	1 965.6	1 915.2	2 004.3	2 200.5	2 271.0	2 355.7
31.Other taxes on production	VQEB	−84.5	−88.9	−92.4	−92.2	−84.9	−80.6	−82.8	−96.5	−102.3	−98.4	−101.3
32.Other subsidies on production	VQEC	370.4	379.2	470.1	462.1	695.7	722.7	782.6	778.0	2 787.7	2 913.7	2 899.9
Animal disease compensation	LUOM	15.3	14.3	19.8	29.4	23.2	54.1	60.6	49.4	53.6	..	..
Set-aside	LUON	90.2	87.7	170.0	127.3	180.1	142.5	176.7	129.5	–	..	..
Agri-environment schemes[9]	ZBXC	83.4	107.5	128.5	140.3	164.1	198.0	224.5	262.0	279.0	..	..
Other including Single Payment Scheme[10]	VQED	–	–	–	–	164.9	170.7	159.9	153.4	2 503.7	..	..
33.Net value added at factor cost	LUOQ	5 591.1	4 881.8	4 832.6	4 251.9	4 420.4	4 929.6	5 473.0	5 313.4	5 135.1	5 389.8	5 801.9
34.Rent	KCPV	255.8	250.1	239.6	224.5	250.5	252.9	267.9	240.7	215.4	234.4	222.1
Paid[11]	ZBXE	335.8	330.6	322.0	303.3	328.5	338.5	363.8	345.8	301.9	318.1	316.6
Received[12]	ZBXF	−80.1	−80.5	−82.4	−78.8	−78.1	−85.6	−95.9	−105.1	−86.5	−83.7	−94.5
35.Interest[13]	KCPU	622.4	688.6	594.2	628.2	559.6	483.5	450.5	510.5	547.7	581.1	686.3
Total income from farming (33-30-34-35)	KCQB	2 783.3	1 968.1	1 970.4	1 498.9	1 660.6	2 227.7	2 839.4	2 557.9	2 171.4	2 303.2	2 537.8

1 See chapter text.
2 Provisional.
3 Output is net of VAT collected on the sale of non-edible products. Figures for total output include subsidies on products, but not other subsidies.
4 Includes straw and minor crops.
5 Landlords' expenses are included within 'Total maintenance', 'Other goods and services' and 'Total consumption of Fixed Capital of buildings'.
6 Includes livestock and crop costs, water costs, insurance premiums, bank charges, professional fees, rates and other farming costs.
7 A more empirically based methodology for calculating landlords' consumption of fixed capital was introduced in 2000. The new series has been linked with the old one using a smoothing procedure for the transition year of 1996.
8 Excludes the value of work done by farm labour on own account capital formation in buildings and works.

9 Includes Environmentally and Nitrate Sensitive Areas, Countryside Stewardship and other management schemes, and Moorland, Habitat, Farm Woodland and Organic Farming Schemes.
10 Land area based schemes which replaced the Hill Livestock Compensatory Allowance Scheme in 2001. These are Tir Mynydd in Wales, Less Favoured Area Compensatory Scheme in Northern Ireland, Less Favoured Areas Support Scheme in Scotland and Hill Farm Allowance in England.
11 Rent paid on all tenanted land (including 'conacre' land in Northern Ireland) less landlords' expenses, landlords' consumption of fixed capital and the benefit value of dwellings on that land.
12 Rent received by farming landowners from renting of land to other farmers less landlords' expenses. This series starts in 1996 following a revision to the methodology of calculating net rent.
13 Interest charges on loans for current farming purposes and buildings and works less interest on money held on short term deposit.

Source: Department for Environment, Food and Rural Affairs: 01904 455080

21.2 Output and input volume indices[1]
United Kingdom

Indices (2000=100)

		1996	1997	1998	1999	2000	2001	2002	2003	2004	2005	2006
Outputs[2]												
1. Total cereals:	VQAN	102.5	97.7	95.0	92.1	100.0	79.5	95.9	89.9	93.0	88.3	86.6
Wheat	LUKH	96.5	89.5	92.4	89.0	100.0	70.2	95.9	86.0	93.3	89.4	88.5
Rye	VQAO	131.8	131.8	104.5	104.5	100.0	104.5	90.9	86.4	86.4	86.4	86.4
Barley	LUKI	119.1	120.1	102.2	100.8	100.0	102.2	94.3	97.8	89.0	85.2	81.6
Oats and summer cereal mixtures	LUKJ	92.7	90.8	92.1	84.2	100.0	97.0	103.5	113.3	116.0	84.7	81.4
Other cereals	VQAP	68.6	64.4	53.1	82.4	100.0	74.5	109.1	107.3	104.6	105.1	102.1
2. Total industrial crops:	VQAQ	109.5	111.9	113.5	117.5	100.0	93.3	105.7	109.3	105.7	103.7	95.3
Oil seeds	VQAR	127.2	139.2	145.7	166.7	100.0	100.3	124.1	153.3	139.9	168.0	161.4
Oilseed rape	VQAS	124.2	135.1	138.9	148.5	100.0	100.7	127.2	153.8	140.6	165.8	163.0
Other oil seeds	LUKN	202.7	248.8	335.5	708.3	100.0	90.2	42.7	138.1	121.3	208.8	114.6
Sugar beet	C5X4	114.8	122.1	110.2	116.6	100.0	91.8	105.3	101.0	99.6	95.7	78.8
Other industrial crops	VQAU	101.4	90.2	103.4	95.2	100.0	91.2	97.2	91.9	93.1	75.5	72.4
Fibre plants	VQAV	167.9	169.5	138.3	139.6	100.0	69.3	40.3	67.3	47.7	31.4	39.3
Hops	LUKP	203.1	192.5	131.9	112.4	100.0	94.3	94.5	72.4	72.4	61.9	51.1
Others[3]	VQAW	96.8	85.4	102.1	94.4	100.0	91.2	97.6	92.5	94.0	76.1	73.2
3.Total forage plants	VQAX	86.6	97.9	93.1	96.7	100.0	117.0	117.2	115.6	111.4	113.4	100.2
4.Total vegetables and horticultural Products:	VQAY	104.4	102.9	100.4	102.4	100.0	96.8	96.1	93.5	95.2	95.0	89.8
Fresh vegetables	LUKX	112.8	107.5	105.4	106.2	100.0	96.6	88.3	87.8	88.1	91.1	89.7
Plants and flowers	LUKZ	93.8	97.0	94.1	97.5	100.0	97.0	106.6	101.3	104.8	100.4	90.3
5.Total potatoes (including seeds)	LUKW	114.0	108.3	95.6	113.4	100.0	105.9	106.8	92.1	101.3	92.2	95.0
6.Total fruit	LUKY	122.2	81.3	103.9	108.2	100.0	105.8	99.8	109.7	127.7	149.6	160.3
7.Other crop products including seeds	VQAZ	89.8	98.5	91.3	101.8	100.0	101.2	69.0	83.0	84.6	81.9	80.3
8.Total crop output	VQBA	105.6	101.5	99.6	102.4	100.0	92.1	98.9	95.7	98.7	96.8	93.8
9.Total livestock production	VQBB	102.6	108.2	109.1	105.4	100.0	94.4	97.4	95.9	98.1	99.1	100.2
Mainly for meat processing	LULH	101.3	106.5	107.9	104.7	100.0	91.9	95.3	95.1	97.5	99.4	100.0
Cattle	LULC	94.5	98.5	101.2	103.1	100.0	88.6	102.6	105.9	104.3	112.6	118.1
Pigs	LULE	116.1	127.4	129.1	118.4	100.0	91.7	87.4	77.5	78.3	78.5	77.9
Sheep	LULD	93.3	98.4	104.2	104.1	100.0	71.7	81.8	83.4	88.5	89.5	88.7
Poultry	LULF	103.9	106.4	104.5	99.2	100.0	103.5	99.4	101.0	106.8	104.2	101.8
Other animals	LULG	100.1	100.5	100.6	100.0	100.0	99.7	99.8	99.3	99.1	99.6	98.9
Gross fixed capital formation	LULR	114.2	123.3	121.0	113.2	100.0	115.8	115.9	106.6	107.1	102.0	105.8
Cattle	LULN	118.4	116.7	113.8	114.5	100.0	116.0	110.6	109.4	101.6	104.2	106.7
Pigs	LULP	165.3	173.7	131.0	147.1	100.0	84.5	127.6	101.0	94.7	80.3	101.5
Sheep	LULO	145.1	188.3	196.0	147.5	100.0	155.6	173.6	126.4	149.4	117.2	132.3
Poultry	LULQ	101.2	108.5	102.3	96.7	100.0	95.7	95.3	95.0	98.0	94.0	93.3
10.Total livestock products	LULM	100.7	102.0	100.7	102.8	100.0	101.6	102.9	104.1	101.7	101.2	100.0
Milk	LULI	101.0	102.0	100.4	102.8	100.0	101.2	102.3	103.5	100.3	99.6	98.7
Eggs	LULJ	96.8	101.3	102.3	101.1	100.0	107.3	107.0	105.3	114.0	115.1	111.1
Raw wool	LULK	103.7	105.7	112.6	103.9	100.0	83.1	86.3	84.4	85.7	87.9	82.1
Other animal products	LULL	106.8	112.4	100.1	118.7	100.0	88.2	139.6	173.9	105.3	105.2	105.3
11.Total livestock output	VQBC	101.8	105.6	105.7	104.4	100.0	97.2	99.6	99.1	99.5	100.0	100.2
12.Total other agricultural activities	VQBD	115.9	111.0	110.6	116.2	100.0	99.0	100.7	101.5	106.5	96.2	95.7
Agricultural services	VQBE	92.7	94.0	99.1	105.9	100.0	102.9	102.5	100.9	106.3	103.3	103.3
Leasing out quota	VQBF	399.3	311.3	243.4	234.5	100.0	54.0	80.9	107.4	107.2	19.6	13.6
13.Total inseparable non-agricultural Activities	LULX	82.5	82.0	90.3	91.1	100.0	124.4	108.2	110.9	113.5	120.4	123.6

21.2
Output and input volume indices[1]
United Kingdom

continued

Indices (2000=100)

		1996	1997	1998	1999	2000	2001	2002	2003	2004	2005	2006
14.Gross output at market prices	VQEG	102.9	103.5	103.1	103.7	100.0	96.4	99.7	98.4	100.1	99.4	98.6
15.Total subsidies (less taxes) on product	VQEE	..	..	..	..	..	..	..	..	..	..	..
16.Output at basic prices	LULY	102.3	103.7	103.6	104.3	100.0	94.9	99.5	98.5	100.0	99.8	98.9
of which transactions within the agricultural industry												
Feed wheat	LULZ	101.2	146.4	174.7	145.6	100.0	95.8	103.2	163.3	221.7	218.0	192.7
Feed barley	LUMA	93.8	112.1	110.1	101.2	100.0	108.2	114.9	108.1	98.0	101.9	107.1
Feed oats	LUMB	82.0	75.0	92.1	108.6	100.0	103.3	97.1	96.7	93.7	75.6	80.5
Seed potatoes	LUMC	165.7	116.9	114.5	114.2	100.0	109.3	110.7	56.2	77.6	100.5	159.9
Straw	LUMD	97.4	84.4	102.9	93.9	100.0	89.8	95.8	89.9	90.9	71.3	67.5
Contract work	LUME	92.7	94.0	99.1	105.9	100.0	102.9	102.5	100.9	106.3	103.3	103.3
Leasing of quota	LUMF	399.3	311.3	243.4	234.5	100.0	54.0	80.9	107.4	107.2	19.6	13.6
Total capital formation in livestock	LUMG	114.1	123.3	121.0	113.2	100.0	115.8	116.0	106.7	107.2	102.0	105.9
Intermediate Consumption												
17.Seeds	LUMO	112.9	109.5	105.0	104.9	100.0	104.2	99.1	98.8	99.9	100.9	103.4
Cereals	LUMM	..	..	..	..	..	..	..	..	..	..	..
Other	LUMN	..	..	..	..	..	..	..	..	..	..	..
18.Energy	VQEH	106.3	103.3	108.3	101.6	92.8	94.0	93.4	79.4	82.0	76.5	..
Electricity	VQEI	106.2	104.0	113.7	108.1	100.0	108.2	110.3	89.6	86.6	85.4	83.4
Fuels	VQEJ	119.8	115.9	118.2	110.1	100.0	97.8	95.8	83.5	89.0	81.2	76.9
19.Fertilisers	VQEK	119.6	130.3	122.1	114.2	100.0	87.4	91.2	78.2	79.4	71.2	68.9
20.Pesticides	LUMQ	96.6	100.1	104.3	101.4	100.0	93.9	95.8	90.5	99.4	92.1	91.9
21.Veterinary expenses	LUMW	118.1	120.4	111.4	104.3	100.0	95.6	100.0	97.6	104.6	104.2	95.9
22.Animal feed	LUML	106.8	103.1	103.4	104.2	100.0	103.8	101.3	105.5	107.4	110.8	106.1
Compounds	LUMH	113.0	108.6	105.9	108.8	100.0	102.9	102.3	102.2	103.3	99.8	105.4
Straights	LUMI	98.5	88.4	92.8	93.2	100.0	105.2	96.7	107.9	110.2	127.8	101.8
Feed purchased from other farms	LUMJ	94.5	117.1	122.8	111.2	100.0	105.2	111.2	120.0	125.8	126.6	125.3
23.Total maintenance[4]	VQEL	124.8	121.2	112.9	110.6	100.0	102.1	96.2	92.7	93.1	86.3	85.7
Materials	LUMU	120.1	115.4	112.1	109.5	100.0	98.5	91.0	86.4	85.5	78.8	78.1
Buildings	LUMT	135.1	134.1	114.7	113.1	100.0	110.4	108.3	107.0	110.8	103.8	103.6
24.Agricultural services	VQEM	92.7	94.0	99.1	105.9	100.0	102.9	102.5	100.9	106.3	103.3	103.3
25.Other goods and services[4,5]	VQEO	121.7	121.0	115.1	111.4	100.0	93.9	92.4	99.0	103.7	95.5	91.3
26.Total intermediate consumption	LUNE	112.9	112.3	110.0	108.0	100.0	98.4	97.0	96.4	99.6	95.5	92.5
27.Gross value added at market prices	LUNF	87.3	89.2	91.5	96.3	100.0	93.0	104.1	101.8	100.8	106.8	110.3
28.Total consumption of Fixed Capital	LUNN	106.0	103.5	102.7	101.3	100.0	98.2	93.9	93.2	92.3	93.4	90.9
Equipment	LUNI	106.5	106.4	104.4	102.3	100.0	97.7	96.1	94.7	94.1	92.6	90.8
Buildings[4,6]	LUNG	105.9	107.7	107.0	104.3	100.0	101.2	103.0	100.2	97.8	94.2	91.6
Livestock	VQES	101.9	91.3	92.8	94.3	100.0	96.0	81.2	83.4	83.3	92.3	88.8
Cattle	LUNJ	98.6	87.0	86.1	88.1	100.0	86.4	76.0	81.0	80.9	92.2	87.8
Pigs	LUNL	111.4	121.3	130.0	117.4	100.0	68.2	99.3	79.4	79.6	69.3	64.5
Sheep	LUNK	99.4	82.9	85.1	95.1	100.0	120.7	78.9	78.1	79.0	86.6	85.5
Poultry	LUNM	102.3	102.8	110.3	105.0	100.0	98.0	98.8	96.2	94.7	98.1	95.6
29.Net value added at market prices	LUNO	71.9	76.1	80.6	91.0	100.0	86.9	116.6	112.2	111.2	123.6	135.8

1 See chapter text.
2 Output is net of VAT collected on the sale of non-edible products. Figures for total output include subsidies on products, but not other subsidies.
3 Includes straw and minor crops.
4 Landlords' expenses are included within 'Total maintenance', 'Other goods and services' and 'Total consumption of Fixed Capital of buildings'.

5 Includes livestock and crop costs, water costs, insurance premiums, bank charges, professional fees, rates, and other farming costs.
6 A more empirically based methodology for calculating landlords' depreciation was introduced in 2000. The new series has been linked with the old one using a smoothing procedure for the transition year of 1996.

Source: Department for Environment, Food and Rural Affairs: 01904 455080

21.3 Agriculture land-use
United Kingdom
Area at the June Survey[1]

Thousand hectares

		1997	1998	1999	2000	2001	2002	2003	2004	2005	2006	2007
Total agricultural area	BFAH	18 653	18 604	18 579	18 311	18 594	18 537	18 464	18 432	18 502	18 713	18 602
Crops	BFAA	4 990	4 971	4 709	4 665	4 493	4 604	4 475	4 589	4 437	4 340	4 350
Bare fallow	BFAB	29	34	33	37	43	33	29	29	164	197	165
Total tillage	KIJR	5 020	5 005	4 742	4 702	4 536	4 636	4 504	4 619	4 600	4 536	4 515
All grass under 5 years old	KFEM	1 405	1 301	1 226	1 226	1 205	1 243	1 200	1 246	1 193	1 137	1 176
Total arable land	KFEN	6 425	6 306	5 968	5 928	5 741	5 879	5 705	5 864	5 794	5 673	5 691
All grasses 5 years old and over	KFEO	5 282	5 364	5 449	5 364	5 584	5 519	5 683	5 620	5 711	5 967	5 965
Total tillage and grass	KFEP	11 706	11 671	11 417	11 292	11 325	11 397	11 388	11 485	11 505	11 641	11 656
Sole right rough grazing	BFAD	4 657	4 621	4 575	4 445	4 435	4 488	4 329	4 326	4 354	4 491	4 313
Set aside	DMNF	306	313	572	567	800	611	689	559	535	466	440
All other land on agricultural holdings including woodland	BFAE	763	773	789	780	801	802	792	825	872	874	954
Total land on agricultural holdings	BFAF	17 432	17 377	17 352	17 083	17 361	17 303	17 227	17 195	17 266	17 472	17 363
Common rough grazing (estimated)	BFAG	1 221	1 227	1 227	1 228	1 232	1 234	1 236	1 237	1 236	1 241	1 238
Crops	BFAA	4 990	4 971	4 709	4 665	4 493	4 604	4 475	4 589	4 437	4 340	4 350
Cereals	BFAJ	3 514	3 418	3 141	3 348	3 014	3 245	3 057	3 130	2 919	2 861	2 871
Wheat	BFAK	2 036	2 045	1 847	2 086	1 635	1 996	1 837	1 990	1 867	1 833	1 816
Barley	BFAL	1 359	1 253	1 179	1 128	1 245	1 101	1 076	1 007	938	881	898
Oats	BFAM	100	98	92	109	112	126	121	108	90	121	129
Mixed corn	BFAN	2	2	2	2	3	4	4	..	..	..	..
Rye[2]	BFAO	9	10	8	7	5	5	4	6	..	..	..
Triticale[3]	DMNH	8	11	13	16	14	14	15	15	13	13	16
Other arable crops (excluding potatoes)	DMNI	1 125	1 210	1 211	979	1 141	1 024	1 098	1 136	1 211	1 172	1 170
Oilseed rape	BFAP	445	507	417	332	404	357	460	498	519	500	602
Sugar beet not for stock feeding[2]	BFAQ	196	189	183	173	177	169	162	154	148	130	125
Hops[4]	DMNJ	3	3	3	2	2	2	2	2	1	1	..
Peas for harvesting dry and field beans	DMNK	197	213	202	208	276	249	235	242	239	231	161
Linseed	DMNL	73	100	209	71	31	12	32	30	45	33	11
Other crops	DMNM	210	200	197	192	214	204	201	203	252	278	272
Potatoes	BFAR	166	164	178	166	165	158	145	148	137	140	140
Horticultural	BFAV	184	180	179	172	173	176	176	175	170	166	169
Vegetables grown in the open	DMNN	126	125	126	119	120	124	125	125	121	119	121
Orchard fruit[5]	BFBG	30	30	28	28	28	26	25	24	23	23	23
Soft fruit	DMNO	11	10	9	10	9	9	9	9	9	10	9
Ornamentals	DMNP	14	14	13	14	14	15	14	15	14	12	13
Glasshouse crops	DMNQ	2	2	2	2	2	2	2	2	2	2	2

1 Includes estimates for minor holdings for all countries. See chapter text.
2 Figures are for England and Wales only.
3 Figures for 2004 do not include Wales.
4 Figures are for England only from 2005. From 2007 are included in Other Crops.
5 Includes non-commercial orchards.

Source: Agricultural Departments: 01904 455332

21.4 Estimated quantity of crops and grass harvested[1]
United Kingdom

Thousand tonnes

		1996	1997	1998	1999	2000	2001	2002	2003	2004	2005	2006
Agricultural crops												
Wheat	BADO	16 100	15 020	16 449	14 867	16 704	11 580	15 973	14 288	15 473	14 863	14 735
Barley (Winter and Spring) .	BADP	7 790	7 830	6 623	6 581	6 492	6 660	6 126	6 370	5 816	5 495	5 239
Oats	BADQ	590	575	586	541	640	621	753	749	627	532	728
Sugar beet[2]	BADR	10 420	11 084	10 002	10 584	9 079	8 335	9 557	9 168	9 042	8 687	7 400
Potatoes	BADS	7 228	7 128	6 422	7 131	6 636	6 649	6 966	6 058	6 246	5 979	5 727

		1996 /97	1997 /98	1998 /99	1999 /00	2000 /01	2001 /02	2002 /03	2003 /04	2004 /05	2005 /06	2006 /07
Horticultural crops												
Field vegetables												
Brussels sprouts	BADT	82.6	74.2	72.5	78.5	67.3	54.8	42.7	55.8	45.1	46.1	44.8
Cabbage (including savoys and spring greens)	BADU	360.1	309.7	283.6	269.1	254.3	282.1	244.0	229.2	222.0	262.7	274.9
Cauliflowers	BADV	217.1	191.0	191.7	172.4	156.1	107.4	115.8	126.3	168.3	133.2	123.7
Carrots	BADW	624.4	623.1	617.6	673.2	725.8	760.0	718.4	602.4	671.1	710.1	701.3
Turnips and swedes	BADX	135.6	106.9	117.5	123.3	132.1	141.8	104.7	96.5	97.0	103.1	105.7
Beetroot	BADY	72.1	72.4	69.5	63.4	67.1	68.6	56.3	58.8	53.9	51.0	57.3
Onions, dry bulb	BADZ	313.3	329.3	342.0	391.4	392.7	374.9	283.4	373.6	340.9	413.6	358.8
Peas, green for market (in pod weight)	BAEA	6.7	8.2	7.0	7.0	6.7	6.2	7.2	5.9	5.9	5.9	5.9
Peas, green for processing (shelled weight)	BAEB	215.5	167.9	152.0	143.1	184.5	161.0	169.3	167.6	131.1	129.0	124.4
Lettuce	BAEC	187.5	157.7	151.8	155.2	135.8	123.9	109.9	125.6	140.9	131.7	126.4
Protected crops												
Tomatoes	BAED	115.5	114.0	107.6	116.6	113.0	109.1	100.9	75.6	78.6	78.8	83.6
Cucumbers	BAEE	85.6	81.7	83.8	83.8	79.8	71.5	73.6	77.0	61.4	59.9	56.5
Lettuce	BAEF	26.5	24.1	20.6	19.9	18.7	20.9	16.0	16.6	10.4	8.1	8.2
Fruit												
Dessert apples	BFCD	105.4	96.0	97.8	133.9	101.3	104.4	84.0	69.0	92.2	118.0	129.3
Cooking apples	BFCE	118.5	91.1	85.9	112.4	107.5	107.4	95.3	74.9	78.2	100.1	111.5
Soft fruit	BFCF	83.4	60.6	60.8	67.2	65.4	64.6	67.1	79.6	86.0	105.4	107.7
Pears	BFBQ	35.8	33.0	26.3	22.7	26.6	38.5	34.2	29.6	22.7	23.4	28.4

1 See chapter text.
2 Figures are adjusted to constant 16% sugar content.

Source: Agricultural Departments: 01904 455332

21.5 Cattle, sheep, pigs and poultry on agricultural holdings[1]
United Kingdom
At June each year

Thousands

		1997	1998	1999	2000	2001	2002	2003	2004	2005	2006	2007
Total cattle and calves[2]	BFCG	11 637	11 519	11 423	11 135	10 602	10 345	10 508	10 588	10 770	10 579	10 304
of which:												
dairy cows	BFCH	2 478	2 439	2 440	2 336	2 251	2 227	2 191	2 129	2 063	2 066	1 954
beef cows	BFCI	1 862	1 947	1 924	1 842	1 708	1 657	1 698	1 736	1 762	1 733	1 698
heifers in calf	BFCJ	848	787	763	718	701	728	679	690	638	645	..
Total sheep and lambs	BFCM	42 823	44 471	44 656	42 264	36 716	35 834	35 812	35 817	35 416	34 722	33 946
of which:												
ewes and shearlings	CKUQ	20 696	21 260	21 458	20 449	17 921	17 630	17 580	17 630	16 935	16 637	16 064
lambs under one year old	BFCP	21 032	22 138	22 092	20 857	17 769	17 310	17 322	17 238	17 488	17 058	16 855
Total pigs	BFCQ	8 072	8 146	7 284	6 482	5 845	5 588	5 046	5 159	4 862	4 933	4 834
of which:												
sows in pig and other sows for breeding	CKUU	683	675	603	537	527	483	442	449	403	401	398
gilts in pig	CKUR	116	103	85	73	71	74	73	66	67	67	57
Total fowls	KPSV	..	..	..	..	..	..	165 285	167 825	160 509	158 202	157 513
of which:												
table fowls including broilers	CKUT	..	98 244	101 625	105 689	112 531	105 137	116 738	119 888	111 475	110 672	108 753
laying fowls[3]	CKUV	34 286	29 483	29 258	28 687	29 895	28 778	29 274	29 655	29 544	28 632	27 321
growing pullets	CKUW	11 510	9 860	9 583	9 461	9 367	9 784	8 286	8 156	10 928	9 625	8 936

1 Includes estimates for minor holdings for all countries. See chapter text.
2 In 2007 the cattle figures were sourced form the Cattle Tracin System (CTS) in England and Wales, the equivalent APHIS system in Northern Ireland and survey data in Scotland and are therefore no directly comparable with earlier years. To see comparable data for 2005-2007 please go to: http://statistics.defra.gov.uk/esg/statnot/june_uk.pdf
3 Excludes fowls laying eggs for hatching.

Sources: Department for Environment, Food and Rural Affairs;
Farming Statistics: 01904 455332

21.6 Forestry[1]
United Kingdom

		1980	1990	2000	2002	2003	2004	2005	2006	2007
Woodland area[2] - (Thousand hectares)										
United Kingdom	C5OF	2 175	2 400	2 793	2 800	2 807	2 816	2 825	2 829	2 837
England[3]	C5OG	948	958	1 103	1 104	1 110	1 114	1 119	1 121	1 124
Wales[3]	C5OI	241	248	289	288	285	286	286	285	285
Scotland[3]	C5OH	920	1 120	1 318	1 324	1 327	1 330	1 334	1 337	1 341
Northern Ireland	C5OJ	67	74	83	84	85	86	85	86	87
Forestry Commission/Forest Service	C5OK	946	956	886	855	848	842	838	832	827
Other[5]	C5OL	1 230	1 443	1 907	1 945	1 960	1 974	1 987	1 997	2 010
Conifer	C5OM	1 372	1 576	1 663	1 658	1 652	1 651	1 647	1 642	1 640
Broadleaved[6]	C5ON	804	824	1 131	1 143	1 155	1 165	1 178	1 187	1 197

		1996 /97	1997 /98	1998 /99	1999 /00	2000 /01	2001 /02	2002 /03	2003 /04	2004 /05	2005 /06	2006 /07
New Planting[7] - (Thousand hectares)												
United Kingdom	C5OO	17.6	16.9	17.0	17.9	18.7	14.4	13.5	12.4	11.9	8.7	10.7
England	C5OP	4.7	4.4	5.1	5.9	5.9	5.4	5.9	4.6	5.3	3.7	3.2
Wales	C5OR	0.4	0.5	0.6	0.7	0.4	0.3	0.3	0.5	0.5	0.5	0.4
Scotland	C5OQ	11.8	11.4	10.5	10.4	11.7	8.0	6.7	6.8	5.7	4.0	6.6
Northern Ireland	C5OS	0.8	0.6	0.7	0.8	0.7	0.7	0.6	0.5	0.4	0.6	0.5
Forestry Commission/Forest Service	C5OT	0.6	0.2	0.2	0.3	0.3	0.8	0.9	0.3	0.1	0.3	0.2
Other[8]	C5OU	17.0	16.7	16.8	17.6	18.4	13.6	12.6	12.1	11.8	8.4	10.4
Conifer	C5OV	7.7	7.0	6.6	6.5	5.1	3.9	4.0	2.9	2.1	1.1	2.1
Broadleaved	C5OW	9.9	9.9	10.4	11.4	13.6	10.5	9.5	9.5	9.8	7.6	8.5
Restocking[7] - (Thousand hectares)												
United Kingdom	C5OX	15.1	14.2	14.1	15.2	15.3	13.8	14.5	14.9	14.8	14.8	17.7
England	C5OY	4.3	4.4	4.1	3.9	4.0	3.4	3.4	3.2	2.8	3.2	2.7
Wales	C5P2	3.0	2.7	3.0	2.6	2.2	1.9	1.9	1.8	1.6	2.5	2.7
Scotland	C5OZ	7.2	6.3	6.3	8.0	8.0	7.8	8.5	8.9	9.5	8.2	11.4
Northern Ireland	C5P3	0.6	0.7	0.6	0.6	1.1	0.8	0.7	1.0	1.0	0.9	0.8
Forestry Commission/Forest Service	C5P4	8.4	8.5	8.5	8.8	8.9	9.1	9.1	9.9	9.4	9.3	9.7
Other[8]	C5P5	6.7	5.7	5.6	6.4	6.4	4.7	5.3	5.0	5.5	5.5	8.0
Conifer	C5P6	11.6	11.2	11.3	11.9	12.2	11.4	12.0	12.1	12.0	11.6	14.2
Broadleaved	C5P7	3.5	3.0	2.8	3.3	3.0	2.4	2.5	2.8	2.9	3.3	3.5

		1998	1999	2000	2001	2002	2003	2004	2005	2006
Wood Production (volume - Thousand green tonnes[9])										
United Kingdom	C5P8	7 540	7 960	8 090	8 140	8 270	8 900	9 040	9 080	8 940
Softwood total	C5PA	6 830	7 280	7 430	7 500	7 650	8 330	8 530	8 490	8 500
Forestry Commission/Forest Service	C5PB	4 190	4 730	4 850	4 600	4 650	4 820	4 890	4 580	4 580
Non-Forestry Commission/Forest Service	C5PC	2 640	2 550	2 580	2 900	3 000	3 520	3 630	3 910	3 920
Hardwood[10]	C5PD	720	680	660	640	620	560	510	590	440

1 See chapter text.
2 Areas as at 31 March.
3 For England, Wales and Scotland, 1980 woodland area figures are the published results from the 1979-1982 Census of Woodlands and Trees and figures for 1990 are adjusted to reflect subsequent changes. From 1998 onwards they are based on results from the 1995-1999 National Inventory of Woodlands and Trees, adjusted to reflect subsequent changes.
4 The apparent fall in woodland cover in 2001 is due to the reclassification of Forestry Commission open land within the forest.
5 Includes private woodland and non-Forestry Commission / Forest Service public woodland.

6 Broadleaved includes coppice. For data based on 1979-82 Census, all scrub and other non-plantation woodland have been assumed to be broadleaved.
7 Figures shown are for the areas of new planting and restocking in the year to 31 March.
8 Includes grant aided planting on non-Forestry Commission/ Forest Service woodland and estimates for areas planted without the aid of grants.
9 Figures have been rounded to the nearest 10 thousand green tonnes.
10 Hardwood is timber from broadleaved species. Most hardwood production comes from non-FC/FS woodland; the figures are estimates based on reported deliveries to wood processing industries.

Source: Forestry Commission: 0131 314 6171

21.7 Sales for food of agricultural produce and livestock
United Kingdom

			1997	1998	1999	2000	2001	2002	2003	2004	2005	2006	2007
Cereals:		Thousand											
Wheat[1]	KCQK	tonnes	5 535	5 707	5 668	5 617	5 672	5 628	5 611	5 600	5 642	5 625	5 702
Barley	KCQL	"	5 498	5 548	5 280	5 363	5 714	5 771	5 438	5 418	4 962	4 971	4 904
Oats[2]	KCQM	"	259	272	266	261	287	312	322	321	343	373	420
Potatoes[3]	KCQN	"	6 279	5 997	6 209	6 129	6 605	6 803	6 560	6 449	5 868	5 674	5 816
Milk:													
Utilised for liquid consumption	KCQO	Million litres	6 778	6 767	6 889	6 793	6 748	6 825	6 752	6 693	6 652	6 736	6 698
Utilised for manufacture	KCQP	"	7 039	6 806	6 973	6 628	6 902	7 056	7 271	6 827	6 568	6 343	6 131
Total available for domestic use[4]	KCQQ	"	14 258	13 973	14 234	13 730	13 940	14 101	14 294	13 769	13 488	13 366	13 202
Hen eggs in shell	KCQR	Million dozens	794	774	738	712	753	746	733	778	772	743	714
Animals slaughtered:													
Cattle and calves:													
Cattle	KCQS	Thousands	2 274	2 270	2 220	2 267	2 051	2 191	2 199	2 261	2 298	2 578	2 615
Calves	KCQT	"	20	31	75	152	92	98	87	101	111	125	108
Total	KCQU	"	2 293	2 301	2 296	2 419	2 143	2 289	2 286	2 361	2 409	2 702	2 723
Sheep and lambs	KCQV	"	17 714	19 578	20 801	19 635	13 322	15 342	15 436	15 493	16 539	16 590	15 979
Pigs:													
Clean pigs	MBGD	"	15 097	15 539	14 310	12 165	10 383	9 983	8 760	8 597	8 496	8 520	8 862
Sows and boars	KCQZ	"	381	414	379	325	182	317	247	244	213	211	222
Total	KCRA	"	15 479	15 954	14 690	12 490	10 565	10 300	9 007	8 841	8 709	8 731	9 084
Poultry[5]	KCRB	Millions	850	857	863	843	866	862	882	882	903	880	871

Note: The figures for cereals and for animals slaughtered relate to periods of 52 weeks

1 Flour millers' receipts of home-grown wheat.
2 Oatmeal millers' receipts of home-grown oats.
3 Total sales for human consumption in the UK. Figures for 2007 are provisional.

4 The totals of liquid consumption and milk used for manufacture may not add up to the total available for domestic use because of adjustments for dairy wastage, stock changes and other uses, such as farmhouse consumption, milk fed to stock and on farm waste.
5 Total fowls, ducks, geese and turkeys.

Source: Department for Environment, Food and Rural Affairs: 01904 455332

21.8 Estimates of producers of organic and in-conversion livestock[1]
United Kingdom

At January each year

Thousand head

		2004	2005	2006	2007
Cattle	IDR8	126.8	174.8	214.3	244.8
Sheep	IDR9	440.7	571.6	691.0	747.3
Pigs	IDS2	48.8	43.7	30.0	32.9
Poultry	IDS3	2 166.2	2 431.6	3 439.5	4 421.3
Goats	IDS4	0.7	0.5	0.5	0.6
Other Livestock	IDS5	1.0	1.2	1.5	4.3

1 Certification bodies record production data at various times of the year so figures should be treated with care as they will not represent an exact snapshot of organic livestock farming.

Sources: Department for Environment, Food and Rural Affairs; Organic Statistics Team: 01904 455557

21.9 Producers of organic and in-conversion livestock, Organic producers, growers, processors and importers

United Kingdom

		2003[1]	2004	2005	2006	2007
Producers of organic and in-conversion livestock						
North East	IDZ2	..	49	44	54	46
North West	IDZ3	..	122	87	102	104
Yorkshire and Humberside	IDZ4	..	82	54	82	82
East Midlands	IDZ5	..	135	110	125	121
West Midlands	IDZ6	..	196	162	196	174
Eastern	IDZ7	..	99	69	86	91
South West	IDZ8	..	761	553	724	706
South East (including London)	IDZ9	..	220	162	201	179
England	IE22	..	1 664	1 241	1 570	1 503
Wales	IE23	..	469	402	502	493
Scotland	IE24	..	385	293	296	285
Northern Ireland	IE25	..	119	110	140	167
United Kingdom	IE26	..	2 637	2 046	2 508	2 448
		2003[1]	2004	2005	2006	2007
Producers and growers businesses						
North East	IE27	73	74	83	101	116
North West	IE28	171	169	176	168	173
Yorkshire and Humberside	IE29	136	134	149	138	155
East Midlands	IE2A	220	218	237	221	236
West Midlands	IE2B	330	325	337	335	351
Eastern	IE2C	248	258	259	253	267
South West	IE2D	1 026	1 020	1 123	1 152	1 282
South East (including London)	IE2E	418	409	463	417	423
England	IE2F	2 622	2 607	2 827	2 785	3 003
Wales	IE2G	618	623	667	688	710
Scotland	IE2H	725	689	653	595	686
Northern Ireland	IE2I	139	153	174	217	240
United Kingdom	IE2J	4 104	4 072	4 321	4 285	4 639
Processors and/or importers businesses[2]						
North East	IE2K	34	31	19	28	45
North West	IE2L	122	130	107	143	159
Yorkshire and Humberside	IE2M	118	126	121	141	164
East Midlands	IE2N	175	191	154	195	210
West Midlands	IE2O	138	139	114	143	169
Eastern	IE2P	224	249	209	255	289
South West	IE2Q	333	353	242	380	450
South East (including London)	IE2R	393	450	387	484	516
England	IE2S	1 537	1 669	1 353	1 769	2 002
Wales	IE2T	103	112	85	112	125
Scotland	IE2U	152	174	152	197	225
Northern Ireland	IE2V	33	35	36	50	52
United Kingdom	IE2W	1 825	1 990	1 626	2 128	2 404

1 As at March in 2003.
2 Processers and importers include abattoirs, bakers, stores and wholesalers. The recorded location depends on the address registered with the Sector Bodies and so larger businesses may be recorded at their headquarters.

Sources: Department for Environment, Food and Rural Affairs; Organic Statistics Team:01904 455557

21.10 Organic and in-conversion land and land use United Kingdom

Thousand hectares

		2003[1]	2004	2005	2006	2007
Land, in-conversion						
North East	IDS6	15.3	6.8	4.6	6.6	6.9
North West	IDS7	7.7	2.6	2.5	3.2	1.8
Yorkshire and Humberside	IDS8	2.3	1.7	1.3	2.3	3.4
East Midlands	IDS9	2.9	1.6	1.2	2.4	2.1
West Midlands	IDT2	6.0	3.7	2.4	3.2	4.0
Eastern	IDT3	4.1	3.0	2.4	2.6	3.6
South West	IDT4	18.0	10.8	9.1	22.0	31.6
South East (including London)	IDT5	11.5	6.5	5.4	10.7	13.2
England	IDT6	67.8	36.8	28.8	53.2	66.5
Wales	IDT7	13.7	8.0	8.6	12.8	15.4
Scotland	IDT8	121.3	20.4	13.7	16.7	35.2
Northern Ireland	IDT9	1.5	0.8	1.6	3.2	4.0
United Kingdom	IDU2	204.3	66.0	52.7	86.0	121.1
Land, fully organic						
North East	IDU3	12.4	20.5	25.3	29.3	22.6
North West	IDU4	15.1	19.9	19.8	18.9	19.4
Yorkshire and Humberside	IDU5	7.0	8.1	8.6	9.0	9.0
East Midlands	IDU6	12.0	16.1	13.4	13.2	12.5
West Midlands	IDU7	23.4	25.5	26.8	27.0	26.3
Eastern	IDU8	7.8	9.7	10.3	11.8	10.8
South West	IDU9	78.1	86.2	90.5	94.0	93.4
South East (including London)	IDV2	28.3	34.3	34.9	35.2	35.8
England	IDV3	184.0	220.2	229.6	238.4	229.9
Wales	IDV4	41.4	50.2	55.6	58.0	63.5
Scotland	IDV5	307.3	351.9	331.6	231.2	200.1
Northern Ireland	IDV6	4.1	6.6	5.0	6.3	5.1
United Kingdom	IDV7	536.9	629.0	621.8	533.9	498.6

		2003[1]	2004	2005	2006	2007
Land, in-conversion						
Cereals	IDV8	11.2	7.0	4.1	10.3	11.9
Other Crops	IDV9	6.5	1.9	2.7	3.5	3.4
Fruit and Nuts[2]	IDW2	0.4	0.2	0.2	0.2	0.2
Vegetables (including potatoes)	IDW3	3.0	1.9	1.3	1.3	2.1
Herbs and ornamentals[3]	IDW4	0.1	0.1	–	0.2	0.1
Temporary pasture	IDW5	18.1	12.7	10.4	15.9	22.9
Set aside	IDW6	3.5	2.3	1.3	1.4	1.1
Permanent pasture[4]	IDW7	159.1	38.1	27.2	47.5	72.1
Woodland	IDW8	1.1	0.7	0.6	3.5	4.2
Non cropping	IDW9	0.2	0.3	2.9	1.1	2.3
Other	IDX2	0.4	0.3	1.7	1.1	0.2
Unknown	IDX3	0.8	0.5	0.1	0.1	0.8
Total	IDX4	204.3	66.0	52.7	86.0	121.1
Land, fully organic						
Cereals	IDX5	25.7	35.4	35.1	37.4	35.5
Other Crops	IDX6	14.1	7.5	10.2	7.3	6.8
Fruit and Nuts[2]	IDX7	1.5	1.4	1.5	1.5	1.6
Vegetables (including potatoes)	IDX8	9.7	11.7	12.7	12.4	13.5
Herbs and ornamentals[3]	IDX9	0.2	0.2	0.2	0.6	0.6
Temporary pasture	IDY2	58.9	77.3	80.3	82.0	79.8
Set aside	IDY3	3.4	4.6	4.6	2.3	1.3
Permanent pasture[4]	IDY4	413.9	481.3	467.8	380.9	350.5
Woodland	IDY5	5.6	4.8	5.2	3.3	4.0
Non cropping	IDY6	1.4	0.9	1.3	2.4	4.0
Other	IDY7	0.2	3.0	2.4	3.2	0.4
Unknown	IDY8	2.4	0.8	0.4	0.4	0.6
Total	IDY9	536.9	629.0	621.8	533.9	498.6

1 As at March in 2003.
2 Nuts not included in 2003.
3 Included Nuts in 2003.
4 Includes rough grazing.

Sources: Department for Environment, Food and Rural Affairs;
Organic Statistics Team: 01904 455557

21.11 Average weekly and hourly earnings and hours of full-time male agricultural workers[1]

England and Wales: At September each year

		2002	2003	2004	2005	2006	2007
Average weekly earnings (£)	LQML	366.82	352.88	380.75	422.15	359.48	359.62
95% confidence interval		(+/-£18.88)	(+/-£30.30)	(+/-£28.79)	(+/-£29.39)	(+/-£34.99)	(+/-£25.17)
Average weekly hours worked	LQMM	54.1	51.1	51.0	55.7	48.0	48.6
95% confidence interval		(+/-2.1)	(+/-3.0)	(+/-2.8)	(+/-3.2)	(+/-3.1)	(+/-2.4)
Average earnings/hours (£)	LQMN	6.78	6.91	7.46	7.58	7.48	7.40
95% confidence interval		(+/-£0.19)	(+/-£0.31)	(+/-£0.31)	(+/-£0.26)	(+/-£0.43)	(+/-£0.27)
Number of workers in the sample		204	72	94	76	50	68

1 See chapter text.

Source: Department for Environment, Food and Rural Affairs: 01904 455332

21.12 Average weekly and hourly earnings and hours of agricultural workers[1] : by type, aged 20 and over

England and Wales: At September 2007

	Full-time		Part-time		Casual		Managers
	Male	Female	Male	Female	Male	Female	
Average weekly earnings (£)	359.62	287.92	143.13	147.33	245.53	168.00	491.12
95% confidence interval	(+/-£25.17)	(+/-£16.99)	(+/-£34.31)	(+/-£29.89)	(+/-£38.20)	(+/-£54.13)	(+/-£30.55)
Average weekly hours worked	48.6	43.0	21.5	23.0	35.6	28.2	..
95% confidence interval	(+/-2.4)	(+/-1.5)	(+/-5.1)	(+/-4.2)	(+/-4.8)	(+/-8.9)	
Average earnings/hour (£)	7.40	6.69	6.64	6.41	6.89	5.96	..
95% confidence interval	(+/-£0.27)	(+/-£0.27)	(+/-£0.73)	(+/-£0.47)	(+/-£0.53)	(+/-£0.61)	
Number of workers in the sample	68	58	16	23	42	11	48

1 See chapter text.

Source: Department for Environment, Food and Rural Affairs: 01904 455332

21.13 Workers employed in agriculture [1,2]: by type

United Kingdom

At June each year

Thousands

	Regular					Seasonal or casual			All			Salaried managers[3]
	Total	Full - time		Part - time		Total	Male	Female	Total	Male	Female	
		Male	Female	Male	Female							
	BANC	BAMY	BAMZ	BANA	BANB	BANF	BAND	BANE	BANI	BANG	BANH	KAYG
1993	165.3	96.5	13.7	29.8	25.3	85.4	55.0	30.4	250.7	181.3	69.4	7.6
1994	161.0	93.6	13.2	30.0	24.2	82.2	53.9	28.4	243.2	177.5	65.7	7.8
1995	157.4	90.4	13.0	30.0	24.1	83.7	56.5	27.2	241.2	176.8	64.3	7.7
1996	156.4	89.2	12.6	31.2	23.4	81.5	55.6	25.8	237.9	176.0	61.9	7.8
1997	154.4	87.5	12.6	31.2	23.1	80.9	55.3	25.5	235.2	174.0	61.2	7.8
1998[4,5]	155.6	88.0	13.1	29.7	24.7	79.5	55.6	23.8	235.0	172.8	62.2	12.1
1999	144.7	82.7	11.9	27.5	22.6	73.0	51.8	21.2	217.7	162.0	55.6	13.8
2000	128.9	73.4	10.3	24.6	20.6	64.4	45.9	18.5	193.3	143.9	49.4	11.1
2001[6]	120.8	69.0	10.9	22.0	18.9	63.2	44.6	18.6	184.0	135.6	48.5	13.4
	123.5	70.3	11.2	22.5	19.4	64.1	45.4	18.8	187.6	138.2	49.4	14.1
2002	116.3	64.7	11.5	21.7	18.4	64.2	46.2	18.0	180.6	132.6	47.9	13.4
2003	108.4	60.4	10.0	21.0	17.0	62.6	44.8	17.8	170.9	126.2	44.8	12.7
2004 Jun	108.8	58.1	9.8	23.5	17.4	68.3	49.6	18.6	177.0	131.2	45.8	15.2
2005 Jun	109.2	57.2	10.3	24.5	17.2	65.1	46.4	18.7	174.3	128.1	46.2	15.7
2006 Jun	105.4	53.6	10.4	24.3	17.1	64.0	44.4	19.6	169.4	122.3	47.1	14.6

1 See chapter text. Includes estimates for minor holdings for all countries.
2 Figures exclude schoolchildren, farmers, partners, directors and their spouses and most trainees.
3 Great Britain only.
4 Results from 1998 onwards are not comparable with previous years, due to changes in the labour questions on the June Agricultural and Horticultural Census in England, Wales and Scotland.

5 From 1998, all farmers managing holdings for limited companies or other institutions in England and Wales were asked to classify themselves as salaried managers.
6 Due to an English register improvement only the top figure for 2001 is directly comparable with 2000, while the bottom figure for 2001 is only comparable with data from 2002.

Sources: Department for Environment, Food and Rural Affairs;
Farming Statistics: 01904 455332

21.14 Summary of UK fishing industry
United Kingdom

£ million (unless otherwise stated)

		1997	1998	1999	2000	2001	2002	2003	2004	2005	2006
GDP for fishing[1]											
current pricegross value added at basic prices	QTUF	412	400	406	398	376	374	376	389	399	469
Output index (chain volume measures)2003 = 100	EWAC	132.4	136.5	124.2	112.0	110.4	109.0	100.0	96.5	95.9	93.4
GDP for agriculture, forestry and fishing											
Current price gross value added at basic prices	QTOP	10 213	9 457	9 270	8 788	8 566	9 218	10 032	10 323	10 253	10 577
Output index (chain volume measures) 2003 = 100	GDQA	95.8	97.9	101.1	100.3	90.9	102.1	100.0	99.0	103.3	106.2
GDP at market prices											
Current price GDP at market prices	YBHA	815 881	865 710	911 945	958 931	1 003 297	1 055 793	1 118 245	1 184 296	1 233 976	1 303 915
Chain volume measures index 2003 = 100	YBEZ	84.3	87.1	89.7	93.1	95.3	97.3	100.0	103.3	105.2	108.2
Percentage contribution of GVA from fishing to GVA for agriculture, hunting, forestry & fishing											
Current prices		4.0%	4.2%	4.4%	4.5%	4.4%	4.1%	3.7%	3.8%	3.9%	4.4%
Current price gross value added for fishing[2]											
2003=100	I3X3	109.6	106.4	108.0	105.9	100.0	99.5	100.0	103.5	106.1	124.7

		1997	1998	1999	2000	2001	2002	2003	2004	2005	2006
Fleet size at end of year[3]											
number of vessels	I3TC	7 812	7 639	7 448	7 242	7 169	7 033	6 735	6 642	6 342	6 372
Employment											
Number of fishermen	I3TD	18 604	17 889	16 896	15 649	14 958	14 205	13 122	13 453	12 831	12 934
Total landings by UK vessels[4]											
quantity ('000 tonnes)	I3TE	891.3	923.8	836.2	748.1	737.8	685.5	639.7	653.7	707.8	614.2
value	I3TF	621.9	661.5	587.6	550.3	574.4	545.6	528.3	513.0	571.3	610.3
Imports											
quantity ('000 tonnes)	I3TG	503.2	533.3	552.0	550.2	626.6	621.4	631.5	671.3	720.4	753.0
value[5]	I3TH	1 055.2	1 065.6	1 301.6	1 325.2	1 435.1	1 438.7	1 438.7	1 473.9	1 696.0	1 919.1
Exports											
quantity ('000 tonnes)	I3TI	299.8	376.9	351.4	364.9	391.0	389.1	479.5	477.8	461.4	416.3
value[5]	I3TJ	605.2	354.7	746.3	696.0	744.6	762.2	891.4	885.7	938.5	944.0

		1997	1998	1999	2000	2001	2002	2003	2004	2005	2006
Household consumption											
('000 tonnes)[6])	I3TK	448.0	450.5	446.8	442.9	482.5	479.0	484.6	486.9	493.5	524.9
Population ('000 persons)	I3TL	58 314	58 475	58 684	58 886	59 113	59 322	59 554	59 834	60 209	60 349
Consumer expenditure											
on fish	I3TM	1 947	2 009	2 063	2 172	2 298	2 405	2 397	2 447	2 661	2 987
on food	I3TN	53 812	55 162	57 040	58 628	59 804	61 310	63 174	65 521	67 539	70 809
Fish as a % of food[7]	I3TO	3.6	3.6	3.6	3.7	3.8	3.9	3.8	3.7	3.9	4.2
Landed Price index 1987 = 100	I3TP	122.6	138.3	144.1	148.6	156.4	153.1	157.2	166.0	181.8	204.4
Retail Price Index[8]	I3TQ	125.2	135.7	147.8	151.0	153.4	157.9	156.3	153.6	154.2	163.9

1 GDP for fish includes landings abroad.

2 Year on year comparisons may be affected by changes in the industrial classification of some contributors. For most businesses data are appropriate to a single activity heading; where information covers a mixture of activities, the business is classified according to the main activity.

3 The number of vessels excludes those registered in the Channel Islands and the Isle of Man.

4 The quantity of landed fish is expressed in terms of liveweight. The figures relate to landings both into the UK and abroad.

5 Imports are valued at cost, including insurance and freight terms whereas exports are valued at free on board terms.

6 Data are derived from the National Food Survey prior to 2001, and from the Expenditure and Food Survey from 2001 onwards. Figures for 2001 onwards are based on financial year data.

7 Including non-alcoholic beverages.

8 The fish component of the RPI which includes canned and processed fish. The index is calculated on a monthly basis with January 1987 = 100.

Source: Fisheries Statistics Unit: 020 7272 8096

21.15 Fishing fleet[1]
United Kingdom
At 31 December each year

Numbers

		1996	1997	1998	1999	2000	2001	2002	2003	2004	2005	2006
By size												
10m and under	KSNF	5 606	5 474	5 487	5 409	5 273	5 227	5 287	5 113	5 092	4 833	4 896
10.01 - 12.19m	KSNG	800	732	628	577	547	536	514	486	465	449	445
12.20 - 17.00m	KSNH	540	523	491	468	467	442	409	405	393	387	384
17.01 - 18.29m	KSNI	164	162	154	154	131	143	129	121	115	112	111
18.30 - 24.38m	KSNJ	509	471	443	414	406	405	322	271	257	253	244
24.39 - 30.48m	KSNK	223	227	226	224	219	218	185	156	147	143	139
30.49 - 36.58m	KSNL	114	104	89	80	77	75	65	63	60	55	56
over 36.58m	KSNM	117	119	121	122	122	123	122	120	112	109	97
Total over 10m	KSNN	2 467	2 338	2 152	2 039	1 969	1 942	1 746	1 622	1 549	1 508	1 476
Total UK fleet[2]	KSNO	8 073	7 812	7 639	7 448	7 242	7 169	7 033	6 735	6 641	6 341	6 372
By segment												
Pelagic gears	KSNP	58	49	50	46	44	47	45	42	31	23	16
Beam trawl	KSNQ	215	153	123	114	111	116	113	162	102	96	93
Demersal, Seines and Nephrops	JZCI	..	1 428	1 318	1 235	1 208	1 158	969	853	852	812	785
Lines and Nets	KSNR	224	214	187	172	165	146	136	118	123	114	111
Shellfish: mobile	KSNS	265	227	241	243	211	229	228	191	166	155	151
Shellfish: fixed	KSNT	339	352	311	301	297	301	304	307	253	236	230
Distant water	KSNU	15	13	14	12	13	11	10	8	10	10	8
Under 10m	KSNV	6 091	6 022	6 027	5 916	5 769	5 713	5 773	5 587	5 395	4 276	4 131
Other: Mussel Dredgers	JZCJ	..	3	2	2	2	7	15	15	13	7	6
Total UK fleet[3]	KSNX	8 658	8 461	8 273	8 041	7 820	7 728	7 593	7 283	7 022	6 716	6 752

1 See chapter text.
2 Excluding Channel Islands and Isle of Man.
3 Including Channel Islands and Isle of Man.

Source: Department for Environment, Food and Rural Affairs: 01904 455332

21.16 Estimated household food consumption[1]

Grammes per person per week

		Great Britain						United Kingdom					
		1996	1997	1998	1999	2000		2001 /02	2002 /03	2003 /04	2004 /05	2005 /06	2006
Liquid wholemilk[2] (ml)	KPQM	776	712	693	634	664	VQEW	599	555	585	484	460	477
Fully skimmed (ml)	KZBH	137	158	164	167	164	VQEX	160	166	154	158	159	163
Semi skimmed (ml)	KZBI	935	978	945	958	975	VQEZ	931	919	926	975	1 008	974
Other milk and cream (ml)	KZBJ	259	248	243	248	278	VQFA	333	350	358	366	385	395
Cheese	KPQO	111	109	104	104	110	VQFB	112	112	113	110	116	116
Butter	KPQP	39	38	39	37	39	VQFC	42	37	35	35	38	40
Margarine	KPQQ	36	26	26	20	21	VQFD	13	13	12	11	20	18
Low and reduced fat spreads	KZBK	79	77	69	71	68	VQFE	72	70	71	68	55	57
All other oils and fats (ml for oils)	KPQR	71	62	62	58	58	VQFF	70	70	68	68	70	69
Eggs (number)	KPQS	2	2	2	2	2	VQFG	2	2	2	2	2	2
Preserves and honey	KPQT	41	41	38	33	33	VQFH	35	34	33	34	35	34
Sugar	KPQU	144	128	119	107	105	VQFI	112	111	102	99	94	92
Beef and veal	KPQV	101	110	109	110	124	VQFJ	118	118	119	123	120	128
Mutton and lamb	KPQW	66	56	59	57	55	VQFK	51	51	49	50	53	54
Pork	KPQX	73	75	76	69	68	VQFL	61	61	56	56	52	55
Bacon and ham, uncooked	KPQY	77	72	76	68	71	VQFM	68	69	70	70	68	66
Bacon and ham, cooked (including canned)	KPQZ	33	41	40	39	41	VQFN	45	45	47	43	44	45
Poultry uncooked	JZCH	233	221	218	201	214	VQFO	206	199	200	197	212	207
Cooked poultry (not purchased in cans)	KYBP	23	33	33	35	39	VQFQ	43	44	11	10	12	12
Other cooked and canned meats	KPRB	62	52	49	48	51	VQFR	54	59	60	58	56	53
Offals	KPRC	7	7	5	5	5	VQFS	6	6	7	5	5	5
Sausages, uncooked	KPRD	63	63	60	58	60	VQFT	66	66	70	67	64	65
Other meat products	KPRE	207	209	216	221	239	VQFU	313	319	335	330	323	315
Fish, fresh and processed (including shellfish)	KPRF	72	70	70	70	67							
Canned fish	KPRG	31	31	29	31	32							
Fish and fish products, frozen	KPRH	50	46	46	42	44							
Fish, fresh chilled or frozen							VQAI	51	48	45	42	45	47
Other fish and fish products							VQAJ	105	106	111	115	122	123
Potatoes (excluding processed)	KPRI	805	745	715	673	707	VQFY	647	617	600	570	587	565
Fresh green vegetables	KPRJ	233	251	246	245	240	VQAK	229	231	228	225	235	221
Other fresh vegetables	KPRK	489	497	486	500	492	VQAL	502	505	505	536	567	566
Frozen potato products	KYBQ	113	106	111	113	120							
Other frozen vegetables	KPRL	94	94	88	87	80							
Potato products not frozen	JZCF	92	90	89	86	82							
Canned beans	KPRM	125	122	118	112	114							
Other canned vegetables (excl. potatoes)	KPRN	113	104	99	92	97							
Other processed vegetables (excl. potatoes)	LQZH	55	52	54	59	54							
All processed vegetables							VQAM	620	613	611	597	608	601
Apples	KPRO	175	179	181	169	180	VQGN	175	172	171	173	179	180
Bananas	KPRP	185	195	198	202	206	VQGO	203	208	211	217	225	226
Oranges	KPRQ	63	62	63	50	54	VQGP	55	62	64	57	59	55
All other fresh fruit	KPRR	263	276	274	290	304	VQGS	318	351	343	358	392	394
Canned fruit	KPRS	43	44	37	38	38	VQGT	40	39	40	38	36	39
Dried fruit, nuts and fruit and nut products	KPRT	36	35	34	30	35	VQGU	39	41	40	46	51	53
Fruit juices (ml)	KPRU	258	277	304	284	303	VQGX	327	333	322	280	350	366
Flour	KPRV	70	54	55	56	67	VQGY	55	61	52	55	60	54
Bread	KPRW	752	746	742	717	720	VQGZ	769	756	728	695	701	692
Buns, scones and teacakes	KPRX	47	43	41	40	43	VQHA	37	41	44	47	46	45
Cakes and pastries	KPRY	87	93	88	87	89	VQHB	139	122	120	117	122	120
Biscuits	KPRZ	150	138	137	132	141	VQHC	166	174	163	165	165	165
Breakfast cereals	KPSA	140	135	136	134	143	VQHE	133	132	134	131	135	135
Oatmeal and oat products	KPSB	13	16	11	13	15	VQHF	12	13	12	14	19	17
Other cereals and cereal products	JZCG	304	293	270	284	291	VQHG	345	366	360	354	378	378
Tea	KPSC	38	36	35	32	34	VQHK	34	34	31	31	33	30
Instant coffee	KPSD	13	11	12	11	11	VQHL	13	12	13	13	13	14
Canned soups	KPSE	72	70	71	67	71	VQHM	79	80	77	76	82	79
Pickles and sauces	KPSF	84	92	96	91	107	VQHN	121	123	121	120	125	128

1 See chapter text.
2 Including also school and welfare milk.

Sources: Expenditure and Food Survey;
Department for Environment Food and Rural Affairs: 01904 455067

Production

Chapter 22

Production

Annual Business Inquiry

(Table 22.1)

The Annual Business Inquiry (ABI) estimates cover all UK businesses registered for Value Added Tax (VAT) and/or Pay As You Earn (PAYE), classified to the 2003 Standard Industrial Classification (SIC(2003)) headings listed in the tables. The ABI obtains details on these businesses from the Office for National Statistics (ONS) Inter-Departmental Business Register (IDBR).

As with all its statistical inquiries, ONS is concerned to minimise the form-filling burden of individual contributors and as such the ABI is a sample inquiry. The sample was designed as a stratified random sample of about 77,000 businesses, the inquiry population is stratified by SIC(2003) and employment using the information from the register.

The inquiry results are grossed up to the total population, so that they relate to all active UK businesses on the IDBR for the sectors covered.

The results meet a wide range of needs for government, economic analysts and the business community at large. In official statistics the inquiry is an important source for the national accounts and input-output tables, but also provides weights for the indices of production and producer prices. Inquiry results also enable the UK to meet statistical requirements of the European Union.

Data from 1995 and 1996 were calculated on a different basis from those for 1997 and later years. In order to provide a link between the two data series, the 1995 and 1996 data were subsequently reworked to provide estimates on a consistent basis.

Revised Annual Business Inquiry results down to SIC(2003) 4 digit class level for 1995–2005, giving both analysis and tabular detail, are available from the National Statistics Website at www.statistics.gov.uk/abi, with further extracts and bespoke analyses available on request. This service replaces existing publications.

Manufacturers' sales by industry

(Table 22.2)

This table shows the total manufacturers' sales for products classified to SIC(2003) and collected under the Products of the European Community Inquiry since its introduction in 1993. Some data are not available for confidentiality reasons or where data have not been published for a given period. Detailed product sales data together with exports and imports data are available in ONS's Product Sales and Trade quarterly and annual reports (PRQ and PRA series).

Number of local units in manufacturing industries in 2003

(Table 22.3)

The table shows the number of local units (sites) in manufacturing by employment size band. The classification breakdown is at division level (2 digit) as classified to SIC(2003) held on the Inter-Departmental Business Register (IDBR). This register became fully operational in 1995 and combines information on Value Added Tax traders and Pay As You Earn employers in a statistical register comprising 2.1 million enterprises (businesses), representing nearly 99 per cent of economic activity. UK Business: Activity, Size and Location 2007 provides further details and contains detailed information on enterprises in the UK including size, classification and local units in the UK including size, classification and location.

For further information on the IDBR see the National Statistics website at: www.statistics.gov.uk/idbr.

Production of primary fuels

(Table 22.4)

This table shows indigenous production of primary fuels. It includes the extraction or capture of primary commodities and the generation or manufacture of secondary commodities. Production is always gross; that is, it includes the quantities used during the extraction or manufacturing process. Primary fuels are coal, natural gas (including colliery methane), oil, primary electricity (that is, electricity generated by hydro, nuclear wind and tide stations and also electricity imported from France through the interconnector) and renewables (includes solid renewables such as wood, straw and waste and gaseous renewables such as landfill gas and sewage gas). The figures are presented on a common basis, expressed in million tonnes of oil equivalent. Estimates of the gross calorific values used for converting the statistics for the various fuels to these are given in the Digest of UK Energy Statistics available at: www.berr.gov.uk/energy/statistics/publications/dukes/page39771.html

Total inland energy consumption

(Table 22.5)

This table shows energy consumption by fuel and final energy consumption by fuel and class of consumer. Primary energy consumption covers consumption of all primary fuels (defined above) for energy purposes. This measure of energy consumption includes energy that is lost by converting primary fuels into secondary fuels, that is, the energy lost burning coal to generate electricity or the energy used by refineries to separate crude oil into fractions, in addition to losses in distribution. The other common way of measuring energy consumption is to measure the energy content of the fuels supplied to consumers. This is called final energy consumption. It is net of fuel used by the energy industries, conversion, transmission and distribution losses. The figures are presented on a common basis, measured as energy supplied and expressed in million tonnes of oil equivalent. Estimates of the gross calorific values used for converting the statistics for the various fuels to these are given in the *Digest of UK Energy Statistics* available at: www.berr.gov.uk/energy/statistics/publications/dukes/page39771.html

So far as practicable the user categories have been grouped on the basis of the SIC(2003) although the methods used by each of the supply industries to identify end users are slightly different. Chapter 1 of the *Digest of UK Energy Statistics* gives more information on these figures.

Coal

(Table 22.6)

Since 1995, aggregate data on coal production have been obtained from the Coal Authority. In addition, main coal producers provide data in response to an annual Department for Business, Enterprise & Regulatory Reform (BERR) inquiry which covers production (deepmined and opencast), trade, stocks and disposals. HM Revenue & Customs (HMRC) also provide trade data for solid fuels. BERR collects information on the use of coal from UK Iron and Steel Statistics Bureau, and consumption of coal for electricity generation is covered by data provided by the electricity generators.

Gas

(Table 22.7)

Production figures, covering the production of gas from the UK Continental Shelf offshore and onshore gas fields and gas obtained during the production of oil, are obtained from returns made under the BERR's Petroleum Production Reporting System. Additional information is used on imports and exports of gas and details from the operators of gas terminals in the UK to complete the picture.

It is no longer possible to present information on fuels input into the gas industry and gas output and sales in the same format as in previous editions of this table. As such, users are directed to Chapter 4 of the 2002 edition of the *Digest of UK Energy Statistics*, where more detailed information on gas production and consumption in the UK is available.

BERR carry out an annual survey of gas suppliers to obtain details of gas sales to the various categories of consumer. Estimates are included for the suppliers with the smallest market share, since the BERR inquiry covers only the largest suppliers (that is, those known to supply more than 1,750 GWh per year).

Electricity

(Tables 22.8–22.10)

Tables 22.8 to 22.10 cover all generators and suppliers of electricity in the UK.

The relationship between generation, supply, availability and consumption is as follows:

Electricity generated

less	electricity used on works
equals	electricity supplied (gross)
less	electricity used in pumping at pumped storage stations
equals	electricity supplied (net)
plus	imports (net of exports) of electricity
equals	electricity available
less	losses and statistical differences
equals	electricity consumed

In Table 22.8 'major power producers' are those generating companies corresponding to the old public sector supply system:

- AES Electric Ltd.
- Baglan Generation Ltd.
- Barking Power Ltd.
- BNFL British Nuclear Group
- British Energy plc
- Centrica Energy
- Coolkeeragh ESB Ltd.
- Corby Power Ltd.
- Coryton Energy Company Ltd.
- Derwent Cogeneration Ltd.

Production

- Drax Power Ltd.
- EDF Energy plc
- E.ON UK plc
- Energy Power Resources Ltd.
- First Hydro Company
- Immingham CHP
- International Power plc.
- Premier Power Ltd.
- RGS Energy Ltd.
- Rocksavage Power Company Ltd.
- RWE Npower plc
- Scottish Power plc
- Scottish and Southern Energy plc
- Seabank Power Ltd.
- SELCHP Ltd.
- Spalding Energy Company Ltd.
- Teesside Power Ltd.
- Uskmouth Power Company Ltd.
- Western Power Generation Ltd.

In Table 22.10 all fuels are converted to the common unit of million tonnes of oil equivalent, that is, the amounts of oil which would be needed to produce the output of electricity generated from those fuels.

More detailed statistics on energy are given in the *Digest of United Kingdom Energy Statistics 2003*. Readers may wish to note that the production and consumption of fuels are presented using commodity balances. A commodity balance shows the flows of an individual fuel through from production to final consumption, showing its use in transformation and energy industry own use.

Oil and oil products

(Tables 22.11–22.13)

The data on the production of crude oil, condensates and natural gases given in Table 22.11 are collected by BERR direct from the operators of production facilities and terminals situated on UK territory, either onshore or offshore, that is, on the UK Continental Shelf. Data are also collected from the companies on their trade in oil and oil products. These data are used in preference to the foreign trade as recorded by HMRC in *Overseas Trade Statistics*.

Data on the internal UK oil industry (that is, on the supply, refining and distribution of oil and oil products in the UK) are collected by the UK Petroleum Industry Association. These data, reported by individual refining companies and wholesalers, and supplemented where necessary by data from other sources, provide the contents of Tables 22.12 and 22.13. The data are presented in terms of deliveries to the inland UK market. This is regarded as an acceptable proxy for actual consumption of products. The main shortcoming is that, while changes in stocks held by companies in central storage areas are taken into account, changes in the levels of stocks further down the retail ladder (such as stocks held on petrol station forecourts) are not. This is not thought to result in a significant degree of difference in the data.

Iron and steel

(Tables 22.14–22.16)

Iron and steel industry

The general definition of the UK iron and steel industry is based on groups 271 'ECSC iron and steel', 272 'Tubes', and 273 'Primary Transformation' of the UK SIC(92), except those parts of groups 272 and 273 which cover cast iron pipes, drawn wire, cold formed sections and Ferro alloys.

The definition excludes certain products which may be made by works within the industry, such as refined iron, finished steel castings, steel tyres, wheels, axles and rolled rings, open and closed die forgings, colliery arches and springs. Iron foundries and steel stockholders are also considered to be outside of the industry.

Statistics

The statistics for the UK iron and steel industry are compiled by the Iron and Steel Statistics Bureau (ISSB) Ltd from data collected from UK steel producing companies with the exception of trade data which is based on HMRC data.

Crude steel is the total of usable ingots, usable continuously cast semi-finished products and liquid steel for castings.

Production of finished products is the total production at the mill of that product after deduction of any material which is immediately scrapped.

Deliveries are based on invoiced tonnages and will include deliveries made to steel stockholders and service centres by the UK steel industry.

For more detailed information on definitions etc please contact ISSB Ltd. on 020 7343 3900.

Minerals

(Table 22.19)

Table 22.19 gives, separately for Great Britain and Northern Ireland, the production of minerals extracted from the ground. The figures for chemicals and metals are estimated from the quality of the ore which is extracted. The data come from an annual census of the quarrying industry which, for Great Britain, is conducted by ONS for Communities and Local Government and BERR.

Building materials

(Table 22.20)

Table 22.20 gives the production of a number of building materials which are closely associated with material extracted from the ground. The data come from surveys conducted by ONS on behalf of BERR.

Construction

(Tables 22.21–22.22)

Figures for the construction industry are based on SIC(2003).

The value of output represents the value of construction work done during the quarter in Great Britain and is derived from returns made by private contractors and public authorities with their own direct labour forces. The series (and the accompanying index of the volume of output) include estimates of the output of small firms and self employed workers not recorded in the regular quarterly output inquiry.

The new orders statistics are collected from private contractors and analysed by the principal types of construction work involved. The series includes speculative work for eventual sale or lease undertaken on the initiative of the respondent where no formal contract or order is involved.

Engineering turnover and orders

(Tables 22.23–22.24)

The figures represent the output of UK-based manufacturers classified to Subsections DK and DL of the SIC(2003). They are derived from the monthly production inquiry (MPI) and include estimates for non-responders and for establishments which are not sampled.

Passenger cars

(Table 22.25)

The figures represent the output of UK based manufacturers classified to Class 34.10 (motor vehicles) of the SIC(2003).

They are derived from the Motor Vehicle Production Inquiry (MVPI). This inquiry ceased at July 2007.

These figures include vehicles produced in the form of kits for assembly. The value of the kit must be 50 per cent or more of the value of a corresponding complete vehicle.

Drink and tobacco

(Tables 22.26–22.27)

Data for these tables are derived by HMRC from the systems for collecting excise duties. Alcoholic drinks and tobacco products become liable to duty when released for consumption in the UK. Figures for releases include both home-produced products and commercial imports. Production figures are also available for potable spirits distilled and beer brewed in the UK.

Alcoholic drink

(Table 22.26)

The figures for imported and other spirits released for home consumption include gin and other UK produced spirits, for which a breakdown is not available.

Since June 1993 beer duty has been charged when the beer leaves the brewery or other registered premises. Previously duty was chargeable at an earlier stage (the worts stage) in the brewing process, and an allowance was made for wastage. Figures for years prior to 1994 include adjustments to bring them into line with current data. The change in June 1993 also led to the availability of data on the strength; a series in hectolitres of pure alcohol is shown from 1994.

Made wine with alcoholic strength from 1.2 per cent to 5.5 per cent is termed 'coolers'. Included in coolers are alcoholic lemonade and similar products of appropriate strength. From 28 April 2002, duty on spirit-based 'coolers' (ready to drink products) is charged at the same rate as spirits per litre of alcohol. Made wine coolers include only wine based 'coolers' from this period.

Tobacco products

(Table 22.27)

Releases of cigarettes and other tobacco products tend to be higher in the period before a Budget. Products may then be stocked, duty paid, before being sold.

22.1

Production and construction:[1] summary table
United Kingdom
Standard Industrial Classfication 2003: Estimates for all firms

£ million

	Total turnover	Gross value added	Stocks and work in progress		Capital expenditure *less* disposals	Total employment costs
			At end of year	Change during year		

Standard Industrial Classification: Revised 2003

Production and construction
Sections C-F

	ZIYQ	KSCD	KSCE	KSCF	KSCG	AWKC
2001	674 274	229 773	65 831	713	28 823	117 560
2002	669 855	228 613	70 233	520	27 116	119 037
2003	678 072	228 976	67 044	1 845	25 663	118 540
2004	704 450	242 834	67 027	3 339	23 989	120 512
2005	740 168	257 002	70 790	4 229	26 064	122 722

Production industries (Revised definitions)
Sections C-E

	ZIYR	KSCL	KSCM	KSCN	KSCO	AWKH
2001	544 210	182 243	52 732	−824	25 716	93 993
2002	529 380	178 828	50 261	−753	23 182	93 098
2003	527 180	175 826	49 122	−401	22 448	91 317
2004	546 426	187 199	48 831	1 180	20 598	92 423
2005	572 837	193 806	50 065	1 814	22 682	92 639

Mining and quarrying
Section C

	ZIYS	KSCT	KSCU	KSCV	KSCW	AWKI
2001	37 057	22 560	958	64	4 272	2 698
2002	32 950	19 279	882	30	4 813	2 682
2003	32 329	18 173	814	−29	4 420	2 782
2004	34 159	17 890	798	30	3 992	2 755
2005	44 103	24 981	973	101	5 746	3 199

Mining and quarrying of energy producing materials
Subsection CA

	ZIYT	KSDB	KSDC	KSDD	KSDE	KSDF
2001	32 237	20 765	658	33	4 008	1 945
2002	28 406	17 827	612	7	4 563	1 974
2003	27 506	16 682	506	−47	4 116	1 957
2004	29 012	16 163	492	12	3 680	1 975
2005	37 479	22 785	627	84	5 432	2 184

Mining and quarrying except energy producing materials
Subsection CB

	ZIYU	KSDJ	KSDK	KSDL	KSDM	KSDN
2001	4 820	1 795	300	31	264	752
2002	4 544	1 452	271	23	249	708
2003	4 823	1 491	308	18	304	825
2004	5 147	1 728	307	17	312	780
2005	6 624	2 195	346	17	314	1 015

Manufacturing (Revised definition)
Section D

	ZIYV	KSDR	KSDS	KSDT	KSDU	AWKL
2001	461 898	145 230	50 038	−816	16 278	87 574
2002	450 090	144 149	47 669	−667	13 237	86 691
2003	447 637	142 207	46 914	−371	12 677	84 597
2004	459 880	148 864	46 807	975	11 689	85 243
2005	466 731	146 487	47 697	1 452	10 886	84 853

22.1
continued

Production and construction:[1] summary table
United Kingdom
Standard Industrial Classfication 2003: Estimates for all firms

£ million

	Total turnover	Gross value added	Stocks and work in progress		Capital expenditure *less* disposals	Total employment costs
			At end of year	Change during year		

Standard Industrial Classification: Revised 2003

Manufacture of food; beverages and tobacco
  Subsection DA

	ZIYW	KSDZ	KSEA	KSEB	KSEC	AWKM
2001	74 692	20 324	7 633	87	2 638	10 045
2002	76 764	20 721	7 557	53	2 161	10 416
2003	78 759	21 870	7 677	63	2 364	10 564
2004	81 985	22 516	7 846	177	1 966	10 632
2005	82 618	22 766	7 935	−17	2 098	11 030

Manufacture of textile and textile products
  Subsection DB

	ZIYX	KSEH	KSEI	KSEJ	KSEK	AWKN
2001	13 229	5 051	2 046	41	258	3 096
2002	12 203	4 480	1 881	41	307	2 894
2003	11 396	4 147	1 713	23	234	2 553
2004	10 840	3 825	1 639	7	117	2 333
2005	10 318	3 891	1 474	20	132	2 336

Manufacture of leather and leather products
  Subsection DC

	ZIYY	KSEP	KSEQ	KSER	KSES	AWKO
2001	1 758	595	230	−28	23	320
2002	1 541	571	228	−3	18	275
2003	974	375	145	−1	11	198
2004	920	326	138	−6	20	197
2005	770	301	112	4	−	167

Manufacture of wood and wood products
  Subsection DD

	ZIYZ	KSEX	KSEY	KSEZ	KSFA	AWKP
2001	6 571	2 315	585	−17	219	1 374
2002	7 016	2 459	658	37	186	1 626
2003	7 134	2 669	713	49	211	1 444
2004	7 421	2 958	702	6	177	1 662
2005	7 462	2 943	699	46	187	1 555

Manufacture of pulp, paper and paper products; publishing and printing
  Subsection DE

	ZIZA	KSFF	KSFG	KSFH	KSFI	AWKQ
2001	44 922	19 425	2 606	25	1 657	10 856
2002	45 317	19 294	2 651	104	1 477	10 927
2003	44 767	18 684	2 637	78	1 338	11 056
2004	45 924	19 413	2 750	−30	1 251	11 063
2005	44 086	18 612	2 411	37	1 756	10 881

Manufacture of coke, refined petroleum products and nuclear fuel
  Subsection DF

	ZIZB	KSFN	KSFO	KSFP	KSFQ	AWKR
2001	25 369	2 401	1 000	−190	705	898
2002	24 255	2 502	1 287	190	473	1 099
2003	25 348	2 213	1 269	−13	604	1 160
2004	27 881	2 651	1 362	97	484	1 131
2005	34 273	2 094	2 200	505	285	1 065

22.1

continued

Production and construction:[1] summary table
United Kingdom
Standard Industrial Classfication 2003: Estimates for all firms

£ million

	Total turnover	Gross value added	Stocks and work in progress		Capital expenditure *less* disposals	Total employment costs
			At end of year	Change during year		

Standard Industrial Classification: Revised 2003

Manufacture of chemicals, chemical products and man-made fibres
  Subsection DG

	ZIZC	KSFV	KSFW	KSFX	KSFY	AWKS
2001	48 915	15 821	6 205	−8	2 473	7 959
2002	48 759	15 847	6 208	−14	2 147	8 295
2003	49 779	15 700	6 190	−119	1 926	7 964
2004	51 375	17 240	5 941	−15	1 915	8 313
2005	50 225	16 582	5 887	−72	1 112	8 125

Manufacture of rubber and plastic products
  Subsection DH

	ZIZD	KSGD	KSGE	KSGF	KSGG	AWKT
2001	19 869	7 716	1 833	−1	742	4 769
2002	19 637	7 536	1 769	27	690	4 694
2003	19 803	7 533	1 779	78	751	4 762
2004	20 790	7 799	1 878	116	579	4 960
2005	21 328	7 821	1 850	−23	427	4 848

Manufacture of other non-metallic mineral products
  Subsection DI

	ZIZE	KSGL	KSGM	KSGN	KSGO	AWKU
2001	11 656	4 895	1 332	−4	488	2 828
2002	12 139	5 011	1 354	21	602	2 755
2003	12 573	5 315	1 321	11	579	2 779
2004	13 715	5 846	1 434	87	525	3 041
2005	12 534	5 244	1 398	80	549	2 881

Manufacture of basic iron and of ferro-alloys
  Subsection DJ

	ZIZF	KSGT	KSGU	KSGV	KSGW	AWKV
2001	40 660	15 316	3 920	−43	1 122	10 098
2002	38 360	14 640	3 626	88	1 179	9 649
2003	38 125	14 623	3 744	216	1 121	9 584
2004	40 873	15 234	3 963	540	1 049	9 498
2005	43 154	15 375	4 289	294	972	9 724

Manufacture of machinery and equipment not elsewhere specified
  Subsection DK

	ZIZG	KSHB	KSHC	KSHD	KSHE	AWKW
2001	32 825	11 770	4 460	−73	792	8 302
2002	32 247	11 841	4 118	−141	673	8 114
2003	32 078	11 785	4 913	134	644	7 914
2004	33 838	12 170	5 020	118	505	8 040
2005	34 744	12 206	4 992	63	521	8 077

Manufacture of electrical and optical equipment
  Subsection DL

	ZIZH	KSHJ	KSHK	KSHL	KSHM	AWKX
2001	63 227	15 813	7 280	−1 130	1 950	12 576
2002	53 048	15 960	6 107	−693	868	11 292
2003	46 638	15 302	5 228	−265	773	10 024
2004	41 545	15 206	5 210	160	703	9 389
2005	40 831	15 057	5 090	120	558	9 112

22.1
continued

Production and construction:[1] summary table
United Kingdom
Standard Industrial Classfication 2003: Estimates for all firms

£ million

	Total turnover	Gross value added	Stocks and work in progress		Capital expenditure *less* disposals	Total employment costs
			At end of year	Change during year		

Standard Industrial Classification: Revised 2003

Manufacture of transport equipment
Subsection DM

	ZIZI	KSHR	KSHS	KSHT	KSHU	AWKY
2001	61 366	17 322	9 206	444	2 740	10 740
2002	61 550	16 925	8 581	−473	2 028	10 808
2003	63 338	15 838	7 975	−688	1 659	10 963
2004	64 870	16 963	7 198	−429	1 913	11 274
2005	66 558	17 074	7 582	331	1 920	11 409

Manufacture not elsewhere classified
Subsection DN

	ZIZJ	KSHZ	KSIA	KSIB	KSIC	AWKZ
2001	16 839	6 468	1 701	81	471	3 714
2002	17 254	6 361	1 643	94	428	3 846
2003	16 923	6 153	1 608	61	463	3 633
2004	17 902	6 718	1 724	147	486	3 710
2005	17 829	6 520	1 777	65	368	3 642

Electricity, gas and water supply
Section E

	ZIZK	KSIH	KSII	KSIJ	KSIK	AWLA
2001	45 256	14 453	1 736	−72	5 165	3 721
2002	46 341	15 399	1 709	−116	5 132	3 725
2003	47 214	15 446	1 393	−1	5 351	3 938
2004	52 386	20 445	1 227	175	4 917	4 425
2005	62 003	22 339	1 395	261	6 050	4 587

Construction
Section F

	ZIZL	KSIP	KSIQ	KSIR	KSIS	AWLB
2001	130 064	47 530	13 099	1 537	3 107	23 567
2002	140 475	49 785	19 973	1 272	3 934	25 939
2003	150 892	53 150	17 923	2 246	3 215	27 223
2004	158 025	55 636	18 195	2 159	3 391	28 088
2005	167 331	63 196	20 725	2 415	3 382	30 083

1 See chapter text.

Source: Office for National Statistics: 01633 812435

22.2 Manufacturers' sales: by industry[1]
United Kingdom
Standard Industrial Classification 2003

£ million

Industry		SIC (03)	2003	2004	2005	2006
Other mining and quarrying						
Quarrying of stone for construction	KSPF	14110	..	..	..	..
Quarrying of limestone, gypsum and chalk	KSPG	14120	..	..	..	..
Quarrying of slate	KSPH	14130	..	..	..	..
Operation of gravel and sand pits	KSPJ	14210	..	..	..	..
Mining of clays and kaolin	KSPK	14220	..	..	..	..
Mining of chemical and fertilizer minerals	KSPL	14300	..	..	..	..
Production of salt	KSPM	14400	..	..	..	..
Other mining and quarrying not elsewhere classified	KSPN	14500	62	46	52	44
Manufacture of food products and beverages						
Production and preserving of meat	KSPO	15110	3 659	3 937	4 159	4 281
Production and preserving of poultry meat	KSPP	15120	1 933	..	2 064	2 123
Bacon and ham production	KSPQ	15131	1 274	1 365	1 466	1 600
Other meat and poultry meat processing	KSPR	15139	3 884	3 966	4 151	4 009
Processing and preserving of fish and fish products	KSPS	15200	1 706	1 741	1 802	1 859
Processing and preserving of potatoes	KSPT	15310	..	1 233	..	..
Fruit and vegetable juice	KSPU	15320	557	570	589	737
Processing and preserving of fruit and vegetables not elsewhere classified	KSPV	15330	2 324	2 451	2 504	2 617
Crude oils and fats	KSPW	15410	431	399	237	144
Refined oils and fats	KSPX	15420	616	914	889	831
Margarine and similar edible fats	KSPY	15430	471	..	..	416
Operation of dairies	KTEH	15510	5 602	5 457	5 798	6 043
Ice cream	KSPZ	15520	..	..	467	431
Grain mill products	KSQA	15610	2 672	2 788	2 573	2 755
Starches and starch products	KSQB	15620	389	380	429	355
Prepared feeds for farm animals	KSPI	15710	2 108	2 419	2 178	2 376
Prepared pet foods	KSQC	15720	928	1 189	..	1 235
Bread; fresh pastry goods and cakes	KSQD	15810	4 345	4 407	4 186	4 348
Rusks and biscuits; preserved pastry goods and cakes	KSQE	15820	..	..	3 294	3 132
Sugar	KSQF	15830	1 153	1 133	1 077	1 058
Cocoa; chocolate and sugar confectionery	KSQG	15840	3 533	3 384	3 036	3 431
Macaroni, noodles, couscous and similar farinaceous products	KSQH	15850	496	..	..	499
Processing of tea and coffee	KSQI	15860	..	1 420	1 502	..
Condiments and seasonings	KSQJ	15870	1 023	1 129	1 129	1 270
Homogenised food preparations and dietetic foods	KSQK	15880	..	..	42	47
Manufacture of other food products not elsewhere classified	KSQL	15890	2 039	2 200	2 301	2 520
Distilled potable alcoholic beverages	KSQM	15910	2 123	2 216	..	..
Production of ethyl alcohol from fermented materials	KSQN	15920	..	..	..	..
Wines	KSQO	15930	..	52	..	..
Cider and other fruit wines	KSQP	15940	524	416	490	518
Other non-distilled fermented beverages	KSQQ	15950	–	–	–	–
Beer	KSQR	15960	3 769	4 073	3 805	3 774
Malt	KSQS	15970	253	255	239	242
Mineral waters and soft drinks	KSQT	15980	..	..	3 021	3 204
Manufacture of tobacco products						
Tobacco products	KSQU	16000	1 829	1 838	1 718	1 875
Manufacture of textiles						
Preparation and spinning of textile fibres	KSQV	17100	438	486	434	400
Textile weaving	KSQW	17200	666	690	609	559
Finishing of textiles	KSQX	17300	409	472	478	468
Soft furnishings	KSQY	17401	592	576	582	655
Canvas goods, sacks etc	KSQZ	17402	113	101	81	109
Household textiles	KSRA	17403	730	654	642	616
Carpets and rugs	KSRB	17510	751	690	715	763
Cordage, rope, twine and netting	KSRC	17520	87	76	85	78

22.2

Manufacturers' sales: by industry[1]
United Kingdom

Standard Industrial Classification 2003

£ million

Industry	SIC (03)	2003	2004	2005	2006
Manufacture of textiles continued					
Nonwovens and articles made from nonwovens, except apparel	KSRD 17530	153	149	150	160
Lace	KSRE 17541	18	16	19	15
Narrow fabrics	KSRF 17542	160	145	131	124
Other textiles not elsewhere classified	KSRG 17549	439	435	446	411
Knitted and crocheted fabrics	KSRH 17600	203	197	..	..
Knitted and crocheted hosiery	KSRI 17710	241	230	..	..
Knitted and crocheted pullovers, cardigans and similar	KSRJ 17720	307	219	201	181
Manufacture of wearing apparel; dressing and dyeing of fur					
Leather clothes	KSRK 18100	9	7	5	3
Workwear	KSRL 18210	287	263	219	215
Men's outerwear	KSRM 18221	292	249	182	157
Other women's outerwear	KSRN 18222	709	792	654	657
Men's underwear	KSRO 18231	195	171	..	107
Women's underwear	KSRP 18232	458	392	343	368
Hats	KSRQ 18241	37	35	..	32
Other wearing apparel and accessories	KSRR 18249	362	315	301	290
Dressing/dyeing of fur; articles of fur	KSRS 18300	4	4	4	3
Tanning and dressing of leather; manufacture of luggage, handbags, saddlery, harness and footwear					
Tanning and dressing of leather	KSRT 19100	..	..	..	..
Luggage, handbags and the like, saddlery and harness	KSRU 19200	166	140	152	143
Footwear	KSRV 19300	292	250	227	212
Manufacture of wood and of products of wood and cork, except furniture; manufacture of articles of straw and plaiting materials					
Sawmilling and planing of wood, impregnation of wood	KSRW 20100	757	750	784	828
Veneer sheets	KSRX 20200	767	808	796	843
Builders' carpentry and joinery	KSRY 20300	2 992	3 222	3 516	3 713
Wooden containers	KSRZ 20400	349	413	438	439
Other products of wood	KSSA 20510	368	385	417	371
Articles of cork, straw and plaiting materials	KSSB 20520	6	6	5	4
Manufacture of pulp, paper and paper products					
Paper and paperboard	KSSC 21120	3 103	2 748	2 715	2 747
Corrugated paper and paperboard, sacks and bags	KSSD 21211	596	551	513	461
Cartons, boxes, cases and other containers	KSSE 21219	1 024	1 158	1 195	1 216
Household and sanitary goods and toilet requisites	KSSF 21220	..	2 069	..	1 488
Paper stationery	KSSG 21230	..	592	602	553
Wallpaper	KSSH 21240	188	184	..	102
Manufacture of printed labels	EQ2T 21251	477	467	445	421
Manufacture of unprinted labels	EQ2U 21252	40	44	..	..
Manufacture of other articles of paper and paperboard not elsewhere classified	EQ2V 21259	357	290	221	197
Publishing, printing and reproduction of recorded media					
Publishing of books	KSSJ 22110	3 033	3 247	3 118	3 228
Publishing of newspapers	KSSK 22120	4 122	4 320	4 135	4 125
Publishing of journals and periodicals	KSSL 22130	7 118	7 303	7 633	7 385
Publishing of sound recordings	KSSM 22140	215	..	296	247
Other publishing	KSSN 22150	516	549	576	567
Printing of newspapers	KSSO 22210	205	235	..	..
Printing not elsewhere classified	KSSP 22220	9 037	9 168	8 807	8 580
Bookbinding and finishing	KSSQ 22230	439	414	422	378
Composition and plate-making	KSSR 22240	400	346	..	344
Other activities related to printing	KSSS 22250	667	822	712	642
Reproduction of sound recording	KSST 22310	260	209	244	128
Reproduction of video recording	KSSU 22320	220	272	197	118
Reproduction of computer media	KSSV 22330	..	..	26	..
Manufacture of chemicals and chemical products					
Industrial gases	KSSW 24110	525	528	525	565
Dyes and pigments	KSSX 24120	971	936	912	900
Other inorganic basic chemicals	KSSY 24130	1 084	1 090	1 169	1 171
Other organic basic chemicals	KSSZ 24140	4 451	5 825	5 752	6 925
Fertilizers and nitrogen compounds	KSTA 24150	789	786	772	721

22.2
Manufacturers' sales: by industry[1]
United Kingdom

Standard Industrial Classification 2003

£ million

Industry		SIC (03)	2003	2004	2005	2006
Manufacture of chemicals and chemical products continued						
Plastics in primary forms	KSTB	24160	3 394	3 740	3 812	3 858
Synthetic rubber in primary forms	KSTC	24170	..	..	..	..
Pesticides and other agro-chemical products	KSTD	24200	431	470	427	461
Paints, varnishes and similar coatings, printing ink and mastic	KSTE	24300	2 745	2 776	2 684	2 708
Basic pharmaceutical products	KSTF	24410	740	734	895	1 054
Pharmaceutical preparations	KSTG	24420	9 194	8 761	9 863	9 830
Soap and detergents, cleaning and polishing preparations	KSTH	24510	1 718	1 805	1 656	1 649
Perfumes and toilet preparations	KSTI	24520	2 314	2 171	1 772	1 835
Explosives	KSTJ	24610	105	110	120	..
Glues and gelatines	KSTK	24620	371	400	433	456
Essential oils	KSTL	24630	..	..	504	556
Photographic chemical material	KSTM	24640	..	250	260	244
Prepared unrecorded media	KSTN	24650	127	..	..	33
Other chemical products not elsewhere classified	KSTO	24660	1 754	1 992	1 972	2 062
Man-made fibres	KSTP	24700	618	587	482	616
Manufacture of rubber and plastic products						
Rubber tyres and tubes	KSTQ	25110	647	569	..	551
Retreading and rebuilding of rubber tyres	KSTR	25120	..	99	..	..
Other rubber products	KSTS	25130	1 562	1 608	1 566	1 598
Plastic plates, sheets, tubes and profiles	KSTT	25210	3 554	3 756	4 186	4 354
Plastic packing goods	KSTU	25220	..	..	..	..
Builders' ware of plastic	KSTV	25230	4 670	4 452	4 347	4 428
Other plastic products	KSTW	25240	3 411	3 425	3 283	3 421
Manufacture of other non-metallic mineral products						
Flat glass	KSTX	26110	278	..	..	..
Shaping and processing of flat glass	KSTY	26120	969	1 033	940	929
Hollow glass	KSTZ	26130	627	638	632	537
Glass fibres	KSUA	26140	340	325	361	389
Manufacturing and processing of other glass including technical glassware	KSUB	26150	235	251	177	129
Ceramic household and ornamental articles	KSUC	26210	423	..	..	..
Ceramic sanitary fixtures	KSUD	26220	..	..	180	175
Ceramic insulators and insulating fittings	KSUE	26230	..	..	22	24
Other technical ceramic products	KSUF	26240	22	21	20	21
Other ceramic products	KSUG	26250	18	..	..	..
Refractory ceramic products	KSUH	26260	344	340	335	335
Ceramic tiles and flags	KSUI	26300	91	97	98	89
Bricks, tiles and construction products in baked clay	KSUJ	26400	..	656	644	652
Cement	KSUK	26510	778	763	..	..
Lime	KSUL	26520	61	..	78	..
Plaster	KSUM	26530	123	125	131	148
Concrete products for construction purposes	KSUN	26610	..	2 278	2 207	2 177
Plaster products for construction purposes	KSUO	26620	..	394	429	..
Ready mixed concrete	KSUP	26630	..	1 017	898	737
Mortars	KSUQ	26640	132	143	146	..
Fibre cement	KSUR	26650	86	96	109	..
Other articles of concrete, plaster and cement	KSUS	26660	106	113	96	95
Cutting, shaping and finishing of stone	KSUT	26700	445	..	..	455
Abrasive products	KSUU	26810	157	167	180	174
Other non-metallic mineral products not elsewhere classified	KSUV	26820	642	713	754	814
Manufacture of basic metals						
Cast iron tubes	KSUW	27210	..	164	190	..
Steel tubes	KSUX	27220	939	1 096	1 159	1 219
Cold drawing	KSUY	27310	113	141	146	132

22.2
continued

Manufacturers' sales: by industry[1]
United Kingdom
Standard Industrial Classification 2003

£ million

Industry	SIC (03)	2003	2004	2005	2006
Manufacture of basic metals continued					
Cold rolling of narrow strip	KSUZ 27320	82	125	117	120
Cold forming or folding	KSVA 27330	104	..	..	..
Wire drawing	KSVB 27340	231	..	235	..
Precious metals production	KSVD 27410	197	247	280	288
Aluminium production	KSVE 27420	1 783	1 780	1 780	2 341
Lead, zinc and tin production	KSVF 27430	258	..	305	457
Copper production	KSVG 27440	625	766	683	..
Other non-ferrous metal production	KSVH 27450	460	639	757	996
Casting of iron	KSVI 27510	440	440	438	404
Casting of steel	KSVJ 27520	107	108	136	142
Casting of light metals	KSVK 27530	307	289	278	308
Casting of other non-ferrous metals	KSVL 27540	356	292	250	224
Manufacture of fabricated metal products, except machinery and equipment					
Metal structures and parts of structures	KSVM 28110	4 910	5 390	5 882	6 081
Builders' carpentry and joinery of metal	KSVN 28120	964	1 012	1 202	1 164
Tanks, reservoirs and containers of metal	KSVO 28210	290	291	314	347
Central heating radiators and boilers	KSVP 28220	580	652	804	..
Steam generators, except central heating hot water boilers	KSVQ 28300	..	..	..	..
Forging, pressing, stamping and roll forming of metal	KSVR 28400	1 833	1 816	1 900	1 889
Treatment and coating of metals	KSVS 28510	1 089	1 162	1 268	1 344
General mechanical engineering	KSVT 28520	2 500	2 832	2 972	3 356
Cutlery	KSVU 28610	..	25	21	23
Tools	KSVV 28620	801	805	795	726
Locks and hinges	KSVW 28630	575	600	568	552
Steel drums and similar containers	KSVX 28710	113	122	138	121
Light metal packaging	KSVY 28720	1 079	1 079	1 093	1 160
Wire products	KSVZ 28730	482	503	537	629
Fasteners, screw machine products, chain and spring	KSWA 28740	607	612	609	587
Other fabricated metal products not elsewhere classified	KSWB 28750	1 636	1 694	1 659	1 718
Manufacture of machinery and equipment not elsewhere classified					
Engines and turbines, except aircraft, vehicles and cycle engines	KSWC 29110	2 082	2 295	2 437	2 598
Pumps	KSWD 29121	1 133	1 157	1 239	1 217
Compressors	KSWE 29122	1 079	1 177	1 087	1 231
Taps and valves	KSWF 29130	1 103	1 164	1 229	1 264
Bearings, gears, gearing and driving elements	KSWG 29140	844	887	962	1 014
Furnaces and furnace burners	KSWH 29210	259	273	258	260
Lifting and handling equipment	KSWI 29220	2 761	2 964	3 150	3 207
Non-domestic cooling and ventilation equipment	KSWJ 29230	2 727	2 840	2 805	2 938
Other general purpose machinery not elsewhere classified	KSWK 29240	2 028	2 021	2 176	2 249
Agricultural tractors	KSWL 29310	764	739	658	698
Other agricultural and forestry machinery	KSWM 29320	476	528	499	536
Manufacture of portable hand held power tools	EQ2W 29410	229	146	148	..
Manufacture of other metal working machine tools	EQ2X 29420	541	537	557	560
Manufacture of other machine tools n.e.c.	EQ2Y 29430	361	339	327	303
Machinery for metallurgy	KSWO 29510	82	72	82	78
Machinery for mining	KSWP 29521	432	524	804	671
Earth-moving equipment	KSWQ 29522	1 016	..	1 287	1 423
Equipment for concrete crushing and screening and roadworks	KSWR 29523	562	..	..	..
Machinery for food, beverage and tobacco processing	KSWS 29530	609	667	621	635
Machinery for textile, apparel and leather production	KSWT 29540	129	106	95	100
Machinery for paper and paperboard production	KSWU 29550	222	203	159	..
Other special purpose machinery not elsewhere classified	KSWV 29560	1 570	1 663	1 600	1 596
Weapons and ammunition	KSWW 29600	1 638	2 095	107	95

22.2
continued

Manufacturers' sales: by industry[1]
United Kingdom
Standard Industrial Classification 2003

£ million

Industry	SIC (03)	2003	2004	2005	2006
Manufacture of machinery and equipment not elsewhere classified continued					
Electric domestic appliances	KSYR	29710	1 898	2 038	1 673	1 728
Non-electric domestic appliances	KSWX	29720	476	496	454	478
Manufacture of office machinery and computers					
Office machinery	KSWY	30010	..	376	..	418
Computers and other information processing equipment	KSWZ	30020	5 222	4 007	3 626	2 189
Manufacture of electrical machinery and apparatus not elsewhere classified					
Electric motors, generators and transformers	KSXA	31100	1 951	2 150	2 319	2 652
Electricity, distribution and control apparatus	KSXB	31200	2 320	2 403	2 401	2 466
Insulated wire and cable	KSXC	31300	872	985	926	1 103
Accumulators, primary cells and batteries	KSXD	31400	329	317	266	236
Lighting equipment and electric lamps	KSXE	31500	1 046	1 095	1 107	1 052
Electrical equipment for engines and vehicles not elsewhere classified	KSXF	31610	1 060	924	871	802
Other electrical equipment not elsewhere classified	KSXG	31620	1 747	1 752	1 787	1 943
Manufacture of radio, television and communication equipment and apparatus					
Electronic valves and tubes and other electronic components	KSXH	32100	2 958	3 007	2 711	2 358
Telegraph and telephone apparatus and equipment	KSXI	32201	944	931	870	983
Radio and electronic capital goods	KSXJ	32202	..	1 707	1 755	..
Television and radio receivers, sound or video recording etc	KSXK	32300	2 297	2 510	2 021	2 032
Manufacture of medical, precision and optical instruments, watches and clocks					
Medical and surgical equipment and orthopaedic appliances	KSXL	33100	2 093	2 234	2 412	2 505
Instruments and appliances for measuring, checking, testing etc	KSXM	33200	5 098	4 814	4 941	5 118
Industrial process control equipment	KSXN	33300	649	709	819	810
Optical instruments and photographic equipment	KSXO	33400	810	947	939	961
Watches and clocks	KSXP	33500	50	50	52	38
Manufacture of motor vehicles, trailers and semi-trailers					
Motor vehicles	KSXQ	34100	22 501	22 447	23 876	22 599
Bodies (coachwork) for motor vehicles (excluding caravans)	KSXR	34201	900	771	712	764
Trailers and semi-trailers	KSXS	34202	914	1 052	1 146	999
Caravans	KSXT	34203	..	593	..	..
Parts and accessories for motor vehicles and their engines	KSXU	34300	9 975	9 804	9 673	9 541
Manufacture of other transport equipment					
Building and repairing of ships	KSXV	35110	1 423	1 551	467	491
Building and repairing of pleasure and sporting boats	KSXW	35120	602	641	768	812
Railway and tramway locomotives and rolling stock	KSXX	35200	1 688	2 099	..	..
Aircraft and spacecraft	KSXY	35300	11 761	11 918	9 585	9 780
Motorcycles	KSXZ	35410	..	..	..	..
Bicycles	KSYA	35420	59	55	49	44
Invalid carriages	KSYB	35430	113	..	..	106
Other transport equipment not elsewhere classified.	KSYC	35500	..	83	..	..
Manufacture of furniture; manufacturing not elsewhere classified					
Chairs and seats	KSYD	36110	2 923	2 871	2 790	2 734
Other office and shop furniture	KSYE	36120	1 060	1 046	1 096	1 090
Other kitchen furniture	KSYF	36130	958	972	959	1 050
Other furniture	KSYG	36140	2 270	2 018	1 962	2 014
Mattresses	KSYH	36150	568	591	542	548
Striking of coins and medals	KSYI	36210	..	..	..	..
Jewellery and related articles not elsewhere classified	KSYJ	36220	426	388	342	419
Musical instruments	KSYK	36300	41	43	42	32
Sports goods	KSYL	36400	325	336	327	285
Games and toys	KSYM	36500	364	354	352	318
Imitation jewellery	KSYN	36610	..	27	33	31
Brooms and brushes	KSYO	36620	..	130	111	108
Miscellaneous stationers' goods	KSYP	36631	189	..	174	177
Other manufacturing not elsewhere classified	KSYQ	36639	448	383	420	416

1 See chapter text. PRODCOM data is published on the ONS website in the PRA and PRQ series of reports.

Source: Office for National Statistics: 01633 456746

22.3

Number of local units in manufacturing industries, March 2007[1]
United Kingdom
Standard Industrial Classification 2003 Division by Employment Sizeband

Numbers

		Employment size								Total
		0 - 4	5 - 9	10 - 19	20 - 49	50 - 99	100 - 249	250 - 499	500+	
Division										
15/16	Food products; beverages and tobacco	3 200	1 870	1 355	1 125	545	530	245	175	9 045
17	Textiles and textile products	2 400	760	550	425	220	120	20	5	4 500
18	Wearing apparel; dressing and dyeing of fur	2 075	650	370	265	60	25	10	0	3 455
19	Leather and leather products	340	130	85	65	25	15	0	0	660
20	Wood and wood products	4 585	1 545	970	570	170	75	10	5	7 930
21	Pulp, paper and paper products	845	285	265	310	185	160	30	10	2 090
22	Publishing, printing and reproduction of recorded media	18 255	3 895	2 450	1 560	560	345	105	55	27 225
23	Coke, refined petroleum products and nuclear fuel	95	45	20	20	20	20	5	10	235
24	Chemicals, chemical products and man-made fibres	1 475	595	505	525	330	255	120	60	3 865
25	Rubber and plastic products	2 680	1 310	1 205	1 090	515	350	75	20	7 245
26	Other non-metallic mineral products	3 185	985	680	600	275	185	50	5	5 965
27	Basic metals	660	265	210	275	155	95	30	15	1 705
28	Fabricated metal products, except machinery and equipment	14 830	4 900	3 520	2 505	840	330	45	10	26 980
29	Machinery and equipment not elsewhere classified	6 290	2 140	1 780	1 430	555	360	120	50	12 725
30	Office machinery and computers	510	100	75	80	25	35	10	10	845
31	Electrical machinery and apparatus not elsewhere classified	2 510	795	670	605	265	190	60	20	5 115
32	Radio, television and communication equipment and apparatus	1 355	310	225	245	105	80	35	20	2 375
33	Medical, precision and optical instruments, watches and clocks	2 010	750	595	550	275	145	45	20	4 390
34	Motor vehicles, trailers and semi-trailers	1 200	370	335	350	175	155	90	55	2 730
35	Other transport equipment	1 285	365	265	190	120	120	45	55	2 445
36/37	Manufacturing not elsewhere classified	11 360	3 090	1 635	995	335	185	50	15	17 665
Total manufacturing (15/37)		81 145	25 155	17 765	13 780	5 755	3 775	1 200	615	149 190

1 The data in this table is taken from the NS publication,
UK Business: Activity, Size and Location 2007.
The count of units refers to local units, i.e. individual sites, rather than whole
businesses. All counts have been rounded to avoid disclosure.

Source: Office for National Statistics: 01633 812293

22.4 Production of primary fuels[1]
United Kingdom

Million tonnes of oil equivalent

		1996	1997	1998	1999	2000	2001	2002	2003	2004	2005	2006
Coal	HFZQ	31.1	30.3	25.8	23.2	19.6	20.0	18.8	17.6	15.6	12.7	11.4
Petroleum[2]	HGCY	142.1	140.4	145.3	150.2	138.3	127.8	127.0	116.2	104.5	92.9	84.0
Natural Gas[3]	HGDB	84.2	85.9	90.2	99.1	108.4	105.9	103.6	102.9	96.4	88.2	80.0
Primary electricity[4]	HGDN	22.4	23.5	24.0	22.9	20.2	21.2	20.6	20.4	18.7	19.0	17.7
Renewable energy[5]	HGDO	1.8	1.9	2.1	2.2	2.3	2.5	2.8	3.0	3.1	3.6	3.6
Total Production	HGDP	281.6	282.1	287.2	297.7	288.7	277.4	272.9	260.2	238.4	216.4	196.7

1 See chapter text.
2 Includes crude oil, natural gas liquids and feedstocks.
3 Includes colliery methane.

4 Nuclear, natural flow hydro-electricity and generation at wind stations.
5 Includes solar and geothermal heat, solid renewable sources (wood, waste, etc), and gaseous renewable sources (landfill gas, sewage gas).

Source: Department for Business, Enterprise and Regulatory Reform: 020 7215 2710

22.5 Total inland energy consumption
United Kingdom
Heat supplied basis

Million tonnes of oil equivalent

		1996	1997	1998	1999	2000	2001	2002	2003	2004	2005	2006
Inland energy consumption of primary fuels and equivalents[1]	KLWA	230.0	226.8	230.8	230.7	233.7	236.3	229.9	232.0	233.5	234.9	232.1
Coal[2]	KLWB	45.7	40.8	40.9	36.7	38.6	41.0	37.7	40.5	39.0	39.8	43.4
Petroleum[3]	KLWC	77.8	75.5	76.0	75.2	75.9	75.4	74.0	73.5	75.3	77.3	77.1
Primary electricity	KLWD	23.8	24.9	25.0	24.2	21.4	22.1	21.3	20.6	19.4	19.8	18.4
Natural gas	KLWE	81.0	83.5	86.9	92.5	95.6	95.4	94.2	94.5	96.6	94.0	89.2
Renewables and waste	GYUY	1.8	1.9	2.1	2.2	2.3	2.5	2.8	3.1	3.5	4.0	4.1
less Energy used by fuel producers and losses in conversion and distribution	KLWF	73.0	72.9	74.7	74.1	74.5	75.4	73.2	73.8	73.6	74.7	74.3
Total consumption by final users[1]	KLWG	157.0	153.9	155.9	156.5	159.2	160.9	156.5	158.0	159.8	160.1	157.8
Final energy consumption by type of fuel												
Coal (direct use)	KLWH	4.4	4.3	3.7	3.5	2.7	2.7	2.2	2.1	2.0	1.7	1.6
Coke and breeze	KLWI	1.0	0.8	0.9	0.9	0.8	0.8	0.7	0.7	0.6	0.6	0.5
Other solid fuel[4]	KLWJ	0.8	0.7	0.7	0.6	0.4	0.5	0.5	0.3	0.3	0.4	0.4
Coke oven gas	KLWK	0.4	0.5	0.4	0.2	0.2	0.2	0.1	0.1	0.1	0.1	0.1
Natural gas (direct use)	KLWL	56.5	54.2	55.9	55.1	57.1	57.8	55.2	56.7	57.1	55.5	52.8
Electricity	KLWM	26.5	26.8	27.1	27.8	28.3	28.6	28.7	28.9	29.1	29.7	29.5
Petroleum (direct use)[5]	KLWN	66.1	65.4	66.1	65.1	66.3	67.1	66.1	66.8	68.6	70.4	71.0
Renewables	GYVA	1.0	0.9	0.9	0.7	0.7	0.7	0.7	0.7	0.7	0.6	0.6
Final energy consumption by class of consumer												
Agriculture	KLWP	1.4	1.3	1.4	1.3	1.2	1.3	1.2	1.0	0.9	1.0	0.9
Iron and steel industry	KLWQ	4.2	4.2	4.0	3.8	2.2	2.3	2.0	1.9	1.9	1.8	1.8
Other industries	KLWR	30.3	30.4	30.5	30.5	33.1	33.2	32.0	32.2	31.3	31.8	30.7
Railways[6]	KLWS	1.3	1.2	1.3	1.4	1.4	1.4	1.4	1.5	1.4	1.4	1.5
Road transport	KLWT	40.8	41.3	41.0	41.4	41.1	41.1	41.9	41.8	42.2	42.4	42.5
Water transport	KLWU	1.3	1.3	1.2	1.1	1.0	0.8	0.7	1.2	1.2	1.4	1.8
Air transport	KLWV	8.9	9.3	10.2	11.0	12.0	11.8	11.7	11.9	12.9	13.9	14.0
Domestic	KLWW	48.1	44.8	46.1	46.1	46.9	48.2	47.0	47.7	48.6	47.2	45.6
Public administration	KLWX	8.8	8.4	8.1	8.2	8.1	8.0	7.0	6.7	7.2	7.2	7.1
Commercial and other services	KLWY	11.9	11.7	12.0	11.8	12.2	12.8	11.6	12.0	12.2	12.1	11.9

1 Includes heat sold from 1999.
2 Includes net trade and stock change in other solid fuels.
3 Refinery throughput of crude oil, *plus* net foreign trade and stock change in petroleum products. Petroleum products not used as fuels (chemical feedstock, industrial and white spirits, lubricants, bitumen and wax) are excluded.

4 Includes briquettes, ovoids, Phurnacite, Coalite, etc., and wood, waste etc., used for heat generation.
5 Includes manufactured liquid fuels from 1994.
6 Includes fuel used at transport premises.

Source: Department for Business, Enterprise and Regulatory Reform: 020 7215 2710

22.6 Coal: supply and demand[1]
United Kingdom

Million tonnes

		1995	1996	1997	1998	1999	2000	2001	2002	2003	2004	2005	2006
Supply													
Production of deep-mined coal	KLXA	35.2	32.2	30.3	25.7	20.9	17.2	17.3	16.4	15.6	12.5	9.6	9.4
Production of opencast coal	KLXB	16.4	16.3	16.7	14.3	15.3	13.4	14.2	13.1	12.1	12.0	10.4	8.6
Total	KLXC	51.5	48.5	47.0	40.0	36.2	30.6	31.5	29.5	27.8	24.5	20.0	18.1
Recovered slurry, fines, etc	KLXD	1.5	1.7	1.5	1.1	0.9	0.6	0.4	0.5	0.5	0.6	0.5	0.4
Imports	KLXE	15.9	17.8	19.8	21.2	20.3	23.4	35.5	28.7	31.9	36.2	44.0	50.5
Total	KLXF	68.9	68.0	68.3	62.4	57.4	54.6	67.5	58.7	60.2	61.3	64.5	69.0
Change in stocks at collieries and opencast sites	KSOL	−4.2	−3.0	0.7	−0.2	0.6	−3.5	−0.1	0.9	−0.9	−0.4	−0.1	−0.3
Total supply	KLXI	73.1	70.9	67.6	62.7	56.8	58.2	67.5	57.8	61.0	61.7	64.6	69.3
Home consumption													
Total home consumption	KLXW	76.9	71.4	63.1	63.2	55.7	59.9	63.9	58.6	63.0	60.5	61.9	67.4
Overseas shipments and bunkers	KLXX	0.9	1.0	1.1	1.0	0.8	0.7	0.5	0.5	0.5	0.6	0.5	0.4
Total consumption and shipments	KLXY	77.8	72.4	64.2	64.1	56.5	60.6	64.4	59.1	63.6	61.1	62.4	67.8
Change in distributed stocks[2]	KLXZ	−2.2	−0.9	3.0	−1.2	0.6	−2.3	3.5	−1.4	−2.4	0.5	2.2	1.6
Balance[3]	KLYA	−2.5	−0.6	0.3	−0.3	−0.3	−0.1	−0.3	0.1	−0.2	0.1	−0.1	−0.1
Stocks at end of year													
Distributed[2]	KLYB	13.1	12.3	15.3	14.1	14.7	12.3	15.8	14.5	12.1	12.6	14.8	16.4
At collieries and opencast sites	KSOM	7.1	4.2	4.8	4.6	5.2	1.6	1.6	2.5	1.6	1.2	1.1	0.8
Total stocks	KLYE	20.2	16.4	20.1	18.7	19.8	14.0	17.4	17.0	13.7	13.8	15.9	17.2

1 See chapter text. Figures relate to periods of 52 weeks. For 1998, figures relate to 52 weeks estimate for period ended 26 December 1998.
2 Excludes distributed stocks held in merchant yards etc., mainly for the domestic market, and stocks held by the industrial sector.
3 This is the balance between supply and consumption, shipments and changes in known distributed stocks.

Source: Department for Business, Enterprise and Regulatory Reform: 020 7215 2717

22.7 Fuel input and gas output: gas consumption[1,2]
United Kingdom

Giga-watt hours

		1998	1999	2000	2001	2002	2003	2004	2005	2006
Analysis of gas consumption										
Transformation sector	I77I	267 733	341 678	349 454	336 525	351 856	344 410	362 668	351 586	332 522
Electricity generation	I77G	267 733	315 493	324 563	312 939	329 847	324 580	340 824	329 103	310 355
Heat generation[3]	I77H	−	26 185	24 891	23 586	22 009	19 830	21 844	22 484	22 167
Energy industry use total	I77N	75 993	76 973	77 941	91 451	91 260	88 907	88 468	86 273	79 535
Oil and gas extraction	I77J	65 500	64 634	65 555	78 457	79 364	76 837	77 753	74 187	70 130
Petroleum refineries	KIKN	3 753	4 155	3 641	4 189	3 350	2 773	3 076	4 274	2 573
Coal extraction and coke manufacture	I77K	338	265	241	220	196	188	150	114	114
Blast furnaces	I77L	527	643	712	375	222	539	728	941	611
Other	I77M	5 875	7 276	7 792	8 210	8 128	8 570	6 761	6 757	6 106
Final consumption total	I77F	661 580	654 312	678 142	683 753	653 151	669 457	673 860	654 623	623 044
Iron and steel industry	KIKR	20 105	21 622	8 953	8 502	8 791	10 327	9 715	8 410	8 172
Other industries	KIKS	155 979	155 193	174 488	171 341	156 375	155 890	144 238	144 615	135 594
Domestic	KIKT	355 895	358 066	369 909	379 426	376 372	386 486	396 411	384 009	364 555
Public administration	KIKU	51 976	43 253	44 552	46 232	42 998	44 362	51 934	50 317	48 853
Commercial	I77D	40 722	36 622	36 216	37 098	36 224	39 537	37 595	35 134	34 279
Agriculture	KIKV	953	1 155	1 522	2 329	2 346	2 324	2 355	2 261	2 013
Miscellaneous	KIKW	23 973	25 457	28 166	27 452	19 265	20 510	21 591	20 156	20 079
Non energy use	I77E	11 977	12 944	14 336	11 373	10 780	10 021	10 021	9 721	9 500
Total gas consumption	I77O	1 005 306	1 072 963	1 105 537	1 111 729	1 096 267	1 102 774	1 124 996	1 092 482	1 035 101

1 See chapter text. The breakdown of consumption by industrial users is made according to the 2003 Standard Industrial Classification.
2 Natural gas plus colliery methane.
3 Heat generation data are not available before 1999. For earlier years gas used to generate heat for sale is allocated to final consumption by the sector producing the heat.

Source: Department for Business, Enterprise and Regulatory Reform: 020 7215 2717

22.8 Electricity: generation, supply and consumption[1]
United Kingdom

Gigawatt-hours

		1996	1997	1998	1999	2000	2001	2002	2003	2004	2005	2006
Electricity generated												
Major power producers: total	KLUA	326 235	324 133	333 764	336 608	341 783	353 066	353 994	362 600	358 313	362 212	361 657
Conventional thermal and other[2]	AWLC	160 791	133 591	134 009	118 762	131 062	132 744	126 694	139 147	139 105	140 399	157 382
Combined cycle gas turbine stations	KJCS	65 880	86 974	93 832	114 620	117 935	123 846	132 016	128 311	131 182	130 689	118 495
Nuclear stations	KLUC	94 671	98 146	99 486	95 133	85 063	90 093	87 848	88 686	79 999	81 618	75 451
Hydro-electric stations:												
Natural flow	KLUE	2 801	3 337	4 237	4 431	4 331	3 215	3 927	2 568	3 908	3 826	3 727
Pumped storage	KLUF	1 556	1 486	1 624	2 902	2 694	2 422	2 652	2 734	2 649	2 930	3 853
Renewables other than hydro	KLUG	536	599	576	761	698	738	856	1 154	1 471	2 746	2 750
Other generators: total	KLUH	24 632	26 534	28 938	31 543	35 285	31 721	33 252	35 609	35 554	36 160	36 670
Conventional thermal and other[2]	AWLD	18 334	18 629	19 091	19 419	19 094	16 621	15 788	17 244	16 359	16 341	17 378
Combined cycle gas turbine stations	KJCT	3 535	4 412	5 428	7 141	10 859	8 979	10 577	10 879	11 852	11 854	11 216
Hydro-electric stations (natural flow)	KLUK	592	832	881	905	755	840	860	660	936	1 096	878
Renewables other than hydro	KILA	2 171	2 661	3 538	4 078	4 577	5 283	6 028	6 825	6 407	6 869	7 197
All generating companies: total	KLUL	350 867	350 667	362 702	368 151	377 068	384 787	387 246	398 209	393 867	398 372	398 327
Conventional thermal and other[2]	AWYH	179 125	152 220	153 100	138 181	150 156	149 365	142 482	156 391	155 464	156 744	174 760
Combined cycle gas turbine stations	KJCU	69 415	91 386	99 260	121 761	128 794	132 825	142 593	139 190	143 034	142 543	129 711
Nuclear stations	KLUN	94 671	98 146	99 486	95 133	85 063	90 093	87 848	88 686	79 999	81 618	75 451
Hydro-electric stations:												
Natural flow	KLUP	3 393	4 169	5 118	5 336	5 086	4 055	4 787	3 228	4 844	4 922	4 605
Pumped storage	KLUQ	1 556	1 486	1 624	2 902	2 694	2 422	2 652	2 734	2 649	2 930	3 853
Renewables other than hydro	KLUR	2 707	3 260	4 114	4 839	5 275	6 021	6 884	7 979	7 878	9 615	9 947
Electricity used on works: Total	KLUS	16 078	16 560	17 408	16 706	16 304	17 394	17 126	18 136	17 030	17 872	18 566
Major generating companies	KLUT	14 967	15 411	16 140	15 461	14 952	16 066	15 746	16 747	15 582	16 265	17 073
Other generators	KLUU	1 111	1 149	1 268	1 245	1 352	1 328	1 380	1 389	1 448	1 608	1 495
Electricity supplied (gross)												
Major power producers: total	KLUV	311 268	308 722	317 624	321 147	326 831	336 999	338 248	345 854	342 731	345 947	344 584
Conventional thermal and other[2]	AWYI	155 086	127 419	127 788	112 919	124 828	126 434	120 495	132 053	132 240	133 407	148 868
Combined cycle gas turbine stations	KJCV	65 604	86 682	93 005	112 768	116 110	121 344	129 384	125 630	128 983	128 179	116 398
Nuclear stations	KLUX	85 820	89 341	90 590	87 672	78 334	82 985	81 090	81 911	73 682	75 173	69 237
Hydro-electric stations:												
Natural flow	KLUZ	2 763	3 299	4 225	4 409	4 316	3 203	3 914	2 559	3 901	3 821	3 714
Pumped storage	KLVA	1 507	1 439	1 569	2 804	2 603	2 340	2 562	2 641	2 559	2 776	3 722
Renewables other than hydro	KLVB	488	542	447	574	640	692	802	1 059	1 367	2 592	2 645
Other generators: total	KLVC	23 521	25 385	27 670	30 298	33 933	30 393	31 873	34 220	34 106	34 522	35 175
Conventional thermal and other[2]	AWYJ	17 492	17 815	18 250	18 643	18 499	15 996	15 211	16 711	15 925	15 961	16 999
Combined cycle gas turbine stations	KJCW	3 358	4 192	5 157	6 785	10 318	8 531	10 049	10 336	11 260	11 262	10 657
Hydro-electric stations (natural flow)	KLVF	584	822	869	894	743	829	849	653	919	929	865
Renewables other than hydro	KIKZ	2 085	2 555	3 393	3 977	4 374	5 037	5 764	6 519	6 002	6 400	6 654
All generating companies: total	KLVG	334 789	334 107	345 294	351 445	360 764	367 392	370 121	380 074	376 837	380 469	379 759
Conventional thermal and other[2]	AWYK	172 578	145 234	146 038	131 562	143 327	142 430	135 706	148 764	148 165	149 368	165 867
Combined cycle gas turbine stations	KJCX	68 962	90 874	98 162	119 553	126 428	129 875	139 433	135 966	140 243	139 441	127 055
Nuclear stations	KLVI	85 820	89 341	90 590	87 672	78 334	82 985	81 090	81 911	73 682	75 173	69 237
Hydro-electric stations:												
Natural flow	KLVK	3 347	4 121	5 094	5 303	5 059	4 032	4 763	3 212	4 820	4 750	4 579
Pumped storage	KLVL	1 507	1 439	1 569	2 804	2 603	2 340	2 562	2 641	2 559	2 776	3 722
Renewables other than hydro	KLVM	2 573	3 097	3 840	4 551	5 014	5 729	6 566	7 578	7 369	8 992	9 299
Electricity used in pumping												
Major power producers	KLVN	2 430	2 477	2 594	3 774	3 499	3 210	3 463	3 546	3 497	3 707	4 918
Electricity supplied (net): Total	KLVO	332 359	331 630	342 700	347 671	357 266	364 182	366 657	376 528	373 340	376 793	374 841
Major power producers	KLVP	308 838	306 245	315 030	317 373	323 332	333 789	334 785	342 308	339 234	342 241	339 666
Other generators	KLVQ	23 521	25 385	27 670	30 298	33 933	30 393	31 873	34 220	34 106	34 552	35 175
Net imports	KGEZ	16 755	16 574	12 468	14 244	14 174	10 399	8 414	2 160	7 490	8 321	7 517
Electricity available	KGIZ	349 114	348 203	355 168	361 915	371 440	374 581	375 072	378 687	380 830	385 114	382 358
Losses in transmission etc	KGKW	29 335	27 138	29 818	29 862	31 146	32 077	30 963	32 070	33 115	31 297	30 998
Electricity consumption: Total	KGKX	319 779	321 065	325 350	332 053	340 294	342 504	344 109	346 617	347 715	353 817	351 360
Fuel industries	KGKY	9 211	8 624	8 406	8 037	9 703	8 625	10 060	9 752	8 142	8 275	7 896
Final users: total	KGKZ	310 567	312 441	316 944	324 016	330 593	333 879	334 049	336 865	339 573	345 542	343 464
Industrial sector	KGLZ	107 631	108 102	108 443	112 250	115 286	112 495	113 296	114 006	116 467	119 206	116 988
Domestic sector	KGMZ	107 513	104 455	109 410	110 308	111 842	115 337	114 534	115 761	116 526	116 811	116 449
Other sectors	KGNZ	95 423	99 884	99 091	101 457	103 465	106 047	106 219	107 098	107 580	109 525	110 027

1 See chapter text.
2 Includes electricity supplied by gas turbines and oil engines and plants producing electricity from renewable resources other than hydro.

Source: Department for Business, Enterprise and Regulatory Reform: 020 7215 5190

22.9 Electricity: plant capacity and demand
United Kingdom

At end of December | Megawatts

		1998	1999	2000	2001	2002	2003	2004	2005	2006
Major power producers:[1]										
Total declared net capability	GUFY	68 312	70 245	72 193	73 382	70 369	71 465	73 293	73 941	75 016
Conventional steam stations	GUFZ	35 081	35 647	34 835	34 835	30 687	30 327	31 982	32 292	33 628
Combined cycle gas turbine stations	GUGA	14 618	16 110	19 349	20 517	21 800	23 577	23 783	24 263	24 859
Nuclear stations[2]	GUGB	12 956	12 956	12 486	12 486	12 240	11 852	11 852	11 852	10 969
Gas turbines and oil engines	GUGC	1 434	1 301	1 291	1 291	1 433	1 537	1 495	1 356	1 444
Hydro-electric stations:										
Natural flow	GUGD	1 327	1 327	1 327	1 348	1 304	1 267	1 276	1 273	1 294
Pumped storage	GUGE	2 788	2 788	2 788	2 788	2 788	2 788	2 788	2 788	2 726
Renewables other than hydro	GUGF	108	117	117	117	117	117	117	117	96
Other generators:										
Total capacity of own generating plant[3]	GUGG	4 990	5 388	6 258	6 296	6 336	6 829	6 829	7 452	8 029
Conventional steam stations[4]	GUGH	3 248	3 315	3 544	3 464	3 325	3 480	3 275	3 303	3 626
Combined cycle gas turbine stations	GUGI	1 005	1 243	1 709	1 777	1 854	1 927	1 968	2 182	2 200
Hydro-electric stations (natural flow)	GUGJ	148	150	158	160	162	165	132	127	130
Renewables other than hydro	GUGK	589	680	847	895	995	1 257	1 454	1 840	2 073
All generating companies: Total capacity[3]	GUGL	73 302	75 633	78 451	79 678	76 705	78 294	80 122	81 393	83 045
Conventional steam stations[4]	GUGM	38 329	38 962	38 379	38 299	34 012	33 807	35 257	35 595	37 254
Combined cycle gas turbine stations	GUGN	15 623	17 353	21 058	22 294	23 654	25 504	25 751	26 445	27 059
Nuclear stations	GUGO	12 956	12 956	12 486	12 486	12 240	11 852	11 852	11 852	10 969
Gas turbines and oil engines	GUGP	1 434	1 301	1 291	1 291	1 433	1 537	1 495	1 356	1 444
Hydro-electric stations:										
Natural flow	GUGQ	1 475	1 477	1 485	1 508	1 466	1 432	1 408	1 400	1 424
Pumped storage	GUGR	2 788	2 788	2 788	2 788	2 788	2 788	2 788	2 788	2 726
Renewables other than hydro	GUGS	697	797	964	1 012	1 112	1 374	1 571	1 957	2 169
Major power producers:[1]										
Simultaneous maximum load met[5]	GUGT	56 312	57 849	58 452	58 589	61 717	60 501	61 013	61 697	59 071
System load factor[6] (percentages)	GUGU	68.0	67.0	67.0	69.0	65.0	67.0	67.0	66.0	69.0

1 See chapter text.
2 Nuclear generators are now included under "major power producers" only.
3 Capacity figures for other generators are as at end-December of the previous year.

4 For other generators, conventional steam stations cover all types of stations not separately listed.
5 Maximum load in year to end of March.
6 The average hourly quantity of electricity available during the year ending March expressed as a percentage of the maximum demand.

Source: Department for Business, Enterprise and Regulatory Reform: 020 7215 5190

22.10 Electricity: fuel used in generation
United Kingdom

Million tonnes of oil equivalent

		1996	1997	1998	1999	2000	2001	2002	2003	2004	2005	2006
Major power producers:[1] total all fuels	KGPS	74.60	71.50	74.90	73.60	74.40	77.38	75.79	77.53	76.82	78.19	78.68
Coal	FTAJ	32.40	27.10	28.70	24.50	27.80	30.60	28.60	31.60	30.40	31.70	34.90
Oil[2]	FTAK	3.00	1.20	0.80	0.80	0.80	0.80	0.70	0.70	0.60	0.90	1.00
Gas	KGPT	15.2	19.3	20.3	24.2	24.4	23.8	25.0	24.5	26.2	25.4	23.9
Nuclear[3]	FTAL	22.20	22.00	23.40	22.20	19.60	20.80	20.10	20.00	18.20	18.40	17.10
Hydro (natural flow)	FTAM	0.20	0.30	0.40	0.40	0.40	0.30	0.30	0.20	0.30	0.30	0.30
Other fuels used by UK companies	KGPU	0.1	0.2	0.2	0.2	0.2	0.3	0.3	0.4	0.5	0.8	0.7
Net imports	KGPV	1.4	1.4	1.1	1.2	1.2	0.9	0.7	0.2	0.6	0.7	0.6
Other generators: total all fuels	KGPW	6.4	6.7	7.1	7.3	8.0	7.6	8.0	8.7	8.4	8.9	8.8
Transport undertakings												
Gas	KGPX	0.200	0.200	0.200	0.200	0.200	0.200	0.200	0.008	0.002	0.003	0.002
Undertakings in industrial sector												
Coal	KGPY	1.2	1.2	1.2	1.0	0.9	1.0	1.0	1.0	0.9	0.9	0.9
Oil	KGPZ	0.9	0.8	0.7	0.7	0.8	0.6	0.6	0.5	0.5	0.5	0.4
Gas	KGQM	1.9	2.2	2.5	2.7	3.3	2.9	3.2	3.4	3.1	2.8	2.7
Hydro (natural flow)	KGQO	0.1	0.1	0.1	0.1	0.1	0.1	0.1	0.1	0.1	0.1	0.1
Other fuels	KGQP	2.037	2.186	2.420	2.640	2.770	2.740	2.968	3.660	3.800	4.600	4.600
All generating companies: total fuels	KGQQ	81.03	78.20	82.00	80.90	82.40	84.90	83.80	86.20	85.20	87.10	87.50
Coal	KGQR	33.6	28.3	29.9	25.5	28.7	31.6	29.6	32.5	31.3	32.6	35.9
Oil	KGQS	4.0	2.0	1.5	1.5	1.5	1.4	1.3	1.2	1.1	1.4	1.4
Gas	KGQT	17.4	21.7	23.0	27.1	27.9	26.9	28.4	27.9	29.3	28.2	26.6
Nuclear[3]	KGQU	22.2	22.0	23.4	22.2	19.6	20.8	20.1	20.0	18.2	18.4	17.1
Hydro (natural flow)	KGQV	0.3	0.4	0.4	0.5	0.4	0.3	0.4	0.3	0.4	0.4	0.4
Other fuels used by UK companies[4]	KGQW	2.183	2.351	2.597	2.863	3.007	2.993	3.242	4.041	4.300	5.400	5.400
Net imports	KGQX	1.4	1.4	1.1	1.2	1.2	0.9	0.7	0.2	0.6	0.7	0.6

1 See chapter text.
2 Includes oil used in gas turbine and diesel plant for lighting up coal fired boilers and Orimulsion.

3 Nuclear generators are now included under "major power producers" only.
4 Main fuels included are coke oven gas, blast furnace gas, waste products from chemical processes and sludge gas.

Source: Department for Business, Enterprise and Regulatory Reform: 020 7215 5190

Production

22.11 Indigenous petroleum production, refinery receipts, imports and exports of oil[1]

Thousand tonnes

		1996	1997	1998	1999	2000	2001	2002	2003	2004	2005	2006
Total indigenous petroleum production[2]	KMBA	129 742	128 234	132 633	137 099	126 245	116 678	115 944	106 073	95 374	84 721	76 578
Crude petroleum:[3] Refinery receipts total	KMBB	96 660	97 023	93 797	88 286	88 014	83 343	84 784	84 585	89 821	86 135	83 213
Foreign trade[4]												
Imports	KMBF	50 099	49 994	47 958	44 869	54 387	53 551	56 968	54 177	62 516	58 886	59 443
Exports	AXRB	81 563	79 400	84 610	91 797	92 918	86 930	87 144	74 898	64 504	54 098	50 195
Net imports	AXRC	−31 464	−29 406	−36 652	−46 928	−38 531	−33 378	−30 176	−20 720	−1 988	4 787	9 249
Petroleum products Foreign trade												
Imports[4]	BHMI	9 315	8 705	11 418	13 896	14 212	17 234	14 900	16 472	18 545	22 510	26 828
Exports[4]	AXRD	23 681	26 755	24 375	21 730	20 677	19 088	23 444	23 323	30 495	29 722	29 009
Net imports[4]	AXRE	−14 366	−18 049	−12 957	−7 834	−6 464	−1 854	−8 544	−6 851	−11 950	−7 211	−2 181
International marine bunkers	BHMK	2 664	2 961	3 080	2 329	2 079	2 274	1 913	1 764	2 085	2 055	2 348

1 See chapter text. The term 'indigenous' is used in this table to cover oil produced on the UK Continental Shelf. This includes small amounts produced onshore.

2 Crude oil *plus* condensates and petroleum gases derived at onshore treatment plants.

3 Includes process (partly refined) oils.

4 Foreign trade as recorded by the petroleum industry and may differ from figures published in *Overseas Trade Statistics*.

Source: Department for Business, Enterprise and Regulatory Reform: 020 7215 6072

22.12 Throughput of crude and process oils and output of refined products from refineries[1]

United Kingdom

Thousand tonnes

		1996	1997	1998	1999	2000	2001	2002	2003	2004	2005	2006
Throughput of crude and process oils	KMAU	96 661	97 024	93 797	88 285	88 014	83 343	84 784	84 585	89 821	86 135	83 213
less: Refinery fuel:	KMAA	6 623	6 572	6 177	5 538	5 252	5 059	5 677	5 456	5 417	5 602	4 728
Losses	KMAB	152	86	1 004	1 550	1 632	1 233	788	58	−5	132	133
Total output of refined products	KMAC	89 885	90 366	86 616	81 197	81 130	77 051	78 319	79 071	84 409	80 402	78 352
Gases:												
Butane and propane	KMAE	1 828	1 950	1 961	1 975	1 917	1 764	2 139	2 281	2 152	2 424	2 304
Other petroleum	KMAF	144	139	394	361	288	272	537	715	520	427	610
Naphtha and other feedstock	KMAG	2 824	2 854	2 316	2 430	3 082	3 428	3 153	3 503	3 168	3 019	2 734
Aviation spirit	KMAH	–	–	–	16	30	101	28	26	31	32	25
Motor spirit	KMAJ	28 046	28 260	27 166	25 230	23 445	21 455	22 944	22 627	24 589	22 620	21 443
Industrial and white spirit	KMAK	136	128	135	129	122	121	121	104	100	136	107
Kerosene:												
Aviation turbine fuel	KMAL	8 305	8 342	7 876	7 249	6 484	5 910	5 365	5 277	5 615	5 167	6 261
Burning oil	KMAM	3 510	3 336	3 442	3 553	3 078	3 088	3 506	3 521	3 613	3 325	3 374
Gas/diesel oil	KMAN	28 903	28 778	27 542	25 755	28 229	26 748	28 343	27 380	28 647	28 486	26 038
Fuel oil	KMAO	11 479	11 747	11 125	10 446	10 296	10 179	8 507	9 495	11 308	10 155	11 280
Lubricating oil	KMAP	1 111	1 231	1 125	907	702	656	509	576	1 136	936	617
Bitumen	KMAQ	2 189	2 258	2 172	1 644	1 438	1 707	1 918	1 925	2 196	1 912	1 749
Petroleum wax	KMAR	41	65	59	261	437	416	430	460	94	98	16
Petroleum coke	KMAS	714	598	678	648	657	513	441	612	633	660	606
Other products	KMAT	655	680	625	593	927	692	378	569	607	1 005	1 189

1 See chapter text. Crude and process oils comprise all feedstocks, other than distillation benzines, for treatment at refinery plants. Refinery production does not cover further treatment of finished products for special grades such as in distillation plant for the preparation of industrial spirits.

Source: Department for Business, Enterprise and Regulatory Reform: 020 7215 6072

22.13 Deliveries of petroleum products for inland consumption[1]
United Kingdom

Thousand tonnes

		1996	1997	1998	1999	2000	2001	2002	2003	2004	2005	2006
Total (including refinery fuel)	KMCA	82 013	79 073	78 438	77 974	77 196	76 413	76 233	77 154	79 053	81 035	79 990
Total (excluding refinery fuel)	KMCB	75 390	72 501	72 261	72 436	71 944	71 354	70 556	71 697	73 636	75 433	75 262
Butane and propane	ECAQ	2 439	2 426	2 368	2 249	2 070	2 097	2 553	3 017	3 114	3 554	3 327
Other Petroleum Gases (includes Ethane)	ECAR	1 482	1 561	1 752	2 041	1 886	2 077	2 181	2 114	1 918	2 021	1 870
Naphtha	ECAS	3 010	2 640	2 882	3 100	2 344	1 592	1 592	2 332	2 029	1 916	2 279
Aviation spirit	KMCI	32	37	36	45	52	59	50	46	49	52	46
Motor spirit:												
Retail deliveries:												
Leaded Premium / Lead Replacement Petrol	KMCK	7 043	6 138	4 595	2 629	1 462	838	401	183	74	25	19
Super Premium Unleaded	KMCL	698	506	409	473	403	420	706	861	810	924	719
Premium Unleaded	KMCM	14 228	15 188	16 432	18 307	19 008	19 100	19 167	18 291	17 795	16 954	16 704
Total Retail Deliveries	ECAT	21 969	21 832	21 436	21 409	20 873	20 358	20 274	19 335	18 679	17 903	17 442
Commercial consumers:												
Leaded Premium / Lead Replacement Petrol	KMCO	135	112	91	61	44	34	19	19	14	1	2
Super Premium Unleaded	KMCP	11	9	4	6	6	9	17	22	26	16	63
Premium Unleaded	KMCQ	294	298	318	311	480	538	499	542	765	811	637
Total Commercial Consumers	ECAU	440	419	413	378	530	581	535	583	805	828	702
Total Motor spirit	BHOD	22 409	22 251	21 849	21 787	21 403	20 939	20 809	19 918	19 484	18 731	18 144
Industrial and white spirits	KMCS	184	195	179	174	170	151	157	147	281	284	156
Kerosene:												
Aviation turbine fuel	BHOE	8 049	8 411	9 241	9 939	10 806	10 614	10 519	10 765	11 637	12 497	12 641
Burning oil	KMCT	3 336	3 343	3 575	3 633	3 839	4 236	3 578	3 569	3 950	3 869	4 016
Gas/diesel oil:												
Derv fuel:												
Retail Deliveries	ECAV	5 537	6 127	6 602	7 137	7 181	7 846	8 153	9 057	9 517	10 679	11 453
Commercial Consumers	ECAW	8 828	8 849	8 541	8 371	8 451	8 213	8 774	8 655	8 997	8 757	8 693
Total Derv fuel	BHOI	14 365	14 976	15 143	15 508	15 632	16 059	16 927	17 712	18 514	19 436	20 146
Other gas/diesel oil (includes Mdf)	ECAX	8 349	8 053	7 908	7 454	7 576	6 960	6 099	6 326	6 017	6 797	6 565
Fuel oil	BHOK	6 854	3 936	3 105	2 701	2 119	2 578	1 721	1 540	2 063	2 023	2 151
Lubricating oils	BHOL	864	872	813	790	801	846	829	868	914	750	713
Bitumen	BHOM	2 146	2 015	1 967	1 928	1 975	1 935	2 002	1 959	1 991	1 906	1 610
Petroleum wax	KMCU	44	44	18	37	32	33	51	57	50	72	48
Petroleum coke	KMCV	1 210	1 095	887	660	776	702	893	880	1 145	1 042	925
Miscellaneous products	KMCW	617	646	537	388	463	475	596	449	476	484	628

1 See chapter text.

Source: Department for Business, Enterprise and Regulatory Reform: 020 7215 6072

Production

22.14 Iron and steel:[1] summary of steel supplies, deliveries and stocks
United Kingdom

		1996	1997	1998	1999	2000	2001	2002	2003	2004	2005	2006
Supply, disposal and consumption - (Finished product weight - Thousand tonnes)												
UK producers' home deliveries	KLTA	8 383	8 626	8 260	7 652	7 255	6 762	6 506	6 227	7 083	6 279	6 757
Imports excluding steelworks receipts	KLTB	5 147	5 894	6 466	6 014	6 387	6 978	6 793	6 893	7 272	6 297	7 403
Total deliveries to home market (a)	KLTC	13 530	14 520	14 726	13 666	13 642	13 740	13 299	13 120	14 355	12 576	14 160
Total exports (producers, consumers, merchants)	KLTD	8 917	9 060	8 008	7 623	7 446	6 512	6 320	7 007	7 455	8 408	7 862
Exports by UK producers	KLTE	8 305	8 534	7 876	7 416	7 163	6 182	5 594	6 202	6 275	6 594	6 852
Derived consumers' and merchants' exports (b)	KLTF	612	526	132	207	283	330	708	806	1 179	1 814	1 010
Net home disposals (a)-(b)	KLTG	12 918	13 994	14 594	13 460	13 359	13 410	12 591	12 314	13 176	10 762	13 150
Estimated home consumption	KLTI	12 918	13 994	14 594	13 460	13 359	13 410	12 591	12 114	13 176	10 762	13 150
Stocks - (Finished product weight - Thousand tonnes)												
Producers												
- ingots & semis	KLTJ	767	946	717	747	727	705	690	706	765	869	790
- finished steel	KLTK	1 515	1 358	1 495	1 318	1 039	981	932	917	901	947	876
Estimated home consumption - (Crude steel equivalent - Million tonnes)												
Crude steel production[2]	KLTN	17.99	18.50	17.32	16.28	15.15	13.54	11.53	13.13	13.77	13.23	13.90
Producers' stock change	KLTO	..	0.03	..	..	..	..	..	..	..	0.18	—
Re-usable material	KLTP	0.07	0.06	0.02	..	..	..	..	..	..	..	—
Total supply from home sources	KLTQ	18.13	18.53	17.45	16.47	15.48	13.68	11.61	13.13	13.77	13.20	13.90
Total imports[3]	KLTR	7.01	7.49	8.38	7.81	8.43	9.11	9.86	9.32	10.31	9.82	10.30
Total exports[3]	KLTS	10.26	10.43	9.25	8.70	8.61	7.53	7.39	8.65	9.15	8.93	10.40
Net home disposals	KLTT	14.88	15.59	16.58	15.58	15.30	15.26	14.08	14.20	14.99	13.09	14.70
Estimated home consumption	KLTV	14.88	15.59	16.58	15.58	15.30	15.26	14.08	14.20	14.99	13.09	14.70

1 See chapter text. The figures relate to periods of 52 weeks.
2 Includes liquid steel for castings only up to 2003.

3 Based on HM Customs Statistics, reflecting total trade rather than producers' trade.

Source: Iron and Steel Statistics Bureau: 020 8686 9050 ext 126

22.15 Iron and steel:[1] iron ore, manganese ore, pig iron and iron and steel scrap
United Kingdom

Thousand tonnes

		1996	1997	1998	1999	2000	2001	2002	2003	2004	2005	2006
Iron ore[2]	KLOF	19 720	20 820	19 532	18 754	16 991	15 113	13 185	15 766	16 013	15 991	16 539
Manganese ore[2]	KLOG	48	37	22	14	36	4	4	..	6	3	6
Pig iron (and blast furnace ferro-alloys)												
Average number of furnaces in blast during period	KLOH	9	9	9	9	8	7	5	6	6	6	7
Production Steelmaking iron	KLOI	12 830	13 054	12 746	12 139	10 890	9 870	8 561	10 228	10 180	10 189	10 696
In blast furnaces: total	KLOL	12 830	13 054	12 746	12 139	10 890	9 870	8 561	10 228	10 180	10 189	10 696
In steel works	KLOM	12 753	13 044	12 746	12 139	10 890	9 870	8 561	10 228	10 180	10 189	10 696
Consumption of pig iron: total	KLOO	12 753	13 044	12 746	12 139	10 890	9 870	8 561	10 228	10 180	10 189	10 696
Iron and steel scrap												
Steelworks and steel foundries Circulating scrap	KLOQ	2 639	2 459	2 380	2 488	2 287	2 019	1 882	1 926	1 787	1 737	1 669
Purchased receipts	KLOR	4 130	5 418	4 045	3 433	3 327	3 001	2 271	2 617	3 371	2 779	3 171
Consumption	KLOS	6 828	7 207	6 408	5 884	5 675	5 006	4 216	4 469	5 123	4 531	4 811
Stocks (end of period)	KLOT	260	236	253	290	229	224	161	234	242	228	257

1 See chapter text. The figures relate to periods of 52 weeks.
2 Consumption.

Source: Iron and Steel Statistics Bureau: 020 8686 9050 ext 126

22.16 Iron and steel:[1] furnaces and production of steel
United Kingdom

Number and thousand tonnes

		1996	1997	1998	1999	2000	2001	2002	2003	2004	2005	2006
Steel furnaces (numbers[2])	KLPA	192	192	190	181	181	181	173	..	..	..	..
Oxygen converters	KLPC	11	11	11	11	11	11	8	..	..	..	..
Electric	KLPD	181	181	179	170	170	170	165	..	..	..	..
Production of crude steel	KLPF	17 992	18 499	17 315	16 284	15 155	13 543	11 667	13 268	13 766	13 239	13 905
by process												
Oxygen converters	KLPH	13 758	13 986	13 426	12 634	11 551	10 271	8 956	10 630	10 667	10 550	11 203
Electric	KLPI	4 234	4 513	3 889	3 650	3 604	3 272	2 711	2 639	3 099	2 685	2 702
by cast method												
Cast to ingot	KLPK	1 892	1 660	784	534	539	369	339	354	383	281	206
Continuously cast	KLPL	15 912	16 653	16 346	15 637	14 470	13 024	11 182	12 766	13 383	12 958	13 698
Steel for castings	KLPM	188	186	185	127	146	150	146	148	..	..	..
by quality												
Non alloy steel	KLPN	16 708	17 193	16 145	15 263	14 004	12 482	10 657	12 294	12 809	12 376	..
Stainless and other alloy steel	KLPO	1 284	1 306	1 170	1 035	1 151	1 061	1 010	974	957	863	760
Production of finished steel products												
(All quantities)[3]												
Rods and bars for reinforcement (in coil and lengths)	KLPP	1 182	1 118	1 133	893	812	755	487	294	769	730	902
Wire rods and other rods and bars in coil	KLPQ	1 536	1 565	1 492	1 407	1 408	1 389	1 394	1 316	1 392	1 035	962
Hot rolled bars in lengths	KLPR	1 499	1 716	1 791	1 542	1 545	1 449	1 267	1 107	1 179	1 142	1 249
Bright steel bars[4]	KLPS	357	385	336	311	337	296	271	273	277	233	226
Light sections other than rails	KLPT	298	302	318	264	183	201	188	116	136	130	149
Heavy sections	KGQZ	2 557	2 397	2 346	2 303	1 915	1 931	1 873	1 774	1 694	1 414	1 527
Hot rolled plates, sheets and strip in coil and lengths	KLPW	8 512	8 956	8 454	7 893	7 293	5 841	5 756	6 145	6 437	5 823	6 010
Cold rolled plates and sheets in coil and lengths	KLPX	4 221	4 437	4 288	3 914	3 612	2 944	2 951	2 958	3 001	2 769	2 726
Cold rolled strip[4]	KLPZ	246	255	259	233	218	201	179	186	156	131	98
Tinplate	KLQW	739	754	772	736	753	602	562	493	507	471	421
Other coated sheet	KLQX	2 366	2 534	2 610	2 475	2 471	1 773	1 786	1 811	1 713	1 644	1 773
Tubes and pipes[4]	KLQY	1 317	1 310	1 276	1 100	1 061	1 096	940	1 066	1 076	932	993
Forged bars[4]	KLQZ	3	3	3	2	1	1	1	..	..	..	..

1 See chapter text. The figures relate to periods of 52 weeks.
2 Includes steel furnaces at steel foundries, only up to 2003.
3 Includes material for conversion into other products listed in the table.
4 Based on producers' deliveries.

Source: Iron and Steel Statistics Bureau: 020 8686 9050 ext 126

22.17 Non-ferrous metals
United Kingdom

		1996	1997	1998	1999	2000	2001	2002	2003	2004	2005	2006
Copper												
Production of refined copper:												
Primary	KLAA	13.0	9.1	6.4	1.7	–	–	–	–	–	–	–
Secondary	KLAB	43.6	51.3	47.4	48.6	–	–	–	–	–	–	–
Home consumption:												
Refined	KLAC	396.0	408.3	374.1	305.3	322.7	285.9	260.8	242.2	243.4	165.4	172.1
Scrap (metal content)	KLAD	81.0	69.0	64.6	112.5	132.4	127.0	120.0	120.0	120.0	120.0	120.0
Stocks (end of period)[1,2]	KLAE	6.6	12.8	7.5	7.3	10.4	7.3	..	..	..	..	..
Analysis of home consumption (refined and scrap):[3,4] total	KLAF	477.3	477.4	438.7	417.8	455.5	212.7	..	..	..	..	..
Wire[5]	KLAG	309.4	312.5	287.2	276.1	310.2	151.8	..	..	..	..	..
Rods, bars and sections	KLAH	58.3	58.3	53.6	46.9	43.6	21.6	..	..	..	..	..
Sheet, strip and plate	KLAI	34.0	36.5	30.5	27.7	32.3	16.9	..	..	..	..	..
Tubes	KLAJ	75.6	70.1	67.4	67.1	69.4	22.4	..	..	..	..	..
Zinc												
Slab zinc:												
Production	KLAL	96.9	107.7	99.6	132.8	99.6	99.6	99.6	16.6	–	–	–
Home consumption	KLAM	195.7	194.8	187.9	198.9	206.5	197.1	202.4	176.2	150.1	161.7	161.7
Stocks (end of period)	KLAN	10.5	10.1	10.6	10.9	10.9	9.5	9.2	8.9	8.9	8.9	8.9
Other zinc (metal content):												
Consumption	KLAO	41.3	41.5	37.3	41.6	46.3	48.2	51.8	52.3	55.4	–	–
Analysis of home consumption (slab and scrap): total	KLAP	237.1	236.5	221.6	232.1	237.9	226.6	230.4	226.8	232.0	..	..
Brass	KLAQ	39.1	41.6	36.6	33.6	34.4	32.2	30.0	30.0	31.2	..	..
Galvanized products	KLAR	110.3	108.4	103.8	116.6	120.9	111.8	117.3	113.3	116.2	..	..
Zinc sheet and strip	KLAS	3.0	3.3	3.3	3.3	3.3	3.3	3.4	3.3	3.3	..	..
Zinc alloy die castings	KLAT	46.5	46.5	46.5	46.5	46.5	46.5	46.5	46.5	46.5	..	..
Zinc oxide	KLAU	20.7	20.6	20.4	21.1	21.8	21.8	22.2	22.7	23.8	..	..
Other products	KLAV	17.5	16.1	11.0	11.0	11.0	11.0	11.0	11.0	11.0	..	..
Refined lead												
Production[6,7]	KLAW	351.4	384.1	349.7	351.0	328.0	366.3	366.3	364.6	245.9	304.3	306.7
Home consumption[7,8]												
Refined lead	KLAX	272.8	270.4	275.5	283.3	294.0	298.3	298.3	314.7	330.3	281.6	300.0
Scrap and remelted lead[7]	KLAY	43.4	39.1	38.4	32.2	39.5	40.6	40.7	34.1	40.8	..	..
Stocks (end of period)[9]												
Lead bullion	KLAZ	32.9	15.5	20.9	17.1	10.0	17.2	17.2	24.0	23.0	23.0	23.0
Refined soft lead at consumers	KLBA	28.8	29.1	27.4	25.7	25.8	26.1	26.1	25.3	25.9	25.9	25.9
In LME Warehouses (UK)	KLBB	3.0	2.4	0.1	0.1	0.1	0.1	0.1	0.1	0.1	0.1	..
Analysis of home consumption (refined and scrap): total	KLBC	316.2	309.5	313.9	315.5	333.5	338.9	339.0	348.8	371.1	281.6	300.0
Cables	KLBD	9.8	9.7	9.7	9.7	9.6	9.6	9.7	9.7	9.7	..	..
Batteries (excluding oxides)	KLBE	52.3	54.7	51.6	47.4	50.5	48.2	48.2	51.9	54.1	..	..
Oxides and compounds:												
Batteries	KLBF	54.9	56.1	54.4	53.1	55.9	54.7	54.7	55.9	59.0	..	..
Other uses	KLBG	56.1	54.5	56.4	57.0	56.8	53.8	53.8	60.6	64.5	..	..
Sheets and pipes	KLBH	94.1	91.1	96.1	94.9	102.3	102.3	102.3	109.8	111.4	..	..
Solder	KLBJ	7.4	7.4	7.4	7.4	7.4	7.4	7.4	7.2	7.4	..	..
Alloys	KLBK	12.1	9.4	9.4	11.9	15.2	24.3	24.3	25.7	33.3	..	..
Other uses	KLBL	29.5	26.6	28.9	34.1	35.8	38.6	38.6	28.0	31.7	..	..

Production

22.17 Non-ferrous metals
United Kingdom
continued

Thousand tonnes

		1996	1997	1998	1999	2000	2001	2002	2003	2004	2005	2006
Tin												
Tin ore (metal content):												
Production	KLBM	2.1	2.3	0.4	0.4	..	..	1.9	1.9	–	–	–
Tin metal:[10]												
Production[11]	KLBO	–	..	..	..	..	..	1.9	1.9	–	–	–
Home consumption[11]	VQIX	10.5	10.4	10.6	9.6	10.0	10.3	6.9	7.1	5.3	3.2	4.1
Exports and re-exports[12]	KLBQ	0.6	0.3	3.4	0.1	0.1	0.4	1.9	0.3	0.6	1.7	11.8
Stocks (end of period):												
Consumers	KLBR	1.0	1.0	1.0	1.0	1.0	1.0	1.0	1.0	1.0	1.0	1.0
Analysis of home consumption												
(excluding scrap): total	KLBT	10.5	10.4	17.5	16.5	17.0	18.8	18.8	1.9	18.4	..	..
Tinplate	KLBU	3.6	2.8	2.6	3.0	3.0	3.0	1.9	1.9	3.0	..	..
Alloys	KLBV	3.5	3.4	12.1	11.2	11.6	2.6	1.9	1.9	2.6	..	..
Solder	KLBW	1.1	1.1	1.1	0.6	0.8	1.5	1.9	1.9	1.5	..	..
Other uses	KLBX	0.4	0.4	0.4	0.4	0.4	0.4	1.9	1.9	0.4	..	..
Aluminium												
Ingot production												
Primary	KLBY	240.0	247.7	258.4	269.7	305.1	340.8	344.3	342.7	359.6	368.5	360.3
Secondary[13]	KLCA	260.0	242.7	274.8	285.3	237.7	248.6	205.4	205.4	205.4	205.3	197.9
Wrought remelt production[14]	C6EW	500.0	490.4	533.2	555.0	542.8	589.4	549.7	548.1	565.0	573.8	558.2
Wrought and cast despatches												
Bar, section and tube[15]	C6EX	149.6	160.8	168.0	181.7	184.7	177.1	168.3	158.7	157.0	–	–
Plate, sheet, strip and circles	C6EY	327.9	350.4	352.5	349.7	419.1	384.8	312.2	274.3	267.3	–	–
Castings	KLCH	156.0	152.4	148.0	137.3	134.9	138.2	159.4	127.5	139.7	–	–
Exports												
Primary ingot	C6EZ	53.1	219.6	68.7	233.6	347.7	203.4	214.7	244.3	305.1	–	–
Secondary ingot	KLCC	152.2	153.3	156.6	143.1	84.2	59.9	35.7	26.9	30.8	–	–
Extruded products	C6F2	45.8	56.8	59.7	47.5	25.5	20.7	15.3	14.2	15.8	–	–
Rolled products	C6F3	155.5	157.7	160.1	166.6	222.9	198.3	208.8	193.9	192.2	–	–
Refined nickel												
Production (including ferro-nickel)	KLCM	38.6	36.1	39.1	39.5	38.0	33.8	33.8	26.8	38.6	37.6	36.8

1 Unwrought copper (electrolytic, fire refined and blister).
2 Reported stocks of refined copper held by consumers and those held in London Metal Exchange (LME) warehouses in the United Kingdom.
3 2001 figures only cover the period January to June.
4 Copper content.
5 Consumption for high-conductivity copper and cadmium copper wire represented by consumption of wire rods, production of which for export is also included.
6 Lead reclaimed from secondary and scrap material and lead refined from bullion and domestic ores.

7 Figures for production and consumption of refined lead include antimonial lead, and for scrap and remelted lead, exclude secondary antimonial lead.
8 Including toll transactions involving fabrication.
9 Excluding goverment stocks.
10 Including production from imported scrap and residues refined on toll.
11 Primary and secondary metal.
12 Including re-exports on toll transactions.
13 Predominantly from old scrap.
14 Predominantly using recycled scrap from fabrication.
15 Excluding forging bars

Sources: World Bureau of Metal Statistics: 01920 461274;
Aluminium Federation: 0121 456 1103

22.18 Fertilisers
Years ending 30 June

Thousand tonnes

		1997	1998	1999	2000	2001	2002	2003	2004	2005	2006	2007
Nutrient Content												
Nitrogen (N):												
Straight	KGRM	957	912	819	819	714	751	664	662	691	631	656
Compounds	KGRN	483	463	465	449	448	446	467	463	370	372	352
Phosphate (P_2O_5)	KGRO	412	383	347	317	279	283	282	278	259	235	224
Potash (K_2O)	KGRP	501	487	451	409	369	391	375	375	352	325	317
Compounds - total product	KGRQ	3 238	3 037	3 013	2 851	2 471	2 511	2 558	2 550	2 221	2 134	2 039

Source: Agricultural Industries Confederation: 01733 385230

22.19 Minerals: production[1]
United Kingdom

Thousand tonnes

		1996	1997	1998	1999	2000	2001	2002	2003	2004	2005	2006
Great Britain												
Limestone	KLEA	82 442	84 252	85 382	82 714	80 810	83 492	88 013	84 445	86 846	81 830	82 598
Sandstone	KLEB	12 581	12 457	13 545	11 870	12 056	11 897	11 788	11 665	11 929	11 609	11 827
Igneous rock	KLEC	43 731	42 370	39 838	45 294	44 633	45 053	44 544	45 305	46 193	45 992	47 867
Clay/shale	KLED	11 804	11 322	12 230	11 355	10 838	10 426	10 306	10 680	11 164	10 898	10 432
Industrial sand	KLEE	4 861	4 704	4 662	4 092	4 095	3 848	3 833	4 073	5 011	4 146	5 174
Chalk	KLEF	9 239	9 550	9 934	9 667	9 213	8 205	8 587	8 066	7 997	7 105	7 376
Fireclay	KLEG	536	338	577	545	595	459	491	528	402	395	228
Barium sulphate	KLEH	93	57	64	59	54	70	56	..	..	62	44
Calcium fluoride	KLEI	..	58	52	46	21	46	22	..	..	44	133
Copper	KLEJ	–	–	–	–	–	–	–	–	..	–	–
Lead	KLEK	..	..	1	1	..	1	..	..	..	1	4
Tin	KLEL	2.1	2.0	–	–	–	–	–	–	..	–	–
Zinc	KLEM	..	–	–	–	–	–	–	–	..	–	–
Iron ore: crude	KLEN	1	2	2	1	1	1	1	–	..	–	–
Iron ore: iron content	KLEO	1	1	1	1	1	..	..	–	..	–	–
Calcspar	KLEP	..	13	15	..	..	12	..	–	..	–	..
China clay	KILC	2 654	2 798	2 866	2 841	2 779	2 804	2 467	2 378	2 148	1 908	..
Ball clay	KIMS	..	..	..	..	..	..	..	..	..	..	..
Chert and flint	KLER	..	..	..	6	..	2	2	..	2	2	..
Fuller's earth	KLES	183	162	111	83	103	..	33	19	11	–	–
Lignite	KLET	–	–	–	–	–	–	–	–	..	–	–
Salt[2]	I8AV	..	..	..	..	..	..	..	..	..	5 770	5 224
Anhydrite	KLEX	–	–	–	–	–	–	–	–	..	–	–
Dolomite	KLEY	16 555	17 282	15 632	13 698	13 069	14 314	12 946	..	..	11 514	12 100
Gypsum	KLEZ	..	..	..	..	..	..	..	..	1 686	..	..
Slate[3]	KLFA	408	347	425	361	479	551	742	832	901	928	865
Soapstone and talc	KLFB	5	5	5	6	5	5	6	6	4	6	4
Sand and gravel (land-won)	KLFC	70 489	74 362	73 016	74 785	74 877	74 599	69 889	68 090	73 061	69 368	66 268
Sand and gravel (marine dredged)	KLFD	11 508	12 004	12 952	13 424	14 356	13 611	12 832	12 131	12 996	13 024	13 974
Northern Ireland												
Sand and gravel	KLFG	7 684	5 138	5 300	5 517	5 073	6 194	5 512	4 894	5 084	5 803	5 150
Basalt and igneous rock (other than granite)	KLFH	6 974	6 286	6 107	7 861	9 480	6 448	6 681	6 051	6 844	7 112	6 087
Limestone	KLFI	4 122	3 500	3 892	4 219	3 538	4 746	4 514	4 887	5 634	5 588	6 385
Sandstone[4]	KLFJ	4 941	6 042	6 584	3 615	2 844	8 070	6 574	6 594	6 915	7 076	6 211
Granite	KLFL	–	–	–	–	–	–	–	–	..	..	..
Others[5]	KLFN	1 392	625	473	1 579	3 098	753	242	1 055	1 266	2 090	1 698

1 See chapter text.
2 Includes rock salt, salt from brine and salt in brine.
3 Roofing and vertically hanging slates, includes 'true' slate and stone slates produced from thinly bedded sandstones and limestones. Also includes 'true' and stone slates sold as sawn slabs for decorative cladding.

4 Prior to 1993 the 'Sandstone' heading was called 'Grit and conglomerate'. The new heading is all encompassing and was confirmed as correct with the Geological Survey in Northern Ireland.
5 Rock salt, Chalk, Diatomite and Fireclay.

Source: Office for National Statistics: 01633 812082

22.20 Building materials and components: production[1]
Great Britain

			1997	1998	1999	2000	2001	2002	2003	2004	2005	2006	2007
Building bricks[2]	KLGA	Millions	2 997	3 000	2 939	2 864	2 754	2 750	2 772	2 868	2 748	2 510	2 478
Common bricks	GRTD	"	422	385	367	342	320	332	315	318	319	304	312
Facing bricks	GRTE	"	2 386	2 411	2 369	2 287	2 211	2 209	2 244	2 327	2 202	2 013	1 950
Engineering bricks	GRTF	"	190	204	204	235	223	210	213	224	227	193	216
Clay bricks (including sand-lime)	GRTG	"	2 828	2 830	2 759	2 694	2 595	2 600	2 606	2 707	2 601	2 359	2 313
Concrete bricks	GRTH	"	169	171	180	170	159	150	167	161	147	150	165
Cement (grey Portland)[3]	KLGB	Thousand tonnes	12 638	12 409	12 697	12 452	11 090	11 089	11 215	11 405	11 216	11 469	..
Sand and gravel	GRTI	"	86 366	85 968	88 209	89 234	88 210	82 721	80 221	86 057	82 392	80 242	75 506
Building sand[4]	KLGC	"	15 337	13 810	13 941	14 219	13 772	13 221	13 617	13 125	13 730	12 555	10 360
Concreting sand	KLGD	"	30 130	30 244	31 730	31 167	31 656	31 224	31 411	32 529	29 848	29 815	29 787
Gravel[5]	KLGE	"	40 899	41 914	42 538	43 847	42 782	38 276	35 193	40 404	38 814	37 871	35 359
Crushed rock	GRTJ	"	133 787	131 716	132 598	130 307	133 759	126 568	122 885	127 674	121 860	126 895	..
Coated roadstone	KLGF	"	23 906	23 131	22 260	21 785	23 340	23 281	23 139	18 721	20 136	21 367	..
Uncoated roadstone	KLGG	"	40 186	36 816	38 114	36 509	34 638	27 323	28 950	25 260	25 902	27 234	..
Fill and ballast	KLGH	"	51 396	51 623	52 144	53 417	47 225	49 622	42 208	62 460	58 945	58 431	..
Concrete aggregate	KLGI	"	18 300	20 146	20 080	18 595	28 556	26 342	28 588	21 231	16 876	19 863	..
Ready mixed concrete[6]	GRXA	Thousand cubic metres	22 327	22 983	23 550	23 043	23 008	22 597	22 289	22 856	22 432	23 029	23 548
Concrete building blocks	GRTK	Thousand square metres	82 537	84 662	87 767	90 219	87 922	91 474	95 645	96 256	89 997	87 510	89 958
Dense aggregate	KLGN	"	37 250	39 439	38 439	37 629	36 598	35 744	36 745	37 677	36 188	34 956	36 698
Lightweight aggregate	KLGO	"	17 783	19 110	20 830	22 991	22 684	23 478	24 991	25 462	25 561	25 345	25 960
Aerated concrete	KLGP	"	27 505	26 113	28 497	29 599	28 639	32 252	33 909	33 117	28 248	27 209	27 300
Concrete roofing tiles	KLGM	"	24 958	24 981	25 972	26 765	24 825	25 023	21 437	20 739	25 719	23 730	23 551
Roofing and architectural slates	GRXB	Tonnes	44 578	46 159	46 998	41 214	45 604	50 530	50 094	..	..	..	..
Fibre cement products	KLGK	Thousand tonnes	164.0	161.0	156.0	..	..	..	..	..	..	..	..

1 See chapter text.
2 Excluding refractory and glazed bricks.
3 United Kingdom up until 2000. Great Britain for 2001 onwards.
4 Includes sand and gravel used for coating.
5 Includes hoggin.
6 United Kingdom.

Source: Department for Business, Enterprise and Regulatory Reform: 020 7215 1555

22.21 Volume of construction output by all agencies[1] by type of work at constant 2000 prices (seasonally adjusted)

Standard Industrial Classification 2003. Great Britain.

£ millions

	New work							Repair and maintenance						All work (seasonally adjusted volume index numbers)
	New housing for		Infrastructure	Other new work for	Private sector		Total new work	Housing		Other work for		Total repair and maintenance	Total all work	
	Public sector	Private sector		Public sector	Industrial	Commercial		Public	Private	Public sector	Private sector			
	BLAC	BLAD	BAXF	BLAE	BLAF	BLAG	BLAB	BLBK	BLBL	BLAJ	BLAK	BLAH	FGAY	SFZX
2005	1 831	11 232	5 328	7 341	3 582	12 888	42 202	6 730	12 044	7 003	11 562	37 338	79 540	114.2
2006	2 238	11 433	4 930	6 969	3 981	14 616	44 167	6 527	11 674	6 483	11 576	36 260	80 426	115.4
2007[2]	2 612	11 360	4 985	6 622	4 002	16 485	46 065	6 336	11 746	5 777	12 500	36 359	82 424	118.3
2005 Q1	485	2 669	1 297	1 867	819	3 053	10 189	1 930	3 015	1 905	2 902	9 752	19 941	114.5
Q2	482	2 875	1 322	1 844	874	3 221	10 618	1 778	3 069	1 712	2 872	9 432	20 049	115.1
Q3	431	2 873	1 386	1 796	909	3 241	10 636	1 530	2 941	1 711	2 958	9 140	19 776	113.5
Q4	434	2 815	1 323	1 833	980	3 373	10 758	1 492	3 019	1 674	2 830	9 015	19 773	113.5
2006 Q1	563	2 755	1 301	1 807	976	3 398	10 801	1 707	2 961	1 730	2 775	9 174	19 975	114.7
Q2	596	2 834	1 223	1 741	961	3 540	10 895	1 589	3 019	1 647	2 848	9 103	19 998	114.8
Q3	562	2 937	1 235	1 711	978	3 778	11 201	1 653	2 804	1 636	2 844	8 935	20 136	115.6
Q4	517	2 907	1 170	1 710	1 066	3 900	11 270	1 578	2 890	1 471	3 109	9 047	20 317	116.8
2007 Q1	670	2 811	1 140	1 650	1 037	3 868	11 176	1 712	2 886	1 501	3 095	9 194	20 370	116.9
Q2	693	2 868	1 216	1 608	1 025	4 045	11 455	1 542	3 031	1 431	3 064	9 069	20 523	117.8
Q3	650	2 908	1 332	1 647	970	4 236	11 743	1 482	2 820	1 446	3 168	8 917	20 660	118.6
Q4[2]	599	2 774	1 297	1 717	969	4 335	11 691	1 600	3 010	1 399	3 172	9 180	20 872	119.8

1 Estimates of unrecorded output by small firms and self-employed workers, and output by the public sector's direct labour department are included.
2 Provisional

Sources: Office for National Statistics;
Tel : 020 7215 1953

Note: Responsibility for these statistics transferred from BERR (formerly DTI) to the ONS on 1st March 2008.

22.22 Value of new orders obtained by contractors for new work[1] at current prices

Great Britain

£ millions

	New housing[2]			Other new work					New work total
	Public and housing association	Private	Total	Infrastructure	Other public	Private industrial	Private commercial	Total	
	BLBC	BLBD	FGAU	BAWT	BAWU	BAWV	BAWW	BLBE	FHAA
2005	1 951	13 171	15 122	5 532	6 694	3 421	13 163	28 811	43 932
2006	2 653	13 468	16 121	4 319	6 162	3 634	17 528	31 643	47 764
2007	2 968	13 115	16 084	5 622	7 338	3 281	18 244	34 485	50 569
2005 Q1	552	3 203	3 756	1 483	1 606	679	3 283	7 052	10 807
Q2	448	3 605	4 053	1 463	1 693	856	3 248	7 259	11 312
Q3	390	3 626	4 016	1 488	1 867	842	3 114	7 311	11 328
Q4	560	2 737	3 297	1 098	1 528	1 044	3 518	7 188	10 485
2006 Q1	833	3 333	4 166	1 025	1 625	961	4 410	8 021	12 187
Q2	586	3 704	4 290	1 279	1 375	804	5 133	8 590	12 880
Q3	696	3 317	4 014	1 089	1 672	955	4 386	8 102	12 116
Q4	537	3 114	3 651	926	1 491	914	3 599	6 929	10 581
2007 Q1	1 056	3 473	4 529	1 677	1 651	876	4 189	8 393	12 922
Q2	707	3 547	4 254	1 533	1 912	851	5 386	9 680	13 934
Q3	568	3 150	3 718	1 225	1 992	756	4 588	8 562	12 279
Q4	638	2 946	3 583	1 187	1 783	799	4 081	7 850	11 433
2007 Jul	241	1 119	1 360	312	866	281	1 433	2 892	4 253
Aug	122	1 096	1 218	309	521	276	1 680	2 786	4 004
Sep	205	935	1 140	604	604	199	1 476	2 883	4 022
Oct	193	992	1 185	403	588	333	1 197	2 521	3 707
Nov	198	1 181	1 379	410	599	271	1 700	2 980	4 358
Dec	246	773	1 019	374	596	195	1 184	2 349	3 368
2008 Jan[3]	241	1 005	1 246	375	890	230	1 082	2 577	3 824

1 Including the value of speculative building when work starts on site.
2 Excluding orders for home improvement work.
3 Provisional.

Sources: Office for National Statistics;
Tel : 020 7215 1953

Note: Responsibility for these statistics transferred from BERR (formerly DTI) to the ONS on 1st March 2008.

22.23 Total engineering: total turnover of UK based manufacturers[1]
Standard Industrial Classification 2003

£ millions

	Total			Home			Export		
	Orders on Hand	New Orders	Turnover	Orders on Hand	New Orders	Turnover	Orders on Hand	New Orders	Turnover
	HP62	HP65	HP5X	HP64	HP67	HP5Z	HP63	HP66	HP5Y
2003	27 538.2	76 096.0	76 099.8	20 361.6	47 801.0	47 153.7	7 176.6	28 295.2	28 946.0
2004	27 256.9	79 680.2	79 961.2	19 980.7	48 174.6	48 555.3	7 276.2	31 505.3	31 405.7
2005	28 502.9	79 077.7	77 831.5	20 436.9	48 276.8	47 820.8	8 066.0	30 801.0	30 011.0
2006	29 131.0	81 089.5	80 461.3	19 729.9	47 417.5	48 124.5	9 401.1	33 672.2	32 336.9
2007	32 970.9	88 268.7	84 428.9	23 141.9	53 780.8	50 368.8	9 829.0	34 487.7	34 059.9
2005 Q4	28 502.9	19 591.2	19 890.0	20 436.9	11 845.4	12 023.3	8 066.0	7 745.8	7 866.7
2006 Q1	28 734.3	19 776.9	19 545.6	20 321.3	11 481.7	11 597.3	8 413.0	8 295.3	7 948.3
Q2	29 249.4	20 506.9	19 991.6	20 479.5	12 217.7	12 059.4	8 769.9	8 289.2	7 932.3
Q3	29 640.0	20 343.9	19 953.2	20 437.6	12 166.6	12 208.5	9 202.4	8 177.4	7 744.7
Q4	29 131.0	20 461.8	20 970.9	19 729.9	11 551.5	12 259.3	9 401.1	8 910.3	8 711.6
2007 Q1	29 652.1	21 396.6	20 875.5	20 295.9	13 169.4	12 603.5	9 356.2	8 227.0	8 271.9
Q2	30 249.3	21 416.1	20 819.0	20 582.8	12 459.4	12 172.5	9 666.5	8 956.7	8 646.4
Q3	32 721.7	23 467.5	20 995.1	22 389.6	14 388.6	12 581.7	10 332.1	9 078.9	8 413.4
Q4	32 970.9	21 988.5	21 739.3	23 141.9	13 763.4	13 011.1	9 829.0	8 225.1	8 728.2
2006 May	29 129.0	6 660.1	6 723.3	20 270.0	3 752.9	4 025.5	8 859.0	2 907.2	2 697.8
Jun	29 249.4	7 396.2	7 275.7	20 479.5	4 620.0	4 410.4	8 769.9	2 776.2	2 865.3
Jul	29 295.7	6 427.5	6 381.2	20 512.5	3 956.6	3 923.6	8 783.2	2 471.0	2 457.6
Aug	29 473.1	6 685.7	6 508.3	20 726.0	4 273.7	4 060.2	8 747.0	2 412.0	2 448.1
Sep	29 640.0	7 230.7	7 063.7	20 437.6	3 936.3	4 224.7	9 202.4	3 294.4	2 839.0
Oct	29 490.7	6 762.1	6 911.4	20 245.2	3 839.3	4 031.8	9 245.6	2 922.7	2 879.6
Nov	29 341.5	7 217.0	7 366.2	19 765.0	3 877.9	4 358.1	9 576.5	3 339.1	3 008.1
Dec	29 131.0	6 482.7	6 693.3	19 729.9	3 834.3	3 869.4	9 401.1	2 648.5	2 823.9
2007 Jan	28 916.1	6 263.9	6 478.8	19 568.8	3 734.8	3 895.9	9 347.2	2 529.0	2 582.9
Feb	28 788.6	6 376.6	6 504.1	19 729.2	4 106.1	3 945.7	9 059.4	2 270.5	2 558.3
Mar	29 652.1	8 756.1	7 892.6	20 295.9	5 328.5	4 761.9	9 356.2	3 427.5	3 130.7
Apr	30 030.1	6 851.0	6 473.1	20 546.2	4 150.9	3 900.6	9 483.9	2 700.1	2 572.4
May	30 020.4	6 962.9	6 972.6	20 574.1	4 148.9	4 121.0	9 446.2	2 813.9	2 851.6
Jun	30 249.3	7 602.2	7 373.3	20 582.8	4 159.6	4 150.9	9 666.5	3 442.7	3 222.4
Jul	32 209.7	8 880.5	6 920.1	22 105.8	5 669.5	4 146.5	10 103.9	3 211.0	2 773.6
Aug	32 426.8	7 016.4	6 799.3	22 480.2	4 484.2	4 109.8	9 946.6	2 532.2	2 689.5
Sep	32 721.7	7 570.6	7 275.7	22 389.6	4 234.9	4 325.4	10 332.1	3 335.7	2 950.3
Oct	32 418.1	7 077.1	7 380.7	22 237.1	4 222.8	4 375.3	10 181.0	2 854.3	3 005.4
Nov	32 457.5	7 539.7	7 500.3	22 413.4	4 652.6	4 476.3	10 044.1	2 887.1	3 024.0
Dec	32 970.9	7 371.7	6 858.3	23 141.9	4 888.0	4 159.5	9 829.0	2 483.7	2 698.8
2008 Jan	34 365.9	8 187.2	6 792.2	23 826.1	4 764.4	4 080.2	10 539.9	3 422.9	2 712.0

1 New methodology was introduced from January 2008 affecting all historic estimates. See details in February ELMR in-brief page 3 found at: http://nswebcopy/elmr/02_08/downloads/ELMR_Feb08.pdf published on 11 February.

Source: Office for National Statistics 01633 812126

22.24 Manufacture of machinery and equipment not elsewhere classified[1]
Values at current prices

£ million

	Total			Home			Export		
	Orders on Hand	New Orders	Turnover	Orders on Hand	New Orders	Turnover	Orders on Hand	New Orders	Turnover
	HP6B	HP6E	HP68	HP6D	HP6G	HP6A	HP6C	HP6F	HP69
2003	13 965.3	32 262.8	31 006.2	10 603.3	21 283.7	19 636.0	3 362.0	10 979.3	11 370.4
2004	13 669.4	33 228.0	33 524.0	10 192.8	20 242.2	20 652.8	3 476.6	12 985.8	12 871.3
2005	13 484.9	35 353.8	35 538.4	9 515.9	20 975.7	21 652.4	3 969.0	14 378.6	13 885.9
2006	14 095.2	38 110.7	37 500.3	9 260.9	22 047.4	22 302.1	4 834.3	16 063.6	15 198.2
2007	15 098.8	42 282.3	41 278.8	10 173.9	25 646.1	24 733.3	4 924.9	16 636.1	16 545.5
2002 Q4	12 708.9	8 576.1	7 855.2	8 955.8	5 542.9	4 947.0	3 753.1	3 033.2	2 908.0
2003 Q1	13 879.0	8 579.9	7 409.6	9 946.3	5 805.1	4 814.6	3 932.7	2 774.8	2 595.2
Q2	13 646.0	7 344.0	7 576.9	9 639.7	4 443.3	4 749.8	4 006.3	2 900.7	2 827.1
Q3	13 822.0	7 924.6	7 748.7	10 086.1	5 405.1	4 958.7	3 735.9	2 519.6	2 790.0
Q4	13 965.3	8 414.3	8 271.0	10 603.3	5 630.2	5 112.9	3 362.0	2 784.2	3 158.1
2004 Q1	14 596.6	8 563.2	7 932.0	10 709.1	5 030.8	4 925.1	3 887.5	3 532.3	3 006.8
Q2	15 099.6	8 749.2	8 246.2	10 931.1	5 179.2	4 957.2	4 168.5	3 570.0	3 288.9
Q3	14 652.4	7 827.9	8 275.1	10 745.3	4 878.9	5 064.8	3 907.1	2 949.0	3 210.5
Q4	13 669.4	8 087.7	9 070.7	10 192.8	5 153.3	5 705.7	3 476.6	2 934.5	3 365.1
2005 Q1	14 361.2	9 200.2	8 508.3	10 349.8	5 455.7	5 298.6	4 011.4	3 744.6	3 209.7
Q2	14 482.6	8 972.7	8 851.2	10 367.1	5 404.6	5 387.3	4 115.5	3 568.1	3 463.9
Q3	13 961.1	8 343.8	8 865.5	9 998.9	5 030.8	5 398.9	3 962.1	3 313.3	3 466.6
Q4	13 484.9	8 837.1	9 313.4	9 515.9	5 084.6	5 567.6	3 969.0	3 752.6	3 745.7
2006 Q1	13 854.0	9 176.5	8 807.3	9 374.6	5 032.7	5 173.9	4 479.5	4 143.9	3 633.4
Q2	14 196.0	9 558.4	9 216.5	9 607.2	5 698.3	5 465.7	4 588.8	3 860.3	3 750.9
Q3	14 239.9	9 555.5	9 511.5	9 571.9	5 727.1	5 762.2	4 668.0	3 828.4	3 749.3
Q4	14 095.2	9 820.3	9 965.0	9 260.9	5 589.3	5 900.3	4 834.3	4 231.0	4 064.6
2007 Q1	13 894.2	9 613.7	9 814.7	9 336.6	6 077.0	6 001.3	4 557.6	3 536.7	3 813.4
Q2	14 427.4	10 605.6	10 072.5	9 656.3	6 302.0	5 982.4	4 771.1	4 303.6	4 090.1
Q3	15 429.3	11 453.8	10 452.0	10 312.3	6 922.0	6 266.1	5 117.0	4 531.8	4 185.8
Q4	15 098.8	10 609.2	10 939.6	10 173.9	6 345.1	6 483.5	4 924.9	4 264.0	4 456.2
2006 Jan	13 558.8	2 741.2	2 667.3	9 083.4	1 104.6	1 537.0	4 475.3	1 636.6	1 130.3
Feb	13 857.2	3 072.6	2 774.2	9 489.2	2 059.2	1 653.4	4 368.0	1 013.5	1 120.8
Mar	13 854.0	3 362.7	3 365.8	9 374.6	1 868.9	1 983.5	4 479.5	1 493.8	1 382.3
Apr	14 086.9	3 007.4	2 774.6	9 364.7	1 622.4	1 632.3	4 722.1	1 385.0	1 142.3
May	14 259.0	3 259.5	3 087.4	9 493.6	1 932.4	1 803.4	4 765.4	1 327.2	1 284.0
Jun	14 196.0	3 291.5	3 354.5	9 607.2	2 143.5	2 030.0	4 588.8	1 148.1	1 324.6
Jul	14 234.3	3 099.4	3 061.1	9 677.1	1 928.7	1 858.7	4 557.1	1 170.7	1 202.4
Aug	14 266.8	3 043.4	3 010.8	9 780.8	1 954.7	1 851.0	4 486.1	1 088.7	1 159.8
Sep	14 239.9	3 412.7	3 439.6	9 571.9	1 843.7	2 052.5	4 668.0	1 569.0	1 387.1
Oct	14 276.7	3 333.6	3 296.9	9 594.2	1 965.0	1 942.7	4 682.5	1 368.6	1 354.1
Nov	14 283.6	3 457.4	3 450.4	9 283.8	1 747.5	2 057.9	4 999.8	1 709.9	1 392.5
Dec	14 095.2	3 029.3	3 217.7	9 260.9	1 876.8	1 899.7	4 834.3	1 152.5	1 318.0
2007 Jan	13 814.6	2 718.1	2 998.7	9 087.7	1 653.6	1 826.8	4 726.9	1 064.5	1 171.9
Feb	13 751.2	3 019.7	3 083.1	9 354.6	2 162.7	1 895.9	4 396.6	857.0	1 187.2
Mar	13 894.2	3 875.9	3 732.9	9 336.6	2 260.7	2 278.6	4 557.6	1 615.2	1 454.3
Apr	14 040.8	3 288.9	3 142.3	9 497.3	2 072.0	1 911.4	4 543.6	1 216.9	1 230.9
May	14 042.0	3 369.2	3 368.1	9 509.7	2 037.0	2 024.6	4 532.3	1 332.2	1 343.5
Jun	14 427.4	3 947.5	3 562.1	9 656.3	2 193.0	2 046.4	4 771.1	1 754.5	1 515.7
Jul	15 254.5	4 257.4	3 430.4	10 409.9	2 792.4	2 038.9	4 844.6	1 465.0	1 391.5
Aug	15 256.6	3 361.1	3 359.0	10 358.1	1 984.1	2 035.9	4 898.5	1 377.0	1 323.1
Sep	15 429.3	3 835.3	3 662.6	10 312.3	2 145.5	2 191.3	5 117.0	1 689.8	1 471.2
Oct	15 401.6	3 683.0	3 710.7	10 414.7	2 267.3	2 164.9	4 986.9	1 415.7	1 545.8
Nov	15 273.2	3 706.3	3 834.7	10 161.9	2 003.5	2 256.3	5 111.3	1 702.7	1 578.4
Dec	15 098.8	3 219.9	3 394.2	10 173.9	2 074.3	2 062.3	4 924.9	1 145.6	1 332.0
2008 Jan	16 266.4	4 657.7	3 490.0	10 796.7	2 663.2	2 040.4	5 469.7	1 994.5	1 449.7

1 Note: New methodology was introduced from January 2008 affecting all historic estimates. See details in February ELMR in-brief page 3 found at: http://nswebcopy/elmr/02_08/downloads/ELMR_Feb08.pdf published on 11 February.

Source: Office for National Statistics : 01633 812126

Production

22.25 Passenger cars
United Kingdom

Number

	Total production					Production for export				
	1000cc and under	Over 1000cc and not over 1600cc	Over 1600cc and not over 2500cc	Over 2500cc	Total	1000cc and under	Over 1000cc and not over 1600cc	Over 1600cc and not over 2500cc	Over 2500cc	Total
	GKAB	GKAD	GKAF	GKAH	JCYM	GKAC	GKAE	GKAG	GKAI	JCYL
2000	96 043	676 438	723 294	145 677	1 641 452	56 556	375 528	509 591	121 315	1 062 990
2001	93 695	632 747	634 573	131 350	1 492 365	56 426	329 944	400 648	107 236	894 254
2002	79 545	711 553	720 067	118 579	1 629 744	35 866	442 975	470 285	98 158	1 047 284
2003	23 985	750 840	740 486	142 247	1 657 558	12 380	503 950	509 050	118 379	1 143 759
2004	15 471	796 174	690 759	144 346	1 646 750	10 316	560 505	492 564	116 371	1 179 756
2005	6 111	854 687	546 744	188 155	1 595 697	4 925	625 929	405 204	148 445	1 184 503
2006	–	792 187	446 143	203 755	1 442 085	–	622 205	324 880	159 008	1 106 093
2006 Feb	–	74 048	38 871	18 274	131 193	–	53 830	27 236	14 145	95 211
Mar	–	88 834	46 000	24 154	158 988	–	67 774	32 449	19 499	119 722
Apr	–	65 103	37 156	16 313	118 572	–	52 814	28 855	13 504	95 173
May	–	74 864	39 886	17 566	132 316	–	60 704	30 835	13 901	105 440
Jun	–	78 055	42 280	18 991	139 326	–	61 508	30 749	14 566	106 823
Jul	–	66 528	37 241	14 060	117 829	–	51 223	26 995	10 692	88 910
Aug	–	35 223	23 067	14 669	72 959	–	25 963	15 333	10 810	52 106
Sep	–	67 981	37 354	16 977	122 312	–	53 839	25 365	13 083	92 287
Oct	–	66 536	35 526	14 081	116 143	–	56 995	27 157	11 620	95 772
Nov	–	68 181	38 726	21 656	128 563	–	56 623	28 557	17 085	102 265
Dec	–	44 381	29 740	10 641	84 762	–	35 789	22 513	7 615	65 917
2007 Jan	–	58 476	44 747	20 974	124 197	–	45 690	32 511	16 683	94 884
Feb	–	50 765	45 021	19 863	115 649	–	35 745	34 582	14 634	84 961
Mar	–	60 556	57 299	20 154	138 009	–	43 991	39 465	16 697	100 153
Apr	–	51 685	52 171	16 584	120 440	–	39 791	41 062	13 694	94 547
May	–	52 566	55 754	19 063	127 383	–	42 253	44 341	15 687	102 281
Jun	–	58 890	58 327	20 312	137 529	–	46 020	45 812	16 984	108 816
Jul	–	61 021	52 489	16 178	129 688	–	47 046	38 221	12 964	98 231

*Note: The survey and publication of motor vehicle production ceased at July reference period.

Source: Office for National Statistics: 01633 812394

22.26 Alcoholic drink[1]
United Kingdom

			1997	1998	1999	2000	2001	2002	2003	2004	2005	2006	2007
Spirits[2]		Thousand hectolitres of alcohol											
Production	KMEA	"	5 297	5 145	4 705	4 210	4 368	4 508	4 553	4 081	4 365	4 485	5 673
Released for home consumption													
Home produced whisky	KMEE	"	312	289	323	314	321	321	318	319	301	283	286
Spirit-based Ready-to-drink[3]	SNET	"	..	..	..	..	..	105	124	114	84	65	52
Imported and other	KMEG	"	533	505	596	615	647	689	744	792	822	767	832
Total	KMEH	"	845	794	919	929	968	1 115	1 187	1 226	1 207	1 114	1 170
Beer		Thousand hectolitres											
Production	BFNK	"	59 139	56 652	57 854	55 279	56 802	56 672	58 014	57 459	56 255	53 763	50 511
Released for home consumption	BAYL	"	61 114	58 835	58 917	57 007	58 234	59 384	60 301	59 195	57 572	55 748	53 315
Production	JYXJ	Thousand hectolitres of pure alcohol	2 406	2 333	2 364	2 299	2 358	2 352	2 414	2 433	2 338	2 249	2 133
Released for home consumption	JYXK	"	2 504	2 439	2 428	2 382	2 429	2 473	2 515	2 499	2 398	2 335	2 247
Wine of fresh grapes													
Released for home consumption		Thousand hectolitres											
Fortified	KMEM	"	323	370	316	289	287	325	296	298	306	302	305
Still table	KMEN	"	7 653	7 979	8 391	8 864	9 534	10 319	10 647	11 768	12 117	11 655	12 559
Sparkling	KMEO	"	382	416	576	543	515	578	640	676	721	715	838
Total	KMEP	"	8 358	8 765	9 284	9 696	10 336	11 222	11 584	12 742	13 143	12 672	13 702
Made-wine													
Released for home consumption													
Other than coolers	KMEQ	"	485	406	416	431	364	367	339	351	334	317	348
Coolers[3]	KJDD	"	1 153	1 244	1 802	2 800	3 712	1 606	423	508	597	528	720
Cider and perry													
Released for home consumption	KMER	"	5 513	5 548	6 022	6 006	5 911	5 939	5 876	6 139	6 377	7 523	8 046

1 See chapter text.
2 Potable spirits distilled.
3 Made wine with alcoholic strength 1.2% to 5.5%. Includes alcoholic lemonade of appropriate strength and similar products. From 28 April 2002, duty on spirit-based "coolers" is charged at the same rate as spirits per litre of alcohol. Coolers for calendar year 2002 includes only wine based "coolers".

Sources: HM Revenue & Customs UK Trade Information website:;
http://www.uktradeinfo.com/index.cfm?task=bulletins

22.27 Tobacco products: released for home consumption[1]
United Kingdom

			1997	1998	1999	2000	2001	2002	2003	2004	2005	2006	2007
Cigarettes:		Thousand million											
Home produced	KMFA	"	71.1	67.8	28.2	49.3	47.7	49.6	49.1	48.2	45.9	44.4	42.0
Imported	KMFB	"	9.9	7.5	6.0	7.3	6.8	6.5	4.9	4.5	4.3	4.6	3.8
Total[2]	KMFC	"	81.0	75.3	34.2	56.6	54.5	56.1	54.0	52.6	50.2	49.0	45.7
Cigars:		Million kg											
Home produced	KMFD	"	1.3	1.2	0.9	1.0	0.9	0.9	0.8	0.7	0.6	0.6	0.5
Imported	KMFE	"	0.1	0.1	0.1	0.1	0.1	0.1	0.1	0.1	0.1	0.1	0.1
Total[2]	KMFF	"	1.4	1.3	1.0	1.1	1.0	1.0	0.9	0.8	0.8	0.7	0.6
Hand-rolling tobacco:													
Home produced	KMFG	"	1.8	1.7	2.0	2.1	2.8	2.8	2.9	3.0	3.2	3.4	3.6
Imported	KMFH	"	0.1	0.1	–	–	–	–	–	–	–	–	–
Total[2]	KMFI	"	1.9	1.8	2.0	2.2	2.8	2.8	2.9	3.1	3.2	3.5	3.6
Other smoking and chewing tobacco:													
Home produced	KMFJ	"	1.1	1.0	0.6	0.7	0.7	0.6	0.5	0.5	0.4	0.4	0.3
Imported	KMFK	"	0.1	0.1	0.1	0.1	0.1	0.1	0.1	0.1	0.1	0.1	0.1
Total[2]	KMFL	"	1.2	1.1	0.7	0.8	0.8	0.7	0.6	0.6	0.5	0.5	0.4

1 See chapter text.
2 Any apparent discrepency between totals and the sum of the constituents is due to rounding.

Sources: HM Revenue and Customs UK Trade Information website:;
http://www.uktradeinfo.com/index.cfm?task=bulletins

Banking, insurance

Chapter 23

Banking, insurance

Other banks balance sheet

(Table 23.3)

Carrying out the review of banking statistics at the end of September 1997 resulted in several changes to this table:

(a) The table now includes the business of all monthly and quarterly reporting banks in the UK. It previously covered only the business of monthly reporting institutions.

(b) The Channel Islands and Isle of Man are no longer treated as part of the UK for statistical purposes. Banking institutions in the Channel Islands and Isle of Man no longer have the option of being within the UK banking sector and their business, along with the business of offshore island branches of UK mainland banks, is now excluded from the figures within this table. Additionally, the business of the UK banking sector with offshore island residents and entities has been reclassified from UK residents to non-residents.

(c) The table now contains more comprehensive detail of business with building societies. This business wasn't previously distinguished within the UK private sector elements of the table.

(d) The aggregate balance sheet of the banking sector has been inflated because it is now reported on an accrual basis rather than a cash basis (accrued amounts that are payable and receivable are shown under liabilities and assets respectively). Additionally, acceptances have been brought onto the balance sheet and are shown under both liabilities and assets.

With effect from 1998, the balance sheet of the Banking Department of the Bank of England is excluded from this table, and other banks business with the Issue Department is reclassified from 'UK public sector' to 'UK banks'.

Data for 1999 reflect the acquisition of Birmingham Midshires Building Society by Halifax during that year.

Data for the end of 2000 reflect the entry of Bradford and Bingley plc to the banking sector during the year. Data for the end of 2000 also reflect the new reporting during the year of agency business as a result of collateral management via repurchase agreements (repos) and reverse repos.

Bank lending to, and bank deposits from, UK residents

(Tables 23.4 and 23.5)

These are series statistics based on the Standard Industrial Classification (SIC) 1992.

Table 23.4. Until the third quarter of 2007, the analysis of lending covered loans, advances (including under reverse repos), finance leasing, acceptances and facilities (all in Sterling and other currencies) provided by reporting banks to their UK resident non-bank non-building society customers, as well as bank holdings of Sterling and Euro commercial paper issued by these resident customers. Following a review of statistical data collected, acceptances and holdings of Sterling and Euro commercial paper are no longer collected at the industry level detail with effect from fourth quarter 2007 data. Total lending therefore reflects loans and advances (including under reverse repos) only, from fourth quarter 2007 data.

Table 23.5 includes borrowing under sale and repo. Adjustments for transit items are not included.

Figures for both tables are supplied by monthly reporting banks and grossed to cover quarterly reporters. Following the transition of building societies' statistical reporting from the Financial Services Authority to the Bank of England on 1st January 2008, both tables will include data reported by building societies from the first quarter of 2008 onwards. They exclude lending to building societies and to residents of the Channel Islands and Isle of Man.

Building societies

(Table 23.13)

Building society figures are sourced from societies' annual returns and for each year relate to accounting years ending on dates between 1 February and 31 January of the following year. Figures are society-only as opposed to group consolidated.

Consumer credit

(Table 23.14)

Figures for net lending refer to changes in amounts outstanding adjusted to remove distortions caused by revaluations of debt outstanding, such as write-offs. Class 3 loans are advanced under the terms of the Building Societies Act 1986.

A high proportion of credit advanced in certain types of agreement, notably on credit cards, is repaid within a month. This reflects use of such agreements as a method of payment rather than a way of obtaining credit. As from December 2006 the Bank of England has ceased to update the separate data on consumer credit provided by other specialist lenders, retailers and insurance companies previously contained in these tables. These categories have been merged into 'other consumer credit lenders'.

23.1 Bank of England Balance Sheet
Liabilities and assets outstanding at end of period

£ million

Consolidated statement

	Notes in circulation	Reserve balances	Standing facility deposits	Short term open market operations	Foreign currency public securities issued	Cash ratio deposits	Other liabilities	Standing facility assets	Short term open market operations	Of which 1 week sterling reverse repo	of which fine-tuning sterling reverse repo	of which other maturity within maintenance period reverse repos	Longer term sterling reverse repo	Ways and Means advances to HMG	Bonds and other securities acqured via market transactions	Other assets	Total assets/liabil
	B55A	B56A	B57A	B58A	B59A	B62A	B63A	B65A	B66A	B67A	B68A	IGL6	B69A	B72A	B73A	B74A	B75A
2007	45 022	25 768	–	–	4 727	2 936	23 789	–	14 358	4 360	–	9 998	23 500	13 370	7 481	43 533	102 241
2007 Jan	38 465	18 437	–	–	4 666	2 568	15 703	–	31 110	31 110	–	–	15 000	13 370	7 073	13 286	79 839
Feb	38 214	17 716	–	–	3 314	2 568	15 180	–	30 110	30 110	–	–	15 000	13 370	6 727	11 784	76 991
Mar	38 541	18 310	–	–	4 373	2 568	15 746	–	31 260	31 260	–	–	15 000	13 370	7 827	12 082	79 539
Apr	39 134	19 011	–	–	4 345	2 568	16 029	–	32 870	32 870	–	–	15 000	13 370	7 746	12 103	81 088
May	39 271	18 475	–	–	4 393	2 568	16 662	–	31 990	31 990	–	–	15 000	13 370	7 790	13 220	81 369
Jun	39 571	18 623	–	–	4 333	2 716	15 784	–	32 550	32 550	–	–	15 000	13 370	7 668	12 438	81 026
Jul	39 984	17 769	–	–	4 314	2 716	15 246	–	32 440	32 440	–	–	15 000	13 370	7 554	11 666	80 030
Aug	41 219	19 023	–	–	4 390	2 716	15 875	1 556	33 400	33 400	–	–	15 000	13 370	7 739	12 158	83 222
Sep	40 425	29 226	–	–	4 521	2 716	21 192	–	40 950	40 950	–	–	15 000	13 370	7 865	20 897	98 081
Oct	40 817	20 062	–	–	4 492	2 716	24 447	–	20 610	20 610	–	–	14 900	13 370	7 663	35 991	92 533
Nov	41 716	23 469	–	–	4 602	2 716	24 307	–	18 349	18 349	–	–	15 000	13 370	7 814	42 277	96 810
Dec	45 022	25 768	–	–	4 727	2 936	23 789	–	14 358	4 360	–	9 998	23 500	13 370	7 481	43 533	102 241

Issue Department

	Notes in circulation	Notes in Banking Department	Short term open market operations	Of which 1 week sterling reverse repo	of which fine-tuning sterling reverse repo	Longer term sterling reverse repo	Ways and Means advances to HMG	Bonds and other securities acqured via market transactions	Other assets	Total assets/liabilities
	AEFA	AEFB	BL29	BL32	BL33	BL34	B54A	BL35	BL36	BL37
2007	45 022	–	14 358	4 360	–	13 500	13 370	–	3 794	45 022
2007 Jan	38 465	–	10 052	10 052	–	15 000	13 370	–	44	38 465
Feb	38 214	–	9 795	9 795	–	15 000	13 370	–	49	38 214
Mar	38 541	–	10 122	10 122	–	15 000	13 370	–	49	38 541
Apr	39 134	–	10 712	10 712	–	15 000	13 370	–	52	39 134
May	39 271	–	10 853	10 853	–	15 000	13 370	–	48	39 271
Jun	39 571	–	11 151	11 151	–	15 000	13 370	–	50	39 571
Jul	39 984	–	11 563	11 563	–	15 000	13 370	–	52	39 984
Aug	41 219	–	12 805	12 805	–	15 000	13 370	–	44	41 219
Sep	40 425	–	11 989	11 989	–	15 000	13 370	–	66	40 425
Oct	40 817	–	12 497	12 497	–	14 900	13 370	–	50	40 817
Nov	41 716	–	13 294	13 294	–	15 000	13 370	–	52	41 716
Dec	45 022	–	14 358	4 360	–	13 500	13 370	–	3 794	45 022

Banking Department

	Reserve balances	Standing facility deposits	Short term open market operations	Foreign currency public securities issued	Cash ratio deposits	Other liabilities	Standing facility assets	Short term open market operations	Of which 1 week sterling reverse repo	of which fine-tuning sterling reverse repo	of which other maturity within maintenance period reverse repos	Longer term sterling reverse repo	Bonds and other securities acqured via market transactions	Bank of England notes	Other assets	Total assets/liabilit
	BL38	BL39	BL42	BL43	BL44	BL45	BL47	BL48	BL49	BL52	IGL7	IGL8	BL53	BL54	BL55	BL56
2007	25 768	–	–	4 727	2 936	27 583	–	–	–	–	–	10 000	7 481	–	43 533	61 013
2007 Jan	18 437	–	–	4 666	2 568	15 747	–	21 059	21 059	–	–	–	7 073	–	13 286	41 418
Feb	17 716	–	–	3 314	2 568	15 229	–	20 315	20 315	–	–	–	6 727	–	11 784	38 826
Mar	18 310	–	–	4 373	2 568	15 796	–	21 138	21 138	–	–	–	7 827	–	12 082	41 048
Apr	19 011	–	–	4 345	2 568	16 081	–	22 158	22 158	–	–	–	7 746	–	12 103	42 006
May	18 475	–	–	4 393	2 568	16 710	–	21 137	21 137	–	–	–	7 790	–	13 220	42 146
Jun	18 623	–	–	4 333	2 716	15 833	–	21 399	21 399	–	–	–	7 668	–	12 438	41 505
Jul	17 769	–	–	4 314	2 716	15 297	–	20 877	20 877	–	–	–	7 554	–	11 666	40 097
Aug	19 023	–	–	4 390	2 716	15 919	1 556	20 595	20 595	–	–	–	7 739	–	12 158	42 048
Sep	29 226	–	–	4 521	2 716	21 259	–	28 961	28 961	–	–	–	7 865	–	20 897	57 723
Oct	20 062	–	–	4 492	2 716	24 497	–	8 113	8 113	–	–	–	7 663	–	35 991	51 767
Nov	23 469	–	–	4 602	2 716	24 359	–	5 055	5 055	–	–	–	7 814	–	42 277	55 146
Dec	25 768	–	–	4 727	2 936	27 583	–	–	–	–	–	10 000	7 481	–	43 533	61 013

Source: Bank of England

23.2 Value of inter-bank clearings
United Kingdom

£ billion

		1997	1998	1999	2000	2001	2002	2003	2004	2005	2006	2007
Bulk paper clearings[1]												
Cheque (formerly general)	KCYY	1 200	1 214	1 226	1 214	1 210	1 178	1 141	1 111	1 062	1 076	1 062
Credit	KCYZ	94	92	88	82	80	75	69	63	57	56	54
High-value clearings												
Town	KCZA	–	–	–	–	–	–	–	–	–	..	..
CHAPS Sterling only	KCZB	36 032	41 501	44 704	49 146	52 913	51 896	51 613	52 348	52 672	59 437	69 352
Electronic clearing (BACS)	KCZC	1 432	1 602	1 761	1 922	2 166	2 382	2 574	2 883	3 150	3 429	3 696

1 Excludes inter-branch clearings and clearings in Scotland and Northern Ireland.

Source: APACS - The UK payments association: 020 7711 6223

Banking, insurance

23.3 Other banks' balance sheet[1]

£ million

		1998	1999[2]	2000[3,4]	2001	2002	2003	2004	2005	2006	2007
Sterling liabilities											
Notes outstanding & cash loaded cards	TBFA	2 929	3 311	3 359	3 866	3 957	4 207	4 338	4 534	4 987	5 265
Sight deposits[5]											
UK banks[6]	TBFB	37 839	33 463	40 054	59 573	101 905	99 208	109 866	148 202	165 479	91 322
UK building societies	TBFC	1 277	841	1 168	1 466	2 403	1 736	1 697	2 314	2 277	2 653
UK public sector[7]	TBFD	3 003	3 450	3 403	4 283	3 997	5 679	6 635	7 341	9 046	8 190
Other UK residents	TBFE	295 068	325 392	372 725	415 180	457 077	502 359	566 524	638 684	701 743	765 752
Non-residents	TBFF	43 528	44 581	55 489	55 837	57 218	65 157	72 452	83 608	94 822	107 795
Time deposits											
UK banks[6]	TBFG	111 970	112 530	110 955	125 261	141 401	164 433	230 749	289 656	455 672	116 025
UK building societies	TBFH	4 361	4 253	4 688	4 856	4 487	3 643	4 045	4 098	3 573	4 182
UK public sector[7]	TBFI	9 748	8 064	8 241	8 306	8 936	8 934	10 872	11 378	16 504	16 820
Other UK residents	TBFJ	295 924	282 789	301 007	302 715	306 453	313 244	322 603	353 481	433 436	496 697
of which TESSAs	TBFK	21 568	22 868	24 265	9 752	5 235	1 832	–	–	–	..
of which SAYE	TBFL	2 604	2 840	2 726	2 439	2 367	2 226	2 301	2 164	1 900	1 049
of which cash ISAs	TFDG	..	5 210	13 684	31 298	42 269	52 118	61 033	68 584	76 323	83 827
Non-residents	TBFM	97 953	116 967	134 844	150 964	151 304	166 449	177 381	203 777	234 754	420 637
Acceptances granted	TBFN	16 658	12 854	10 012	10 627	9 954	2 856	1 446	928	1 105	1 860
Liabilities under sale and repurchase agreements											
of which British govt. securities[8]	TBFU	55 561	56 145	83 819	83 330	78 155	114 468	109 692	180 087	234 606	..
UK banks[7]	TBFP	43 314	48 213	56 408	60 551	52 079	95 922	86 876	133 938	190 384	167 057
UK building societies	TBFQ	32	200	36	–	107	170	62	345	–	175
UK public sector[7]	TBFR	–	–	14 351	5 127	1 402	1 521	113	155	35	3 792
Other UK residents	TBFS	20 918	17 165	22 974	25 732	19 759	19 906	35 038	55 378	58 312	71 150
Non-residents	TBFT	5 469	5 542	9 849	8 643	19 072	18 475	26 669	40 012	54 240	68 660
CDs and other short-term paper issued	TBFV	138 248	158 826	151 153	153 768	157 354	148 606	160 173	165 923	179 554	199 834
Total sterling deposits	TBFW	1 125 311	1 175 130	1 297 356	1 392 890	1 494 908	1 618 298	1 813 197	2 139 217	2 600 935	2 542 600
Sterling items in suspense and transmission	TBFX	15 714	17 307	15 261	16 702	13 318	18 371	17 923	27 479	34 047	29 469
Net derivatives	TBFY	8 342	8 324	10 992	4 029	2 491	−10 672	−15 457	9 894	−33 397	−26 271
Accrued amounts payable	TBFZ	24 632	22 122	23 726	22 836	21 541	22 624	26 262	27 108	35 267	44 916
Sterling capital and other internal funds	TBGA	103 868	100 575	133 436	148 294	173 320	204 295	265 344	243 392	299 359	274 180
Total sterling liabilities	TBGB	1 280 796	1 326 769	1 484 130	1 588 618	1 709 535	1 857 123	2 111 607	2 451 625	2 941 199	2 870 160
Foreign currency liabilities											
Sight and time deposits											
UK banks[9]	TBGC	77 128	77 684	99 447	106 368	111 536	139 018	151 946	153 024	184 880	179 934
UK building societies	TBGD	639	681	233	279	373	550	310	615	658	726
UK public sector[7]	TBGE	149	126	1 808	926	833	865	898	1 098	2 279	616
Other UK residents	TBGF	60 513	65 203	79 627	95 666	81 590	89 034	111 035	137 651	162 328	207 907
Non-residents	TBGG	766 934	736 792	914 888	1 001 321	997 398	1 055 183	1 185 037	1 427 857	1 551 892	1 994 259
Acceptances granted	TBGH	729	619	689	638	754	751	890	846	1 270	1 394
Sale and repurchase agreements											
UK banks	TBGJ	30 669	25 170	38 901	54 499	90 407	224 743	243 933	265 239	259 088	251 867
UK building societies	TBGK	–	–	–	–	–	–	–	–	–	–
UK public sector	TBGL	–	–	468	1	71	844	858	391	1	1 077
Other UK residents	TBGM	26 742	21 997	35 145	52 438	54 463	73 477	67 544	79 689	83 379	108 075
Non-residents	TBGN	118 909	115 357	139 656	154 976	211 276	289 674	379 695	433 712	419 744	526 493
CDs and other short-term paper issued	TBGO	124 151	151 009	199 510	224 225	234 731	255 590	278 440	341 866	406 487	530 751
Total foreign currency deposits	TBGP	1 206 562	1 194 637	1 510 373	1 691 336	1 783 432	2 129 730	2 420 587	2 841 988	3 072 007	3 803 098
Items in suspense and transmission	TBGQ	25 026	30 548	46 678	47 363	38 355	60 465	92 173	108 217	95 421	123 779
Net derivatives	TBGR	2 656	3 704	−4 472	−3 854	5 816	14 774	22 765	3 347	66 215	30 761
Accrued amounts payable	TBGS	25 184	18 080	18 568	17 756	16 312	15 708	18 214	23 015	36 279	42 640
Capital and other internal funds	TBGT	46 952	69 798	89 359	85 489	87 047	81 778	45 835	93 991	50 759	93 472
Total foreign currency liabilities	TBGU	1 306 380	1 316 767	1 660 506	1 838 090	1 930 961	2 302 455	2 599 575	3 070 557	3 320 680	4 093 750
Total liabilities	TBGV	2 587 177	2 643 536	3 144 636	3 426 708	3 640 497	4 159 579	4 711 182	5 522 182	6 261 879	6 963 910

23.3 Other banks' balance sheet[1]
continued

£ million

		1998	1999[2]	2000[3,4]	2001	2002	2003	2004	2005	2006	2007
Sterling assets											
Notes and coins	TBGW	6 699	9 047	8 007	6 566	6 621	7 464	10 559	9 500	9 279	7 798
With UK central bank											
Cash ratio deposits	TBGX	1 068	1 141	1 275	1 386	1 495	1 609	1 759	1 953	2 271	2 597
Other	TBGY	383	676	117	143	249	54	100	1 388	17 645	21 268
Market loans											
UK banks[5,6]	TBGZ	148 138	144 537	149 174	181 350	237 771	263 004	342 699	438 572	618 742	185 858
UK bank CDs	TBHB	65 510	75 071	65 156	68 868	68 728	55 053	59 505	58 780	63 236	50 856
UK bank commercial paper	TBHC	130	208	8	52	62	5	54	75	410	399
UK building societies CDs etc and deposits	TBHD	4 505	5 093	4 748	3 933	4 293	7 200	7 222	5 655	7 481	7 827
Non-residents	TBHE	84 162	74 403	94 381	102 404	89 848	109 665	102 286	128 343	166 599	268 090
Acceptances granted											
UK building societies	TBHF	–	–	–	–	–	–	–	–	–	–
UK public sector[7]	TBHG	–	–	–	–	–	–	–	–	–	–
Other UK residents	TBHH	15 394	11 933	9 496	9 992	9 111	2 777	1 348	817	956	1 032
Non-residents	TBHI	1 264	920	516	635	842	79	99	111	148	828
Bills											
Treasury bills	TBHJ	779	2 749	1 612	8 474	18 752	18 265	14 507	15 707	11 984	4 837
UK bank bills	TBHA	14 110	11 426	7 011	8 098	8 491	1 265	646	24	103	51
UK building societies	TBHK	–	–	–	–	–	–	–	–	375	–
Other UK	TBHL	1 221	818	1 202	1 601	485	1 013	955	779	1 636	320
Non-residents	TBHM	207	206	287	744	979	733	702	1 063	1 831	4 099
Claims under sale and repurchase agreements											
of which British govt. securities[8]	TBHT	56 639	64 943	86 362	84 068	77 460	114 091	116 652	187 606	237 177	..
UK banks	TBHO	41 969	39 667	46 088	46 585	37 197	77 691	64 353	113 540	160 380	140 564
UK building societies	TBHP	134	91	116	327	86	114	263	1 048	76	3 885
UK public sector	TBHQ	–	–	9 067	4 692	5 159	5 231	10 801	11 695	9 168	8 025
Other UK residents	TBHR	23 803	30 338	35 058	36 222	31 363	35 885	50 371	61 311	65 569	103 692
Non-residents	TBHS	5 907	6 310	7 266	7 010	14 271	12 981	20 456	36 261	52 300	68 570
Advances											
UK public sector	TBHU	3 403	2 567	2 746	2 442	3 783	4 414	6 078	6 838	8 092	9 589
Other UK residents[10]	TBHV	672 812	732 649	823 787	891 790	986 835	1 062 650	1 159 833	1 252 836	1 376 190	1 555 617
Non-residents	TBHW	21 039	23 364	24 494	29 483	31 380	34 603	38 447	49 223	62 314	82 026
Banking dept. lending to central govt. (net)	TBNU	–	–	–	–	–	–	–	–	..	..
Investments											
British government stocks	TBHX	14 714	9 243	2 867	499	–3 545	–8 525	–4 210	–6 203	–11 173	–12 950
Other public sector	TBHY	215	124	88	116	158	385	328	459	569	767
UK banks[11]	TBHZ	13 415	13 584	22 935	23 965	23 542	34 971	34 664	36 365	36 655	37 633
UK building societies	TBIA	2 223	2 506	2 251	2 099	1 835	1 702	1 889	2 068	1 891	1 009
Other UK residents[12]	TBIB	48 781	57 391	77 647	82 013	76 773	84 813	100 892	112 593	165 898	165 949
Non-residents	TBIC	11 834	13 775	20 572	23 462	22 821	22 505	26 029	30 487	39 000	46 211
Items in suspense and collection	TBID	23 888	23 441	21 982	24 024	19 577	22 434	22 066	29 714	34 629	40 301
Accrued amounts receivable	TBIE	17 352	15 173	15 919	13 528	15 486	17 204	19 987	19 510	24 909	30 816
Other assets	TBIF	12 593	13 036	12 654	12 876	12 685	11 955	12 875	15 522	14 430	14 749
Total sterling assets[13]	TBIG	1 257 652	1 321 486	1 468 527	1 595 380	1 727 136	1 889 200	2 107 562	2 436 032	2 943 591	2 852 313

23.3 Other banks' balance sheet[1]

continued

£ million

		1998	1999[2]	2000[3,4]	2001	2002	2003	2004	2005	2006	2007
Foreign currency assets											
Market loans and advances											
UK banks[9]	TBIH	72 263	74 250	93 269	104 107	114 809	137 417	149 119	146 316	173 211	177 957
UK banks' CDs etc	TBII	11 065	14 364	13 171	13 298	10 128	13 162	11 026	18 412	13 023	12 851
UK building societies CDs etc. and deposits	TBIJ	259	451	173	354	357	591	448	411	422	608
UK public sector[7]	TBIK	45	20	30	13	83	91	50	153	105	170
Other UK residents	TBIL	83 968	88 847	107 707	118 106	117 669	134 894	153 574	161 488	199 147	279 600
Non-residents	TBIM	616 832	599 146	743 781	783 057	783 168	779 983	839 535	1 013 764	1 104 494	1 492 863
Claims under sale and repurchase agreement											
UK banks	TBIO	31 900	28 008	41 801	61 188	91 488	225 027	250 209	272 361	257 856	248 960
UK building societies	TBIP	–	–	–	–	–	–	–	100	67	2 152
UK public sector[7]	TBIQ	–	–	737	23	486	1 420	1 590	1 125	1	1 118
Other UK residents	TBIR	39 764	33 027	57 876	73 237	86 866	100 817	106 973	135 018	131 709	171 482
Non-residents	TBIS	147 562	146 756	199 990	219 449	256 663	382 672	506 157	612 065	595 615	751 407
Acceptances granted	TBIT	729	619	689	638	754	751	890	846	1 270	1 394
Bills	TBIU	15 239	19 508	21 878	25 399	20 803	31 429	24 250	24 230	25 917	35 841
Investments											
British government stocks	TBIV	4 755	4 473	3 518	890	226	19	−20	−30	104	9
Other public sector	TBIW	–	–	–	4	18	7	–	–	1	–
UK banks	TBIX	4 310	8 607	11 706	10 633	10 298	11 688	13 187	13 176	12 384	13 805
UK building societies	TBIY	526	631	939	850	1 170	1 570	2 400	2 974	2 683	2 590
Other UK residents	TBIZ	4 584	5 679	12 298	18 129	20 130	21 846	32 882	45 283	57 858	68 537
Non-residents	TBJA	234 563	243 147	297 404	324 073	326 035	334 371	398 040	484 874	566 025	662 101
Items in suspense and collection	TBJB	30 229	29 706	44 885	55 026	44 037	60 804	81 937	112 089	117 498	122 409
Accrued amounts receivable	TBJC	27 821	20 163	21 279	18 969	19 434	18 129	19 561	22 397	32 639	42 051
Other assets	TBJD	3 111	4 648	2 978	3 880	8 735	13 683	11 802	19 089	26 251	23 691
Total foreign currency assets[14]	TBJE	1 329 525	1 322 050	1 676 109	1 831 322	1 913 355	2 270 372	2 603 610	3 086 141	3 318 281	4 111 597
Total assets	TBJF	2 587 177	2 643 536	3 144 636	3 426 702	3 640 491	4 159 572	4 711 173	5 522 173	6 261 872	6 963 910
Holdings of own sterling acceptances	TBJG	2 137	1 725	1 231	916	1 220	411	265	24	19	20
Holdings of own FC acceptances	TBJH	170	150	135	118	58	104	170	222	247	526
Eligible banks' total sterling acceptances	TBJI	18 722	14 523	10 597	11 320	10 805	3 035	1 217	152	..	..
Eligible liabilities	TBJJ	807 803	849 289	952 062	1 012 194	1 087 877	1 163 917	1 266 726	1 420 348	1 636 053	1 874 899

1 See chapter text.
2 Data for 1999 reflect the acquisition of Birmingham Midshires Building Society by Halifax during that year.
3 Data for 2000 reflect the entry of Bradford & Bingley plc to the banking sector during the year.
4 Data for 2000 reflect the new reporting during the year of agency business as a result of collateral management via repos and reverse repos.
5 Sterling sight deposits from UK banks and sterling market loans to UK banks in 2003 were depressed by £19 bn following the consolidation of two banks balance sheets.
6 Sterling deposits (sight plus time) from, and lending to banks in 2007 were reduced by £386bn following changes in the reporting population.
7 From 2000 the UK public sector series reflects assumption by the Debt Management Office (an executive agency of HM Treasury) of responsibility for government cash management.
8 Due to changes to the forms completed by reporting institutions, the breakdown of sale and repurchase agreements into gilt and non-gilt collateral is not available after 2006.

9 Foreign currency sight and time deposits from UK banks and foreign currency market loans and advances to UK banks in 2001, 2003 and 2004 were each depressed by £14.5 bn, £0.5 bn and £4.7 bn respectively as a result of positions being consolidated out on the merger of two banks.
10 During 2000, 2001, 2002, 2003, 2004 and 2005 sterling advances to other UK residents were reduced by £10.3 bn, £12.9 bn, £16.2 bn, £29.1bn, £30.4bn and £33.6 bn respectively as a result of securitisations and other loan transfers to non-banks or non-residents.
11 Sterling investments in UK banks in 2000 were boosted by Barclay's £5.8 bn investment in Woolwich.
12 Sterling investments in other UK residents in 2000 were boosted by Lloyds TSB's £5.8 bn investment in Scottish Widows Group.
13 Changes in the reporting populations in 1998, 1999, 2000, 2001, 2003 and 2004 account for a net decrease of £7.3 bn, £11.3 bn £0.8 bn, £0.7bn, £0.2 bn and £4.5 bn respectively in sterling assets outstanding.
14 Changes in the reporting populations in 1998, 1999, 2000, 2001, 2003 and 2004 account for a net decrease of £4.6 bn, £6.6 bn, £0.2 bn, £0.2 bn £0.2 bn and £5.2 bn of foreign currency assets outstanding.

Source: Bank of England: 020 7601 3236

23.4 Industrial analysis of bank lending to UK residents[1]
Not seasonally adjusted

£ million

	UK residents					Manufacturing			
	Total	of which sterling	Agriculture, hunting and forestry	Fishing	Mining & quarrying	Total	Food, beverages & tobacco	Textiles & leather	Pulp, paper, publishing & printing

Amounts outstanding (sterling & other currencies)

Loans & advances (including under repo & sterling commercial paper)

	TBOA	TBOB	TBOC	TBOD	TBOE	TBOF	TBOG	TBOH	TBOI
2005	1 632 663	1 333 243	9 363	371	3 262	48 485	11 817	1 641	6 931
2006	1 793 840	1 460 380	9 620	413	4 205	47 476	11 434	1 512	6 405

Acceptances

	TBQA	TBQB	TBQC	TBQD	TBQE	TBQF	TBQG	TBQH	TBQI
2005	1 015	816	–	1	2	83	7	26	1
2006	1 190	956	–	–	1	104	5	28	1

Total

	TBSA		TBSC	TBSD	TBSE	TBSF	TBSG	TBSH	TBSI
2006	1 795 030		9 620	413	4 206	47 579	11 439	1 540	6 406
2007	2 129 758		9 939	401	13 229	51 331	13 510	1 407	7 021

of which in sterling

	TBUA		TBUC	TBUD	TBUE	TBUF	TBUG	TBUH	TBUI
2006	1 461 336		9 375	399	1 934	32 396	8 630	1 015	4 916
2007	1 676 924		9 590	394	1 827	31 682	8 563	925	4 573

Facilities granted

	TCAA		TCAC	TCAD	TCAE	TCAF	TCAG	TCAH	TCAI
2006	2 177 763		12 146	504	11 358	88 919	25 048	2 501	11 636
2007	2 569 437		12 840	488	29 562	100 352	25 715	2 288	11 962

of which in sterling

	TCCA		TCCC	TCCD	TCCE	TCCF	TCCG	TCCH	TCCI
2006	1 746 462		11 834	490	2 586	54 208	15 251	1 689	7 496
2007	1 966 032		12 436	478	2 924	51 412	13 015	1 476	6 925

	Manufacturing					Electricity, gas and water supply		
	Chemicals, man-made fibres, rubber & plastics	Non-metallic mineral products & metals	Machinery, equipment & transport equipment	Electrical, medical & optical equipment	Other manufacturing	Electricity, gas & heated water	Cold water purification & supply	Construction

Amounts outstanding (sterling & other currencies)

Loans & advances (including under repo & sterling commercial paper)

	TBOJ	TBOK	TBOL	TBOM	TBON	TBOO	TBOP	TBOQ
2005	6 253	5 242	7 085	4 267	5 250	4 992	1 163	19 154
2006	5 681	6 122	6 678	3 741	5 903	7 075	4 235	20 671

Acceptances

	TBQJ	TBQK	TBQL	TBQM	TBQN	TBQO	TBQP	TBQQ
2005	5	9	8	7	19	–	2	2
2006	4	10	8	14	33	–	–	15

Total

	TBSJ	TBSK	TBSL	TBSM	TBSN	TBSO	TBSP	TBSQ
2006	..	6 132	6 686	..	5 936	7 075	4 235	20 686
2007	..	6 593	7 460	..	6 481	6 484	2 449	27 183

of which in sterling

	TBUJ	TBUK	TBUL	TBUM	TBUN	TBUO	TBUP	TBUQ
2006	2 962	3 763	4 497	2 078	4 534	6 113	3 924	20 141
2007	2 864	3 841	3 819	1 994	5 102	5 558	2 435	26 058

Facilities granted

	TCAJ	TCAK	TCAL	TCAM	TCAN	TCAO	TCAP	TCAQ
2006	..	10 193	12 381	6 466	9 810	15 024	11 441	33 381
2007	..	10 793	14 122	7 873	10 092	12 930	6 452	40 256

of which in sterling

	TCCJ	TCCK	TCCL	TCCM	TCCN	TCCO	TCCP	TCCQ
2006	5 361	6 072	8 395	3 508	6 436	10 407	10 110	30 912
2007	5 104	6 568	7 445	3 344	7 536	8 966	5 568	36 716

Banking, insurance

23.4 Industrial analysis of bank lending to UK residents[1]
Not seasonally adjusted

continued

£ million

		Wholesale and retail trade					Real estate, renting, computer and other business activities		
	Total	Sale & repair of motor vehicles & fuel	Other wholesale trade	Other retail trade & repair	Hotels and restaurants	Transport, storage & communication	Total	Development, buying, selling, renting of real estate	Renting of machinery & equipment

Amounts outstanding (sterling & other currencies)

Loans & advances (including under repo & sterling commercial paper)

	TBOR	TBOS	TBOT	TBOU	TBOV	TBOW	TBOX	TBOY	TBPA
2005	40 548	9 293	13 312	17 943	25 064	20 836	177 152	137 281	6 661
2006	42 368	10 167	14 401	17 800	25 707	26 361	209 942	162 332	6 881

Acceptances

	TBQR	TBQS	TBQT	TBQU	TBQV	TBQW	TBQX	TBQY	TBRA
2005	151	7	120	25	–	–	721	714	–
2006	160	4	99	58	1	1	812	800	–

Total

	TBSR	TBSS	TBST	TBSU	TBSV	TBSW	TBSX	TBSY	TBTA
2006	42 528	10 171	14 499	17 858	25 707	26 362	210 754	163 132	6 881
2007	53 503	9 427	20 100	23 975	28 555	26 876	252 861	196 152	9 123

of which in sterling

	TBUR	TBUS	TBUT	TBUU	TBUV	TBUW	TBUX	TBUY	TBVA
2006	35 836	9 508	10 238	16 090	25 042	21 589	201 020	160 970	5 818
2007	42 429	8 925	12 254	21 251	27 758	20 085	240 992	193 033	7 628

Facilities granted

	TCAR	TCAS	TCAT	TCAU	TCAV	TCAW	TCAX	TCAY	TCBA
2006	68 254	13 960	22 076	32 217	32 487	46 499	272 051	206 171	8 444
2007	77 691	12 773	28 204	36 715	34 081	43 250	314 320	237 110	10 547

of which in sterling

	TCCR	TCCS	TCCT	TCCU	TCCV	TCCW	TCCX	TCCY	TCDA
2006	53 580	12 565	15 464	25 550	30 081	32 882	253 070	200 110	6 670
2007	58 755	11 361	17 289	30 105	31 764	27 862	292 344	230 385	8 589

	Real estate, renting, computer and other business activities				Recreational, personal & community service activities		Financial intermediation (excl. insurance & pension funds)	
	Computer & related activities	Legal, accountancy, consultancy & other business activities	Public administration & defence	Education	Health & social work	Recreational, cultural & sporting activities	Personal & community services activities	Total	Financial leasing corporations

Amounts outstanding (sterling & other currencies)

Loans & advances (including under repo & sterling commercial paper)

	TBPB	TBPC	TBPD	TBPE	TBPF	TBPH	TBPG	TBPI	TBPJ
2005	3 752	29 458	19 590	6 317	12 729	10 025	5 304	422 947	36 770
2006	4 431	36 299	17 227	7 498	15 854	12 255	5 594	491 121	41 068

Acceptances

	TBRB	TBRC	TBRD	TBRE	TBRF	TBRH	TBRG	TBRI	TBRJ
2005	–	7	–	–	–	–	4	48	–
2006	–	12	–	–	–	–	5	90	–

Total

	TBTB	TBTC	TBTD	TBTE	TBTF	TBTH	TBTG	TBTI	TBTJ
2006	4 431	36 311	17 227	7 498	15 854	12 255	5 599	491 211	41 068
2007	4 590	42 996	18 536	8 719	19 230	14 305	7 037	663 564	42 282

of which in sterling

	TBVB	TBVC	TBVD	TBVE	TBVF	TBVH	TBVG	TBVI	TBVJ
2006	2 933	31 298	17 120	7 431	15 643	10 894	5 051	246 302	35 832
2007	2 829	37 502	17 334	8 625	18 805	13 271	6 419	354 296	35 464

Facilities granted

	TCBB	TCBC	TCBD	TCBE	TCBF	TCBH	TCBG	TCBI	TCBJ
2006	6 371	51 065	19 587	10 046	19 182	17 407	7 925	547 402	43 617
2007	7 294	59 368	21 243	11 658	22 652	19 342	9 288	739 356	44 275

of which in sterling

	TCDB	TCDC	TCDD	TCDE	TCDF	TCDH	TCDG	TCDI	TCDJ
2006	4 209	42 081	19 479	9 947	18 667	14 459	6 886	275 459	37 890
2007	4 383	48 988	20 044	11 415	21 860	16 903	8 305	380 241	37 268

23.4 Industrial analysis of bank lending to UK residents[1]
Not seasonally adjusted

continued

£ million

	Financial intermediation (excl. insurance & pension funds)								
	Non-bank credit grantors, excl. credit unions	Credit unions	Factoring corporations	Mortgage & housing credit corporations	Investment & unit trusts excl. money market mutual funds	Money market mutual funds	Bank holding companies	Securities dealers (f)	Other financial intermediaries

Amounts outstanding (sterling & other currencies)

Loans & advances (including under repo & sterling commercial paper)

	TBPK	TBPL	TBPM	TBPN	TBPO	TBPP	TBPQ	TBPR	TBPS
2005	17 833	28	4 633	62 869	20 394	1 377	19 707	165 421	93 916
2006	21 496	60	5 593	84 959	20 131	674	17 969	183 551	115 620

Acceptances

	TBRK	TBRL	TBRM	TBRN	TBRO	TBRP	TBRQ	TBRR	TBRS
2005	15	5	–	–	–	–	–	–	27
2006	15	5	–	–	–	–	–	–	69

Total

	TBTK	TBTL	TBTM	TBTN	TBTO	TBTP	TBTQ	TBTR	TBTS
2006	21 511	66	5 593	84 959	20 131	674	17 969	183 551	115 689
2007	23 678	80	6 523	99 216	20 975	327	44 382	219 265	206 835

  of which in sterling

	TBVK	TBVL	TBVM	TBVN	TBVO	TBVP	TBVQ	TBVR	TBVS
2006	20 205	65	4 673	74 403	6 972	91	12 472	25 830	65 759
2007	21 439	80	5 520	82 563	6 132	77	32 358	37 996	132 667

Facilities granted

	TCBK	TCBL	TCBM	TCBN	TCBO	TCBP	TCBQ	TCBR	TCBS
2006	23 625	89	5 916	92 587	33 310	752	18 902	186 663	141 942
2007	25 527	92	6 774	103 965	47 525	391	44 612	228 585	237 610

  of which in sterling

	TCDK	TCDL	TCDM	TCDN	TCDO	TCDP	TCDQ	TCDR	TCDS
2006	21 977	88	4 946	81 888	13 042	106	12 413	26 540	76 568
2007	22 869	89	5 724	87 071	12 775	88	32 153	38 565	143 640

	Activities auxiliary to financial intermediation			Individuals & individual trusts		
	Insurance companies & pension funds	Fund management activities	Other	Total	Lending secured on dwellings inc. bridging finance	Other loans & advances

Amounts outstanding (sterling & other currencies)

Loans & advances (including under repo & sterling commercial paper)

	TBPT	TBPU	TBPV	TBPW	TBPX	TBPY
2006	26 355	34 316	55 836	729 712	587 069	142 643
2007	..	..	..	749 174	605 186	143 988

Acceptances

	TBRT	TBRU	TBRV			
2005	1	–	–			
2006	1	–	–			

Total

	TBTT	TBTU	TBTV	TBTW	TBTX	TBTY
2006	26 356	34 316	55 836	729 712	587 069	142 643
2007	30 301	52 769	93 312	749 174	605 186	143 988

  of which in sterling

	TBVT	TBVU	TBVV	TBVW	TBVX	TBVY
2006	24 373	20 732	27 964	728 057	..	141 413
2007	27 960	15 771	58 145	747 490	..	142 827

Facilities granted

	TCBT	TCBU	TCBV	TCBW	TCBX	TCBY
2006	38 596	37 898	57 901	829 754	640 095	189 660
2007	57 824	55 907	94 807	865 139	667 412	197 727

  of which in sterling

	TCDT	TCDU	TCDV	TCDW	TCDX	TCDY
2006	31 340	22 775	29 474	827 817	639 663	188 154
2007	37 959	17 672	59 275	863 134	666 884	196 250

1 See chapter text.

Source: Bank of England: 020 7601 3236

23.5 Industrial analysis of bank deposits from UK residents[1]

£ million

					Manufacturing			
	Total from UK residents	Agriculture, hunting and forestry	Fishing	Mining & quarrying	Total	Food, beverages & tobacco	Textiles & leather	Pulp, paper, publishing & printing
Amounts outstanding (sterling & other currencies)								
Deposit liabilities (including under repos)								
	TDAA	TDAB	TDAC	TDAD	TDAE	TDAF	TDAG	TDAH
2006	1 467 063	4 147	192	5 692	39 978	3 686	1 175	3 710
2007	1 679 929	5 096	208	6 336	40 578	3 632	1 393	4 760
of which in sterling								
	TDCA	TDCB	TDCC	TDCD	TDCE	TDCF	TDCG	TDCH
2006	1 219 076	4 063	170	3 136	30 083	3 031	957	3 175
2007	1 362 254	4 969	176	3 149	30 692	2 738	1 042	4 246

	Manufacturing					Electricity, gas and water supply		
	Chemicals, man-made fibres, rubber & plastics	Non-metallic mineral products & metals	Machinery, equipment & transport equipment	Electrical, medical & optical equipment	Other manufacturing	Electricity, gas & heated water	Cold water purification & supply	Construction
Amounts outstanding (sterling & other currencies)								
Deposit liabilities (including under repos)								
	TDAI	TDAJ	TDAK	TDAL	TDAM	TDAN	TDAO	TDAP
2006	4 083	5 612	9 280	6 283	6 150	5 368	3 681	17 520
2007	4 531	4 851	10 427	6 103	4 880	5 292	2 840	19 639
of which in sterling								
	TDCI	TDCJ	TDCK	TDCL	TDCM	TDCN	TDCO	TDCP
2006	2 752	4 792	7 511	3 533	4 333	4 564	3 486	17 263
2007	3 012	4 152	7 731	3 752	4 020	4 713	2 141	18 604

	Wholesale and retail trade						Real estate, renting, computer and other business activities		
	Total	Sale & repair of motor vehicles & fuel	Other wholesale trade	Other retail trade & repair	Hotels and restaurants	Transport, storage & communication	Total	Development, buying, selling, renting of real estate	Renting of machinery & equipment
Amounts outstanding (sterling & other currencies)									
Deposit liabilities (including under repos)									
	TDAQ	TDAR	TDAS	TDAT	TDAU	TDAV	TDAW	TDAX	TDAY
2006	29 012	3 531	12 952	12 530	5 069	20 352	113 658	33 331	1 568
2007	32 478	4 008	14 592	13 878	5 339	20 753	123 626	36 580	1 623
of which in sterling									
	TDCQ	TDCR	TDCS	TDCT	TDCU	TDCV	TDCW	TDCX	TDCY
2006	24 735	3 251	9 819	11 664	4 935	16 440	105 300	32 067	1 448
2007	27 713	3 558	11 110	13 045	5 042	16 350	113 982	35 531	1 419

23.5 Industrial analysis of bank deposits from UK residents[1]

continued

£ million

	Real estate, renting, computer and other business activities					Recreational, personal & community service activities		Financial intermediation (excl. insurance & pension funds)	
	Computer & related activities	Legal, accountancy, consultancy & other business activities	Public administration & defence	Education	Health & social work	Recreational, cultural & sporting activities	Personal & community services activities	Total	Financial leasing corporations

Amounts outstanding (sterling & other currencies)

Deposit liabilities (including under repos)

	TDAZ	TDBA	TDBB	TDBC	TDBD	TDBF	TDBE	TDBG	TDBH
2006	7 969	70 791	22 260	7 800	11 685	14 016	14 067	349 446	5 416
2007	9 163	76 260	26 003	9 163	13 653	16 203	15 627	440 612	4 164

of which in sterling

	TDCZ	TDDA	TDDB	TDDC	TDDD	TDDF	TDDE	TDDG	TDDH
2006	6 795	64 989	21 169	7 479	11 332	13 076	13 637	195 096	3 895
2007	7 600	69 432	24 641	8 907	13 254	15 217	15 094	247 703	3 252

	Financial intermediation (excl. insurance & pension funds)							
	Non-bank credit grantors, excl. credit unions	Credit unions	Factoring corporations	Mortgage & housing credit corporations	Investment & unit trusts excl. money market mutual funds	Money market mutual funds	Bank holding companies	Securities dealers	Other financial intermediaries

Amounts outstanding (sterling & other currencies)

Deposit liabilities (including under repos)

	TDBI	TDBJ	TDBK	TDBL	TDBM	TDBN	TDBO	TDBP	TDBQ
2006	10 433	400	890	13 508	35 089	254	25 719	115 581	142 157
2007	9 557	438	768	12 887	36 033	489	39 870	154 351	182 056

of which in sterling

	TDDI	TDDJ	TDDK	TDDL	TDDM	TDDN	TDDO	TDDP	TDDQ
2006	7 712	399	529	13 239	16 022	236	13 700	34 075	105 289
2007	7 753	438	631	12 601	19 093	358	27 013	41 855	134 709

	Insurance companies & pension funds	Activities auxiliary to financial intermediation		Individuals & individual trusts
		Placed by fund managers	Other	

Amounts outstanding (sterling & other currencies)

Deposit liabilities (including under repos)

	TDBR	TDBS	TDBT	TDBU
2006	62 561	65 595	71 090	603 872
2007	67 759	88 179	94 639	645 906

of which in sterling

	TDDR	TDDS	TDDT	TDDU
2006	54 396	43 742	44 141	600 834
2007	59 180	49 295	59 367	642 064

1 See chapter text.

Source: Bank of England: 020 7601 3236

Banking, insurance

23.6 Public sector net cash requirement and other counterparts to changes in money stock during the year

Not seasonally adjusted

£ million

		1997	1998	1999	2000	2001	2002	2003	2004	2005	2006	2007
Public sector net cash requirement (surplus)	ABEN	12 011	−6 622	−1 609	−37 389	−2 750	18 316	38 832	41 445	41 008	33 058	32 303
Sales of public sector debt to M4 private sector	IDH8	−16 157	1 698	−1 448	13 639	7 716	−9 258	−32 438	−32 007	−11 257	−20 082	−16 293
M4 lending[1]	AVBS	68 186	63 926	78 029	111 202	82 574	107 553	127 820	156 084	158 086	218 446	238 831
External and foreign currency finance of the public sector	VQDC	−2 452	−4 717	6 199	3 616	3 875	2 486	−13 441	−2 395	−30 708	−33 556	−23 067
Other external and foreign currency flows[2]	AVBW	24 565	14 033	−44 911	7 153	−21 607	−25 113	−27 161	4 364	31 307	−1 528	−45 715
Net non-deposit liabilities (increase)	AVBX	−5 880	−8 222	−2 936	−31 025	−10 815	−25 149	−20 341	−67 477	−37 567	−30 688	−3 116
Money stock (M4)	AUZI	80 271	60 097	33 329	67 198	58 994	68 834	73 271	100 014	150 868	165 648	181 867

1 Bank and building society lending, plus holdings of commercial bills by the Issue Department of the Bank of England.
2 Including sterling lending to non-residents sector.

Source: Bank of England: 020 7601 5468

23.7 Money stock and liquidity

£ million

		1997	1998	1999	2000	2001	2002	2003	2004	2005	2006	2007
Amounts outstanding at end-year												
Notes and coin in circulation with the M4 private sector[1]	VQKT	22 242	23 705	26 269	28 174	30 450	31 889	34 010	36 410	38 508	40 565	44 606
UK private sector sterling non-interest bearing sight deposits[2]	AUYA	38 578	36 765	42 130	45 867	50 548	45 594	51 274	50 845	55 208	54 800	62 050
Money stock (M2)[3]	VQXV	484 300	514 508	558 334	597 523	649 980	703 920	777 347	845 654	922 687	996 671	1 073 021
Money stock M4	AUYM	722 133	783 354	816 601	884 873	942 594	1 008 751	1 081 299	1 179 192	1 328 320	1 497 559	1 673 736
Changes during the year[4]												
Notes and coin in circulation with the M4 private sector[1]	VQLU	1 609	1 501	2 582	1 957	2 284	1 493	2 189	2 461	2 156	2 079	4 202
UK private sector sterling non-interest bearing sight deposits[2]	AUZA	4 399	−754	5 354	3 533	4 914	−6 761	5 321	−227	5 699	−409	9 292
Money stock (M2)[3]	AUZE	35 078	30 781	41 992	39 123	52 813	53 698	72 255	68 901	78 428	72 806	66 128
Money stock M4	AUZI	80 271	60 097	33 329	67 198	58 994	68 834	73 271	100 014	150 868	165 648	181 867

1 The estimates of levels of coin in circulation include allowance for wastage, hoarding, etc.
2 Non-interest bearing deposits are confined to those with institutions included in the United Kingdom banks sector (See Table 23.3).

3 M2 comprises the UK non-monetary financial institutions and non-public sector, i.e. M4 private sector's holdings of notes and coin together with its sterling denominated retail deposits with UK monetary financial institutions.
4 As far as possible the changes exclude the effect of changes in the number of contributors to the series, and also of the introduction of new statistical returns. Changes are not seasonally adjusted.

Source: Bank of England: 020 7601 5468

23.8 Selected retail banks' base rate[1]
Operative between dates shown

Percentage rates

Date of change	New rate	Date of change	New rate	Date of change	New rate
1986 Jan 9	12.50	Nov 25	13.00	Nov 6	7.25
Mar 19	11.50				
Apr 8	11.00-11.50	1989 May 24	14.00	1998 Jun 4	7.50
Apr 9	11.00	Oct 5	15.00	Oct 8	7.25
Apr 21	10.50			Nov 5	6.75
May 23	10.00-10.50	1990 Oct 8	14.00	Dec 10	6.25
May 27	10.00				
Oct 14	10.00-11.00	1991 Feb 13	13.50	1999 Jan 7	6.00
Oct 15	11.00	Feb 27	13.00	Feb 4	5.50
		Mar 22	12.50	Apr 8	5.25
1987 Mar 10	10.50	Apr 12	12.00	Jun 10	5.00
Mar 18	10.00-10.50	May 24	11.50	Sep 8	5.00-5.25
Mar 19	10.00	Jul 12	11.00	Sep 10	5.25
Apr 28	9.50-10.00	Sep 4	10.50	Nov 4	5.50
Apr 29	9.50				
May 11	9.00	1992 May 5	10.00	2000 Jan 13	5.75
Aug 6	9.00-10.00	Sep 16[2]	12.00	Feb 10	6.00
Aug 7	10.00	Sep 17[2]	10.00-12.00		
Oct 23	9.50-10.00	Sep 18	10.00	2001 Feb 8	5.75
Oct 29	9.50	Sep 22	9.00	Apr 5	5.50
Nov 4	9.00-9.50	Oct 16	8.00-9.00	May 10	5.25
Nov 5	9.00	Oct 19	8.00	Aug 2	5.00
Dec 4	8.50	Nov 13	7.00	Sep 18	4.75
				Oct 4	4.50
1988 Feb 2	9.00	1993 Jan 26	6.00	Nov 8	4.00
Mar 17	8.50-9.00	Nov 23	5.50		
Mar 18	8.50			2003 Feb 6	3.75
Apr 11	8.00	1994 Feb 8	5.25	Jul 10	3.50
May 17	7.50-8.00	Sep 12	5.75	Nov 6	3.75
May 18	7.50	Dec 7	6.25		
Jun 2	7.50-8.00			2004 Feb 5	4.00
Jun 3	8.00	1995 Feb 2[2]	6.25-6.75	May 6	4.25
Jun 6	8.00-8.50	Feb 3	6.75	Jun 10	4.50
Jun 7	8.50	Dec 13	6.50	Aug 5	4.75
Jun 22	8.50-9.00				
Jun 23	9.00	1996 Jan 18	6.25	2005 Aug 4	4.50
Jun 28	9.00-9.50	Mar 8	6.00		
Jun 29	9.50	Jun 6	5.75	2006 Aug 3	4.75
Jul 4	9.50-10.00	Oct 30	5.75-6.00	Nov 9	5.00
Jul 5	10.00	Oct 31	6.00		
Jul 18	10.00-10.50			2007 Jan 11	5.25
Jul 19	10.50	1997 May 6	6.25	May 10	5.50
Aug 8	10.50-11.00	Jun 6	6.25-6.50	Jul 5	5.75
Aug 9	11.00	Jun 9	6.50	Dec 6	5.50
Aug 25	11.00-12.00	Jul 10	6.75		
Aug 26	12.00	Aug 7	7.00	2008 Feb 7	5.25

1 Data obtained from Barclays Bank, Lloyds/TSB Bank, HSBC Bank and
  National Westminster Bank whose rates are used to compile this series.
2 Where all the rates did not change on the same day a spread is shown.

Source: Bank of England: 020 7601 3644

23.9 Average three month sterling money market rates[1]

Percentage rates

	1997	1998	1999	2000	2001	2002	2003	2004	2005	2006	2007
Treasury bills:[2] KDMM											
January	6.01	6.80	5.28	5.72	5.49	3.83	3.80	3.90	4.66	4.39	5.30
February	5.81	6.88	5.04	5.83	5.46	3.87	3.50	3.98	4.69	4.38	5.34
March	5.92	6.95	4.92	5.86	5.23	3.97	3.47	4.10	4.77	4.40	5.33
April	6.09	7.00	4.90	5.92	5.12	3.97	3.45	4.19	4.70	4.42	5.43
May	6.15	7.01	4.93	5.95	4.98	3.95	3.44	4.34	4.66	4.50	5.55
June	6.37	7.29	4.76	5.85	4.99	3.98	3.47	4.58	4.62	4.54	5.67
July	6.63	7.22	4.76	5.83	5.01	3.84	3.31	4.64	4.46	4.53	5.77
August	6.83	7.19	4.85	5.81	4.72	3.77	3.40	4.72	4.41	5.75	5.79
September	6.88	6.94	5.12	5.78	4.43	3.79	3.52	4.69	4.40	4.84	5.69
October	6.94	6.54	5.23	5.75	4.16	3.75	3.65	4.68	4.40	4.94	5.61
November	7.09	6.31	5.20	5.68	3.78	3.80	3.81	4.66	4.42	5.01	5.50
December	7.07	5.72	5.46	5.62	3.83	3.84	3.83	4.68	4.43	5.08	5.30
Eligible bill: KDMY[3]											
January	6.15	7.28	5.63	5.90	5.64	3.91	3.87	3.94	4.75	..	..
February	5.99	7.24	5.28	6.01	5.56	3.92	3.65	4.06	4.78	..	..
March	6.01	7.25	5.11	5.98	5.37	3.99	3.54	4.19	4.88	..	..
April	6.26	7.24	5.02	6.05	5.21	4.04	3.52	4.28	4.84	..	..
May	6.31	7.20	5.08	6.09	5.06	4.01	3.52	4.42	4.80	..	..
June	6.50	7.42	4.94	6.03	5.08	4.04	3.45	4.68	4.76	..	..
July	6.80	7.49	4.89	5.97	5.07	3.94	3.39	4.75	4.57	..	..
August	6.95	7.40	4.94	5.97	4.82	3.86	3.42	4.85	4.51	..	..
September	7.02	7.20	5.16	5.95	4.57	3.86	3.59	4.83	..	..	..
October	7.10	6.91	5.42	5.92	4.26	3.82	3.69	4.79	..	..	..
November	7.27	6.52	5.43	5.88	3.85	3.84	3.88	4.78	..	..	..
December	7.31	6.05	5.59	5.78	3.88	3.71	3.90	4.77	..	..	..
Interbank rate: AMIJ											
January	6.32	7.48	5.80	6.06	5.76	3.98	3.91	3.99	4.80	4.54	5.45
February	6.19	7.46	5.43	6.15	5.69	3.98	3.69	4.10	4.82	4.52	5.52
March	6.20	7.48	5.30	6.15	5.47	4.06	3.58	4.23	4.92	4.53	5.50
April	6.38	7.44	5.23	6.21	5.33	4.11	3.58	4.33	4.88	4.57	5.61
May	6.45	7.41	5.25	6.23	5.17	4.08	3.57	4.46	4.83	4.65	5.72
June	6.66	7.63	5.12	6.14	5.19	4.11	3.57	4.73	4.78	4.69	5.83
July	6.96	7.71	5.07	6.11	5.19	3.99	3.42	4.79	4.59	4.68	5.98
August	7.15	7.66	5.18	6.14	4.93	3.92	3.45	4.89	4.53	4.90	6.34
September	7.21	7.38	5.32	6.12	4.65	3.93	3.63	4.87	4.54	4.98	6.58
October	7.26	7.14	5.94	6.08	4.36	3.90	3.73	4.83	4.53	5.09	6.21
November	7.54	6.89	5.78	6.00	3.93	3.91	3.91	4.82	4.56	5.18	6.36
December	7.62	6.38	5.97	5.89	3.99	3.95	3.95	4.81	4.59	5.25	6.35
Certificate of deposits: KOSA											
January	6.27	7.44	5.74	6.02	5.73	3.96	3.90	3.98	4.80	4.54	5.45
February	6.14	7.42	5.38	6.10	5.66	3.96	3.68	4.09	4.82	4.52	5.51
March	6.15	7.43	5.26	6.09	5.44	4.04	3.57	4.22	4.91	4.53	5.52
April	6.33	7.40	5.19	6.17	5.30	4.08	3.57	4.32	4.86	4.57	5.69
May	6.39	7.37	5.22	6.19	5.15	4.06	3.56	4.45	4.82	4.65	5.84
June	6.62	7.59	5.09	6.10	5.16	4.09	3.56	4.72	4.78	4.69	5.94
July	6.92	7.66	5.03	6.08	5.17	3.97	3.41	4.79	4.60	4.68	6.11
August	7.12	7.61	5.14	6.09	4.90	3.90	3.44	4.89	4.53	4.89	6.35
September	7.17	7.34	5.28	6.08	4.62	3.91	3.62	4.87	4.54	4.98	6.54
October	7.22	7.09	5.86	6.05	4.33	3.88	3.72	4.83	4.53	5.09	6.21
November	7.50	6.82	5.72	5.98	3.91	3.89	3.90	4.81	4.57	5.18	6.34
December	7.57	6.32	5.89	5.85	3.96	3.93	3.94	4.80	4.59	5.24	6.35
Local authority deposits: KDPX[4]											
January	6.27	7.43	5.76	6.03	5.73	3.85	3.87	3.91	..	..	..
February	6.15	7.40	5.38	6.09	5.62	3.88	3.61	4.08	..	..	..
March	6.14	7.40	5.27	6.08	5.39	4.01	3.55	4.12	..	..	..
April	6.33	7.38	5.17	6.12	5.26	4.05	3.54	4.31	..	..	..
May	6.38	7.34	5.19	6.14	5.13	4.06	3.54	4.45	..	..	..
June	6.57	7.56	5.07	6.09	5.10	4.05	3.57	4.75	..	..	..
July	6.90	7.64	5.01	6.04	5.12	3.95	3.39	4.82	..	..	..
August	7.11	7.55	5.11	6.06	4.86	3.87	3.43	4.92	..	..	..
September	7.19	7.35	5.19	6.05	4.58	3.88	3.61	4.90	..	..	..
October	7.21	7.08	5.83	6.03	4.29	3.86	3.71	4.85	..	..	..
November	7.49	6.85	5.64	5.96	3.82	3.87	3.90	4.84	..	..	..
December	7.56	6.35	5.88	5.80	3.87	3.93	3.92	4.82	..	..	..

1 A full definition of these series is given in Section 7 of the ONS Financial Statistics Explanatory Handbook.
2 Average rate of discount at weekly (Friday) tender.
3 This series discontinued at end of August 2005.
4 This series discontinued at end of December 2004.

Source: Bank of England: 020 7601 3644

23.10 Average foreign exchange rates[1]

	1997	1998	1999	2000	2001	2002	2003	2004	2005	2006	2007
Sterling exchange rate index (1990 = 100)[2] AGBG											
January	95.9	104.7	99.6	108.5	104.4	106.9	104.0	102.4	102.1	102.7	..
February	97.4	104.7	100.8	108.4	104.1	107.4	102.4	104.8	103.3	102.8	..
March	97.4	106.8	102.8	108.4	105.0	106.5	100.6	105.0	103.2	102.1	..
April	99.5	107.1	103.4	110.1	105.8	107.1	99.8	105.2	104.4	101.9	..
May	99.0	103.4	104.2	108.5	106.6	105.3	97.9	104.6	103.6	104.1	..
June	100.4	105.4	104.7	104.6	106.8	103.6	99.6	105.8	104.9	..	..
July	104.5	105.3	103.5	105.6	107.2	105.3	99.4	105.9	102.1	..	..
August	102.5	104.6	103.3	107.4	105.1	105.4	99.0	105.2	102.8	..	..
September	100.4	103.3	104.7	106.2	106.1	106.5	99.2	103.3	103.9	..	..
October	101.1	100.7	105.4	109.2	105.8	106.7	99.8	102.2	103.1	..	..
November	103.8	100.6	105.7	107.3	106.1	105.9	100.4	101.7	103.2	..	..
December	104.4	100.4	106.7	106.4	106.5	105.5	100.3	103.2	103.3	..	..
Effective Sterling exchange rate index (Jan 2005 = 100) BK67											
January	92.4	100.6	96.5	103.0	98.6	100.6	99.9	100.2	100.0	99.1	105.4
February	93.3	100.3	97.3	102.6	98.1	100.9	98.5	102.5	101.0	99.0	104.9
March	93.2	102.0	99.0	102.4	98.9	100.2	96.8	102.3	101.1	98.4	103.4
April	95.0	102.3	99.0	103.8	99.5	100.9	96.1	102.3	102.0	98.4	104.1
May	94.8	99.2	99.8	101.8	99.8	99.5	94.9	101.8	101.0	101.2	103.7
June	96.0	101.1	99.8	98.8	99.7	98.3	96.6	103.1	101.8	100.9	104.4
July	99.5	101.0	98.6	99.5	100.2	100.4	96.1	103.2	98.9	100.9	105.0
August	97.4	100.6	98.8	100.7	98.8	100.4	95.5	102.4	99.8	102.9	104.3
September	95.7	99.9	100.0	99.2	100.0	101.5	95.8	100.7	100.7	102.9	103.0
October	96.7	97.7	100.9	101.8	99.8	101.7	96.9	99.8	99.7	103.1	102.5
November	99.6	97.5	100.8	100.1	99.9	101.1	97.5	99.7	99.5	103.4	101.5
December	100.1	97.4	101.4	99.9	100.5	100.9	97.9	101.3	99.6	104.4	99.7
Sterling/US Dollar AUSS											
January	1.6587	1.6353	1.6509	1.6402	1.4769	1.4323	1.6169	1.8234	1.8764	1.7678	1.9587
February	1.6246	1.6407	1.6276	1.5998	1.4529	1.4231	1.6046	1.8673	1.8871	1.7470	1.9581
March	1.6063	1.6620	1.6220	1.5802	1.4454	1.4225	1.5836	1.8267	1.9078	1.7435	1.9471
April	1.6295	1.6733	1.6105	1.5837	1.4350	1.4434	1.5747	1.8005	1.8960	1.7685	1.9909
May	1.6334	1.6366	1.6154	1.5075	1.4259	1.4593	1.6230	1.7876	1.8538	1.8702	1.9836
June	1.6446	1.6507	1.5950	1.5089	1.4014	1.4863	1.6606	1.8275	1.8179	1.8428	1.9864
July	1.6702	1.6437	1.5747	1.5088	1.4139	1.5546	1.6242	1.8429	1.7509	1.8447	2.0338
August	1.6034	1.6320	1.6073	1.4910	1.4365	1.5377	1.5950	1.8216	1.7943	1.8944	2.0111
September	1.6015	1.6822	1.6243	1.4355	1.4635	1.5561	1.6131	1.7922	1.8081	1.8847	2.0185
October	1.6329	1.6952	1.6572	1.4511	1.4517	1.5574	1.6787	1.8065	1.7640	1.8755	2.0446
November	1.6890	1.6620	1.6214	1.4256	1.4358	1.5723	1.6901	1.8603	1.7341	1.9119	2.0701
December	1.6597	1.6705	1.6132	1.4625	1.4409	1.5863	1.7507	1.9275	1.7462	1.9633	2.0185
Sterling/Euro THAP											
January	1.3559	1.5166	1.4236	1.6201	1.5753	1.6222	1.5222	1.4447	1.4331	1.4582	1.5079
February	1.3906	1.5196	1.4534	1.6266	1.5786	1.6348	1.4893	1.4774	1.4499	1.4637	1.4969
March	1.3944	1.5507	1.4902	1.6377	1.5901	1.6224	1.4649	1.4890	1.4440	1.4500	1.4703
April	1.4243	1.5490	1.5051	1.6730	1.6084	1.6282	1.4505	1.5022	1.4652	1.4402	1.4713
May	1.4217	1.4834	1.5185	1.6655	1.6304	1.5914	1.4030	1.4894	1.4611	1.4637	1.4677
June	1.4499	1.5110	1.5374	1.5882	1.6434	1.5515	1.4234	1.5050	1.4952	1.4560	1.4805
July	1.5247	1.5091	1.5204	1.6052	1.6433	1.5665	1.4277	1.5023	1.4547	1.4540	1.4821
August	1.5043	1.4912	1.5146	1.6478	1.5955	1.5723	1.4286	1.4933	1.4592	1.4785	1.4762
September	1.4591	1.4617	1.5458	1.6471	1.6060	1.5861	1.4338	1.4676	1.4761	1.4811	1.4515
October	1.4623	1.4200	1.5491	1.6994	1.6024	1.5868	1.4334	1.4455	1.4674	1.4869	1.4370
November	1.4914	1.4290	1.5706	1.6664	1.6166	1.5694	1.4426	1.4311	1.4719	1.4834	1.4106
December	1.5053	1.4254	1.5953	1.6302	1.6151	1.5566	1.4246	1.4401	1.4725	1.4860	1.3863

1 Working day average. A full definition of these series is given in Section 7 of the ONS Explanatory Handbook.
2 Series discontinued from 31 May 2006.

Source: Bank of England: 020 7601 3644

23.11 Average zero coupon yields[1]

Percentage rates

	1997	1998	1999	2000	2001	2002	2003	2004	2005	2006	2007
Nominal Five Year Yield ZBRG											
January	7.15	6.18	4.30	6.28	5.07	4.90	4.15	4.61	4.43	4.11	5.06
February	6.82	6.10	4.46	6.13	5.04	4.94	3.85	4.63	4.53	4.17	5.08
March	7.07	6.09	4.69	5.89	4.86	5.22	3.93	4.56	4.73	4.33	5.00
April	7.28	5.93	4.66	5.80	4.96	5.21	4.09	4.80	4.54	4.48	5.20
May	6.94	5.95	4.95	5.82	5.14	5.22	3.85	5.01	4.31	4.67	5.32
June	6.96	6.04	5.28	5.61	5.25	5.05	3.72	5.15	4.17	4.69	5.59
July	7.01	6.12	5.49	5.58	5.26	4.88	3.98	5.07	4.16	4.69	5.55
August	6.97	5.80	5.75	5.65	5.03	4.54	4.36	4.96	4.23	4.74	5.25
September	6.72	5.32	6.00	5.65	4.90	4.31	4.46	4.83	4.12	4.67	5.02
October	6.51	4.94	6.25	5.46	4.74	4.36	4.73	4.65	4.26	4.76	4.95
November	6.69	4.92	5.86	5.33	4.55	4.38	4.91	4.58	4.29	4.73	4.64
December	6.46	4.51	5.90	5.14	4.88	4.34	4.71	4.43	4.21	4.80	4.57
Nominal Ten Year Yield ZBRH											
January	7.52	5.96	4.24	5.62	4.75	4.85	4.39	4.76	4.50	4.02	4.76
February	7.15	5.91	4.39	5.44	4.90	4.90	4.22	4.78	4.54	4.10	4.79
March	7.41	5.85	4.60	5.18	4.64	5.18	4.34	4.67	4.74	4.26	4.72
April	7.58	5.69	4.53	5.14	4.90	5.19	4.48	4.92	4.58	4.46	4.94
May	7.08	5.73	4.83	5.23	5.05	5.22	4.23	5.06	4.38	4.58	5.03
June	7.04	5.60	5.07	5.05	5.11	5.05	4.13	5.13	4.25	4.60	5.31
July	6.92	5.65	5.24	5.09	5.10	4.95	4.43	5.04	4.28	4.59	5.29
August	6.97	5.41	5.25	5.18	4.88	4.68	4.59	4.95	4.29	4.58	5.05
September	6.70	5.03	5.51	5.25	4.91	4.47	4.68	4.86	4.17	4.47	4.91
October	6.37	4.93	5.68	5.09	4.77	4.60	4.88	4.72	4.31	4.53	4.88
November	6.46	4.83	5.11	4.98	4.58	4.62	5.03	4.65	4.26	4.45	4.67
December	6.22	4.44	5.19	4.80	4.83	4.55	4.87	4.49	4.17	4.53	4.65
Nominal Twenty Year Yield ZBRI											
January	7.74	5.94	4.36	4.45	4.33	4.69	4.46	4.69	4.45	4.05	4.87
February	7.39	5.88	4.44	4.38	4.42	4.72	4.40	4.72	4.45	4.13	4.90
March	7.59	5.78	4.60	4.25	4.45	4.99	4.56	4.61	4.65	4.29	4.82
April	7.73	5.61	4.53	4.35	4.76	5.02	4.69	4.79	4.53	4.48	5.04
May	7.16	5.67	4.75	4.40	4.87	5.08	4.49	4.89	4.36	4.62	5.14
June	7.08	5.42	4.77	4.37	4.98	4.93	4.44	4.87	4.23	4.64	5.42
July	6.80	5.45	4.67	4.38	4.90	4.82	4.70	4.80	4.24	4.63	5.40
August	6.86	5.30	4.53	4.49	4.69	4.57	4.68	4.69	4.27	4.64	5.13
September	6.64	4.91	4.62	4.63	4.88	4.40	4.74	4.65	4.16	4.54	4.96
October	6.36	4.87	4.56	4.61	4.92	4.54	4.81	4.59	4.30	4.61	4.92
November	6.37	4.73	4.07	4.39	4.53	4.60	4.87	4.50	4.28	4.55	4.68
December	6.17	4.47	4.20	4.30	4.65	4.59	4.76	4.42	4.19	4.62	4.64
Real Ten Year Yield ZBRJ											
January	3.45	3.10	2.00	2.10	2.22	2.52	2.00	1.94	1.75	1.29	1.78
February	3.27	3.06	1.91	2.17	2.27	2.50	1.74	1.96	1.77	1.32	1.80
March	3.43	3.00	1.85	2.05	2.33	2.53	1.79	1.81	1.87	1.41	1.70
April	3.56	2.91	1.70	2.08	2.56	2.43	1.96	1.93	1.76	1.54	1.91
May	3.57	2.92	1.91	2.14	2.58	2.43	1.81	2.05	1.70	1.63	2.05
June	3.66	2.85	1.89	2.12	2.54	2.33	1.67	2.10	1.65	1.68	2.21
July	3.62	2.77	1.90	2.14	2.56	2.42	1.85	2.07	1.65	1.65	2.19
August	3.60	2.65	2.19	2.25	2.42	2.33	1.95	2.03	1.61	1.55	1.97
September	3.52	2.59	2.31	2.28	2.51	2.20	2.05	1.97	1.51	1.49	1.79
October	3.23	2.67	2.26	2.33	2.53	2.36	2.15	1.89	1.57	1.57	1.75
November	3.25	2.40	2.05	2.34	2.39	2.33	2.21	1.88	1.54	1.47	1.48
December	3.11	2.11	1.98	2.23	2.58	2.24	2.03	1.76	1.47	1.56	1.50
Real Twenty Year Yield ZBRK											
January	3.67	3.06	2.07	2.01	1.88	2.26	2.07	1.96	1.59	0.97	1.23
February	3.49	3.05	1.99	1.95	1.88	2.30	1.98	1.90	1.59	0.99	1.25
March	3.59	2.98	1.93	1.78	1.99	2.32	2.07	1.77	1.72	1.10	1.19
April	3.68	2.85	1.81	1.84	2.25	2.25	2.12	1.85	1.64	1.28	1.36
May	3.66	2.83	1.99	1.91	2.32	2.25	2.03	1.88	1.57	1.33	1.46
June	3.69	2.63	1.97	1.87	2.27	2.17	1.97	1.88	1.53	1.39	1.54
July	3.57	2.58	2.00	1.90	2.24	2.24	2.16	1.87	1.54	1.31	1.52
August	3.57	2.53	2.14	1.96	2.16	2.15	2.14	1.82	1.49	1.21	1.31
September	3.48	2.49	2.26	1.96	2.31	2.06	2.18	1.80	1.40	1.12	1.24
October	3.22	2.59	2.22	1.99	2.32	2.22	2.22	1.76	1.40	1.13	1.25
November	3.18	2.36	1.92	1.94	2.12	2.25	2.21	1.71	1.29	1.03	1.09
December	3.06	2.14	1.87	1.87	2.24	2.21	2.08	1.60	1.20	1.11	1.08

1 Working day average. Calculated using the Variable Roughness Penalty (VRP) model.

Source: Bank of England: 020 7601 3644

23.12 Average rates on representative British Government Stocks[1]

Percentage rates

	1997	1998	1999	2000	2001	2002	2003	2004	2005	2006	2007
5 Year Conventional Rate[2] KORP											
January	7.19	6.33	4.25	6.36	5.17	4.94	4.15	4.59	4.43	4.27	..
February	6.86	6.24	4.41	6.23	5.13	4.96	3.88	4.46	4.61	4.34	..
March	7.08	6.26	4.65	6.01	4.94	5.23	3.93	4.44	4.77	4.41	..
April	7.30	6.11	4.66	5.95	4.97	5.26	4.08	4.66	4.58	4.44	..
May	6.98	6.14	4.93	5.97	5.15	5.48	3.83	4.89	4.36	4.44	..
June	7.01	6.31	5.27	5.78	5.32	5.10	3.68	5.08	4.24	4.66	..
July	7.09	6.14	5.49	5.75	5.34	4.92	3.72	4.98	4.11	4.62	..
August	7.02	5.84	5.80	5.81	5.09	4.57	4.30	4.88	4.22	4.84	..
September	6.78	5.34	6.04	5.81	4.94	4.25	4.42	4.76	4.18	4.91	..
October	6.59	4.88	6.24	5.66	4.78	4.38	4.70	4.57	4.23	5.00	..
November	6.79	4.86	5.89	5.50	4.59	4.40	4.88	4.52	4.31	4.39	..
December	6.60	4.45	5.91	5.27	4.88	4.34	4.68	4.42	4.27	–	..
10 year Conventional Rate KORQ											
January	7.53	6.07	4.16	5.75	4.86	4.84	4.37	4.78	4.51	4.19	5.21
February	7.17	6.02	4.32	5.56	4.88	4.91	4.25	4.75	4.60	4.25	5.25
March	7.41	5.97	4.54	5.29	4.75	5.15	4.51	4.65	4.79	4.39	5.15
April	7.60	5.81	4.48	5.25	4.95	5.23	4.64	4.91	4.60	4.47	5.34
May	7.13	5.85	4.77	5.35	5.13	5.51	4.26	5.07	4.38	4.39	5.39
June	7.10	5.77	5.02	5.15	5.09	5.06	4.38	5.19	4.23	4.74	5.74
July	7.01	5.67	5.20	5.18	5.16	4.94	4.23	5.10	4.20	4.73	5.70
August	7.05	5.56	5.24	5.27	4.92	4.66	4.59	4.99	4.25	4.78	5.39
September	6.77	5.10	5.52	5.32	4.92	4.46	4.69	4.89	4.16	4.74	5.13
October	6.47	4.93	5.70	5.15	4.76	4.57	4.89	4.73	4.31	4.85	5.07
November	6.59	4.87	5.16	5.06	4.58	4.59	5.04	4.66	4.33	4.84	4.70
December	6.34	4.49	5.24	4.88	4.88	4.52	4.94	4.50	4.27	4.93	4.60
20 Year Conventional Rate KORR											
January	7.71	6.04	4.36	4.91	4.52	4.81	4.46	4.73	4.55	4.05	4.77
February	7.35	5.98	4.47	4.80	4.58	4.83	4.37	4.80	4.58	4.13	4.80
March	7.58	5.90	4.64	4.64	4.56	5.12	4.51	4.69	4.79	4.28	4.73
April	7.74	5.73	4.58	4.71	4.84	5.14	4.64	4.91	4.63	4.38	4.95
May	7.21	5.79	4.83	4.77	4.98	5.45	4.44	5.03	4.43	4.59	5.08
June	7.15	5.59	4.92	4.68	5.10	5.03	4.38	5.07	4.30	4.60	5.32
July	6.93	5.63	4.88	4.70	5.05	4.92	4.59	4.99	4.33	4.60	5.28
August	6.98	5.43	4.82	4.79	4.83	4.65	4.67	4.88	4.34	4.58	5.04
September	6.74	5.02	4.97	4.90	4.94	4.46	4.74	4.83	4.24	4.49	4.89
October	6.45	4.92	4.97	4.84	4.80	4.59	4.85	4.73	4.37	4.53	4.92
November	6.50	4.79	4.46	4.64	4.55	4.65	4.93	4.64	4.31	4.48	4.73
December	6.32	4.49	4.56	4.51	4.75	4.61	4.80	4.53	4.22	4.41	4.71
10 Year Index-Linked Rate KORS											
January	3.44	3.01	2.00	2.11	2.21	2.61	2.07	1.88	1.73	1.48	2.24
February	3.23	2.94	1.94	2.16	2.30	2.53	1.81	1.90	1.81	1.54	2.27
March	3.41	2.89	1.90	2.06	2.34	2.55	1.88	1.76	1.99	1.65	2.18
April	3.55	2.80	1.74	2.08	2.55	2.45	1.90	1.94	1.83	1.65	2.61
May	3.52	2.83	1.96	2.15	2.61	2.58	1.74	2.10	1.71	1.96	2.59
June	3.62	2.81	1.93	2.13	2.56	2.35	1.59	2.17	1.67	1.94	2.73
July	3.68	2.67	1.93	2.14	2.57	2.46	1.67	2.12	1.66	1.92	2.68
August	3.59	2.55	2.20	2.25	2.45	2.37	1.89	2.04	1.63	1.80	2.37
September	3.47	2.59	2.32	2.29	2.56	2.24	1.99	1.95	1.49	1.76	2.01
October	3.17	2.66	2.26	2.33	2.55	2.42	2.08	1.83	1.89	1.89	1.99
November	3.23	2.39	2.03	2.32	2.42	2.39	2.16	1.85	1.64	1.87	1.70
December	3.01	2.11	1.99	2.20	2.65	2.30	1.97	1.74	1.27	1.96	1.80
20 Year Index-Linked rate KORT											
January	3.62	3.01	2.06	2.01	1.96	2.35	2.10	1.95	1.68	1.17	1.63
February	3.43	3.01	1.97	1.98	1.99	2.36	1.99	1.94	1.72	1.22	1.65
March	3.55	2.92	1.93	1.83	2.09	2.39	2.07	1.80	1.89	1.34	1.57
April	3.65	2.80	1.81	1.90	2.35	2.32	2.10	1.91	1.77	1.38	1.77
May	3.61	2.79	1.99	1.97	2.41	2.43	2.00	1.99	1.67	1.56	1.91
June	3.65	2.61	1.97	1.94	2.38	2.23	1.93	2.01	1.63	1.61	2.07
July	3.68	2.56	1.97	1.96	2.36	2.30	2.05	1.99	1.63	1.55	2.07
August	3.54	2.51	2.12	2.03	2.25	2.21	2.09	1.93	1.58	1.45	1.83
September	3.43	2.51	2.23	2.04	2.39	2.12	2.13	1.89	1.48	1.37	1.67
October	3.17	2.58	2.18	2.08	2.38	2.29	2.17	1.84	1.51	1.44	1.65
November	3.16	2.35	1.91	2.02	2.19	2.31	2.16	1.80	1.45	1.34	1.41
December	3.02	2.12	1.88	1.94	2.33	2.26	2.04	1.69	1.38	1.43	1.41

1 Working day average.
2 Discontinued from 6 December 2006.

Source: Bank of England: 020 7601 3644

23.13 Building societies[1,2]
United Kingdom

		1997[3]	1998[3]	1999[3]	2000[4]	2001	2002	2003	2004	2005	2006
Number and balance sheets											
Societies on register (numbers)	KRNA	82	78	72	68	65	65	63	63	63	60
Share investors (thousands)	KRNB	19 234	21 195	21 774	22 237	20 311	20 724	20 901	20 734	22 090	22 396
Depositors (thousands)	KRNC	882	820	642	660	501	440	452	446	370	391
Borrowers (thousands)	KRND	2 703	2 934	2 868	2 925	2 579	2 520	2 520	2 570	2 617	2 626
Assets and liabilities (£ million)											
Liabilities:											
Shares	KRNE	90 092.8	103 289.8	109 137.7	119 298.5	119 815.2	132 372.9	142 477.1	153 844.0	171 935.0	188 943.0
Deposits and loans	KRNF	31 033.7	33 311.2	34 746.6	44 262.4	37 358.9	37 933.0	49 552.6	64 025.2	70 845.1	75 443.0
Taxation and other	KRNG	1 338.8	1 586.4	1 665.4	1 664.0	1 244.9	1 088.4	1 179.0	1 394.9	2 619.4	6 838.5
General reserves	KRNH	7 331.2	7 926.4	8 301.5	8 987.1	8 511.2	9 043.4	9 489.8	10 123.9	10 677.4	10 845.3
Other Capital	KRNI	1 643.9	1 550.7	1 529.2	1 861.0	1 416.1	1 709.2	2 534.7	3 599.1	4 566.5	5 510.9
Assets:											
Mortgages	KRNK	107 531.5	118 288.4	123 183.4	137 072.3	130 229.6	140 839.7	159 938.2	184 191.0	207 621.4	231 198.9
Investments and cash	KHVZ	21 869.8	27 102.0	29 917.8	36 574.2	35 925.9	38 952.7	43 067.9	46 234.1	49 240.3	52 349.4
Other	KRNN	2 039.1	2 274.1	2 279.2	2 426.6	2 190.7	2 354.4	2 226.9	2 562.0	3 781.7	4 032.3
Total	KRNJ	131 440.4	147 664.5	155 380.4	176 073.0	168 346.2	182 146.8	205 233.1	232 987.1	260 643.3	287 580.6
Current transactions (£ million)											
Mortgage advances	KRNU	28 771.7	21 988.3	23 997.9	28 233.6	29 320.0	33 077.0	43 392.4	51 089.0	50 059.4	52 327.5
Management expenses	KRNX	2 270.5	1 501.7	1 573.8	1 640.7	1 528.0	1 623.6	1 746.4	1 844.2	1 939.9	2 116.2

1 See chapter text.
2 The figures for each year relate to accounting years ending on dates between 1 February of that year and 31 January of the following year.
3 The societies which have converted to the banking sector, namely Cheltenham & Gloucester (August 1995), National & Provincial (August 1996), Alliance & Leicester (April 1997), Halifax (June 1997), Woolwich (July 1997), Bristol & West (July 1997), Northern Rock (October 1997), and Birmingham Midshires (April 1999) have been included in flow figures (using flows up to the date of conversion), but have been excluded from the end of year balances.

4 Bradford & Bingley, which converted to the banking sector in December 2000, is included within flow figures and the end of year balances.

Source: Financial Services Authority: 020 7066 1000

23.14 Consumer credit
United Kingdom

£ million

		1998	1999	2000	2001	2002	2003	2004	2005	2006	2007
Total amount outstanding	VZRD	106 341	121 547	135 168	150 802	169 209	180 649	198 856	211 037	212 785	224 352
Total net lending	VZQC	15 503	16 133	15 969	19 673	23 443	22 401	25 337	19 666	13 006	12 592
of which											
Credit cards	VZQS	4 858	5 676	6 686	6 229	7 579	8 710	9 998	6 166	1 951	2 251
Other	VZQT	10 647	10 457	9 284	13 445	15 867	13 692	15 340	13 497	11 052	10 045
Banks	AIKN	11 738	11 057	13 217	16 055	17 452	15 269	19 370	11 316	9 348	5 751
Building societies' class 3 loans	ALPY	–	12	112	63	180	177	172	238	217	260
Other consumer credit lenders	BM59	3 764	5 065	2 640	3 554	5 811	6 954	5 796	8 111	3 440	6 346
Total gross lending	VZQG	134 847	148 623	160 744	177 452	196 451	207 255	221 318	217 466	207 460	205 514

As from Dec 2006 the Bank of England has ceased to update the separate data on consumer credit provided by other specialist lenders, retailers and insurance companies previously contained in these tables. These categories have been merged into 'other consumer credit lenders'.

Source: Office for National Statistics: 01633 456635

23.15 End-year assets and liabilities of investment trust companies, unit trusts[1] and property unit trusts[2]

United Kingdom

£ million

		1996	1997	1998	1999	2000	2001	2002	2003	2004	2005	2006
Investment trust companies												
Short-term assets and liabilities (net):	CBPL	1 076	1 157	2 263	71	423	161	–	73	866	921	..
Cash and UK bank deposits	AHAG	1 424	1 577	2 647	1 227	2 202	2 513	1 821	1 346	1 756	1 483	1 785
Other short-term assets	CBPN	794	1 445	1 734	1 097	1 082	656	805	1 189	1 344	1 549	353
Short-term liabilities	-CBPS	−805	−1 865	−2 118	−2 253	−2 861	−3 008	−2 626	−2 462	−2 234	−2 111	..
Medium and long-term liabilities and capital:	-CBPO	−50 911	−54 117	−49 985	−57 616	−60 412	−54 630	−38 054	−48 076	−48 627	−55 076	..
Issued share and loan capital	-CBPQ	−8 330	−8 625	−8 837	−8 565	−8 934	−8 796	−8 711	−9 873	−8 210	−7 155	−5 492
Foreign currency borrowing	-CBPR	−638	−658	−607	−880	−994	−933	−780	−682	−607	−839	−1 043
Other borrowing	-CBQA	−823	−1 296	−1 723	−1 716	−2 503	−3 251	−2 246	−2 181	−1 728	−1 420	..
Reserves and provisions, etc	-AHBC	−41 120	−43 538	−38 818	−46 455	−47 981	−41 650	−26 317	−35 340	−38 082	−38 082	−43 444
Investments:	CBPM	50 034	53 076	46 313	56 491	59 948	54 822	37 748	48 035	47 212	53 265	50 052
British government securities	AHBF	1 422	1 052	815	1 217	821	645	471	303	466	769	533
UK company securities:												
Loan capital and preference shares	CBGZ	832	1 320	1 351	1 425	1 654	1 516	946	1 079	1 270	673	1 071
Ordinary and deferred shares	CBGY	25 046	29 082	24 729	28 010	33 456	30 338	19 475	23 292	23 941	25 037	22 870
Overseas company securities:												
Loan capital and preference shares	CBHA	279	1 165	768	979	963	1 143	458	603	682	937	741
Ordinary and deferred shares	AHCC	21 047	17 747	17 741	23 330	21 355	19 476	14 453	20 294	18 967	23 065	21 659
Other investments	CBPT	1 408	2 868	1 051	1 530	1 699	1 704	1 945	2 464	1 886	2 784	3 178
Unit trusts												
Short-term assets and liabilities:	CBPU	3 822	5 048	6 883	5 894	8 340	7 979	8 041	10 256	10 229	13 944	..
Cash and UK bank deposits	AGYE	3 895	4 731	6 020	4 797	6 969	5 748	5 321	5 243	6 302	7 740	12 336
Other short-term assets	CBPW	1 201	869	1 343	1 545	2 319	2 763	3 072	5 990	4 390	7 420	6 990
Short-term liabilities	-CBPX	−1 274	−552	−480	−448	−948	−532	−352	−977	−463	−1 216	..
Foreign currency borrowing	-AGYK	−	−	−	−	−	−	−	−	−	−	−
Investments:	CBPZ	125 841	144 038	162 929	213 553	222 844	204 899	210 002	245 516	269 064	351 645	420 153
British government securities	CBHT	2 716	3 087	3 771	3 627	4 693	4 690	7 077	9 125	9 768	25 181	31 603
UK company securities:												
Loan capital and preference shares	CBHU	5 029	6 494	9 290	13 322	14 654	16 318	21 152	23 972	22 467	29 293	29 876
Ordinary and deferred shares	RLIB	67 509	85 742	93 291	119 496	116 808	103 704	82 851	116 407	130 230	157 149	185 637
Overseas company securities:												
Loan capital and preference shares	CBHV	1 288	1 834	1 801	3 032	3 212	4 113	5 916	9 840	13 142	16 057	25 617
Ordinary and deferred shares	RLIC	47 346	42 898	51 119	70 256	79 601	71 329	63 152	75 074	81 034	105 443	127 409
Other assets	CBQE	1 953	2 518	3 657	3 820	3 876	4 800	9 997	11 098	12 801	18 522	20 011
Property unit trusts												
Short-term assets and liabilities (net)	AGVC	255	328	176	205	285	247	242	459	466	686	1 258
Property	CBQG	2 582	3 895	2 740	2 722	3 488	2 078	4 026	5 125	5 909	9 623	12 781
Other assets	AGVL	11	168	202	436	380	151	677	373	1 366	1 864	2 713
Long-term borrowing	-AGVM	−45	−247	−106	−75	−391	−90	−75	−76	−63	−250	−90

Note: Assets are shown as positive: liabilities as negative.
1 Including open ended investment companies (OEICs).
2 Investments are at market value.

Source: Office for National Statistics: 01633 812789

23.16 Self-administered pension funds: market value of assets

United Kingdom

End year

£ million

		1994	1995	1996	1997	1998	1999	2000	2001	2002	2003	2004	2005	2006
Total pension funds[1]														
Total net assets	AHVA	443 467	508 581	543 879	656 874	699 191	812 228	765 199	711 572	610 441	692 694	761 066	914 955	1 010 794
Short-term assets	RYIQ	22 617	26 114	31 521	35 368	39 005	32 703	36 638	31 337	30 700	46 091	57 476	73 649	98 691
British government securities	AHVK	41 854	52 659	57 783	80 533	91 084	98 882	92 458	83 754	84 461	88 803	87 579	94 325	104 910
UK local authority long-term debt	AHVO	250	83	89	156	183	133	177	125	42	8	4	4	2
Overseas government securities	AHVT	11 092	11 721	11 800	13 079	15 493	16 684	19 206	20 383	16 031	16 340	15 075	19 037	21 776
UK company securities														
Ordinary shares	AHVP	219 189	256 625	276 001	339 687	334 648	357 230	299 318	260 696	186 437	186 426	180 561	199 199	208 473
Other	AHVQ	3 935	7 064	6 180	5 618	8 168	9 258	16 978	22 301	30 450	37 082	43 027	48 065	54 902
Overseas company securities														
Ordinary shares	AHVR	74 813	82 164	84 163	104 187	108 884	148 335	135 514	127 893	104 392	125 740	140 282	183 060	192 978
Other	AHVS	3 045	1 184	4 909	3 851	3 842	5 099	12 736	11 781	11 386	12 475	15 996	20 502	31 536
UK loans and mortgages	RLDQ	44	34	83	160	22	14	7	3	..	35	44	6	6
UK land, property and ground rent	AHWA	24 353	21 317	21 637	24 176	24 355	31 107	32 945	30 617	31 658	30 619	30 552	31 613	34 394
Authorised unit trust units	AHVU	13 345	15 212	21 767	21 979	30 596	33 731	34 587	38 083	36 530	62 029	67 482	86 660	94 638
Property unit trusts	AHVW	2 463	2 485	2 666	3 219	3 211	5 498	4 835	5 280	5 869	6 761	10 444	16 687	20 689
Other assets	RKPL	31 318	36 352	30 628	32 978	47 136	82 273	90 841	90 139	82 490	107 229	152 170	..	..
Total liabilities	GQFX	4 852	4 412	5 347	8 118	7 436	8 719	11 041	10 819	10 005	26 944	39 626	..	..

1 These figures cover funded schemes only and therefore exclude the main superannuation arrangements in the central government sector.

Source: Office for National Statistics: 01633 812726

23.17 Insurance companies: balance sheet market values
United Kingdom
End year

£ million

		1997	1998	1999	2000	2001	2002	2003	2004	2005	2006
Long-term insurance companies											
Assets											
Total current assets (gross)	RYEW	42 795	46 165	56 360	62 937	63 855	58 122	58 518	63 407	72 754	77 748
Agents' and reinsurance balances (net)	AHNY	155	1 383	508	384	620	6 373	4 720	3 755	3 933	5 100
Other debtors[1]	RKPN	15 708	18 210	18 613	21 045	27 285	34 391	35 414	30 504	27 591	52 253
British government securities	AHNJ	107 847	127 903	126 223	116 734	119 513	131 305	142 920	157 019	161 906	161 641
UK local authority securities etc	AHNN	914	1 722	1 456	1 170	1 407	1 427	1 547	2 044	1 840	1 614
UK company securities[2]	RKPO	386 734	438 666	539 834	557 293	505 691	443 535	468 910	487 034	601 681	643 433
Overseas company securities	RKPP	73 428	82 122	120 665	107 439	127 259	110 738	110 193	130 098	165 452	194 997
Overseas government securities	AHNS	8 471	17 515	18 494	18 004	21 285	19 762	20 561	20 161	16 065	21 078
Loans and mortgages	RKPQ	8 271	11 027	10 914	9 687	10 048	10 994	12 107	12 917	13 502	15 330
UK land, property and ground rent	AHNX	42 275	45 903	50 387	49 705	53 726	52 658	57 174	60 502	61 037	58 918
Overseas land, property and ground rent	RGCP	98	252	206	1 975	498	158	184	94	27	61
Other investments	RKPR	3 416	5 654	8 334	8 385	7 420	9 513	17 985	26 480	18 146	27 783
Total	RFXN	690 112	796 522	951 994	954 760	938 609	878 979	930 233	994 015	1 143 934	1 259 956
Net value of direct investment in:											
Non-insurance subsidiaries and associate companies in the United Kingdom	RYET	3 426	3 035	3 045	6 133	4 486	4 577	4 191	3 971	8 390	13 016
UK associate and subsidiary insurance companies and insurance holding companies	RYEU	−239	148	2 245	3 586	4 206	4 569	5 054	3 473	2 528	6 114
Overseas subsidiaries and associates	RYEV	1 104	1 087	3 638	4 002	5 581	5 463	6 330	2 181	4 455	3 341
Total assets	RKBI	694 403	800 792	960 922	968 481	952 882	893 588	945 808	1 003 640	1 159 307	1 282 427
Liabilities											
Borrowing:											
Borrowing from UK banks	RGDF	3 027	3 252	6 064	8 272	8 790	4 958	4 164	5 358	5 037	2 862
Other UK borrowing	RGDE	786	1 040	3 070	2 823	5 350	7 406	10 923	8 385	9 036	9 542
Borrowing from overseas	RGDD	104	148	159	38	81	800	530	793	1 151	1 965
Long-term business:											
Funds	RKDC	581 009	669 301	800 184	838 485	831 051	794 177	824 766	873 071	1 037 658	1 125 221
Claims admitted but not paid	RKBM	1 436	1 712	2 032	2 249	2 547	3 234	3 699	3 579	3 481	3 513
Provision for taxation net of amounts receivable:											
UK authorities	RYPI	4 207	5 443	6 344	5 381	3 951	2 803	4 055	4 881	8 225	7 908
Overseas authorities	RYPJ	25	67	314	67	45	−20	2	−13	−2	199
Provision for recommended dividends	RYPK	368	359	201	183	87	32	27	93	22	13
Other creditors and liabilities	RYPL	8 083	12 509	17 042	19 031	18 468	23 261	15 870	16 738	16 907	33 192
Excess of assets over above liabilities:											
Excess of value of assets over liabilities in respect of long-term funds	RKBR	89 790	96 456	116 951	79 173	63 337	36 517	62 546	65 641	59 132	71 017
Minority interests in UK subsidiary companies	RKTI	2	–	25	–	–	–	1	267	–	–
Shareholders' capital and reserves in respect of general business	RKBS	3 862	6 299	6 139	10 287	17 044	18 629	15 698	20 719	18 717	27 315
Other reserves including profit and loss account balances	RKBT	1 704	4 206	2 396	2 492	2 130	1 791	3 527	4 129	−57	−320
Total liabilities	RKBI	694 403	800 792	960 922	968 481	952 882	893 588	945 808	1 003 640	1 159 307	1 282 427

23.17
continued

Insurance companies: balance sheet market values
United Kingdom
End year

£ million

		1997	1998	1999	2000	2001	2002	2003	2004	2005	2006
Other than long-term insurance companies											
Assets											
Total current assets (gross)	RYME	12 628	8 524	10 468	8 772	12 264	17 671	20 036	29 258	26 561	24 942
Agents' and reinsurance balances (net)	AHMX	9 405	10 528	12 177	8 362	7 941	9 492	9 890	9 858	7 996	10 782
Other debtors[1]	RKPS	5 998	6 277	7 059	7 179	9 056	14 437	13 255	12 618	13 310	16 881
British government securities	AHMJ	15 666	16 409	15 938	14 561	15 064	18 390	19 645	19 662	19 818	19 296
UK local authority securities etc	AHMN	16	14	10	8	6	10	10	49	44	–
UK company securities[2]	RKPT	18 845	18 440	18 800	18 585	17 101	15 362	15 153	20 561	21 879	22 983
Overseas company securities	RKPU	6 594	8 676	6 284	8 190	6 402	7 394	7 124	11 520	12 645	18 636
Overseas government securities	AHMS	8 215	10 459	7 980	6 849	7 134	7 156	5 720	6 662	7 341	8 035
Loans and mortgages	RKPV	1 385	1 335	1 070	1 429	1 348	1 063	1 400	2 412	3 040	3 319
UK land, property and ground rent	AHMW	2 842	1 146	1 085	1 069	860	805	859	893	1 470	1 569
Overseas land, property and ground rent	RYNK	149	107	83	45	4	1	4	5	13	137
Other investments	RKPW	2 465	2 366	2 638	2 294	1 608	2 182	1 408	1 858	2 083	2 010
Total	RKAL	84 208	84 281	84 027	77 343	78 789	93 965	94 504	115 356	116 200	128 590
Net value of direct investment in:											
Non-insurance subsidiaries and associate companies in the United Kingdom	RYNR	6 950	5 553	7 074	7 038	10 456	11 706	13 408	19 028	20 530	20 111
UK associate and subsidiary insurance companies and insurance holding companies	RYNS	4 204	6 424	5 617	5 400	8 837	7 190	2 918	2 280	6 071	4 745
Overseas subsidiaries and associates	RYNT	16 402	14 239	17 775	15 993	14 260	9 014	5 718	5 507	6 446	9 657
Total assets	RKBY	111 764	110 497	114 493	105 774	112 342	121 875	116 548	142 171	149 247	163 103
Liabilities											
Borrowing:											
Borrowing from UK banks	RYMB	3 029	1 825	1 392	783	481	1 384	2 046	4 519	893	3 148
Other UK borrowing	RYMC	2 996	1 551	3 186	4 239	10 621	10 472	9 342	10 261	11 080	10 445
Borrowing from overseas	RYMD	1 202	1 600	3 045	1 867	1 964	2 916	2 918	2 476	2 817	5 459
General business technical reserves	RKCT	59 527	60 775	59 455	60 236	60 995	62 776	63 463	67 241	71 710	77 221
Long-term business:											
Funds	RKTF	–	–	–	–	–	–	–	–	–	–
Claims admitted but not paid	RKTK	–	–	–	–	–	–	–	–	–	–
Provision for taxation net of amounts receivable:											
UK authorities	RYPO	1 253	1 197	939	874	594	941	834	1 094	1 796	2 376
Overseas authorities	RYPP	7	11	11	11	7	5	84	24	5	10
Provision for recommended dividends	RYPQ	2 048	1 318	1 817	2 682	1 957	958	1 082	1 311	5	270
Other creditors and liabilities	RYPR	3 873	3 793	4 981	6 293	6 410	8 025	9 567	10 817	10 718	16 226
Excess of assets over above liabilities:											
Excess of value of assets over liabilities in respect of long-term funds	RKCG	–	–	–	–	–	–	–	–	–	–
Minority interests in UK subsidiary companies	RKCH	60	68	29	33	276	4	6	6	–	–
Shareholders' capital and reserves in respect of general business	RKCI	35 172	34 397	35 372	24 699	26 190	31 982	25 153	39 695	43 264	42 186
Other reserves including profit and loss account balances	RKCJ	2 597	4 215	4 265	4 056	2 847	2 411	2 053	4 727	6 959	5 762
Total liabilities	RKBY	111 764	110 497	114 493	105 774	112 342	121 875	116 548	142 171	149 247	163 103

1 Including outstanding interest, dividends and rents (net).
2 Including authorised unit trust units.

Source: Office for National Statistics: 01633 812726

23.18 Individual insolvencies
United Kingdom

Numbers

		1997	1998	1999	2000	2001	2002	2003	2004	2005	2006	2007
England and Wales												
Bankruptcies[1]	AIHW	19 892	19 647	21 611	21 550	23 477	24 292	28 022	35 898	47 291	62 956	64 480
Individual voluntary arrangements[2,3]	AIHI	4 549	4 902	7 195	7 978	6 298	6 295	7 583	10 752	20 293	44 332	42 165
Total	AIHK	24 441	24 549	28 806	29 528	29 775	30 587	35 604	46 650	67 584	107 288	106 645
Scotland												
Sequestrations[4]	KRHA	2 502	3 016	3 195	2 965	3 048	3 215	3 328	3 297	4 965	5 430	6 219
Protected Trust Deeds	GJ2I	686	1 449	2 144	2 801	3 779	5 174	5 452	6 024	6 881	8 208	7 595
Total	GJ2J	3 188	4 465	5 339	5 766	6 827	8 389	8 780	9 321	11 846	13 638	13 814
Northern Ireland												
Bankruptcies[5]	KRHB	393	394	401	349	292	334	517	666	821	1 036	897
Individual voluntary arrangements[3,6]	KJRK	84	123	172	267	176	207	318	449	633	774	440
Total	KRHD	477	517	573	616	468	541	835	1 115	1 454	1 810	1 337

1 Comprises receiving and administration orders under the Bankruptcy Act 1914 and bankruptcy orders under the Insolvency Act 1986. Orders later consolidated or rescinded are included in these figures.
2 Introduced under the Insolvency Act 1986.
3 For statistical purposes deeds of arrangement are now included with individual voluntary arrangements.
4 Sequestrations awarded but not brought into operation are included in these figures.

5 Comprises bankruptcy adjudication orders, arrangement protection orders and orders for the administration of estates of deceased insolvents. Orders later set aside or dismissed are included in these figures.
6 Introduced under the Insolvency Northern Ireland order 1989.

Source: Insolvency Service: 020 7637 6504/6443

23.19 Company insolvencies
United Kingdom

Numbers

		1997	1998	1999	2000	2001	2002	2003	2004	2005	2006	2007
England and Wales												
Compulsory liquidations	AIHR	4 735	5 216	5 209	4 925	4 675	6 231	5 234	4 584	5 233	5 418	5 165
Creditors' voluntary liquidations	AIHS	7 875	7 987	9 071	9 392	10 297	10 075	8 950	7 608	7 660	7 719	7 261
Total	AIHQ	12 610	13 203	14 280	14 317	14 972	16 306	14 184	12 192	12 893	13 137	12 426
Scotland												
Compulsory liquidations	KRGA	254	338	364	344	378	556	436	431	420	416	439
Creditors' voluntary liquidations	KRGB	223	228	208	239	224	232	195	190	149	133	100
Total	KRGC	477	566	572	583	602	788	631	621	569	549	539
Northern Ireland[1]												
Compulsory liquidations	KRGD	..	..	..	..	..	49	95	76	85	78	122
Creditors' voluntary liquidations	KRGE	..	..	..	..	..	53	47	45	53	50	42
Total	KRGF	..	..	..	..	..	102	142	121	138	128	164

1 Prior to 2002, the quality of the statistics on company liquidations in Northern Ireland are not robust enough and have been removed from this table.

Source: Insolvency Service: 020 7637 6504/6443

23.20 Selected financial statistics[1]

£ million

| | Building societies | | | Net equity of households in life assurance and pension funds' reserves |
| | Advances[2] | | Unit trusts[3] | |
	Not seasonally adjusted	Seasonally adjusted		
Amount outstanding as at 31 Dec	AHIF		AGXB	
2007	266 897		468 000	
Transactions	AAMN	AHHU	AGXE	NBYD
2004	22 078	21 886	5 718	40 582
2005	20 419	20 439	12 030	51 994
2006	27 057	27 147	20 678	59 318
2007	24 975	24 861	645	83 747
2007 Q1	6 319	7 270	−1 427	18 594
Q2	6 916	6 733	3 406	15 699
Q3	6 129	4 799	287	31 419
Q4	5 611	6 059	−1 621	18 035
2007 Feb	1 441	2 241	987	..
Mar	1 912	2 094	−3 095	..
Apr	1 797	2 257	1 738	..
May	1 380	1 800	828	..
Jun	3 739	2 676	840	..
Jul	1 361	1 171	−1 842	..
Aug	2 081	1 018	989	..
Sep	2 687	2 610	1 140	..
Oct	2 057	2 847	421	..
Nov	2 231	1 587	−1 184	..
Dec	1 323	1 625	−858	..
2008 Jan	..	..	−644	..

| | Banks[4] | | | | Consumer credit[5] | | of which Credit cards[5] | |
| | UK private sector deposits | | Lending to the private sector | | | | | |
	Sterling (Not seasonally adjusted)	Other currencies	Sterling (Not seasonally adjusted)	Other currencies	Not seasonally adjusted	Seasonally adjusted	Not seasonally adjusted	Seasonally adjusted
Amount outstanding as at 31 Dec	AEAS	AGAK	AECE	AECK	VZRD	VZRI	VZRE	VZRJ
2007	1 440 779	393 694	1 836 000	522 007	224 352	223 766	56 086	54 913
Transactions					Net lending	Net lending	Net lending	Net lending
	AEAT	AEAZ	AECF		VZQC	RLMH	VZQS	VZQX
2004	86 098	27 697	133 774		25 337	25 413	9 998	9 948
2005	137 241	39 710	137 554		19 666	19 743	6 166	6 115
2006	148 695	58 393	191 018		13 006	13 104	1 951	1 963
2007	158 091	70 679	213 279		12 592	12 234	2 251	2 189
2007 Q1	42 860	21 883	57 770		1 471	2 329	−1 321	339
Q2	51 750	40 191	51 343		2 954	2 572	598	218
Q3	38 002	−3 024	81 355		3 737	3 586	941	775
Q4	25 479	11 629	22 811		4 430	3 747	2 033	857
2007 Mar	37 215	87	12 370		215	854	−312	212
Apr	11 429	28 359	17 160		1 234	653	482	105
May	21 181	17 055	22 633		921	914	−235	−174
Jun	19 140	−5 223	11 550		800	1 005	351	287
Jul	122	5 724	23 939		1 389	1 128	354	281
Aug	18 295	−655	28 551		480	1 063	162	152
Sep	19 585	−8 093	28 865		1 868	1 395	425	341
Oct	−7 825	−1 127	12 476		2 046	1 732	−41	225
Nov	9 595	32 319	4 758		1 213	1 300	698	354
Dec	23 709	−19 563	5 577		1 171	715	1 375	278
2008 Jan	3 435	24 948	29 818		976	879	−743	120
Feb	..	..	..		1 729	2 353	58	350

1 For further details see *Financial Statistics,* Tables 1.2E, 3.2B, 4.2A, 4.3A, 4.3B, 5.2D, 6.2A, 10.5D.
2 Total administered by the Department for National Savings.
3 Including open ended investment companies (OEICs).
4 Monthly figures relate to calendar months.

5 Data have been revised back to February 2003 due to the inclusion of some additional other specialist lenders and the removal of some non-resident based securitisation vehicles.

Sources: Office for National Statistics;
Department for National Savings;
Building Societies Commission;
Association of Unit Trusts and Investment Funds;
Bank of England;
Department for Business, Enterprise and Regulatory Reform

23.21 Selected interest rates, exchange rates and security prices

	Selected retail banks' base rate	Average discount rate for 91 day Treasury bills	Inter bank 3 months bid rate	Inter bank 3 months offer rate	British government securities 20 years yield[1]	Exchange rate US spot
	ZCMG	AJNB	HSAJ	HSAK	AJLX	LUSS
2004 Jan	3.75	3.96	4.05	4.10	4.75	1.8202
Feb	4.00	4.07	4.11	4.16	4.78	1.8556
Mar	4.00	4.19	4.30	4.33	4.67	1.8379
Apr	4.00	4.26	4.35	4.39	4.87	1.7735
May	4.25	4.49	4.56	4.59	4.98	1.8336
Jun	4.50	4.60	4.77	4.79	5.00	1.8137
Jul	4.50	4.74	4.86	4.89	4.92	1.8187
Aug	4.75	4.71	4.88	4.90	4.81	1.7992
Sep	4.75	4.68	4.82	4.86	4.76	1.8094
Oct	4.75	4.68	4.81	4.84	4.68	1.8324
Nov	4.75	4.64	4.77	4.80	4.58	1.9119
Dec	4.75	4.69	4.81	4.84	4.44	1.9199
2005 Jan	4.75	4.65	4.79	4.81	4.44	1.8859
Feb	4.75	4.73	4.87	4.90	4.53	1.9257
Mar	4.75	4.76	4.90	4.93	4.74	1.8904
Apr	4.75	4.69	4.86	4.88	4.60	1.9100
May	4.75	4.65	4.79	4.81	4.41	1.8225
Jun	4.75	4.52	4.69	4.73	4.29	1.7925
Jul	4.75	4.43	4.54	4.56	4.33	1.7607
Aug	4.50	4.38	4.52	4.54	4.34	1.7990
Sep	4.50	4.40	4.52	4.55	4.26	1.7688
Oct	4.50	4.42	4.54	4.56	4.36	1.7700
Nov	4.50	4.40	4.55	4.58	4.25	1.7304
Dec	4.50	4.43	4.57	4.59	4.14	1.7166
2006 Jan	4.50	4.40	4.52	4.54	3.81	1.7775
Feb	4.50	4.39	4.51	4.53	3.96	1.7511
Mar	4.50	4.41	4.54	4.56	4.15	1.7345
Apr	4.50	4.45	4.60	4.63	4.32	1.8179
May	4.50	4.51	4.66	4.68	4.43	1.8712
Jun	4.50	4.54	4.71	4.73	4.46	1.8494
Jul	4.50	4.58	4.73	4.74	4.45	1.8671
Aug	4.75	4.77	4.94	4.95	4.42	1.9018
Sep	4.75	4.87	5.02	5.05	4.29	1.8682
Oct	4.75	4.98	5.14	5.16	4.35	1.9073
Nov	5.00	5.04	5.20	5.22	4.27	1.9670
Dec	5.00	5.11	5.26	5.29	4.33	1.9570
2007 Jan	5.25	5.37	5.54	5.55	4.51	1.9574
Feb	5.25	5.31	5.48	5.50	4.59	1.9600
Mar	5.25	5.38	5.56	5.58	4.52	1.9613
Apr	5.25	5.47	5.66	5.70	4.72	1.9997
May	5.50	5.59	5.76	5.78	..	1.9782
Jun	5.50	5.77	5.93	5.98	..	2.0064
Jul	5.75	5.75	6.00	6.02	..	2.0322
Aug	5.75	5.77	6.55	6.65	4.80	2.0171
Sep	5.75	5.61	6.18	6.28	4.74	2.0374
Oct	5.75	5.57	6.17	6.25	4.74	2.0774
Nov	5.75	5.44	6.53	6.58	4.59	2.0561
Dec	5.50	5.24	5.95	5.95	4.59	1.9909
2008 Jan	5.50	5.01	5.50	5.58	4.46	1.9882
Feb	5.25	4.98	5.68	5.72	4.62	1.9892

1 Average of working days.

Source: Bank of England

23.22 Mergers and acquisitions in the UK by UK companies: category of expenditure

£ million

	Number of companies acquired	Total[1]	Cash Independent companies	Cash Subsidiaries	Issues of ordinary shares[2]	Issues of fixed interest securities[2]
	AIHA	DUCM	DWVW	DWVX	AIHD	AIHE
1997	506	26 829	6 851	4 072	15 583	323
1998	635	29 525	10 471	5 298	13 160	595
1999	493	26 163	12 605	3 615	9 592	351
2000	587	106 916	33 906	6 168	65 570	1 272
2001	492	28 994	8 489	6 704	12 356	1 445
2002	430	25 236	9 574	7 991	6 780	891
2003	558	18 679	8 956	7 183	1 667	873
2004	741	31 408	12 080	7 822	10 338	1 168
2005	769	25 134	13 425	8 510	2 768	431
2006	777	28 501	..	8 125	..	335
1997 Q4	129	16 730	1 525	2 287	12 798	120
1998 Q1	140	4 790	1 760	1 761	1 156	113
Q2	155	11 956	3 091	738	7 932	195
Q3	178	6 193	3 530	1 618	817	228
Q4	162	6 586	2 090	1 181	3 255	59
1999 Q1	117	8 735	2 299	625	5 735	76
Q2	127	7 212	4 893	728	1 509	82
Q3	145	6 479	2 618	1 682	2 098	81
Q4	104	3 737	2 795	580	250	112
2000 Q1	139	33 739	17 483	1 136	14 960	160
Q2	133	21 469	4 224	1 881	15 045	319
Q3	163	16 852	6 934	2 237	7 367	314
Q4	152	34 856	5 265	914	28 198	479
2001 Q1	131	6 181	2 606	2 255	982	338
Q2	108	4 890	1 679	2 214	555	442
Q3	129	16 079	3 457	1 526	10 649	447
Q4	124	1 844	747	709	170	218
2002 Q1	83	3 853	2 201	1 298	104	250
Q2	120	4 228	801	3 179	78	170
Q3	88	6 333	4 695	1 426	184	28
Q4	139	10 822	1 877	2 088	6 414	443
2003 Q1	107	3 857	1 003	1 892	609	353
Q2	122	3 753	1 437	1 713	258	345
Q3	153	4 700	2 495	1 919	153	133
Q4	176	6 369	4 021	1 659	647	42
2004 Q1	151	12 639	2 819	655	8 807	358
Q2	169	5 359	2 555	1 682	822	300
Q3	211	8 109	3 469	4 026	240	374
Q4	210	5 301	3 237	1 459	469	136
2005 Q1	166	3 516	1 334	1 918	166	98
Q2	215	8 983	4 869	2 715	1 285	114
Q3	211	7 287	4 106	1 878	1 207	96
Q4	177	5 348	3 116	1 999	110	123
2006 Q1	207	6 969	4 069	2 427	431	42
Q2	208	4 222	3 298	527	384	13
Q3	163	11 372	..	4 579	..	216
Q4	199	5 938	4 689	592	593	64
2007 Q1	191	5 637	2 817	346	2 332	142
Q2	203	9 539	3 576	3 821	1 862	280
Q3	216	7 262	5 375	612	331	944

Missing data for any series have been suppressed to avoid the disclosure of information relating to individual enterprises.
1 Includes deferred payments.
2 Issued to the vendor as payment.

Source: Office for National Statistics

Service industry

Chapter 24

Service industry

Annual Business Inquiry

(Tables 24.1, 24.3 and 24.4)

For details of the Annual Business Inquiry, see the text accompanying Table 22.1.

Retail trade: index numbers of value and volume

(Table 24.2)

The main purpose of the Retail Sales Inquiry (RSI) is to provide up to date information on short period movements in the level of retail sales. In principle, the RSI covers the retail activity of every business classified in the retail sector (Division 52 of the 2003 Standard Industrial Classification (SIC)) in Great Britain. A business will be classified to the retail sector if its main activity is one of the individual four digit SIC categories within Division 52. The retail activity of a business is then defined by its retail turnover, for instance the sale of all retail goods (note that petrol, for example, is not a retail good).

The RSI is compiled from the information returned to the statutory inquiries into the distribution and services sector. The inquiry is addressed to a stratified sample of 5,000 businesses classified to the retail sector, the stratification being by 'type of store' (the individual four digit SIC categories within Division 52) and by size. The sample structure is designed to ensure that the inquiry estimates are as accurate as possible. In terms of the selection, this means that:

- each of the individual four digit SIC categories are represented, their coverage depending upon the relative size of the category and the variability of the data

- within each four digit SIC category, the larger retailers tend to be fully enumerated with decreasing proportions of medium and smaller retailers

The structure of the inquiry is updated periodically, by reference to the more comprehensive results of the Annual Business Inquiry. The monthly inquiry also incorporates a rotation element for the smallest retailers. This helps to spread the burden more fairly, as well as improving the ability to represent between successive benchmarks.

During 2003, the retail sales index was rebased using detailed information from the 2000 annual business inquiry. The reference year is currently set at 2000=100. The next rebasing exercise is due to take place during 2008 when the base year will be updated to 2005=100.

The latest summary statistics are published each month by First Release. More disaggregated indices (not seasonally adjusted) are published each month in the Business Monitor SDM28, via the National Statistics website: www.statistics.gov.uk/rsi

24.1 Retail businesses[1]
United Kingdom

£ million and percentages

		2001	2002	2003	2004	2005
Number of businesses	ZABE	210 691	207 513	202 604	200 606	201 420
Total turnover[2]	ZABL	251 624	265 577	278 373	288 716	295 682
Value Added Tax in total turnover	ZABM	25 249	26 907	28 505	29 420	29 860
Retail turnover[2]	ZABN	227 298	238 456	250 849	258 903	263 859
Non-retail turnover[2]	ZABO	24 327	27 121	27 524	29 812	31 823
Other income						
Value of commercial insurance claims received	ZABP	89	105	65	40	76
Subsidies received from UK government sources and the EC	ZAEN	24	4	5	10	16
Employment costs[3]	ZABQ	28 036	29 779	31 367	32 806	34 721
Gross wages and salaries	ZABR	25 320	26 933	28 294	29 481	30 929
Redundancy and severance payments	ZABS	130	130	134	158	251
Employers' National Insurance contributions	ZABT	1 733	1 805	1 991	2 142	2 281
Contributions to pension funds	ZABU	853	911	948	1 026	1 260
Stocks						
Increase during year	ZABV	900	1 284	978	957	766
Value at end of year	ZABW	21 509	22 400	23 024	23 527	24 345
Total turnover[3] divided by end-year stocks (Quotient)	ZABX	10.5	10.7	10.9	11.0	10.9
Purchases of goods, materials and services[3]	ZABY	175 593	185 875	194 169	199 773	204 911
Goods bought for resale without processing	ZABZ	147 791	155 608	161 304	165 667	169 089
Energy and water products for own consumption	ZACA	2 028	1 918	2 048	2 191	2 516
Goods and materials	ZACB	3 544	3 845	3 917	4 166	4 394
Hiring, leasing or renting of plant, machinery and vehicles	ZACC	788	924	946	727	575
Commercial insurance premiums	ZACD	688	827	1 001	1 061	1 039
Road transport services	ZACE	1 945	2 137	2 545	2 557	2 721
Telecommunication services	ZACF	603	561	624	626	607
Computer and related services	ZACG	581	756	765	915	823
Advertising and marketing services	ZACH	2 881	3 047	3 378	3 298	3 544
Other services	ZACI	14 745	16 252	17 642	18 565	19 603
Taxes, duties and levies	ZACJ	4 432	4 576	4 715	4 896	5 834
National non-domestic (business) rates	ZACK	3 616	3 726	3 859	3 937	4 340
Other amounts paid for taxes, duties and levies	ZACL	816	850	855	958	1 495
Capital expenditure						
Cost of acquisitions	ZACM	8 469	9 355	8 776	9 936	10 157
Proceeds from disposals	ZACN	1 606	1 240	1 328	1 590	1 517
Net capital expenditure	ZACO	6 863	8 115	7 448	8 346	8 640
Amount included in acquisitions for assets under finance leasing arrangements	ZACP	474	587	304	332	301
Work of a capital nature carried out by own staff (included in acquisitions)	ZACQ	144	128	142	149	176
Gross margin						
Amount	ZACR	78 913	83 708	88 904	93 830	96 253
As a percentage of adjusted turnover[4]	ZACS	*34.9*	*34.9*	*35.6*	*36.2*	*36.2*
Approximate gross value added at basic prices	ZACT	51 201	53 545	56 104	59 764	60 507

24.1

Retail businesses[1]
United Kingdom

continued

£ million

		2001	2002	2003	2004	2005
Total turnover	ZABL	251 624	265 577	278 373	288 716	295 682
Retail turnover	ZABN	227 298	238 456	250 849	258 903	263 859
1 Fruit (including fresh, chilled, dried, frozen, canned and processed)	DSSX	4 112	3 997	4 507	4 499	4 647
2 Vegetables (including fresh, chilled, dried, frozen, canned and processed)	DSSY	6 662	6 871	8 354	8 470	9 183
3 Meat (including fresh, chilled, smoked, frozen, canned and processed)	DSSZ	11 133	11 671	13 505	13 727	13 484
4 Fish, crustaceans and molluscs (including fresh, chilled, frozen, canned and processed)	DSTA	2 200	2 299	2 549	2 671	2 860
5 Bakery products and cereals (including rice and pasta products)	DSTC	9 424	9 661	12 314	11 880	12 941
6 Sugar, jam, honey, chocolate and confectionery (including ice-cream)	DSTD	6 289	6 469	6 446	6 534	6 387
7 Alcoholic drink	DSTE	10 625	11 301	12 297	12 931	13 073
8 Non-alcoholic beverages (including tea, coffee, fruit drinks and vegetable drinks)	DSTF	5 717	6 476	6 713	7 386	7 499
9 Tobacco (excluding smokers requisites, eg pipes, lighters, etc)	DSTG	8 616	9 016	9 204	9 020	8 932
10 Milk, cheese and eggs (including yoghurts and cream)	DSTH	7 032	7 233	7 390	7 995	8 335
11 Oils and fats (including butter and margarine)	DSTI	1 314	1 222	1 162	1 287	1 327
12 Food products not elsewhere classified (including sauces, herbs, spices and soups)	DSTJ	9 986	9 185	4 112	4 399	4 319
13 Pharmaceutical products	DSTK	2 744	2 911	2 963	2 987	3 086
14 National Health Receipts	DSTL	6 981	7 740	8 647	9 006	9 669
15 Other medical products and therapeutic appliances and equipment	DSTN	2 737	2 753	3 122	3 388	3 362
16 Other appliances, articles and products for personal care	DSTO	8 543	9 611	10 698	11 111	11 393
17 Other articles of clothing, accessories for making clothing	DSTP	1 253	1 293	1 955	2 089	2 548
18 Garments	DSTQ	26 777	28 331	29 691	30 375	31 313
19 Footwear (excluding sports shoes)	DSTR	4 629	5 270	5 622	5 904	5 959
20 Travel goods and other personal effects not elsewhere classified	DSTT	848	1 007	1 175	1 120	1 125
21 Household textiles (including furnishing fabrics, curtains, etc)	DSTV	3 568	3 656	3 799	3 890	3 698
22 Household and personal appliances whether electric or not	DSUA	6 499	6 580	6 776	6 798	6 666
23 Glassware, tableware and household utensils (including non-electric)	DSUB	2 748	2 823	2 843	2 743	3 211
24 Furniture and furnishings	DSUC	11 065	12 094	13 285	13 493	13 615
25 Audio and visual equipment (including radios, televisions and video recorders)	DSUE	4 500	4 781	4 818	5 130	5 830
26 Recording material for pictures and sound (including audio and video tapes, blank and pre-recorded records, etc)	DSUG	3 304	3 591	3 788	4 488	4 362
27 Information processing equipment (including printers, software, calculators and typewriters)	DSUL	3 175	3 056	3 077	3 743	3 731
28 Decorating and DIY supplies	DSUM	6 279	6 548	6 631	7 427	6 925
29 Tools and equipment for house and garden	DSUN	2 669	3 007	3 452	2 838	2 976
30 Books	DSUP	2 366	2 752	2 748	3 004	2 646
31 Newspapers and periodicals	DSUQ	3 652	3 709	4 067	4 053	4 042
32 Stationery and drawing materials and miscellaneous printed matter	DSUW	3 601	3 864	3 824	3 989	4 193
33 Carpets and other floor coverings (excluding bathroom mats, rush and door mats)	DSUX	3 182	3 411	3 757	3 386	3 469
34 Photographic and cinematographic equipment and optical instruments	DSUZ	1 059	1 402	1 670	1 842	2 045
35 Telephone and telefax equipment (including mobile phones)	DSVA	2 398	2 238	2 293	3 272	3 204
36 Jewellery, silverware and plate; watches and clocks	DSVB	3 774	4 387	4 312	4 681	4 787
37 Works of art and antiques (including furniture, floor coverings and jewellery)	DSVF	1 820	1 509	1 493	1 619	1 711
38 Equipment and accessories for sport, camping, recreation and musical instruments	DSVH	3 861	3 624	3 803	3 732	3 578
39 Spare part and accessories for all types of vehicle and sales of bicycles	DSVI	752	1 082	572	610	550
40 Games, toys, hobbies (including video game software, video game computers that plug into the tv, video-games cassettes and CD-ROMs)	DSVM	4 624	5 468	5 962	5 920	5 727
41 Other goods not elsewhere classified (including sale of new postage stamps and sales of liquid and solid fuels)	DSVN	3 745	3 359	3 134	2 884	2 605
42 Non-durable household goods (including household cleaning, maintenance products) and paper products and other non-durable household goods	DSVO	4 352	4 405	5 017	5 429	5 279
43 Natural or artificial plants and flowers	DSVQ	3 028	3 266	3 745	3 117	3 228
44 Pets and related products (including pet food)	DSVR	2 724	2 497	2 681	3 012	3 196
45 Repair of household and personal items	DSVS	927	1 031	875	1 021	1 138

1 See chapter text.
2 Inclusive of VAT.
3 Exclusive of VAT.
4 Turnover is adjusted to take out VAT.

Source: Office for National Statistics: 01633 812435

24.2 Retail trade: index numbers of value and volume of sales[1]
Great Britain

Not seasonally adjusted

Weekly average (2000=100)

		Sales in 2000 £ million	1997	1998	1999	2000	2001	2002	2003	2004	2005	2006	2007
Value													
All retailing	EAFY	207 149	89.9	93.4	96.5	100.0	105.9	110.6	113.7	118.8	119.9	123.3	127.7
Large	EAFZ	153 022	87.4	91.7	95.8	100.0	106.5	112.2	118.2	123.9	126.0	130.8	135.9
Small	EAGA	54 128	97.4	98.6	98.5	100.0	104.1	105.8	101.1	104.1	102.9	102.2	104.7
Predominantly food stores	EAFS	89 041	88.9	93.4	96.6	100.0	106.0	110.4	114.8	119.6	123.6	128.3	132.5
Predominantly non-food stores	EAFT	106 359	90.6	93.2	96.3	100.0	106.8	111.8	114.8	119.9	119.1	121.6	125.8
Non specialised predominantly non-food stores	EAGE	18 781	91.5	92.6	95.2	100.0	105.0	107.4	109.2	111.2	110.8	114.0	118.0
Textiles, clothing, footwear and leather	EAFU	27 880	93.4	93.8	96.0	100.0	108.4	114.9	118.9	124.7	126.5	131.8	136.3
Household goods stores	EAFV	27 699	86.8	91.6	95.7	100.0	107.6	113.1	113.4	117.2	112.9	114.2	117.6
Other specialised non-food stores	EAFW	31 999	89.3	93.1	96.8	100.0	105.7	110.5	115.6	123.0	123.0	123.5	128.3
Other retail sale (non-store) and repair	EAFX	11 749	91.8	97.1	98.8	100.0	97.0	100.5	96.2	102.7	99.1	100.6	108.5
Volume													
All retailing	EAHC	207 149	89.9	92.5	95.7	100.0	106.1	112.2	116.3	123.3	125.8	129.8	135.2
Predominantly food stores	EAGW	89 041	92.9	95.5	97.2	100.0	104.1	108.2	111.9	116.5	119.7	122.7	124.0
Predominantly non-food stores	EAGX	106 359	87.4	89.9	94.3	100.0	108.5	116.2	121.3	129.6	131.8	136.4	143.9
Non specialised predominantly non-food stores	EAHI	18 781	91.5	91.5	94.0	100.0	106.0	110.5	113.8	118.0	119.3	124.1	129.9
Textiles, clothing, footwear and leather	EAGY	27 880	88.1	88.8	92.9	100.0	112.1	123.7	129.6	139.3	143.9	150.9	156.8
Household goods stores	EAGZ	27 699	80.3	85.8	92.6	100.0	109.6	117.8	122.3	130.8	131.2	137.7	147.7
Other specialised non-food stores	EAHA	31 999	90.7	93.6	97.1	100.0	105.9	111.6	117.5	127.0	129.2	130.0	137.5
Other retail sale (non-store) and repair	EAHB	11 749	88.2	93.2	96.2	100.0	99.6	106.5	105.4	117.1	118.0	123.6	141.1

1 See chapter text.

Source: Office for National Statistics

£ million and percentages

		Sale, maintenance and repair of,motor vehicles and motorcycles; retail sale of automotive fuel (SIC 2003 50.00)					Sale of motor vehicles (SIC 2003 50.10)			
		2002	2003	2004	2005		2002	2003	2004	2005
Number of businesses	MKEQ	70 338	70 080	70 265	70 993	MKER	25 856	24 895	24 199	23 924
Total turnover	CMRH	141 867	150 629	153 447	157 409	EWRI	96 968	102 242	103 594	106 901
Motor trades turnover	CMRI	136 346	145 739	147 850	152 616	FDFZ	95 885	101 377	102 579	105 881
Retail sales of:										
New cars	CMRJ	28 433	31 050	30 645	30 152	FDGA	27 065	28 597	28 427	28 188
Other new motor vehicles and motorcycles	CMRK	4 404	4 070	5 223	4 963	FDGB	3 876	3 592	4 358	3 996
Sales to other dealers of:										
New cars	CMRL	20 867	22 855	23 209	23 734	FDGC	20 773	22 336	22 790	23 415
Other new motor vehicles and motorcycles	CMRM	3 703	3 949	3 692	3 456	FDGD	3 085	3 486	3 074	2 897
Gross sales of used motor vehicles and motorcycles	CMRN	27 939	32 050	32 951	35 823	FDGE	26 337	30 106	30 560	33 565
Turnover from sales of petrol, diesel, oil and other petroleum products	CMRO	16 978	17 738	17 998	18 145	FDGF	782	1 184	806	826
Other motor trades sales and receipts (including parts and accessories, workshop receipts)	CMRP	14 256	34 027	34 131	36 342	FDGG	4 916	12 076	12 564	12 993
Non-motor trades turnover	CMRQ	5 521	4 890	5 598	4 793	FDHJ	1 083	865	1 015	1 021
Purchases of goods, materials and services										
Total purchases	CMNR	120 819	127 823	131 600	135 360	FDGH	84 354	89 198	91 714	94 363
Energy, water and materials	CMRS	1 379	1 631	1 696	2 017	FDGI	542	666	704	816
Used motor vehicles and motorcycles	COBU	24 391	27 910	29 352	31 083	FDGJ	22 939	26 239	27 397	29 192
Parts used solely in repair and servicing activities	CMRT	6 397	6 481	7 079	7 601	FDGK	2 616	2 521	2 682	2 980
Other goods for resale	CMRU	80 726	83 396	84 679	85 437	FDGL	53 512	55 108	55 864	56 129
Hiring, leasing and renting of plant, machinery and vehicles	CMRV	326	349	369	301	FDGM	131	72	84	79
Commercial insurance premiums	CMRW	465	572	561	600	FDGN	198	224	215	235
Road transport services	CMRX	740	778	753	845	FDGO	373	368	415	446
Telecommunication services	CMRY	278	335	295	302	FDGP	129	150	128	140
Computer and related services	CMRZ	306	329	388	350	FDGQ	174	170	187	199
Advertising and marketing services	CMSA	1 847	2 076	2 267	2 413	FDGR	1 611	1 742	1 897	1 970
Other services	CMSB	3 964	3 967	4 161	4 411	FDGS	2 130	1 939	2 140	2 178
Taxes, duties and levies										
Total taxes and levies	CMSC	1 002	1 048	972	1 054	FDGT	519	520	516	605
National (non-domestic business) rates	CMSD	536	611	613	644	FDGU	245	278	280	331
Other amounts paid for taxes, duties and levies	CMSE	466	437	359	409	FDGV	275	243	236	274
Capital expenditure										
Cost of acquisitions	CMSF	2 216	2 290	2 346	2 413	FDGW	1 374	1 380	1 425	1 529
Cost of disposals	CMSG	846	778	987	1 337	FDGX	593	566	671	720
Net capital expenditure	CMSH	1 370	1 512	1 359	1 076	FDGY	781	813	755	809
Work of a capital nature carried out by own staff (included in acquisitions)	CMSI	12	31	5	10	FDGZ	6	1	5	9
Stocks										
Increase during year	CMSJ	886	1 363	1 344	530	FDHA	661	1 191	1 138	263
Value at end of year	CMSK	13 217	14 437	14 923	15 528	FDHB	9 913	10 632	11 104	11 276
Total turnover divided by end-year stocks (Quotient)	CMSL	10.7	10.4	10.3	10.1	FDHC	9.6	9.6	9.3	9.5
Employment costs										
Total employment costs	CMSM	9 400	9 726	10 238	10 674	FDHD	5 024	5 056	5 327	5 546
Gross wages and salaries paid	COBP	8 409	8 669	9 062	9 361	FDHE	4 470	4 487	4 701	4 811
National insurance and pension contributions	COBQ	991	1 056	1 175	1 313	FDHF	554	569	625	735
Gross margin										
Amount	COBR	31 064	34 080	33 580	33 679	FDHG	18 536	19 556	18 770	18 822
As a percentage of adjusted turnover	COBS	*22.0*	*22.6*	*21.9*	*21.4*	FDHH	*19.7*	*19.1*	*18.1*	*17.6*
Approximate gross value added at basic prices	COBT	21 777	24 072	23 125	22 463	FDHI	13 259	14 242	13 011	12 778

24.3 Motor trades[1]
United Kingdom
continued

£ million and percentages

		Maintenance and repair of motor vehicles (SIC 2003 50.20)					Sale of motor vehicle parts and accessories (SIC 2003 50.30)			
		2002	2003	2004	2005		2002	2003	2004	2005
Number of businesses	MKES	28 438	29 188	30 050	30 973	MKET	7 715	7 799	7 952	8 066
Total turnover	FDHK	11 964	12 542	13 337	14 530	FDIW	11 068	13 801	13 694	13 666
Motor trades turnover	FDHL	11 658	12 147	13 023	14 158	FDIX	10 567	13 304	12 702	12 720
Retail sales of:										
New cars	FDHM	1 206	1 081	939	1 008	FDIY	19	1 168	1 241	..
Other new motor vehicles and motorcycles	FDHN	162	153	213	164	FDIZ	161	..	172	..
Sales to other dealers of:										
New cars	FDHO	4	8	..	..	FDJA	89	509	..	..
Other new motor vehicles and motorcycles	FDHP	–	3	..	..	FDJB	–	..	..	..
Gross sales of used motor vehicles and motorcycles	FDHQ	1 079	1 109	1 380	1 296	FDJC	143	..	374	352
Turnover from sales of petrol, diesel, oil and other petroleum products	FDHR	334	117	100	126	FDJD	85	70	86	1
Other motor trades sales and receipts (including parts and accessories, workshop receipts)	FDHS	7 891	9 674	10 386	11 541	FDJE	1 029	11 085	10 362	10 884
Non-motor trades turnover	FDHT	306	396	314	372	FDJF	501	497	992	945
Purchases of goods, materials and services										
Total purchases	FDHU	7 806	8 100	8 795	9 507	FDJG	8 611	11 062	10 958	11 273
Energy, water and materials	FDHV	528	572	652	750	FDJH	171	220	227	334
Used motor vehicles and motorcycles	FDHW	892	897	1 041	1 073	FDJI	91	..	371	347
Parts used solely in repair and servicing activities	FDHX	3 053	3 374	3 980	4 237	FDJJ	544	410	183	201
Other goods for resale	FDHY	2 170	1 774	1 453	1 727	FDJK	6 657	..	9 000	8 955
Hiring, leasing and renting of plant, machinery and vehicles	FDHZ	75	77	111	120	FDJL	60	151	136	61
Commercial insurance premiums	FDIA	139	204	227	245	FDJM	85	89	78	84
Road transport services	FDIB	13	49	104	81	FDJN	228	267	126	206
Telecommunication services	FDIC	70	97	103	97	FDJO	57	60	45	45
Computer and related services	FDID	34	61	72	39	FDJP	78	75	107	96
Advertising and marketing services	FDIE	109	127	125	113	FDJQ	70	165	208	291
Other services	FDIF	724	868	926	1 025	FDJR	568	643	478	654
Taxes, duties and levies										
Total taxes and levies	FDIG	194	197	215	217	FDJS	90	102	116	128
National (non-domestic business) rates	FDIH	142	162	152	145	FDJT	74	84	89	97
Other amounts paid for taxes, duties and levies	FDII	52	35	63	71	FDJU	16	19	27	31
Capital expenditure										
Cost of acquisitions	FDIJ	376	433	442	431	FDJV	170	221	199	193
Cost of disposals	FDIK	84	87	98	108	FDJW	106	47	54	75
Net capital expenditure	FDIL	292	346	345	323	FDJX	64	173	144	118
Work of a capital nature carried out by own staff (included in acquisitions)	FDIM	2	1	–	–	FDJY	3	29	–	–
Stocks										
Increase during year	FDIN	51	102	36	23	FDJZ	66	76	81	127
Value at end of year	FDIO	805	881	835	1 006	FDKA	1 498	1 750	1 807	1 814
Total turnover divided by end-year stocks (Quotient)	FDIP	14.6	14.2	16.0	14.4	FDKB	7.8	7.9	7.6	7.5
Employment costs										
Total employment costs	FDIQ	2 298	2 480	2 581	2 700	FDKC	1 348	1 427	1 565	1 637
Gross wages and salaries paid	FDIR	2 075	2 233	2 315	2 432	FDKD	1 209	1 268	1 391	1 440
National insurance and pension contributions	FDIS	223	247	266	268	FDKE	139	159	174	197
Gross margin										
Amount	FDIT	5 878	6 597	6 857	7 466	FDKF	3 833	4 501	4 199	4 269
As a percentage of adjusted turnover	FDIU	*49.0*	*52.6*	*51.4*	*51.4*	FDKG	*30.6*	*32.6*	*30.7*	*31.2*
Approximate gross value added at basic prices	FDIV	4 187	4 552	4 548	4 999	FDKH	2 514	2 831	2 796	2 499

24.3 Motor trades[1]
United Kingdom
continued

£ million and percentages

		Sale, maintenance and repair of motorcycles and related parts and accessories (SIC 2003 50.40)					Retail sale of automotive fuel (SIC 2003 50.50)			
		2002	2003	2004	2005		2002	2003	2004	2005
Number of businesses	MKEU	2 513	2 710	2 948	3 157	MKEV	5 816	5 488	5 116	4 873
Total turnover	FDKI	1 812	1 955	2 116	2 229	FDLV	20 056	20 089	20 708	20 083
Motor trades turnover	FDKJ	1 737	1 887	2 102	2 218	FDLW	16 500	17 024	17 444	17 639
Retail sales of:										
New cars	FDKK	–	49	–	37	FDLX	142	154	38	39
Other new motor vehicles and motorcycles	FDKL	194	215	479	570	FDLY	11	19	–	–
Sales to other dealers of:										
New cars	FDKM	–	–	–	–	FDLZ	–	1	1	2
Other new motor vehicles and motorcycles	FDKN	618	419	564	484	FDMA	–	2	–	–
Gross sales of used motor vehicles and motorcycles	FDKO	186	333	499	531	FDMB	193	160	138	79
Turnover from sales of petrol, diesel, oil and other petroleum products	FDKP	–	–	–	–	FDMC	15 776	16 367	17 006	17 191
Other motor trades sales and receipts (including parts and accessories, workshop receipts)	FDKQ	172	872	558	596	FDMD	248	319	261	328
Non-motor trades turnover	FDKR	75	68	14	11	FDME	3 556	3 065	3 263	2 444
Purchases of goods, materials and services										
Total purchases	FDKT	1 493	1 512	1 705	1 916	FDMF	18 554	17 951	18 428	18 301
Energy, water and materials	FDKU	39	59	13	21	FDMG	99	115	100	96
Used motor vehicles and motorcycles	FDKV	142	252	409	420	FDMH	328	140	134	51
Parts used solely in repair and servicing activities	FDKW	112	87	163	76	FDMI	72	90	71	108
Other goods for resale	FDKX	1 049	967	1 016	1 277	FDMJ	17 338	16 946	17 346	17 349
Hiring, leasing and renting of plant, machinery and vehicles	FDKY	4	7	1	2	FDMK	56	41	37	38
Commercial insurance premiums	FDKZ	9	23	8	12	FDML	34	32	32	25
Road transport services	FDLA	33	15	21	18	COBV	93	79	86	95
Telecommunication services	FDLB	5	9	5	6	COBW	17	20	14	14
Computer and related services	FDLC	3	4	3	5	COBX	17	18	19	11
Advertising and marketing services	FDLD	35	21	22	28	COBY	22	22	14	11
Other services	FDLE	63	67	42	50	COBZ	479	449	574	504
Taxes, duties and levies										
Total taxes and levies	FDLF	15	29	32	30	COCA	183	200	92	74
National (non-domestic business) rates	FDLG	..	..	..	..	COCB	..	..	..	..
Other amounts paid for taxes, duties and levies	FDLH	..	..	..	..	COCC	..	..	..	..
Capital expenditure										
Cost of acquisitions	FDLI	34	46	65	34	COCD	263	211	215	225
Cost of disposals	FDLJ	5	7	20	8	COCE	58	71	144	425
Net capital expenditure	FDLK	29	39	45	26	COCF	205	140	71	−201
Work of a capital nature carried out by own staff (included in acquisitions)	FDLL	1	–	–	–	COCG	–	–	–	–
Stocks										
Increase during year	FDLM	35	−8	−1	−24	COCH	72	2	90	140
Value at end of year	FDLN	302	432	391	406	COCI	698	741	786	1 026
Total turnover divided by end-year stocks (Quotient)	FDLO	6.2	4.5	5.4	5.5	COCJ	28.8	27.1	26.3	19.6
Employment costs										
Total employment costs	FDLP	144	151	155	165	COCK	587	611	610	626
Gross wages and salaries paid	FDLQ	127	136	136	148	COCL	528	545	519	529
National insurance and pension contributions	FDLR	17	15	19	16	COCM	59	66	91	97
Gross margin										
Amount	FDLS	542	630	517	422	COCN	2 275	2 796	3 238	2 701
As a percentage of adjusted turnover	FDLT	*31.0*	*32.2*	*24.4*	*18.9*	CMQN	*11.4*	*13.9*	*15.6*	*13.4*
Approximate gross value added at basic prices	FDLU	353	424	400	279	CMQO	1 464	2 022	2 370	1 908

1 See chapter text. Figures are exclusive of VAT.

Source: Office for National Statistics: 01633 812435

24.4 Catering and allied trades[1]
United Kingdom

£ million and percentages

		Total catering and allied trades (SIC 2003 55.00)					Hotels and motels (SIC 2003 55.11 and 55.12)			
		2002	2003	2004	2005		2002	2003	2004	2005
Number of businesses	MKEK	122 714	123 491	126 706	130 180	MKEL	10 800	10 535	10 417	10 252
Total turnover[2]	CMKX	60 603	63 412	70 199	71 334	CMLW	11 824	12 172	13 009	12 898
Taxes and levies[3]										
Total taxes and levies	CMLM	1 594	1 622	1 848	1 928	CMML	373	395	427	446
National (non-domestic business) rates	CMLJ	1 481	1 495	1 673	1 733	CMMI	359	380	400	425
Other amounts paid for taxes, duties and levies	CMLL	113	126	175	195	CMMK	14	15	27	22
Capital expenditure[3]										
Capital acquisitions	CMLP	4 491	4 068	4 122	4 591	CMMO	1 127	960	934	1 085
Capital disposals	CMLQ	670	850	612	1 169	CMMP	225	144	150	360
Net capital expenditure	CMLK	3 820	3 217	3 510	3 422	CMMJ	902	815	783	725
Work of a capital nature carried out by your own staff (included in acquisitions)	CMLR	25	31	12	31	CMMQ	13	12	4	5
Stocks[3]										
Increase during year	CMLN	44	42	75	60	CMMM	−12	2	2	5
Value at end of year	CMLO	1 132	1 106	1 253	1 463	CMMN	231	169	168	153
Purchases of goods and services[3]										
Total purchases	CMLI	27 408	29 230	31 813	33 190	CMMH	4 327	4 521	4 838	4 966
Energy, water and materials	CMKZ	10 608	12 130	13 374	12 786	CMLY	1 729	2 015	2 043	2 000
Goods for resale	CMLA	8 173	8 851	9 555	11 408	CMLZ	468	489	583	690
Hiring, leasing of plant, machinery etc.	CMLB	350	275	303	259	CMMA	51	54	66	45
Commercial insurance premiums	CMLC	430	494	545	522	CMMB	106	124	135	129
Road transport services	CMLD	115	96	103	146	CMMC	19	22	8	10
Telecommunication services	CMLE	239	260	265	249	CMMD	61	71	68	56
Computer and related services	CMLF	141	149	169	193	CMME	45	50	45	68
Advertising and marketing services	CMLG	661	686	713	721	CMMF	178	183	203	196
Other services	CMLH	6 691	6 289	6 786	6 905	CMMG	1 670	1 513	1 687	1 772
Employment costs[3]										
Total employment costs	CMKY	13 504	14 116	15 287	16 414	CMLX	3 021	3 159	3 270	3 520
Gross wages and salaries paid	CMKV	12 475	12 998	14 075	15 021	CMLU	2 760	2 865	2 993	3 171
National insurance and pension contributions	CMKW	1 029	1 118	1 212	1 393	CMLV	260	294	277	350
Gross margin[4]										
Amount	CMQP	43 943	45 747	51 047	50 268	CMQS	9 610	9 889	10 525	10 312
As a percentage of turnover	CMQQ	*84.2*	*83.7*	*84.1*	*81.4*	CMQT	*95.5*	*95.3*	*94.6*	*93.7*
Value added at basic prices[4]	CMQR	24 786	25 435	28 833	28 511	CMQU	5 759	5 864	6 272	6 044
Accommodation										
Number of establishments	CMLS	23 559	28 209	28 332	83 134	CMMR	12 874	13 974	14 190	24 367
Letting bedplaces	CMLT	2 071 308	2 214 366	2 676 991	2 441 159	CMMS	1 022 079	1 198 410	964 733	1 589 498

24.4 Catering and allied trades[1]
United Kingdom
continued

£ million and percentages

		Camping sites and other provision of short-stay accommodation (SIC 2003 55.21 to 55.23)					Restaurants or cafes, take-away food shops (SIC 2003 55.30)			
		2002	2003	2004	2005		2002	2003	2004	2005
Number of businesses	MKEM	4 175	4 370	4 703	5 027	MKEN	54 340	55 475	57 674	60 539
Total turnover[2]	CMMV	2 631	3 032	3 620	3 696	CMNU	18 843	20 145	21 731	22 612
Taxes and levies[3]										
Total taxes and levies	CMNK	74	79	90	91	CMOJ	508	515	556	627
National (non-domestic business) rates	CMNH	73	75	81	83	CMOG	468	469	483	544
Other amounts paid for taxes, duties and levies	CMNJ	1	4	8	7	CMOI	40	46	73	83
Capital expenditure[3]										
Capital acquisitions	CMNN	364	345	336	444	CMOM	1 222	1 117	1 153	1 341
Capital disposals	CMNO	38	192	55	47	CMON	112	187	130	254
Net capital expenditure	CMNI	326	153	281	397	CMOH	1 110	930	1 023	1 088
Work of a capital nature carried out by your own staff (included in acquisitions)	CMNP	–	2	–	17	CMOO	4	3	4	8
Stocks[3]										
Increase during year	CMNL	4	2	10	19	CMOK	25	5	12	13
Value at end of year	CMNM	89	102	137	194	CMOL	295	313	326	340
Purchases of goods and services[3]										
Total purchases	CMNG	1 184	1 461	1 747	1 753	CMOF	8 637	9 546	10 056	10 607
Energy, water and materials	CMMX	249	360	449	442	CMNW	4 144	4 775	5 080	4 810
Goods for resale	CMMY	390	411	594	585	CMNX	2 067	2 345	2 399	3 118
Hiring, leasing of plant, machinery etc.	CMMZ	9	8	14	10	CMNY	62	54	47	38
Commercial insurance premiums	CMNA	29	59	59	48	CMNZ	119	117	140	138
Road transport services	CMNB	10	7	11	17	CMOA	38	30	51	55
Telecommunication services	CMNC	12	19	17	18	CMOB	67	71	72	71
Computer and related services	CMND	7	8	13	15	CMOC	28	34	41	46
Advertising and marketing services	CMNE	73	112	111	101	CMOD	248	231	251	268
Other services	CMNF	405	476	480	516	CMOE	1 865	1 888	1 975	2 063
Employment costs[3]										
Total employment costs	CMMW	488	554	578	682	CMNV	4 031	4 276	4 642	5 137
Gross wages and salaries paid	CMMT	450	507	523	617	CMNS	3 751	3 971	4 305	4 731
National insurance and pension contributions	CMMU	38	47	55	65	CMNT	280	305	337	406
Gross margin[4]										
Amount	CMQV	1 921	2 260	2 586	2 739	CMQY	14 085	14 936	16 289	16 366
As a percentage of turnover	CMQW	*83.2*	*84.7*	*81.4*	*83.2*	CMQZ	*87.6*	*86.3*	*86.9*	*83.8*
Value added at basic prices[4]	CMQX	1 128	1 212	1 435	1 573	CMRA	7 544	7 744	8 660	8 885
Accommodation										
Number of establishments	CMNQ	4 247	6 962	6 255	43 033	CMOP	1 809	1 965	1 604	4 195
Letting bedplaces	CMRR	895 191	857 489	1 533 656	674 684	CMOQ	55 406	51 974	42 383	65 339

24.4 Catering and allied trades[1]
United Kingdom

continued

£ million and percentages

		Licensed clubs with entertainment, independent, tenanted, managed public houses or wine bars (SIC 2003 55.40)[5]					Canteen operator, catering contractor (SIC 2003 55.51 and 55.52)			
		2002	2003	2004	2005		2002	2003	2004	2005
Number of businesses	MKEO	47 914	47 475	48 147	48 400	MKEP	5 485	5 636	5 765	5 962
Total turnover[2]	CMOT	20 681	21 392	24 455	23 826	CMPS	6 624	6 670	7 383	8 302
Taxes and levies[3]										
Total taxes and levies	CMPI	611	602	748	726	CMQH	27	31	28	38
National (non-domestic business) rates	CMPF	557	548	688	652	CMQE	24	23	21	28
Other amounts paid for taxes, duties and levies	CMPH	54	53	59	73	CMQG	3	8	8	10
Capital expenditure[3]										
Capital acquisitions	CMPL	1 634	1 482	1 489	1 572	CMQK	144	164	211	148
Capital disposals	CMPM	284	317	260	483	CMQL	12	11	17	25
Net capital expenditure	CMPG	1 350	1 166	1 229	1 090	CMQF	132	153	194	123
Work of a capital nature carried out by your own staff (included in acquisitions)	CMPN	8	13	4	1	CMQM	–	–	–	–
Stocks[3]										
Increase during year	CMPJ	19	28	41	8	CMQI	8	6	9	15
Value at end of year	CMPK	414	409	512	639	CMQJ	102	112	109	138
Purchases of goods and services[3]										
Total purchases	CMPE	10 222	10 675	11 844	12 001	CMQD	3 037	3 028	3 328	3 863
Energy, water and materials	CMOV	2 408	2 959	3 458	3 013	CMPU	2 078	2 022	2 344	2 521
Goods for resale	CMOW	4 836	5 151	5 522	6 425	CMPV	411	455	457	591
Hiring, leasing of plant, machinery etc.	CMOX	188	116	138	120	CMPW	42	44	38	45
Commercial insurance premiums	CMOY	148	150	182	170	CMPX	27	44	30	37
Road transport services	CMOZ	26	25	17	44	CMPY	23	13	15	20
Telecommunication services	CMPA	79	79	86	77	CMPZ	20	20	23	28
Computer and related services	CMPB	39	33	48	39	CMQA	22	24	22	26
Advertising and marketing services	CMPC	136	127	129	122	CMQB	26	32	19	35
Other services	CMPD	2 362	2 036	2 264	1 993	CMQC	389	374	380	561
Employment costs[3]										
Total employment costs	CMOU	3 745	3 834	4 294	4 373	CMPT	2 219	2 293	2 503	2 702
Gross wages and salaries paid	CMOR	3 484	3 566	3 974	4 034	CMPQ	2 029	2 090	2 281	2 469
National insurance and pension contributions	CMOS	260	268	320	339	CMPR	190	204	222	233
Gross margin[4]										
Amount	CMRB	12 819	13 182	15 408	13 941	CMRE	5 508	5 480	6 238	6 911
As a percentage of turnover	CMRC	*72.7*	*71.9*	*73.6*	*68.3*	CMRF	*90.9*	*92.3*	*93.2*	*92.3*
Value added at basic prices[4]	CMRD	7 469	7 708	9 098	8 370	CMRG	2 885	2 907	3 368	3 639
Accommodation										
Number of establishments	CMPO	3 970	5 018	6 046	11 288					
Letting bedplaces	CMPP	71 214	77 371	110 130	84 174					

1 See chapter text.
2 Inclusive of VAT.
3 Exclusive of VAT.

4 The total turnover figure used to calculate these data excludes VAT.
5 Includes figures for managed public houses owned by breweries.

Source: Office for National Statistics: 01633 812435

Sources

This index of sources gives the titles of official publications or other sources containing statistics allied to those in the tables of this *Annual Abstract*. These publications provide more detailed analyses than are shown in the *Annual Abstract*. This index includes publications to which reference should be made for short-term (monthly or quarterly) series. Further advice on published statistical sources is available from the National Statistics Customer Contact Centre on the numbers provided on page ii.

Table number in Abstract	Government department or other organisation	Official publication or other source

Chapter 1: Area

1.1	Ordnance Survey Ordnance Survey of Northern Ireland	
	Office for National Statistics	Regional Trends (annual, Palgrave Macmillan)

Chapter 2: Parliamentary elections

Elections

2.1	University of Plymouth for the Electoral Commission	British Electoral Facts 1832-1999 (Ashgate) Dod's Parliamentary Companion (annual)

By-elections

2.2	University of Plymouth for the Electoral Commission	Vachers Parliamentary Companion (quarterly) Social Trends (annual, Palgrave Macmillan)

Chapter 3: International development

3.1 – 3.2	Department for International Development	Statistics on International Development 2002/03-2006/07, Tables 1, 2, 3, 14 and 18

Chapter 4: Defence

4.1 – 4.11	Ministry of Defence/DASA	UK Defence Statistics 2005 (The Stationery Office (TSO))

Chapter 5: Population

Population **Census**

5.1, 5.2, 5.3, 5.5	Office for National Statistics	*England and Wales*: Census reports 1911, 1921, 1931, 1951, 1961, 1971, 1981, 1991 and 2001 Key Population and Vital Statistics; Great Britain, Digest of Welsh Statistics (annual, Welsh Assembly Government)
	General Register Office Scotland	*Scotland*: Census reports 1951, 1961, 1971, 1981, 1991 and 2001

Table number in Abstract	Government department or other organisation	Official publication or other source
	Northern Ireland Statistics and Research Agency	*Northern Ireland*: Census of population 1951, 1961, 1966, 1971, 1981, 1991 and 2001
		Resident population: mid-year estimates
5.1, 5.2, 5.3, 5.5	Office for National Statistics	*England and Wales*: Series FM (Family statistics), DH (Death), MB (Morbidity), PP (Population estimates and projections), MN (Migration) and VS (Key population and vital statistics) Series PP1, Population estimates: The Registrar General's estimates of the population of regions and local government areas of England and Wales Population Trends (quarterly Palgrave Macmillan)
		Health Statistics Quarterly (Palgrave Macmillan)
	General Register Office Scotland	*Scotland*: Annual report of the Registrar General for Scotland Annual estimate of the population of Scotland
	Northern Ireland Statistics and Research Agency	*Northern Ireland*: Annual report of the Registrar General
5.6	Office for National Statistics	
Projections		
5.1, 5.2, 5.3	Office for National Statistics Government Actuary's Department	Series PP2, Population projections – national figures
Migration		
5.7, 5.8, 5.9	Office for National Statistics	International Migration - first release of 2006 estimates Series MN (International migration) Population Trends (quarterly, Palgrave Macmillan)
5.10	Home Office	Control of immigration statistics United Kingdom (annual) Asylum Statistics United Kingdom (annual)
Vital statistics		
5.4, 5.12 – 5.22	Office for National Statistics	*England and Wales*: Series FM (Births, marriages and divorce statistics) DH (Deaths), MB (Morbidity), PP (Population estimates and projections), MN (International migration) and VS (Key population and vital statistics)
	General Register Office Scotland	*Scotland*: Annual report of the Registrar General for Scotland Quarterly return of births, deaths and marriages
	Northern Ireland Statistics and Research Agency	*Northern Ireland*: Annual report of the Registrar General Quarterly return of births, deaths and marriages
5.14	Northern Ireland Court Service	Northern Ireland Judicial Statistics (annual)
5.18	Scottish Government Department of Health	

Sources

Table number in Abstract	Government department or other organisation	Official publication or other source
5.22	Government Actuary's Department	*England and Wales*: Interim Life Table Scotland: Interim Life Table *Northern Ireland*: Annual Report of the Registrar General
5.23	Office for National Statistics General Register Office (Scotland) Northern Ireland Statistics and Research Agency	

Chapter 6: Education

6.1 – 6.11	Department for Children, Schools and Families (DCSF)	Education and Training Statistics for United Kingdom (Internet only) (annual, DCSF)
	Department For Innovation, Universities And Skills (DIUS)	United Kingdom higher education statistics (annual and ad-hoc, DIUS/Higher Education Statistics Agency (HESA))
	Welsh Assembly Government (WAG)	*Wales*: Statistics of education and training in Wales (annual and ad-hoc, WAG)
	Scottish Government (SG)	*Scotland*: Scottish educational statistics (annual and ad-hoc, SG)
	Northern Ireland Department of Education (DENI) Northern Ireland Department for Employment and Learning (DELNI)	*Northern Ireland*: Northern Ireland education statistics (annual and ad-hoc, DENI) Northern Ireland further and higher education statistics (annual and ad-hoc, DELNI)

Chapter 7: Labour market

Labour force survey

7.1 – 7.3, 7.6, 7.9, 7.10, 7.11, 7.13, 7.16 – 7.18	Office for National Statistics	Economic and Labour Market review (monthly, Palgrave Macmillan)
7.4, 7.5	Office for National Statistics	
7.7	Office for National Statistics	Labour Market Statistics
7.8	Cabinet Office	Civil Service Statistics Monthly Digest of Statistics (Palgrave Macmillan)
7.9	Office for National Statistics Home Office	Economic and Labour Market review (monthly, PalgraveMacmillan)
	Scottish Executive	

Claimant count

7.12, 7.14, 7.15, 7.25	Office for National Statistics	Economic and Labour Market review (monthly, Palgrave Macmillan)

Table number in Abstract	Government department or other organisation	Official publication or other source
7.19	Office for National Statistics	Economic and Labour Market review (monthly, Palgrave Macmillan) Monthly Digest of Statistics (Palgrave Macmillan)

Annual Survey of Hours and Earnings

7.20, 7.21, 7.24, 7.25	Office for National Statistics	Annual Survey of Hours and Earnings (annual, ONS)

Average Earnings Index

7.22, 7.23	Office for National Statistics	Economic and Labour Market review (monthly, Palgrave Macmillan) Monthly Digest of Statistics (Palgrave Macmillan)
7.26	Certification Office	Certification Officers Annual Report

Chapter 8: Personal income, expenditure and wealth

8.1	Board of HMRC	HMRC National Statistics www.hmrc.gov.uk www.statistics.gov.uk/cci/article.asp?ID=1804
8.2	Office for National Statistics	National Statistics (www.statistics.gov.uk/cci/article.asp?ID=1804)
8.3 - 8.5	Office for National Statistics	Expenditure and Food Survey, (annual) (1990 onwards edition-Family Spending) (annual, Palgrave Macmillan)

Chapter 9: Health

National Health Service

9.1	Information Centre for health and social care	Hospital Episode Statistics, England (Annual) General Pharmaceutical Services in England and Wales 1996 – 2006
	Department of Health	*England*: Appropriation Accounts (annual) Health and Personal Social Services Statistics for England (annual)
	Welsh Assembly Government	*Wales*: Health Statistics Wales (annual)
9.2	The Scottish Government, ISD Scotland part of NHS National Services Scotland	
9.3	Department of Health, Social Services and Public Safety (Northern Ireland)	Summary of Health and Personal Social Services (Northern Ireland) Accounts (annual) Hospital Statistics (annual)
9.4, 9.5	NHS Information Centre for health and social care	*England*: Health and Personal Social Services Statistics for England (annual) NHS Hospital and Community Health Services (HCHS):

Table number in Abstract	Government department or other organisation	Official publication or other source
	Welsh Assembly Government	*Wales*: Health Statistics Wales (annual)
	The Scottish Government, ISD Scotland part of NHS National Services Scotland	

Public Health

9.6	Office for National Statistics	*England and Wales*: Mortality statistics cause series DH2
	General Register Office Scotland	*Scotland*: Annual Report of the Registrar General for Scotland
	Northern Ireland Statistics and Research Agency	*Northern Ireland*: Annual Report of the Registrar General for Northern Ireland
9.7	HPA Centre for Infections	*England and Wales*: Communicable Disease Statistics Series MB2 (annual) Annual Review of Communicable Diseases
	NHS in Scotland NHS National Services Scotland	*Scotland*: Scottish Health Statistics (annual)
	Communicable Disease Surveillance Centre (NI)	*Northern Ireland*: Annual report of the Registrar General Northern Ireland
9.8 – 9.10	Health and Safety Executive	Health and Safety Statistics (annual)

Chapter 10: Social protection

Social security pensions, benefits and allowances

10.1	Department for Work and Pensions HM Revenue and Customs Department of Health, Social Services and Public Safety (Northern Ireland)	National Insurance Fund Account (annual)
10.2	Department for Work and Pensions HM Revenue and Customs	
10.3	HM Revenue and Customs	
10.4, 10.5	Department for Work and Pensions (Information and Analysis Directorate) Ministry of Defence/DASA (Pay and Pensions)	Work and Pensions Longitudinal Study (WPLS, 100% sample)
	HM Revenue and Customs	
10.6 – 10.8, 10.12 – 10.19	Department for Work and Pensions (Information and Analysis Directorate)	Work and Pensions Longitudinal Study (WPLS, 100% sample)
10.9, 10.11	HM Revenue and Customs	
10.15	Ministry of Defence/DASA (Health Information)	

Table number in Abstract	Government department or other organisation	Official publication or other source
Working Family Tax Credit		
10.10	Working Family Tax Credit Department for Work and Pensions (Information and Analysis Directorate)	Quarterly Enquiry United Kingdom (quarterly)
Social services		
10.20 – 10.24	Office for National Statistics Department for Education and Skills	Appropriation (annual) Northern Ireland Annual Abstract of Statistics
10.20	HM Treasury	HM Treasury Expenditure Statistical Analyses
Housing and community amenities		
10.25	Office for National Statistics	

Chapter 11: Crime and justice

11.1	Home Office	*England and Wales*: Police Service Strength England and Wales 2007 Home Office Statistical Bulletin 02/08
	Scottish Government Justice Analytical Services	
	The Police Service of Northern Ireland	*Northern Ireland*: The Chief Constable's Annual Report
11.3	Home Office	Crime in England and Wales 2003/04 (Home Office Statistical Bulletin 10/04) Crime in England and Wales 2005/06 (Home Office Statistical Bulletin 12/06) Crime in England and Wales 2006/07 (Home Office Statistical Bulletin 11/07)
11.4 – 11.9	Office for Criminal Justice Reform	Criminal Statistics, England and Wales (annual) (TSO) Offender Management Caseload Statistics 2003 (annual) Digest of Welsh Statistics (annual, Welsh Office)
11.2, 11.10, 11.11	Ministry of Justice	Sentencing Statistics 2006 England & Wales Offender Management Caseload Statistics 2006
11.12	Ministry of Justice	HM Prison Service Annual Report and Accounts April 2006 – March 2007
11.13	Scottish Government Justice Analytical Services	Recorded Crime in Scotland, 2005/06
11.14 – 11.17	Scottish Government Justice Analytical Services	Criminal Proceedings in Scottish Courts, 2005/06
11.18, 11.19	Scottish Government Justice Department	Prison Statistics Scotland, 2002 Scottish Prison Service Annual Report and Accounts

Table number in Abstract	Government department or other organisation	Official publication or other source
11.20	The Police Service of Northern Ireland	
11.21 – 11.24	Northern Ireland Office	A Commentary on Northern Ireland Crime Statistics 2004 'Court Prosecutions and Sentencing 2005' NIO Research and Statistical Bulletin 3/2008 The Northern Ireland Prison Population in 2006

Chapter 12: Lifestyles

12.1	Department for Culture, Media and Sports	
12.2	Department for Culture, Media and Sports	
12.3	Department for Culture, Media and Sports	
12.4	CAA Nielsen EDI	
12.5	UK Film Council	
12.6	Visit Britain	United Kingdom Tourism Survey
12.7 – 12.8	Office for National Statistics	International Passenger Survey Overseas Travel & Tourism MQ6 Overseas Travel & Tourism First Release Travel Trends
12.9	Target Group Index, BMRB International	
12.10	Department for Culture, Media and Sports Gaming Board for Great Britain	www.gbgb.org.uk

Chapter 13: Environment

13.1, 13.2, 13.5, 13.18, 13.22	Office for National Statistics	Environmental Accounts Autumn 2007 www.statistics.gov.uk/downloads/theme_environment/EADec2007.pdf
13.3, 13.4, 13.6, 13.7, 13.8, 13.11, 13.16	Department for Environment Food and Rural Affairs	e-Digest of Environmental Statistics (annual) www.defra.gov.uk/environment/statistics/index.htm The Environment in your Pocket (annual)
13.9, 13.13	Centre for Ecology and Hydrology, Wallingford	www.ceh-nerc.ac.uk/data/NWA.htm
13.10	The Met Office	www.met-office.gov.uk

Table number in Abstract	Government department or other organisation	Official publication or other source
13.12	Scottish Environment Protection agency	www.sepa.org.uk/pdf/data/classification/water_qual_class_2006.pdf
13.14	Water Services Regulation Authority (OFWAT)	Companies 2007 June Return to OFWAT (annual)
13.15	Environment Agency	*England and Wales*: www.environment-agency.gov.uk
	Scottish Environment Protection agency	*Scotland*: www.sepa.org.uk
	Environment & Heritage Services Northern Ireland	*Northern Ireland*: www.ehsni.gov.uk
13.17	Environment Agency	www.environment-agency.gov.uk
13.19, 13.20	Department for Environment Food and Rural Affairs	*England*: www.defra.gov.uk/environment/statistics/index.htm
	Welsh Assembly Government	*Wales*: www.wales.gov.uk/statistics
	Scottish Environment Protection agency	*Scotland*: www.sepa.org.uk
	Environment & Heritage Services Northern Ireland	*Northern Ireland*: www.ehsni.gov.uk
13.21	The Chartered Institute of Environmental Health	
	The Royal Environmental Health Institute of Scotland	

Chapter 14: Housing

14.1	Communities and Local Government	
	Welsh Assembly Government	
	Scottish Government	
	Department for Social Development, Northern Ireland	
14.2	Office for National Statistics	General Household Survey
14.3	Communities and Local Government	
	Welsh Assembly Government	*Wales*: Welsh Housing Statistics (annual, WAG)
	Scottish Government	*Scotland*: Statistical Bulletins on Housing (SG)

Table number in Abstract	Government department or other organisation	Official publication or other source
	Department for Social Development, Northern Ireland	*Northern Ireland*: Northern Ireland Housing Statistics (annual)
14.4	Communities and Local Government	
14.5	Communities and Local Government	
	Welsh Assembly Government	
14.6	Council of Mortgage Lenders	
14.7	HM Court Service	
	Northern Ireland Court Service	
14.8	Communities and Local Government	
	Welsh Assembly Government	
	Scottish Government	
14.9	Communities and Local Government	Statutory Homelessness Statistical Release (quarterly) www.communities.gov.uk/index.asp?id=1156302

Chapter 15: Transport and communications

General

15.1, 15.2, 15.4	Department for Transport	
15.3	Office for National Statistics	

Road Transport

15.5 – 15.12	Department for Transport	Office for National Statistics (annual, TSO) Vehicle Licensing Statistics (annual, TSO) Monthly Digest of Statistics (Palgrave Macmillan) Road Casualties Great Britain (annual, TSO) Road accidents Wales (annual, National Assembly for Wales) Office for National Statistics: Department for Transport
15.11		Driving Standards Agency
15.13, 15.14	Department for Regional Development, Northern Ireland	Publication: Transport Statistics NISource: Driver and Vehicle Agency

Rail Transport

15.20, 15.21	Department for Transport	Office for National Statistics (annual, TSO) Health and Safety Executive: Industry and Services (annual) Bulletin of Rail Statistics (quarterly)
15.22, 15.23	Department for Regional Development, Northern Ireland	Translink

Table number in Abstract	Government department or other organisation	Official publication or other source
Air Transport		
15.24 – 15.28	Civil Aviation Authority	Monthly Digest of Statistics (Palgrave Macmillan) Civil Aviation Authority; Annual Statements of Movements, Passengers and Cargo Civil Aviation Authority; Monthly Statements of Movements, Passengers and Cargo
Sea Transport		
15.29, 15.30	Department for Transport	Maritime Statistics (annual, TSO) Monthly Digest of Statistics (Palgrave Macmillan)
Communications		
15.31	Royal Mail Parcel Force Capita Business Services Ltd Post Office Counters Ltd	Monthly Digest of Statistics (Palgrave Macmillan) Post Office report and accounts (annual)

Chapter 16: National accounts

16.1 – 16.22	Office for National Statistics	United Kingdom National Accounts (annual, Palgrave Macmillan) Monthly Digest of Statistics (Palgrave Macmillan)

Chapter 17: Prices

Producer Prices		
17.1, 17.2	Office for National Statistics	Producer Price Index Press Notice (monthly) Business Monitor MM22, Producer Price Indices Monthly Digest of Statistics (Palgrave Macmillan)
Consumer Prices		
17.3 – 17.6	Office for National Statistics	Monthly Digest of Statistics (Palgrave Macmillan) Economic and Labour Market review (monthly, Palgrave Macmillan) Focus on Consumer Price Indices (monthly, National Statistics website)
17.7, 17.8	Department for Environment, Food and Rural Affairs	Agriculture in the UK (annual) Agricultural Price Indices, Statistical notice (monthly) Monthly Digest of Statistics (Palgrave Macmillan)
17.9	Department for Environment, Food and Rural Affairs	Agriculture in the UK (annual) Economic & Labour Market Review (monthly, Palgrave Macmillan) UK Economic Accounts (quarterly, Palgrave Macmillan)

Chapter 18: Government finance

Central Government		
18.1 – 18.3	Office for National Statistics	Financial Statistics (monthly, Palgrave Macmillan)

Sources

Table number in Abstract	Government department or other organisation	Official publication or other source
18.4	HM Treasury Office for National Statistics	Consolidated Fund and National Loans Fund Accounts Financial Statistics (monthly, Palgrave Macmillan)
18.5	HM Treasury Office for National Statistics	United Kingdom National Accounts (annual, Palgrave Macmillan)
18.6 – 18.7	HM Treasury	Consolidated Fund and National Loans Fund Accounts Financial Statistics (monthly, Palgrave Macmillan)
18.8	Office for National Statistics	
18.9, 18.10	HM Revenue & Customs	www.hmrc.gov.uk

Rateable values

18.11	HM Revenue & Customs	www.hmrc.gov.uk

Local Authorities

18.12, 18.13	Communities and Local Government Welsh Assembly Government Public Works Loan Board Scottish Executive Statistical Support for Local Government Department of Finance and Personnel for Northern Ireland Department of the Environment for Northern Ireland Chartered Institute of Public Finance and Accountancy	Local government financial statistics (England) (annual) Welsh local government financial statistics (annual) Annual report of the Public Works Loan Board Local Financial Returns (Scotland) (annual)
18.14	Communities and Local Government Welsh Assembly Government	Local government financial statistics (England) (annual) Welsh local government financial statistics (annual)
18.15, 18.16	Communities and Local Government	Local government financial statistics (England) (annual)
18.17 – 18.19	Scottish Executive Statistical Support for Local Government (Scotland)	Local financial returns (Scotland) (annual) Capital Returns (annual)
18.20	Department of the Environment for Northern Ireland	District Council - Summary of Statement of Accounts (annual)

Chapter 19: External trade and investment

19.1 – 19.8	HM Revenue & Customs	OTS1 – Overseas Trade Statistics – Extra EC, (formerly MM20) (monthly) OTS2 – Overseas Trade Statistics – Intra EC and World (formerly MM20A) (monthly) OTSQ – Overseas Trade Statistics – Intra EC, (formerly MQ20) (quarterly) OTSA – Overseas Trade Statistics – Extra and Intra EC (formerly MA20) (annual)

Table number in Abstract	Government department or other organisation	Official publication or other source
	Office for National Statistics	Business Monitor MM24, Monthly Review of External Trade Statistics (monthly, Palgrave Macmillan) Overseas Trade Analysed in Terms of Industries MQ10 (quarterly, Palgrave Macmillan) Monthly Digest of Statistics (monthly, Palgrave Macmillan)
19.9 – 19.18	Office for National Statistics Bank of England	United Kingdom Balance of Payments (annual, Palgrave Macmillan) (quarterly, Palgrave Macmillan) figures: UK Economic Accounts Financial Statistics (monthly, Palgrave Macmillan) Foreign Direct Investment MA4 (annual, National Statistics website)

Chapter 20: Research and development

20.1 – 20.5	Office for National Statistics	Business Monitor MA14, Research and Development in UK Business (annual, ONS)

Chapter 21: Agriculture, fisheries and food

Agriculture

21.1, 21.2	Department for Environment Food and Rural Affairs	Agriculture in the United Kingdom 2007 (annual)
21.3 – 21.5 21.7 – 21.13	Department for Environment Food and Rural Affairs	Agriculture in the United Kingdom 2007 (annual)
21.6	Forestry Commission Department of agriculture and Rural Development (Northern Ireland)	Forestry Statistics (annual) Northern Ireland Annual Abstract of statistics

Fisheries

21.14, 21.15	Department for Environment Food and Rural Affairs Scottish Government Agricultural Departments	

Family food

21.16	Department for Environment Food and Rural Affairs	Expenditure and Food Survey (annual) (1990 onwards edition-Family Spending) (annual, Palgrave Macmillan)

Chapter 22: Production

Production and construction

22.1	Office for National Statistics	Annual Business Inquiry (www.statistics.gov.uk/abi)

Sources

Table number in Abstract	Government department or other organisation	Official publication or other source
Manufacturers sales		
22.2	Office for National Statistics	ProdCom: Product Sales and Trade Annual Reports - PRA series (annual, ONS) Product Sales and Trade Quarterly Reports - PRQ series (quarterly, ONS)
22.3	Office for National Statistics	UK Business: Activity, Size and Location (www.statistics.gov.uk/ukbusiness)
Energy		
22.4 – 22.13	Department for Business, Enterprise and Regulatory Reform (Energy Strategy and International Unit)	Digest of United Kingdom Energy Statistics (annual) Energy Trends (monthly and quarterly) Annual Business Inquiry (www.statistics.gov.uk/abi)
Iron and steel		
22.14 – 22.16	Iron and Steel Statistics Bureau	Iron and steel industry: annual statistics published by the Iron and Steel Statistics Bureau Corporation Regional Trends (annual, Palgrave Macmillan)
Industrial materials		
22.17	World Bureau of Metal Statistics Aluminium Federation	World Metal Statistics (monthly) Annual Business Inquiry (www.statistics.gov.uk/abi)
22.18	Agricultural Industries Confederation	Annual Business Inquiry (www.statistics.gov.uk/abi)
Minerals		
22.19	Communities and Local Government	Minerals (Business Monitor PA 1007) (annual, ONS)
	Department for Business, Enterprise and Regulatory Reform	Natural Environment Research Council: United Kingdom
	Department of Economic Development (Northern Ireland)	Minerals Yearbook Northern Ireland Annual Abstract of Statistics
Building materials		
22.20	Department for Business, Enterprise and Regulatory Reform	Monthly Statistics of Building Materials and Components (BERR) Monthly Digest of Statistics (Palgrave Macmillan)
Construction		
22.21, 22.22	Office for National Statistics	Monthly Digest of Statistics (Palgrave Macmillan)
Engineering		
22.23, 22.24	Office for National Statistics	Annual Business Inquiry (www.statistics.gov.uk/abi) UK Business: Activity, Size and Location (www.statistics.gov.uk/Ukbusiness)
Motor vehicle production		
22.25	Office for National Statistics	Monthly Digest of Statistics (Palgrave Macmillan)

Table number in Abstract	Government department or other organisation	Official publication or other source
Drink and tobacco		
22.26	HM Revenue & Customs	Annual report of the Commissioners of HM Revenue and Customs (www.hmrc.gov.uk/stats/tax_receipts/menu.htm) and HMRC Statistical Bulletins on UK Trade Information website (www.uktradeinfo.com/index.cfm?task=bulletins) Monthly Digest of Statistics (Palgrave Macmillan)
22.27		Office for National Statistics

Chapter 23: Banking, insurance etc

Banking		
23.1	Bank of England	Bank of England Annual Report and Accounts
23.2	Association for Payment Clearing Services	Yearbook of Payment Statistics 2004
23.3 – 23.7	Bank of England	Bank of England, Statistical Interactive Database
23.8	Bank of England	Bank of England Quarterly Bulletin
23.9 – 23.12	Bank of England	Monthly Digest of Statistics (Palgrave Macmillan) Financial Statistics (monthly, Palgrave Macmillan)
Other financial institutions		
23.13	Financial Services Authority	Building Societies: Statistical Tables www.fsa.gov.uk/pages/Library/Other_publications/ Miscellaneous/2007/bs_stats.shtml
23.14	Office for National Statistics	Business Monitor SDQ7, Assets and Liabilities of Finance Houses and Other Credit Companies (quarterly, ONS)
23.15	Office for National Statistics	Financial Statistics (monthly, Palgrave Macmillan) Monthly Digest of Statistics (Palgrave Macmillan) Business Monitor MQ5, Insurance Companies; Pension Funds and Trusts Investments (quarterly, ONS) First Release
23.16, 23.17	Office for National Statistics	Financial Statistics (monthly, Palgrave Macmillan) Business Monitor MQ5, Insurance Companies; Pension Funds and InsolvencyTrusts Investments (quarterly, ONS)
23.18 – 23.19	Insolvency service	
23.20	Association of Unit Trusts and Investment Funds	
	Bank of England	
	Building Societies Commission	

Table number in Abstract	Government department or other organisation	Official publication or other source
	Department for Business, Enterprise and Regulatory reform	
	Department for National Savings	
	Office for National Statistics	
23.21	Bank of England	
23.22	Office for National Statistics	

Chapter 24: Service industry

Retail trades

24.1	Office for National Statistics	Annual Business Inquiry (www.statistics.gov.uk/abi)
24.2	Office for National Statistics	Business Monitor SDM 28, www.statistics.gov.uk/rsi

Motor trades

24.3	Office for National Statistics	Annual Business Inquiry (www.statistics.gov.uk/abi)

Catering

24.4	Office for National Statistics	Annual Business Inquiry (www.statistics.gov.uk/abi)

Index

Index

Index

Office for National Statistics

Social Reporting
from the Office for National Statistics

Family Spending
A report on the 2006 Expenditure and Food survey

One of the most accurate pictures of what households in the UK spend their money on today, this report presents a comprehensive overview of all aspects of household expenditure and income for 2006-2007. It is derived from the Expenditure and Food Survey and based on around 7000 households in the UK. Published annually, *Family Spending* provides analysis of household expenditure broken down by age, income, household composition, socio-economic characteristics and geography.

This year's report will feature a dedicated chapter commemorating 50 years of the long-running Family Expenditure and National Food Survey, highlighting key trends since 1957 and examining how household expenditure has changed over time.

Jan 2008
216pp   297 x 210mm
Paperback   £49.50
978-0-230-54561-8

Social Trends
38th edition

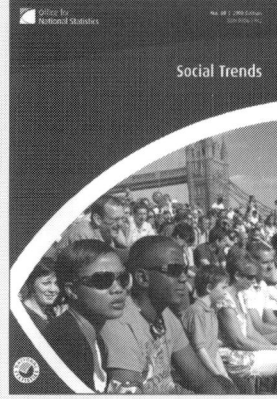

Often referred to as 'the biography of Britain', *Social Trends* provides a unique picture of life and lifestyle in the UK. An established reference source, this annual publication draws together the most up-to-date social and economic data from a wide range of government departments and other organizations.

This year's theme is 'societal wellbeing', or perceived quality of life, looking at factors like economic growth, financial security, quality of health and housing and survey-based data on life satisfaction and happiness. Data are presented clearly in a combination of tables, figures and text, providing the ideal tool for researching life and lifestyles in the UK.

April 2008
264pp   297 x 210mm
Paperback   £49.50
978-0-230-54564-9

Key Population and Vital Statistics 2006

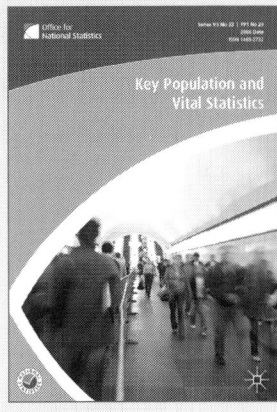

This annual publication draws together the United Kingdom's key population and vital statistics into a single source, summarizing population, births, mortality and migration data. It includes breakdowns by countries, unitary authorities, local government districts, London boroughs, health authorities and health boards.

April 2008
112pp   297 x 210mm
Paperback   £49.50
978-0-230-54562-5

Regional Trends
40th edition

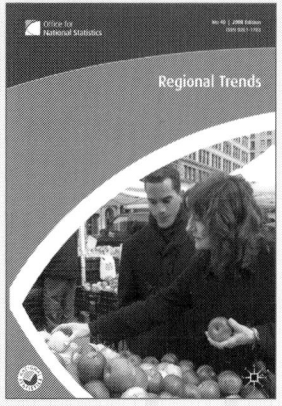

A comprehensive source of official statistics at a regional level for all the countries of the United Kingdom, *Regional Trends* is the ideal tool for researching on locations in the UK and comparing between them. The 40th edition includes a wide range of demographic, social, industrial and economic statistics, covering aspects of life within all areas of the UK. The data are presented clearly in a combination of tables, maps and charts with footnotes explaining differences in coverage where appropriate.

May 2008
272pp   297 x 210mm
Paperback   £45.00
978-1-4039-9386-1

Keep up to date with National Statistics from Palgrave Macmillan

Palgrave Macmillan's e-newsletter brings you the most up-to-date information on publication dates, prices and forthcoming products from the Office for National Statistics.

Register at **www.palgrave.com/ONS/mailinglist** to receive this monthly newsletter.

www.palgrave.com/ons